THE OXFORD HANDBOOK OF

LEGAL
STUDIES

THE OXFORD HANDBOOK OF

LEGAL STUDIES

Edited by

PETER CANE

AND

MARK TUSHNET

OXFORD

UNIVERSITY PRESS

OXFORD
UNIVERSITY PRESS

Great Clarendon Street, Oxford OX2 6DP

Oxford University Press is a department of the University of Oxford.
It furthers the University's objective of excellence in research, scholarship,
and education by publishing worldwide in

Oxford New York

Auckland Cape Town Dar es Salaam Hong Kong Karachi
Kuala Lumpur Madrid Melbourne Mexico City Nairobi
New Delhi Shanghai Taipei Toronto

With offices in

Argentina Austria Brazil Chile Czech Republic France Greece
Guatemala Hungary Italy Japan Poland Portugal Singapore
South Korea Switzerland Thailand Turkey Ukraine Vietnam

Oxford is a registered trade mark of Oxford University Press
in the UK and in certain other countries

Published in the United States
by Oxford University Press Inc., New York

First published 2003
Published new as paperback, 2005

British Library Cataloguing in Publication Data

Data available

Library of Congress Cataloging in Publication Data

Data available

Typeset by Newgen Imaging Systems (P) Ltd., Chennai, India
Printed in Great Britain
on acid-free paper by
Biddles Ltd., Guildford and King's Lynn

ISBN 0-19-924816-8 (Hbk.)
ISBN 0-19-924817-6 (Pbk.)

1 3 5 7 9 10 8 6 4 2

CONTENTS

PART III WEALTH REDISTRIBUTION AND WELFARE

PART VI PROCESSES

PART VII RESEARCH AND RESEARCHERS

Introduction and
Guide for the Reader

....

This volume in the series of Oxford legal handbooks is about legal scholarship. This superficially straightforward statement needs some explanation. The prime focus of the chapters in this book is not on law, legal rules, and legal institutions but on *scholarship about* law, legal rules, and legal institutions. As Upendra Baxi notes (see Ch. 22), in global terms the vast majority of published legal scholarship originates in countries of the developed 'North'; and this volume inevitably reflects that fact. More particularly, the main orientation of the essays is towards scholarly activity in what might loosely be called 'the common law world', made up of those legal systems that are more or less closely related, in terms of their conceptual and institutional structure, to the English. A corollary of this orientation is a focus on scholarship written in English. The explanation and justification for these limitations on the scope of the book are purely pragmatic. And it is, of course, our hope and expectation that this volume will prove to be accessible, and of interest and use, to lawyers both within the academy and outside it, and to people interested in legal scholarship wherever they might be within the common law world or beyond.

The basic idea for a volume of essays on scholarship about law came from John Louth, who is Senior Editor responsible for 'academic and scholarly' law publishing at Oxford University Press's 'mother house' in Oxford. Obviously, such a large idea could be developed in various ways, and we take responsibility for the shape of the project as defined by the table of contents and the brief given to the authors—of which, more later. The field of legal scholarship is as large and diverse as the social phenomena which legal scholars attempt to map and interpret; and the forms and styles of scholarly output are many and varied. This volume can make no claim to comprehensiveness either in terms of the subject-matter of legal scholarship or in terms of its forms and styles. Our aim was to cover a broad range of legal topics that seemed to us to have generated significant and important bodies of legal scholarship. No doubt, there are other topics that could profitably have been included—one that sprang to our minds rather too late was 'evidence and proof'. More importantly, perhaps, there are certainly other illuminating ways in which the field of legal scholarship could be divided up into manageable chunks. If the chosen coverage and arrangement of this volume stimulate readers to imagine other helpful ways of portraying and understanding the rich and complex doings of legal scholars, so much the better.

Each of the chapters in Parts I to VI deals with scholarship about a particular sub-stantive area of law. Although a conscious attempt was made to avoid compiling a list of textbook titles (*The Law of Contract*, *Corporations Law*, *Environmental Law*, and so on), inevitably the scope of many of the chapters reflects the pedagogical imperatives by which the professional life of the typical legal researcher is constrained. The chapters in Part VII deal with various issues related to the activities of legal researchers (including pedagogy) but which cut across the substantive areas dealt with in the other parts of the book. It will be immediately obvious to the critically observant reader that there are no chapters on scholarly 'movements' such as legal realism or law and economics, and none on general concepts such as responsibility and precedent. Apart from the fact that no single volume of sensible length could deal with the whole range of legally related scholarship, a conscious editorial decision was made to carve out for this collection an identity and focus distinctly different from that of volumes (including the one in this series edited by Jules Coleman and Scott Shapiro) devoted to 'legal theory', 'jurisprudence', and 'philosophy of law'. Because areas covered by the various chapters in this handbook are large, the discussions they contain are typically conducted at quite a high level of abstraction from the details of particular legal pro-visions and the law of particular jurisdictions. However, no attempt has been made to survey scholarship that defines itself as concerned with the *theory* or *philosophy* of law as opposed to *law* and *legal institutions* as such.

The authors were given a set of guidelines which it is important that the reader understand in order to get the most out of the book and not to expect more than is on offer. Authors were asked to focus not on the law in the substantive areas respectively allocated to them, but on scholarship about the law in those areas. Concentration on scholarship published since 1960 was recommended (except in relation to Chs 38 and 42). This temporal limit was suggested partly in order to make the authors' task more manageable, but also because it seemed to us that 1960 represented a watershed of sorts in the life of the legal academy, marking the beginning of a period in which the quantity and quality of legal scholarship has increased enormously. The rate of pro-duction of scholarship seems unlikely to abate; and in surveying the past, authors were asked to keep an eye on likely trends in the preoccupations of legal scholars in the early years of the twenty-first century.

Authors were encouraged to take a comparative, or at least a multi-jurisdictional, approach. In other words, they were asked to look beyond the scholarship with which they were most familiar in their own respective jurisdictions and to find distinctive scholarly contributions to our understanding of law and legal institutions from any-where and everywhere in the common law world. Of course, we did not expect authors to (be able to) survey the whole body of legal scholarship published in any area since 1960, nor to write accounts that were jurisdictionally neutral. We were con-tent for authors to privilege what they knew best, while at the same time pushing out the frontiers of their knowledge. Nor did we ask or expect authors to conceal or suspend their personal intellectual commitments, or to be impartial as between different styles or schools of scholarship or competing views about law and legal institutions. Rather, each contributing scholar was encouraged to write a personal reflection on a body of legal research and a set of legal ideas related to the area of law loosely defined by the title of the chapter for which he or she was responsible. We did not want, and we did not get, a set of substantively and structurally uniform 'reports' of various bodies of legal scholarship.

More technically, authors were instructed to eschew footnotes in order to maximize readability and the accessibility of the various contributions to a mixed audience. Each author was given a word limit, in some cases 8,000 words, in others 10,000, and in yet others 12,000. These length allocations reflect undoubtedly contestable editorial judgements about the relative significance and vibrancy of various bodies of scholarship. Somewhat to our surprise, and to our great relief, authors were generally and cheerfully punctilious in observing their personal word limits.

More controversial was the instruction to cite a maximum of thirty pieces of academic writing. We owe it to our authors to explain to readers this initially surprising constraint, which at least some of them found irksome and most found challenging—even though all managed in the end to work within or close to it. In some social-science disciplines (but not in law), the 'literature review' is a well-known and respected genre of academic writing. Literature reviews can be extremely valuable, especially when the topic addressed is relatively narrow and the time-frame quite short. The practicability and worth of a review of forty years of literature on topics as broad as those dealt with in each of the chapters of the *Handbook* are much more questionable. More importantly, what we wanted from each of the authors was his or her personal perspective on scholarship in the relevant area; and we wanted to relieve them of the burden of giving a comprehensive or 'balanced' account. One of the criteria for choosing authors was that each should be an authority in the field they were asked to write about. So we encouraged them to tell the reader not what others have said, but what they think about what others have said—to identify and comment upon themes and trends rather than to recount or focus on individual scholarly contributions. In different ways, each chapter in this book is itself an original contribution to, rather than an account of, an area of legal scholarship. Without putting too fine a point on the matter, we would say that there will almost inevitably be considerable room for disagreement about the items that should or should not have been included in the list of works referred to in the various chapters, as there will be about the authors' vision of the areas they discuss. The lists of references should not be thought of as encapsulating the author's answer to an (impossible and worthless) question such as, 'what are the thirty most significant scholarly contributions to your field in the last forty years?' Rather the references will most likely have been chosen for their aptness to support the particular argument that the author has chosen to make about scholarship in that field.

When first the outlines, and later the drafts, of chapters were submitted, we were considerably surprised by the variety of interpretations of the brief we had given to authors. As readers will find, there is considerable variation between chapters within the volume in the way that our authors strike the balance between, on the one hand, explaining what things scholars are talking about and, on the other, what they are saying about those things. For us, this is a cause for celebration rather than regret. If the intellectual posture of this volume could be summarized, the injunction to 'let a thousand flowers bloom' would do the job well enough. We hope that the chapters presented here will provoke some readers to offer their own perspectives on the fields discussed, approaching the work of our authors in a spirit of constructive criticism.

Partly because of this diversity of approach, we have made no attempt to integrate the various chapters by adding cross-references to discussions of related topics elsewhere in the volume. Instead, the *Handbook* has been provided with a detailed index which, we hope, will enable the reader to trace themes and topics across the boundaries of particular chapters.

As is true of many other areas of life, the world of anglophone legal scholarship can, for some purposes at least, be divided between the United States and 'the rest'. In relation to most of the chapters in the *Handbook*, 'the rest' effectively refers to major jurisdictions such as England, Canada, Australia, and New Zealand. Whereas 'US legal scholarship' can be conveniently referred to as such, it is not so obvious how best to refer generically to 'the rest'. We have encouraged authors to use the term 'Commonwealth' for this purpose. When used in this way, it refers to non-US, anglophone, common-law legal scholarship with particular reference to the larger jurisdictions in the 'developed' world.

A word about Chapter 41 (The Role of Academics in the Legal System) is in order. Unfortunately, the author who had agreed to write this chapter was ultimately not able to do so. It occurred to us that we might turn the consequent logistical problem into an opportunity to ask several scholars to write about the system with which each was most familiar. This also made it possible for us to focus on the international legal system as a phenomenon of independent importance and interest. Moreover, although the *Handbook* is primarily concerned with common law systems, we seized the chance to ask a European scholar to provide insights into the role of scholars in civil law systems. We believe that although the division of this chapter into four discrete sections creates a certain discontinuity, it more than compensates by the breadth of coverage that it offers of this relatively unexamined topic.

This volume would not have come into being without John Louth's initial vision and continuing confidence that the project was both doable and worth doing, and we are very grateful to him for his support and commitment. An undertaking of this size requires a considerable investment of organizational time and energy, and it would not have been possible without the help of Chris Treadwell, the administrator of the Law Program in the Research School of Social Sciences at the Australian National University, to whom we owe a large debt of thanks.

P.C.
M.T.

Notes on the Contributors

Richard L. Abel is Connell Professor of Law at the University of California at Los Angeles. He has written extensively on the sociology of legal professions; law, lawyers, and social change; disputing; harmful speech; and torts. Oxford University Press will publish *English Lawyers between Market and State: The Politics of Professionalism* in 2003.

Edwin Baker is Nicholas F. Gallicchio Professor of Law at the University of Pennsylvania Law School, where he has taught since 1981. Earlier he taught at the University of Toledo and the University of Oregon and has visited at the University of Texas, Cornell, Kennedy School at Harvard, University of Chicago, and New York University. His works on free expression and the regulation of the media include *Media, Markets, and Democracy* (Cambridge University Press, 2002), *Advertising and a Democratic Press* (Princeton University Press, 1994), and *Human Liberty and Freedom of Speech* (Oxford University Press, 1989).

John Baldwin is Professor of Judicial Administration in the Law School, University of Birmingham, and has been Director of the Institute of Judicial Administration since 1982. In the past thirty years, he has conducted a great number of empirical research projects, concerned in particular with the administration of justice, both criminal and civil. His latest book is *Small Claims in County Courts in England and Wales: The Bargain Basement of Civil Justice?* (Clarendon Press, 1997).

Robert Baldwin is a Professor of Law at the London School of Economics and Political Science where he teaches regulation and criminal law. He is the author/editor of numerous articles and books on public law and regulatory issues, including *Rules and Government* (Oxford University Press, 1995), *Law and Uncertainty* (Kluwer, 1996), *Understanding Regulation* (with M. Cave, Oxford University Press, 1999), and *The Government of Risk* (with C. Hood and H. Rothstein, Oxford University Press, 2001). He has advised numerous bodies on regulation, including HM Treasury, the National Audit Office, the Cabinet Office, the European Commission, and the International Labour Organization.

Mark Barenberg is Professor of Law at Columbia University Law School. He joined the Columbia faculty in 1987 after practising labour, constitutional, and international law in New York. He has been a Tutor in comparative labour studies at Harvard and a Visiting Professor of labour law at Yale Law School, the University of Tokyo, Peking

University, and the European University Institute. He is a member of the International Commission on Labor Rights, and his scholarship concentrates on issues of US and transnational labour law.

Upendra Baxi is Professor of Law at Warwick University in the UK. Between 1973 and 1995 he held posts at Indian universities, including that of Vice-Chancellor of the University of Delhi from 1990–4. His areas of specialist interest include comparative constitutionalism, social theory of human rights, and law in globalization. His recent publications include *The Future of Human Rights* (Oxford University Press, 2002). He has been actively engaged with the struggle of the Bhopal violated and has innovated social action litigation in India.

John Bell is Professor of Law (1973) at the University of Cambridge. He was Pro-Vice Chancellor for Teaching in the University of Leeds (1992–4) and has undertaken a number of projects in British legal education, including developing Benchmark statements for Law for the Quality Assurance Agency. He has taught extensively in France and Belgium.

Brian H. Bix is the Frederick W. Thomas Professor of Law and Philosophy at the University of Minnesota. He received a JD from Harvard University and a D.Phil. from Balliol College, Oxford. Prior publications include *Law, Language, and Legal Determinacy* (Oxford University Press, 1993) and *Jurisprudence: Theory and Context* (Sweet & Maxwell, 2nd edn., 1999; 3rd edn., forthcoming).

Linda Bosniak is a Professor at Rutgers Law School–Camden. She has written widely on the subjects of citizenship, alienage, and national membership, and is currently completing a book on these themes.

John Braithwaite is a Professor in the Law Program, Research School of Social Sciences, Australian National University and Chair of the Regulatory Institutions Network (RegNet). His most recent books are *Global Business Regulation* (Cambridge University Press, 2000), *Information Feudalism* (Earthscan Publications, 2002) (both with Peter Drahos), *Shame Management through Reintegration* (Cambridge University Press, 2001) (with Eliza Ahmed, Nathan Harris, and Valerie Braithwaite), and *Restorative Justice and Responsive Regulation* (Oxford University Press, 2002).

Peter Cane is Professor of Law and Head of the Law Program in the Research School of Social Sciences at the Australian National University. Between 1978 and 1997 he taught law at Corpus Christi College, Oxford. His main research interests are in the law of obligations (especially tort law) and public law (especially administrative law). His most recent book is *Responsibility in Law and Morality* (Hart, 2002).

Deborah Z. Cass teaches International Economic Law in the Law Department at the London School of Economics. She has recently co-edited (with Brett G. Williams and George Barker) *China and the World Trading System: Entering the New Millennium*

(Cambridge University Press, 2003) and is currently writing a book on the constitutionalization of the World Trade Organization. Contact: d.z.cass@lse.ac.uk

Brian R. Cheffins has been, since 1998, the S. J. Berwin Professor of Corporate Law at the Faculty of Law, University of Cambridge. He was a member of the Faculty of Law at the University of British Columbia from 1986 to 1997. He has held visiting appointments at Duke, Harvard, Oxford, and Stanford. Professor Cheffins is author of *Company Law: Theory, Structure and Operation* (Oxford University Press, 1997) and various articles on corporate law and corporate governance.

Jane Maslow Cohen is the Edward Clark Centennial Professor of Law at the University of Texas School of Law.

Gwynn Davis is Emeritus Professor and Senior Research Fellow attached to the Department of Law, University of Bristol. Over the past twenty-five years he has conducted over forty empirical research projects in the fields of family law and practice, criminal justice, and developments in the legal profession. He is the author of *Partisans and Mediators* (Clarendon Press, 1988) and, most recently, *Child Support in Action* (with Nick Wikeley and Richard Young, Hart, 1998).

John Dewar is Dean and Professor of Law at Griffith University in Queensland, Australia. He is Director of the Families, Law and Social Policy Research Unit, hosted by the Socio-Legal Research Centre at Griffith University, and Director of Studies for the World Congress on Families, Youth and the Rights of the Child. He is Chair of the Family Law Council and was a member of the Australian Federal Government's Family Law Pathways Advisory Group. His current research interests include self-represented litigants in family law proceedings, superannuation on divorce, and post-separation parenting.

Neil Duxbury teaches law at the University of Manchester. He is the author of *Patterns of American Jurisprudence* (Clarendon Press, 1995), *Random Justice* (Clarendon Press, 1999), and *Jurists and Judges* (Hart, 2001). His long-term research focuses on the development of law as an academic discipline in England.

Keith Ewing has been Professor of Public Law at King's College, University of London since 1989, having taught previously at the Universities of Edinburgh and Cambridge. He has held visiting appointments in Australia, Canada, and Japan, and has written in the fields of constitutional law, human rights, and labour law. His writings include (with C. A. Gearty) *Freedom under Thatcher: Civil Liberties in Modern Britain* (Oxford University Press, 1990) and *The Struggle for Civil Liberties: Political Freedom and the Rule of Law in Britain 1915-1945* (Oxford University Press, 2000). With A. W. Bradley he is also editor of A. W. Bradley and K. D. Ewing, *Constitutional and Administrative Law* (13th edn., Longman, 2002).

Ward Farnsworth is an Associate Professor at the Boston University School of Law. He previously served as a law clerk to Hon. Anthony M. Kennedy of the Supreme

Court of the United States and to Hon. Richard A. Posner of the United States Court of Appeals for the Seventh Circuit. His writings include 'Talking Out of School: Notes on the Transmission of Intellectual Capital from the Legal Academy to Public Tribunals', *Boston University Law Review* 81 (2001), 13.

Malcolm M. Feeley is the Claire Sanders Clements Dean's Professor of Law in the Jurisprudence and Social Policy Program at the University of California at Berkeley. He has held positions at New York University, Yale Law School, the University of Wisconsin. He is the author of several books, including *The Process is the Punishment* (Russell Sage Foundation, 1979) (recipient of the ABA's Silver Gavel Award for 'best book'), (with Austin Sarat); *The Policy Dilemma* (University of Minnesota Press, 1981), *Court Reform on Trial* (Basic Books, 1983), and most recently, (with Edward Rubin), *Judicial Policy Making and the Modern State* (Cambridge University Press, 1998). His articles have focused on various aspects of law and politics, including methodology, the criminal process, prison privatization, and most recently women and crime.

Phil Fennell is a Reader in Law in Cardiff Law School in Wales where he teaches Medical Law and European Community Law. He is a member of the Law Society's Mental Health and Disability Committee and was a member of the Mental Health Act Commission from 1983–9. He has published many articles on law and psychiatry. He is an editor of Butterworths Medico-Legal Reports, and is honorary legal adviser to Wales Mind. He is co-author of Lawrence O. Gostin and Phil Fennell, *Mental Health: Tribunal Procedure* (Sweet and Maxwell, 1992) and author of *Treatment without Consent: Law, Psychiatry and the Treatment of Mental Disorder since 1845* (Routledge, 1996).

Sandra Fredman is Professor of Law at Oxford University and Fellow of Exeter College, Oxford. She has written widely on equality, labour law, public law, and human rights. Her book *Women and the Law* was published by Clarendon Press in 1997, and her most recent book *Discrimination Law* appeared in the Clarendon Law Series in 2002. She has written two other books *The State as Employer* with Gillian Morris (Mansell, 1989), and *Labour Law and Industrial Relations in Great Britain* with Bob Hepple (Kluwer Law and Taxation, 2nd edn., 1992).

David J. Gerber is Distinguished Professor of Law and Director of the Program in International Law and Comparative Law at Chicago-Kent College of Law. He specializes in comparative law with an emphasis on competition law and business regulation. He has been a Visiting Professor at the law schools of the University of Pennsylvania, Northwestern University, and Washington University in the United States as well as in the law faculties of Munich and Freiburg in Germany and Stockholm and Uppsala in Sweden. His book *Law and Competition in Twentieth Century Europe* was published by Oxford University Press in 1998 (paperback, 2001).

H. Patrick Glenn is the Peter M. Laing Professor of Law, McGill University.

John C. P. Goldberg is Professor at Vanderbilt University Law School. Professor Goldberg received Masters degrees in Politics from Oxford and Princeton Universities, and his JD from New York University Law School. He has published numerous articles and essays on tort law and tort theory and has been an active participant in the drafting of the Third Restatement of Torts as a member of the American Law Institute. He is currently completing a casebook on torts with Professors Anthony Sebok and Benjamin Zipursky entitled *Tort Law: Responsibilities and Redress*, to be published by Aspen Law and Business.

James Gordley is Shannon Cecil Turner Professor of Jurisprudence at the University of California at Berkeley School of Law, where he has taught since 1978. He specializes in comparative law, and is the author of *The Enforceability of Promises in European Contract Law* (Cambridge University Press, 2001) and *The Philosophical Origins of Modern Contract Doctrine* (Oxford University Press, 1991).

Wendy J. Gordon is Professor of Law and Paul J. Liacos Scholar in Law at Boston University. Her articles include 'An Inquiry into the Merits of Copyright', *Stanford Law Review*, 41 (1989), 1343, 'Fair Use as Market Failure', *Columbia Law Review*, 82 (1982), 1600, 'A Property Right in Self-Expression', *Yale Law Journal*, 102 (1993), 1533, and 'On Owning Information', *Virginia Law Review*, 78 (1992), 149. Professor Gordon has been a Fulbright Scholar, and Visiting Senior Research Fellow at St John's College, Oxford. She is the recipient of several grants and honours, most recently an award from the Ronald A. Cass Fund for Teaching Excellence.

Lawrence O. Gostin is Professor of Law at Georgetown University; Professor of Public Health at the Johns Hopkins University; and the Director of the Center for Law & the Public's Health. He is an elected lifetime Member of the National Academy of Sciences and serves its Board on Health Promotion and Disease Prevention. He works internationally with the World Health Organization and UNAIDS. He is Health Law and Ethics Editor of the *Journal of the American Medical Association*. Professor Gostin's latest books are both published by the University of California Press: *Public Health Law: Power, Duty, Restraint* (2000) and *Public Health Law and Ethics: A Reader* (2002).

Lisa Heinzerling is Professor of Law at the Georgetown University Law Center. She received an AB from Princeton University and a JD from the University of Chicago Law School, where she was editor-in-chief of the Law Review. She clerked for Judge Richard A. Posner on the United States Court of Appeals for the Seventh Circuit and for Justice William J. Brennan, Jr. on the United States Supreme Court. She served as an assistant attorney general in Massachusetts, specializing in environmental law. She has been a Visiting Professor at the Yale and Harvard law schools.

Michael A. Heller is the Lawrence A. Wien Professor of Real Estate Law at Columbia Law School. He joined Columbia after eight years on the faculty at the University of

Michigan Law School. Before entering teaching, he worked for the World Bank and the Urban Institute on housing policy in developing and post-socialist countries.

Jeremy Horder is Porjes Foundation Fellow, and Reader in Criminal Law, Worcester College, Oxford.

David Ibbetson is Regius Professor of Civil Law at the University of Cambridge.

Benedict Kingsbury is Professor of Law and Director of the Institute for International Law and Justice at New York University Law School. He also directs the Law School's Program in the History and Theory of International Law. He held a permanent teaching position in the Law Faculty at Oxford before moving to Duke University in 1993, and New York University in 1998. He is a member of the Editorial Board of the *American Journal of International Law*, and the Advisory Boards of the *European Journal of International Law* and the *New York University Journal of International Law and Politics*. He is completing a book on indigenous peoples in international law.

Beverly I. Moran is Professor of Law and Sociology at the Vanderbilt University Law School. She is a graduate of the New York University Law School LL M programme in taxation as well as of the University of Pennsylvania Law School and Vassar College. Professor Moran has taught public finance, development, and tax-related subjects in North America, Europe, Asia, and Africa. She has received a number of grants including a Ford Foundation grant and a Fulbright award.

David Nelken After teaching Law at Cambridge, Edinburgh, and London Universities, David Nelken moved in 1990 to be Distinguished Professor of Legal Institutions and Social Change at the University of Macerata in Italy. He is also Distinguished Research Professor in Law at the University of Wales, Cardiff, UK, and Visiting Professor of Law at the London School of Economics. He was awarded the 1985 Distinguished Scholar prize of the American Sociological Association (Criminology section). Recent books include *Contrasting Criminal Justice* (Dartmouth, 2000), *Adapting Legal Cultures* (Hart Publishing, 2001) and *Law's New Boundaries* (Dartmouth, 2001). He is a Trustee of the Law and Society Association (USA), and Vice-President of its European equivalent.

Christine Parker is a Senior Lecturer in the Law Faculty, University of Melbourne, Australia, where she teaches legal ethics and corporate law and regulation. Parker researches and writes on the relationship between legal regulation and self-regulation in the normative context of deliberative democracy. Her first book, *Just Lawyers* (Oxford University Press, 1999), evaluated the regulatory and self-regulatory regimes governing the legal profession. *The Open Corporation: Effective Self-Regulation and Democracy* (Cambridge University Press, 2002) examines corporate regulatory compliance systems and the 'meta-regulation' of corporate self-regulation. Parker also speaks and consults widely on regulatory compliance for industry and the public sector.

Jordan Paust is Law Foundation Professor of International Law at the Law Center of the University of Houston. He has served on several committees on international law, human rights, terrorism, and the use of force in the American Society of International Law, the American Branch of the International Law Association, and the American Bar Association. He is currently Co-Chair of the American Society's International Criminal Law Interest Group. He was also Chair of the Section on International Law of the Association of American Law Schools and was on the Executive Council and the President's Committee of the American Society of International Law.

Judith Resnik is the Arthur Liman Professor of Law at Yale Law School, where she teaches and writes about procedure, federalism, and feminism. She serves on committees of the ABA and the National and International Association of Women Judges, and is a member of the American Law Institute, the American Academy of Arts and Sciences, and the American Philosophical Society, and is a consultant to RAND. She has chaired the Sections on Federal Courts, Civil Procedure, and Women in Legal Education of the American Association of Law Schools. She has authored many books (most recently, *Adjudication and its Alternatives: An Introduction to Procedure*, Westbury, N.Y.: Foundation Press, 2003, with Owen M. Fiss) and articles and has testified many times before congressional and judicial committees and has been a court-appointed expert as well as an occasional litigator.

Kent Roach is a Professor of Law and Criminology at the University of Toronto. His books include *Due Process and Victims*: *The New Law and Politics of Criminal Justice* (University of Toronto Press, 1999), *The Supreme Court on Trial*: *Judicial Activism or Democratic Dialogue* (Irwin Law, 2001), and *September 11: Consequences for Canada* (McGill Queens Press, 2003). He edits the *Criminal Law Quarterly* and co-edited recent collections of essays on restorative justice and anti-terrorism law. His present research includes work on anti-terrorism politics and policy, regulatory offences, and wrongful convictions.

Jo Shaw is Salvesen Chair of European Institutions and Senior Research Fellow at the Federal Trust.

Lionel Smith is William Dawson Scholar in Law at McGill University. He studied Zoology and Philosophy at the University of Toronto, and Law at the Universities of Western Ontario, Cambridge, and Oxford. He was a law clerk to Justice Sopinka at the Supreme Court of Canada and taught Law at the Universities of Alberta and Oxford before joining McGill in 2000. He is the author of *The Law of Tracing* (Clarendon Press, 1997) and numerous articles, including 'Restitution: The Heart of Corrective Justice', *Texas Law Review*, 79 (2001). He is a member of the Common Core of European Private Law project in Trent, and is Canadian Editor of the *Restitution Law Review*.

Michael Taggart teaches at the Faculty of Law, The University of Auckland, New Zealand. His latest book is *Private Property and Abuse of Rights in Victorian England: The Story of Edward Pickles and the Bradford Water Supply* (Oxford University Press, 2002). Contact: mb.taggart@auckland.ac.nz

Fernando Tesón is Tobias Simon Eminent Scholar at Florida State University. He is the author of *Humanitarian Intervention: An Inquiry into Law and Morality* (2nd edn., Transnational Publishers, 1997), and *A Philosophy of International Law* (Westview Press, 1998). He has published many articles on international law and political philosophy, most recently 'Self-Defeating Symbolism in Politics' (with Guido Pincione), *The Journal of Philosophy*, 98 (Dec. 2001), and 'The Liberal Case for Humanitarian Intervention', forthcoming in J. Holzgrefe and R. Keohane (eds.), *Humanitarian Intervention: Ethical, Legal, and Political Dilemmas* (Cambridge University Press). Professor Tesón has taught and lectured widely in the United States, Europe, and Latin America.

Gerald Thain is Professor of Consumer Law at the University of Wisconsin Law School (Madison). His numerous articles for law reviews and other scholarly journals include, 'The E.C. Directive on Unfair Contract Terms: A Perspective From the U.S', *Consumer Law Journal*, 2 (1994), 127. He has directed many academic conferences, is a frequent consultant or expert witness for federal and state agencies, and is one of the US members of the US–EU Transatlantic Consumer Dialogue which seeks the adoption of uniform consumer-friendly rules for international electronic commerce. Professor Thain spent three years as an Air Force Judge Advocate, and eleven years at the Federal Trade Commission in various legal and administrative positions.

Mark Tushnet has taught at Georgetown University Law Center since 1981. He served as a law clerk to Justice Thurgood Marshall of the United States Supreme Court in 1972–3, after which he began teaching at the University of Wisconsin Law School. He has published widely in American legal history and US constitutional law. His most recent book is *The New Constitutional Order* (Princeton University Press, 2003).

William Twining was Quain Professor of Jurisprudence from 1983–96 at University College London, where he is now Research Professor of Law. He has been President of the Society of Public Teachers of Law (SPTL), Chairman of the Commonwealth Legal Education Association, and is a Fellow of the British Academy. His recent books include *Blackstone's Tower: The English Law School* (Hamlyn Lectures, 1994), *Law in Context: Enlarging a Discipline* (Oxford University Press, 1997), *Globalisation and Legal Theory* (Butterworth, 2000), and *The Great Juristic Bazaar* (Ashgate, 2002).

Stefan Vogenauer is Fellow at the Max Planck Institute for Foreign Private Law and Private International Law, Hamburg.

Nick Wikeley holds the John Wilson Chair in Law at the University of Southampton, UK. His books include *Compensation for Industrial Disease* (Dartmouth 1993),

Judging Social Security (with John Baldwin and Richard Young, Clarendon Press, 1992), *Child Support in Action* (with Gwynn Davis and Richard Young, Hart, 1998), and *The Law of Social Security* (2002). He holds a part-time judicial appointment as a deputy Social Security Commissioner and is Honorary Secretary of the Society of Legal Scholars (formerly SPTL). He also co-edits the *Journal of Social Security Law* with Professor Neville Harris.

Sarah Worthington is Reader in Law, London School of Economics and Political Science.

PART I

PROPERTY AND OBLIGATIONS

CHAPTER 1

....

CONTRACT

....

JAMES GORDLEY

1 INTRODUCTION: THE BREAKDOWN OF 'CLASSICAL' CONTRACT LAW

....

IN contemporary contract law, much of the work of scholars and judges has a common feature. It has been written in response to the breakdown of a system of doctrines built, largely by scholars, in the nineteenth and early twentieth centuries, a system which has sometimes been called 'classical contract law'. This chapter will describe this response.

Before the nineteenth century, Anglo-American contract law did not have a systematic doctrinal organization. There was little scholarly literature aside from a few pages in Blackstone (Simpson, 1975: 247). It is somewhat misleading to say there was a law of contract. The law was organized around forms of action such as covenant or *assumpsit* which could be brought for what we now call breach of contract. Within these forms of action, the case law was often precise as to particulars but unclear about general doctrine and the underlying principles.

'Classical' contract law was built on a substantive premise about contract law and two premises about legal method. The substantive premise was voluntaristic: the business of contract law is to enforce the will or choice of the parties. Eventually, some jurists, such as Oliver Wendell Holmes, found the concept of will so empty that they proposed a so-called 'objective' theory in which contract law merely consisted of consequences which the law attached to the parties' outward manifestations of consent. But for followers of Holmes such as Samuel Williston, the theory meant, primarily, treating these outward manifestations as though they genuinely manifested consent. One wonders how much influence the 'objective' theory had upon doctrine.

The first methodological premise was positivistic: the law is found, implicitly or explicitly, in the decisions of common law judges. Sometimes, this premise worked, or was made to work, in harmony with the substantive premise. The case law was mined for rules about fraud, mistake, duress, and offer and acceptance. The rules discovered in the case law supposedly gave effect to the will of the parties. Nevertheless, sometimes the common lawyers had to admit that the case law contained doctrines that failed to respect the will of the parties. An example was the doctrine of consideration.

The second methodological premise was conceptualistic: the law should be stated in general formulas which can be tested by their coherence. Each formula should be internally coherent and consistent with every other formula and with the case law. So far as possible, this premise was made to harmonize with the others just described. As A. W. B. Simpson has said, the will of the parties became a *Grundnorm* from which other rules were to be derived (Simpson, 1975: 266). The doctrine of consideration was understood by seeking a general formula that would fit all the decided cases.

Finally, 'classical' contract law reflected an attitude about how best to steer a course—as every legal system must—between strict rules and equitable considerations. The preference was for strict rules. They should be clear and hard-edged. If a contracting party did not express himself fully, or consider all contingencies, or understand what he signed, or look out for his own interests, the problem lay with him. To describe this characteristic as a preference for rigor is to view the matter with the benefit of hindsight. At the time, it was not regarded as a preference but as required by respect for the will of the parties, or as implicit in the case law, or as necessary for coherence.

Since the early twentieth century, classical contract law has been breaking down. Allegiance to its premises has weakened as has the preference for rigor. At the same time, scholars have found the classical law to be inconsistent even in its own terms. Nevertheless, much of it has remained in place *faute de mieux* while contemporary jurists have tried to see what is really at stake in particular legal problems. This chapter will describe their work.

2 WHAT PROMISES ARE ENFORCEABLE

2.1 Consideration

Traditionally, courts would only enforce a promise in an action of *assumpsit* if it was 'supported by consideration'. Before the nineteenth century, they found 'consideration' for a variety of promises with little in common except that judges wished to enforce them. Bargains such as sale had consideration, but so did promises of marriage settlements and a variety of gratuitous loans and bailments. In the nineteenth century, however, treatise writers tried to formulate the doctrine in a way that would, on the one hand, be general, and, on the other, fit the decided cases. They identified consideration with bargain or exchange. That suggested that the common law doctrine was based on a principle already ancient in civil law: that bargains should be enforced more freely than gifts. Then Sir Frederick Pollock in England followed by Oliver Wendell Holmes in the United States defined bargain in a way that could explain even those cases in which courts enforced promises which were not bargains in any ordinary sense. According to them, bargain meant that one party made a promise, at least in part, in order to induce the other to surrender some legal right (Pollock, 1876: 150–1, 1936: 164; Holmes, 1881: 293–4). This formula and variants of it could be manipulated to find consideration, for example, for the promise of a father to give money to his prospective son-in-law upon his marriage (although English courts eventually refused to enforce one); the promise of a gratuitous bailee to look after the object loaned to him; or (in the United States) a promise to give money to a university that would name a scholarship fund after the donor. One merely characterized the marriage, the loan of the object, or the naming of the fund as one reason the promise was made. In the nineteenth and early twentieth centuries, courts also began to deny that certain commercial promises had consideration: for example, a promise to hold an offer open, or to sell at an agreed price any quantity of a commodity the other party chose to order, or to pay the other party more than originally agreed. The Pollock/Holmes formula could explain these results as well. The promisee had not given up a legal right.

In the nineteenth and early twentieth centuries, scholars debated whether and why the law should enforce bargains more easily than gifts. These debates have continued. Charles Fried, like many earlier scholars, sees the doctrine as an unwarranted limitation on a party's freedom to bind himself (Fried, 1981: 35). Some economists see it as an interference with the parties' attempts to do what they both regard as beneficial (Cooter and Ulen, 2000: 183–4). Other economists have tried to explain it in terms of efficiency. According to Richard Posner, promises of gifts may be poorly evidenced or trivial (Posner, 1998: 109) although that hardly explains why courts do not enforce them when they are well evidenced and large. Both Posner and non-economists have repeated the traditional explanation: that such promises may be inadvertant or carelessly phrased as promises (Posner, 1998: 109). Melvin Eisenberg has a 'positive theory': legal enforcement of such a promise may be incompatible with the relationship of love or trust between the parties which inspired it; moreover, they may be subject to tacit conditions which a court is not able to appreciate (Eisenberg, 2001: 230). Ultimately, what must be explained is that commitments to make gifts are enforced selectively. While a promise to give is not generally enforceable, a commitment to give, even in the future, can be made so by using a trust instead of a contract. In the United States, marriage settlements and charitable subscriptions have traditionally been enforced. The reason, according to Gordley, is that in these cases, there is reason to believe that wealth is being transferred in a sensible direction, either because the donor forced to use a trust will have had more time to reflect, or because the donee seems particularly deserving (Gordley, 2001: 298–307). This view supposes that some transfers of wealth are more sensible than others: to some that might seem a matter of common sense (see Farnsworth, 1995: 364).

Newer is the recognition that much of the doctrine of consideration is not only about enforcing bargains more freely than gifts. It is also about fairness. That may seem strange since the fairness of the amount given in consideration does not legally matter. Indeed, the courts that first applied the doctrine to commercial promises denied, as English courts still do, that a contract can be unenforceable simply because it is unfair. Yet courts manipulated the doctrine of consideration to prevent unfair results. It is often unfair for one party to be bound when the other is not; or for one party to be able to change the quantity he may demand in response to price changes; or for one party to take advantage of the other's change of position to charge more than they originally agreed. Such contracts were not enforced.

The trouble is that as Eisenberg, Gordley, and others have pointed out, the doctrine of consideration is a crude tool for preventing unfairness since it will also strike down fair promises. The attempt to resolve this problem while keeping the doctrine in place has led to reforms which are merely piecemeal. For example, in the United States, the Uniform Commercial Code (UCC) enforces some promises to hold offers open (§ 2-205). The English Law Commission has recommended doing so as well (Working Paper 60 (1975)). The UCC enforces contracts to buy or sell however much one requires or produces provided the quantity is demanded or offered in good faith (§ 2-306(1)). It also enforces some promises to take more or do less than originally agreed if the promisee acted in good faith (§ 2-209(1)). American courts have enforced such promises when they were a response to changed conditions (e.g. *Angel v Murray* 322 A 2d 630 (RI 1974)). English courts say they will do so if the promisor received 'practical benefits' although no one is sure what that actually means (*Williams v Roffey Bros & Nichols (Contractors) Ltd* [1991] 1 QB 1).

American scholars such as Eisenberg and Gordley argue that piecemeal reform is unsatisfactory if the object is to prevent unfairness. As we will see, American courts are now willing to strike down unfair contracts as 'unconscionable'. When courts can examine the fairness of a contract directly, they should no longer do so indirectly by a doctrine of consideration that had to be manipulated to consider unfairness at all. Eisenberg and Gordley would abolish the doctrine of consideration and apply that of unconscionability although Gordley thinks that the older applications of the doctrine have much to teach us about the kinds of promises that are unfair (Eisenberg, 1982; Gordley, 1995: 582–613).

2.2 Reliance

Williston noted that there were a few cases which the Pollock/Holmes formula for consideration could not explain. For example, a woman quit her job after her grandfather promised her $2,000 so she could do so. The court enforced the promise after he died solvent without changing his mind (*Ricketts v Scothorn* 77 NW 365 (Neb 1898)). He suggested that in these cases and in enforcing marriage settlements and charitable subscriptions, courts were allowing the reliance of the promisee to substitute for the requirement of consideration (Williston, 1920: 307–14). He incorporated this doctrine of 'promissory estoppel' into the first Restatement of Contracts (§ 90) of which he was Reporter. It has now been universally adopted by US courts and applied in a vast number of cases. The English doctrine is much more restrictive. The promisee who relied has a defense against an action by the promisor but not an action against him. English scholars such as Atiyah would like the courts to go further (Atiyah, 1995: 137–52).

The orthodox position, taken, for example, by Farnsworth and Atiyah, is that the purpose of the doctrine is to protect the promisee from being harmed by the promisor's failure to keep his promise (Farnsworth, 1999: 99; Atiyah, 1995: 119–21, 137–41). This is also the view of economists such as Posner who regard the promisee's harm as a 'cost' to be avoided (Posner, 1998: 106–7). As a result, in the United States, the dominant academic opinion is that the promisee should recover only the amount by which he was harmed, not any larger amount he was promised. That suggestion was incorporated into the second Restatement by providing that a court should award the amount which 'justice requires' (§ 90(1)). By this view, reliance-based recovery is much like recovery for harm in tort. Indeed, Grant Gilmore suggested that ' "contract" is being reabsorbed into the mainstream of "tort" ' (Gilmore, 1974: 87).

Yet Farber and Matheson found in 1985 that courts applying the doctrine not only enforce a promise to its full extent but often do so without any proof that the promisee relied, a finding later confirmed by Wangerin, Feinman, Becker, Yorio, and Thel. Indeed, the second Restatement provides that no proof of reliance is required to enforce marriage settlements or charitable subscriptions (§ 90(2)). Moreover, the vast bulk of the cases concern promises made in commercial transactions, not promises of gifts. Farber and Matheson have suggested that 'any promise made in furtherance of an economic activity is enforceable' (Farber and Matheson, 1985: 905). But that clearly goes too far.

In Gordley's view, courts' use of the doctrine has less to do with protecting the promisee from harm than with curing two problems with the doctrine of consideration that have already been mentioned. One is that, although promises of gifts may be sensible or foolish, the doctrine refuses to enforce all of them. As mentioned, marriage settlements and charitable subscriptions are particularly likely to be sensible, and so it is not surprising that US courts twisted the doctrine of consideration to enforce them even before the rise of promissory estoppel. Similarly, it is not surprising that a court stretched to enforce the promise of a person who died solvent without ever repudiating the promise. A second difficulty mentioned earlier is that some promises are fair even though only one party is bound, and yet the doctrine of consideration strikes them all down. In commercial transactions, the promise, though important to the promisee, may have been virtually costless to the promisor or it may benefit the promisor by inducing the promisee to incur some expense to evaluate or finance a deal the promisor has proposed. In these and similar cases, courts apply the doctrine of promissory estoppel (Gordley, 1995).

3 The Content of Contractual Obligation

Long before the nineteenth century, Continental jurists had known that contracts are made by consent. As Simpson said, the nineteenth-century innovation was to turn consent or will into a sort of *Grundnorm* from which as many rules of contract law as possible were to be derived. The parties were not only obligated because they consented. In principle, their will was the source of all the obligations to which they were bound. This innovation created two problems which are still with us. First, if the will of the parties is the source of their obligations, why are they bound to the terms which the law reads into their contract to govern matters which they had not expressly decided? Secondly, why does a court sometimes refuse to enforce the terms on which the parties did agree on the grounds that they are unfair?

3.1 Implied Terms

The terms the law will read in to govern matters the parties did not decide for themselves compose the bulk of the law of sales, leases, partnership, and so forth. Randy Barnett has suggested that the parties give 'subjective consent' to these terms when they conform to their 'commonsense or conventional expectations' (Barnett, 1992: 876–7). But while these terms may not contradict their expectations, their expectations cannot include all the terms which these bodies of law contain. Many scholars have concluded that implied terms cannot be rooted in the intention of the parties (e.g. Treitel, 1999: 189–90), including Charles Fried whose theory centers on consent (Fried, 1981: 60). Consequently, as Fried's critics have noted, his theory cannot explain most of contract law. Indeed, this problem, noted decades before, led the American jurists Oliver Wendell Holmes and Samuel Williston to adopt a so-called 'objective theory' of contract: the implied terms are not willed by the parties but are simply consequences attached to their agreement by the law. But then the question arises, why does the law attach one set of consequences rather than another?

According to those who take an economic approach, the reason the parties do not include all the terms in their contracts is because some contingencies are hard to foresee or so remote that it would be too costly to deal with them in advance. Therefore it may be 'cheaper' for a court to 'draft' terms to deal with these contingencies when they arise, reading into the contract the terms the parties would have chosen themselves (Posner, 1998: 104–5; Cooter and Ulen, 2000: 201). These terms will place the risks and burdens of the contract on the party who can most easily bear them, thus maximizing the value of the contract to the parties. This economic approach brings a new precision to the analysis of what the parties would have done which is much appreciated even by people who disagree on other matters. Nevertheless, it is hardly novel to say that a court should read into a contract the terms the parties would themselves have provided. The problem traditionally was to explain why a court should do so if the will of the parties is the source of their obligations. According to the economic approach, the reason is a gain in efficiency: it may be cheaper for a court to provide the terms. But if the only reason courts read such terms into an agreement is to spare the parties the cost of drafting them, then there is a gain only if the parties would otherwise have incurred this cost. Often they would not. To understand why courts should read in these terms, we need to understand that these terms are also fair.

3.2 Fairness

Courts and legislatures do give relief when a contract is unfair. Most scholars agree that they should but have trouble explaining why. Traditionally, courts of equity gave relief when a bargain was so unfair as to be 'unconscionable'. In the United States, this doctrine has been extended to allow all courts to refuse to enforce the express terms of a contract if they are seriously unfair (UCC § 2-302; Restatement (Second) of Contracts § 208). In English courts, however, the doctrine withered (Treitel, 1999: 223–4) but the legislature stepped in. Relief for unfairness is given under the Unfair Contract Terms Act 1977 or the Unfair Terms in Consumer Contracts Regulations 1994. The 1977 Act deals with exemption and indemnity clauses. The Regulations, enacted to give effect to an EC Council Directive (93/13/EEC), contain a general clause invalidating an 'unfair term' which is defined as one 'contrary to the requirement of good faith' which 'causes a significant imbalance in the parties' rights and obligations'. The Regulations are nevertheless narrower than the American unconscionability doctrine. They apply only to standardized terms in contracts for the provision of goods and services to consumers. Also, Regulation 3(2) provides that no relief will be given if a price is unfair. In contrast, US courts have sometimes held a price to be 'unconscionable' (e.g. *American Home Improvement Co v MacIver* 201 A 2d 886 (NH 1964)).

However broad or narrow, the refusal to enforce unfair terms is hard to explain by a consent-based theory such as Fried's, though Fried himself concedes that some contracts are simply too unfair to enforce (Fried, 1981: 109). It is hard to explain by a law and economics approach. Posner suggests that bargains are rarely one-sided because, on a competitive market, the harm to the supposed victim of 'unconscionable' terms will be offset by the benefit of paying a lower price (Posner, 1998: 126–30). The fundamental problem, however, is that the economic approach is concerned, not with fairness, but with efficiency. To explain why, under admiralty law, a rescuer cannot charge 99 per cent of the value of a ship in distress, Posner claims that the transaction costs of negotiating such an arrangement will be high (why?) and that too many resources would then be devoted to rescue operations. But the reason that relief is given by admiralty law, US courts, and English and European legislators is not to reduce transaction costs or optimize expenditures on rescue equipment. It is that they believe some contracts are unfair. If contracts were merely expressions of consent, or if all that mattered were efficiency, it is hard to see how a contract could be unfair or why it should matter.

American jurists have analyzed unconscionability by distinguishing 'procedural' from 'substantive' fairness (Craswell, 1993: 17; Slawson, 1996: 38). The former means that one party had difficulty protecting himself. The latter means that the terms of the contract are unfair. But, presumably, if the terms are unfair, the disadvantaged party had some sort of difficulty protecting himself. And if the terms were fair, no court would give relief. So the question again arises, what it means for terms to be unfair.

A clue to the problem is that, as economists have observed, rational parties would agree to terms that place risks and burdens on whichever party can most easily bear them. That party would then be compensated by adjusting the price in his favor. Posner notes the parties would do so in a competitive market. Indeed, one would think even a monopolist would offer such terms if the other party understood the risks and burdens they entail, for roughly the same reason that he would put leather upholstery in cars if he could charge more than the cost of doing so. Suppose, then, that a court can see that a contract places a risk or burden on the party who is less able to bear it. It can conclude, not only that this party did not understand its cost, but also that he was not compensated by a corresponding adjustment in the price. Rather than make the adjustment, the other party would have chosen to bear the risk or burden himself. The contract is therefore unfair in the way a bet would be unfair if the odds did not reflect one party's greater chance to win. An unfair price is unfair in the same sense. If markets work as economists say they do, prices are as likely to rise as to fall, and the party who gains if they rise was as likely to lose. A contract at the market price is like a fair bet. But the bet is no longer fair if one party can buy below the market price because the other is ignorant of that price or lacks access to the market. Courts have a reason, then, to refuse to enforce contracts that deviate from the market price or place risks and burdens on the party less able to bear them (Gordley, 2001: 310–23).

3.3 Implied Terms Reconsidered

The same question therefore arises whether rational parties with their eyes open are drafting terms for themselves, whether a court is implying terms to cover matters they did not deal with expressly, or whether a court is deciding whether the express terms are fair. The question is which party is best able to bear a risk or burden. Returning to the problem discussed earlier, we can now see a legitimate sense in which the implied terms of a contract are rooted in the will of the parties. They are the terms that fair-minded parties would want to govern their agreement. They would want these terms in the same sense that a car buyer who has never heard of a camshaft would want his car to have one. He wants the car to have whatever it needs to accomplish the purpose he consciously has in mind when he buys it (Gordley, 2001: 323–6).

3.4 Terms in 'Transactional' and 'Relational' Contracts

This analysis also shows what is the matter with a more radical approach urged by some scholars. They distinguish between 'transactional' contracts, in which the parties can realistically hope to deal with all contingencies in advance, and 'relational' contracts, in which they cannot. Typically, the former are short-term one-shot arrangements while the latter endure in time and govern an ongoing course of dealing. According to these scholars, 'classical' or traditional contract law was concerned with the former kind of arrangement, and needs considerable modification to deal successfully with the latter (Macneil, 1978). Nevertheless, rather than liberating us from 'classical' contract law, this approach perpetuates a narrow classical conception of will in which the will of the parties is deemed to include only those matters the parties consciously considered. The concept of 'transactional' contracts is based on such a conception. These scholars fail to suggest what conception of will or choice could work for 'relational contracts', or whether the problems of these contracts could really be solved without having such a conception of will.

4 CONSENT

4.1 Mistake and Unforeseen Circumstances

In the nineteenth and early twentieth centuries, common lawyers borrowed two doctrines which had long been familiar to Continental jurists: that a contract was not binding if the parties made a sufficiently important mistake, or if circumstances had sufficiently changed. At the same time, the common lawyers subscribed to the narrow conception of the will just mentioned. It included only those matters which the parties had consciously considered, and was distinguished sharply from whatever motives or considerations had led to this choice, and from the question of whether the choice was reasonable or fair. They had difficulty seeing what else the will could mean, and in any case, conceiving of the will in this way seemed consonant with their preference for strict law over considerations of equity. This narrow conception of the will made problems of mistake and changed circumstances intractable because these doctrines deal with situations the parties did not anticipate and as to which they could not have willed anything in this limited sense.

That these problems remain difficult can be seen by the efforts of leading authorities to deal with them. Treitel wants to solve both of them by asking how the parties would have identified the performance for which they were contracting. In the case of a mistake over whether a picture was a Rembrandt, would they have said, if asked immediately after contracting, that they had bought or sold 'a Rembrandt' or 'a picture' (Treitel, 1999: 676–78)? If the king's coronation processions are cancelled after a person has rented a flat to view them at a suitably enhanced price, is the contract 'on its true construction' one for 'the flat' or one for 'facilities for viewing the coronation processions' (Treitel, 1999: 824)? The trouble is, unless the criterion is to be the economic importance of the quality in question, the parties might have described the performance in either way. And if the criterion were its economic importance, any party could escape whenever the mistake was important economically.

The Restatement (Second) of Contracts asks whether the mistake or change of circumstances is contrary to a 'basic assumption' of the parties (§§ 152(1), 261). But what counts as a 'basic assumption'? According to the Official Comment, a party can make such an assumption without being consciously aware that he has done so (§ 152 Comment b). Moreover, his assumption may not be 'basic' even if the matter assumed were of great importance to him: for example, he will not get relief for a mistake about market conditions (ibid.). So we are left with the strange rule that the parties must have made an assumption, whether they consciously assumed anything or not, and that it must be basic, whether or not it is of great importance.

Atiyah believes these doctrines should be applied by asking what allocation of risk between the parties is reasonable (Atiyah, 1995: 226–7, 240–3), and that is the approach of scholars who take an economic approach to law (Posner, 1998: 114–21). Where it is clear the parties have made an agreement and the performance has merely become less valuable or more onerous than expected, this approach has merit for reasons already discussed. One can follow the same procedure as with any implied term of the contract by asking which party can best bear a risk or burden.

Nevertheless, it is hard to see how this approach will work when the question is whether the parties have made anything that can meaningfully be called an agreement. If a party ordered item 1152 in a catalog, thinking it is a bicycle pump, and it turns out to be a bird cage, he did not agree to buy a bird cage. It would not seem to matter if he happens to run a pet store and is in the best position to bear the risk of being stuck with one after it has been delivered. An earlier edition of Posner's *Economic Analysis of Law* illustrates the difficulty. Suppose a cow, which would have great value if she could be made to breed, is thought to be sterile but, in fact, is pregnant at the moment she is sold. In the earlier edition, Posner said that to ask which party can best bear the risk of the mistake 'in effect, decomposes the contract into two distinct agreements: an agreement respecting the basic performance (the transfer of the cow) and an agreement respecting a risk associated with the transfer (that the cow will turn out to be different from what the parties believed)' (Posner, 1977: 73–4). That is quite right, but why should we think that the parties agreed on the basic transaction of transferring the cow (be she sterile or pregnant) anymore than in the case of the catalog they agreed on transfer of item 1152 (be it a bicycle pump or a bird cage)? It seems, then, that we are inevitably forced to confront a question we do not know how to answer: when is it meaningful to say that the parties did agree? We are not likely to answer it until we have a considerably more sophisticated theory of consent.

4.2 Offer and Acceptance

In classical contract law, the parties were bound because they had given their consent. The consent of one party was the offer. That of the other was the acceptance. By definition, it seemed, a contract was binding as soon as an offer was accepted.

4.2.1 *Liability before Acceptance*

As conceptualism waned and scholars placed less emphasis on the will, they recognized that it is not a logical impossibility for the parties to be liable before an offer is accepted. Indeed, the law of Germany, France, Holland, and other civil law countries will now hold a party liable for failing to negotiate in good faith. His liability is regarded, sometimes as contractual, sometimes as delictual, and sometimes as *sui generis*. Nevertheless, neither English nor American law recognizes such a ground for liability. E. Allan Farnsworth has shown why it is not necessary to do so. He has noted that in three types of cases US courts will impose liability for conduct during negotiations. A party can be held liable who would otherwise be unjustly enriched, for example, when a secret formula has been confided to him which the other party wants him to buy. He can be held liable when he has misrepresented something, for example, when he has misrepresented his intention to contract. And he can be held liable when he has made a promise, for example, that if the other party incurs trouble and expense, he will receive a franchise (Farnsworth, 1999: 197–205). In fact, the vast bulk of continental cases of 'pre-contractual liability' are of these three types. But one hardly needs a new principle to justify holding people liable who are unjustly enriched, who misrepresent, or who break promises. Moreover, if a party never made a promise, never misrepresented anything including the likelihood that he would make a promise, and wasn't unjustly enriched, it is hard to see why he should be held liable. Farnsworth concludes he should not be.

4.2.2 *The Moment of Acceptance*

According to classical contract law, the parties should be bound as soon as they both consented, that is, as soon as an offer was accepted. Yet, in the nineteenth century, English courts hit on an apt rule as to when an offer was accepted that has little to do with consent. Before much theorizing had been done, they decided that an offer or its revocation were effective when the offeree received them, but the acceptance of an offer was effective when it was mailed (*Adams v Lindsell* 1 Barn. & Ald. 681 (KB 1818)). Later, some judges and scholars tried unsuccessfully to explain these rules by the requirement that both parties must consent. According to Thesiger, LJ, the parties had made the post office their common agent (*Household Fire & Carriage Acc Ins Co v Grant* 4 Exch Div 216 (1879)). Others merely accepted them as part of the case law. Today, there is fairly widespread agreement that these rules do make sense, not because of the need for mutual consent, but because of the desirability of protecting the offeree. He knows when he mails his acceptance that he has a contract (Farnsworth, 1999: 176–7). A similar solution has been adopted by the Unidroit Principles of International Commercial Contracts (art. 2.4(1)).

Less clear is why the offeree should be protected. Some have found no reason (Eisler, 1990–1: 566) or too many conflicting policies to justify the rule (MacNeil, 1964: 953). A good reason is that one of the parties must assume the burden of committing himself before he knows if the other party will. If the offeror is unwilling to do so, he can invite an offer on terms he proposes instead of making one himself. The offeree does not have this choice (Gordley, 1995: 608–9).

4.3 The Effect of a Writing

In contrast to doctrines of mistake, changed circumstances, and offer and acceptance, which were borrowed from Continental jurists, the problem of the effect of a writing was governed by a traditional common law rule. It excluded 'parol evidence' offered to prove that the parties had an understanding that contradicted, or, sometimes, one that added to the terms of a written document to which they had subscribed. 'Parol' evidence was evidence, whether written or oral, apart from the document itself. According to nineteenth and early twentieth-century writers such as Williston, the parol evidence rule rested on respect for the intentions of the parties. If they intended a document to be the final or the complete expression of their agreement, it should be treated as such. Moreover, the rule appealed to the courts' preference for hard-edged rules. The rule allowed the parties to govern their affairs by inserting hard-edged rules in a document and giving them final effect.

Beneath the surface, however, was a paradox, and one that has become the focus of contemporary controversy. As the English Law Commission put it, the rule seems 'no more than a circular statement'. For if the document was intended to contain terms that could not be contradicted or varied, evidence of other terms would be irrelevant if admitted since they would not form part of the contract, while the rule never excludes evidence of terms that were intended to be part of the contract (Law Commission Report on The Parol Evidence Rule, Law Com. no. 154, para. 2.7). Treitel's response is like Williston's. The rule is not circular because if the contract looks as though it was intended to be complete, the other party cannot introduce evidence to show it is not (Treitel, 1999: 177). But why not? If because the law presumes the parties intended these to be the only terms, we are still in the circle. If for some other reason, the rule does not rest on the parties' intent. In the United States, Judge Roger Traynor, following Arthur Corbin, concluded that because the rule rests on the intention of the parties, extrinsic evidence cannot be excluded merely because the contract looks complete. The extrinsic evidence must be considered to help determine whether the parties intended it to be complete (*Masterson v Sine*, 436 P 2d 561 (Cal 1968)). But then the rule seems to disappear. The underlying problem seems to have been accurately diagnosed by Calamari and Perillo. The parol evidence rule is not based on consent. It gives exclusive force to documents that look complete to promote the security of transactions and to avoid perjury even, in some cases, at the cost of injustice (Calimari and Perillo, 1967). Whether promotion of these objectives is worth the cost is another question.

4.4 The Battle of the Forms

Sometimes, one party responds to another's offer by expressing general agreement but varying the terms. One response to this problem is the so-called 'mirror image rule' which became accepted in England and entrenched in the United States. By this rule, the acceptance must exactly match the offer. If it does not, it is a rejection and a counter-offer. This rule appealed to the narrow conception of the will which then prevailed. If the offeree varied a single particular, how could one say he had agreed? It also appealed to the preference for hard-edged rules. The offeree had either agreed or not, and one could tell simply by inspecting the documents. The result, however, when the parties exchange forms, is that no contract is made until one of them begins performing and is therefore deemed to have accepted the other party's terms. The battle of the forms is won by whoever fires the last shot.

In the United States, under the Uniform Commercial Code, a contract is completed on the offeror's terms if the offeree signifies his acceptance but on terms which are materially different (§ 2-702(2)). In one English case, the court reached a similar result by holding that the sellers had accepted the buyer's terms even though, when they returned the buyer's tear-off slip, they did so with a letter insisting on their own terms (*Butler Machine Tool Co v Ex-Cell-O Corp* [1979] 1 WLR 401). The trouble is, if it is arbitrary for the victor to be whoever fires the last shot, it is equally arbitrary for him to be whoever fires the second to last.

Atiyah has accurately diagnosed the problem. When the parties start to perform, although they have not agreed on a single set of terms, they have in fact agreed on a contract but not on what all the terms of the contract should be (Atiyah, 1995: 69–70). Thus, the mirror image rule actually conflicts with the classical doctrine that what matters is the will of the parties. The better solution would be what has been called a 'knock out rule'. The parties should be bound by the terms to which they both agreed, and to such other terms as would be implied by law in the absence of agreement. American courts have applied this rule by ingenious manipulation of the Uniform Commercial Code (e.g. *Gardner Zemke Co v Dunham Bush, Inc* 850 P 2d 319 (New Mexico 1993)). It has been adopted by the Unidroit Principles of International Commercial Contracts (art. 2.22).

5   REMEDIES

The traditional role of courts of equity was to intervene when the common law courts could not give adequate relief. In *assumpsit*, the common law remedy was damages. Consequently, if damages were not an adequate remedy, equity would order specific performance, that is, it would order the party in breach to perform his promise. A typical case is when the performance is unique—land, or a painting—so that the buyer awarded a sum of money may be worse off than if he obtained it.

In the nineteenth and early twentieth centuries, it seemed axiomatic that a party should receive either what he was promised or the money to buy it. To enforce a contract meant to make sure that a party received what he had been promised. Beneath the surface, however, protection was sacrificed to the preference for hard-edged rules. Specific performance was denied when details of the performance promised were unclear. Damages were denied when they were difficult to compute or sought for emotional distress rather than financial harm. In the twentieth century, courts have been less insistent on hard-edged rules. At the same time, there has been more controversy about why the law gives the remedies it does.

Since the publication of a famous article by Lon Fuller and William Perdue (Fuller and Perdue, 1936), it has been fashionable to say that specific performance or awarding the amount of damages just described are two ways of protecting a party's 'expectation interest'. In contrast, a party's 'reliance interest' would be protected by placing him where he would have been had the contract not been made. His 'restitution interest' would be protected if he received the amount by which the other party had been enriched.

In dispute is why contract law normally protects the so-called 'expectation interest'. The reason suggested by Fuller and Perdue is that a party's reliance interest is often hard to measure. Some economists have suggested that protecting it gives a party the proper incentives to perform his contract (Posner, 1998: 130–3; Cooter and Ulen, 2000: 189–90). Suppose A will lose $5,000 if he performs but B will make a profit of $10,000. There is a net gain if the contract is performed and so breach would be 'inefficient'. Suppose, however, that A agreed to sell something worth $10,000 to B and then discovers C will pay $30,000 for it—far more than it is worth to B. It is now 'efficient' for A to breach. Of course, A could perform and B could resell to C but that, supposedly, involves additional transaction costs (Posner, 1998: 133). Consequently, if A is made to pay B's 'expectation interest', he will have the right incentives to decide whether to breach. One difficulty with this approach is that it is hard to see why the law makes A perform when goods are unique. In any event, other economists have found the problem to be more complex. Richard Craswell notes that to be efficient, the parties must also have the right incentives to ensure that performance will be possible and to minimize the costs of breach. No one measure of damages could get all the incentives right in every case (Craswell, 2000: 107–11).

Daniel Friedmann believes that the problem has been misanalyzed ever since Fuller and Perdue wrote. A party contracts in order to obtain the right to a certain performance. A court does not need any other justification for protecting this right except that it belongs to that party (Friedmann, 1995).

When a performance is unique—land, a painting, or the like—surely the parties themselves usually do think, as Friedmann says, that the buyer is acquiring a right to the object promised him. If that is so, then it is somewhat mysterious that economists cast about for some further reason he should receive it or think that a breach could be efficient. The parties understand that the buyer is acquiring the right, not only to use the object, but to resell it if someone like C appears on the scene. They would not agree to transfer title unless that right were worth more to *B* than *A*. It is hard to see, then, why it matters if *C* appears a bit earlier than expected. On the other hand, if a performance is not unique, normally it wouldn't matter to *B* who performs. Consequently, one cannot see why *B* would insist on the right to make *A* perform even if *A* unexpectedly finds performance difficult, a right for which he would have to pay *A* some extra amount in compensation. Friedmann would say in this situation as well, that *B* has a right to receive what he was promised, and, indeed, he does, for he can obtain it once *A* pays what Fuller and Perdue call 'expectation damages'. But we can see why, in this situation, he should not have the right to force the other party to perform. The law will merely give him damages. The question of what remedy to give is therefore like that of which terms to imply in a contract. Friedmann is correct that what matters is what rights the parties meant to convey. But that question should be analyzed by asking what disposition they would have made for themselves at the time they contracted.

This analysis suggests that a court should not always award so-called 'expectation damages'. Suppose that a customer cancels his reservation; the restaurant has time to offer his table to others but no one wants it. Or suppose that the customer of a retail boat store cancels his order before delivery and that the boat, on order for him from the manufacturer, is sold to someone else (*Neri v Retail Marine Corp.* 285 NE 2d 311 (NY 1972)). If expectation damages are awarded, the restaurant will recover the amount of the profit it would have made on its customer's meal; the boat store will recover the extra profit it would have made by selling two boats instead of one. Supposedly, they can do so under English and American law (see also UCC § 2-708(2)). But as Atiyah notes, it is hard to see why they should. These are not cases in which the point of contracting in advance was to transfer the risk that prices would rise or fall (Atiyah, 1995: 445). Moreover, the restaurant or the boat store will not incur any extra cost if their customers have the right to cancel. The customers may incur costs if they do not have the right to do so. If, as suggested, risks and burdens should be placed where they can most easily be borne, the customers ought to have this right.

6 Conclusion

Speaking of the demise of classical contract law, Grant Gilmore said: 'The systems have come unstuck, and we see presently, no way of glueing them back together again' (Gilmore, 1974: 102). In one sense, the systems remain unstuck. Classical contract law has not been replaced by a generally accepted theoretical account of contract law. Work on such an account has proceeded from quite different directions: for Fried, from the concept of consent; for the law and economics scholars, from that of efficiency; for Peter Benson and Ernest Weinrib, from the philosophy of Hegel; for Gordley, from the concept of commutative justice. Nevertheless, surveying the work of scholars in the quarter-century since Gilmore wrote, one is struck by the progress that has been made toward understanding a range of specific legal problems even in the absence of a generally accepted theory of what contract law is all about.

REFERENCES

Atiyah, P. S. (1995). *An Introduction to the Law of Contract* (5th edn.), Oxford: Clarendon Press.

Barnett, R. (1992). 'The Sound of Silence: Default Rules and Contractual Consent', *Virginia Law Review*, 78: 821–911.

Benson, P. (2001). 'The Unity of Contract Law', in P. Benson (ed.), *The Theory of Contract Law: New Essays*, Cambridge: Cambridge University Press, 118–205.

Calimari, J. D., and Perillo, J. M. (1967). 'A Plea for a Uniform Parole Evidence Rule and Principles of Interpretation', *Indiana Law Review*, 42: 333–54.

Cooter, R., and Ulen, T. (2000). *Law and Economics* (3rd edn.), Reading, Mass.: Addison-Wesley.

Craswell, R. (1993). 'Property Rules and Liability Rules in Unconscionability and Related Doctrines', *University of Chicago Law Review*, 60: 1–65.

—— (2000). 'Against Fuller & Perdue', *University of Chicago Law Review*, 67: 99–161.

Eisenberg, M. A. (1982). 'The Principles of Consideration', *Cornell Law Quarterly*, 67: 640–65.

—— (2001). 'The Theory of Contracts', in P. Benson (ed.), *The Theory of Contract Law: New Essays*, Cambridge: Cambridge University Press, 223–64.

Eisler, B. A. (1990–1). 'Default Rules for Contract Formation by Promise and the Need for Revision of the Mailbox Rule', *Kentucky Law Review*, 79: 557–83.

Farber, D. A., and Matheson, J. H. (1985). 'Beyond Promissory Estoppel: Contract Law and the "Invisible Handshake"', *University of Chicago Law Review*, 52: 903–47.

Farnsworth, E. A. (1995). 'Promises to Make Gifts', *American Journal of Comparative Law*, 43: 359–78.

—— (1999). *Contracts* (3rd edn.), New York: Aspen Publishers.

Fried, C. (1981). *Contract as Promise: A Theory of Contractual Obligation*, Cambridge, Mass.: Harvard University Press.

Friedmann, D. (1995). 'The Performance Interest in Contract Damages', *Law Quarterly Review*, 111: 628–54.

Fuller, L. L., and Perdue, W. R. (1936). 'The Reliance Interest in Contract Damages', *Yale Law Journal*, 46: 52–96, 373–420.

Gilmore, G. (1974). *The Death of Contract*, Columbus, Oh.: Ohio State University Press.

Gordley, J. (1995). 'Enforcing Promises', *University of California Law Review*, 83: 547–614.

—— (2001). 'Contract Law in the Aristotelian Tradition', in P. Benson (ed.), *The Theory of Contract Law: New Essays*, Cambridge: Cambridge University Press, 265–334.

Holmes, O. W., Jr. (1881). *The Common Law*, Boston: Little, Brown & Co.

Macneil, I. R. (1964). 'Time of Acceptance: Too Many Problems for a Single Rule', *University of Pennsylvania Law Review*, 112: 947–79.

Macneil, I. R. (1978). 'Contracts: Adjustment of Long-Term Economic Relations under Classical, Neoclassical and Relational Contract Law', *Northwestern University Law Review*, 72: 854–901.

Pollock, F. (1876). *Principles of Contract* (1st edn.); (1936) (10th edn.), London: Stevens & Sons.

Posner, R. A. (1977). *Economic Analysis of Law* (2nd edn.), Boston: Little, Brown & Co (1998) (5th edn.), New York: Aspen Publishers.

Simpson, A. W. B. (1975). 'Innovation in Nineteenth Century Contract Law', *Law Quarterly Review*, 91: 247–78.

Slawson, W. D. (1996). *Binding Promises: The Late Twentieth Century Reformation of Contract Law*, Princeton: Princeton University Press.

Trebilcock, M. J. (1993). *The Limits of Freedom of Contract*, Cambridge, Mass.: Harvard University Press.

Treitel, G. H. (1999). *The Law of Contract* (10th edn.), London: Sweet & Maxwell.

Weinrib, E. J. (1995). *The Idea of Private Law*, Cambridge, Mass.: Harvard University Press.

Williston, S. (1920). *The Law of Contracts*, New York: Baker, Voorhis & Co.

CHAPTER 2

TORT

JOHN C. P. GOLDBERG

1 INTRODUCTION

1.1 Redress and Regulation

THE word 'tort', like the word 'torque', derives from a Latin root that means 'twisted'. Early English common lawyers sometimes spoke of situations as being 'atort'. Through this locution, they conveyed several related ideas: a person had acted in a manner lacking *rectitude* (in contravention of standards of *right* conduct); another person had suffered an invasion of his *rights*; that other person, or something of his, was no longer *all right*; accordingly, he was entitled to have the situation set *aright*. In this view, the law of torts, which afforded individuals access to courts and, if successful there, monetary damages, was conceived as a means by which a person who is wrongfully injured by another could obtain redress for that wrong and that injury.

In the eighteenth century, jurists began to carve up the civil side of law into now-familiar substantive departments such as tort, property, and contract. Since that time, the terms 'tort' and 'torts' have increasingly been used by lawyers in a more specific sense, namely, to refer to various civil causes of action by which individuals may seek legal remedies for injuries caused to them by others. This collection includes actions for Assault, Battery, Conversion, Defamation, Defective Products (Products Liability), Fraud, Intentional Infliction of Emotional Distress, Intentional

I wish to thank Professors Homer Goldberg, Richard Nagareda, Anthony Sebok, and Benjamin Zipursky for providing numerous helpful comments on drafts of this chapter.

Interference with Contract, Invasion of Privacy, Malicious Prosecution, Negligence, Negligent Misrepresentation, Nuisance, and Trespass to Property.

Scholars writing in the nineteenth century were, for the most part, content to produce taxonomic works that demarcated the elements of, and defenses to, the tort causes of action. However, starting in the 1870s, jurists, including Oliver Wendell Holmes, Jr. and Sir Frederick Pollock, commenced more ambitious efforts to analyze tort's place within Anglo-American law. These efforts coincided with the emergence of industrial accidents, particularly workplace and railroad accidents, as a significant social and political problem. As a result, modern tort scholarship was at its inception devoted largely to analyzing how tort law responds, or ought to respond, to injuries caused *accidentally*, rather than intentionally or knowingly. This emphasis on accidental torts—a category that includes not only workplace mishaps, but slips-and-falls, professional malpractice, vehicle collisions, injuries caused by defective products, and so on—would remain characteristic of torts scholarship throughout the twentieth century.

Given this focus on accidentally-caused injuries, as opposed to injuries arising from more culpable conduct such as intentional wrongdoing, it is not surprising to find that much of modern tort scholarship has aimed to recast the field in a manner that de-emphasizes the common lawyers' notions of wrongdoing and personal redress. Instead, starting with Holmes, scholars have tended to regard tort law as a means by which government deters, and compensates victims of, conduct that is regulated not because it is wrong, but because it is socially undesirable: against the public interest. In this 'regulatory' conception, the function of substantive tort rules is the same as that of traffic ordinances or legislative and administrative safety standards. Tort differs only in that the 'fine' or 'tax' for misconduct is paid to the victim, rather than the government.

As explained more fully in the remainder of this section and Section 2, the Holmesian conception of tort law as accident law, and accident law as a form of regulatory law, dominated twentieth-century tort scholarship. American and Commonwealth judges, however, have never fully accepted it. Moreover, in the last twenty-five years, some tort scholars have sought to revitalize the older common law conception of tort as a law of personal redress for mistreatment by others. For reasons now to be examined, this debate between the regulatory and redress models of tort has largely played itself out as a debate over the proper characterization of one particular tort, namely, the tort of negligence.

1.2 Negligence and Strict Liability

As Holmes framed it, the central issue raised by the application of tort law to accidents concerned the governing liability standard. Specifically, the law faced a fundamental policy choice as to whether, as a threshold matter, the injured victim of an accident (*V*) who seeks compensation from another (*I*) for having caused the accident must establish that the injurer, *I*, was careless, or whether it was enough to show simply that *I*'s conduct played some role in bringing about the accident. The latter constitutes a rule of *strict liability*, under which *I* is held liable even if she took reasonable care to avoid the accident. The former sets a standard of *fault*, under which liability attaches only if the injury was caused by carelessness on *I*'s part.

Reviewing the leading English and American precedents, Holmes concluded that Anglo-American judges—with an important exception, and an important qualification—had consistently settled on fault as a threshold for the imposition of tort liability. Ordinarily, an actor could not be held liable unless he caused injury to another through a failure to exercise reasonable care (Holmes, 1923).

The exception to this rule was found in the continued vitality of the ancient doctrine of *respondeat superior* ('let the master answer'), under which even an employer who carefully screens and monitors employee behavior is held liable for injuries caused by the faulty acts of its employees undertaken within the scope of their employment (ibid. 16–17). (Whether rightly characterized as a doctrine of strict liability, or as a doctrine of agency by which acts are attributed to entities such as corporations, *respondeat superior* continues to provide the primary device through which tort victims obtain access to corporate assets.) The qualification to the rule concerned the legal definition of fault, which, Holmes insisted, is 'objective' rather than 'subjective' (ibid. 107–10). Under this standard, a person could be held to have acted 'unreasonably', in the legal sense, even if he had done his very best not to injure others. The legal metric of due care was set by the care that an 'ordinary' or 'reasonable' person would exercise under the circumstances, not by the capacities of the individual defendant.

Holmes attached huge significance to his 'discovery' that liability for the typical modern tort hinges on the objective fault standard. Indeed, it signaled to him that modern tort law, although it retained the shell of its pre-modern ancestors, was an altogether different creature. In its earliest, ancient incarnations, tort functioned to keep the peace by providing an avenue through which victims of injuries could satisfy their instinctual cravings for vengeance against their injurers. Strict liability was suited to this original mission, because, according to Holmes, the men of that time were superstitious enough to blame even inanimate objects for harms. This revealed a world-view in which the mere causing of injury was itself sufficient to generate a feeling in the victim of violation, and of an entitlement to avenge the injury.

As superstitions waned, Holmes argued, courts began to develop and apply the fault standard as they sought to define a role for tort law more appropriate to a modern state. Consciously or not, they converted tort law from a law of vengeance into regulatory law through which the state achieved certain policy goals. Specifically, they identified a standard of conduct that would permit a broad realm of free action, even action that risked harm to others, but would compensate those who suffer bodily harm and property damage by conduct that poses excessive risks (ibid. 144). For this task, a fault standard was required. The old rule of strict liability threatened to make conduct too expensive, and thereby to inhibit unduly freedom of action and productive activity (ibid. 95–6). Moreover, according to Holmes, the fault standard had to be an objective one. The state could not set rational policy by means of a standard of careful conduct that fluctuated with the capacities and mental states of each individual actor.

In sum, Holmes associated the redress conception of tort with a superstitious notion of vengeance that expressed itself in the principle of strict liability. By contrast, he linked his regulatory conception of tort to the modern, amoralistic idea that government ought to pursue broadly accepted public policy goals. In turn, he concluded that the pursuit of these goals demands the abandonment of strict liability and the adoption of the objective fault standard. These conclusions reflected in part Holmes's acceptance of nineteenth-century liberal-individualist conceptions of the limited role for government. Likewise, his argument that negligence law had to be understood as judicial regulation heralded the emergence of Legal Realism, a jurisprudence which conjoined skepticism about the meaningfulness of legal concepts, particularly concepts referencing moral notions such as rights and wrongs, with a belief that judges could settle on rules that, in the aggregate, promoted the policies undergirding modern law.

Although Holmes's regulatory model would dominate torts scholarship for the next century, his linkage of that model to the fault standard and to a strongly individualistic form of liberalism soon came to be questioned by progressive, socialist and other scholars who argued for more aggressive state regulation of individual conduct. As applied to torts, the progressive critique focused on the ways in which a fault-based regime severely handicapped workers in their efforts to obtain compensation for workplace injuries. First, they were required to hire a lawyer, and to prove 'fault' on the part of the employer. (The plaintiff would usually prove faulty conduct by a fellow employee, whose carelessness would then be charged to the employer via *respondeat superior*.) Also, they would have to overcome various defenses that were sometimes interpreted generously by judges in favor of employers. To take an extreme example, a worker's suit might be barred on grounds of 'contributory negligence' or 'assumption of risk', merely because he continued to show up to work notwithstanding his awareness of the workplace hazard that generated his injury. For these reasons, negligence law tended to permit businesses to fob off a major 'cost' of their business—workplace injuries—onto less well-off workers and their families.

Many progressive scholars argued that a rule of strict liability would correct for this unfairness, and that businesses would not be unduly burdened by such a rule because they could spread the cost of compensating injured workers through liability insurance or small price increases paid by the consuming public. Their campaign was quite successful. Worker-compensation systems were widely adopted through legislation in American and Commonwealth jurisdictions. In removing claims by workers against employers from the jurisdiction of the common law, these schemes imposed strict liability on employers in place of the fault standard, but only on the condition that employers would pay pre-determined damages rather than full compensatory damages awarded on a case-by-case basis.

In the 1940s and 1950s, the progressive critique of negligence as cumbersome, wasteful, and unfair would again be wielded by scholars, this time with regard to the burgeoning realm of automobile accidents. In this context, scholars and commissions designed various 'no fault' first-party and third-party insurance schemes, versions of which were adopted by most of the American states so as to supplant wholly or partially the common law of negligence (Blum and Kalven, 1965: 3–9). Later scholars argued that the experiences of workers' compensation and automobile no-fault schemes logically pointed toward the ultimate goal of replacing the tort system altogether with a general accident fund (Atiyah, 1970). Such a fund would be supported by tax revenues, and would provide need-based compensation to the injured without lawyers, without an inquiry into fault, and with a minimum of bureaucracy. Except in New Zealand, however, this vision of an injury-compensation scheme, completely divorced from the traditional tort inquiry into whether a particular person (or persons) should be held responsible to compensate, has not been realized.

Scholarship advocating workers' compensation, no-fault automobile insurance, and accident funds essentially took it for granted that these schemes, because they departed from the common law's negligence regime, ought to come about through legislative action. In the 1950s and 1960s, however, the supremacy of negligence was challenged from within the domain of the common law itself, this time with respect to injuries caused by mass-produced consumer products. Legal scholars and jurists, including Fleming James, Jr., and Justice Roger Traynor of the California Supreme Court, argued that consumers injured by occasional-yet-inevitable glitches in assembly-line production processes (e.g. soda bottles that were overcharged or contaminated by foreign objects) were no less burdened by the negligence system than workers injured on the job. It was difficult for them to prove that some alternative and safer manufacturing method would have avoided the harm. Moreover, these injury costs could also be treated as a cost of doing business to be shifted from the victim and spread through liability insurance or price increases. Finally, given imbalances in information and power between large manufacturing firms and individual consumers, it was widely thought unfair to permit manufacturers to limit their liability by contract: all products should instead be understood as bearing an un-waivable implied warranty of fitness (*Henningsen v Bloomfield Motors, Inc*, 32 NJ 358 (1960)).

Again, the most novel feature of the scholarly push for strict products liability was not the rationales employed to support it, but the idea that such significant law reform should be undertaken by courts. Yet, under the influence of section 402A of the American Law Institute's Second Restatement of Torts (authored by Dean William Prosser), and Justice Traynor's landmark concurring opinion in *Escola v*

Coca-Cola (24 Cal 3d 453 (1944)), every American jurisdiction would soon adopt the implied warranty/strict liability regime for products liability (Prosser (1966)).

By 1970, then, negligence and strict liability had achieved in US common law a condition of peaceful coexistence through territorial division among types of accident. Strict liability governed injuries caused by product defects (as well as those caused by certain unusually risky activities, such as blasting). The tort of negligence was left to govern all other unintentionally caused injuries still within the purview of the common law. In contrast to their US counterparts, Commonwealth courts clung more steadfastly to notions of warranty and negligence in the area of products liability. However, with the passage in 1985 of the EC Directive on Products Liability, British and other Commonwealth jurisdictions moved substantially toward the American model, although some important differences remain (Stapleton, 1994: 37–66). The timing of that shift carries with it a certain irony. As discussed below, by this time, American scholars and courts were rethinking whether liability for product-related injuries ought to be strict.

2 MODERN NEGLIGENCE SCHOLARSHIP

Even granted the adoption, at least for a time, of strict products liability, the tort of negligence has dominated the modern torts landscape and modern tort scholarship, which has primarily been concerned to analyze its content and operation. This scholarship has been particularly occupied with two issues. The first concerns the content of the fault standard itself. Fault or carelessness has long been identified as standing at an intermediate point between two other liability standards: the standard of strict liability and that of intentional wrongdoing. The question is whether its content can be further specified. Secondly, there remain the various other doctrines that adorn the negligence tort. Indeed, as courts have traditionally formulated it, the tort of negligence contains four 'elements' that must be made out by a plaintiff seeking recovery: (1) duty; (2) breach; (3) actual and proximate cause; and (4) injury. (Confusingly, the breach element is sometimes also referred to as the 'negligence' issue. This chapter uses 'negligence' to refer to the four-element tort, and 'fault' or 'carelessness' to refer to the breach element.) Moreover, claims of negligence are subject to various affirmative defenses. What role do these other elements and defenses play in the operation of the negligence tort? For the most part, scholars have pursued these two questions from within the Holmesian or regulatory framework. Recently, however, a minority have argued that the difficulties Holmesians have faced in tackling these questions suggest the need for a fundamental reorientation that, to some extent, points back to a redress conception of tort.

Contrary to Holmes's equation of redress with crude vengeance and strict liability, these modern redress theories maintain that a tort law built around the tort of negligence *can* function as a law of personal redress for wrongs.

2.1 What is Fault?

Beyond connecting fault to the twin goals of liberty and compensation, Holmes was not much concerned to specify its content. Rather, he seems to have assumed that judges would, over time, provide relatively clear directives as to the care expected of classes of actors in recurrent situations. For example, a car driver approaching a railroad crossing with an obstructed view would be required to stop, get out, and reconnoiter, on pain of being found contributorily negligent if struck by a speeding train and thus barred from recovering from the railroad (*Baltimore & OR Co v Goodman*, 275 US 66 (1927) (Holmes, J.)).

   The next generation of scholars working within the negligence paradigm devoted more attention to fleshing out the concept of fault. In doing so, they moved to an explicitly utilitarian conception. Dean Prosser, for example, following the lead of earlier scholars such as Francis Bohlen and Henry Terry, argued that the reasonableness standard calls on the jury or judge to weigh the magnitude of the risk of loss posed by the actor's conduct against the benefits of that conduct. On this account, loss and benefit are to be measured in terms of the costs to society of particular harms and the value of particular activities. So, for example, the operation of commercial railroad trains at a typical rate of speed, say 30 m.p.h., would usually be deemed not at fault, even though such conduct often produced injuries, because these losses are 'more than counterbalanced by the service which [the trains] render to the public' (Restatement (Second) of Torts § 292, comment a). In principle, the fault standard thus defined, by penalizing conduct that does more harm than good, will promote the greatest welfare of the greatest number by permitting conduct whose aggregate benefits to society outweigh its costs.

   Subsequent scholars began developing a related, yet distinctive, deterrence-based account of fault, one tied not to utilitarianism but to microeconomics. According to this camp, led by Judge Richard Posner, the utilitarian approach asks too much of judges and juries because it requires them to guess as to whether particular activities and risks work to the net benefit of society. For example, they must somehow decide whether society is better off—happier—having slower-moving trains or more injuries and deaths from train accidents. Given the impossibility of making such judgments, judges and juries cannot help but read into the law their own biases as to what is good for society. Implicit in this critique was the sense that judges and juries in the 1960s were too keen to find fault, and hence apt to overdeter productive activity on the basis of subjective assessments of utility.

What was needed, then, was a method for balancing gains and losses that, while retaining utilitarianism's focus on aggregate social goods, was more disciplined and less reliant on value-laden judgments about the net contribution to general welfare of particular activities. The proffered solution was to conceive of fault in economic terms (Posner, 1972). On this view, the fault inquiry concerns whether the monetary cost of precautions that would have prevented plaintiff's injury is less than the monetary value of the losses that the absence of those precautions were expected to generate at the time the decision was made not to take them. If so, the defendant acted 'carelessly' in that he failed to take a precaution that would have used fewer resources than one would have expected to use if it were not taken. Under this conception, the fault standard imposes liability in a manner that, in principle, will maximize societal *wealth*, as opposed to utility or happiness. According to Posner, Judge Learned Hand had already hit upon the economic conception of fault in a 1947 admiralty case (*United States v Carroll Towing Co*, 159 F 2d 169 (2d Cir 1947)), in which Hand noted that fault could be algebraically presented as posing the issue of whether the burden (cost) of precaution (B) was less than the probable losses ($P \times L$) flowing from the absence of the precaution.

More recently, scholars have questioned whether the 'balancing' called for under the fault standard is best captured by either utilitarian or wealth-maximizing principles. Reconnecting fault to notions of wrongdoing, they argue that the fault standard aims to balance the rights of citizens to liberty and bodily security, and that fault is best understood as mediating the conflicting demands of justice by reconciling these basic goods. In this view, like the utilitarian view, courts must be in the business of evaluating the relative 'worth' of the activities in question, not simply their dollar value. The economic approach is therefore rejected because it entitles actors to disregard the well-being of others simply because it is more expensive to society to take steps to avoid injuring them than to cause them injury. But, in contrast to the utilitarian approach, the 'worth' of activities and losses is determined not by an aggregate welfare measure, but by the degree to which they figure (or do not figure) as part of a just distribution of rights. So, imagine a case in which overall utility would be promoted, or societal wealth maximized, by not installing view-inhibiting screens or walls at baseball stadiums or cricket pitches to prevent injuries caused by batted balls. On a justice-based conception of fault, stadium owners might be found at fault for failing to take even precautions that are not utility-maximizing or cost-minimizing given the relative unimportance of cheaper and less-fettered access to sport as compared to the weightier right to security from physical injury (Keating, 1996).

Finally, it is worth noting the existence of an important, somewhat skeptical current in tort scholarship as to the possibility of specifying the content of the fault standard. Here, the reasonable person determination must be understood as a 'black box'—a hidden decision-making process that takes place in the mind of the judge, or the jury's deliberation room (Green, 1928). Fault, on this view, is what the judge or jury says it is. This is not necessarily to condemn use of the fault standard. It may be, for example, that the decisional space created by the fault standard has the healthy effect of permitting judges and juries to introduce tacit knowledge, common sense, or ordinary morality into the legal process. That this process cannot be reduced to anything other than a capacious standard such as the reasonable person formula may set a limit on the ability of scholars to provide an abstract account of fault, but does not necessarily point to a deficiency in the operation of the law itself.

2.2 The Other Elements of Negligence

To say that fault ought to set the threshold for tort liability for accidentally caused harms is to say that it is a *necessary* condition of liability, not that it is *sufficient*. In fact, as it has existed since Holmes's time, the negligence tort contained various restrictions that barred a plaintiff from recovering even when he could locate an at-fault defendant. First, of course, he had to prove that the faulty conduct functioned as a cause of his injury: if a surgeon carelessly failed to sterilize his instruments, yet the patient suffered no infection, then the physician's carelessness would not provide the basis for a tort cause of action. Secondly, the plaintiff had to run the gauntlet of *duty* and *proximate cause*, as well as affirmative defenses such as *contributory negligence* and common law *immunities*.

As explained below, Holmesian scholars have, until recently, assumed that the actual causation element fits comfortably within their conception of the negligence tort as setting a regulatory standard. By contrast, they have been highly suspicious of the other elements, which they regard as vestiges from tort law's moralistic and formalistic past. Accordingly, they have sought either to critique them as empty adornments to the core elements of breach and cause, or to recast them, as referencing certain policy considerations that have nothing to do with notions of 'duty' or 'proximity' as those words are used in ordinary discourse. This section will turn first to the Holmesian critique and reconstruction of duty and proximate cause, then to an analysis of the actual cause element. Along the way it will also elaborate briefly the minority position, here labeled the 'Cardozoan' view. This camp maintains that Holmesians have failed to give an adequate account of the duty, cause, and proximate cause elements, and that a more adequate account is available within a modernized redress conception of tort.

2.2.1 *Duty and Proximate Cause*

In various classes of negligence suits, courts would dismiss claims even against at-fault defendants whose faulty conduct caused injury to the plaintiff on the ground that the defendant owed no duty to take care not to injure them. Infamously, prior to 1916, manufacturers were often freed of liability to consumers injured by carelessly made products on the supposition that they owed no duty of care to persons who obtained the product through middlemen rather than directly from them (the so-called 'privity' rule). Likewise, landowners who were at fault for not correcting dangerous conditions on their properties were often deemed not liable to persons injured by these conditions if the persons were deemed mere 'trespassers' or 'licensees', as opposed to 'invitees'. In addition, plaintiffs complaining of carelessness causing certain types of injury, particularly emotional distress unaccompanied by physical injury, as well as pure economic loss (loss of profits and business opportunities, rather than damage to tangible property), were denied recovery on the grounds that defendants had no duties to take care to prevent these sorts of injuries. Finally, the common law severely limited the circumstances under which an actor could be held liable for failing to fulfill an affirmative duty to render aid or rescue. Even a person so indecent as not to lift a finger to aid a drowning man would not be held liable in negligence, so long as he had nothing to do with creating the peril in the first place.

Other negligence plaintiffs lost because the defendant's fault was held to be too remote from the plaintiff's injuries and thus not a proximate cause of those injuries. Suppose, for example, a defendant drove carelessly, barely avoiding impact with the plaintiff, thereby causing her severe emotional distress, which in turn caused her a physical injury, such as a miscarriage or a heart attack. Late nineteenth- and early twentieth-century courts tended to deny recovery in such cases on proximate cause grounds. Even if one might have expected a person to suffer such an injury in response to the trauma of nearly being run down, because the injury only occurred *indirectly*, through the murky medium of the plaintiff's nervous system, it was deemed 'too remote' from defendant's faulty conduct to count as a legally cognizable consequence of that conduct. Still other plaintiffs' suits were barred under the rule of contributory negligence, which held that *any* carelessness on the part of the plaintiff that contributed to her injuries entirely barred an action against even a comparatively more careless defendant. Claims were also denied on the ground that certain defendants such as government actors, charitable institutions, and family members enjoyed common law immunity for their careless and injurious acts.

Holmes himself, although skeptical that the concepts of duty and proximate cause did any work in justifying these exceptions, did not object to their substance. Indeed, he thought they were sound as a matter of policy. However, progressive Holmesians subsequently condemned them as both unjustified and regressive. Duty and proximate cause, they maintained, were 'labels' behind which reactionary judges could hide politically motivated decisions to limit recoveries for workers and consumers in the name of protecting businesses and the wealthy. During the period 1915–75 courts and legislatures followed the lead of the progressive critics by removing or pruning many of these doctrinal limits. The privity rule for claims of negligence against product manufacturers was eliminated in the leading cases of *MacPherson v Buick*

(217 NY 382 (1916)) and *Donoghue v Stevenson* ([1932] AC 562). In many jurisdictions, persons injured while on another's premises were made eligible to recover in negligence without regard to their legal status as entrants on the property. Courts also recognized new claims for negligence causing pure emotional distress and economic loss, in part by expanding the concept of proximate cause to encompass the class of reasonably foreseeable harms caused by a negligent act, rather than the harms 'directly' caused by that act. Courts and legislatures abolished contributory negligence in favor of comparative responsibility, under which fault on the part of the plaintiff may reduce, but will not bar, plaintiff's recovery. Likewise, they abolished or waived many of the common law immunities. A handful even recognized liability for breach of affirmative duties to rescue.

These developments seemed to herald a day when negligence would attain a purer form, under which a defendant would be deemed prima facie liable to any injured plaintiff so long as two elements could be proved: (1) the defendant engaged in careless conduct; and (2) the careless conduct actually caused some injury to the plaintiff. (Some versions of this formulation add a third element, namely, that the injury must have been a foreseeable (possible) consequence of the defendant's careless conduct. However, this use of foreseeability adds nothing. To say that injury is not a foreseeable consequence of the defendant's being careless is simply to say that the defendant could not possibly be found to have acted carelessly under the circumstances: one cannot be careless with respect to a risk that no one would recognize as a possibility at the time of acting (Holmes, 1923: 95–6)).

And so, in the 1960s and 1970s, decisions such as *Rowland v Christian* (70 Cal Rptr 97 (1968)), issued by the influential California Supreme Court, seemed to herald the arrival of the pure, two-element negligence cause of action in place of the traditional four-element tort. Similarly, in *Anns v London Borough of Merton* ([1977] 2 All ER 492), Lord Wilberforce declared that, prima facie, liability would attach to any faulty conduct that (foreseeably) caused harm to another.

Many late-twentieth-century tort scholars have happily charted and advocated this expansionary trend toward a 'pure' fault principle or a 'full' regime of negligence. As Holmesians, they view the traditional restrictions on the reach of negligence set by 'duty', 'proximate cause', and other doctrines as dysfunctional vestiges of tort law's past: arid concepts, the substance of which consists merely of whatever nineteenth-century judges read into them. Once Holmes placed negligence on its new, policy-oriented footing, they argue, it was inevitable that judges and legislatures would push it toward its pure form. For, cleansed of these doctrinal impurities, negligence law becomes nicely aligned with its twin regulatory functions: it will issue sanctions against all—but only all—unreasonable conduct, on the one hand, and compensate all victims of that conduct, on the other (G. Schwartz, 1992).

The general run of modern negligence scholarship has thus been concerned to chart or advocate the various doctrinal developments that, cumulatively, seem to point toward the implementation of a full negligence regime. However, this scholarship has also had to acknowledge that, in certain areas, courts continue to balk at the unfettered operation of the pure fault principle. Most courts remain reluctant to enforce affirmative duties to rescue. Likewise, although they have permitted a broader range of claims for negligence causing emotional distress and pure economic loss, they continue to impose limits on these claims not imposed on claims for negligence causing physical injury. Thus, in many courts, a plaintiff complaining of emotional distress is required to establish either that she was physically endangered by the defendant's faulty conduct (e.g., subjected to a near-miss by defendant's negligent driving), or that she was caused by the defendant's carelessness to witness a loved one being seriously injured or killed. Likewise, courts hold that a plaintiff complaining of pure economic loss must demonstrate that the defendant had, with respect to particular plaintiffs, 'assumed responsibility' for any such losses caused by its careless conduct (Cane, 1997: 164). So, if a shipowner were negligently to pilot his ship into a local bridge, cutting off traffic in the area for a week, thereby disrupting businesses whose suppliers and customers relied on the bridge, the shipowner typically is not held liable to those businesses for their lost profits, notwithstanding that such lost profits were a foreseeable consequence of the careless operation of a ship in the area.

In sum, modern courts have stopped short of fully implementing the two-element fault principle. As a result, modern commentators cannot simply explain these away as vestiges of pre-modern, 'formalist' thinking about negligence. Instead, they are obligated, as an interpretive and evaluative matter, to make sense of these exceptions in terms consistent with the Holmesian conception of negligence. In the language of the California Supreme Court in *Rowland*, and Lord Wilberforce in *Anns*, they are required to consider whether and when exceptions to the pure fault regime in particular areas are warranted, not for unsound formalistic or reactionary reasons, but for sound reasons of 'public policy'.

Although scholars have identified a 'menu' of such considerations (Stapleton, 1998), the most frequently identified of these policy concerns are a first-order concern over crushing liability, and second-order considerations of administrability. With respect to affirmative misconduct, causing physical injury, there are no special policy considerations at work: the universe of physical injury is relatively self-contained, and hence the pure version of the negligence tort may safely be given free reign. By contrast, emotional distress is supposed to be more easily triggered and potentially widespread. Likewise, as the boat/bridge example suggests, the economic ripple effects of a given accident may be vast. In these cases, permitting the operation of a pure fault system would impose overwhelming and disproportionate liability on actors. A negligent driver would find himself liable to each member of an extended family emotionally devastated by his running down of their loved one. (Perhaps if the event were caught on tape, he would be potentially liable to viewers horrified by seeing the incident on the local news.) The negligent shipowner would find himself liable to an entire community of businesses, their suppliers, and so forth. For the same reasons, claims for these sorts of injuries threaten to flood or overwhelm the courts with litigation and hence need to be contained through doctrinal limitations to recovery. Also, because emotional distress is sometimes less objectively verifiable than physical injuries, recognition of these claims poses the risk of encouraging 'fraudulent' suits. Invocations of policy concerns such as floodgates and fraud are thus the means by which most modern negligence scholars reconcile the fault principle with the continued presence of pockets in which no liability attaches to faulty conduct causing harm. *In principle*, accidents causing harms ought ordinarily be governed by the pure, two-element version of the negligence tort; *in practice*, special policy considerations sometimes warrant ad hoc exceptions to a pure fault regime.

Notwithstanding its popularity among academics, this reconstruction of modern negligence law has never taken hold in the majority of courts. Indeed, many courts have rejected this account of the case law. Most conspicuously, the House of Lords and other Commonwealth courts have renounced Lord Wilberforce's *Anns* opinion in favor of the traditional four-element formulation (*Caparo Industries plc v Dickman* [1990] 1 All ER 569, 573–4). The vast majority of American courts likewise continue to treat elements such as 'duty' as if they have content of their own (Goldberg and Zipursky, 2001).

Although Holmesians are scornful of the courts for their continued recalcitrance, recent scholarship suggests that there may be sound pragmatic and philosophical bases for this judicial reluctance to embrace the fault principle. Pragmatically, as we have seen, the Holmesian approach strips the negligence tort down to the two elements of breach and cause, then relies on the blunderbuss concept of policy to carve out exceptions for which there is no liability despite the existence of breach and causation. Arguably, such a spare description of negligence leaves judges and juries to make standardless discretionary decisions under the guise of applying the unstructured concepts of 'breach' and 'policy'. This in turn can deprive negligence of stability, predictability, consistency, and other rule-of-law virtues (Henderson, 1976).

At a conceptual level, the Holmesian reduction of negligence to breach and cause, tempered by considerations of policy, suggests to some a mistake in Holmes's bedrock claim that modern negligence law must be understood as forward-looking and regulatory, rather than a law that empowers those wronged by the carelessness of others to seek redress (Weinrib, 1995; Goldberg and Zipursky, 2001).

This critique can best be explicated by focusing on the duty element of the negligence tort. As indicated in the Holmesian view, duty is an empty shell. This conclusion, however, follows only if one accepts the Holmesian characterization of tort law as regulatory law. For Holmes and his followers, negligent conduct is akin to littering in a public space: it is subject to (judicial) regulation because it produces *social* harms in the form of broken limbs and destroyed property. This conception of negligence is, to invoke a grammatical analogy, 'intransitive'—it attempts to capture the idea of careless conduct without specifying a direct object of that action. It is for this reason that the concept of duty strikes Holmesians as an empty shell.

The duty owed by every defendant in a negligence action is always the same: a duty to comport oneself as would a reasonable person under the circumstances. It follows, then, that duty cannot do any real work in legal analysis, and that when judges issue no-duty rulings they can only be purporting to justify a decision that is in fact being made on some other, unstated ground of policy, such as a concern for floodgates or fraud.

There is, however, another way to conceptualize the negligence tort. This may be deemed the Cardozoan account, as it takes its inspiration from Judge Benjamin Cardozo's observation that negligence 'imports relation' (*Palsgraf v Long Island RR* (248 NY 339 (1928))). In this account, negligence is conceived of as grammatically 'transitive': it makes little more sense to say, with the Holmesian, that 'X acted carelessly' than it does to say 'X injured'. The verb 'injured', as employed in the preceding sentence-fragment, requires a direct object to convert it into a true sentence ('X injured A or B or C'). So, too, the sentence 'X acted carelessly' requires the specification of at least one other person toward whom X so acted.

With negligence thus conceived, the element of duty no longer seems empty, nor unmotivated, but instead an intelligible feature of a body of law that, contrary to Holmes's suggestion, retains the aim of providing redress to those who have been wronged by others. It is because a negligence plaintiff must show not merely that the defendant engaged in socially undesirable conduct of a sort that warrants regulation, but also that this conduct constituted a *wrong to her*, that she must establish that the defendant's faulty conduct constituted the breach of a duty owed to her. This was precisely Cardozo's point in *Palsgraf*. The state, he conceded, might well have an interest in regulating railroad safety, or in compensating Mrs Palsgraf. But tort law, in contrast to safety codes or compensation funds, does not aim simply to regulate or compensate (although it may do incidentally). Rather, it exists to permit victims of wrongdoing to seek redress from those who have done them wrong. In the area of accidents, one does another wrong when one fails to heed a duty of care owed to that other.

Restoration of the traditional idea of tort as a law of wrongs permits a rehabilitation of the duty element. Likewise, it can help explain why the plaintiff must prove that the defendant's breach of duty owed to her was a *proximate*—meaning nonfortuitous—cause of her injury. Needless to say, the Cardozoan is not thereby committed to defend each historical instantiation of concepts like duty and proximate cause. The privity rule for injuries caused by products, and the directness test for proximate cause are no longer defensible, if they ever were. It is simply to say that the right response to these past mistakes is not necessarily the Holmesian response of jettisoning these concepts altogether, and of abandoning the traditional notion of tort as a law of wrongs and redress. Rather, the task is to update negligence law to reflect modern realities and norms. Thus, the decision to permit a plaintiff to recover from a given defendant for careless conduct causing pure emotional distress or economic loss will not turn—at least not in the first instance—on judicial guesses about the expected volume of liability or litigation. Instead, it will hinge on whether there is a basis in precedent to assert that the defendant was obligated to persons such as the plaintiff to take care not to cause the sorts of harms experienced by the plaintiff.

2.2.2 *The Causation Element: Risk or Harm?*

As indicated, Holmesian scholars have incorporated the actual causation requirement of the traditional four-element description of negligence as the second element of their fault principle. Recently, however, some scholars have argued that the deterrence and compensatory functions of negligence law may sometimes (or even often) be better served by imposition of liability whenever an actor's careless conduct *risks* harm to another, even if no harm is actually realized. So, if a driver can be shown to have driven carelessly in the vicinity of a pedestrian, the fact that the driver was lucky enough not to injure or scare the pedestrian does not of itself provide a reason to refrain from sanctioning him. Moreover, one could argue that the pedestrian is worse off merely for having been exposed to a heightened risk of harm, and is therefore entitled to some compensation from the driver for that loss of welfare. Accepting these premises, it would follow that, absent administrative or other policy concerns, liability in negligence should track risk, not harm. In effect, Holmesians who accept this argument take one step further the project of stripping away the traditional elements of negligence by collapsing the tort into the single element of fault. Many Holmesians, however, take the view that the administrative difficulties associated with assessing risks and valuing the 'harm' associated with exposure to increased risk are too great to warrant the removal of cause as a component of the plaintiff's prima-facie case. In addition, Cardozoan redress theorists have argued that causation is a core component of negligence precisely because negligence law is not to be equated with administrative risk regulation, but instead is a means by which victims of 'realized' wrongs may seek redress from wrongdoers (Goldberg and Zipursky, 2002).

3 CONTEMPORARY ISSUES IN TORT SCHOLARSHIP: A SURVEY

This chapter has sought to highlight the centrality of accidents and the tort of negligence in modern tort law and scholarship, while also noting certain legislatively and judicially created pockets of strict liability. It has also sought to describe the dominant orientation among modern tort scholars by elucidating how the negligence tort is understood on the Holmesian or regulatory model of tort, as contrasted to the minority conception, which has been labeled the Cardozoan or redress model. In the pages that remain, this chapter will change its orientation by briefly describing seven subject areas with which tort scholarship is currently occupied. The goal here is to give the reader a feel for some of the subjects presently in play within the legal academy.

3.1 Frontiers of Negligence

Whether employing a Holmesian or Cardozoan framework, scholars concerned to analyze modern problems in negligence face a number of 'live' issues, three of which may be noted here. First, as indicated above, the scope of liability for negligent infliction of pure emotional distress and pure economic loss remains of central concern. In the former category, courts are struggling to determine when, if ever, plaintiffs exposed by the defendant's carelessness to a known toxin, yet displaying no physical symptoms, should be entitled to bring suit for the emotional distress that attends the heightened risk of disease (Goldberg and Zipursky, 2002). In the area of economic loss, courts and scholars have tended to conclude that the pure fault principle is not appropriate, yet they have struggled mightily to state with any precision the circumstances that will support liability (Cane, 2000).

Secondly, there is the question of whether and how to recognize new forms of negligence liability, such as the emerging class of claims alleging negligent 'enabling' (Rabin, 1999). For example, American gun manufacturers arguably have been careless in not keeping track of how their handguns are re-sold and distributed by other entities. As a result, some criminals perhaps have been enabled to obtain access to guns they might not have obtained had the manufacturers been more careful. Can the manufacturers be sued by gunshot victims for helping to bring about the shootings? To a Holmesian, the pure fault principle would say, 'Yes, so long as the plaintiff can demonstrate unreasonable conduct and a causal link between that conduct and the shootings'. Policy considerations of floodgates or administrability, however, may counsel against liability (*Hamilton v Beretta USA Corp*, 727 NYS 2d 7 (2001)).

A third important contemporary issue concerns the rights of private citizens injured by carelessness on the part of government officials acting within the scope of their official powers and duties. As indicated above, until the mid-twentieth century, sovereign immunity blocked such claims when brought against the federal and state governments in the United States, and the national governments of the Commonwealth countries. By and large, the mid-century statutes abolishing these immunities state that the relevant government entity should now, for purposes of tort liability, be treated like a private employer. In other words, it should be held liable for injuries caused by wrongful acts of its employees acting within the scope of their employment. The underlying ideal is intuitive enough: treat like cases alike. A suit by a pedestrian who is run down by a carelessly driven delivery truck should not come out differently simply because the government, as opposed to a private company, owns the van. The intuition becomes cloudier, however, once it is remembered that government performs many functions not generally performed by private entities. Because it is often asked to do things private entities are not asked to do, it sometimes seems deserving of special rules not as a matter of blanket immunity, but of policy.

In recognition of these differences, courts have been reluctant to treat the abolition of sovereign immunity as automatically entailing an obligation of care owed by government actors to particular citizens. Rather, the possibility of liability will hinge on the nature of the activity in question. Discretionary decisions on economic, education, and housing policies, the allocation of police or fire protection, and the organization of the criminal justice system are still essentially immunized from liability. By contrast, courts are more willing to recognize claims when government officials are careless in performing non-discretionary or ministerial acts in furtherance of these policies. For example, suppose a government implements a policy of housing certain juvenile offenders in correctional institutions that permit them to leave confinement for certain appointed tasks, as a result of which some escape and cause personal injury or property damage. Since the proper approach to the punishment and reform of juvenile offenders is a discretionary policy decision, were the plaintiff's negligence suit to rest exclusively on a claim that the government *policy* was faulty (in that it unduly risked injury to the citizenry), it would fail. By contrast, if the allegation is that a particular correctional institution carried out the policy carelessly—for example, with inadequate staffing or supervision—then the claim may proceed (*Dorset Yacht Co Ltd v Home Office* [1970] AC 1004).

Given the generally lesser role played by government entities in the United States with respect to the provision of housing, health care, and other goods and services, it is not surprising to find Commonwealth scholarship on government liability—particularly liability for breaching statutory duties in a manner that causes individuals to suffer an intangible economic loss—to be more extensive (Feldthusen, 1994: 273). For example, a much-discussed issue in Commonwealth scholarship concerns whether local housing authorities statutorily charged with the task of inspecting buildings to ensure their safety can be held liable for carelessly failing to notice construction defects that turn out not to cause physical injury, but nevertheless diminish the economic value of the structure. Another issue in government liability of concern to US and Commonwealth scholars is the extent to which government entities may be held liable for negligent omissions—for example, for failing to respond to a call for police aid, or failing to remove a child from a household in which he is known by officials to be at risk of serious physical injury at the hands of another household member. On the one hand, the common law remains generally loath to impose such affirmative duties of care. On the other, it would seem to be precisely the duty of the relevant government actors (police and fire departments, social services) to protect at least those known to be in peril.

3.2 Products Liability: Revisiting Strict Liability versus Negligence

From roughly 1960 to 1980, academic consensus in the United States supported the imposition of strict products liability. Since then, however, that consensus has broken down for a number of reasons. First, the nature of product liability claims has changed. Increasingly, plaintiffs complained not of 'manufacturing defects'—assembly-line glitches—but of 'failures to warn' and 'design defects', that is, the failure of the manufacturer to take into account, or warn of, hazards associated with conscious design choices. In contrast to manufacturing defect claims, these seem almost by their nature to demand a negligence-style inquiry into the 'costs' and 'benefits' of including or omitting certain safety features or warnings. Moreover, some of these claims seek to establish not just that particular variations on a given product are defective for being unsafe, but that an entire product genus (above-ground swimming pools, tobacco cigarettes, handguns) are defective for posing certain risks (spinal injuries to divers, lung cancer, criminal shootings). This sort of claim raises significant issues of institutional competence and legitimacy: should courts and juries be in the business of deciding whether consumers are to have access to entire product lines (Henderson, 1973). The concerns generated by these developments were amplified when, starting in the 1980s, American courts began permitting juries to award punitive damages for instances in which they found that a given manufacturer had produced a defective product with 'reckless indifference' to the dangers it posed to life and limb (*Wangen v Ford Motor Co*, 97 Wisc 2d 260 (1980)).

The re-examination of strict products liability was also prompted by various developments outside of the law. By the late 1970s, courts and commentators were taking note of the more fragile state of the industrial and manufacturing sectors of Western economies. This in turn gave rise to concerns that strict products liability was placing these sectors at a serious disadvantage relative to their international competitors. Arguments for loss-spreading that once carried so much sway in mid-century also came under fire. In particular, scholars argued that the elaborate and fickle machinery of litigation, even under a strict liability standard, provides a glaringly inefficient means for spreading the cost of injuries. If loss-spreading is the aim, they reason, it would be better accomplished through private purchases of health insurance by would-be victims, supported, if necessary, by government subsidies (Priest, 1987). Finally, the principle of individual consumer autonomy has reasserted itself, in part because of the re-emergence in the 1980s of the powerful libertarian strand in Anglo-American culture, and in part because Western industries have begun to compete on product safety in the face of global competition. If consumers are routinely permitted to choose among products and product attributes, the argument runs, why should tort law require manufacturers to build in expensive safety features? The effect is to bar consumers from deciding whether, for example, they would rather have the increment of safety provided by automobile airbags or an additional $500 to spend on other items (A. Schwartz, 1992).

With the crumbling of the strict products liability consensus, scholarship in this area has gone in a number of directions. Probably the predominant tack among US tort scholars has been to reassert the primacy of negligence as the appropriate principle to apply to claims of design defect and failure to warn. (Manufacturing defects should, on this view, remain subject to strict liability.) Courts, it is argued, must recognize that they are balancing the costs and benefits of added safety measures in deciding whether a manufacturer's product should be deemed 'defective'. The American Law Institute's Third Restatement of Torts unabashedly adopts a reasonableness standard for design defect and failure to warn claims (Restatement (Third) of the Law of Products Liability § 2 (1997)).

A second view, championed by some scholars influenced by economic and libertarian theory, is that contract—both between manufacturer and consumer, and between injury victim and insurer—should frequently take precedence over tort. Assisted by the Internet, government-required disclosures, and consumer watchdog groups, the consumer, it is supposed, will usually have access to adequate information to make a decision about what portion of her disposable income to spend on safety devices and health insurance.

Some scholars continue to make the original case for strict liability on loss-spreading grounds. Others, including most famously Judge Guido Calabresi, argue for it on the rather different basis of efficiency. As between manufacturers and consumers, he maintains, the former are likely to be in a better position to identify and implement the cheapest solution to a particular safety problem. Moreover, strict liability saves on litigation expenses, since parties need not litigate the issue of fault. Thus, society as a whole is likely to get the most from dollars spent on safety if it operates under a system that gives manufacturers an economic incentive to discover ways to reduce the number and severity of accidents associated with their products (Calabresi and Hirschoff, 1972). Others champion strict products liability on a third ground: as a political check on corporate dominance of the legislative and regulatory process. Strict liability is necessary, on this view, because it empowers juries to take corporations to task for their irresponsibility through orders to pay compensatory and punitive damages. A related argument, perhaps more familiar among Commonwealth scholars, is rooted in the law of restitution. Businesses, the argument goes, profit from injury-producing activities and to that extent are unjustly enriched unless the costs of those injuries are deducted from those profits.

3.3 Mass Torts

Buoyed by the successful course of litigation that put an end to *de jure* segregation in the United States, American scholars in the 1960s began to explore the ability of large-scale 'public law' litigation to respond to various social and political problems, including unequal access to adequate housing and educational opportunities. Such litigations were marked, first, by use of the class action device, by which a handful of plaintiffs were authorized to sue as representatives of a large group of complainants (e.g. all victims of race discrimination in access to housing) and, secondly, by the supervision of a 'managerial' judge whose job was less to resolve a dispute before him than to work with the parties to develop a political solution to the problem that would be enforced either by settlement or an equitable decree ordering specific institutional changes.

Within a decade, the influence of the public law model was felt in US tort law thanks in part to two further developments. First, came the rise in the 1960s of the consumer movement and an attendant distrust of corporate power and decision-making, as heralded by Ralph Nader's *Unsafe at Any Speed* (1965). Secondly, and relatedly, Thalidomide-caused birth defects emerged as the first, large-scale 'toxic tort' of the postwar period. That episode demonstrated the capacity of drugs to cause serious damage against which the pharmaceutical industry and government regulatory agencies could not necessarily be trusted to protect citizens' well-being (Bernstein, 1997).

These developments coalesced in the Agent Orange litigation, brought by veterans of the Vietnam War as a class action proceeding on at theory of strict products liability against the manufacturers of various chemical defoliants. The immediate claim of the suit was that the manufacturers had created and distributed a defective product that caused the veterans to suffer various illnesses, including forms of cancer. The implicit claim was that the US government, although legally 'immune' from liability for its policy decisions as to how to conduct the war, had breached its obligation to its soldiers, not just by needlessly exposing them to carcinogens, but by disowning any responsibility to honor or care for them upon their return simply because of the unpopularity of the war (Schuck, 1987).

Although the Agent Orange case was perhaps unique for its political overtones, it became a blueprint for 'mass tort' class actions. Most of these actions, like the original, have been brought on allegations that a defendant or defendants manufactured or distributed a product—usually a drug—that has caused toxic side-effects in those who used or were exposed to it. Thus, the last thirty years have seen mass tort/product liability claims arising in connection with asbestos, Bendectin (an anti-nausea drug), cigarettes, the Dalkon Shield (a birth control device), DES (an anti-miscarriage drug), Fen-Phen (a combination of two diet drugs), and silicone gel breast implants.

The issues raised and addressed by scholars of mass torts are vast and complex, comprising, among other subjects, bankruptcy, civil procedure, constitutional law, insurance, and professional ethics. In terms of traditional tort doctrine, the most important issue raised and addressed in the context of modern mass tort litigations is that of proving a causal link between a defendant's tortious conduct and a plaintiff's injuries. According to the traditional rule (applicable to claims of negligence and strict liability), a plaintiff may not recover unless she can prove by a preponderance of the evidence that the defendant's conduct more likely than not played a role in bringing about the injury of which she complains. The toxic tort claims that lie at the heart of most mass tort actions can present two challenges on this score. First, some plaintiffs will lack the ability to identify the manufacturer of the particular product that injured them. This has been the case for many DES plaintiffs, because that drug was manufactured by scores of companies and marketed generically through physicians without brand-identifying characteristics.

Secondly, unless the toxic product or substance is linked by science to a particular illness (as the disease asbestosis is linked to asbestos exposure), individual toxic tort plaintiffs face a serious problem of proof. Typically, the class representative can produce experts who hypothesize why, as a matter of biology, there might be a correlation between a given product and an injury. Sometimes this testimony is supplemented by epidemiological evidence showing a statistical correlation between exposure to the product and a heightened incidence of a certain illness as compared to the general population. Courts, however, including the US Supreme Court, have been concerned about the willingness of juries to find causal relationships based on expert-witness speculations. Thus, in *Daubert v Merrell Dow Pharmaceuticals* (509 US 579 (1993)), the Supreme Court instructed federal trial courts aggressively to screen proffered expert testimony regarding causation to determine if it was sufficiently well-grounded to be admitted into evidence. (Whether this is something judges are equipped to do is an important and much-discussed question.) Beyond the admissibility issue is that of the quantum of evidence sufficient to carry the plaintiff's burden of proof. Even when admitted, expert statistical and biological evidence can only establish an aggregate correlation between a product and injuries suffered by a class of persons; it does not demonstrate that the illness of any given plaintiff was caused by the product. The leeway granted juries to infer proof of particular causation from evidence of general causation has become a much contested issue.

Given these problems of proof, drug manufacturers who have sold a product with a possible link to an injury or illness may often bear no liability because no individual plaintiff will be able to prove a causal link between the product and her injuries by a preponderance of the evidence. (Of course to ignore these problems and permit all plaintiffs to recover would pose the opposite problem: a defendant would be made to pay for more harm than it probably caused.) In response, courts and scholars have proposed various solutions to the causation conundrum. Some have suggested that burden-shifting rules can alleviate the difficulty in certain cases. Most famously, in the DES cases, the California Supreme Court adopted the concept of market share liability under which each defendant is held liable for a percentage of the plaintiff's damages caused by DES corresponding to the percentage share of the DES market enjoyed by that manufacturer at the time the plaintiff purchased or consumed the DES (*Sindell v Abbott Labs*, 163 Cal Rptr 132 (1980)).

Other scholars have advocated abandoning the traditional causation requirement in favor of a purely probabilistic approach. Under this view, the defendant would pay into a fund an amount of money equivalent to the aggregate amount of harm its product is likely to have caused, and each member of the class of plaintiffs exposed to the product would be entitled to recover a portion of that fund based on various criteria, such as severity of injury and wealth (Rosenberg, 1984). Others suggest that the causation hurdle can be side-stepped in some instances by re-conceiving the nature of the injury being sued upon and compensated. Suppose a case in which a mass tort claim is predicated on a manufacturer's failure to warn, or on its suppression of information about risks associated with a product. One could argue that the tort is complete upon the wrongful non-disclosure, because it is an indignity in itself for a business wrongfully to deprive its customers of material information concerning health risks posed by its products. With the injury thus redefined, causation ceases to be difficult to determine, although damages become harder to quantify (Berger, 1997). Finally, some skeptics of mass tort law have concluded that the difficulties posed by causation issues sometimes provide a reason to conclude that such matters are better left to legislative solution and administrative regulation than to the tort system (Nagareda, 1996).

3.4 Tort Reform

Another major development in modern tort law and scholarship, again emerging primarily in response to peculiar features of the American system, has been the rise of the modern 'tort reform' movement. As indicated below, scholars who emphasized the desirability of loss-spreading and reliable compensation have argued since before the beginning of the twentieth century for replacement of common law negligence with either industry-specific or general compensation schemes. The modern reform movement, however, does not seek a more rational and comprehensive injury compensation system. Instead, it invokes the twin banners of economic productivity and individual responsibility (i.e. victim responsibility) as grounds for limiting the scope of liability faced by corporate and other actors.

Inklings of modern tort reform first emerged in response to the liability insurance crises of the 1970s and 1980s, particularly in connection with rising medical malpractice insurance premiums (Fleming, 1988: 25). During the Reagan and first Bush administrations, a more generalized reform movement emerged as a key component of the Republican political platform. This movement has spurred various changes through judicial decision and statute. Some states have adopted caps on the dollar amount of damages certain categories of plaintiffs, such as medical malpractice victims, may recover. Other jurisdictions have eliminated the rule of 'joint and several liability', which holds that a plaintiff whose injury is caused by multiple tortfeasors may collect the entirety of her damages from any one of them. In a somewhat surprising development, the US Supreme Court—a court that, in other areas of its constitutional jurisprudence is wary of interfering with states' prerogatives and of relying on abstract rights guarantees—decided in *BMW of North America, Inc v Gore* (517 US 559 (1996)) that the Due Process Clause of the Fifth Amendment sets a constitutional standard of excessiveness against which courts must measure jury awards of punitive damages. As a result, jury discretion to set punitive damages likely has been significantly reduced.

Although it has mostly played out as a battle of pro-business and pro-consumer interest groups, the tort reform movement has placed a number of empirical issues on the scholarly agenda. First, there is the general issue of litigation finance. Does the American contingent-fee system, and its lack of a 'loser pays' framework, make litigation too easy to bring or, worse, too easy to foment? Is the American plaintiffs' bar's steadfast defense of contingent fee arrangements an effort to ensure court access, or a device for charging high fees and preventing the implementation of more efficient compensation systems?

Secondly, there is the perennial question of the American system's unique reliance on the jury. Some have argued that lay jurors tend in their liability and damage findings to punish defendants for engaging in cost-benefit analysis, notwithstanding that this cost-benefit analysis is exactly what the fault standard (at least in some interpretations) requires of them. Would the abolition of the jury in tort cases lead to sounder law? Or is the jury a necessary device for fending off the biases of judges toward defendants, and for infusing tort with common-sense morality (Symposium, 1998)?

Thirdly, tort reform movements have highlighted the importance of scale in the award of pain and suffering and punitive damages. Is it the case that, when successful American plaintiffs obtain awards for these intangibles, the dollar amounts they receive are an order of magnitude larger than the amounts received by Commonwealth plaintiffs? If so, is this a function of economics, political culture, or other factors? Also worth knowing would be the effects of changes in doctrine, such as the imposition of damage caps, on settlement amounts. The overwhelming majority of tort cases 'settle' rather than go to verdict. To what extent do legislative and judicial efforts to control damages affect settlement amounts?

Fourthly, the debates engendered by the tort reform movement have led scholars to examine the degree to which tort affects businesses' bottom line. At the most general level, the question is whether the prospect of tort liability actually does influence individual or corporate behavior. Although some studies have expressed skepticism about the general deterrent effect of tort law (Dewees *et al.*, 1996), tort's deterrent effects probably vary significantly depending on the activity in question, the type of actors involved, and so on. Related empirical issues in need of examination concern other potential effects of liability beyond deterrence. For example, which segments of the population are made worst off by price increases associated with increased liability? Are liability insurance crises prompted by expanding tort liability, or inherent in the business cycle of the relevant industry?

3.5 Other Torts

This chapter has focused on the subject that has been of most concern to twentieth-century torts scholars, namely accident law. Yet tort is broader than accident, and there is a wealth of important issues raised by torts such as fraud, defamation, invasion of privacy, trespass, and nuisance. Indeed, it is perhaps one of the major shortcomings of mainstream modern Anglo-American torts scholarship that it has treated tort law as if it were synonymous with accident law, and thus overlooked how analysis of these other areas of tort might inform our understanding of negligence and strict liability. One might speculate that, as the Western economies move further into the post-industrial, computer-driven economy, this single-minded focus will change as issues such as harassment, invasion of privacy, and interference with contract come to the fore.

In addition, torts scholarship, like any mode of scholarship that works within departmental boundaries, has tended to be somewhat provincial. There is no doubt much to be learned from an effort to integrate tort with related common law subjects such as contract and restitution. Given the ever-expanding body of law within each of these departments, such a task is no small order. Moreover, the natural tendency of such efforts is to adopt a reductionist strategy, by which each can be seen as instantiating some more general or abstract principle or set of principles. (Holmes, for example, thought that crime, tort, and contract could be unified around the objective fault liability standard.) Still, one hopes that scholars with appreciation of the subtleties in areas such as contract and restitution will build toward a nuanced account of tort in relation to these other areas.

Finally, there is need for further study of the comparative advantages and disadvantages of tort versus tort-replacement schemes. The twentieth century has witnessed the United States and Commonwealth countries experiment with or adopt a variety of schemes to replace or supplement tort. These include workers compensation systems, national health care, 'no-fault' auto insurance, New Zealand's general no-fault accident compensation system, other industry-specific tort replacement schemes (such as applies to American vaccine manufacturers), and administrative safety regulations. Although scholars have examined these efforts, much more remains to be done before judgments can be made about whether or when modification or abandonment of the tort system will serve particular goals such as compensation, deterrence, or the dispensation of justice.

3.6 Tort Theories

Holmesian theory, which conceives of tort as a species of public, regulatory law, dominated twentieth-century accounts of tort. To be sure, Holmesians have come in various guises. Fleming James took American tort law to be a gerry-rigged scheme of national health insurance for accidents. Prosser took it to be a decentralized administrative apparatus by which judges could regulate particular activities in the public interest. Posner takes it to be a system for promoting an efficient allocation of dollars spent on safety. Each, however, agreed or agrees with Holmes that modern tort has left behind its roots as a body of law designed to redress wrongs.

As indicated earlier, however, scholars have begun to challenge the Holmesian consensus. Some, such as Jules Coleman, Stephen Perry, and Ernest Weinrib, have done so by examining tort in light of the Aristotelian conception of 'corrective justice'. Others, such as George Fletcher, Gregory Keating, and Arthur Ripstein, have argued that tort law embodies a Kantian notion of reciprocal or fair terms of interaction (Goldberg, forthcoming (surveys these and other theories)). Still others, such as Peter Cane, suggest that tort law is first and foremost an expression in law of ethical principles of individual responsibility (Cane, 1997: at 211). In this respect, deep theoretical questions about the proper domain of, and justifications for, tort are 'on the table' in a way that they have not been for some time.

3.7 Comparative Tort Law

Comparative torts scholarship is in its infancy. Such studies might begin with the formal, doctrinal differences among tort rules of various jurisdictions. For example, Anglo-American negligence law has long incorporated 'duty' as an element of the tort, whereas civil law systems apparently do not. Is this merely a semantic or superficial difference, or does it reflect a deeper divergence over the character of negligence law? (In this regard, it would be interesting to assess how identical fact patterns would be resolved under the laws of different jurisdictions.) Comparative institutional analysis also holds significant promise. Again, the significance of the American jury would be an important object of study. More broadly, there is the question of the relatively greater reliance on, and importance attributed to, tort in the United States as compared to all other Anglo-American jurisdictions. Only in America, one suspects, would the abomination of African-American slavery end up being litigated, 150 years after its formal abolition, in a civil suit on behalf of slave descendants seeking compensation from the corporate successors of companies involved in slave trafficking. Is the United States' possibly-excessive reliance on tort explicable in terms of the nation's affluence, its long-standing distrust of bureaucracy, its fervent individualism, or other factors? Is it in any respects a healthy phenomenon? If so, is it exportable to other polities, or is it best left where it is, an exotic growth best left in its current environment?

REFERENCES

Atiyah, P. (1970). *Accidents, Compensation and the Law*, London: Weidenfeld & Nicolson.

Berger, M. (1997). 'Eliminating General Causation: Notes toward a New Theory of Justice and Toxic Torts', *Columbia Law Review*, 97: 2117–52.

Bernstein, A. (1997). 'Formed by Thalidomide: Mass Torts as a False Cure for Toxic Exposure', *Columbia Law Review*, 97: 2153–76.

Blum, W., and Kalven, H., Jr. (1965). *Public Law Perspectives on a Private Law Problem: Auto Compensation Plans*, Boston: Little, Brown & Co.

Calabresi, G., and Hirschoff, J. (1972). 'Toward a Test for Strict Liability in Torts', *Yale Law Journal*, 81: 1055–85.

Cane, P. (1997). *The Anatomy of Tort Law*, Oxford: Hart Publishing.

—— (2000). 'The Blight of Economic Loss: Is there Life after *Perre v. Apand*?' *Torts Law Journal*, 8: 246–62.

Dewees, D., Duff, D., and Trebilcock, M. (1996). *Exploring the Domain of Accident Law*, New York: Oxford University Press.

Feldthusen, B. (1994). *Economic Negligence* (3rd edn.), Scarborough: Carswell.

Fleming, J. (1988). *The American Tort Process*, Oxford: Clarendon Press.

Goldberg, J. (forthcoming). 'Twentieth-Century Tort Theory', *Georgetown Law Journal*, 91.

—— and Zipursky, B. (2001). 'The *Restatement (Third)* and the Place of Duty in Negligence Law', *Vanderbilt Law Review*, 54: 657–750.

—— and —— (2002). 'Unrealized Torts', *Virginia Law Review*, 88: 1626–1719.

Green, L. (1928). 'The Negligence Issue', *Yale Law Journal*, 37: 1029–47.

Henderson, J., Jr. (1973). 'Judicial Review of Manufacturers' Conscious Design Choices: The Limits of Adjudication', *Columbia Law Review*, 73: 1531–78.

—— (1976). 'Expanding the Negligence Concept: Retreat from the Rule of Law', *Indiana Law Journal*, 51: 467–527.

Holmes, O. W., Jr. (1923). *The Common Law* (repr. of 1st edn., 1881), Boston: Little Brown & Co.

Keating, G. (1996). 'Reasonableness and Rationality in Negligence Theory', *Stanford Law Review*, 48: 311.

Nagareda, R. (1996). 'In The Aftermath of the Mass Tort Class Action', *Georgetown Law Journal*, 85: 295–368.

Posner, R. (1972). 'A Theory of Negligence', *Journal of Legal Studies*, 1: 29–96.

Priest, G. (1987). 'The Current Insurance Crisis and Modern Tort Law', *Yale Law Journal*, 96: 1521–90.

Prosser, W. (1966). 'The Fall of the Citadel (Strict Liability to the Consumer)', *Minnesota Law Review*, 50: 791–848.

Rabin, R. (1999). 'Enabling Torts', *DePaul Law Review*, 49: 435–54.

Rosenberg, D. (1984). 'The Causal Connection in Mass Exposure Cases: A "Public Law" Vision of the Tort System', *Harvard Law Review*, 97: 849–929.

Schuck, P. (1987). *Agent Orange on Trial: Mass Toxic Disasters in the Courts* (2nd edn.), Cambridge, Mass.: Belknap Press.

Schwartz, A. (1992). 'The Case against Strict Liability', *Fordham Law Review*, 60: 819–42.

Schwartz, G. (1992). 'The Beginning and the Possible End of the Rise of Modern American Tort Law', *Georgia Law Review*, 26: 601–702.

Stapleton, J. (1994). *Product Liability*, London: Butterworths.

——(1998). 'Duty of Care Factors: A Selection from the Judicial Menus', in P. Cane and J. Stapleton (eds.), *The Law of Obligations: Essays in Celebration of John Fleming*. Oxford: Clarendon Press, 59–95.

Symposium (1998). 'The American Civil Jury: Illusion and Reality', *DePaul Law Review*, 48: 197–502.

Weinrib, E. (1995). *The Idea of Private Law*, Cambridge, Mass.: Harvard University Press.

CHAPTER 3

RESTITUTION

LIONEL SMITH

1 INTRODUCTION

THE great interest of the law of restitution as a subject of academic study for common lawyers is that it has yet to take a definitive modern shape. This contrasts sharply with the situation in civilian legal systems. In the common law, the subject is still not far removed from its roots in pleading fictions. Although most agree that the language of 'quasi-contract' and 'money had and received' is out of date and must be replaced by more transparent and defensible concepts, there is still much room for argument about the basic floor plan of the field. What is its function? What are its basic principles and analytical tools?

The subject-matter of restitution is agreed by many to comprise two parts. The first part deals with the obligation to return a benefit received pursuant to a defective transfer, as where a defendant who has received a mistaken payment must return it. The transfer may be defective for a variety of other reasons, such as compulsion or duress, or undue influence, or because its receipt violates some principle of public law. In such cases, the law requires the giving back of the transfer. The second part deals with gain-based remedies for wrongful conduct, as where a defendant who commits a breach of fiduciary obligation or a patent infringement can be required to disgorge the profits so acquired. This is not so much

I acknowledge with gratitude the financial support of the Social Sciences and Humanities Research Council of Canada.

a matter of giving back, as of giving up, since the gain came from someone other than the plaintiff.

In the common law, the history of restitution as a subject of academic study is relatively short. In the days of the forms of action, most claims were pleaded in *assumpsit*, the form whose chief feature was an allegation of an undertaking or promise by the defendant, and part of whose role was the enforcement of promises not under seal. In most cases now studied under the heading of restitution, the promise was a pleading fiction, the goal and effect of which was to allow the use of *assumpsit* to enforce a debt arising by operation of law. But the result was that as contract and tort took their modern shape in the later part of the nineteenth century, the law of restitution naturally gravitated to contract, due to the affinity in pleading practices. The basis of liability was said to be an 'implied promise'. Even today, in some common law jurisdictions, a claim to recover a mistaken payment of money is pleaded in the obscure language which identifies a sub-species of *indebitatus assumpsit*, itself a sub-species of *assumpsit*, which in turn is a type of trespass: the plaintiff sues for 'money had and received to the use of the plaintiff'.

Although they were building on earlier work, in particular that of William Keener, which in turn built on that of James Barr Ames, the process of overcoming the burden of this historical legacy was really begun by Warren Seavey and Austin Scott, the reporters of the *Restatement of the Law of Restitution: Quasi-Contracts and Constructive Trusts* (1937). The general decline of doctrinal scholarship in the United States, and with it the marginalization of private law (Langbein, 1998), meant that the subject was not developed there. It was re-founded in England by Gareth Jones and Robert Goff, with the publication of the first edition of *The Law of Restitution* in 1966 (see now Goff and Jones, 1998). The next landmark in the development of the subject was Peter Birks's seminal book, *An Introduction to the Law of Restitution* (Birks, 1985/1989). Birks did for the law of restitution what had been done for contract law in the nineteenth century: he set out a framework by which a huge mass of case law could be integrated and understood. In so doing, he unleashed a torrent of academic energy in the Commonwealth. Not everyone agrees with his framework, but the effect of his efforts has been that competing visions must be articulated. The *Restitution Law Review* was founded in 1993, and many textbooks and collections of essays have appeared since then. The subject has also shown signs of rebirth in the United States. Certainly one reason for this is George Palmer's magisterial four-volume treatise (Palmer, 1978). Currently Andrew Kull is working to produce the Restatement (Third) for the American Law Institute, the Restatement (Second) having failed to get past the drafting stage. Restitution scholarship has also started to re-emerge in the US periodical literature.

It remains the case, even so, that there is a striking dichotomy between the state of the scholarship in the Commonwealth and that in the United States. Very little attention is paid to restitution in the United States. Even given the general paucity of doctrinal scholarship, one might expect that other, more fashionable, theoretical approaches would be addressed to the field of restitution. This has not happened. One explanation is that the absence of doctrinal work meant that the subject was lost to the law school curriculum, which in turn meant that it was not on the radar screens of scholars as they turned new modes of analysis to familiar legal subjects. Taking the case of the law and economics movement, consider the seminal article by Calabresi and Melamed (1972). Analyzing the fields of property and tort, the authors noted that an entitlement could be protected in three ways: by a rule of inalienability; by a 'property rule', meaning that a transfer or infringement can occur only with the holder's consent; or by a 'liability rule', meaning that a transfer or infringement can be effected against the wishes of the holder, subject only to the payment of compensation. The terminology and the analytical framework have been enormously influential, so much so that many scholars in the United States today understand the defining feature of 'property' to be the availability of injunctive relief, rather than the operability of the right against an undefined class of third parties. But the terminological scheme made no mention of a 'disgorgement rule', by which the consequence of a wrongful transfer or infringement would be that the defendant would have to give up any gains. The possibility of disgorgement was well-established by then, as the Restatement made clear, but clearly it did not have a high profile. This gap in the framework, recently noted (Levmore, 1997), seems to have caused a genuine lacuna in the economic literature. As for the other part of restitution, the reversal of defective transfers of wealth, it seems also to have largely escaped the attention of economic analysts.

By contrast, in the Commonwealth, restitution is attracting the attention of a lot of scholars, and an enormous volume of periodical literature, monographs, treatises, and collections of essays is being generated. This work is overwhelmingly doctrinally oriented. There is some comparative and some historical work. Examples of other theoretical approaches, such as economic or sociological or feminist analysis, or high-level theory, are very rare. Part of the explanation for the difference must be that doctrinal scholarship has always remained a credible and arguably a dominant form of scholarly discourse in the Commonwealth. Moreover, at this relatively early stage in its development, the field of restitution presents unparalleled opportunities for creative doctrinal scholarship, and for doctrinal comparative law. The relatively undeveloped state of restitution may go some way towards explaining another feature of Commonwealth scholarship, which is that it is quite preoccupied with taxonomic issues: the structure or organization of the field, and its relationship to other fields. At least part of the explanation for the shape of the literature is that the scholarship of Birks plays a large part in setting the agenda in the Commonwealth. He takes a doctrinal approach and is very much concerned with taxonomic issues. Not everyone agrees with his views, but no one ignores them.

2 ORGANIZATION

Even the basic organization of the subject is contested. The Restatement is illustrative of the argument that all of restitution is about unjust enrichment:

§1. A person who has been unjustly enriched at the expense of another is required to make restitution to that other.

This approach was accepted by Palmer and by Goff and Jones. Birks (1985), in his seminal analysis, challenged the unity of the subject. He argued that restitution is a legal response, like compensation; unjust enrichment is the cause of this response. Moreover, he argued that there is a crucial difference between 'unjust enrichment by wrongdoing' and 'autonomous unjust enrichment'. In the former case, an example of which is a profitable breach of copyright, the enrichment is unjust because it is wrongful. The enriched defendant has committed a wrong against the plaintiff. The plaintiff in such a case has not necessarily suffered any loss, as the long line of cases on fiduciary obligations shows. In this type of case, the cause of action, or the basis of liability, or the source of the obligation, is the wrongful act of the defendant. The only thing unusual about these cases is that the plaintiff has asked, not for compensation of a loss suffered, but for a giving up of the defendant's gain. In autonomous unjust enrichment, by contrast, the defendant need not have done anything wrong. An example is the case of a mistaken payment. The defendant must refund, however innocent he may be (unless perhaps he has since spent the money in good faith). What makes the enrichment unjust in this case is that it came defectively from the plaintiff. The mistake vitiates the plaintiff's consent to the transfer. Here, the cause of action or basis of liability cannot be found in wrongdoing, because liability can arise without wrongdoing. The cause of action, or the source of the obligation as a civilian would say, is unjust enrichment. This is why Birks called it 'autonomous unjust enrichment'.

Developing this idea, Smith (1992) argued that the difference between autonomous unjust enrichment and restitution for wrongdoing should be taken even more seriously than Birks proposed. Restitution is the response to unjust enrichment: that is, to a legally untenable transfer of wealth. Restitution is the reversal of a transfer, and so involves undoing not only a gain by a defendant but also a corresponding loss to the plaintiff. In cases of gainful wrongdoing, by contrast, the response is not the reversal of a transfer, but simply gain-stripping from the defendant. Hence he proposed that the response of stripping gains from wrongdoers should not be called restitution at all, but rather 'disgorgement', a term of some pedigree in this connection. Further, he suggested that the term 'unjust enrichment' should be confined to the autonomous cause of action, and should be altogether avoided in the case of disgorgement for wrongdoing. Many scholars have adopted the terminology of disgorgement and restitution (see e.g. the developments by Virgo, 1999 and McInnes, 1999), although some, including Birks, still prefer 'restitution' for giving up as well as giving back. For all of these scholars, 'unjust enrichment' is a better name for most of the subject-matter than 'restitution', since 'unjust enrichment' identifies the cause of action, like breach of contract, while restitution identifies a legal response, like compensation. According to this view, however, unjust enrichment does not include gain-based remedies for wrongdoing; this belongs analytically to the various wrongs that may give rise to it.

Beatson (1991) and Friedmann (1980) are not at all persuaded that there is such a clear analytical difference between disgorgement for wrongdoing and restitution of defective transfers; their view is that the concept of unjust enrichment can unite both. Burrows (2000) finds the analytical difference convincing, but even so takes the view that both parts of the field can properly be described as restitution for unjust enrichment.

This kind of structural debate therefore takes place on at least two levels. One is whether it is necessary to make an analytical distinction between 'giving back' and 'giving up'. Another is the proper scope of the idea of unjust enrichment. Sometimes maturity leads to dismemberment. When the law of contract matured, in the sense that some foundational organizing principles were agreed, then some material was seen not to belong: in particular, the law of restitution. A similar process is unfolding with unjust enrichment. It is not just a question of organization within the field, but also of what belongs. On the view that a gain-based remedy for a wrong is neither restitution nor unjust enrichment, it does not belong. Similarly, other material may in the end prove to be best understood as belonging elsewhere. There is also a reverse phenomenon. The recognition that there is a generalized claim in unjust enrichment, which analytically unites a large number of established claims, can lead to argument that material traditionally understood to belong elsewhere is actually best understood as sourced in unjust enrichment. For example, it is arguable that claims to rescind contracts for mistake or undue influence—the same factors that can allow the restitution of non-contractual transfers—are actually claims for restitution based on unjust enrichment. This can breed fears of 'restitution imperialism'.

The uncertain scope of the idea of unjust enrichment has led some to take the position that it properly has no content at all (e.g. Dietrich, 1998); but as those scholars have discovered, this line of thought requires the generation of multiple novel principles to explain the material. The presence throughout the civil law tradition of unjust enrichment as a source of obligations suggests that discarding unjust enrichment is an unnecessarily radical approach to take, especially considering that in terms of broad categories, the common law and civil law traditions are generally similar. There are two common objections to unjust enrichment as a source of legal relationships. The first is that unjust enrichment is a useless term because it merely states a conclusion; this has long since been shown to be spurious (Hand, 1897). 'Negligence' and 'breach of contract' are names of other causes of action, which on their face merely state a conclusion as to liability. It is doctrine that helps provide an answer to the question of whether someone has been negligent, just as it helps to say whether someone has been unjustly enriched. And it is good doctrine which helps us to be sure that we are treating differently cases which are different in a defensible way, and helps us to be sure we are treating cases alike which are only different in unimportant ways.

The second objection is that unjust enrichment is potentially so large as to be incoherent. If I wrongfully cause you loss, there is a sense in which I am too well off; until I compensate you, I am richer than I should be, and unjustly so. So I am unjustly enriched. It is true that if this were a case of unjust enrichment, then almost every set of facts to which the law attaches some consequence would be a case of unjust enrichment. But no one who uses the term unjust enrichment intends it to be so wide.

But what do they intend? On the whole, common law scholars have recognized the explanatory power of the idea of unjust enrichment, when it is understood as a technical term with boundaries. The challenge now is to define those boundaries. Those who believe that unjust enrichment is a source of legal relationships have to articulate a vision of its defining characteristics; and this exercise will have implications as to the scope of the subject. Some of the recent literature that attempts to expose the philosophical foundations of the subject arguably marks another stage in its development. Weinrib (2000) has shown how the law relating to the disgorgement of wrongful gains can be explained within a theory of corrective justice. Smith (2001) has argued in a similar vein that the law of restitution for unjust enrichment is explicable under Weinrib's theory of corrective justice. On this view, restitution for unjust enrichment is about reversing transfers of wealth that are legally defective. Although they can be defective for many reasons, this view confines unjust enrichment to giving back. Since liability can arise without wrongdoing, both a defendant's gain and a plaintiff's loss are required, in order for the plaintiff to have a sufficient normative connection with the defendant's gain to generate liability. This view therefore excludes from the purview of unjust enrichment any claim that a plaintiff may have in excess of the plaintiff's loss, while also excluding any claim that is in excess of the defendant's gain.

3 INTERACTION WITH OTHER FIELDS

In every legal system, understanding the interaction of restitution with other legal categories presents a challenge. Many civilian systems incorporate a principle of 'subsidiarity', by which the law of unjust enrichment is subsidiary to other legal regimes, but the meaning of this varies widely from system to system. Common law scholars have begun to examine whether such a principle is necessary, and if so what should be its implications (Grantham and Rickett, 2001).

3.1 Restitution and Equity

Perhaps the most vibrant controversies surround the interaction of restitution with the doctrines of equity. A clear example is the case of property held in trust that has been misappropriated or misdirected. The trust beneficiary claims against the third party recipient. If the third party still has the trust property, then the only question is whether or not he took free of the beneficiary's interest, being a bona-fide purchaser for value without notice. The controversial case is the one in which the third party no longer has the property. The traditional doctrine of equity is that this third party can only be personally liable if he has committed some kind of wrongdoing. Another view is that the third party should be strictly liable in unjust enrichment, which does not depend on wrongdoing (Birks, 1985). Still others seek a middle way (Smith, 2001), arguing that the distinctive structural character of the trust prevents the straightforward application of defective transfer reasoning to the trust beneficiary's claim against a recipient from the trustee of misdirected trust property.

The view that equity has nothing to learn from unjust enrichment is strongest in Australia, where the solution to such cases, and others, is said by many to be found in equity's test as to whether the facts reveal unconscionability. This dispute is illustrative of a deeper tension, which is most clearly visible in the modern world in the field of restitution and also in the study of the remedies available for wrongs, including breaches of contract. That deeper tension is the uncertainty surrounding the proper understanding of the relationship between the common law and equity in the twenty-first century. The springboard of restitution has in this way launched an argument about the proper role of judicial discretion. The traditionalist view remains that solutions emanating from the Court of Chancery are properly discretionary. The opposing view says that this is a historical relic, and that in the modern world the proper role of judicial discretion is slight. This view is partly based on the claim that wide judicial discretion is inconsistent with the rule of law (Birks, 2000). Again, there is room (and much deep traditional and analytical underpinning, in both the common law and the civilian traditions) for a middle view. Llewellyn (1960), for example, formulated a Law of Lawful Discretion. For the moment at least, the judges seem largely unaware of this debate, and generally assume that they have a fairly high degree of discretion, at least in matters equitable.

More specifically, the interaction between restitution and equity comes to the fore in the context of the constructive trust. The courts of Canada and the

United States seem to accept that this is a remedy that the court may, in its discretion, grant to reverse an unjust enrichment or to effect the disgorgement of a wrongful gain. This therefore raises all of the concerns about judicial discretion, heightened in this context because the trust, with its proprietary implications, seems liable to affect non-parties to the dispute (as in the case of a bankrupt defendant). In reality, the courts in Canada and the United States are not at all consistent, and they disown the possibility of this application of the constructive trust as frequently as they apply it. The courts in other jurisdictions seem to forswear this possibility, and yet ironically they employ it equally frequently, often with a smokescreen of terminology that only conceals the issues. The constructive trust has been the subject of serious academic attention for many years (Waters, 1964), and yet the confusion remains. It is arguable that the debates in the literature regarding the constructive trust as a remedy for unjust enrichment have not advanced for some time. One way forward may be the recognition of the *resulting* trust as a tool to reverse unjust enrichment (Chambers, 1997). Subrogation is another equitable doctrine that can be understood as reversing unjust enrichment in some situations (Mitchell, 1994). But a deep analysis of the normative underpinnings of all forms of proprietary relief is still needed.

Discussion of the constructive trust gives occasion to notice that the law of unjust enrichment has taken on a role in the common law jurisdictions of Canada which, to date, has not been adopted elsewhere: that is, the resolution of property disputes on the breakdown of a domestic relationship, often but not always by the imposition of a constructive trust. Other jurisdictions have solved these disputes with other bodies of doctrine (for example, unconscionability in Australia, proprietary estoppel in England (Gardner, 1993)); but interestingly, the solution is invariably one that is laden with judicial discretion. It seems fairly clear that in most such cases, the goal of the court is not to reverse a defective transfer but rather to divide fairly property held at the end of the relationship. On many views of the scope of unjust enrichment, it follows that these cases are not about unjust enrichment (which does not entail that they are bad law, but only that they are better explained in other ways). The Canadian courts may be reluctant to acknowledge this, because the foundational case in Canadian common law for the modern shape of unjust enrichment was just such a case (*Pettkus v Becker* [1980] 2 SCR 834). But there has been some movement towards recognizing that there is something special about the domestic property disputes (*Peter v Beblow* [1993] 1 SCR 980).

3.2 Restitution and Contract

The interaction of the law of restitution with the law of contract creates a number of controversial questions. One arises at the stage of contract formation. Contracts may be voidable for mistake induced by misrepresentation, for economic duress, for undue influence, and so on. This generates a minor 'border skirmish', with some scholars claiming that all of this 'belongs' to contract law, while others say that the setting aside of a contract because of a mistake or pressure is simply a case of restitution for unjust enrichment, just like recovering a payment made by mistake or under pressure. The issue is important inasmuch as a recognition that rescission of a contract is a kind of restitution for unjust enrichment would entail that the shape of the law of rescission should at least approximate the shape of the general law of unjust enrichment. Beyond the question of classification, the substance of the law relating to economic duress is a matter of continuing debate. The recognition of this form of duress has opened up an intractable issue as to its scope, since the currency of economic activity is economic pressure of various kinds, most of which are entirely permissible. The most controversial cases relate to the renegotiation of contracts under a threat of breach (S. Smith, 1997).

More recently, questions have been asked about whether it is possible to have restitution of a benefit conferred within the framework of an existing contract. Another issue, of longer standing, arises after the contract has been breached. The plaintiff in such a case may try to recover whatever benefit he transferred by way of performance; this is largely uncontroversial, although there is still some question about whether an innocent victim of such a breach can have a larger claim in restitution than he could have in breach of contract, thereby escaping a bad bargain (Kull, 1994). Another question is whether and when it is appropriate to allow such recovery by a plaintiff who himself breached the contract. Much more difficult is whether the non-breaching party can require the breaching party to disgorge any gain which he made through the breach. Running into issues of 'efficient breach' and hence market ideology, this has been hugely controversial, with academic writing far exceeding decided cases. Even so, the UK courts have recently begun to allow such claims, discarding the old orthodoxy that claims for breach of contract are solely compensatory in nature.

3.3 Restitution, Change of Position, and Estoppel

The recognition of unjust enrichment has brought with it the recognition of the defence of change of position. There is some evolving debate about the nature of this defence, in particular how it interacts with the doctrine of estoppel (Fung and Ho, 2001). The defence of change of position will allow the defendant to resist a claim to the extent that he has reasonably relied on the enrichment being his (or, it seems, to the extent that the defendant has been the victim of some disaster which destroyed some of the enrichment). The logic of estoppel as a rule of evidence is that it works in an all-or-nothing way. So in the case of a mistaken payment of $100, assume that the defendant asks the plaintiff to confirm that the money was properly paid, and the plaintiff confirms this. The defendant then spends $50 before the plaintiff realizes that it made a mistake and reclaims the money. The defence of change of position would apply only as to $50 and would require the defendant to pay $50. But if the defendant can deploy an estoppel by representation, he can prevent the plaintiff from asserting (contrary to its earlier representation, on which the defendant relied) that the money must be repaid. The courts that have considered the issue to date have simply said that in the light of the defence of change of position, estoppel should not be allowed; but no court has explained how it takes away the applicability of this general doctrine or rule of evidence.

3.4 Restitution and Wills

When a solicitor is negligent in drafting a will, the estate may go to the 'wrong' beneficiary. It now seems clear that the disappointed non-beneficiary, the 'right' person who would have inherited in the absence of the solicitor's negligence, can recover in negligence against the solicitor. This potentially doubles the estate; both the 'right' and the 'wrong' beneficiaries end up getting the same amount of money. This illustrates a distinguishing characteristic of many claims for pure economic loss, that the loss is not a loss to society as a whole (as is the case when people are hurt or property is destroyed), but in fact is just a misdirection of wealth. Can this doubling problem be solved by allowing the 'right' beneficiary, or indeed the negligent solicitor, to sue the wrong beneficiary in unjust enrichment? Or does this inappropriately undermine the result given by the law of wills? This is a thorny question that requires an evaluation, necessarily largely by inference, as to what the 'law of wills' says or means.

Frequently the law of unjust enrichment reverses the effects that seem to be dictated by other parts of the law. In a mistaken payment, for example, the law of property says that the money belongs to the payee. Restitution for unjust enrichment reverses this. It must be right that this happens sometimes; it is the function of unjust enrichment. Unjust enrichment seems to contradict the disposition given by property law, but the contradiction is not significant because unjust enrichment is not undermining any significant policy that the property disposition protects. The property disposition makes it clear that the defendant has been enriched, and the disposition might have important implications for third parties, but it is not undermined by the existence of an obligation to make restitution of an equivalent sum. Sometimes, however, the legal disposition that creates the defendant's enrichment goes beyond that role, and also provides a legal justification for the enrichment. For example, if the plaintiff enriches the defendant by providing building services, but the contract is void due to a lack of formality, there is a serious question whether the disposition that makes the contract void should also go further and exclude any claim in unjust enrichment.

It is largely a matter of inference to determine on which side of the line a particular case falls. This phenomenon has been particularly noticed in the literature as regards illegal and unenforceable transactions, but in fact it is a general concern. It particularly applies to defective wills. The law of wills identifies, as a matter of form, what counts as the testator's intentions as to the disposition of his property. This leads to the enrichment of the 'wrong' beneficiaries. If it be proven that the testator had changed his mind before death, we might think that the enrichment was unjust. But a contrary argument would be that the legislative decision about the form of wills goes beyond determining who gets the property (in a way which might be reversed by a claim in unjust enrichment), and actually implies that this person or persons get the benefit in a way that the law of unjust enrichment is not to reverse.

4 RESTITUTION AND THIRD PARTIES

The paradigm case of restitution for unjust enrichment is the simple case of a mistaken payment. Deeper waters are encountered when more than two parties are involved in the dispute. The common law and its scholarship have only just begun to address some of these issues.

4.1 Liability of an Indirect Recipient of the Enrichment: Recovery of Substitutes

If the original recipient transfers the enrichment to another party, can the plaintiff recover from the third party? And if so, what is the basis of the recovery? This opens up the complex vista of tracing and following. The common law differs significantly from the civilian tradition in this field. Building on roots in the law of trusts, the common law has accepted that if a plaintiff has certain rights, notably rights of ownership, in a particular asset, then it should also be possible to assert those rights in other assets acquired with the asset. This is broadly what is known as tracing. One of the crucial contributions of Birks (1985) was to observe that there were two distinct questions. The first is the question of what asset is the traceable product of the plaintiff's asset. This is largely a factual inquiry, coloured by certain policy choices in situations of mixing, especially in relation to bank accounts. The second issue is the question of what rights can be asserted in the assets so identified as traceable products. These rights are typically equitable rights, under a constructive trust or perhaps a lien, but there are other possibilities as well. This kind of claim is increasingly important in civil litigation, as the most potent weapon in private law against fraud and misappropriation.

There are difficult questions about the justification for this whole idea (Rotherham, 1996; L. Smith, 1997). Underlying these arguments is the issue whether the ability to make a claim to a traceable product is best understood as sourced in unjust enrichment or not. It is often assumed that it is, but when unjust enrichment is understood as being concerned with reversing defective transfers of wealth, it is more difficult to accept this position. The claim to traceable proceeds may be greater than the plaintiff's loss, as where the defendant has made a profitable investment. It may be difficult to find a loss suffered by the plaintiff in the same way that such a loss is present in a mistaken payment. Again, if the matter was simply one of unjust enrichment, the tracing rules should focus on whether the defendant was enriched in some abstract or causal way; instead, they focus entirely on transactional links. Further inquiry may support the argument that such cases are based not on the logic of defective transfer, but on interference with the plaintiff's rights in particular assets (Virgo, 1999; Smith, 2001). Alternatively, if it is true that such claims can be built on the same logic as that which underlies defective transfers, then it may be possible to make remote recipients liable even when the plaintiff cannot establish any proprietary rights in the property received. Currently this seems unsupported by the cases.

4.2 Defence of Passing On

The cases on indirect enrichment can be seen as cases in which an initial recipient passes the enrichment on to another party. Conversely, what if the defendant argues that the plaintiff did not really suffer any deprivation in making the transfer to the defendant, because the loss was 'passed on' to someone else? This kind of claim is most frequently made by a defendant which is a taxing authority which has collected an unlawful tax. The logic initially seems impeccable: if the loss was passed on by the plaintiff, then somebody else should be suing. In practice, it does not really work. As a number of authors have noticed, the economics of the market tell us that a simple raising of the plaintiff's prices cannot mean that any loss has automatically been 'passed on' to someone else, since there will be a loss of business volume.

4.3 Third Party Contracts

In many cases, the enrichment which is the subject-matter of the dispute will have been transferred to the defendant pursuant to the plaintiff's contract with a third party. The classic case is that of a building contract. A subcontractor performs work that enriches the owner. But the subcontractor is contractually bound to the main contractor to do this work. Conversely, the owner has a contractual obligation to pay the main contractor for the building work. If something goes wrong (say, the main contractor is insolvent), can the subcontractor sue the owner in unjust enrichment? Another frequent example is that the plaintiff has contracted with someone (now insolvent) who was in possession of some property, and has improved the property, and then later has learned that the property is owned by someone else. Can he recover from the owner?

This raises questions as to whether a plaintiff should be able to escape the consequences of the insolvency of the party with whom it made a contract, by suing another party in unjust enrichment. A similar question sometimes arises in tort law. If the plaintiff contracts with some party, can it sue in negligence some other party whose performance it was indirectly purchasing? The answer there seems to be that the contractual relationship can be ignored in cases of personal injury or property damage, but in a case of pure economic loss the plaintiff must sue its contractual counterparty. Claims in unjust enrichment for defective transfers are effectively always claims in pure economic loss. Although some legal systems have evolved doctrinal apparatus within the law of unjust enrichment to solve these problems, the common law remains immature. On the whole, the cases deny recovery, but the issue is complex and difficult (Rendleman, 2001).

5 CONCLUSION

Just as in all legal fields, there are many unresolved debates and issues throughout the field of restitution. But the battles at the core are the most interesting. The floor plan is still a matter of debate. Almost everything else will follow from the results of that debate. It is as though we were still arguing about whether contracts are formed by offer and acceptance, or by some other mechanism. This is no doubt part of the reason that the field has attracted a lot of attention and energy in recent years, a level of energy that shows no signs of abating. As Langbein (1998) has written, 'Restitution is still in many ways an open book, and what fun it is to write on blank pages'.

REFERENCES

Beatson, J. (1991). 'The Nature of Waiver of Tort', in J. Beatson, *The Use and Abuse of Unjust Enrichment*, Oxford: Clarendon Press, 206–43.

Birks, P. (1985/1989). *An Introduction to the Law of Restitution*, rev. edn., Oxford: Clarendon Press, 1989; 1st. pub., 1985.

—— (2000). 'Rights, Wrongs, and Remedies', *Oxford Journal of Legal Studies*, 20: 1–37.

Burrows, A. (2000). 'Quadrating Restitution and Unjust Enrichment: A Matter of Principle?' *Restitution Law Review*, 8: 257–69.

Calabresi, G., and Melamed, A. D. (1972). 'Property Rules, Liability Rules, and Inalienability: One View of the Cathedral', *Harvard Law Review*, 85: 1089–128.

Chambers, R. (1997). *Resulting Trusts*, Oxford: Clarendon Press.

Dietrich, J. (1998). *Restitution: A New Perspective*, Annandale, NSW: Federation Press.

Friedmann, D. (1980). 'Restitution of Benefits Obtained through the Appropriation of Property or the Commission of a Wrong', *Columbia Law Review*, 80: 504–58.

Fung, E., and Ho, L. (2001). 'Establishing Estoppel after the Recognition of Change of Position', *Restitution Law Review*, 9: 52–66.

Gardner, S. (1993). 'Rethinking Family Property', *Law Quarterly Review*, 109: 263–300.

Goff, R., and Jones, G. (1998). *The Law of Restitution* (5th edn.), London: Sweet & Maxwell.

Grantham, R., and Rickett, C. (2001). 'On the Subsidiarity of Unjust Enrichment', *Law Quarterly Review*, 117: 273–99.

Hand, L. (1897). 'Restitution or Unjust Enrichment', *Harvard Law Review*, 11: 249–57.

Kull, A. (1994). 'Restitution as a Remedy for Breach of Contract', *Southern California Law Review*, 67: 1465–518.

Langbein, J. (1998). 'The Later History of Restitution', in W. Cornish, R. Nolan, J. O'Sullivan, and G. Virgo (eds.), *Restitution: Past, Present and Future*, Oxford: Hart, 57–62.

Levmore, S. (1997). 'Unifying Remedies: Property Rules, Liability Rules, and Startling Rules', *Yale Law Journal*, 106: 2149–273.

Llewellyn, K. (1960). *The Common Law Tradition: Deciding Appeals*, Boston and Toronto: Little, Brown & Co.; repr. 1996, Buffalo: Hein & Co.

McInnes, M. (1999). 'Restitution, Unjust Enrichment and the Perfect Quadration Thesis', *Restititution Law Review*, 7: 118–27.

Mitchell, C. (1994). *The Law of Subrogation*, Oxford: Clarendon Press.

Palmer, G. (1978). *Law of Restitution*, Boston and Toronto: Little, Brown & Co.

Rendleman, D. (2001). 'Quantum Meruit for the Subcontractor: Has Restitution Jumped Off Dawson's Dock?' *Texas Law Review*, 79: 2055–81.

Rotherham, C. (1996). 'The Metaphysics of Tracing: Substituted Title and Property Rhetoric', *Osgoode Hall Law Journal*, 34: 321–54.

Seavey, W., and Scott, A. (1937). *Restatement of the Law of Restitution: Quasi-Contracts and Constructive Trusts*, St Paul, Minn.: American Law Institute.

Smith, L. (1992). 'The Province of the Law of Restitution', *Canadian Bar Review*, 71: 672–99.

—— (1997). *The Law of Tracing*, Oxford: Clarendon Press.

—— (2001). 'Restitution: The Heart of Corrective Justice', *Texas Law Review*, 79: 2115–75.

Smith, S. (1997). 'Contracting under Pressure' *Cambridge Law Journal*, 56: 343–73.

Virgo, G. (1999). *The Principles of the Law of Restitution*, Oxford: Oxford University Press.

Waters, D. (1964). *The Constructive Trust*, London: Athlone (repr. 1996), Holmes Beach, Fl.: Gaunt.

Weinrib, E. (2000). 'Restitutionary Damages as Corrective Justice', *Theoretical Inquiries in Law*, 1: 1–37.

CHAPTER 4

....

PROPERTY

....

MICHAEL A. HELLER

1 INTRODUCTION

....

IN recent years, the idea of property as a legal concept may have lost its unifying
thread (Grey, 1980), perhaps as an unintended consequence of advances within
property theory itself. With the work of Hohfeld (1923) and Honoré (1961), twentieth-century lawyers came to see property as a 'bundle of rights' rather than viewing
it through the old image of property as a 'thing'. Where property law once was concerned primarily with an individual's relation to land (on property in land, see
Ellickson, 1993), now it may be understood to include a broad array of social relations
in resources ranging from the radio spectrum to gene fragments. Property may
appear to be just an umbrella term corralling increasingly disparate bodies of law—
real estate, landlord-tenant, intellectual property, environmental, secured credit, and
so on—with each area animated by divergent scholarly concerns. If consensual
relations among people are the focus of contracts, and accidental relations the core of
torts, then where does property fit?

This chapter argues that despite its seeming disintegration, property is more
vibrant than ever—it is a field that has focused on understanding the formal and
informal institutions by which society channels decision-making for scarce resources
(see e.g. Ellickson, 1991; Ostrom, 1990). Many exciting recent innovations in property
theory have arisen through dialogue between US and Commonwealth scholars and
legislatures. Much of the work has been in reconceptualizing the core analytic tools
of property, such as the bundle of rights view of ownership. In addition to the bundle
of rights approach, this chapter will consider a handful of property concepts, each

with a distinguished pedigree and continuing usefulness, such as the '*numerus clausus*' of private property forms and Hardin's metaphor of the 'tragedy of the commons' (Hardin, 1968: 1244–5). This handful of concepts is the main prism through which legal scholars address the 'what is property?' question and through which legislators frame debate when they seek to implement changes in the law.

The first part of this chapter explains my focus on what I call analytic property theory, which I pose in distinction to a jurisprudential approach. The second part introduces the familiar division of ownership into a trilogy of ideal types: private, commons, and state. The next three parts use this trilogy to show how defining, integrating, and constructing these ideal types can lead to useful innovation in property theory. In sum, property theory scholarship seems to work cyclically—reasoning from real-world contests over scarce resources, to analytic tools that translate these struggles into useful conceptual terms, to jurisprudential debates regarding the rightness of resulting allocations, to practical politics that implement one property regime or another, and then back to new on-the-ground struggles.

2 ANALYTIC VERSUS JURISPRUDENTIAL APPROACH

Some property theorists may be impatient with this chapter's focus on conceptual tools and may, indeed, challenge the premise of this essay that this focus offers much that is useful in prompting legal innovation. If the conceptual framework is understood just to mean a workable taxonomy, then little fundamental would be gained by a renewed focus on analytic work; indeed, such theory would have a marginal role, simply cutting and pruning the well-tended vineyard of property terms. Further work on property concepts would quickly translate into mind-numbing parsing of taxonomic detail.

I call this view of property analytics the 'good enough' approach. According to this view, we just need a reasonably consistent and intelligible common language of property that is good enough to sustain the more important normative and practical debates that follow. To give an example, note Lawrence Becker's plea for more work on pluralist justifications for property in an article where he bluntly summarizes the current state of theory:

What has been left undone? What has been done to death? . . . [An inquiry that has] been done enough (perhaps even overdone) . . . is the extensive recapitulation and dissection of the now-standard conceptual analysis of property theory: Hohfeld's analysis of rights,

Honoré's analysis of ownership, and typologies of justificatory arguments. Tinkering with these matters has become a sort of benign addiction. (Becker, 1992: 197–8)

In Becker's view, adding a new term to the list of property concepts may be 'benign', rather than pernicious, because 'we would lose a great deal of clarity and rigor if [the conceptual apparatus] were ignored' (ibid. 198). Still, for Becker, the conceptual front has been adequately covered—it is good enough—and the main work for property theory lies elsewhere.

Similarly, Jeremy Waldron suggests in his jurisprudential work a good enough approach to property analytics (Waldron, 1996). As he puts it, the standard analytic framework 'respects both the technician's sensitivity to legal detail and the philosopher's need for a set of well-understood "ideal types" to serve as the focus of justificatory debate' (ibid. 3). In this view, unsettling the familiar categories may be counterproductive because it would scramble the relatively stable, transparent, and neutral-seeming ideal types that allow people to argue productively with each other regarding more substantive issues (see also Michelman, 1980). The point for these scholars is to ready the field for the power-lifting political philosophy that follows. The lively debates within this group could form the basis for a wholly alternative 'property jurisprudence' chapter for this volume, one that would center on the important work of Harris (1996), Munzer (1990), and Waldron (1988).

Property theorists also challenge the *raison d'être* of property analytics from the other end of the spectrum, deploying what I call the 'never good enough' approach. This approach rejects not just the existing analytic framework, but also the possibility of an improved version. For example, Thomas Grey once suggested that private property is, in the end, indefinable in any useful or determinate way and that the categories we use to talk with one another collapse on themselves upon closer examination (Grey, 1980). Similarly, Bruce Ackerman's conception of the layman's view of property partakes of the never good enough approach (Ackerman, 1977). In this view, property analytics may be understood to be about mystifying real power relations that, in essence, resist categorization. Like the good enough approach, the never good enough criticism does not seem to leave much room for further work.

So the challenge from existing property theory is substantial: to thread between, on the one hand, a view that the taxonomies we have already are good enough so that further work amounts to, at best, a benign addiction, and, on the other hand, a position that conceptual work in property is hopelessly indeterminate, obfuscatory, normatively pernicious, and likely a waste of time. Situating the analysis in this chapter between those views, I suggest that we look at recent scholarship that bases its methodology on close observation of on-the-ground, emerging property relations; asks whether the existing framework facilitates understanding of and support for these new forms of ownership; and proposes new analytic tools where the present ones fail. Because people are constantly creating new types of property, there remains substantial room for analytic innovation which, in turn, may carry a normative punch when it redirects jurisprudential and practical debates to new questions.

3 The Property Trilogy and its Discontents

Consider the preeminent analytic tool of property theory, that is, the well-worn trilogy of ownership forms—private, commons, and state property. The trilogy has long formed the focal point for normative and practical property debates (Waldron, 1988: 44). As Frank Michelman states, 'We need some reasonably clear conceptions of regimes that are decidedly not [private property], with which [private property] can be compared' (Michelman, 1980: 5). This process of working from ideal types pervades property theory stretching back past Locke's discussion of the State of Nature and forward to the modern law-and-economics debates. Theorists push reforms towards one ideal type or the other, but none subjects the trilogy itself to much challenge. The trilogy is so entrenched as to seem almost natural, beyond serious contestation or elaboration. Before we go about constructing new ideal types or synthesizing existing ones, let us briefly recapitulate the trilogy itself.

3.1 Private Property

Private property is a complicated idea to pin down precisely; its boundaries fray at the edges. For property theorists (and for ordinary layfolk), the term seems reasonably coherent and capable of simple definition, despite Grey's arguments. For example, Michelman focuses his definition on rules for initial acquisition and reassignment. He defines sole ownership to mean 'the rules must allow that at least some objects of utility or desire can be fully owned by just one person' and freedom of transfer to mean 'owners are immune from involuntary deprivation or modification of their ownership rights and empowered to transfer their rights to others at will, in whole or in part' (Michelman, 1980: 5).

This standard definition can be multiplied many times over, but all such definitions partake of and help keep current William Blackstone's talismanic definition of private property as 'that sole and despotic dominion which one man claims and exercises over the external things of the world, in total exclusion of the right of any other individual in the universe'. While the image of sole dominion has never adequately described any real world property ownership, as even Blackstone recognized (Rose, 1998), the idea rings through the ages and continues to block clear thinking about private property.

3.2 Commons Property

Commons property has been the residual category that theorists usually use when they describe a regime that is not private or state property. Michelman defines a commons property regime as one where 'there are never any exclusionary rights. All is privilege. People are legally free to do as they wish, and are able to do, with whatever objects (conceivably including persons) are in the [commons]' (Michelman, 1980: 5). To restate, this definition means that every individual may use any object of property and no individual has the right to stop someone else from using the object. As used in this chapter, commons property refers to the latter of two distinct subgroups, what have been called 'open access' and 'group property'. Open access includes resources, such as the ocean, from which no one at all may be excluded and for which it is difficult to imagine property-based solutions to the tragedy of the commons. On the other hand, group property—held in common by insiders but private as to outsiders—is much more amenable to property law intervention. Because open access and group property are often mistakenly lumped together in the catch-all category of 'commons property', their distinctive characteristics have been largely overlooked. Open access is a losing game. Group property is the type of commons on which recent property theory has focused.

Although this is not the place to elaborate the point, a useful distinction could be drawn between the utilitarians' image of commons property and the liberals' notion of a State of Nature: the two images share the core definition, but have different emphases and contexts. Liberal property theorists usually deploy the State of Nature image to describe an 'open access' pre-political commons, the world from which a generalized private property regime emerges; while modern law-and-economists use the commons metaphor to focus attention on creation of private property out of specific group property resources (Smith, 2000). For both groups, the transition from 'commons' to private property is a core problem that property theory seeks to explain.

3.3 State Property

State property, also sometimes called collective property, can be defined as a property regime in which

In principle, material resources are answerable to the needs and purposes of society as a whole, whatever they are and however they are determined, rather than to the needs and purposes of particular individuals considered on their own. No individual has such an intimate association with any object that he can make decisions about its use without reference to the interests of the collective. (Waldron, 1985: 328–9)

As Jeremy Waldron notes, a state property regime is similar to commons property in that no individual stands in a specially privileged position with regard to any resource, but is distinguished from commons property in that the state has a special status or distinct interest—that of owner of all resources, able to include or exclude all individuals according to the rules of that particular state (ibid. 329). In other words, the collective, represented usually by the state, holds all rights of exclusion and is the sole locus of decision-making regarding use of resources. So, a subsidiary set of questions needs to be answered to specify a state property regime fully, including what is the 'collective interest' and what procedures will be used to apply that conception to a particular case.

Today, for most property theorists, state property has become a less and less important category, particularly since the decline of socialist states and rise of the worldwide movement towards privatization. For liberal, communitarian, and utilitarian theorists alike, the trilogy may effectively reduce down to a dichotomy—private and commons—so that all theoretical work takes place in the interplay of these two regimes. For example, Michelman says that a commons can be seen as 'a scheme of universally distributed, all-encompassing privilege . . . that is opposite to [private property]' (Michelman, 1980: 5, 9). Similarly, the economist Yoram Barzel notes that the standard economic analysis of property has 'tended to classify ownership status into the categories all and none, the latter being termed "common property"—property that has no restrictions put on its use' (Barzel, 1989: 71).

3.4 Three Approaches to Innovating around the Property Trilogy

The ideal-typic trilogy straitjackets analysis. For example, when people share access to resources in a commons and then proceed to waste the resources through overuse, theorists see an instance of Hardin's metaphor of the 'tragedy of the commons'—another core concept of property theory. By looking to the trilogy, liberals and utilitarians see conservation solutions that require either privatization or state control (Demsetz, 1967: 354); while communitarians search for those limited circumstances in which close-knit groups can avoid tragedy (Ostrom, 1990: 35–6). The tragedy of the commons metaphor may be deployed alternatively to provide moral justification for private property regimes, to promote state regulation, and to disparage the practical possibilities for cooperative use of resources. While the trilogy has helped in the ongoing justificatory debates among theorists, and has suggested an impressive range of policy reforms, the familiar framework also has rendered emerging problems invisible and made creative solutions hard to imagine.

Despite the trilogy's seeming inevitability, there are at least three productive ways to move beyond it, what I call the *definitional*, *constructive*, and *integrative* approaches. The definitional approach takes familiar terms and gives them new meaning, for example, by revisiting the standard metaphors for property (e.g. Demsetz, 1967). The constructive approach builds new ideal types that challenge the imaginative limits imposed by the existing trilogies (e.g. Calabresi and Melamed, 1972). Finally, the integrative approach shows how the existing ideal types can be combined to reveal and indeed to help policy-makers implement the underlying social values that animate property (e.g. Radin, 1993).

4 THE DEFINITIONAL APPROACH: FROM NUMERUS CLAUSUS TO BUNDLE OF RIGHTS

First, the definitional approach. 'Private property' as an ideal type has proven quite problematic, and the effort to understand the ideal type is generating renewed interest from both US and Commonwealth scholars. The most lively recent definitional work has focused on two fundamental aspects of the meaning of private property—as thing and bundle. First, prompted by the work of Bernard Rudden (1987), several scholars have been examining the '*numerus clausus*' problem, that is, the reasons for the limited number of property forms allowed in Anglo-American legal regimes. This debate seeks to explain why the thing-like quality of property has had such a persistent role. Secondly, recent scholarship explores the limits of and possible replacements for the long-lasting 'bundle of rights' metaphor.

4.1 The Standard Story of Private Property

According to the stylized history taught to generations of law students and applied by judges every day, people understood property as a physical thing or a legal thing until this century, when lawyers recast it as an abstract bundle of legal relations (Alexander, 1997; Penner, 1996). Under the old metaphor, property involves the physical control of discrete, individually owned things, an image symbolized by the medieval ceremony of livery of seisin, which gathered people in a field to exchange ownership by handing over a clod of dirt. Fees, life estates, easements, and leases each represent highly stylized legal forms for controlling physical things. Although superseded in property theory, the thing-ownership metaphor continues today as a theme in popular understanding (Ackerman, 1977). It is easy to think of a house or a field or a farm as a thing because resources defined on this scale can be put to productive use.

During the past century, scholars shifted to the now-standard Hohfeld-Honoré story which is quite a thin account of ownership. Rooted in an early legal realist tradition, the bundle of rights metaphor is an anachronism now ripe for jurisprudential and analytic attention. Neither the old property-as-thing metaphor nor the current property-as-bundle metaphor conveys well the nuanced way law structures control over scarce resources. In particular, the idea of property-as-thing misses the complex internal relations among owners of a thing while the modern bundle metaphor suggests more fluidity than appears in existing property relations.

4.2 The *Numerus Clausus* Debate

Until recently, the *numerus clausus* has been entirely ignored in Anglo-American property theory (though the concept is familiar to civil lawyers). The paucity of allowable property forms in a common law system does not even appear as a puzzle until one reflects on its strangeness. As society becomes more complex, one might expect more forms automatically to emerge. For example, Harold Demsetz argues, '[T]he more extensive specialization becomes, the greater is the variety of private property rights that is needed to accommodate differing production and exchange conditions. The development of private property rights ... [has] mainly been a response to increased gains from specialization of production' (Demsetz, 2001: 16).

Indeed, we do see more and more *comprehensive* governance of scarce resources through private property systems in the post-socialist world, in securities markets, in cyberspace. However, what we do not see with increased specialization is any greater *variety* in core property forms. Even after the breakup of the Soviet Union, to my surprise, the new Russian government created almost the same sharply limited, familiar set of property forms that exists in the United States (Heller, 1998). Perhaps they were trying to copy Western forms as a shortcut to wealth, or perhaps international donors forced their choices. Perhaps, though, the Russians were participating in a more universal phenomenon, one that is at odds with both the familiar understanding of property as an open-ended bundle of rights and Demsetz's argument about rapid property rights evolution.

In his article raising the issue, Rudden wrote, 'In all "non-feudal" systems with which I am familiar (whether earlier, as at Rome, or later), the pattern is (in very general terms) similar: there are less than a dozen sorts of property entitlements'. These entitlements include, for example, the fee simple, easement, and lease. Rudden continued by noting that, '[T]he current literature offers no economic explanation of the *numerus clausus* ... but seems largely to ignore its existence' (Rudden, 1987: 242). Henry Hansmann and Reinier Kraakman also note that 'property law both defines a set of well-recognized standard forms that property rights can take, and burdens the creation of property rights that deviate from those standard forms' (Hansmann and Kraakman, 2002: 3).

More broadly, we lack a theory for what I call the 'economy of property forms', in which economy is read as parsimony. In recent years, three theories have offered partial explanations from a law-and-economics perspective. These include my work on the boundary principle (Heller, 1999), a recent article by Tom Merrill and Henry Smith (2000) on optimal standardization, and Hansmann and Kraakman's (2002) suggestion of a verification approach. Future definitions of property may start with these solutions, but should also reflect our liberal and communitarian intuitions about property, intuitions evoked by the thing and bundle metaphors, respectively.

4.2.1 *The Boundary Principle*

In my view, the limits on existing property forms, what I call the boundary principle, function as one of many crude mechanisms the law has evolved to limit the costs of excessive resource fragmentation (Heller, 1999; Michelman, 1980). For example, the Rule Against Perpetuities restrains some attempts at over-long temporal fragmentation. The boundary principle expands on the idea of anticommons property (Heller, 1998). We have long noted the possibility of a tragedy of the commons, in which people waste a resource through *overuse* when too many have access. Indeed, the image of tragedy forms one of the standard explanations for why we create private property in the first instance, as a mechanism for conservation. The idea of anticommons property focuses on the mirror tragedy, the possibility that people may waste a resource through *underuse* when too many owners have rights in property and can use those rights to block each other's use. The boundary principle suggests that the law has evolved to avoid anticommons tragedy by discouraging people from breaking up ownership on such a scale that the resource will no longer be marketable.

4.2.2 *Communication*

Tom Merrill and Henry Smith (2000) argued that the boundary principle is not sufficient because buyers and sellers who create new property forms would directly bear the costs of those new forms, thus restraining excessive fragmentation. They counter with an argument that focuses attention on costs of communication. Sellers and buyers can communicate with each other directly, but their agreements create rights that third parties must respect. Communicating those obligations is expensive, especially if third parties have to inquire into the details of what has been exchanged. In Merrill and Smith's approach, there must exist some point of optimal standardization, approximated by the *numerus clausus*, because the costs to third parties of measuring their obligations increase with each new form, while the benefits to buyers and sellers of creating some customized form decrease after a while. With just a few property forms, buyers and sellers have inexpensive building blocks for the complex transactions a modern economy requires.

Hansmann and Kraakman (2002) countered Merrill and Smith, arguing that the communication approach may help explain why there exist *some* standard-form property rights and why *clarity* matters, but not why law *limits* creation of non-standard forms. Additional types do not reduce the communicative value of standard forms; rather, like new words in a language, they marginally increase our ability to speak precisely or govern resources efficiently.

4.2.3 *Verification*

Hansmann and Kraakman (2002) propose a focus on the institutional mechanisms that shape new forms, what they call property law's verification function. For them, verification is the primary reason for the *numerus clausus*, indeed what most distinguishes property from contract. Buyers and sellers can negotiate easily over the content of their contract, but without some verification system, which property law provides, buyers have no way of ensuring that a seller has the power to sell. In other words, buyers need to verify *whether* sellers have the power to sell more than they worry about the *content* of rights. Property law is addressed to increasing the transferability of resources by creating a number of verification systems that establish rules for determining who among competing claimants will be awarded control over a resource. Verification systems may include simple possession, branding or labeling, and public registries. To understand what property forms exist, Hansmann and Kraakman ask us to look more closely at verification institutions and to think about the third party information dilemmas they solve.

4.2.4 *Next Steps*

There stands the debate. To understand the strange economy of property forms, we will have to examine not only the forms themselves, but also the acceptable pace of evolution, and rules for when old forms may be destroyed and new ones created. For example, now and then, legislatures or courts retroactively dismiss obsolete forms, such as dower or curtesy, from the *numerus clausus* without people raising a fuss. Why are these legislative acts not takings of private property that require compensation? If existing but obsolete forms do not impose additional fragmentation, communication, or verification costs, and if some people continue to rely on the form, then there is no particular reason to be rid of any form after it has been created. The *numerus clausus* would seem a one-way ratchet. But since feudal times, many quaint forms have been abolished, including not only dower and curtesy, but also fees tail, incorporeal hereditaments such as advowsons and corodies, and so on (Simpson, 1986: 103). Over the past 500 years, despite additions such as the trust and condominium, on balance, the *numerus clausus* has shrunk.

We have a few partial economic explanations—the boundary principle, third-party communication, and verification institutions—oriented towards the utilitarian function of property, and aimed at distinguishing limits on property from freedom of contract. But these explanations are limited indeed. They do not bring to bear insights from history, philosophy, or other disciplines—all elements that would give a richer account of the *numerus clausus*.

4.3 Beyond the Bundle of Rights Definition of Property

The *numerus clausus* debate helps highlight a second area of ongoing theoretical work in property, that is, renewed inquiry into the continuing usefulness of the 'bundle of rights' metaphor as an organizing image for land ownership. The image is perhaps the property concept most in need today of ambitious theoretical work. While the metaphor structures large segments of theoretical and practical debate, it poorly describes emerging property innovations and problems. Though the modern version is usually attributed to Hohfeld, he never mentioned a 'bundle of rights'. Nevertheless, he developed the now standard idea that property comprises a complex aggregate of social and legal relationships made up of rights, privileges, duties, and immunities. This vision of land contrasts with 'the simple and non-social relation between a person and a thing that Blackstone's description suggested' (Alexander, 1997: 319). The Hohfeldian view moved quickly from legal theory into the 1936 Restatement of Property and from there into mainstream scholarship and judicial decision-making. For example, the American Law of Property (1952) defines private property to be an aggregate of legal relations which has economic or sale value if transfer be allowed (§ 26.1 n. 15).

While the modern bundle of legal relations metaphor captures the possibility of complex fragmentation of land, it gives a weak sense of the 'thingness' highlighted by the *numerus clausus* debate. So long as courts and property theorists continue to rely on the modern bundle of legal relations metaphor, and apply it to land as the focus of property, they need some analytical tool to distinguish bundles that count as private property from bundles that do not qualify (see *United States v Craft* (122 S Ct 1414 (2002)). Lacking such a perspective has jurisprudential consequences. For example, the US Supreme Court has adopted uncritically the bundle of rights view of property and used it inadvertently to collapse the idea of private property as a distinct economic and constitutional category (Heller, 1999: 1202–21).

As the bundle of rights view—applied to land as the core resource—waxes in judicial decision-making, it is waning in property theory. J. E. Penner has written caustically that, 'I believe in giving dead concepts [such as the bundle of rights metaphor] a decent burial' (Penner, 1996: 819); and in conversation, property scholars Brian Simpson and Gregory Alexander concur that the time has come for a better core metaphor. Carol Rose extends the critique further and asks:

Why is land—immovable, enduring land—the central symbol for property? Why not, say, water? Water, after all, is in fact the subject of important and valuable property rights, and indeed, concerns about water can substantially modify the rules about land. If water were our chief symbol for property, we might think of property rights—and perhaps other rights—in a quite different way. We might think of rights literally and figuratively as more fluid and less fenced-in; we might think of property as entailing less of the awesome Blackstonian power of exclusion and more of the qualities of flexibility, reasonableness and moderation, attentiveness to others, and cooperative solutions to common problems. (Rose, 1996: 351)

Perhaps we can follow Rose's lead and move away from land as the central resource just as we move away from the bundle of rights as the core metaphor. To be persuasive, any new core definition for the private property ideal type must resonate with existing property debates while it better describes new social practices.

5 THE CONSTRUCTIVE APPROACH: ADDING THE ANTICOMMONS IDEAL TYPE

Secondly, I turn to the constructive approach, which responds to real world property developments by offering a new ideal type rather than redefining old ones. While there are many ways to go outside the usual trilogy, this section will set out just the anticommons ideal type (Heller, 1998). Consider new areas for property law formation, such as the problem of spurring private investment in biomedical research or creating well-functioning markets in post-socialist economies. In both cases, recent reforms aimed to create well-functioning private property regimes, but instead had surprising results, in part by threatening to leave resources stuck in wasteful uses, to deter rather than promote innovation and production. By drawing the wrong property boundaries around resources, by fragmenting ownership too much, it turns out that privatization can destroy resource productivity in enduring ways. Anticommons property, as a fourth ideal type, helps to capture these unexpected results from excessive privatization. The concept goes beyond the old trilogy and crystallizes emerging property relations that had previously remained invisible. Constructing a new ideal type of property can give voice to previously inchoate worries about the progressive march of privatization and explain why too much private property can be as costly as too little.

The ideal type of anticommons property is constructed in such a way as to render it useful for describing real-world property regimes. In theory, in a world of costless transactions, people could always avoid common or anticommons tragedy —overuse from too few owners or underuse from too many—by trading their rights. In practice, however, avoiding tragedy requires overcoming transaction costs, strategic behaviors, and cognitive biases of participants, with success more likely within close-knit communities than among hostile strangers. To have an anticommons, I do not require that everyone hold rights of exclusion, but only that a limited group of owners be able to block one another. Waste through non-use can occur even when a few actors have rights of exclusion in a resource that each wants to use. Also, my definition does not require that non-use be optimal. There are many situations in which non-use results from excessive fragmentation, but is not socially desirable. For most resources that people care about, some level of use is preferable to non-use, and an anticommons regime is a threat to, rather than the epitome of, productive use. Finally, an anticommons may be created even when multiple rights of exclusion are not formally granted through the legal system. Once an anticommons emerges, collecting rights into usable private property is often brutal and slow.

Legal and economic scholars have mostly overlooked this tragedy, in part because it did not fit within the familiar property trilogy, but waste through underuse can appear whenever governments create new property rights. I developed the idea initially from observing privatization in post-socialist economies. One promise of transition to markets was that new entrepreneurs would fill stores that socialist rule had left bare. Yet after several years of reform, many privatized storefronts remained empty, while flimsy metal kiosks, stocked full of goods, mushroomed up on the streets. Why did the new merchants not come in from the cold? One reason was that transition governments often failed to endow any individual with a bundle of rights that represented full ownership. Instead, fragmented rights were distributed to various socialist-era stakeholders, including private or quasi-private enterprises, workers' collectives, privatization agencies, and local, regional, and federal governments. One new owner would be given the right to lease out the store; a second the right to sell it, and a third the right to occupy. No one could set up shop without first collecting rights from each of the other owners back into a coherent bundle.

Privatization of upstream biomedical research in the United States may create anticommons property that is less visible than empty storefronts, but even more economically and socially costly (Heller and Eisenberg, 1998). In this setting, privatization takes the form of intellectual property claims to the sorts of research results that, in an earlier era, would have been made freely available in the public domain. Today, upstream research in the biomedical sciences is increasingly likely to be supported by private funds, carried out in a private institution, and privately appropriated through patents, trade secrecy, or agreements that restrict the use of materials and data. An anticommons in biomedical research may be more likely to endure than in other areas of intellectual property because of high transaction costs of bargaining, heterogeneous interests among owners, and cognitive biases of researchers. But there is little public outcry to fix a biomedical anticommons because the price people pay is in the form of life-saving drugs that are not discovered because too many people hold intellectual property rights that let them block each other from carrying out the necessary research.

Like the transition to free markets in post-socialist economies, privatization of biomedical research offers both promises and risks. It promises to spur private investment, but risks creating a tragedy of the anticommons through a proliferation of fragmented and overlapping property rights. Constructing the anticommons ideal type helps to show why privatization must be more carefully deployed if it is to serve the public goals of biomedical research and post-socialist transition. Otherwise, in the biomedical context, more upstream rights may lead paradoxically to fewer useful products for improving human health, and in post-socialism, excessive privatization can have the unintended effect of turning people against the benefits of market reforms. Adding the idea of anticommons property to our analytic toolkit—going beyond the familiar trilogy—helps to reveal precisely how privatization can cause an unexpected, new form of resource tragedy as it solves an old, familiar dilemma.

6 THE INTEGRATIVE APPROACH: PROPERTY GOVERNANCE THROUGH A LIBERAL COMMONS

Finally, the existing trilogy can be challenged using what I call an integrative approach that brings together elements of the existing ideal types and reveals characteristics of them that are quite distinct. Consider here emerging property regimes that Carol Rose identifies as 'limited commons property' and Hanoch Dagan and I (2001) develop into the 'liberal commons'—complex social relations that we believe may be the future of property. The standard trilogy misses what is most distinctive, perplexing, and important about these regimes, which is the 'property governance' rules people are creating for themselves in new ownership forms, forms not implied either by the image of sole despotic dominion or of a commons. The law governing co-ownership and common interest communities illustrates well success and failure in emerging liberal commons regimes across the US and Commonwealth systems. These regimes open a debate about how property law can and should embody our deepest social values concerning autonomy and community.

The core theoretical issues in co-ownership are not those associated with the Blackstonian image of sole despotic dominion, with atomized owners struggling against each other—problems traditionally covered by laws of nuisance and land use regulation. Nor is co-ownership necessarily characterized by the waste associated with an open access commons, a problem often resolved by state regulation. Despite not fitting within the existing analytic boxes, forms of co-ownership—such as condominium communities—are now among the predominant types of real property organization.

Dagan and Heller's 2001 paper illustrates the integrative approach to property analytics. It looks at the forms of internal self-governance that make cooperation work in new property regimes and then abstracts from those solutions to form a new property construct that integrates the private and commons ideal types of ownership and may be called a 'liberal commons'. A liberal commons is a legal regime that enables a limited group of owners to capture the economic and social benefits from cooperative use of a scarce resource, while also ensuring autonomy to individual members who each retain a secure right to exit.

The idea of a liberal commons challenges entrenched property theory built on oppositions inherent in the existing trilogy. According to these entrenched views, the liberal commons is an oxymoron in theory, impossible in practice, and therefore unworthy of support by law. 'Communitarians', who celebrate successful commons property regimes, openly promote their illiberal character. They emphasize that restrictions on exit are essential in a flourishing community, for only by locking people together can small, close-knit groups develop the informal norms key to conserving commons resources. 'Privatizers' counter that breaking up commons property augurs better for efficiency and autonomy. Most economists join this camp because they worry that rational owners will over-consume commons resources, while most liberals join in because they object to locking people together. 'Regulators' call for state command and control where communitarian or privatization approaches cannot apply. For all, the opposition of commons and private property proves an ideal foil, a shared counterpoint for otherwise competing advocates of community, efficiency, autonomy, and state authority.

The liberal commons approach rejects the oppositions between private and commons property. More precisely, by integrating these types in theory and showing how these types can work together in practice, this approach dissolves the 'tragedy of the commons' conundrum. The tragedy metaphor has long been understood to refer to the problem of tragic outcomes. Seen through the liberal commons prism, the debate between the communitarians and the liberals appears to rely too heavily on a false opposition between commons and private property. Rightly considered, the debate over tragic outcomes should be reframed in terms of the question of tragic choice: are we doomed to choose between our liberal commitments and the economic and social benefits available in a commons? Constructing a liberal commons is, indeed, a challenge, but it is not inherently contradictory or practically unattainable—though the familiar trilogy obscures the meaning of already-existing integrative solutions. Marital property, trusts, condominiums, partnerships, and corporations all belong under a single analytic umbrella: they are forms of liberal commons property. Each is a legal invention that encourages people voluntarily to come together and create limited-access and limited-purpose communities dedicated to shared management of a scarce resource. Each offers internal self-governance mechanisms to facilitate cooperation and the peaceable joint creation of wealth, while simultaneously limiting minority oppression and allowing exit.

By introducing the liberal commons as an analytic tool, already-existing group property regimes become more visible and more tractable for normative and practical property theory work. For example, the idea of a liberal commons helps draw attention to a puzzle: why is there such a sharp contrast regarding cooperation between existing group property regimes, which demonstrate success, and much of the common law of property, which assumes failure? The liberal commons approach can be deployed wherever people want to work together but are prevented from doing so by background property rules premised on the old-fashioned Blackstonian image of private property and the unreflective hostility to cooperation built into the tragedy of the commons image.

The liberal commons idea helps make sense of aspects of US and English property law, including, for example, in the law of co-ownership. Until recently, the English law was uniquely unsupportive of co-owned property. (For the older English law, see Law of Property Act, 1925.) To give one perhaps esoteric example, co-owners in England do not have a right to immediate contribution, even for basic maintenance and other necessary expenses (*Leigh v Dickeson* [1884–5] 15 QBD 60). Delaying such recovery until dissolution increases incentives for ending commons ownership. Not surprisingly, when the US law of co-ownership was formed, it followed the British preference for ending co-ownership rather than supporting its continuation, even though the two systems did not use the same technical forms. (For the American law, see 2 American Law of Property (1952), §§ 6.14–6.18.) Over the past centuries, the autonomy-oriented US law of co-ownership has only further entrenched the lead it took from the English law.

In 1996, however, England passed the Trusts of Land and Appointment of Trustees Act, moving England significantly closer to a more community-supportive regime, influenced perhaps by the relatively pro-cooperation law prevalent throughout the balance of the European Union. The details are complex, but, in some ways, the English law now surpasses its US progeny in supporting the goals of a successful liberal commons. Nevertheless, despite these changes, English law still does not go as far as the Continental systems. (For a comparative law analysis, see Dagan and Heller, 2001: 602–22.) The liberal commons construct helps to make more visible the social values and choices that these legal systems embed in the details of their laws of co-ownership, with the US system most suspicious of and hostile to cooperation, and the British moving towards more support for cooperation.

7 CONCLUSION

Ideal-typical understandings of property frame the normative and practical debates that matter. Across a broad range of recent analytic work, scholars are revisiting the existing trilogy of property forms—private, commons, and state—and showing how these forms hide tragedy and impede innovation at the frontiers of property. Beyond the standard trilogy lie new and useful analytic tools, not just anticommons property and the liberal commons, but also as yet unimagined property types that will respond to new real-world property puzzles. Property theorists are redefining, constructing, and integrating property theory as they update the hoary metaphors of property law.

None of the basic terms for property are stable. This is not to say that they are meaningless or disintegrating, but that property scholarship can gain from pushing these categories to move beyond polarizing oppositions that render problems invisible and jurisprudential debates unresolvable.

REFERENCES

Ackerman, B. (1977). *Private Property and the Constitution*, New Haven: Yale University Press.
Alexander, G. (1997). *Commodity & Propriety: Competing Visions of Property in American Legal Thought, 1776–1970*, Chicago: University of Chicago Press.
Barzel, Y. (1989). *Economic Analysis of Property Rights*, Cambridge: Cambridge University Press.
Becker, L. (1992). 'Too Much Property', *Philosophy & Public Affairs*, 21: 196–206.
Calabresi, G. and Melamed, A. (1972). 'Property Rules, Liability Rules, and Inalienability: One View of the Cathedral', *Harvard Law Review*, 85: 1089–128.
Dagan, H., and Heller, M. (2001). 'The Liberal Commons', *Yale Law Journal*, 110: 549–623.
Demsetz, H. (1967). 'Toward a Theory of Property Rights', *American Economic Review*, 57: 347–58.
—— (2001). 'The Trend Favoring Private Ownership', unpublished.
Ellickson, R. (1991). *Order Without Law: How Neighbors Settle Disputes*, Cambridge, Mass.: Harvard University Press.
—— (1993). 'Property in Land', *Yale Law Journal*, 102: 1305–400.
Grey, T. (1980). 'The Disintegration of Property', *NOMOS*, 22: 69–85, New York: New York University Press.
Hansmann, H., and Kraakman, R. (2002). 'Property Rights, Contract Rights, and Transferability', unpublished.
Hardin, G. (1968). 'The Tragedy of the Commons', *Science*, 162: 1243–8.
Harris, J. (1996). *Property and Justice*, Oxford and New York: Clarendon Press.
Heller, M. (1998). 'The Tragedy of the Anticommons: Property in the Transition from Marx to Markets', *Harvard Law Review*, 111: 621–88.
—— (1999). 'The Boundaries of Private Property', *Yale Law Journal*, 108: 1163–223.
—— and Eisenberg, R. (1998). 'Can Patents Deter Innovation? The Anticommons in Biomedical Research', *Science*, 280: 698–701.
Hohfeld, W. (1923). *Fundamental Legal Conceptions as Applied in Judicial Reasoning and Other Legal Essays*, W. Cook (ed.), New Haven: Yale University Press.
Honoré, A. (1961). 'Ownership', in A. Guest (ed.), *Oxford Essays in Jurisprudence*, Oxford: Oxford University Press, 107–47.
Merrill, T., and Smith, H. (2000). 'Optimal Standardization in the Law of Property: The *Numerus Clausus* Principle', *Yale Law Journal*, 110: 1–70.
Michelman, F. (1980). 'Ethics, Economics and the Law of Property', *NOMOS*, 24: 3–40, New York: New York University Press.
Munzer, S. (1990). *A Theory of Property*, Cambridge: Cambridge University Press.
Ostrom, E. (1990). *Governing the Commons: The Evolution of Institutions for Collective Action*, Cambridge and New York: Cambridge University Press.

Penner, J. (1996). 'The Bundle of Rights Picture of Property', *University of California at Los Angeles Law Review*, 43: 713–820.

Radin, M. (1993). *Reinterpreting Property*, Chicago: University of Chicago Press.

Rose, C. (1996). 'Property as the Keystone Right?', *Notre Dame Law Review*, 71: 329–69.

—— (1998). 'Canons of Property Talk, or, Blackstone's Anxiety', *Yale Law Journal*, 101: 601–32.

Rudden, B. (1987). 'Economic Theory v Property Law: The *Numerus Clausus* Problem', in J. Eekelaar and J. Bell (eds.), *Oxford Essays on Jurisprudence* (3rd edn.), Oxford: Clarendon Press, 239–63.

Simpson, A.W.B. (1986). *A History of the Land Law* (2nd edn.), Oxford: Clarendon Press.

Smith, H. (2000). 'Semicommon Property Rights and Scattering in the Open Fields', *Journal of Legal Studies*, 29: 131–69.

Waldron, J. (1985). 'What is Private Property?' *Oxford Journal of Legal Studies*, 5: 313–49.

—— (1988). *The Right to Private Property*, Oxford: Clarendon Press.

—— (1996). 'Property Law', in D. Patterson (ed.), *A Companion to Philosophy of Law and Legal Theory*, Oxford: Blackwell, 3–23.

EQUITY

PROPERTY AND OBLIGATION

SARAH WORTHINGTON

PROPERTY and obligation lie at the heart of any legal system. The common law's history of divided common law and equitable jurisdictions has produced unique concepts of property and obligation that remain unmatched in civil law jurisdictions. Equitable property, especially as illustrated in the trust, and equitable obligations, especially fiduciary obligations, are without precise civil law counterparts. This ought to have marked these areas out as prime candidates for innovative and inventive common law and comparative scholarship. Instead, even at the turn of the century, modern equity scholarship is still overwhelmingly devoted to doctrinal analysis that seeks simply to define and understand these equitable concepts. There are some notable exceptions, but the focus is largely on narrowly based introspective examination of what the rules are and when they apply, not on more critical and contextual analysis of why the rules should (or should not) be this way, how they can be used, and how they contribute to the evolving common law landscape. This suggests that scholarship in this area is still in its infancy: it is still directed at knowledge and understanding, not at synthesis and evaluation. Moreover, even at this fundamental level, it is not clear that the right questions are being asked if the goal is comprehensive insight into the nature of equitable property and obligation. Indeed, many scholars in non-Commonwealth jurisdictions, perhaps especially those in the United States, would doubt that such pure doctrinal analysis could ever lead to a proper resolution of the issues at stake. In these other jurisdictions there is a long and sophisticated history of concern for social context and circumstances, and to these scholars the prevailing focus of much equity scholarship will seem fundamentally flawed, and maybe even pointless. On the other hand, it is also true that the legal concepts underpinning equitable property and equitable obligation are difficult, and proper definition is important to coherent development of the law's practices.

1 IDEAS OF EQUITABLE PROPERTY

Equity has profoundly affected the idea of property. Very early concepts of property focused on 'things': land and goods were property; other forms of wealth (such as debts due) were merely personal rights enforceable against particular individuals. This undervalued the economic potential of personal rights. Equity changed this. If personal rights were made transferable and protected against interference by third parties, they became usable, tradable, wealth: they became 'property'. This simple fact was recognized first by equity and later by the common law. Debts provide the simplest example: equity elevated debts into tradable assets, not simply personal rights between debtor and creditor. This move from thinking about property as a 'thing' to thinking about it as a bundle of protected, tradable rights, including a bundle of rights relating to intangible forms of wealth, made the legal landscape immediately more sophisticated. It also meant that decisions had to be taken about the dividing line between property and obligation, or between rights that should be accorded this special 'proprietary' status and rights that were deemed merely personal (see Ch. 4). Much general property scholarship is undoubtedly relevant in analysing and evaluating equity's various modes of proprietary intervention, yet property theory is rarely used in this specific way. The approach might prove revealing.

General property theory commonly asks *why* particular rights should be proprietary at all: it asks why rights should be accorded the special privileges and protections traditionally accorded to legal property. If this were the question, then careful analysis might suggest that different types of property rights (common law and equitable property rights, including both ownership and security interests) should be accorded different degrees of protection. This discrimination exists already, although with little supporting theoretical analysis: consider the priority rules that favour the holders of legal property over the holders of equitable property. Modern property theory might be used to good effect not only to compare and contrast legal and equitable property, but also to compare and contrast equitable charges and equitable ownership interests. The intuitive response is that ownership must be more valuable than a security interest, and yet the truth may turn out to be the opposite, at least so far as equitable property is concerned. It is, at least superficially, easier to justify the proprietary status of an equitable security interest than that of an equitable ownership interest.

The commercial objectives underpinning an equitable charge simply will not work without according the chargee's interest strong, protected, privileged proprietary status. The same cannot automatically be said of a trust arrangement. The civilian law approach is a stark reminder of this. Although modern commercial trusts now rely heavily on the proprietary incidents associated with the trust structure, it might do little damage to the commercial success of these trust vehicles if equitable ownership interests were accorded less aggressive proprietary protection than other forms of proprietary interests (whether legal or equitable). This possibility of differentiation between property interests needs to be addressed.

The beginnings of this sort of discriminating scholarship can be seen in Smith (2000). He suggests that there is no necessary reason why owners of legal property and equitable property should be accorded the same rights. However, his suggestion has been staunchly criticized by those seeking simple framework expositions of legal rules. The critics are inclined to view such differentiation as tantamount to advocating internal inconsistencies, where property ownership means something different on either side of an historical but now irrelevant jurisdictional divide. Instead, the critics argue, a consistent rule should deliver the same legal privileges and protections to all owners of wealth, whether their interests are legal or equitable. The issue is critical. Simplicity is clearly a desirable goal, yet it is also clear that an evolving legal system matures by devising increasingly sophisticated distinctions. Many of the distinctions between legal and equitable property, and between ownership and security interests, do not depend upon the jurisdictional divide even though this may have supported their emergence. These differences may make it quite inappropriate to treat all 'property' interests in the same crudely uniform manner.

Until this fundamental issue is resolved, it is impossible to provide defensible answers to the questions that are now beginning to trouble both courts and legislatures. These questions all centre on the degree of protection that should be accorded to equitable property interests (see Sects 1.3 and 1.4 below). The wrong answers will appear defensible, at least superficially, if the initial assumptions are incorrect. It is vital to know whether all property interests, whether common law or equitable, whether ownership or security, should be treated alike. Indeed, the next section makes it clear that this sort of analysis is also essential in satisfactorily distinguishing between different property interests and between property and obligation.

1.1 Identifying Equitable Property

If scholarship has lagged in its theoretical analysis of equitable property, it has more than made up for it in the doctrinal analysis of the incidence of equitable property. Interest has been sparked because there are obvious commercial advantages in having rights that are proprietary rather than personal. Despite this, a property right is often no more than a personal right—maybe even a personal right recognized only in equity and not at law—that the law deems worthy of privileged protection. This boundary between property and obligation has always been hard fought, and yet the divide is now more controversial than it was fifty years ago.

Equity invented both ownership and security interests that differ quite radically from their common law counterparts. Predictably, the nature of the bundle of rights is different; less predictably, equitable property rights can arise both consensually and by operation of law. The nearest the common law comes to interests arising by operation of law is with its rules on money as currency, where title to money can vest in a third party even though the original owner expressed no intention to part with the cash. Consensual arrangements, whether for security or ownership, are easier to understand. An equitable charge agreement not only gives chargees contractual rights against their chargor; it also gives them specifically enforceable and transferable rights to have the charged property dealt with in defined ways and, additionally, rights to exclude third parties from interfering with these specific rights. The chargee's personal contract rights are protected in equity as 'property'. The genius of the trust went even further than this. In a typical express trust arrangement, orthodox common law contract rules of privity and consideration would deny the third party beneficiary any incidental personal rights (never mind proprietary rights) relating to the arrangement. Equity simply ignored these common law impediments. Initially, it regarded the beneficiary as having enforceable personal rights against the trustee, and later it protected these rights to such an extent that they were elevated to the status of property interests. The analogous non-consensual interests are more difficult to explain. These interests are generated by operation of law, in the form of equitable liens and resulting and constructive trusts.

The boundaries of these seemingly simple ideas about property have generated an enormous volume of technical and doctrinal legal scholarship. Most attention has focused on the crucial boundary between property and obligation. In particular, which 'personal' obligations will equity deem worthy of elevating to protected proprietary status? Arrangements that are specifically intended to create express trusts have this status (whether or not they are contractual). So too do contracts for the creation of equitable charges. By contrast, other contractual arrangements to deal with property in particular ways do not deliver a proprietary interest in the underlying property in advance of any agreed legal transfer unless the contract is unconditional, specifically enforceable, and relates to identifiable property (Worthington, 1996). If these conditions are met, then the ownership interests (constructive trusts) arise by operation of law in advance of the agreed obligation to effect a legal transfer. In a similar fashion, many analogous non-consensual obligations designed to effect restitution or to remedy wrongdoing can also generate proprietary interests. Equity's core idea is that an obligation (however generated) to deal with underlying property in certain ways can, of itself, create interests in that property in favour of the party to whom the personal obligation is owed. This idea underpins all of equity's proprietary intervention. It is the basis of express trusts and equitable charges, as well as constructive trusts, resulting trusts, and equitable liens.

The privileges accorded to proprietary status provide the impetus for pushing the boundaries between property and obligation further outwards. First consider consensual arrangements. Because contracts so rarely deliver proprietary interests in advance of the legal transfer of the promised asset (see above), there are obvious advantages in recharacterizing the agreement as one that specifically creates an express trust. This recharacterization is central to *Quistclose* trusts (*Barclays Bank Ltd v Quistclose Investments Ltd* [1970] AC 257). On its face, the arrangement between the parties is a contract for a loan with the added rider that the loan funds must only be used for nominated purposes. The express agreement plainly restricts the rights of the borrower to deal with the loan funds. However, academic analysis has not yet satisfactorily pinpointed what feature in this restriction compels the conclusion that the lender retains equitable ownership of the funds, rather than a security interest (indeed, the facts are always such that this has never even been suggested) or merely the benefit of a personal right against the borrower. Instead, the analyses successfully generate internally consistent conclusions about the personal and proprietary relationships between all the various parties *if* the initial assertion of trust (Millett, 1985; Worthington, 1996) or personal obligation (Chambers, 1997) is accepted as correct. It is the initial boundary assertion that is crucial, and to that extent these analyses remain incomplete.

The shortcomings in doctrinal analysis of consensual arrangements are even more evident in one other much investigated area. This is the scholarship dealing with family homes. The courts routinely use constructive trusts to divide family property. In the UK, this is typically justified as the enforcement of an agreement between the parties. The problem is that express agreements between domestic parties are exceptional and inferred agreements often appear to be instrumental fictions. Added to this, an agreement which is not in writing is now void (Law of Property Act 1925 s 53 (UK); Law of Property (Miscellaneous Provisions) Act 1989 s 2 (UK)). To specifically enforce *any* unwritten arrangement in these circumstances, never mind an arrangement discovered on rather flimsy evidence, seems doctrinally perverse, whatever the social imperatives. It would be far better to solve the problem by statutory means, where judicial discretion can overtly implement identified social expectations (Gardner, 1993).

The conviction that doctrine is being used to disguise instrumentalist judicial discretion in these family homes cases is reinforced by comparisons with other common law jurisdictions. Every jurisdiction manages to deliver similar results on similar facts, and yet each achieves this by adopting different and allegedly more acceptable doctrinal strategies. In Australia the driving force is 'unconscionability', and in New Zealand it is 'reasonable expectations', but in both jurisdictions the analysis appears to lead to much the same contract-styled remedy. In Canada the driving force is 'unjust enrichment'. This is a very different doctrinal analysis (see Ch. 3), but because of the way the enrichment is assessed (seemingly based on expectations of benefit rather than reversal of enrichment) there is little to distinguish the end result from those of other jurisdictions.

If the boundary between property and obligation appears uncertain in these consensual arrangements, it is dramatically more uncertain in non-consensual situations. Disgorgement remedies (also labelled restitutionary damages) for breach of fiduciary duty were, historically, often regarded as personal remedies, but courts in the UK and Australia have recently been persuaded that a proprietary response is more consistent with equity's traditional mode of operation—equity treats as done that which ought to be done (Millett, 1993). But, at least in this area, perhaps the general equitable rule has been generalized too far. Certainly the change from personal to proprietary response has provoked hostility in some quarters (Goode, 1998). Once again, identifying the boundary between property and obligation is crucial (see the approach adopted by Oakley, 1997). The better general rule may be one that is more finely attuned to differences between different types of fiduciary breaches. Constructive trust remedies may be appropriate when the analogy with contract admits of specific performance of an investment obligation embodied in the trust deed, for example. Otherwise, where the fiduciary has merely breached the duty of loyalty by taking bribes or disloyal opportunities, both policy and doctrine suggest that the remedy should perhaps be personal only (Finch and Worthington, 2000). This would leave the Anglo-Australian constructive trust as institutional (i.e. arising on the facts rather than ordered by the court, for whatever that is worth). At the same time, it would align the results with those jurisdictions like the United States and Canada that are more alert to the insolvency consequences of the proprietary response: their 'remedial' constructive trust permits the judges to ensure that the remedy does not impact on vulnerable third parties (Sherwin, 1989).

The other battlefront for non-consensual claims is the scholarship relating to proprietary responses to unjust enrichment claims. Restitutionary obligations require defendants to return value to disappointed claimants (see Ch. 3). The key issue is whether these personal restitutionary obligations can also be analysed on the proprietary model, with the relevant obligation being regarded as one that obliges the defendant to restore specific property to the claimant rather than an obligation simply to restore value. Although there were some promising early judicial precedents and suggestive academic arguments (Birks, 1992), the possibility of a proprietary response has now been vehemently denied by the judiciary, at least in the UK. This judicial reformulation suggested that a presumed resulting trust arose only when there was an unrebutted presumption that the claimant intended to transfer the asset to the defendant *on trust* (a view put by Swadling, 1996, disagreeing with Birks, 1992). If the presumption is of *an intention to create a trust*, then it is rebutted by any evidence which shows that the claimant did not *intend to create a trust*. Importantly, if the transfer was made in ignorance, or by mistake, or according to the terms of an otherwise voidable or void contract, then clearly the claimant did not intend to create a trust. The result is to decrease dramatically the role of proprietary restitutionary remedies.

Yet again, the controversy in these unjust enrichment cases centres on the boundary between property and obligation. If the conceptual landscape is to present a consistent profile, then analysis must necessarily adopt a rationale that is consistent with the property and obligation boundaries presented in other circumstances. This can only be ensured by deliberate comparison across the entire landscape of equitable property interests. This reveals that perhaps the older orthodoxy, or some refinement of it, remains the preferable explanation of resulting trusts. This older view suggests that resulting trusts arise where there is an unrebutted presumption that the transferor did not intend *to benefit* the defendant (Birks, 1992; Chambers, 1997). Indeed, even earlier judicial approaches put the presumption more widely still: a presumed resulting trust arises whenever the claimant makes a gratuitous transfer to the defendant and there is an unrebutted presumption that a gift was not intended. It then follows that the presumption of a resulting trust can only be properly rebutted if the evidence surrounding the gratuitous transfer shows both that the transferor intended the transfer to be absolute (i.e. a beneficial transfer) *and* intended it to be voluntary (i.e. gratuitous). This version then presents the possibility of an alternative analysis of the fault line between property and obligation. The claimant may not have formed a proper (legally recognized) intention to effect the transfer (whether gratuitous or for value)—perhaps the claimant was mistaken, or operating under undue influence. Alternatively, the claimant may have legally intended the transfer, but not intended it to be gratuitous—the circumstances may simply conspire to deliver a gratuitous transfer because the alleged contract is void at law, or the contract is legitimately terminated or frustrated and the claimant's transfer is one made on a total failure of consideration. It would seem imperative that the former category (the unintended transfer) is seen to generate proprietary responses to restitutionary recovery if doctrinal analysis is to remain coherent. Consider the rules that operate in the context of ineffective transfers or conditional transfers such as *Quistclose* trusts. With the second category, however, there may be room for manoeuvre. It is true that presumed resulting trusts and purchase money resulting trusts demonstrate that the traditional means of reversing these unintended gifts in equity was by proprietary means. (The same is true of constructive trusts designed to effect disgorgement of disloyal fiduciary gains—see above.) However, modern judicial analyses suggest that the remedy in these circumstances does not warrant privileged proprietary status. If this proprietary status arose simply because equity could only operate by proprietary means or not at all, then these traditional illustrations may reflect the unacceptable face of the historical jurisdictional divide between the common law and equity. The modern law ought not to be bound by these traditions if the response is inapt and inconsistent with other responses across the common law landscape.

These modern debates over the identification of trusts—whether express trusts or trusts imposed by operation of law—are all, at root, concerned with the dividing line between property and obligation. This general issue permeates much of modern law. In the trust context, the issue is quite specific: which obligations to deal with specific property should be regarded as delivering interests in that property to third parties? The difference is euphonically described as the difference between owing and owning, but it marks the boundary between obligation and property. Indeed, other boundary issues could usefully be fed into this sort of analysis. The floating charge might afford fruitful ground. A hundred years ago, American judges decided that 'floating charges' generated personal rights only, not proprietary interests in any underlying assets. English courts took the opposite view. This difference says something about the issues associated with the dividing line between property and obligation and the protections that ought legitimately to be accorded to different types of property interests.

If the primary focus of scholarship in this area is on the boundary between property and obligation, the second, and narrower, strand of doctrinal scholarship relates to the boundary between ownership and various security interests. Perhaps surprisingly, this has received relatively little attention, and then only on two fronts. Scholars have usually focused on the divide between fixed and floating charges or, alternatively, on retention of title clauses where the parties themselves have attempted to construct products and proceeds ownership clauses, but judges have almost invariably construed them as registrable but unregistered security interests. Practising lawyers regard this scholarship as important because various statutory incursions have made the rights of different interest holders radically different: ownership interests need not be registered, but most security interests by way of charge are ineffective unless registered; furthermore, in many jurisdictions, floating charges are less valuable than fixed charges because of the relative priority accorded by statute to certain personal claims. Analogous boundary issues exist in relation to equitable ownership and security interests that arise by operation of law rather than consensually, yet these have attracted almost no sustained academic attention. All these boundary issues are important to a proper understanding of the underlying concepts, although the conclusions might appear more compelling if the studies were more broadly based.

In summary, despite the sustained scholarly attention devoted to identifying the markers of equitable proprietary interests, especially ownership interests, there is still no simple answer to the apparently simple question of what divides property and obligation, and what divides different property interests. The answer seems unlikely to be offered by scholarship that does not adopt a broad comparative focus, surveying all the circumstances that generate these interests, and looking for a common set of discriminators. Even textbooks with reputations for detailed and comprehensive coverage (such as Meagher *et al.*, 1992) do not adopt this broad comparative perspective. Moreover, although doctrinal analysis is obviously crucial, there will undoubtedly be controversy at the margins, and the preferred approach is likely to be best discovered by testing and evaluating the alternatives against more general theoretical principles and policy objectives. To date this has been largely ignored.

1.2 Uses of Equitable Property

Not all the scholarship in this area has been doctrinal. Relatively recently, American scholars have used law and economics approaches to attempt to identify and explain the most valuable commercial attributes of the trust. Their work suggests that two particular features make the express trust especially valuable as a commercial vehicle: flexibility and asset partitioning (Hansmann and Mattei, 1998; Hansmann and Kraakman, 2000; Langbein, 1995). (They also recognized two other less significant features: the automatic imposition of onerous fiduciary duties, and tax benefits.)

Flexibility, in the trust context, is generally taken to mean flexibility in selecting governance structures and flexibility in structuring the beneficiaries' interests. The second aspect, not the first, gives trusts their real commercial advantages. Trusts permit the slicing up of monolithic property rights in ways that are inconceivable without the trust. They thus enable the creation of new forms of usable wealth. Consider the property in a company share. Shareholders may transfer ownership or security interests in the entire right associated with the entire share, but they cannot sell part of a share, or parcel out the different benefits inherent in shareholding to different transferees, giving one the right to dividends, another the right to vote, and yet another the right to capital gains. Under the umbrella of a trust, all of this is possible. This strategy is now commonly used in 'asset securitization' trusts, where bundles of receivables held on trust are repackaged into high risk and low risk tranches, and then re-sold to third parties. Practitioners are driving these developments, but the potential they afford for academic theorizing about property is readily apparent.

The other significant advantage of trusts is asset partitioning. The trust's unique proprietary structure provides a commercial vehicle where business assets are partitioned from the assets of the owners and managers of the business. This facility lies at the heart of the economic advantages and efficiencies of all organizational law (Hansmann and Kraakman, 2000), and the trust was one of the earliest vehicles to achieve this goal. Remarkably, it did so without the need for separate legal personality (which is corporate law's mechanism) or specific statutory recognition of divided patrimony (which may be the chief reason that civilian jurisdictions did not invent their own versions of the trust).

There are two strategies associated with 'asset partitioning'. Affirmative asset partitioning protects the pool of trust assets from the claims of the owners' and managers' creditors. This remarkable commercial achievement cannot, even now, be replicated by contract or by modern security law. In English trust law, it is critically dependent on two particular features of the trust—divided legal and equitable title, and the concept of a fund. Divided title protects the trust assets from the claims of the trustee's creditors. The 'fund' concept protects trust assets from the claims of the beneficiaries' creditors. A fund achieves this by defining the beneficiaries' entitlements as net interests, assessed net of the entitlements of the trust creditors, not as unencumbered interests in the fixed and circulating assets presently held by the trustees. These asset-partitioning default rules make trusts an attractive 'counter-party' (raising the issue of separate legal personality) in commercial transactions (Hansmann and Kraakman, 2000). The other aspect of asset partitioning, defensive asset partitioning, works in reverse. It protects the beneficiaries' assets from the trust's creditors. This is useful—indeed, in the corporate law context it has been the subject of much scholarly attention—but it could be achieved relatively easily by contract mechanisms.

1.3 Proprietary Protection of Equitable Property and Tracing into Windfall Secondary Profits

As suggested earlier, one of the reasons for wide-ranging sustained doctrinal analysis in this area is the proprietary consequences which follow from the legitimate asser-tion of a primary trust (whether express, constructive, or resulting). Such trusts, whatever their genesis, give the beneficiary valuable insolvency priority in any claims to recover the trust assets from the insolvent trustee or from third parties other than bona fide purchasers for value. Doctrinal and policy debates rage over the extent to which this insolvency priority ought to be preserved, and indeed maybe even enhanced, if the defendant no longer holds the original asset, but instead holds its valuable traceable substitutes.

The rules that regulate these issues were first developed in the context of trustees managing express trusts. The cases paid little regard to the trustee's particular breach of duty, but grounded their remedies in the assertion that an initial fiduciary duty combined with equity's tracing rules (which allowed property to be traced into its exchange products) were sufficient to deliver advantageous proprietary remedies to the claimant. Until the 1990s, these tracing rules could not be utilized unless the defendant was a fiduciary and the claimant could demonstrate an initial equi-table proprietary interest. Only then could the beneficiary claim either an equitable security interest (thus preserving the insolvency priority of the initial claim) or equitable ownership of any profitable exchanges (thus gaining the benefit of windfall secondary profits) (Smith, 1997).

Now there are powerful moves to generalize these tracing rules so that they apply whenever there is any form of proprietary base, whether legal or equitable, and whether or not there is a fiduciary relationship (Smith, 1997). The resulting changes would be dramatic. Any claimant with an initial proprietary claim against the defendant would be entitled to preserved insolvency priority against traceable substitutes, and to claim the enhanced value inherent in those substitutes regardless of whether the defendant had committed any wrong in effecting the substitution. Certain UK cases already support this extended protection. These cases hold that claims to windfall secondary profits derive directly from the claimant's proprietary interest in the initial asset, and are not dependent upon any wrongdoing or proof of unjust enrichment. Other scholars disagree, suggesting that the remedy is more appropriately grounded in unjust enrichment (Smith, 1997) or in proof of some wrong for which the remedy is disgorgement (i.e. a fiduciary wrong or certain breaches of confidence) (Worthington, 2001). The answer matters. Ownership of the substitute asset is at stake. In the headlong rush to advance doctrinally coherent solutions to this problem, few seem to have asked the most fundamental question, which is whether an initial proprietary claim can legitimately generate such exceptional and extended proprietary protection. Once again, the gap in analysis is the failure to focus on the essential attributes of property rights.

1.4 Personal Protection of Equitable Property— Accessory Liability and Recipient Liability

As well as debate on the proprietary front, there is fierce doctrinal debate surrounding the personal obligations that are necessarily imposed on trustees and complicit third parties in the event of a breach of trust. It is not controversial that express trustees are exposed to the whole gamut of common law and equitable obligations in the management of the trust property. Whether trustees holding property under constructive and resulting trusts are similarly constrained is not such an easy question. Academic analysis has largely avoided the issue, although it is conceded that knowledge of the circumstances of the trust must be material. Indeed, there is increasing room for debate about what 'the whole gamut of fiduciary obligations' entails. In particular, when fiduciary obligations are pared down to their essentials, it is not clear what duties are imposed or how far liability should extend when the trust arises by operation of law (see Sect. 2.2 below).

Secondly, in this area of personal liability, still more controversial debates concern the liability of third parties who are associated in some way with a breach of trust. Judicial reassessment of the liability attracted by 'knowing assistance in a breach of trust' has recategorized this wrong as accessory liability. Third parties who dishonestly assist in a breach of trust are made personally liable to compensate for the losses generated by the breach. Until recently, dishonesty seemed to be assessed objectively, as befits a civil wrong. Perhaps surprisingly, then, the most recent UK judicial reassessment suggests that the dishonesty requirement also has a subjective element, so that the defendant must appreciate that the assistance was dishonest. All of this analysis has been provided by the courts.

Lastly, the hardest fought battles concern the personal liability of 'knowing recipients' of trust property. This area of the law is sorely in need of definitive and compelling academic or judicial analysis. At root the difficulty centres on how to categorize the receipt of property by the third party stranger to the trust so that doctrinal analysis delivers the appropriate remedy. If the receipt is classed as an unjust enrichment, then common law analogies suggest that the recipient ought to be strictly liable. The remedy would then be quantified according to restitutionary rules, and would be subject to the defence of change of position (Lord Nicholls, 1998). Alternatively, the receipt may be categorized as the equitable counterpart of common law conversion, with the recipient strictly liable to compensate the owner for any losses caused by the wrong. These analytical options seem quite simple. But the proper approach is not necessarily revealed by such simple analogies with the common law rules. All depends upon the essential attributes of legal and equitable property. If the two are equivalent, then simple analogies should be apt. If they are not equivalent, and some lesser degree of protection is somehow warranted for equitable property, then a different analysis may be needed. It might still be appropriate to categorize the receipt as an unjust enrichment, but to afford a remedy only when the recipient has constructive knowledge that the receipt is trust property (Smith, 2000). Alternatively, it might be more appropriate to characterize the receipt as conversion, but as warranting a remedy only when the recipient knows, or has constructive knowledge, that the receipt is a wrong. The quantification of compensation could even reflect the different degrees of knowledge. If the recipient has constructive knowledge, then liability might be restricted to foreseeable losses; if the recipient has actual knowledge, however, then liability might encompass all incidental losses, no matter how remote. The common law rules relating to misrepresentation could provide a useful model. Yet again, the message is the same: compelling scholarship must consciously address the possibility of important distinctions between legal and equitable property.

2 FIDUCIARY LAW SCHOLARSHIP

Trustees, company directors, and solicitors are all fiduciaries. So too are other parties. Equity subjects these individuals to obligations of loyalty. Fiduciaries are required to put their principal's interests ahead of their own. Unless they have the informed consent of their principal, they cannot enter into transactions that involve a conflict between their personal interests and their duty to their principal; in fact, they cannot profit in any secret way from their position. Without the necessary consent, fiduciaries cannot engage in certain perfectly legitimate activities that would otherwise be open to them. If fiduciaries fail to live up to these standards (and a fiduciary can fail despite acting carefully and in perfect good faith), then equity insists that the profits of the breach be paid over to the principal. The fiduciary has to 'account'. The remedy is available whether or not the principal has suffered a loss and whether or not the principal expected to obtain the gain personally. Because of this, it is often said that the remedy delivers a windfall to the principal.

Sustained scholarly analysis of fiduciary law began relatively late, and even now it remains heavily influenced by a few early writers (Scott, 1949; Sealy, 1962, and 1963; Finn, 1977—this last work remains the *locus classicus*). Indeed, at the end of the nineteenth century, fiduciary law appeared to be more or less settled. In the past forty years, however, that illusion has been exploded. Different common law jurisdictions have developed fiduciary law at different rates in vastly different directions. These developments might be summarized, rather cynically, by suggesting that orthodox fiduciary law is no longer critical in mainstream common law jurisdictions other than England.

Early fiduciary scholarship was concerned to identify a range of status-based fiduciaries, such as agents, company directors, partners and solicitors, and then to describe the common obligations to which this group was subject, and the remedies that fiduciary breaches would attract (Scott, 1949; Sealy, 1962; Finn, 1977). Fiduciary law was attractive to claimants because it delivered better remedies more easily: its remedies included proprietary disgorgement (delivered by way of a constructive trust); limitation periods were more generous; and damages assessment rules were unconstrained by doctrines of remoteness or foreseeability.

Later scholarship focused on pushing out the boundaries of this fiduciary law. Two strategies were adopted. The first looked to how fiduciaries were defined, with the aim of suggesting that other parties could be subjected to the rigours of the fiduciary regime. These parties became known as fact-based fiduciaries, characterized as such because of the context of their relationship with the other party. Alternatively, and more recently, the approach has been to question whether fiduciary remedies are necessarily limited in their application to status-based, or even fact-based, fiduciaries. These two different drives for expansion were prompted by the perceived remedial advantages inherent in orthodox fiduciary law. English scholars alone have resisted these attractions, and have instead focused on refining and paring down the scope and reach of the fiduciary regime. However, even their approach is now being undermined by recent English judicial developments.

2.1 The Fiduciary Role

Despite years of scholarship and judicial activity, there is still no generally accepted definition of a fiduciary. Many possibilities have been advanced, but all seem fatally flawed (for a critique, see Shepherd, 1981). Several characteristics are commonly recognized as being crucial in determining the incidence of fiduciary obligations: one party entrusts property to another; or undertakes to act in the interests of another; or relies on another; or is vulnerable to abuse by another; or is able to exercise a discretion affecting the other (Weinrib, 1975; Frankel, 1983). But the difficulty has always been that these descriptors, although apt to describe relationships where fiduciary obligations *are* imposed, are often equally apt when such obligations are traditionally considered to be absent. In particular, the characteristics are equally apt where contract and tort are seen as providing adequate protection—for example, in the relationship between home-owner and house-painter, or diner and chef, or driver and other road users.

Despite this lack of precision, Canadian judges and scholars have adopted this jurisprudence and used it to radically expand the range of relationships regarded as fiduciary. Doctors and parents may be regarded as fiduciaries, for example (and not simply in the ambiguous sense that there is a relationship of presumed undue influence). The clear aim is to take advantage of fiduciary law's more advantageous remedies, its longer limitation periods, and its useful presumptions against the fiduciary defendant. It is not, unfortunately, to reflect society's changing values and attitudes to medical and parenting roles. Moreover, this expansion has been matched by a willingness to see fiduciary law as designed to protect not only economic rights, but also bodily integrity and other social and political rights, and then necessarily to encompass different duties. With this degree of expansionism, fiduciary law loses its core meaning. The tag is simply being used instrumentally to remedy wrongs where judges perceive that there is no existing remedy available and no more amenable route for judicial law reform. The consequence is an inevitable loss of doctrinal coherence. This expansionist practice is not used where protective strategies are already in place. For example, it has not been necessary to see corporate directors as owing fiduciary duties to bond holders or employees, for example (Frankel, 1983). This Canadian approach (and, to a lesser extent, the New Zealand approach described below) is commonly caricatured as an abandonment of principle.

If fiduciary doctrine is to retain any core meaning, then fiduciaries need to be appropriately defined (see Sect. 2.2 below). Law and economics scholars may help in devising a better definition. These scholars recognize that fiduciary proscriptions (for this is the unique nature of fiduciary obligations of loyalty) and their unusual disgorgement remedies are amply justified by economic analysis simply because the fiduciary relationship is one characterized by unusually high costs of specification and monitoring (Easterbrook and Fischel, 1993). This insight suggests that fiduciary obligations should be imposed not simply when certain descriptors are apt, but when the very function or purpose or reason for one party's role in relationship demands that the party operate on the basis of self-denial. This condition is not met simply because one party would prefer the other to act selflessly, or has assumed this to be the case; nor is the condition denied simply because it is conceivable that the subject's interests can be served notwithstanding selfish behaviour. The rules are needed only if, without them, the subject would be left with no effective legal means of monitoring the relationship because obligations imposed in contract or tort, or by some other equitable duty, would be insufficient for the task. As a defining characteristic, this purpose-based requirement, focusing on reducing agency costs, appears very elastic. However, it ought to prove no more difficult to apply than the search for implied terms in contract, or a duty of care in negligence.

The second development which seems set to deny fiduciary law any significant role attacks the coherence of fiduciary doctrine from the remedial end. Instead of expanding the notion of who is a fiduciary so that almost anyone is caught in the fiduciary net, this tactic suggests that equitable remedies, in particular advantageous fiduciary disgorgement remedies, are available to remedy non-fiduciary wrongs. New Zealand jurists and certain scholars worldwide favour this approach. If this is the correct approach, then there is no need to be concerned about carefully defining the fiduciary role.

The final reason why fiduciary law is losing some of its intense attraction is that the common law is increasingly developing alternative strategies to deal with these and similar cases. There is a growing reliance on notions of good faith and uncon-scionability. Fiduciary loyalty, good faith and unconscionability represent points on an increasingly liberal continuum (Finn, 1989). Unconscionability accepts that one party can act self-interestedly, but proscribes excessively self-interested or exploitative conduct. Good faith permits a party to act self-interestedly, but demands recognition of the legitimate self-interests of the other party. Fiduciary standards enjoin a party to act selflessly and with undivided loyalty. These related doctrines are important to the position of fiduciary law. Civilian law comparisons reinforce this. Because civilian law jurisdictions start from the baseline of specific performance of contracts and impose obligations of good faith as a matter of routine, there is not the sharp divide for them between fiduciary rules and results and non-fiduciary rules and results. In many circumstances where the common law sees fiduciary doctrine as essential, civilian law already has a non-fiduciary remedy based on good faith, even if its detail is not as dramatic as that delivered by the common law (indeed, it is often the drama of the common law response which creates the controversy surrounding fiduciary doctrine).

These civilian law notions of good faith are already prevalent in the United States, where the UCC 1-202 imposes an obligation of good faith. In Australia, the Trade Practices Act 1974 has introduced an equally prevalent notion of unconscionability. Neither approach necessarily delivers the strong fiduciary protection generated by the duty of loyalty and the remedies of profit-stripping and tracing into unauthor-ized transfers, but nevertheless they afford a measure of compensation where ortho-dox contract or tort law would not. To that extent, they relieve the pressure on fiduciary law.

All of these developments reduce the need to resort to fiduciary law. They there-fore reduce the impetus for fiduciary scholarship. Instead, the focus has turned increasingly to defining the limits to discretionary remedialism and articulating the boundaries of good faith, unconscionability, and disgorgement remedies (Finn, 1989).

2.2 Doctrinal Refinement

The English jurisdiction alone seems to have remained true to early fiduciary law. Indeed, this feature has attracted its own critics: English jurists and scholars are sometimes caricatured as unbendingly conservative because modern English doctrine appears to be little more than an ossified version of nineteenth-century principles. The theoretical concern has been to preserve the distinctiveness of the equitable jurisdiction (the views of Meagher *et al.*, 1992 are seen as compelling). Only slowly—perhaps only in the last decade—are long-accepted jurisdictional alignments being regarded with a little more scepticism (see Sect. 3 below).

English fiduciary law has, however, made a substantial contribution to paring down the fiduciary regime to its essential components. At the outset, the early scholarship defined the duties to which status-based fiduciaries were subject, and these were all classed as 'fiduciary duties' (Finn, 1977; Sect. 2.1 above). Only slowly has it come to be recognized that not all these duties are fiduciary duties. The core fiduciary duty is now recognized as the duty of loyalty, with its historically distinctive remedy of disgorgement. It is not yet the case, but it may soon be recognized that the fiduciary's duty of strict compliance will be recognized as contractual; the fiduciary's duty of care will become subsumed within the common law duty of care despite its equitable provenance; and the fiduciary's duty to act bona fide and for proper purposes will be seen as analogous to the duty to act for proper purposes which is evident in several non-fiduciary circumstances. All of these duties attract compensatory remedies, not disgorgement remedies. Disgorgement remedies are the preserve of the fiduciary's breach of loyalty. This process of analysing the fiduciary role is leaving fiduciary law much reduced in scope, but its essential attributes are then better exposed for what they are, and its essential and unique justifications are more readily identified. These core fiduciary obligations might then be usefully compared and contrasted with equity's other major contribution to the obligations landscape, the law on breach of confidence. It might turn out that these two equitable contributions are not analogous: fiduciary obligations may align more coherently with contract, and breach of confidence with tort.

3 THE COMMON LAW–EQUITY DIVIDE

All of this narrowly focused doctrinal analysis of equitable property and obligation stands in stark contrast to one vein of modern scholarship that has, very recently, taken a dramatic turn and questioned the relevance of the historical common law–equity divide (Duggan, 1997; Burrows, 2002). This issue is crucial if legal analysis is to generate a coherent map of the common law. The orthodox view is that the two jurisdictional streams are so fundamentally different that integration is impossible. The inevitable conclusion is that coherence across the boundary is doomed. The typical stance is that equity differs from the common law in both a substantive and a formal sense. Substantively, the goal of equity is allegedly to promote other-regarding behaviour, or altruism, whereas the common law pragmatically concedes, and utilizes, the parties' tendencies towards self-interested behaviour. The formal difference is even more significant: equity allegedly administers individual, discretionary justice while the common law administers universal, rule-based justice. Both claims are becoming increasingly disputed. Duggan (1997) argues that equitable rules, like common law rules, are best explained in efficiency terms. Certainly there appears to be nothing of significance dividing either system's resort to values or discretion. Any eventual demolition of this historical jurisdictional divide is likely to have dramatic consequences for the resolution of the various difficult issues associated with equitable property and obligation.

Take equitable property. The trust, and the pragmatic desire to retain its commercial and social advantages, is commonly seen as an insurmountable impediment to integrating equity and common law. However, the genius of the trust is simply that it makes it possible to divide a bundle of proprietary rights in an asset between different individuals in a novel way so as to create new forms of usable wealth (see Sects 1.1, 1.2 above). It seems unnecessary to this creativity to require constant acknowledgement of its equitable provenance. The different proprietary interests could be recognized and labelled without recourse to an equitable tag. This is not a matter of mere semantics. A coherent legal system needs to ensure that differences in the treatment of legal and equitable property rights mirror acknowledged differences in the underlying rights themselves, so that more valuable rights attract more valuable remedies. Incoherencies cannot be allowed to persist simply because they have been delivered by inconsistent developments on either side of a jurisdictional divide.

The same integrationist concerns are also being directed at equitable obligations. The question is whether these obligations can be absorbed into some category of common law obligations, or whether they are justifiably regarded as distinctive. Again, the goal is to develop a rational and predictable pattern of legal intervention. Reclassification of equitable obligations so that they become more clearly aligned with contracts or civil wrongs might lead to differentiation and reassessment of the proprietary status of fiduciary remedies, for example. If the disgorgement remedy is rooted in specific enforcement of a consensual arrangement, then its proprietary status can be justified relatively easily; on the other hand, if the remedy is justified simply because it is the only workable response to fiduciary wrongdoing in the very special circumstances that attract fiduciary obligations of loyalty, then its especially privileged proprietary status does not sit well with the common law's usual response to civil wrongs. Satisfactory resolution of these jurisdictional distinctions is crucial to the development of a coherent map of the common law.

4 Conclusions

Fundamental doctrinal analysis is an essential part of legal scholarship, but if this is the limit of the work being done, then the clear signal is that scholarship in the area is still in its infancy. Concepts have to be understood before they can be justified or used productively. More mature scholarship is likely to focus increasingly on these higher level issues. The move to assess equitable property and obligation on the basis of broader principle and policy is slowly emerging in some of the most recent work in the area, although still often only peripherally. It is much more common to find discrete, issue-specific islands of doctrinal analysis focused on individual forms of equitable intervention. This is because the fundamentals remain contested and the search is still predominantly directed at defining concepts. Because the disputes centre on the crucial boundary issues between property and obligation, and between obligations that attract disgorgement sanctions and those that do not, it seems essential that scholarship in this area adopts a broadly based perspective. A narrower stance is likely to lead to unacceptable doctrinal inconsistencies in the legal landscape. In this vein, the most basic questions must surely centre on the necessary implications, if any, of the fact that concepts of equitable property and obligation were developed on the equity side of the common law's unique historical divide.

References

Birks, P. (1992). 'Restitution and Resulting Trusts', in S. Goldstein (ed.), *Equity and Contemporary Legal Problems*, Jerusalem: Hamaccabi Press, 335–73.

Burrows, A. (2002). 'We Do This at Common Law and That in Equity', *Oxford Journal of Legal Studies*, 22: 1–16.

Chambers, R. (1997). *Resulting Trusts*, Oxford: Clarendon.

Duggan, A. J. (1997). 'Is Equity Efficient?' *Law Quarterly Review*, 113: 601–36.

Easterbrook, F. H., and Fischel, D. R. (1993). 'Contract and Fiduciary Duty', *Journal of Law and Economics*, 36: 425–51.

Finch, V., and Worthington, S. (2000). 'The Pari Passu Principle and Ranking Restitutionary Rights' in F. Rose (ed.), *Restitution and Insolvency*, London: Mansfield Press, 1–20.

Finn, P. D. (1977). *Fiduciary Obligations*, Sydney: Law Book Co.

—— (1989). 'The Fiduciary Principle', in T. G. Youdan (ed.), *Equity, Fiduciaries and Trusts*, Toronto: Carswell, 1–56.

Frankel, T. (1983). 'Fiduciary Law', *California Law Review*, 71: 795–836.

Gardner, S. (1993). 'Rethinking Family Property', *Law Quarterly Review*, 109: 263–300.

Goode, R. (1998). 'Proprietary Restitutionary Claims', in W. R. Cornish, R. Nolan, J. O'Sullivan, and G. Virgo (eds.), *Restitution: Past, Present and Future*, Oxford: Hart, 63–77.

Hansmann, H., and Kraakman, R. (2000). 'The Essential Role of Organizational Law', *Yale Law Journal*, 110: 387–440.

Hansmann, H., and Mattei, U. (1998). 'The Functions of Trust Law: A Comparative Legal and Economic Analysis', *New York University Law Review*, 73: 434–79.

Langbein, J. H. (1995). 'The Contractarian Basis of the Law of Trusts', *Yale Law Journal*, 105: 625–75.

Meagher, R. P., Gummow, W. M. C., and Lehane, J. R. F. (1992). *Equity: Doctrines and Remedies* (3rd edn.), Sydney: Butterworths.

Millett, P. J. (1985). 'The *Quistclose* Trust: Who can Enforce it?', *Law Quarterly Review*, 101: 269–91.

—— (1993). 'Bribes and Secret Commissions', *Restitution Law Review*, 1: 7–30.

Nicholls, Lord (1998). 'Knowing Receipt: The Need for a New Landmark' in W. R. Cornish, R. Nolan, J. O'Sullivan, and G. Virgo (eds.), *Restitution: Past, Present and Future*, Oxford: Hart, 231–45.

Oakley, A. J. (1997). *Constructive Trusts*, London: Sweet & Maxwell.

Scott, A. (1949). 'The Fiduciary Principle', *California Law Review*, 37: 539–55.

Sealy, L. S. (1962). 'Fiduciary Relationships', *Cambridge Law Journal*, 20: 69–81.

—— (1963). 'Some Principles of Fiduciary Obligation', *Cambridge Law Journal*, 21: 119–40.

Shepherd, J. C. (1981). 'Towards a Unified Concept of Fiduciary Relationships', *Law Quarterly Review*, 97: 51–79.

Sherwin, E. L. (1989). 'Constructive Trusts in Bankruptcy', *University of Illinois Law Review*, 2: 297–365.

Smith, L. (1997). *The Law of Tracing*, Oxford: Clarendon.

—— (2000). 'Unjust Enrichment, Property and the Structure of Trusts', *Law Quarterly Review*, 116: 412–44.

Swadling, W. (1996). 'A New Role for Resulting Trusts?' *Legal Studies*, 16: 110–31.

Weinrib, E. J. (1975). 'The Fiduciary Obligation', *University of Toronto Law Journal*, 25: 1–22.

Worthington, S. (1996). *Proprietary Interests in Commercial Transactions*, Oxford: Clarendon.

—— (2001). 'Justifying Claims to Secondary Profits', in E. J. H. Schrage (ed.), *Unjust Enrichment and the Law of Contract*, London: Kluwer, 451–73.

PART II

CITIZENS AND GOVERNMENT

CHAPTER 6

THE NATURE AND FUNCTIONS OF THE STATE

MICHAEL TAGGART

1 INTRODUCTION

FOR much of last century it was taken for granted in many countries that it was the duty of the State to care for its citizens 'from cradle to grave': to provide education, pensions, medical services, and public utilities, and to hold out a safety net for the less fortunate so that they had food, shelter, and the other necessaries of life. Since the late 1970s, however, these functions of the State have been put in question by the world-wide march towards privatization.

The privatization movement was said to be a response to budget deficits and mounting public debt, perceived inefficiencies in government operations, and a loss of faith in the ability of governments in the developed world to meet the expectations of their citizenry of an ever-increasing standard of living. It was insisted that there was simply no alternative to going down the privatization path. Privatization has since spread to almost every corner of the globe, often at the insistence of the International Monetary Fund and the World Bank. Much of what follows will be recognizable by lawyers everywhere, but the focus is on legal scholarship concerning the

Thanks to David Dyzenhaus for helpful comments.

privatization movement in the common law world, and most particularly the United Kingdom and the United States.

For the moment, 'privatization' will be used as an umbrella term to describe the manifold processes and techniques by which governments (of varying political stripes) have readjusted the balance between private (non-State) and public (State) activity in their economies. The literature on privatization is now enormous, covering large areas of economics, political science, and political theory; it is gargantuan if the privatization movement is placed within the folds of internationalization and globalization. Some of this scholarship has 'trickled down' into legal scholarship but in varying degrees and rates in different common law countries (see Harlow and Rawlings, 1997; Cass, 1988).

2 THE INFLUENCE OF ECONOMIC THEORY

Several strands in the economic literature dating from the 1960s and originating from the United States have powerfully propelled the privatization movement. As John Maynard Keynes quipped many years ago, '[p]ractical men . . . are usually the slaves . . . of some academic scribbler of a few years back'. The most influential 'scribblers' have assembled under the colours of public choice and the new institutional economics. As a broad generalization, these theories have in common a reappraisal of the role of the State in the economy. Central to this theorizing is the view that no function or job is inherently governmental, and that the basis for assigning functions between the government ('the State') and the private sector ('the market') should be economic efficiency.

As many of the policy diagnoses and prescriptions of the privatization movement rest upon these economic and theoretical foundations it may be useful at the outset to expose some of the assumptions (Cass, 1988). The first is that the private order created spontaneously by the decisions of autonomous individuals is the natural and preferred order of things. Such private action can only be displaced by governmental command if intervention is justified, with the burden of justification lying on government. Secondly, it is assumed that the best course of action for society is that which maximizes the aggregate of individual utilities. Thirdly, there is an advantage in gathering information in decentralized decision-making, as opposed to decisions made centrally. Fourthly, private, for-profit enterprises can provide better incentives to perform efficiently than can public enterprise. Fifthly, democratic-representative government creates economic rents, whereby individuals and groups profit at the public expense. Unsurprisingly, these assumptions have proved difficult to prove or refute (contrast Cass, 1988; Wright, 1993; Mashaw, 1997), because at base the debate is about political fundamentals.

The public choice school has been particularly influential in the United States. Public choice is the economic study of non-market decision-making by politicians, public servants, regulatory agencies, and judges. The methodology is that of economics and the fundamental precept is that people act as rational, utility-maximizing individuals. Politicians and public servants are said to be motivated by their own self-interest; politicians attempting to maximize their chances of re-election and public servants seeking to protect and, if possible, expand their empires. This self-seeking behaviour is given the technical label of 'rent seeking'—rent seekers extract profits (or economic rents) at the expense of taxpayers or consumers. Public choice thinkers dispute that politics is concerned with the general welfare or public good; and deny that there is any such thing as the public interest. In short, the exponents of public choice view political and administrative processes in the same way as they are portrayed on the (now 'cult') British television programmes from the 1980s and early 1990s, *Yes, Minister* and *Yes, Prime Minister*. This is a direct attack on the premise of public and administrative law that all public power is created and regulated in the public interest.

Much has been written about public choice, and as with any school of thought there is much variety of opinion within the school. However, some generalizations can be hazarded. As a general rule, public choice theorists prefer the market system to political systems. At best the public choice movement is sceptical about the benefits of government and public administration, and, at worst, it is contemptuous of democracy. The public choice school has had a considerable impact on contemporary political thought in the United States and the United Kingdom. It has influenced considerably public law theorizing in the United States, but it has gained few adherents in the Commonwealth academic legal community (see Wright, 1993; McAuslan, 1988).

In direct response to the public choice critique of the 'public-regarding' premise of administrative law, Commonwealth administrative lawyers began to self-consciously identify public law values, and to emphasize their importance (McAuslan, 1988; Harlow and Rawlings, 1997). The response of many administrative lawyers has been to distil the essence of administrative law (i.e. its values or norms) for transporting to the newly deregulated and privatized areas (see the contributions in Taggart, 1997). No list of these values is exhaustive, but they include openness, fairness, rationality, accountability, participation, independence, transparency, legitimacy, equity, and equality.

Accordingly, much of the scholarly debate about privatization has revolved around whether the newly privatized and corporatized entities are subject to judicial review (in the administrative law sense). Cases such as *R v Panel on Take-overs and Mergers, ex p Datafin* [1987] QB 815 (English Court of Appeal), *Mercury Energy Ltd v Electricity Corporation of New Zealand* [1994] 1 WLR 521 (Privy Council, appeal from New Zealand), *Richardson v McKnight*, 521 US 399 (1997) (US Supreme Court)—dealing (respectively) with judicial review of a self-regulatory body, judicial review of contract termination by a corporatized state-owned business entity, and the denial of qualified immunity to employees of a privately run prison sued by a prisoner for civil rights violations—have attracted considerable academic attention. But other legal scholars believe this emphasis on court-centred judicial review is profoundly mistaken (e.g. Aronson, 1997). It is said to have diverted attention from other vital areas of enquiry, such as institutional design and recognition of the shared regulatory roles of government and private actors. Scott argues that the emphasis should be on 'governance' rather than 'government', and on the networks of influence and interaction up, down, and sideways (Scott, 2000).

There are reasons why many administrative lawyers have navigated the sea of privatization so close to the shoreline of judicial review and constitutional principle. This is not just the lawyers' predisposition to 'court-itis'—an unnatural fascination with legal pathology—but also the fear of interdisciplinary open seas. The currents of thought in many disciplines negate, doubt, or undercut the legitimacy of the State, and want to redistribute its powers and functions to intermediary or private groups or the market.

3 Law and Economic Policy

Economic theorizing has much to say about the impact of law (often used synonymously with government regulation) on the economy (Kitch, 1986); our focus here is a related but distinct issue, what impact have changes in the economy (namely, the privatization movement) had on law, particularly legal scholarship?

As noted above, the privatization movement represents a significant shift in economic policy in almost every country. Until the early 1980s, with some honourable exceptions, the study of economic policy in the light of constitutional and other legal rules was beyond the pale of lawyers in the Commonwealth legal tradition (Daintith, 1982). That staple of Continental European university law curricula, 'economic law', found little or no place in law teaching or scholarship in the Commonwealth legal tradition. It was, of course, different in North America, where the 'law and economics' movement developed earlier and was more readily accepted and deployed in law teaching and research (e.g. Kitch, 1986). The study of 'regulated industries' and 'antitrust' (competition policy) was well established early on in American law schools.

One consequence of this 'head-in-the-sand' attitude to economic policy was that legal scholars outside North America did not play a major role in the development and implementation of the privatization movement. Indeed, legal scholars were slow in responding to the movement. In the United Kingdom, for instance, the earliest sustained legal commentary came from a group of public lawyers who were working in the early 1980s in the Law School (and later, the Centre for Socio-Legal Studies) in the University of Sheffield. This group included Cosmo Graham, Ian Harden, Norman (Douglas) Lewis, and Tony Prosser. This early work did much to alert the legal academic fraternity in the United Kingdom and elsewhere to the public law implications of privatization (e.g. Lewis and Harden, 1983; Graham and Prosser, 1991).

4 Privatization

The term privatization can mean different things in different societies, even ones that share a capitalist ideology and the common law heritage. At its most general, privatization expresses a preference for the private sector ('the market') over the public sector ('the State'). Some usages focus more narrowly on changes from public to private ownership. This is most frequent in the British Commonwealth, where much of the economic infrastructure and many businesses were government-owned and operated. In the United States, where historically there has been very little government ownership at federal level, privatization is generally given a broader meaning, and primarily compasses 'contracting out' of the performance of public functions to private contractors at public expense, deregulation, and the streamlining of government administration. In Commonwealth usage, 'contracting out' or, as it is sometimes known, 'outsourcing' is typically treated separately from privatization (Aronson, 1997).

It is salutary to view these developments in historical perspective. The public utilities privatized in the United Kingdom in the 1980s and early 1990s—telecommunications, gas, electricity, water, railways—started out under private ownership, and subsequently were nationalized or municipalized in the last century or so. Strictly speaking, the most recent process is one of reprivatization. This helps make three points. First, what is or is not a governmental function is socially constructed and hence society-specific, and can (and does) change over time. For example, the much-contested penal policy issue of private prisons—which is infused with difficult legal issues—looks quite different from a historical perspective in different common law countries (Freeman, 2000a). Secondly, economic theorizing grounded in the experience of a large, open economy with many millions of customers (such as that of the United States) may not fit neatly in smaller, more closed economies with populations a fraction the size. Thirdly, there has been a good deal of private sector involvement in the provision of public services for a long time in many sectors of these economies. What distinguished privatization in the late 1970s and beyond was that it was a movement, with broad-based political and electoral support, that helped sweep Ronald Reagan to the presidency of the United States in 1980 and maintained the Thatcher/Major Conservative governments in power in the United Kingdom for eighteen years.

5 PUBLIC/PRIVATE

The scholarly reaction to the privatization movement within the legal academy occurred first in the subdiscipline of administrative law, and this perspective continues to dominate the legal discourse. This is true of both the Commonwealth and American legal literature. These jurisdictions, while sharing the common law landscape, are distinguished by distinctly different public law architecture (Beermann, 1997). The role of the Constitution and the absence of any common law of administrative law at the federal level has made the public/private law divide much harder-edged in the United States, than in the Commonwealth world.

The public/private law divide is critical to an understanding of the legal significance of 'privatization'. The root of the word is 'private', and its original meaning was 'not holding public office or official position'. So the derivative, privatization, well captures the significance of the process: the shift from the public to the private sphere. For common lawyers this entails a mental shift—from the public law sphere, where the starting premise is public or other-regarding behaviour, to the private law sphere, where the starting-point is self-regarding behaviour. The move ends up on 'the level playing field', with all the public law mechanisms of control and accountability bulldozed off.

As for the public/private divide, administrative lawyers in the Commonwealth tradition advocate different tacks. Some, following the lead of A. V. Dicey, do not wish to recognize any distinction between public and private law. They place reliance on private law remedies, and fear that if the State is treated differently than the citizen inevitably the State will be treated more favourably (e.g. Harlow and Rawlings, 1997). Others support firmly distinguishing public law from private law, arguing that otherwise public law values will disappear in the rush to the market (see the contributions to Taggart, 1997). For them, public law duties are usually, and should be, more burdensome on the State and its agents because of the State's monopoly over coercive power. Still others see the two systems of law mixing as the creation and implementation of laws is now shared between public and private actors (Aronson, 1997; Freeman, 2000a), and a search has begun for shared, common values (Oliver, 1999).

Many public lawyers have not got much beyond the articulation of broad public law values. These normative claims are rarely unpacked or prioritized. For example, legal scholars have seldom probed the many different meanings of words like accountability. Although in some quarters the level of abstraction or generalization is increasing (e.g. Oliver, 1999), this can obscure the inevitability of conflict between the articulated values. Writing from a US perspective, Mashaw has observed that administrative lawyers have naively 'tended to ignore behavioural questions about how its concepts are generated, structured and maintained' (Mashaw, 1997). In a similar vein, on the other side of the Atlantic, Daintith has criticized public lawyers for failing to fill the 'normative gap'; this is the gap between the articulation of broad constitutional values (openness, transparency, impartiality, accountability, and so on) and the detail of practice on the ground (Daintith, 1991).

Some in the United Kingdom have looked instead to raid the American public law larder in order to beef up British administrative law to cope with privatization and contracting out. The standard list of 'imports' has included freedom of information legislation, requirements to give reasons, a US-style Administrative Procedure Act, rules about *ex parte* contact between politicians and regulatory agencies, the 'hard look' doctrine, regulatory procedures, negotiated regulation and incentive regulation (Graham and Prosser, 1991). Some of this has come to pass, but it is difficult to get an overall sense of system or appropriate fit.

For their part, the small band of American administrative lawyers who have concerned themselves with privatization have concentrated their attention on two issues. The first is the possible resurrection of the dormant 'non-delegation' doctrine, which might prevent the government delegating the performance of public functions to private persons. The second issue is the ability of the courts to constrain decision-making by a private party exercising a privatized function. In federal constitutional and administrative law this revolves around the scope of the 'State action' doctrine. This limited doctrine, which importantly cleaves the American legal universe into those who are bound by the Constitution and those who are not, provides little comfort that the exercise of privatized functions will be subjected to constitutional standards (Beermann, 1997).

Although not often publicly articulated as a reason in favour of privatization, freeing government business enterprises from the 'shackles' of public law accountability mechanisms was a consequence of placing these entities in private hands (privatization) or (less certainly) in corporate form (corporatization). Upon corporatization or privatization, one or more of the following threads of public-ness are diminished or eliminated—applicability of judicial review of administrative action and/or Bill of Rights, freedom of information legislation, centralized financial audit, executive and/or parliamentary (select committee) oversight, Ombudsmen review, and other complaint resolution mechanisms. This public law regulation was thought to get in the way of efficient market transactions. These inconvenient accountability mechanisms were removed, leaving the competitors (including the State) to operate on 'the level playing field'. So legal/constitutional forms of control and accountability were replaced with market-based forms of control.

6 PRIVATIZATION—UK-STYLE

Many of the ideas behind the privatization movement had been nurtured in other places—particularly the United States—but they found their most dramatic manifestation in the successive terms of Conservative government rule in the United Kingdom (1979-97). It is apparent that privatization in the United Kingdom was not a coherent and systematic application of economic policy, but a pragmatic and improvised policy that fed upon its own success. The programme had several objectives, some of which cut across others and with varying emphasis over time: reducing government involvement in industry, reducing public debt and public sector borrowing, increasing efficiency through competition and regulatory arrangements, widening share ownership, encouraging employee share ownership, enhancing economic freedom, and gaining party political advantage.

One explanation for the United Kingdom's world leadership in privatization is that the flexible, 'unwritten' constitution of the United Kingdom imposed few, if any, restraints on the economic policy choices of the government. In other words, the British Constitution is relatively economically neutral, compared to many other countries in the world (Daintith, 1991; Daintith and Sah, 1993; cf. Gillette and Stephan, 1998). Another explanation (already noted) is simply that more of the economic infrastructure and business activity were in public ownership in the United Kingdom than in the United States. Government enterprises do exist in the United States but they occupy a backseat to regulated private enterprise. Moreover, the fall of communism across Eastern Europe in the late 1980s provoked intense interest in the British privatization experience by the new transformative governments, and influenced considerably the economic reforms in those countries.

The implementation of similar policies in many different countries around the world opened the way for comparative legal analysis. A pioneering work compared the effect of different constitutional and legal cultures on the implementation of privatization programmes in Britain and France, with a sideways glance at public utility regulation in the United States (Graham and Prosser, 1991). The conclusion reached was that constitutional law/culture had been a significant restraint on the way privatization had been implemented in France, but not in the United Kingdom. The explanations for why this was so in the United Kingdom are several and intertwined: the lack of a written Constitution or Bill of Rights in Britain, the concept of parliamentary sovereignty with its corollary of the absence of judicial review of legislation, weakness of parliamentary scrutiny before and after privatization, executive domination of the policy-making process, severe limitations on the role of the courts and a judicial unwillingness to supervise matters seen as falling on the private law side of the public/private law divide, and the absence of a developed concept of the 'State' in British political and legal theory (Graham and Prosser, 1991; Daintith and Sah, 1993).

Privatization of 'public utilities' has been particularly problematic due to the presence or perception of natural monopolistic aspects and the political importance of maintaining universal service obligations. Initially in the United Kingdom reliance was placed on regulation of the privatized utilities, and only latterly on liberalization and promotion of competition. Independent regulatory agencies were late arriving on the British regulatory scene. The model was 'imported' from the United States in the 1980s in order to regulate the newly privatized public utilities. In the United Kingdom, regulatory powers and duties are divided between a government minister, an industry-specific regulatory agency headed by a director general, the Monopolies and Mergers Commission, and now the Office of Fair Trading. There is an ever-growing literature in the United Kingdom about the role of the regulators and competition policy, and the overlay of the increasing 'Europeanization' of British law (Prosser, 1999). The discussion quickly descends to a level of detail that increasingly makes comparative analysis difficult.

McCrudden, evaluating the reviews of public utility regulation undertaken since the Blair Labour government came to power in 1997, has usefully described the battle-lines as drawn between the following three camps (McCrudden, 1999). First, there are the 'social marketeers', for whom the purpose of regulation is to take advantage of the market mechanism where possible, to regulate to achieve competition if achievable, but at the same time to moderate the results achieved for purposes of social integration and the achievement of other 'social' (non-economic) goals. Secondly, there are the 'free marketeers', for whom the purpose of regulation is to establish sufficient competition to enable regulation to wither away or, where competition cannot be established, then to regulate the market to reach results as close as possible to what the market would have reached. Thirdly, the 'good governance' advocates say that, *whatever* the purpose of regulation, the regulator should reach legitimate decisions, and legitimacy is mostly defined in procedural terms.

No discussion of public utility privatization or deregulation, no matter how brief, should ignore market liberalization altogether. 'Liberalization' has a more settled meaning than most of the other 'izations' bandied around. It refers to the removal of barriers to entry and other barriers to competition, so that an industry is opened up to competitive forces. Of course, competition is a means to the end of economic efficiency, not an end in itself. Liberalization often goes hand in hand with privatization, as it did in countries (e.g. New Zealand) that liberalized markets *before* privatizing public utilities or other government businesses. But it need not do so, and, as is well known, early utility privatizations in the United Kingdom were not preceded by liberalization. Hence public monopolies simply became private monopolies subject to regulation by independent agencies, whose job it became to promote competition.

One of the economic assumptions behind the push to privatize is that public ownership of business is less economically efficient than private enterprise. This is disputed in economic circles and appears to turn on the degree of competitiveness in the market. The less competitive the market the greater the assumed need for regulation, and the less clear the evidence of efficiency gains upon privatization; and vice versa. The role of competition policy in the era of privatization has been hugely important, but is beyond the scope of this chapter.

7 CORPORATIZATION AND PUBLIC SECTOR REFORMS

The privatization movement led numerous governments to rethink not only what they did, but also how they did it. The push for better management and efficiency in government led to significant changes in the public service throughout the common law world. Once again, the terminology is not universally accepted.

In the United Kingdom in the late 1980s so-called 'Next Steps' agencies were created for the most part simply by administrative rearrangement within government departments. These executive agencies are charged with achieving economy, efficiency, and effectiveness in delivery of services (the so-called 'three Es'), and are headed by chief executives employed on short-term, performance-based contracts. These agencies are semi-independent of their host departments but have no separate legal status. This creates considerable legal difficulty in subjecting their activities to regulation by contract law (Harden, 1992; Davies, 2001). The framework of policy objectives and resources within which these agencies operate continues to be set by Ministers of the Crown advised on such policy issues by much smaller (down-sized) departments. By 2000 more than three-quarters of all public servants in the United Kingdom worked in Next Steps agencies. The relationship between an executive agency and the department under which it legally shelters is governed by a 'framework document'. The momentum of these reforms has not noticeably been slowed by the election of the Blair Labour government in 1997.

These changes go by the name 'New Public Management' (NPM) in the United Kingdom but variations on the theme can be found in almost all common law countries; indeed, some of the foundations of NPM were cast in New Zealand. In the United States these changes are often associated with the best-selling book *Reinventing Government* (Osborne and Gaebler, 1992), which influenced the Clinton administration. Osborne and Gaebler argued that in an era of budget deficits, increasing public spending, and higher taxes, there was an urgent need for enhancement of the efficiency and productivity of the public sector. This was to be achieved by the application of private sector organizational models to the public sector. They championed the separation of policy advice from service provision, made famous by the phrase 'the State steers, it does not row'.

Public sector reform has been part and parcel of the privatization movement, and may well be one of its most lasting and profound legacies. For these changes have important implications for ministerial responsibility, for parliamentary scrutiny of the executive, and for the structure and ethos of the public service (Drewry, 2000).

In some countries, these ideas have found expression in the creation of semi-autonomous government-owned enterprises in corporate form, with the shares held by designated Ministers and the enterprises run by a Board of Directors usually drawn from the private sector. These enterprises, called GBEs (Government Business Entities) in Australia and SOEs (State-Owned Enterprises) in New Zealand, were founded on the following first principles: State trading activities should have purely commercial objectives; they should operate in a competitively neutral environment, subject to the same rules as any other business; and the enterprises should be organized in a legal form designed to assist in the implementation of the principles of commercialization and competitive neutrality.

Both NPM and corporatization of state-owned businesses have been heavily influenced by economic thinking, particularly the theory of agency problems in firms. In the private firm, the owners of the assets (shareholders) do not manage or control the firm in any direct way; this is done by professional managers (directors). Thus ownership and control are separated, creating a so-called 'agency' problem. The problem is how to ensure that the directors (as agents of the shareholders) run the firm in the most efficient way possible for the maximum benefit of the owner-shareholders. The share market is said to provide many incentives for managers to serve the interests of the owners. The share market will evaluate performance of the firm and its managers, and this assessment will be reflected, to some extent, in the share price. Shareholders dissatisfied with managerial performance can 'exit' from the firm, by selling stock. Alternatively, shareholders may 'voice' their dissatisfaction at the annual general meeting and attempt to vote out management. Also, the threat of takeover provides some incentive for incumbent managers to behave in the shareholders' interests. And, in the extreme case, there is the threat of insolvency.

Economists rightly point out that in merely imitating the corporate form, public enterprise will not be able to replicate the benefits of private enterprise. The monitoring mechanisms of voice and exit are less effective or non-existent in the contexts of NPM and state-owned enterprises. Shares in state-owned enterprises are non-transferable; hence there is no share price and takeovers are impossible. Nor is there a realistic prospect of insolvency. Undeterred by the misfit of public enterprise with the theory of the private firm, the architects of NPM and corporatization attempted to replicate, as far as possible, the share market disciplines and mechanisms that apply in private enterprise. Consequently, the emphasis was on monitoring the performance of agency heads and directors, and on holding them accountable to Ministers for that performance. Incentives were put in place to ensure that agents (agency heads, directors) pursued the interests of their principals (Ministers); including the clear statement of objectives/outputs in agreements or statutes; the regular supply of information to Ministers to allow monitoring of performance; and the ability of Ministers to appoint and, where necessary, to dismiss agency heads or directors.

In some countries it was envisaged that the corporatization phase would be short, with experienced private sector directors quickly putting the businesses on a profitable footing, in preparation for privatization. This did not work out in every instance. In New Zealand, for example, many of the state-owned enterprises lined up for privatization became entangled in claims by the indigenous people (Maori) under the Treaty of Waitangi, and consequently have remained in public ownership.

8 DEREGULATION

For present purposes, regulation can be taken to mean direct government intervention in the market place, and accordingly deregulation means the lessening or removal of some or all such intervention. And now, as the ideological pendulum swings in some countries away from deregulation, the phrase re-regulation has emerged. Each of these phrases or catch-calls, however, either proceeds from or reacts to a vision of a 'free market' economy where willing buyers and sellers trade goods, services, and money, and the primary role of the State is to enforce those agreements. In accordance with this vision, the free market is the natural order of things and regulation can only be justified on the ground of market failure. In the 1970s and 1980s deregulation was argued to lead to competitive markets, with all the assumed benefits for consumers and society.

With most public utilities in government ownership and control in the Westminster-style Commonwealth governments, there was little need for overt regulation. Other sectors of the economy, however, were heavily regulated. In the United States, where privately owned but heavily regulated public utilities were the norm, economists in the 1960s developed conceptual tools that attempted to demonstrate that many forms of regulation harmed consumers and benefited the regulated industries by limiting competition and discouraging efficiency. So regulation, which was meant to correct market failure, was itself argued often to fail. The tide of American public opinion finally caught up and upon the changing tide Ronald Reagan was swept into the Presidency.

As 'command and control' regulation is usually laid down in statute, its democratic pedigree is usually assured; but not so with many of the alternatives. The alternatives to 'command-and-control' regulation have been explored extensively both theoretically and in applied studies. They include: creation or stimulation of competition, incentives, subsidies, imposition of taxes or fees on undesired activities, changes in liability rules, elimination of taxes or granting of tax exemptions, government contracts and franchises, self-regulation, bargaining, marketable/tradable permits, vouchers, mandatory disclosure of information, and consensual restraint (Breyer, 1982). These approaches have in common the desire to shape the behaviour of firms by providing incentives to act in accordance with the purposes of the regulatory scheme.

The debate over deregulation often proceeds from a model that juxtaposes the State and the market. But in the era of 'mixed administration' both State and private (non-State) actors directly or indirectly formulate and implement economic policies, often using similar or broadly analogous techniques or instruments. The State may be unique in that it has a monopoly over force and can give effect to policies by the enactment of generally applicable laws, but that should not blind us to the considerable similarities between State and non-State implementation of economic policy (Bercusson, 1988).

9 CONTRACTING OUT

Contracting out takes different forms. The oldest form is the procurement contract, for government has always had to procure goods and services by contract. The newer form of government contracting usually associated with the term 'contracting out' is where the State accepts responsibility for the performance of a public function or the provision of a public service, but the function is performed or service provided by a private sector contractor. Obviously, a condition precedent to contracting out is the conscious governmental decision that the function or service is necessary and that it would not be provided at all or in the right amount if the government abandoned the field to the market (itself a form of privatization) (Harden, 1992). In the United States and the United Kingdom, as well as elsewhere, there has been a very significant increase in the volume and range of functions and services contracted out at both the national and state levels of government, and especially at the local government levels. A process of competitive tendering has evolved, to ensure efficiency and value for money.

This form of contracting out is premised on two interrelated assumptions. First, that the funding ('purchasing') of the performance of public functions/provision of public services can be split off from service delivery without disadvantage. This is the so-called purchaser/provider split that was also very influential in the reform and downsizing of the core public sector in many countries over this period. This split institutionally separates the responsibility for determining what service there should be (political/policy decisions) from the responsibility of delivering that service (operational decisions). In the United Kingdom, in particular, contracting out has occurred to semi-autonomous state bodies through the 'Next Steps' initiative. The second assumption is that private sector provision of public services/public function is more efficient (cost-effective) than provision by the public sector itself. This, in turn, depends on the competitiveness of the market.

Contracting out usually gives rise to a triangular relationship between government ('purchaser'), private sector provider ('provider'), and the recipient of the service ('customer'). The problem here is how to ensure accountability and ultimately control. The issues raised include: who is responsible for what and when; how is the performance monitored and assessed, and as a consequence modified; what redress is available to a disgruntled customer, and against whom? The reach and adequacy of both private and public law remedies and consumer protection legislation has been much discussed (Aronson, 1997; Davies, 2001; Freeman, 2000*b*; Harlow and Rawlings, 1997).

Once again, the public/private law divide looms large. There is considerable uncertainty and debate as to how best to categorize government contracting (including contracting out). One response is to apply the private law of contract to government contracting without any modification whatsoever. A second response would apply the private law of contract to government contracting but would modify the rules or the remedies in certain respects to reflect inherent differences between State and citizen. Such modifications as prove necessary or expedient to make, would apply only to 'government' contracts, and to that extent 'distinctive' rules may develop for government contracts within the rules of the private law of contract. The remedies awarded, however, would be private law remedies (albeit tempered by public law values). A third response would apply administrative law doctrine and remedies to government contracting to prevent unfairness and abuse of power. This would be in addition to any private law remedies. The fourth response would be to apply public law doctrines and remedies to all contracting, whether governmental or not, and thereby change the law of contract across the board.

Of these four responses to government contracting, all but the first reflect to some degree public law values, although these values are given effect to by differing techniques and mechanisms. The difference of opinion over technique is important. Some scholars prefer to give primacy to private law remedial tools but to integrate public law values into private law rights and remedies, so that the public interest is protected (Harlow and Rawlings, 1997). The difficulty with that position is that if the contest between private law and public law values takes place on private law terrain then it is likely to be an unequal and ultimately unsuccessful struggle. There is a tendency on the part of public lawyers to underestimate the structural and ideological impediments to the 'interpenetration' of public law values in private law (McLean, 2001). Contract law has its own logic and self-regarding premise, and is resistant to other forms of control.

The brilliant *double entendre* in the title of Ian Harden's book, *The Contracting State*—the State transacting increasingly by contract and the shrinking State—summed up the ambivalence of many commentators towards this phenomenon (Harden, 1992). Harden observed that the term 'contract' is deeply symbolic, and pregnant with social, economic, and political significance. He sees in the history and operation of contract law the values of individual and collective 'consumer sovereignty'—entailing equality, freedom, and choice—which Harden believes offers the promise of 'a kind of democratic equality in economic decision-making', and thus is linked to maintenance of the rule of law and citizenship. The competitive tension that the contract form creates between those engaged in bargaining resonates with the rule of law values of minimizing and structuring discretion in order to prevent abuse of power, and the delegation of specific and specified tasks to accountable organizations (Harden, 1992).

The shift from the public sphere to the private sphere in terms of ownership of business enterprises, and the adoption of private law forms, such as contract, in the transaction of public business, has raised issues of control and accountability in the exercise of those powers. Indeed, in Commonwealth law, a predominant focus of legal scholarship has been on the availability and appropriateness of public law accountability mechanisms. In the United States, where the administrative law framework (at least at the federal level) is much more confined than in Commonwealth law (Beermann, 1997), this is less noticeable.

In a series of articles, Jody Freeman has sought to demonstrate the important role that private (non-governmental) actors play in governance (Freeman, 2000a). Adopting Mark Aronson's phrase, Freeman argues that 'mixed administration' better describes the shared responsibility of private and public actors for regulation, service delivery, and policy design and implementation (Freeman, 2000a; Aronson, 1997). Privatization and contracting out are given as the most common examples of the public–private cooperation in governance she describes, and wants to legitimate in theoretical terms. Freeman challenges the public/private distinction, and advocates developing informal and formal accountability mechanisms, emanating not just from government but also from independent third parties and the regulated entities themselves (Freeman, 2000a). While they appear to have similar concerns, and certainly use similar language, it appears that Harden and Freeman may be heading in different directions. Harden is grappling with a world in which the State has—conceptually—been relegated to the margins, and he wants to bring the State back into the centre of the picture. Freeman describes a world in which the private sector increasingly engages in 'governance', and she wants this substantial role reflected in theory (Freeman, 2000b).

10 CONCLUSION

As noted in the introduction, the privatization movement brought about a significant shift in economic policy. As with all policy formation processes, be they economic or otherwise, law usually plays an important but ancillary role. Policy-makers should be made aware of the legal framework, and of the constitutional and other legal rules and principles that may come into play when formulating policy. Law seldom constrains policy choices; unless, of course, there are constitutional provisions that place limits on what can be done, as is the case in the United States (Gillette and Stephan, 1998) and may be the case with the recent incorporation of the European Convention on Human Rights in the United Kingdom (McCrudden, 1999). It is at the implementation stage of the policy-making continuum, however, that law plays a much larger role. Here the issue is, given the settled policy to be pursued, which legal instrument(s) should be deployed to give effect to that policy? What problems are caused by the adoption of various instruments and how might these be resolved?

This is not to say that law is value neutral. If you believe that the legislature is a forum dominated by vested interest groups intent on maximizing their own advantage, then you are unlikely to look to the legislative process in preference to the market. In contrast, if you believe that the market mechanism does not sufficiently reflect social norms encapsulated in the notion of the public interest, then you are more likely to look to the demos and regulatory agencies.

When the political kaleidoscope was turned sharply in the late 1970s, the world of public law was also turned upside down. Many public lawyers opposed the privatization movement and the ideology behind it. Commonwealth administrative lawyers reacted (admittedly belatedly) by seeking to stand up for public law values amid a sea of privatization. Now twenty or so years on, privatization has become part of the 'constitutional furniture' and is largely taken for granted by the current generation of law students and lawyers.

What of the future? Where is legal scholarship likely to head in the next few years? It is possible that law and lawyers will be more successful in future in infiltrating economic policy-making. To do that lawyers will need to know much more about the formation and operation of economic policy, and the choice of economic instruments. And lawyers will need to be able to identify problems in the design and implementation of policy that might be capable of legal solution. Broad concepts, such as 'accountability', need to be unpacked, so that we can see how they actually operate on the ground in various contexts. This suggests that some of the more interesting work to be done will be at the empirical end of socio-legal studies (see Davies, 2001). More generally, the claims made by privatization proponents and opponents need to be tested against reality; in some countries there is now twenty years worth of data to work with. This important interdisciplinary work should be contributed to by lawyers and legal scholars. Perhaps this will lead, on the one hand, to a greater focus on the reality of the privatization movement for customers, clients, and citizens, and, on the other hand, to a renewed interest in the State.

By too many accounts, the State is an endangered species—supposedly too small to deal with global problems and too big to deal with local ones. State sovereignty is under attack from globalization without and privatization within. The literature in other disciplines is full of phrases like the hollowed-out state, the shadow state, the reinvented state, and the virtual state. Much of this influence on lawyers has led them away from the State. Paradoxically, in many countries, the privatization agenda has been implemented by a strong State under the ideological guise of limiting State power and influence.

For too long, common lawyers have ignored the State, and this benign neglect contributed to the marginalization of the State during the privatization blitzkrieg (Graham and Prosser, 1991). In Commonwealth law, 'the Crown' is the closest approximation to the State, but it is nebulous concept. One particular issue that calls for further exploration is the assumption that the State ('the Crown' as well as other public entities) has, by way of prerogative or common law, all the powers of a legal person, and hence is able to trade, contract, and hold and dispose of land, shares ('golden' and otherwise), and other incorporeal property. This assumption is often the legal source of the State's power to contract out. At the same time, property can be privatized at a 'fire sale' price—as occurred in many instances—without fear of legal liability on the part of politicians and officials for breach of public trust. In contrast, acquisition of property usually requires parliamentary appropriation. All this leads us to some deep and unresolved issues about the State (see the contributions to Sunkin and Payne, 1999).

Lastly, there will be a continuing need for historical research. As noted earlier, some of the problems arising from the privatization movement have appeared in other guises in earlier times. For example, the problem of controlling large aggregations of private property is not a new one, and the law has qualified or tempered private property rights in the public interest in many areas of law (see e.g. Craig, 1991). There is a tendency in legal scholarship to herald the 'brave new world', unmindful of lessons to be learnt from the past. Will future historians rank in importance the privatization movement alongside (say) the Black Death or the advent of the railway? The profound impacts of such developments on governance, law, and society throw up lessons for today.

References

Aronson, M. (1997). 'A Public Lawyer's Response to Privatization and Outsourcing', in M. Taggart (ed.), *The Province of Administrative Law*, Oxford: Hart, 40–70.

Beermann, J. M. (1997). 'The Reach of Administrative Law in the United States', in M. Taggart (ed.), *The Province of Administrative Law*, Oxford: Hart, 170–95.

Bercusson, B. (1988). 'Economic Policy: State and Private Ordering', in T. Daintith (ed.), *Law as an Instrument of Economic Policy: Comparative and Critical Approaches*, Berlin: Walter de Gruyter, 359–420.

Breyer, S. (1982). *Regulation and its Reform*, Cambridge, Mass.: Harvard University Press.

Cass, R. (1988). 'Privatization: Politics, Law, and Theory', *Marquette Law Review*, 71: 449–523.

Craig, P. (1991). 'Constitutions, Property and Regulation', *Public Law*: 538–54.

Daintith, T. (1982). 'Legal Analysis of Economic Policy', *Journal of Law and Society*, 9: 191–224.

Daintith, T. (1991). 'Political Programmes and the Content of the Constitution', in W. Finnie, C. Himsworth, and N. Walker (eds.), *Edinburgh Essays in Public Law*, Edinburgh: Edinburgh University Press, 41–55.

——and Sah, M. (1993). 'Privatization and the Economic Neutrality of the Constitution', *Public Law*: 465–87.

Davies, A. C. L. (2001). *Accountability: A Public Law Analysis of Government by Contract*, Oxford: Oxford University Press.

Drewry, G. (2000). 'The New Public Management', in J. Jowell and D. Oliver (eds.), *The Changing Constitution* (4th edn.), Oxford: Oxford University Press, 167–89.

Freeman, J. (2000a). 'The Private Role in Public Governance', *New York University Law Review*, 75: 543–675.

——(2000b). 'The Contracting State', *Florida State University Law Review*, 28: 155–214.

Gillette, C. P., and Stephan III, P. B. (1998). 'Constitutional Limitations on Privatization', *American Journal of Comparative Law (Supplement)*, 46: 481–501.

Graham, C., and Prosser, T. (1991). *Privatizing Public Enterprises: Constitutions, the State, and Regulation in Comparative Perspective*, Oxford: Clarendon Press.

Harden, I. (1992). *The Contracting State*, Buckingham: Open University Press.

Harlow, C., and Rawlings, R. (1997). *Law and Administration* (2nd edn.), London: Butterworths.

Kitch, E. W. (1986). 'Law and the Economic Order', in L. Lipson and S. Wheeler (eds.), *Law and the Social Sciences*, New York: Russell Sage Foundation, 609–49.

Lewis, N., and Harden, I. (1983). 'Privatisation, De-regulation and Constitutionality: Some Anglo-American Comparisons', *Northern Ireland Law Quarterly*, 34: 207–29.

McAuslan, P. (1988). 'Public Law and Public Choice', *Modern Law Review*, 51: 681–705.

McCrudden, C. (1999). 'Social Policy and Economic Regulators: Some Issues from the Reform of Utility Regulation', in C. McCrudden (ed.), *Regulation and Deregulation: Policy and Practice in the Utilities and Financial Services Industries*. Oxford: Clarendon Press, 275–91.

McLean, J. (2001). 'The Ordinary Law of Torts and Contract and the New Public Management', *Common Law World Review*, 30: 387–411.

Mashaw, J. L. (1997). *Greed, Chaos, & Governance: Using Public Choice to Improve Public Law*, New Haven: Yale University Press.

Oliver, D. (1999). *Common Values and the Public-Private Law Divide*, London: Butterworths.

Osborne, D., and Gaebler, T. (1992). *Reinventing Government: How the Entrepreneurial Spirit is Transforming the Public Sector*, Reading, Mass.: Addison-Wesley Publishing Co.

Prosser, T. (1999). *Law and the Regulators*, Oxford: Oxford University Press.

Scott, C. (2000). 'Accountability in the Regulatory State', *Journal of Law and Society*, 27: 38–60.

Sunkin, M., and Payne, S. (eds.) (1999). *The Nature of the Crown: A Legal and Political Analysis*, Oxford: Clarendon Press.

Taggart, M. (ed.) (1997). *The Province of Administrative Law*, Oxford: Hart.

Wright, M. (1993). 'A Critique of the Public Choice Case for Privatization: Rhetoric and Reality', *Ottawa Law Review*, 25: 1–37.

CHAPTER 7

REGULATION

CHRISTINE PARKER
JOHN BRAITHWAITE

1 WHAT IS REGULATION?

FOR some, regulation is about rules. Regulation can mean more than just the enforcement of legal rules. It is normally taken to include the enforcement of informal rules that are not state laws as well as formal rules promulgated by supranational bodies such as the World Trade Organization or the European Union, and subnational bodies such as professional associations. On its broadest reading, regulation means even more than that. Much regulation is accomplished without recourse to rules of any kind. It is secured by organizing economic incentives to steer business behaviour, by moral suasion, by shaming, and even by architecture. On this broadest view, regulation means influencing the flow of events. Conceived in this broad way, regulation means much the same thing as governance or Foucauldian governmentality (as opposed to government, which is more narrowly something state organizations do). Indeed, the distinction between governance and regulation is narrowing as governments shed their responsibilities for service provision and shift more of their energies to regulating the service provision of other types of actors (a development we call the 'new regulatory state').

The study of governance in political science is informed by a progressively narrowing focus, like a set of Russian dolls, from 'intergovernmental networks' studies, to 'whole of government' studies, to national government studies that exclude local and state government, to studies of legislatures that exclude courts and executives, to studies of cabinets, and so on. Julia Black (2001) has argued that for different intellectual purposes there is merit in conceptualizing regulation in different ways—excluding or including regulation by non-government actors, including only administrative action by specific kinds of 'regulatory agencies', excluding or including governance without rules, and so on. Our hope for regulatory studies is that the whole set of Russian dolls will inform big-picture theories of regulation conceived in the broadest way. Moreover, this regulatory theory might become a significant influence on other theoretical frameworks that are broader still in some ways (though narrower in others)—regulatory influences on the theory of governance, economic theory, and psychological theory, for example.

The plan of the chapter is first to lay out a short history of regulation conceived in this broad way. We then consider whether ours is a society that regulates more because it has become a 'risk society'. Next we will use Gunther Teubner's model of the 'regulatory trilemma' and a consideration of the key regulatory mechanisms to review the literature on the finer grain of how regulation works. Finally we return to pluralization of regulation as a crucial dynamic in creating spaces where 'democratic experimentalism' is emerging as a possibility.

2 A Short History of Regulation

Regulation is an older activity than states and law. The regulation of incest was fundamental to the survival of our genes. As soon as money was invented, there emerged a need for macroeconomic regulation of some sort, for example in Babylon from at least a millennium before the Code of Hammurabi. But regulation by taxes (paid in goods and services) is probably older than money; the 5,300-year-old Egyptian fragments of clay and ivory that recently challenged the view that writing was invented by the Sumerians were actually receipts for tax payments. The next major development was formal law. Its most important moment was Justinian's codification of Roman law which has a surviving influence on all the world's formal legal systems. While the latter are what lawyers primarily study, regulatory researchers primarily study the next fundamental development in the history of regulation—the emergence of specialized administrative agencies to enforce particular kinds of standards.

Tax administrations aside, nearly all of the important regulatory agencies emerged in the nineteenth and twentieth centuries. An important moment was Peel's creation of the Metropolitian Police in London in 1829 and the even more internationally influential model of the colonial police in Dublin in a process that ends with every significant city in the world having such a specialized, paramilitary crime-fighting agency. Police until the eighteenth and early nineteenth centuries in Europe continued to mean institutions for the creation of an orderly environment, especially for trade and commerce. In other words, until 1829 police meant regulation. Police certainly included enforcement of rules related to theft and violence, but also of standards for weights and measures. It also included other forms of consumer protection, liquor licensing, health and safety regulation, building, road and traffic regulation, and early forms of environmental regulation. The institution was rather privatized, subject to considerable local control, heavily oriented to self-regulation and infrequent (if sometimes draconian) in its recourse to punishment.

The crime-fighting police came to rival and even surpass tax administrations as the largest regulatory bureaucracies. It was not many decades after the first police forces were established that other new regulatory agencies began to specialize in forms of enforcement that had once counted among general police responsibilities. In the mid-nineteenth century the first inspectorates of factories, food, shipping, mines, and weights and measures emerged. Other types of regulatory agencies came much later. There was very little environmental legislation until the end of the nine-teenth century and most of the environmental agencies of industrialized nations were established in the late 1960s and early 1970s. Still more specialized nuclear inspectorates emerged only after the splitting of the atom. The earliest of the antitrust agencies were established in North America after the first state and federal antitrust laws in the 1890s and now most of the world's nations have them. Yet most of these agencies were established in the 1990s. By the 1980s in a nation such as Australia, there were eight police forces and more than a hundred specialized business regulatory agen-cies, some of them with thousands of officers.

Of course, all nation states and all localities within nation states have distinctive histories of regulation. The comparative literature is limited to comparisons of a small number of states, so it does not help us to understand the differences between Chinese and Russian regulation. The most researched comparison is between the United States and the United Kingdom. On the one hand, Atiyah and Summers (1987) probably correctly claim that American law is more substantive, British law more formal. Paradoxically, we also know, however, that American rule-making is much more procedurally formalized and that American regulatory enforcement across a range of regulatory domains from nursing homes to environmental enforcement is more formal, rule-bound, and less discretionary than British regulation (e.g. Vogel, 1986). It is likely that it is the United States and not the United Kingdom that is excep-tionalist in these respects. Japan is one example of a society much less litigious than the UK that relies on an even less rule-bound form of administrative guidance to achieve regulatory outcomes. Robert Kagan and his co-authors are probably on the right track in identifying US adversarial legalism as distinctive (Kagan, 1991). It is possible that the exceptional distrust Americans have of executive government in the regulation of domestic affairs explains both why regulators are given less discretion to solve problems as they see fit and why courts have felt encouraged to make sub-stantive law that thwarts the decisions of executive governments.

3 RISK SOCIETY OR NEW REGULATORY STATE?

One view of the rise of the regulatory state is that it is a response to new fears and tensions about our relationship to science and technology. This is the risk society thesis most popularized in the academy through the writing of Ulrich Beck and Anthony Giddens (see Garland, 2002). Nuclear energy is the paradigm case. Like genetically modified organisms or Internet transmission of computer viruses, nuclear energy is a completely new twentieth-century technology that has created unprecedented risks and fears, redefined the way we invest in our security, and necessitated the creation of new national and transnational regulatory agencies. Nuclear risks are different from the major risks of previous centuries in that they are the technological creations of human beings and are potentially more catastrophic and mysterious than natural risks. Nevertheless, we do not live in a risk society in the sense of risks being in aggregate greater. On average, people live longer than they ever did.

As David Garland (2002) has pointed out, we are a risk society in the sense that we invest much more in risk management than we once did, and we are better at it. Nuclear risks are a case in point. Nuclear power plant scrams (automatic emergency shutdowns) per unit declined in the United States from over seven per unit in 1980, to one by 1993, to 0.1 by 1997. Rees (1994; see discussion below) has shown how early nuclear safety regulation was less effective because it was oriented to strict rule enforcement. Operators became rule-following automatons who lacked systemic wisdom of the safety systems they were managing. It was a shift to more 'communitarian', less command and control regulation that produced dramatic improvements in safety.

It is true then that much growth in regulatory surveillance is about risk management, yet that escalating intrusiveness from command and control regulation is not necessarily how this is accomplished (Vogel, 1986). Increasingly, contemporary regulation is meta-risk management, risk management of risk management systems (Gunningham and Grabosky, 1998; Parker, 2002). So prudential regulation of banks used to work by mandating how much gold had to be in their vaults. In time these became more complex capital adequacy ratios. But the Asian financial crisis of 1997 taught us that financial risks in a world of derivatives trading are rather more volatile and complex than they used to be. Capital adequacy rules cannot adjust fast enough or be sufficiently contextually attuned to specific markets to do the job. With great difficulty, prudential regulators today are attempting to reorient their work to regulating the risk management systems of major international trading banks. If a particular bank is seen as unusually exposed to the yen, the regulator might say 'Run your risk management software and prove to me that you remain solvent if there is a 40 per cent fall in the value of the yen at midnight'.

While it is correct to say that fundamental to what central banks do is managing the risks of a financial crisis, that is not their only objective. They regulate the macroeconomy not only to avert risks but also to promote growth. Environmental regulators not only seek to prevent pollution catastrophes. They also seek to promote growth in the number of fish in the rivers, whales in the sea, trees that are planted. Labour market regulators seek to manage not only discrimination against women, the disabled, or ethnic minorities. They also tend to seek to affirmatively expand opportunities for such groups. Food standards regulate not only food poisoning but the nutritional properties and freshness of food as well. Indeed, very often the same regulatory technologies that are used to monitor and manage risk are used to monitor and promote quality-of-life improvements. This is also why it can be a poor analytic judgement to marry the concept of regulation too closely to rules. Rules are mostly used to specify a minimum standard below which certain risks are unacceptable; but regulatory monitoring and management is often oriented to continuous improvement. This is often best achieved by enticing the best performing firms to extend themselves further, to invent new self-regulatory technologies that will pull most of their competitors along with them. Regulation can break through ceilings in ways that pull everyone above risk-management floors.

More fundamentally than becoming a risk society, or even a risk-management society (as Garland (2002) might have it), ours is becoming a regulatory society in ways it once was not. While concern to manage risk is an important part of this, so is learning to improve through monitoring and exhortation. Some readers will think this an odd claim. What about deregulation? What about the Thatcher and Reagan revolutions? One answer is to say that some important deregulatory shifts did occur from the late 1970s in Western democracies, but that these pale in significance compared to the regulatory growth that occurred under the New Deal in the United States, and everywhere in the 1960s and early 1970s. Moreover, it is not empirically correct to say that the pages of regulatory laws or even the numbers of business regulatory bureaucrats actually decreased under Reagan or Thatcher (e.g. Tramontozzi and Chilton (1989)). For instance, numbers of police went through the roof, with the number of private police (private security guards) growing even more in recent decades than the number of public police (see Shearing et al., forthcoming).

What did change from the late 1970s onwards was that governments provided less in the way of goods and services. The watchword of the Clinton administration in the United States became that government should be reinvented to do less rowing and more steering. The British in the 1990s called this the 'new public management'. Indeed, this is what even the Reagan and Thatcher governments had been doing in the 1980s. Mrs Thatcher would privatize something such as telecommunications and then create a new regulator—the Office of Telecommunications (Oftel) in this case. Even the supply of water was partially marketized, and regulated by the Office of Water Supply (Ofwat). In Australia when the Keating Labor government moved privatization into the heartland of the Keynesian welfare state by privatizing the

Commonwealth Employment Service's job placement service for the unemployed, it had to create an Employment Service Regulatory Authority. When John Howard's new conservative government decided it could continue the privatization without the new regulatory agency it soon found itself embroiled in fraud scandals involving private providers of job placement services. So in the last decades of the twentieth century, governments learned that privatization and deregulation did not actually go together in the way the Thatcherite ideological package contended. This was an ideological smokescreen for the reality of what was happening. Thatcher herself accompanied most of her privatization initiatives with considerable investment in enhanced steering capability in an attempt to ensure that the privatizations advanced her political objectives. A particularly bitter learning experience for libertarians in the 1990s was the way the inadequately regulated privatization of the Russian economy passed a huge portion of it, including much of the banking system, into the hands of the Russian mafia on the strength of bribes and patronage by exiting nomenclatura.

Michael Dorf and Charles Sabel (1998) describe changes in the nature of public sector governance as 'democratic experimentalism'. Democratic experimentalism is an emergent pragmatic form of management with its origins in the complexity and flux of the post-industrial private sector. Production systems of recent decades in developed economies have increasingly required decentralized, collaborative design of innovations. In these volatile conditions, one of the first things firms do as they explore how to improve their efficiency is to benchmark—survey current or promising products or processes that are superior to those they use. Benchmarking is designed to disrupt expectations of what is feasible by a comparison of actual and potential performance. Benchmarking is thus designed to spur exploration of new possibilities. Then independent production units, some collaborating with other firm insiders, others collaborating with organizations outside the firm, simultaneously engineer competing visions of crucial components of the project. This throws up quite a steering challenge to select which of the collaborating groups will become the producers of the final design and to integrate the different components. Dorf and Sabel see successful firms as accomplishing this through 'learning by monitoring'. Error-detection, error-correction, and continuous pragmatic adjustment of means to ends are features of these innovative production systems. There is a shift from Fordist control of a systematically specialized, broken-down production system to post-Fordist steering of more volatile systems that are partially contracted-out and partly contracted-in to shifting collaborative groups that compete for growth with outsiders and insiders. This competition is part of the error-detection system; work groups watch for flaws in the work of competing groups so they can show how their output can surpass the benchmarks set by these competitors. Excellence is grounded in collaboration, detection of poor performance in competition. Everyone is learning how to continuously improve by monitoring everyone else. Monitoring and steering (regulation) is therefore not only top–down. End-of-century production methods institutionalize more participatory and complex forms of self-regulation of production. Rules and routines shape agendas less than in the past. Of course, Fordist production lines also persist; collaborative learning through monitoring expands alongside older systems of production.

Dorf and Sabel argue that these technologies of governance have begun to infiltrate the public sector in a major way. Contracting-out and continuous improvement supplant command-and-control, freeing up managers from public service rules. There are fewer rules but more monitoring of outcomes and competing collaborations across the whole of government to tackle problems from drug abuse to security against terrorism, where the best collaborations are supposed to attract more funds. Public sector-centred collaborations have more profound possibilities for enriching democracy because learning by monitoring does not only lead to contracting out to the market. It can also lead to extensive collaboration with NGOs in civil society. Learning by monitoring can also involve expanded collaboration between business and civil society and more participatory styles of private–civic governance.

By such processes, the public sector is transformed under the influence of management consultants, and as a result of political demands for partnership from business and NGOs, and the competitive pressures on governments to perform well in order to attract foreign investment and hold domestic capital. The upshot is a world where the private–public divide is increasingly blurred, where steering collaborations is everything, and controlling production by doing it yourself is less important. We see this even with the military and policing, the sphere of governmental activity that is supposed to define what a state is, namely an organization that has a monopoly over the means of violence in a particular territory. In Australia, when you visit military or Australian Federal Police headquarters, it is a private security firm that manages your entrance to the building. Most police in contemporary societies are private police and often they have impressive arsenals. Following the published ideas of one of its members, Clifford Shearing, the Patten Commission on policing in Northern Ireland recommended abolishing the police budget and replacing it with a policing budget that could be contested by local NGOs wanting funding to organize their own nightwatch of a housing estate, for example. For Shearing *et al.* (2003), governance has become and should become more 'nodal' and less statist.

When war breaks out in a serious way, the militaries of various states are likely to be installed by the UN to fracture the indigenous state's monopoly of violence precisely when it counts. Most of the large number of Australian soldiers serving overseas at the time of writing—from Afghanistan to Somalia to Sierra Leone—are not regulars but reservists, part-time soldiers whose main work commitment is in civilian life. Most of the troops on the other side of the barricades are also irregulars in the pay of warlords rather than state commanders-in-chief. And in some economies there are even the beginnings of a debate about cutting defence expenditure to increase international competitiveness, using the cuts to drive down the national debt, while increasing the will to greatly expand that debt in a time of crisis by large loans to hire mercenaries. The final element of that debate is about the need to regulate the professional standards of mercenary armies such as Sandline and Executive

Outcomes to assure compliance with the Geneva Conventions via contractual assurance of democratic accountability. In 2002 the British Home Office issued a Green Paper on the licencing of 'private military companies'; *The Economist* (16 Feb. 2002, 53) quipped that the regulator might be named Ofkill.

With regulatory functions of the post-Keynesian state, such as environmental protection, we see plural paradigms of 'smart regulation' (Gunningham and Grabosky, 1998) that involve energizing third party regulators of many different kinds—private insurance companies, environmental NGOs, non-governmental standard-setting agencies such as the British Standards Institution (the originator of ISO 14,000, the global environmental management system standard), industry association self-regulatory schemes such as the international chemical industry's Responsible Care, hybrid business–NGO international accreditation schemes such as the Forest Stewardship Council, trade unions, even skin-diving networks for monitoring historic shipwrecks! Parker's (2002) work in *The Open Corporation* argues that particularly strategic actors in such collaborative networks that steer environmental protection and other regulatory spaces are compliance professionals—environmental managers, occupational health and safety officers, equal employment opportunity officers, intellectual property managers. Part of their strategic importance is that they translate public regulatory discourses into business discourses (the 'business case for an environmental initiative') and vice versa.

Thus, in the new regulatory state, not only does the state do less rowing and more steering, it also does its steering in a way that is mindful of a lot of steering that is also being done by business organizations, NGOs, and others. In such a world, strategic planning by a single decision-maker (say cabinet) at the apex of a hierarchy of command is passé. Learning by monitoring and partially decentralized steering increasingly supplants command-and-control.

4 THE REGULATORY TRILEMMA

Michel Foucault's corpus of work on the different disciplines and neo-liberal governmentalities that regulate our lives, mostly unhinged from the direct will of any Leviathan ('regulation at a distance'), is a highly relevant theoretical frame for comprehending the kind of regulatory society we have been describing. However, regulatory scholars mostly prefer to rely on a combination of more conventional historical, quantitative, experimental, and ethnographic methods than Foucault's genealogical method of tracing a history of the present. We have seen that the historical work documents the global spread and growth of complex bodies of regulatory law and the rise of a large number of specialized regulatory institutions in the past two centuries.

Much of the earlier regulatory research analyses the genesis of particular regulatory policies, standards, and agencies in the political economy—the political, state-centred process of mediating between the demands of capitalism and interest groups' influence (Snider, 1991). Regulation was seen primarily as a law and state-centred process of legislative action combined with administrative enforcement (now often referred to as 'command-and-control'). The major focus was on the ability of the political process and agencies of the state to deliver appropriately democratic regulation, regulatory decisions that reflected the will of the people, not capture by interest groups.

In the new regulatory state, policy-makers and researchers have lost confidence in the ability of traditional regulation via 'command-and-control' to adequately govern conduct, especially business conduct. Contemporary regulatory research has, to a large extent, been concerned with charting the failures in impact and legitimacy of state-centred regulatory intervention in action. Teubner (1987: 21) pointed out that any regulatory intervention that attempts to change social institutions will face a 'regulatory trilemma'—it is 'either irrelevant or produces disintegrating effects on the social area of life or else disintegrating effects on regulatory law itself'. Much contemporary regulatory scholarship explores the horns of Teubner's trilemma— effectiveness, responsiveness, and coherence. To a large extent, the focus of the research has moved from the 'high' politics of legislative enactment to the 'low' politics of regulation in action—what regulators actually do, the monitoring and enforcement strategies they use, how regulatees respond to enforcement and how they negotiate and avoid the meaning of the rules.

4.1 Effectiveness

Regulation, including legal rules, may fail to shape social practices. Much of the research is concerned with the extent to which target populations comply with the law, why people comply, or fail to comply, and how regulators and the targets of regulation construct the meaning of compliance. Researchers investigate the impact of different styles of rules, legal instruments, monitoring and enforcement techniques on compliance, and attainment of regulatory objectives (see Baldwin *et al.*, 1998: 14–21). One strand of research is concerned with the impact of the cost of compliance on actual compliance levels. Another focuses on whether laws and regulations are put on the books to pacify public concerns, without being effectively enforced. This may occur through lack of availability of adequate resources, or lack of wisdom and leadership to monitor and enforce strategically. From regulatees who are unwilling from the start to act responsibly, legalistic command and control regulation invites evasion through loopholes and 'creative compliance' (McBarnet and Whelan, 1997). Overly technical rules can also increase non-compliance by encouraging evasion and creative adaptation. As the technicality of rules increases so does the possibility for less scrupulous players to find loopholes.

4.2 Responsiveness

Government regulation may be so effective that it subverts and destroys otherwise desirable social practices. Regulatory research therefore looks at the responsiveness of legal regulatory institutions (both rule-making processes and enforcement) to the practices and norms of the targets of regulation, including issues of efficiency and practicality of compliance and the extent to which the values represented in regulation and the techniques used to monitor and enforce compliance with regulatory standards fit with pre-existing norms and social ordering in the target population. Much of the evidence shows that apparently effective legal regulation that is not responsive to non-legal normative orderings will ultimately fail to accomplish the goals of justice because of its failure to connect with social reality (see Selznick, 1992: 463). Cotterrell (1995: 304-5) describes at least five dimensions of the 'moral distance' between the normative expectations of 'law-government' and those of the field of social interaction it attempts to regulate—that regulation is too generalized, absolutist, inflexible, impressionistic, and democratically weak. Empirical research in business regulation has frequently demonstrated the existence of these limitations. It has also shown that non-responsive regulation will not only fail to be just, but also be ineffective as people refuse to comply with legal regulation that does not seriously engage with their concerns, values, and social milieu. Overly legalistic regulation can be ineffective because its very legalism dissipates voluntary responsibility—the will to comply with reasonable regulatory objectives. The normative literature on regulation has specialized in describing, evaluating, and proposing alternative, more responsive strategies for the design, implementation, and enforcement of regulatory instruments. A central concern has been 'to consider how regulation can acquire the qualities of being simultaneously rationally planned and purposeful, and also deeply rooted in social and cultural life' (Cotterrell, 1995: 308). There is an increasing emphasis on styles of government regulation that facilitate and enable private regulation, rather than overriding it. These include enforced self-regulation, co-regulation, corporate compliance systems, incentive-based regimes, harnessing markets, conferring private rights and liabilities, and relying on third party accreditation to standards and insurance-based schemes (e.g. Gunningham and Grabosky, 1998).

4.3 Coherence

Regulation that is too responsive to customs from civil society may subvert the doctrinal coherence of law's analytic framework. Simultaneously, doctrinal coherence can be threatened by the primacy of instrumental policy concerns in legislative regulation (see Cotterrell, 1995: 283–4). Scholars of legal regulation have been parti-cularly concerned with the extent to which constitutional guarantees, human rights and fundamental legal principles of openness, accountability, consistency, propor-tionality, and procedural fairness are observed (or not observed) in the practice of instrumental, policy-oriented public regulation, and also in the diverse sites, methods, and agents of enforcement in the pluralized regulation of the new regu-latory state (e.g. self-regulation). They are also concerned with the potential failure of effective and responsive regulation to secure certainty, consistency, and predict-ability in legal principles and values.

5 REGULATORY MECHANISMS

We have already begun to glimpse something of the new modalities of pluralized and decentralized regulation that are involved in the shift from the Keynesian welfare state to steering of private–public partnerships. Just as private firms and public agencies are abandoning command-and-control as a policy ideal in favour of outsourcing and networks of service delivery combined with monitoring, at the same time the focus of empirical regulatory research has also shifted from regulation by means of formal law to a more pluralized understanding of what regulation is and how social control works. The growing literature that describes and evaluates various regulatory mech-anisms reflects the fact that regulatory pluralism is, and always was, a reality. The state is not, and never has been, the sole font of regulation.

The empirical research on regulatory mechanisms breaks down the classical orthodoxy that regulation only occurs through a mechanism of deterrence that works via commands against misconduct spelled out in legal rules, monitoring of compliance by a state regulatory agency, and application of punitive sanctions for breach. Early empirical studies of how regulatory officials actually enforce the law found that they often prefer in the first instance to use strategies of education, persuasion, and cooperation to coax businesses to comply voluntarily with regula-tory rules (e.g. Hawkins, 1984), rather than to use adversarial and punitive means to sanction non-compliance. Classical deterrence theory assumes an essentially adver-sarial and antagonistic relationship between regulators and regulatees. Therefore cooperative strategies were previously thought to be the result of 'capture' of the regulator by regulatees. In practice 'capture' is multiplex and it is hard empirically to pin down strong structural capture effects. There is limited empirical evidence of capture actually affecting regulators' public interest orientation (Ogus, 1994: 94–5). Indeed, not all social bonds between regulators and regulatees are undesirable. The 'capture' problem is one of orthodox command and control sometimes positing an unachiev-able, and possibly undesirable, social disjunction between regulator and regulatee.

These descriptive findings prompted a fruitful empirical and normative debate about how regulatory agencies should approach enforcement—'compliance' (i.e. a cooperative, persuasive style) versus 'deterrence' (punitive enforcement). The simple compliance/deterrence dichotomy has not stood up to empirical scrutiny. The focus has therefore moved from the evaluation of discrete mechanisms of *legal* regulation to empirical and policy-oriented analysis based on a conception of a regulatory society where *social control* works through webs of regulatory influences.

5.1 The Classical Deterrence Approach

Traditionally, the deterrence approach assumes that enterprises will only comply to the extent that it is in their self-interest to do so. For example, some theorists argue that since all corporations have profit-maximization as their main goal, they will always be 'amoral calculators' who only ever comply with regulatory requirements when the penalties are heavy enough to ensure their calculations come up with the correct answer. Law-and-economics theorists see compliance as a function of the benefits of non-compliance versus the probability of being discovered and punished, and the severity of the penalty (see Ogus, 1994: 90–2 for a summary). On the whole, the assumption is that deterrence motivates via fear of punishment or rational calculations of the potential cost of penalties or sanctions.

While the deterrence approach holds some attraction as an explanation of how targets of regulation decide whether to comply, it is also now clear that it will only apply in some circumstances. Scholz (1997) has argued that the basic model of deterrence is only valid when (*a*) corporations are fully informed utility maximizers; (*b*) legal statutes unambiguously define misbehaviour; (*c*) legal punishment provides the primary incentive for corporate compliance; and, (*d*) enforcement agents optimally detect and punish misbehaviour given available resources. Scholz (1997) and other researchers have concluded from empirical tests of the deterrence model that these assumptions usually do not hold true, and that a simple model of deterrence is therefore generally not a helpful explanation of what motivates organizations to comply with the law.

One reason for this is that regulatory agencies are often not as powerful and efficient as they would need to be in order for the deterrence model to work. The deterrent effect of sanctions will depend on their certainty, severity, celerity, and uniformity, especially certainty. Another reason is that because so many kinds of business law-breaking have high rewards and low penalties, the threatened application of sanctions is not a severe enough threat to deter non-compliance (Ogus, 1994: 93). In order to cope with these realities, researchers have abandoned the simple economic model of deterrence as an explanation for compliance in favour of a more sophisticated analysis of how deterrence mechanisms work, and how they interact with a number of other factors that together accomplish social control.

Research on deterrence also shows that when individuals or management do think about the disadvantages of non-compliance, they do not make a simple calculation based on the direct economic costs of non-compliance. Other factors, particularly the indeterminate costs of bad publicity on the firm's reputation and morale are very significant. This undermines the basic premise of deterrence theory that the size of the expected financial penalty relates directly to the level of compliance. For example, occupational health and safety research (Scholz, 1997) found that although workplace safety in plants improves after penalties are imposed, the size of the penalty has little impact on safety improvements (indeed most of the penalties were very low). Fisse and Braithwaite (1983) studied the impact of publicity on corporate offenders in seventeen high profile cases in great detail. They found that 'Adverse publicity is of concern not so much by reason of its financial impacts but because of a variety of non-financial effects, the most important of which is loss of corporate prestige' and that 'corporations fear the sting of adverse publicity attacks on their reputations more than they fear the law itself' (Fisse and Braithwaite, 1983: 247, 249). Indeed, maintaining or advancing corporate reputation and counteracting negative publicity is an important reason why enterprises are interested in ensuring compliance. Even where regulators only have small penalties at their disposal, actual or potential bad publicity can overcome otherwise bounded rationality (i.e. inability to consider all the costs and benefits of every potential course of action simultaneously) and put compliance issues on management agendas.

5.2 The Significance of Maintaining Legitimacy

Similarly, regulatees are often motivated to comply with the law, or at least to appear to comply, in order to maintain their legitimacy in the eyes of government, industry peers, and the public. The insight here is that the possibility of fines, sanctions, and inspections acts less as a deterrent threat than as a way to focus management attention on institutional expectations that may affect the legitimacy and operation of their enterprise. The 'new institutional' scholarship in economics, political science, and organization theory finds that individuals and enterprises do not always make decisions solely on the basis of atomistic, financial self-interest, and that various other social and environmental factors including their own values and the expectations of others will affect their actions. These institutional influences include historical legacies, cultural mores, cognitive scripts (i.e. taken-for-granted ways of seeing the world), and structural linkages to the professions and to the state.

Thus there are three ways in which regulated organizations adopt practices and structures from their normative environments beyond what is required by the technical and financial parameters under which they operate: they submit to the demands of powerful external actors, such as the regulatory agencies of the state; they import the practices of professionals and other organized value-carriers; and they copy the apparently successful practices of other, similar organizations.

These three mechanisms are respectively regulative, normative, and cognitive (see Hoffman, 1997: 36–8). Hoffman sees regulative institutions as based on legal sanctions and coercion. Their logic is instrumental and their legitimacy based on law. Normative institutions are a matter of social obligation, and are based on values and social expectations. Cognitive institutions are taken for granted. They are seen as 'orthodox', deeply rooted in cultural assumptions and ways of seeing the world. They are a matter of unconscious compliance on the basis that it is almost unthinkable to do anything else. In any particular company's 'organizational field', these three pillars may be consistent or inconsistent with each other, and may affect different groups within the company differently. A regulative institution that fits pre-existing normative and cognitive institutions will be much more 'successful' at achieving compliance than one that is in conflict with them. For example, Prohibition in the United States did not fit the culture of the time. Equally, however, a company or industry may find that it has to change the cognitive institutions of its internal culture in order to avoid conflict with newly emerging normative and regulative institutions adopted by the society at large as these new influences enter its organizational field.

Edelman (1990) has used neo-institutional theory to explain the growth of employee due process rights designed to protect against a wide spectrum of arbitrary management behaviour in US companies, including indiscriminate firing, failure to promote, safety violations, unequal discipline, sexual harassment, and discriminatory employment opportunity structures. She argues that the civil rights movement and legal mandates of the 1960s together created a normative environment that put pressure on employers to create formal protections of due process rights. She shows how novel models of due process were initially accepted by some companies as a matter of legitimacy and survival in an environment in which they felt strong public scrutiny and employee expectations of change. Those that were most exposed to public scrutiny and government control changed first. Others followed in an effort to remain 'up to date'. Due process rights that were unheard of for private companies early in the century eventually became institutionalized in the normal bureaucratic structure of the corporation in the role of the personnel department and the professionalism of personnel officers. Now few large companies lack programmes for safeguarding basic employee rights; they are simply part of the basic operations of a company. However, as Edelman shows, a concern with legitimacy can motivate enterprises to manage their image of compliance, without necessarily complying substantively with the requirements of the regulation.

Hoffman's (1997) study of corporate environmentalism in the US petroleum and chemicals industry also demonstrates the power of institutions on corporate behaviour through the period 1960 to 1993, a period during which 'The corporate environmental management function grew from a small subsection of the engineering department to...a central aspect of corporate strategy driven by a core business constituency' (Hoffman (1997), 143). Hoffman's content analyses of industry journals showed that corporate attention to environmental issues did not follow the linear trends in volume of environmental laws and regulation, nor growth in industrial expenditure on environmental issues. So corporate attention to environmental issues cannot be explained solely by the motivation to regain control of capital and operating expenditure in relation to the environment, nor as a response to the threat of regulatory penalties and punitive damages (see Hoffman (1997), 144). Rather, Hoffman's analysis of the up-and-down trends in public concern for environmental issues between 1960 and 1993 matched exactly his analysis of corporate concern with environmental issues from the trade journals. He also points to the way that organizations made similar shifts in management structures for environmental issues at the same time as each other (not just technological shifts as required by regulation) to illustrate the influence of social factors (1997: 145).

Thus, Hoffman sees the history of corporate environmentalism over the last thirty years in the US petroleum and chemical industries as a 'story of institutional negotiation over corporations' rules, norms, and, ultimately, beliefs regarding legitimate environmental management' (1997: 152). The field moved from being dominated by cognitive institutions in which industry defined its environmental actions in terms of engineering advances to being dominated by regulative institutions when the EPA was established. The EPA was weakened by Reagan, but the public backlash against this weakening showed that environmentalism had now emerged as a normative institution. The chemical and petroleum industries therefore adopted environmentalism as a matter of social obligation. By the twentieth anniversary of the first international Earth Day (in 1990), insurance companies, investors, and competitors had entered the field and prominent environmental events and disasters sharpened public concerns. Environmentalism therefore moved from being an external community concern to an internalized strategic issue for corporations and reached new levels of cultural primacy, bringing it much closer to a cognitive institution: 'The heresy of the 1960s became the dogma of the 1990s' (Hoffman, 1997: 143).

5.3 Informal Sanctions and the Internalization of Compliance

The evidence also suggests that in general informal sanctions have a greater deterrent impact than formal legal sanctions (Paternoster and Simpson, 1996), and that regardless of what kind of social control is attempted it is usually not its formal punitive features that make a difference, but its informal moralizing features (Braithwaite, 2002: 106). Informal sanctions include negative publicity, public criticism, gossip, embarrassment, and shame. Formal sanctions are official sanctions such as fines, compensation, licence revocations and restrictions, and prison sentences. However, formal sanctions often trigger informal sanctions.

Some impressive evidence has been collected suggesting that, although cooperative and persuasive strategies are not always appropriate, when they are successful they are superior to punitive sanctions in effectively and efficiently accomplishing long-term compliance. A large body of empirical sociological and psychological research converges on the finding that non-coercive and informal alternatives are likely to be more effective than coercive law in achieving long-term compliance with norms, and coercive law is most effective when it is in reserve as a last resort (Braithwaite, 2002: 30–4; 106). This is because people are less likely to internalize the virtues of compliance when they see compliance as a response to extrinsic rewards and punishments; reasoning and dialogue promote feelings of self-determination that support internalization. Quantitative research on nursing home regulation suggests that cooperative strategies of trust, restorative shaming, praise, nurturing pride in corporate social responsibilities, and avoidance of stigmatization are more effective at increasing business compliance with regulation than the application of formal sanctions (Braithwaite, 2002: 17–18, 112).

5.4 Trust

A significant sub-theme of research on compliance is the importance of trust in securing compliance. Trust between regulator and regulatee simultaneously builds efficiency and improves the prospect of compliance. If regulatees trust regulators as fair umpires who administer and enforce rules that have important substantive objectives, then the evidence is that compliance levels will be higher, and resistance and challenges to regulatory action will be low. For example, Scholz and Lubell (1998) found that tax compliance increases as trust towards the government increases, and also that the sense of duty to pay taxes increases when government policies prove beneficial to the taxpayer. If regulatees feel that regulators treat them as untrustworthy, then defiance and resistance build up so that inefficiency and non-compliance both increase (see V. Braithwaite, 1995).

5.5 Effective Motivations for Compliance Vary among People and Contexts

The strands of research summarized above give us a more complex picture of what motivates people to comply with regulation than the simple deterrence model. This picture is further complicated by the finding that effective motivations for compliance vary between persons and contexts. Various motivations are likely to apply in different enterprises, in different parts of the same enterprise and at different times in the same enterprise.

Paternoster and Simpson (1996) looked at intentions to commit four types of corporate crime by MBA students, and found that these intentions were affected by sanction threats (formal and informal), moral evaluations, and organizational factors. They found that where people did hold personal moral codes, then these were more significant than rational calculations in predicting compliance. If moral inhibitions were high then cost-benefit calculations were virtually superfluous. But when moral inhibitions were low, then deterrence became relevant. Companies frequently respond to weak sanctions including adverse publicity. This is because there are usually a variety of actors associated with any wrongdoing. Although some will be 'hard targets' who cannot be deterred even by maximum penalties, others will be 'vulnerable targets' who can be deterred by penalties, and still others will be 'soft targets' who can be deterred by the mere exposure of the fact that they have failed to meet some responsibility they bear (Braithwaite, 2002: 109–13). Differing motivations and responses will also be partially determined by economic circumstances and place in the economic and social structure (see Gunningham and Grabosky, 1998) as well as by individual dispositions of particular corporate managers.

Indeed, most accounts that find people to be compliant in response to cooperation, goodwill, and trust also find that deterrence is necessary as a back-up for the minority of organizations that do not voluntarily comply. They also find that cooperative compliance is generally contingent upon persuading those of goodwill that their compliance will not be exploited by free riders who will get away with the benefits of non-compliance without being held to account for it. Thus deterrent and punitive sanctions must still be available in the background.

5.6 Creative Compliance and Regulatory Community

Finally, it is evident that even where regulatees do appear to 'comply' with legal rules, their compliance may be a sham. Because rules can be under- or over-inclusive and always require interpretation (Black, 1997: 6), regulatees can evade the letter of the law through loopholes or creatively interpret its requirements to avoid substantive compliance. For example, Edelman's (1990) work suggests that many companies are highly motivated to preserve legitimacy by responding to external norms and setting up compliance programmes, but these will not necessarily reflect legal norms in substance. Similarly much empirical research, especially that of McBarnet and Whelan (1997), shows that corporate lawyers can ensure that their clients comply scrupulously with legal requirements while completely missing its spirit, substance, and foundation. Indeed 'compliance' with legal regulation is rarely clearly defined, and is created and modified on the ground by a variety of players including regulatory inspectors, company lawyers, industry associations, and many more.

Black (1997: 30, 31–2) argues that one important way in which these problems can be addressed is through ensuring that the context in which rules are formed, followed, and enforced is that of a shared understanding of regulatory goals, norms, and definitions. This type of 'regulatory community' will share a tacit understanding of how regulatory rules should be interpreted and applied in particular circumstances. It occurs where regulators, regulatees, and their advisors have continuing relationships and in their dialogues and disagreements, constitute, define, and redefine appropriate norms of behaviour. Habituated compliance happens when regulatory enactments are communicated into a world of shared understandings in which regulatees can effectively respond to regulatory signals, and the parties deliberate effectively about their responses to them which, in turn, create shared commitments to regulatory goals.

6 PLURALIZED REGULATION IN THE NEW REGULATORY STATE

A central insight in the literature on regulatory mechanisms is that there exist many forms of formal and informal, legal and non-legal ordering in society, and multiple motivations and normative commitments amongst targets of regulation. Regulation is not confined to law. There are plural sources of regulatory ordering, and compliance is often constructed through webs of social controls. For example, Lawrence Lessig (1999: 235–9) proposes the following typology of regulatory mechanisms in *Code and Other Laws of Cyberspace*.

Law defines rights, constitutes or regulates structures of government (e.g. establishing a bicameral legislature), and expresses the values of the community, but its most important role as a regulatory mechanism is that of issuing commands and imposing sanctions for transgressions against them.

Social norms, like law, are commands, but they are enforced according to Lessig by the community rather than the state, by informal social disapproval rather than by formal sanctions.

The *market* constrains through price. To some, it is controversial to describe the market as a regulatory mechanism because in a market there is no regulator who decides on a price in order to regulate something—the market is the antithesis of intentional social engineering (Black, 2001). There is no doubt, however, that public and private policy-makers do make decisions to move transactions 'from hierarchy to market' to steer the achievement of objectives such as efficiency or pollution control.

Architecture is the environment built around an object of regulation that physically constrains it. Disney world regulates by a Foucauldian architecture of bars, guard rails, and other physical barriers (Shearing and Stenning, 1987). A reinforced door to a cockpit is a way of regulating hijackers, as is a lock. Architecture can organize natural surveillance to focus on hot spots of vulnerability to crime—for example, kitchen windows in a housing estate that look out onto children's playgrounds. The basic idea is the same as that which underlies Jeremy Bentham's Panopticon prison design. Lessig's special contribution to regulatory scholarship is to show the profound consequences of software code as an architectural regulator of cyberspace. Both Bill Gates and the US-dominated regime of copyright and trademarks have structured the architecture of the Internet to advantage certain commercial interests and disadvantage others. Lessig argues that a lot of the power of architectural mechanisms of regulation resides in their self-executing properties. Legal constraints need to be mobilized, and this may result in delay and uncertainty. This is why architectural regulation was so favoured a feature of safeguards the United States and USSR put in place to make it impossible for one to activate a warhead without an electronic alert automatically being triggered in the other state.

Further, each form of regulation is itself modified as it refracts through other forms of regulatory ordering. Indeed, it can be fruitful to think of compliance with regulation occurring in a 'regulatory space' in which various regulatory regimes simultaneously operate and compete with each other to secure compliance (Scott, 2001). Government regulators have to compete with, form alliances with, or influence these non-state forms of regulation in order to be effective at gaining compliance with public policy goals. Legal sanctions rarely achieve prime legitimacy and efficacy automatically in social and economic life. In order to understand the impact of legal regulation, it is therefore necessary to understand how law connects or fails to connect with the other sources of normative ordering. The different modalities of regulation may be mutually constitutive or destructive. For example, a market cannot be constituted without laws and norms about honouring contracts and eschewing cartels, or without the architectural feature of an electronic or bricks-and-mortar stock exchange.

Regulatory effects always depend on the extent to which regulatory norms are incorporated into informal and self-regulation, whether at the level of a corporation's management, an industry, a local community, or socialization within a family. One strand of regulatory research focuses on the possibilities for enterprise and industry self-regulation to improve compliance with government policy objectives in a way that satisfies both business and communities (e.g. Parker, 2002). Another emerging theme in regulatory scholarship is the role of third parties and civil society in regulation and compliance either because they are (*a*) coopted into the formal regulatory system via government regulation, or (*b*) responsible for regulatory orderings distinct from or subordinate to government regulation. For example, can standards developed by national and international standardization organizations be adequate alternatives to regulatory requirements in some situations, and to what extent can we expect markets to spontaneously make compliance with these standards widespread? The ISO 14,000 series on environmental management systems has attracted particular interest (Gunningham and Grabosky, 1998: 172–87). A further emerging theme is the effectiveness of regimes that attempt to coopt market mechanisms to regulatory purposes in improving overall regulatory policy outcomes such as the creation of trading regimes or tax incentives to control total allowable emissions of sulphur dioxide or greenhouse gases.

6.1 Capacity Building

There is a constitutive relationship between regulatory institutions and developmental institutions. Developing human capacity and regulating it are both generically important activities to understand if we are to grasp how the world functions. Citizens are not born democratic; democracy is something we learn in developmental institutions, particularly schools. Citizens must learn democratic virtues such as respectful listening during collaborative deliberation through, for example, restorative justice programmes to confront school bullying and create norms about it (see Sect. 6.2 on restorative justice).

Crucial roles of developmental institutions are the creation of citizens who are (a) self-regulating and (b) collaborators in creating spaces where we leave ourselves open to the normative regulation of communities. This is why developmental criminology has been such a booming subfield of criminology during the past decade or so. Many criminologists have the belief—perhaps extreme but not totally devoid of foundation—that investing in early developmental interventions to solve the learning difficulties of children in pre-school, in school, and in families, is the best way to reduce crime. The evidence is that by unblocking learning difficulties, preferably early, but even late in adult prison education programmes, we can improve self-regulatory capacities at a cost that is much less than the benefits. Learning how to learn not only has the advantage of enhancing self-regulation, it also enhances societal capabilities for learning through monitoring. Collaborative education also builds social capital (learning how to trust) as it builds human capital. Educational interventions also enrich people's lives, of course, whereas punitive interventions make them more miserable.

Developmental institutions not only achieve regulatory objectives by enhancing self-regulation; they also do so through self-capacitation, capacity building. Psychologists call this self-efficacy. Jenkins (1994) showed that sustaining the self-efficacy of managers for improving quality of care was critical to improved compliance with nursing home regulatory standards. While defiance (participation in a business subculture of resistance to regulation) did reduce compliance (Sherman, 1993), disengagement was the bigger problem (V. Braithwaite, 1995). Strategies such as praise and avoiding stigmatization were important to sustaining self-efficacy and engagement with continuous improvement.

At a more macro level, capacity building is also an important mechanism for the globalization of regulatory regimes. For example, developing countries find it difficult to join the global intellectual property regime until international organizations such as the World Intellectual Property Organization have trained their professionals in the principles of intellectual property law, in how to run a patent office, and so on.

6.2 Restorative Justice

Scholarly interest has turned towards research that evaluates alternatives to traditional 'command-and-control strategies' that relied on a simple theory of deterrence. In particular this research takes a more holistic approach towards regulation and examines the effectiveness of mixes of regulatory strategies that utilize the complexity and variety of motivations underlying compliance. The study of regulation is developing more scientific integrity, not least by the deployment of actual experiments which pass methodological tests such as random assignment. Restorative justice is one field where we have seen randomized controlled trials combined with the paradigmatic features of Dorf and Sabel's (1998) democratic experimentalism—bottom-up collaborations between state, business, and civil-society actors to solve specific crime problems and to use crime as an opportunity to confront underlying social problems, such as a school environment that is unsupportive to its students, with ultimate accountability to courts which have a duty to protect rights and police limits.

The central idea of restorative justice is that the purpose of intervention is to give the offender a chance to proactively put things right. In criminal process, restorative justice asks offenders to confront their responsibility for wrongdoing by facing their victim(s) so that together they can decide how to put the wrong right, for example, by the payment of restitution or the doing of community service. The aim is not only to provide a better remedy and healing for the victim than imprisonment or a fine would provide, but also to help transform the offender into a more law-abiding person in the future, and to assist communities to be more just and compassionate.

Nothwithstanding the safeguarding role of the courts in securing accountability for the conduct of restorative justice processes, jurisprudential traditionalists have deep trouble with restorative justice. Unlike utilitarians who say crime control or deterrence is their clear objective and deontologists who say that honouring just deserts is theirs, restorativists slip and slide across seemingly dozens of objectives. For example, they want to fix up a school culture that does not support its students, use a crime as an opportunity to heal rifts in a family, compensate a victim, prevent future recurrence of the crime, confront an underlying substance abuse problem, build community, and enrich democracy! One advocate has even suggested destabilizing and transforming the entire legal system as a long-term objective (Braithwaite, 2002).

Restoring victims, restoring offenders, and restoring communities covers a cascade of objectives in tension.

Dorf and Sabel (1998) state that the philosophical underpinning of their democratic experimentalism is pragmatism. The pragmatist account of thought and action is of a world 'bereft of first principles and beset by unintended consequences, ambiguity and difference' (Dorf and Sabel, 1998: 12). According to Dorf and Sabel, this is what leads to the central pragmatist theme in the writing of Peirce, Dewey, and Mead of reciprocal adjustment of means and ends—learning through monitoring. Objectives get transformed in the light of experience of their pursuit. With restorative justice, the transformations can be profound: participants in a restorative justice circle might begin with a shared objective of deciding on a just punishment for a crime. Yet the experience of the dialogue often transforms the needs of the victim to a need to forgive, sometimes to the point where the victim requests of the other stakeholders not only the grace of forgiveness but of a gift for the offender instead of the exaction of punishment. In one famous case in New Zealand, an armed robbery victim who had been bound and gagged at the point of a knife was so touched by the life circumstances of her assailants that she invited them to live and work on her family farm, which one of them did. For Dewey, democracy was the method for collaborative investigation of differences in response to doubt, for transforming our conception of justice in light of the experience of its pursuit.

Institutional innovations in restorative justice are akin to Dorf and Sabel's (1998) descriptions of collaborative innovations in military hardware—concurrent and parallel engineering of component parts and individual machines before the weapons system as a whole has been designed. In restorative justice projects, the collaborations are rather competitive with other collaborations as well—groups developing competing models of restorative justice watch eagerly for empirical evidence of the failures of variants developed by other groups. As Dorf and Sabel point out, there is considerable irony in the military-industrial complex pioneering methods of governance that create spaces for the new forms of democracy that are manifest in restorative justice.

An example of the success of restorative justice in regulation is the Institute of Nuclear Power Operators (INPO), a US self-regulatory organization for nuclear utilities set up after the Three Mile Island accident to develop standards, conduct inspections, and investigate accidents. Safety has increased significantly since Three Mile Island across a number of indicators (see Sect. 3 above). One of the restorative mechanisms that has contributed to this success is a meeting in which senior nuclear officials from all companies gather together to hear three vice-presidents give a detailed explanation of a recent accident at their utility and what went wrong. This 'confession' of wrongdoing within the occupational community arouses remorse and repentance in the wrongdoer and reacceptance by the other members of the community, with a powerful continuous improvement effect (Rees, 1994: 106–7; see Braithwaite, 2002: 62–6 for other examples).

6.3 Meta-regulation and Learning by Monitoring

The new regulatory state's move from command and control towards indirect governance explicitly recognizes what has always been true—that policy outcomes are not solely the product of central government but a complex interaction between law, local government, administrative agencies, the voluntary sector, the private sector, schools, families, each of which in turn interacts with one another. What is new is that there is an increasing emphasis on styles of government regulation that facilitate and enable private regulation, rather than overriding it. In this style, government tries to work with the grain of things, to co-opt and form alliances with non-state orderings. For independent government regulators, this can mean a normative preference for winning influence through alliances with or co-optation of non-government regulatory institutions through strategies that include (Grabosky, 1995):

- Enforced self-regulation: legislation or regulatory action forces industry associations or individual firms to introduce self-regulatory programmes that meet certain standards and goals set by the government and that can be publicly enforced.
- Co-regulation: government and self-regulatory agencies work together to set and enforce standards.
- Third party oversight: third parties are required to act as whistle-blowers to ensure compliance (e.g. banks are required to report suspiciously large cash deposits to a regulatory agency) or are required to guarantee or accredit a certain level of compliance with standards (e.g. corporate financial reports must be audited to accounting standards by accredited auditors).
- Equipping consumers and competitors to take formal or informal enforcement action: private parties are encouraged to take action to receive compensation if a regulatory standard is breached or are given information and standing to enforce public interests.

The idea is that government leverages its resources by facilitating activity in markets and civil society to help accomplish public policy objectives. These forms of regulation can be characterized as 'meta-regulation' (Grabosky, 1995) not solely state regulation, not solely market ordering, but government regulation of plural regulation in the private sector and civil society.

Just as we argued earlier that the emergence of a risk management society is a less fundamental development than the movement from a Keynesian welfare state to a new regulatory state that rows less and steers more, now we must concede that the development of democratic experimentalism is more fundamental still. The role of the state is more than steering, it is also an important source of democratic accountability, albeit in a decentred demos. With the emergence of democratic experimentalism, the chief role of the legislature should be to authorize and finance experimental reform by partnerships between different levels of government, business, and civil society. The legislature provides one especially important form of democratic accountability and it legitimates more participatory forms of bottom-up collaboration as it seeks to energize them. This model also means that the courts should have a significant role in ensuring that collaborations respect fundamental human rights and fundamental constitutional and legal values (Dorf and Sabel, 1998; Lessig, 1999: 215).

The final piece of the Dorf and Sabel analysis of democratic experimentalism takes us back to the fundamental importance of a new regulatory state that gives more emphasis to steering than to delivering government services. Learning by monitoring occurs piecemeal by watching our own organization's performance and benchmarking the performance of our collaborators and competitors. It follows that national coordination is needed to ensure that those interested in innovating will be able to find one another and pool their learnings, and that those wanting to build competing models will be guaranteed by the State a window that makes the errors of their competitors transparent to them. Especially when the greatest burden of innovation rests in civil society, as in restorative justice, substantial state funding of democratic experiments is needed with strings attached which require information pooling, evaluation, and transparency of the evaluation results. State funding is needed for the websites for the Campbell Collaboration (modelled on medicine's Cochrane Collaboration) which publishes continuously updated literature reviews and meta-analyses of the efficacy of crime prevention, educational and other social interventions. State courts are needed to enforce rights and limits. Specialist regulatory agencies have a role here as well. While democratic experimentalism favours the overthrow of centralized curriculum development in education bureaucracies in favour of school-level curriculum innovation, something like the British Ofsted, the Office of Standards for Education, is needed to enforce benchmarks and the human right of children to certain educational basics.

It is the central task of the new regulatory state to connect the private capacity and practice of pluralized regulation to public dialogue and justice. Ultimately, coordinating state agencies need to keep track of what issues suggest the need for legislative change, regulatory enforcement action, legal aid funding for test case litigation, and so on. They need to look for patterns of injustice that arise from reliance on private regulation in order to determine where extra rights need to be given to protect or promote the bargaining power of stakeholders, or where legal regulation needs to be amended to promote better pluralized regulation. In other words, we need to build institutional capacity for regulators and legislators to learn about the regulatory space in which they act, and to change law and regulatory strategy in response. This means that a fundamental strategy of the new regulatory state should be to gather and disclose information, to report it to stakeholders, and to ensure that it is adequately verified/audited so that it is reliable. This provides a basis of information on which private regulation and its impacts can be judged (by regulators and stakeholders), and a type of society where individual capacity, organizational capacity, and the capacity of states to regulate are linked through democratic participation, collaboration, and learning by monitoring.

7 CONCLUSION

We started out by conceiving of regulatory studies as a set of Russian dolls, moving from a core of studies of specific regulatory agencies out to the entire field of governance. Now we have conceived of regulatory studies itself as a middling Russian doll in a set that moves from studies of the anxieties of a so-called risk society to the practices of a risk-management society, to the more generic practices of a regulatory society, to the even more generic learning through monitoring of an experimental democracy. There is something to all these shifts, but they can all be overstated and doubtless in some respects have been in this chapter. If we look at a typical police force, command and control is still their core business. Certainly they might espouse a community-policing philosophy at meetings of their police–community consultative committee, and might even do some restorative justice in their cautioning of juveniles. They might do a good bit of collaboration with business, local ethnic communities, and private security organizations in efforts to regulate risks, for example, in the architecture and security systems of housing estates. But even if they spend only a small proportion of their time trying to arrest bad guys, their mentality remains that this is the core of what they do. Ditto with the even older regulatory agency of the tax authority: shifts towards meta-risk management there might be, but their mentality remains that the core of what they do is finding unpaid taxes through audits. Evidence that police arrests can be counterproductive by creating defiance (Sherman, 1993) or that audits can help taxpayers learn what they can get away with (Kinsey, 1986) only chips away at the old mentalities.

Nevertheless, the study of regulation is making some particularly exciting contributions to the radically reconfigured social science that democratic experimentalism implies. This is a social science organized around theories about the dynamics that are driving change in contemporary conditions, not around received disciplines that represent static descriptive categories—economics (the study of money transactions), political science (the study of political transactions), law (the study of political transactions that occur through statutes and courts), international relations (the study of transactions between nation states), and so on. Our hope is that ideas like democratic experimentalism will help usher in a re-energizing of the social sciences in the twenty-first century akin to the re-energizing of the biological sciences in the twentieth century as a result of substantially abandoning descriptively unified disciplines including anatomy, zoology, botany, microbiology, and entomology in favour of theoretically dynamic organization around ecology, molecular biology (the DNA revolution), and evolutionary biology.

While a good case can be made that at the technological cutting edge of the private sector, command and control has been partially supplanted by participatory, collaborative learning by monitoring, the inroads of democratic experimentalism into the work of the mainline regulatory agencies has been modest. Courts have embraced efficiency elements of the New Public Management through, for example, Case Flow Management, but mostly reject experimentalism as a threat to the consistency of justice and scotch most kinds of collaboration as a threat to the independence of the judiciary. In some, but not all, respects this may be as it should be. But beyond court-rooms, in the rooms where most of the justice and injustice is done, it can be argued that it is with regulatory institutions that some of the most innovative work of democratic experimentalism is happening—for example, in South Africa from nodal governance of security in the squatter settlement of Zwelethemba ('place of hope') (Shearing *et al.*, forthcoming) to further refinement of the idea of the Truth and Reconciliation Commission and the restorative justice philosophy it embodies.

REFERENCES

Atiyah, P. S., and Summers, R. S. (1987). *Form and Substance in Anglo-American Law*, Oxford: Clarendon Press.

Baldwin, R., Scott, C., and Hood, C. (1998). *A Reader on Regulation*, Oxford: Oxford University Press.

Black, J. (1997). *Rules and Regulators*, Oxford: Clarendon Press.

——(2001). 'Decentring Regulation: Understanding the Role of Regulation and Self-Regulation in a Post-Regulating World', *Current Legal Problems*, 54: 103–47.

Braithwaite, J. (2002). *Restorative Justice and Responsive Regulation*, New York: Oxford University Press.

Braithwaite, V. (1995). 'Games of Engagement: Postures within the Regulatory Community', *Law and Policy*, 17: 225–55.

Cotterrell, R. (1995). *Law's Community: Legal Theory in Sociological Perspective*, Oxford: Oxford University Press.

Dorf, M., and Sabel, C. (1998). 'A Constitution of Democratic Experimentalism', *Columbia Law Review*, 98: 267–473.

Edelman, L. (1990). 'Legal Environments and Organisational Governance: The Expansion of Due Process in the American Workplace', *American Journal of Sociology*, 95: 1401–40.

Fisse, B., and Braithwaite, J. (1983). *The Impact of Publicity on Corporate Offenders*, Albany, NY: State University of New York Press.

Garland, D. (2002). 'The Rise of Risk', in R. Ericson (ed.), *Risk and Morality*, Toronto: University of Toronto Press.

Grabosky, P. (1995). 'Using Non-governmental Resources to Foster Regulatory Compliance', *Governance: An International Journal of Policy and Administration*, 8: 527–50.

Gunningham, N., and Grabosky, P. (1998). *Smart Regulation: Designing Environmental Policy*, Oxford: Clarendon Press.

Hawkins, K. (1984). *Environment and Enforcement: Regulation and the Social Definition of Pollution*, Oxford: Clarendon Press.

Hoffman, A. (1997). *From Heresy to Dogma: An Institutional History of Corporate Environ-mentalism*, San Francisco: The New Lexington Press.

Jenkins, A. (1994). 'The Role of Managerial Self-Efficacy in Corporate Compliance', *Law and Human Behaviour*, 18: 71–88.

Kagan, Robert A. (1991). 'Adversarial Legalism and American Government'. *Journal of Policy Analysis and Management*, 10/3: 369–406.

Kinsey, K. A. (1986). 'Theories and Models of Tax Cheating'. *Criminal Justice Abstracts*, Sept.: 402–25.

Lessig, L. (1999). *Code and Other Laws of Cyberspace*, New York: Basic Books.

McBarnet, D., and Whelan, C. (1997). 'Creative Compliance and the Defeat of Legal Control: The Magic of the Orphan Subsidiary', in K. Hawkins (ed.), *The Human Face of Law*, Oxford: Clarendon Press.

Ogus, A. (1994). *Regulation: Legal Form and Economic Theory*, Oxford: Clarendon Press.

Parker, C. (2002). *The Open Corporation: Effective Self-Regulation and Democracy*, Cambridge: Cambridge University Press.

Paternoster, R., and Simpson, S. (1996). 'Sanction Threats and Appeals to Morality: Testing a Rational Choice Model of Corporate Crime', *Law and Society Review*, 30: 549–83.

Rees, J. (1994). *Hostages of Each Other: The Transformation of Nuclear Safety since Three Mile Island*, Chicago and London: University of Chicago Press.

Scholz, J. (1997). 'Enforcement Policy and Corporate Misconduct: The Changing Perspective of Deterrence Theory', *Law and Contemporary Problems*, 60: 253–68.

—— and Lubell, M. (1998). 'Trust and Taxpaying: Testing the Heuristic Approach to Collective Action', *American Journal of Political Science*, 42: 398–417.

Scott, C. (2001). 'Analysing Regulatory Space: Fragmented Resources and Institutional Design', *Public Law*, Summer: 329–53.

Selznick, P. (1992). *The Moral Commonwealth*, Berkeley: University of California Press.

Shearing, C., and Stenning, P. (1987). 'Say "Cheese!": The Disney Order that is Not So Mickey Mouse', in C. Shearing and P. Stenning (eds.), *Private Policing*, Newbury Park, Calif.: Sage Publications, 309–23.

—— Wood, J., with Cartwright J., and Jenneker, M. (2003). 'Nodal Governance, Democracy and the New "Denizens": Challenging the Westphalian Ideal', *Journal of Law and Society* (forthcoming).

Sherman, L. W. (1993). 'Defiance, Deterrence and Irrelevance: A Theory of the Criminal Sanction', *Journal of Research in Crime and Delinquency*, 30: 445–73.

Snider, L. (1991). 'The Regulatory Dance: Understanding Reform Processes in Corporate Crime', *International Journal of the Sociology of Law*, 209–36.

Teubner, G. (1987). 'Juridification: Concepts, Aspects, Limits, Solutions', in G. Teubner (ed.), *Juridification of Social Spheres: A Comparative Analysis of the Areas of Labor, Corporate, Antitrust and Social Welfare Law*. Berlin: Walter de Gruyter, 3–48.

Tramontozzi, P. N., and Chilton, K. W. (1989). *US Regulatory Agencies under Reagan, 1960–1988*. St. Louis: Center for the Study of American Business, Washington University.

Vogel, D. (1986). *National Styles of Regulation: Environmental Policy in Great Britain and the United States*. Ithaca, NY: Cornell University Press.

CHAPTER 8

....

REVIEW OF
EXECUTIVE ACTION

....

PETER CANE

PUT at its broadest, this chapter is about accountability for public decision-making. Thus, it is not confined to scholarship concerned with scrutiny of the executive branch of government narrowly understood, or with the activities of judges and courts. Nor is the chapter confined to scholarship concerned with the exercise of 'review' (or 'supervisory'), as opposed to 'appellate', jurisdiction, or with legal accountability for decision-making and conduct as opposed to legal liability for harm resulting from decisions and conduct.

The chapter has three main sections. The first develops two themes: that mainstream administrative law scholarship is mainly concerned with the legitimacy of the administrative process; and that the preoccupations of scholars are partly a function of the constitutional, legal, and political landscape in which administrative law operates. The second section explores the ways in which administrative law scholarship has been affected by trends in legal scholarship more generally. The third section discusses government tort liability in the wider context of the distinction between public law and private law.

1 THE PROVINCE OF ADMINISTRATIVE
LAW SCHOLARSHIP

....

In terms of the categories of legal thought, judicial review of executive action is identified as part of administrative law. The theoretical foundation of administrative law is the tripartite division of government into the legislative, executive, and judicial branches. Understood in these terms, the province of administrative law encompasses the structure, powers, and duties of the executive branch (see Ch. 6), and scrutiny of the executive by the judiciary. Other aspects of the legal framework of government activity, such as the powers of the legislature, the relationship between the executive and the legislature, and judicial review of legislation (see Ch. 9), are traditionally treated as parts of constitutional law. At one level, such division of subject-matter between categories of scholarly endeavour is no more than a matter of organizational and pedagogical convenience. However, like the division of academic studies into various 'disciplines', the categories of legal thought may hinder our understanding of social phenomena by artificially screening off important parts of the object of study. This helps to explain the persistent theme in administrative law scholarship to the effect that administrative law needs to be viewed from a wider constitutional perspective that takes account, for instance, of the role of the legislature in scrutinizing the executive. This broader approach may be expressed in use of the term 'public law' to refer to an amalgam of constitutional and administrative law (e.g. Mashaw *et al.*, 1992).

More particularly, administrative law scholars who concentrate in their research on judicial review are often criticized for various deficiencies of vision. One accusation is that they pay too little attention to other 'external' accountability mechanisms such as scrutiny by the legislature, auditing, inspection, investigations by ombudsmen, and so on. Secondly, they are accused of focusing unduly on legal rules and principles of judicial review at the expense of questions about the impact of those rules, relative to other influences and constraints, on administrative behaviour. A third criticism points to the importance of 'internal' and 'informal' review mechanisms within executive agencies relative to external and formal modes of review through the courts, for instance. Fourthly, it is said, administrative lawyers should be at least as interested in the way executive agencies conduct their business—with issues of administrative 'process'—as with *ex post facto* checking and review of administrative decisions and actions. Fifthly, scholars who concentrate on judicial review are sometimes attacked for being focused on process and procedure at the expense of the substance and outcomes of administrative decisions and programmes. A sixth accusation is directed at scholars who, in the opinion of their critics, pay too much attention to the law of judicial review and too little to its 'context', represented by political and constitutional theory on the one hand, and the political system described by political scientists on the other.

In the Commonwealth literature, criticisms of this sort have been influentially encapsulated in a distinction between 'red-light' and 'green-light' approaches to administrative law (Harlow and Rawlings, 1984/1997). In the view of red-lighters (so the story goes), the prime concern of administrative law is (and should be) formal, external review mechanisms such as courts and tribunals. According to red-lighters, the main function of such external control is protection of individual rights against undue encroachment in the name of the public interest. Consequently, they favour restrictive interpretation of the scope of public powers. At the same time, they consider the proper focus of external control to be the process and procedures of public decision-making, not its substance. In the United States, this red-light spirit infuses the compromise that was struck between supporters of the New Deal and their critics in the shape of the Administrative Procedure Act of 1946.

By contrast, in the view of green-lighters, the prime concern of administrative law is (and should be) to facilitate the execution of public programmes and the promotion of government policies. Consequently, they favour generous interpretation of the scope of public powers; and they emphasize the role of law in regulating the distribution of public powers between different organs of power as opposed to the relationship between public organs and the individual. Green-lighters favour internal control mechanisms (such as intra-departmental complaint and appeal mechanisms) over external mechanisms, and political control (by the legislature, for instance) over control in the name of law. Political control is preferred because it is more concerned with outcomes than with procedures and because it is more 'democratic'.

Of course, the difference between the two positions is only one of degree. The typical green-lighter does not advocate the abolition of judicial review of the exercise of public power any more than the typical red-lighter denies the value of non-judicial review mechanisms and of judicial restraint in the exercise of the review jurisdiction. More importantly, whether any particular scholar espouses red-light or green-light views is likely to depend to some extent at least on his or her personal ideology. Thus, Harlow and Rawlings suggest an association between red-lightism and liberal individualism; and there is some reason to think that green-light views may be particularly attractive to those of a communitarian or welfarist persuasion. However, such coincidence of commitments (to the extent that it exists) is likely to be contingent. For instance, communitarians are more likely than liberal individualists to be concerned about the 'accountability deficit' allegedly generated by neo-liberal reforms of the modes of delivery of public services, designed to replace traditional 'public' forms of accountability with market(-type) forces.

To some extent the various criticisms of scholars who focus on judicial review can be seen as particular applications of more general attacks on legal scholarship which is rooted in the assumption that law is a more or less autonomous social institution, and that it is not just a 'dependent variable' that can only be understood in terms of some other social institution (such as politics), some other set of norms (such as morality), or some other disciplinary perspective (such as economics or philosophy). But at another level, uncertainty about the province of administrative law as a category of legal thought and a field of scholarly activity may be related to the fact that compared with other basic legal categories around which scholarship is organized, such as property, contract, and tort, administrative law is relatively young. In the United States, for instance, its genesis is usually traced to the period that witnessed the surge of legislative activity associated with the New Deal, and that ended with the enactment of the Administrative Procedure Act in 1946. It was at this time that the focus of legal concern shifted from the constitutionality of the independent regulatory agency as a vehicle of executive government to the procedures and judicial control of agency decision-making.

In England, the awakening of sustained academic interest in legal control of the executive can reasonably be traced to a new judicial activism manifested, for instance, in decisions of the House of Lords in *Ridge v Baldwin* ([1964] AC 40) and *Conway v Rimmer* ([1968] AC 910). Perhaps even more important were reforms of the procedure for applying for judicial review which were introduced in 1978 following the 1976 Law Commission *Report on Remedies in Administrative Law* (Law Com No 73, Cmnd 6407). These reforms are widely considered finally to have freed English law from the legacy of the renowned Victorian jurist, Albert Venn Dicey, who is best known, and most widely reviled, for his view that unlike civil law systems, the common law recognized no distinction between public law and private law. In Australia, the catalytic events were various committee reports that led to the introduction of a federal 'administrative law package' comprising the establishment of an Administrative Appeals Tribunal in 1975, creation of the office of Commonwealth Ombudsman in 1976, statutory codification of the law of judicial review in the Administrative Decisions (Judicial Review) Act 1977, and enactment of a Freedom of Information Act in 1982.

These observations about the genesis of administrative law as an academic subdiscipline support the unsurprising hypothesis that trends in public law scholarship reflect, at least in part, political and legal developments outside the academy. This hypothesis is consistent with the strong bias in US administrative law scholarship towards regulation and the relationship between regulatory agencies and the courts. Regulation by 'independent' (appointed rather than elected) agencies has been the characteristic form of government intervention in social and economic life in the United States since the late nineteenth century. The decade of the New Deal saw the creation of ten new agencies in addition to the fourteen already in existence; and by 1979 there were more than fifty such bodies. In Britain, by contrast, the main political reactions to the Depression were the Welfare State and 'nationalization' of key industries. As a result, British administrative law scholarship has been much more concerned than US scholarship with government as service provider and direct participant in the economy, and with elected government—departments of central government and local authorities. It was not until the 1970s and onwards that independent regulators began to assume a prominent role in British governmental arrangements, especially (in the 1980s and 1990s) as a concomitant of the privatization of monopolistic utilities—gas, water, electricity, and so on.

However, regulation has not become anything like as central a topic in British administrative law scholarship as it has always been and continues to be in the United States. Various factors may be suggested in explanation. One is that in Commonwealth countries in the last fifteen or twenty years, regulation has itself become a separate category of legal thought and a subdiscipline within legal studies (see Ch. 7). Topics such as regulatory standard-setting and agency rule-making procedure, which are staples of US administrative law scholarship, are likely to be dealt with by British scholars under the rubric of regulation rather than administrative law. Indeed, regulation scholarship has become so imperialistic in its aspirations that it can subsume judicial review as just one amongst many mechanisms for 'regulating government'. Whereas traditional administrative law scholarship is conducted in the language of constitutional and political values (such as rule of law, separation of powers, procedural fairness, and so on), this new regulatory scholarship is essentially instrumentalist in orientation. A second explanatory factor may be that in Britain, despite the Thatcherite neo-liberal revolution, central and local government is still very heavily involved in the provision of services to the public through the National Health Service and the social welfare system, and of financial benefits through the social security system.

There is, perhaps, a more fundamental reason why the link between administrative law scholarship and regulation is much stronger in the United States than in Britain. Ever since the establishment of the first independent regulatory agency—the Inter-state Commerce Commission—in 1887, the legitimacy of such bodies as a mode of governance has been controversial (Freedman, 1978). The first line of attack was that multifunctional agencies, exercising a mix of legislative, executive, and judicial powers, represented a 'fourth branch' of government that breached constitutional principles of separation of powers. The New Deal revolution more or less put an end to such complaints, and attention shifted to agency procedure leading, in 1946, to the enactment of the Administrative Procedure Act. After the last great wave of regulatory expansion in the 1960s and 1970s, the focus of criticism shifted again, this time to inadequacies and inefficiencies of the command-and-control style of regulation associated with the independent agencies (Sunstein, 1991). The chief political manifestations of this concern with outcomes were financial deregulation (removal of price and entry controls) and the introduction of cost-benefit scrutiny of regulatory initiatives. We may speculate that because administrative law scholarship has historically been centrally concerned with the legitimacy of executive government decision-making, the emergence of regulation as a separate category of legal thought in Britain and elsewhere in the last quarter of the twentieth century was a result, in part at least, of this new focus on styles and outcomes of regulation.

The centrality of the issue of legitimacy to administrative law suggests why British scholars have shown little interest in regulation as such. For one thing, by comparison with the powers of US independent agencies—which have been dubbed 'governments in miniature'—those of British agencies, particularly to make rules and enforce compliance, have historically been modest. Furthermore, in late twentieth century Britain, independent regulation was widely considered to be desirable and, indeed, essential to counteract the effects of lack of competition in sectors of the economy in which newly privatized utilities were operating. As a result, in Britain independent regulatory agencies are not seen as being problematic in terms of separation of powers and due process to the extent that they are in the United States. Much more troubling to British (and Commonwealth) scholars have been other aspects of the neo-liberal agenda—contracting-out of the provision of public services; joint public/private funding of infrastructural ventures; 'corporatization'; the creation of quasi-autonomous government agencies for the delivery of public services; and the 'contractualization' of relationships between units of executive government (Taggart, 1997). In other words, Commonwealth administrative law scholarship has been much more preoccupied with the legitimacy of government as provider than as regulator.

The basic ideological presupposition of these various neo-liberal developments in modes of governance was that markets and quasi-markets provide better ways of facilitating and controlling the provision of public benefits and services than do public law techniques such as judicial review and scrutiny by the legislature. Many administrative lawyers have found this ideology unacceptable, and have reacted against it by attempting to find ways of subjecting new forms of governance to the discipline of traditional public law rules, values, and techniques of accountability (e.g. Davies, 2001). By contrast, scholars who approach issues of accountability instrumentally challenge the preoccupation of public lawyers with centralized, hierarchical, and *ex post* forms of accountability and suggest that new patterns of governance bring with them new modes of and opportunities for accountability (Freeman, 2000; Scott, 2000).

Earlier I hypothesized that trends in administrative law scholarship reflect legal and political developments outside the academy. The story that has emerged in the process of developing that suggestion hints at a further hypothesis, namely that the preoccupations of administrative law scholars are partly a function of the constitutional background of administrative law. For instance, ideas of separation of powers play a much more prominent role in the US Constitution than they do in British constitutional arrangements; and this has had a significant effect on the identification, by scholars in the two systems, of concerns about legitimacy. This second hypothesis gains further support by consideration of Australian administrative law scholarship.

At the federal level, Australian constitutional arrangements are an amalgam of British and US elements. The relationship between the legislature and the executive follows the Westminster model even though the Australian Constitution (like the US Constitution) contains separate chapters dealing respectively with the legislature, the executive, and the judiciary, thus entrenching a stronger form of separation of powers than pertains in Britain. Unlike the US Supreme Court, the Australian High Court has interpreted the structure of the Constitution to require that 'the judicial power of the Commonwealth' be exercised only by courts established under the judiciary chapter (Ch. III) of the Constitution, and that such courts not perform functions that fall outside this concept. One such function is 'merits review' of decisions of officers and bodies established under the executive chapter (Ch. II) of the Constitution.

As a result, the Administrative Appeals Tribunal (AAT), which 'stands in the shoes of the decision-maker' when it reviews decisions of the executive and of first-tier tribunals, was established under Chapter II of the Constitution, not Chapter III. The AAT is technically part of the executive, not of the judiciary. However, in practice, it functions very much like a court, and it is viewed by the executive as an organ of external rather than internal review. The uneasy position of the AAT, perched as it is between the executive and the judiciary, has guaranteed that ever since it began its work in 1977, its legitimacy has been a subject of great interest and concern to Australian administrative lawyers.

Because the AAT was one of the pillars of the administrative law package introduced in the 1970s and 1980s, and because of the importance it has assumed in the Australian system, administrative law scholarship in Australia is preoccupied with tribunals and with external 'non-judicial review' of administrative decision-making to a far greater extent than in the United States or Britain. In Britain, 'court-substitute' tribunals are less systematized than in Australia, and tribunals are generally not seen to present serious issues of *constitutional* legitimacy. As a result, tribunals appear only marginally in mainstream administrative law scholarship. Similarly in the United States, 'administrative law judges' receive short shrift even from scholars who have written extensively about the internal workings of executive agencies (e.g. Mashaw, 1983: 41–4). That having been said, it is striking to the Commonwealth lawyer how little attention is paid in the mainstream US literature to administrative adjudication (i.e. non-judicial review) relative to administrative rule-making. An explanation for this lack of interest in adjudication amongst US scholars may be that adjudicatory procedures are generally perceived to comply with due process principles, thus raising few legitimacy concerns that they can get their teeth into. The best explanation for the relative lack of concern shown by Commonwealth scholars about the legitimacy of administrative rule-making is probably structural: in Westminster systems, non-parliamentary rule-making has predominantly been the province of the elected executive as opposed to appointed officials. As a result, academics have focused on the adequacy of parliamentary scrutiny of the substance of executive rule-making rather than on legitimacy-related issues such as the credentials of the rule-maker, constitutional separation of powers, and judicial control of executive rule-making. For the same reason, the expertise-versus-politics debate, which looms large in the US literature about agency rule-making, is a minor strand in Commonwealth scholarship.

Another explanation for the obsession of US scholarship with rule-making is the fact that, under US law, administrative rule-making procedures are highly regulated, formal, and elaborate compared with the more informal and legally unconstrained consultative processes that are typical of administrative rule-making in Commonwealth jurisdictions. Once again, this procedural difference reflects differing degrees of concern about the constitutional and political legitimacy of administrative rule-making. Indeed, to the outsider it appears that the engine of US administrative law scholarship is the perception of chronic and more-or-less irresolvable tension between concern about the legitimacy of agency rule-making on the one hand, and of judicial review of agency rule-making on the other (Cross, 1999a).

As might be expected, in Commonwealth administrative law scholarship discussion of procedural issues is biased towards administrative adjudication—decisions of regulatory and benefits agencies in relation to individuals, and review of such decisions by tribunals. From this perspective, procedural requirements are viewed not so much as a way of constraining the power of agencies as a protection for the rights and interests of individuals. Three matters have dominated the debates. One is whether and to what extent interests other than those recognized by private law ought to receive procedural protection. In this respect, Charles Reich's famous concept of 'the new property' (Reich, 1964) has been as influential outside the United States as within it. A second matter is the extent to which administrative procedures ought to be modelled on judicial procedures. On this point, the overwhelming balance of academic opinion has been that adversarial trial-type procedures are more or less inappropriate as a model for administrative decision-making by reason of their formality and complexity, and their cost in time and resources. Thirdly, while scholars have agreed that both instrumental goals and non-instrumental, 'dignitary' values may support the imposition of procedural requirements on administrative decision-makers, they have disagreed about how tensions and conflicts between instrumental and non-instrumental values ought to be resolved (Galligan, 1996).

If I am right in arguing that the *idée fixe* of administrative law scholarship is the legitimacy of executive decision-making, this discussion of procedure suggests that whereas in the American political, legal, and scholarly tradition, the key to legitimacy is found in institutional design, in the British tradition it is thought to lie in striking the right balance between the rights of the governed and the powers of the governors. This contrast can be illustrated by reference to the law of standing. From an institutional-design perspective standing rules are primarily concerned with the balance between public and private law enforcement; but from a rights perspective they regulate access to the courts as an avenue for protecting the rights and interests of individuals (and more latterly, groups and 'the public' at large) against undue encroachment in the name of 'the public interest'. More generally, there seems no doubt in the American tradition that the prime task of administrative law is to constrain, and thereby to legitimize, the exercise of power. By contrast, in the British tradition there is a real tension between the view that administrative law is a law of rights—a protection for citizens against the state—and the alternative view that it is a law of wrongs, focused on ensuring that government acts within the law.

History may help to explain this difference of approach. The main institutions of American (as of Australian) federal government were consciously created at a particular 'historical moment' as an integrated and internally balanced whole, amidst vigorous and quite sophisticated debate about fundamental questions of institutional design. By contrast, evolution has played a much more significant role than revolution in the development of British government. Moreover, although it is often said that British public law lacks a concept of 'the state' as an entity set against civil society, the hereditary monarchy—the 'Crown'—is arguably its functional equivalent. A central theme of British constitutional history is the relationship between the monarch and the people, the Crown and its subjects, the government and its citizens (or, in the neo-liberal world of the late twentieth and early twenty-first centuries, its 'clients' or 'customers'). It is for this reason, I would suggest, that 'the rule of law' has a more prominent place than 'separation of powers' in British political and legal thought. Over the past thirty years, constitution-building has played an unprecedented role in the British polity. Membership of the European Union, devolution, enactment of the Human Rights Act 1998, and other developments, have transformed the constitutional and legal landscape. Such changes have greatly enhanced the constitutional power and importance of courts, and they pose deep questions about the interaction between a new constitutional legalism and the traditional predominance of political institutions in the constitution.

My basic argument, then, is that the central, motivating idea of administrative law scholarship is the legitimacy of administrative decision-making and action. The province of administrative law scholarship in any particular jurisdiction—or, in other words, the scholarly understanding of the requirements and conditions of legitimacy—is, to some extent, a reflection of the constitutional and political arrangements and traditions in that jurisdiction. For this reason, it is more difficult and dangerous in this area of scholarship than it may be in some others (criminal or contract law, perhaps) to treat 'the common law world' as a useful frame within which to interpret and understand scholarly empirical, doctrinal, and theoretical preoccupations.

2 RULES, VALUES, FACTS, AND THEORIES IN ADMINISTRATIVE LAW SCHOLARSHIP

As well as the political and constitutional environment of administrative law, trends in legal scholarship more generally have a significant impact on administrative law scholarship. According to its critics, one of the characteristics of the 'red-light' approach to administrative law (mentioned in Sect. 1) is 'positivism'. This charge associates red-light scholarship with a 'scientific' or 'black-letter' or 'formalist' methodology that treats legal rules and principles (whether made by legislatures, courts, or other entities with legal rule-making power) as major premises of syllogistic arguments. 'Positivist' methodology is underpinned by an assumption that law is an autonomous universe of normative discourse. Its practitioners are prepared to criticize the law, but according to criteria of internal coherence and consistency rather than of substance. The archetypal 'positivist' literary forms are the casenote and the text-book. The prime target audience (apart from students) for scholarship in this genre is the appellate judiciary. 'Positivist' methodology is best understood as rooted in a view about the function of the legal academic that sees legal scholarship as essentially parasitic on administration of the law.

That view has become deeply unfashionable, at least in the 'élite' sector of the legal education system. Perhaps the dominant style of administrative law scholarship at the turn of the twenty-first century is one that seeks to uncover the values 'inherent' or 'immanent' in legal rules and principles (in the sense that they best explain 'the law' as it is); to expound and develop those principles systematically; and then to assess particular legal rules and principles critically in terms of those values. The archety-pal 'normativist' literary forms are the law review article and the monograph. Scholarship in this 'normative' genre shares with work in the 'positivist' mould the assumption that law is a relatively autonomous universe of normative discourse. But whereas the 'positivist' methodology provides the scholar with no *substantive* basis for evaluating legal rules and principles, the abstract values that the 'normativist' scholar finds immanent in legal rules and principles provide resources from within the law itself for criticizing legal rules and principles on the ground that they do not respect and promote fundamental legal values. For the 'normativist', what the law ought to be can itself be a legal issue, whereas for the 'positivist' the question of what the law ought to be can only be answered in non-legal ('political' or 'moral') terms. Both 'positivist' and 'normativist' methodology is conservative in the sense that it is rooted in respect for society's established legal culture. The normative methodology can be seen at work, for instance, in attempts (mentioned in Sect. 1) to subject neo-liberal reforms to the discipline of 'public law values'. Jurisprudential underpinnings for 'normativism' can be found in Ronald Dworkin's 'law as interpretation' and in the concept of law as an 'autopoietic system' developed by Niklas Luhmann and Gunther Teubner.

'Normativism' is the methodology of what is known in the United States as the 'legal process' approach to public law. This is widely regarded as having reached its apotheosis in the famous Harvard Law School course materials on legal process prepared by Henry Hart and Albert Sacks in the 1950s. The legal process 'school' took on board the realist, anti-formalist argument that legal rules cannot be understood or applied without reference to purposes underlying them and values they promote (Eskridge and Peller, 1991). The approach had two other key components: a concept of comparative institutional competence, and a focus on procedure. The first informs (for instance) the huge body of administrative law scholarship about the grounds and intensity of judicial review of agency decision-making spawned by the decision of the Supreme Court in *Chevron USA Inc v Natural Resources Defense Council Inc* (467 US 837 (1984)). The second supports the universally accepted (though often unarticulated) idea that, however intensive judicial control of executive agencies may be, it is nevertheless the role of courts to review rather than to second-guess agency decisions. More positively, it expresses the conviction that people who cannot agree about ends may nevertheless agree about means.

The legitimizing power of procedure received its most important formal affirmation in the enactment of the Administrative Procedure Act in 1946. Its centrality to the development of public law as a separate category of legal thought is reflected in two of the most influential pieces of administrative law scholarship ever published—Reich's 'The New Property' (Reich, 1964), and Richard Stewart's 'The Reformation of American Administrative Law' (Stewart, 1975). Reich's basic argument—which bore spectacular fruit in the US Supreme Court's decision in *Goldberg v Kelly* (397 US 254 (1970))—was that the constitutional guarantee of due process should be interpreted to protect not only private law property and contractual rights, but also welfare and other benefits provided by the state to its citizens. Stewart's focus was on the use of *law* to expose administrative agencies to the sort of pluralistic pressures that the *political system* imposed on the legislature. If legitimacy is the *leitmotif* of administrative law scholarship, due process and fair procedure are the values that lie at its heart.

A story commonly told about US public law scholarship is that the legal process approach came under attack in the 1970s and 1980s from two different camps—on the one side, critical legal studies (CLS) and on the other, economic analysis. The main thrust of the critical attack returned to, and relentlessly elaborated, a realist theme which legal process scholars had not fully taken on board—the 'indeterminacy' and 'manipulability' of legal rules. From a 'critical' perspective, the idea that judicial review can control and legitimize agency decision-making is pure deception because the legal rules according to which judicial review is exercised can be manipulated, in any and every case, either to facilitate or to frustrate agency action (Frug, 1984). Because of its indeterminacy, law can provide citizens with no reliable protection against bureaucratic power. Beyond this negative deconstruction of legal discourse, CLS had little to offer. Those of a pessimistic disposition tended to retreat into abstract epistemological theory, while the optimists advocated vague and impractical objectives such as 'participatory democracy'. Not surprisingly, therefore, CLS had little long-term impact on the nature and content of administrative law scholarship other than to reinforce the realist message that law is normative and value-laden.

The economic attack on the legal process approach had two main prongs. One (associated primarily with Chicago-style law and economics) was directed at its focus on means at the expense of ends, on process at the expense of outcomes. The other, under the banner of 'public choice' theory, challenged the assumption that government institutions form a balanced mechanism working towards the public interest. On the contrary, said public choice theorists, the public sector is as much driven by individual self-interest as is the private market. Some notable exceptions aside (see especially Sunstein, 1990), the first criticism has had much more impact on instrumentalist regulatory scholarship than on mainstream, court-focused, legitimacy-based administrative law scholarship. Nor has the second criticism reached its target, partly as a result of widespread scepticism about its validity, and partly because public-choice theorists have been slow to apply the logic of their argument to the courts, viewing them instead as altruistic promoters of the public interest—defined, of course, in terms of economically efficient outcomes (Cross, 1999*b*). Even agency-cost theory (Bishop, 1990), which seems at first sight to map many of the traditional concerns of administrative law, has made little or no impact. Mainstream administrative law scholarship has been similarly impervious to 'outsider theory'—outcome-oriented, distributive critiques rooted in issues of race, gender, class, and sexual orientation. Indeed, such has been the clarity and durability of the legal process vision that the most influential response to the intellectual ferment of the 1980s and 1990s has been deliberative republicanism—the 'new legal process'.

Legal process ideas also lie at the heart of mainstream Commonwealth administrative law scholarship, despite the absence of explicit recognition of the fact. Indeed, a striking difference between US scholarship on the one hand and Commonwealth scholarship on the other lies in the latter's lack of interest in grand unifying theories, whether descriptive or normative. Paul Craig's encyclopaedic excursion into political theory (Craig, 1990) was greeted with a surprising level of hostility, and stands more or less alone. There has been some flirtation with Habermasian democratic proceduralism (Prosser, 1982), but with distinct notes of caution bred of a concern that it be of practical use (Black, 2000, 2001). How might we account for this difference of scholarly style? Once again, it may be relevant that the US Constitution was the product of a 'historical moment', and that the *Federalist Papers* have been widely treated as a historically authoritative commentary on its most important structural features. Britain's less formal (although far from completely 'unwritten') constitution, by contrast, developed much more organically and pragmatically. No wonder, then, that Margaret Thatcher's ideologically driven programme of constitutional reform came as such a shock, and generated considerable suspicion and opposition amongst British public law scholars (as in many other quarters). However, constitutional form and history cannot be the whole story because Australian administrative law scholarship also exhibits a lack of interest in grand theorizing.

Another possibility is that American legal scholars as a group are more 'fashion conscious' and more inclined to 'herd behaviour' than Commonwealth scholars. In a profession as large as the US legal academy, the adoption of ideologically charged and intellectually polarized positions may be perceived as the best way of making a mark. The sheer size and complexity of the US legal system and the huge volume of written law may encourage a resort to abstract theory as a way of cutting through the dense thicket of institutional activity and of being heard above the background noise of the legal system. The fact that law is a postgraduate course in the United States is no doubt significant. This surely encourages legal scholars (and students) to think about law in a broader interdisciplinary frame. The role of US philosophers such as John Rawls, Robert Nozick, and Ronald Dworkin in the revival of normative theory in the second half of the twentieth century has, one might speculate, created an intellectual atmosphere in which theorizing about law comes much more naturally. Whatever the reasons, élite administrative law scholarship is much more theory-driven in the United States than in the Commonwealth.

It is not surprising, therefore, that empirical studies of the operation of decision-making institutions and the impact of administrative law have a relatively high profile in administrative law scholarship in the United Kingdom (Richardson and Sunkin, 1996). The British version of legal realism (the 'law in context' movement) generated more interest in the social context and day-to-day operation of legal doctrine ('the law in action') than in its theoretical underpinnings. In the 1980s the establishment by Joseph Raz of a new Oxford postgraduate course—Philosophical Foundations of the Common Law—sparked a renaissance of interest in doctrinally grounded legal theory; but it focused on tort, contract, and criminal law and largely ignored public law. Empirical public law research has generated three main bodies of scholarship. One is concerned with the 'epidemiology' of judicial review. Before this research was done, scholars had little idea about the relative frequency with which various areas of government activity were subject to challenge by way of judicial review. Perhaps the most important conclusion supported by the statistics was that judicial review is a last resort, and that the areas in which it is most frequently used are those in which alternative avenues of redress (internal reviews and tribunal appeals, for instance) are least available or satisfactory. Researchers are now setting their sights on much more difficult questions, such as the incidence and dynamics of out-of-court settlement of judicial review applications.

A second area of empirical research concerns the impact of judicial review on bureaucratic behaviour. In terms of theory and methodology, this type of research is complex, and the conclusions drawn may be tentative, or difficult to generalize, or both. Typically, the motivating intuition (if not hypothesis) is that judicial review has little direct influence on decision-making procedures and processes, and that other legal and non-legal factors possess much more explanatory power. And so the research, on the whole, suggests. More or less unconsidered is whether and why this matters. Debate on the instrumentalist assumptions underlying such research is noticeable by its absence. The values-based and social-scientific strands of public law scholarship run in parallel streams.

A third significant body of empirical work has investigated regulatory enforcement and, to a lesser extent, standard-setting. For legitimacy-minded administrative lawyers (as opposed to instrumentally minded regulation lawyers), the chief interest of this research lies in its concern with rule-making procedures, and with the relationship between discretion and rules. In this context, it is also worth observing that US administrative lawyers seem to have accepted Kenneth Culp Davis's case in favour of rule-making over 'discretion' (Davis, 1971) more uncritically than have their colleagues on the other side of the Atlantic (Baldwin and Hawkins, 1984). This may reflect the greater level of distrust of government in the United States compared with the United Kingdom.

What I have described as the 'dominant style' of administrative law scholarship is partly motivated by a desire to make sense of a body of legal doctrine in terms of the assumption that law can play an important part in legitimizing the exercise of political power. The mainstream methodological reaction to the anti-formalist, realist argument that legal rules are 'indeterminate' was to develop a set of procedural and institutional values (or normative principles) analogous to canons of statutory or constitutional interpretation. As the neo-realist, CLS critique made clear, however, this move does not overcome the problem. The explanatory power of values is a function of their abstractness relative to the rules they supposedly support. As a result, they are less likely than those rules to yield determinate solutions to concrete disputes. More than that, they are likely to conflict with one another. For instance, the principle of citizen access to the courts may conflict with the value of judicial fidelity to legislation in the face of a statutory preclusion of judicial review; and the value of protection of the individual may conflict with the value of promoting the 'public interest'. The problem is even worse with 'theories' such as pluralism and republicanism. Such theories may be understood as sets of values worked into a system in order to show how the values relate to one another and how conflicts between them ought to be resolved. Such theories are inevitably even more abstract than the values they systematize. As a result, people who profess to hold the same theory may disagree about the details of the theory—that is, about how the values they hold relate to one another, and about how conflicts between them ought to be resolved.

Empirical investigation of the operation of legal rules may be interpreted as an attempt to overcome this problem. By shifting the focus from values to outcomes, the hope would be that the 'art' of law-making could be transformed into a 'science' based on a sophisticated understanding of social processes and human psychology. The problem here, of course, is that no amount of knowledge about how the world works can settle, or resolve disagreements about, goals, purposes and desirable outcomes. Another common move in the face of perceived indeterminacy in legal rules is to argue that instead of focusing on 'general principles of administrative law' applicable across the whole range of bureaucratic activity, administrative lawyers should pursue their interest in legitimacy in the context of particular government activities—social security, housing, education, financial regulation, and so on. It is only by understanding the substantive 'policy objectives' of these various areas of law (so the argument goes) that we can understand how general ideas about accountability and legitimacy will apply in individual cases. However, it is by no means clear that this 'sectoral' or 'functionalist' strategy helps much either. Rules, no matter how detailed, are, by their very nature, abstractions from the particular, inherently prone to under- and over-inclusiveness and, hence, to uncertainty of application, at least at the margins.

The point is that interpreting and applying rules, as much as making rules, involves the exercise of power. The administrative lawyer's concern with the legitimacy of the making, interpretation, and application of rules by bureaucrats seems often to blind them to the problem of legitimizing the very same activities when undertaken by the judiciary. For instance, the 'counter-majoritarian difficulty' gets a lot more attention in the constitutional law literature than from administrative law scholars. Witness, too, the focus in the public choice literature on the legislature and the executive at the expense of the judiciary. In the United Kingdom in recent years, there has been a vigorous debate about whether, in controlling the executive, the courts do the bidding of the legislature or march to their own tune (Forsyth, 2000). Either way, the gap remains between rules, principles, values, and theories on the one hand, and the particularities of situations, relationships, and disputes on the other. By constraining and supervising decision-makers, law and legal institutions can help to allay our worst qualms about government and combat the worst pathologies of power. But there is no complete cure for indeterminacy. Agency costs can be minimized but not eliminated. In the face of endemic disagreement about values there can, in the end, be no legitimacy without trust. To the production of trust, law has little to contribute.

3 Government Liability and the Public/Private Divide

Fundamental to the construction of administrative law as a separate category of legal thought in common law systems has been the public/private distinction—or, more accurately, set of distinctions. In Commonwealth scholarship, at least, A.V. Dicey's aversion to written constitutions, bills of rights, and administrative tribunals separate from the 'ordinary courts' is widely credited with having delayed the development of a 'proper system' of administrative law (and hence, of scholarly interest in the subject) for the best part of a century. There is a deep irony in this story. On the one hand, Dicey has been repeatedly and harshly criticized for failing to observe the variety of adjudicative bodies that existed in his day; and his work certainly did not stunt the growth of the British 'administrative state' or of administrative adjudication in the first half of the twentieth century. On the other hand, in the past forty years a major growth area in administrative law, and arguably the chief preoccupation of administrative law scholarship in the Commonwealth as much as in the United States, has been judicial review. Another paradox in attitudes to Dicey's work and in the assessment of his influence lies in the fact that although, from one perspective, he can be criticized for distorting or ignoring the truth in the service of his political agenda, from another perspective his account of the British constitution can be seen as postmodern in its appreciation of the interaction of fact and value in law, politics, and life.

In my view, Dicey understood the British constitution better than his critics typically allow. The causes of the late flowering of public law in common law systems, and its early institutionalization in France, lie deep in the political and constitutional soil (Allison, 1994). Ironically, too, no sooner had administrative law won its academic spurs than the public/private distinction came under attack from feminists and others who saw it as a cloak for hiding the role of politics and government in certain areas of life; and from critical legal scholars, who offered it as a glaring example of the indeterminacy of legal categories. More importantly, perhaps, many legal scholars interpreted the neo-liberal process of 'hollowing-out the state' that took place in the 1980s and 1990s as disintegration of the public/private divide rather than relocation of the boundaries between the two sectors; as more like the scrambling of an egg than the weaving of a two-stranded rope. The apotheosis of this approach is found in the neo-Diceyan argument that there is no public law–private law divide because all decision-making is subject to a common set of normative demands or 'values' (Oliver, 1999). In extreme versions, such views are both descriptively inaccurate and normatively undesirable. Buzzwords such as 'privatization' and 'partnership' attest to the former point; and even the most uncompromising liberal individualists acknowledge the need for a 'night-watchman state'. Amongst legitimacy-minded administrative lawyers, the strongest critics of the public/private distinction are people who, like Dicey, see it as a formula for bureaucratic privilege and immunity from laws that govern the lives of citizens (Harlow, 1980). What this position fails to acknowledge is the potential of law to impose on governments and their delegates duties and obligations that recognize the state's monopoly of legitimate force.

It is in the context of the tort liability of public authorities that Dicey's views have had their greatest resonance and impact. Government immunity from tort liability (including vicarious liability) was abolished by statute in the United Kingdom in 1946 (and much earlier in Australia). This reform effectively shielded government officials from being personally sued for damages. The equivalent US provisions (the Federal Tort Claims Act in particular) are somewhat narrower in scope, and as a result have generated a large body of case law dealing with the personal liability of public officials for harm inflicted in the course of performing their official functions. Whereas the development of judicial review (and of other accountability mechanisms offering non-monetary remedies) has involved extending legal protection to interests not recognized by private law, and imposing obligations and responsibilities different from those developed by private law, the effect of these statutes was to discourage a similar departure from the private law model in respect of monetary remedies. As a result, much scholarly debate (especially in the Commonwealth) about the role of damages as a remedy for breaches of public law has been conducted indirectly in terms of whether principles of tort liability (predominantly liability for negligence) should be modified in their application to 'public' defendants.

The orientation of US administrative law scholarship to issues of regulation has had an impact in this area, too. Whereas Commonwealth scholars typically view tort liability in terms of compensation, US scholars (both tort lawyers and administrative lawyers) are much more likely to view it instrumentally in terms of behaviour modification (e.g. Schuck, 1983). From this perspective, the central questions relate to the relative strengths and weaknesses of courts and regulatory agencies as standard-setters, and the balance between public and private monitoring and enforcement of regulatory standards (e.g. Rose-Ackerman, 1992, ch. 8). Although the hollowing-out of the state raises important issues in this context which scholars (especially those adopting a tort-oriented perspective) have yet seriously to consider, the continued vitality and utility of the public/private distinction is not one of them.

The context in which the idea of a truly public law of damages has received most discussion is liability for breaches of constitutional provisions, especially bills of rights. In the European context, scholarly interest in this topic focuses on the provision for 'just satisfaction' contained in the European Convention on Human Rights and now, in Britain, under the Human Rights Act 1998. The rapid development of damages as a remedy for breaches of European law by Member States of the EU has also attracted a great deal of scholarly attention. In the United Kingdom at least, the days of the private model of public tort law seem numbered.

4 THE FUTURE

In US scholarship, the next big intellectual waves are already on the rise. One is behavioural law and economics (see e.g. the Symposium, 'Getting Beyond Cynicism: New Theories of the Regulatory State' in *Cornell Law Review*, 87), and another is its sibling, social norms theory. Whether either of these academic fashions will have greater impact on mainstream administrative law scholarship than their law-and-economics parent remains to be seen. In the United Kingdom, administrative law scholars are likely to be preoccupied for the foreseeable future with working out the implications of the judicialization of the constitution that has accompanied membership of the EU, devolution, and the Human Rights Act in particular. The Australian scene is set to be dominated by the issue of constitutionalization of judicial review. In recent years, the Federal government has been engaged in a long-term project to reduce access to courts, especially for immigrants. However, the High Court of Australia, unlike the US Supreme Court, possesses entrenched original judicial review jurisdiction. The Court has just begun to explore the scope and characteristics of this jurisdiction; and given the importance of the issues at stake, scholars are likely to be absorbed by them for some years to come.

REFERENCES

Allison, J. W. F. (1994). *A Continental Distinction in the Common Law: A Comparative and Historical Perspective on English Public Law*, Oxford: Clarendon Press.
Baldwin, R., and Hawkins, K. (1984). 'Discretionary Justice: Davis Reconsidered', *Public Law*: 570–99.

Bishop, W. (1990). 'A Theory of Administrative Law', *Journal of Legal Studies*, 19: 489–530.

Black, J. (2000). 'Proceduralizing Regulation: Part I', *Oxford Journal of Legal Studies*, 20: 597–614.

—— (2001). 'Proceduralizing Regulation: Part II', *Oxford Journal of Legal Studies*, 21: 33–58.

Craig, P. P. (1990). *Public Law and Democracy in the United Kingdom and the United States of America*, Oxford: Clarendon Press.

Cross, F. B. (1999*a*). 'Shattering the Fragile Case for Judicial Review of Rulemaking' *Virginia Law Review*, 85: 1243–334.

—— (1999*b*). 'The Judiciary and Public Choice', *Hastings Law Journal*, 50: 355–82.

Davies, A. C. L. (2001). *Accountability: A Public Law Analysis of Government by Contract*, Oxford: Oxford University Press.

Davis, K. C. (1971). *Discretionary Justice: A Preliminary Inquiry*, Urbana, Ill.: University of Illinois Press.

Eskridge, W. N., Jr., and Peller, G. (1991). 'The New Public Law Movement: Moderation as a Postmodern Cultural Form', *Michigan Law Review*, 89: 707–91.

Forsyth, C. (ed.) (2000). *Judicial Review and the Constitution*, Oxford: Hart.

Freedman, J. O. (1978). *Crisis and Legitimacy*, Cambridge: Cambridge University Press.

Freeman, J. (2000). 'The Private Role in Public Governance', *New York University Law Review*, 75: 543–675.

Frug, G. E. (1984). 'The Ideology of Bureaucracy in American Law', *Harvard Law Review*, 97: 1276–388.

Galligan, D. J. (1996). *Due Process and Fair Procedures: A Study of Administrative Procedures*, Oxford: Clarendon Press.

Harlow, C. (1980). '"Public" and "Private" Law: Difference without Distinction', *Modern Law Review*, 43: 241–65.

——and Rawlings, R. (1984/1997). *Law and Administration*, London: Weidenfield and Nicolson (1st edn. (1984), 2nd edn. (1997)), London: Butterworths.

Mashaw, J. L. (1983). *Bureaucratic Justice: Managing Social Security Disability Claims*, New Haven: Yale University Press.

——, Merrill, R. A., and Shane, P. M. (1992). *Administrative Law: The American Public Law System*, St Paul, Minn.: West Publishing Co.

Oliver, D. (1999). *Common Values and the Public/Private Divide*, London: Butterworths.

Prosser, T. (1982). 'Towards a Critical Public Law', *Journal of Law and Society*, 9: 1–19.

Reich, C. A. (1964). 'The New Property', *Yale Law Journal*, 73: 733–87.

Richardson, G., and Sunkin, M. (1996). 'Judicial Review: Questions of Impact', *Public Law*: 79–103.

Rose-Ackerman, S. (1992). *Rethinking the Progressive Agenda: The Reform of the American Regulatory State*, New York: The Free Press.

Schuck, P. H. (1983). *Suing Government: Citizen Remedies for Official Wrongs*, New Haven: Yale University Press.

Scott, C. (2000). 'Accountability in the Regulatory State', *Journal of Law and Society*, 27: 38–60.

Stewart, R. B. (1975). 'The Reformation of American Administrative Law', *Harvard Law Review*, 88: 1669–813.

Sunstein, C. R. (1990). *After the Rights Revolution: Reconceiving the Regulatory State*, Cambridge, Mass.: Harvard University Press.

—— (1991). 'Administrative Substance', *Duke Law Journal*: 607–46.

Taggart, M. (ed.) (1997). *The Province of Administrative Law*, Oxford: Hart.

CHAPTER 9

JUDICIAL REVIEW
OF LEGISLATION

MARK TUSHNET

1 INTRODUCTION

THE global expansion of judicial power (Tate and Vallinder, 1995) has transformed long-standing debates about judicial review of legislation. Until the late 1970s those debates concerned the fundamental question of whether judicial review of legislation could be reconciled with democratic self-governance. Proponents of parliamentary sovereignty argued that review of legislation by judges not immediately responsible to the people, even review for conformity of legislation with fundamental norms endorsed at some point by a majority of the people in a constitution or similar foundational document, was inconsistent with majority rule. Advocates of judicial review contended, in contrast, that the people having once committed themselves to restricting their own power to act through legislation, judicial review was compatible with, and perhaps even compelled by, democratic premises.

Democratic transitions throughout the world in the 1980s and 1990s produced a consensus, shared in established democracies, in favor of some form of judicial review of legislation. A residue of skepticism about the ability of judicial review as a mechanism for protecting liberal democratic rights remains (Campbell *et al.*, 2001; Waldron, 1999), but the contemporary debates are over the form that judicial review should take. The longest established system of judicial review, that of the United States, involves what can be called *strong-form* judicial review. A constitutional court's decision that legislation is unconstitutional prevails unless the Constitution is amended. Beginning with the Canadian Charter of Rights (1982), constitutions came to include variations on *weak-form* judicial review. These variations range from the Canadian Charter's 'notwithstanding' clause to the practice authorized by the British Human Rights Act (1998) of a judicial declaration that a statute is incompatible with fundamental legal norms to even weaker forms of judicial review. Contemporary debates deal with the characteristics of strong-form and weak-form judicial review, their respective advantages and disadvantages, and whether in the end they will in fact operate differently.

Although pure parliamentary supremacy has few defenders today (but see Waldron, 1999), the precise contours of the constraints on legislative power are to some degree controversial. That courts should limit legislative power in the service of individual rights is uncontroversial; that they should enforce constitutional guarantees of social welfare rights is not. One can expect increased scholarly attention to the enforceability of social welfare rights because contemporary constitutions often combine guarantees of such rights with some form of judicial review.

2 JUDICIAL REVIEW AND PARLIAMENTARY SUPREMACY

Judicial review of legislation came into being with the adoption of the US Constitution (1789). Building upon well-established practices, the US Supreme Court took upon itself the duty to determine whether a statute was compatible with the Constitution. The Supreme Court argued that judicial review for constitutionality was implicit in a popularly adopted written constitution that specified limits on legislative power. According to the Court, the people in adopting the constitution must have meant that legislatures, acting as representatives of the people who elected them, should respect constitutional limits, and, by enacting the constitution as law, the people must have relegated enforcement of those limits to the courts, who would apply the constitution as supreme law just as they would apply statutory law as subordinate law.

Only in the United States was judicial review of legislation an important practice through the nineteenth and early twentieth centuries. Few other nations had written constitutions, and France, which did, drew upon a historical experience in which judges were so closely aligned with the discredited royalty that its constitution writers considered judicial review deeply inconsistent with majority rule. By the twentieth century, the US experience confirmed the judgment among social democrats in particular that judicial review was a conservative institution hostile to democratic initiatives. French scholars decried *gouvernement des juges*. Facing unfavorable decisions in common law cases, the British Labour Party became deeply suspicious of judges as well.

The difficulty, as these critics saw it, was that judicial review was a form of political decision-making parading as law. To them, courts invoked fundamental (and conservative) principles to override legislation supported by contemporary majorities. Austrian legal theorist Hans Kelsen agreed that judicial review of legislation was a political activity, but argued that constitutional systems could devise a form of judicial review that explicitly acknowledged the practice's political aspects while still taking advantage of judicial expertise in interpreting fundamental law. Constitutional courts in the United States were also courts of general jurisdiction, dealing with ordinary questions of statutory interpretation and, when Kelsen wrote, with applying and developing the common law. Treating judges of such courts as primarily legal specialists might have made sense, but, Kelsen argued, responsibility for judicial review required decision-makers selected as much with an eye to their capacity for political decision-making as to their legal ability. Kelsen urged that specialized constitutional courts be created, to which people with particular sensitivity to the political aspects of judicial review could be appointed.

For about fifty years, the central question in designing institutions of judicial review was the choice between the generalist court with constitutional review power, on the US model, and the specialized constitutional court. With minor variations, common-law systems that adopted judicial review followed the US model and civil law systems adopted the Austrian model propounded by Kelsen and briefly adopted in Austria in the late 1920s. The German Constitutional Court, on the Austrian model, is perhaps the most successful post-1945 constitutional court. The French *Conseil Constitutionnel* was conceptualized as almost another stage in the ordinary political process, and its political aspects are symbolized by a provision authorizing former Presidents of France, by reason of their station, to sit on the *Conseil Constitutionnel*, although in fact none do.

Another difference among constitutional courts emerged as new ones were created. The US model came to be known as one involving *concrete* review, because the Supreme Court justified judicial review as incidental to the application of law in actual cases. The competing model allowed *abstract* review. The forms of abstract review vary. Sometimes a government may request the constitutional court to interpret the constitution. The French *Conseil Constitutionnel* was designed initially to resolve conflicts between the president and parliament over their respective powers, and it was authorized to determine, before a statute became effective, whether legislation would infringe on presidential prerogatives. Other systems allow substantial legislative minorities (typically, 30% of one house) to challenge legislation that they failed to block in the legislature, again prior to its application in any particular case. In their purest form, systems of abstract review deny courts the power to consider constitutional objections when pressed in actual cases.

The differences between specialized and generalist constitutional courts, and abstract and concrete review, are no longer matters of central scholarly concern. As judicial review spread, experience showed that structural features, including the appointment process, are less important than was initially thought. For example, although US courts remain nominally committed to concrete review, in practice, judicial review in the United States approaches abstract review, as a result of court-devised modifications of rules on what amounts to an injury allowing a person to bring a lawsuit, and on the timing of when such lawsuits can be brought. As in abstract review systems, then, in the United States the vast majority of newly enacted statutes can be challenged in courts shortly after their enactment. Similarly, systems initially committed to pure versions of abstract review have gradually adopted rules allowing citizens to lodge constitutional complaints, sometimes in the ordinary courts, which then refer the complaints to the constitutional court, and sometimes in the constitutional court directly. Differences among the systems remain, but the differences are narrower than they were when the systems were first put in place.

2.1 Reconciling Judicial Review and Majority Rule: Procedural and Substantive Accounts

There is now consensus on the proposition that legislatures should be constrained by fundamental principles, ordinarily principles written in some authoritative document. Supporters of parliamentary supremacy remain concerned that enforcing such constraints through judicial review is in tension with democratic self-rule.

Alexander Bickel coined the term *counter-majoritarian difficulty* for this concern (Bickel, 1962). As Bruce Ackerman pointed out, the term was somewhat misleading, and proposed the alternative term *intertemporal difficulty* to describe the concern more accurately (Ackerman, 1991). Putting aside questions of interpretation, Ackerman pointed out that courts exercising the power of judicial review purported to be applying the will of a majority at one time—that is, the majority that created the limitations on legislative power—against the will of a later majority, the one supporting the enacted legislation. The question therefore was to explain why the views of the earlier majority should prevail over those of the later one.

Generalizing from the US experience, Ackerman offered the following solution (Ackerman, 1998). People properly devote most of their attention in the ordinary course to their routine and daily concerns. Ordinarily, then, they act in politics to advance those concerns. The legislation that results will be focused on advancing particular interests. Sometimes, though, periods of crisis displace ordinary politics. During these constitutional moments, as Ackerman calls them, the people focus attention on fundamental questions of principle and institutional design, taking a longer-range view of what they ought to do. Constitutions are made or amended during these moments. Ackerman argues that the longer-range focus and more deliberative discussion during constitutional moments gives the solutions chosen then greater normative force than attaches to the legislation adopted during periods of ordinary politics. Political deliberation during constitutional moments is simply better than that which occurs during the more extended periods of ordinary politics.

Ackerman's solution to the intertemporal difficulty is ingenious, and captures important aspects of the project of constitutionalism and judicial review. Critics have identified two main problems with it. First, Ackerman concedes that courts must enforce constitutional amendments adopted even when there is no constitutional moment. This positivism sits uneasily with his explanation for the normative priority of constitutions over ordinary legislation. Secondly, Ackerman offers a formal set of characteristics to help courts identify when constitutional moments have occurred. Those characteristics inevitably map inaccurately onto the underlying reality of deep deliberation and ordinary politics. In the United States, for example, Ackerman's analysis does not deal well with the retreat after 1876 from efforts to transform race relations in the South nor with the transformation of race relations that accompanied the civil rights movement of the 1960s.

Ackerman's is one of a class of procedural efforts to reconcile judicial review with parliamentary supremacy. The most prominent alternatives are substantive, in which courts justifiably displace legislation that is inconsistent with the premises of democracy itself. John Hart Ely (Ely, 1980) offers an account that appears primarily procedural but that actually rests on important substantive assumptions about what democracy means. Ely argues that courts should set aside legislation that is inconsistent with democracy understood as the unobstructed operation of majority rule. Laws disfranchising people without strong justification are one example; laws impairing the ability of people to communicate their views on matters of public policy are another. Ely also develops a theory of discriminatory legislation that courts can invalidate on the ground that the statutes being challenged result from prejudice, which Ely carefully defines as the imputation to a disadvantaged group of characteristics, such as criminality, at a higher rate than actually exists.

Ely's account makes sense of important aspects of the practice of judicial review in the United States and elsewhere, but it has been criticized as overly procedural, ignoring the possibility that democracy may require more than the procedures on which Ely focuses. Ely's definition of discrimination does not capture fundamental moral concerns about impermissible discrimination, for example. He appears to assume, without defense, that democracy, properly understood, would prevail once the obstacles he identifies are removed, and does not consider the possibility that some guarantees of basic social welfare rights are essential predicates for participation in governance.

More purely substantive theories are associated with Ronald Dworkin (Dworkin, 1977) and the German Constitutional Court. Dworkin argues that democracy rests on a commitment to treating people equally, and that courts can invalidate legislation inconsistent with that commitment. Dworkin offers a relatively comprehensive theory of equality, with quite strong implications about legislation across a wide range of policy matters, from abortion to distributive justice. The German Constitutional

Court takes the position that Germany's Basic Law embodies an objective order of values, which the courts enforce.

The difficulties with substantive theories that seek to reconcile judicial review with parliamentary supremacy arise from what John Rawls describes as the ineradicable persistence of reasonable disagreement over what justice entails. In the context of constitutional law, the very fact of judicial review brings reasonable disagreement to the fore. A legislature enacts a statute that, in the legislature's often-reasonable view, is consistent with the constitution as the legislature interprets it. A constitutional court invalidating the legislation may rest on another, also reasonable interpretation of the constitution. But, as long as the legislature's view is reasonable, why should the court's different view prevail? Dworkin has a specific account of equality, but others have alternative accounts that are, if not correct in some transcendent sense, suffi-ciently reasonable for their adherents to be concerned that imposing Dworkin's, or any other, account on them would be incompatible with Dworkin's own ideas about the equal worth of every person. This concern can be brought to ground in the context of judicial review by asking, What reason do we have to think that courts will systematically be better at identifying the requirements of substantive justice, equality, and the like than legislatures will?

By introducing concern about the comparative capacities of alternative institu-tions, we return to procedural accounts. Jürgen Habermas (Habermas, 1996) in the German context and Frank Michelman in the US context (Michelman, 1999) have defended some forms of judicial review on the ground that, in the presence of persistent disagreement on substantive issues of justice and the like, democratic self-rule requires that institutions be open to what Michelman calls the 'full blast' of competing views, and that courts are better structured than legislatures to receive and deliberate about such views. Michelman illustrates the argument by devoting attention to what he calls the law of law-making, that is, the rules according to which public policy is made, such as the rules governing financing of political campaigns. People disagree not only over the details of such rules, but over whether one or another set of rules is consistent with the very premises of democratic self-governance: Some think that strict regulation of campaign finance interferes with free expression, while others think that strict regulation promotes political equality. Any substantive resolution, whether by the legislature or the courts, will devalue the position reasonably taken by some about what democracy requires. Michelman argues that people who disagree over the results none the less have reason to accept results issuing from institutions that deliberate seriously about all the available substantive positions, and that courts that understand their task in the right way can be such institutions. Michelman acknowledges, however, that whether courts actually operate in the way he thinks will reconcile judicial review with parliamentary supremacy is inevitably an empirical question.

Whatever its basis, judicial review of legislation seems now well established. It exists even in nations without written constitutions expressly or implicitly authorizing

courts to exercise that power. Australia's High Court developed a constitutional freedom of political communication, relying on the Ely-like argument that such a right was
necessary to protect the institutions of representative government. Although the Court
has adhered to this doctrine, and some judges have indicated in dicta their willingness
to expand it, the scope of constitutional protection of free expression has remained significantly narrower than similar protections in the United States. With few exceptions,
courts have come to treat international human rights norms as applicable to domestic
legislation, and evaluate legislation for its consistency with those norms.

2.2 Problems of Interpretation

Ackerman's solution to the intertemporal difficulty works only if courts in fact are
enforcing the views of the earlier majority, enacted during constitutional moments,
against the views of contemporary majorities. Bickel was concerned with a different
problem, the capacity of courts to engage in whatever interpretive task was appropriate for a constitutional court. Bickel catalogued a number of proposals, including
substantive (moral) approaches, before settling on a quasi-procedural view that
courts should interpret constitutions with what he called 'the ways of the scholar'. As
Bickel's thought evolved, Bickel concluded that these ways involved the exercise of
prudence and practical judgment about government.

   One version of the problem with which Bickel was concerned is that of constraint
on adjudication. He and others sought methods of constitutional interpretation that
would limit the ability of judges to enact their personal preferences in the guise of
interpreting the Constitution. Constitutional scholarship in the United States was
dominated in the 1980s by efforts to identify a method of constitutional interpretation that would impose the required constraints. These efforts were provoked by conservative reaction to the liberal decisions of the Warren Court. Conservatives
believed that the Warren Court had improperly imposed its members' liberal views
on society because the justices interpreted the Constitution to advance the justices'
controversial judgments about what justice and equality required. Conservatives
argued that judicial review could be justified only if courts interpreted the
Constitution in light of its original meaning. This position was related to debates in
general legal theory that had less overt political content. Some contend, for example,
that all interpretation must rest on original meaning. Any other practice, whatever its
merits, cannot fairly be described as interpretation. For US conservatives since the
1980s, interpretations that did not rest on original meaning were illegitimate.

   Original-meaning jurisprudence came in several variants. Some were highly
focused on text, others on what the Constitution's drafters meant, and still others on
what the terms used in the Constitution meant to an informed public at the time the
Constitution was adopted. Critics suggested several reasons for rejecting original-
meaning jurisprudence in all its variants. They argued that proponents of that
jurisprudence erroneously claimed that inquiries into original meaning would
resolve many important controversies; the critics found more ambiguity in the

history than original-meaning proponents did (Rakove, 1996). One could take the position that where the original meaning could not reliably be determined, courts should not invalidate legislation. US conservatives were in general unwilling to do so, and conservative judges based some decisions invalidating statutes on highly contested versions of the original understanding. Critics also argued that original-meaning jurisprudence was inconsistent with the meaning given the Constitution by its authors (Powell, 1985). Finally, critics pointed out that original-meaning jurisprudence was inconsistent with long-standing practice, including *stare decisis* in constitutional cases, and might require the repudiation of precedents like *Brown v Board of Education* (1954) (invalidating racial segregation) that were not only well-settled but were also universally regarded as correctly decided.

Original understanding approaches to constitutional interpretation also confront difficulties when novel problems, which were not and indeed could not have been anticipated by a constitution's framers, arise. Again, one could say that legislative power to deal with such problems is simply unrestricted, and again original-understanding theorists are usually unwilling to do so. Alternatively, one could invoke the more abstract principles that justify the particular restrictions the framers imposed on government, and then apply those principles to the new problems. One prominent formulation is that contemporary interpreters must 'translate' the framers' understandings into contemporary terms (Lessig, 1995). This, however, threatens to eliminate original understanding as a constraint on judges.

The debate over original-meaning jurisprudence may have resulted from the peculiar circumstances of US judicial review, where the courts must interpret constitutional provisions adopted many years earlier. Constitutional courts dealing with more recently adopted constitutions are more likely to find it natural to interpret their constitutions with reference to original meaning, which will be for those courts a matter of almost personal memory, but will also find it natural to believe that original meaning coincides with contemporary views of justice and equality. The debate in the United States generated valuable scholarship on legal interpretation and its relation to other practices of interpretation (Levinson and Mailloux, 1988), but in the end the debate ended with no clear resolution. Probably the prevailing view in the United States is that the search for constraint through interpretive method is misguided. Courts do, and should, deploy a number of interpretive techniques, the importance of which will vary depending on the specific problem: text, precedent, history, notions of justice and equality past and present—all can play a role (Fallon, 1987).

2.3 Problems of Judicial Selection

The question of constraint does not disappear once interpretive technique is found inadequate. Perhaps it makes sense to allow judges to enforce a prior generation's views on the present generation, but allowing them to enforce their personal views of justice and equality against a popular majority's is more questionable. The inconclusive outcome of the US debates over interpretation in the 1980s appeared to rule out agreement that judges were actually implementing anyone's views other than their own. What, then, limited judges?

Bickel's answer was that judges should exercise practical wisdom. That only shifted the inquiry back one step. How should we go about ensuring that judges would do so? The answer seems to lie with developing appropriate methods of judicial selection. Here long-standing concerns about the judiciary's elitism recur (Griffith, 1997). Judges will be lawyers, and they will reflect the demographic and ideological composition of the bar, which is likely to be atypical of the societies in which the judges sit. Further, specialization in the law is no guarantee of practical wisdom. Indeed, some scholars argue that specialization in law gives a particularly conservative cast to decision-making by constitutional courts whose judges think of themselves primarily as lawyers rather than as participants in a complex policy-making process.

Demographic changes in the bar may undermine some criticisms of an unrepresentative judiciary. The legal profession worldwide appears to be becoming more diverse demographically, and that diversity is likely to be reflected on constitutional courts. Ensuring that judges have practical wisdom is more difficult. Here the Austrian model of a specialized constitutional court conceptualized as containing an important political element may be preferable to models that treat constitutional courts as institutions that deal with law alone, albeit supreme law. The Austrian and related models make fairly natural the selection of constitutional court judges with an eye, not simply to their ideological views but also to their experience in politics. Where courts interpret constitutions and do ordinary law-work as well, concern may be raised that looking for political experience in judges may impair the courts' ability to perform their other tasks, a concern sometimes mistakenly expressed as one about 'politicizing' the judiciary.

As constitutional courts come to play increasingly large roles in their societies, we can expect continued scholarly attention to the connection, if any, between the characteristics of judges and the processes by which they are chosen, on the one hand, and the ideological tilt of the judges' decisions.

2.4 Conditions for the Emergence and Maintenance of Judicial Review

The consensus on including judicial review in the constitutions created in the last quarter of the twentieth century obscured issues concerning the political conditions under which judicial review is created and maintained. These issues have been of more concern to political scientists than to legal academics, but the fact that legal academics acknowledge the political dimensions of judicial review makes the issues important to them as well.

In general, political scientists attribute the creation and maintenance of judicial review to the interests of political elites. For example, elites currently controlling legislative and executive power may foresee that they will soon be displaced from those positions, with no expectation that they will return to power in the near future; they may create or expand judicial review to ensure that some component of the political system will continue to respond to their concerns (Hirschl, 2000). In contrast, states where one party is clearly dominant and likely to remain so are unlikely to have vigorous judicial review.

Political elites can take advantage of judicial review once it is established, which gives them reason to maintain it even when sometimes the courts rule against their transient interests. In particular, elites can use judicial review to resolve policy questions that would fracture the governing coalition (Graber, 1993). By passing off contentious issues like abortion to the courts, a political coalition can satisfy one of its elements while not taking responsibility for an outcome opposed by another element. A similar analysis might be available to account for decisions by the Hungarian and South African Constitutional Courts, handed down shortly after their nations' constitutions were adopted, holding the death penalty unconstitutional; and for Australia's acceptance of a decision by an international human rights body that state legislation violated the rights of gay men.

This analysis suggests that judicial review will be maintained in societies where political elites are divided between two or more parties, each of which can see some advantage in having the courts available on occasion. As positive political theory suggests, it is precisely when political elites are farthest apart that courts have the largest role in determining public policy. So, to preserve their own political coalitions, political elites may end up creating an institution that significantly displaces the policy-making role of institutions directly controlled by those elites.

2.5 The Role of International Human Rights Law

Constitutional courts can find legislation unconstitutional because the legislation violates either some structural provisions or some individual rights provisions in the constitution. The Canadian Supreme Court, before the adoption of the Charter of Rights in 1982, and the Australian High Court, prior to its innovations in free expression law, generally confined themselves to reviewing national legislation with an eye to determining whether it intruded on domains reserved to subnational governments, and subnational legislation with an eye to determining whether it intruded on national domains. The French *Conseil Constitutionnel* was, as noted earlier, designed to adjudicate controversies between the president and parliament over their constitutional powers.

Constitutional change, sometimes in the form of amendment as in Canada and sometimes in the form of judicial interpretation as in the cases of Australia and

France, has led courts to expand their purview to include individual rights. In addition, the development of international human rights law has had an important effect on many constitutional courts. Taking their nations to be committed to complying with international law, these courts have held legislation unconstitutional because it violated international human rights norms. (The US Supreme Court stands almost alone in resisting the trend of taking such norms as relevant to interpreting the domestic constitution.) Scholars primarily interested in international human rights law have increasingly turned their attention to domestic constitutional law, and scholars of constitutional law in nations with relatively new systems of judicial review draw upon the scholarship of international human rights law to inform their work on domestic law.

3 STRONG-FORM AND WEAK-FORM JUDICIAL REVIEW

Concerns about the countermajoritarian difficulty were pressing when the only model of judicial review was strong-form judicial review. In such a model, rulings by constitutional courts are conclusive unless overturned by a later constitutional amendment. Until the 1980s, scholars generally assumed that judicial review, whether by a generalist court or by a specialist one, whether abstract or concrete, had to be of this form. Since then, however, various types of weak-form judicial review have been created, raising new questions about judicial review of legislation (Gardbaum, 2002). Scholars have contended that weak forms of judicial review provide a novel resolution of the countermajoritarian difficulty. One important question that constitutional scholarship will address in the next decade is whether the differences between strong-form and weak-form judicial review are indeed sufficient to dissolve or at least weaken the countermajoritarian difficulty.

3.1 Examples of Strong-Form and Weak-Form Review

The United States has a strong form of judicial review. The US Supreme Court's constitutional interpretations are final and definitive, in the sense that, constitutional amendment aside, legislatures have no formal mechanism of responding within the law to a Supreme Court decision finding a statute unconstitutional. Legislatures may pass resolutions disapproving the Court's decisions; they may attempt to enact new statutes that attempt to implement the policy of an invalidated statute within the confines the Court has specified; and Congress and the president may attempt to influence the Court's future actions by their decisions about whom to nominate and confirm to the Supreme Court. All these are indirect methods of responding to a decision of which the legislature disapproves. In a strong-form system, the legislature has no direct way to respond.

It is important to emphasize that this is so even though in many contexts the Supreme Court exercises *deferential* review, sometimes called rationality review or low-level scrutiny. Deferential review is a form of judicial review in which a constitutional court interprets the constitution to impose loose limits on legislative discretion. It is also important to distinguish between strong-form review and judicial exclusivity in constitutional interpretation. Judicial exclusivity comes into play in situations where the courts initially find that the constitution does not protect some activity from regulation, the legislature responds with a statute predicated on an interpretation of the constitution according to which the constitution *does* protect that activity, and the courts respond by denying the legislature the authority to act on constitutional interpretations different from the courts'.

Where review is deferential, no occasion for judicial exclusivity will likely arise, because the legislature can first enact a statute, then repeal it, all within the range of discretion the court finds in the constitution. Where review is less deferential, though, judicial exclusivity can matter a great deal. In 1991, the US Supreme Court held that the Constitution's protection of religious freedom did not require that governments provide exemptions from generally applicable laws for practices that were integral parts of religious exercise. Congress responded with the Religious Freedom Restoration Act, requiring governments to make such accommodations. The structure of the US Constitution meant that this statute was justified only if Congress had the power to determine that the constitutional guarantee of freedom of religion was broader than the Supreme Court had held. The Court then held the statute unconstitutional, denying that Congress had any role in constitutional interpretation.

Weak-form judicial review comes in several variants, but all have the characteristic of allowing a legislative and executive response, within the law, to a decision by the constitutional court interpreting the constitution. Section 33 of Canada's Charter of Rights provides that a legislature may declare that a statute take effect notwithstanding its inconsistency with certain Charter guarantees, with the proviso that the notwithstanding clause insulates a statute from invalidity for no longer than five years, a period during which, under Canadian law, there must be a parliamentary election. The notwithstanding clause was designed to allow a legislature to respond to judicial invalidation of its work by invoking the clause in re-enacting the statute. It was thought that this sort of interaction between court and legislature would promote a productive dialogue about the Charter's meaning, with both the Court and the legislature putting before the public their alternative reasonable interpretations of the Charter's guarantees, allowing the public then to decide which it preferred. In practice the notwithstanding clause has not operated in that manner. The Canadian Supreme Court held that a legislature could use the notwithstanding clause prospectively, prior to any judicial interpretation, thereby allowing the legislature to pre-empt any dialogic interaction. In addition, legislatures have been quite reluctant to invoke the clause (see Sect. 3.3).

The British Human Rights Act (1998) uses a different type of weak-form review. The Act directs courts to interpret primary (i.e. parliamentary) legislation in a manner compatible with the provisions of the European Convention on Human Rights. If a court is unable to do so, that is, if no fair reading of the statute is possible that makes it compatible with the Convention, the court is to uphold or enforce the statute but issue a declaration of incompatibility. Although experience with the Act is limited as yet, its proponents expect that ordinarily a minister will respond to a declaration of incompatibility by introducing legislation to amend the statute. (In urgent cases, the minister may make a remedial order amending the legislation directly; the order lapses unless approved by Parliament within 120 days.) The Act does not compel the government to respond at all to a declaration of incompatibility, but the possibility of review in the European Court of Human Rights, coupled with the declaration by a domestic court of incompatibility, is likely to place substantial pressure on the government to amend the legislation. (In some circumstances legislation may be insulated from a declaration of incompatibility by an express derogation from the Convention, which the Convention itself authorizes. In that event, the statute is not incompatible with the Convention because the Convention has been suspended *pro tanto* for the statute.)

The New Zealand Bill of Rights offers an even weaker form of judicial review, in imposing on the courts only the obligation to interpret statutes in ways that make them consistent with the Bill of Rights. Finally, for completeness it is worth mentioning the 'directive principles of public policy' contained in the Irish and Indian Constitutions. These provisions do not require anything from the courts, although they can be read to encourage the courts to interpret statutes and develop the common law in ways that promote principles that, in the main, deal with social and economic 'rights' (see Sect. 4).

3.2 Asserted Differences between Strong-Form and Weak-Form Review

Proponents of strong-form judicial review argue that it is the only way to ensure that constitutional limitations on government power do not degenerate into mere 'parchment barriers', as James Madison called bills of rights. Legislatures cannot be trusted to adhere to limitations on their own power, because, acting out of self-interest, legislatures will respond to the immediate political pressures on their members rather than take seriously the longer-term commitments expressed in constitutional limitations.

Madison and supporters of pure parliamentary systems believed that well-designed constitutions could use institutional arrangements other than strong-form judicial review to ensure that constitutional limitations would be honored. For Madison, separation of powers and federalism would give politicians political incentives to respect constitutional limitations. For later scholars working in the Madisonian tradition, sociological factors were more important. Robert Dahl, for example, emphasized ideological commitments to limited government by political elites and, perhaps more important, what he called cross-cutting pluralism, that is, the fact that each person was a member of many interest groups that might differ among themselves on particular issues of public policy (Dahl, 1956).

Proponents of strong-form judicial review rely on historical experience, which, they believe, shows that Madisonian and other devices to ensure that governments respect constitutional limitations are not reliable guarantees. Most scholars agree that some form of institutionally constrained parliamentarism (Ackerman, 2000) is desirable. The creation of weak-form judicial review changes the terms of discussion, however.

Proponents of weak-form judicial review point out that, more often than not, judicial invalidations of legislation arise not from legislative irresponsibility but rather from simple disagreement between courts and legislatures over what restrictions the constitution, reasonably read, actually places on legislatures. That is, legislatures do not typically simply disregard the limitations placed on them by constitutions, but rather act on their frequently reasonable interpretations of those limitations. Courts may be enforcing an equally reasonable interpretation when they invalidate the ensuing legislation, but proponents of weak-form judicial review argue that there is no reason to prefer courts' interpretation to a legislature's, in circumstances of reasonable disagreement.

Weak-form judicial review has the advantage of creating an institutional framework that allows reasoned deliberation over alternative interpretations of constitutional provisions. Strong-form review, it is said, leads to a debilitation of the legislative process, as legislators come to believe that only the courts have responsibility for considering whether a proposal is constitutional, or to believe that the courts will rescue the legislators from any improvident action by finding the statutes they enact unconstitutional. The fact that legislatures *might* disregard constitutional limitations makes some institutional check valuable, which is why weak-form judicial review is preferable to no judicial review at all. But, the fact that legislatures might hold reasonable views about the constitution suggests that the courts' alternative views need not be taken as final. Weak-form judicial review allows legislatures to consider the courts' views and respond without going through elaborate processes of constitutional amendment.

3.3 Experience with the Two Forms of Judicial Review

The US experience with strong-form judicial review is the longest and most informative. Critics point to various historical periods—for some, the time during the early twentieth century when the US Supreme Court invalidated significant amounts of legislation emerging out of the Progressive political movement, for others, the Warren Court era when the Court promoted a politically liberal agenda by invalidating state and national legislation—to demonstrate that strong-form judicial review has not consistently served to enforce widely agreed upon limitations on government power (Tushnet, 1999). Political scientists suggest that strong-form judicial review does not impede a determined political majority that secures political victories over a reasonably sustained period (Dahl, 1957), and that effective implementation of strong-form judicial review ultimately requires support from the legislature and executive anyway (Rosenberg, 1991). These observations take the sting out of the claim that strong-form judicial review is countermajoritarian, but they also weaken the claim that it is the only way to ensure that legislatures respect constitutional limitations.

Experience with weak-form judicial review is more limited, and scholars will provide more definite evaluations as experience accumulates. In Canada, scholars disagree over whether the notwithstanding clause has in fact given Canada a system with weak-form review. Critics of the Canadian Supreme Court argue that the Charter has given rise to a 'Court party', a set of interest groups and academics who encourage the Court to adopt Charter interpretations that promote a generally liberal political agenda (Morton and Knopff, 2000). The Court's defenders reply that the critics overlook the precise contours of Charter jurisprudence, which expressly seeks to accommodate disagreement between courts and legislatures through the Canadian Supreme Court's interpretation of the Charter clause allowing legislatures to limit rights when doing so is 'demonstrably justified in a free and democratic society'. Furthermore, defenders argue, critics fail to take account of the effects of the notwithstanding clause in tempering the Court's willingness to reach beyond the point where its decisions have substantial public support (Roach, 2001).

An important issue for scholarly consideration over the next decade will be whether the differences in practice between strong-form and weak-form judicial review are as large as might initially appear. One possibility, suggested by the literature on US and Canadian judicial review, is that strong-form judicial review is not quite as strong, nor weak-form review as weak, as each system's most vigorous proponents think.

4 JUDICIAL REVIEW AND SOCIAL WELFARE RIGHTS

There is a scholarly consensus on one important aspect of constrained parliamentarism: that there should be judicial review for violations of individual rights, including freedom of expression and religion, voting rights, and equality rights. There is of course a wide range of views about what precisely those rights are, and how they are defined in particular constitutional systems. For example, the US Constitution's protection of free speech as interpreted by the Supreme Court makes it quite difficult to enact legislation making 'hate speech' a criminal offense, while such regulation is widespread in other nations with constitutional guarantees of free expression, and indeed is mandated by some international human rights treaties. Despite this sort of disagreement about what particular constitutional guarantees actually protect, the need for judicial review in the area of individual rights is widely conceded.

The situation is quite different with respect to social welfare rights. The idea of constitutionalism took root during the Enlightenment, and in its initial versions held that the point of constitutions was to limit government power in the service of human well-being. Classical constitutionalism, that is, was also classically liberal. Socialist movements in the nineteenth century helped change the meaning of constitutionalism. Socialists argued that threats to human well-being arose not merely from government action, as liberals believed, but from aggregations of private power as well. They argued that constitutionalism sometimes required government action. Prodded by socialist movements, German chancellor Otto von Bismarck and the Roman Catholic Church initiated and supported governmental social welfare programs. The Irish Constitution of 1937 placed social welfare rights in a constitution, through the 'directive principles of public policy'. Nearly every constitution adopted after World War II included some protection of social welfare rights as well. The round of constitution-making in the 1980s and 1990s continued to incorporate social welfare rights in new constitutions; the people of nations emerging from Communist rule had expectations about government's proper role that could not be satisfied by purely liberal constitutions.

Analytically, questions of social welfare rights arise even under classically liberal constitutions, in the guise of the state action doctrine in the United States and Canada and of the issue of the horizontal effect of constitutional guarantees elsewhere. These doctrines deal with problems that occur when an individual or corporation exercises the rights it has under the legal system's background rights of property and contract to refuse to deal with another person or corporation at all, or to deal with them on terms that seem inconsistent with substantive constitutional norms. The doctrines of state action and horizontal effect define the circumstances under which the background rules of property and contract are themselves constitutionally problematic (Tushnet, 1988). The beneficiary of a judicial remedy for unconstitutional background rules obtains precisely what the beneficiary of social welfare rights does, an entitlement to resources.

Social welfare rights deal with the level and distribution within society of goods like food, housing, and education. Scholars steeped in the tradition of strong-form review imagine a lawsuit challenging a government's housing program on the ground that it violates a constitutional guarantee that each person shall have adequate housing. In arguing that a constitutional court could not order that housing be provided to the litigant, they draw on Lon Fuller's classic distinction between bipolar and polycentric problems (Fuller, 1978) to argue that a court could not sensibly address the merits of such a claim, which, for reasoned resolution, would require consideration of available techniques for building housing, budget priorities, the degree to which market provision of housing is inadequate, and much more. Problems so polycentric are beyond the capacity of courts, according to this view (Sunstein, 1996). At the most, courts could intervene when a government pursues a program of social provision that cannot be defended on any ground whatever; that is, courts can exercise only rationality review in cases involving social and economic rights.

The argument against judicial enforcement of social welfare rights loses some force once weaker forms of judicial review are possible. The court need not order that this particular litigant be placed in adequate housing that the government must provide. It might declare the government's program inadequate and invite a response, perhaps in the form of a plan developed by the government to address the inadequacies of social provision within some foreseeable period. The South African Constitutional Court's decision in *Grootboom* (2001) is likely to become a model for this sort of judicial review. There the Court found that the government's program for providing housing violated the constitutional guarantee of adequate housing for all, because the program did not include a component specifically addressed to the requirements of those in desperate need. It did not direct the government to provide housing to that group, but ordered it to develop a plan that included the component the Court found was constitutionally required. United States courts engaged in similar efforts as they grappled with inadequacies in education at the state level (Reed, 2001) and with the conditions under which prisoners were confined (Feeley and Rubin, 1998). The experience in the United States is mixed at best, but it does not foreclose the possibility that courts might protect social welfare rights through some version of weak-form judicial review.

5 CONCLUSION

Judicial review of legislation is now a well-established practice in most constitutional democracies. Many of the theoretical issues have been fully explored, primarily in the literature emerging from the United States, where the practice has been in place the longest. New forms of judicial review, and new constitutional commitments to social welfare rights, raise important empirical questions about the performance of courts and legislatures (Sadurski, 2002). The largest gains in scholarly understanding to be made in the next decade are likely to come not from further theoretical explorations but from empirical inquiries into the actual operation of various systems of judicial review, with respect to a range of constitutional issues.

REFERENCES

Ackerman, B. (1991). *We the People: Foundations*, Cambridge, Mass.: Harvard University Press.
—— (1998). *We the People: Transformations*, Cambridge, Mass.: Harvard University Press.
—— (2000). 'The New Separation of Powers', *Harvard Law Review*, 113: 633–729.
Bickel, A. M. (1962). *The Least Dangerous Branch: The Supreme Court at the Bar of Politics*, Indianapolis: Bobbs-Merrill.
Campbell, T., Ewing, K. D., and Tomkins, A. (2001). *Sceptical Essays on Human Rights*, Oxford: Oxford University Press.
Dahl, R. A. (1956). *A Preface to Democratic Theory*, Chicago: University of Chicago Press.
—— (1957). 'Decision-Making in a Democracy: The Supreme Court as a National Policy-Maker', *Journal of Public Law*, 6: 279–95.
Dworkin, R. M. (1977). *Taking Rights Seriously*, Cambridge, Mass.: Harvard University Press.
Ely, J. H. (1980). *Democracy and Distrust: A Theory of Judicial Review*, Cambridge, Mass.: Harvard University Press.
Fallon, R. H., Jr. (1987). 'A Constructivist Coherence Theory of Constitutional Interpretation', *Harvard Law Review*, 100: 1189–286.
Feeley, M., and Rubin, E. L. (1998). *Judicial Policy-Making and the Modern State: How the Courts Reformed America's Prisons*, New York: Cambridge University Press.
Fuller, L. L. (1978). 'The Forms and Limits of Adjudication', *Harvard Law Review*, 92: 353–409.
Gardbaum, S. (2002). 'The New Commonwealth Model of Constitutionalism', *American Journal of Comparative Law*, 49: 707–60.
Graber, M. A. (1993). 'The Nonmajoritarian Difficulty: Legislative Deference to the Judiciary', *Studies in American Political Development*, 7: 35–73.
Griffith, J. A. G. (1997). *The Politics of the Judiciary* (5th edn.), London: Fontana Press.
Habermas, J. (1996). *Between Facts and Norms: Contributions to a Discourse Theory of Law and Democracy*, Cambridge, Mass.: MIT Press.
Hirschl, R. (2000). 'The Political Origins of Judicial Empowerment through Constitutionalization: Lessons from Four Constitutional Revolutions', *Law & Social Inquiry*, 25: 91–149.
Lessig, L. (1995). 'Understanding Changed Readings: Fidelity and Theory', *Stanford Law Review*, 47: 395–472.
Levinson, S. and Mailloux, S. (1988). *Interpreting Law and Literature: A Hermeneutic Reader*, Evanston, Ill.: Northwestern University Press.
Michelman, F. I. (1999). *Brennan and Democracy*, Princeton: Princeton University Press.
Morton, F. L., and Knopff, R. (2000). *The Charter Revolution and the Court Party*, Peterborough, Ont.: Broadview Press.
Powell, H. J. (1985). 'The Original Understanding of Original Intent', *Harvard Law Review*, 98: 885–948.

Rakove, J. N. (1996). *Original Meanings: Politics and Ideas in the Making of the Constitution*, New York: Alfred A. Knopf.

Reed, D. (2001). *On Equal Terms: The Constitutional Politics of Educational Opportunity*, Princeton: Princeton University Press.

Roach, K. (2001). *The Supreme Court on Trial: Judicial Activism and Democratic Dialogue*, Toronto: Irwin Law.

Rosenberg, G. N. (1991). *The Hollow Hope: Can Courts Bring about Social Change?* Chicago: University of Chicago Press.

Sadurski, W. (2002). 'Judicial Review and the Protection of Constitutional Rights', *Oxford Journal of Legal Studies*, 22: 275–99.

Sunstein, C. R. (1996). 'Against Positive Rights', in A. Sajó (ed.), *Western Rights? Post-Communist Application*, The Hague: Kluwer Law International.

Tate, C. N., and Vallinder, T. (1995). *The Global Expansion of Judicial Power*, New York: New York University Press.

Tushnet, M. V. (1988). '*Shelley v. Kraemer* and Theories of Equality', *New York Law School Law Review*, 33: 383–408.

——(1999). *Taking the Constitution away from the Courts*, Princeton: Princeton University Press.

Waldron, J. (1999). *The Dignity of Legislation*, Cambridge: Cambridge University Press.

CHAPTER 10

··

CITIZENSHIP

··

LINDA BOSNIAK

1 INTRODUCTION

··

THE past decade and a half have seen a tremendous resurgence of interest in the
subject of citizenship. There is probably no subject commanding more persistent
attention across the disciplines. The 'return of the citizen' is manifest in constitutional theory, in political philosophy, in social theory, in cultural studies, and in legal
studies more generally. Nor does any other concept better satisfy so many kinds of
normative appetites at once: citizenship is championed by civic republicans, participatory democrats, cultural radicals, communitarians, egalitarian liberals, and sometimes social conservatives, all of whom claim citizenship as a fulfillment of their
particular moral vision.

Any concept that can mean so much to so many is bound to be highly enigmatic.
And citizenship surely is that. Indeed, it is possible to argue that the idea is more symbol than substance, and that in analytical terms, our understandings of citizenship
are highly fragmented, if not incoherent. As Judith Shklar aptly observed, 'there is no
notion more central in politics than citizenship, [yet] none more variable in history
nor contested in theory' (Shklar, 1991).

Yet while citizenship's precise meaning is often contested, its normative valence is
never in question. Citizenship is a word of the greatest approbation. To designate
institutions and practices and experiences in the language of citizenship is not merely

This chapter was written during a Fellowship year at the Program in Law and Public Affairs at Princeton
University (2001–2).

to describe them; it is also to accord them a kind of honor and political recognition. In fact, it is precisely because of the concept's immense normative value and resonance that people disagree so sharply over the conditions for its proper application. Struggles over citizenship's meaning are, in fundamental respects, struggles over competing normative visions of collective life.

This is not to say that citizenship is entirely indeterminate in its scope and meaning. There are, in fact, common themes and common divides which have come to organize the citizenship discourse both within and beyond legal studies. Broadly speaking, questions about citizenship can be divided into three (inevitably overlapping) categories: those that concern the substance of citizenship (what citizenship is), those that concern its domain or location (where citizenship takes place), and those that concern citizenship's subjects (who is a citizen). Each of these questions, in turn, has received a range of conventionally acceptable answers which have served to structure the citizenship debates.

This chapter sketches out some of the main responses conventionally offered to each of these questions. It contends, however, that pressure has recently been brought to bear by scholars across the disciplines on the prevailing approaches to each of these questions in ways that seek to significantly redefine citizenship's scope and meaning. Briefly, scholars have sought to take the concept of citizenship beyond the strictly political, beyond the nation-state, beyond the individual, and beyond the ethical particularist and even humanist commitments usually associated with the concept. These efforts at redefinition are often supported by way of an appeal to citizenship's own expansive logic and ethics; the challengers purport to capture the normative heart of the citizenship idea better than prevailing approaches have thus far done.

Whether these alternative conceptions of citizenship recently pressed by scholars will stick remains to be seen. Some have argued that acceptance of the kinds of arguments the challengers have made would amount to an abandonment of the idea of citizenship altogether. This chapter maintains, in contrast, that citizenship is a flexible enough concept to take on new meanings, even some that appear sharply in tension with earlier understandings. It also contends that the idea of citizenship contains enough universalist normative content that it can plausibly be used (though perhaps paradoxically) as a resource for challenging narrower and more exclusive understandings.

In the end, however, arguments about citizenship are less about the scope and meaning of the term itself than they are about the value and legitimacy of the political practices and ideals the word is used to represent. Whether and how citizenship can be redefined will depend on the shape and the outcomes of various substantive debates in legal and political thought in which the conceptual debate is embedded—those concerning the proper domains of political life, the future of the nation-state, and the rightful scope of ethical solidarity, among them. The citizenship debates are best regarded as debates about these questions.

2 CITIZENSHIP AS MEMBERSHIP: MULTIPLE UNDERSTANDINGS

Despite the strikingly broad uses to which the idea of citizenship has been applied, the term may be said to possess a common substantive core. Most commentators approach citizenship as a concept that designates some form of community membership—membership in a political community (the political theorists) or a common society (the sociologists). Yet this answer to citizenship's 'what' question begs its own questions in turn, for the nature and character of this membership still remain to be specified. As it happens, the membership that citizenship is understood to represent has been quite diversely conceived, from its earliest invocations to the present day.

J. G. A. Pocock's well-known account of citizenship's conceptual origins counterposes the early Athenian and Roman conceptions. On one side, the Athenians approached the membership associated with citizenship as the practice of collective self-governance; this is the Aristotelian conception of citizenship as the process of 'ruling and being ruled'. Early Roman thought, in contrast, approached citizenship as entitlement possessed by the individual to protection by the rulers themselves (Pocock, 1998; Walzer, 1989).

This early division in prevailing conceptions of citizenship has, in some respects, carried forward to our own time. From the Roman model, we have derived two contemporary conceptions of citizenship. We first of all understand citizenship to be a matter of formal legal standing: to be a citizen is to possess the legal status of citizenship—one that brings with it certain privileges and obligations. In this usage, citizenship designates formal membership in an organized political community. In today's world, the site of such membership is ordinarily the political community of the nation-state, although citizenship status is also sometimes possessed at the subnational and (now in Europe) at the supranational levels as well.

The Roman legalist conception of citizenship gave us, in addition, our widely shared understanding of citizenship as rights. In this conception, the enjoyment of rights under law is the defining feature of social membership. Citizenship requires the possession of rights (to non-interference, originally, and now to other goods as well) and those who possess the rights are usually presumed thereby to enjoy citizenship. In this century, the tradition is closely associated with the work of British sociologist T. H. Marshall, who is best known for his description of contemporary citizenship as constituted by a tripartite structure of civil, political, and social rights. But this tradition has been elaborated and extended as well by a range of contemporary constitutional and political and social theorists (Karst, 1989; Shklar, 1991; Smith, 1998).

The Aristotelian conception of active citizenship, on the other hand, also continues to shape prevailing understandings. This conception was reclaimed by figures including Machiavelli and Rousseau, and played a critical role in shaping both US and French revolutionary thought. This tradition of 'high citizenship' (Flathman, 1995) was revived again early in the twentieth century by Hannah Arendt, but, on the whole, it lay dormant during this period, having been supplanted by liberal conceptions largely concerned with the rights and status of individuals. During the past two decades, however, civic republican theory has made a comeback in the academy and brought with it a revitalized interest in citizenship's classically political dimension. Today, as political and constitutional theorists often use the term, citizenship denotes the process of democratic self-government, and the practice of active engagement in the life of the political community.

For some republicans, citizenship is closely tied to conceptions of civic virtue which extend beyond political participation and deliberation. Here, citizenship's touchstone is 'responsibility', defined partly in antithesis to liberal, rights-oriented discourse. Among other things, citizenship is understood to entail obligations to earn a living, and in more general terms, to foster moral character and a common culture. Ensuring that people possess the disposition to meet such obligations, in turn, requires inculcation through 'education for citizenship' (Sherry, 1995).

In addition to these liberal and republican-derived conceptions of citizenship, we have today a fourth understanding which broadly refers to the way in which people experience themselves in collective terms. The term citizenship is here deployed to evoke the affective ties of identification and solidarity that people maintain with others in the wider world; it conveys the quality of belonging—the felt aspects of community membership. This subjective conception of citizenship finds its roots in the Greeks as well, though not in Aristotle: the Stoics spoke of being 'citizens of the world' (Nussbaum in Cohen, 1996) and in so doing, meant to convey the sense of psychological membership to which the term citizenship is sometimes applied. Today, the experience of national identity and patriotism is often described in the language of citizenship as well.

Thus, status, rights, political engagement, responsibilities, and identity/solidarity together define the contours of our contemporary understandings of citizenship-as-membership. Some commentators describe these conceptions (or some similar set) as distinct, though overlapping, dimensions, of a larger, unitary phenomenon. This is plausible in certain respects: it seems clear that we define ourselves at times along each of these parameters, that they are not mutually exclusive and, indeed, that each is sometimes intimately related to the others in ways that contribute to the broader constitution of political and social subjects.

There are times, however, when the social ontologies and normative commitments associated with these various dimensions of citizenship appear more incommensurable than complementary. The largely liberal tradition of citizenship-as-rights and the largely republican tradition of citizenship-as-politics, in particular, might be said to be highly incompatible on some readings. There are, in addition, distinct disciplinary divides in the uses of the term. As a general rule, social theorists tend to employ

Marshallian rights-based conceptions of citizenship while political theorists usually invoke republican conceptions. Often these groups seem to be talking past one another entirely.

In any case, each of these understandings of citizenship finds expression today in contemporary legal thought. Some legal scholars—particularly those with an interest in questions of immigration and nationalism—are concerned with citizenship as a formal legal status. Others increasingly employ the language and concepts of republican citizenship to address the subjects of deliberative democracy and collective identity in their scholarship. The conception of citizenship *qua* rights is also widely invoked by legal scholars, particularly by constitutional scholars. Once again, however, the idea of citizenship is understood in each case to be a matter of membership, with the various approaches conveying distinct understandings of how membership is enacted within the institutions and the affective bonds of a particular social community.

3 THE DOMAINS OF CITIZENSHIP: POLITICS AND BEYOND

Despite the significant variation in substantive approach, the major conceptions of citizenship have traditionally tended to converge on one point: they have assumed that the domain of citizenship—the sphere in which it is enacted, and to which it is relevant—is broadly political in nature. Republican theorists have specifically treated citizenship as representing the process of political self-governance, while in liberal understandings, citizenship has been defined in relationship to the state—the entity which both guarantees rights and defines legal status. It is true that the jurisprudential, rights-based conception of citizenship is concerned—as in the well-known formulation of T. H. Marshall—not only with rights of political participation but with civil rights (rights to legal personality, to 'sue and be sued', as Pocock puts it) and with social rights (rights to enjoyment of a minimum level of social welfare). But these rights are defined as broadly public in nature, and in any event, they are understood as entirely creatures of positive, state law.

Specifically excluded from each of these conceptions of citizenship, in contrast, are the domains of social life traditionally defined as private in character, including—most significantly—the spheres of the market and the economy at large. Indeed, citizenship has been famously criticized as a formalist construct that purports to extend formal equality in the public sphere but which simultaneously obscures relations of domination in the private economic realm. Marxist thought, in particular, is well-known for counterposing citizenship to economy by maintaining that the formal equality of citizenship status masks relations of drastic inequality prevailing in what Marx himself called the domain of 'material life'.

Over the past several decades, however, the notion that a private domain exists distinct and insulated from state and law has itself been contested and importantly discredited. In the first place, it is now widely recognized that public power serves both to frame and to constitute relationships in these ostensibly private spheres. At the same time, many scholars have sought to redefine the domain of the political itself to include sites that had hitherto been treated as private in nature. Coercive power, it has been argued, is exercised in the economy, the university, the workplace, the family, the media, and elsewhere, and all of the relationships which take place in these domains have consequently been redescribed as fundamentally political in both character and significance.

It is in this intellectual context that some scholars have begun to press against traditionally statist conceptions of citizenship. Theorists of both left and right have sought to reclaim spheres of social life that have often been excluded from conventional understandings of the political as sites of citizenship. This literature has two principal strands. The first applies republican conceptions of active citizenship to new domains. Political and legal theorists urge recognition of citizenship practices in the workplace, in the marketplace, in the neighborhood, in unions, in political movements, in cultural arenas, and even in the family (e.g. Okin, 1992; Pateman, 1970). Some authors employ the concept of citizenship here largely descriptively to refer to actual practices of self-government and community-mindedness in these spheres; others are particularly concerned with fostering the necessary conditions for 'good citizenship', or civic virtue, in these arenas. In either case, the practice of citizenship is held to be no longer limited to the confines of the demos, as it has been traditionally conceived.

Significantly, this redeployment of the republican conception of citizenship to apply to various non-state domains is closely linked to the ongoing debate in political and social thought over the status of civil society. Many of the sites claimed as alternative domains of citizenship have been characterized as constituting aspects of the sphere of civil society. Though a contested concept itself, civil society is often described as the sphere of association or sociability—the sphere in which people engage with one another and forge relationships independent of the constraints or demands of state governance. (The question of whether the economy constitutes a part of civil society remains a contested question in the literature.) Traditionally, citizenship and civil society have been treated in opposition, with citizenship regarded as a practice that occurs only at the level of the political community and, therefore, outside of civil society. Nevertheless, a number of scholars have recently insisted that politics and/or citizenship are integral to, and inevitable in, the domain of civil society (Barber, 1999). Social movements are the paradigmatic example; they have been described as civil society citizenship in its purest form. Certainly, such activity fulfills the normative criteria of republican and participatory conceptions of citizenship very well: it is active and robust and reflects a commitment to the common good and to engaged participation in public affairs.

In a second strand of literature, exponents of rights-based conceptions of citizenship have sought to extend their entitlement claims to arenas traditionally viewed as insulated from public intervention. Some scholars, including many in the law, have recently pressed for understandings of citizenship that would ensure a basic measure of economic well-being in society. 'Economic citizenship', in the prevailing language, might encompass a right to decent work, or a right to earn (Forbath, 1999; Shklar, 1991), a right to a financial 'stake' in society, and to more complete and meaningful social welfare schemes (Fraser and Gordon, 1994).

Another group of scholars, especially those concerned with rights of ethnic and sexual minorities, have urged attention to the idea of 'cultural citizenship'. Cultural citizenship is described as recognition of 'the right to be different' without marginalization or subordination in the membership community at large (Young, 1989).

A final group has pressed arguments on behalf of 'multicultural citizenship', pursuant to which minority groups would be afforded social and cultural recognition of their group identities, and would sometimes obtain rights to political autonomy as well (Kymlicka, 1995). The multicultural citizenship literature, notably, posits the cultural group, rather than the liberal individual, as the central protagonist in the struggle for citizenship rights.

In each of these cases, the claims of citizenship have been transposed from the domains of state and politics to spheres which have traditionally been regarded as insulated from direct public concern. This is a far cry from the Aristotelian conception of citizenship, according to which citizenship is distinctly political by nature, and it departs from the traditional liberal rights-based conception as well to the degree that it insists upon dramatically expanding the scope of legitimate state involvement to previously off-limit domains. While some purists have objected to these recent efforts (e.g. Miller, 2000), it seems fair to say that the innovators have been relatively successful: the coupling of the idea of citizenship with economy, culture, corporation, university, workplace, and civil society more broadly, no longer sounds as jarring and paradoxical as it must once have sounded. It is common, by now, even in colloquial discourse, to conjoin the idea of citizenship with activities and spheres that once seemed remote from citizenly concern.

This development can be read as either a broadening of citizenship's range of application or an expansion of our understandings of what constitutes the domain of the political. In either reading, citizenship has clearly gained substantial release from its conventional association with the traditionally defined public sphere. In the process, the range of claims for rights and self-governance and solidarity that are regarded as worthy of political recognition has been substantially enlarged as well.

4 LOCATING CITIZENSHIP: THE NATION-STATE AND THE POSTNATIONAL CHALLENGE

Yet while citizenship is now understood by many scholars to extend to new social domains, the nature and the parameters of the broader community in which citizenship is located are almost always treated as given. Citizenship is presumed, with little question, to be a national enterprise—a set of institutions and practices that necessarily take place within the political community (or the social world) of the nation-state. Of course, citizenship was not always understood this way. Citizenship has an important history that predates the nation-state's development: the idea of citizenship began its career as a concept linking membership to the city-state. Today, however, citizenship's national character and national location are treated as axiomatic—so much so that they are rarely specified, much less defended.

In the past several years, however, the national assumption in the citizenship literature has come under increasing challenge. A growing number of scholars across the disciplines have lately begun to press new understandings of citizenship's location. They have coined new phrases: 'transnational citizenship', 'global citizenship', 'postnational citizenship', and have revived the classic notion of 'cosmopolitan citizenship'. For some, these terms represent empirical claims about the changing nature of citizenship in practice: citizenship, they maintain, is becoming increasingly decoupled from the nation-state as a matter of fact. Others contend that citizenship *should* be conceived in ways that are divorced or distanced from state-belonging. The particulars of each of these kinds of arguments vary, but the common theme is that exclusively state-centered conceptions of citizenship are unduly narrow or parochial in this age of intensive globalization. Citizenship is described as increasingly denationalized, with new forms of citizenship (both above and below the state) actually, or ideally, displacing the old (Falk, 1994; Soysal, 1994; Linklater, 1999).

Efforts by scholars across the disciplines to talk about citizenship in ways that decouple it from the nation-state have met, in turn, with substantial resistance among mainstream citizenship theorists. Many agree with the view articulated half a century ago by Hannah Arendt that a citizen 'is *by definition* a citizen among citizens of a country among countries. His rights and duties must be defined and limited, not only by those of his fellow citizens, but also by the boundaries of a territory' (Arendt, 1968: 81). This view has been reaffirmed recently by a number of theorists, perhaps most succinctly by historian Gertrude Himmelfarb, who has written that citizenship 'has little meaning except in the context of a state' (Himmelfarb in Cohen, 1996: 74).

This traditionalist view continues to dominate the debate concerning citizenship's actual and proper location, with those seeking to either describe or promote citizenship's denationalization remaining largely marginalized. Yet blanket rejection of their claims is overly facile.

To begin with, because citizenship possesses multiple understandings in substantive terms, the question whether citizenship is in fact taking non-national form is actually several questions, to which different answers may apply (Bosniak, 2000). It is surely true that the formal legal status of citizenship remains closely bound to nation-state membership. As a practical matter, citizenship status is almost always conferred by nation-states and as a matter of international law, it is national citizenship that is recognized and honored. Yet even here there are exceptions, as the emerging development of European Union citizenship demonstrates (though it is also true that EU citizenship remains grounded in, and derivative of, the citizenships of the Union's constituent nation-states).

Where citizenship is understood as the enjoyment of basic rights and entitlements, the idea of transnational or global citizenship seems even less implausible. This is because the various rights associated with citizenship in this tradition—including civil, political, social, and cultural rights—are no longer exclusively guaranteed at the national level. As is well known, the international human rights regimes that have developed in the post-World War II period are designed to implement supranational standards for the treatment of individuals by states. Certainly, there are real limits to the international human rights system, and people surely continue to face serious constraints in enforcing internationally guaranteed rights. But there is no disputing that many of the rights commonly associated with citizenship are no longer entirely circumscribed by nation-state boundaries (Baubock, 1994; Soysal, 1994). While this incipient form of citizenship may be more symbolic than real, this has often been true of citizenship rights within nation-states as well.

To the extent, moreover, that we approach citizenship in its republican sense as active political (and now, civic) engagement, the claims of transnational citizenship seem more plausible still. Increasing numbers of people are engaged in democratic political practices across national borders in the form of transnational social movements, including those of labor rights activists, environmentalists, feminists, and human rights workers. Characterizing this sort of activism as 'citizenship', of course, requires recognition of citizenship practices in the domain of civil society—a recognition (I have argued) that many commentators have begun to extend. What is distinct, in this context, is that the civil society at issue is not nationally bounded but takes transnational form; its domain is the arena of 'global civil society' (Falk, 1994).

Finally, when citizenship is approached psychologically, as an experience of identity and solidarity, anthropologists and others have shown that people increasingly maintain central identities and commitments that transcend or traverse national boundaries. This includes not merely the solidarities and identifications that may develop among members of transnational social movements and transnational elites, but also the experiences of migrants who live in various diasporic and other cross-national communities. These individuals 'lead dual lives', as sociologist Alejandro Portes observes. 'Members are at least bilingual, move easily between different cultures, frequently maintain homes in two countries, and pursue economic, political, and cultural interests that require a simultaneous presence in both'

(Portes, 1996: 77). The proliferation of transnational communities has resulted in the production of plural identities and solidarities among their members which are often not reducible to unitary statist models of social belonging.

A number of critics have responded to these various efforts to extend the idea of citizenship beyond the state by contending that proponents are not describing citizenship at all, but events and processes that either directly undermine citizenship or are, in any event, distinguishable from it. Sociologist David Jacobson, for example, maintains that the rise of international human rights law represents not a relocation of citizenship but rather citizenship's 'devaluation' or displacement (Jacobson, 1996). Political theorist David Miller has argued, correspondingly, that while Greenpeace activists may well be doing something laudable, they are not engaged in the practice of citizenship—among other reasons, because citizenship requires 'rooted[ness] in a bounded political community' (Miller, 2000: 96).

These responses begin with an a priori state-centered definition of citizenship, and then categorically rule out any institutions or practices that depart from this framework. An alternative approach would begin by treating citizenship as a core political concept that is conventionally used to designate a variety of different practices and experiences and institutions, and would then recognize that some of the practices and experiences and institutions conventionally described by the concept of citizenship have in fact begun to take transnational or non-national or extra-national form or direction. In this approach, the ideas of postnational or transnational citizenship cannot be regarded as incoherent *per se*, and they are at least sometimes plausible in descriptive terms. As with the case of civil society citizenship, I see no compelling logical or empirical reason to refuse to allow the term citizenship to evolve along with its referents (Bosniak, 2000).

Perhaps the deeper debate goes to the normative question of where citizenship *should* be located. Much of this debate is centered around questions of citizenship understood as ethical identification and solidarity. A number of theorists have recently argued on behalf of cosmopolitan conceptions of citizenship solidarity, or 'world citizenship'. These are ethical universalist notions which are meant to express the fundamental moral duties we owe to humanity at large (Linklater, 1999: 36; Nussbaum in Cohen, 1996). Others—including activists in the globalization protests in Seattle and elsewhere—have begun to argue for a cross-border, anti-corporate, class-based solidarity of the marginalized, which they have characterized as a form of 'global citizenship' or 'globalization from below' (Falk, 1994). In each case, the claim is that citizenship solidarity—particularly in the domain of distributive justice—need not, and cannot legitimately, be constrained by national boundaries.

Some critics have protested, in turn, that national conceptions of citizenship-as-solidarity must remain primary for at least two reasons. First, liberal institutions and practices depend on it: redistributive projects have been, and are likely, to remain national in scope, grounded in relations of mutual solidarity that cannot be developed on a global scale. Others have maintained that national conceptions of citizenship are not merely necessary but intrinsically desirable; the nation-state, they contend, is the only large-scale contemporary institutional setting in which people may develop the sense of common good and shared fate that is so vital to human flourishing.

Yet these kinds of arguments have been subject to challenge, not least on grounds that they represent an unjustifiably parochial vision of ethical commitment. Normatively privileging identification with, and solidarity toward, compatriots presumes the existence of a class of non-national others who are necessarily excluded from the domain of normative concern. Some outsiders are located beyond the national territory and are routinely denied access to it; others reside within the national territory as aliens or as perceived foreigners. In either case, the question arises as to why the people with whom we happen to share nation-state territory and formal membership should be the objects of our identification and solidarity to a greater extent than others with whom we are joined by other kinds of status or affiliative ties. Some scholars have argued that liberal-egalitarian principles require abandonment of nationalist ethics in favor of ethical universalism or other forms of cross-national solidarity (Linklater, 1999; Nussbaum in Cohen, 1996; Falk, 1994).

In addition to the question of the scope of citizenship's ethical community, the national conception of citizenship raises important concerns of democratic political theory. Here, republican conceptions of citizenship as political engagement emerge as central. With increasing globalization of social and economic life, the capacity of nation-states to regulate in ways that can effectively respond to many of today's most pressing policy problems has notoriously diminished. The enormous growth and influence of globalized corporate activity is of special concern. A growing number of democratic theorists have recently warned that many fundamental processes which determine people's life-chances both within and across political communities are now beyond the reach of nation-states. To the extent that one supports development of institutions that permit people to have a meaningful voice in the process of democratic self-governance, establishing mechanisms of democratic accountability, and cultivating forms of transnational participatory politics more generally, would seem to be essential (Bosniak, 2000).

These debates—both ethical and institutional—between supporters of nationalism and forms of cosmopolitanism are complex and ongoing. What is significant is that they have increasingly taken the form of debates over *citizenship*. At one level, this is a debate over definitions—over the question of when and how the idea of citizenship is properly applied. But it is also clear that given citizenship's power as a great honorific, both sides have substantial incentive to claim the term as their own.

5 THE SUBJECTS OF CITIZENSHIP

One of the persistent themes in the academic literature on citizenship concerns the question of how far citizenship extends in social terms: this is the question of who will constitute the class of citizenship's subjects. Because citizenship is conceived as representing political or social membership (almost always, as we have seen, in the context of the nation-state), the question of citizenship's subjects is consequently the question of who it is that will be counted as (usually national) political or social members.

But because membership is very differently conceived in different understandings of citizenship, the answer to citizenship's 'who' question may quite possibly vary as well. The class of republican participatory citizens, for instance, will not necessarily correspond—and has not always corresponded—with the class of rights-bearing citizens more generally, nor with the class of people having the legal status of citizenship, nor with the class of psychological citizens. Even rights-bearing citizens themselves are not a monolithic group: the class of persons enjoying civil citizenship, for example, is not always—and has not always been—the same as the class of people enjoying political or social or cultural citizenship (Cott, 1998).

Most discussions of citizenship's subjects tend not to acknowledge distinctions in the meanings of citizenship; the usual approach is to treat citizenship as an undifferentiated whole. Scholars of citizenship tend to diverge, on the other hand, in the way in which they approach citizenship's normative orientation. Some treat citizenship principally as a universalist project while others emphasize its exclusionary attributes. Much of the literature on citizenship's 'who' question can be divided this way.

5.1 Universal Citizenship

On one side, the story of citizenship is often recounted as a tale of progressive incorporation, with new social classes increasingly demanding, and ultimately achieving, inclusion as citizens over time. T. H. Marshall expressly contemplated this kind of expansion in his work: he wrote that '[s]ocieties in which citizenship is a developing institution [have strived for] a fuller measure of equality, an enrichment of the stuff of which the status is made, *and* an increase in the number of those on whom the status is bestowed' (Marshall, 1949). Likewise Michael Walzer, who writes that 'the number and range of people in [citizenship's] commonality grows by invasion and incorporation. Slaves, workers, new immigrants, Jews, Blacks, women—all of them move into the circle of the protected, even if the protection they actually get is still unequal or inadequate' (Walzer, 1989). This is citizenship's 'expanding. . . circle of belonging', in Kenneth Karst's phrase (Karst, 1989).

These accounts of citizenship's progressive inclusiveness over time give voice to what Iris Marion Young has called 'the ideal of universal citizenship'. This ideal, she writes, has 'driven the emancipatory momentum of modern political life'. It stands for 'the inclusion and participation of everyone' (Young, 1989). And indeed, the claim of 'citizenship for all' has been a very powerful normative touchstone in most liberal democratic societies in the modern period. But it is an aspirational value, and tells only part of the story.

As a historical matter, for one thing, the progressive trajectory has been interlaced with other, more regressive social narratives. In the US context, Rogers Smith has recently shown that the liberal universalist citizenship story has always been accompanied by a regressive strand—what he calls ascriptive Americanism—which has served to justify the exclusion of African-Americans, women, and ethnic and religious minorities from recognition as full citizens (Smith, 1999; Cott, 1998). Beyond this and other histories of overt exclusion, critics have also charged that even where citizenship has been made available to ever-widening groups of people, the citizenship they enjoy in substantive terms is often strikingly narrow. Some critics characterize this as citizenship formalism: while citizenship has been extended horizontally to increasing numbers of social groups, the citizenship they enjoy in substance is often an empty shell. The best-known version of this claim is the neo-Marxist critique that the grossly unequal distribution of resources in capitalist societies renders many formal citizenship rights largely empty, since most citizens are not in a position to avail themselves of those rights in any meaningful way (Fraser and Gordon, 1994).

Others have emphasized existing inequalities in the enjoyment of citizenship rights among formally equal citizens. This claim lies at the heart of the well-known and rhetorically powerful critique of 'second-class citizenship' (Karst, 1989). The argument is that certain marginalized social groups may now enjoy nominal citizenship status, but their members are, in fact, afforded less in the way of substantive citizenship than others in society—either by way of directly unequal treatment (e.g. gays and lesbians in the United States) or through a legal system which treats certain social domains where *de facto* inequality prevails (e.g. the ostensibly private spheres of family, economy, and culture) as falling beyond the constraints of citizenship altogether.

There is, finally, the charge that despite the increasingly widespread extension of citizenship to community residents, levels of civic and political engagement are exceptionally low. From a civic republican perspective, the universal availability of citizenship status means little in the context of a society of citizens who live pervasively passive and privatized lives, with little engagement in community and the process of self-government (Barber, 1999).

Each of these critiques makes clear that even when citizenship is formally extended to ever-broader groups of subjects, widespread enjoyment or practice of citizenship is not thereby guaranteed. Rather, there is often a gap between possession of citizenship status and the enjoyment or performance of citizenship in substantive terms. Indeed, each of these critiques suggests that expansion in the class of citizenship's subjects has more or less outrun the expansion and deepening of its substance.

Nevertheless, in political and legal theory on citizenship, universalism remains the defining normative touchstone. It is no longer disputed that citizenship—meaningful, substantive citizenship—should be available to 'everyone'. As always, however, the notion of universality is itself subject to pressure and renegotiation. Recently, for instance, some advocates and commentators have pressed for recognition of the citizenship of non-human animals and of members of future generations, often under the rubric of 'ecological citizenship' (Turner, 1986). Others have sought to extend the recognition and protections imparted by citizenship to fetuses or the 'unborn'. While relatively marginal formulations, the entry of these claims into the discourse attests to the power, and the perceived expansiveness, of citizenship's universalist ethic.

5.2 Bounded Citizenship

Universalism is the prevailing ethic within a political community whose boundaries and identity are taken as given. And most legal and political theorists do take these boundaries as given: they presume a fixed national citizenry and devote themselves to inquiring about the nature of the relations that do or ought to prevail among its members. Yet the study of citizenship is not confined to these internal questions, and universalism does not exhaust citizenship's fundamental commitments. On the contrary, for another group of legal and political scholars—usually scholars of immigration and nationality—citizenship is the core analytical concept for thinking about the way in which the community's membership and boundaries are constituted in the first instance. And in the context of this scholarly enterprise, citizenship stands not for universalism but for closure.

Citizenship in this latter understanding is concerned not with the interior life of the political community but with its threshold. And in most versions, the community's threshold with which citizenship is concerned is that of the nation-state. Citizenship is a status which assigns persons to membership in specific nation-states. At the same time, citizenship status in any given nation is almost always restricted, available only to those who are recognized as its members.

Different states, of course, have different policies regarding admission to citizenship. Virtually all states assign citizenship to children born of the state's nationals (*jus sanguinis*), while only some—though increasing numbers—grant citizenship to children born within the state's territory (*jus soli*). Most states, furthermore, make provision for naturalization of foreigners into citizenship after birth. In each case, however, citizenship status is not automatically granted either to anyone who seeks it, nor, necessarily, to anyone who enters into or resides within state territory, but is, instead, subject to rationing by the state. This kind of rationing is accepted as a matter of international law: states are deemed fully sovereign with respect to decisions about who to admit to membership (though there are some constraints on forcible expatriation).

Legal scholars have devoted much attention to questions concerning acquisition and loss of citizenship. The debate over the propriety of *jus soli* assignment of citizenship has garnered particular attention in recent years. In the US context, some prominent American scholars urged in the 1980s that birthright citizenship no longer be accorded to children born in the United States of undocumented immigrant parents (Schuck and

Smith, 1985). This proposal was highly controversial, partly in light of that nation's history of denying citizenship to blacks through the Civil War and the specific repudiation of that exclusion through the Fourteenth Amendment of the US Constitution. Most commentators agree that a state's denial of citizenship to persons born and raised within its territory presents significant problems of political legitimacy—though again, not all states have embraced the principle of automatic birthright citizenship.

Dual or multiple nationality has been another subject of intense scholarly interest. In recent years, more people than ever hold citizenship in more than one nation. This is the result, in part, of recent liberalization of different national rules on naturalization, expatriation, and assignment of citizenship at birth which together make multiple citizenship legally possible and often routine. It is also due to the availability of dramatically improved transportation and communications technologies, which make the pursuit of life in more than one nation-state increasingly possible in practical terms. This increase in the incidence of dual nationality has led to widespread debate. While some critics have insisted that national citizenship must remain a unique commitment (Brubaker, 1992), others have increasingly celebrated the rise in cases of multiple allegiances and identities that multiple citizenships often entail (Spiro, 1997).

In addition to issues involving the allocation and distribution of the status of citizenship, scholars have devoted substantial attention to questions about the status's legal significance. The concern here is what, exactly, possession or lack of possession of citizenship status should rightfully entail within the national society. Because citizenship is an exclusive status, and because in most states, foreigners enter the territory in some status short of citizenship, the question arises as to how those without citizenship status should be treated, to what extent should enjoyment of basic rights depend on being a status citizen, and to what extent should it depend on the fact of personhood and territorial presence alone? Legal theorist Alexander Bickel famously launched the modern version of this debate in the United States by arguing that possession of citizenship status has long been, and should remain, fundamentally insignificant in the American constitutional order. The American Constitution, he writes, presents 'the edifying picture of a government that bestow[s] rights on people and persons, and [holds] itself out as bound by certain standards of conduct in its relations with people and persons, not with some legal construct called citizen' (Bickel, 1973). Others, by contrast, have disputed this account in historical terms, and have urged, in any event, that the status of citizenship has been wrongly 'devalued' and deserves constitutional prominence and honor (Schuck, 1998). This debate has enormous practical implications for the treatment and condition of aliens in the national society in which they reside (about which more below).

There is, finally, a vast scholarship in law and policy on the regulation of the border itself. The concern here is national immigration policies in all their dimensions: those pertaining to substantive admission, exclusion, and deportation criteria, those concerned with procedures at the border, and those with refugee and asylum policy. While these subjects do not involve citizenship directly, they are the indispensable backdrop and corollary to any study of citizenship in its threshold dimension.

The regulation of immigration presumes the non-citizenship of national outsiders; it is their lack of citizenship that allows the state to limit and otherwise place conditions on their territorial ingress and membership. Immigration control is thus the policy expression of bounded citizenship in its purest form.

The great majority of commentators endorse the right of nation-states to restrict their membership. Communitarians maintain that such a right is an essential part of a community's process of self-definition, while liberal theorists tend to endorse restrictions at least to the extent necessary to preserve the liberal order. But state control of access to territory and to national membership status is not entirely uncontroversial at the level of normative theory. A few commentators have challenged the prevailing commitment to closure. Joseph Carens, in particular, has argued that a commitment to liberal principles entails, necessarily, support for a policy of relatively open borders (Carens, 1987). Carens's position still represents an outlying view, however, and in most legal and political theory, the issue of the legitimacy of barriers to territorial entry and to national citizenship is not even on the table.

5.3 Alien Citizenship

The question of who it is that constitutes citizenship's subjects thus has two kinds of answers: a universalist answer (everybody) and a nationally particularist answer (members of the nation). In most circumstances, the radical divergence between these two answers is hardly noticed, apparently because each answer is viewed as relevant to a different domain. Universality is understood to govern life within the community, while exclusivity is assumed to govern the community at its threshold. This is mostly accurate, but there is one significant context in which the two commitments are not divided jurisdictionally but have come to occupy the same terrain.

This context involves the condition of non-citizens residing within a national political community. On the one hand, the status of non-citizens, or aliens, is constituted by citizenship's exclusionary regime. These are people who are legally defined as lacking in full national membership, and are subject to certain disabilities, including lack of political rights and potential deportation, as a result. In the case of alienage, citizenship's exclusionary threshold moves inside to operate directly within the territory of the national political community (Bosniak, 1994).

Yet some commentators have remarked that, in many respects, the status of aliens in liberal democratic societies is hardly distinguishable from that of citizens (Soysal, 1994; Schuck, 1998). By virtue of their territorial presence and their personhood, aliens in most liberal democratic societies are, in fact, commonly entitled to a broad range of important civil and social rights—rights of a kind that are commonly described in the language of citizenship. These are citizenship rights which are distributed according to citizenship's internally universalist logic, which means their extension (no doubt paradoxically) to non-citizens as well. In most liberal democratic societies, many non-citizens are entitled, among other things, to full due process rights in criminal proceedings, to expressive and associational rights and religious freedom, to the protections of the state's labor and employment laws, and to the right to education and to other social benefits. And while they remain subject to potential deportation, non-citizens are often entitled to important procedural rights which serve to constrain state power over them in the expulsion process as well.

Aliens can thus be described as both outsiders to citizenship and subjects of citizenship simultaneously. This dual location can make for legal uncertainty and sometimes conflict, because in any given case it is not always clear which regime—exclusive national citizenship or universal citizenship—should and will prevail. While immigration protectionists invoke the national interest to justify use of citizenship as an 'instrument of social closure' (Brubaker, 1992: 31), advocates of immigrant's rights press to extend citizenship's universalist promises beyond the class of nationals to further protect aliens—or non-citizens—themselves.

What is significant, for analytical purposes, is that alien status represents an arena in which both the universalist and particularist commitments of citizenship are relevant and determinative. The condition of aliens makes clear that citizenship at the border and citizenship within the community are not always jurisdictionally separate projects but are, instead, sometimes deeply imbricated with one another. And it is not always clear where the boundary lies between them (Bosniak, 1994).

The case of alienage is also significant for a different reason: it highlights the segmented, even fractured, quality of conventional understandings of citizenship. To the extent that non-citizens can, comprehensibly, be described as governed by the norms of universal citizenship—to the extent that making citizenship claims on behalf of aliens is not entirely incoherent—it becomes clear that the class of citizenship's subjects and the domain of citizenship's substance are not always in alignment. In the same way that there are some status-citizens who are denied many aspects of rights-citizenship (and are thereby understood to be second-class citizens), a person need not possess status-citizenship in order to enjoy many of the incidents of rights-citizenship. Citizenship, in this respect, is not a unified condition but a set of different institutions and practices which converge in some respects but are relatively autonomous in others (Bosniak, 2002). Any answer to the question 'who is a citizen?' will depend, in large part, on which particular institutions and practices are under discussion.

6 Conclusion: Citizenship's Future

If so many aspects and concerns of our collective lives can be articulated in the language of citizenship, how useful can the term be in scholarly discourse, including legal studies? On one view, the concept is simply too multivalent to play the kind of central analytical and aspirational role that it has come to play in the work of many contemporary scholars. Citizenship too often seems to represent all things to all people; in the process it is often hard to know what is at stake and how the concept advances discussion at all.

Yet it is also true that citizenship's meaning is not entirely indeterminate. Status, rights, political participation, and identity represent the core of its analytical concerns. Moreover, citizenship's long association with egalitarian and democratic ideals in at least some of its understandings make it a powerful term of progressive political rhetoric. It is this aspect of citizenship that has led to the many ongoing efforts to reshape and extend the term to new subjects and new domains. 'Cultural citizenship', 'economic citizenship', 'minority group citizenship', 'postnational/global citizenship', 'citizenship of non-human animals', 'ecological citizenship', 'alien citizenship': these all represent efforts to press the idea of universality beyond its currently given boundaries. Notice, however, that while these attempts generally reflect the concerns of the political left, there is nothing intrinsically emancipatory about this process, as current efforts to recognize and protect 'fetal citizenship', among other things, make clear.

It is not yet certain which of these new formulations will become part of our conventional understandings of citizenship. Those which seek to sever citizenship from its presumed association with the nation-state and national forms of belonging are among the deepest challenges to conventional understandings today, and will face especially strenuous resistance. Still, citizenship is nothing if not a pliable concept. And in its universalist aspect, it appears to contain the seeds of its own transformation.

REFERENCES

Arendt, H. (1968). *Men in Dark Times*, New York: Harcourt, Brace & World.

Barber, B. (1999). 'Clansmen, Consumers and Citizen: Three Takes on Civil Society', in Robert K. Fullinwider (ed.), *Civil Society, Democracy and Civic Renewal*, Lanham, Md.: Rowman and Littlefield.

Baubock, R. (1994). *Transnational Citizenship: Membership and Rights in Transnational Migration*, Aldershot: Edward Elgar.

Bickel, A. (1973). 'Citizenship in the American Constitution', *Arizona Law Review* 15: 369–87.

Bosniak, L. (1994). 'Membership, Equality and the Difference that Alienage Makes', *New York University Law Review*, 69: 1047–149.

—— (2000). 'Citizenship Denationalized', *Indiana Journal of Global Legal Studies*, 7: 447–509.

—— (2002). 'Constitutional Citizenship through the Prism of Alienage', *Ohio State Law Review*, 63/5: 1285–325.

Brubaker, R. (1992). *Citizenship and Nationhood in France and Germany*, Cambridge, Mass.: Harvard University Press.

Carens, J. (1987). 'Aliens and Citizens: The Case for Open Borders', *Review of Politics*, 49: 251.

Cohen, J. (ed.) (1996). *For Love of Country*, Boston: Beacon Press.

Cott, N. (1998). 'Marriage and Women's Citizenship in the United States, 1830–1934', *American Historical Review* (Dec.)

Falk, R. (1994). 'The Making of Global Citizenship', in B. van Steenbergen (ed.), *The Condition of Citizenship*, London: Sage.

Flathman, R. (1995). 'Citizenship and Authority: A Chastened View of Citizenship', in R. Beiner (ed.), *Theorizing Citizenship*, Albany, NY: State University of New York.

Forbath, W. (1999). 'Class, Caste and Equal Citizenship', *Michigan Law Review*, 98/1 (Oct.).

Fraser, N., and Gordon, L. (1994). 'Civil Citizenship against Social Citizenship? On the Ideology of Contract-Versus-Charity', in B. van Steenbergen (ed.), *The Condition of Citizenship*, London: Sage.

Jacobson, D. (1996). *Rights across Borders: Immigration and the Decline of Citizenship*, Baltimore: Johns Hopkins University Press.

Karst, K. (1989). *Belonging to America: Equal Citizenship and the Constitution*, New Haven: Yale.

Kymlicka, W. (1995). *Multicultural Citizenship: A Liberal Theory of Minority Rights*, Oxford: Oxford University Press.

Linklater, A. (1999). 'Cosmopolitan Citizenship', in K. Hutchings and R. Dannreuther (eds.), *Cosmopolitan Citizenship*, Columbia, SC: St Martins.

Marshall, T. H. (1949). *Citizenship and Social Class*, Cambridge: Cambridge University Press.

Miller, D. (2000). *Citizenship and National Identity*, Cambridge: Polity Press.

Okin, S. M. (1992). 'Women, Equality and Citizenship', in *Queens Quarterly*, 99 (spring).

Pateman, C. (1970). *Participation and Democratic Theory*, Cambridge: Cambridge University Press.

Pocock, J. G. A. (1998). 'The Ideal of Citizenship since Classical Times', in G. Shafir (ed.), *The Citizenship Debates*, Minneapolis: University of Minnesota Press.

Portes, A. (1996). 'Global Villagers: The Rise of Transnational Communities', *American Prospect*, Mar.–Apr.

Schuck, P. (1998). 'The Devaluation of Citizenship', in Schuck, *Citizens, Strangers, and In-Betweens: Essays on Immigration and Citizenship*, Boulder, Colo.: Westview Press.

—— and Smith, R. (1985). *Citizenship without Consent: Illegal Aliens in the American Polity*, New Haven: Yale University Press.

Sherry, S. (1995) 'Responsible Republicanism: Educating for Citizenship', *University of Chicago Law Review*, 62: 131–208.

Shklar, J. (1991). *American Citizenship: The Quest for Inclusion*, Cambridge, Mass.: Harvard University Press.

Smith, R. M. (1998). *Civic Ideals: Conflicting Visions of Citizenship in U.S. History*, New Haven: Yale.

Soysal, Y. N. (1994). *Limits of Citizenship: Migrants and Postnational Membership in Europe*, Chicago: Cornell University Press.

Spiro, P. (1997). 'Dual Nationality and the Meaning of Citizenship', *Emory Law Review*, 46: 1411–85.

Turner, B. (1986). *Citizenship and Capitalism*, London: Allen and Unwin.

Walzer, M. (1989). 'Citizenship', in T. Ball, J. Farr, and R. Hanson, *Political Innovation and Conceptual Change*, Cambridge: Cambridge University Press.

Young, I. M. (1989). 'Polity and Group Difference: A Critique of the Ideal of Universal Citizenship', *Ethics*, 99/2: 250–74.

CHAPTER 11

DISCRIMINATION

SANDRA FREDMAN

EQUALITY is a principle which is widely and often passionately held. Its precise meaning, however, has been the site of conflict between the major ideologies of our time. Liberal, neo-liberal, and radical theorists have all fought vigorously over the same terrain. Legal scholarship has, nevertheless, reflected rather than directly influenced the development of equality law. Instead, legal progress has been primarily the result of turbulent social forces. Thus in the United States, discrimination law was born out of the struggle of black communities for civil and political rights. In Europe, by contrast, despite the legacy of the Holocaust, it was the women's movement which was in the vanguard of the equality crusade.

Social currents have been channelled too by the differing constitutional frameworks of particular jurisdictions. In the United States, the constitutional structure framed equality as a civil liberties question. In the European Union, by contrast, the fact that the remit of the Community was limited to the creation of a common labour market meant that equality law had to be formulated in terms of labour market regulation. It is only as the Union matured, and the social dimension became more prominent, that the equality principle was transformed into a social right. In Britain, the absence of a written constitution has meant that change has come through the legislature rather then the courts. Instead of being viewed as a civil liberty, the equality principle has taken the form of anti-discrimination legislation in the employment field. In examining legal scholarship, these differences need to be kept in mind.

Legal scholarship on discrimination derives from a strongly liberal source, despite its avowed link with Aristotelian philosophy. Early liberalism has more recently bifurcated. While one influential set of writers has buttressed liberal principles with market-based theories, a second has softened the contours of liberalism by adding an extra dimension drawn from notions of distributive justice and social theory. Opposing the fundamentals of liberal theory are the critical theorists, which include both feminism and critical race theory. The chapter therefore begins with an examination of early liberalism, turning then to neo-liberalism, modified liberalism, feminists, and critical race theorists. It ends by considering new developments into areas where theorizing has yet to catch up.

1 Liberal Theories

1.1 Background

Discussions about equality usually begin with the familiar aphorism, derived from Aristotle, that likes should be treated alike. Aristotelian philosophy was, however, far removed from political or social equality. To the contrary, order and hierarchy were the ideal. Slavery was seen as a beneficial and just system, and men were depicted as naturally fitter to command than women (Barnes, 1982). It was not difficult to reconcile these views with the aphorism that likes should be treated alike. Women and slaves, according to Aristotle, were not rational, and therefore, were not 'like' free men. Thus it appeared fully justifiable to treat them less favourably.

It was the liberal ethic which was necessary to infuse the aphorism with broader egalitarian meaning. Only with the end of feudalism did equality come to eclipse hierarchy. Instead of the belief that each person's destiny was dictated by his or her pre-ordained status, liberalism asserted the key value of individual autonomy, or the freedom of individuals to make their own choices as to their moral values and the objectives they would pursue in their lives. Crucially, and in contrast to Aristotle, this autonomy is predicated on the notion that all individuals have an equal capacity for reason. Individual autonomy has its correlative in State neutrality. The State should be neutral as between the preferences and moral decisions of individuals. State intervention is justified only where necessary to prevent individuals harming one another.

1.2 Individual Autonomy and State Neutrality

These seminal values of rationality, autonomy, individualism, and a neutral abstentionist State have been highly influential in the development of equality law; and there remains a group of writers committed to their defence (Abram, 1986; Brest, 1976; Waldron, 1996). At its heart is the assertion of the values of individual autonomy and State neutrality. Individuals should be free to choose their own version of the 'good life', and the State should not prefer any individual's choice over any other. Laws should be of general application, and all should be equal before the law. Because State intervention is justified only by the 'harm' principle, equality translates into a negative prohibition of discrimination, rather than a positive requirement to promote or facilitate equality. Thus Abram rejects any notion that the State should have a role in guaranteeing social and economic rights. For him, 'eliminating discrimination and providing a safety net for the truly needy constitute the limits of what the law in the American system should do if that system is to remain free' (Abram, 1986: 1326).

Also of central importance is the value accorded to individualism. The individual's intrinsic rationality means that she should be treated according to her individual merit, not her status. Conversely, individuals should only be responsible for their own actions. Thus discrimination is characterized as an interaction between two parties, the victim and the perpetrator. Correspondingly, the role of the law is one of corrective justice, to provide a remedy for the individual against the perpetrator. This strident individualism militates against any theory based on groups. For Brest, the basic premise of the anti-discrimination principle is that no moral significance should be attached to membership in racial groups. 'If a society can be said to have an underlying political theory, ours has not been a theory of organic groups, but of liberalism, focussing on the rights of individuals' (Brest, 1976: 49). Race, as well as being a poor proxy for merit, is also considered to be a poor proxy for need. Thus while the State may intervene to assist the needy, it cannot legitimately do so by classifying according to race. Abram similarly rejects what he calls the social engineers' 'invitation to view people as statistics, submerging personality, effort and character under the blanket concerns of race, sex and ethnicity' (Abram, 1986: 1322).

1.3 Rationality

The use of rationality is more complex and ambiguous. For Brest, race-dependent decisions are irrational in so far as they reflect the assumption that members of one race are less worthy than others. Used in this way, it is clear that rationality, while retaining the appearance of an objective concept, is in fact no more than a moral statement. Thus both Brest and Aristotle rely on rationality as the basis of their equality principles, but reach radically different results because they infuse rationality with differing moral content. This demonstrates that rationality is unable, on its own, to generate principles to decide which groups should be protected by anti-discrimination law. It is not from theory but from practical politics that race came to be recognized as irrational in the United States. It is striking that Brest and many other American theorists focus on race as the paradigm. Brest merely mentions in passing that the extent to which his anti-discrimination principle covers gender or other grounds is a reason for further inquiry. However, it is this inquiry which is basic to the current development of anti-discrimination law. To what extent should other groups also be protected? Current debates over discrimination based on sexual orientation, age, and religious discrimination cannot be resolved by reference to the notion of rationality on its own. As a result, modern jurisprudence has turned away from rationality, to other basic concepts such as dignity.

A more formal way of using rationality is to focus on the relationship of means to ends. In their seminal work, Tussman and tenBroek, recognizing that not all distinctions or classifications are invidious, argue that the key to distinguishing between illegitimate and legitimate distinctions lies in an evaluation of the extent to which the classification can be said to be a rational means of achieving a governmental end (Tussman and tenBroek, 1949). A classification is irrational if it is too wide or too narrow for the purpose specified. Formulated in this apparently mechanical way, the test seems to ask 'no more of the judiciary than that it engage in what at first seems to be the near mathematical task of determining … whether there is the right "fit" between means and ends' (Fiss, 1976: 120). In this way, it claims to avoid the charge that judges are illegitimately substituting their opinion for that of the democratically elected legislature.

However, in this sense too, it is misleading to think of rationality as a value-free notion. As Fiss points out, several auxiliary concepts are necessary to give meaning to the notion of means–end rationality. Most importantly, 'ill-suitedness' is a question of degree. Some margin of ill-fit can be discovered in any classification (Fiss, 1976: 113). Therefore, it is necessary to decide how poor the relationship between criterion and purpose must be before it is deemed arbitrary. Should reasonably large margins of over- or under-inclusiveness be tolerated ('mere rational relationship'), or must the fit between means and ends be tight ('strict scrutiny')? One of the key developments in the jurisprudence of the US Supreme Court was to characterize racial classifications as suspect and therefore subject to strict scrutiny. But this cannot be derived solely from the notion of means–end rationality. This can clearly be seen from the different approaches taken by the US Supreme Court to the intensity of scrutiny applicable to other classifications, such as sex, sexual orientation, religion, or disability.

1.4 Applications to the Law

The continued emphasis on liberal principles of autonomy, individualism, and State neutrality has specific implications for the translation of the equality principle into law. This manifests itself in at least three ways. First, liberalism is more comfortable with the notion of direct discrimination or disparate treatment than indirect discrimination or disparate impact. This is because direct discrimination seems to be based primarily on the individual's right to be treated according to her merit and not on the grounds of her race or gender. Indirect discrimination, with its emphasis on the impact of apparently equal treatment on a group, threatens to move too far away from individual rights. For Brest, therefore, disparate impact can only be a valid application of the anti-discrimination principle to the extent that it remains firmly based in the individual's right not to be discriminated against. Disparate impact should only be held to breach the anti-discrimination principle if it is evidence of a decision which is in fact race dependent, or can be shown to be causally connected to past discrimination. The mere fact that it detrimentally affects a group in the present, without evidence of past or current acts of discrimination, is not sufficient.

Secondly, the emphasis on individual autonomy entails the rejection of minority group rights. Thus Waldron dismisses the view that an individual is partly constituted by the group or culture within which she belongs, arguing instead that culture is really a matter of personal choice. Such a choice is enhanced if individuals can move freely through a 'kaleidoscope' of culture, picking and choosing a range of cultural fragments. Any notion of group rights, which extends beyond the right of the individual not to be discriminated against, in his view, merely stultifies individual autonomy (Waldron, 1996).

The third concrete manifestation of liberalism in its application to the law concerns reverse discrimination. As a start, reverse discrimination infringes the notion of State neutrality. 'Without doing violence to the principles of equality before the law and neutral decision-making, we simply cannot interpret our laws to support both colour blindness for some citizens and colour-consciousness for others' (Abram, 1986: 1319). Reverse discrimination also violates liberal individualism, both in respect of merit and of fault. Thus reverse discrimination permits race or gender to override individual merit in the allocation of benefits in society. It also infringes the fault principle, imposing a cost on a white person or a man (for instance) even though he or she is in no way responsible for the history of discrimination against black people or women. The equality principle is fundamentally breached by according favoured status to any particular group, and a move from the individual to the group is bound to degenerate into a crude political struggle between groups seeking favoured status.

2 Market Liberalism

2.1 Background

While many liberal thinkers have been concerned to develop the tenets of liberalism in the direction of social justice, market liberals have moved in the opposite direction, combining liberal political theory with neo-liberal economic analysis. In neo-liberal hands, the major tenets of liberalism, namely rationality, autonomy, neutrality, individualism, and equality, are imbued with a market-oriented meaning. Rationality becomes the ability to maximize self-interest; autonomy denotes freedom within the market; and State neutrality means lack of intervention in market outcomes. Individuals are interchangeable market agents and society is no more than a group of atomistic individuals. Similarly, equality is simply the formal equality of individuals to enter into contracts. The result is that while the debates between liberal thinkers concern the content of anti-discrimination law, proponents of neo-liberalism contest whether anti-discrimination law can be justified at all.

Possibly the most influential thinker in this school is Hayek (1960). Hayek defines liberty in the essentially negative form of freedom from coercion. The extent to which a person can exercise real choice from a range of acceptable options is irrelevant. 'Liberty describes the absence of particular obstacles—coercion by other men . . . It does not assure us of any particular opportunities, but leaves it to us to decide what use we shall make of the circumstances in which we find ourselves' (Hayek, 1960: 11). Inevitably then, the role of the State is limited to the prevention of coercion by individuals against each other. It is in order to limit the power of the State that equality comes into play. One of the most important means of restraining State power is that it should only be permitted to act according to known general rules, which do not differentiate between individual citizens.

For Hayek, the central mechanism for ensuring freedom of the individual is through a spontaneous market order. The market does not dictate any particular end-state, but gives the individual the freedom to pursue his or her own ends 'by increasing the prospects of everyone of a greater command over the various goods . . . than we are able to secure in any other way' (Hayek, 1960: 107). There is no such thing as 'social justice'. Justice is only about rules of procedure; market outcomes, provided procedural rules of exchange are followed, cannot be characterized as just or unjust. Hayek concedes that the initial chances of individual actors within the market order can be very different, for reasons beyond the individual's control. But any State intervention to correct inequalities is an illegitimate interference, an insistence on a 'single order of ends' which reflects a notion of social justice which does not exist. Thus the role of the State is limited to providing services for the smooth running of the market. It can also make provision against the extremes of poverty, simply to protect individuals against the 'consequences of the extreme misery of their fellows' (Hayek, 1960: 286).

2.2 Autonomy, Rationality, and State Neutrality

These theories are specifically applied to the discrimination law field by Posner (1989), Epstein (1992), and Polachek and Siebert (1993). For all these thinkers, autonomy, rationality, and State neutrality, imbued with market-oriented meanings, produce a potent mix. Rationality is defined as consisting of actions which maximize an individual's self-interest; and all people are rational in that they act consistently to maximize the excess of their private benefits over their private costs (Posner, 1989: 1315). This relates directly both to autonomy and State neutrality. In maximizing their own self-interest, individuals' preferences are entirely their own choice. Subject only to the harm principle, the State should not interfere with this autonomy. If some individuals' preferences include a distaste or aversion for associating with members of different groups, such as blacks, these tastes should be respected with all others. Epstein takes this further, arguing that civil rights law is a 'dangerous form of government coercion', where the State illegitimately abandons its neutrality and gives primacy to the preferences of those who reject discrimination over the preferences of those in favour of discrimination (Epstein, 1992). Instead, the individual's freedom of association should be respected, and, *a fortiori*, his or her right to choose those with whom they enter into contractual relationship.

In the context of gender discrimination, rationality and autonomy are given a slightly different meaning. Posner argues that lower wages for women are a direct result of rational choices women make, namely to invest less than men in their own human capital in the expectation of taking time out of the paid labour market to bear and raise children (Posner, 1989). This in turn causes their wages to be lower than the average man's, 'since a part of every wage is repayment of the worker's investment in human capital' (Posner, 1989: 1315). Similarly, for Polachek and Siebert, 'much of the difference between men and women can be explained as a rational response to differences in labour force intermittency, in mathematical abilities and in tastes' (Polachek and Siebert, 1993: 208). Rationality is also reflected in the 'rational (family-wealth-maximising) division of labour in the home due to women's comparative advantage in child-bearing and rearing' (Polachek and Siebert, 1993: 166). They acknowledge that the human capital theory cannot explain the whole difference between men and women's pay. To fill the gap, they assert that maximization of self-interest includes not only monetary rewards. Thus women choose to supply their labour more cheaply than men to caring occupations because the opportunity to 'care' is seen as a good in itself, compensating for lower wages (Polachek and Siebert, 1993: 206).

All these thinkers believe, with Hayek, that the State should not interfere with market outcomes. However, they differ as to what outcomes a rational market would produce. Polachek and Siebert (1993) maintain that in a competitive market, prejudice against women would be eradicated. 'In a competitive market, if men were paid more than similarly productive women, some firms would be able to lower their costs by hiring women instead of men. These firms would expand their market share, bidding up the pay of women. Men's and women's wages would thus be brought into equality' (Polachek and Siebert, 1993: 141). Therefore, for them 'competition is the greatest tool for fighting unequal opportunity' (Polachek and Siebert, 1993: 139). Epstein (1992), by contrast, argues that this only holds in a world in which transaction costs are not taken into account. Once account is taken of such costs, he asserts, it becomes clear that all groups have rational incentives to discriminate on the grounds prohibited by anti-discrimination law. For example, if an employer has a white

workforce which is racist and refuses to work with blacks, then it is rational and efficient for employers to exclude blacks. To prohibit such rational discrimination not
only imposes unwarranted costs on employers, but also infringes on the freedom and
autonomy of all. Posner goes further, and argues that discrimination laws are counterproductive. Since, according to his theory, the market ensures that women are paid
according to their productivity, anti-discrimination laws force the level of women's
pay up beyond their real productivity, giving them more than their share of the total
wage bill. This leads to lower pay for other, more productive workers, who, on
Posner's hypothesis, are primarily married men. Adding this to his assumption that
married couples pool their earnings, he concludes that married women will on average be worse off than if there were no anti-discrimination laws (Posner, 1989: 1327–8).

2.3 Individualism

The neo-liberal approach takes a paradoxical view of individualism. On the one hand,
the individual is depicted as the primary focus. Individuals are prior to society, which
in turn is no more than a conglomeration of individuals. Individual freedom to make
choices which maximize individual self-interest is pivotal. On the other hand, the definition of rationality in terms of market efficiency is distinctly utilitarian. In order to
decide whether a market is efficient, it is necessary to consider the sum of individual
utilities. Epstein argues that it is by considering utilities that one can maintain a neutral stance as between individual preferences. Thus in trying to determine whether a
given action will increase or decrease overall levels of social satisfaction, subjectively
measured for all persons, it is necessary to consider utilities rather than determining
whose preferences are legitimate and whose are not. However, Epstein finds it difficult
to stay within his own rubric. He is quick to exclude from the calculus the utility of
those who oppose discrimination not because they are victims but for a sense of moral
outrage. 'Society should exclude all instances of mere offence born of moral outrage
or bruised sensibilities from the class of actionable harms, however deeply felt'
(Epstein, 1992: 43). Altruism is therefore regarded as distorting cost-benefit analyses.

2.4 Critique of Neo-liberalism

Neo-liberalism was embraced as a dominant political ideology in both the United
States and Britain during the 1980s. In order to defend anti-discrimination laws
against this ideology, several theorists have begun to dispute it on its own premises.
In particular, these writers contest the claimed inefficiency of anti-discrimination
laws. Thus Donohue, while accepting the view that in the long term the market will
drive out discriminators, argues that anti-discrimination laws can speed up the
process by reducing the profits of discriminators more quickly. Achieving welfare

more quickly is itself an improvement in efficiency (Donohue, 1986). Deakin and Wilkinson go further and demonstrate that low labour standards buttress inefficient management, while fair labour standards, including equality laws, enhance labour market efficiency (Deakin and Wilkinson, 1991).

Other critics of neo-liberalism point to inconsistencies within the economic model itself (Humphries, 1995). Thus the notion that the market is perfectly competitive is shown to be an idealized vision. At least three problems are identified. First, incomplete information may prevent competition from driving out under-valuation of labour. Secondly, firm-specific skills mean that there is often no perfect labour mobility. Thirdly, employers do not always properly assess and therefore reward productivity based on investment in human capital. Moreover, it is pointed out that discrimination itself is defined in unduly narrow, economistic terms. In defining gender discrimination, neo-classical economists define discrimination as including only the portion of the gender gap which cannot be attributed to productivity. Yet discrimination itself might be the cause of ostensibly low productivity.

The critique of neo-liberalism from outside the economic school is more fundamental. Economics, far from being a science, it is argued, is socially constructed (Humphries, 1995). Feminists, in particular, take issue with the underlying assumptions which permeate the neo-liberal analysis of rationality, individualism, and autonomy. The neo-liberal notion of rationality is deeply problematic because it negates the emotional and social ties which legitimately constrain the activities of individuals within the market. For women, the denial of the value of unpaid caring responsibilities limits their meaningful participation in the market; for men, the same denial limits their meaningful participation in the family. Similarly, the notion that women make a rational choice to invest less in their own human capital than men presupposes that there is a range of choices open to women. Women are often faced with the invidious choice between caring for their children at the expense of progress in the paid workforce or progressing in the workforce at the expense of caring for their children. Barriers to a meaningful combination of the two, both generated by the structure of the labour market and the structure of the family, are ignored (Fredman, 1997). Finally the assumption behind State neutrality, namely that market outcomes are desirable unless proved otherwise, is deeply problematic.

3 Modified Liberalism

3.1 Background

Pulling in the opposite direction have been those liberal thinkers whose concern has been to reformulate liberal tenets to take into account principles of distributive justice and egalitarianism. Such thinkers have moved beyond the demand for an abstentionist State, and discrimination is no longer regarded simply as an interaction between two individuals. Corrective justice is seen as legitimately allied with distributive justice. There are, however, important nuances as between different thinkers who fall within this broad group. This section considers the ways in which these liberals have developed the notions of State neutrality, autonomy, individualism, and equality and the influence of these developments on discrimination law.

3.2 State Neutrality

For Dworkin, the key development within liberalism is signified by the change in the relative values accorded to State neutrality, on the one hand, and equality on the other. Traditional liberalism considers State neutrality to be the prime value, with equality merely derivative. It is for this reason that it easily supports a neo-liberal position whereby economic inequalities which arise from the market should not justify State intervention. Modified liberalism, however, regards it as fundamental that the State treat its citizens as equals. Neutrality is derivative; and therefore only required to the extent that it supports equality in this sense (Dworkin, 1985).

Beyond this, however, modified liberals differ in their views as to the legitimate role of the State. For Dworkin, the positive commitment to an egalitarian morality still entails that the State should remain neutral on the question of what constitutes the good life. 'Since the citizens of a society differ in their conceptions [of what gives value to life], the government does not treat them as equals if it prefers one conception to the other, either because the officials believe that one is intrinsically superior, or because one is held by the more numerous or powerful' (Dworkin, 1985: 191). Moral neutrality in this sense does not, however, entail non-intervention in the market. Dworkin recognizes that the market does not allocate resources entirely according to people's free choices. Individuals differ widely in their ability to exercise free choice, whether because of their educational and socio-economic background, their race or class, or even their natural talents. Thus to treat people as equals the State must intervene in the market to the extent necessary to bring some people closer to the share of resources they would have had but for differences in initial advantage, luck, and inherent capacity (Dworkin, 1985: 207). This intervention is, however, a limited one. Treating people as equals requires that each be permitted to use no more than an equal share of the resources available to all, and this can only be accomplished by a market relatively free of State intervention.

The attempt to preserve a moral abstentionism while at the same time permitting State intervention for redistributive aims, is challenged by other liberal thinkers. Dworkin considers that it is a conservative, and not a liberal, who argues that a State may take a position as to which version of the good life is the preferred version

(Dworkin, 1985). Raz, however, argues explicitly for a perfectionist principle, according to which the good can be distinguished from the bad. The State, therefore, has a positive role in promoting the good (Raz, 1986). It is by defining the 'good' according to the primacy of valuable individual autonomy that his liberalism asserts itself. State promotion of the good life is not through authoritarian imposition of a particular value system, but through the creation of conditions of valuable autonomy. Autonomy necessarily requires the acceptability of a plurality of sets of values, within a framework of moral acceptability, derived from a set of shared cultural understandings. Nor is choice simply a formal notion. Raz, recognizing the inherent constraints on choice, argues that personal autonomy requires the existence of a range of acceptable and realistic options. The State's duties therefore include ensuring the availability of an adequate range of options (Raz, 1986: 406). This means that the State is justified in using coercion, not just to stop people from acting to diminish others' autonomy, but also to force people to take actions which are required to improve people's options and opportunities.

The acknowledgement that the State, instead of being under an injunction to remain neutral, may legitimately promote particular values has led to further consideration of what these values might be. A prime contender has been that of human dignity. Drawing on the Kantian injunction that a person should always be treated as an end, and never as a means only, the notion of dignity has been strongly endorsed in both constitutional texts and judicial exposition. This is particularly evident in the jurisprudence of the Canadian Supreme Court and the South African Constitutional Court. However, a closer look at the concept itself reveals that it could have a range of meanings. Various scholars have depicted dignity as connoting innate and indefeasible human worth. Alternatively, dignity could entail, as the Canadian Supreme Court has stated, 'the development of human potential based upon individual ability' (*Miron v Trudel* [1995] 2 SCR 418 at 489). This highly individualistic view can be contrasted with a notion of dignity which entails a decent standard of living, a fair share of the communal resources, and a right to participate as citizens in shaping the moral direction of the community. The malleability of the concept has led other theorists to argue that the principle of equality is weakened by reducing it to dignity. Instead, the complexity of equality needs to be recognized and appropriate legal tools fashioned.

3.3 Individualism

As well as challenging State neutrality, modified liberalism contests its intense individualism. Instead, Fiss substitutes a 'group-disadvantaging principle' (Fiss, 1976). For him, a social group is more than a collection of individuals. It has an identity and a distinct existence apart from its members; and there is an interdependence between the identity and well-being of individual members of the group and the group itself.

Individual members cannot be truly free while the group remains enslaved or perse-cuted; and similarly the group can only continue to exist if members continue to iden-tify or be identified with it. For a group to be within the reach of the equal protection clause, he argues, a further characteristic of a social group is needed—it must have been in a position of perpetual subordination and its political power as a group must be severely circumscribed. Fiss acknowledges that there may be difficulties in defining groups; but he maintains that these definitional disputes do not deny the validity or importance of the idea. Blacks are the prototype of such specially disadvantaged groups; but any other group with the same characteristics would qualify.

Kymlicka's analysis takes this further, concentrating on the positive and affirming aspects of group membership. In developing a 'distinctively liberal defence' of group-differentiated rights, he argues that for meaningful individual choice to be possible, individuals need access to their own societal culture (Kymlicka, 1995: 84). Group membership is crucial to an individual's well-being because of its role in supporting and shaping self-identity. Identification with a societal culture is particularly impor-tant to individual identity because it is based on belonging, not accomplishment; it provides the safety of 'effortless secure belonging' (Margalit and Raz, 1990: 447). This remains, in Kymlicka's view, a liberal rather than a communitarian approach, because the element of choice as to the extent of adherence of a societal culture remains. Communitarians regard some aspects of group or community as constitu-tive of the self, defining who she is. There is therefore no scope for renunciation or revision of those community values. For Kymlicka, by contrast, the individual cru-cially retains the choice (albeit often a costly one) of revising her allegiance to some or all of those ends (Kymlicka, 1995: 91). This analysis has important implications for the conceptualization of equality. Kymlicka rejects the idea that true equality entails no more than equal rights of each individual regardless of race or ethnicity. Instead, group-specific rights are needed to eliminate unfair disadvantage in the cultural marketplace. Like Fiss, however, he emphasizes the need for actual disadvantage, which the group right must in practice mitigate.

The move from an abstentionist State, combined with the acceptance of the group dimension of discrimination, leads to a wider conception by modified liberals of the function of equality laws. Brest, it will be recalled, argued that the function of anti-discrimination law is to prohibit irrational decision-making. Redistribution is not legitimate in respect of race because, argues Brest, race is a poor proxy for poverty. Fiss, by contrast, argues that it is not poverty but the social fact of special disadvan-tage which legitimates State intervention in respect of race and other similar groups. Gardner reinforces this point by demonstrating that in any event the harm principle is insufficient to legitimate anti-discrimination laws. Discrimination on grounds of race or gender is not 'harmful' in any abstract sense, but only when judged against the social and political context. Because the harm is the perpetuation of a social system which has used colour or gender as a reason to subordinate a group of people, the harm principle has significant redistributive elements (Gardner, 1989).

The move from individual to group is not, however, without problems. Two of these loom particularly large. First, how does equality for the group as a whole interact with equality as between members of the group? If the group does not accord some of its own members the same status as others, what is the role of the equality principle? This is particularly true for women, who in countless examples find themselves accorded an inferior position within their own ethnic, religious, or cultural group. The dilemma can be characterized either as a clash between the individual and the group, or as a clash between two different aspects of equality, ethnic equality and gender equality. Kymlicka navigates this dilemma by maintaining that a liberal view requires *freedom within* the minority group and *equality between* the minority and the majority groups (Kymlicka, 1995: 152). But does this not impose the liberal ethic of the majority on the minority, and so contradict the principle that minority groups are entitled to equal treatment with the majority group? For Kymlicka, the clash is not between principles of tolerance and autonomy. Instead, liberal tolerance specifically protects the right of individuals to dissent from their group, as well as the right of groups not to be persecuted by the State. In this sense, autonomy underpins tolerance.

Equally difficult is the question of how the group *qua* group is defined. In asserting that the group as a group has rights, it is tempting to view a group as a fixed category, with a rigid boundary and a set of defined characteristics. Yet this raises a host of difficulties. Are the group characteristics subjectively defined or defined by a set of external criteria? An aspect of group autonomy is surely lost if the group is externally defined, but subjective definition raises questions about the internal hierarchy and decision-making mechanisms of the group. Similarly, the presumption of fixed characteristics ignores the very real dynamism of ethnicity and culture. Moreover, the presumption of rigid boundaries immediately creates a sense of 'absolute otherness': that an individual is defined entirely by the group. In practice, people can belong to more than one group and people move in and out of groups. Young therefore argues that the meaning of group identity needs to be revised. Instead of characterizing a group on the basis of apparently fixed attributes, she argues, a group is constituted by means of a social process of interaction and a subjective affirmation of affinity of individuals. Groups need to define themselves, rather than being subjected to a devalued essence imposed from outside. This in turn entails a re-conceptualization of the equality–difference dichotomy. Instead of difference connoting deviance from a single norm, difference is about relationships between and within groups (Young, 1990).

Other theorists concentrate their attack on individualism by challenging the concept of merit. Thus Fallon and Weiler (1985) contest the view that individuals have a moral right to benefits which their talents and efforts otherwise would bring them. This assumes that personal autonomy requires the operation of a free market which distributes benefits entirely on the basis of merit. However, they demonstrate that this argument is flawed. Merit is not an objective yardstick, but is itself based on transient market-based appetites and technological development. More importantly, the market does not in fact reward merit *per se*. The ultimate distribution of resources depends as much on the material and educational advantages an individual brings to the market (Fallon and Weiler, 1985: 41). Similarly, Dworkin argues that there is no combination of abilities and qualities that constitutes 'merit' in the abstract; it all depends on a judgement as to which abilities are useful for the job or training in question. If a woman or a black person may because of their gender or race do a particular job better (for example, as a medical doctor), then gender or race counts as 'merit'. 'That argument may strike some as dangerous; but only because they confuse its conclusion—that black skin may be a socially useful trait in particular circumstances—with the very different and despicable idea that one race may be inherently more worthy than another' (Dworkin, 1985: 299).

Fallon and Weiler stop short of wholly endorsing the group-disadvantaging principle advocated by Fiss. Respect for the individual, they argue, cannot be entirely subordinated to respect for the group. Thus they prefer a model of 'social justice' which has a dual aim. On the one hand, an equality principle should recognize that discrimination goes beyond individual acts of prejudice directed against individual victims. 'Rectification expresses a moral rejection, not only of wilful, individual wrongs, but of the pervasive systematic discrimination that has left blacks as a class in a status of economic deprivation' (Fallon and Weiler, 1985: 30). On the other hand, fairness to individuals should also be considered, in particular, in allocating the cost of rectification. In the context of affirmative action, therefore, it is possible to justify reverse discrimination in terms of the first aim, but only if the cost to individual whites is not disproportionately large.

Raz challenges individualism from a different and equally fundamental angle. Although for Raz, individual autonomy remains the prime value, such autonomy is not based on a presumption of atomistic individuals who should be free to pursue their own self-interest, limited only by the injunction that such pursuits should not harm others. Personal well-being is based as much on collective public values as individual values. Such collective goods are valuable in themselves; they are not simply instrumental in enhancing individual self-interest (Raz, 1986: 18, 193–206). Personal autonomy can only be enhanced within a social context, one which includes the institutions and network of human relationships which are essential to human existence. In his view, it is crucial for the development of normal relationships that an individual understands his or her own tastes and goals in ways which relate to others and incorporate the mosaic of values inherent in social life (Raz, 1985: 215).

3.4 Application to the Law

Modified liberal theory provides a strong theoretical basis for modern anti-discrimination law. First, it makes it possible to develop the scope of protection beyond the paradigm of race discrimination. By focusing on actual social and political disadvantage rather than on abstract notions of justice, it is possible to develop principles, as Fiss has done, for identifying groups which should be protected. The advantages of this strategy are that they do not depend on criteria such as immutable characteristics, which are of dubious validity; and they permit courts to develop the coverage of the equality concept in a principled fashion. Nevertheless, there is still room for deep controversy over which groups fulfil these characteristics. Notably, Fiss puts women in the category of those which do not fall within his category of 'pure' specially disadvantaged groups. By contrast, in Europe, as we have seen, it is gender which is seen as the paradigm group warranting protection, a protection which was only very recently extended to race.

Secondly, modified liberalism justifies the development of the discrimination concept beyond direct discrimination, which focuses on less favourable treatment by one individual of another, to indirect discrimination, or disparate impact which is concerned with the disproportionate impact, of apparently equal treatment. Modified liberalism has no difficulty with a group-based analysis. Modified liberal theory similarly provides a coherent defence of reverse discrimination. Since colour-blindness or gender neutrality is not an end in itself, but instead the yardstick is actual disadvantage, an asymmetric approach is inevitable. As Dworkin argues: 'The difference between a general racial classification that causes further disadvantage to those who have suffered from prejudice and a classification framed to help them is morally significant' (Dworkin, 1985: 314). Thus to appoint or promote a person because of their colour or gender is not anathema, provided it is framed to alleviate rather than cause disadvantage.

In both these contexts, discrimination is characterized as more than just an interaction between an individual perpetrator and an individual victim. This means that it is necessary to justify placing the remedial burden on employers or others who are not 'at fault'. For Raz, the failure to improve the situation of another is a kind of harm (Raz, 1986: 416). Anyone who is capable of remedying a social ill is 'at fault' if he or she fails to do so. Thus it is entirely legitimate to expect employers to remedy institutional discrimination even if they have not personally caused it. This merges the 'fault' and the 'redistributive' principles: it is because employers are in control of the very valuable resource of jobs and employment opportunities that they can legitimately be required to take action to reduce disparate impact (Gardner, 1989). Liberals within this camp nevertheless disagree on the extent to which the burden should be borne by those who have had no part in causing structural discrimination. As we have seen, Fallon and Weiler, while recognizing the power of pervasive discrimination, also assert that fairness to individuals should be considered, particularly in allocating the cost of rectification. They are therefore prepared to justify reverse discrimination in favour of blacks only if the cost to individual whites is not disproportionately large.

4 CRITICAL THEORY

We have seen that, within the liberal camp, the basic tenets of liberalism have been stretched in different directions, to embrace market ideology on the one hand, and to incorporate social welfare and distributive issues on the other. There is, however, a substantial body of critique which distances itself altogether from the liberal camp, challenging the basic tenets of liberalism in all their forms. Although feminists and critical race theorists have much in common, it is convenient to deal with them separately.

4.1 Feminism

Faced with the imperviousness of gender inequality to liberal anti-discrimination laws, feminist writers argue that the central concepts of liberalism are incapable of pushing the boundaries of emancipation any further (Jaggar, 1983; Lacey, 1998; Fredman, 1997). Particularly problematic is the aura of Truth and Justice which attaches to law and legal reasoning (Smart, 1989). Under the guise of objectivity and neutrality, feminists argue, law in fact embodies the standards of the dominant culture, which are inescapably male. In the vivid words of Catharine MacKinnon, man is the measure of all (MacKinnon, 1990). One of the chief tasks of feminist critique, therefore, is to unmask the male perspective in law. At the same time, legal ideology is regarded as important social text, one that can illuminate cultural constructions of gender, as well as influence them (Rhode, 1990: 198).

4.1.1 *Rationality, Individualism, and Choice*

Feminists also challenge the notions of rationality, individualism, and choice which underpin liberal ideology. The conception of rationality as the pursuit of one's own self-interest or conception of the good ignores a core reality of human existence, namely the dependence of young children, of the aged, the sick, and the disabled (Jaggar, 1983: 45). It is no accident that the altruism which is negated by this conception of rationality has historically been primarily the function of women. Indeed, for feminists, one of the most fundamental flaws of liberalism is its failure to address the crucial role of the family. Characterizing the citizen as a rational individual exercising free choice within the public arena, liberals negate the family while simultaneously depending on women to continue to perform the invisible role of supporting paid labour and reproducing the species. Liberals are able to assert the prime value of individual autonomy only because they ignore the constraints created by relationships of dependency. Equally seriously, this analysis obscures power relationships within the family, particularly the possibility of men's domination of women within the family. Neo-liberal analysis, in particular, despite resting on a strong assertion of the liberty and formal equality of individuals within the market, nevertheless takes the power structures within the family as an unalterable given.

The advances represented by modified liberalism do not, from the feminist perspective, go far enough. Many liberal thinkers continue to depict the family as an individual by equation with the 'head of household'. Even more disturbing, argue feminist theorists, is Dworkin's analysis. Dworkin depicts the family as an association based on reciprocal obligations. 'I have special responsibilities to my brother by virtue of our brotherhood, but these are sensitive to the degree to which he accepts such responsibilities toward me' (Dworkin, 1986: 198). The notion that family ties arise from an expectation of reciprocity simply fails to capture the relationship of dependency by children on their parents. Dworkin's emphasis on individual choice of the good life is similarly problematic. In a dependency situation, whereby one person's activities are dictated by another's needs for care, or indeed survival, choice in this sense is simply an irrelevant concept. It is therefore not sufficient to characterize a mother's care for her baby as a manifestation of her choice of the good, which includes caring for babies. Care for babies is neither a choice, nor a constraint on choice. It is both a value in itself, and a necessary activity, not just for the baby and its parents, but for society as a whole. Feminists argue, therefore, that caring responses to dependence should be considered as primary values in themselves, rather than squeezed into a paradigm of self-interest (Fredman, 1997). Because of these features, the response of the law should be to require the workplace and other institutions of society to be adapted to accommodate child-bearing and child-care; rather than, under the guise of respect for individual choice, to neglect them.

4.1.2 Equality or Difference?

Also central to the feminist project is the critique of the notion of equality. One of the key achievements of feminism has been to unmask the underlying normative premises of equality. Equality is a relative concept, depending fundamentally on a comparative yardstick. Thus, in order to decide if a woman has a right to equal treatment, it is first necessary to answer the question: equal to whom? The answer, inevitably is, 'equal to a man' (MacKinnon, 1987: 33). Seen in this light, it is clear that the liberal strategy of equality amounts to the assimilation of women to a norm set by and for men. This critique also applies to more developed notions of equality as equality of opportunity or equality of results (Lacey, 1998: 240).

This insight has led many feminists to opt instead for an assertion of women's difference. In a highly influential empirical study, Gilligan found that, when addressing moral problems, or describing relationships between the self and others, women tended to speak in a different voice from men. The contrast between the male and female perceptions appears most significantly in the depiction of the self: the male as a self defined through separation; the female as a self delineated through connection. In the male voice, relationships with others are depicted as adversarial. Responsibility is therefore characterized in terms of limiting your own interference with others in order to ensure that others limit their interference with you. Autonomy is protected through reciprocity (see Dworkin, 1986: 198). In the female voice, responsibility signifies response, extension rather than limitation, doing what others are counting on you to do rather than what you yourself want (Gilligan, 1982: 38). The expression of care is seen as the fulfilment of moral responsibility (ibid. 73). This leads to an apparent conflict between 'a morality of rights that dissolves natural bonds and a morality of responsibility that knits such claims into a fabric or relationship, blurring the distinction between self and other through the representation of their interdependence' (ibid. 132).

The work of Gilligan and others, and the disappointment in the practical ineffectiveness of discrimination laws based on an equality principle, have led feminists to argue for a rhetoric of difference, based in part on special rights for women. This is particularly apposite in the context of pregnancy, where equality as a foundation for proper treatment has repeatedly been proved blatantly inappropriate. However, the reliance on difference as a substitute for equality has some fundamental problems. Indeed, the difference–equality debate itself falls into the trap, dating back to Aristotle, of conceiving the world in terms of a set of dichotomies. For Aristotle, the male is active, the female passive; the male contributes the soul, the female the body; the male is strong, the female weak. These dualisms have been extrapolated into contemporary thought: opposing reason with emotion, self with other, individual with community, public with private. In each dualism, the second is conceived of as inferior, and the feminine is equated with the less valued of the pair (Lacey, 1998: 194). The assumption that they are mutually exclusive makes it impossible to conceive of both sets of qualities co-existing in a single individual, or the accommodation of both within a legal system.

Even if the male norm can be replaced by a female norm of comparison, a further problem remains: that of assuming that all women share an 'essence'. This essence is itself a social construction and can be permeated with problematic assumptions. In particular, the 'woman' is often constructed as white, middle class, Western, Christian, heterosexual, and able-bodied. This has the effect of negating the needs and experiences of women who do not fall into these categories. Gilligan herself stresses that the different voices she describes are characterized not by gender but by theme, and that their association with gender is an empirical observation. In addition, she shows that as children grow up, they are able to establish a dialectical connection between the two modes of thought.

4.1.3 *Beyond the Equality–Difference Debate*

Instead of becoming trapped in this debate, therefore, it is necessary to look beyond equality and difference to the underlying power structures. 'Viewing gender as a matter of sameness and difference—as virtually all existing law and theory does in one way or another—is a way of covering up the reality of gender, which is a system of social hierarchy. Gender is an imposed inequality of power first, a social status based on who is permitted to do what to whom ... Differences are inequality's post hoc excuse' (MacKinnon, 1990: 213; Rhode, 1990). However, the project of reconstructing rights to reflect feminist insights remains a challenging one. Lacey argues that feminism has made a crucial contribution in exposing the gendered nature of law's power, but the task of reconstructing the law must not be abandoned (Lacey, 1998: 219). This is a complex and paradoxical task, since the very use of legal instruments could amount to co-option to its ideology. Thus any legal change must be premised on 'massive changes in the configuration of social power at every level' (ibid. 248).

4.2 Critical Race Theory

Critical race theory was generated not only as a critique of mainstream liberal ideology, but also by a need for a minority perspective on the critical legal studies movement (CLS). While some critical race theorists feel able to derive their critique direct from CLS, others argue trenchantly that CLS had not only paid far too little attention to minorities, but also that its basic assumptions misunderstand and therefore fail to be of relevance to the real-life problems of racial discrimination. This brief discussion therefore begins with critical legal theory and its bearing on racial discrimination, and then moves on to the critique of critical legal theory.

4.2.1 *State Neutrality*

Like feminist theory, CLS powerfully contests the apparent neutrality of the law and legal rights. Instead, the law is portrayed as largely serving to legitimize the existing social structure and, especially, class relations within that structure. At the same time law serves as part of the process of forming and crystalizing dominant moral positions. Freeman (1978) draws on this central insight to expose the dissonance between the discourse of civil liberties and the reality of disadvantage and inequality. 'As surely as the law has outlawed racial discrimination, it has affirmed that Black Americans can be without jobs, have their children in all-black, poorly funded schools, have no opportunities for decent housing and have very little political power, without any violation of anti-discrimination law' (Freeman, 1978). Legal doctrine is manipulated to legitimate continuing domination: the persuasiveness of legal discourse convinces individuals of the efficacy of the law; but in reality, law obstructs change or maintains the status quo. This is centrally revealed through the adoption by the law of a 'perpetrator perspective' in defining a violation of discrimination law. In other words, rather than recognizing the conditions of actual social existence as a member of a perpetual underclass, the law's task is merely to neutralize the inappropriate conduct of the perpetrator. Ultimately, since the main aim of law is to legitimize and preserve the existing structure, it cannot be expected to be an engine of change (Freeman, 1978).

4.2.2 *Rights*

Rights rhetoric is a further target of CLS critique. Tushnet (1984) argues that rights construct individuals as isolated rights-bearers; and since rights are invariably concerned with property and security, rights necessarily place individuals in conflict with one another. Thus rights inevitably alienate individuals from each other. By filtering our experience of solidarity and individuality through the abstract and ulti- mately indeterminate filter of rights, we lose sight of our real ideals. Rights discourse impedes advances by progressive social forces and real demands are absorbed into a vacuous discourse. The language of rights should therefore be abandoned, and pop- ular aspirations for change be recast in the language of solidarity and individuality.

Delgado (1987) and Crenshaw (1988), however, argue that CLS does not constitute, on its own, a sufficient theoretical basis to capture the real issues of racial discrimi- nation. For Crenshaw, there are three major flaws in the CLS approach. First, CLS thinkers see the key problem as the power of ideology to achieve domination by con- sent. This ignores the real experience of black people, which is that racial domination is achieved by coercion, not by ideologically induced consent. Secondly, CLS theor- ists assume that racial domination is merely an aspect of class domination. By contrast, critical race theorists see it as essential to recognize the ways in which racism operates in its own right to maintain hegemony. Thirdly, by 'trashing' rights consciousness, CLS theorists disregard the transformative potential of rights.

For Crenshaw, it is this third issue that is key to her distinctive critical race theory. Crenshaw takes issue with the view that thinking in terms of rights is incompatible with feelings of solidarity. Instead, she argues, the expression of rights was a central organizing feature of the civil rights movement. Because blacks had been routinely denied rights, their assertion of their rights constituted a serious ideological challenge to white supremacy. For the very reason that rights have such strong ideo- logical power, the assertion by an excluded group of their own rights, the turning of the society's logic against itself, can be a powerful weapon in the hands of the politic- ally dispossessed (Crenshaw, 1988). In the same way as women in Britain exposed the contradictions in liberal logic by demanding that rights be extended to all human beings (Fredman, 1997), so blacks during the civil rights period were able to force institutional change on the basis of the very ideology which Americans believed fundamental to its culture (Crenshaw, 1988). 'Casting racial issues in the moral and legal rights rhetoric of the prevailing ideology helped create the political controversy without which the state's coercive function would not have been enlisted to aid Blacks' (Crenshaw, 1988).

However, in the same way as women in Britain discovered that the gains made through formal entitlements were ultimately limited, so the extent to which civil rights in the United States can bring about real equality is demonstrably circumscribed. Crenshaw acknowledges that the attainment of formal equality is not the end of the story. She also acknowledges the risks associated with engaging in 'inherently legitimating discourse'. For Crenshaw, a new approach should not 'be defined and thereby limited by the possibilities of dominant political discourse, but should maintain a distinctly progressive outlook that focuses on the needs of the African-American community' (Crenshaw, 1998: 1387). As in the case of feminist theorists, the challenge of devising such an approach is raised but not resolved in her work. It is perhaps in the new generation equality rights that some of these issues are addressed, albeit only in their formative stages. It is with a brief description of this approach that this chapter ends.

5 A New Generation?

In the past decade, a new approach to discrimination law has been emerging and theorizing is hastening to catch up with practical legal change (McCrudden, 1999; Hepple *et al.*, 2000). This approach takes on board the critique of liberalism and attempts to move beyond it by positing positive duties to promote equality, rather than just the negative requirement to refrain from discriminating. Positive duties are based on the recognition that societal discrimination extends well beyond the acts of individual perpetrators against identifiable victims. Instead, the problem is embedded in many social institutions and practices. Responsibility for change therefore lies with those who are in a position to bring about change, rather than those who have 'caused' the problem. Consequently too, positive duties are proactive. Instead of simply responding to a complaint by an individual victim, the new approach requires responsible agents to identify the problem and take proactive measures to address it. Positive duties are frequently expressed in the concept of mainstreaming, which requires policy-makers to incorporate a gender or other equality perspective in all policies at all levels and at all stages (McCrudden, 1999). 'Mainstreaming approaches are intended to be anticipatory, rather than essentially retrospective, to be extensively participatory, rather than limited to small groups of the knowledgeable and to be integrated into the activities of those primarily involved in policy-making' (McCrudden, 1999: 1697). Raz's theory provides the best account of the duty positively to promote equality. Because it legitimates the State's role in providing the conditions of valuable flourishing for its citizens, there is no need to justify either State intervention, or the placing of burdens on individuals.

A particularly important dimension of positive duties is their potential to encourage participation from affected parties. Because the duty is prospective, and should be fashioned to fit the problem at hand, it requires a continuing process of diagnosis, strategic decisions, and evaluation of progress. Participation not only makes it likely that strategies will be more successful, but the very process of achieving equality becomes a democratic one. This in turn potentially transforms the nature of rights. Instead of functioning as a barricade around individual interests, the right to equality becomes a pathway to belonging. Mary Robinson recently emphasized

how crucial to the concept of rights is the concept of participation. People should not be just docile subjects of rights: rights are never 'given' to people. Rights must be asserted, and they must be asserted on one's own behalf and on behalf of all other human beings, without decision. [This] has produced an understanding of participation which allows people to become agents of their own change. (McCrudden, 1999: 1771)

Changing the structure of equality laws in these ways is an important step forward. However, having moved away from the notion of corrective justice, they throw open the question of exactly what equality means and what are the aims to be achieved. Many positive duties appear to be furthering a redistributive aim in that they are formulated in terms of improving the representation of minorities or women in a given sector. These aims themselves require further scrutiny. Is diversity an end in itself, or does a change in colour or gender outcomes signify that equality of opportunity has been achieved? If the representation pattern has changed this might be because strategies of assimilation have been successful in some cases, rather than because underlying structures have changed. Representation of minorities might improve because some of its members have felt compelled to assimilate to dominant cultures. More women might be in higher positions because they have chosen not to have children or delegated their child-care responsibilities to other women who remain low paid and are given little social status. There remains much work for legal theorists and policy-makers to do in order to provide a full theoretical explanation of the new developments.

REFERENCES

Abram, M. (1986). 'Affirmative Action: Fair Shakers and Social Engineers', *Harvard Law Review*, 99: 1312–26.

Barnes, J. (1982). *The Complete Works of Aristotle*, Oxford: Oxford University Press.

Brest, P. (1976). 'In Defence of the Anti-discrimination Principle', *Harvard Law Review*, 90: 1–54.

Crenshaw, K. (1988). 'Race, Reform and Retrenchment: Transformation and Legitimation in Anti-discrimination Law', *Harvard Law Review*, 101: 1331–87.

Deakin, S., and Wilkinson, F. (1991). *The Economics of Employment Rights*, London: Institute of Employment Rights.

Delgado, R. (1987). 'The Ethereal Scholar: Does Critical Legal Studies Have What Minorities Want?' *Harvard Civil Rights—Civil Liberties Law Review*, 22: 301–22.

Donohue, J. III. (1986). 'Is Title VII Efficient?' *University of Pennsylvania Law Review*, 134: 1411–31.

Dworkin, R. (1985). *A Matter of Principle*, Oxford: Oxford University Press.

—— (1986). *Law's Empire*, London: Fontana.

Epstein, R. (1992). *The Case against Employment Discrimination Law*, Cambridge, Mass.: Harvard University Press.

Fallon, R. H., and Weiler, P. C. (1985). 'Firefighters v Stotts: Conflicting Models of Racial Justice', *Supreme Court Review*: 1–68.

Fiss, O. M. (1976). 'Groups and the Equal Protection Clause', *Philosophy and Public Affairs*, 5: 107–77.

Fredman, S. (1997). *Women and the Law*, Oxford: Oxford University Press.

Freeman, A. D. (1978). 'Legitimizing Racial Discrimination through Anti-discrimination Law', *Minnesota Law Review*, 62: 1049–119.

Gardner, J. (1989). 'Liberals and Unlawful Discrimination', *Oxford Journal of Legal Studies*, 9: 1–22.

Gilligan, C. (1982). *In a Different Voice*, Cambridge, Mass.: Harvard University Press.

Hayek, F. A. (1960). *The Constitution of Liberty*, London: Routledge & Kegan Paul.

Hepple, B., Coussey, M., and Choudhury, T. (2000). *Equality: A New Framework*, Oxford: Hart.

Humphries, J. (1995). 'Economics, Gender and Equal Opportunities', in J. Humphries and J. Rubery (eds.), *The Economics of Equal Opportunities*, London: Equal Opportunities Commission.

Jaggar, A. M. (1983). *Feminist Politics and Human Nature*, Totona, NJ: Rowman & Allanheld; Brighton: Harvester.

Kymlicka, W. (1995). *Multicultural Citizenship: A Liberal Theory of Minority Rights*, Oxford: Oxford University Press.

Lacey, N. (1998). *Unspeakable Subjects*, Oxford: Hart.

McCrudden, C. (1999). 'Mainstreaming Equality in the Governance of Northern Ireland', *Fordham International Law Journal*, 22: 1697–774.

MacKinnon, C. A. (1990). 'Legal Perspectives on Sexual Difference', in D. L. Rhode (ed.), *Theoretical Perspectives on Sexual Difference*, New Haven: Yale University Press.

Margalit, J., and Raz, J. (1995). 'National Self Determination', in W. Kymlicka (ed.), *The Rights of Minority Cultures*, Oxford: Oxford University Press.

Polachek, S. W., and Siebert, W. S. (1993). *The Economics of Earnings*, Cambridge: Cambridge University Press.

Posner, R. A. (1989). 'An Economic Analysis of Sex Discrimination Law', *University of Chicago Law Review*, 56: 1311–35.

Raz, J. (1986). *The Morality of Freedom*, Oxford: Clarendon Press.

Rhode, D. L. (1990). 'Definitions of Difference', in D. L. Rhode (ed.), *Theoretical Perspectives on Sexual Difference*, New Haven: Yale University Press.

Smart, C. (1989). *Feminism and the Power of the Law*, London: Routledge.

Tushnet, M. (1984). 'An Essay on Rights', *Texas Law Review*, 62: 1363–403.

Tussman, J., and tenBroek, J. (1949). 'The Equal Protection of the Laws', *California Law Review*, 37: 341–81.

Waldron, J. (1996). 'Minority Cultures and the Cosmopolitan Alternative', in W. Kymlicka (ed.), *The Rights of Minority Cultures*, Oxford: Oxford University Press.

Young, I. M. (1990). *Justice and the Politics of Difference*, Princeton: Princeton University Press.

CHAPTER 12

CRIMINAL LAW

JEREMY HORDER

SCHOLARS coming afresh to the study of criminal law are indeed fortunate. Over the last twenty years, important and sophisticated new theoretical approaches have evolved, and much new theoretical life has been breathed into more traditional approaches, to their mutual benefit. I hope to convey at least a flavour of these developments here, but my overarching theme has a different focus. My story is that of over-ambition and (all-too-often) under-achievement on the part of those who believe the task of 'theory' is to give very detailed and definite shape to the 'universalizable' part of the criminal law. As we shall see, it may be possible to devise a set of simplified and general universalizable maxims of criminal liability, to which all States could be urged to adhere in their criminal codes and case law. Beyond the formulation of such simplified maxims, however, richness and diversity in criminal law theory should go hand in hand with richness and diversity in criminal law doctrine. Whatever the strength of the case for, say, a uniform commercial law code, the belief that there needs to be a uniform criminal code is founded on theoretical error as well as political naivety.

1 LAW REFORM, AND THE SPIRIT OF BENTHAM'S POSITIVISM

For a great number of criminal law scholars worldwide, the intellectual legacy of the late nineteenth century was a codified system of doctrine as an object of study. To give

I am very grateful to John Gardner, for his efforts in helping me to shape the direction of my contribution, and improve it more generally. Naturally, responsibility for the final product rests with me.

an eclectic selection of examples, criminal codes were first enacted (or substantially revised) in India in 1860, in California in 1872, in Japan in 1880, in New York in 1881, in the Netherlands in 1886, in Brazil and in Italy in 1890, in Argentina (based on the Dutch code of 1886) in 1891, in Canada in 1892, in New Zealand in 1893, in Bangladesh in 1898, in Queensland in 1901, and in Imperial Russia in 1903. These criminal codes rarely embodied revolutionary new legal thinking, most amounting to little more than consolidation of the pre-existing law, the codification occasionally reflecting a wish to assert legislative freedom from a former colonial power. Even so, the late nineteenth-century codification movement testified, in some measure, to the growing influence of utilitarian philosophy, and of an early strain of positivist legal theory.

Early positivist thinking (given wide intellectual currency through the influence on his followers of the utilitarian radical, Jeremy Bentham) placed the primary emphasis in the development of a mature legal system on turning law into a clear, comprehensive, and independent system of conduct-guidance. In practice, the realization of early positivist codifiers' ambitions entailed switching responsibility for major substantive changes to the criminal law from the higher courts to the legislature. As indicated above, in much of the common law world and beyond, significant steps had been taken towards this end by the beginning of the twentieth century. However, there is plenty of life left in the codification movement, particularly if measured by Bentham's test of whether, at the end of the codification process, there was 'no terrae incognitae, no blank spaces: nothing is at least omitted, nothing unprovided for'. For example, for reasons discussed below, there was much less enthusiasm for legislative inroads on the common law in the jurisdictions within the United Kingdom. Moreover, in the United States and in Australia (as well as within the European Union), where individual States have separate criminal jurisdictions, there is pressure to move to a more uniform system (Robinson *et al.*, 2000). In countries such as New Zealand, where the existing criminal codes predate the enactment of a Bill of Rights, criminal codes have begun to look in some respects outdated and in need of substantial reform. What is now the driving intellectual force behind the continuing pressure for further codification or re-codification of the criminal law?

In part, it has been the wish to snuff out once and for all the flickering flame of judicial creativity in the field of criminal law, creativity preserved in part by the perceived need to adopt expansive interpretations of older codified crimes, to meet new circumstances. Recommending codification of the criminal law, in his famous letter to the US President, Bentham derided the courts' role in the development of the criminal law. For Bentham, it had led to nothing but 'uncertainty and uncognoscibility . . . and, instead of compliance and obedience, the evil of transgression, mixed with the evil of punishment . . . and in the hands of the judge, power everywhere arbitrary, with the semblance of a set of rules to serve as a screen to it' (Schofield and Harris, 1998: 20).

Unbending hostility to judge-made criminal law has continued to inspire many of the more radical academic codifiers in the modern era, who have more or less self-consciously donned Bentham's mantle, a mantle of special significance to English criminal lawyers. As indicated above, in England, and to a greater or lesser extent in the separate jurisdictions of Scotland and Ireland (as, for a long time, in some African states), piecemeal legislative innovation or reform of particular areas of law was never followed by overarching codification, even of a consolidating kind. Despite the tireless efforts of the great Victorian judge and jurist Sir James Fitzjames Stephen—who himself drafted criminal codes in 1878 and 1879 that shaped legislation in other common law jurisdictions such as Queensland and Canada—proposals for a criminal code for England and Wales repeatedly failed to make the statute-book, although there were some legislative consolidations. Why? The fault lay in part with the zealously protective attitude adopted by judges (even those in favour of conservative and modest codification, like Stephen himself) towards existing criminal law doctrines fashioned through the so-called 'common law method' of legal development. Stephen claimed that the virtue of English criminal law was that it was 'formed by very slow degrees and with absolutely no conscious adaptation of means to ends', that its trials were characterized by 'dignity, order and calmness', and that it possessed 'an internal organic unity ... wanting in the [French] system' (Stephen, 1883, i: 565).

Perhaps unsurprisingly, this idealistic characterization of judge-made criminal law has been firmly rejected by the modern, more radical criminal law codifiers. So, for Glanville Williams, 'the expansion of the law is unavowed ... the judges keeping up the pretence that they are mere mouthpieces of the law', whereas in reality, 'to the discerning eye [a judicial decision] is often no more than ... rationalisation accompanied by misdirection and legerdemain' (Williams, 1983: 16). Such sentiments are commonly shared across the Atlantic, where Paul Robinson speaks for many in claiming that, 'It is imperative ... that a code include all appropriate defences and leave nothing to the whim of the judiciary' (Robinson et al., 2000: 17).

In spite of these strong sentiments, however, there has been a growing sense of unease about the lofty ambitions of the more radical academic codifiers. Some blame the codification movement for damping down the philosophical interest in doctrine that might be sparked by a more open-textured and revisable criminal law. So, for George Fletcher, the heavy-handed comprehensiveness of Bentham-style codification (what he dismisses as the 'dogmas of the Model Penal Code') 'stifles theoretical enquiry', inhibiting the investigation of 'the philosophical issues that lie behind the code' (Fletcher, 1998: 284). He does not say much, however, about why codification might have this effect. Worse still, even for enthusiastic supporters of comprehensive codification, there is the worry about what a modern legislature that embarked on a radical programme of codification might feel itself empowered to do. The worry stems from disillusionment with the way in which the legislature uses (and, in truth, always has used) the criminal law. For Robinson (Robinson et al., 2000: 64), 'The very immediacy and import of [US] criminal law render it all the more susceptible to mere politicking rather than deliberate craftsmanship' (the entrenchment of constitutional guarantees and protections for the individual in the United States seems to have done little to prevent this). For Glanville Williams, 'Statutes, which are generally drafted by Government officials, often neglect juristic principles' (Williams, 1983: 18). The contrast being drawn here—'mere politicking', as opposed to 'deliberate crafts-manship' or 'juristic principles'—is revealing. One senses a touching faith, held by all radical would-be codifiers, in the existence of a realm of law reform beyond politics. In this technocratic realm held together by conservative or social democratic consensus (according to taste), laws are forged through 'open government using the best brains of the legal profession', and shaped by 'reasoned consideration and consensual amendment' (Williams, 1983: 18).

In the meantime, of course, the governments to whom codifiers appeal have become increasingly disdainful of so-called 'expert advice', as the full implications of their ability to rule without seeking to heal social divisions—through vulgar popu-larism and shallow appeals to sentiment—have become clear. The worry must be that the codifiers' 'noble dream' will turn into a nightmare, in which an all-embracing criminal code becomes the vehicle for authoritarian legislative repression, rather than a bastion against it. Lest we be too quick to condemn, however, some considera-tion must be given to the so-called 'juristic principles' held dear by radical codifiers who reject Stephen's more conservative project of placing most of the common law on a legislative footing. What are these principles?

2 SUBJECTIVISM AND THE SPIRIT OF LIBERTY

For Stephen, the English approach of limited codification of the criminal law, embodying common law rules and principles, meant that 'it is unnecessary to distin-guish between the morality of the Legislator and that of the persons legislated for, for the two may be considered practically identical'. By way of contrast, he thought 'the spirit of French legislation ... is very favourable to persons in authority', and 'a dictator like Napoleon [is] placed in such circumstances that he can practically impose his own will on a great nation' (Stephen, 1883, ii: 77). In this contrast, we find implicit a Blackstonian patriotic appeal to defend 'THE LIBERTY OF BRITAIN' (Blackstone's phrase, and his capitals in the original (Smith, 1998: 24)), enshrined in common law prin-ciples, against the bogy of unrestrained legislative tyranny. Such sentiments—it is worth noting—would also certainly have struck a chord in the hearts of many early nineteenth-century American criminal lawyers, self-conscious heirs to the Blackstonian tradition. Bombastic claims of this kind, about the 'Englishness' of English criminal law's supposed emphasis on the liberty of the subject, inspired the early generations of modern criminal law scholars, particularly those in what one might call the 'Cambridge school' (C. S. Kenny; J. W. C. Turner; L. Radzinowicz;

Glanville Williams). For Sir Leon Radzinowicz, writing in 1945, English criminal law was 'definitely anti-authoritarian', whereas the criminal law in Germany (Germany having by now supplanted France as the new intellectual as well as military enemy) was 'unanimously recognised as a classical embodiment of the authoritarian conception of criminal policy' (Radzinowicz, 1945: 34). Even so stern a critic of the judiciary's handling of the criminal law as Glanville Williams claimed that, 'We enjoy a blessed degree of political liberty, and part of the credit for this is due to the judges' (Williams, 1983: 16–17).

Such claims about the link between liberty and the (Anglo-American) common law, whatever their (de)merit, form an essential part of the background when assessing the development, begun in earnest by the aforementioned scholars, of perhaps the most important intellectual influence on modern criminal law thinkers in the Benthamite positivist tradition, namely 'subjectivism', defined below (Smith, 1998, ch. 4). For Williams, requirements of subjective (advertent) fault in serious offences are a mark of 'advancing civilization', because such offences involve 'so drastic an interference with the liberty of the subject' (Williams, 1983: 70). For Andrew Ashworth, the judges should adopt a 'defensive' approach to interpreting criminal statutes to reflect 'the importance of protecting individuals from undue State power' (Ashworth, 1999: 28). For him, such an approach entails subjectivism, as an aspect of 'The principle of autonomy [that] assigns great importance to liberty and individual rights in any discussion of what the state ought to do in a given situation' (ibid.). A previous generations of judges like Stephen, of course, saw a need to preserve—through consolidating codification, if need be—the *common law* to defend liberty against the potentially tyrannous excesses of legislative means–end rationality. For late-twentieth-century thinkers it is (ironically) *legislation* that is ideally needed to defend and promote liberty, in spite of such thinkers' misgivings (discussed earlier) about the character of current legislative forays into criminal law reform. This is to be done through the adoption of subjectivist principles of liability hitherto consistently ignored in judicial development of the criminal law. So, in Robinson's proposed criminal code for US states (Robinson, 1997: 42–9) as in the Draft Criminal Code for England and Wales, conduct is not criminal unless (with some important exceptions, considered below) it is committed intentionally or recklessly, recklessness being defined as conscious disregard (Robinson), or awareness (Law Commission for England and Wales) of a risk that it is unreasonable to take. What does it mean to say that such principles are 'subjectivist' in character, and what is the link with the defence of liberty?

There are a number of subtly different ways in which one might claim to be a defender of 'subjectivism', in different parts of the criminal law. Subjectivists typically build their attack on what they perceive to be the 'objectivist' or 'moralistic' common law of crimes around one or more of the following four propositions (loosely expressed):

1. *The 'pure mens rea' principle.* One should be criminally liable for one's wrongful choices. Liability should turn on whether one intended to commit a crime, or on

whether one consciously and wrongfully disregarded the risk that the *actus reus* might occur. In this regard, *whether the prohibited outcome intended or risked in fact occurred is not relevant to criminal liability*.

2. *The 'advertent wrongdoing' principle*. One should be criminally liable in respect of harm or wrong done if one 'chose' to do that harm or wrong. *What matters is whether one was subjectively at fault when committing (or attempting or risking) the harm or wrong*, that is, whether one did it, in all its aspects, intentionally, knowingly, recklessly, or dishonestly, and so on.

I have phrased these two principles as if they were principles of what one might call an 'inculpatory' subjectivism, a subjectivism that provides a justification for criminal liability in certain very restricted circumstances. This might be thought perversely to overlook the historical thrust of subjectivism, just outlined above, as a *defensive* approach to criminal liability, meant to keep the State at bay by saying a good deal about when criminal liability is unjustified, but saying little about when and why it is justified. It is, however, one of the marks of modern subjectivism that inculpatory principles have now been squeezed into what was originally a more unashamedly exculpatory framework, making that framework far less capable of containing the divergent forces at work in modern subjectivist theory. Even so, alongside these inculpatory principles are two clearly exculpatory ones, more consistent with the traditional defensive approach adhered to by many subjectivists:

3. *The 'relative standards' principle*. The standards by which the defendant is to be judged, in assessing his or her entitlement to excuse or justification, must be standards that the defendant him or herself—with his or her particular characteristics and capacities—could have met in the circumstances known to him or her.

4. *The 'benevolent construction' principle*. Statutory provisions creating criminal offences should be restrictively construed, in favour of the accused, and against the background of a strong presumption that there can be no liability without subjective fault.

I do not want to spend time here considering which particular subjectivist theorists adhere only to some, and which to all, of these principles, to what degree they do so, and with what modifications. I can only hope that the principles' general importance can be detected in much broadly subjectivist scholarship in the Anglo-American tradition, and beyond (Williams, 1983; Ashworth, 1999; Robinson, 1997; Brudner, 1993). Why should anyone be attracted by subjectivism in his or her approach to criminal liability?

In answering this question, we find that the historical link between the defence of liberty and the development of the substantive criminal law has acquired a very modern philosophical justification. As Ashworth expresses it:

individuals should be respected and treated as agents capable of choosing their acts and omissions, [because] without allowing independence of action to individuals they could hardly be regarded as moral persons . . . individuals should be protected from official censure, through the criminal law, unless they can be shown to have chosen the conduct for which they are being held liable . . . (Ashworth, 1999: 28).

The link between respecting freedom of action and criminalizing only wrongdoing that has been *chosen*, has been thought to support the radical 'pure *mens rea*' principle (not further considered here). Less dramatically, such a link has been commonly taken to lend support to the 'advertent wrongdoing' principle (Brudner, 1993). In this regard, Herbert Hart's famous claim that one could justly be found liable when one had the 'capacity' and a 'fair opportunity' to do otherwise is allocated only a minor, exculpatory role, particularly in relation to the 'relative standards' principle, rather than a positive, inculpatory role in justifying liability based on negligence. So, the defences of automatism, insanity, diminished capacity, and infancy are to be explained by lack of capacity, whereas the defences of duress, necessity, and (possibly) provocation and mistake are to be explained by lack of fair opportunity (Ashworth, 1999: 254).

   In practice, subjectivists find it difficult to justify staying consistently within the theoretical structure of liability they have created. So, for Robinson, an exception must be created for manslaughter cases: 'negligence is punished only in exceptional situations, as where death is caused' (Robinson, 1997: 44). For Ashworth, by way of contrast, whereas manslaughter is perhaps the last place one would hope to find negligence-based liability, it turns out that negligence-based liability can be supported where the fault element in rape and in sexual offences against children is in issue (Ashworth, 1999: 370–1). In retrospect, one may wonder whether the intellectual heat generated by subjectivism can ever match in significance the light shed by Stephen's justly famous observation, that the 'mental element var[ies] according to the different nature of different crimes . . . [and] the only means of arriving at a full comprehension of the expression "*mens rea*" is by a detailed examination of the definitions of particular crimes' (Stephen, 1883, ii: 95).

3 BEYOND SUBJECTIVISM: FREEDOM THROUGH AND ACCOUNTABILITY TO REASON

There is another purpose for which subjectivists press into service Hart's notion of a 'capacity and fair opportunity to do otherwise' in the criminal law. As the passage cited above from Ashworth's work implies, the notion has been thought to underpin the links subjectivists wish to establish between criminal responsibility, blame, and an autonomous choice to do wrong. On this view, responsibility and criminal blame-worthiness are related as follows:

Prima-facie responsibility condition: capacity for choice.
Blame condition: choice to do wrong.

In so far as it is meant to say anything about prima-facie responsibility, however, the notion of a 'fair opportunity to do otherwise' does not imply a *choice* made between alternatives. It requires only a certain kind and degree of control over the nature of one's actions and reactions (that they be responsive to reason), whether or not these were, or could have been, chosen from alternatives. Consider an example.

Suppose that I kill someone upon spontaneously losing self-control, in response to provocation. How much I am to blame for reacting in this way will depend—assuming I am not suffering from some mental abnormality—on how grave the provocation was to me. I might try to assert, however, not merely that blame is inappropriate (the provocation was exceptionally grave), but that I should not even be regarded as a candidate for blame in the first place. My claim, then, is that I was not responsible for the loss of my temper at all: the provoker was. However grave the provocation, the latter claim looks far-fetched. Prima-facie *responsibility* for the loss of temper is shared between the two of us (the provoker sparked it off, but on another day perhaps I would have kept my feelings in check, so my role is not wholly passive), even if the *blame* for it—at least in cases involving grave provocation—must be shouldered largely by the provoker. It is difficult, though, to account for the idea that I am partly responsible for my losses of temper, on the 'choice' model of responsibility.

According to the 'choice' model, the focus in point of responsibility must be on a capacity to choose between options, between keeping and losing my temper; but such a focus is unattainable because I did not choose to lose my temper. The idea that someone might 'choose' to lose their temper (as opposed to deciding to put on a display of temper), is at odds with the very spontaneity of provoked losses of self-control that makes them plausible candidates for excuse in the first place. In fact, I may be responsible for losing my temper, in spite of the absence of choice at the time. This is because (being mentally normal) I am not wholly passive with regard to my emotional make-up, including my disposition to feel angry (Raz, 1999, ch. 1). Even if any ordinary person would have lost self-control in the circumstances in which I lost mine, I can intelligibly still reproach myself for losing it and wish that I had kept my anger in check (perhaps I had hitherto prided myself on what I had thought was my complete imperturbability). Underpinning this insight is an evaluation of my conduct not in terms of choices available and known to me, but in terms of my continuing responsiveness to the demands of reason.

Sensitivity, or responsiveness, to reason is central to questions of responsibility. Until we have decided that, at the time, I was in principle responsive to the demands of reason, it does not even begin to make sense to ask questions about the degree to which (if at all) I was to blame for my reaction, given the gravity of the provocation.

Crucially, though, this 'degree of blame' question should be framed in what looks like the same terms as the prima-facie responsibility question: how insensitive was my reaction (given the gravity of the provocation) to the demands of reason? Here, judgement in accordance with 'reason' means reason in its famously Aristotelian sense of proportionate or well-measured; but acting 'reasonably' in this sense may involve no more choice, at the moment of the fact, than did being responsive to considerations of reason in the first place. Those who spontaneously lose control only when the provocation is very grave, are less to blame when they do lose control than those who lose it for trivial reasons, because the reaction of the former is less disproportionate, even if neither chooses their reaction. Moreover, the absence of choice does not entail that it is mere brute luck when one's response is less disproportionate. An even-tempered disposition robust enough to withstand trivial provocation is, in part, itself a product (over time) of reason, and is thus something by reference to which the criminal law's standards can be set for all mentally normal people.

This way of thinking about the link between responsibility, blame, and the ways in which one is responsive to reason, has implications for how one should view the status of liability for negligently caused harm, in criminal law. To be found negligent, one must first be found to be (broadly speaking) mentally normal, in the sense of responsive to reason. When that has been established (or at least, not challenged by the defence), it will be natural and proper to go on to consider whether one's actions reflected *sufficient* attention paid to the relevant reasons against acting as one did: the Aristotelian question of judgement in accordance with the 'mean'. From this two-stage process, one may then go further, by considering whether one's conduct displayed a certain kind of bad attitude towards those reasons (carelessness; indifference, and so forth).

On this view, there is a very different understanding of the relationship between responsibility and criminal blameworthiness, one gained without reliance on choice or a capacity to choose:

(*a*) *Prima-facie responsibility condition*: responsiveness to reason.
(*b*) *Minimum blame condition*: a departure from the 'mean'.
(*c*) *Possible direct inferences from* (*b*): indifference; carelessness; ill-temperedness; cowardice; and so on.

At no point in this three-stage process does 'choice', or a 'capacity to choose', enter the equation. A *choice* to ignore a relevant reason brings into play a related but quite different set of judgements: that one acted 'knowingly', 'maliciously', 'wilfully', 'dishonestly', 'subjectively recklessly', and so forth (although these judgements also rely, for the moral purchase they gain in any individual case, on the assumption that a defendant met condition (*a*) above). Negligence-based liability (including liability based on indifference, or a 'depraved heart', in North American homicide law) is focused on one's sensitivity to the demands of reason, to how others' legitimate concerns should impact on one's own thinking and one's attitudes. This is one of the moral *strengths* that negligence-based liability can bring to criminalization, however sparingly—for a variety of reasons—it ought to be used. The thought that, by way of contrast, the existence of such liability is a weakness in the criminal law, because negligent conduct is not 'chosen', simply betrays reliance on a misconception about the relationship between responsibility and blame.

4 RECONSIDERING THE CODIFICATION PROJECT

For Bentham, an important aim of codification was clarification of existing offences and defences. For him, what was important was that, instead of having to guess at one's obligations from the language of 'Treason, unclergyable felony, clergyable felony, praemunire and misdemeanour', there would be 'matter descriptive of the offence in its ordinary state, and matter indicative of the several causes of justification, aggravation and extenuation, with the grounds of exemption from punishment which apply to it' (Schofield and Harris, 1998: 10). The Model Penal Code drafters, like many of their nineteenth-century predecessors, had similarly modest aims. In the hands of some influential subjectivists, however, the codification movement has become overshadowed and politicized by the wish to entrench subjectivist principles of liability. Their aim has become to ensure that politicians are not let loose on proposals for criminal law reform until such proposals have been subjected to 'deliberate craftsmanship' by the 'best brains of the legal profession', drawing on subjectivist 'juristic principles' (see above). In practice, of course, Williams's very general sounding 'juristic principles', especially the 'advertent wrongdoing' and 'benevolent construction' principles, turn out to be geared to an attack on particular crimes that have for a long time been the *bêtes noires* of subjectivists. It turns out that what legislating for subjectivism entails is that some crimes—involuntary manslaughter, felony murder, offences with any element of strict liability, and so forth—must automatically disappear from the law reformer's menu. There are sometimes important and telling criticisms that can be made of such crimes, often along broadly subjectivist lines, but such criticisms can and should be detached from, because they do not entail, a commitment to an all-embracing subjectivism masquerading as a set of general, rationally demonstrable and supposedly distinctively 'juristic' principles (Norrie, 2000).

So, whither codification, and the wish to entrench guiding general principles of liability? No one could seriously doubt the need to improve the clarity of the substantive criminal law, as a whole, through codification and periodic re-codification. Rather than just assume the a priori correctness of academic subjectivist views on these issues, however, a different way to address them would be to pay closer attention to the research now emerging on ordinary people's understanding of blame and excuse, wherein subjective fault is an *aggravating* feature rather than a threshold condition of liability (Robinson and Darley, 1998). Should codification none the less take place against a background of more or less well-entrenched general principles of criminalization? There may be something to be gained from this, but only if such principles can be detached from the obsession with opposing particular crimes, such as felony murder, or manslaughter. A list of such principles might run as follows:

1. The creation of any crime or offence involving a more than merely minor penalty shall not be regarded as a proportionate response to wrongdoing where a minor penalty would prove adequate.
2. No crime or offence involving a more than merely minor penalty shall be created other than through primary legislation.
3. No crime or offence involving a more than merely minor penalty shall create liability without fault, although the burden of proving an absence of fault may lie on the defendant.
4. In any crime or offence, a defendant may not be found criminally liable for harm done greatly in excess of that which he was (or should have been) aware that he might do.
5. A penalty is not a minor penalty if it involves compulsory detention of any kind.
6. Those with responsibility for law-making shall develop defences that reflect a defendant's lack of capacity, or a defendant's lack of fair opportunity, to conform his or her conduct to the law.

In these general principles there are strong echoes of the subjectivist principles listed earlier; but they are detached, in a way subjectivist principles are not, from an opposition to particular crimes. In a way that subjectivists have not been sufficiently willing to grant, in any codification of general principles of criminal liability there must be an element of '*determinatio*', moral 'elbow-room', for legislatures. If the defendant rapes the victim, and the victim dies in consequence of the trauma suffered, is convicting the defendant of manslaughter or felony murder the unacceptable face of constructive liability, something that must be ruled out from the start? Or is it rather perfectly permissible, within the limits of principle 4, above? If the defendant can be fined $10 for failing to produce a driving licence when it is demanded by a police officer, whatever the reason for the failure, is that an example of the grotesque injustice wrought by any form of strict liability? Or is it really a legitimate use of principle 3, above, recognizing that the fault principles appropriate for harmful invasions of others' interests are out of place in a regulatory framework aimed at securing (partly through minor penalties and the judicious use of prosecutorial discretion) a common good? These should be important questions for legislators operating within a framework of general principle; they are not questions whose answers should have already been given by the (subjectivist) shape of the framework itself.

5 FROM CAMBRIDGE PAST OXFORD: THE RISE OF THE 'PHILOSOPHER-KING'

The influence of genuinely philosophical critique came late to an Anglo-American tradition of thinking about criminal law that was, for a long time, dominated by anti-theoretical, anti-comparative, 'common law' pragmatism. On mainland Europe, by way of contrast, philosophically inspired thinking can be found from a much earlier time in—for example—both Germany and Italy; and it is still highly influential. In Johannes Wessels's leading work on the general part of German criminal law, for example, one finds entries on 'epistemology', 'the natural unity of action', and 'the object of norms' (Wessels, 1990), entries that are about as likely to turn up in an equivalent modern English language treatise as a reference to gay people's rights. In America and England, the influence of academics on the process of criminal law reform did not begin in earnest until the 1950s, with (in America) the ten-year-long project of formulating what is now the Model Penal Code, and (in England) the foundation of the Criminal Law Revision Committee in 1959. Self-consciously 'philosophical' analysis of criminal law doctrines has its modern origins in the influence of linguistic ('Oxford school') philosophy in the mid-twentieth century (e.g. Austin, 1956/7). However, the apparently dry (albeit subtle and nuanced) character of such philosophical work made it unattractive to mainstream criminal lawyers, ever anxious to find significant normative pay-offs from the intellectual labour they were being required to invest by immersing themselves in 'interdisciplinary' scholarship. Moreover, the methodology of at least some champions of this kind of philosophy was open to question.

Suppose, like many theorists worldwide, my interest has been kindled by the phenomena of justifications, denials of responsibility, excuses, and exemptions. Some theorists in the older tradition of philosophy held that I ought sharply to distinguish between the interest I might have in 'analysis', directed at establishing proper usage of each term, and the interest I might have in 'evaluation', in exploring the role (if any) each term—having been properly analysed—should play within the criminal law. This aspiration rigidly to compartmentalize the tasks of philosophy has been heavily criticized (Lacey, 1998a). I will find, for example, that most theorists support the contention that whilst justifications focus on the act, denials of responsibility, exemptions, and excuses focus on the actor (Robinson, 1997). I might wonder, however, how this claim can be squared with the common idea that some acts (genocide; torturing someone to death) are not only unjustifiable but inexcusable, or with the judicial view (Aristotelian in origin) that exactly how much force it is justifiable to use in self-defence in a particular set of circumstances may ultimately lie inescapably with the defendant's own perception. Can one identify these points as being of purely 'analytical' significance, important solely for their implications as to how to classify a given defence as an excuse or justification? Surely, one cannot. The significance of these points is that they suggest that the very idea of an excuse is bound up with an evaluative concern that defences should uphold decency (so, no excuse for genocide, even if there might be an insanity or infancy-based denial of responsibility); just as the very idea of a justification is bound up with an evaluative concern that defences should operate in a humane way (so, justifications should sometimes have an agent-relative dimension).

In this regard, a key turning-point was the publication (at about the same time) of George Fletcher's justly celebrated work on philosophical and comparative aspects of the criminal law (Fletcher, 1978), and the publication of Ronald Dworkin's attack on positivist accounts of law. The significance of Fletcher's work was his insistence that to engage critically with criminal law doctrine is to engage in a 'species of moral philosophy' (Fletcher, 1978, introd.; and 1998: 287), just as for Dworkin, to try to give an account of law *just is* to give it a certain kind of moral and political (philosophical) account. As Dworkin was later to put it, 'it falls to philosophers . . . to work out law's ambitions, the purer form of law within and beyond the law we have' (Dworkin, 1986: 407). So, perhaps for the first time, lawyers were now being urged to think that analysis of criminal law in the light of moral and political philosophy is not an optional 'interdisciplinary' kind of scholarship after all. For Fletcher and Dworkin, it is the only intellectually significant kind of analysis of such doctrine that there is; and the influence of such thinking on major recent works of criminal law scholarship is there for all to see (e.g. Ashworth, 1999; Brudner, 1995; Moore, 1997; Duff, 1990).

It would be easy to dismiss Fletcher's claim as involving a simple confusion between a kind of analysis (philosophy), and a kind of institutionalized system for generating authoritative conduct-guidance and decision-making, that could be subject to such analysis (law); but this would be to miss the point. Since Fletcher took the pioneering steps, there can now be little doubt that the search for light shed by philosophical analysis of criminal law has inspired some of the most influential scholarship in the field in the last twenty years. Few would cast doubt on the importance to criminal law of the insights recently gained, through philosophical reflection, on (say) voluntary conduct (Simester, 1996), and the general part of the criminal law (Gardner, 1998). However, the importance of such philosophical work (as of the work done in the 1950s and 1960s) is most emphatically not that it fulfils Dworkin's ambitions for philosophical thinking about law. Indeed, the value in philosophical analysis may lie in just those respects in which it lacks Dworkinian credentials, as when it is meant to highlight a sharp *contrast* between legal and philosophical concerns when it comes to defining, say, intention (Gardner, 1994; Duff, 1990). More broadly, it has never been a criterion for the success of philosophical analysis that the insights about the law it yields are capable of being knitted together by a single author, to express a coherent moral and political philosophy, as Dworkin claims it should be (Dworkin, 1986). In her magisterial review of modern philosophical analysis of the criminal law, Nicola Lacey claims that it is only very recently that its exponents have given up on the aspiration to present criminal law as expressing a single, coherent rationality (Lacey, 1998*a*). She thus associates this development with the rise of a fashionable postmodernism, 'a general trend in [modern] intellectual culture away from the pretensions of "grand theory" ' (ibid. 319). In fact, nothing in the older work of professional philosophers examining the criminal law, such as that of Austin or Hart and Honoré, ever embodied that aspiration. Its fulfilment was really the pet project of a few influential criminal lawyers who mistakenly thought that developing an all-encompassing and coherent rationale for the criminal law was what it truly meant to be arguing in a theoretical, rather than simply in a pragmatic way. It must be conceded, however, that there is perceived by some to be a good deal of mileage left in 'grand theory', principally by those determined to explain (or, sometimes, to explain away) the criminal law in terms of the arguments of particular philosop*h*ers, rather than by simply employing one or more of the analytical or investigative methods of philosoph*y*. It is to their theories that I now turn.

6 'FORMAL' FREEDOM, AND THE POSSIBILITY OF 'NATURAL' CRIMINAL LAW

Although he thought that forward-looking utilitarian considerations provided the best justification for the institution(s) of punishment, H. L. A. Hart famously regarded the imposition of criminal prohibitions on at least some kinds of wrong as tantamount to a species of natural law. As he put it:

the most important [prohibitions] for social life are those that restrict the use of violence in killing or inflicting bodily harm. The basic character of such rules may be brought out in a question: If there were not these rules what point could there be for beings such as ourselves in having rules of *any* other kind? (Hart, 1994: 192–4, emphasis in original)

This—essentially pragmatic—way of framing the issue rightly leaves open, as a matter of *determinatio*, the question of just what kind or range of prohibitions (including fault requirements, defences, and so forth) would satisfy the 'natural law' requirement that violence etc. be prohibited. By way of contrast, inspired by a theoretically far more ambitious tradition of thinking associated with Kant and Hegel, some modern criminal law theorists have sought to go much further.

For Alan Brudner (1993, 1995), there is a vital theoretical connection between the near universality of crimes that are *mala in se* (murder, theft, and so forth), the appeal of subjective fault requirements (like intention and recklessness), and the importance of certain defences (such as, duress and insanity). As he puts it, 'All of these . . . flow from the basic norm of the pure agency paradigm . . . they follow logically from a normative standpoint that takes the choosing self as the sole absolute end' (Brudner, 1995: 239). This is the standpoint of formal freedom. On Brudner's view, harm done is not wrongful in a truly criminal sense, unless it is done deliberately or recklessly: where the wrongdoer '*knowingly* exercises a degree of freedom inconsistent with the equal freedom of the other' (Brudner, 1993: 32; my emphasis). For, only in such circumstances will it be right to say that the wrongdoer, 'challenges the intersubjective foundation of valid claims to respect, claiming an absolute worth for his singular self and denying worth to the other' (Brudner, 1993: 32), thus violating the basic norm of formal freedom. Accordingly, defences in the criminal law reflect not the absence of a wrongful interference with another, but an absence of *a fully knowing and wilful* breach of the duty to respect personality as an absolute end. So, 'insanity excuses if . . . there is lacking the devaluation of personality that alone implies the nugatoriness of one's own rights' (Brudner, 1995: 238). Similarly, for Brudner, duress excuses where 'the accused is entitled to treat his life or health as inalienable when they conflict with another's property in a particular thing', that is, where the wrong done to avoid the evil threatened reflects 'an objective scale of value based on the importance of an object for the expression of freedom' (ibid. 1995: 243).

Such an ambitious attempt to forge a conception of supposedly truly *criminal* law (combining subjectivism, and a traditional view of the nature and scope of excuses, with an exclusive concentration on murder, rape, and pillage), finds a natural source of support in other theories that regard state-sponsored retribution for wrongdoing as in principle an intrinsic good. For 'just deserts' theorists, the proper instantiation of the good of retribution for wrongdoing, through punishment, would be perverted by a criminal law that (unless wholly exceptionally) licensed punishing purely for its consequential benefits. For Michael Moore, for example, taking the (supposed) intrinsic value of retributivism seriously leads to an understanding of criminal law 'properly so called' strikingly similar to that of Brudner (although Moore defends criminal liability for negligent wrongdoing), even though he (Moore) makes telling criticisms of the purely deontological version of retributivism favoured by Brudner (Moore, 1997). Significantly, however, Moore seeks to place this understanding in the context of the common theoretical and legislative practice of dividing the criminal law into a general (or universal) part, and a special (or particular) part (Fletcher, 1978; Moore, 1997). An appreciation of how artificial and distorting this division really is, sets the scene for the rejection of the idea that securing just deserts through criminal law and punishment has intrinsic, as opposed to instrumental, value.

7 On the Hallowed 'General Part' of the Criminal Law

The philosophical work of nineteenth-century German and Italian scholars (alluded to above) brought to prominence in the Western world what was held to be an important distinction between a 'general' and a 'special' part of the criminal law, a distinction then adopted in criminal codes elsewhere as, for example, in the revised Japanese Criminal Code of 1907. The 'general part' of the criminal law is concerned with doctrines that are analytically detachable from connection to a specific crime, and are hence in principle applicable to almost any crime. On Moore's view, these doctrines include, for example, '*actus reus, mens rea*, and causation . . . conspiracy, attempt, solicitation, and complicity' (Moore, 1997: 30). The 'special part' is supposedly concerned with the unique elements of any given crime's *actus reus* or *mens rea*, such as the requirement of 'indecency' in indecent assault, 'causing death' in homicide, or 'dishonesty' in theft.

In one way, this distinction might be thought to have little significance: at best, a way of dividing up the subject analytically for the benefit of law students. However, the distinction between the 'general' and the 'special' part can be made central to two rather more substantial, normative claims. The first is that, to be considered general, doctrines of the 'general part' must apply to *all* crimes. On this view, for example, someone who claims to be a supporter of the idea of the 'general part' must agree that, to avoid theoretical inconsistency, duress should be a complete excuse for all crimes (including murder), or none. The assumption, evident here, that 'special part' concerns—such as the sanctity of human life—should not be permitted to infect or adulterate the purity and universality of the 'general part', is also a feature of the second normative claim about the relationship between the two. This is the claim that doctrines of the 'general part' act as side-constraints, restricting the shape and character of crimes that may appear in the 'special part'. It is here that we the find the link with the retributivist theory of punishment. The supposition that criminal liability is warranted only where it is, in a retributive sense, justly deserved has been held to imply the need to show, in any truly 'criminal' proceedings, an *actus reus malum in se*, and a (subjective) *mens rea*. As we have seen, only these together (in the right relation) are thought to instantiate 'criminal' wrongdoing (Moore, 1997; Brudner, 1993, 1995).

However, the attempt to mark off a universalizable 'general part' of the criminal law, and to assign to it a constraining role in determining what the 'special part' may contain, has turned out to be of little theoretical or practical value. The attempt almost inevitably ends up presenting an impoverished picture of the 'special part', in which the latter's moral richness and diversity have been airbrushed out. Rape (unlike murder), for example, defies analysis in terms of 'causing' a prohibited result. One cannot 'cause' penetration to occur; there is simply 'penetration'. The crime of rape also assigns a special role to consent, as a denial of the harm or wrong itself, rather than as a general defence following some harm admittedly done. So, in the crime of rape (as elsewhere), both causation and consent look like issues whose normative (in)significance comes from their 'special part' context. Similarly, in some crimes (conspiracy; attempt) but not in others (rape; criminal damage), the role of intention is as a constitutive part of the very definition of the offence. Intention is what makes the former crimes the crimes that they are, whereas its (dispensable) role with the latter crimes may simply be to satisfy the subjectivist demands of retributivism (no one doubts that the wrong of rape or of criminal damage *could* be regarded as done when done through carelessness).

Finally, even Moore himself concedes that justifications (the same is true of some excuses) cannot plausibly be regarded as belonging exclusively to the 'general part' (Moore, 1997: 32 n 53). This is because whether one was or was not justified in harming another turns in part on how one's proffered justification stands up, ethically, once one has a grasp of the moral detail of the crime purportedly justified; and a grasp of the latter entails reference to the 'special', not to the 'general', part. Necessity, for example, might readily justify inflicting minor bodily harm, in some circumstances, but would much more rarely justify torture, even if the nature of the torture in question involves doing something like the same kind of minor bodily harm.

I am not claiming that it is impossible to say something of general importance about, say, causation, necessity, or intention. Indeed, one can even find substance in the claim that there *is* a 'general part' of the criminal law, if one confines one's focus to the universal applicability of denials of responsibility, like insanity, and of exemptions, like infancy (Gardner, 1994). What cannot be done, without gross moral over-simplification of the 'special part', is to insist that the retributive principles of criminalization conjured from neo-Kantian or neo-Hegelian moral theory must shape the character of wrongdoing, if it is to be properly described as 'criminal'. As we shall now see, whether wrongdoing is properly regarded as 'criminal' can be as much a reflection of the procedure put in place to prove it, and of the responses to its proof at the judge's disposal, as of nature (and definition) of the wrongdoing itself. Recognizing this demands the reconnection of substance and procedure in criminal law theory, and the reassertion of the importance of consequentialism as against retributivism.

8 QUESTIONING RETRIBUTIVISM: RECONNECTING SUBSTANCE AND PROCEDURE

There is good reason to doubt Brudner's and Moore's claims that state-sponsored retribution for 'truly criminal' wrongdoing always has intrinsic moral worth.

Suppose, as Douglas Husak argues, that the infliction of an appropriate degree of consequential suffering, *whether or not* this suffering is inflicted through state punishment, is what is morally deserved by wrongdoers (Husak, 2000). If, then, someone has by some means 'suffered enough', in any individual case (suppose the relatives of a rape victim castrate the convicted offender before the authorities can deal with him), there will be no reason whatever—moral or legal—for the State to inflict punishment itself. This suggests that the value of state punishment resides in the way it (instrumentally) serves a supposedly intrinsic value, this being the infliction of appropriate suffering on the wrongdoer which might not otherwise be inflicted; for unless it will realize this value, state punishment is pointless.

Husak would leave it there, but unfortunately things are not that simple. The institutions and practices of state punishment are—perhaps primarily—justified by the way in which they serve through systematically *replacing*, with a new normative order, the ways (like taking private vengeance) that suffering may otherwise be inflicted on an offender. Within this new normative order (let us call it 'responding officially to wrongdoing'), the infliction through state punishment of carefully considered, humane, and proportionate suffering, will loom large. However, the very redefinition ('appropriation') of punishment as a manifestation of an official response to wrongdoing necessarily connects punishment to the State's broader vision for governance, a vision going well beyond a concern for retribution. Let me define this broader vision in terms of a question that—for a consequentialist liberal—must be asked of all official responses to wrongdoing, including the structuring of substantive offences and defences. The question is: to what extent do those responses contribute to a more civilized and cultured, as well as more tolerant and humane, society, to that end helping to shape the ways in which, and the attitudes with which, individuals flourish in common (Raz, 1986)? In so far as particular criminal procedures, offences, defences, and punishments make such a contribution, then they may—instrumentally—be justified. However, so characterized, such an instrumental justification is obviously not a crudely utilitarian justification, of the kind opposition to which has historically lent to retributivism much of its intuitive appeal. This being so, much wind is taken out of retributivism's sails.

As we have seen, for retributivists there is a crucial distinction to be drawn between 'real' crime (murder; rape; pillage) and 'regulatory offences' (transgressions inimical to what has broadly been called 'public welfare', in some sphere of, say, transport or commerce). For the retributivist, only the former justly deserve truly retaliatory suffering (to use Aristotle's term), although administrative penalties and fines may be tolerable where the latter are concerned (e.g. Brudner, 1993). For the liberal consequentialist, however, there is no particular need to regard the much-criticized distinction between 'real' and 'regulatory' crime as crucial to an account of criminal law. She can happily adopt some version of the orthodox, content-independent, understanding of laws as criminal simply 'when persons who violate them are subject to punishment' (Husak, 2000: 960). This is because what matters to the liberal consequentialist is not simply the stark fact of conviction but whether, all things considered, the State's response to the conduct to be outlawed is civilized, tolerant, and humane. No doubt, that the conduct in question may be met with punishment ought to indicate that it is neither wholly trivial, nor something that might be better dealt with by use of the civil law. So long, however, as the nature of the proceedings leading to conviction, the way the offence is defined, the defences available (if any), and the measures that may be taken following conviction, are—*taken together*—within the bounds of reasonableness as an official response to the wrongdoing, neither the 'public welfare' character of the conduct to be outlawed nor (even) the absence of fault in its definition, need necessarily undermine the appropriateness of treating the wrongdoing as 'criminal'.

If the 'liberal' part of liberal consequentialism is what generates the need for criminal laws to be civilized, tolerant, and humane as official responses to wrongdoing, it is perhaps more the 'consequentialist' part that demands the reconnection of substance, procedure, and punishment in that response, as Bentham (never Britain's most ardent liberal) himself recognized (Smith, 1998: 40). These had become separated as, in the second half of the twentieth century, people felt that they could write books or draft law proposals with 'criminal law' in the title which said barely anything about criminal procedure or punishment at all. Yet, all along, scholars should have known that truly penetrating critique requires an examination of how procedure, substance, and punishment relate to and affect one another (as some critical legal theorists and theorists of corporate criminal liability have been quick to recognize). There is little point, for example, to the provision of a substantive defence of insanity, if the adversarial nature of the procedure put in place to prove it distorts the necessarily expert-diagnostic character of any inquiry into the defendant's state of mind at the time of the offence, thus degrading the forensic process as a whole.

In setting down what he has described as the 'principled core of criminal law', Andrew Ashworth has taken steps towards (re)formulating the kind of approach to criminal liability that liberal-consequentialists might well favour (Ashworth, 2000: 253–5). For him, there are four main principles:

1. The criminal law should only be used to censure people for substantial wrongdoing.
2. Criminal laws should be enforced with respect for equal treatment and proportionality.
3. Persons accused of substantial wrongdoing/crimes should be afforded at least the protections declared by articles 6.2 and 6.3 of the European Convention on Human Rights (fair trial provisions).
4. Maximum sentences and effective sentence levels should be proportionate to the seriousness of the wrongdoing.

There is naturally plenty of room for disagreement over whether further principles are needed to supplement these (such as the principles set out at the end of Sect. 4 above), and over what their exact implications for any given criminal law really are.

None the less, what is important is that, whilst motivated by a retributivist approach, the spirit of these principles is consequentialist, and liberal-consequentialist into the bargain.

9 Subjectivism and Objectivism again: Critical Criminal Law Theory

No one would cast doubt on the existence of inconsistencies in criminal law doctrine. However, the 'critical' project of finding important contradictions at the heart of an explanatory account of the criminal law implausibly presupposes a one-dimensional commensurability between the values that inform the criminal law (Lacey, 1998a). Such an over-simplification of morality has been convincingly refuted by the more sophisticated liberal theories that 'critical' theory purports to oppose (Raz, 1986). The best critical theorists take a different track. Their claim, directed mainly but not solely against the retributivists, is that liberal thinkers are theoretical prisoners of the individualism that permeates their moral, political, and legal culture (Norrie, 2000; Lacey, 1998b). This individualism manifests itself in enthusiasm for exculpatory subjectivism, and in liberals' portrayal of an expanding criminal law as little more than State authoritarianism (see Sect. 2 above). In this, liberal subjectivists suppress not only social—as opposed to individual—excuses (like poverty), but also communitarian or collective justifications for, say, regulatory offences and corporate criminal liability (Norrie, 2000).

In response, one could point out that sophisticated liberal theories leave plenty of scope for collective goals to be pursued though the criminal law (see Sect. 8 above), and that since poverty is relative more than it is absolute—and intellectual, emotional, or moral as often as it is economic—its status as a potential excuse is likely to be as problematic in thoughtful non-liberal theory as it is for liberals. I wish to conclude, however, with a focus on a different point. For Lacey, the problem with liberal theory lies in its supposedly universalizing aspirations: 'at large philosophising, which is not addressed to any particular system or practice of criminal law, is, like a map of imaginary terrain . . . a stimulating intellectual . . . exercise, but . . . not one which particularly claims the attention of those interested in criminal law . . .' (Lacey, 1998a: 310). Ironically, this claim puts her in conflict with other 'critical' scholars for whom it is the alleged *parochialism* of liberal scholarship, focused almost exclusively on problems arising in some (but far from all) Anglo-American jurisdictions, from which radical—'realist'—scholarship should break free (Leiter, 2001). Lacey's 'jurisdiction specific' view of how theorizing should be done carries an inherent risk

Table 12.1. Wessels's Categorization of Criminal Law Theories

Doctrinal system	Classical system	Neoclassical system	Teleological system	'Final' system
	(= pure causal conception of criminality)	(= causal starting-point, subject to recognition of discrete subjective elements of crime)	(= strives for a workable solution within the framework of a value-laden outlook, falling back on the social meaning of legal norms)	(= derives from the goal-directness of human behaviour and the supposed authority of the lawgiver the *ontological* character of the concept of action)
Represented by	Beling, Binding, von Liszt	Baumann, Kienapfel, Weber	Gallas, Jescheck, Lackner, Eser, Cramer, Lenckner, Roxin, Rudolphi, Wessels, Wolter	Welzel, Maurach, Armin, Kaufmann, Hirsch, Gossel, Schroeder, Stratenwerth, Zipf
Deed	Taking away of another's movable property	Taking away of another's movable property with intention of unlawful acquisition	(a) objective element: taking away of another's movable property (b) subjective elements: intention as to the taking away *plus* intention of unlawful acquisition	(a) objective element: taking away of another's movable property (b) subjective elements: intention as to the taking away *plus* intention of unlawful acquisition

	Lack of justifying grounds (with *objective/formal* criteria)	Possible involvement of justifying grounds in objective and subjective respects	Possible involvement of justifying grounds (a) objective elements of justification (b) subjective elements of justification	Possible involvement of justifying grounds (a) objective elements of justification (b) subjective elements of justification
Unlawfulness				
Culpability	(a) causal responsibility (b) intent (i.e. deliberateness of action) as a mode of culpability (c) further intention of unlawful acquisition as extra culpability element (d) lack of excuse	(a) susceptibility to blame (b) intent (i.e. deliberateness of action) as basis of culpability (c) knowledge of law-breaking as further element of culpability (d) lack of excuse	(a) susceptibility to blame (b) intention/culpable state of mind as basis of culpability (c) knowledge of law-breaking as further element of culpability (d) lack of excuse	(a) susceptibility to blame (b) knowledge of law-breaking as element of culpability (c) lack of excuse

Source: From Johannes Wessels, *Strafrecht: Allgemeiner Teil* (20th edn.), Heidelberg, 1990: 257–8.

that any narrowness of vision within the liberal approach will be reflected in an equal and opposite narrowness of 'critical' response. For example, the fierce conflict in Anglo-American criminal law theory between subjective and objective approaches to liability has provided the background against which Alan Norrie has powerfully characterized liberalism as wedded to seeking resolution of an unresolvable conflict between its equally implausible views of individual (subjective) and collective state (objective) interests (Norrie, 2000).

Few would doubt that the relationship between the individual and the State has indeed preoccupied many liberal theorists; but in mainland European jurisdictions, this has not been associated with the same kind of division between objective and subjective approaches to liability that Norrie regards as the almost inevitable concomitant of such a preoccupation. In Wessels's helpful characterization of the differences between German theorists (including himself), for example, the main dispute is over where to locate culpability elements—be they subjective or objective—within the overall theoretical structure, rather than over whether those culpability elements should be subjective or objective (see Table 12.1). So, if German criminal law is to be characterized as 'liberal' (a term frequently wrongly equated by 'critical' theorists with the championing of individual interests *at the expense of* collective goals), it cannot be because the hallmark of liberal criminal law is a rather sterile and narrowly focused debate familiar to Anglo-American writers, between the irresistible force of subjectivism and the immovable object that is objectivism.

References

Ashworth, A. (1999). *Principles of Criminal Law* (3rd edn.), Oxford: Oxford University Press.
—— (2000). 'Is the Criminal Law a Lost Cause?' *Law Quarterly Review*, 116: 225–56.
Austin, J. L. (1956/7). 'A Plea for Excuses', *Proceedings of the Aristotelian Society*, 57: 1–27.
Brudner, A. (1993). 'Agency and Welfare in the Penal Law', in S. C. Shute, J. Gardner, and J. Horder (eds.), *Action and Value in Criminal Law*, Oxford: Oxford University Press, 21–53.
—— (1995). *The Unity of the Common Law*, Berkeley: University of California Press.
Duff, R. A. (1990). *Intention, Agency and Criminal Liability*, Oxford: Blackwell.
Dworkin, R. M. (1986). *Law's Empire*, London: Fontana.
Fletcher, G. P. (1978). *Rethinking Criminal Law*, New York: Little Brown.
—— (1998). 'The Fall and Rise of Criminal Law Theory', *Buffalo Criminal Law Review*, 1: 275–94.
Gardner, J. (1994). 'Criminal Law and the Uses of Theory: A Reply to Laing', *Oxford Journal of Legal Studies*, 14: 217–28.
—— (1998). 'On the General Part of the Criminal Law', in R. A. Duff (ed.), *Philosophy and the Criminal Law: Principle and Critique*, Cambridge: Cambridge University Press, 205–55.
Hart, H. L. A. (1994). *The Concept of Law* (2nd edn.), Oxford: Oxford University Press.
Husak, D. N. (2000). 'Retribution in Criminal Theory', *San Diego Law Review*, 37: 959–86.

Lacey, N. (1998a). 'Philosophy, History and Criminal Law Theory', *Buffalo Criminal Law Review*, 1: 295–328.

—— (1998b). 'Contingency, Coherence and Conceptualism', in A. Duff (ed.), *Philosophy and the Criminal Law: Principle and Critique*, Cambridge: Cambridge University Press, 9–59.

Leiter, B. (2001). 'Legal Realism, Hard Positivism, and the Limits of Conceptual Analysis', in J. Coleman (ed.), *Hart's Postscript*, Oxford: Oxford University Press, 355–70.

Moore, M. (1997). *Placing Blame*, Oxford: Oxford University Press.

Norrie, A. (2000). *Punishment, Responsibility and Justice*, Oxford: Oxford University Press.

Radzinowicz, L. (1945). 'Present Trends of English Criminal Policy: An Attempt at Interpretation', in Sir L. Radzinowicz and J. W. C. Turner (eds.), *The Modern Approach to Criminal Law*, London: Macmillan, 27–38.

Raz, J. (1986). *The Morality of Freedom*, Oxford: Oxford University Press.

—— (1999). *Engaging Reason*, Oxford: Oxford University Press.

Robinson, P. (1997). *Structure and Function in Criminal Law*, Oxford: Oxford University Press.

—— Cahill, M., and Mohammed, U. (2000). 'The Five Worst (and Five Best) American Criminal Codes', *Northwestern University Law Review*, 94: 1–90.

—— and Darley, J. M. (1998). 'Objectivist versus Subjectivist Views of Criminality: A Study on the Role of Social Science in Criminal Law Theory', *Oxford Journal of Legal Studies*, 18: 409–47.

Schofield, P., and Harris, J. (1998). *'Legislator of the World': Writings on Codification, Law and Education*, Oxford: Oxford University Press.

Simester, A. P. (1996). 'Agency', *Law and Philosophy*, 15: 159–81.

Smith, K. J. M. (1998). *Lawyers, Legislators and Theorists*, Oxford: Oxford University Press.

Stephen, J. (1883). *History of the Criminal Law of England* (3 vols.), London: Macmillan.

Wessels, J. (1990). *Strafrecht: Allgemeiner Teil* (20th edn.), Heidelberg: C. F. Müller.

Williams, G. (1983). *Textbook of Criminal Law*, (2nd edn.), London: Stevens.

CHAPTER 13

CRIMINOLOGY

CRIME'S CHANGING BOUNDARIES

DAVID NELKEN

THE reader should not expect to find in this chapter anything like a survey of criminology over the last forty years. Even if we limited ourselves to English language criminology such an enterprise would need to cover such a wide range of scientific disciplines and myriad of specialized topics that it would be quite impossible in the space available (readers wishing to go deeper into specific aspects of the subject may consult selected volumes of *The Dartmouth International Library of Crime, Criminal Justice and Penology*. The leading single-volume British guide is *The Oxford Handbook of Criminology* (ed. Maguire *et al.*), now in its third edition). It would also be beyond the reach of any one author, itself testimony to what has been described as 'the fragmentation of criminology' (Ericson and Carriere, 1994). In this chapter, I shall limit myself to recent sociological work on developments in crime and crime control. I shall be considering, in particular, the ways in which concern about different types of unacceptable behaviour is affected by changes in political and geographical boundaries.

Calling something crime presupposes that we accept or at least expect that the state or government will try to reduce that form of misbehaviour. But by examining which behaviours a society chooses to call crime, why it does so, and what it actually does about them, we can also learn a great deal about the distribution of power. In a period of increasing global interconnections, responses to crime help express and shape the regulation of social conflict and the construction of social order at a series of intersecting local, regional, national, and international levels. In particular, crime, crime control, and criminology increasingly play themselves out on a wider than national stage as frontiers are bypassed or restructured by trade, travel, and communication.

Crime, crime control, and criminology are themselves interrelated in complex ways; hence the increasing emphasis on a global perspective is an aspect of the behaviour which is being studied as well as of the approach used to combat or to study it. As cause and consequence of larger socio-economic changes such as deregulation, we are witnessing a reconfiguration of the responsibilities for crime control between government and civil society, between state and non-state actors, and between the public and private spheres. At the same time, it has become more difficult to know how, when, and where to draw the boundary line between crime and politics (Cohen, 1996), and, after the terrorist attacks on the United States of 11 September 2001, between crime and war ('the pursuit of politics by other means'). The risks associated with crimes related to state-sponsored terrorism must now be added to those affecting the environment and financial systems. Sometimes, in what Beck now describes as the 'world risk society', the three types of risks interact—as when terrorists deliberately threaten or inflict damage on the ecosystem or financial markets (Beck, 2002).

In the rest of this chapter, I shall discuss in turn trends in crime, criminal justice, and criminology, and the relationship between these and the changing role of the state in national and international crime control. The advantage of putting these topics together in this way is that it allows us to trace connections and see unexpected links. A major theme running through this chapter is the need to relate transformations in crime control to shifts in forms of governance (in this way, underlining the appropriateness of placing this chapter in the part of the *Handbook* which deals with public law). Another issue that links the various parts of this chapter is the central importance of the victim. The move to define crime from the point of view of the victim was originally encouraged by the development of victim surveys which were invented in an attempt to deal with criminology's long-standing problem of measuring the unknown 'dark figure' of crime. This instrument made it possible to count and document crime (or at least crimes with identifiable and aware victims) independently of the actions of law enforcement agencies. But, as we shall see, victims have now become an ever more important focus for crime prevention and the criminal process in general as well as serving as the justification and legitimation for new forms of global criminological expertise.

1 LIVING WITH HIGH CRIME RATES

Most criminologists agree that the single most important fact about crime rates in industrialized societies over the past forty years is that they have been steadily rising.

The disproportionate growth in violent crimes (now around a tenth of the number of property crimes) gives rise to particular anxiety. The evidence for this comes not only from official statistics but is also supported by national and international victim surveys. Victim surveys do tend to show more constant trends as compared to the annual variations revealed by police statistics. But they also suggest that even an apparent decline in crime rates such as that registered in Britain over the past few years may be as much due to changes in recording by the police as to an actual decline in crime (Reiner, 2000).

But, despite the empirical basis of the concern over rising crime, because of the political consequences which are made to follow from such 'facts', it is important to remember that care needs to be exercised in interpreting all data about crime. It is often not easy to determine how far we are measuring changes in behaviour, or in enforcement activity, or even in levels of general tolerance or intolerance of (mis)-behaviour (see Maguire, 1997). The impression of increasing youth violence, for instance, may in large part be manufactured by the police and the media, and represent a sign of reduced tolerance for any sort of violent behaviour rather than an increase in the real level of serious violence (Estrada, 2001). Decreasing tolerance levels (in part, the result of feminist criminological writings) certainly also seem best to account for the increasing number of cases of domestic assault brought to court, even if this behaviour is still regrettably too common.

On the other hand, over the last generation there has been considerable growth in tolerance for some sorts of deviance, especially those involving sexual orientation (though this could itself also be viewed as more *intolerance* for those expressing discrimination). But, as Jock Young has suggested, greater tolerance for some sorts of deviance has gone in parallel with declining concern for the 'inclusion' of the less-advantaged and unsuccessful (Young, 1999). More generally, whilst some crimes have been decriminalized, others have become more prominent. Important examples include 'hate crimes'; crimes against the environment; financial crimes such as money-laundering and insider trading, and crimes involving information techno-logy (about which more will be said later). Although most police and criminological attention continues to be focused on youth, street crimes, burglary, and drugs (and the same is true of victim surveys), increasingly, crimes are also committed by, for, and against organizations (Heiland *et al.*, 1992). And a cynical public, ever less respectful of authority, provide a ready audience for any accounts the media get hold of regarding crimes by the powerful and cases of government and official corruption (Levi and Nelken, 1996).

Given that this increase in crime coincided with a period of unparalleled economic prosperity, it has become more difficult for criminologists to argue that the answer to crime lies in increasing economic opportunities. Instead, the political and crimino-logical conventional wisdom has shifted to reducing the 'opportunities' to commit crime. Crime is now treated less as a sign of the tensions produced by an unjust society with unequally distributed resources and more as an inevitable consequence of the weakening of formal and informal 'controls' in a culture increasingly dominated by individualistic consumerism. The new realities of social structure and culture are largely taken as a given. As David Garland puts it, governments and ordinary people have adopted strategies to deal with the risk of crime which means that in some sense high crime rates have been 'normalized'. The exceptional cases, which are magnified out of all proportion by media attention, regard those offenders accused of committing horrific or serial crimes (Garland, 2001).

It is true that crime and incivilities cannot always be explained by situations of disadvantage; and many people living in such conditions do not resort to crime. But, as against the claims of so-called 'right realist' criminologists such as J. Q. Wilson, there are others who continue to emphasize the relationship between crime, inequality, and blocked opportunities (Currie, 1998). Longitudinal studies, such as those by West and Farrington in the United Kingdom which follow up samples of children over a long period to see which of them become criminal, demonstrate beyond doubt that the hard core of juvenile delinquents and young-adult criminals are those who are disadvantaged with respect to social and economic opportunities. These children have usually experienced socio-economic deprivation, poor housing, and disorganized inter-city communities. They are often impulsive, hyperactive, of low intelligence and low school attainment, and they have disproportionately suffered from inconsistent and uncaring parenting and parental conflict. Equally, the recent significant fall in crime rates in major US cities has been linked, among other things, to the increase in unskilled (legal and semi-legal) employment opportunities. So-called 'control' theories of crime causation are right to emphasize the importance of building and maintaining attachments between individuals, families, and social institutions. But feelings of 'investment' in legitimate society are not unaffected by changing opportunities to participate in it.

In the countries of Continental Europe, the obsession with personal security and anxiety about 'street crime' is of more recent origin and always discussed in the context of increases in immigration. The way political discourse so often confuses immigrants with criminals is a good illustration of the way criminalization is linked to the tightening of boundaries. Approaches based on objective and relative deprivation are again relevant here. Because of the limits on legal immigration in countries like Italy or Spain, unregistered 'irregular' immigrants have little choice but to live by illegal expedients. In France and Germany, which have longer-standing immigrant communities, the disproportionate level of crime of second-generation immigrant youth (in so far as this is not merely a result of differential responses by the forces of order) can be linked to relative social disadvantage and a strong sense of exclusion. More generally, a recent global survey commissioned by the United Nations (Newman, 1999) argues that worldwide, both theft and contact crimes are associated with deprivation and with strain between means and available goals. In developing countries, it is said, more education goes together with less crime, and urbanization and affluence generally reduce crime levels. Certainly, the 'opportunity' to commit crimes is also relevant. Serious violence, for example, is a more likely outcome of criminal events where, as in the United States or some South American countries, handguns are easily available. But except perhaps for high-volume crimes such as theft of cars and bikes, opportunity is rarely by itself a sufficient cause.

The police are increasingly impotent in the face of 'high crime societies'. They are able to solve only a small proportion of the enormous number of property crimes and only a tiny proportion of offenders are sentenced (though those committing crimes of violence are more likely to be known to their victim and thus more likely to be caught). Historically speaking, it has been claimed, the severity of sanctions has certainly declined (Heiland *et al.*, 1992). But in the United States especially, practices such as 'zero tolerance', mandatory sentencing, and the increasing tendency to treat juveniles like adults have produced an inflated population in prison or under some sort of supervision which is now almost the highest in the world. Some scholars argue that this has only been a response to the exceptional level of crime and that it has helped to keep crime rates down. But others argue that states such as California cannot continue to shift so much of their public funds from education to building prisons without creating enormous problems for the future. Prison numbers have also gone up throughout Europe—to a large extent reflecting the incarceration of immigrants and ethnic minorities. Otherwise, there is wide variety in such rates in the rest of the world from a maximum in Russia to almost none in some Arab countries, which often use other means of deterrence, and civil law and religious modes of treating crimes, including murder (Newman, 1999).

2 The Criminologies of Everyday Life

In addition to its scientific pretensions, criminology is also an arm of the administration of justice. From the eighteenth century onwards, criminological data was sought by government-sponsored empirical enquiries aimed at improving the state's grip on populations by charting the patterns of crime and monitoring the practice of police and prisons. Hence we can only properly understand the narrow field of crime control by going outside it to the spheres of economics and politics, and examining the relationship between crime control and governance (what Foucault called 'Governmentality'). Criminologists have broken this down into a variety of questions. What is the political agenda behind crime control? How is crime governed? What is the role of the state, of private agencies, of the 'community', or the potential victim? When, why, and how do governments seek to reduce crime, to gain legitimacy through crime control, or even, in some societies, to govern in collusion with crime? How does the response to crime help construct the difference between those considered actual and potential citizens as compared to those who must be treated as actual or potential outsiders? Empirical evidence can be sought by showing how the response to crime and criminals is symbolized and communicated through the different types of strategies used in responding to deviance and disorder. Important recent examples include the use of 'contracts' with juvenile delinquents, or the adoption of 'zero-tolerance' policing of low-level disorderly behaviour.

There is widespread agreement that the most salient development in crime control in the past generation has been the centrality which has now been assumed by strategies and techniques of crime prevention. For crime to occur, there must be motivation, opportunity, and a lack of guardians. Over the last forty years, criminologists have come to give less attention to motivation and more to the other two conditions. For ideological and fiscal reasons, many governments adopted a superficial reading of research which was said to show that 'nothing worked' in the sphere of reforming delinquents. Right-wing and even left-wing forms of so-called 'realistic' criminology gave up on trying to solve the problem of crime through understanding the motivations of offenders and seeking to rehabilitate them, and concentrated much more on meeting the priorities of victims looking for protection from crime. Policy-makers were particularly influenced by the 'criminologies of everyday life', advanced by Marcus Felson (1998) and others, whose approaches deal with crime not as if it were a result of social deprivation or psychological inadequacy but as a matter of 'rational choice'. For these approaches, the criminal exploits the opportunities available to steal mass-produced, easily movable and anonymous, hard-to-identify, cars and consumer goods. Attention is therefore given to the routines and lifestyles of offenders and victims—the way, for example, that modern two career families are less likely to provide 'guardians' of their homes during the day.

So-called 'supply-side criminology' seeks to make crime more difficult, more risky, and less rewarding to potential offenders through means such as 'target hardening' and increased surveillance. Likewise, crime-prevention initiatives involve a number of local agencies in an attempt to mobilize potential victims to take more precautions as well as offering the assistance of various technological and human aids (Crawford, 1997). Private police and corporate interests and private-public partnerships are increasingly involved in providing security (and private business organizations are also among the most important consumers of such services). Criminologists have documented how crime control is now a fast-expanding and lucrative international industry, sometimes involving American multinational firms.

In the concern to reduce the consequences of crime and 'incivilities' for victims and potential victims, efforts are also made to alleviate the 'fear of crime' as a problem in its own right. But the apparently technical decision to conduct regular surveys of the fear of crime also illustrates the way criminology helps construct the phenomena it studies. Interest in this issue originated as part of the backlash against increased legal protections given to (often black) defendants in the 1960s in the United States. As Ditton and Farrall explain, this 'general if bigoted societal concern about crime has been transformed into a personal problem of individual vulnerability' (Ditton and Farrall, 2000, p. xvi). Early research based on survey data about the fear of crime showed that old people and women were more afraid of crime, though it was the young—especially young men—who suffered the highest incidence of victimization. But it was soon noted that the apparent irrationality of these fears can be explained if we recognize both that older people and women are more vulnerable if crime actually happens to them, and that their risk statistics may be reduced because fear means they have already limited their movements. Other findings are less than obvious. Research shows that survey respondents nearly always tend to think there is more crime in other neighbourhoods than in those of which they have direct know-ledge. In general, feelings about the neighbourhood as such are often more important than direct experience of crime. The fear of crime, criminologists now believe, often condenses or serves to distract from larger feelings (including anger) about unwel-come changes in the neighbourhood. In today's 'risk society' the pursuit of security and personal and community safety becomes an end in itself whose success or failure is not identical with the reduction of crime rates. But since the pursuit of security requires an apparatus of surveillance, this serves as a visible reminder of insecurity. Some criminologists have also reminded us that there may also be an unacknow-ledged fascination with criminal behaviour which is transformed by reaction into the desire for exemplary punishment.

3 THE STATE UNDER PRESSURE

The shift to devolve responsibility for crime prevention from the state illustrates and is embedded in changing forms of governance. At one level, the state has to meet political challenges from regions and local government as well as from supranational political groupings. But even where its rule is unchallenged, crime is less and less linked to the state's task of maintaining public order and more and more to the needs and rights of victims. Especially in the United States, it is the victim rather than the offender who is individualized and seen as in need of rehabilitation. The current reluctance to sympathize with the offender, as also in some sense a victim, is all the more significant in the light of the many cases in which offenders involved in serious violence perceive *themselves* to be the wronged party. The move to tie crime control to the victim appeals broadly to both the political right and left, much as the ideal of punishment by, in, and for the 'community' did before. In many cases it is the com-munity itself which is seen as a 'collective victim'. But it is far from obvious that the type and degree of punishment for an offender should be allowed to depend on the existence of an identifiable victim or on the priorities of that victim. We should also bear in mind that the category of victim is not self-evident and is ultimately a normative not a descriptive designation. When the status of victim becomes crucial in the allocation of material and symbolic resources, we should expect to find prospective victims increasingly fighting for recognition—sometimes also against each other. The increasing centrality of the victim in the criminal-justice system, and, in particular, the growing importance of restitution and mediation as operational goals, raise a variety of difficult questions. In what ways, if at all, are the traditional criteria of harm and culpability, fairness, proportionality, and consistency, still relevant? How can sufficient allowance be made for considerations of deterrence, protection, and prevention (especially for more serious crimes)? Can and should the offender and the victim be allowed to settle between themselves the interests of the wider community? What counts as this community? Can there be local justice without social justice?

In his influential recent writings, David Garland (e.g. Garland, 2000) links the rise of the criminologies of everyday life to what he calls 'the limits of the sovereign state'. Until the 1970s the crime problem was assumed by governments to require expert advice so as to construct interventions which could then be put into practice by welfare professionals. But as governments recognized that they could do relatively little to reduce crime rates, they increasingly came to devolve their responsibilities onto the local community, to private organizations, and to victims and potential victims themselves. Garland offers a pessimistic account of the way 'penal welfarism' has been displaced by the politicization of popular punitiveness. He notes the privileging of public protection and the claim that 'prison works', and describes the changes in the emotional tone of crime policy from decency and humanity to insecurity, anger, and resentment.

A number of factors, he and others argue, have combined to produce 'the crisis in penal welfarism'. Criticisms of state-sponsored rehabilitation proved convenient at a time when Keynesian methods of running the economy gave way to deregulation and privatization. Less control over economic actors under neo-liberalism went together with a move to more authoritarian forms of social control and the rise of a right-wing politics which placed emphasis on individual responsibility. Instead of the state protecting all its citizens, social control increasingly came to be exerted by commercial organizations—in shopping malls, theme parks, transport systems, and other forms of public-private property. In practice, penal welfarism had actually relied on an everyday environment of norms which depended on the informal social controls exerted by families, neighbours, churches, and communities and the disciplines of schools and workplaces. By contrast, late modernity is characterized by more relaxed informal social controls in families, neighbourhoods, streets, and schools, plus the economic freedoms of neo-liberalism. Social control now depends more on the attractions of consumer goods and on the threat of unemployment connected to the increase of flexible working and insecurity at work.

Garland distinguishes between the criminology of 'the self' and 'the other'. Opportunistic crimes, those committed by people 'like us', are dealt with according to managerial and actuarial considerations. They rely on situational disincentives, the 'designing out' of crime, and (to a lesser extent) social crime prevention. On the other hand, a moralizing criminology of 'the other', accompanied by public shaming and exclusionary punishment, is mobilized to deal with such politically high-profile crimes as those of the serial killer, the paedophile, or the recidivist. The dramatization of punishment in the mass media has little to do with everyday crime and is increasingly rooted in larger insecurities characteristic of late modern times. Put in terms of the argument of this chapter, we could say that the normalizing response is more geared to reducing misbehaviour, while the dramatizing reaction is more concerned with marking moral boundaries. On a day-to-day basis, however, the two responses are interconnected and symbiotic. They may be aimed at different types of crimes and offenders, or be differentially emphasized at successive stages of law enforcement and punishment. Crime control may be relatively instrumental and inclusive at the local level, whilst more expressive and exclusionary at the level of national politics. Above all, these two approaches are directed to different constituencies, on the one hand, to professionals within the criminal justice system and on the other, to the diffuse public.

For some writers, the recognition that crime control is political, that it is shaped as much by techniques of governance as by a determination to reduce crime, shows the need to imagine a new sort of 'political criminology' (Scheingold, 1998). In mapping this field, Scheingold distinguishes three theoretical positions, each with a different diagnosis of high modern society and the existing (and ideal) role of government. The first of these characterizes high modernity in terms of the way a concern with risk has displaced traditional methods of crime control. In risk society, the police, for example, increasingly become a clearing house for communicating information about risk and allocating to others the responsibility for handling it (Ericson and Haggerty, 1997). Actuarial strategies emerge which are targeted not at deviant individuals (as in positivism), or at rational actors (as with classicism), but at designated dangerous 'sub-populations' and places. Dangers are identified in terms of generalized clues and profiles, and people are subjected to preventive policing geared to minimizing risk rather than changing behaviour. Extending the logic of insurance to the penal sphere has serious implications for procedural rights and accountability to the courts (Feeley and Simon, 1994).

A second approach, adopted by critical criminologists, argues that, as Western societies have undergone processes of commodification and individualization, the modern state has abandoned any project for overcoming divisions in society. Crime control is less and less accompanied by considerations of social justice. It has become, rather, an agent and site for producing fragmentation along class and race lines. In many circumstances, the underprivileged find themselves at cross-purposes, as in the case of violence against women. But crime may also offer the opportunity for resistance, as in the case of entrepreneurial crime by marginalized groups. Finally, however, a third approach claims that the way out of the problems of high modernity lies in recovering the idea of community (Braithwaite, 1989). Unlike the critical criminologists, who celebrate conflict and difference, those favouring this approach look to overcome these by using methods of reintegrative shaming (rather than exclusionary stigmatization) so as to maintain a healthy social consensus. At the same time, however, they envisage a strong role for the State in maintaining and extending the liberty of the individual.

But it would be a mistake to characterize high modernity as if it represented a complete break with the past. Even Garland admits that the state is often making no more than a tactical retreat—what he calls 'governing at a distance'. Often the use of other agencies can be a way of relieving the state from certain burdens without giving up overall control. The contrast is often presented metaphorically as one in which the state now seeks to 'steer' rather than 'row' civil society. When government encourages private agencies or potential victims to deal with crime, it is often the private which is being co-opted by the state and not vice versa. For example, those offering victim support have to meet government-defined charter standards of service delivery, and voluntary organizations such as the UK National Association for the Care and Resettlement of Offenders (NACRO) regularly carry out government-sponsored inspections of private services for offenders. This will apply less, of course, to the growth of private security paid for by commercial interests. New forms of regulation may even sometimes be more effective than more obviously penal methods of crime control, as in the successful use of restrictions on licences to run businesses as a method of weakening the hold of organized crime in New York.

Likewise, the idea that politicians find it convenient to rely on the slogan that 'nothing works' is already outdated. In a recent survey, already on its way to becoming canonical, Sherman and his colleagues have summarized what (they claim) is now known about the success of rehabilitative and preventative measures on the basis of competent evaluations in terms of their effects on recidivism (Sherman *et al.*, 1998). Their report distinguishes those projects or interventions which have not been demonstrated to work, from those which are promising, and those which are definitely known to work. The (otherwise plausible) initiatives which fall into the first category include community mobilization against crime in areas of high crime and poverty, drug abuse resistance education, 'scaring-straight' programmes of visits to prison, and home detention with electronic monitoring. On the other hand, those schemes which do work include courses in teaching social competency and coaching in thinking skills, home visits by teachers and others to give advice to young parents, work training for ex-offenders, arresting domestic abusers, drug treatment in prison, and policing 'hot spots' where crime events are recurrent.

Many of those working in the criminal justice system still think in terms of welfare even where they are obliged to talk the language of managerialism. The extent to which penal welfarism has been discredited also varies greatly by society. Formal and informal social controls in civil society in common law countries have a different relationship to the state than in Continental state societies such as France or Germany.

There the new criminologies of everyday life or the introduction of mediation are much less emancipated from the guiding role of the State or from traditional criminal-justice procedures. In some southern European countries such as Spain and Italy, on the other hand, penal welfarism hardly ever got started. The same applies to populist punitiveness. In Continental Europe, exclusion is still aimed less at the underclass and much more at those seen to be threatening the state. Above all, it is reserved for recent immigrants—even where they are only engaged in opportunistic crimes. In some European societies, there are second-generation immigrants who are seen by much of the population to form part of an underclass. The unexpected support for far right populism in the first round of the 2002 French Presidential election may be attributed in part to the reduced 'credibility' of the security policies, still fundament-ally based round 'inclusion', which were put forward by the principal candidates. We must learn to talk of *cultures* of control not *the* culture of control. In so far as criminology is itself part of the developments it analyses, arguing that other societies will go the same way as the United States (and to a lesser extent the United Kingdom) could become a self-fulfilling prophecy.

4 CRIME AND GLOBALIZATION

Any discussion of 'the limits of the sovereign state' in dealing with crime must also be linked to the way this is affected by the various processes of increasing trade, travel, and communication which have come to be known as globalization. The nation state is being weakened as economic actors become more independent of it and as the locus of political decisions, including those to do with crime control, moves else-where. And the 'uncoupling' of the economic from the political creates an anomic situation of deregulation in which both upper-world business malpractice and ordin-ary street crime flourish. But not all the consequences of globalization for the nation state are so univocal. The State's response to organized crime and terrorism can also offer a way of (re)legitimating itself, even if this may often also require some pooling or relinquishing of sovereignty in order to collaborate with other states and organi-zation. This can be seen in the American reply to the Al Qa'ida attack on the centre of international finance in New York and military headquarters in Washington on 11 September 2001. The re-nationalization of airline security and the creation of the office for homeland security are only two of the most obvious manifestations of the re-found centrality of the Federal state.

Globalization is a name for complex and contradictory developments regarding the overcoming of economic, political, and cultural boundaries. It has objective and subjective features which do not always coincide. Surveys have suggested that many in the Muslim world refuse to accept the Western version of the events of September 11. For some, globalization itself is experienced as a sort of crime because it spreads models of behaviour which threaten or do not respect boundaries. More widely yet, the American response to terror was often seen as unjustified aggression rather than 'policing'. Both the terrorist attack and the response to it offer a dangerous foretaste of what some writers see as the coming worldwide culture clash of 'Macworld v Jihad'. Much of globalization is not without precedent, especially in the area of crime and crime control. Illegal immigration and drug trading (often involving European countries) has a long history. And as far as crime control is concerned, it is enough to think of the spread of Beccaria's ideas about punishment in the eighteenth century, or the flurry of international exchange visits in the nineteenth century to compare styles of prison building. Nor is globalization inevitable, even though talking about as if it is may try to make it so. There are increasing signs of 'resistance', such as the beginnings of a nationalist backlash against the trend towards stronger regional and global groupings and signs of a return to protectionism rather than open markets. But it is significant that even so-called 'no global' groups committed to fighting the evils of globalization are forced, or choose, to adopt many of the techniques and logos developed by globalizing companies.

It is often assumed that globalization inevitably leads to increases in crime. But we should remember that globalization also affects crime control. This is well illustrated by the link between new forms of information technology and crime. Flows and exchanges in cyberspace serve both as a support and as an environment for crime beyond boundaries. 'Cyberspace crimes' include trespass and hacking (not yet unambiguously criminal), the theft of data (for example, of credit card numbers or trade secrets), the harassment of individuals, fraud and deception, obscenity and pornography. On the one hand, the Internet does lead to more crime opportunities. It spreads knowledge of new crime techniques and facilitates the possibilities for organizing or committing crimes, especially where images, speech, or information are themselves part of the *actus reus* of the crime (as with paedophilia, money-laundering, terrorism, bomb making, violent racism, and hate crimes). Though some damaging computer viruses have been put about, major military or terrorist attacks using information technology have not so far materialized. But the potential is there. More generally, it also offers new opportunities for crimes spawned by familiar motives of greed and power (Wall, 2002). Yet, on the other hand, the same technological progress which facilitates crime beyond boundaries can also be used for the purposes of crime control. Cryptography is used by governments even more than by criminals. Governments increase surveillance of international traffic through ECHELON and other unaccountable forms of listening devices. More and more criminals are traced through their incautious use of mobile phones.

Cyberspace represents a new challenge to policy-makers and law enforcers. The evidence so far is that the police do not give computer crime a high priority. Successful prosecution of net crime will also require changes in trial processes and types of acceptable evidence. But the initial euphoria over the unregulated communal togetherness which could be created across political and social boundaries has now largely been dissipated. The high proportion of sex sites on the Internet, for example, offers an easy excuse for censorship. While Western nations will probably seek a balance between censure and creativity, more authoritarian regimes will be less tolerant when considering the possible challenges the Internet represents. Virtual relationships, like all relationships, may sometimes be abused or abusive, but the evidence shows that so called 'netizens' usually bring with them their existing normative values rather than treating the net as a moral wilderness. There are also signs of increasing informal control and regulation by, in, and for this 'virtual community'.

While some writers emphasize the crime threat which globalization brings in from 'outside', others rightly argue that the locus of most crime, even organized crime, continues to be local, or at least 'glocal'. It is often assumed that the process(es) of globalization must produce convergence, and that therefore methods of crime and cultures of crime control must become more similar. But it is at least as important to see globalization as a process of growing interdependence which presupposes and produces differences. Both organized crime and international responses, like globalized manufacturing and services themselves, require the specialization and integration of differentiated units. Illegitimate as well as legitimate businesses gain from customs frontiers being reduced, as in the North Atlantic Free Trade Association (NAFTA) or the European Union. Companies can shop around for more favourable regimes of regulation so as to gain impunity for what would be white-collar crimes at home, and organized criminals look for the softest penal regimes. On the other hand, the reduction of economic barriers can also reduce some opportunities for organized crime, for example, smuggling or subsidies frauds within the European Union (Nelken, 1997). And some aspects of globalization, such as the way money goes to where the returns are best, may be out of anyone's control (including that of organized criminals).

There are a variety of other ways of linking globalization and crime. Greater contacts through trade, travel, and communication can give rise to new types of crime such as those connected to transnational organized crime or to sexual tourism. But, more typically, globalization affects the way more ordinary crimes can be committed, and has implications for the levels and distribution of such crimes. One important way globalizing trends can contribute to crime is by exacerbating the differences between more or less economically successful or favoured countries, regions, and even parts of cities. In its impact on developed societies, globalization can be seen as an aspect of the relative exhaustion of the home market for mass-produced manufactured goods. It is thereby held responsible for the reduced opportunities, ghettoization, marginalization, and social exclusion which provide both the conditions and alibi for much crime. As areas decline, there is less factory and industrial work for young men; much work that is still available is more suited to women. This can lead to a crisis in masculinity, the gender order, and parenting. With so many women working, there are also fewer people around to exercise surveillance and provide unpaid voluntary work in and for the community. As locally based social control declines, property crime and black economy activity increases and escapist routes of alcohol and drugs become tempting (Taylor, 1999). On the other hand, those fortunate enough to benefit from the better economic opportunities presented by globalization seek to safeguard their families in bubbles of security in defined areas of housing and shopping. These are then fortified against the risks posed by those members of the population who have been displaced from the economy by processes of global change (Bottoms and Wiles, 1996).

Globalization, as we have said, also affects crime control. This may be by means of political alliances, through technological collaboration, or via the spread of models and ideas. But there are also other less obvious connections. Sometimes globalization helps bring an offence into existence. The laws against what is aptly named 'insider trading', introduced at the time of the so-called 'big bang' liberalization of the London stock exchange, were required so as to maintain the impression of predictability and trustworthiness of the globalized City of London once it was opened up to outsiders. Globalization here led to the criminalization of behaviour which not long before had been considered as acceptable, or at least containable within acceptable limits, as long as it was confined to 'insiders'. 'Globalizing moral panics' about crime problems range from paedophilia to political corruption. These may not necessarily have any common denominator but their very existence is indicative of the way crime reconstructs moral boundaries beyond the nation state. It is interesting in this connection that some states have passed laws reducing the burden of proof in criminal cases dealing with sex tourism. Whether this increased protection for victims abroad is a sign of a broadened definition of who counts as my 'neighbour', or only an emotional reaction to the danger represented by returning sex criminals, is less than clear. On the other hand, a key feature of the current approach to the globalization of crime control is the cruel and contradictory attempt to increase the circulation of goods and money whilst blocking the transfer of people from less favoured to more favoured countries. From the 1970s onwards this has meant that international police collaboration and databases have been overwhelmingly focused on illegal immigration.

In relation to the theme of changing forms of governance, two arguments stand out in much current writing about globalization (Nelken, 1997). The first of these repeatedly insists that globalization is a process out of control, or even beyond control, which is creating enormous opportunities for business and organized crime. Starting in the 1990s, there has been a major campaign concerned with the menace of ex-communist transnational organized criminals. These concerns are shared not only by sympathizers with the American secret services (who were in search of a new role) but also by otherwise anti-establishment sociologists such as Manuel Castells in his description of what he calls 'The Perverse Connection; the Global Criminal Economy' (Castells, 1998). Locally based criminal-justice systems, it is said, are struggling to keep up with this challenge and perhaps are always destined to be behind.

There is a long list of so-called transnational crimes. These include terrorism; espionage, including industrial espionage; theft of intellectual property; fraud; criminal bankruptcy; infiltration of legal business; drugs and arms trafficking; aircraft hijacking; the international wholesaling of pornography and prostitution; smuggling and trade in children, women, immigrants, bodily organs, cultural artefacts, flora and fauna; nuclear materials and cars; counterfeiting; crimes related to computer technology; international fraud and other financial crimes; tax evasion; theft of art, antiques, and other precious items; piracy; insurance fraud; crimes against the environment; trade in endangered species; and internationally coordinated racial violence. Radical conclusions are drawn from this challenge. The legal institutions of the world, it is claimed, are still bound to the nation state, but existing state-based legal systems cannot protect citizens from the new authoritarian threat provided by transnational organized crime. According to this view, the globalization of crime thrives on the inability of the criminal law to globalize.

But there are also mirror-image fears. The claim here is that police forces are in fact using these worries about transnational crime to forge democratically unaccountable alliances. America has long given a lead by exporting its war against drugs and terrorism, but the attempts by the European Union to organize police cooperation in the absence of European-wide parliamentary accountability is another good example. Even before the events of September 2001, European Community members, individually and collectively, had already developed a 'fortress' mentality. One author claims that it is by looking at the enforcement practices of the transnational law-enforcement enterprise that we can best come to understand the political form of the emergent transnational world system (Sheptycki, 1995). There is evidence that powers and techniques which are demanded or taken in order to deal with the threat of menacing forms of organized crime often end up being used against more low-level or local forms of criminality (Sheptycki, 2002). Often they are adapted to keeping out those immigrants who in the present economic climate are once again assumed to be surplus to requirements. It is noticeable that illegal immigration is always now included alongside drugs and terrorism as a major threat against which 'Fortress Europe' needs to be defended.

For these writers, the solution of transnational policing is often worse than the problem, not only because it is authoritarian on its own account but also because there is ample evidence that unaccountable policing can itself involve illegality or engage in crime in its own account. We should not exaggerate the extent to which the police have managed to organize themselves on a European or international basis. The European Union is now creating a coordinated prosecution service for a limited number of serious crimes. The International War Crimes Court at The Hague is increasingly being granted powers to deal with the most serious international crimes. On the other hand, we are still far from anything approaching a system of international criminal law. In the meantime, individual states also take drastic measures, allegedly aimed at responding to transnational criminality, which have serious implications for civil liberties. The current crackdown on terrorism is used increasingly so as to justify controls over groups and social movements campaigning against globalization. Even if some members of these groups do not always do all they should to prevent protest action from escalating into violent confrontation, the threat they pose has little in common with Al Qa'ida terrorism.

5 The Global Penal Gaze

In seeking to understand the implications of globalization for crime and criminology, it is important to appreciate that what we could call the 'global penal gaze' is not limited to those transnational organized crimes and other crimes for which international collaboration is essential. Economic and political developments are also promoting the trend towards a European or worldwide homogeneous understanding and control of more ordinary and conventional crimes such as mugging and burglary. In this final section, I shall attempt to show how criminology is itself part of this larger project through which local ideas about crime, like the discourses of rights and victimization with which they are of course connected, are seeking to become a universal language.

Given its auspices and likely influence, the recently published United Nations-sponsored global survey of crime and crime control provides an intrinsically important example of globalizing criminology (Newman, 1999). It well illustrates its impressive scope and ambition, and also its biases and blind spots. I shall devote special attention to this volume here because it both purports to synthesize the current state of criminological knowledge and also to summarize the results of an unprecedented international survey of the views and experiences of no less than 155,000 victims in fifty-four countries.

The UN Report argues that nation states are now subjected to the competing pressures of the fragmentation of states and the homogenization of culture. At the same time, the Report insists, 'one of the unifying or common features of all countries examined in this book is crime and the response to it' (Newman, 1999: 1). The Report starts out by seeking to prove that the crime problem is experienced more or less similarly throughout the world. Worldwide, it says, opinion polls show the crime problem to be a worry second in importance only to unemployment. It builds its vision for a (re)ordered world on the idea of 'crime as a universal concept' (this subtitle is not even given a question mark). The evidence for this is found in an alleged worldwide 'almost perfect correspondence in ranking of crimes' as reflected in similar ideas about the seriousness of car theft, robbery with a weapon as compared to robbery without a weapon, and so on (ibid. 28).

In my judgement, questions can and should be raised about the validity of this premise. Only a limited choice of crimes are included; there is nothing, for example, about corruption, white-collar crime, crimes of the middle classes, or victimless crimes. Elsewhere the Report makes clear that there are very different evaluations of assaults against women in Europe as compared to some countries in Africa, Asia, and Latin America. Focusing only on victim responses to surveys of comparative serious-ness has the effect of de-contextualizing crime. It does little, for example, to explain the willingness of those in poorer countries to take the risks of prostitution and drug dealing abroad as a way of paying the costs of escaping from political conflict or economic hopelessness. The Report does not (and could not) deny the existence of diversity; but it takes this as precisely the stimulus to its globalizing mission. A large part of the Report is taken up with categorizing differences between countries in crime rates, victimization rates, arrest rates for juveniles, prison rates, levels of fear of crime, and so on. But there is little interest in exploring the cause and meaning of such differences. The goal is rather to impose a homogeneous idea of what is and should be treated as crime, and hence what the response to crime should be. The model is what (some) Western countries describe as the criminal-justice system, and the focus is on reducing those differences which evidence a departure from the minimum (normal and normative) standards of criminal justice.

Globalizing criminology of this sort draws on all the world indifferently for its data. We are told, for example, that 'over a five year period two out of three inhabit-ants in big cities will be victims of crime at least once'. Much the same explanations of crime, it is proposed, can be applied to both poor and rich countries—and this forms part of a determined effort to reappraise the link between crime and modernity. It used to be thought that a growth in levels of property crime was the inevitable price to be paid for modernization. But the new conventional wisdom put forward in this Report claims that the level of theft in less economically developed countries, espe-cially in large towns, has been underestimated because where people do not trust the police they report less. The Report argues therefore that increasing the level of affluence in poorer countries would indeed lead to *less* crime. The exceptions are where rich and poor live alongside each other, or where affluence leads to more going out at night and hence, just as in more developed societies, increases the risk of exposure to crime.

It is important to see how globalizing criminology not only documents but also *produces* 'global facts'. Even the apparently objective task of gathering comparative statistics, without ulterior purpose, can itself have an independent effect on systems of criminal justice. Thus, after comparative figures on relative rates of incarceration emerged in the 1970s, Finland sought to reduce its prison population, whilst other nations such as Italy felt able to do the opposite. But those responsible for organizing large scale cross-national victim surveys sometimes deliberately deploy their find-ings more as a tool for achieving social change than as a search for understanding variability. The political goal, which is seen to be applicable on a worldwide scale, is the need to increase the status of the victim and especially that of 'repeat victims'. The views of victims are assumed to be *the* appropriate basis for determining how well police and other aspects of the criminal justice system are operating and how they should be made to operate (see Van Dyke, 2000).

As far as the issue of governance is concerned, there is some ambiguity (or is it contradiction?) about the implications of globalizing criminology for state monopoly of crime control. On the one hand, what is prescribed is the universal introduction of the Western model of the criminal-justice state—what the UN Report calls 'policing plus prevention'. The appropriate way of dealing with crime is taken to be a well-organized mix of public policing, private crime prevention, and community initiatives. As opposed to those who announce the end of penal welfarism, the global penal gaze offers a 'top–down' and easy (too facile?) mixing of the older rehabilitative approach with more 'state of the art' advice about crime prevention. As the Report puts it, 'promoting social control and responsibility, investing in youth and family, breaking the cycle of violence, city action and innovative policing have become synonymous with best practice in crime reduction' (Newman, 1999: 220).

The Report indicates a range of projects which it is claimed will work effectively in reducing crime; but there is no discussion of the many reasonably sounding interventions which do not in fact work. Although it cites the Sherman survey, it also continues to recommend warmly crime prevention initiatives that Sherman *et al.* found to be quite unsupported by satisfactory evidence. On the other hand, like Sherman, the Report assumes as universals what are often specifically American patterns of crime causation. It is unlikely, for example, that home visiting by teachers to give advice to negligent or incompetent parents is always relevant to reducing crime (in Italy, for example, the family is, if anything, over-protective; and it is the State which is negligent and distrusted). Nor do they hint at the difficulties even the most economically developed societies have in organizing unbiased and effective methods of evaluation so as to be able to distinguish what 'works' from what is (merely) politically plausible or instrumental. The emphasis on the need to centralize social control in the state also seems to give too little attention to the important role played by types and forms of social control within social groups, workplaces, and neighbourhoods. Indeed, it goes in the opposite direction to the conclusion which has been reached in those societies, such as the United States, which have most experience of governmentally organized criminal-justice remedies. Here we are told that those who respond to crime 'can no longer rely on "state knowledge", on unresponsive bureaucratic agencies, and upon universal solutions imposed from above' (Garland, 2000: 285).

On the other hand, and at the same time, there are many ways in which the Report also undermines the sovereignty of the state. This is implicit above all in the way the Report presupposes that states need to accept the requirements of the United Nations as a supranational body and the universal criterion and standards it claims should be applied. The Report also bypasses the state by speaking, in the name of victims and their priorities, for crime control rather than in terms of the state's claim to monopoly authority as regulator of disputes. The state is not being encouraged to 'govern through crime control' but rather to improve its services to victims.

In general, the Report tries to give the impression that organizing an appropriate response to crime is much like setting up a successful health or road system. Perhaps because of the diplomatic requirements of UN sponsorship, there is no discussion of the problem of state crime, or the participation or collusion of governments in the crimes of their citizens (Cohen, 2001; Friedrichs, 1998). There is also no acknow-ledgement of the ambiguous role of states in politically, ethnically, religiously, or otherwise deeply divided societies. No allowance is made for the intensely political stakes in the construction of consensus for criminal justice interventions, whether, as in the past, against the 'dangerous classes', or, as now, against immigrants and ethnic minorities. Reading this report it is easy to forget that what is good for some may not be in everyone's interest. Private sector involvement in crime prevention is seen as only a good thing. No problems are raised about potentially conflicting public and private interests, the danger that private security only goes to those who can pay for it, or that those who supply it may have a vested interest in increasing rather than reducing fear of crime.

Globalizing criminology, like the related discourse of human rights, whatever its good intentions, is also part of a scheme of world governance. In trying to make the world safe for all (but, we need to ask, against whom?) it is also trying to make the world safe for us (but, we should also ask, safe to do what?). In practice, whether or not the Report acknowledges this, the struggle against crime at the international, national, subnational, or local level regularly overlaps with the attempt to tame diversity and nul-lify threats to established power. Despite its global reach, the United Nations Report presupposes Western (and even what are largely Anglo-American) models of criminal justice and discourses of criminology. This is not to deny that models taken from else-where, for good or bad reasons, continue to play a large part in the process of introduc-ing legal change (see Nelken and Feest, 2001). But the United States and even Europe are hardly models of success when it comes to crime control. And in a globalized world we can no longer assume any Archimidean point of leverage for change (Coombe, 2000). We must face up to the challenge of trying to understand—and even learn from—the different forms taken by crime and crime control in other places (Nelken, 1994, 2000a, 2002b). To do this wisely, we will need to take much more care to avoid the opposing errors of presuming either that other societies are—and should be—necessarily like ours, or assuming that they are—and always will be—inherently different (Cain, 2000).

References

Beck, U. (2002). 'The Politics of World Risk Society', Public Lecture given at Cardiff University, 6 Feb.

Bottoms, A., and Wiles, P. (1996). 'Crime and Insecurity in the City', in C. Finjaut, J. Goetals, T. Peters and L. Walgrave (eds.), *Changes in Society, Crime and Criminal Justice in Europe*, i, Amsterdam: Kluwer.

Braithwaite, J. (1989). *Crime, Shame and Integration*, Cambridge: Cambridge University Press.

Cain, M. (2000). 'Orientalism, Occidentalism and the Sociology of Crime', *British Journal of Criminology*, 40: 239–60.

Castells, M. (1998). *The Information Age: Economy, Society and Culture*, 111: *End of Millennium*, Oxford: Blackwell.

Cohen, S. (1996). 'Crime and Politics: Spot the Difference', *British Journal of Sociology*, 47: 2–21.

—— (2001). *States of Denial*, Oxford: Polity Press.

Coombe, R. J. (2000). 'Contingent Articulations: A Critical Studies of Law', in A. Sarat and T. Kearns (eds.), *Law in the Domains of Culture*: Ann Arbor: University of Michigan Press, 21–64.

Crawford, A. (1997). *The Local Governance of Crime*, Oxford: Oxford University Press.

Currie, E. (1998). *Crime and Punishment in America*, New York: Holt.

Ditton, J., and Farrall, G. (eds.) (2000). *Fear of Crime*, Aldershot: Dartmouth.

Ericson, R., and Carriere, K. (1994). 'The Fragmentation of Criminology', in D. Nelken (ed.), *The Futures of Criminology*, London: Sage, 89–109.

—— and Haggerty, K. (1997). *Policing the Risk Society*, Oxford: Oxford University Press.

Estrada, F. (2001). 'Juvenile Violence as a Social Problem', *British Journal of Criminology*, 41: 639–55.

Feeley, M., and Simon, J. (1994). 'Actuarial Justice: The Emerging New Criminal Law', in D. Nelken (ed.), *The Futures of Criminology*, London: Sage, 173–201.

Felson, M. (1998). *Crime and Everyday Life* (2nd edn.), Thousand Oaks, Calif: Pine Forge.

Friedrichs, D. (1998). *State Crime* (2 vols.), Aldershot: Dartmouth.

Garland, D. (2001), *The Culture of Control*, Oxford: Oxford University Press.

Heiland, H. G., Shelley, L. I., and Katoh, H. (eds.) (1992), *Crime and Control in Comparative Perspectives*, Berlin: de Gruyter.

Levi, M., and Nelken, D. (1996). *The Corruption of Politics and the Politics of Corruption*, special issue of the *Journal of Law and Society*, Oxford: Blackwell, 23 Jan.

Maguire, M. (1997). 'Crime Statistics, Patterns and Trends: Changing Perceptions and their Implications', in M. Maguire, R. Morgan, and R. Reiner (eds.), *The Oxford Handbook of Criminology*, Oxford: Oxford University Press (2nd edn.): 135–88.

Nelken, D. (1994). 'Whom can you Trust: The Future of Comparative Criminality', in D. Nelken (ed.), *The Futures of Criminology*, London: Sage, 220–44.

—— (1997). 'The Globalization of Crime and Criminal Justice: Prospects and Problems', in M. Freeman (ed.), *Law at the Turn of the Century*, Oxford: Oxford University Press, 251–79.

—— (ed.) (2000a). *Contrasting Criminal Justice*, Aldershot: Dartmouth.

—— (2002b). 'Comparing Criminal Justice', in M. Maguire, R. Morgan, and R. Reiner (eds.), *The Oxford Handbook of Criminology* (3rd edn.), Oxford: Oxford University Press, 175–202.

—— and Feest, J. (2001). *Adapting Legal Cultures*, Oxford: Hart.

Newman, G. (ed.) (1999). *Global Report on Crime and Justice*, Oxford: Oxford University Press.

Reiner, R. (2000). 'Crime Control in Britain', *Sociology*, 34: 71–94.

Scheingold, S. A. (1998). 'Constructing the New Political Criminology: Power, Authority, and the Post-liberal State', *Law and Social Inquiry*, 23: 857–95.

Sheptycki, J. (1995). 'Transnational Policing and the Makings of a Postmodern State', *British Journal of Criminology*, 35: 613–35.

Sheptycki, J. (2002). *In Search of the Transnational Police*, Aldershot: Dartmouth.

Sherman, L. W., Gottfredson, D. C., Mackenzie, D. L., Eck, J., Reuter, P., and Bushway, S. D. (1998). 'Preventing Crime: What Works, What Doesn't, What's Promising', *Research in Brief*, National Institute of Justice, Washington: US Department of Justice.

Taylor, I. (1999). *Crime in Context*, Oxford: Polity Press.

Young, J. (1999). *The Exclusive Society*, London: Sage.

Van Dyke, J. (2000). 'Implications of the International Crime Victims Survey for a Victim Perspective', in A. Crawford and J. Goodey (eds.), *Integrating a Victim Perspective within Criminal Justice: International Debates*, Aldershot: Dartmouth, 97–124.

Wall, D. (ed.) (2002). *Cyberspace Crime*, Aldershot: Dartmouth.

CHAPTER 14

THE INTERNATIONAL LEGAL ORDER

BENEDICT KINGSBURY

CONTROVERSIAE (disputes) is the first word in book I of Hugo Grotius's foundational text *De Jure Belli ac Pacis* (The Law of War and Peace, 1625). Much modern scholarship in international law has followed this strand of Grotius's thought in orienting the subject to the problem of managing disputes. Since the late nineteenth century, generations of leading scholar-practitioners have shaped a view of international law which emphasizes legal doctrines and materials related to disputes: the specific rules one party to a dispute may invoke against another, the sources (e.g. treaty, custom) to which an international court will look to identify international law rules, the general principles (e.g. acquiescence, abuse of rights) that international courts have borrowed from national legal systems to help deal with international cases, the foundational principles of international law (e.g. state responsibility) enunciated by courts, the precedential implications of a specific decision or a specific settlement agreement. This focus owes much to the sociological model of the successful international lawyer as it developed in the English and French traditions of international law over the past century: that of the academically respected practitioner, primarily the world-wise professor-counsel or the erudite lawyer-civil servant, whose career involved both scholarship and representing litigants in the management of disputes, and might eventually culminate in becoming a judge or arbitrator in an international tribunal and an author of learned general courses and essays. Naturally these scholar-practitioners are committed also to the enunciation of general norms and the assertion of community values. But the interwoven practice and scholarship of settlement of international disputes has tilted the subject toward specific questions of whether one state has become bound by a particular rule which the other state may invoke (the question of opposability of particular norms between the parties), and away from what might otherwise have been an overwhelming preoccupation with the construction of a global normative order. Similarly, a focus on dispute settlement gives higher priority to solving bilateral problems than to vindicating other kinds of community interest. It has tended also to encourage legal-positivist scholarship that emphasizes materials already generated by recognized sources of law (treaties, the custom-creating legal practice of relevant actors, judicial decisions, scholarly opinions, and so on), and strictly separates statements of the *lex lata* from suggestions for reform *de lege ferenda*.

The English-French dispute settlement-focused model and its accompanying practice-inspired positivist jurisprudence never took hold as strongly in the United States. Many imbued with Wilsonian or New Deal ideals invested themselves in constructing or writing about international institutions as means not simply of dispute settlement but of problem-solving more generally (Kennedy, 1987). The jurisprudential ideas influencing these problem-solvers in the period between the Wilson and Truman administrations were above all those of American legal realism, emphasizing the role of policy in framing law and producing legal decisions. Upon this platform, Myres McDougal and others built the New Haven 'policy science' approach to international law, which repudiated the positivist notion of law as a body of rules and sought instead to systematize the different tasks of lawyers as decision-specialists in a process of authoritative decision aimed at clarifying and implementing the community interest in world public order. Abram Chayes and others sought to develop a less prescriptive account of international law as process. While the pragmatic problem-solving agenda, with its interdisciplinary view of relevant materials and its more explicit engagement with policy and politics, has been widely influential, the distinctive jurisprudential theories underpinning it in the United States have not been broadly accepted elsewhere. The dominant jurisprudential approach to the global practice of international law continues to be positivist. But it is a positivism attenuated by the pragmatic needs to ameliorate disputes, ensure international institutions can operate effectively, and respond to demands of global governance. To adherents of this approach, the positivist state-centered system is increasingly stretched and strained, but neither in theory nor in practice has it been displaced by another. Its resilience has been greater than expected because in international law, practice continues to shape theory, and deeply embedded theory continues to shore up practice.

The task of this chapter is to assess major themes and approaches in the recent scholarship of international law, and to identify likely future directions and problems. It proceeds from the starting-point that the Anglo-French focus on dispute settlement and litigation, and the US focus on managerial problem-solving, are manifestations of a recurrent feature of international law writing since two of its founding scholar-practitioners, Alberico Gentili (1552–1608) and Grotius (1583–1645). This feature is the nexus between the aspirations of scholarship to engage closely with practice, and of practitioners to work within the frameworks transmitted through scholarship.

The problem of how to contribute at once to practice and theory has been central in defining both the scholarly discipline of international law and some of the main lines of debate within it. The work of Martin Wight, Hedley Bull, and other leaders of the 'English School' of international relations theory (Butterfield and Wight, 1966) distinguishes Hobbesian realism, Grotian rationalism, and Kantian cosmopolitanism as three distinctive approaches whose interplay captures much of the history of Western ideas about international politics. The three approaches elucidated by the 'English school' can be mapped to three different views of the relations between theoretical inquiry in international law and the legal practice of relevant actors. A realist approach emphasizes consistency with practice as the criterion for assessing good theory, and in developing theory seeks to approximate the understandings or behavior of relevant decision-makers. A Grotian approach seeks to temper theory with practice, and practice with theory. As Wight put it, Grotian international law 'sings a kind of descant over against the movement of diplomacy' (Butterfield and Wight, 1966: 29). A normative cosmopolitan approach holds out the possibility of re-making the world through theory: in a sense, theory is practice (Allott, 2001).

It will be argued that the specific focus on disputes and on third-party settlement, with its associated positivist theory, has dovetailed with broader problem-solving approaches in encouraging the development of several useful legal concepts (Sect. 1), but that the dominant positivist theoretical structure that has held international legal practice together now encounters so many internal critiques and external challenges (Sect. 2) that its viability is seriously in question, unless it can be deepened and renovated (Sect. 3). A proposal for rethinking the concept of international law will be outlined in summary fashion (Sect. 4). It will be argued that the Grotian integration of theory and practice is a valuable and distinctive feature of international law, that there are ethical arguments for the predominant positivist positions which this problem-solving engagement with practice has fostered, that problems such as moral injustice and lack of legitimacy now require a richer approach to international law rules and process in an era of deepening international governance, and that a Grotian conception of international law which integrates sources-based and content-based criteria provides a promising way forward.

1 Scope of Pragmatic International Law Scholarship: Recent Conceptual Developments

The question 'What is international law?' does not have anything approaching an agreed theoretical answer (for further discussion see the final section of this chapter). Yet a large cadre of scholars and practitioners around the world share the identification of a set of treaties, customary rules, international judicial decisions, formal institutions, and practices of reasoning and argument that together constitute the nucleus of international law. This core is reflected in the remarkable degree of commonality of structure and method among the most influential textbooks in different languages, a structure and method that was already largely in place by the beginning of the twentieth century in the work of textbook writers such as Franz von Liszt and Lassa Oppenheim. The degree of agreement reflects the centrality for these text writers of a body of prac- tice that is for them both constitutive of international law and the principal source of meaning in the field. International law is thus a field of legal study unified by the grav- itational pull of a core set of materials and commitments that holds together a diverse group of participants whose individual subject-matter interests, interdisciplinary borrowings, theoretical inclinations, and political orientations may not be well reflected in this core. In so far as this core set of materials is structured by a generally recognized theory, that theory is a legal positivism that bases international legal obligation on some form of state consent. Most participants recognize that, in practice, international legal rules are frequently formed, applied, and changed without such developments being the will of all the states concerned. The processes and institutions of international law cannot be comprehensively and convincingly explained simply in positivist terms.

   But many useful international law concepts have been constructed and to some extent made operational within this positivist gravitational field. These include several basic concepts: subjects (legal persons) in international law, sovereignty, equality, consent, custom, jurisdiction, state responsibility, recognition, the common interest, regionalism, good faith, freedom of the seas, and self-defense (see the useful survey in Macdonald and Johnston, 1983). They include also conceptual structures relating to such matters as: the relations of international and municipal law; the nature and process of legal development; the impact of international organizations; majoritari- anism and consensus in law-making; the international constitutional role of the UN Charter; the efficacy and morality of sanctions; universality and particularism in human rights (each covered in Macdonald and Johnston, 1983). The post-Cold War Western policy agenda has brought to prominence other notions which, through the dynamics of practice, have in a pragmatic if not highly coherent way become legal ideas, including terrorism, narcotics traffic, trafficking in people, money-laundering, corruption, protection of particular notions of intellectual property. The interrelated post-Cold War security and humanitarian agendas have given new life to such older legal notions as: intervention for humanitarian purposes; international governance of territory, as in Kosovo after 1999 or in East Timor prior to its 2002 independence; the decisional and legitimizing powers of the UN Security Council and regional organ- izations; the interplay in military contexts of international human rights and interna- tional humanitarian laws of war; and verification and mandatory inspection in arms control. This section focuses on five more systemic concepts that have emerged in recent years and are shaped by, and shaping, practice.

1.1 The Decline of the 'Third World' and of Distributive Justice, and the Rise of Sustainable Development

The decline of the 'Third World' as a legal concept owes much to differences in interests that became manifest after the common projects of European decolonization and Cold War 'non-alignment' lost salience. This decline was also promoted by Western policies and by broad acquiescence in neo-liberal economic arrangements. This decline has been accompanied by a precipitate diminution in normative international legal scholarship directed specifically toward global distributive justice or curbing global inequality (Pogge, 2002). This reflects a loss of confidence in the ability of international law to address fundamental issues such as poverty and social violence. The decline of the Third World as an operational concept has played out in many areas of international legal practice and scholarship. Information and innovation policy provides one illustration. In the 1970s, a significant struggle was that of developing countries to change the Western-dominated structure of the global media and establish greater control over a new information order, an effort that foundered against the principle of press freedom. By the 1990s, the dominant struggles were those of the West to globalize intellectual property rights and to promote privatization and foreign corporate involvement in information services. Developing countries have achieved solidarity in resistance on specific issues such as manufacture of low-cost AIDS drugs, but have been unable to marshal a comprehensive programmatic alternative to the Western agenda. The success of the Internet, with accompanying problems of criminality, legitimate content control and governance, would in earlier decades have been addressed partly as a North-South issue, but in the current era the debate has been framed in terms of a Western agenda of blending and controlling state and non-state regulation and market forces. Beyond the agenda-setting group of prosperous Organization for Economic Cooperation and Development (OECD) countries, some individual states, most notably China, have been able to preserve appreciable policy autonomy. But these and many other areas of international law are generally characterized by a marked imbalance in favor of Western influence, heightened by the relative paucity of expert scholars, practitioners, regulators, and leading corporations based outside the OECD.

If the Third World designation has diminished as a practical concept, it has survived in a network of mainly US-based migrant scholars pursuing 'Third World Approaches to International Law' (Anghie, 1999). This consortium is unified by vestigial solidarity rather than a single research program, but the movement shares a general skepticism about neo-liberal dimensions of globalization. One iteration of this is a renewal of the long-standing developing country critique of the imposition of an 'international minimum standard' of protection for foreign investors. The critique is now applied to efforts to protect foreign investors and intellectual property rights holders through the Trade-Related Aspects of Intellectual Property (TRIPS) agreement of the World Trade Organization (WTO), the North American Free Trade Agreement (NAFTA), the lattice of over two thousand mainly North–South bilateral investment treaties, and the draft Multilateral Agreement on Investment (MAI) that failed in the OECD but laid the ground for related work in the WTO. The Third World critiques of transnational regimes for foreign investment continue to focus on traditional themes of inequity and the injustices of transnational alliances with comprador elites. They have begun also to highlight the adverse consequences, for the rule of law and for local investors in developing countries, of ignoring the need to develop ordinary national legal processes and simply bypassing these to provide special direct remedies for aggrieved foreign interests.

As the concept of the Third World has declined, along with its specific legal claims relating to colonial wrongs and distributive justice, the concept of sustainable development has risen. While lacking in precision, it has become almost ubiquitous in global policy platforms since the 1992 Rio Conference on Environment and Development. It has had a shaping effect on the formation of new legal regimes, such as those addressing climate change and desertification. It has influenced interpretation of existing legal rules, as in the 1997 International Court of Justice (ICJ) decision in the Hungary/Slovakia case on the post-communist future of communist-era dam projects in the Danube river (Boyle and Freestone, 1999). It draws from the more technical field of international environmental law, a field which increasingly brings regulation and markets together through such mechanisms as tradable permits and liability insurance, and which now has highly detailed rules on matters ranging from oil tanker design and air and water quality measurement, through to environmental impact assessment and access to official information. Whereas much of the impetus for the elaboration of international environmental law comes from the OECD countries, international development law has not had the same Western political or academic support. Its academic decline is in part the continuing result of a loss of confidence within the 1960s law and development movement, buttressed by skepticism about liberal triumphalism and about evasion of rich-state responsibilities in the revival of that movement since the 1990s. Insufficient theorization of this important field of practice has left the theory of sustainable development more oriented to environment than development, and more of a moderate statement of global values than a basis for justice claims and for serious international legal obligations for transborder poverty alleviation.

1.2 International Criminal Responsibility

The concept of international criminal responsibility, long established for military personnel in the laws of war, was broadened in the Nuremberg and Tokyo tribunals and related proceedings. Since the 1990s a newly influential cadre of scholar-practitioners has been created by its sudden operationalization and extension through the International Criminal Court (the ICC, fully constituted in 2003), tribunals created by the UN Security Council for former Yugoslavia (in 1993) and Rwanda (in 1994), proceedings in foreign courts such as the *Pinochet* proceedings in Spain and the United Kingdom, as well as a wide array of national criminal trials, courts martial, truth commissions, and the controversial military commissions authorized after terrorist attacks on the United States in 2001. (See generally Chapter 36 of this *Handbook*, and the defense of military commissions in Bradley and Goldsmith, 2003.) Scholars have of necessity endeavored to strike balances within a series of tensions that are not comprehensively resolvable: between criminal responsibility and the political strategy of amnesty in ending brutal regimes or civil wars, between legally upright but remote international trials and troubling but perhaps reparative local engagement, between prosecution of small numbers of malefactors and notions of collective responsibility for mass atrocities, between righteous pursuit of justice and the realities of military action in very nasty contexts. A feature of the scholarship and of the practice has been the separation of individual responsibility from requirements of state action and from defenses of act of state. This separation, while in some respects promoted by the United States, has also heightened US concern about the potential of the ICC to reach actions by US service personnel.

1.3 Transnational Civil Responsibility

Epitomized by the 1980 decision of the US Second Circuit Court of Appeals in *Filartiga*, in which plaintiffs were awarded damages against a Paraguayan police inspector for the torture and killing of their Paraguayan son in Paraguay, the concept of transnational civil responsibility has animated hundreds of cases brought in US courts against alleged individual abusers of basic civil rights in other countries. Only in unusual situations, such as the US suits by Filipino victims against the estate and family of former President Ferdinand Marcos, have the plaintiffs in such cases had much prospect of actually receiving payment of damages. Such litigation may aim to give voice to victims of injustices, and to establish the submerged facts of atrocities (Koh, 1991). But while such litigation has multiple agendas, the animating concept that gives it form and purpose is transnational civil responsibility. US courts have also made massive damages awards to victims of state terrorism, under highly selective 1996 amendments to the Foreign Sovereign Immunities Act that limit recovery to actions by American plaintiffs or victims against specified states to which the United States is hostile. These tort precedents have generally not been followed elsewhere, although English courts have begun to consider the possibilities, holding for example that South African victims of asbestos poisoning could sue in UK courts in the absence of an adequate legal aid system for them in South Africa. More national courts have, however, been willing to uphold or even to impose substantial direct or indirect civil costs on states responsible for contract breaches and other commercial losses arising from unlawful war-like acts. This strategic use of transnational civil responsibility to raise the cost of illegal action has been augmented by the creation of international bodies, such as the UN Compensation Commission dealing with claims against Iraq after the 1990–1 conflict, with the power to issue binding awards enforceable in national courts.

The development of transnational civil responsibility has been so intertwined with the US judicial system and US lawyering as to appear to many to be a unilateralist imposition of US interests and of a litigious US culture. The engagement of the US system with other countries' courts and with international tribunals is uneven. This has meant that some meritorious suits that could not proceed anywhere else have been dismissed on *forum non conveniens* grounds. Conversely, US courts might disrupt legitimate arrangements reached in other jurisdictions, although well-briefed judges will be reluctant to do so. For example, it is theoretically possible that US civil proceedings might be taken against someone who had received an amnesty abroad as part of a genuine political settlement, such as the kinds of amnesty-for-confession arrangements that enabled the South African Truth and Reconciliation Commission to obtain conclusive evidence of many apartheid-era atrocities.

Aspects of the transnational civil responsibility agenda are opposed by some US civil procedure experts concerned about extra-jurisdictional overreaching or judicial overload, by some isolationists on ideological grounds, and by business interests vulnerable to suit. Various branches of the US government are likely to react with hostility if comparable proceedings against US interests are successful elsewhere. Much concern was expressed in Washington at the (ultimately unrealized) prospect that the NAFTA tribunal in the *Loewen* case might order the US government to compensate a Canadian company allegedly subjected to a gross injustice as a foreign defendant in a Mississippi tort suit brought by a private plaintiff. The US Supreme Court has deliberately chosen not yet to rule on the *Filartiga* line of cases, nor has it considered the constitutionality of US submission to NAFTA tribunals.

Without the momentum supplied by the US legal system, pressure for stronger civil accountability for major breaches of international law would be much weaker. The transnational human rights movement, and increasingly activist judiciaries and lawyers in other countries, make likely the transplantation of this agenda, even if it eventually encounters checks in the United States. (For advocacy of a transnational tort responsibility agenda in other common law jurisdictions see Scott, 2001.)

1.4 The Decline and Possible Revival of Claims to Exclusive Domestic Jurisdiction

The decline of exclusivity of domestic jurisdiction as a ground for limiting the reach of international law has been anticipated, promoted, and applauded by many international lawyers since 1945. Most see this decline as inevitable in the context of globalization, with no sign of any revival. Like the related concept of sovereignty, however, which for over a century has seemed to be at once an obstacle to progress in international law and a source of the potential of the international legal order (Kennedy, 1987), exclusive domestic jurisdiction has proven much more polyvalent and enduring than its poor prognoses suggested. Ironically, some of the old Third World ideas of exclusive jurisdiction that were deployed as legal counters to European and US interventionism, while now repudiated for neo-liberal reasons in their regions of origin, are currently being asserted by the United States. An example is the 'Calvo clause', devised in the late nineteenth century by Argentina and long incorporated in many Latin American constitutions, which requires that agreements by the state with foreign investors provide for jurisdiction only in the country's own courts and exclude foreign courts and international arbitral tribunals. The Calvo clause has almost no currency in contemporary Latin American practice. But, concerned by claims in NAFTA tribunals by foreign investors seeking compensation for environmental restrictions imposed by national or local governments, an increasing number of US scholars have argued that the United States should confine jurisdiction over such matters to US courts. A second example is the intense late-nineteenth-century opposition in Asian and Mediterranean countries to 'consular' courts, in which European and US officials stationed overseas adjudicated disputes involving their own nationals. This opposition led in the following decades to grudging Western agreement to abolish consular courts and to accept the principles of territorial sovereignty and jurisdictional equality. Contemporary US objections to the exercise by the International Criminal Court of jurisdiction over US nationals for crimes committed outside the United States revive that earlier consular-era US preference for exclusive jurisdiction over US nationals. But in favoring trials *in situ* or in the United States, they also echo the old developing-country skepticism about delocalized judicial power.

International law scholarship has been a vehicle of an internationalist morality, expressing ideas of shared responsibility for human rights, for basic human needs, and for the realization of environmental values. To give such a morality legal purchase through international law has involved crafting concepts that justify and make necessary the erosion of exclusive jurisdiction for each state in determining how to legislate and how to act on such matters. Efforts to find justifications for external involvement beyond formal consent refer increasingly to a 'common interest' or to matters being of 'common concern'. Such justifications are invoked to press some states to adopt or follow values held by others, and to authorize pressure on smaller or weaker states not to allow their territories to be used to undermine a favored international policy. Further studies are required to determine why some such efforts succeed and others do not, and what the roles of specific legal considerations are in shaping outcomes. 'Anecdata' suggest that very large states are more insistent than most other states on retaining their own jurisdictional primacy, and more hesitant to authorize systematically binding jurisdiction for international tribunals over internal matters (other than matters related to trade). For example, of the ten most populous states, China, India, the United States, Indonesia, Brazil, Pakistan, Russia, Bangladesh, Nigeria and Japan, none has accepted the jurisdiction of the UN Human Rights Committee over individual cases against them, and only Brazil and Russia have accepted the competence of a regional human rights court, and this only in the late 1990s. The European Union itself, albeit a special case, has not been made subject to the jurisdiction of the European Court of Human Rights. By contrast, the majority of smaller states are within one or other of these human rights institutional structures.

The reluctance to accept international jurisdiction is a statement of opposition to the prospect of international integration leading eventually to international rule-of-law federalism. Federations such as the United States and the EU have been premised on the loss for most purposes of the exclusive domestic jurisdiction of the member states of the federation, and the establishment of supremacy of federal or EU law. As demands for multi-level governance and transfers of competence grow, so do demands for overlapping or nesting of jurisdiction. The insistence on exclusive domestic jurisdiction, or failing that on the primacy of domestic jurisdiction, is not simply a living fossil that survives from the old order, it is a statement of intent about the future international legal order (see Sect. 3.2 below).

1.5 The Expanding but Precarious Concept of the International Legal System

The questions whether there exists, or should exist, a unified international legal system have been posed with new intensity by the dramatic increase in the number as well as the workload of international courts and tribunals. In the 1970s it seemed reasonably clear to most international lawyers that an international legal system could be identified in terms of H. L. A. Hart's union of primary and secondary rules. All participants acknowledged a large number of primary rules of state conduct. Enough agreement on sources of international law existed to satisfy in at least a rudimentary way Hart's requirement of a rule of recognition. The system struggled with a theory of legal change but was at least able to consolidate and memorialize change through global conferences or authoritative decisions. A reasonably orderly structure of adjudication had emerged centered on the ICJ and complemented by some arbitral jurisprudence and by a few specialist regional adjudicatory bodies.

As the volume and scope of the practice falling within the domain of international law have grown, however, the complacent assumption that it all forms part of a single system has seemed increasingly precarious. In particular, any group of states is generally free to establish a new adjudicative body, with almost any jurisdiction and any composition the parties involved specify, without it being placed in a hierarchical relationship with any existing body. A few formal hierarchies exist, arising, for instance, from the special status of the UN Charter and the binding powers of the Security Council, or in the EU from the supremacy of EU law and of the European Court of Justice, but for the most part international law is horizontal.

The proliferation of tribunals carries a prospect of fragmentation of international law, with different courts reaching conflicting interpretations, and no hierarchical mechanism of judicial control. So far this has not materialized as a serious problem. Divergences of doctrine have occurred—for instance, human rights tribunals have been more expansive than the ICJ in utilizing teleological approaches to treaty interpretation, in reading down territorial limits incorporated by a state into its acceptance of an international court's jurisdiction, and in imposing state responsibility for failure to take active measures to prevent international law violations. But these examples reflect the distinctive nature of human rights issues and the special responsibilities felt by human rights tribunals, rather than deep divergence or interjudicial competition (Charney, 1998). Some institutional rivalry between different courts and tribunals may be expected as they compete for business. This may help stimulate reforms. For example, the rapid procedures now available in the WTO Dispute Settlement Body or in the UN Law of the Sea Tribunal may have spurred other institutions to accelerate. The ICJ's decision in the *LaGrand* case (*Germany v USA*, 2001), resolving in the affirmative the long-avoided question whether its pre-judgment provisional measures orders create binding obligations, was rendered all the more necessary and palatable by the experience of other tribunals, such as the Law of the Sea Tribunal, which have binding provisional measures powers.

In standard positivist theory, the unity of the legal system depends on the capacity of states to create legal obligations by acts of willing. But this does not provide an answer where a state assumes irreconcilable obligations toward different groups of other states, or where two tribunals issue irreconcilable binding decisions. An alternative theory would unify the legal system by reading the UN Charter as a constitution, and seeking there answers to problems of hierarchy or norm conflict. But for the time being, this provides at most a partial answer, because so much of international law is in theory and in practice prior to or autonomous from the United Nations. Others have argued in anti-foundationalist terms that there can be no legal system, just a lot of activities by people who share the identity of international lawyers; and that in any event the pursuit of a system will introduce a ponderous structure that cuts off many flourishing and valuable initiatives and excludes marginal voices. But in practice, states have remained unitary enough in their legal policy to avoid egregious conflicts of obligations, the members of international tribunals have shown a commitment to systemic coherence and to comity, and the sense of a unified legal system connected with a unified international political order has generally been preserved.

In sum, pragmatic problem-solving has been used to prevent any system-threatening crisis of fragmentation—but the theoretical problems can be expected eventually to unsettle this temporizing practical resolution.

2 CHALLENGES TO PREVAILING POSITIVIST CONCEPTS AND ASSUMPTIONS

If a core set of practical materials and concepts exerts a unifying gravitational pull, such an attraction is no longer exerted so strongly by the loose positivist theory that is still most commonly used to order this set of materials. The changing sociology of international lawyers, shifts in prevalent academic ideas, and changes in the circumstances and needs of international society have made long-standing theoretical challenges to this traditional positivism more and more acute. Some of the most important current critiques are considered in this section.

2.1 Internal Critiques of Positivist Concepts: Statism, National Interest, and Instrumental Rationality

Approaches to international law are embedded in theories or intuitions about the nature of international politics. The English school places international lawyers in a middle Grotian strand, rejecting on the one side a realist world-view of states in the posture of gladiators governed not by laws but by survival and maximization of relative power (Hobbes), and on the other side an emancipatory cosmopolitanism centered on the ethics and self-realization of individuals and societies in a league of republican states or even a universal state (Kant). Under this conception the Grotian *via media* is a very wide middle way, prompting the English School writers further to subdivide Grotian views of international politics into pluralist and solidarist positions (Butterfield and Wight, 1966). Pluralist Grotians (often diplomats or others directly engaged in governmental affairs) tend toward realism and to caution against extending international law beyond what the power configuration of inter-state politics will support. Solidarist Grotians, who see in international law possibilities to realize more expansive agendas of justice and social change, tend toward cosmopolitanism and the construction of a new world through ideas. These enduring patterns are overlain by the specific context of politics and ideas in any particular period, the immediacy of which provides the energizing imperative for much international legal scholarship. The specific context of recent scholarship includes the consequences of the collapse of the USSR and command economy policies, struggles in an era of markets and privatization over the roles of the state and inter-state institutions, the wider politics of globalization, and specific demands for intervention or other action against conduct ranging from ethnically motivated killing to anthropogenic climate change. This context has given a distinctive cast to enduring debates about the nature and purpose of international society or community, the meaning and relevance of 'national interest', and the possibilities of explaining and structuring international law on the basis of game-theoretic models that presuppose the instrumental rationality of collective actors.

2.1.1 *Statism and International Community*

The realist view that international relations is a Hobbesian anarchy, in which states as unitary and rational actors seek to maximize their relative power and the realization of their defined national interests within the constraints imposed by the power and interests of other states, continues to exert strong effects on international law theory (see e.g. Ladreit de Lacharrière, 1983), even while few international law scholars accept it in its entirety (Combacau and Sur, 1999 is among the more Hobbesian of academic international law texts). Many Grotian pluralists continue to take statist positions, treating states as pre-legal political facts, with governmental institutions that are strong *vis-à-vis* the society, and a tightly held foreign affairs structure that enables the state to function in international law as a univocal corporate body (Combacau and Sur, 1999). International law is then theorized as the norms that emerge by agreement or consensus in the interactions among these entities. Even the most realist-inclined among the pluralists accept that some sort of international society exists, but they regard it as a society of states in which the Hobbesian problem of anarchy has been assuaged but not overcome.

Attacking such pluralist statism has been one of the most prevalent objectives in the literature of recent decades. A cluster of German and Austrian scholars has argued that the problem of anarchy has been partially overcome by international constitutionalism, above all the adoption of the United Nations Charter (e.g. Verdross and Simma, 1984). Several North American scholars have argued that international law is made by transnational networks formed among specialist state organs (Slaughter, 2000) or amongst a combination of state and private actors, and have endeavoured to disaggregate 'the state' into its many components with distinct agendas and interests. This has carried forward a view, widely held in US scholarship, that sovereignty should be approached in functional rather than in categorical terms (Koh, 1991). In such functionalist thinking, the state is simply one contender among many to be considered when the allocation of governance powers is made as part of the optimal functional design of each governance regime. Feminist scholars concentrated in Australia and North America have attacked the gendered imagery of pluralist statism, and highlight its adverse implications for women (Charlesworth and Chinkin, 2000; Knop, 2002). An assortment of European scholars, inspired by the trajectory of the EU or (as in the case of Allott, 2001) perturbed that the imagery of the state remains so dominant in the EU, have argued for an international community of overlapping communities (Paulus, 2001) or a society of all societies (Allott, 2001) that transcends statism. Yet many scholars in developing countries have defended the traditional state-centered system of international law, and have worked hard to try to increase the influence of these states within it (Maluwa, 1999). The government of India, a country with a flourishing civil society and vast numbers of activists and intellectuals not co-opted by government power, is one of many to argue against a comprehensive opening of the inter-state WTO to NGOs, and to oppose the admissibility of amicus briefs by non-state groups in WTO dispute settlement proceedings. While some defenders of statism are doubtless beneficiaries of the privileges of power and access to transnational capitalism that statism entrenches, many are genuinely concerned that weakening of the state and empowering of 'transnational civil society' will further heighten global inequality.

Statism is giving way to a richer conception of international society. But neither in theory nor in practice is the widening conception of international society keeping pace with the rapidly rising demands for more participation and more legitimacy in global governance. Three reasons for this slowness may be noted. First, the starting-points for theorizing international legitimacy vary across countries, regions, and political traditions. Secondly, patterns of political decision and law-making that are entrenched within large or long-stable states are not easily changed to accommodate a new politics of global governance or a new role for international law. Proponents of such internationalist changes are encountering both political resistance and increasingly sophisticated theoretical opposition (e.g. Bradley and Goldsmith, 2003). Thirdly, states fulfil important roles that are not easily replicated outside a statist framework.

2.1.2 National Interest

The challenges to statism carry within them a range of objections to the notion that international politics can or should be predicated on the pursuit of 'national interest'. The disaggregation of inter-state interactions, and the networks of integration resulting from the increasing density and range of cross-border transactions, make processes of interest calculation so complex that a single 'national' interest may often seem undefinable. Yet while government and democratic politics remain so much dependent on the state as the key form of political and legal organization, politicians whose continuing power derives from state political systems are only rarely able to transcend the language of 'national interest' when challenged by rivals for their constituencies. This constraint is reflected in the structure and operation of international law. The model of inter-state bargaining in pursuit of perceived national interests thus remains a persuasive starting-point in explaining the formation and design of many international legal regimes, and in explaining why substantial gains in aggregate global welfare that ought morally to be pursued are not in fact achieved because of the inability to capture these gains through the limited processes of bargaining among self-interested states. This bargaining model of regime theory does not in itself explain, however, how particular interests come to be identified as 'national' interests, how such 'interests' or 'preferences' are constructed and reconstructed through social processes that are not reducible to simple aggregation of the diverse interests that wield influence in political processes within each state, or how constitutive norms and social processes shape the design and operation of regimes in ways not covered by the express bargaining process (Hurrell, 1993). Constructivist or reflectivist alternatives to rationalist bargaining models have been proposed within regime theory as means to consider these questions (e.g. Kratochwil, 1989). These have significant implications for theorizing the role of international law. But the problems of developing robust methodologies for testing such constructivist or reflectivist theories have limited the progress of the empirical studies that are needed to give these theories practical purchase.

The long cosmopolitanist tradition of positing a global societal interest which differs from the interplay of national or sectoral interests has continuing vitality as a source of normative challenges to the pre-eminence of 'national interest'. Modern cosmopolitanists seek to embed international law in an international society of societies (e.g. Allott, 2001), or in transnational civil society. But the continuing practical need for state action, and the enduring importance of national sources of political motivation, have more often provoked intermediate Grotian scholarly responses that respond to, but temper, this cosmopolitanist impulse. One Grotian claim is that international institutions, such as international human rights treaty bodies, are trustees of a global interest. Another is the argument that states in some circumstances act as representatives of an international community interest. This argument was used to support NATO's 1999 use of force against Serbia in relation to Kosovo, as well as the international governance regime subsequently applied in Kosovo.

The long campaign waged by free-trade liberals in the tradition of the English publicist Richard Cobden (1804–65), arguing that transnational commerce should be freed from regulatory or military interference by nationalistic politicians, has been remarkably effective in undermining mercantilist notions of 'national interest'. This liberal ideology is evident in much legal scholarship on the design of international economic institutions. It underpins restrictions on protectionism, and on the invocation of national interest clauses such as the national security exception in the General Agreement on Tariffs and Trade (GATT). But the scholarly application of sophisticated liberal economic analysis to the design of international law rules and institutions has remained surprisingly rare, with a few notable exceptions concentrated mainly in trade and finance (e.g. Sykes, 1999). The Marxist proposition that 'national interest' is a myth obscuring the unity of transnational capitalist interests (a view that overlaps in part with Cobdenite liberalism) has not been incorporated into a substantial reconstruction of international law theory nor into a robust agenda of research on the international legal implications of capitalist structures. The possibilities of such an agenda have, however, been suggested, in 'post-colonial' literature and in some of the lines of critique of globalization and neo-liberalism, including work focused on intergovernmental international financial institutions and on transnational 'rule of law' initiatives (see Chimni, 1999).

Against such an array of theoretical challenges, few modern international lawyers have been willing to venture strong normative defenses of the concept of 'national interest', and those who have, such as then legal adviser to the French Ministry of Foreign Affairs Guy Ladreit de Lacharrière (Ladreit de Lacharrière, 1983), have been castigated by others in the field as Machiavellian parochialists. Yet it must not be overlooked that the concept of 'national interest' emerged in part to counter and eclipse tendencies to act purely in the dynastic or personal interests of a monarch or tyrant, and the concept continues to have a democratic appeal, especially because the international legal effects of a state's actions may endure long after the incumbent regime is gone. An understanding of international law in Grotian pluralist terms as a balancing of national interests has the attraction of attenuating inter-state inequalities and doubtful claims of the powerful to be custodians of universal values. This pluralist view appears in concurring opinions in the ICJ in the *Yerodia* case (*Democratic Republic of the Congo v Belgium*, 2002). The ICJ declared unlawful Belgium's issuance of an arrest warrant against the DRC Minister of Foreign Affairs, while he was in office, for crimes against humanity he had allegedly committed in the DRC against DRC nationals. While the Court's judgment on the narrow issue imposed only modest limitations on the increasingly vigorous human rights-inspired claims for universal jurisdiction, several judges took broader positions in emphasizing that the interest of all in preventing and punishing crimes against humanity does not totally supersede the particular national interest of the DRC. Some of the judges emphasizing the DRC's national interest noted the history of Belgian colonialism and neo-colonialism in the Congo, and also expressed the suspicion that the exercise of universal jurisdiction by Third World states over the leaders of rich countries would be met with much less Western enthusiasm.

2.1.3 *Instrumental Rationality*

Realist and rationalist theories of international relations assume that states are instrumentally rational actors, such that each state will act so as to maximize the realization of its interests within the constraints of limited information and uncertainty about the intentions of others. All recognize that this is simply an assumption, convenient for modeling regularities in international affairs but not universally realized in practice. Many also make the normative argument that rationality of policy decisions ought to be a goal of decision-makers and decision-making processes—several leading works in the history of realism are both counsels to rationality and efforts to manage the gap between the aspiration for rationality and the idiosyncratic irrationalities of practice. International law is concerned with structuring patterns of behavior and increasing the predictability of behavior in international society. In this respect, international law serves rationalist purposes. Rational institutionalist theory has focused on analyzing specific non-normative functions served by law and international legal institutions (Keohane, 1997; Slaughter, 2000). In line with this rationalist functionalism, but for different reasons, positivist international law theory also embraces rationality as both a feature and a desideratum of the international legal system. This is manifest in the positivist view that international legal obligation is a result of state willing; and also in specific doctrinal structures, such as the rules of attribution in the law of state responsibility (Crawford, 2002).

Any modern theory of international law is bound to place a premium on rationality. Accepting that, some challenges to the assumption of instrumental rationality may be noted. First, unless international institutions are simply endogenous to the interests of the member states, the dynamics of rule interpretation, authoritative decision, and institutional policy formation are likely to be different in an international institutional context than they would be if left entirely to the member states. Institutions develop their own patterns of meaning and value, and their own structures of decision-making. Organization theorists have argued persuasively that institutions are seldom structured to maximize achievement of a single goal through processes characterized by Weberian rationality. Institutions are more likely to involve the interplay of mutually checking features (such as a logic of action and a logic of rhetorical justification), and their structures are as likely to be determined by mimesis or path dependence as by pure rationalist efficiency. Secondly, in international affairs, rationality is notably bounded, and subject to severe limitations of informational uncertainty, limited capacity, and cultural dissonance. Thirdly and most importantly, international law has expressive functions, and objectives such as symbolic legitimation, that are not readily reducible to instrumental rationality. Neglect of this complex range of functions has overly narrowed the important research agenda of compliance with international law. Robust studies of variations in correspondence between rules and behavior have provided valuable insights, but for many purposes the research issues must be framed more broadly. The concept of compliance with law does not have meaning independent of the questions of what is meant by 'law', how legal rules relate to legal processes, and how the rules and process of law relate to other normative systems.

2.2 External Critiques and Alternatives to the Dominant Positivist Approach: Critical, Marxist, and Constructivist Scholarship

The separation of the goals of codification and progressive development, embodied in the provisions of the United Nations Charter establishing the International Law Commission (ILC), has a long pedigree in analytic positivist writing about international law. The separation itself incorporates a positivist commitment to firm distinctions between 'fact' and 'value', and 'is' and 'ought'. Influenced by the interpretive turn in the humanities, as well as the tenets of American Legal Realism, scholarship in critical, Marxist, and constructivist traditions has challenged the confidence with which this set of positivist distinctions is asserted in international law.

The best of the early critical scholarship utilized anti-foundationalist ideas to challenge positivist jurisprudential concepts and assumptions such as the existence and completeness of an international legal system (e.g. Carty, 1986), or the separability of particular legal strategies such as international institutionalization from the political and intellectual engagements of their proponents (e.g. Kennedy, 1987). Upon this base have been built illuminating accounts of the history (Koskenniemi, 2002; Anghie, 1999; Berman, 2000) and sociology (Kennedy, 2000) of the discipline of international law, an increasingly suggestive engagement of international law with the discipline of comparative law, and valuable explorations of the scope and human implications of such fundamental concepts as self-determination (Knop, 2002).

Marxist writing on international law, having dwindled in the last decades of the twentieth century, began to revive in response to perceived injustices of global economic arrangements. The renewal of the critique of international law as an ideology connected to the global expansion of liberal capitalism has been accompanied by calls to recast international law in terms of transnational economic forces and institutions rather than the relations of formally independent and equal states (Chimni, 1999). But little progress has yet been made in carrying forward this agenda or developing the legally oriented counter-hegemonic discourse its proponents call for.

Like critical theory and the less-materialistic strands of Marxist thought, constructivist scholarship has emphasized the social construction of international legal concepts, and the inseparability of scholarly description from this process of construction. Constructivists have tended to accept the internal value of positivist explanatory methodologies and doctrinal structures, but to regard these as inherently too limited. They have focused on building conceptual accounts of the wider social relations and intersubjective community which shape and make possible particular structures of positive law. Some have sought to do this in Habermasian fashion through the claimed universality of speech acts (Habermas, 1996), arguing, for example, that a Hobbesian focus on threats and sanctions has overemphasized the perlocutionary force of speech acts as compared to the evident significance of illocution in social norm formation (Kratochwil, 1989). Others have made idealist arguments for the self-constitution of a universal social consciousness in order to create, through ideas, a truly universal society of societies with its own constitutionalism and layered legal system (Allott, 2001). But 'constructivism' is a very loose designation for a variety of ideas and methods, and no unified constructivist school or research program has emerged.

The methodological self-consciousness stimulated by these and other movements has problematized the claim, made, for instance, by Lassa Oppenheim at the beginning of the twentieth century, that scholarship can and should separate the tasks of presenting an analytic report of practice, then if necessary critiquing rules or institutions and suggesting improvements. Yet at the same time, judicialization and legalization in some areas of international political practice are creating more and more situations where the profession and vocation of the international lawyer entails working within this established framework. This work has generated an increasing volume of materials that provide a credible basis for positivist statements of legal doctrine and critique on many issues of practical importance (see e.g. the ILC's work on state responsibility, Crawford, 2002). The scholarly styles of serving or aspiring government legal advisers, counsel, judges, and international civil servants continue to dominate the field, and sustain a progress-oriented positivist approach to practice. Yet these same participants are conscious of the need to respond to current problems of theory that will necessarily shape scholarship.

3 FUTURE AGENDAS OF INTERNATIONAL LEGAL SCHOLARSHIP

Many of the most challenging themes in the future of international legal scholarship are enduring ones in the history of international law that call not so much for solution as for re-engagement. These include the roles of international law in accentuating or alleviating poverty and inequality (Pogge, 2002); social violence and transnational violence, including arms sales and financing; nuclear obliteration; the legal structures for the movement of people and for political expression through citizenship or self-determination (Knop, 2002); the marginalization or (re-)integration of religiosity and religious power structures in the law of the global political order; the roles and responsibilities of corporations and of networks; the roles of states and the implications of variations in state formations and in national legal cultures. Other pressing themes are more technical and manageable as the discipline evolves: the development of international administrative law; the relations between international, transnational, and state law; the integration of international economic law with global and local social and environmental policy; rethinking the structures of jurisdiction and arrangements for enforcement to better address the Internet, transnational crime, global commons, and other non-territorial issues. This section will highlight two broad research agendas that will likely be at the center of Grotian approaches to the theory and practice of the discipline: legitimacy and democracy in international governance; and the roles of normativity in international order.

3.1 Legitimacy, Democracy, and Justice in International Governance

Among the most pressing problems of the international legal order are those of legitimacy, democracy, and justice in emerging governance regimes. Efforts to address comparable problems in the European Union—through such initiatives as the directly elected European Parliament, strong judicial institutions led by the European Court of Justice, the recondite but participatory committee system studied under the 'comitology' rubric, and an increasingly rights-oriented constitutionalism—provide relevant diagnostics and useful precedents for global governance. But the EU is an exceptional case. European integration as a political project has had sufficient enduring public support in the EU member and applicant states to carry the institutions through periods of technocratic European Commission governance, then of state domination via the European Council, and into the present era of legitimacy-enhancing reform.

The governance of global integration cannot depend on such a level of global popular or political support to overcome shortfalls in public participation and democratic accountability. Most theories of democracy within states presuppose not only an organized polity akin to a state, but also a strong identity-community (demos) and the concentrated institutional powers of a government. These and other features of national democratic theory render improbable its simple transposition to global governance.

A particular European social consciousness is reflected in proposals directed toward the emergence of a kind of universal state predicated on mutuality as to incontrovertible principles of justice and the consequent possibility of submitting to third-party judgment. A similar particularity characterizes proposals to develop a global public sphere of deliberative democracy structured around constitutive process rules of participation and reasoned dialogue (Habermas, 1996), or to construct regional and global rights-respecting democratic institutions to supplement states and overcome the limitations of states as organs of global cosmopolitan democracy. It is doubtful that these proposals will provide principles for an architecture robust enough to cope with the harder politics, violence, and heterogeneity that confronts global governance.

If these cosmopolitanist solutions are implausible, the traditional realist alternatives of balance of power or hegemony are starkly insufficient. The most likely ways forward are Grotian efforts to shape agreed principles of international legitimacy and pursue their implementation. Procedural rule-of-law principles of legitimacy already attract broad support: international rules that satisfy tests of sources-pedigree, determinacy, perceived fairness, and coherence with other rules and with systemic principles, exert a greater compliance-pull than other rules (Franck, 1990). More far-reaching substantive concepts of legitimacy, buttressed by more effective systems of accountability and popular participation, will be essential for the implementation and sustainability of the kinds of international governance that are now emerging or proposed.

The Western sense of living in a post-political age after the fall of the Berlin Wall in 1989 renewed amongst many international lawyers an instinctive aspiration to technocratic progress. In this era, the old topic of political revolution has almost entirely disappeared from the literature of international law, eclipsed in the 1990s by studies of the roles of international law in national democratization, and thereafter by studies of the roles of international law in the context of non-state terrorism and related political pathologies. Yet fundamentally different world-views, and deep disagreement, inevitably remain central to international politics. Lasting solutions to problems of governance and legitimacy cannot in the long run be pursued without a theory of real politics that serves internationally at least some of the functions fulfilled nationally by democracy, and that confronts the possibilities of revolution. The tendency to renewed interest in stark politics and in critiques of liberalism, most notably the writings of Carl Schmitt (Koskenniemi, 2002), is a reaction against this dearth, but not one likely to provide normatively attractive solutions.

3.2 Normativity and International Order

A determination to make the emerging professional discipline of international law truly normative formed part of the shared sensibility and civilizing mission that animated activists in the formation and early work of the Institut de Droit International and the International Law Association in the late nineteenth century (Koskenniemi, 2002). This is exemplified in Lassa Oppenheim's *International Law* (1905), stressing that the progress of international law would depend on whether the legal school of international jurists prevailed over the diplomatic school. For Oppenheim, both the diplomat and the international jurist were directly engaged with practical problems, but he understood progress through international law as entailing a more principled and rule-governed conduct of international politics than would result if each question were left simply to the diplomatic considerations of the moment. Many European international lawyers perceive a contemporary iteration of this struggle between a normative international community and a traditional diplomatic case-by-case approach to international order in debates between the United States and Europe over adherence to major multilateral treaties. While the United States is party to many such treaties and is a prime mover in many multilateral initiatives, it has conspicuously refused to participate in such widely accepted regimes as the Kyoto Protocol on climate change, the International Criminal Court statute, the Landmines Convention, the Biodiversity Convention, and the Convention on the Rights of the Child.

If the United States is indeed a special case, at least five explanatory variables are involved. First, as a single superpower, it can afford to stay outside some agreements that might constrain its freedom of action—but while the configuration of power clearly matters, doubts arise about this as a complete explanation because the United States has been reluctant to enter constraining agreements at times in its history when it was not the leading power. Secondly, the US domestic ideology of popular sovereignty may be so strong as to raise major concerns about any transfer of significant powers to an extra-national body. If this is so, current international concerns about

US attitudes may reflect not a change in US behavior but a change in the international system, characterized by the adoption of more agreements with deeper governance implications than existed hitherto. Thirdly, US constitutional structure and political understandings, including the minority veto rule under which the approval of two-thirds of the Senate is thought to be required for certain treaties, provide a large number of opportunities for special interest groups to intervene to derail a proposed treaty.

Fourthly, US governmental processes and public culture may be more legalistic than in some other countries—treaties are scrutinized with great intensity by phalanxes of lawyers from numerous government agencies whose concerns about a minor detail or a remotely conceivable interpretation of the treaty may cause the government to back away. European governments in the EU may be more willing to trust to good sense and flexibility to work out such issues once a treaty is in force. But egregious US non-compliance, including the widespread failure to notify foreign defendants in US capital cases of their rights to contact their consulate as required by the Vienna Convention on Consular Relations, makes some observers skeptical about the consistency of the legalism of the Washington bureaucracy. Fifthly, on some issues, the United States holds positions fundamentally at odds with those embraced by international institutions, for example, on the moral question of the death penalty, or on the market-philosophy question of the use of tradable emissions permits in global environmental policy.

Oppenheim's European successors use essentially his terminology in regarding the European inclination to multilateralism as championing the modern legal school which represents the hope of progress, while US case-by-case evaluation of unilateral and power political options alongside legalist strategies is the modern diplomatic school from which only occasional inspired contributions can be expected. Many adherents of this view, like many of their critics in the United States, frame the contemporary US hesitancy about multilateralism in terms of US exceptionalism. This framing was adopted and reinforced in much of the debate about US determination to act militarily against Iraq in 2003. But it can also be understood as involving EU exceptionalism. The EU is extraordinary in that very deep integration among formerly hostile sovereign states has been organized not through conquest or colonial unification but through the initial mechanism of treaties grounded in public international law. The use of treaties to structure cooperation on matters bearing intrusively on internal national policy-making is thus not only normal but advantageous for the EU and its member states. The difficulties the EU finds in pursuing a common military policy or even a unified foreign policy represent a weakness for the EU in traditional diplomacy, but one that can be potentially offset by international legalism and institutionalism. If the EU is becoming a quiet superpower, many of its techniques of external influence are law-structured: enlargement negotiations, conditional external aid, and multilateral agreement. The United States, by contrast, does well enough in traditional diplomacy and coercion for some of its leaders to feel confident in staying outside, or opposing, multilateral treaty initiatives.

Drawing comparisons and contrasts between European and US approaches has been a particularly attractive project to scholars in Europe anxious to promote a pan-European identity. But in global terms, the United States and the EU together set the parameters for most major governance questions. The OECD zone as a whole provides the initiative and the framing for almost every global governance regime that comes into being. Consultation takes place with other states whose support is needed to make the regime work, and the major Western NGOs usually have local partners in non-OECD areas, as indeed do multinational corporations in some cases. But, whereas the ambition of international law is global, full participation in the construction of the current international order is not. The project for a truly normative international law has adherents all over the world, and individuals from all regions have long played significant roles in international institutions. Even in the most pacific of governance regimes, however, the sense of profound inequalities of voice and unevenness in representation confront the normative project with serious problems of legitimacy, democracy, and justice (Charlesworth and Chinkin, 2000; Chimni, 1999; Maluwa, 1999). These are problems which the pragmatic problem-solving approach, with its diplomatic sensibility and case-by-case orientation, has perhaps made more acute as global governance regimes have proliferated and deepened. The concerns are heightened where global regimes seem to trade off lives in poor countries for wealth preservation in rich countries, or to reproduce and intensify gross gender inequities, or to encompass the use by some states of military force in other states.

The framework of peaceful settlement of disputes, which the problem-solving approach incorporates, utilizes for war-avoidance purposes the concepts of bilaterality and opposability that had long been central to war. This structural parallel was prefigured in the close analogy drawn by Grotius between lawsuits and war. But the integration of war and peace in texts such as *De Jure Belli ac Pacis* has been supplanted by their sharp separation in modern texts. The modern problem-solving approach to war and other fundamental perturbations of order is accompanied by a stark Grotian-pluralist sense of the limits of what can be done through international law. Here even the elusive aspirational claims for global normativity seem to run out. This is illustrated in the extreme case by the profound problems of nuclear weapons, which continue to be addressed in international law scholarship not so much even in managerial terms but rather as problems touching the limits of the discipline. This tendency was accentuated by the holding of the ICJ (in the 1996 *Advisory Opinion on the Legality of the Threat or Use of Nuclear Weapons*), on the President's casting vote, that it 'cannot conclude definitively whether the threat or use of nuclear weapons would be lawful or unlawful in an extreme circumstance of self-defence, in which the very survival of a State would be at stake'.

4 THE CONCEPT OF INTERNATIONAL LAW

Any useful theoretical concept of international law must reflect the different functions international law plays in theory and in practice. The function of dispute management, which has received particular emphasis in the English and French traditions and in much Commonwealth scholarship, is only one of many functions of international law. As Grotius's *De Jure Belli ac Pacis* manifests, the discipline of international law has historically been impelled by other systemic objectives, including the expression of essential values of the international political system, the development of a normative language for international politics, and the articulation and propagation of an international morality (Koskenniemi, 2002; Knop, 2002; Habermas, 1996; Anghie, 1999). Contemporary scholarship has highlighted many further functions of international law. With intensified patterns of transnational mimesis and borrowing, international law plays roles in the construction and transmission of the cognitive scripts and the technologies of a world culture, from the organization of a foreign ministry in virtually every state to the standardization of economic statistics and Internet protocols. In a context of increasingly dense international institutional governance, the theory of international law must take account of law's functions in regime design and maintenance: establishing rules as focal points that provide an equilibrium in situations requiring coordination, where thereafter no participant has an incentive to defect from the rule; providing transparency and monitoring and some sanctioning in ways that make possible the capture of gains from cooperation without excessive cost; embedding international agreements in national law that can have more direct purchase on relevant actors; drawing systemic linkages among otherwise unrelated issues so as to raise the cost of violation; aiding powerful states to make commitments that others have confidence will be adhered to, by enmeshing them in deeper structures of legal obligations (Keohane, 1997).

Three simple jurisprudential approaches to the concept of international law were delineated in the seventeenth century and remain relevant. The most influential has been the Hobbesian command theory of law, which was applied also by Samuel Pufendorf to ground natural law in divine command. In command theories, the source of any particular norm is determinative of its validity as law. Under some other theories of natural law, it is not the source of the rule but the agreeability of the content of the proposed rule with some set of governing principles that determines its validity. Grotius provided the third alternative, a hybrid concept of international law that encompassed both the source of a rule (usually consent of the relevant actors) and the content of the rule (identification of rules from nature by use of right reason) as criteria in evaluating the validity of the rule.

Both strict sources-based positivism and content-focused policy science or political approaches now seem inadequate to meet the legal needs of a deepening international society. No longer is international society simply a minimum structure of basic order—it is more and more a purposive association based on solidarity, with more searching legal needs (Hurrell, 1993). This purposive quality is most evident in the structures of economic governance, but also in the assertion and transmission of values, in occasional collective mobilization of force or sanctions, and in pressing demands for global structures of equal concern and respect and for global distributive justice (largely unmet). For international law to instantiate and carry forward such a purposive society, international law requires a stronger theoretical structure.

An adequate theoretical approach to international law must continue to engage with and seek to shape practice. It must become more concerned with participation, and with managing inequality—the domination by the OECD world may be prolonged, but is not ultimately sustainable. It must (re-)integrate peace and force. It is likely to be more value-pluralist, and more dependent on democratic consent than at present. Its justifications will depend on showing its superiority to contending theories in achieving the fundamental normative objectives of international society. This justificatory case will likely depend more on legitimacy and functional attributes than on the normative authority and technocratic expertise of an invisible college of international lawyers. It will be required to be an effective and parsimonious theory. This entails resisting the current tendency to overload international law that results from the continuous accretion to it of all kinds of transnational norms and private standards and overlapping national regulations. The focus of international law theory should instead be on systematization of the relations between different normative structures, including social norms. Such a theory will define and differentiate international law, separating the subject with clarity from other intellectual disciplines in order then to engage coherently with them. It will integrate an ethically justified normative positivism with theories going to the processes and content of international law, including a nested set of theories of governance, institutions, and community. It will be a hybrid of sources-based criteria and content-based criteria. In short, it will be Grotian.

REFERENCES

Note: see Chapter 36 for additional references on aspects of International Law.

Allott, P. (2001). *Eunomia: New Order for a New World* (2nd edn.), Oxford: Oxford University Press.

Anghie, A. (1999). 'Finding the Peripheries: Sovereignty and Colonialism in Nineteenth-Century International Law', *Harvard International Law Journal*, 40: 1–81.

Berman, N. (2000). 'Modernism, Nationalism, and the Rhetoric of Reconstruction', in C. Lynch and M. Loriaux (eds.), *Law and Moral Action in World Politics*, Minneapolis: University of Minnesota Press, 108–39 (1st pub. 1992).

Boyle, A., and Freestone, D. (eds.) (1999). *International Law and Sustainable Development*, Oxford: Oxford University Press.

Bradley, C., and Goldsmith, J. (eds.) (2003). *Foreign Relations Law: Cases and Materials*, Boston: Aspen.

Butterfield, H., and Wight, M. (eds.) (1966). *Diplomatic Investigations*, London: George Allen and Unwin.

Carty, A. (1986). *The Decay of International Law? A Reappraisal of the Limits of Legal Imagination in International Affairs*, Manchester: Manchester University Press.

Charlesworth, H., and Chinkin, C. (2000). *The Boundaries of International Law*, Manchester: Manchester University Press.

Charney, J. (1998). 'Is International Law Threatened by Multiple International Tribunals?' *Recueil des Cours de l'Académie de Droit International*, 271: 101–382.

Chimni, B. (1999). 'Marxism and International Law: A Contemporary Analysis', *Economic and Political Weekly*, 34: 337–49.

Combacau, J., and Sur, S. (1999). *Droit international public* (4th edn.), Paris: Montchrestien.

Crawford, J. (2002). *The International Law Commission's Articles on State Responsibility*, Cambridge: Cambridge University Press.

Franck, T. (1990). *The Power of Legitimacy among Nations*, Oxford: Oxford University Press.

Habermas, J. (1996). *Between Facts and Norms: Contributions to a Discourse Theory of Law and Democracy*, Cambridge, Mass.: MIT Press.

Hurrell, A. (1993). 'International Society and the Study of Regimes: A Reflective Approach', in V. Rittberger (ed.), *Regime Theory and International Relations*, Oxford: Oxford University Press, 49–72.

Kennedy, D. (1987). 'The Move to Institutions', *Cardozo Law Review*, 8: 841–988.

—— (2000). 'When Renewal Repeats: Thinking against the Box', *New York University Journal of International Law and Politics*, 32/2 (Winter), 335–500.

Keohane, R. (1997). 'International Relations and International Law: Two Optics', *Harvard International Law Journal*, 38: 487–502.

Knop, K. (2002). *Diversity and Self-Determination in International Law*, Cambridge: Cambridge University Press.

Koh, H. (1991). 'Transnational Public Law Litigation', *Yale Law Journal*, 100: 2372–402.

Koskenniemi, M. (2002). *The Gentle Civilizer of Nations: The Rise and Fall of International Law 1870–1960*, Cambridge: Cambridge University Press.

Kratochwil, F. (1989). *Rules, Norms, and Decisions: On the Conditions of Practical and Legal Reasoning in International Relations and Domestic Affairs*, Cambridge: Cambridge University Press.

Ladreit de Lacharrière, G. (1983). *La Politique juridique extérieure*, Paris: Economica.

Macdonald, R., and Johnston, D. (eds.). (1983). *The Structure and Process of International Law*, Dordrecht: Martinus Nijhoff.

Maluwa, T. (1999). *International Law in Post-colonial Africa*, The Hague: Kluwer.

Paulus, A. (2001). *Die internationale Gemeinschaft im Völkerrecht: Eine Untersuchung zur Entwicklung des Völkerrechts im Zeitalter der Globalisierung*, Munich: Beck.

Pogge, T. (2002). *World Poverty and Human Rights: Cosmopolitan Responsibilities and Reforms*, Cambridge: Polity Press.

Scott, C. (ed.) (2001). *Torture as Tort: Comparative Perspectives on the Development of Transnational Human Rights Litigation*, Oxford: Hart.

Slaughter, A. (2000). 'International Law and International Relations', *Recueil des Cours de l'Académie de Droit International*, 285: 13–249.

Sykes, A. (1999). 'Regulatory Protectionism and the Law of International Trade', *University of Chicago Law Review*, 66: 1–46.

Verdross, A., and Simma, B. (1984). *Universelles Völkerrecht: Theorie und Praxis* (3rd edn.), Berlin: Duncker & Humblot.

CHAPTER 15

....

HUMAN RIGHTS

....

KEITH EWING

1 INTRODUCTION

....

UNIVERSAL interest in human rights is matched only by a universal failure to respect them. The interest is overwhelming, not only on the part of lawyers but also on the part of philosophers, political scientists, sociologists, social anthropologists, theologians, and others. In the law schools there are few areas which have grown so rapidly in the years since 1960, and few issues which cover so many pages of law reviews as human rights. This reflects the growth in the number of human rights instruments at international and regional level since 1960 (when many of the great instruments had yet to be conceived), but also the great cascade of human rights from the international to the national level throughout the common law world. With the exception of the United States, at the beginning of 1960 no major common law jurisdiction enjoyed or endured the constitutional protection of fundamental rights or human rights. With the exception of Australia, by the end of 2000 no major common law jurisdiction was without some form of constitutional protection of fundamental rights or human rights. But this cascade has not stopped at the level of constitutional law, and part of the reason why there is such a great interest in human rights is that the discipline has implications for all other areas of law, affecting them by its principles and standards, whether directly or indirectly.

Before addressing some of the main developments in this area since 1960, it may be helpful at the outset to deal with linguistic differences which appear across jurisdictions. This is an area where the same term is used to mean different things, and where different terms are used to mean much the same thing. In the United States in particular, human rights are associated with international law, yet paradoxically the United States has longer experience of the constitutional protection of the rights to be found in international treaties than any other country in the common law tradition. Many of the issues discussed in this chapter are dealt with in their US context elsewhere in this volume. In other countries—such as Australia and Canada—where human rights are part of the currency of domestic law, the term is sometimes used to refer to issues which in the United Kingdom might be referred to as discrimination or equality law. These issues are also dealt with elsewhere in this volume. The starting-point for this chapter is the international treaties which have emerged to protect human rights in national legal systems, and the aim is to consider aspects of the scholarship which has developed alongside the cascade of these rights from international law to constitutional law to ordinary municipal law. This is a process which has been controversial as human rights and democracy are seen by some to be mutually dependent (Habermas, 1994), but by others to be engaged in an abrasive struggle for superiority on the battleground of ideas.

2 What are Human Rights?

The modern legal scholarship on human rights can be traced back to the aftermath of World War II. It is at this point that we encounter the great human rights instruments which have become the frame of reference for the discipline. The starting-point is the UN Declaration of Human Rights which was proclaimed in 1948 'as a common standard of achievement for all peoples and all nations'. Drawing on a large canvas, the Declaration deals with a broad range of civil, political, social, economic, and cultural rights, though there were a number of gaps in the coverage. The Declaration is now accompanied by the two international covenants of 1966, which in dealing with civil and political rights and with economic, social, and cultural rights, in a sense linked the opposing ideologies separated by the Berlin Wall. To this extent, the peoples of the West were the vicarious beneficiaries of communism in the East. The 1948 Declaration and the 1966 Covenants may be said to be the core instruments of the international human rights code, which demonstrates a 'clear bias in favour of the kind of society that displays a specific coherent set of civilized values: tolerance of diversity; plurality of belief, ideas, and culture; reasonableness and rationality; the peaceable resolution of conflicts under the rule of law; and, above all, respect for the dignity, autonomy, and integrity of every single one of its individual members' (Sieghart, 1986: 42).

2.1 Civil and Political Rights

These treaties fall initially within the domain of international human rights lawyers, who have had to develop lines of scholarly inquiry in response. The first response has been to describe and inform, and in the process to analyse the scope and content of these instruments, and of the sometimes not easily accessible jurisprudence of the bodies which supervise their application. This essentially educational role of the scholar is important for a number of reasons: it is necessary to inform governments and parliaments of the nature, scope, and extent of international human rights obligations; it is necessary to inform public opinion about the extent to which governments are complying with obligations which they voluntarily accepted; and it is necessary to empower activists and their advisers who may wish to bring complaints in international or domestic forums for the ventilating of grievances about alleged violations of international standards. Joseph, Schultz, and Castan (2000) is an important example of work in this tradition, relating specifically to the International Covenant on Civil and Political Rights, and providing a detailed overview which is suitable for use in all common law countries and beyond.

The second task of the international human rights lawyer has been in-depth country studies, in which international treaties are given meaning by reference to the practice of the individual countries to which they are addressed. The most important work of this nature is Harris and Joseph (1996) which is a detailed comparison of 'United Kingdom law with the standards set by the Covenant across the board'. A book of nineteen chapters and eighteen contributors, it is in a real sense a template for similar work in other jurisdictions and on other international treaties, as well as a template for follow-up work in the United Kingdom. It is a particularly valuable feature of this book that international human rights lawyers work in conjunction with constitutional lawyers and other experts in national law. In the meantime, other important work on national failures to comply with international human rights standards has been conducted by the NGOs (non-governmental organizations) which have proliferated and become more prominent in the period under review: bodies such as the International Commission of Jurists, Amnesty International, Human Rights Watch, and the International Centre for Trade Union Rights, all of which have commented unfavourably on the national human rights standards of common law countries.

2.2 Economic, Social, and Cultural Rights

Much of the international human rights scholarship is thus concerned with civil and political rights, though its boundaries are extending to include not just concern about specific rights but also wider issues of democratic engagement. But this is not to suggest that social and economic rights have been less than well treated: there is both valuable analysis of the International Covenant on Economic, Social and Cultural Rights, as well as valuable expositions of the economic and social rights generally in the literature. International human rights lawyers have also been concerned with other instruments and with specialist agencies dealing with social and economic rights. The most important of these agencies is the International Labour Organization, a remarkable tripartite body in which trade unions and employers participate as equals with governments. Now a UN body responsible for labour standards, the ILO has a human rights dimension to its work, which is pursued through instruments dealing with freedom of association, child labour, forced labour, and discrimination. Study of the ILO (standing as it does on the border of a number of disciplines) has attracted human rights scholars approaching from international law, constitutional law, and labour law, with labour lawyers being particularly active in assessing the extent to which the domestic laws of Australia, Canada, and the United Kingdom comply with core ILO Conventions. Similar work in the United States has been undertaken by NGOs.

This interest has become more urgent as labour standards have become vulnerable to neglect in the Western liberal democracies following strategies of economic liberalism based on deregulation and privatization; and in developing countries in the context of globalization. Interest in the ILO as a human rights agency has been fuelled by the debate about labour standards and world trade, and the proposals for a social clause in the proceedings of the WTO which would tie tariff reform to respect for core labour standards. One suggestion is that the ILO should have responsibility within this framework to determine whether labour standards have been observed. Yet although this is a debate which continues, it is all but over, with the human rights advocates having failed to make any significant ground. The visibility of the ILO has been enhanced, however, by the ILO Declaration on Fundamental Principles and Rights at Work of 1998 by which the International Labour Conference declared that all 180 or so member states of the ILO have a duty 'to respect, to promote, and to realize' the 'principles concerning the fundamental rights' which are the subject of the different Conventions dealing with freedom of association and collective bargaining, the elimination of all forms of forced or compulsory labour, the effective abolition of child labour, and the elimination of discrimination in employment.

3 REGIONAL INSTRUMENTS

The UN is not the only international agency concerned with the development of human rights standards, there being a number of regional instruments which in many cases cover much of the same territory. Here there are key treaties to be found in Europe, the Americas, and Africa. These have been inspired by the UN Declaration, and are clearly important for the purposes of this study, with common law jurisdictions being covered by each of these regional instruments. Indeed, the only common law jurisdictions which are not yet covered by a regional human rights instrument are Australia and New Zealand. Of these instruments, the European Convention on Human Rights is the oldest and the most fully developed in terms of the range of rights protected and the manner of their supervision and enforcement. It is also the most extensively examined, now the subject of exhaustive historical research (Simpson, 2001), comparative study, and detailed analysis, as befits a document which has influenced the structure of human rights instruments in the constitutions of a number of nations outside the Council of Europe, and which may now be enforced in the national courts of both the United Kingdom and Ireland.

3.1 The European Convention on Human Rights

For all the historical, political, and legal significance of the Convention, it is not to be forgotten that it is first and foremost an international treaty which uniquely creates a court (the European Court of Human Rights) which hears complaints from individuals against nation states. The work of the Court has grown enormously as the Council of Europe has expanded to the east to include the countries of the Warsaw Pact, and following the overhaul of the enforcement procedures in 1998. Indeed, it has been pointed out that 'the full-time European Court of Human Rights' established by these new procedures announced that it had 'delivered more judgments (838) in the first two years of its existence than its part-time predecessor gave in 39 years (837 judgments)' (Mowbray, 2001: p. i). The growing prominence of the Court has generated some quite remarkable scholarship about the Convention and its jurisprudence. Much of it is expository and much of it proselytizes. But particularly important is the emergence of scholarship which subjects the jurisprudence of the Court to rigorous conceptual analysis, in order to identify the theoretical underpinnings of the Court's decisions, and the trends to be discerned in the case law. The great explosion in the number of cases decided by the Court means that it is time for writing of this kind to be updated and developed, and also for work to be done on the personnel of the Bench who remain largely unknown despite the quite remarkable powers which they wield over the law of the forty-four countries in the Council of Europe.

In one of the earliest examples of this kind of writing, Gearty (1993) contends that the Court has developed a coherent jurisprudence around the theme of 'due process', which 'has to be understood in three senses, in ascending order of generality, as covering the trial type situation, the protection of minorities and the fairness of the political process itself'. With strong echoes of Ely (1980), it is claimed that this understanding of the purpose of the Convention 'sets limits to the activism of the Court, since it suggests that decisions beyond these parameters are wrong'. Mowbray (1999) has also written about the role of the Court in advancing democratic participation, and how it has promoted a 'contemporary European model of democracy' which it has 'generally developed and applied' in 'a progressive manner' to 'enhance and safeguard the vitality of the political process operating in Member States'. These arguments about the role of the Court in reinforcing democracy lead to difficult questions about whether 'the whole Strasbourg process, with its oversight of national law, is an illegitimate contamination of democracy' (Gearty, 1993: 126). But general satisfaction with the Court—'the gains have so far exceeded the costs' (ibid. 127)—means curiously that the answer to this question has never been fully developed, despite the strong resistance to the incorporation of the ECHR into domestic law by at least some British-based lawyers, for precisely this reason.

3.2 The Social Charter and the Revised Social Charter

The attention devoted to the European Convention on Human Rights has tended to deflect attention from its siblings, the European Social Charter of 1961, and the Revised Social Charter of 1996. Although these latter instruments have not been ignored, they have been wholly overshadowed by the ECHR. There is only one book which deals with the Social Charters in depth, and only a handful of articles which are concerned in different ways to draw attention to the existence of the Charters, or to highlight problems of non-compliance with their terms. It has been left mainly to labour lawyers to engage with these instruments, which indeed barely register even in the international law texts which deal with human rights (a fate, it may be said, that the Social Charters share with the ILO, which is often covered in the most cursory terms). By the same token, the Social Charters have been largely overlooked by European lawyers who have advocated the accession of the European Community to the ECHR. This is despite the fact that the ECHR and the Council of Europe's Revised Social Charter of 1996 are said in the preamble to the latter to be 'indivisible'. The case for the adoption of the Social Charters by the EC has, however, been made convincingly by labour lawyers.

Together with the ECHR, both the Council of Europe's Social Charters have been expressly acknowledged as sources of inspiration of the new EU Charter of Fundamental Rights which is discussed below. This is rather surprising in view of the fact that the Revised Social Charter of 1996 has not been ratified by all member states. Nevertheless, an explanation for lack of interest in the Charters by a larger body of scholars is difficult to fathom. It may be that social and economic rights are thought to be less important than civil and political rights, though the universality of the latter is dependent upon the universality of the former. There is little point in having a right to protection of one's home or correspondence if one is homeless; or the right to form and join trade unions for the protection of one's interests if one is unemployed; or of the right to freedom of expression if one is without education. The explanation may be that the ECHR is administered by a court before which lawyers appear, whereas the Social Charters are administered by a Social Rights Committee, albeit one staffed by eminent jurists. Or it may be that social rights are considered to be non-justiciable, even though the Collective Complaints Protocol of 1995 would tend to indicate otherwise. It remains the case that although there are a growing number of decisions of the Social Rights Committee under the 1995 protocol, there has not been a single law review article in a common law jurisdiction in which any of these cases has been discussed. The fact that the protocol has not been accepted by the leading common law jurisdiction on the Council of Europe provides a good excuse, but hardly a satisfactory explanation.

4 The Cascade from International Law to Constitutional Law

It would be safe to say that in 1960 in many—if not most—common law jurisdictions human rights was a subject for the international lawyer. But even then not a great deal had been done in developing the reporting and supervisory systems of the international treaties, and indeed many treaties had yet to be born. In 1960 too, as already pointed out, surprisingly few countries in the common law tradition had any kind of effective constitutional protection of human rights, even though it was not the practice then to refer to constitutional rights as human rights. The US Supreme Court had only just awoken from its own long sleep, and was on the threshhold of judicial activism, with scholars now beginning to engage with this process. Elsewhere, only Canada had introduced a Bill of Rights (in 1960 itself), though this was to prove to be the dampest of squibs. The increased role of human rights in constitutional law since then unquestionably has been one of the most significant legal developments in common law jurisdictions, described by one writer as an 'irresistible worldwide movement in the direction of entrenching human rights' (Tushnet, 2001: 374).

4.1 The Cascade of Human Rights

There is probably no single explanation for these developments. Indeed the reasons why different countries have adopted instruments for the protection of human rights in national law are probably to be found in the particular politics or circumstances of the country in question, though we ought not to underestimate the impact which the adoption of a Bill of Rights in one country has on others. Much of the explanation lies in nation building and national identity, around which there are a number of different themes. In the Caribbean jurisdictions—Antigua, Jamaica, and Trinidad and Tobago, for example, Bills of Rights accompanied independence from the colonial power. The Canadian Charter of Rights and Freedoms of 1982 accompanied the patriation of the Canadian Constitution, and was designed in part to restore a sense of national identity at a time of 'accelerating regionalism, especially from Quebec' (Fudge, 2001: 336). The South African Bill of Rights was seen as an agent for the transformation of society in the wake of apartheid (Jagwanth, 2001). The proposed Bill of Rights for Northern Ireland may serve a similar function in a community divided on other grounds.

Yet although nation building provides part of the answer, it is not the whole story. The debate about the constitutional protection of human rights in some countries has also arisen at a time when political life has moved to the Right, with governments in the post Cold-War era moving quickly to privatize public authorities, deregulate national economies, and remove or dilute social protection. These concessions to the liberal free market have been accompanied in some countries by restrictive laws extending police powers and the powers of state authorities. In such circumstances, the entrenchment of rights was advocated by scholars and others as a way of restraining the illiberal tendencies of the State, an initiative—paradoxically—of progressive forces resisted for the most part by the Right at a time of deeply conservative governments. Such advocacy was a feature of much scholarly writing in the United Kingdom, and appears to lie behind some of the scholarship engaging with the Bill of Rights movement in Australia. It was true, in the British context, that individuals could seek a remedy in international law under the European Convention on Human Rights. But (it was argued) why should they be forced to endure the expense and inconvenience of travelling to enforce rights in an international forum, when the same rights could be enforced much more quickly and much more cheaply in the domestic courts?

4.2 Controlling the Human Rights Cascade

Although there may thus be different explanations for change, the outcome has been to produce documents in national law which are generally confined to civil and political rights, with social and economic rights typically excluded. Given the circumstances of the introduction of such measures, this is not surprising, particularly in view also of the changing ideological context in which these instruments were placed. Much scholarly interest has focused not only on the case for instruments of this kind, but also on more technical questions relating to the scope of their application. Although these instruments are generally directed to the State, the way in which they apply to state action varies from country to country, leading to vigorous debates in some countries about the need for measures with greater penetration. Some of the literature in

New Zealand in particular has been scornful of the New Zealand Bill of Rights which gives the courts the power to interpret legislation consistently with its terms, but which falls some way short of the Human Rights Act in the United Kingdom (where the courts may declare primary legislation incompatible with its terms but not quash or refuse to apply such legislation), and the Charter of Rights and Freedoms in Canada (where the courts may quash primary legislation). But for some New Zealand lawyers, even the weakest of all the contemporary Bills of Rights in the common law jurisdictions is a measure too far.

The other issue of scope and content raised by scholars relates to whether domestic bills of rights should apply only to state action, or whether they should also apply to action between private parties. This is a hugely important question given the fact that powerful private agencies (such as transnational corporations) are just as likely to violate human rights as powerful public authorities (such as the police and the security services). Legislative purpose divined by cautious judges has generally confined the application of bills of rights to public action, and has excluded private action. This has been justified on the ground that 'a constitution establishes and regulates the institutions of government, and it leaves to those institutions the task of ordering the private affairs of the people'. Indeed 'if private abuse exists, the democratic political process can drive the legislative bodies to produce the laws that are needed to provide a remedy' (Hogg, 1997: 859, 860). But in a vigorous debate, in the Canadian and South African literature in particular, not everyone is convinced, with Hutchinson and Petter (1988) drawing attention to the remarkable paradox that private power excluded from constitutional scrutiny is able to enlist the constitutional protection of human rights to restrain government authorities who seek to hold that power to account in the public interest. This is a matter to which we return.

5 QUESTIONS OF LEGITIMACY: HUMAN RIGHTS AND DEMOCRACY

Most common law countries were given one or both of the fundamental aspects of the British Constitution: parliamentary sovereignty and responsible government. This means simply that Parliament can make or unmake any law whatsoever, and that ministers are responsible to Parliament for the manner in which they execute the responsibilities of office. Bills, Charters, and Conventions of Rights create potential conflicts with these arrangements, particularly to the extent that they empower the courts to challenge Acts of Parliament. Parliament would no longer be sovereign in any real sense; and although ministers would continue to be accountable to

Parliament, it is to the courts that real accountability would lie in practice. It is no argument against constitutional reform that it will disturb constitutional tradition: that is the circular route to perpetual reaction. But it is an argument against constitutional reform that the reforms in question are in fact a violation of constitutional principle which the constitutional traditions defend (Goldsworthy, 2001). Although parliamentary sovereignty is a principle which was developed in the pre-democratic era to limit the power of the King, it is a principle the purpose of which has metamorphosed with the advent of democracy to give legal and constitutional expression to the principle of popular sovereignty: it enables the people through their elected representatives to make the laws by which they wish to be governed, and for the people through regular elections to hold these representatives to account. The Bill of Rights in national constitutional law thus raises important issues of constitutional and political principle about the final source of legal authority in a democracy, issues which have been hotly contested in the scholarly literature.

5.1 Human Rights and Democracy

The debate about human rights and democracy is deeply polarized, and takes place in the shadow of subtle and sophisticated debates about rights generally amongst legal philosophers, notably Dworkin and Rawls, though others such as Ely and Gewirth have been influential in some circles. Much of this writing coincides with the awakening of the US Supreme Court and the jurisprudence of the Warren Court and its progeny, and is concerned in different ways to justify and defend the court, or to question and criticize it. But these debates have had a huge influence throughout the common law world, as legal philosophers and legal scholars face up to the role of rights and the role of judicial review in the protection of rights in a liberal democracy. Timely descents from the ivory tower by influential figures have proved to be very effective. On the one side are those who see human rights as a precondition of democracy, which can be sustained only if the right to liberty, the right to privacy, the right of freedom of expression, and the right to freedom of association are sustained and respected. According to Feldman (2002: 32–3),

citizens must have certain guaranteed rights if an effective democratic structure is to be put in place and maintained. It is impossible to imagine a properly functioning democracy in a country where people by and large are not guaranteed freedom of expression, a free press, a right to vote, a right to petition Parliament, freedom of protest, and freedom from arbitrary arrest and detention by government agencies. Such rights are fundamental to the notion of democracy, and the development of the very idea of citizenship. They should not be abrogated by democratic decision-makers in the public sphere without undermining the very democracy which is said to legitimize public decision-making.

An important weakness of this argument, however, is that it leaves to the courts the power not only to police restraints on the democratic process, but also to determine the nature and meaning of democracy for this purpose. If the former is controversial, the latter would render inconsolable those social democrats critical of review of legislation by a 'judicial upper house' (Neumann in Kirchheimer and Neumann, 1987).

On the other side are the rights sceptics. It is not clear how far scepticism extends to the concept of rights as such, or whether it extends only to the concept of entrenched rights. So far as the former is concerned, such scepticism would be difficult to sustain in a common law system. In the absence of statutory rights, we are thrown back on the liberties protected by the common law, liberties which are rooted in contract and property, which sustain inequality. It would also tend to contradict the commitment of many sceptics to democratic principles, in the sense that statutory rights are one of the ends of democracy, which exists not only as an end in itself, but also to serve the movable goals of temporal majorities. In this sense, it is not revocable rights which are the enemy of democracy, so much as entrenched irrevocable rights of indeterminate scope and generous open texture. With that caveat, a particularly effective critic is Waldron who writes as 'a theorist of rights' to argue that 'people have a right to participate in the democratic governance of their community, and that this right is quite deeply connected to the values of autonomy and responsibility that are celebrated in our commitment to basic liberties'. He writes, moreover and more specifically, that 'the right to democracy is a right to participate on equal terms in social decisions on issues of high principle and that it is not to be confined to interstitial matters of social and economic policy'. That 'right of rights' is diminished if the source of decision-making authority is shifted from 'the legislature to the courtroom', that is to say from 'the people and their admittedly imperfect representative institutions to a handful of men and women supposedly of wisdom, learning, virtue and high principle' (Waldron, 1993: 20).

5.2 Human Rights and Democracy: Searching for a Synthesis

These doubts about the legitimacy of judicial review are a serious irritant to the rights project: a constant itch on the body politic which periodically has to be scratched. As such, it needs to be addressed by those who support the constitutional protection of rights. Is there an answer to the claim that judicial review of legislation is undemocratic? One answer is provided by Hogg and Bushell (1997) who respond in an influential article by adopting the metaphor of dialogue, and arguing that the Canadian Charter 'can act as a catalyst for a two way exchange between the judiciary and legislature on the topic of human rights and freedoms, but it rarely raises an absolute barrier to the wishes of democratic institutions' (1997: 81). This explanation of the new relationship between the legislature and the judiciary was endorsed by the Supreme Court of Canada in *Vriend v Alberta* [1998] 1 SCR 493, and it is seen as the most important attempt to reconcile conflicting values and to justify the role of the courts in policing the political process. The metaphor of dialogue has also been adopted for use in the British context, for which it may appear peculiarly well suited, given the nature of the powers of the British courts under the Human Rights Act by which they may draw Parliament's attention to, but may not refuse to apply, legislation which violates Convention rights.

Yet for all its attraction, it is by no means clear that the metaphor of dialogue fully addresses the concerns of opponents of entrenched rights: apart from the fact that not all court decisions in Canada are easily reversible by legislation, it remains the case that the judges still have a privileged position to challenge the outcome of the democratic process, which may already have spoken with a muted voice in order to avoid any Charter challenge in the first place. Whatever metaphor is used and however the relationship between courts and legislature plays out in practice, there is no escape from the fact that judicial review of legislation empowers unelected and unaccountable political actors (the judges) to constrain the wishes of the people speaking through their elected representatives (Parliament), either by pre-legislative restraint, or by post-legislative scrutiny. The fact that Parliament still has room for manoeuvre after the judges have spoken is simply another way of saying that there are certain things which Parliament is disabled by the courts from doing. If judicial review of legislation is to be justified, it must be for reasons of principle which are intrinsic to the process itself, and not because the process is not as intrusive or as expansive in practice as might otherwise be claimed by the opponents of judicial review of legislation. The dialogue metaphor does not address the question of the legitimacy of unelected and unaccountable officials being elevated to the status of legislative interlocutors in the first place.

6 Questions of Legitimacy: The Politics of the Judiciary

What do the judges make of this challenge to their authority? A remarkable feature of the period under review is their willingness to engage with the political controversy about the constitutional protection of human rights. Judges are in big demand in law schools for speeches; and judicial speeches are in big demand by law review editors. There are now many pages of judicial writing in the law reviews, by no means confined to issues relating to the debate about the constitutional protection of human rights. But so far as the latter is concerned, the writing has taken several forms, with judges engaging as advocates in a political debate to promote a bill of rights, or to give an account of or to explain the nature of the judicial function in constitutional adjudication, or to justify particular decisions or their role in these decisions. In some cases, the judges intervene through the pages of the law reviews to express concerns and criticisms, as in the case of Wilson (1990) who raised concerns as a justice of the Supreme Court of Canada about the gender balance of the court. In other cases, the judges intervene through the pages of the law reviews to think aloud, as in the case of Gonthier (2000), another justice of the Supreme Court of Canada who argued, in an unusually interesting and unpredictable contribution, for fraternity to be recognized as a third principle of constitutional law.

6.1 On the Offensive: The Judge as Political Activist

There have been a number of leading judicial activists for political change who have used the law reviews as a platform for their advocacy. The three English judges who campaigned most vigorously for the Human Rights Act 1998 were Bingham, Laws, and Sedley, at the time of writing all prominent members of the English bench. In an article advocating the incorporation of the European Convention on Human Rights into English law, Bingham was to write provocatively that the case for doing so was 'clear', and that the burden lay 'on the opponents to make good their grounds of opposition' (1993: 399). Other contributors to the debate were Woolf (now Lord Chief Justice) and Browne-Wilkinson. The only British judge to campaign or speak against a Bill of Rights was McCluskey who, as a result, was held to be disqualified from taking part in legal proceedings in which an accused person asserted his rights under the Human Rights Act: *Hoekstra v HM Advocate (No 3)* 2000 JC 391. At the time of writing, no similar fate had befallen any of the judicial proponents of the same Act, which they were now administering. Indeed, Lord Bingham has been made the 'senior law lord', and some judges are campaigning for a new Supreme Court.

Political advocacy of this kind (in which the senior judges are in effect seeking a greater share of political power and questioning the ultimate source of legal and political sovereignty) is a troublesome development which raises important questions about judicial independence and judicial accountability. Yet although it has attracted some criticism (Griffith, 2001), this has been mainly on account of the content of the judicial writings rather than their implications for constitutional principle. Nevertheless, similar work is to be found in other jurisdictions where serving and retired judges have been at the forefront of the debates about the protection of human rights in the courts. In Australia, the work of Mason stands out, while in New Zealand, Cooke has been prominent. A variation on this theme is the writing of those judges who add their weight to the campaigns for incorporation in other countries. The world has become a much smaller place since 1960. Judges travel widely, and they are constantly invited to participate in meetings and conferences about human rights, or to explain how their own system of human rights protection operates. Important contributions to the debate in the United Kingdom were made by Justice

William Brennan from the United States, and Chief Justice Beverley McLachlan from Canada.

6.2 On the Defensive: The Judge as Political Philosopher

The extension of entrenched rights to more jurisdictions has inevitably led to a change in the nature of extra-judicial writing, which in those countries where human rights have been entrenched is more concerned to explain the nature of the process of judicial decision-making, to justify the process of judicial review, and to engage with debates about the nature and scope of the entrenching document. This is most marked in Canada where the Charter has been operational for twenty years, and where there has been criticism of the Supreme Court from both the Right and Left of the political spectrum, as well as in the press. It is true that there is curiously little extra-judicial writing by the Canadian judges before 1982, perhaps reflecting their inability to make much of the Bill of Rights of 1960, a measure which had little impact until the introduction of the Charter. But there have been a number of significant pieces since, including those by Wilson and Gonthier already referred to. Perhaps even more interesting than these is the judicial writing which seeks to explain and justify the role of the courts under the Charter, in direct recognition of the fact that in 'the age of the Charter where judicial output is often perceived in highly-charged political terms', there is a need to 'convince Canadians that the courts are not administering anti-democratic fiats from behind judicial robes' (Bastarache, 1998: 419).

The prominent example of this last kind of judicial writing is McLachlan (1999), at the time Chief Justice of Canada. In a remarkably defensive speech published in the *University of British Columbia Law Review*, the Chief Justice denied that judges and legislator were 'adversaries', 'locked in an embrace of eternal and inevitable opposition' (1999: 35). Rather, 'the relationship between the elected legislators and the courts in a constitutional democracy' is 'symbiotic', in which the three branches of government 'work together' (though not in an 'active sense') to 'produce justice'. In her view

A just society is not the product of the elected legislators alone, nor is it the product of effective administration and enforcement of the laws. A just society is the product of responsible action by all three segments of government—the elected legislators, the executive charged with enforcing and administering the law, and the courts. (ibid.)

It is not clear whether public engagement of this kind will be beneficial to the judiciary in the long term. Nor is it clear that it is the job of the judges to defend the Charter (or similar texts) and to expose alleged myths about it which appear in the press. It is true that there needs to be a theory of the role of the courts in a democracy, and that there needs to develop a theoretical framework as a basis for judicial review. But in a democracy, it is not clear that these are matters for the judges alone to determine. Similar attempts to explain the judicial role were made from the bench in *Vriend v Alberta* above, but were not universally well received by scholars:

> In *Vriend v Alberta*, the Supreme Court took the opportunity to speak about its place in the Canadian polity. Unhappily, as appears so often to be the case, the Court spoke on the basis of too little reflection. Whereas it should have offered informed history and theory, it instead offered a discourse impoverished by clichés and disfigured by misinformation and misunderstanding. The rule of law minimally requires that each branch understands its proper place in democratic politics. It is the Supreme Court's failing in this regard that, in the final analysis, renders *Vriend* an opportunity lost, and the Court's decision a matter of so much regret. (DeCoste, 1999: 253)

British judges in the meantime are 'particularly comfortable with the fact that, for example, the law on abortion has been made by the elected representatives of the people rather than being deduced from some very general statements in the Bill of Rights' (Hoffman, 1999: 161). But this will not absolve the judges for long from the criticism which has been heaped onto the Canadian courts, in response to which a few mumbled words by two of Lord Hoffmann's colleagues in extra-judicial writings about 'common sense' (Lord Steyn) and 'balance' (Lord Hope of Craighead) may provide inadequate reassurance or protection.

7 THE JUDICIAL RECORD

These concerns about the legitimacy of the judicial function exist partly because the courts are placed in a position of political power by human rights instruments. It is true that the nature of that power is different in the case of each instrument, and that not all courts have the power to strike down legislation. But all courts (with the possible exception of those in New Zealand) have the power to thwart the wishes of an elected, responsible, and accountable government. Part of the difficulty about giving such power to the courts is the remarkable indeterminacy and open texture of bills or charters of rights for which judges have lobbied and which they are asked by parliaments to administer. The question which much of the literature is concerned with is how this power is exercised in practice. Here we find that there is general dissatisfaction with the courts: the Right are critical because of decisions on what are referred to as recognition (or formal equality) claims; the Liberal rights enthusiasts because the courts appear to be unduly conservative; and the Left because the courts are generally hostile to redistributionist claims or indeed the claims of redistributionist institutions such as trade unions. The possible exception to this picture of dissatisfaction is found in the United States where, with notable dissenters (such as Tushnet on the Left and Bork on the Right), most (though by no means all) scholars appear quite satisfied, if not complacent, about the Supreme Court's performance, although there is criticism of particular decisions or lines of decision.

7.1 The Judicial Record and Human Rights

Assessment of the overall record of the courts depends to a large extent on the expectations of the process which the author had when embarking upon the assessment. There are those who believe that the judicial record has been positive, either generally or in specific areas. But it is striking that, as indicated, outside the United States many leading figures associated with constitutional review of rights have lamented the performance of the courts. This is true in Canada where Beatty (1999: 21–2) has remarked that:

Summarising the evolution of Canadian constitutional law since the entrenchment of the Charter is a relatively straightforward affair. There really is no disagreement among those who study the judgments of the Court that, after an initial flurry of activity, increasingly over time and as new justices took their seats on the bench, the Court adopted a highly deferential even submissive posture towards the other two branches of government. Caution, restraint and a very attenuated standard of review are widely acknowledged to be the leitmotif of Canadian constitutional law.

As might be expected, those who were initially sceptical feel fully vindicated by the experience of judicial review (Ison, 1997). But it is also true that in the United Kingdom some of those who were strongly committed to the Human Rights Act are now publicly confessing serious concerns. It is perhaps premature to be drawing meaningful conclusions after the experience of only one year when the judges are still feeling their way around the new instrument, and are perhaps untested on the big controversial questions. A review by Wadham (2001) of the cases decided in the first year of the Act's operation was nevertheless damning, and concluded: 'Perhaps those who lobbied for the Human Rights Act were a little naive because despite [some] optimistic signs from the courts Liberty does not think that overall the judiciary have followed the principles of the Convention as well as they should'. The author was writing as the Director of Liberty, a civil rights group that campaigned for the Human Rights Act.

Other commentators have tried to assess the winners and losers from constitutional jurisprudence. Here the message is mixed, though a sophisticated analysis of the Canadian experience has concluded that 'the courts are disposed to recognition claims but inclined against redistribution ones' (Fudge, 2001: 357). The former cover claims by groups 'who are subject mainly to cultural and symbolic injustice' (such as gays and lesbians), while the latter covers those whose claims are 'primarily political and economic' (such as labour unions) (ibid. 340). But although it is believed by some that constitutional protection has advanced the cause of women's rights and gay and lesbian rights, others have been much more cautious. Yet there have been few challenges to the claim that while trade unions have gained little at the altar of adjudication, corporations have fared rather better (Hutchinson and Petter, 1988). A curious feature of human rights adjudication—pointed out in Section 4.2 above— is that it is open to legal as well as natural persons to assert human rights claims, in some cases even where the right allegedly violated is one which cannot conceivably be exercisable by a legal person (such as freedom of religion). So although rights may operate to protect minorities—which is one of the principal justifications for this kind of review (Ely, 1980)—they are also available for the defence of those who are already advantaged, and wish to retain the advantages which they enjoy. One colourful conclusion about the Canadian Charter asserts that:

It is possible that the Charter may have had some broad-scale beneficial effects. The values enumerated in the Charter might possibly have received more media attention than they otherwise would, and perhaps this may have had some permeating influence in public policy decision-making; but one has to clutch at straws like this to find any broad-scale public benefit. About the only groups in society that have clearly benefited from the Charter are constitutional and criminal lawyers, drug traffickers and transnational corporations. The Charter might also meet the needs of any politician or official who needs to explain inertia. (Ison, 1997: 511)

7.2 The Judicial Record and Judicial Appointments

Commitment to entrenched rights nevertheless remains very robust, with some of those (particularly the Liberal rights enthusiasts) disappointed by the judicial record taking the view that the problems are not systemic but remediable. One of the suggested remedies is for greater care to be taken in the appointment of judges to office. Indeed, Beatty (1999) writes that under the Canadian system of executive appointments, Prime Ministers have been 'able to favour people who were inclined to take a very cautious approach to their role as "guardians of the constitution" and whose instinct was to give [them and their] government a wide "margin of appreciation" to choose whatever policies and programmes they preferred' (1999: 26). According to Beatty:

For countries considering whether to incorporate a written bill of rights into their constitutions, I have no doubt that the single most important lesson to be learned from Canada's experience is that the extent to which human rights are protected in a society depends, more than anything else, on the way judges are appointed to its courts. (ibid. 27)

Beatty's concern was that there should be a greater role for the legislature in the making of judicial appointments on the ground that 'legislatures in which minority parties play a meaningful role, and where decisions are taken after open, public hearings, are institutionally less inclined to want to neutralise the Court and more likely to see it as an ally and friend' (ibid. 26).

Measures such as the Canadian Charter of Rights and Freedoms, and the United Kingdom Human Rights Act have unquestionably generated concern about the accountability and representativeness of the courts, and these are not concerns which the judges find uncontroversial. It is important to emphasize, however, that these have always been difficult questions which have lain largely unasked and certainly unanswered. Quite apart from their power of constitutional veto under charters or bills of rights, the courts have always exercised a legislative function through the common law and through the interpretation of statutes. It is nevertheless uncontestable that the judicial power of legislative veto or review increases the case for courts which are not only independent, but also representative and accountable. Yet it is not clear that a more open appointments system will lead to a more liberal and less conservative judiciary, as Beatty and others contemplate. The problem may be the process as much as the personnel. Lessons to be drawn from the United State are hardly propitious (Tushnet, 2001), though the Senate did contrive to block Robert Bork. But even if reforms to the appointments system were to produce more 'liberal' judges, there are still hurdles of legitmacy to be overcome, no matter how open and accountable the procedures for the appointment of those endowed with a democratic veto.

8 ALTERNATIVES TO JUDICIAL REVIEW: DEMOCRATIC PROTECTION OF HUMAN RIGHTS

Questions of judicial legitimacy and judicial performance have led some to look for alternatives to judicial review, as a way of protecting human rights within the context of national constitutional law. This is a matter to which the attention of lawyers and others is beginning to turn in a number of jurisdictions (Hiebert, 1998, 1999; Tushnet, forthcoming), with alternatives being proposed for different reasons, and in different forms. Initial interest in countries such as the United Kingdom which were contemplating a bill of rights (in the era before the Human Rights Act) was pre-emptive: designed to discourage a rights model based on judicial enforcement. But given the onward march of the rights movement this was hugely optimistic, and it is striking that Sweden—the jurisdiction which provided a model of parliamentary scrutiny—has moved to incorporate the ECHR by making it legally enforceable. In other countries—such as Canada and the United States—where there are already bills or charters of rights, part of the attraction of alternatives to judicial review is to allow the legislature to take back responsibility for the protection of rights. According to Hiebert (1999: 29), a 'clearly documented parliamentary record', in which a specialist parliamentary committee and the government 'address specific Charter concerns and explain the reasons and rationale for the legislative objective, will be difficult for judges to discount'.

8.1 Executive Scrutiny and Reporting

The case for 'taking the constitution away from the courts' has been elegantly made, as has the case for the better parliamentary scrutiny of legislation to ensure better compliance with human rights standards without the need for judicial review. A number of different practices have developed for this purpose, including executive scrutiny of legislation, and executive reporting to the legislature of consistency or inconsistency of legislation with the national bill of rights or human rights instrument. Executive scrutiny in the United States is discussed by Tushnet (forthcoming) who considers the operation of the Office of Legal Counsel in the US Department of Justice. In the United Kingdom, the Ministerial Code has for some time required ministers to ensure that bills brought to Cabinet are consistent with the requirements of the ECHR. The impact of this procedure ought not to be underestimated. For although it is true that there have been many successful complaints against the United Kingdom before the European Court of Human Rights, most of the high profile and controversial cases have related to administrative action and the common law, rather than primary legislation. It is nevertheless true that in recent years, a number of declarations of incompatibility relating to Acts of Parliament have been made by the courts under the Human Rights Act 1998.

So far as executive reporting is concerned, the starting-point is Canada's pioneering Bill of Rights of 1960 which provided for the Minister of Justice to scrutinize both primary and secondary legislation and report any inconsistency with the Bill of Rights to the House of Commons. The purpose was to require the Minister to advise the Cabinet and Parliament of any inconsistency, leaving it to them 'to accept his advice or take the responsibility of overriding it', the expectation being that 'the Legislative Division of the Department of Justice would make every attempt to resolve any inconsistency between the Bill of Rights and a draft Bill at a much earlier stage', in order to avoid any embarrassment for the government (Tarnopolsky, 1976: 126, 128). A similar obligation exists in relation to the Charter of Rights (Hiebert, 1998: 123), and this was a model for New Zealand's Bill of Rights 1990, which is said to be designed to ensure that 'Parliament does not legislate in ignorance of the Bill of Rights, and to exact political accountability for government legislation that would derogate from the substantive guarantees' (Joseph, 2002: 1048). In the United Kingdom, the Human Rights Act 1998 now requires all bills to state on their face that their provisions are compatible with Convention rights, and that if they are not that the minister nevertheless wishes to proceed with them. This may be seen as another example of executive reporting.

8.2 Parliamentary Scrutiny

The New Zealand experience of government reporting has been the subject of some scepticism. Although it was 'hoped that the reporting procedure would have a salutary effect on Ministers promoting legislation', it has been concluded that the procedure 'has not fulfilled its promise as a key feature of the legislation' and 'has not had the deterrent effect that was expected' (Joseph, 2002: 1053). It is perhaps rather early to make judgements about the British reporting procedures, though it is doubtful whether all of the ministerial statements of compatibility with Convention rights would bear close forensic scrutiny. Indeed the Anti-terrorism, Crime and Security Act 2001 was passed in the wake of the events in the United States on 11 September despite parliamentary concerns about compatibility with Convention rights. It is nevertheless the case that the government's critics were able to win important concessions, and it remains the case that this reporting procedure (together with the Joint Committee discussed below) requires more careful consideration of human rights in the preparation of legislation than might otherwise take place, while the statement on the face of the bill provides an invitation for confrontation and debate which otherwise might not exist.

A significant feature of the New Zealand Bill of Rights is the rejection by the government of a Bill of Rights Standing Committee to review and examine bills, and it is not clear what difference this decision has made to the nature of parliamentary scrutiny. A Committee of this kind was in fact introduced in the United Kingdom in 2000. A Joint Committee of both Houses, it has wide terms of reference which include the examination of all bills to determine whether statements of compliance with Convention rights can stand up to scrutiny. But although parliamentary scrutiny of legislation operates in a number of countries, it was pioneered in the common law world (in relation to primary legislation) in Australia, where there is no judicially enforceable bill of rights (Hiebert, 1998). A study of the operation of the scrutiny committees in Australia has identified a number of constraints on parliamentary scrutiny, not the least being 'political cultures in which governments are resistant to perceived obstacles to the fulfilment of their mandates and policy programs' (Hiebert, 1998: 126). Further work on this issue will determine the full potential of such scrutiny, and will assess how far—if at all—it does or can contribute to revitalizing the work of parliamentary institutions.

9 EXPANDING HORIZONS: RECLAIMING SOCIAL RIGHTS

The case for a more effective parliamentary scrutiny is in part a response to concerns about the institutional legitimacy of the courts in enforcing human rights instruments. But there are also concerns about the way in which the powers of the courts are used in practice which lead paradoxically to arguments for an extension of human rights instruments to include social and economic rights as well as civil and political rights. From this perspective, the extension of human rights instruments to include such rights is seen as purely defensive: not so much to provide a guarantee of such rights and not in response to a suspicion of representative institutions, but on the contrary to protect legislation dealing with these matters from being undermined by the courts applying the narrowly conceived instruments that we find for the most part in the common law world. The argument for extension is partly a response to the concerns that Anglo-American instruments can be used by corporate interests to challenge social legislation, and extension is seen as giving an instruction to the courts that social and economic rights on the one hand, and civil and political rights on the other, are to be given an equal weight, and that the latter are not to be regarded as trumping the former.

9.1 The Argument about Social Rights

There are of course other reasons for the constitutional protection of social rights. Curiously there is a democratic argument. It is not simply that social equality or a measure of 'equality of rank and fortune' are regarded by many as a precondition of democracy, but also that the effect of a bill of social rights would be to socialize the common law, by providing a statutory basis to replace the common law as the default rules for private relationships (for example, those between workers and employers). In this way a bill of social rights is designed not only to regulate the exercise of public power, but also to regulate the exercise of private power. But it would also impose duties on the State, in relation to education, health care, and housing. In embracing the constitutional model of many of the social democracies of Western Europe, the social rights proposals in the human rights era are also taking an important step which recognizes the indivisibility of human rights: the need to protect the right to be housed as a precondition of the right to respect for one's home; the right to work as a precondition of the right to form and join trade unions for the protection of one's interests; and the right to education as a precondition of the right to freedom of expression.

This is a debate which is beginning to ignite. But there is also a great deal of scepticism about the protection of social rights, from both human rights enthusiasts and critics alike. Questions of principle relate to the familiar concerns about constraining the powers of elected, representative, and accountable governments and parliaments, while questions of practice relate to the issue of justiciability which is thought to be a particularly acute problem in the context of social rights. The existence of social rights depends on resources being available, and the rights can hardly be demanded when the resources are not there. More work is required to determine whether this is an exaggerated concern. It may overlook the fact that there is already a procedure at international level for NGOs to enforce social and economic rights in quasi-judicial forums, and it may also overlook the relative nature of social rights (there can be no absolutes), as well as the fact that many social rights of a procedural nature addressed to relationships in private law do not present problems of this kind. But even to the extent that social rights instruments are addressed to the State, the aim is to guarantee a minimum standard of protection, not that all needs are met. Otherwise the aim is to ensure that rights are denied only where there are rational grounds.

9.2   From Argument to Action: The South African Bill of Rights

The South African Bill of Rights of 1996 includes a number of social and economic rights. It has been said that

The inclusion of economic, social and cultural rights as directly enforceable rights in South Africa's final Constitution, signals a decisive break with the idea that a Bill of Rights is only a shield which protects citizens against government interference. This means that the Bill of Rights will require judges, lawyers and academics to scrutinise and reject many of the accepted practices and assumptions in relation to judicial review. (Vos, 1997: 66)

But although other recently introduced instruments have not made this break (with the exception of Quebec where chapter IV of the Charter of Human Rights and Freedoms contains a number of derogable 'economical and social rights'), this is not to say that the issue has not been considered in other jurisdictions. A proposal in Canada to include a number of social and economic principles as amendments to the Charter of Rights and Freedoms was included in a package of constitutional reform which foundered in a referendum in 1992. The problem was not the inclusion of social rights so much as the distribution of powers which haunts Canadian politics like no other. It would be true to say, nevertheless, that there was little scholarly enthusiasm for this initiative which was criticized as 'a snare and a delusion', and 'a way for government and others to avoid having to engage in transformative politics' (Glasbeek, 1992).

The South African experience provides an opportunity to assess some of this scepticism. The Bill of Rights now to be found in chapter 2 of the Constitution of 1996 provides for a range of rights and freedoms, including rights relating to trade union membership and activities, housing, health care, food and water, social security, and education. Although it is very early to be drawing meaningful conclusions about the effectiveness of these measures, initial views are that the 'judicial enforcement of socio-economic rights has had a mixed success' (Jagwanth, 2001: 311). Much will be heard of *Soobramoney v Minister of Health* (1997) 12 BCLR 1696 where it was held that the denial of dialysis treatment to an unemployed man suffering from kidney failure was not a breach of the constitutional right of access to health care services. The treatment had been denied because of a scarcity of resources, and it was not for the court to decide how these resources were to be allocated. But on the other hand, it was held that the eviction of homeless squatters from public land to make way for a public housing development in *Government of the Republic of South Africa v Grootboom* (2000) 11 BCLR 1169 violated the constitutional right of access to adequate housing. The State was required by the decision of the court to devise and implement within its available resources a comprehensive and coordinated programme progressively to realize the right of access to adequate housing.

10 Human Rights, Globalization, and the Multinational Corporations

These concerns with social rights in constitutional law anticipate the direction of future scholarship, as they emerge at a time of growing concern with social rights in international law, in an era of globalization. It is at this point that we return to and conclude with the challenges faced by the international lawyer, whose human rights concerns must now relate as much to the activities of the multinational corporation, as of the nation state and international institutions. Globalization is a hotly contested phenomenon, 'ordinarily understood as economic and, as its root suggests, involving connections that span the world' (Giddens, 1998: 29), and described by one pair of sceptics addressed by Giddens as meaning the emergence of a 'truly global economy' in which 'distinct national economies and therefore domestic strategies of national economic management are increasingly irrelevant'. But for some, globalization is 'misunderstood' if it is treated as if it were only or primarily economic. According to Giddens (1998: 33), globalization is 'a complex range of processes, driven by a mixture of political and economic influences', which is 'creating new transnational systems and forces', and 'transforming the institutions of the societies in which we live'.

10.1 Globalization and Human Rights

The threat to human rights in a globalized economy is caused in part by the multinational corporations with great powers of economic investment, and by international institutions such as the IMF and the World Bank through media such as economic structural adjustment programmes. So far as the multinationals are concerned, political sociologists remind us that many of the largest economies in the world are corporations not countries. Yet human rights instruments are addressed to countries rather than corporations, even though the latter are also liable to violate international human rights standards, as a number of academic studies have revealed. So far as international institutions are concerned, an emerging problem is that not all parts of the international community insist on compliance with international human rights standards in the conduct of their activities. Indeed, for bodies such as the World Bank and the IMF, these instruments may be an irritant. It has been claimed that 'while opportunities for enhanced human rights protection can emerge from pressure on globalised economic institutions to take more account of human rights issues, so far this pressure (and the resultant impact) has been piecemeal and inconsistent' (McCorquodale and Fairbrother, 1999: 757).

Initial work on the impact of globalization on human rights is rather bleak: external investment, privatization, and liberalization have not been kind either to civil and political rights, or to social and economic rights. There is some evidence that some multinationals are impatient and even intolerant of corrupt regimes in which human rights are likely to be violated, but there is also evidence that 'many of the funding conditions imposed by the globalised economic institutions . . . require strong government action for smooth implementation', with authoritarian and military governments being favoured by external investors as the best suited to implement these policies successfully (McCorquodale and Fairbrother, 1999: 755). Many multinational companies have adopted codes of conduct under which they undertake to respect human rights, and the revised OECD Guidlelines on Multinational Enterprises make oblique reference to human rights generally, though more direct reference to social rights in particular (including a reference to the ILO Declaration of 1998). But the former are treated with scorn by many scholars and activists, while the latter are the softest of soft law which may yet have little impact in the host countries where the companies are welcomed. Space does not permit a full examination of the human rights problems associated with globalization. But the matter has been summarized in the following way:

it is possible to argue that there is a positive relationship between economic globalisation and the protection of political rights. Certainly, the globalised economic institutions have been seeking to make the relationship a positive one by placing democratic governance conditions on investment and by taking some account of non-economic factors in their decision-making. However, the arguments that the relationship is a negative one are also strong. These arguments raise questions about the legitimacy of the democratic governance conditions and the seriousness with which human rights issues, and the nebulous concept of 'democracy', are taken into account by both the global economic institutions and transnational corporations. It would appear that instead of creating order, the rule of law, and the protection of human rights, globalisation can create conditions for disorder, authoritarian rule, and the disintegration of the state entity with consequent violations of human rights. (McCorquodale and Fairbrother, 1999: 758)

10.2 Human Rights Responses to Globalization

Much of the concern about the human rights implications of globalization has been with the failure of countries and corporations to respect international human rights instruments dealing with social and economic rights in particular. An emerging development has been the prominence which has been given to these rights at a number of levels. Apart from the ILO Declaration on Fundamental Principles and Rights at Work 1998, a development of great importance has been the EU Charter of Fundamental Rights which was solemnly declared at Nice on 7 December 2000. Human rights in the EU is an issue beginning to generate a significant body of literature, reflecting a number of different political and legal developments. The power of the Union is increasing as its borders expand. At the same time, the European Court of Justice is developing a line of jurisprudence which requires the Community institutions and the member states in the implementation of Community law to respect fundamental rights of the kind found in national constitutions and in the ECHR. There is also concern about racism and xenophobia in the member states which has led to the production of new legal instruments in response. All of which are in addition to the meandering social policy of the Community which led to the EC Charter of the Social Rights of Workers in 1989 and the revisions to the EC Treaty at Amsterdam in 1997 to enable social rights to be introduced more easily by qualified majority voting rather than with the approval of all member states.

The EU Charter of Fundamental Rights is inspired by several of the existing treaties to which EU member states are already party, such as the ECHR, the Council of Europe's Social Charter of 1961, and the Revised Social Charter of 1996. But the wide sweep of the EU Charter is such that it includes measures which were previously unknown as fundmental rights, thereby revealing that the category of human rights is not closed. This is not to say that all of these measures are necessarily welcome additions to the family, with the right to conduct business being a fundamental right with more than a touch of the cuckoo about it. The great uncertainty about the legal status of the EU Charter has generated an impressive literature which is likely to develop still further as the ECJ takes account of the Charter, and as the process of European constitutional revision continues. At the time of writing a Convention chaired by Valerie Giscard D'Estaing has been given the responsibility to determine the role of fundamental rights within the treaty structure of the Union. Yet there remain those who are doubtful about the exercise, contending that Europe already has enough Charters of Rights, a sentiment with which it is not difficult to disagree. There is nevertheless much for common law jurisdictions to learn from a document, such as the EU Charter, which recognizes the indivisibility of human rights, not only by including both civil and political rights and social and economic rights in the same text, but by doing so in a manner which recognizes that each should have an equal status with the other.

REFERENCES

Bastarache, M. (1998). 'The Challenge of the Law in the New Millennium', *Manitoba Law Journal*, 25: 411–19.

Beatty, D. (1999). 'The Canadian Charter of Rights: Lessons and Laments', in G. W. Anderson (ed.), *Rights and Democracy: Essays in UK—Canadian Constitutionalism*, London: Blackstone Press.

Bingham, T. H. (1993). 'The European Convention on Human Rights: Time to Incorporate', *Law Quarterly Review*, 109: 390–400.

DeCoste, F. C. (1999). 'The Separation of Powers in Liberal Polity: Vriend v Alberta', *McGill Law Journal*, 44: 231–53.

Ely, J. H. (1980). *Democracy or Distrust: A Theory of Judicial Review*, Cambridge, Mass.: Harvard University Press.

Feldman, D. (2002). *Civil Liberties and Human Rights in England and Wales* (2nd edn.), Oxford: Oxford University Press.

Fudge, J. (2001). 'The Canadian Charter of Rights: Recognition, Redistribution and the Imperialism of the Courts', in T. Campbell, K. D. Ewing, and A. Tomkins (eds.), *Sceptical Essays on Human Rights*, Oxford: Oxford University Press.

Gearty, C. A. (1993). 'The European Convention on Human Rights and the Protection of Civil Liberties: An Overview', *Cambridge Law Journal*, 89–127.

Giddens, A. (1998). *The Third Way*, Cambridge: Polity.

Glasbeek, H. (1992). 'The Social Charter: Poor Politics for the Poor', in J. Bakan and D. Schneiderman (eds.), *Social Justice and the Constitution: Perspectives on a Social Union for Canada*, Ottawa: Carleton Press.

Goldsworthy, J. (2001). 'Legislative Sovereignty and the Rule of Law', in T. Campbell, K. D. Ewing, and A. Tomkins (eds.), *Sceptical Essays on Human Rights*, Oxford: Oxford University Press.

Gonthier, C. D. (2000). 'Liberty, Equality, Fraternity: The Forgotten Leg of the Trinity, or Fraternity: The Unspoken Third Pillar of Democracy', *McGill Law Journal*, 45: 567–89.

Griffith, J. A. G. (2000). 'The Brave New World of Sir John Laws', *Modern Law Review*, 63: 159–75.

Habermas, J. (1994). 'Human Rights and Popular Sovereignty: The Liberal and Republican Versions', *Ratio Juris*, 7: 1–13.

Harris, D. J., and Joseph, S. (1996). *The International Covenant on Civil and Political Rights and United Kingdom Law*, Oxford: Oxford University Press.

Hiebert, J. (1998). 'A Hybrid Approach to Protect Rights? An Argument in Favour of Supplementing Canadian Judicial Review with Australia's Model of Parliamentary Scrutiny', *Federal Law Review*, 26: 115–38.

—— (1999). 'Wrestling with Rights: Judges, Parliament and the Making of Social Policy', *Choices*, 5: 31–36.

Hoffmann, Lord (1999). 'Human Rights and the House of Lords', *Modern Law Review*, 62: 159–66.

Hogg, P. W. (1997). *Constitutional Law of Canada*, Scarborough, Ont.: Carswell.

—— and Bushell, A. A. (1997). 'The *Charter* Dialogue between Courts and Legislators', *Osgoode Hall Law Journal*, 35: 75–124.

Hutchinson, A., and Petter, A. (1988). 'Private Rights/Public Wrongs: The Liberal Lie of the Charter', *University of Toronto Law Journal*, 38: 278–97.

Ison, T. (1997). 'The Constitutional Bill of Rights—The Canadian Experience', *Modern Law Review*, 60: 499–512.

Jagwanth, S. (2001). 'The South African Experience of Judicial Rights Discourse: A Critical Appraisal', in T. Campbell, K. D. Ewing, and A. Tomkins (eds.), *Sceptical Essays on Human Rights*, Oxford: Oxford University Press.

Joseph, P. S. (2002). *Constitutional and Administrative Law in New Zealand* (2nd edn.), Wellington: Brookes.

Joseph, S., Schultz, J., and Castan, M. (2000). *The International Covenant on Civil and Political Rights: Cases, Materials, and Commentary*, Oxford: Oxford University Press.

Kirchheimer, O., and Neumann, F. (1987). *Social Democracy and the Rule of Law*, ed. K. Tribe and trans. L. Tanner and K. Tribe, London: Allen & Unwin.

McCorquodale, R., and Fairbrother, R. (1999). 'Globalisation and Human Rights', *Human Rights Quarterly*, 21: 735.

McLachlan, B. (1999). 'Charter Myths', *University of British Columbia Law Review*, 33: 23–36.

Mowbray, A. (1999). 'The Role of the European Court of Human Rights in the Promotion of Democracy', *Public Law*, 703–25.

——(2001). *Cases and Materials on the European Convention on Human Rights*, London: Butterworths.

Sieghart, P. (1986). *The Lawful Rights of Mankind*, Oxford: Oxford University Press.

Simpson, A. W. B. (2001). *Human Rights and the End of Empire*, Oxford: Oxford University Press.

Tarnopolsky, W. S. (1976). *The Canadian Bill of Rights* (2nd edn.), Ottawa: McClelland and Stewart Ltd.

Tushnet, M. (2001). 'Scepticism about Judicial Review: A Perspective from the United States', in T. Campbell, K. D. Ewing, and A. Tomkins (eds.), *Sceptical Essays on Human Rights*, Oxford: Oxford University Press.

——(forthcoming). 'Non-Judicial Review', in A. Stone, T. Campbell, and J. Goldsworthy (eds.), *Human Rights Protection: Boundaries and Challenges*, Oxford: Oxford University Press.

Vos, P. de (1997). 'Pious Wishes or Directly Enforceable Human Rights?: Social and Economic Rights in South Africa's 1996 Constitution', *South African Journal on Human Rights*, 13: 67–101.

Wadham, J. (2001). 'The Human Rights Act: One Year On', *European Human Rights Law Review*, 620–39.

Waldron, J. (1983). 'A Right-Based Critique of Constitutional Rights', *Oxford Journal of Legal Studies*, 13: 18–51.

Wilson, B. (1990). 'Will Women Judges Really Make a Difference?' *Osgoode Hall Law Journal*, 28: 507–22.

CHAPTER 16

THE EUROPEAN UNION

DISCIPLINE BUILDING MEETS POLITY BUILDING

JO SHAW

1 INTRODUCTION: LAW, EUROPE AND THE EU

THERE is no such thing as 'European' law in a purely legal sense. It is neither a conceptual category recognized in legal doctrinal usage (cf. national law or international law) nor a territorial or functional designation with precise external boundaries (cf. French law or WTO (World Trade Organization) law). European law is certainly not coterminous with the law of the European Union (or European Community law as it once was), although it is the latter which is the focus of this chapter. EU law is a distinctive and territorially based jurisdictional framework, based on international treaties and the interactions between those treaties and a range of national legal orders. But it is only one facet of 'European' law. Other legal orders operating within Europe are similarly part of a loose corpus of 'European law', including the law of the

Many thanks to those who have helped me to untangle my thoughts on the discipline of EU legal studies over many years, and thanks in particular for reading a draft and making comments to Neil Duxbury, Christian Joerges, and Neil Walker. The usual caveat applies with a particular intensity to this chapter, as the views set out here are mine and mine alone, although I have learnt a great deal from conversations with others.

European Convention on Human Rights, other aspects of the legal work of the Council of Europe, for example, on local democracy or gender equality, the international law frameworks provided by the United Nations Economic Commission for Europe, the Organization for Security and Cooperation in Europe, and the 'European' work of wider international organizations such as the OECD (Organization for Economic Cooperation and Development), the WTO, or the United Nations High Commissioner for Refugees (UNHCR). Furthermore, as a field of research and study, European law includes the interactions and interdependencies between these different sources of law, as well as relevant national laws, although probably not comparisons between national legal orders, or specifically domestic issues, even with a 'European' dimension. Yet that process of comparison can produce another potential candidate to be 'European law', a putative 'Common law of Europe' based on the identification of a common core of principles both informing and also transcending the national legal orders.

It is also pertinent that the regional boundaries of 'Europe' in geographical and geo-political terms are not closed. In April 2002, Italian Prime Minister Silvio Berlusconi invited Russian President Vladimir Putin to bring Russia into the European Union, showing that he could in future see the boundaries of the EU stretching from the Atlantic Ocean to the Pacific Ocean, and from the Barent Sea to the Caspian Sea. It is certainly the case that since the end of the Cold War—and in the shadow of the violent breakup of Yugoslavia in particular—the European Union has been managing a range of accession and stabilization/association processes right across the Euro-Mediterranean area in the south and south-east and far into the territory of the former Soviet Union in the east and north-east. These are likely to continue throughout and beyond the first decade of the twenty-first century.

At best, then, European law can only be an amalgam with uncertain conceptual and functional boundaries, and with no precise jurisdictional core. Yet despite the inherent definitional difficulties, scholars persist in using the term European law— for example, in the designation of the chairs they occupy, the titles of some of the journals they write in, and the subject they purport to study. This is only problematic where it is unclear whether they are referring (adequately, perhaps, but imprecisely, certainly) to the conceptual and jurisdictional amalgam sketched out here, or whether they are in fact conflating the term with 'European Union law', just as many observers and scholars similarly conflate 'Europe' with the 'European Union'. The title of Joseph Weiler's otherwise sharply observed book *The Constitution of Europe* (Weiler, 1999) is such a case of uncertainty in terminological usage, since it focuses essentially on the development of the European Union. But Weiler is intensely aware of the fact that there may be 'One or Several Europes' (the title of a research programme funded by the UK's Economic and Social Research Council, 1999–2004). Timothy Garton Ash's spicy term 'EU-rope' is the best example of terminological innovation which highlights the risks and challenges inherent in the conflation.

The focus in this chapter is the law, legal order, and institutional framework of what we now term the 'European Union', which was created in 1993 by the Treaty of Maastricht. This entity encompasses also the older European Communities, dating back to the 1950s. Incidentally, even those who agree that writing on the EU itself should not be termed plain 'European' do not all agree on precisely what its law should be called. After 1993, many lawyers and legal scholars were reluctant to abandon terms such as Community law or EC law, and to adopt the 'European Union' terminology which the media, in contrast, took up quite happily from the very first. Indeed, the Court of Justice even now generally refers only to Community law; after all, that institution is still formally the Court of Justice of the European Communities, confined in its jurisdiction for the most part to the span of the supranational European Community Treaties (the so-called 'first pillar'), and largely excluded from the predominantly intergovernmental European Union and its two 'pillars' of Common Foreign and Security Policy and Police and Judicial Cooperation in Criminal Matters. Legally, therefore, its appellation is correct. The term Community law, however, cannot effectively capture the scope of the legal analysis of the EU's constitution, which encompasses elements of the Treaty on European Union itself, even if these are not always formally justiciable. Consequently, as textbook writers have engaged ever more intensely with the EU's constitutional dimension as well as gradually turning to some of the legal issues raised by the intergovernmental second and third pillars, so they have successively renamed their textbooks 'law of the European Union', or 'European Union law'. EU law is what we shall mainly call it here. However, whenever a historical analysis of the law or legal scholarship is made, it is perverse to attempt to relabel what was—at the time—the law of the Communities into the law of the Union. Hence, where appropriate, terms such as EC law and Community competence will be used, especially to preserve historical depth, and the combination 'EC/EU' will be used to capture the overall frame of reference.

In contrast to certain of the definitional uncertainties identified here, the time span of EC/EU law is precise. It matches the historical span of the existence of the European Communities and the European Union, since the entry into force of the Treaty of Paris establishing the European Coal and Steel Community on 1 January 1952 to the present day. Coincidentally, ECSC law as a separate entity died fifty years later—the treaty having been concluded for a limited duration of fifty years— with the functions of the ECSC being subsumed into the EC Treaty. A bare fifty years is a short time span for a legal order which constitutes the raw material for the construction of an entire subdiscipline of legal studies. Yet, for a legal or constitutional order as such, it is not necessarily so short—especially when it is compared to time spans such as those of the Weimar Republic (1919–33), the various French Republics (even the current Fifth Republic is of more recent date (1958)), the pre-WTO General Agreement on Tariffs and Trade (GATT) (1948–94) or the international order based on the League of Nations (1919–46, although the last ten years did not really count).

The temporal aspect of the evolution of the EC/EU as legal and constitutional order, and especially the shifting basic conditions as a result of major Treaty change which had occurred four times in the sixteen years leading up to the time of writing (i.e. 1986–2002), has been fundamental to the way EU legal studies have developed as a subdiscipline of both legal studies and of 'European studies' more generally. It is a feature which suffuses the second section of this chapter which constructs a picture of EU legal studies by outlining its defining characteristics and the contexts which have shaped its evolution; in other words, it helps to show where and how discipline building has met polity building. The point is not to attempt to present a single cohesive picture of the subdiscipline, but to hint at its richness and variety by showing many of the pressures and forces operating upon and within it. The third section provides necessarily abbreviated tasters of some key areas of study for EU lawyers. It concentrates on how scholars have dealt with questions of constitutionalism and constitutionalization in a non-state context, and with understanding and defining the role of the law in the (single) market order, in Euroland (i.e. the group of states which have so far adopted the euro as their currency), in the nascent 'European social space', and in the Area of Freedom, Security, and Justice. It is easy to gain the impression when reviewing some fields of EU legal activity that the production of EU law is overwhelmingly a top–down activity, with obligations being imposed upon the Member States and indeed individual economic actors or even citizens by a legal authority—the EU—which is somehow separate from the national legal orders. This impression is fundamentally false—at every level of analysis. At the constitutional level, the EU's constitution comprises a system of 'multi-level constitutionalism' (Pernice, 1999), embracing both the EU's own emerging but still incomplete constitutional framework and the national constitutional orders of the Member States. The interaction between the different orders along both horizontal and vertical lines results in a continuous process of mutual transformation. Where EU law is primarily judge-made—as in the case of the 'negative' single market freedoms (goods, services, capital, persons)—the rules now in place result from dynamic conversations involving a wider community of actors, especially the Court of Justice and the national courts. Finally, in the legislative domain, the adoption of EU-level regulatory solutions to socio-economic problems generally results from the identification *at national level* of the need for coordinated action, not from an autonomous decision on the part of the EU's own institutions to change the nature of the regulatory burden upon the Member States and upon individual economic actors. Both of the two sections which follow focus primarily on English-language literatures, in order to ensure that the discussion is fully accessible to readers from the Anglo-American legal sphere. However, as Sections 2.2 and 2.3 will show, language is in fact a critical question in the evolution of EU legal studies.

2 Building the Discipline: Contexts and Characteristics of European Union Legal Studies

2.1 Polity Building: Moving Target or Stable Framework?

The pace of change in EU constitutional and institutional developments in the early twenty-first century has remained as rapid as ever. For example, a book published in early 2000 on EU constitutional and institutional law would already lack coverage of the Treaty of Nice (agreed December 2000, signed February 2001, came into force 15 February 2003) and the important post-Nice constitutional debate. This culminated in the establishment in February 2002 of a Convention on the Future of the Union, charged with preparing options for a planned intergovernmental conference on constitutional questions in 2004. Contributions to this debate helped to sharpen understandings of what the EU is at present, as well as what it might become in the future.

And yet, in other respects, the EC/EU has been a remarkably stable entity throughout its existence. From 1958 until 1985, no major Treaty-based changes were introduced. The Single European Act, which came into force in 1986, heralded the beginning of a new phase of frequent Treaty change, as well as underpinning the political programme to complete the internal market by the end of 1992. The triptych of political institutions, namely the Council, the Commission, and what we now know as the European Parliament, has remained essentially unchanged since the Treaty of Rome 1957, especially in relation to functions and activities, although the balance of powers between the institutions has evolved dramatically (de Búrca, 1999). The Court of Justice, although now assisted in its work by the Court of First Instance, still has the same 'mission' (to ensure that the law is observed: art. 220 EC) and the same jurisdictional bases (especially arts. 226, 230, and 234 EC—enforcement actions by the Commission, direct actions for judicial review of EU measures, and references for preliminary rulings from national courts) as it had in 1958. Integration in economic and some social affairs remains at the heart of the 'European' project, although it is accompanied ever more closely by a political integration project framed by notions of internal and external security and by the political imperative of developing institutions and—many would argue—a constitutional framework to match the economic power of the EU in the global economy.

The co-existence of longer-term stability of purpose and institutional reference points with rapid change in certain areas, such as the development of new competences (widening), the intensification of legislative activity (deepening), or the emergence of parliamentary control over many aspects of EU law-making (democratization), highlights the risks which the development of simple prognoses about the EU can involve. It is wrong to stick solely to the lens of Treaty-based change in order to judge the speed and extent of change overall. The 1960s and 1970s saw the period of heightened judicial activism, characterized by Eric Stein and Joseph Weiler amongst others as the period of the 'constitutionalization of the treaties', when the Court of Justice developed key doctrines such as the supremacy of EU law over national law, the concept of direct effect allowing certain norms of EU law to be directly enforceable by individuals in national courts, the protection of fundamental rights within EU law, and the principles which govern the scope and exercise of the EU's powers and competences. These doctrines in turn, although refined in subsequent case law, have proved to be the enduring pillars of the EU legal order, studied by succeeding generations of students. However, as the following subsections will show, a Court-centred focus for EU legal studies itself offers an inadequate picture of the reality of EU legal development, bearing in mind the intensive levels of legislative and administrative activity within the institutions, in some ways since the very beginning (for example, the construction of the complex legislation-heavy Common Agricultural Policy) and certainly since the inception in the mid-1980s of the programme to complete the Single Market by the beginning of 1993.

2.2 A Multinational and Multilingual Domain for Scholarship

At present, the European Union has fifteen Member States and eleven official languages. Wherever there is a 'full language regime' in force, this means that documents must be translated into all official languages—at considerable cost, of course. This applies not only to the treaties, the Official Journal, and the case law of the Court of Justice, but also to numerous other preparatory documents which are internal to one institution or are passed between the institutions and/or the Member States. Where there are meetings of officials or politicians, there needs to be simultaneous interpretation across every language combination. It is not uncommon to find, however, that interpretation from Finnish to Portuguese, for example, occurs via an intermediary language such as French or English. Furthermore, as the next wave of enlargement moves ever closer, the multilingual domain for scholarship grows ever more complex. Substantial tranches of the so-called *acquis communautaire*, or body of EU law, have already been translated into the ten or more anticipated new official languages. Language is just one feature of EU law and policy-making which makes it a rich multinational and multilingual domain for legal scholarship. Other factors include patterns of legal education, the organization and funding of higher education and research, academic career structures, and the needs of legal practice, all of which vary across the Member States.

Each year, in preparation for professional qualification, thousands of undergraduate law students across the Member States will study one or more compulsory modules on basic aspects of EU law, including its relationship with their own 'home' legal order, as well as perhaps advanced optional modules. To that end, they need to be kept supplied with at least a minimum of adequate learning materials in their own language, especially textbooks. In the accession states, new teaching activities in EU law are being established, often with support from the European Commission's Jean Monnet Project, or with the PHARE and TACIS programmes, which provide technical assistance and funding to the states of Central and Eastern Europe and the former Soviet Union. Likewise, legal practitioners in the different Member States whose work touches upon EU law need 'domesticized' materials, such as commentaries and manuals of procedure in their own language and written especially with reference to the still primarily nationally-based practices of most lawyers.

Of course, there are huge variations in the extent and sophistication of EU legal scholarship in the various Member States and in the different languages, but the separate domains of study and research on EU law within the Member States continue to exercise an influence today. Anecdotally, members of the Law Department of the European University Institute in Florence report that applicants for admission for Ph.D. study will most often cite literature in the language in which they undertook their undergraduate studies when presenting their research proposals on aspects of EU law. Advocates General in the Court of Justice also generally cite a preponderance of literatures in their own language when drafting the Opinions which they place before the Court of Justice; they work initially in their own languages before their Opinions are translated into all the official languages. The English language was a slight latecomer to the party, since the United Kingdom was not one of the original six members of the European Communities, and Community law scholarship in French, German, Dutch, and Italian obtained something of a head start. French was for a long time the dominant institutional language, although it has lost ground in recent years to English within the Commission in particular. It still remains the general working language of the Court of Justice, and knowledge of French is a baseline competence needed by all those who work there. Textbooks, commentaries (especially in German), and periodical literatures were all developed from the early days and the very earliest contributors to the literature were inevitably 'converted' international or national public lawyers, rather than scholars trained from the beginning in Community law. In Germany, the first *Habilitation* theses in Community law—marking the access point to the professorial rank—date from the mid and late 1960s.

However, given the level of interest in matters of Community law in the United States from the early years onwards (Eric Stein at the University of Michigan and Werner Feld at the University of New Orleans were pivotal figures) as well as in the UK even before accession (key figures included Kurt Lipstein, Dominik Lasok, D. C. Valentine, Brian Wortley, and Edward Wall), an English-language literature on aspects of Community law was not slow to develop, from the 1960s onwards at least. The very first article in the multidisciplinary *Journal of Common Market Studies* (first published in 1963) was by J. M. McMahon on the Court of Justice. The prestigious US journals, the *American Journal of International Law* and the *American Journal of Comparative Law* carried important early work in English by scholars from many disciplinary and national backgrounds. Interestingly, Stein, Lipstein, and Lasok were all originally 'outsiders', immigrants, often refugees from political repression, as well as law professors, like so many major contributors to twentieth-century Anglo-American legal scholarship. The contributions of such scholars to the very beginnings of European legal scholarship in English is particularly poignant, in view of the political goals of European integration, namely peace, prosperity and supranationalism, to quote the words of Joseph Weiler. These goals were evident from the very first, in the Schuman Plan of 1950, even if the instruments were primarily economic. Many of the writers cited here contributed in important ways to the federal and functionalist strands of European legal studies, which often had a normative underpinning focusing on the ethics of European integration (often described as 'building Europe') as contributing to the avoidance of violent conflict and the promotion of human well-being.

Feld—also a refugee from Nazi Germany—was not in fact a lawyer, but contributed substantially to legal journals, initiating another marked tradition of European Union legal studies, namely the contribution of non-lawyers, particularly to the task of figuring out what the significance of the law might be in this emerging international order, and whether the 'normal' rules of international relations and international law might apply. The importance of cross-disciplinary studies for the construction of European Union legal studies becomes a primary focus of the presentation later in this section.

The development of English-language scholarship was assisted by the fact that English was the language used in a number of crucial Netherlands-based publications, such as the *Common Market Law Review* (first published in 1963), which was published by Kluwer and edited by members of the Europa Instituut at Leiden University. The *Common Market Law Review* offered a forum for English-language publications in the 1960s from some of the major early figures of Community law such as Hans Peter Ipsen, Dennis Tallon, and Robert Kovar, whose writings would otherwise only be available to those with an understanding of German or French. Henry Schermers, the distinguished Director of the Europa Instituut of Leiden, regularly published in English from the early 1960s, as did Gerhard Bebr and Laurens Jan Brinkhorst, and a number of Dutch Ph.D. theses on European law were written in English (e.g. by Piet-Jan Slot). A number of Belgians also moved into English-language publishing, such as Pierre Mathijsen and Michel Waelbroeck, the latter in conjunction with Eric Stein and Peter Hay, in an influential US-published 'text, cases and readings' venture (Stein *et al.*, 1976).

A discernible UK-based contribution to thinking about Community law only really emerged after accession in 1973, with notable contributions from Francis Jacobs (already a Professor of European Law at Kings College London in 1976 and responsible with Neville Brown for a seminal work on the Court of Justice, now in its fifth edition), Alan Dashwood and Derek Wyatt (still responsible for a leading textbook), John Usher, Dominik Lasok and John Bridge, Trevor Hartley (from 1980 onwards) and public lawyers such as J. D. B. Mitchell, and latterly Carol Harlow and Paul Craig. The UK-based *European Law Review* was established in 1975. From the early 1970s, European law centres and postgraduate programmes were put in place in Exeter and Edinburgh, and they played an important role in diffusing the emerging UK-based expertise to a wider international audience. These effects mirrored those of the earlier centres of excellence in European legal studies established in the original 'Six' Member States such as CERES in Paris, the Institut des Etudes Européennes at the Université Libre de Bruxelles, and the Europa Institutes in Leiden and Saarbrücken, which always did more than merely educate the domestic European Community law elite, and from the first welcomed international students.

2.3 Towards an Anglo-American or English-Language Core?

While it is true that there remains a vibrant multilingual dimension to European Union legal studies in which authors continue quite naturally to perpetuate national traditions and focuses by citing a majority of literature and legal sources drawn from their own primary languages of scholarship and 'home' jurisdiction, it is arguable that there is a gradually emerging tradition of 'Europeanized' European Union legal studies (von Bogdandy, 2000: 237). In 'Europeanized' work, English-language writing certainly dominates, but it is furthermore arguable that the meta-structure of Anglo-American legal institutions is beginning to acquire a central defining place in the canon of legal studies. In developing this argument, Armin von Bogdandy likens this to the acceptance of German monetary and fiscal philosophy as the price paid in countries such as France, Belgium, and Italy for achieving a single European currency. In the era of the globalization of cultures and economies, it would hardly make sense to argue that the English language is not increasing in importance as the predominant linguistic frame within which ideas about law, legal norms, and legal institutions are communicated across different states and legal traditions. The trend towards English-language writing is obviously *not* limited to writing by those for whom English is their first language, since there are many German, Belgian, and Dutch contributors to this body of work, as well as substantial numbers of French, Portuguese, Spanish, Scandinavian, Italian, and Central and Eastern European participants. Moreover, von Bogdandy himself is one of a number of writers whose work cuts across both the domestic and the Europeanized paradigms of EU legal scholarship, along with scholars such as Christian Joerges, who writes predominantly on economic law and Bruno de Witte, best known for work rethinking some of the foundation stones of EU law such as direct effect and supremacy. Not only do these three scholars write in their own languages as well as in English, but their writings can also feed the differing needs of the different 'consumers' of domestic and Europeanized European Union legal studies. Even so, it is not absolutely clear that the meta-structure of Anglo-American legal thinking and legal institutions is emerging as the new intellectual paradigm which dominates Europeanized European law. There are, after all, lively cross-fertilization processes taking place at the level of doctrine between *inter alia* UK public law, European Union public law, and influential national public laws such as those of Germany and France. The danger is, of course, that some of the subtleties of cross-fertilizing jurisdictions may sometimes be lost, if EU law scholarship simply becomes a cacophony of competing voices, with those working in English making the most noise, simply because they are greatest in number.

Whether limited to language or not, there is certainly a number of important factors contributing to this Europeanization process around an Anglo-American paradigm. First, there are the publication opportunities, offering a wide audience, provided by the many publishers of journals and books in English (including many publishers which are neither British nor American). In addition to the conventional print media, there are, of course, myriad opportunities to publish via the Internet, where English is generally the preferred medium of communication. Secondly, there is the institutional role of the European University Institute in Florence in creating a culture of European Union legal studies which is uniquely detached from the reach of any one national legal culture and which is quite anglophone in its approach to teaching. A counterweight might still be the similarly multinational College of Europe in Bruges—historically more francophone, in particular since it was a creature of the Hague Congress of 1948 and hence more closely linked to the 'wider' Europe of the Council of Europe rather than the EU as such. It has also become increasingly English-language-based, especially since the creation of its Central European branch at Natolin in Poland; English—it should be noted—is very definitely the second language of the accession states. A more general point here would be the widespread internationalization of postgraduate legal experiences, especially at the level of the Masters degree, where many new and old providers of postgraduate legal education self-consciously market 'European' Masters of Laws programmes, including a number involving multiple sites and institutions. A focus of such programmes is often opening up access for graduates from many different national backgrounds to the increasingly 'Europeanized' big law firms, especially those based in London and Brussels. The cross-national experience of study is not limited to the postgraduate level and there are substantial numbers of undergraduate students who benefit from the EU's SOCRATES programme of exchanges. Many who choose to travel to a state which has a relatively 'minority' language in EU law terms (e.g. in Scandinavia or Central and Eastern Europe) do so because there are study programmes in English available.

One can cite—thirdly—the frequency of English-language academic conferences and other opportunities to present research, and—fourthly—a related point about the availability of research funding from both national and international funders to support English-language-based research into aspects of EU law (the Ford Foundation in the United States and beyond, the Volkswagen and Thyssen Stiftungen in Germany and beyond, the European Science Foundation and the social science strands of the European Commission's Framework programmes all accept applications in English). The intensity of these newer possibilities of transnational networking and their contribution to the development of a 'meta-science' of European Union legal studies dwarf those offered by some of the older institutions for transnational cooperation, such as the *Fédération Internationale de Droit Européen* (FIDE). FIDE, a federation intended to draw together national European law societies in the various Member States and other countries, continues to hold its biennial conferences—mainly in various European capital cities—but these have always been rather expensive and inaccessible to most academic lawyers (FIDE has always attracted many practitioners in private practice, as well as judges and public officials), and the results have been generally very poorly disseminated (von Bogdandy, 2000).

2.4 Building the Legal Order: The Law/Integration Interface

The earliest steps in the construction of the new academic discipline were primarily descriptive and legal doctrinal in nature, employing familiar methodologies of legal positivism and doctrinal reconstruction. However, for the first ten years of the existence of the European Communities as a legal order, there was relatively little raw material for scholars to make use of in their various commentaries—little case law before what was initially the Court of Justice of the Coal and Steel Community, and relatively little secondary law adopted on the basis of the founding treaties either by the High Authority (Commission) which was charged with implementing the ECSC Treaty or by the Council of Ministers, which was the dominant legislative organ under the original version of the EEC Treaty.

The incisive contributions of the Court of Justice from the early 1960s onwards, and the ground-breaking cases of *Van Gend en Loos* (Case 26/62 [1963] ECR 1) and *Costa v ENEL* (Case 6/64 [1964] ECR 585) in particular, constitute an extremely well known—if not always uncontested—narrative. These cases suggested for the first time a more 'federal' future for the Community legal order rather than a limited future as a 'mere' international legal order. As the cases on the effects of Community law and the relationship between Community law and national law emerged piecemeal in the 1960s and 1970s, and were later joined by case law on the scope and nature of powers or 'competence' of the Communities and the institutions and on the doctrine of Community fundamental rights, the focus of commentary gradually shifted from footnoting the judges and sorting out their conceptual categories (e.g. Jan Winter's distinction between 'direct effect' and 'direct applicability' (Winter, 1972), Trevor Hartley's conceptually sure-footed exposition of Community public law (Hartley, 1981)) to an enquiry into the significance of what the Court of Justice was doing. Eric Stein's 'Lawyers, Judges and the Making of a Transnational Constitution' (originally published in the 1981 *American Journal of International Law* but reprinted in Stein, 2000) was probably the first authoritative attempt to rephrase in explicitly 'constitutional' terms the Court's work in relation to the 'transformation of Europe' (Weiler's equally influential phrase in a paper originally published in 1991 in the *Yale Law Journal*, and reprinted in Weiler, 1999). Even so, a cautionary word about the truly innovatory character of this vocabulary can be sounded, since the German government report to the *Bundestag* on the Treaty of Paris of 1951 spoke even then of 'a European model of a constitutional type' (Ophuls, 1966), a wording which doubtless owes something to the influence of Walter Hallstein, who contributed at that time as leader of the German government delegation negotiating that Treaty but who later became the influential first President of the Commission of the European Economic Community in 1958.

Be that as it may, what is interesting about Stein's approach—which begins with some famously purple prose about the Court 'tucked away in the fairyland Duchy of Luxembourg'—is his attempt to disaggregate the various interests which feed into any given conclusion about the scope and nature of EU law on the part of the Court of Justice, notably the views of the Commission, the Member States, and the Advocates General. Stein chose to simplify his findings on approaches to 'constitutional' issues into tabular form, phrased in terms of yes/no answers of particular actors to particular questions (e.g. the very possibility of direct effect, whether the Treaty should take precedence over national law regardless of the national constitutional conditions on the reception of international law, whether direct effect should be expanded and developed beyond the vertical direct effect of Treaty provisions, and so on). The findings appear to show an activist court working—with an intensity shared not even to that degree by the traditionally supranationalist Commission—towards what Stein called the 'legal integration of the Community'. The investigation of this concept has spawned a vigorous cottage industry of studies—both legal and political—about the role of the Court of Justice and of the law in the EC/EU system, especially in relation to national law, national courts, and national authorities, and about judicial activism and its effects more generally.

The fact that the Court has, at particular points in the history of the EU and in response to specific fact situations requiring some form of adjudication, more often than not adopted positions which tend to extend rather than to restrict the effects and scope of EU law raises a number of research challenges for scholars such as how and why this has occurred, and why Member States comply with the dictates of a Court backed only by the rhetorical and normative force of the 'rule of law' and lacking the violence of the state. The early scholarship on the Court did not always generate sufficient 'critical distance'—a point eloquently made by Martin Shapiro in a critique of a paper adopting the classic 'close to the Court' approach (1980: 538):

[the work] is a careful and systematic exposition of the judicial provisions of the 'constitution' of the [EEC] . . . But it represents a stage of constitutional scholarship out of which American

constitutional law must have passed about seventy years ago ... It is constitutional law without politics. [The work] presents the Community as a juristic idea; the written constitution as
a sacred text; the professional commentary as a legal truth; the case law as the inevitable working out of the correct implications of the constitutional text; and the constitutional court as
the disembodied voice of right reason and constitutional teleology ... [S]uch an approach has
proved fundamentally arid in the study of individual constitutions ...

There has been a tendency on the part of some commentators to characterize the
Court in almost heroic terms, as sustaining the entire momentum of European integration through its efforts. Some writers have treated the law/integration relationship as cosy, inevitable, and even immutable:

The European Community's legal order simultaneously presupposes and creates unity—and
vice versa. The Community is above all a 'Community based on law' in the sense that the
relations between the Community's subjects are relations between subjects of law and
'legalised' to a high degree under the control of the Court, which must 'ensure that ... the law
is observed' (Article 164 EEC [now art. 220 EC]). For this reason Community law is important as a unifying factor, especially because not only the Member States, but also individuals,
have been recognised as directly subject to that law. (Dagtoglou, 1981: 40)

A significant element of responsibility for the development of this understanding
of the law/integration interface must be attributed to the self-conscious leadership
function which the members of the Court (judges and Advocates General) and other
practitioners of EU law, such as lawyers in the Commission and European Parliament
as well as legal secretaries at the Court, have taken in 'explaining' the nature of the
EC/EU. They have taken this role both when in office or working in the institutions—
a matter of some surprise to a lawyer working in the United States such as Eric Stein
who would not have expected such open pronouncements about cases they were
involved in from judges—and later after reverting or moving to academia, national
legal practice, or the national public service. The Proceedings of the 1976 Judicial and
Academic Conference held in Luxembourg provide fertile evidence of the sense that
the judges, in particular, needed both to explain and to defend the sometimes quite
controversial positions which they took:

The special nature of the Community, which must be regarded, not as an association of States
subject to international law, but as a community *sui generis* orientated to the future and
designed with a view to the alteration of economic and social relationships and progressive
integration, rules out a static and requires a dynamic and evolutionary interpretation of
Community law. The Community judge must never forget that the Treaties establishing the
European Communities have laid the foundations of an ever closer union among the peoples
of Europe and that the High Contracting Parties were anxious to strengthen the unity of their
economies and to ensure their harmonious development (Preamble to the EEC Treaty). The
principle of the progressive integration of the Member States in order to attain the objective
of the Treaty does not only comprise a political requirement; it amounts rather to a
Community legal principle, which the Court of Justice has to bear in mind when interpreting
Community law, if it is to discharge in a proper manner its allotted task of upholding the law
when it interprets and applies the Treaties. (Kutscher, 1976)

The judges often felt the need to point out the special features of the Court such as its multinational and multilingual nature, and the fact that in the early years it was not operating within the 'robust' environment of an established domestic legal order, but in an emerging and as yet uncertain legal order. Amongst the most active 'explainers' can be counted Kutscher, Donner, Everling, Pescatore, and Due, as well as Mancini in more recent years, all judges whose extra-judicial pronouncements were always accorded high respect. When Hjalte Rasmussen published his famous critique of the Court of Justice in 1986, his criticism of the Court of Justice for acting well beyond the text of the Treaty and the boundaries of permissible judicial interpretation was itself the subject of sharp criticism, notably by Mauro Cappelletti and Joseph Weiler in book reviews. To students of the discipline itself, such as Harm Schepel and Rein Wesseling (1997), even more engaging than the debate about judicial activism itself has been the dense network of contacts between academia and practice, in its broadest sense, which has served to structure the early years of the development of the discipline, and perhaps helps to explain why so many academic commentators so readily leap to the defence of the Court of Justice, even while presenting in more recent years an increasingly nuanced picture of the Court's so-called activism (Weiler, 1999; Dehousse, 1998).

Beyond the judicial politics of an emerging 'constitutional'-type court, the wider politics of European integration have also exerted a substantial influence upon the law/integration interface. 'Integration through law', the title of a substantial American-European comparative project of the 1970s and 1980s led from the European University Institute in Florence, is not confined to the judicial domain. Few debates on what is now commonly termed the 'governance' of the European Union fail to refer to the so-called 'Monnet' method, that is, the classic supranational policy-making mode associated with one of the Communities' founding fathers, Jean Monnet. Monnet was the first president of the High Authority (i.e. Commission) of the European Coal and Steel Community from 1952. Few accounts of the development of the legal order as an emerging constitutionalized polity beyond the state omit references to the federalist politics of Altiero Spinelli who led early plans in the European Parliament for a proto-European constitution, to Robert Schuman's Plan for supranational union via functionalist means (drafted in large measure by Monnet), and to Jacques Delors's various programmes for completing the internal market and establishing a single currency. Less often is reference made to the work and writings of Walter Hallstein, the first President of the EEC Commission, and a German law professor as well as a politician, but his extended analyses of the role of law in place of force (a chapter heading in his 1972 book) and of the key features of a 'Community of law' including the role of legislation as well as adjudication certainly deserve greater attention on the part of modern-day commentators. An interesting example of the interpretative contribution of translation is evident from Hallstein's most influential book. It was published originally in German in 1969 as *Der unvollendete Bundesstaat* ('the unfinished federal state'); in English it appeared in 1972 as *Europe in the Making* (Hallstein, 1972), creating an altogether different impression of the entity which it placed under scrutiny.

In sum, the concept of integration has cast a long shadow over EU legal studies, contributing in both positive and negative ways to the construction of this new subdiscipline. However, its role is all the more surprising in view of the fact that thus far it has only twice been explicitly mentioned in the Treaties. First, it appears in the context of the role of transnational political parties (article 191 included by the Treaty of Amsterdam in 1999); and second, the new article 11*a* EC on enhanced cooperation makes reference to the objective of integration as underpinning the Treaties. It is remarkable that this taken-for-granted if contested concept was such a late-comer to the formal text of the treaties and that it plays such a marginal role in their texts.

2.5 Building the Discipline: Paradigms, Approaches, and Meta-theories

One of the problems with approaching the task of understanding EU law via a primary focus on the law/integration interface is that it tends to override other ways of 'cutting' into the discipline of EU legal studies via the full variety of different paradigms which legal studies generally would normally offer. Looking back at the nature of the critique of European law scholarship entered by Shapiro, it will be clear that it was concerned as much as anything with the failure by scholars to take the necessary steps backwards in order to generate a greater objectivity and distance when examining the role of the Court of Justice.

Since 1987, when Francis Snyder first published his paper 'New Directions in European Community Law', the case for developing critical analysis in the field of EC/EU legal studies has been well known and has received increasingly wide acknowledgement. Snyder argued that 'European Community law represents, more evidently perhaps than most other subjects an intricate web of politics, economics and law' (Snyder, 1990: 9). Moreover, it 'virtually calls out to be understood by means of a political economy of law or an interdisciplinary, contextual or critical approach'. Instead, 'it has often been regarded (and taught) simply as a highly technical set of rules, a dense doctrinal thicket into which only the ignorant or foolish would "jump in and scratch out their eyes" [a reference to Karl Llewellyn's *Bramble Bush*], still less try to understand in terms of social theories of law'.

The constant flow of 'new' EU law—Treaty revisions, legislative programmes, administrative action, judicial interpretation, and so on, plus all the associated proposals, opinions, and reports which are attendant upon the complex EU law-making process—continues to create a healthy marketplace for predominantly expository work presenting and interpreting the law. Since the judgments of the Court of Justice and, to a lesser extent, the Court of First Instance are generally rather terse, adopting an approach to judicial reasoning which draws most heavily upon the French tradition of elliptic judgments, there is plenty of room for experts, self-appointed or otherwise, to offer explanations and elucidation for a wider audience. That said, scholarship on EU law in English now draws upon the same range of paradigms and theories of law and legal institutions which underpin the other subdisciplines of legal studies—postmodernism, socio-legal approaches, the broad range of 'law-in-context' approaches, and so on, alongside work informed by a range of liberal and critical legal and political theories, especially, in recent years, Habermassian social theory and neo-republican/deliberation-based political theory. Substantively, this turn to theory (or 'normative turn' as Richard Bellamy and Dario Castiglione have termed it) has been accompanied by a quantum increase in writing about topics such as constitutionalism, democracy and accountability, citizenship, and, latterly, 'governance', especially in its 'new governance' variants. Certainly, in terms of focus, the heavy court-centred emphasis of the early years of scholarship in the EU has generally been transcended. Legal phenomena beyond the Court are commonly a focus of analysis. These include legislative and administrative action of the more conventional type familiar from harmonization programmes in the single market or social affairs arenas or from executive action by the Commission in fields such as competition law or the Common Agricultural Policy. Legal studies have also encompassed more and more so-called 'soft law' or 'new governance' approaches to regulation such as the Open Method of Coordination (OMC) or 'Lisbon process'. What is involved in areas such as labour market policy or economic policy, where OMC is applied, is the setting of guidelines at the EU level, the use of benchmarks and standard-setting to facilitate the transfer of best practice between Member States, and systems of periodic monitoring and peer review, rather than coercive action by the Commission to 'persuade' Member States to move towards policy convergence. The very legal nature of such policy instruments is therefore called into question. Much work also seeks to situate the Court of Justice (or, better, the EU Courts, including also the Court of First Instance) explicitly in a wider network of legal and political institutions, such as the EU's very complex legislative process or the contested phenomenon of 'comitology' or myriad networks of committees which operate within the Commission, or to examine the relationship between the Courts and non-governmental organizations or strategic litigants who use national courts to achieve policy-oriented goals.

In addition, as the next subsection will show, the very close interactions between EU legal studies and other disciplines which focus on the EU and on the study of regional integration, such as political science and the study of international relations, raise the additional challenge of meshing together the epistemological and methodological paradigms of different disciplines which typically ask different questions about legal and socio-economic phenomena.

2.6 EU Legal Studies and Other (EU-Focused) Disciplines

In 1998, Kenneth Armstrong (1998: 155) noted that 'political science had discovered the European Court of Justice'. Had it, he queried, also 'discovered law'? This comment illustrates the dissonances which have sometimes entered into the relationships between the different disciplines which seek to explain and understand the phenomenon of EU-based integration. There is no shortage of political scientists, especially those working in the international relations end of the discipline, posing questions about the 'judicialization' of EU-based integration. Why do Member States generally comply with EU law—especially when the demands of compliance on national legal and administrative orders are so much more intense and indeed intrusive when compared to what is involved in national compliance with international law? The Court seems, from that perspective, a novel institution to be given the task of constructing the glue to hold together what looks, especially from the perspective of realist international relations scholarship, very much like a grouping of states similar to an international organization. From that same realist perspective, the delegation to the Court of the capacity to constrain states' freedom of action in international relations is a puzzle which many scholars have taken up. Many have, for example, examined how the Court has worked 'strategically', with other actors, to promote its goal of legal integration between EU law and national law. They have also questioned whether the phenomenon of legal integration is generalizable to other experiments in regional economic integration (e.g. NAFTA), or even quasi-global trade-based integration (e.g. the WTO). Is it part of a general move towards the legalization of world politics?

Reading the case law of the Court of Justice and looking at this question from the Court's own perspective, it is easy enough to see why Member States comply. It is because of the supremacy of EU law, which decrees that as a source of law EU law takes precedence over national law, including national constitutions, in any circumstances falling within the scope of the Community competence. Added to this is the apparently inherently cohesive force of the 'rule of law', referred to by Dagtoglou in the quotation which appears in Section 2.4. Such 'legalist' explanations—so-called by Anne-Marie Burley (now Slaughter), publishing with Walter Mattli, and by Karen Alter amongst others—were never likely to satisfy political scientists for whom the primacy of politics over law is a cardinal principle. Slaughter, herself a lawyer, but with a training in international relations as well, has provided an important neo-functionalist and actor-based account of the EU's legal order focusing on the interactions between the Court of Justice and the national courts, and showing the variegated pattern of acceptance of the Court of Justice's core principles of the legal order: supremacy and direct effect. This goes beyond the limitations of a functionalist account which sees the Court as simply acting from the demands of integration (Mattli and Slaughter, 1998 with references also to their earlier work). Their work has added to a rich tradition of comparative judicial and constitutional politics, in which scholars such as Mary Volcansek and Alec Stone Sweet have sought to place the Court of Justice in a wider comparative frame.

It is not just political scientists, however, who will not be satisfied that the single word answer of 'supremacy' provides an adequate account of 'why EU law works as well as it does'. To many lawyers, also, this will be an oversimplistic account of law's operation in a complex interconnected domain such as the EU. Lawyers have examined many other principles and instruments which bind the EU and its Member States, such as the principle of mutual loyalty between the Member States and the institutions contained in article 10 EC, or indeed the subsidiarity principle contained in article 5 EC, and they have not always done so purely from a positivist or doctrinalist point of view alone. Scholars are also well aware of the evident contradiction between a Court of Justice which asserts 'competence-competence' (that is, the power to determine the scope of EU law in relation to national law), and the positions adopted by a range of key national actors such as the German Federal Constitutional Court which insist that competence-competence remains at the national level. The adoption of a systems-theoretic account of the nature of the EU legal order (e.g. Maher, 1998) produces a very different set of preconceptions of how we might expect a multi-level legal order such as the EU to operate, bearing in mind systems theory's focus on interactions between and perturbations amongst contiguous, but separate, legal orders. In fact, moving away from the preoccupations of international relations scholars with the ties which bind sovereign states towards comparative politics approaches which study the EU as an evolving if incomplete polity helps to carve out a research territory where lawyers can examine the nature of legal and institutional change in a way which is sensitive to the variables of both law and politics. New institutionalism's concept of path dependency, for example, has provided a useful framework for studying the emergence and evolution of legal regimes, such as the single market programme. Lawyers are fascinated about differences, or dissonances, between legal regimes and governance regimes, and have produced numerous sector-specific accounts in fields such as labour law or environmental law which comfortably blend legal and non-legal sources, in terms of both primary and secondary materials.

In sum, to suggest that a 'legalist' account of the nature and force of EU law dominates legal science's treatment of the EU law/national law distinction is—at best— a gross simplification of the varieties of theoretical paradigms which inform EU legal studies work. At worst, it reinforces an age-old dialogue of the deaf between legal scientists and political scientists: 'law matters!'; 'oh no, it doesn't!'; 'oh yes, it does!'. It does considerable disservice to the richness of EU legal studies, so far as it concentrates on the full panoply of hard and soft legal phenomena within the EU.

In particular, recent years have seen academic lawyers participating fully in cross-disciplinary, interdisciplinary, and transnational debate about the whole panoply of issues coming under the umbrella of 'governance beyond the state'. The debate has ranged from local governance to global governance and back, taking in also the role of private non-state agencies in the regulation of socio-economic affairs as well as the particular legitimacy challenges facing a quasi-government such as the EU which lacks the conventional structures of input legitimacy which operate within the confines of a liberal democratic state. The particular focus is the future of governance more generally in the EU, with specific questions about the governance of the internal market and of Euroland, the development of 'new' forms of governance such as the Open Method of Coordination as well as—as Scott and Trubek (2002: 2) term it—'new, old governance', where the old 'classic' policy-making systems of the Community method are used, for example, to generate non-binding policy instruments such as recommendations or flexible framework directives. Both 'new governance' and its older variants are applied in emerging sectors where EU policy choices increasingly affect national choices, such as labour market policy, social exclusion policy, economic policy, and policy on asylum and immigration. These developments are well summed up by a special issue of the *European Law Journal* published in 2002, edited by Joanne Scott and David Trubek and involving a transatlantic and cross-European team of lawyers and political scientists offering a range of descriptive and theoretical assessments of what is, and is not, innovatory about so-called 'new governance', and its potential effects on key actors such as the social partners and civil society (see also Hodson and Maher, 2001).

3 European Union Legal Studies: The 'State of the Art'

3.1 The Nature of the Beast: The Emerging Euro-polity

Perhaps the most acute and pressing research questions facing those who seek to characterize the nature of this beast, the emerging Euro-polity, are whether or not to compare it with other polities (states or international organizations) and whether the tools and methodologies of national public law or public international law should be used in the analysis. Formally, it is an international organization (based on Treaties). In certain respects, it appears and behaves like a state (territorial jurisdiction, impact of the law on individuals, regulation of many aspects of socio-economic affairs within the component entities, claim to exclusive competence in certain areas). Yet neither analogy is perfect and neither fully captures the liminality and ambiguity of many aspects of the current EC/EU system, and its capacity to generate both vertical and horizontal integration. Comparisons have been undertaken above all with the United States as federal system, although in view of many aspects of its contested nature, the federal system of Canada, complete with the secessionist ambitions of Quebec nationalists, may represent a more useful point of comparison. The alternative to comparison is, of course, to treat the EU as *sui generis* and unique, and to analyse it solely on its own terms, perhaps deploying micro-level comparisons only, for example, of its institutions, its systems of representation or accountability, or its approach to external relations and the conclusion of international agreements. In German academic circles, Hans-Peter Ipsen's characterization of the three original European Communities as 'purposive associations for functional integration' has been both influential and suggestive. It can be used to sustain a limited *economic* vision of EC/EU-based integration in which an ordo-liberal economic theory focused on economic freedoms as opposed to deliberate integration of markets is the dominant *leitmotiv* while remaining open to what is often termed the neo-functionalist 'spillover' paradigm of integration, involving progressive transfers of societal functions and indeed sovereignty to the supranational level. As an academic explanation of the progress of European integration, this paradigm enjoyed a significant revival in the 1980s alongside the more general revival of the fortunes of the European Communities.

The concept of 'federalism' can provide a useful framework to capture the EU as a divided power system, but 'federal' remains a contested term both because it is conventionally only attached to federal *states* and also because it has traditionally been anathema to the dominant political class in the United Kingdom. The fact that the UK—and indeed other Member States—are gradually transforming themselves internally in a direction which could be described as proto-federal lends grist to the mill that the 'F' word needs to be brought urgently into the lexicon for thinking about the Euro-polity. In systemic terms, Ingolf Pernice's elaboration of the EU as a multi-level constitutional polity offers perhaps the most suggestive framework for the purposes of disaggregating the contested elements of that constitutional structure (Pernice, 1999).

Those who regularly face the task of explaining the EU—especially to students whose law studies are generally dominated in the early years by an almost exclusively national legal diet—find that one of the most challenging tasks is that of explaining the so-called pillar system, based on the EU and EC Treaties. The initial task is simply to master its different elements, but the complexity factor spirals almost out of control when the added element of flexibility is thrown in. There are the opt-outs and opt-ins which bedevil many policy areas such as Justice and Home Affairs and Economic and Monetary Union, not to mention the possibility that limited groups of states may engage in what is called 'enhanced cooperation' to deepen the integration project in certain areas where they cannot find unanimity. For all of these reasons, it is hard to find an intellectually satisfying rationale or explanation of the current system. German legal science has seen a lively debate between those who view the EC and EU together as a single unit and those who insist that the EU is a separate entity from the EC, distinguished in particular by the fact that the former is does not have internal or external legal personality and so can barely be described even as an international organization (von Bogdandy, 1999). Drawing on the theory of institutional normative order elaborated by Neil MacCormick, Deirdre Curtin and Ige Dekker (1999) suggest a focus on the legal practices of the Union, rather than its legal form as such. In any event, the question may become purely academic if, as is widely anticipated, the Constitutional Convention of 2002/3 and the Intergovernmental Conference of 2004 lead to a substantial fusion of the three current pillars and the creation of a more unitary system.

3.2 The Contested Constitutional Framework

The pattern of scholarship on the EU's constitutional framework is shaped by three key factors. On the one hand, there is a marked reluctance to separate out the normative question of whether the EU *should* have a constitution from the analytical question of whether it *does* have one, and if so how it should be approached (Shaw, 1999). Secondly, there is an absence of consensus about what constitutions are, whether they are by definition confined to states, and whether there is a difference between the study of constitutions (whether formal written ones, or diffuse unwritten ones like the EU's current arrangement) and the study of *constitutionalism* as the science of the possible in terms of values and principles. Neil Walker's work on constitutional pluralism brings a welcome intellectual clarity by placing the study of the EU's putative constitution beyond the state into the wider context of other non-state 'meta-constitutional' developments, including the WTO (Walker, 2002). Thirdly, the image of the 'constitutionalized Treaty', and hence the debates about the role of the Court of Justice and the relationship between national law and EU law already referred to in this chapter have themselves shaped much debate about what the EU constitution currently comprises. Yet apart from the question of competence, or the division of powers between the EU and the Member States, these questions are not an explicit part of the agenda for the 2002/3 Constitutional Convention, an agenda which was shaped by the Laeken Declaration of December 2001. One of the most contested aspects of any attempt to write a simple citizen-friendly constitutional document for the European Union would be the task of rendering into constitutional form the relationship between EU law and national law. What is simple and straightforward to the Court of Justice is—theoretically, if not always in practice—anathema to national constitutional courts brought up on a rigorous diet of state sovereignty. Joseph Weiler has argued that one key element of the principle of constitutional tolerance, which he thinks both does and should underpin the current system, is the avoidance of unnecessary constitutional conflicts (Weiler, 2001). To use the words of Miguel Poiares Maduro, a set of principles enunciated by the Court of Justice and a widespread practice amongst courts at the national and EU levels of avoiding open constitutional conflicts may be 'As good as it gets' in terms of creating a constitutional framework for the EU and fixing the relationship between EU law and national law.

For those writing on the EU's constitutional past, present, and future, one of the most acute challenges is to distil the essence or value of much of the liberal constitutionalism which underpins its founding Member States, such as the balance between the rule of law, majoritarianism, and the principle of democracy, and to apply it to the complex governance arrangements through which the EU does its business. This means not only evaluating and auditing the formal institutional system against principles such as democracy and accountability (and thinking about ways to fill the deficits which almost invariably seem to appear when these terms are applied to the EU) but also examining the dynamic and constantly changing policy-making system, with its complex combinations of actors, inputs, and outputs and 'new' concepts such as partnerships and networks. Where, it still remains to be seen, does the concept of democracy fit in here? Can the turn to neo-republican thinking in political theory offer concrete solutions to challenges such as the role of civil society or the public disillusionment with conventional representative institutions?

3.3 The Evolving Area of Freedom, Security, and Justice

Whereas the arena of scholarship on EU constitutional law and politics is bursting at the seams with competing theoretical frameworks and insights, the theory surplus has yet to spill over into a new and challenging field of EU policy-making, that of the Area of Freedom, Security, and Justice. EU Justice and Home Affairs law and policy-making had been developing in the slow lane from the 1980s onwards, largely hidden from view and based on intergovernmental cooperation between Interior Ministry officials. In the 1980s, some of the Member States embarked upon an experiment to create a laboratory of integration in relation to the free movement of persons and the elimination of border controls, endeavouring to achieve the removal of internal borders between the participating states through the Schengen Agreement and associated intergovernmental arrangements (the Schengen *acquis*). The Treaty of Maastricht formally recognized the significance of the Justice and Home Affairs area for the EU generally, through the creation of the third pillar, but it failed to provide an effective institutional system, and consequently 'progress' (i.e. policy-making of an intergovernmentalist nature) continued outside the Treaties. The Treaty of Amsterdam gave a massive shock to the system of Justice and Home Affairs Law. A new title on free movement was created in the EC Treaty, to create the conditions for the removal of internal borders, and the erection of a single external border. The third pillar was slimmed down and focused on criminal justice cooperation. Finally, Schengen—most unexpectedly—was shoehorned into the EU system with the hope and intention—in the longer term—of it being transformed into a more transparent and democratically accountable system for the regulation of borders (or the absence thereof), and the associated security and control issues. Meanwhile, the UK and Ireland continue to opt out of the borderless Europe initiatives, while involving themselves in many of the initiatives which facilitate police and criminal justice cooperation (i.e. the security dimension). Justice and Home Affairs law involves new policy instruments in the third pillar, a novel but still changing institutional mix in the new title on free movement, and—most significantly—the creation of new independent agencies, such as Europol and Eurojust, providing EU-wide cooperation structures for the police and criminal prosecution authorities. These bodies act substantially independently of the control of the European Parliament and indeed national parliaments, as well as the Court of Justice.

The pace of change (and the complexity of much of that change, especially in view of the UK opt-out), the challenges which much of the new legal framework throws up to cherished systems of fundamental rights and civil liberties at the national level, and the asymmetrical focus on security at the expense of freedom and justice at the EU level have spawned lively polemical debates about the desirability of EU action. NGOs have been as involved as academics, and many academics have contributed to the work of NGOs. Security is—after all—a profound voter concern. But security, the critics say, at what cost? The debate after the terrorist attacks of 11 September 2001 was—as would be expected—particularly intense. Beyond the threat to rights, liberties, access to justice and even citizenship, however, there is as yet little evidence of a conceptualization or theorization of EU Justice and Home Affairs law. For example, scholars have yet to develop a rich scholarship on the conceptual challenges offered by the framing of immigration law and policy *beyond the state*, in a scenario in which the core of immigration law is no longer the reciprocal attempts by courts and executives to assert control. The major exception to this theoretical lacuna is the area of citizenship. It may be that work in this area owes much both to the enquiry into citizenship's place in the constitutional canon and, furthermore, to the relationship between citizenship and free movement, and hence the socio-economic foundation stones of EU law.

3.4 Regulation, Governance, and Socio-economic Policy-Making in the EU from the Single Market to the Euro

While academic commentators still remain unsure of what to make of the trajectory of EU Justice and Home Affairs law, they are on much safer ground when dealing with the legal regulation of economic affairs, trade, and exchange both within the EU, and across the EU's external borders. There is a well-trodden path leading from the EC Treaty's economic freedoms (goods, services, persons, and capital), via the interpretative and transformative work of the Court of Justice in partnership with national courts, to the legislative programme for the completion of the internal market (the '1992 Programme') and beyond. Until the mid-1980s, the key milestones were invariably those established by the Court of Justice, notably the *Cassis de Dijon* case (Case 120/78 *Rewe-Zentrale AG v Bundesmonopolverwaltung für Branntwein*

(Cassis de Dijon) [1979] ECR 649). This judgment instituted a novel approach to the treatment of non-discriminatory indistinctly applicable barriers to trade in goods, involving a basic principle of mutual recognition of goods lawfully marketed in one Member State, offset by the possibility of justification of trade barriers by Member States on grounds of the public interest, such as consumer protection or protection of the environment. With its case law on all four freedoms, the Court had by the 1990s substantially remodelled the legal environment established by the founding Treaties, and had contributed in a major way to the range of legislative possibilities taken up by the Commission in its 1985 White Paper on completing the internal market.

Inevitably, the contribution of the Court of Justice to the construction of the internal market and to some sort of economic constitution within the EU has been the focus of close attention on the part of those scholars who have sought to take their work beyond legal doctrinal reconstruction. The German intellectual and political tradition of ordo-liberalism provides a radically different explanation of the very existence and nature of EU law, rooted in private rather than public law traditions. On that view, EU law is not captured by a vision of its hierarchical relationship with national law (or indeed, as the better view currently has it, a heterarchical networked view of interlocking legal systems), but by a private law vision based on economic freedoms and economic constitutionalism, which in turn guarantees political freedoms. Subsequently, authors such as Miguel Poiares Maduro and Christian Joerges have introduced networked views of the economic constitution, with the Court of Justice seen as a partner rather than a driver in an interactive constitutionalization process.

The establishment of monetary union, and the moves towards a single fiscal and economic policy—at least in 'Euroland' if not yet in every aspect right across the EU—has raised new challenges. The Member States and the institutions have developed novel institutional solutions for the management of a variegated integration process involving 'ins' and 'outs' such as the Euro-12 Council which develops strategies for governing economic policy in Euroland, and have introduced new types of legal instruments, such as the Stability and Growth Pact, to assist with cross-national economic management in accordance with the disciplines of the Treaty of Maastricht settlement on EMU. As yet, however, legal scholarship on this aspect of EU polity-building has largely concentrated on following the legal complexities of the monetary union regime.

3.5 The Social Dimension of the EU

Traditionally, social law and policy has been designated the Cinderella of EU law and policy. This comment has been regularly justified by reference to the relative paucity of provisions dealing with harmonization of national provisions on social law and employment law in the original treaties, and the general exclusion of national welfare states from the scope of Community competence. The fairy tale of Cinderella has, of course, a happy ending. In the case of social law and policy, more recent scholarship such as that collected in a recent edited volume (Shaw, 2000) reinforces the view that the incremental growth of Treaty-based competences, case law interventions of the Court of Justice, and EU 'legislation' of both a soft and hard law character have resulted in a widespread recognition that the social dimension is now a core aspect of the EU's overall project to promote peace and prosperity. The intrinsic interest of the social dimension has been its availability as a laboratory for new policy instruments or the development of new policy domains, such as health care policy (e.g. Hervey, 2002). Furthermore, gender equality law—as perhaps the most developed field of EU social law—ensured that EU law scholarship engages directly with other legal scholarship on the politics of rights, law, and legal institutions in liberal states. Forms of what Scott and Trubek (2002) call 'new, old governance', which represent an incremental development of the 'classic Community method' but involving its investiture with flexibility, soft law instruments, lower degrees of policy prescriptiveness for Member States, and a variety of institutional innovations including 'partnership' are very familiar to scholars of the social dimension, especially environmental policy. Environmental regulators were early converts to the proposition that 'traditional' forms of command and control regulation were not successful in enhancing environmental standards and both regulators and commentators quickly turned their attention to developing other means of using law to achieve policy goals. New governance in its classic form of the Open Method of Coordination, involving policy learning, loose goal-setting, and cooperation rather than coercion for Member States is rooted firmly in the social dimension. This is especially true of labour market policy since the Lisbon European Council of March 2000 and more recently of social exclusion policy.

In sum, no study of the EU as an integration could plausibly begin and end with the economic vocation to create a single market. The signal intrusiveness of the single market concept into the national organization of welfare states (see Hervey in Shaw, 2000) is ample testimony of that point. The point is also well reflected in an increasingly complex theoretical and empirical literature in this field.

4 FUTURE PERSPECTIVES

After fifty years it is not possible to do more than draw interim conclusions about how EU legal studies is shaping up. The time span of the discipline has not yet encompassed two full academic 'generations'. There are very few—if any—key figures on whose contribution a cross-section of EU lawyers from a variety of national backgrounds (even limiting the sample to those working substantially in the English language) would be likely to agree. To those working on the Court and on constitutional/citizenship questions generally, it would be hard to find widespread agreement on names other than Eric Stein and Joseph Weiler. Neil MacCormick's contribution from the perspective of legal theory is weighty—but comes very much from an outsider to the discipline, bringing, of course, a fresh breeze of new insights. Emerging contributions in the field of EU constitutionalism from Neil Walker, Gráinne de Búrca, and Ingolf Pernice can also be acknowledged. The law of the internal market owes much to those who have sought to theorize aspects of the economic constitution, such as Christian Joerges, Miguel Poiares Maduro, and Francis Snyder, the latter meriting a particular mention because of his endeavours to break out of received doctrinalist paradigms from the 1980s onwards. Much of this, however, invidiously ignores non-English-language contributions and also those without whose work our capacity to systematize EU legal doctrine would be immeasurably poorer (Hans-Peter Ipsen, Claus-Dieter Ehlermann, Guy Isaac, Koen Lenaerts, to name but four key figures). Many others, whose works have been cited or whose names have been mentioned in this chapter, are likewise part of an extraordinarily diverse and rather loose 'canon' of core literature in EU legal studies.

It is always misleading and perhaps even unfair to cite some contributors to the development of the discipline, and to omit others. In recent years, in particular, it is fair to say that the challenge of discipline-building in an environment where policy-building is a major political preoccupation is one that has been taken up very cooperatively amongst multinational groups of EU law scholars, often in close conjunction with political scientists and scholars of international relations. In moving to a conclusion, it is important to stress, alongside the features discussed in Section 2 of this chapter which contribute to shaping the domain, the overwhelming complexity of EU law. EU law is not in general much loved by the majority of law students. They find the complexity of the legal order, and the sheer variety of fields of law which studying even the outlines of EU law brings them into contact with (constitutional law, administrative law, economic law, trade law, and so on) a barrier to easy understanding. Efforts to simplify the EU and its legal and constitutional orders— more for citizens than for students it has to be said—continue at a number of different levels. It was one of the issues raised in Declaration No. 23 on the Future of the Union appended to the Treaty of Nice of December 2000, taken up by the Laeken Declaration of December 2001, and thus on the agenda of the Convention on the Future of the Union sitting in Brussels in 2002–3. This, like the many academic simplification projects, focuses on the Treaties. Simplification, consolidation, and codification of the legislative corpus has long been a goal of the Commission. Institutional innovations on the agenda have included the suggestion that the EU should adopt the model of the American Restatement and create a 'European Law Institute' (Schmid, 1999). Academic scholarship clearly has a role to play in such an enterprise, alongside policy-makers and representative organs charged with constitutionalist endeavours including legislatures, governments, and—arguably—courts. As this chapter has sought to show, EU legal studies already has a rich and varied history, peopled with distinguished figures whose contributions would grace any field of legal studies. Its future, like its past, will involve the complex intertwining of discipline-building and polity-building, whether at the macro-constitutionalist or more banal day-to-day policy-making levels.

REFERENCES

Armstrong, K. (1998). 'Legal Integration: Theorizing the Legal Dimension of European Integration', *Journal of Common Market Studies*, 36: 155–74.

Curtin, D., and Dekker, I. (1999). 'The EU as a "Layered" International Organization: Institutional Unity in Disguise', in P. Craig and G. de Búrca (eds.), *The Evolution of EU Law*, Oxford: Oxford University Press, 83–136.

Dagtoglou, P. (1981). 'The Legal Nature of the European Community', in Commission of the European Communities (ed.), *Thirty Years of Community Law*, Luxembourg: Office for Official Publications of the European Communities, 33.

de Búrca, G. (1999). 'The Institutional Development of the EU: A Constitutional Analysis', in P. Craig and G. de Búrca (eds.), *The Evolution of EU Law*, Oxford: Oxford University Press, 55–81.

Dehousse, R. (1998). *The European Court of Justice*, London: Palgrave.

Hallstein, W. (1972). *Europe in the Making*, London: George Allen and Unwin.

Hartley, T. C. (1981). *The Foundations of European Community Law: An Introduction to the Constitutional and Administrative Law of the European Community*, Oxford: Clarendon Press.

Hervey, T. K. (2002). 'Mapping the Contours of European Union Health Law and Policy', *European Public Law*, 8: 69–105.

Hodson, D., and Maher, I. (2001). 'The Open Method as a New Mode of Governance', *Journal of Common Market Studies*, 39: 719–46.

Kutscher, H. (1976). 'Methods of Interpretation', in Court of Justice of the European Communities (ed.), *Judicial and Academic Conference 27–28 Sept. 1976: Reports*, Luxembourg: Office for Official Publications of the European Communities.

Maher, I. (1998). 'Community Law in the National Legal Order: A Systems Analysis', *Journal of Common Market Studies*, 36: 237–54.

Mattli, W., and Slaughter, A.-M. (1998). 'Revisiting the ECJ', *International Organization*, 52: 177–209.

Ophuls, C. F. (1966). 'Zur ideengeschichtlichen Herkunft der Gemeinschaftsverfassung', in E. von Caemmerer, H.-J. Schlochauer, and E. Steindorff (eds.), *Probleme des Europäischen Rechts: Festschrift für Walter Hallstein zu seinem 65. Geburtstag*, Frankfurt-am-Main: Vittorio Klostermann.

Pernice, I. (1999). 'Multilevel Constitutionalism and the Treaty of Amsterdam: European Constitution-Making Revisited', *Common Market Law Review*, 36: 703–50.

Rasmussen, H. (1986). *On Law and Policy in the European Court of Justice: A Comparative Study in Judicial Policymaking*, Dordrecht: Martinus Nijhoff.

Schepel, H., and Wesseling, R. (1997). 'The Legal Community: Judges, Lawyers, Officials and Clerks in the Writing of Europe', *European Law Journal*, 3: 165–88.

Schmid, C. U. (1999). 'Ways Out of the Maquis Communautaire: On Simplification and Consolidation and the Need for a Restatement of European Primary Law', European University Institute, Working Paper RSC No. 99/6.

Scott, J., and Trubek, D. (2002). 'Mind the Gap: Law and New Approaches to Governance in the European Union', *European Law Journal*, 8: 1–18.

Shapiro, M. (1980). 'Comparative Law and Comparative Politics', *Southern California Law Review*, 53: 537–42.

Shaw, J. (1999). 'Postnational Constitutionalism in the European Union', *Journal of European Public Policy*, 6: 579–97.

—— (ed.) (2000). *Social Law and Policy in an Evolving European Union*, Oxford: Hart.

Snyder, F. (1990). *New Directions in European Community Law*, London: Weidenfeld and Nicolson.

Stein, E. (2000). *Thoughts from a Bridge: A Retrospective of Writings on New Europe and American Federalism*, Ann Arbor: University of Michigan Press.

——, Hay, P., and Waelbroek, M. (1976). *European Community Law and Institutions in Perspective*, Indianapolis and New York: Bobbs-Merrill.

von Bogdandy, A. (1999). 'The Legal Case for Unity: The European Union as a Single Organisation with a Single Legal System', *Common Market Law Review*, 36: 887–910.

—— (2000). 'The European Union as a Supranational Federation: A Conceptual Attempt in the Light of the Amsterdam Treaty', *Columbia Journal of European Law*, 6: 27–54.

Walker, N. (2002). 'The Idea of Constitutional Pluralism', *Modern Law Review*, 65: 317–59.

Weiler, J. H. H. (1999). *The Constitution of Europe*, Cambridge: Cambridge University Press.

—— (2001). 'Federalism without Constitutionalism: Europe's *Sonderweg*', in K. Nicolaïdis and R. Howse (eds.), *The Federal Vision: Legitimacy and Levels of Governance in the United States and the European Union*, Oxford: Oxford University Press, 54–70.

Winter, J. (1972). 'Direct Applicability and Direct Effect: Two Distinct and Different Concepts in Community Law', *Common Market Law Review*, 9: 425–38.

CHAPTER 17

COMPLEX POLITIES

MALCOLM M. FEELEY

CONVENTIONAL political wisdom from Aristotle to Dahl (1971) onwards has held that a prerequisite for stable government is cultural homogeneity. However, modern governments in culturally diverse, complex polities have sought to devise a number of different structural arrangements in an effort to guarantee both democratic participation and political stability. No doubt there are limits to the cultural heterogeneity that a society can endure without losing its stability or its democratic character and splitting apart. Still, as Arend Lijphart (1977) has shown, there are numerous states with heterogeneous populations that also have stable democratic governments.

It is beyond the scope of this chapter to review the literature on all such political arrangements and theories, let alone to try to identify the conditions that foster success. However, this chapter will explore several of the more widely used constitutional devices used to structure political life in complex societies in ways that give voice to each distinct segment of society while at the same time fostering stable democratic government. Constitutional devices here are understood in a broad sense of the term, to include both formal provisions in constitutions and law, as well as established political 'arrangements' that are part of a 'living constitution'. The emphasis, however, will be on planned structural devices—formal constitutional architecture—that have been consciously adopted with specific objectives in mind.

These several devices are: (1) consociational political arrangements; (2) majoritarian democracy with limited government; (3) federalism; (4) devolution and decentralization; (4) voting systems (e.g. single-member representative districts, proportional representation, preferential voting); and (5) multiculturalism recognized in bills or charters of rights that extend rights to individuals or groups. Consociational arrangements have been used to structure political representation in polities that are segmented into a handful of different and distinct groups. Federalism is a special type of consociational arrangement designed to foster political representation of those in different geographical areas. Decentralization and devolution is a decision in a unitary governmental structure to grant more decision-making authority to at least some of its component regions. Various complex voting systems have been used in some heterogeneous societies in an effort to foster fair and proportional representation. Finally, bills or charters of rights or other similar provisions, while they cannot guarantee minorities a voice in the political process, can assure that minorities are free to pursue their own distinct concerns, and arrangements recognizing group rights can invest cultural groups with limited political autonomy.

1 Consociational and Majoritarian Democracies

In *Polyarchy: Participation and Opposition*, political scientist Robert Dahl (1971) examined the political structures and stability of 114 different countries. He found that stable representative government was highly correlated with low levels of what he termed 'pluralism'. In other words, countries with relatively homogeneous cultures or low levels of political or cultural cleavages were more likely to have stable democratic politics than those countries with deep cultural and political cleavages. In particular, many countries, particularly non-Western countries, are plagued by the twin problems of sharp political cleavages and political instability. But as Arend Lijphart (1994) has noted, there are important exceptions to Dahl's generalization. Among them are Austria, Belgium, the Netherlands, and Switzerland. Each of these countries, and particularly from the mid-nineteenth century up through the 1960s, 'provide concrete examples of how democracy can be a stable and effective system of government in plural societies' (p. 2). Lijphart offers consociational democracy as a structural ideal, and the experiences of these countries at least during extended periods of the twentieth century as a concrete expression of this ideal. By 'plural society', Lijphart (1997: 4) means a society with segmental cleavages, which may consist of deep divisions based along religious, ideological, linguistic, cultural, or ethnic lines, and that are reinforced by separate political parties, voluntary association, interest groups, media, and schools for each of the groupings. Under such circumstances, Dahl's theory of pluralism and politics would predict instability. But, Lijphart shows, consociational arrangements in these societies offset a tendency towards instability and instead have fostered political stability.

As Lijphart (1977: 9) defines it, consociational democracy is a political arrangement in segmented or deeply divided societies that in its most robust form is distinguished by four characteristics: (1) government by a 'grand coalition' of political leaders from all significant segments of society rather than a government of the majority with minorities confined to the role of opposition; (2) the principle of a 'concurrent majority' which allows all significant segments the power to veto or significantly modify government action (thereby protecting minority interests); (3) proportional representation (so that all significant segments are included in the representative assembly—and in the grand coalition consisting of all major parties, the civil service, and in receipt of government funds—in rough proportion to their size in the polity; and (4) some degree of autonomy for each 'segment' to mange its own internal institutions and affairs (e.g. political parties, schools, newspapers, sports and professional associations, public housing programs, and the like).

Consociational democracy seeks stability through inclusiveness. The governing coalition consists of representatives of all segments of society by means of proportional representation and grants each segment some degree of veto power. It is government through coalition, negotiation, and consensus. This does not require that every policy is hammered out in ways that all can agree on it, but it assumes that in the long run, all participating groups receive their 'fair share of goods provided by the legislative process'. Thus, in an otherwise deeply divided society, all segments are induced to join together in an alliance of mutual benefit. This cooperative model stands in contrast to the adversarial, winner-take-all 'majoritarian democracy' that is common to many English-speaking countries.

Consociational democracy has its roots in the Middle Ages. Throughout Europe, the modern nation state emerged through long struggle among various powerful institutions, the church, great landowners, commercial interests, the military, and various other politically organized groups. National political formation was often effected by bringing together or co-opting these institutions, establishing them as 'pillars' in the emerging new national government and giving them a place at the governing table. Modern consociational democracy extends this tradition, but rests to various degrees on democratic rather than hereditary institutions.

Although the grand coalition rests upon an implied constitutional understanding that emerges organically from a political culture, many of its particular arrangements are embedded in explicit provisions of written constitutions. While proportional representation does not guarantee that the representatives of smaller segments of society will be represented in a 'grand coalition', it does facilitate the likelihood that they will be proportionately represented, and this may be a necessary though not sufficient condition for consociational democracy.

2 Majoritarian Democracy

Majoritarian democracy stands in sharp contrast to consociational arrangements. Here it is defined as a structural arrangement which allows simple majorities (or pluralities in many instances) to control the gains of victory, with no need to share their gains with others (as is the case in consociational democracies). It operates on the principle of winner take all. Majoritarian democracy can rely on PR, but often relies on majority or plurality voting for individual representatives in single-member electoral districts.

Although majoritarian democracy is presented here as a contrast to consociational democracy, it too tends to be defended as a way of fostering harmony or at least stability in diverse, though perhaps not deeply divided, polities. In the former case, parties will engage in strategic behavior to form a governing coalition, and once formed distribute the benefits to members of this coalition. In majoritarian democracies with single member districts, the person elected can choose to represent only that party or interest which backed her in the election, although the governing coalition in the legislature will be determined in much the same way as it is under proportional representation. In multi-party systems, parties will engage in strategic behavior to form a (minimum) winning coalition, and in a two-party system, the party with the greatest number of victors will control the reins of government (Epstein, 1980). This is thought to guarantee effectiveness in governing during the period in office.

Advocates of majoritarian democracy point to several features that tend to moderate the potential threat posed by its winner-take-all electoral system: divided government (a bicameral legislature and the attendant principle of separation of powers); the principle of limited government, the constitutional protections of minorities; and, most importantly, a tradition of competitive parties and turnover in governmental regimes.

Majoritarian democracy as defined here tends to be associated most strongly with Anglo-American political systems, which have single member districts and, for the most part, two-party systems. Single member districts, with their winner-take-all arrangements, are often justified on the ground that they reflect political stability and moderation, and also foster it. Societies with deep cleavages and sharp divisions may very well benefit from an electoral system that guarantees each significant segment or division in society some voice and some representation in the governmental process, and at least an opportunity to participate in the governing coalition. However, in homogeneous societies with strong two-party systems, candidates and parties must offer moderate programs if they want to attract electoral majorities. Consider an electorate with a range of political preferences that can be graphed as a bell-shaped curve, a political system with two competitive parties, and a structural arrangement for single member districts. Although both parties might want to reach out to voters on the two tails of the distribution, one to the right and the other to the left, they will, in fact, moderate their platforms to appeal to the large middle group, and in so doing reinforce moderation and stability. Moderation is further enhanced, so argue proponents, by other structural features identified in the paragraph above.

Such structural arrangements work well to the extent that members of society are members of overlapping groups, hold moderate views that fit a bell-shaped rather than bimodal distribution, have these views reflected in the dominant political discourse and policies, and there is in fact rotation among parties controlling the reigns of government. But to the extent that some voters or groups hold distinctly different views and their identity is formed by this, they may not be well served by majoritarian democratic politics in two-party, winner-take-all electoral systems.

3 Federalism

Federalism, Daniel Elazar (1968: 370) has written, is a 'mode of political organization which unites separate polities within an overarching political system so as to allow each to maintain its fundamental political integrity'. It is then a limited and distinct type of consociational arrangement. Consociational arrangements provide for a place at the political table for each significant segment of society. Federalism is a special instance of this general principle and one that is embodied in a polity's constitution. It guarantees a special place and role for geographical areas—or more properly for all those living within defined political units. Thus, distinct interests or segments of society are understood in terms of place or location. In federal systems, states or provinces enjoy constitutional recognition and a degree of autonomy. One view is that distinct locations, or at least those who reside in them—by virtue of residence alone—have distinct interests that warrant representation and special constitutional protection. In federal systems, the constituent units are geographical units as opposed to functional or social units, segments of society with distinct interests and concerns. Thus, in the United States, the Constitution guarantees each state two senators, regardless of the size of the state or the size of its population, in contrast to the consociational 'arrangement' in the Netherlands that assures that each significant segment of society is part of the governing coalition. Still, there are similarities; unless the areal unit in a federal system is understood as a convenient way of identifying a distinct segment of society or a functional group, the rationale for federalism is diminished and its appeal elides into a rationale for decentralization. Thus, for instance, when one considers the position of Quebec in Canada, the appeal of the idea of federalism is obvious and powerful in a way it is not when one considers the position of Kansas or Oregon in the United States or New South Wales or Queensland in Australia. Quebec stands out as a culturally distinct polity in a way these other places do not.

   Still, the idea of federalism has shortcomings that are readily apparent. If it is meant to protect the interests of culturally distinct groupings, a necessary condition is that these cultural groupings must be concentrated within the designated federal boundaries. Although federalism functions to protect the interests of French-speakers in

Quebec, it does not protect French-speakers in Ontario and New Brunswick. More generally, as distinct cultural groups are dispersed throughout the larger society, functional representation of the sort embraced in consociational arrangements may be more effective than the area-based representation of federalism.

Federalism has a long history. It has been traced to Biblical times, and some form of it was institutionalized in the league of Greek city states, medieval Spain, the Austro-Hungarian and other empires, as well as other associations of autonomous polities in various times and places (Elazar, 1968). Still, modern usage makes a sharp distinction between 'confederations' or leagues of mutual interests (groups of states united by treaties and mutual agreement) and 'true' federations (single polities with two levels of government each with its own sphere of responsibility) (Riker, 1964). Moreover, the contemporary understanding of federalism comes in large part from the American experience, which sharply distinguishes federalism from confederation, and from indirect and home rule often permitted under colonialism, and decentralization. However, another form of federalism may be evolving in contemporary Europe, one that may empower subnational regions and cultural groups and a new supranational government and shrink national (state) sovereignty, though it is much too early to establish long-term trends or structural arrangements (Burgess, 2000; Weiler, 1999).

As indicated, both the idea and the practice of federalism have existed for millennia. Despite its durability, however, there is no enduring theory that underlies it. It is obviously an important political arrangement and federal systems have grown by leaps and bounds in the wake of postwar, post-colonial independence (Elazar, 1994). And since the late 1980s, it has re-emerged as both an important scholarly and political issue in Australia, Canada, the United States, and elsewhere. In the United States, interest was rekindled in the early 1990s when the Supreme Court rejected an earlier ruling that issues of federalism are non-justiciable because states are adequately represented in the national political process (*Garcia v San Antonio Metropolitan Transit Authority*, 469 US 528 (1985)). Since then rulings permit the Court to review such questions, and in fact it has held several Acts of Congress unconstitutional on grounds that they violate states' powers. In Australia and Canada, renewed interest in federalism is a result of debates over the adoption of a constitution, a bill of rights, and increased concerns with cultural minorities (Galligan, 1995: 133).

Despite its popularity, federalism tends to be an idea without a strong theory or rationale (Feeley and Rubin, 1998). By theory, I mean a general defense of the structural arrangement of dual levels of government. In contrast to other core features of the modern state, such as democracy, representation, and separation of powers, federalism is under-theorized. These concepts have generated a vast theoretical literature that links them to ideas of human nature, liberty, freedom, individual autonomy, and the like. In contrast, federalism has only generated theories that ask: 'What functions does federalism serve?' Like functional theories generally, these discussions begin with a given structure (federalism), assume that it serves some function, and then set out to identify what it is. In some cases, as is the case with Switzerland, federalism does serve important functions. But there is no reason to think that all federal systems serve similarly important functions, or that having once served important functions, they continue to do so.

What follows is a partial list of what appear to be main claims made by contemporary proponents of federalism. The claims can be divided into two types, first, that federalism promotes one or more *instrumental* values; and secondly, that it promotes *affective* values of community. These two types can be further divided. There are four distinct instrumental arguments for federalism. They are, that federalism: (1) increases public participation in the political process; (2) maximizes citizen utility by fostering competition among jurisdictions; (3) achieves economic efficiency through competition among jurisdictions; and (4) encourages experimentation in ways that foster innovation in public policies. There are two different affective or expressive arguments in favor of federalism. The first holds that federalism protects liberty by diffusing governmental powers, in effect weakening the national government and establishing state units that do not permit strong central authority. The second holds that federalism fosters community in any of three different ways. Federalism can foster (1) personal identity and the social self by creating and sustaining meaningful communities; (2) a sense of fulfillment and a realization of the public self by facilitating participation in a meaningful political unit; and (3) by identifying, recognizing, valuing, and sustaining a pre-existing community or distinct segment of society that provides meaning and coherence for individuals' lives. These three justifications for federalism are not clear-cut; they overlap among themselves and at times with one or more of the instrumental justifications. Furthermore, defenders of federalism usually employ several and not just one single argument to defend the principle of federalism. Still, it is useful to consider each of the arguments separately.

3.1 Instrumental Arguments Favoring Federalism

3.1.1 *Federalism Increases Public Participation in the Political Process*

This argument has been made forcefully by Justice Sandra Day O'Connor of the US Supreme Court, as well as many scholars, including Vicki Jackson (1998) in the United States, and Andrew Fraser (1990) for Canada and Australia. The argument is appealing. But it is not true. Federalism is a structural principle; it establishes dual levels of government, but it is silent on participation, and there is nothing in the structural principle *per se* that encourages or prohibits policies that enhance participation in the political process. Indeed, the history of American—and Australian, and with perhaps one notable exception, Canadian—federalism suggests that on balance national governments and the national political process has been much more active and effective in promoting public participation. In the United States, national, not state, institutions have been responsible for expanding political participation (e.g. Amendments XIV, XIX, XXIV, XVI, and a number of Civil Rights Acts). Similar developments have taken place in other federal systems as well. In short, the appeal of the idea of civic republicanism and small-scale democracy is strong, but the primary mechanisms for expanding and assuring increased political participation in the United States and other federal systems have tended overwhelmingly to come from national and not local initiatives. Indeed, in most instances, they have been necessary to overcome local impediments to participation.

This does not mean, however, that federalism could not in some places and at some times enhance democratic participation and civic republicanism. When state boundaries incorporate and thus preserve distinct and 'natural' cultural communities distinguished by religion or language and tradition, federalism enhances civic participation, at least of a certain type. This has been the case in Switzerland which throughout the twentieth century has continued to establish cantons to preserve and enhance culturally distinct political units, and in Canada where federalism has facilitated the distinctiveness of Quebec (Elazar, 1994: 246).

Still, it should be recalled that federalism is a structural principle that establishes dual sovereignties. Under any robust theory of federalism, this means that if they so choose, the smaller units might favor less rather than more participation, as, for instance, the Southern states did in the pre-Civil Rights era. Conversely, a unitary government might foster democratic participation at both the national and local levels as has, say, Great Britain, and as national governments have in many federal systems where states have been reluctant to act on their own. It is therefore by no means obvious that federalism, by preserving the autonomy of local units, fosters democratic participation. Indeed, Weingast (1995) argues that federalism fosters economic development precisely because it is a political structure that restricts political action, and thus political participation, and preserves a robust free market. However, it is important to remember that federalism is a structural principle that can have a great variety of effects. As with functional analysis generally, there is a tendency among supporters of federalism to generalize too broadly and too quickly. This problem with the argument that federalism fosters political participation holds for all the other functional arguments for federalism as well.

3.1.2 Federalism Maximizes Citizen Utility by Fostering Competition among the States

This argument appears to be distinctively American, although similar arguments arise in support of the European Union, which some believe is evolving into a federal system (Burgess, 2000; Weiler, 1999). The statement is put succinctly by Justice Sandra Day O'Connor, when she claims that federalism 'makes government more responsive by putting states in competition for a mobile citizenry'. Apart from undermining the argument that federalism increases public participation in politics, this argument holds that politics is a market with government as supplier and citizens as consumers. It is one readily familiar to theories of public finance (Tiebout, 1956). Certainly, at the national level, it is clear that immigration is motivated by people's desire to relocate in areas with greater opportunities, including government goods and services, and that this accounts for the migration of Southern Europeans to Northern Europe, Latin Americans to North America, and the like. But much of this migration is motivated by economic opportunities unrelated directly to government policies. The same holds true for internal migration, from one region of the country to another, or one state or province to another. The mixture of government goods and services is just one of many factors that include economic opportunity, weather, family ties, and inertia, and these factors are likely to dwarf considerations of the mix of government services.

Indeed Tiebout's 'theory of local expenditures', upon which this justification of federalism rests, assumes as much. It does not predict that people will move from one *state* to another in order to obtain the mix of governmental goods and services that maximizes their interests. Rather, it assumes that people move to a particular area to pursue employment opportunities, and once in an area, the theory of *local* expenditures holds that people will then move into the *local* community—the neighborhood or the suburb—that best fits their needs, say either a community with low taxes, or one with high taxes but excellent schools. Such choices, then, do not involve issues of federalism, except coincidentally when metropolitan areas happen to straddle state lines. In short, the theory of local expenditures is in fact a theory of *local* and not state or provincial expenditures, and thus, in fact, may even undermine the theory of competitive federalism (in that local communities are creatures of the state and not sovereign entities).

3.1.3 *Fiscal Federalism: Competition among Jurisdictions*

A closely related argument in favor of federalism holds that it fosters competition among the states rather than competitive choice by citizens. This theory holds that states, like firms in a competitive market, compete with each other and in so doing will reduce costs and improve services. On balance, this theory holds, such competition fosters efficiencies, and businesses (and people) will migrate to the more efficient states. This idea has considerable appeal, but it too, dissolves upon inspection. It rests upon the idea that states provide the same sorts of goods and services and thus are competing for the same consumers. But there is nothing in the theory or practice of federalism to lead us to believe this is the case. In Switzerland, Jura offers its citizens French, Ticino Italian, and Zurich German. In the United States, Colorado offers mountains and Rhode Island the seashore. New Jersey offers easy access to New York, and Wyoming solitude. Similarly, Alberta offers wheat and Nova Scotia fish. Indeed, if subnational units of government are to be designed to enhance competition among themselves, it would be better to have a unitary not federal government;

conditions for competition could be set by the central government and then implemented through decentralization, just as General Motors has established separate autonomous divisions to compete with one another.

3.1.4 *States as Laboratories*

This felicitous phrase, coined by US Supreme Court Justice Louis Brandies has done a great deal to popularize the idea of federalism. He argued, 'It is one of the happy incidents of the federal system that a single courageous state may, if its citizens choose, serve as a laboratory; and to try novel social and economic experiments without risk to the rest of the country'. Although appealing and all the more so because of the prestige of its author, the argument in fact is weak. It is certainly true that Oregon imposed minimum age and maximum hour limits on employees in dangerous occupations before other states did, and that Saskatchewan was the first Canadian province to establish universal health care for its residents, that Florida fosters citrus production, and that New South Wales favors private prisons. It is also true that at times other governments have followed suit and adopted policies first tried elsewhere.

Yet, such policies are experiments in only a loose and metaphorical sense; the structural principle of federalism permits states freedom to do what they want. No laboratory director is likely to grant complete freedom to his staff scientists without first having set out the objectives and goals. Experimentation can only be understood in light of common objectives; an experiment is a process of sorting out the best solution to a problem from various alternatives, not allowing researchers to go off to pursue different problems altogether.

4 DEVOLUTION AND DECENTRALIZATION

Devolution was the term coined to describe the process of the imperial powers recognizing independence of their colonies following World War II. More recently, it has been used to characterize central governments relinquishing some degree of control to the periphery by granting limited 'home rule'. Two well-known examples are Great Britain's recognition of limited local autonomy for Scotland, Wales, and Greater London, and Quebec's 'special status' that goes beyond what other provinces possess under Canadian federalism. Devolution has been unsuccessful as a means of creating stable political structures in Northern Ireland, although interest in it continues. Spain has granted the Basque region and Catalonia a degree of autonomy, although it has not gone far enough to dampen the independence movement in the Basque region (Elazar, 1994: 229).

Devolution has a close affinity with federalism in that it recognizes a degree of autonomy for provinces within the larger polity. However, it has some sharp differences. Federal systems, such as the United States, Australia, Canada, throughout Latin America, and perhaps in the emerging European Union were 'federal' from the outset, or were formed as a joining together of separate political entities from the outset (Burgess, 2000; Weiler, 1999). In contrast, devolution is a process by which a recognized unitary sovereign relinquishes central power to sub-units. Such partial autonomy for troublesome locales is often achieved as a result of intense and often violent political struggle, and is likely to represent an unstable compromise between national authority and regional independence movements. It may be unsatisfactory to nationalists because it represents a step towards dissolution. It may be interpreted as a sign of weakness of the nation-state, and it may simply be a strategically adopted ceasefire in a continuing struggle against what is seen as an illegitimate occupying power.

Furthermore, in contrast to the ways many successful federal systems function, devolution is a type of forced decentralization, one grudgingly granted by central authority to only some regions under its control. There is the continuing concern: what has been given may subsequently be taken back. The history of 'home rule' for cities in the United States is a case in point. States have expanded and contracted the authority they have allowed cities over time (Briffault, 1997). Thus it is probably better to think of modern devolution (in contrast to the process of recognizing the independence of colonies immediately following World War II) as a form of decentralization—the center granting greater authority to some peripheral sections, but 'granting' in such a way as not to foreclose the possibility of rescinding the agreement.

Despite its instability, devolution or decentralization has significant advantages. Unlike federalism which implies that an entire polity be divided into two levels, devolution or decentralization can pinpoint particular regions and grant them special status in an otherwise unitary state. Thus the City of New York, Scotland, Wales, Greater London, Quebec, and still other regions have been granted special 'status'. Elsewhere, areas populated by insular and indigenous groups have been granted varying degrees of political autonomy (e.g. the First Nations in Canada, Native Americans in the United States, Aborigines and Torres Strait Islanders in Australia, the Maori in New Zealand, the Lapps in Scandinavia). The obvious advantage of such arrangements is that an otherwise unitary national government can craft special arrangements suitable for the distinctive features of each region.

A more limited but also more common form of devolution is the administrative principle of decentralization. Size alone is a factor in administration and many theories of public administration suggest the value of decentralization, allowing administrative sub-units considerable freedom to fashion responses to policies prescribed by the center. As suggested earlier, defenses of 'fiscal federalism' might in fact better be understood as defenses of decentralization on efficiency grounds.

5 ALTERNATIVE VOTING SYSTEMS

Since Duverger's classic analysis of the effects of various voting systems, it has been a staple of political and legal studies to show that electoral systems 'matter', and that rules for aggregating votes can have profound consequences for the outcome of the election and the formulation of political agendas. Douglas Rae (1967) was perhaps the first scholar who set out to measure the consequences of different types of voting systems. Since then there has been a small library of articles and books devoted to the subject, some 2,500 by one survey published in 2001 (Bowler *et al.*, 2001), and there is a small but important body of theoretical analysis of the mathematics of various electoral systems (Brams and Fishburn, 1991). We cannot here begin to review the large and diverse literature, but it is possible to identify some of the electoral systems and major issues in this field.

There are two main systems for counting votes and organizing electoral systems in Western democracies, majority voting in single member districts (SMDs) and proportional representation (PR). These systems were addressed briefly in the discussion of consociational structures and majoritarian single member districts earlier in this chapter, so this issue will be treated briefly here. We will then turn to consider other less-used systems, and explore some of the literature about them.

Typically, under a system of proportional representation, each party draws up a list of its candidates and ranks them. The numbers of representatives each party receives is dependent upon its proportion of the total vote cast. Such an arrangement assures some degree of political representation for all but the smallest organized segments of society (minimal thresholds and absolute numbers of representatives limit the numbers of parties that can be represented), and, all things equal, is likely to facilitate distinct political expression of the various distinct segments of society. Once their numbers in the assembly are established, the various parties engage in strategic negotiations to form a government.

Proportional representation can be contrasted to representation in single member districts. Here individuals are elected to represent a geographical area. Typically (though not always) there is only one representative per district. So, the party (or faction) that gains the most votes wins the election in a winner-take-all system. Under this scheme, the party that garners the most votes obtains full victory and every other party receives nothing. Of course, different parties may win in different districts, but within each district only one party wins, and all others lose—regardless of the margin of victory. Although there are benefits to such an arrangement, particularly in homogeneous societies (to be discussed below), one obvious shortcoming is that the 'losers' have no representation at all. This can pose significant problems. Consider: in a four-way race, the winner might only receive 26 percent of the vote, while each of the three losers obtained 24.7 percent of the vote. This defect can be rectified to some extent by holding a run-off election if the winner of the first election does not receive a clear majority or some designated percentage of the votes (Epstein, 1980).

There is a seemingly endless debate among legal studies and political scholars about the pros and cons of these two voting systems. Advocates of PR with party lists argue that this process is fairer because it assures political representation in the legislature in rough proportion to the percentage of popular support in the electorate at large, and thus ensures that minority views will be formally represented (Barber, 2000). Opponents charge that PR leads to fragmentation, difficulty in forming governing coalitions, and political instability. They see value in fewer larger parties that are less ideological, and thus more likely to compromise and represent stable majority consensus. As we shall see, there are numerous variations on PR and plurality voting with SMDs, along with theoretical debates of their pros and cons as vehicles for aggregating voter preferences, and empirical studies of their actual operations. (For a succinct summary of both the philosophy and history of various voting schemes, see Barber, 2000.)

There are several alternatives to SMDs and simple PR. Among them are the Hare system of single transferable vote (STV), the Borda count, cumulative voting, additional-member systems, and approval voting. All but approval voting are variations of proportional representation. The 'Hare system' of single transferable vote (STV) was first proposed by Thomas Hare and Carl George Andrae in the 1850s, and has been used in Australia (where it is known as the 'alternative vote'), Malta, the Republic of Ireland, Northern Ireland, and in local elections in Cambridge, Massachusetts, and New York City. Since the US Supreme Court ruling in *Shaw v Reno* (1993), in which the Court sharply limited the use of race-based districting to remedy minority vote dilution, experiments with alternative election systems, such as cumulative and limited voting, have given renewed impetus to PR (Barber, 2000: 58). Several of the more prominent variations are discussed below.

Under a system designed in the late eighteenth century, the 'Borda' system assigns points to candidates so that the lowest-ranked candidate of each voter receives 0 points, the next-lowest 1 point, and so forth. Points for each candidate are summed up across votes, and the candidate with the most points wins. The Borda count system remains largely of theoretical interest in that it is not used in public elections, though they are widely used by private organizations (Brams and Fishburn, 1991). Cox (1997) has shown that all systems of voting are susceptible to strategic voting, but that the Borda system is particularly susceptible. In a multi-candidate race, it can lead to a situation in which the candidate receiving a majority of first-place votes is not elected (if others rank her lower and there is a concentration of preferences for the candidate ranked second).

Cumulative Voting (CV) is a system that creates at-large voting in multi-member districts in ways that facilitate opportunities for minority representation. It, and other related systems, such as limited voting (LV) and single non-transferable voting (SNTV), gives voters up to the same number of votes as positions to be filled, but permits electors to vote for only some candidates rather than requiring them to vote for as many candidates as there are open seats. This option facilitates strategic voting. For example, in a multi-member district with five seats, organized members of a minority group enhance their candidate's chances of election if they vote for her and no one else. In the United States, CV has been used only occasionally in local elections, but Lani Guinier (1994) has vigorously championed it as a way of averting racial polarization and gerrymandering, while at the same time increasing the likelihood of minority representation. In the United States, interest in CV has increased in the wake of *Reno v Shaw* (1993) which held that bizarrely shaped black majority districts were unconstitutional (Bybee, 2002).

The additional-member system (AMS) combines features of both SMDs and PR. It provides for legislators to be elected from single member districts, but permits additional members to be *added* to the legislature, to ensure that parties underrepresented on the basis of their proportions of the national vote are represented proportionally in the legislature. For instance, in a standard single member district with two parties, if one party's candidates receive 51 percent of the votes in all districts, that party wins 100 percent of the seats in the assembly. However, under AMS, membership in the assembly would be adjusted by the proportion of total votes nationally cast for each party; seats would either be reserved for (or added to) the assembly so that the parties would be represented proportionally. Although complicated, such a scheme is used for elections in the German Bundestag, Iceland's Parliament, and the upper house in Puerto Rico (Brams and Fishburn, 1991).

One problem with single member districts when there are three or more candidates is that a 'minority' candidate can be elected, that is, someone who would not win if there were a set of paired contests (this is known as the Condorcet problem, named after the mathematician who first demonstrated the dilemma). Although run-off elections can ameliorate this problem, they do not solve it. They can still produce the Condorcet dilemma in that the electorate's first choice (if there were paired comparisons) might not be elected. To rectify this, some students of electoral systems have proposed approval voting (AV). It allows electors to vote for, or approve of, as many candidates as they wish. Each candidate receives one vote, and each voter can vote for as many candidates as she likes. The candidate with the highest vote total wins. Proponents of AV claim that it results in the election of candidates (or adoption of issues) with the greatest overall support, and thus eliminates the possibility that 'minority' candidates in a divided field can win, as is the case in plurality voting. As of 2002, AV has been restricted largely to private associations, although it has been used in some internal political party elections in the United States, in electing members of the House of Representatives in North Dakota and in the old Soviet Union; and it is under active consideration in other places (Brams and Fishburn, 1991).

6 MULTICULTURALISM: DEVICES TO PROTECT GROUP RIGHTS

Since the 1980s there has been a flurry of scholarly writing on multiculturalism and a growing interest in seeking new and creative ways to structure political and legal arrangements that are sensitive to diverse cultures. This development has occurred for a number of reasons: globalization and unprecedented immigration has increased multicultural diversity in polities throughout the world; a resurgence of cultural nationalism (in former colonies, as well throughout Europe, the United States, Canada, Australia, and elsewhere); increased sensitivity to, and legal and political power of cultural minorities and native peoples in the Western industrialized societies; growing disenchantment with the liberal legal tradition and liberal theory as it has been interpreted to protect and accommodate culture diversity; and the rise of feminism, whose opposition to patriarchy has led to a vast array of new ways of thinking about the state. The challenge of all of this, as Ayelet Shachar (2001: 4) has pointed out, is to find ways to accommodate cultural differences or group-based rights while at the same time respecting individual rights.

Concern with multiculturalism and efforts to protect cultural groups are not wholly new. Consociational arrangements, federalism, devolution, and voting systems have all been devised, in part, to accommode cultural diversity. But federalism and devolution can work only to the extent that the distinct cultures coincide with geographical units. And voting schemes may foster more choices for members of targeted groups, but cannot guarantee that the distinct interests of these groups will be represented. Similarly, limited government may protect minorities to some degree, but it does not necessarily empower them politically.

It is for these reasons that some political theorists have sought a more robust conception of group and cultural rights (Kymlicka, 1995; Taylor, 1994). Some have proclaimed liberalism inadequate to the task (Tully, 1995), and others, most notably feminists, have advocated radically new ways of thinking about political association, the public/private distinction, and individual rights in complex societies (Shachar, 2001; Young, 1997). One of the first orders of business of the new theorists of multiculturalism and group rights was to critique traditional liberal responses to cultural diversity. This traditional position might be termed the 'bill of rights' model (often coupled with a majoritarian system). It holds that the liberal state protects minorities in two ways, by embracing the idea of a limited role of government, with a limited public sphere (thereby placing restraints on majorities and fostering an expansive private sphere), and by providing constitutional guarantees of rights and liberties. Such an arrangement, liberal constitutional theory holds, fosters a robust civil society that encourages individuals to come together in 'private' associations to pursue their common concerns. Indeed, one of the central duties of the courts is to protect the boundaries of the public/private sphere in order to permit the private sphere to flourish.

One weakness of this arrangement, the new critics emphasize, is that liberalism imposes serious impediments to developing compensatory policies (Walzer, 1983) for members of historically oppressed groups. Thus, for instance, affirmative action programs to address historic wrongs suffered by various groups are challenged on the basis that they violate liberalism's individualist premises. Although this is hotly debated, it is clear that such policies do not fit neatly within traditional liberal theory and policies.

Such concerns have led many rights theorists to abandon traditional liberal theory altogether, and to search for new theoretical frameworks that recognize group rights as well as individual rights. Some want to recognize cultural groups as distinct political entities with jurisdiction over their members and *vis-à-vis* the national government. None of this is entirely new. Historically, colonial and imperial powers have granted considerable autonomy to the various peoples they have conquered, and usually sought to sustain their legitimacy by building on indigenous authority structures. And modern democratic governments have recognized limited autonomy for indigenous groups within their borders, although such arrangements have often been honored in the breach.

At the beginning of the twenty-first century, multiculturalism is both a burning practical political issue and a vibrant theoretical issue. It is probably fair to say that new theories have outstripped the construction of new political arrangements, although changes have taken place in both arenas. For historical reasons, both political change and theoretical developments may have been most pronounced in Canada. In Canada, three factors emerged at roughly the same time to reinforce both the practice and the theory of cultural or group-based rights. The move to sever formal constitutional ties with Great Britain and establish its own national constitution forced recognition of the diverse cultures in Canada. Proposed constitutional language that recognized the special character of French-speaking Canada, not only introduced the issue of the rights of cultural groups in ways that are distinct from protections accorded under federalism or traditional liberal conceptions of individual rights, it also triggered claims by other cultural groups, the First Nations and the Inuit, and increasingly by still other groups of new immigrants from the Middle East, Asia, and elsewhere. Canadian recognition of cultural rights has led both to important political developments and to a robust Canadian legal literature and political theory (Kymlicka, 1995; Taylor, 1994). What has occurred in Canada has been echoed, but usually not as strongly, in other regions of the world. Native American tribes in the United States, for instance, are now guaranteed a limited degree of sovereignty under legislation adopted in the 1970s and implemented a decade later (Frickey, 1999).

These developments have led to important new developments among political and legal theorists. As Ayelet Shachar (2001: 25) has observed, if political and legal theory was once dominated by the problem of the relationship of the individual to the state, contemporary legal and political theory is preoccupied with parceling out autonomy to the individual, the group, and the state, as well as to various combinations among these three competing centers of autonomy. She identifies two major traditions, discussed below, that embrace the idea of group rights or recognition of some substantial degree of autonomy for cultural and religious groups in societies with Western liberal traditions, that is, societies with both philosophical and political traditions that have been hostile to the idea of group rights and autonomy.

A 'strong' version of both group rights and group-based political organization is proposed by Tully (1995), who holds that political arrangements should recognize, within limited spheres, the autonomy of cultural and linguistic groupings over their members so that the distinctive features of the culture can be preserved. This would mean granting groups authority to apply traditional cultural norms in areas close to the heart of the cultural tradition, such as determining who is and is not a member of the group, administering educational and religious (and at times religious educational) institutions, articulating and enforcing law pertaining to the family (marriage, divorce, custody, adoption, and the like), and regulating other social practices closely associated with the defining features of the culture (instruction in the language of the culture, and the like). Although Tully and other strong multiculturalists would all permit group members to opt out and join the larger assimilated majority that might be governed by the more familiar liberal division between the individual and the state, those within a designated cultural group would live in a setting where autonomy was divided between the individual, the group, and the state. Traditional ideas of individual rights would be radically affected. Group autonomy might involve power to establish and impose religious obligations on members. Patriarchy might be sanctioned, freedom of expression might be curtailed. Access to the dominant national language might be limited. For instance, parental authority to arrange marriages might be sanctioned by a group, patriarchal rules for granting divorces (and child custody and spousal support) might be respected, and even some forms of punishment (e.g. corporal punishment) not sanctioned by the larger culture and the state might be accepted. Although admitting that extending such spheres of authority to autonomous groups clearly works injustice in some instances in terms of the values of the majority culture, it is, strong multiculturalists argue, the price one pays for true multiculturalism and for the preservation of group autonomy. Indeed, it might be argued that it is only in the face of such hard cases that one can test a society's resolve to accept multiculturalism and the separate spheres of autonomy that it envisions. Opponents of particularism have also raised the converse issue—whether there is a place for nationalism in liberal theory at all—and ask whether all claims to national and cultural self-determination must be rejected under a robust theory of cosmopolitanism or liberalism (Tamir, 1993).

A 'weaker' version of multiculturalism and group rights has attempted to devise a scheme that mitigates injustices within semi-autonomous groups. Kymlicka (1995), for instance, attempts to construct a liberal theory of group rights that provides for ample and repeated opportunity for members to opt out, or to transfer disputes or rights claims to national institutions. He would allow national state institutions to set minimum standards and monitor practices within cultural groups in order to protect against abuses (as defined by the majority culture). In contrast to political and legal arrangements in most, if not all, contemporary multicultural societies, his proposal would vastly expand powers of cultural groups beyond what they are today. Not only could groups have policy-making powers over substantial areas of public life, they could also serve as the basis for representation in the national assembly. Cultural groups rather than (or in addition to) geographical areas could be the basis for selecting representatives and public officials of all sorts. To a certain extent, some of this is already provided in some polities by means of consociational arrangements, federalism, and proportional representation. Still, stronger versions of contemporary multiculturalism would grant autonomy to groups and recognize many more groups than is likely to be the case under most existing structural arrangements. They would allow group jurisdiction to travel outside geographical boundaries, and contemplate group-based representation in national assemblies (and other national institutions).

As suggested above, some of these ideas are readily familiar to those with some knowledge of colonial administration which often granted vast autonomy to cultural groups, especially as they touched on the family, religious norms, ownership of personal property, and the administration of petty criminal matters. (However, in areas touching on political organization, national taxation, foreign policy, land policy, and other areas of obvious interest to colonial masters, native autonomy was severely limited.) 'Weak' multiculturalists would no doubt take issue with the comparison to colonial policy, and argue that under their theory, the purpose of the national government is benign—to embrace the challenge of finding solutions to problems arising between deeply held minority cultural norms and majority cultural norms, and between individuals and the groups to which they belong. However, 'strong' multiculturalists are likely to accept the comparison to colonialism, and argue that the only way to guard against colonial-like domination is to allow cultural groups to have extensive powers to enforce cultural norms, even if they are repugnant to majority values. Indeed, some would want a complete reconfiguration of state and group power in ways that would locate primary or basic authority in the group, and then assign primary political sovereignty to cultural groups and only limited authority to the nation-state, treating it something like the general authority in a confederation where most significant authority remains in its constituent member units (Tully, 1995). Interestingly, there are suggestions of such developments in the emerging federalism in Europe, as the EU and its judicial institutions reach out to protect subnational cultural minorities in ways that enhance both supranational and subnational political organization at the expense of traditional national jurisdiction.

This review of multiculturalism has only touched the topic, but it is enough to demonstrate one important observation. In contrast to the other devices and institutional arrangements examined above, as of the early twenty-first century, concern with robust culture-group-based subnational polities exists more as a theoretical construct than an actual institutional arrangement. Contemporary politics seem to be pulling in two somewhat opposite directions, towards greater internationalism and greater cosmopolitanism on the one hand, and towards greater appreciation for distinct cultures and traditions. Over the past two centuries, small insular cultures have gone the way of a great many natural species and have either been eradicated or placed on the endangered list. It is not clear that the new wave of theorizing about ways to better preserve distinct cultures in larger complex polities will in fact be any more successful than have various proposals to preserve many of the endangered natural species in the modern world.

7 CONCLUDING OBSERVATIONS

This chapter has focused on structural arrangements—both institutionalized and proposed—to foster fairness and stability in complex, heterogeneous democracies. Most of these arrangements deal with forms of representation in national legislative assemblies or structural arrangements to foster political autonomy. As important as these institutional arrangements are, it should be emphasized that they do not exhaust the issue. Indeed, they may detract from it to some extent. The modern state is a bureaucratic state, and in a bureaucratic state, policy is made through administrative—and not legislative—processes. Indeed, it is not too far off the mark to say that administrative agencies and not legislatures are the primary sources of policy-making in the modern state. Theorists of representation in heterogeneous, complex societies have paid far less attention to this matter than they have to the more traditional forms of political structures, and any complete account of complex polities must rectify this omission. They must tackle the problem of gaining access to and voice in the administrative process. Although there is a vast literature in public administration and administrative law detailing how the administrative process can become more transparent, more accessible, and more responsive, theory and practice in this area remain vastly underdeveloped in comparison to the theory and practice of representative structures examined in this chapter. Still, there are some serious efforts. Public administration scholars have developed important theories of 'representative bureaucracy'. And feminists influenced by postmodernism have offered penetrating critiques of the modern bureaucratic state, and outlined radical alternatives. Any comprehensive analysis of complex polities would include a review of these developments as well.

References

Barber, K. L. (2000). *A Right to Representation: Proportional Representation Systems for the Twenty-First Century*, Columbus, Oh.: Ohio University Press.

Bowler, S., Carter, E., and Farrell, D. M. (2001). *Studying Electoral Institutions and their Consequences: Electoral Systems and Electoral Laws*, Irvine, Calif.: Center for the Study of Democracy, University of California.

Brams, S. J., and Fishburn, P. C. (1991). 'Alternative Voting Systems', in L. Sandy Maisel (ed.) *Political Parties and Elections in the United States*, i, New York: Garland.

Briffault, R. (1997). 'The Rise of Sublocal Structures in Urban Governance', *Minnesota Law Review*, 82: 503–34.

Burgess, M. (2000). *Federalism and European Union: The Building of Europe: 1950–2000*, London: Routledge.

Bybee, K. (2002). 'Mistaken Identity: The Supreme Court and the Politics of Minority Representation', Princeton: Princeton University Press.

Cox, G. W. (1997). *Making Votes Count*, New York: Cambridge University Press.

Dahl, R. (1971). *Polyarchy: Democracy and Opposition*, New Haven: Yale University Press.

Elazar, D. (1968). 'Federalism', in David Sills (ed.), *International Encyclopedia of the Social Sciences*, iv, New York: Macmillan, 353–67.

—— (1994). *Federal Systems of the World: A Handbook of Federal, Confederal and Autonomy Arrangements* (2nd edn.), London: Longman Current Affairs.

Epstein, L. (1980). *Political Parties in Western Democracies*, New Brunswick, NJ: Transaction Books.

Feeley, M. M., and Rubin, E. (1998). *Judicial Policy Making and the Modern State*, New York: Cambridge University Press.

Fraser, A. (1990). *The Spirit of the Laws: Republicanism and the Unfinished Project of Modernity*, Toronto: University of Toronto Press.

Frickey, P. P. (1999). 'A Common Law for our Age of Colonialism: The Judicial Divestiture of Indian Tribal Authority over Nonmembers', *Yale Law Journal*, 109: 1–85.

Galligan, B. (1995). *A Federal Republic: Australia's Constitutional System of Government*, Cambridge: Cambridge University Press.

Guinier, L. (1994). *The Tyranny of the Majority*, New York: Free Press.

Jackson, V. (1998). 'Federalism and the Uses and Limits of the Law: Printz and Principle?' *Harvard Law Review*, 111: 2181–258.

Kymlicka, W. (1995). *Multicultural Citizenship: A Liberal Theory of Minority Rights*, Oxford: Clarendon Press.

Lijphart, A. (1977). *Democracy in Plural Societies: A Comparative Exploration*, New Haven: Yale University Press.

—— (1994). *Electoral Systems and Party Systems: A Study of Twenty-Seven Democracies, 1945–1990*, New York: Oxford University Press.

Rae, D. (1967). *The Political Consequences of Electoral Laws*, New Haven: Yale University Press.

Riker, W. H. (1964). *Federalism: Origin, Operation, Significance*, Boston: Little Brown.

Shachar, A. (2001). *Multicultural Jurisdictions: Cultural Differences and Women's Rights*, New York: Cambridge University Press.

Tamir, Y. (1993). *Liberal Nationalism*, Princeton: Princeton University Press.

Taylor, C. (1994). 'The Politics of Multiculturalism', in A. Guttman (ed.), *Multiculturalism: Examining the Politics of Recognition*, Princeton: Princeton University Press.

Tiebout, C. M. (1956). 'A Pure Theory of Local Expenditures', *Journal of Political Economy*, 64: 416–32.

Tully, J. (1995). *Strange Multiplicity: Constitutionalism in an Age of Diversity*, Cambridge: Cambridge University Press.

Walzer, M. (1983). *Spheres of Justice: A Defense of Pluralism and Equality*, New York: Basic Books.

Weiler, J. H. H. (1999). *The Constitution of Europe*, New York: Cambridge University Press.

Weingast, B. (1995). 'The Economic Role of Political Institutions: Market-Preserving Federalism and Economic Development', *The Journal of Law, Economics, and Organization*, 7: 1–31.

Young, I. M. (1997). *Intersecting Voices: Dilemmas of Gender, Political Philosophy, and Policy*, Princeton: Princeton University Press.

PART III

WEALTH REDISTRIBUTION AND WELFARE

CHAPTER 18

....

TAXATION

....

BEVERLY I. MORAN

1 INTRODUCTION: THE NATURE
OF THE PROJECT

....

PRESENTING the last forty years of tax scholarship in the common law world presents at least six challenges.

1.1 The First Challenge: Common Misconceptions about Taxation

To judge a subject's scholarship, one must first have some sense of the underlying topic. Without this sense, one might completely miss, or at least misunderstand, a body of literature's lack of focus on a particular matter, or its obsession with another. For the non-tax specialist, the danger lies in a host of common misconceptions about taxation. These misconceptions include the notions that:

- governments raise all their revenues through taxation;
- taxes are always used to raise revenues;
- taxes are always demanded and paid in cash; and
- the largest tax in terms of revenues raised (and in terms of what individuals pay) is the income tax.

Although taxation has become ever more central to public finance, it is not the only way that governments raise revenues. Other popular means of raising revenues include sales of natural resources, fines, penalties, licenses, interest on investments, borrowing, and confiscations through conquest. Thus, not all government revenue raising counts as taxation.

Some taxation is redistributive in nature. One United States example of a redistributive tax is the earned income credit in which the working poor can receive back more in taxes than they have paid.

Nor do all taxes have revenue raising as their primary purpose. Taxes are also imposed to control, penalize, or even encourage, behavior. One example is the Australian land tax, which was enacted in 1910 by the Commonwealth government to encourage large landholders, many of whom were wealthy Englishmen who rarely visited, to subdivide and sell to settlers.

Further, it is not true that all taxation is demanded (or paid) in cash. Throughout most of human history, taxes were paid 'in kind', in the form of property or labor. This trend continues today (Moran, 2001). Outside of the OECD universe, many oil-rich countries tax domestic oil producers by taking a share of the extracted petroleum and, even within the 'developed world' forced military service is a form of 'in kind' tax.

Although this chapter begins with the novice's misconceptions, it is also true that, sometimes, novices have insights that are missed by insiders. Non-tax specialists know an important fact that is generally absent from the specialist tax literature, that is, that taxation can have severe, even fatal, political consequences. Two recent examples include the British poll tax, which is sometimes credited with weakening the Thatcher government in the United Kingdom and the Ghanaian value added tax of the mid-1990s, which almost brought down the Rawlings regime (Terkper, 1996; Jones, 1990).

1.2 The Second Challenge: No Single Tax

Although a perfect definition is somewhat elusive, we can say that a tax occurs when a government requires contributions for its operations from individuals, firms, or groups within its jurisdiction without returning a clear quid pro quo. Within this universe, there are a number of different types of taxes that are used to a greater or lesser extent depending on each nation's history, administrative capacity, and culture.

1.2.1 *Types of Taxes in the Commonwealth and the United States*

Governments employ many different types of taxes. Not every country uses every tax, and the amount and percentage of revenue raised from a particular tax differs from nation to nation. Within the Commonwealth and the United States we see income taxes, sales taxes, excise taxes, wealth and wealth transfer taxes, wage taxes, value-added taxes, customs duties, per capita taxes, goods and services taxes, and entity taxes.

In tax literature, a distinction is made between direct taxes, that is, a tax on the thing, and indirect taxes, that is, a tax on a transaction in the thing. Thus, a wealth tax is a direct tax while a wealth transfer tax is an indirect tax. Excise and sales taxes are other forms of indirect taxes while the income tax is a direct tax. Besides the distinction between direct and indirect taxes, each tax's definition is further derived from what the system attempts to tax and how the tax reaches its object.

Thus, an income tax attempts to tax income broadly defined, while a wage tax or a capital gains tax only attempts to tax one type of income, that is, wages earned through labor or income from investments. Sales taxes are based on the amount paid for a good, while excise taxes are based on the amount of the good purchased. Thus, for example, a 10 percent tax on sales of gasoline will raise 10 cents a gallon if gasoline sells for $1 a gallon and 15 cents per gallon if the price rises to $1.50 per gallon. On the other hand, a 10-cent per gallon excise tax on gasoline will remain the same 10 cents per gallon even as the price of gasoline rises and falls. Value-added taxes are a form of sales tax in which each step of the production process creates a new opportunity to tax. In this form of tax, manufacturing a car results in several taxes as the manufacturing process goes from the extraction of ore, to the creation of steel, to the production of various components (seats, radio, tires, and so on). At each step, a tax is laid on the added value created by the manufacturing process. A wealth tax is a tax on the value of property whether or not the property is transferred. One example of a wealth tax is a yearly tax on the value of real estate. Whether the property is kept or sold, its owners pay a tax on its value each year. A wealth transfer tax also reaches value but only when transferred. An example is the US gift and estate tax where the value of property is not taxed until it is given away or inherited. Entity taxes appear in many forms. The point is that a firm rather than its human owners is subject to tax. Per capita taxes are also known as head taxes. These are a single amount charged to each person. The British poll tax under Margaret Thatcher is an example of this type. Customs duties (also known as tariffs) are charges made on the privilege of taking goods across country borders. They can be based on value, like a sales tax, or volume, like an excise tax. Depending on how each government is structured, sometimes these taxes are imposed by the central government and sometimes by smaller governmental subdivisions.

1.3 The Third Challenge: No Common History

A third challenge in drawing together forty years of tax scholarship is the lack of a shared history among common law countries. While it is true that the Commonwealth countries and the United States share a British colonial heritage, it is also true that each country's tax system is a function of its individual history.

1.3.1 *Britain*

The Crown financed medieval Britain through feudalism, in which rights and reciprocal duties were focused on land (Douglas, 1999). As Britain moved to a modern economy, customs duties were added to the revenue mix, followed by excise taxes in the seventeenth century. These were then followed by land taxes, income taxes, social security taxes (national insurance), and a host of other taxes. Present-day Britain raises approximately one-third of its revenues from income tax, one-sixth from social security contributions, another sixth from value-added tax, a tenth from customs and excise duties, another tenth from corporation taxes, 1 percent from capital taxes, and one-sixth from other taxes.

1.3.2 *Commonwealth and the United States*

The rest of the Commonwealth and the United States have a common British colonial history that shaped their early tax history, albeit not always along the same course.

The United States was born of a tax revolt that was followed, after its creation, by other violent tax protests. This political experience, combined with constitutional limitations on Congress's ability to impose direct taxes, prevented a successful income tax until the twentieth century. The United States raised most of its pre-twentieth-century revenues through sale of natural resources, conquest, borrowing, and a series of indirect taxes (Moran, 1992). This was followed in the twentieth century by income taxes and a wealth transfer tax on estates. In the twenty-first century, the United States raises half of its tax revenues from income tax, one-third from social security contributions, one-tenth from corporation taxes, 2 percent from the wealth transfer tax (Gift and Estate Tax), 4 percent from excise duties, and 1 percent from customs duties.

Canada has a mixed colonial tax history. Prior to 1663, French control was exercised through chartered companies. This era saw Canada's first excise tax on the exportation of beaver furs. After 1663, France's North American possessions came under direct royal rule. During this period, both the Catholic Church and the Crown laid taxes. With the unification of the British and French colonies, British colonial taxation dominated. As in the United States, British taxation focused on controlling Canadian trade and manufacturing for the benefit of British industry (Douglas, 1999). As Canada moved to independence, it created a tax system very different from that of the United States in terms of the power to tax.

In Canada, the central government has unlimited power to tax while provincial governments may only impose direct taxes. The exact opposite is true in the United States. Under the US Constitution as originally drafted, the state governments had unlimited powers to tax while the federal government could only impose indirect taxes. This is why the United States needed a constitutional amendment before the federal government could impose an income tax.

Today, Canada raises half its tax revenues from income tax, one-sixth from corporation taxes, another sixth from the goods and services tax, and approximately one-tenth from excise duties.

Australia's colonial tax history begins in the eighteenth century with import duties and excise taxes. As in colonial Canada, these taxes were raised at the local level and not by a central government. By the twentieth century, each state was collecting income taxes. The central government followed in 1915. A land tax that was meant to encourage English landowners to sell their colonial holdings to permanent settlers followed the income tax. The land tax was then followed by a series of sales and other indirect taxes on wool, on fringe benefits, and on capital gains. In 2000, Australia introduced a goods and services tax to replace the wholesale sales tax. The Australian GST is a form of expanded value-added tax. Although it taxes everything that a value-added tax would, the Australian GST also reaches services that do not necessarily add value to a transaction. The Australian GST is not listed in the national budget because the revenues raised belong to the local governments. Australia raises half its tax revenues from the income tax, one-sixth from indirect taxes, another sixth from corporation taxes, and one-tenth from other taxes.

Like the United States, India's independence was tied to a tax revolt. The famous Salt marches lead by Gandhi in the 1930s were a massive show of civil disobedience aimed at the British Salt Tax. In addition to the Salt Tax, Britain introduced many other taxes to its Indian colony. The first income tax came to India in the mid-nineteenth century. At first, state governments laid income taxes. A centralized income tax was introduced in 1922. Modern sales taxes followed in the 1930s, also at the state level.

India raises one-third of its tax revenues from the Union Excise Duties Tax, one-quarter from custom duties, one-fifth from the corporate tax, one-sixth from the non-corporate income tax and 3 percent from other taxes. Article 272 of the Indian Constitution requires the central government to share union excise duties with the states. The Indian emphasis on customs duties and excise taxes makes India's tax system more closely related to Anglophone Africa than to the United States and the rest of the Commonwealth.

Colonial Africa faced many of the same problems as the rest of the British world. Britain extracted revenues from all of its colonies by limiting local manufacturing and controlling local resources. As in its other colonies, this strategy included excise taxes and import restrictions. However, because Anglophone Africa achieved independence later than Australia, Canada, India, and the United States, it entered the modern tax world more quickly. After independence, income taxes, corporate taxes, and the like came at once rather than over time. This is a feature of African taxation that affects other countries as well, through the move to tax harmonization discussed later in this chapter.

What sets modern-day Anglophone Africa and India apart from their British colonial brothers is their tax mix. Australia, Canada, the United Kingdom, and the United States raise most of their revenues from income, wage, and corporate taxes while the Anglophone African nations and India raise more of their tax revenues from customs duties. To illustrate, Botswana, the Gambia, Ghana, Lesotho, and Sierra Leone raise less than one-fifth of their revenues from income taxes. Namibia and Zambia hover at one-third. Kenya and Zimbabwe are more in line with Australia, Canada, India, the United Kingdom, and the United States with income tax contributing close to one-half of tax revenues. Only South Africa's income tax raises more than half of that nation's tax revenues. The fact that customs duties are a very important part of their tax mix puts Anglophone Africa and India in conflict with the global economy and its increasing pressure to do away with barriers to trade. Further, Anglophone African countries tend to centralize their tax systems more than the rest of the Commonwealth and the United States. In Africa there is little, if any, taxing power residing in the provinces or states.

1.4 Challenge Four: No Common Law of Taxation

Having reviewed the many types of taxes and the different histories that shaped each nation's tax structure, it will now come as less of a surprise that our fourth challenge is that there is no common law of taxation that crosses national boundaries in the way that there is a common law of contracts or torts. For a variety of historical reasons, modern taxation is a twentieth-century phenomenon that rests on particular statutes that are quite country-specific. To get around the problem of writing about the common law in an area without one, this chapter focuses on similarities and differences between tax scholarship in the Commonwealth countries and the United States, specifically writings on taxation in Anglophone Africa, Australia, Canada, India, the United Kingdom, and the United States.

1.5 Challenge Five: What Constitutes Relevant Tax Scholarship?

The fifth challenge is what scholarship to present. This issue arises because there are several types of tax scholarship in each nation which take different forms and serve different purposes, most of which are far removed from the purposes of this book.

1.5.1 *Practitioner Scholarship*

At the forefront, in terms of sheer volume alone, are the technical writings that are directed to practitioners. These writings are extremely important because, by its nature, taxation in the twentieth century evolved through complex statutes that require a breadth and depth of technical knowledge. As a result, there is a vast wealth of writings on the workings of various sub-sub-sections and their relationship to sub-sub-sub-sections that are equally obscure (to the outsider) (Schneider, 1999). Clearly those writings, while significant both in terms of content and number, are not central to this book's concerns. Because tax law tends to change fairly rapidly, they are often obsolete within a matter of years. Further, such scholarship is meant to address issues of no importance here, such as describing how to plan transactions for specific clients or presenting calls for minor legislative reforms.

1.5.2 *Academic Scholarship for the Cognoscenti*

Next, there are specialized academic writings that appear in books and journals that contain nothing but tax pieces. These journals and books are another important part of the tax scholarship landscape primarily because they are where tax academics speak to one another. Although these pieces are on a higher level than those of their more practitioner-oriented brethren in terms of the depth and breadth of the issues addressed, they too are often dominated by technical discussions, albeit on a broader plane. Rather than parse a single sub-part of one statutory section, for example, these pieces look at larger statutory schemes, such as the entire system that allows partnerships to allocate income to their partners, or corporate rules allowing mergers without tax liability. Once again, these writings form an important part of the scholarly literature but, as even this brief description demonstrates, they are not of a type to bring a person without extensive prior knowledge into the last forty years of conversation.

1.5.3 *'Cross-Over' Literature*

Instead of the technical pieces both specific and general, I have chosen to discuss the last forty years of writings in what I term 'cross-over' literature, that is, journals and other writings that are aimed at a general academic legal audience rather than at tax specialists. So, for example, I have surveyed the tax scholarship that appears in the *New York University Law Review* but not in the *Tax Law Review*, even though the New York University Law School produces both. While the *Tax Law Review* has produced some noteworthy pieces, it is not read by non-tax academics and so does not count as a 'cross-over' journal.

I attempted to survey the top three journals in terms of prestige in each country. Because of disagreements about which journals fit within the top three, I ended up surveying eight journals in the United States, six journals from the United Kingdom, five journals from Australia, and five journals from Canada. Thus, in the discussions of tax scholarship that follow, the focus is on pieces that are read by both tax and non-tax legal academics. They represent a small part of the scholarly universe but the part most visible to those outside the inner circle of tax cognoscenti.

1.6 The Sixth Challenge: Tax Scholarship and Real World Problems

We now come to the sixth challenge, that is, the fact that the topics discussed in the 'cross-over' literature have very little to do with real-world problems. For example, based on revenue alone, tax scholarship should cover entity taxation, wealth transfer taxes, excise and sales taxes, and the relationship of taxing powers between various levels of government. Yet, rather than cover a broad spectrum of tax issues, 'cross-over' scholarship in each country focuses primarily on only a few parts of the tax universe while almost completely ignoring other, equally relevant, areas. To introduce one instance of this phenomenon, the effect of globalization on taxation and sovereignty is almost completely ignored in this type of tax scholarship, although the interrelationship of globalization and local law is recognized in other areas such as labor and environmental law. An exception to this result is worth noting (Avi-Yonah, 2000).

Adding to the problem of introducing a novice to the last forty years of tax scholarship is the fact that, even in the subject areas that are blessed with abundant writings, it is sometimes hard to see how the topics covered are relevant to the subjects they address. Perhaps the best illustration of this dilemma is the US scholarship on the individual income tax. Within that scholarship, the most covered areas concern the search for a perfect tax system. These discussions, sometimes in the form of works on the comprehensive income tax base and, more recently, in championing the consumption tax, are interesting as matters of philosophy, but have little impact on actual legislation or reform.

To address this sixth problem, I have set aside Section 3 to highlight topics that are not yet addressed in the 'cross-over' literature but which might become popular in the future.

2 THE SCHOLARSHIP

Just as the common law countries have different tax systems, laws, histories, and cultures, they also have varied approaches to tax scholarship. These differences range from how much scholarship is produced to how that literature looks. In the discussion below, I have segregated these differences in four ways, by structure, substance, focus, and, finally, in Section 3, by what is missing from each nation's literature.

Structure tries to guide a reader who wishes to write an article for each market by discussing standards for length, referencing, and whether the scholarship is primarily descriptive, doctrinal, policy-oriented, or interdisciplinary. Substance explains the subjects addressed in the literature and how those topics differ from jurisdiction to jurisdiction. Focus asks if the literature looks out beyond the home country or, in contrast, is almost exclusively focused on local issues. Finally, what is missing from the literature looks at topics we would expect to find in each country's scholarship but do not.

2.1 Structure of Tax Literature across the Common Law Countries

The structure of tax literature across the common law countries raises issues of volume, length, and audience as well as approach.

2.1.1 *Volume*

The first major difference among the common law countries is the volume of scholarship produced. The United States is clearly the leader in volume with more articles (and significantly more pages) than the entire Commonwealth combined. From a US perspective, this is particularly interesting because one of the complaints of US tax academics is that the high prestige 'cross-over' journals are closed to their scholarship. Given what academics in the Commonwealth face, US tax scholars are lucky indeed. Australia produces the most tax works after the United States, followed by Canada and the United Kingdom. There are significantly fewer articles on India and Africa. Works on these nations are more likely to appear in edited books or practitioner-oriented journals.

2.1.2 *Length*

Next, there are differences of length. Once again, the United States takes the lead with articles that are often three or four times as long as their Commonwealth cousins'. Part of this length is related to style because the US reviews require extensive referencing not found in the other nations' tax literature. Thus, footnotes alone account for at least a fifth of the difference in size between US scholarship and the rest of the common law world. But more than style is at work here. There is also the question of audience.

2.1.3 *Audience*

The target audience is not consistent among the Commonwealth countries and the United States. In general, there is one audience for the less developed countries' literature, which sometimes includes India and sometimes not, another for Australia, Britain, and Canada, with India sometimes included, and a third audience in the United States.

   The literature on African taxation is focused on an international community of consultants who move from country to country working on legislation. The interests of this community are comparative because it is made up of people who are working outside their own legal systems while drawing to a large extent on their home country knowledge. These people are like Machiavelli's Prince. They need someone to give them a quick in-depth analysis of the present situation and how the issue at hand is resolved in a variety of systems. Further, the analysis they desire has prompt application in new environments. As Machiavelli did hundreds of years ago, these authors serve their readers' purpose with straightforward reporting and analysis that is filled with comparative examples.

Indian tax scholarship is of two types. Some falls under the same category as the African scholarship, that is, pieces produced by outsiders for the benefit of outsiders who are in some way trying to manipulate the local tax system either for the benefit of India itself or as part of another country's tax program. Indian scholars produce the rest of the tax scholarship, although sometimes in their capacity as employees of international organizations such as the United Nations, the International Monetary Fund, or the World Bank. This scholarship is more along the lines of what one finds in Australia, Canada, and Britain and is discussed below.

Tax literature in Australia, Canada, India, and the United Kingdom seems directed at academics without substantial prior knowledge who want to quickly understand a particular problem and its possible solutions. Thus, a great deal of the difference in length between these pieces and their US counterparts comes from the fact that a person in this position does not have several days to absorb a single piece of scholarship and appreciates the direct and accessible.

US 'cross-over' tax literature is very different from the Commonwealth 'cross-over' tax scholarship in length, referencing, and audience. US tax articles are long, heavily footnoted, and often extremely dense. Not only are many of the pieces hard for an outsider to understand, they are baffling to trained tax professionals as well. It is common for a single piece to take more than a day for a trained tax academic to read and digest. This lack of accessibility is especially odd because, unlike the rest of the scholarship discussed above, the people selecting US pieces for publication have no prior knowledge themselves.

In the rest of the common law world, articles are selected for publication by professional editors and are often peer-reviewed. In contrast, US 'cross over' tax pieces are selected by students who have not had a single tax class and have no sense of the canon they help shape with their selections. Given their profound lack of information, one would expect that the student editors of US law reviews would select pieces more like those found in the Commonwealth nations, that is, accessible, informative works that give the reader a sense of the field. Even a quick review of the US tax literature would show that this is far from the case.

2.1.4 *Approach: Descriptive, Doctrinal, Policy Oriented*

When it comes to approach, there are significant differences between each nation's tax literature. The Australians produce almost as much tax scholarship in 'cross-over' journals as the Canadians and the British combined. Most of this scholarship is doctrinal and descriptive. Very little draws on other disciplines, such as economics or sociology, and, with some exceptions, it does not tend towards policy orientation. There is very little British tax scholarship, at least in the 'cross-over' journals. What appear in these works is both straightforward and policy oriented. Although there are some pieces that draw on economic analysis, there is not much other interdisciplinary focus. Instead, most of the works rely more on describing a major problem, such as the nature of tax avoidance, looking at possible solutions from a variety of social and legal perspectives, and offering a legislative or interpretive solution.

Canadian tax scholarship is primarily doctrinal and descriptive. So doctrinal and descriptive, in fact, that a Canadian academic has written:

Most tax articles in Canadian academic legal journals treat the law as a knowable body of rules and simply describe it. No serious effort is made to analyse, synthesize, or evaluate the rules or to identify and resolve ambiguities or gaps in them. Indeed, in the tax law area much of this kind of legal writing is not much more than a straightforward paraphrasing of the relevant sections of the *Income Tax Act*. (Brooks, 1985: 446)

Further, when this author called for a move to more policy-oriented scholarship, he stated: 'Since Canadian legal scholars have done very little writing on tax policy, I will largely refer to the work of U.S. legal scholars in making this comparison and in suggesting future areas of study for Canadian scholars'. Ironically, Professor Brooks's criticism seems to have had a large but limited effect. Based on a burst of social policy pieces written in the late 1980s, shortly after Professor Brooks's call to arms, Canada actually leads Australia, Britain, and the United States in scholarship on tax and social policy.

By contrast, scholarship on African and Indian tax issues is far more theoretical than what we typically find in the Australian, British, or Canadian literature. Such authors as Richard Goode, Richard Bird, and Vito Tanzi write about taxation almost exclusively from a policy perspective, albeit in a straightforward, accessible way (Blejer and Ter-Minassian, 1997; Bird and Oldman, 1990). Their goal is to create perfect tax systems for their client states and so they are often concerned with problems of administration, the question of proper tax structure, and the impact on tax structures of various communities within each nation. For a complete bibliography of the works of Richard Goode, see Cnossen (1983).

Although the vast majority of US tax scholarship is doctrinal and descriptive, this trend is not reflected in the 'cross-over' literature. In the 'cross-over' journals, US tax scholarship is heavily policy oriented. A significant, albeit minority, portion relies on economic analysis and a much smaller percentage has a nodding acquaintance with history or sociology.

2.2 Substance

Substance refers to the topics addressed by the tax literature. As one might imagine, with so many different ways to tax and so many historical and cultural differences within the Commonwealth and the United States, substance ranges widely across national boundaries.

2.2.1 *A Search for a Perfect Tax System*

If there is one topic that takes up a significant amount of space, it is the search for a perfect tax system. Particularly in the United States and the less developed countries, there is an obsession with creating a system that fits some philosophical ideal.

Next to the less-developed countries, US scholarship is the most obsessed with the search for perfection. This obsession is primarily addressed in two ways. In the earlier writings, there is much written about the comprehensive income tax base. Starting in the late 1970s, the emphasis switches to a concentration on the consumption tax. Taken together, these two topics comprise close to a sixth of all US tax scholarship in the last forty years.

The comprehensive tax base is focused exclusively on the income tax. It is based on an article of faith in US tax policy, that people who earn the same income should pay the same amount of tax. This concept is also known as horizontal equity and it is one of the basic understandings of fairness in the US Income Tax system. To achieve horizontal equity, all income must be subject to tax. Otherwise, some people will have large amounts of income and no tax, while others have small amounts of income all subject to tax. Thus, those who favor the comprehensive tax base spend their time either looking at the income or the deduction side in order to make sure that each taxpayer is including all that he (or she) should in the tax base.

To give one example from the income side, in the United States, appreciation in the value of property is not taxed until that appreciation has been harvested or, in tax parlance, realized. One illustration of this practice concerns the value of corporate shares. A taxpayer can buy a share for $10, see the value rise to $110 and not pay any tax until the share is sold. On the other hand, $10 placed in an interest-bearing savings account will incur tax on that interest every year whether or not the taxpayer withdraws that interest for consumption or retains it for future savings. The interest is considered realized as earned, but the stock appreciation is not realized until harvested through a sale. This difference in treatment gives a tremendous advantage to those with property who are able to defer a taxing event until it is most convenient. Thus, there is a body of literature in the United States that questions realization and tries to find ways of including certain types of income in the tax base more quickly. On the deduction side, Stanley Surrey introduced the concept of the tax expenditure budget more than fifty years ago (Surrey, 1970, 1973). It was Surrey's position that every deduction for personal expenses is a type of government subsidy. So, for example, Surrey opined that it would be politically impossible for Congress to pass a bill that subsidized the homes of the wealthy to a greater extent than the homes of the poor and yet this is done each day with the home mortgage interest deduction. Accordingly, another part of the comprehensive income tax base movement is the search for deductions that are inappropriate because they allow some taxpayers to reduce their tax base more than others.

Starting in the early 1970s, a movement arose in opposition to the US income tax. These authors argued that a fairer tax would be based on consumption rather than earnings. One of the first people to discuss this concept was William Andrews (Andrews, 1972). In other words, these authors claim that the US income tax is not actually taxing income because, by adding all earnings to the tax base, the system taxes both what is earned and saved and what is earned and consumed. According to these scholars, what is earned and saved is not income and should not be taxed until consumed. This argument has been made with more and more economic modeling but, at its base, it is a normative assertion. Those opposed to the consumption tax fear that it is regressive, that is, a tax in which the poor pay a higher percentage of their income than the rich. This occurs because the rich have to spend less of their total income to survive in comparison with the poor who have to spend all of their earnings each year. With a consumption tax, the poor find all of their earnings subject to tax as consumption and the rich find most of their earnings sheltered from tax as investments. For a discussion of a progressive consumption tax, see Gratz (1979). More by far has been written on this topic in US 'cross-over' literature than anything else. In a sense, it is amazing that a tax that does not exist in the United States occupies so much scholarly imagination. In Canada, Australia, and Britain, where there is a flourishing consumption tax in the form of value-added taxes, hardly anything is written about consumption taxes and their normative superiority (or inferiority) to an earnings-based income tax.

The literature most focused on a perfect tax system is based in the less developed countries. The authors who focus on Africa and India have one purpose in mind, that is, to create a tax system that can work in unfavorable conditions, that can raise sufficient revenues, and that can meet some ideal of fairness. Administration is important because many of these countries have poor administrative infrastructures with government workers who are either under-trained, underpaid, or both. Corruption is but one challenge, along with other flaws in the underlying systems that make revenues elusive. Thus, there is considerable work on the nature of tax avoidance, and speculation on ways to curb particular tax-avoidance activities. Although a focus on administration implies a lack of a larger philosophical bent, these authors, many of whom serve as consultants either to the nations themselves or through the World Bank or the International Monetary Fund, are not mere technocrats. They seek more than a system that works. They want fairness as well. Having an administrative structure that works well is seen as part of fairness. By eliminating corruption and spreading the tax burden over larger segments of the population, these authors see infrastructure as an important path to fairness.

What counts as fairness outside of good administration is perhaps the most interesting part of this work. It is certainly not centered on the cultures of the countries explored. Rather, as the meaning of fairness shifts in the more developed nations, consultants trained in those states bring new concepts of fairness to their less developed clients (Goode, 1993). Thus, when Europe and the United States were concerned with a comprehensive income tax base, we see the same concerns in writings on Third World tax problems. This is true even though there is much to be said against an income tax in these regions (Moran, 2001). As Europe began to shift toward consumption taxes, particularly in the form of value-added taxes, the same shift became part of this literature's understanding of fairness, even though value-added taxes have caused more than their share of problems in Africa, if not in the other states (Terkper, 1996).

The rest of Commonwealth scholarship shares the US and less developed countries' interest in perfect tax systems in two respects: Australian, British, and Canadian scholarship all devote substantial space to what constitutes income and to tax avoidance and evasion. In Australia, Britain, and Canada one-tenth of all scholarship is devoted to the question: 'What is income?' Although there is no focus on a consumption tax, as in the United States and the less developed countries, this spotlight on income is a central question in the search for a comprehensive income tax base. The major difference between the Australian, British, and Canadian work on these subjects and the US, African, and Indian literature is that the Australian, British, and Canadian tax scholarship focuses on specific items of income while the US, African, and Indian literature tries to develop broad principles. So, for example, in Canada, there are several articles on the taxation of securities, and in Australia and Britain there is a focus on whether damages are income. In contrast, in the United States, in addition to discussions of specific items, there are also a number of articles on the entire concept of a comprehensive income tax base.

The Australians devote a sixth of their 'cross-over' scholarship to tax evasion and the British follow with a tenth of their scholarship. Of course, this does not mean that there is no Canadian or US literature on this issue. All it means is that the North American 'cross-over' journals are not interested in discussions of tax avoidance and evasion. There are certainly many government-sponsored studies of tax avoidance and evasion in the United States, and I have no reason to believe that the Canadian government is not equally interested in the subject. What is more interesting is why British and Australian readers with no specialized tax knowledge are interested enough in this matter to make it one of the most discussed issues in their 'cross-over' scholarship.

2.2.2 *Constructing the Corporate Tax*

The next topic with significant coverage in the literature is the corporate tax. More than a fifth of the US and a sixth of the Canadian 'cross-over' tax scholarship is devoted to the corporate tax. As with the consumption tax debate and the controversy over the comprehensive income tax base, this focus on the corporate tax is not related to the corporate tax's impact on Canadian or US revenues. In fact, the corporate tax accounts for only a sixth of Canadian tax revenue and only a tenth of US federal tax revenues. Instead, what appears to be going on, at least from the US perspective, is another variation of the search for a perfect tax. In US scholarship, the core of this quest is an attempt to understand the nature of the firm and why it should, or should not, be subject to tax.

The problem of the corporation as taxpayer is, in some sense, a story of the history of corporations. Until fairly recently (within the last two hundred years), the common law did not allow owners of businesses to avoid personal liability through the use of business forms. If two or more people joined together to start a business, that operation was considered a partnership and each partner was individually liable for all partnership debts, torts, and crimes. It was not until the nineteenth century that corporations provided their owners with limited liability on a routine basis. The leap towards accepting a legal fiction with separate rights and obligations was not easy for the common law. Just as the idea of a corporation with a separate legal identity was difficult for non-tax law, it was a challenge to the tax laws as well. The way that the United States and the Commonwealth countries solved this problem was to recognize the corporation as a separate legal actor with its own liability and its own legal rights and responsibilities. Tax law followed the non-tax law by treating the corporation as a separate taxpayer. This decision to make the corporation a separate taxpayer had the consequence of creating two taxes on what is arguably one transaction. To illustrate, Joseph and Mary form a partnership that earns $100,000. Because a partnership is not a legal entity separate from its owners, Joseph and Mary are taxed on the $100,000 whether they keep the funds in the firm for expansion or distribute the funds for their personal use. In contrast, Sarah and Abraham form a corporation that earns $100,000. Because the corporation is a separate legal entity, it is a separate taxpayer as well. The corporation is taxed on the $100,000. Should the corporation then decide to distribute some of its earnings to Sarah and Abraham, they will be taxed on that distribution: hence the double tax.

Most of US corporate tax law is devoted to enforcing this double tax regime or to providing exceptions to the double tax. Most US tax scholarship is devoted to arguments against the double tax or to strategies for avoiding the double tax. The basic argument against the double tax is that the firm is not a separate entity but merely a legal fiction. A subsidiary argument is that the corporation does not pay the tax either because the corporation does not actually exist or because it does exist but is able to pass the tax on to someone else, for example, labor or the consumer. The scholarship devoted to avoiding the double tax tends to focus on the use of techniques that arise from the specific provisions of the tax statute.

Canadian corporate tax scholarship is less related to questions of the double tax as a philosophical matter and more towards specific statutory provisions and their application. In both the United States and Canada, the interest in the corporate tax might come from the famous saying, 'That's where the money is'. Although neither government takes in a great deal of revenue from the corporate tax, corporate taxpayers are often wealthier than individuals with more opportunity to purchase tax advice and to train tax practitioners. Many tax academics in both countries started their careers as lawyers working on corporate tax matters, and so it is no surprise that their early training influences their choice of subject in their later academic careers.

2.2.3 *Wealth Transfer Taxes*

Wealth transfer taxes take up almost a tenth of the US scholarship and a twentieth of the Australian and are not mentioned much elsewhere. Given that the United States raises less than 2 percent of its tax revenues from the gift and estate tax, it is puzzling at first that so much scholarship is devoted to this tax. Unlike the US literature on corporate taxation, which is almost evenly divided between theoretical pieces on the nature of the firm, policy pieces on the corporate tax, and doctrinal/planning pieces, the US 'cross-over' tax scholarship on the wealth transfer tax is more oriented to doctrine and planning with less emphasis on theory and policy. Nevertheless, in keeping with the US tendency for large policy pieces, there are a number of works questioning whether a wealth transfer tax is justifiable at all or attacking major aspects of the tax. In contrast, the Australian pieces are all thirty to fifty years old, and almost exclusively concerned with planning and doctrine.

As to why either country should have significant scholarship in this area, I suspect that deep pockets are once again key. Although few people are affected by wealth transfer taxes, those who are have the wherewithal to hire sophisticated legal counsel who then enter the academy.

2.2.4 *Social Policy*

A tenth of Canadian tax scholarship is devoted to social policy issues, which includes works on sex discrimination, low-income taxpayers, differences in tax based on sexual preference, and distributive justice. Even in terms of absolute numbers, the Canadians have produced more works on tax and social policy than the United States. In the large set of US tax literature, there are only eight pieces on social policy, of which five concern low-income taxpayers. Australia has two pieces on sex discrimination and Britain has not a single work in this area.

2.2.5 *Process of Tax Creation*

Australians devote a significant amount of their scholarship to the process by which legislatures develop tax statutes. The United States devotes less attention to this issue as a percentage of total scholarship but more in absolute numbers. Britain and Canada are absent from this field. Given that tax legislation is significant to nations and their citizens, and that the use of influence, lobbying, media, and all forms of politics play a role in its creation, it is odd that so little attention is paid to how tax laws are made in comparison to the space devoted to their interpretation.

2.3 Focus

How much of each country's tax literature looks outside its own jurisdiction varies from nation to nation. This variance seems more related to how each country's scholars are trained than to the nation's place in the global economy. Thus, for example, the United States, whose citizens have many international investments, has very little comparative or international tax scholarship in contrast to the less developed countries with their extensive comparative literature and relatively isolated economies.

2.3.1 *The United States: Is There Anyone Else Out There?*

Although the United States dominates in terms of number of articles and pages overall, it does less well in comparative and international topics. Here I use 'comparative' to refer to literature that looks at the same question from the perspective of two or more national jurisdictions, and 'international' to refer to scholarship on how transnational transactions are treated. At least in the US 'cross-over' tax literature, there is barely a hint that there is a world outside the United States. I suspect that the reason for this absence has more to do with the way that US scholars are trained than with the nature of tax inquiry. While Europe excels in producing comparative legal scholars, the field is a bit of a backwater in the United States. As you review the other chapters in this book, I suspect that you will find this theme repeated in many other fields.

2.3.2 *Australia and Canada: United States Focused*

Australian authors have produced substantial comparative and international literature. But that scholarship is more focused on the United States than on their Asian neighbors or their Commonwealth brothers. Perhaps this has something to do with similarities between the two countries' tax systems. At least some of the focus on the United States seems to come from a combination of Australian tax academics who have trained in US law programs and US academics teaching in Australian law schools. Some other portion of the focus might be explained by the US dominance in tax scholarship in general.

In contrast with the Australians, whose work is more international than comparative, the Canadians write in both fields but with twice as much emphasis on the comparative. In addition to a strong emphasis on US law, Canadians also write about Europe and Asia. There is much less interest in South America despite the fact that Canada and Latin America share the same hemisphere.

2.3.3 *Britain: Focused on Europe*

International and comparative issues dominate British tax scholarship. Almost half of British 'cross-over' tax literature is concerned with international transactions, comparative analysis, or the European Union. Almost all of these writings are concerned with Europe and European transactions. Given the increasing pressure of global trade, especially in Europe, this trend is no surprise. Nevertheless, the fact that British writings in this area are fairly evenly distributed throughout the decades argues that Britain's colonial past plays a role here as well. More than many other nations, Britain has been at the forefront of international trade for centuries.

3 WHAT'S MISSING FROM
THE SCHOLARSHIP?

Although each nation surveyed employs many different types of taxes and each tax raises numerous issues, the scholarship as a whole tends to focus on only a few areas. In this section, I explore what is missing that one would expect to find given the statutes, systems, and histories at work in each country.

3.1 The Capital Gains Tax

The capital gains tax is a way of applying a lower rate of tax to income derived from property than to income generated from labor. In the United States, at least a third of the provisions in the Internal Revenue Code are devoted to keeping this differential-rate system in place. Yet, the fact that capital gains are so important in terms of their contribution to complexity and their reduction of progressivity, has not inspired a great deal of scholarship. For a general discussion of progressive rates in the United States, see Blum and Kalven (1952).

This is especially odd because a large portion of the political rhetoric about taxation in the United States concerns the capital gains tax. Australia, with a third of the scholarship of the United States has produced almost as much literature on capital gains.

3.2 Non-income Taxes

With the exception of some writings on the wealth transfer tax, there is very little written about any of the other tax systems that contribute to the revenue of various countries. For example, between Australia, Britain, Canada, and the United States, we find five articles on excise taxes. Because excise taxes are computed on the amount of a good sold, they are often used as 'sin' taxes to punish indulgences in alcohol, cigarettes, gasoline, and other materials that countries do not make illegal but want to control. In that one purpose of taxation is the control, discouragement, and encouragement of behavior, the success or failure of the various excise taxes would seem an interesting topic of study. Nevertheless, there is little written about these taxes in any of the countries surveyed. The same is true of sales taxes and stamp taxes. Even the value-added tax does not get much consideration. Ironically, half the articles on the value-added tax are from the United States, a country with no value-added tax. This is in line with the many articles in the United States on the consumption tax, another system not employed in the United States.

3.3 Non-central Government Taxes

Outside the Anglophone African nations, the countries surveyed here all have tax systems maintained at the local level. Often these taxes can raise significant revenues. Yet, there is very little written on state and local taxation. The United States has the largest selection of articles; but even there the subject does not produce even a tenth of the overall scholarship. In Australia, Canada, and the United Kingdom, the subject is practically non-existent in the 'cross-over' literature.

3.4 Tax Harmonization

The most striking absence from the literature is a body of work on tax harmonization. As we enter the twenty-first century, this is clearly the tax issue with the most impact on every country in the world, at least as it relates to the question of sovereignty.

Tax harmonization results from the pressure that each country faces to shape its tax laws for the benefit of international trade. In Africa, the pressure comes from the World Bank and the International Monetary Fund, when a country is forced to adopt certain taxes or abandon others in exchange for finance. In the United Kingdom, pressure comes into play as the European Union makes greater and greater demands for uniform tax systems among its members. In Canada and the United States, the pressure comes from OECD membership and the attempts of OECD countries to create tax cartels that dictate to other countries the 'acceptable' tax rules for so called 'tax havens'.

Taxation is perhaps the greatest sign of sovereignty that any country has. How tax laws are shaped affects the balance of power within a society and reflects each nation's cultural constructs of fairness. Now, with the increasing dominance of international trade and globalization, pressure is building on nations to shape their laws for the benefit of multinational companies who desire one uniform tax system wherever they travel. The increasing mobility of capital makes this demand compelling. As noted above, countries are already caught up in this call for harmonization. At present, the more developed countries, led by the OECD, have the upper hand in their insistence that less developed countries shape their tax laws for the benefit of Western capital. Soon, this capital will be able to enforce its requirements without relying on countries to push its agenda. When that happens, as it is already happening in such areas as environmental and labor law, even the OECD nations will have to give up part of their sovereignty in favor of harmonization.

This is the most striking absence from the literature. It is certainly where tax scholarship must proceed in the near future.

REFERENCES

Andrews, W. (1972). 'Personal Deduction in an Ideal Income Tax', *Harvard Law Review*, 86: 309–85.

Avi-Yonah, R. S. (2000). 'Globalization, Tax Competition, and the Fiscal Crisis of the Welfare State', *Harvard Law Review*, 113/7: 1573–676.

Bird, R. M., and Oldman, O. (eds.) (1990). *Taxation in Developing Countries*, Baltimore: Johns Hopkins University Press.

Blejer, M. I., and Ter-Minassian, T. (eds.) (1997). *Fiscal Policy and Economic Reform: Essays in honor of Vito Tanzi*, London and New York: Routledge.

Blum, W. J., and Kalven, H., Jr. (1952). 'Uneasy Case for Progressive Taxation', *University of Chicago Law Review*, 19: 417–520.

Brooks, N. (1985). 'Future Directions in Canadian Tax Scholarship', *Osgood Hall Law Journal*, 3: 441–76.

Cnossen, S. (1983). 'Comparative Tax Studies: Essays in Honor of Richard Goode', Amsterdam: North-Holland.

Douglas, R. (1990). *Taxation in Britain since 1660*, Basingstoke: Macmillan.

Goode, R. (1993). 'Tax Advice to Developing Countries: An Historical Survey', *World Developments*, 21/1: 37–53.

Gratz, M. (1979). 'Implementing a Progressive Consumption Tax', *Harvard Law Review*, 92: 1575–661.

Jones, M. (1990). 'How long can she last?' *The Sunday Times*, 25 Mar.

Moran, B. I. (1992). 'Income Tax Rhetoric (Or Why Do We Want Tax Reform?)', *Wisconsin Law Review*, 2063–7.

—— (2001). 'Homogenized Law: What the United States Can Learn from African Mistakes', *Fordham International Law Journal*, 25/2: 361–90.

Schneider, D. (1999). 'Interpreting the Interpreters: Assessing Forty-five Years of Tax literature', *Florida Tax Review*, 4: 483–536.

Surrey, S. (1970). 'Tax Incentives as a Device for Implementing Government Policy: A Comparision with Direct Government Expenditures', *Harvard Law Review*, 83: 705–38.

—— (1973). *Pathways to Tax Reform: The Concept of Tax Expenditures*, Cambridge, Mass.: Harvard Univesity Press.

Terkper, S. (1996). 'VAT in Ghana: Why it Failed', *Tax Notes International*, 12: 1801–16.

CHAPTER 19

THE WELFARE STATE

NICK WIKELEY

At the outset it must be recognized that the corpus of *legal* scholarship about the Welfare State remains somewhat limited when contrasted with the extensive literature in other academic disciplines. For many economists, historians, political scientists, sociologists, and scholars of social policy, the Welfare State is at the core of their endeavour. In such disciplines, books and learned journal articles are regularly devoted to analyses of competing conceptions of the purpose, scope, and effectiveness of the Welfare State. Given that welfare spending is the largest single component of public expenditure in most advanced economies, this hive of scholarly activity is hardly surprising. Yet, in contrast, the Welfare State is seen as a marginal area of scholarship by the great majority of academic lawyers. Connections may be made from time to time by scholars in public law and the law of torts—most notably by Atiyah's path-breaking work on compensation systems (Atiyah, 1970)—but the subject is approached from the perspective of the core legal discipline. Thus scholarly writing by jurists which has the Welfare State at its heart is the exception rather than the rule. This disciplinary imbalance is starkly illustrated in the volume edited by Robson (1992) on *Welfare Law* in the International Library of Essays in Law and Legal Theory: just five of the twenty-five contributions, drawn from the period from 1954 to 1988, were the work of legal scholars.

But what do we mean by the Welfare State? For present purposes, a useful starting-point is the definition provided by the social historian Derek Fraser (1984), whilst

Professor Neville Harris's invaluable comments on a draft of this chapter are acknowledged.

recognizing that a range of other conceptions have been developed. Fraser describes the Welfare State as a system of social organization which restricts the operation of the free market in three principal ways. First, the Welfare State designates certain groups within society as in need of protection (e.g. children at risk). Secondly, it delivers services such as education and health care to members of the community irrespective of means. Thirdly, the Welfare State operates a system of transfer payments which serve to maintain an individual's income in times of need, for example, when earnings are interrupted by sickness or unemployment, or as an extra source of financial support during parenthood.

Fraser's paradigm undoubtedly has its weaknesses, not least as it is heavily influenced by the British experience. In particular, his model highlights the role of cash transfer payments whilst, as Titmuss (1968) observed, fiscal measures in the form of tax allowances and reliefs should be seen as a mechanism for delivering welfare (see further below). Moreover, Fraser's typology assumes that the delivery of welfare is predominantly, if not exclusively, the function of central and local government. But Titmuss (1968) also noted the growing importance in the advanced Welfare State of occupational welfare through job-related fringe benefits and pensions. We return later to the intersections with occupational benefits and the tax system in particular and their implications for legal scholarship. The late twentieth century has also seen an increasing shift towards other forms of delivery for welfare. This is particularly evident in the United States, where the Personal Responsibility and Work Opportunity Reconciliation Act of 1996 allowed states to contract out the administration of welfare through the Temporary Assistance for Needy Families (TANF) programme to private organizations.

The coverage of the Welfare State may thus be seen in still broader terms. For Cranston (1985)—one of the few major works of legal scholarship which has sought to undertake a more comprehensive approach—the essence of the Welfare State revolves around 'government-protected minimum standards of income, nutrition, health, housing and education, assured to every citizen as a political right, not as charity'. Cranston's own study of the legal foundations of the Welfare State concentrated on such minimum standards in so far as they related to rented housing, social welfare benefits, and access to legal services. Seen in this way, evidently choices have had to be made about the coverage of legal scholarship in this chapter. The primary focus here is on income maintenance by cash transfers, or social security. This is the most important common theme in the studies by both Fraser and Cranston and is moreover, in popular discourse, seen as the principal business associated with the Welfare State.

The social security function of the Welfare State was quintessentially the product of (and a response to) the pressures generated by the development of mass democracies in the advanced economies of the early part of the twentieth century. However, with a handful of notable exceptions, it is only in the last forty years that serious legal scholarship on the modern Welfare State has emerged. Relatively little had been written on the subject prior to 1960 and most of that corpus of work was fundamentally descriptive rather than analytical in nature. This chapter seeks to explore the nature, direction, and future of such scholarship and accordingly has three main sections.

The first outlines the development of legal scholarship since 1960 on the principles and operation of the main arm of the Welfare State, namely income maintenance systems, and how that scholarship reflects national welfare structures. The second explores the central themes in that scholarship and the third endeavours to highlight the principal issues for future research in this field.

1 THE DEVELOPMENT OF LEGAL SCHOLARSHIP ON THE WELFARE STATE

It is axiomatic that we are all prisoners of our past. Legal scholarship about the Welfare State is no different in that within various countries there is a tendency for such writing to reflect the prevalent and jurisdiction-specific Welfare State model. For example, in the United Kingdom the framework for the modern Welfare State was established by the National Insurance Act 1911, which introduced sickness and unemployment insurance. These schemes in turn formed the basis for the creation of a 'universal' British system of social insurance by the post-World War II Labour government, following the recommendations of the Beveridge Report in 1942. However, the first scholarly monographs on the subject of social security law appeared in the United Kingdom only in (relatively) recent years. Thus, the first edition of Calvert's *Social Security Law* was published in 1974 and the first edition of Ogus and Barendt's *The Law of Social Security* followed in 1978, the same year as the second (and indeed last) edition of Calvert's book appeared. Both books were structured around a conception of the Welfare State in the terms of Beveridge's ideal vision: in particular, the central role of the contributory system and the primacy of national insurance benefits (such as those established by the 1911 Act and subsequent reforms). General means-tested benefits, such as supplementary benefits, for those marginalized members of society who failed to qualify for one of the main contributory benefits, were relegated to the final chapters of each book. In the United Kingdom at least, most of the early journal literature on social security law adopted the same approach. Thus, throughout the 1960s and the greater part of the 1970s, much of the juristic analysis of social security law which appeared in periodicals was primarily concerned with the mainstream national insurance benefits. Indeed, well into the 1970s social security law was typically seen as a subset of labour law—for many years the *Industrial Law Journal* was alone in the United Kingdom in providing a regular home to legal scholarship about social security issues. Standard labour law texts of the time typically included a 'bolt-on' section devoted to social security, but driven by its relationship to employment status.

Since the late 1970s, the focus of much British writing on the law of the Welfare State has moved away from this preoccupation with the labour market aspects of social security provision. This may be a response to the empirical social research agenda which had identified the problem of family and child poverty in the 1960s and the growing dependence of many low-income families on means-tested benefits. There was also an increasing realization, engineered by feminist scholarship (Wilson, 1977), that the system of contributory benefits, the mainstay of Beveridge's scheme of social insurance, perpetuated the gendered nature of the Welfare State. Typically, women with children failed to build up an adequate national insurance record and so were less likely to be able to establish an independent right to a contributory benefit. If living with a partner, a woman would be regarded as a dependant of the male 'head of household'. If living alone, she would be reliant on means-tested benefits.

This shift towards a wider conception of the Welfare State was reflected, somewhat belatedly in British academic legal circles, with the establishment of the *Journal of Social Welfare Law* (or *JSWL*) in 1978. The *JSWL* sought to cover a wide spectrum of material relating to law and social policy but with a strong emphasis on applied rather than theoretical issues. The journal's remit, modelled on Fraser's conception of the British Welfare State, was from the outset *social welfare* and not just *social security*, and included such matters as education, family law, housing, and juvenile justice. Indeed, the journal's increasing emphasis on the family law and social policy aspects of welfare law led to its renaming in 1991 as the *Journal of Social Welfare and Family Law* (or *JSWFL*). The first British academic legal journal to be devoted exclusively to the core activity of the modern Welfare State, the *Journal of Social Security Law* (or *JSSL*) did not appear until 1994.

The contents of a typical issue of the *JSSL* demonstrate how far British legal scholarship in this area has moved from the industrial or labour law model of social security. Extensive coverage is given to means-tested benefits, tax credits, and general disability benefits, whilst the modern-day British equivalent of unemployment benefit, contribution-based jobseeker's allowance, barely merits a mention. A similar approach to the Welfare State, reflecting the reality of the modern benefits system today, is evident in the first substantial new British textbook in the area since Ogus and Barendt, Harris's *Social Security Law in Context* (2000). Indeed, the most recent edition of Ogus and Barendt itself has been radically restructured to shift the prime focus away from the paradigm of contributory benefits (Wikeley *et al.*, 2002). But it is not simply that such scholarship adopts a broader conception of the scope of social security law; it is also avowedly interdisciplinary in its approach. Harris (2000), for example, engages with the literature from social policy and to a lesser extent from economics in order to set the framework for the book's analysis of social security law. However, the adoption of this broader perspective is challenging for the legal scholar, given that the literature on the Welfare State in these other disciplines is vast, diverse (covering the whole range from highly theoretical to unashamedly empirical studies with everything in between) and indeed, in places, uneven in terms of its quality.

Thus it remains the case that most scholarship on social security law emanating from British universities is firmly rooted in the technical tradition (Robson, 1992). There may be a number of further reasons for this. First, in some jurisdictions—most

notably the United States—federal and state governments enjoy different competencies in delivering welfare programmes (e.g. unemployment insurance is a state
responsibility). Consequently, American scholars are more naturally drawn to teas-
ing out theoretical issues rather than concentrating on an analysis of a myriad of
detailed regional arrangements. In contrast, the existence of a unitary system of
social security across Great Britain, with comparatively little scope for diversity in
local provision, has encouraged a focus on the content of such national legislation.
Moreover, once jurists adopt that perspective, the rapid pace of change in the statutory provisions governing social security means that their scholarship is typically in
responsive mode. Secondly, and compounding this tendency towards technicalism,
Great Britain is relatively unusual in having both a well-established specialized system of local social security tribunals and an expert appellate tier at national level (the
Social Security Commissioners). The origins of both date back to the original 1911
scheme and the jurisdiction of the latter is almost exclusively confined to points of
law (the Commissioners have a peculiar original jurisdiction to determine cases of
forfeiture, typically where a widow convicted of the murder or manslaughter of her
late husband is denied a bereavement benefit). To a greater extent, therefore, than
other common law systems, the British Welfare State has developed its own extensive
body of judicial precedent. Yet, unlike in private law, this body of doctrine is wholly
parasitic upon the statutory superstructure. In contrast, relatively few social security
cases in America proceed beyond the stage of a hearing before an administrative law
judge and there is no specialist national welfare court. In Australia, social security
appeal tribunals are a relatively recent innovation (dating only from 1980; between
1975 and 1980 they had a purely 'advisory' function) and appeals from these tribunals
are simply one aspect of the work of the Administrative Appeals Tribunal (AAT).
Additionally, the AAT exercises a jurisdiction based on merits review, rather than
being confined to points of law. (In addition, owing to a curiosity of the Australian
constitutional system, the AAT does not formally exercise a judicial function.)
Consequently, in contrast to the position in the other main common law systems,
doctrinal analysis of the decisions of the Social Security Commissioners has been
assumed by British social security scholars to be one of their core functions.

This positivist influence is apparent in both legal periodicals and books on the
Welfare State. For example, for many years the *JSWL* carried a regular section
analysing 'Recent Social Security Commissioners' Decisions'. Although the *JSWFL*
no longer retains that section, half of each issue of the *JSSL* is devoted to its 'Digest',
summarizing both the many changes to social security law by primary and more particularly secondary legislation and Commissioners' decisions. These journals have
served a valuable function, given the haphazard reporting of social security decisions
in the United Kingdom (indeed, for the greater part of the 1990s, the official series of
Commissioners' decisions simply dried up altogether, hindering both scholarship
and teaching in this area). As regards books, the major publication on social security
law (in terms of both sales and the level of detail in its technical analysis) is the

comprehensive *Social Security Legislation* (Bonner, 2002). This is published annually in three weighty volumes amounting, in 2002, to a total of over 3,200 pages of annotated primary and secondary legislation—not counting the separate volumes on child support and housing benefit law. This positivist bias in British legal scholarship about the Welfare State has resulted in an increasingly close relationship between academics working in the field of social security law and the specialist judiciary in the appeal tribunals and amongst the Commissioners. Since its reconfiguration in the late 1970s, the tribunal system has relied heavily on university law teachers and researchers for the delivery of its in-house training programmes. Moreover, in recent years, academics have been appointed to part-time tribunal chairman or Commissioner posts, or indeed have left the academy altogether for full-time judicial appointments in these jurisdictions. This symbiosis undoubtedly has its advantages, not least in terms of providing a practical judicial insight into the resolution of doctrinal issues and by way of assisting in securing access for empirical research projects. But this focus has arguably been at the cost of an undue focus on doctrine over theory in the British literature.

In the light of these factors, it is no surprise that much legal scholarship about the Welfare State emanating from British jurists is ethnocentric in character (but, in fairness, the same can also be said of the United States: Robson, 1992). For example, we have seen that British legal scholarship in this area is heavily focused on domestic provision of social security. True, the intranational and international impact of European law is acknowledged, both in terms of ensuring equal treatment for men and women in social security under national law and for migrant workers who move round the European Union. Similarly, the profile of the Strasbourg jurisprudence in the domain of social security has inevitably been enhanced by the incorporation of the European Convention on Human Rights into British law by the Human Rights Act 1998. That said, it is rare to see any reference to other forms of international norms relating to social security provision in either the scholarly literature or the case law. It is as though the European Social Charter is implicitly seen as the exclusive province of texts on European human rights law. Certainly, it is rarely referred to in the domestic social security literature, even where British social security legislation has been found to be in breach of the Charter. For example, domestic law imposes a 'habitual residence' test, which stipulates that claimants should have completed an 'appreciable' period of time in the country before they can qualify for any of the main means-tested benefits. The European Committee of Social Rights has held that such a requirement, applied to non-nationals with a legal right of abode, is inconsistent with the right to social assistance under article 13(1) of the Charter.

As in Great Britain, much of the legal scholarship about the Welfare State within the other advanced economies typically reflects prevailing welfare ideologies and systems. Within the rest of Western Europe, the origins of the Welfare State are usually traced back to the 1880s and Bismarck's introduction of invalidity and old age pensions and a workers' compensation scheme in the nascent German state. Today, in both France and Germany, the 'social partners', in the form of capital and labour, retain a powerful role in the realm of social protection. In both countries, although there are some national and universal schemes, social insurance is organized in large part on a sectoral basis (thus, membership is based on occupational classification, with separate schemes for professionals, civil servants, agricultural workers, and so on), whilst regional administrations have a much enhanced role in the provision of social assistance (see e.g. on France, Dupeyroux, 2001). In several European states (e.g. Spain), there is a joint Ministry of Labour and Social Affairs. These structures continue to influence the shape of legal scholarship on the Welfare State in mainland Europe, where social security law is still seen as closely allied to collective labour law. This tradition is reflected in the fact that the main European network for legal scholarship in this field is the International Society for Labour Law and Social Security. For example, the third (and only social security-inspired strand) of the three principal themes of its 2002 Congress in Stockholm (freedom of movement and transfer of social security rights) demonstrates the parasitical nature of such legal scholarship.

Indeed, this approach, focusing on the Welfare State through the prism of the labour market relationship, has also been central to the development of European Union social policy over the last half century. One of the Union's very first legislative acts (Regulation 3/58) established a mechanism for the protection of migrant workers' social security rights; it was then another two decades before the next major practical initiative in social security protection was to take place. Council Directive 79/7 requires equal treatment of men and women in matters of social security, but again its scope is limited to those benefits which are in some way linked to labour market status. Thus, it has no application to social assistance benefits designed solely to relieve poverty, irrespective of cause. Legal scholarship about the Welfare State on the pan-European level remains locked into this way of thinking. Hence the major topic of juristic debate in the new *European Journal of Social Security* revolves around the European Commission's controversial proposals for a radical recasting of Regulation 1408/71 on the social security rights of migrant workers (the immediate successor to Regulation 3/58).

A very different picture of Welfare State legal scholarship is apparent in North America, or, to be precise, the United States (Canada's Welfare State is in many respects closer to those that exist in Europe, as reflected in its legal scholarship). The European model of the Welfare State—whether in its predominant Bismarckian form in mainland Western Europe, or in the somewhat attenuated Beveridge version in Britain—is premised on a shared political value of social solidarity. True, both the Beveridge and Bismarckian forms prioritize the worker's 'earned' right to contributory benefits over any citizen's access to 'gratuitous' means-tested and tax-funded social assistance. Yet the discourse of America's residualist Welfare State has traditionally been even more individualistic, drawing a much firmer distinction between social security (meaning principally disability and old-age social insurance) and welfare (in the narrow sense of means-tested public assistance). According to this value system, the latter connotes 'the morally inferior status of reliance on income not acquired through effort and exchange' (Simon, 1986). Indeed, it was not until the Great Depression of the interwar years that the United States introduced a rudimentary form of social security through the Social Security Act 1935. There are aspects of the American literature on the Welfare State which are similar to the technical and labour law approaches commonly found in Europe, for example, much of the writing about the legal aspects of unemployment insurance and workers' compensation. But the best scholarly work from the United States has been by academicians in the field of public law. Their work has tended to operate at a more sophisticated level of theoretical analysis, certainly than that typically found in Great Britain. The reasons for this are, no doubt, in part the converse of those factors discussed above that have resulted in a more technical approach in the latter jurisdiction. It may also, in any event, reflect the greater emphasis on theoretical approaches in American public law scholarship (see Ch. 8). Bearing that intellectual baggage in mind, we now turn to consider the influence of one of the principal American contributions to the jurisprudence of the Welfare State, Reich's concept of new property rights, along with some of the other main themes in this area of legal scholarship.

2 Central Themes in Legal Scholarship on the Welfare State

This section explores three central themes which may be identified in legal scholarship on the Welfare State over the past half-century: the scope of welfare rights; the role of discretion; and the use of law as an instrument of social control. Of these the first and arguably the dominant theme—associated with the work of Reich (1964 and 1965)—has concerned the notion of rights to welfare.

The citizen's significant encounter now is not with the policeman or the criminal magistrate but with the official representing a regulatory authority, an administration of social insurances, or a state-operated economic enterprise. It is this dramatically increased incidence of encounter that sets the task of the rule of law in the welfare state . . . New expectations progressively brought into existence by the welfare state must be thought of not as privileges to be dispensed unequally or by arbitrary fiat of government officials but as substantial rights in the assertion of which the claimant is entitled to an effective remedy, a fair procedure, and a reasoned decision.

This extract is in fact from Jones (1958), who receives one footnoted reference in two seminal articles by Reich (1964 and 1965). Thus the fundamental concept underlying the latter's analysis of rights in the Welfare State was not, of itself, original. Jones, however, approached the question from a conventional 'rule of law' perspective. Reich's work developed and popularized the idea in legal discourse at a time when governments on both sides of the Atlantic were expanding social security programmes. Moreover, as Simon (1986) has observed, Reich's critical innovation was to blur the distinction between social insurance and public assistance and to extend the concept of rights to the latter type of programme. The notion of rights in social insurance programmes was relatively unproblematic, given the contractual private law analogy—however tenuous in practice—with contributions to a public law insurance scheme. The proposition that benefits by way of public assistance, which had conventionally been seen as mere gratuities, could also be allied to private law norms as a form of 'new property' was more radical.

The primary emphasis in both Jones's preliminary sketch and in the more panoramic landscapes by Reich was on *procedural* rather than *substantive* rights. At the very least, this reflects the lawyer's traditional concerns with issues of due process. Reich's concept of a 'new property' soon had an impact on US public law. In *Goldberg v Kelly* (397 US 254 (1970)) the Supreme Court accepted that the receipt of welfare was not simply a privilege to be withdrawn at the will of the executive; instead a welfare claimant was entitled to a fair hearing before benefits could be terminated. The 'new property' analysis was acknowledged in a footnote to that opinion. But the influence of Reich's work was limited to that of a footnote; indeed, *Goldberg v Kelly* was arguably the highpoint of this judicial approach. Other landmark decisions in the United States have demonstrated that the 'new property' philosophy has had only a limited impact on judicial reasoning, with the result that the notion that a claimant has a substantive right to welfare remains at best fragile. True, in *Shapiro v Thompson* (394 US 618 (1969)) the Supreme Court had struck down residence clauses in state welfare schemes, that is, those which bar recent arrivals from access to public assist-ance for a year (redolent of the Law of Settlement which was a central feature of the British Poor Law, whereby parishes sought to remove paupers to their parish of ori-gin). But this was on the basis of the constitutional (and market-driven) right to inter-state travel, not on any principles drawn from the ideology of 'new property' (Bussiere, 1997). Furthermore, in subsequent decisions, the Supreme Court declined to acknowledge welfare as a fundamental right (*Dandridge v Williams* (397 US 471 (1970)) and restricted the due process requirement for a pre-termination hearing (*Mathews v Eldridge* (424 US 319 (1976)). That said, more recently the Supreme Court has struck down restrictions in California law which had sought to limit welfare pay-ments in the first year of residence to the (typically lower) levels paid in the recipient's previous state of residence (*Saenz v Roe* (526 US 489 (1999)). This decision, based on the rarely invoked Privileges or Immunity Clause of the Fourteenth Amendment, expresses a more solidaristic concept of entitlement derived from notions of citizenship.

The preoccupation with procedural over substantive rights has also been mirrored in British scholarship on the Welfare State. Throughout the 1970s and the 1980s, scholars—often from outside the narrow legal academy—debated the respective roles of 'law' and 'discretion' in the Welfare State. From a social policy perspective, there were dangers inherent in the 'pathology of legalism' (Titmuss, 1971). On the other hand, the analysis of the philosopher and political scientist indicated that the application of both rules and discretion could generate precisely the same types of problem (e.g. arbitrariness, unpredictability, and intrusiveness) (Goodin, 1986). Much of the British socio-legal scholarship of this period tended to focus on the one feature of the Welfare State in which the two issues of procedural justice and the 'law versus discretion' debate came to the fore: the operation of social security tribunals (as in Adler and Bradley, 1976; see also Fulbrook, 1978, a classic study which also exemplifies the labour law roots of social security law in Great Britain). This has remained a recurrent and arguably unique theme of the British scholarship on the work of tribunals, which has always had a strong applied orientation (Prosser, 1977, being one of the best illustrations of a more theory-driven approach). In contrast, although overall there appears to have been relatively little activity by American scholars in the field of dispute resolution in the Welfare State, the study by Mashaw (1983) has been hugely influential in terms of setting the agenda for subsequent research (especially in the United Kingdom). Mashaw's major contribution, aside from developing different theoretical models of administrative justice, was to emphasize the importance of first-tier decision-making within welfare bureaucracies. In Australia, however, although the function and role of tribunals has assumed much greater significance in public law scholarship than in other common law jurisdictions (see Ch. 8), the debate has largely been conducted in an environment in which the claimant's voice is notably absent. Thus, whereas there is a considerable body of socio-legal work on the actual operation of British tribunals, especially those adjudicating claims on the Welfare State, the Australian literature is conspicuous for the fact that there are no major empirical studies examining the operation of social security tribunals. It is, of course, by no means unknown for policy-makers elsewhere to seek to implement significant changes to appeals systems by pursuing a managerialist agenda with little regard for the existing empirical evidence as to appellants' perceptions of fairness and justice (Wikeley, 2000).

There has also, I would argue, been a tendency at times for the 'law versus discretion' debate to distort the scholarly agenda on the Welfare State, especially in the United Kingdom. This was particularly the case with the Fowler Reviews of the mid-1980s, when Margaret Thatcher's Conservative government launched a major overhaul of social security provision. Legal scholars—the present writer included—focused their attention on the controversial proposal to abolish the statutory right of supplementary benefit claimants to 'single payments'. This form of benefit was paid to meet the costs of 'one-off' lump-sum costs (e.g. the cost of a new cooker or bed) which could not be met from normal weekly benefit levels. In its place, the Social Security Act 1986 introduced the social fund, a system of discretionary loans (and, in limited cases, grants) with a capped budget, unlike the demand-led single payments scheme. As the social fund also involved the abolition of the right of appeal to an independent tribunal, this change challenged two precepts fundamental to the lawyer's mind-set: the twin values of entitlement enshrined in law and procedural justice.

Indeed, on the basis of the pages of the *Modern Law Review* and *Public Law*, the reader could be forgiven for thinking that the social fund *was* the Social Security Act 1986. Yet the social fund accounts for less than 1 per cent of all social security expenditure in Great Britain. (And, in any event, although the social fund remains seriously flawed, discretion has been replaced by formulaic computer-driven assessments of eligibility as a result of the Social Security Act 1998, and the review system for social fund decisions has generally been regarded by analysts as a success.) The major issue in the 1986 Act for the social security system was the government's decision to cut back on the generosity of the State Earnings Related Pension Scheme (SERPS). However, pensions provision has rarely featured prominently in the scholarly legal literature, a neglect that has continued to the present day. This is not just a failing of scholars who specialize in the Welfare State: how many undergraduate public law courses in British universities still make tired references to the Crichel Down affair of 1953? But arguably by far the most significant (and undoubtedly the most costly) example of official maladministration in the latter half of the last century involved the DSS's persistent failure, throughout the 1990s, to provide contributors with accurate information about the implications of the 1986 SERPS changes—a neglect which it is estimated will cost about £12 billion to rectify.

The third recurring theme in legal scholarship around the institutions and practices of the Welfare State is that of law as an instrument of social control. Many of the concerns which dominated public discourse about the poor and the Poor Law in earlier centuries—the need to maintain work incentives, the growth of an 'underclass', the problems of lone parenthood—thus remain the fundamental currency of contemporary debates about the modern Welfare State. The 'social control' model is especially evident in the US literature (a prime example being Piven and Cloward, 1993). The focus on the operation of the 'cohabitation rule' in both the United States and the United Kingdom during the 1960s and 1970s demonstrates the enduring influence of this theme in the literature. The effect of the 'cohabitation rule' rule was that a woman who was found to be living together with a male partner 'as husband and wife' would be treated as a member of an unmarried couple. If he was in work, she would lose any entitlement to means-tested benefits and be regarded in the eyes of social security law as his dependant—whilst private family law would recognize no obligation of support. The cohabitation rule inevitably raised issues of privacy as well as the proper place for the exercise of discretion in decision-making in the Welfare State. The American courts ruled on challenges to the 'man in the house' rules in welfare schemes (e.g. *King v Smith* 392 US 309 (1968)), as did the Australian and British courts a decade or so later (e.g. *Lambe v Director-General of Social Services* (1981) 57 FLR 262 and *Crake v Supplementary Benefits Commission* [1982] 1 All ER 498).

The 'social control' model also explains (if it has not already been adequately explained by the intellectual roots of the subject in Great Britain) the attention given by scholars to the role of social security law in labour disputes in the 1970s. There is, however, a danger that social control interpretations can 'degenerate into crude functionalism, lacking explanatory power' (Cranston, 1985). Arguably the most valuable analysis to adopt a social control perspective is found in the literature which has explored the legally prescribed boundaries of capacity and incapacity for work for the purpose of entitlement to benefit. An overriding concern of the Poor Law was to differentiate between the 'deserving' and 'undeserving' poor, a legacy which continues to impact upon contemporary social security policy. As Handler (1990) has argued, 'the heart of poverty policy centers on the question of who is excused from work'. Some of the most impressive work in this field has drawn on theories of the social construction of disability and incapacity to show how the boundaries drawn in benefit schemes ultimately reflect moral choices about the nature and extent of the social obligation to work (Diller, 1996).

Yet the 'social control' school of legal scholarship about the Welfare State remains fundamentally reactive in nature. This stands in marked contrast to the corpus of literature emanating from social policy analysts which has been so influential in recent years in shaping governmental welfare policy. Conservative administrations, especially in the United Kingdom and the United States, were swift to adopt the language of Charles Murray (1984) in identifying welfare dependency as the fundamental problem facing the modern Welfare State, arguing that long-term receipt of benefits eroded individual initiative and personal responsibility. In the United States in particular, 'workfare' programmes (with work requirements being linked to the receipt of benefits) became a key instrument of official welfare policy. These ideas were developed by other writers, principally Lawrence Mead (1987) and David Ellwood (1988). Mead's explanation for poverty focused on individual rather than structural reasons: the prime reason for poverty is identified as non-work; the long-term poor lack 'competence' in the labour market; ergo official policy should be directed towards enforcing the work obligation. Ellwood's approach shares with Mead and Murray the emphasis on the primacy of the individual responsibility to engage in paid employment. However, Ellwood then advocates that the state should stipulate a minimum wage policy and operate benefits and tax policies to ensure that a family is left with an income above the official poverty line. This analysis has been instrumental in more recent years in the development of in-work benefits and other welfare-to-work strategies by centre-left governments.

3 CONTEMPORARY QUESTIONS FOR MODERN LEGAL SCHOLARSHIP ON THE WELFARE STATE

There are a number of major challenges which need to be addressed by scholars working on the Welfare State today. This section identifies three such areas. The first is the need to develop the legal literature in relation to the largest part of the Welfare State's activity (i.e. pensions). The second is to respond to significant changes in the administration and delivery of welfare, for example, through so-called 'activation programmes' and via the taxation system. The third goal should be to integrate the rich literature on the legal theory of rights in the Welfare State into the applied legal scholarship in the same sphere.

First, much of the literature to date is concerned, directly or indirectly, with social security as a form of income transfer to the socially excluded. The archetypal recipient—the claimant—is the disabled person, the lone parent, or the individual who is either jobless or on the fringes of the labour market. Yet arguably this approach ignores the main business of the Welfare State. Thus between two-thirds and three-quarters of such social expenditure in the United Kingdom takes the form of life-cycle redistribution, whereas only a third (or less) is devoted to poverty relief. In quantitative terms, as Barr (2001) has demonstrated, the Welfare State's key function is as a piggy-bank. The starting-point for Barr's analysis is familiar territory: for the past half-century social policy in the industrialized world has been based on three implicit assumptions: first, that constraints on economic policy were principally domestic; secondly, that employment was binary (an individual was either employed full-time or out of work); thirdly, that the 'nuclear family' was the typical (and stable) social relationship. All three assumptions have been undermined. Globalization has limited the extent to which governments can pursue independent fiscal policies; labour markets have become more flexible, with 'atypical work' becoming a normal feature of the labour market; divorce and separation have likewise become commonplace. Barr's conclusion is that 'to a greater extent than previously, people need to be able to carry their welfare state on their back like a snail shell'. For economists, therefore, pensions, being central to individuals' long-term financial security, are the key issue in the modern Welfare State. Yet in much of the legal literature on the Welfare State pensions are invisible. Such scholarship as there is has tended to focus on equality of treatment in pension rights, reflecting the activity in the European Union case law on the point. Other contributions by jurists have tended to be somewhat fragmented, focusing on the trusts law or collective labour law aspects of pensions provision, rather than analysing private and public sector pension regimes in a holistic manner.

Secondly, and drawing on Barr's emphasis on individualization, the notion of a homogeneous, monolithic Welfare State can be seen very much as a twentieth-century construct which appears increasingly difficult to sustain in the modern era. For example, governments across the globe are placing much greater emphasis on 'activation programmes' for those outside the labour market. Initially, and especially during the 1980s, such programmes were typically instigated by right of centre governments and were confined to the long-term unemployed, involving greater emphasis on monitoring compliance with eligibility criteria (e.g. that claimants be available for and actively seeking employment; see, on the Canadian experience, Campeau, 2001). In more recent years, there has been a qualitative change in the nature of these initiatives in two respects. First, claimants who previously would have been seen as outside the labour market have been included within their scope—most notably lone parents. This is exemplified by the Clinton administration's Personal Responsibility and Work Opportunity Reconciliation Act of 1996 and the Blair government's introduction of 'work-focused interviews' for lone parents. These developments have taken place along side efforts to improve child support collection rates as part of a 'stick and carrot' welfare-to-work strategy. Secondly, governments have attempted to transform the role of front-line staff in welfare bureaucracies from passive administrators of benefit schemes to case managers seeking to facilitate the claimant's eventual escape from the 'dependency culture'. Closely associated with this phenomenon has been a trend towards imposing greater conditionality on benefit entitlement, drawing on the thinking of Murray (1984) and Mead (1987). Reflecting how far we have moved from Reich's analysis, the argument is that receipt of benefits brings with it responsibilities as well as rights. For example, at the time of writing, the British government appears to be actively considering measures such as the withdrawal of the 'universal' child benefit from parents who fail to prevent their children's persistent truancy, and of housing benefit from those tenants whose families engage in 'anti-social behaviour'. Today, therefore, the 'new property' ideology appears increasingly static and unable to respond to these modern developments in social security. Instead, welfare contractualism or reciprocity, rather than entitlement based on citizenship, is seen as one of the core values of the Welfare State. The challenge for contemporary legal scholars is to work through the implications of these developments. In particular, the legal architecture of the traditional Welfare State dispute-resolution process, based on claims adjudication by merits review tribunals, may require modification to accommodate the new way of delivering welfare (Carney, 1998).

In addition, returning to Titmuss's (1968) analysis of the scope of welfare, the increasing importance of fiscal measures as a means of furthering governmental social policy objectives needs to be recognized. Australia, Britain, and the United States have all seen a shift towards the tax system as a means of delivering welfare. In the United States, the Clinton administration introduced and rapidly expanded the Earned Income Tax Credit at the same time as traditional welfare programmes were cut back, in keeping with the analysis by Ellwood (1988). Both Australia and Britain have also seen similar initiatives with the introduction of the Family Tax Payments scheme and tax credits respectively. At the very least, the traditional boundaries of scholarship on social security law will have to be redrawn to reflect these changes. For example, British scholars will have to recognize that social security law is not just a study of the legal aspects of the work of the Department of Social Security (renamed in 2001, with a telling ideological resonance, as the Department for Work and Pensions). Instead, and especially with the advent of the Tax Credits Act 2002, the role of the Inland Revenue has become central to the British Welfare State.

Finally, we have already seen that a central theme of much legal scholarship in social security has been the role of welfare rights. Typically, welfare rights are seen in the context of citizenship theory developed by scholars of social policy. Yet, there is a rich literature on social justice in the realm of moral and political philosophy which is also of relevance (e.g. in the work of Dworkin and Rawls). Dworkin's principles of egalitarian justice would certainly support the argument that it is entirely appropriate to attach conditions to the receipt of benefit. The Rawlsian *Theory of Justice*, on the other hand, would appear to allocate primary goods unconditionally through the Difference Principle. Leaving aside these overarching theories of justice, there has been a great deal of work specifically on the philosophical justifications for a basic income (see e.g. Van Parijs, 1992). The work of many social security scholars is remarkable for the absence of connections with this theoretical literature. At the very least, there is scope for an analysis of the growing trend towards conditionality or reciprocity in benefit entitlement in the context of these theoretical models.

4 CONCLUSION

The last section outlined some of the fundamental issues facing contemporary and future legal scholarship on the Welfare State. Many of the policy developments in the advanced Welfare States, whether in the common law world or not, share common themes—activation programmes for the jobless, greater emphasis on fiscal welfare and private pension provision, 'streamlining' of decision-making and appeals systems. However, legal scholarship in this area remains obstinately ethnocentric. At the same time, this branch of academic research faces a number of serious challenges in the early part of the twenty-first century. The most pressing is the sheer question of survival. Few British law schools have treated the Welfare State as a central issue for their research mission or as a core part of their undergraduate curriculum. Certainly, in the United Kingdom at least, only a minority of law schools offer either social security or more generally welfare law as part of the regular diet for undergraduate law degrees. Typically, the average law student and future practitioner's exposure to social security and the Welfare State will perhaps be little more than a passing reference to the role of tribunals in public law courses. Given the centrality of the Welfare State for the experience of the modern citizen, this says much about the practitioner-based paradigm of the standard law degree. Those British academics who remain active in researching and writing in the field—and have not taken up full-time appointments in the specialized tribunal judiciary—are all well known to one another and could comfortably fit into a small seminar room. The acute shortage of academics working in the field necessarily places a greater burden on those who are active in the area, so leaving less capacity to deal with the issues discussed in this chapter. These problems may be especially acute in the United Kingdom, but appear to be evident in other jurisdictions too. The ever-present danger is that legal scholarship on the Welfare State, in seeking to keep pace with the rapid developments in governmental activity, becomes ever more positivist in nature, eschewing any normative perspective.

REFERENCES

Adler, M., and Bradley, A. (1976). *Justice, Discretion and Poverty*, Milton, Oxon.: Professional Books.

Atiyah, P. S. (1970). *Accidents, Compensation and the Law* (1st edn.), London: Weidenfeld & Nicolson.

Barr, N. (2001). *The Welfare State as Piggy Bank*, Oxford: Oxford University Press.

Bonner, D. (ed.) (2002). *Social Security Legislation 2002* (3 vols.), London: Sweet & Maxwell.

Bussiere, E. (1997). *(Dis)Entitling the Poor: The Warren Court, Welfare Rights and the American Political Tradition*, Pennsylvania: Pennsylvania State University Press.

Calvert, H. (1974). *Social Security Law* (1st edn.), London: Sweet & Maxwell.

Campeau, G. (2001). *De l'assurance-chômage à l'assurance emploi, l'histoire du régime canadien et de son détournement*, Montreal: Les Éditions de Boréal.

Carney, T. (1998). 'Merits Review of "Contractual" Social Security Payments', *Journal of Social Security Law*, 5: 18–43.

Cranston, R. (1985). *Legal Foundations of the Welfare State*, London: Weidenfeld & Nicolson.

Diller, M. (1996). 'Entitlement and Exclusion: The Role of Disability in the Social Welfare System', *University of California at Los Angeles Law Review*, 44: 361–465.

Dupeyroux, J.-J. (2001). *Droit de la sécurité sociale* (14th edn.), Paris: Dalloz.

Ellwood, D. (1988). *Poor Support: Poverty in the American Family*, New York: Basic Books.

Fraser, D. (1984). *The Evolution of the British Welfare State* (2nd edn.), London: Macmillan.

Fulbrook, J. (1978). *Administrative Justice and the Unemployed*, London: Mansell.

Goodin, R. (1986). 'Welfare, Rights and Discretion', *Oxford Journal of Legal Studies*, 6: 232–61.

Handler, J. (1990). '"Constructing the Political Spectacle": The Interpretation of Entitlements, Legalization and Obligations in Social Welfare History', *Brooklyn Law Review*, 56: 899–974.

Harris, N. (ed.) (2000). *Social Security Law in Context*, Oxford: Oxford University Press.

Jones, H. W. (1958). 'The Rule of Law and the Welfare State', *Columbia Law Review*, 58: 143–56.

Mashaw, J. (1983). *Bureaucratic Justice*, New Haven: Yale University Press.

Mead, L. (1987). *Beyond Entitlement: The Social Obligations of Citizenship*, New York: The Free Press.

Murray, C. (1984). *Losing Ground: American Social Policy, 1950–80*, New York: Basic Books.

Piven, F. F., and Cloward, R. A. (1993). *Regulating the Poor: The Functions of Public Welfare* (rev. edn.), New York: Pantheon.

Prosser, T. (1977). 'Poverty, Ideology and Legality: Supplementary Benefit Appeals Tribunals and their Predecessors', *British Journal of Law and Society*, 4: 39–60.

Reich, C. A. (1964). 'The New Property', *Yale Law Journal*, 73: 733–87.

——(1965). 'Individual Rights and Social Welfare: The Emerging Legal Issues', *Yale Law Journal*, 74: 1245–57.

Robson, P. (1992). *Welfare Law*, Aldershot: Dartmouth Publishing (International Library of Essays in Law and Legal Theory).

Simon, W. H. (1986). 'Rights and Redistribution in the Welfare System', *Stanford Law Review*, 38: 1431–516.

Titmuss, R. (1968). *Commitment to Welfare*, London: Allen & Unwin.

——(1971). 'Welfare "Rights", Law and Discretion', *Political Quarterly*, 42: 113–32.

Van Parijs, P. (ed.) (1992). *Arguing for a Basic Income*, London: Verso.

Wikeley, N. (2000). 'Burying Bell: Managing the Judicialisation of Social Security Tribunals', *Modern Law Review*, 63: 475–501.

——Ogus, A., and Barendt, E. (2002). *The Law of Social Security* (5th edn.), London: Butterworths.

Wilson, E. (1977). *Women and the Welfare State*, London: Tavistock.

CHAPTER 20

....

FAMILIES

....

JOHN DEWAR

1 INTRODUCTION

....

THE boundaries of the academic discipline of family law are imprecise and are likely to vary with the constitutional and jurisdictional particulars of any given legal system. At its core lies the definition of particular familial relations, the attaching of legal consequences to those relationships and to their dissolution, and the transition of individuals into new family formations. In concrete terms, this translates into marriage and its effects, divorce, the law of the parent–child relationship, including post-separation parenting and child support, and the 'recognition' of non-marital relationships. Other matters often included in family law include domestic violence, adoption, and child protection.

Family law and family law scholarship do not exist in isolation from the empirical facts of family life and legislative responses to it. Demographic trends over the last forty years have pointed inexorably in the same direction—to decreased marriage rates, lower fertility rates, increased divorce rates, rising rates of non-marital cohabitation and parenting, and the growing acceptability of family forms other than the traditional heterosexual, two-parent household (Gibson, 2000; Morrison, 2000). This demographic context helps to shape the agendas of national legislators. Much family law scholarship has been concerned to describe and analyse the way in which these demographic changes have led to legislative or judicial responses, and to examine the effects of those responses. The power of family law scholarship itself to influence those changes is less certain. Although family law has provided a rich seam for empirical investigation, which has sometimes had a decisive impact on legislative policy, it is more often the case that legislative change proceeds with little regard for the state of empirical knowledge. Empirical work is more often than not confined to examining the effects of change.

Family law is therefore largely an aggregation of instrumental legislation, designed to achieve specific social and political purposes. Unlike disciplines that take a legal concept as its starting-point—such as contract, trust, or restitution—family law tends to be more than usually susceptible to shifts in politics and social behaviour, and the complex interplay between the two. This means that a dominant theme of family law scholarship has been that of change and transformation (e.g. Glendon, 1989; Dewar and Parker, 2000). This chapter will offer a brief history of these transformations in family law, and will describe how change has been described and analysed. This historical narrative will provide a framework for a discussion of the debates that have characterized the discipline in the latter part of the twentieth century.

2 Three Eras of Family Law: Formalism, Functionalism, and Complexity

In the last forty years family law has passed through three 'eras', resulting from two pivotal transformations. Much scholarship has been devoted to identifying and describing the nature and effects of these transformations. The first occurred during the 1960s and early 1970s, and was marked by the transition from the formalist fault-based era to a functionalist no-fault era (Glendon, 1989; Grossberg, 2000). The second transformation, more difficult to pinpoint with accuracy and harder to describe, but occurring somewhere towards the end of the 1980s or early 1990s, is perhaps still under way. For the moment, we can call this a transformation to the third era of complexity (Dewar and Parker, 2000). This second transformation from a functionalist to a complex era has not consisted of any single event or legislative initiative comparable to no-fault divorce. Instead, it involves a loosely connected set of developments that together mark a profound change in the assumptions, techniques, and objectives of family law regimes—the 'how and why' of family law. Family law scholarship continues to articulate and describe the nature and effects of this era.

In summary, then, we can say that postwar family law has passed through three 'eras': formalist, functionalist, and complex. However, these eras are best regarded as schematic devices rather than as marking neat divisions of legislative and social policy. In practice, the eras have merged or overlapped with each other to some degree, so that ideas, practices, or techniques from an earlier era often linger on beyond the end of the era as I describe it. Indeed, this is one of the factors contributing to the complexity of the current era.

2.1 From Formalism to Functionalism

Before the introduction of no-fault divorce, family law rested on an identifiable legal-conceptual structure. Marriage was a contract in the sense of being a set of voluntarily assumed rights and obligations, but in the nature of a contract of adhesion and thus not freely negotiable. Under this model, spouses had identifiable rights and obligations, and remedies were available for breach of marital entitlements. Thus, divorce was available only on proof of commission by a spouse of one of a closely defined list of matrimonial offences; and innocence or guilt of matrimonial misconduct affected the consequences of a divorce in terms of money and children. This model of marriage also affected the civil status of the parties to it, especially the wife. For example, a husband could not be prosecuted for raping his wife; spouses were not compellable witnesses against each other; and spouses could not sue each other in tort.

The introduction of no-fault divorce profoundly altered this conceptual apparatus. Marriage was terminable without proof of fault, merely on proof of irretrievable breakdown, usually evidenced by a period of separation. To many, this change meant simply that divorce was more freely available. However, it also meant that the objectives of the law relating to property adjustment and child custody were immediately placed in question. For, if they were not to be used to protect the innocent or punish the guilty, what was their purpose? The most common legislative response to this normative vacuum was to confer wide-ranging discretions on judges to adjust property rights and to make orders relating to children's living arrangements coupled with generally specified objectives for their exercise (e.g. that orders be made that were 'just and equitable' in the light of specified factors). This gave rise to what could be called the 'functionalist' era of family law, in which the task of the legal system was seen as being to assist parties to negotiate transitions, and to employ judicial order-making power to achieve certain welfare-defined outcomes, rather than being to allocate punishment or blame (Eekelaar, 1978, was a powerful exponent of a functionalist account of family law in the 1970s). This functionalist model was seen to be supportive of family life, and of the institution of marriage in general, because it enabled individuals to move on from bad marriages to more satisfying ones. It thus marked a shift in techniques of family governance, from control through restriction to control through managed change (Smart, 2000).

Although not directly linked to no-fault divorce, many of the rules limiting spouses' legal capacities (e.g. to sue each other, or to give evidence against each other) were steadily removed, in keeping with the egalitarian and individualistic spirit of the age (Grossberg, 2000). Yet at the same time, marriage (and, by necessary implication, divorce) was the chief vehicle for the implementation of these transition-assisting measures; and in terms of more general state policy towards the family, the marital family continued to retain pre-eminence in terms of taxation and welfare benefits. Other family forms received little recognition in the functionalist scheme of things.

2.2 From Functionalism to Complexity

If the first transition was from a formalist to a functionalist model of family law, of what has the second consisted? As already suggested, this second transformation cannot be tied to any single legislative event, or to a big idea analogous to no-fault divorce. Instead, it consists of a series of loosely connected shifts in assumptions about family and divorcing behaviour that has fed into a changed set of objectives for managing family transition through law, and a new set of legal techniques. The net result is that we now find ourselves in an era of complexity.

2.2.1 *The Changing Context*

It may help to set out some of the changing context of ideas in which all of this is taking place.

First, there has been a continued anxiety about the seemingly inexorable rise in the rate of divorce and at the levels of family instability this seems to indicate. The blame for this is often laid at the door of no-fault divorce, which is said to make divorce too easy and to set up incentives for family instability.

Secondly, governments have been alarmed at the similarly inexorable rise in the costs to government of marriage and relationship breakdown. Those costs arise from state welfare payments made to single parents, and from the cost of providing a legal system and associated legal services through legal aid budgets. Governments have sought to contain those costs, by defining and enforcing post-separation child support obligations more forcefully and by seeking alternatives to conventional legal processes for resolving family disputes.

Thirdly, there is a growing sense that neither women nor men have done well out of no-fault divorce. For women, it is argued that they suffer financially from divorce, and that the heavily discretionary regime of financial adjustment accompanying no-fault divorce laws is inadequate to the task of protecting women's economic investments in marriage (Ellman, 1989). For men, the increasing emphasis on parental obligations of financial support has refocused attention on post-separation parenting, and in particular on the perceived inequities of traditional custody and access arrangements.

Fourthly, there has been a growing willingness to invoke rights arguments in debates about family law. This is perhaps a more established feature of US law, where the constitutional aspects of family law have been explored over a long period of time going back to rulings of the Supreme Court in the 1960s on issues of marriage and legitimacy, invoking the equality provisions of the Fourteenth Amendment (e.g. *Loving v Virginia* 388 US 1 (1967)). It is, however, an increasingly common feature of other jurisdictions, driven in part by new international declarations of rights (such as the UN Convention on the Rights of the Child) and by new bill of rights instruments (such as the Human Rights Act 1998 in the UK). At any rate, the discretionary techniques of the functionalist model have come under sustained scrutiny from this constitutional and rights-based perspective.

Finally, the privileged position of marriage (and divorce) in the functionalist model is called into question by the growing diversity of family forms. Marriage is no longer the only arena in which family life is played out. There is a sense in which this has always been true, and the privileging of marriage could, in a longer historical sweep, be seen merely as an effect of eighteenth- and nineteenth-century familial capital accumulation. But it is now true in a way that legislators can no longer ignore. If techniques of modern family law governance are more about regulating through enabling rather than through restriction (see above), then legislative techniques need to be more finely attuned to the ways of life that it is sought to regulate. Thus, non-marital relations become more visible in law, as have relationships centred on parenting—in particular, post-separation parenting across households, and step-parenting.

2.2.2 *New Objectives and Techniques: The Complex Era*

So how does all of this play out in terms of the second transformation of family law in the late twentieth century? We can identify a number of trends and patterns flowing from the factors just described. Taken together, they amount to at least a significant revision, and perhaps a complete rejection, of the features of the functonalist no-fault model described earlier. Yet, the changes described below do not always sit easily together—indeed, they may be directly contradictory. This is why the term 'complexity' is used to characterize the era in which we now find ourselves.

First, marriage has been displaced as the central concept linking law to families. Instead, legislation increasingly 'recognizes' other relationships, such as unmarried cohabitation, or attaches greater significance to existing ones, such as parenthood. Some jurisdictions have gone further and have created new forms of marriage or legal partnership to accommodate those who cannot enter marriage in its conventional sense. This trend suggests a continuation and extension of the modes of governance that the functionalist model itself exemplified—that is, regulation through tolerance and empowerment rather than control and restriction—but is distinct from that model in its broader focus and its techniques. At the same time, concerns about the instability of marriage have led to calls for a return to fault-based divorce laws, or for offering couples the option of entering marriages that are harder to exit than 'normal' ones. Ironically, perhaps, these seem to offer a return to an older— pre-functionalist—mode of family governance.

Secondly, there has been a retreat from the discretionary legislation that was a centrepiece of the functionalist model. Increasingly, family law legislation is drafted in more specific, rule-like, terms. For example, child support legislation, whether drafted as judicial guidelines or as legislation creating a separate agency charged with assessment and enforcement of child support, is drafted in terms of fixed entitlements rather than discretionary awards. Rules on property adjustment are similarly debated increasingly in terms of clearer rules rather than broad discretions (Blumberg, 2000); while legislation on post-separation parenting often includes statements of principles of equality between parents, or of rights of children, in mandatory rather than discretionary terms.

The explanation for the shift towards rules lies in the factors described above— governmental concern to control the costs of family breakdown to the welfare state; an increased tendency to conceive of parties in family law disputes as bearers of rights rather than as objects of welfarist interventions; and a perceived need to state legal principles more clearly so that parties can negotiate their own arrangements without going to court. This is not to suggest that family law has become a seamless code of rules, but rather that new techniques are steadily being superimposed on old. In any case, the question of which technique is best, and of the costs and benefits of each, is yet to be settled. Indeed, it has been suggested that 'the continuing search for the third way between discretion and rules is a key feature of modern family law' (Douglas, 2001: 19). The ramifications of this shift in legislative objectives and techniques run through Sections 4 to 6 below.

Thirdly, there is a greater emphasis on family autonomy in decision-making, through promotion of binding pre-nuptial agreements, and non-judicial forms of dispute resolution for those who have no ready-made agreements to fall back on. Once again, this trend is informed by a wish to remove family disputes from costly judicial fora as far as possible, while at the same time drawing on the language of individual empowerment, responsibility, and autonomy as self-sufficient justifications for parties to agree without court or professional involvement. Indeed, it seems that the role of lawyers is sometimes in question. Research evidence relating to lawyers' work in family law (e.g. Maclean *et al.*, 2000; Hunter, 2000) generally paints a positive picture of the work lawyers do. But the positive role of lawyers in dispute management needs to be communicated, and its implications theorized, more effectively than it has been to date. These issues are discussed in Section 6 below.

A final shift of emphasis has been in the area of post-divorce parenting. Under the functionalist model, the emphasis was on assisting parties to move on from one relationship, and household, to the next. The language was that of the clean break, of 'looking to the future'. In this context, little prominence was given to the issue of how ongoing relationships were to be maintained or managed between children and their non-resident parent. That issue has now moved to centre-stage, with policy-makers increasingly concerned to respond to demands from non-resident parents, often framed in terms of fathers' rights, for greater participation and involvement in the lives of children. Indeed, much attention is now focused on how best to manage post-separation relationships centred on children, including (and perhaps especially) those relationships characterized by high conflict.

The reasons for this change of emphasis are complex, and include a revival of fatherhood claims in law, possibly linked to enhanced child support obligations that usually fall on men (Collier, 1995); psychological evidence pointing towards the harm caused by the loss of relationships with fathers, which has in turn fuelled official concerns with preserving contact or access arrangements (see Smart *et al.*, 2001, ch. 2, for a summary); and a recognition that family instability and fluidity is a permanent feature of the landscape and has to be managed rather than ignored. In short, it is now recognized that a complex of parent–child relations, often within and between households, has to be allowed for and, indeed, encouraged.

Taken together, then, it is suggested that family law now has altered significantly in its objectives, techniques, and underlying assumptions from the functionalist model of the late 1960s and early 1970s. We turn now to exploring in more detail the trajectory taken by this second transformation in some specific areas.

3 Relationship Definition: Entries and Exits, But To and From What?

A central concern of modern family law is how familial relationships should be defined, and for what purpose. This is now a much more complex question that it used to be.

Under the functionalist model, as we have seen, marriage was the chief means by which families were linked to law. Marriage conferred a status, in the sense of rights not available to others, in private and public law. There was only limited recognition of other forms of family organization as having legal significance. Marriage is a convenient conceptual device for making families visible in law, provided that most family life is conducted within marriage. The difficulty facing legal policy in this area, however, has been the dramatic shift in attitudes and social practices in relation to non-marital cohabitation and other family forms. Demographic evidence from developed countries suggests that people are marrying less, while living together and having children outside marriage in larger numbers, than in the first half of the twentieth century (Lewis, 2001). This leads to two consequences, both of which have de-centred marriage as a legal concept.

The first is growing practical and political pressure to grant non-marital relationships some form of legal 'recognition'. The terms and consequences of that recognition, however, are not settled. For example, should such recognition be a matter of choice by the parties, or is it to be imposed; and in either case, how far should recognition extend and with what consequences? In some cases, it is argued that marriage itself, or something like it, should be extended to embrace couples previously excluded from it (e.g. same-sex couples); but in most jurisdictions, legislation is confined to criteria-based recognition of unmarried cohabitation, with consequences less far-reaching than those attaching to marriage.

The second is an increased prominence for the legal status of *parenthood*—for if relationships between adults are increasingly fragile and transitory, at least the parent–child relationship is susceptible of clear proof, and is enduring. Indeed, in many jurisdictions, the legal consequences of being a parent are of far greater practical significance (especially in the area of child support) than are the consequences of marriage.

The developments just mentioned could both be seen as examples of a new mode of family governance through law, namely regulation through tolerance and empowerment. This is the subtle mode of the exercise of power through enhanced and differentiated understandings of human behaviour identified by Foucault and others, and sometimes termed 'governmentality' (Smart, 2000). At the same time, and perhaps in reaction to the seeming dissolution of traditional marriage, there has been a revival of interest in a return to fault-based divorce, either for marriages across the board, or for particular types of marriage that parties may elect to enter (Wardle, 1999). The best example of the latter is the 'covenant' marriage, discussed below, and encountered in a small number of US jurisdictions. This seems to hark back to an earlier pre-functionalist era of regulation by restriction and punishment.

The net result is that there is no privileged legal perspective on families—instead, the law now offers a variety of lenses through which family relations may be understood, whether between adults, or between adults and children. Much scholarship in this area has been concerned to make the case for (or against) recognition of new entry and exit points from legally recognized unions, and academics have often been active in campaigns for specific reforms to the law on relationship recognition.

3.1 Recognition of Relationships outside Marriage

The progress of legislation recognizing non-marital cohabitation has been uneven. 'Recognition' for this purpose means equating non-marital relationships with marriage in legislation covering a variety of social entitlements, such as housing, welfare, employment, and superannuation, as well as the core family law concern of property distribution at the end of a relationship.

A central concern in this area has been how non-marital families are to be defined for this purpose (Graycar and Millbank, 2000). It is often the case that legislation extending such recognition does so by measuring the extent to which the relationship in question measures up to the ideal of marriage, or to some other heterosexual standard. This need not mean, however, that relationships defined in this way are exclusively heterosexual. There are instances of judicial decision and legislation that explicitly incorporate same-sex relationships within definitions that apply also to heterosexual ones. An example of this is the English case of *Fitzpatrick v Sterling Housing Association* [2000] 1 FLR 271, in which the House of Lords held that a gay man was a member of the 'family' of his partner, thereby entitling him to succeed to a statutory tenancy. Yet it is suggested that the price paid for this recognition is a high one, in that relationships will only qualify if they conform to a heterosexist model of intimate relations, and if they celebrate rather than challenge the ideology associated with 'family values'. This presents a dilemma for those seeking greater recognition for gay and lesbian couples in law—should they take what is being offered through forced conformity to dominant (and heterosexist) models of 'family', or should they seek more thoroughly to subvert that model by seeking recognition on their own terms (Diduck, 2001)?

In some jurisdictions, legislation recognizes relationships in broader terms, rather than by reference to a particular marriage-like model of domestic relations. In Australia, for example, which has a long tradition of relationship-recognition legislation, New South Wales has introduced the concept of the 'domestic relationship' to its property adjustment statute, a term that covers not only couples who live together, but also a much broader category of 'close personal relationship': Property (Relationships) Act 1984 (NSW), s 5. This term is certainly broad enough to cover same-sex relationships, and covers many others in addition—including, for example, relationships of purely financial or emotional dependence. However, the breadth of relationships that might be covered by this term is such that reliance on judicial discretion to tailor solutions to the nuances of such relationship is unavoidable. This raises the question of whether other 'opt-in' private-ordering mechanisms should be available to parties in such relationships—marriage, perhaps, or something like it?

3.2 Should Marriage, or Something Like It, be more Widely Available?

The common law defined marriage as heterosexual, a legal relationship between a male and female. Legislation on marriage usually reflects this common law definition. Marriage, in most jurisdictions, greatly affects the civil rights of parties to it, in terms of taxation, pension and welfare entitlements, and in other ways. While the relationship-recognition legislation just discussed (where it exists) may ameliorate this in specific instances, it remains the case that marriage is a privileged condition in many respects, not least because it confers generic rather than case-by-case status. This may be justified where parties have exercised a deliberate choice to remain unmarried. But what of those, such as gay and lesbian couples, for whom heterosexual marriage is not available? Although it is open to such couples to regulate their obligations to each other by contract, no contract will bind the State or other third parties (e.g. employers) to recognize the parties as having any special status.

This has led to increased pressure on the legal definition of marriage. For example, there have been constitutional and other rights-based challenges to the legal definition of marriage, the best known of which was litigation in Hawaii (*Baehr v Lewin* 852 P 2d 58 (1993); *Baehr v Miike* 23 Fam L Rep). The Hawaiian Supreme Court held that a state law that restricted marriage to men and women was a violation of the constitutional right of equal protection, and it was subsequently held that the State could demonstrate no pressing reason justifying the discrimination.

However, perhaps as a warning to those seeking to advance political causes by such means, this chain of events triggered a chain of counter-reactions. First, the Federal government passed the Defense of Marriage Act in 1996, which relieved US states of the obligation to grant 'full faith and credit' to enactments of other states so far as they purported to treat relations between persons of the same sex as a marriage, or as creating any rights and duties. Secondly, a referendum proposing an amendment to the Hawaiian constitution reserving marriage as a heterosexual union was overwhelmingly endorsed by voters (see Barron, 2000, for an account of these developments). It is unlikely, though, that events will end there. More recently, the Supreme Court of Vermont (*Baker v State of Vermont*, Dec. 1999) has held that the limitation of marriage to heterosexual couples violates the 'common benefits' provision in the Vermont state constitution. At the same time, some writers have expressed doubts, analogous to those outlined above in relation to relationship-recognition laws, as to whether seeking entry into marriage is an appropriate political strategy for those seeking more radical social change (Polikoff, 1993).

Another legislative response to the demand for equality of treatment has been the introduction of statutory 'registered partnerships'. These are analogous to marriage in that they are 'opt-in' arrangements and confer civil status on the parties; but they are open to same-sex couples. They are currently found in Europe, Scandinavia, and at local government level in the United States (e.g. in San Francisco and Cambridge, Massachusetts). The legal consequences of such arrangements, especially their effectiveness across jurisdictional borders and their relationship with conventional marriage, have yet to be worked out.

Of course, it is possible that the extension of marriage, or its analogues, to wider groups merely reflects the fact that marriage is no longer a legally significant status. As Glendon has put it, 'the ideologising of the freedom to marry has appeared on the scene just at the moment when legal marriage is losing much of its traditional significance' (Glendon, 1989: 83). Instead, as we shall see in the next section, marriage has become increasingly a matter of private ordering, of setting one's own ground rules—in short, of contract rather than status. If this is so, then achieving access to state-sanctioned marriage for gay and lesbian couples would be a hollow victory. Yet there remain numerous ways in which marriage automatically creates a significant legal status. News of the 'death of marriage' may be premature.

3.3 Strengthening Families and Marriage

A strong tradition in family law scholarship, especially in the United States, has been concerned to articulate the case for law's role in strengthening families. Perhaps the most eloquent exponent of this view has been Mary Ann Glendon, whose masterly comparative survey of family law, first published in 1977 and updated in 1989, led her to take the 'communitarian' position that law may have a role in supporting and strengthening families by supporting the communities and other 'mediating structures' in which families exist (Glendon, 1989, ch. 7). More recent variants of such an approach have called more directly for a return to a pre-functionalist model of legal regulation of families (Wardle, 1999). In particular, it is suggested that there should be a return to fault-based divorce. The argument here is that no-fault divorce has led to two undesirable consequences—growing poverty for women and a rapidly rising divorce rate—and that this necessitates a return to the fault-based system it replaced. As a variant of this, it is argued that there should be an optional version of marriage terminable only on proof of fault—the so-called 'covenant' marriage that now exists in slightly different forms in Louisiana and Arizona.

However, there is little evidence to support the claims made in support of a return to fault-based divorce (Ellman, 2000). For example, there is no conclusive evidence pointing to financial hardship to women flowing *exclusively* or even significantly from no-fault divorce. Instead, the causes of hardship facing women and children after divorce are deep-rooted and systemic, implicating the welfare state, and the labour market, as well as family law. The focus should be on what the law says about financial adjustment on divorce, rather than on the ground of divorce itself. Further, there is no evidence that fault-based divorce would stem the flow of family breakdown or marital instability, because these are tied to wider economic and cultural factors that divorce law can only marginally influence. The case for abandoning the fault-based system, and in particular the procedural game-playing that it induces, remains persuasive. Nevertheless, it is an interesting symptom of the anxieties induced by perceptions of family instability that such proposals should receive serious attention.

3.4 Parenthood

Alongside the growing recognition of non-marital relations between adults has been the growth in the significance of parenthood as a legal status. The most obvious evidence of this is the growth in child support schemes which create significant financial obligations on separated parents whether they are married to the other parent or not. It is the presence or absence of children that will make the biggest difference.

3.4.1 *Why is Parenthood Becoming More Significant?*

The increased significance of parenthood can be seen as a function of three separate developments. First, it is a necessary consequence of a policy of removing any distinction in the legal treatment of marital and non-marital children, and of eradicating the common law concept of illegitimacy. One effect of this is that, from the child's point of view, the marital status of the parents is, or should be, irrelevant—what matters, in other words, is parenthood, not marriage.

Secondly, as already noted, the decline in marriage as a social practice has meant that some other legal technique was needed to link men to children, and to impose parental obligations on men, especially obligations of support. Parenthood is a way of tying men into the non-marital family. As Richard Collier has suggested, the rise of parenthood can be seen as a 'widening of the net of paternal authority through facilitating the making of links between men and children just at the time when rising trends of divorce, cohabitation, step-parenthood and serial marriage might appear to have been breaking down the traditional family unit' (Collier, 1995: 207).

Thirdly, parenthood has become a means by which family law maintains a notional set of links between family members after separation. I will suggest later that family law is increasingly emphasizing the maintenance of economic and legal ties between parents and children after separation, as if to create the illusion of permanence in the face of instability. Since, by definition, neither marriage nor cohabitation is available for the purpose, these continuing links are founded on parenthood. I will return to this point later.

3.4.2 Parenthood: Meaning and Effects

If it is the case that parenthood is an increasingly important legal status, what does it mean? It is easy to assume that parenthood is a simple question of biology—that a child's parents are those who have provided the genetic material that created the embryo that grew into the child. Yet there are at least two reasons why this may not be as straightforward as it appears.

The first is that the creation of embryos is increasingly a matter of human intervention. One consequence of this is that a focus on nature or biology may be at odds with the social arrangements we wish to create. For example, a woman who has had a fertilized egg created from donated genetic material implanted in her womb, which she then carries to term, will usually wish to do so because she (and, often, her partner) want to be considered the resulting child's 'parent', legally and otherwise. Jurisdictions with legislative regimes governing assisted reproduction typically assist in maintaining this fictive parenthood, by specifying that the woman carrying the child to term will be deemed the child's mother, while her husband or (male) partner will be the father. Donors of genetic material will be exonerated from parenthood, and would no doubt be alarmed if it were otherwise.

The second complicating factor stems from the culturally specific nature of biological understandings of parenthood. A child has two biological parents, and this mirrors the social expectation that child-rearing will be discharged in a nuclear, two-parent, heterosexual household. To that extent, biology underpins notions of kinship, and much of the legal structure of parenthood shares this two-parent, heterosexual premise. Yet this sits uneasily with the child-rearing practices of, for example, indigenous or ethnic communities, for whom parenthood may be indistinguishable from subtle and extended notions of kinship, so that a child may be regarded as having many 'parents', and parenting may be regarded as a communal rather than individual responsibility. It also sits uneasily with other non-traditional family forms, such as families with same-sex parents where children have been brought into existence by the creative use of low-tech procedures of assisted reproduction. In both cases, legal definitions of parenthood may fail to capture what those involved feel to be the reality of their circumstances; and there is a danger that a shift towards parenthood in its crude biological sense will amount to the imposition of a specific set of cultural values on a racial or social group.

3.5 Where Next?

To the extent that a focus on marriage was a feature of the functionalist model, that feature has now well and truly disappeared. This, it has been suggested, is a playing out of a functionalist regulatory logic—of controlling through permissive regulation rather than prohibition. As a result, it is clear that marriage no longer offers a privileged legal perspective on the family. Instead, and for a variety of reasons, there is now a proliferation of ways in which intimate relationships will be recognized or given effect in law; yet the abandonment of marriage as the sole or dominant legal framework immediately poses the question of what should take its place, how, and for what purpose. That debate can be expected to preoccupy family law scholarship for some time to come.

4 FAMILY FINANCES

Empirical research almost invariably finds that women and children are most adversely affected economically by divorce and separation. Because of the uneven distribution of child-rearing tasks and wage inequalities in the labour market, women tend to bear the costs of failed marriages more heavily than men; and because women continue to bear a disproportionate share of child-rearing tasks after divorce, those costs are passed onto the children. In addition, the parties' greatest asset is usually the earning capacity of one party (often the man), and it is also one to which the other party perhaps has the strongest claim; yet the law has only limited means to capture and redistribute this. Child support regimes, which seek to correct unfairness to children by guaranteeing children a portion of their parents' incomes, could be seen as a way of splitting future earning potential; and legislation splitting super-annuation and pension entitlements is another. Their effectiveness in achieving this aim is yet to be proven, however.

Some have laid the blame for the inequalities on divorce at the door of no-fault divorce itself, yet the evidence does not support this claim. Although studies have found little difference in financial outcomes related to the divorce laws (Brinig, 2000: 58–163), it could be argued that no-fault divorce regimes tend to be unclear about the rationale for post-divorce property distribution and spousal support obligations. As we have seen, the removal of fault from its central place in divorce left a normative vacuum in relation to these financial matters that is not always filled. This has led to a search for clearer rationales for these obligations that rest in something other than fault-based logic or contractual analogy.

4.1 Looking for a Rationale

Many jurisdictions rely on a combination of the concepts of 'contribution' and 'need' in the distribution of assets on divorce. Under such regimes, the spouses' property is divided in accordance with their contributions to property and, more generally, to the family, and then adjusted in the light of disparities in their future needs. Sometimes 'need' is the governing or dominant criterion. There are numerous varia-tions on this theme, including regimes that apply presumptions of equal division only to property defined as 'marital' as distinct from separate, before applying some form of needs-based adjustment. Yet there is a growing consensus that these concep-tual tools are inadequate to explain or justify what is taking place. At the same time, most jurisdictions include provision for spousal maintenance, but evidence suggests that these powers are rarely used. For that reason, many couples are unable to divide what may be their most significant asset—namely, their future earning capacity.

An increasingly popular model for reform, advocated by a number of writers (e.g. Funder, 1992), is that marriage should be treated as a form of partnership or joint investment enterprise and that, on dissolution, the partners should be recompensed for any losses flowing from the partnership or joint enterprise itself. Thus, a partner who has undertaken a disproportionate share of child-care responsibilities during the marriage, and who has suffered a loss of future earning capacity in consequence, should be entitled to be compensated for that loss from joint assets or future earn-ings. Equally, a partner who has contributed to the other's enhanced earning capac-ity, and who is deprived by divorce of the opportunity to enjoy the fruits of that earning capacity, should be similarly recompensed for that loss.

Those who advocate these models have mixed motives. While some are concerned to address the clear inequities in the current financial consequences of divorce, others see a potential for such a model to influence marital behaviour. For if divorce law is concerned to protect partners' investments in their marital partnership, then it may 'cause some spouses to work harder on their marriages' while maximizing choices for women (Brinig, 2000: 172–3). Even those who resist the partnership analogy may arrive at similar conclusions for similar policy reasons—namely, that compensation for these sorts of loss is essential if marital investments are to be encouraged (e.g. Ellman, 1989). Echoes of the 'strengthening marriage' agenda may be discerned here.

One consequence of these models is that the current distinction between property adjustment and spousal maintenance becomes less relevant. The debt could be regarded as one to be repaid over a period of time, from whatever assets come to hand. In the case of periodic payments, such a conceptual shift would transform these payments from resting on a rationale of ongoing dependency and proof of future need, to resting on one of past entitlement.

No doubt these simple statements of principle conceal all sorts of detailed difficulties that would require resolution. For example, how would losses be calculated and how much of that loss would be chargeable to the joint venture or partnership? How would the value of existing property be compared to that of future income? How would the practical difficulties of extracting future payments be dealt with? It is on these rocks that proposals of this sort have often foundered when considered by legislators.

Nevertheless, there is an observable trend in thinking and practice in this direction. How does this illustrate the theme of a second transformation? In two ways, I would suggest—one related to objectives, the other to technique. First, contrary to the functionalist model, these schemes for financial adjustment have an explicit behaviour-modification objective. By making certain assumptions about what motivates family behaviour, they seek to encourage and protect marital investments, and thereby encourage marriage and discourage divorce. This is not to suggest that there is a socially conservative force at work here—far from it, given that the same proposals could probably be supported from a feminist perspective. What is different from the functionalist model is that the task of promoting family stability is seen to lie in the preservation of existing marriages rather than in granting permission to divorce. Secondly, in relation to technique, these proposals represent a marked constraining of the judicial discretion we have seen to be characteristic of the functionalist model.

4.2 Contractualization

While there is a trend towards the public enunciation of more detailed and prescriptive rules for financial adjustment, there is a parallel trend towards greater contractualization of marriage and divorce. 'Contractualization' refers to the use of private contracting as a way of ordering domestic relationships, both while they are ongoing and when they end. As a legal technique, it has long been available to unmarried couples (subject to issues of enforceability, long since resolved—see e.g. *Marvin v Marvin* 557 P 2d 106 (Cal, 1976)); but legislators now seem keen to extend its possibilities to married couples as well, pointing to the control that enforceable contracts provide parties over their own affairs. Each relationship may potentially acquire its own 'proper law', determined by the parties themselves rather than by an outsider armed with discretionary powers of distribution. In this way, private contracting is set to become an autonomous, or semi-autonomous, source of legal norms.

Family lawyers have long been aware that much law-related activity takes place well away from the courtroom, and there has been considerable analysis of the factors influencing negotiations between parties 'in the shadow of the law'. However, most of this literature has looked at negotiations about matters that might otherwise go to court. The significance of contractualization is that one of its chief purposes is to exclude the jurisdiction of courts altogether. For some, this opens up new possibilities for couples to define the terms of their relationship for themselves, free from what some might consider an oppressive and unwelcome legal 'shadow'. For others, however, it raises the danger that the inequalities in bargaining power between parties, that might be checked if set against a background of potentially enforceable legal entitlements or court scrutiny, may be allowed free rein in a contractual negotiation that is hermetically sealed from any other source of background norm.

We need only note just how complex are the patterns emerging from this. For contract offers a different model of family relations from the joint enterprise or partnership model prominent in discussions of legislative reform of property adjustment laws. Contract seems to imply an intensification of the process of individualization, rather than a reaction against it. It seems to provide incentives for opportunistic behaviour, rather than incentives to make marital investments.

In terms of future scholarship, the challenge lies in reconciling these competing tendencies at the level of policy while assessing their empirical impact at the level of practice and outcomes.

5 SUSTAINING THE POST-DIVORCE FAMILY

A prominent feature of the second transformation of family law is that there is now a greater emphasis on maintaining relationships between parents and children after separation. The reasons for this have already been discussed.

What form does this emphasis take? One obvious form is the creation of child support liabilities by statute. Another is the increased legislative emphasis on post-separation contact between a child and the parent with which it is not living, and on the sharing of parental responsibilities. This finds expression in different ways—in joint custody laws, in legal presumptions of access, visitation, or contact, and in more funding for community agencies involved in supervising or supporting contact arrangements.

5.1 Shared Parenting

Decisions relating to children have come to be dominated in the twentieth century by the 'best interests' standard—that is, that decisions will be made according to the child's best interests. This is a quintessential instance of the sort of discretionary decision-making that, it is suggested, was a characteristic feature of the functionalist model. In its pure form, the best interests standard does not prescribe any particular outcome, nor create any hierarchy of factors to be taken into account. The decision is one to be made only once in possession of all the facts. However, there has been a steady process, admittedly not universal across jurisdictions, of controlling that discretion and specifying that certain outcomes are desirable. This process has taken a number of forms, including statutory presumptions of shared parenting (or 'joint custody') and presumptions of contact or visitation between the child and the non-resident parent.

A good example of this sort of legislation is the Children Act 1989 in the UK, and legislation derived from it elsewhere. This replaced the common law language of guardianship and custody (which, it was said, created a 'winner takes all' mentality) with the concept of 'parental responsibility'. This responsibility is shared between parents, which means that each potentially has a power of veto over decision-making by the other, irrespective of the actual living arrangements for the child. This sharing of parental responsibility led to a strong presumption in the English courts in favour of contact with the non-resident parent (see Douglas, 2001, ch. 5). A presumption in favour of contact has found a firmer statutory footing in Australia, where a child is stated (using the language of article 9 of the UN Convention on the Rights of the Child) to have a 'right' of ongoing contact with both parents.

The issue of post-separation child-care arrangements, and in particular visitation or contact, has become a key site for feminist engagement with family law issues. In its seeming attempts to 'shift the balance' away from mothers towards fathers, such legislation has attracted opposition and heightened attention. Research in Australia has suggested that the new regime has led to contact being ordered in inappropriate circumstances, and to women being harassed by men through abuse of court processes, thereby confirming the worst fears of its detractors (Rhoades et al., 2000). Legislation of this sort is said to grant power without responsibility, to place women at the mercy of former partners.

For present purposes, the significance of this lies in the fact that divorce no longer represents the effective termination of parent–child relationships. As Smart and Neale have put it

fragments of families are to be found in various households linked by biological and economic bonds, but not necessarily by affection or shared life prospects. We might say that family law is trying to hold the fragments together through the imposition of a new norma-tive order based on genetics and finances, but not on a state-legitimated heterosexual union with its roots in the ideal of Christian marriage. (Smart and Neale, 1999: 181)

This implies a move away from functionalist assumptions, and supports the thesis of a second transformation, in two ways. The first is that divorce or separation no longer marks the end of the pre-divorce family. Instead, family relations are preserved across and between households. Increasing legislative attention and resources are being devoted to sustaining these relationships. Secondly, the conceptual vehicle by which this is achieved is a newly invigorated concept of parenthood, which is increasingly characterized as continuing and shared. At the same time, the concept of parenthood is increasingly differentiated and capable of being distributed around a wider net-work of individuals than just the biological parents, in order to cater for the subtleties of reconstituted and blended family arrangements.

5.2 A Future Direction? Giving Children a Say

Much of the policy debate around post-separation parenting has been conducted as if it consisted of a zero-sum game of gains and losses to be distributed between moth-ers and fathers. The language of 'shifting the balance' exemplifies this way of think-ing. Researchers, though, are increasingly suggesting that one way to break out of this seemingly intractable debate is to focus more squarely on the expressed needs and desires of the children involved (e.g. Smart *et al.*, 2001).

In some ways, it is surprising that a child-focused approach has taken so long to emerge. Article 12 of the UN Convention on the Rights of the Child states that chil-dren who are capable of forming their own views have a right to express those views freely in all matters affecting the child. In particular, a child has a right to have their views heard in judicial proceedings affecting the child. Yet, in those jurisdictions in which an attempt has been made to give effect to article 12, it has usually been by means of adding the child's views to the check list of factors to be taken into account in deciding where a child's best interests lie (e.g. under s 1(5) of the Children Act 1989 in the UK or s 79E of the Family Law Act 1975 in Australia). In other words, a child's views are not determinative of the issue in their own right, but are merely a factor to be weighed along with others. Whether this satisfies the requirements of article 12 may be questioned; but in any case, taking children's views properly into account requires procedures that are equipped to do that. There is a proliferation of models being used to achieve this, such as the mandatory filing of expert reports and the use of specialist child lawyers, for example. There is also a growing awareness of the need to change rules of evidence and court processes themselves to make them more accommodating of children (Woodhouse, 2000: 436–7). Research is increasingly likely to investigate the best ways of discovering what children want, and how best to feed that information into the decision-making process (Lowe and Murch, 2001). At a more general level, though, there will be a need to reconceptualize the obligations of family lawyers towards children, and a rethinking of the professional development of those lawyers to ensure that they are more familiar with children's needs on divorce. There is an opportunity for family law scholars and researchers to articulate what that role should be.

6 THE FAMILY LAW COMPLEX: COURTS, LAWYERS, AND PROCESSES

Family law is an area of law and practice characterized by high levels of out-of-court activity. There are two reasons for this. One is that the comparatively high cost of litigation means that there are strong incentives for divorcing couples to make their own arrangements, and to avoid going to court at all. The second is that there is a growing movement in support of mediation and other forms of non-judicial dispute resolution. This is partly because of the claimed therapeutic merits of less polarized modes of dispute resolution in which the parties themselves are able to take responsibility for resolving their disputes; but also because governments, keen to reduce the costs of providing judicial resources to decide family disputes and of legal aid, have been eager to promote non-judicial alternatives. It is often said, using the language of a well-known article by Mnookin and Kornhauser, that this out-of-court activity takes place in 'the shadow of the law' (Mnookin and Kornhauser, 1979). Much scholarship has been devoted to exploring this penumbral activity.

The work in this area falls into three groups. The first considers the work that family lawyers do on behalf of their clients (e.g. Sarat and Felstiner, 1995; Maclean et al., 2000). The second considers mediation and other forms of assisted dispute resolution. The third considers the delivery of legal services in family law generally, especially through legal aid and other sources of publicly funded assistance, including courts (e.g. Hunter, 2000). The growing phenomenon of self-represented, or pro se, litigants in family law matters would fall under this third head.

Three themes emerge from this complex body of literature. The first is that family lawyers are often less adversarial, and more settlement-minded, than their popular image would suggest; but that they are also powerful actors in the family law process, playing a pivotal role in the 'translation' of law into terms comprehensible by a client, and in the construction of their clients' perceptions of entitlement. A second is that non-judicial forms of dispute resolution, while often effective in achieving agreement, are not always as empowering of the individuals as their supporters sometimes claim, and that a neutral third-party mediator is often an active participant in the shaping and pursuit of outcomes. Concerns are also often expressed about the ability of mediation adequately to guard against power imbalances between mediating parties. The third is that the task of ensuring that parties meet each other on a level playing field in the family law system is an exceedingly difficult one to realize in practice.

It is possible to draw two conclusions from this, both related to the theme of complexity—which, I have suggested, is characteristic of family law in its second transformation. The first is that the metaphor of 'bargaining in the shadow of the law', so dominant for so long in the way we conceive of out-of-court activity in family law, may now be a misleading one. In so far as it suggests that law casts a single shadow over the whole of the legal system, it is almost certainly inaccurate. Instead, the research cited above suggests that there are now multiple sites for the production of legal meaning in family law systems, interacting with each other in complex and often unpredictable ways. Conventional notions of authority and hierarchy in a legal system—for example, that the will of legislators as interpreted by judges is the pre-eminent source of norms—are demonstrated to be false. Instead, we should see the family law system as a horizontalized network of interacting components (Dewar, 2000).

The explanation for this is linked to the second conclusion, which is that the family law system has developed in this way as a response to the wide range of needs presented by divorcing or separating couples. Family law systems have sought to respond by creating different pathways to, or arenas for, dispute resolution in the light of the complex demands placed on it.

The challenge now, for both family law scholars and policy-makers (whose work is increasingly informed by research), is to identify how to coordinate a systemic response to these complex needs, in a way that rests on a clearly articulated vision of what law and lawyers are, and are not, good for. This entails balancing responsiveness to individual requirements with a firm commitment to uphold basic principles of legality, such as equal access to justice. The complexity of this task is significant, yet it is the defining one of modern family law administration. Family law scholars have an important role in articulating a response to these issues.

References

Barron, J. (2000). 'The Constitutionalisation of American Family Law: The Case of the Right to Marry', in S. Katz, J. Eekelaar, and M. Maclean (eds.), *Cross-Currents: Family Law and Policy in the US and England*, Oxford: Oxford University Press, 257–78.

Blumberg, G. (2000). 'The Financial Incidents of Family Dissolution', in S. Katz, J. Eekelaar, and M. Maclean (eds.), *Cross-Currents: Family Law and Policy in the US and England*, Oxford: Oxford University Press, 387–404.

Brinig, M. (2000). *From Contract to Covenant: Beyond the Law and Economics of the Family*, Cambridge, Mass.: Harvard University Press.

Collier, R. (1995). *Masculinity, Law and the Family*, London: Routledge.

Dewar, J. (2000). 'Family Law and its Discontents', *International Journal of Law, Policy and the Family*, 14: 59–85.

—— and Parker, S. (2000). 'English Family Law since WW II: From Status to Chaos', in S. Katz, J. Eekelaar, and M. Maclean (eds.), *Cross-Currents: Family Law and Policy in the US and England*, Oxford: Oxford University Press, 123–42.

Diduck, A. (2001). 'A Family By Any Other Name … or Starbucks™ comes to England', *Journal of Law and Society*, 28: 290–310.

Douglas, G. (2001). *An Introduction to Family Law*, Oxford: Oxford University Press.

Eekelaar, J. (1978). *Family Law and Social Policy*, London: Weidenfeld and Nicholson.

Ellman, M. (1989). 'The Theory of Alimony', *California Law Review*, 77: 3–81.

—— (2000). 'Divorce in the United States', in S. Katz, J. Eekelaar, and M. Maclean (eds.), *Cross-Currents: Family Law and Policy in the US and England*, Oxford: Oxford University Press, 341–62.

Funder, K. (1992). 'Australia: A Proposal for Reform', in L. Weitzman and M. Maclean (eds.), *Economic Consequences of Divorce: An International Perspective*, Oxford: Oxford University Press.

Gibson, C. (2000). 'Changing Family Patterns in England and Wales over the Last Fifty Years', in S. Katz, J. Eekelaar, and M. Maclean (eds.), *Cross-Currents: Family Law and Policy in the US and England*, Oxford: Oxford University Press, 31–56.

Glendon, M.-A. (1989). *The Transformation of Family Law: State, Law and Family in the United States and Western Europe*, Chicago: University of Chicago Press.

Graycar, R., and Millbank, J. (2000). 'The Bride Wore Pink … to the Property (Relationships) Legislation Amendment Act 1999: Relationships law reform in New South Wales', *Canadian Journal of Family Law*, 17: 227–82.

Grossberg, M. (2000). 'How to Give the Present a Past? Family Law in the United States 1950–2000', in S. Katz, J. Eekelaar, and M. Maclean (eds.), *Cross-Currents: Family Law and Policy in the US and England*, Oxford: Oxford University Press, 1–32.

Hunter, R. (2000). *Legal Services in Family Law*, Sydney: Law Foundation of New South Wales.

Lewis, J. (2001). 'Debates and Issues regarding Marriage and Cohabitation in the British and American Literature', *International Journal of Law, Policy and the Family*, 15: 159–84.

Lowe, N., and Murch, M. (2001). 'Children's Participation in the Family Justice System— Translating Principles into Practice', *Child and Family Law Quarterly*, 13: 137–58.

Maclean, M., Eekelaar, J., and Beinart, S. (2000). *Family Lawyers: The Divorce Work of Solicitors*, Oxford: Hart.

Mnookin, R., and Kornhauser, L. (1979). 'Bargaining in the Shadow of the Law: The Case of Divorce', *Yale Law Journal*, 88: 950–97.

Morrison, D. (2000). 'A Century of the American Family', in S. Katz, J. Eekelaar, and M. Maclean (eds.), *Cross-Currents: Family Law and Policy in the US and England*, Oxford: Oxford University Press, 57–80.

Polikoff, N. (1993). 'We will Get What we Ask For: Why Legalising Gay and Lesbian Marriage will Not "Dismantle the Structure of Gender in Every Marriage"', *Virginia Law Review*, 79: 1535–50.

Rhoades, H., Graycar, R., and Harrison, M. (2000). *The Family Law Reform Act 1995: The First Three Years*, Sydney: University of Sydney/Family Court of Australia.

Sarat, A., and Felstiner, W. (1995). *Divorce Lawyers and their Clients*, Oxford: Oxford University Press.

Smart, C. (2000). 'Divorce in England 1950–2000: A Moral Tale?' in S. Katz, J. Eekelaar, and M. Maclean (eds.), *Cross-Currents: Family Law and Policy in the US and England*, Oxford: Oxford University Press, 363–86.

—— and Neale, B. (1999). *Family fragments?* Cambridge: Polity Press.

—— —— and Wade, A. (2001). *The Changing Experience of Childhood: Families and Divorce*, Cambridge: Polity.

Wardle, L. (1999). 'Divorce Reform at the Turn of the Millennium: Certainties and Possibilities', *Family Law Quarterly*, 33: 783–800.

Woodhouse, B. (2000). 'The Status of Children; A Story of Emerging Rights', in S. Katz, J. Eekelaar, and M. Maclean (eds.), *Cross-Currents: Family Law and Policy in the US and England*, Oxford: Oxford University Press, 423–40.

CHAPTER 21

HEALTH

THE HEALTH CARE SYSTEM, THERAPEUTIC RELATIONSHIPS, AND PUBLIC HEALTH

LAWRENCE O. GOSTIN

PHIL FENNELL

HEALTH law is a vast and complex field, difficult to define and conceptualize. It relates to a wide range of public and private activities designed to protect and preserve health. When the health of individuals or the public is concerned, government almost inevitably accepts the responsibility either to provide or fund the service itself or regulate the ways in which services are provided in the private and voluntary sectors.

It is possible to think of health law as comprising several distinct, but overlapping, areas of interest: the health care system, the therapeutic relationship, and the public health system. These three spheres do not represent the entire range of issues dealt with by health law scholars, but they are among the most prominent.

In this chapter, we analyze the major tensions and trade-offs that occur, explicitly or implicitly, in each of these three areas. Our theory is that individual liberty interests often clash with collective interests in health and security. The law mediates between these two sets of interests. On the one hand, individuals claim an entitlement to self-determination—the right to make health decisions for themselves and to be free from external interference. Individuals have personal interests such as autonomy, privacy, and liberty. They also have proprietary interests such as the freedom to pursue professions, make contracts, and use private property. On the other hand, governments, acting on behalf of society, seek to regulate personal and business activities to improve the health and longevity of individuals and populations. The pursuit of the common good is one of the fundamental justifications for the formation and operation of government.

This chapter first examines the health care system—that is, the organization, financing, and delivery of personal medical services. Governments in the various common law countries make noticeably different calculations about health care. The United Kingdom (UK) and New Zealand directly provide health care services through a national health service; Canada and Australia pay for most of their citizens' health care services; and the United States has a mixed system of publicly and privately financed services.

Government policy with respect to health care can be understood as favoring one or more of the following values: universal access, equitable allocation of resources, consumer choice among health care professionals and institutions, quality of services, and cost-effectiveness of services. Countries differ on how they make these critical choices among the various values of access, equity, choice, quality, and cost. By emphasizing universal access and equity, countries adopt a more communitarian approach to health care. And, by emphasizing personal choice, high quality, and the ability to pay, countries adopt a more individualistic approach to health care.

This chapter next examines the therapeutic relationship—that is, the complex ways in which patients and health care professionals (principally doctors) interact. Much of common law jurisprudence is devoted to a detailed supervision of the doctor–patient relationship. The case law in various common law countries determines the extent to which individuals have the right to informed consent to medical treatment and to confidentiality of patient information. The courts also regulate the therapeutic relationship through the tort system, applying concepts of negligence and battery to treatment decisions.

Jurisprudence regulating the doctor–patient relationship also reveals a preference in the country either for protecting individual freedoms or promoting the common good. Countries that have robust doctrines of informed consent and confidentiality stress personal rights of autonomy and privacy. These countries also typically have a body of case law permitting malpractice claims against doctors and hospitals. Countries that allow health care professionals to act without fully informing patients and to use health information for therapeutic or research purposes stress paternalism and the collective good. These countries typically limit malpractice claims, preferring to give physicians greater discretion in making treatment decisions.

Finally, this chapter discusses public health law, which principally involves government duties and powers to assure the conditions in which populations can be healthy. The government asserts its influence in many spheres to protect and promote the public's health: informational (e.g. labeling and advertising restrictions), physical (e.g. zoning and regulation to create liveable cities), environmental (e.g. clean air and water), and biological (e.g. control of infectious diseases).

Government has many tools at its disposal to protect and promote the public's health, but in each case there is a potential conflict with personal or proprietary interests. For example, labeling and advertising restrictions interfere with freedoms of expression; zoning and business regulation interfere with freedoms of contract and private property; and infectious disease controls (e.g. compulsory vaccination, treatment, and quarantine) interfere with personal freedoms such as autonomy, privacy, and liberty. Whenever government acts to safeguard the population's health there is a trade-off between individual and collective interests. Common law countries make different sorts of calculations in matters of public health. Some governments embark on vast social projects for the population's well-being, while others are far more hesitant to tax and regulate for the public good.

1 THE HEALTH CARE SYSTEM

Effective health care services are fundamental to the welfare of societies and their citizens, and hence all governments use law to regulate the market. In charting a policy course, states make various political and economic decisions including whether and to what extent to employ legal tools to regulate and promote access, choice, and quality, and to control cost. Governments in the common law jurisdictions have different beliefs about providing, and financial abilities to fund, cost-effective high quality health services to their populations. We identify important trends and tensions that have occurred with the rise of market ideology in the late twentieth century, even in countries that established universal entitlements to health care after World War II. This has resulted in an important body of legal scholarship either supporting government intervention to achieve greater access and equity or supporting free markets to achieve greater choice and efficiency (Kennedy and Grubb, 1998).

1.1 Access to Health Care

Common law countries vary considerably in their willingness to assure access to health care services. The archetypal universalist system is the National Health Service (NHS) in the UK, a publicly based service, free at the point of delivery. The NHS's central value is universal access to services designed to cover the population's basic health care needs. This egalitarian value is shared in many common law countries such as New Zealand (which operates a health service) and Canada (which has a 'single payer' system where federal and provincial governments share health care costs).

Scholars, particularly those from the law and economics school of thought, claim that government-dominated national health or single payer systems are inherently inefficient. They point to the rigidity and lack of competition in these systems, leading to restricted choice and explicit rationing of services. Long wait times for non-emergency services, for example, are characteristic of national health and single payer systems.

Scholars have suggested reform based on free market theories such as 'managed competition' (Enthoven, 1993). This almost paradoxical term means that government encourages competition within structured and well-regulated markets. Under this theory, the state would continue to provide or fund health care services, but would introduce internal competition. For example, successive governments in the UK have restructured the NHS by requiring key players in the market (e.g. general practitioners, hospitals, and health authorities) to compete. In this way, the essence of the NHS does not change (e.g. universal access and global budgets), but competition arguably enhances consumer choice and improves quality. The ongoing scholarly debates focus on the extent to which private competition should supplant government control of resource allocations (Newdick, 1995). Private competition is seen by some as inevitably improving efficiency. However, to others, it undermines government's unique obligation to provide universal care on an equitable basis.

By contrast the United States provides the best illustration of an individualistic system based on private health care insurance for the majority. Publicly supported safety nets are available in the form of Medicare (federally subsidized health insurance for the elderly) and Medicaid (federally and state subsidized health insurance for the eligible poor, children, and disabled). There are also special health benefits for certain populations such as veterans (Veterans Administration) and Native Americans (Indian Health Service). Approximately two-thirds of the population are covered by employer-sponsored health plans, with most of the remainder covered by Medicare or Medicaid.

Scholars critique the United States principally for its failure to meet the health care needs of the entire population. American political thought does not share the universalist value found in other common law countries, but prefers personal choice and high quality. Consequently, approximately 14 percent of the population—over 38.7 million people—lacked health insurance in 2000, and many more were under-insured (Mills, 2000).

Theories for expanding health care access abound in the United States, ranging from emulation of a single or multiple payer system in Canada or Germany to solutions unique to America's employer-dominated system (Marmor and Boyum, 1992).

In the United States, as in other common law countries, social welfare and free enterprise ideologies frequently clash. Scholars proposing social welfare approaches seek either total reform or incremental reforms. President Clinton, for example, urged universal access to health care based on managed competition theory, but his plan did not pass Congress. Others have proposed expansion of existing government programs such as covering all children under Medicaid or providing prescription drug benefits to the elderly under Medicare. Finally, many commentators propose employment-based solutions, believing that it is politically expedient to improve the existing system rather than to create a new one. These scholars propose mandates (requiring employers to offer health insurance) or so-called 'play or pay' schemes (requiring employers to pay a tax if they do not offer health insurance).

The scholarly debate over state regulation centers on the economic effects on employers, wages, and the national economy. Economists argue that employer mandates make businesses less competitive, as increased health care costs are passed on in the form of decreased wages or increased prices. This is particularly true of small businesses that often cannot obtain low-priced health insurance because they lack economic clout in the health insurance market. Employer mandates, economists argue, could exacerbate the health care crisis by increasing poverty and unemployment, thus making insurance less affordable.

Economists often prefer tax incentives to achieve social policy objectives. To a large extent, the United States already does this by providing sizeable tax deductions for employers and individuals for purchasing health insurance. Social welfare theorists, however, point out that tax expenditures for health care, which currently exceed $50 billion per annum, are inequitable, distributing financial benefits disproportionately to higher income groups. Tax deductions, moreover, create incentives for increased health care spending as those in upper income groups purchase elaborate insurance products subsidized by the taxpayer.

The debate over tax system approaches has extended to the health care equivalent of 'IRAs' (individual retirement accounts), used in the United States to supplement publicly and employer-funded pensions, whereby individuals would be permitted to set aside non-taxable income to use for health care. Economists argue that if consumers paid the cost of their own health care (rather than rely on third-party reimbursement) they would become more cost-conscious. Social welfare theorists counter that health care IRAs are no answer to the health insurance crisis because individuals could not save sufficiently to pay for catastrophic needs. Health care IRAs, they argue, have no more than cosmetic effects.

A key question for health law scholars is the extent to which legal redress is available to secure or speed up access to medical services. Market-oriented scholars argue that the courts should rarely interfere with allocation decisions, whether 'rights' of access arise under private or public law. In private systems, they argue, entitlements should be almost exclusively governed by the terms of the health care contract—that is, the treatments that are covered and the circumstances in which they are reimbursed. In this way, health plans can effectively insulate themselves from judicial scrutiny by executing contracts that confer discretion on administrators to make final eligibility determinations. The courts, according to this reasoning, should find such determinations to be lawful unless they are arbitrary or capricious. Social welfare proponents, however, believe that negotiations between insurers and consumers are inherently unequal and that, in any event, health care is too important to be left to the unfettered market. Patients' Bill of Rights legislation in the United States, for example, seeks greater external accountability for health plans in the form of independent arbitration or external review of administrator decisions.

There are also debates about entitlements to access in public systems. To some, health authority refusals to provide treatment should be upheld because they are in the best position to make political choices. Courts in the UK and other common law countries agree, striking down allocation decisions only if *Wednesbury* irrational— so arbitrary that no reasonable health authority would have made them (*Associated Provincial Picture Houses v Wednesbury Corporation* [1948] 1 KB 223).

There has been an interesting academic debate about whether access rights could be promoted through the human right to life or health under international law or domestic constitutional law (Bhagwati, 1992). This scholarship has been fueled by the Human Rights Act 1998, which requires UK public authorities to act compatibly with the European Convention of Human Rights. (Ireland is also a signatory to the Convention). Commentators have pondered whether the right to life under article 2 affords an entitlement to necessary medical treatment. The European Court has said that a contracting state might violate article 2 if a person's life was placed at risk by denying health care the state has undertaken to make available to the population (*Cyprus v Turkey* [GC], no 25781/94, § 219, ECHR 2001-IV). Nevertheless, article 2 probably does not afford individuals a certain level of health care.

The human right to life or health conferred under some national constitutions also could be read to create an entitlement. The enforcement of social and economic rights has been a thorny issue in legal journals. Most scholars believe that positive entitlements involve political and economic judgments that are not easily susceptible to judicial resolution. They note that social and economic rights entitle individuals primarily to a fair, non-arbitrary system of resource allocation. For example, in *Shortland v Northland Health Ltd* (1997) 50 BMLR 255, the Court of Appeal found no violation of the right to life under article 8 of the New Zealand Bill of Rights Act despite a government refusal to give life-saving kidney dialysis.

In rare cases, governments act so egregiously that courts are compelled to find a violation of the right to health. For example, the Supreme Court of India found an entitlement to adequate medical services (*Paschim Banga Khet Mazdoor Samity v State of West Bengal*, AIR (1996) Supreme Court 2426). More recently, South Africa's Constitutional Court found an entitlement to anti-retroviral drugs for pregnant women living with HIV/AIDS (*Treatment Action Campaign v Minister of Health and*

Others (2002) (4) BCLR 356). Still, even in South Africa, with an express constitutional right to health care, the courts are reluctant to impose an obligation to provide specific services (*Soobramoney v Minister of Health, KwaZulu-Natal* (1997) 50 BMLR 224). There exists a burgeoning literature in health and human rights seeking to find more precise standards for enforcement of social and economic entitlements (Kinney, 2001).

1.2 Quality and Choice in Health Care

Access to services, of course, is not the only value in health care. Government is also concerned to help ensure that services are of sufficiently high quality, with a range of consumer choice, and not inordinately expensive. All common law countries have mechanisms in place to promote high quality services including clinical guidelines, self-regulation and direct regulation, and consumer disclosure requirements.

Clinical practice guidelines have become an important, and much discussed, method of improving health care (Furrow *et al.*, 2000). Governmental or quasi-governmental bodies publish evidence-based standards with which doctors and hospitals are expected to comply. There is often no explicit sanction for failure to conform, but (as explained below) tort law offers indirect regulation. Practice guidelines evoke considerable debate in the academic community. Many scholars support guidelines because they establish a science base for practice. These scholars note that medicine has been practiced without empirical support and external criteria to measure quality. Clinical guidelines could markedly improve outcomes by providing standards for practice based on objective data. Other scholars, however, stress the importance of clinical autonomy, believing that doctors should have discretion to act in the patient's best interests. These scholars emphasize the sanctity of the clinical relationship and the doctor's fiduciary duty to patients, without external restraints.

Common law countries have also established or facilitated external reviews of health care institutions to ensure high quality. For example, legally constituted bodies exist in the UK (e.g. Commission for Health Improvement and National Care Standards Commission) and the United States (National Committee for Quality Assurance) to inspect and accredit service providers. Law furnishes powers to self-regulatory bodies such as the General Medical Council in the UK and the Joint Commission on Accreditation of Healthcare Organizations in the United States. These and other bodies have powers to set standards, ensure their implementation, and, ultimately, to accredit health care institutions or license health care professionals. Few scholars doubt the importance of a regulatory system for inspection and quality assurance. The debates mostly center on the rigor and independence of the oversight. Predictably, market-oriented scholars do not favor burdensome external regulation, believing that the market better ensures quality. Others note, however, that consumers are not in a position to judge the quality of medical services and a rigorous independent review is essential.

Where there is a large private market in health care such as in the United States, patients' rights often take the form of consumer protections. The provision of information on which rational and informed choices among health plans, institutions, and professionals can be made is a key feature of developed private health care markets. In the United States, rights to information are seen as pivotal, with quality assurance institutions like the National Committee for Quality Assurance evaluating services, publishing reports, and 'empowering customers through compelling information'. Again, scholars disagree about the efficacy of disclosures to promote quality (Sage, 1999). Consumers can misinterpret published data due to their complexity. For example, there are several explanations for poor outcomes among doctors and hospitals. Poor ratings may reflect inferior quality, but they may also mean that the institution admits older, sicker, or more complex cases. To a certain extent, more sophisticated disclosures can account for such variables, but there is still debate as to the ability of consumers to interpret data accurately.

1.3 Controlling Cost in Health Care

All health care systems are embedded within national economies and global markets for medical technologies and pharmaceutical products, and this fact has created the problem of spiraling costs in common law countries. Despite similar pressures on cost everywhere, there are startling differences in the amounts that countries spend on health care, ranging from approximately 7 percent of GDP in the UK to 13 percent in the United States.

Countries have different methods of controlling cost. The most common among nations that guarantee some form of universal access is the global budget. Countries such as Australia, Canada, and the UK control cost by setting annual limits on public spending for health care. Since health authorities operate with finite resources, there is often explicit rationing such as long wait times or differential treatment based on age. Commentators often criticize global budgets for their inflexibility and explicit rationing. Care is distributed within strict economic parameters, irrespective of the population's needs, sometimes leading to increased morbidity or mortality.

The United States has far less control over health care costs, which is one reason that it spends so much more than other countries. Medicare and Medicaid are entitlement programs, making it difficult to limit public expenditures, and the government has not found it politically expedient to strictly regulate the private sector. The United States spent approximately $1.3 trillion in 2000, with an average per-capita cost of $4,358, compared with an average of $1,764, in the other 29 industrialized nations (Levit *et al.*, 2002).

Some argue that the substantial health care expenditures in the United States obviate the need for rationing. This is not quite true, however, because services are rationed implicitly through the ability to pay. If individuals cannot afford health insurance, their access to quality services is reduced. The State of Oregon explicitly rations Medicaid benefits, which has caused considerable controversy. Some scholars argue that rationing offers a rational method of allocating scarce resources, while others believe it is unfair to ration only among the poor (Elhauge, 1994).

The most promising approach to cost containment in America has been the rapid development of managed care organizations (MCO) during the late twentieth century. Managed care is a system that manages or controls what it spends on health care by closely monitoring how health care professionals treat patients. Managed care has been politically charged. Supporters argue that professionally managing patient care can lower cost while maintaining quality. Others have criticized MCOs for their bureaucratic interference with physician autonomy (e.g. administrators second-guessing doctors), limits on patient care (e.g. strict interpretations of 'medical necessity' eligibility criteria), and reduction in patient choice among doctors and hospitals (Jacobson, 2002).

Managed care was initially successful in controlling cost, but the savings were short-lived. Their costs per patient are now nearly equivalent to other forms of health insurance. Due to the unending political critique, many MCOs changed markedly and barely resemble their original structures. Managed care now offers more choice and less patient management, making it indistinguishable in some cases from traditional health plans.

America is still struggling with the high cost of health care as premiums have begun to rise dramatically in the early twenty-first century. As costs rise, so does the problem of uninsured people who cannot afford the premiums. The uninsured have poorer health outcomes, leading to significant disparities in health based on socio-economic status. Despite its wealth, and expenditures for health care and research, the United States compares unfavorably in health outcomes. Leading health indicators such as life expectancy in the United States lag behind most other industrialized countries. For example, the United States ranks twenty-seventh in infant mortality among thirty-nine industrialized nations. At the same time, the United States has marked disparities in health care access and outcomes. Lower socio-economic groups, particularly ethnic minorities, experience considerably greater morbidity and premature mortality (Institute of Medicine, 2002).

There are several important values in health care: access, equity, choice, quality, and cost. It should be clear from this discussion that political choices involve trade-offs. Some common law countries value universal access and equity, but are prepared to compromise on choice and quality. Other countries value choice and quality and are prepared to pay large amounts to achieve those goals, even if it means erecting financial barriers to access and creating inequalities within the population. Although the choices are political, the means used to achieve the goals are often legal, and have engaged the sustained attention of scholars.

2 THE THERAPEUTIC RELATIONSHIP

The therapeutic relationship is viewed as critically important to the compassionate and effective practice of health care. The law actively regulates the doctor–patient relationship, particularly in three key areas: malpractice, consent, and confidentiality.

2.1 Medical Malpractice: The Link between Regulation and Liability

Common law countries take noticeably different positions relating to medical malpractice, ranging from a robust tort system in the United States, to greater deference in the UK, to no-fault compensation in New Zealand (Giesen, 1988). Tort law is intended to accomplish several objectives such as deterrence, compensation, and punishment. However, empirical studies demonstrate that the tort system is a deeply flawed mechanism to achieve these objectives. Legal researchers have demonstrated that there is an imperfect fit between true medical error and successful litigation. In most cases of medical error, there is no litigation; in most cases where malpractice awards are made, there is no medical error. The best predictor of a malpractice award is the patient's disability and not medical negligence (Weiler et al., 1993). As a result, American scholars have proposed a number of ideas for insurance reform, including a cap on damages and no-fault compensation (Furrow et al., 2000).

The introduction of evidence-based clinical practice guidelines, as discussed above, may help secure one goal of medical malpractice litigation, namely quality improvement. In most common law countries, a complex web of hard and soft law regulates health care. Hard law is mainly in the form of mandatory directions, and soft law is mainly in the form of circulars and policy guidance. This provides what can only be described as 'the unsubtle link' between the regulatory framework and civil liability. The UK, for example, has stressed that 'failure to take due account of the contents of guidelines could result in medico-legal complications'.

The charming but deeply minatory medical metaphor of 'medico-legal complications' can only mean one thing—liability in negligence. In the period since the NHS market reforms of the 1990s, the standard of care expected of doctors has been raised considerably. In 1957, McNair J enunciated the infamous *Bolam* test, which has been roundly criticized by scholars for its failure to hold doctors accountable for medical error. McNair J instructed the jury that a doctor would not be negligent if she acts in accordance with a responsible body of medical opinion skilled in the specialty (*Bolam v Friern Barnet Hospital Management Committee* [1957] 1 WLR 582). For the next forty years doctors had a defense if they could produce any responsible expert medical evidence, even if it was the minority view.

In 1998, the House of Lords modified this approach in *Bolitho* [1998] AC 232, finding that, despite a body of professional opinion supporting the doctor's conduct, she could still properly be held liable in negligence. This significant change in the negligence standard, in conjunction with increased use of clinical protocols, means that inevitably there will be more malpractice litigation. It will be hard to argue that a body of medical opinion is 'responsible' if it contravenes evidence-based guidelines. This then enables a model of legislating by clinical guidance, enforced through the tort system.

Not all UK scholars are encouraged by the prospect of increased litigation following *Bolitho*. They argue that common law countries should not emulate the United States where malpractice law has caused doctors to practice defensively—for example, ordering excessive diagnostics and treatments. The influential Bristol Inquiry Report in the UK argued that malpractice litigation works against the interests of patients' safety by providing an incentive to cover up an error. 'And once covered up, no-one can learn from it and the next patient is exposed to the same or a similar risk' (Kennedy, 2001). The UK government is already proposing tort reform options including no-fault compensation, with the aim of moving away from a deterrence-based model. Although no-fault compensation is not as seriously discussed in the United States, the malpractice system has been demonized for contributing to the problem of medical error, which accounts for more deaths per annum than automobile crashes (Institute of Medicine, 2000).

Scholars, therefore, disagree on the utility of medical malpractice. In theory, it ought to provide economic incentives to practice safely and, used in conjunction with clinical guidelines, it might begin to have this effect. However, there is little empirical evidence that the tort system provides the right kinds of incentives. There is the nagging concern that it actually encourages doctors to over-treat (which is costly and potentially dangerous) and cover up their errors (preventing effective external scrutiny).

2.2 Consent to Medical Treatment

The classic common law statement of the right of self-determination was made in *Schloendorff v Society of New York Hospitals*, 105 NE 92, 93 (NY 1914), when Judge Cardozo laid down a principle often quoted in the common law world: 'Every patient of adult years and sound mind has a right to determine what shall be done with his own body; and a surgeon who performs an operation without his patient's consent commits an assault for which he is liable in battery'. Although personal autonomy is taken as a fundamental principle of liberty in common law jurisdictions, there are sharp differences in approach.

The United States has been the most steadfast in upholding the right of self-determination. Most states adopt the 'prudent patient' standard for informed

consent famously enunciated in *Canterbury v Spence*, 464 F 2d 772 (DC Cir 1972)—
that is, the doctor must disclose all risks a reasonable patient would regard as relevant
in deciding whether to consent. The House of Lords in *Sidaway* explicitly rejected the
'transatlantic doctrine of informed consent' and decreed that actions against a doctor for failure adequately to warn of risks would sound in negligence, not battery
(*Sidaway v Board of Governors of the Bethlehem Royal Hospital and the Maudsley
Hospital* [1985] AC 871). This meant that doctors had the *Bolam* defense—that is, they
could argue that failure to fully inform patients was in accordance with a responsible
body of medical opinion.

The prudent patient test has been adopted in Canada (*Reibl v Hughes* [1980] 114
DLR 3d 1) and Australia (*Rogers v Whitaker* (1992) 175 CLR 479), both of which
rejected *Bolam* as applicable in cases of patient consent. Despite having adopted the
prudent patient test, the Australian High Court was anxious to avoid reiterating
the expressions used in the American authorities, such as 'the patient's right to self-
determination' or the amorphous phrase, 'informed consent'. The Court went on to
affirm the rectitude of the Anglo-Australian approach that an action for failure to warn
must sound in negligence. Although the UK courts were hostile to informed consent
when it was a 'transatlantic doctrine', they have been more receptive to its Australian
version, which, for all its protestations to the contrary, is essentially informed consent
because it adopts the 'prudent patient' test. In the UK, there has been a dramatic shift
away from the responsible doctor towards the reasonable patient standard (*Pearce v
United Bristol Healthcare NHS Trust* (1998) 48 BMLR 118, per Woolf MR).

Scholars have considered the difficult issue of treating those who are incapable
of giving consent, such as persons with mental or learning disabilities. Complex
problems are posed such as the threshold for incompetence, the standard for substituted judgments, and appropriate proxy decision-makers (e.g. relatives, doctors, or
courts). The UK Law Commission (1995) proposed fundamental reform to ensure
clear rules for treating incapacitated patients, and scholars have urged government to
introduce legislation to implement the Law Commission report.

2.3 Privacy and Access to Medical Records

One of the most enduring aspects of the doctor–patient relationship is the confidentiality of medical information. Confidentiality is protected through international
human rights law, statute, and common law. It is also one of the most discussed topics
in the health law literature.

The European Court of Human Rights has held that health information privacy is of
'fundamental importance' to a person's enjoyment of 'a private and family life' under
article 8 (*Z v Finland* (1998) 25 EHRR 371). Article 8 extends also to the right of access to
personal information. Rights to privacy and to access to records may be limited to safeguard health, national economic well-being, and the rights and freedoms of others.

Health information privacy is often protected within a country or region's data protection policy. The Data Protection Act 1998 in the UK gives effect to the European Directive on Personal Data. The Act sets out data protection principles such as: (i) fair, legal, and accurate processing; (ii) limits on unauthorized access; and (iii) restrictions on unnecessary data transfers. A Data Processing Commissioner oversees the application of the Act. Similarly, the Bush administration promulgated the first nationwide privacy protection for health information. The rule requires (i) notice of privacy practices, (ii) consumer access to medical records, and (iii) patient consent for specified data uses (67 *Fed Reg* 53, 181, 14 August 2002).

Tort actions for breach of confidence are available in most common law jurisdictions. For example, the equitable remedy of breach of confidence under English law has three elements: the information must have the quality of confidence, be imparted in circumstances importing an obligation of confidence, and there must be an unauthorized use of that information to the person's detriment (*Coco v AN Clark (Engineers) Ltd* [1969] RPC 41, 47; *Attorney General v Guardian Newspapers* [1988] 3 All ER 545 (HL)).

Privacy rules throughout the common law world, like other aspects of the therapeutic relationship, have split the legal academy (Gostin, 1995). Some academics adamantly claim that doctor–patient confidences are inviolable, requiring strict privacy enforcement in tort and by statute. These scholars point to autonomy as the applicable principle—that is, patients have an interest in controlling who has access to their health data. To others, however, privacy protection should give way to achieve important aggregate benefits. Overly strict privacy laws, they argue, can interfere with effective health services research, medical audits, and disease surveillance. As with all aspects of the therapeutic relationship, society faces trade-offs between individual and collective goods, with the law playing a pivotal role in choosing which interests should prevail.

3 PUBLIC HEALTH: ASSURING THE CONDITIONS FOR HEALTHY POPULATIONS

Public health law is quite different from health care law and has emerged as a distinct field of legal study (Gostin, 2002). As indicated above, health care law concerns primarily the provision and regulation of medical care. High quality medical care is certainly important, but it is only one of many conditions necessary for improving the population's health and longevity. Governments in all common law countries engage in a broad range of activities to protect and promote the public's health and safety,

including health education, providing clean air and water, pure food and drugs legislation, occupational health and safety rules, and infectious disease control. When
government acts to preserve or promote health, however, it frequently has to restrict
personal or proprietary interests. Public health law has been defined as:

The study of the legal powers and duties of the state to assure the conditions for people to be
healthy (e.g., to identify, prevent, and ameliorate risks to health in the population), and the
limitations on the power of the state to constrain the autonomy, privacy, liberty, proprietary,
or other legally protected interests of individuals for protection or promotion of community
health. (Gostin, 2000)

A systematic understanding of public health law requires a careful examination of
what is 'public'. A public entity acts on behalf of the people and gains its legitimacy
through a political process, as the following discussion demonstrates.

3.1 Public Health and Theories of Democracy

Legal philosophers have inquired about the obligations of a political, or governmental, entity to protect and promote public's health (Walzer, 1983). Theories of
democracy help to explain the primacy of government in matters of public health.
A political community stresses a shared bond among members: organized society
safeguards the common goods of health, welfare, and security, while members subordinate themselves to the welfare of the community as a whole. Public health can be
achieved only through collective action, not through individual endeavor. Acting
alone, individuals cannot assure even minimum levels of health. Individuals may
procure personal medical services and many of the necessities of living; any person of
means can purchase a home, clothing, food, and the services of a physician or hospital. Yet no single individual, or group of individuals, can assure his or her health.
Meaningful protection and assurance of the population's health require communal
effort. Communities as a whole have a stake in environmental protection, hygiene
and sanitation, clean air and surface water, uncontaminated food and drinking water,
safe roads and products, and control of infectious disease. These collective goods, and
many more, are essential conditions for health. Yet these goods can be secured only
through organized action on behalf of the population.

3.2 Public Health and the Constitution

Constitutions in most common law countries have something to say, explicitly or
implicitly, about government's power or duty to protect the public's health. The
'police power' is the most famous expression of the natural authority of sovereign

governments to regulate private interests for the public good. Legal historians have demonstrated the close association between 'police' and civil society: politia (the state), polis (city), and politeia (citizenship) (Novak, 1996). 'Police' traditionally connoted social organization, civil authority, or formation of a political community. The term was meant to describe those powers that permit sovereign government to control its citizens, particularly for the purpose of promoting the general comfort, health, morals, safety, or prosperity of the public. The word had a secondary usage as well: cleansing or keeping clean. This use resonates with early twentieth-century public health connotations of hygiene and sanitation. Blackstone conceived of 'public health' and 'public police' as of 'highest importance'.

Scholarly disputes in common law countries center on the level of government that may exercise police powers—whether federal, provincial, tribal, state, territorial, or local. American constitutional scholars differ about whether the 'limited' powers of the federal government should extend to areas of traditional state authority such as firearm regulation. In Australia, the Commonwealth Constitution provides federal authorities with specified powers, yet there is ongoing debate about the appropriate distribution of power among the levels of government (Bidmead and Reynolds, 1998). These kinds of disagreements are complex, involving judgments about federal supremacy, harmonization of policy, state experimentation, and local autonomy (Opeskin, 1998). Like other areas of law, scholars claim support from constitutional text, the framer's original design, and flexible constitutional interpretation to meet the modern needs of the state.

3.3 Law as a Tool to Safeguard the Public's Health

The state's role in preserving and protecting the population's health is governed principally by statute. In many common law countries, public health law has not been systematically reformed since the early to mid-twentieth century. This is particularly troubling given the need for rapid detection and response to bioterrorism and naturally occurring health threats. As a result, Australia, the United States, and the UK are planning major reforms of their communicable disease laws (Monaghan, 2002).

There are at least five models for legal intervention designed to prevent injury and disease and promote the public's health. Although legal interventions can be effective, they often raise social, ethical, or constitutional concerns that have attracted considerable attention in the legal literature.

Model 1 is the power to tax and spend. This power, found in most constitutions, provides government with an important regulatory technique. The power to spend enables government to set conditions for the receipt of public funds. For example, the United States grants highway funds to states on condition that they set the drinking age at 21. The power to tax provides strong inducements to engage in beneficial behavior or refrain from risk behavior. For example, taxes on cigarettes significantly reduce smoking, particularly among young people. Many public health scholars have strongly supported spending and taxation as inducements to risk reduction because of their powerful effects.

Although the spending and taxing powers appear relatively benign, they are sometimes criticized as coercive and unfair. Commentators observe that economic incentives or disincentives can be so powerful that they are hard to resist. Seen in this way, behavior change induced through conditional spending or taxation has an element of involuntariness. At the same time, commentators point out that many taxes on risk behavior are highly regressive. For example, the ubiquitous cigarette tax falls disproportionately on the lower socio-economic classes. Spending and taxation, therefore, have problems relating to coercion and inequity that trouble some in the legal academy.

Model 2 is the power to alter the informational environment. Government can add its voice to the marketplace of ideas through health promotion activities such as health communication campaigns; provide relevant consumer information through labeling requirements; and limit harmful or misleading information by regulating advertisements of hazardous products. Government control over the informational environment certainly is beneficial, but it does implicate the freedom of expression. Consequently, it has captured the attention of constitutional law scholars.

Health communication campaigns, of course, rarely infringe on the freedom of expression (Tushnet, 1984). Government's concern with 'healthy messages' is thought to be an inherent good, and most scholars are prepared to give the state considerable leeway. When government presents its view concerning unsafe sex, abortion, smoking, high-fat diet, or sedentary lifestyle, there is no formal coercion. Yet, some scholars claim that public funds should not be expended, or the veneer of government legitimacy used, to prescribe particular social orthodoxies (Lessig, 1995).

Most common law countries do not regard corporate speech as deserving of constitutional protection. However, a vigorous debate has ensued in the United States about First Amendment protection of advertising hazardous products. Law and economics scholars often urge strict First Amendment scrutiny, arguing that a citizen's interest in the price, content, and quality of commercial products is just as strong as his interest in social and political discourse. Public health scholars, however, believe that hazardous product advertising is misleading and deceptive, often targeted at minors. For example, smoking cigarettes and drinking alcoholic beverages are depicted as rugged, athletic, adventuresome, and sexual. Alluring images and associations, according to public health advocates, do not inform consumers but may induce them to act against their self-interest in maintaining health.

Model 3 is direct regulation of individuals (e.g. seatbelt, helmets), professionals (e.g. licenses), or businesses (e.g. inspections, nuisance abatements). Public health authorities regulate pervasively to reduce risks to the population. There is a tension in legal scholarship between broad acceptance of public health regulation and resistance on grounds of civil liberties or property rights.

The exercise of compulsory powers deeply affects individual interests. Personal interests include privacy (e.g. disease reporting), autonomy (e.g. vaccination), and liberty (quarantine). Proprietary interests include freedom to contract (e.g. occupational health and safety), pursue a profession (e.g. licenses), and conduct a business (e.g. food and drugs). Powers that undermine individual interests are bound to be controversial. For example, scholars fiercely debated the compulsory powers in the Model State Emergency Health Powers Act developed in response to 11 September (Gostin *et al.*, 2002). Civil libertarians claimed that infectious disease powers were rarely needed and economic libertarians claimed that businesses should not be intensely regulated in an emergency.

Although many scholars recognize the need to regulate individuals and businesses to prevent harm to others, they have more difficulty accepting regulation of self-regarding behavior. Government regulates paternalistically in many realms such as seatbelt and motorcycle helmet laws, fluoridation of water, and prohibition of gambling. Although most common law jurists nominally reject hard paternalism, some have been willing to uphold it, based on the assumption that individual behavior inevitably affects the community by burdening families, emergency services, and the health care system.

Model 4 is indirect regulation through the tort system. Tort litigation can provide strong incentives for professionals and businesses to engage in less risky activities. Tort litigation can be an effective public health tool to influence behavior in activities ranging from medical practice to automobiles, pharmaceuticals, and children's toys. Perhaps the most famous use of tort law for the public's health was the extensive litigation in America against cigarette and firearm manufacturers.

There is intense debate in the legal literature. Some scholars claim that tort litigation is essential to promote public goods, while others claim it is inequitable, inefficient, and undemocratic (Parmet and Daynard, 2000). The tort system is regarded as inequitable because some injured people receive generous compensation, while others receive nothing. It is regarded as inefficient because considerable resources go to the judicial process (e.g. lawyers' fees and court costs). And it is regarded as undemocratic because the judiciary, a largely unelected branch of government, makes allocation decisions.

The final model is deregulation. Sometimes laws are harmful to public health and stand as an obstacle to effective action. For example, criminal laws proscribe the possession and distribution of sterile syringes and needles. These laws, therefore, make it more difficult for public health authorities to engage in HIV prevention activities.

Deregulation is often controversial among commentators because public health goals clash with other government objectives such as law enforcement. In countries like the United States, the law bans the use of federal funds for needle exchanges believing that they condone drug use. However, other common law countries such as Australia and the UK have innovative programs for the free distribution of sterile drug injection equipment. Scholars often base their arguments for syringe deregulation on the theory of 'harm reduction'—the law should permit interventions to reduce risk even for those engaging in otherwise unlawful conduct.

The government, then, has many legal 'levers' designed to prevent injury and disease and promote the public's health. Law and regulation can be highly effective and need to be part of government's agenda. At the same time, legal interventions can be controversial, raising important ethical, social, constitutional, and political issues. Seen in this way, public health law entails a series of trade-offs, just like other areas of health law. When government acts to promote collective interests in health and safety of populations, it almost invariably curtails personal interests (e.g. autonomy, privacy, expression, or liberty) or proprietary interests (e.g. pursuit of a profession, contracts, and property rights). These trade-offs are complex, important, and fascinating for students of public health law.

4 CONCEPTUALIZING HEALTH LAW

This chapter has examined the field of health law in three spheres: health care systems, the doctor–patient relationship, and public health. Although these three areas do not exhaust the varied subjects that occupy the field, they are among the most common concerns. We have conceptualized each sphere in terms of a series of trade-offs between personal and property interests on the one hand, and collective interests in health and safety on the other.

In the case of health care systems, we have noted the marked differences in approach among common law countries. The key values in some countries are universal access and equity, while in others they are personal choice and high quality. All countries express concern about cost, but spend vastly different percentages of their GDPs on health care. In the case of the doctor–patient relationship, we have noted the trade-offs between clinical discretion, sharing information, and research on the one hand, and patient autonomy and confidentiality on the other. Although all common law countries recognize the importance of patient consent and confidentiality, they differ in the extent to which they prefer clinical paternalism (doctors can be trusted to act wisely and beneficently) and self-determination (individuals have the right to make choices concerning treatment and data uses). Finally, in the case of public health, governments engage in hard trade-offs. Government's role in public health is broad, encompassing foundational areas of law and policy such as taxation, regulation, and the tort system. The state has to balance its powers to protect the common good with its responsibility to defend individual freedoms. Striking an appropriate balance is bound to be complex and politically difficult.

In each of these three spheres, common law countries pay lip service to the protection of rights and freedoms. Ostensibly, all countries adopt a Millian philosophy of individual freedom, except where necessary to prevent discrete harms. But beyond the rhetoric of individual rights are the wide divergences in how these rights are to be protected and in what circumstances. The tension between individual rights and common goods pervades the field of health law in its numerous dimensions.

REFERENCES

Bhagwati, P. N. (1992). 'The Role of the Judiciary in the Democratic Process: Balancing Activism and Judicial Restraint', *Commonwealth Law Bulletin*, 18: 1262–71.

Bidmead, I., and Reynolds, C. (1998). *Public Health Law in Australia: Its Current State and Future Directions*, Canberra: Commonwealth of Australia.

Elhauge, E. (1994). 'Allocating Health Care Morally', *California Law Review*, 82: 1451–544.

Enthoven, A. C. (1993). 'The History and Principles of Managed Competition', *Health Affairs*, 12: 24–39.

Furrow, B. R., Greaney, T. L., Johnson, S. H., Jost, T. S., and Schwartz, R. L. (2000). *Health Law*, St Paul, Minn.: West Group.

Giesen, D. (1988). *International Medical Malpractice Law: A Comparative Law Study of Civil Liability Arising from Medical Care*, Dordrecht: Nijhoff.

Gostin L. O. (1995). 'Health Information Privacy', *Cornell Law Review*, 80: 101–84.

—— (2000). *Public Health Law: Power, Duty, Restraint*, Berkeley: University of California Press.

—— (ed.) (2002). *Public Health Law and Ethics: A Reader*, Berkeley: University of California Press.

—— Sapsin, J. W., Teret, S. P., Burris, S., Mair, J. S., Hodge, J. G., and Vernick, J. S. (2002). 'The Model State Emergency Health Powers Act: Planning for and Response to Bioterrorism and Naturally Occurring Infectious Diseases', *Journal of the American Medical Association*, 288: 611–21.

Institute of Medicine (2000). *To Err is Human: Building A Safer Health System*, Washington: National Academy Press.

—— (2002). *Unequal Treatment: Confronting Racial and Ethnic Disparities in Health Care*, Washington: National Academy Press.

Jacobson, P. D. (2002). *Strangers in the Night: Law and Medicine in the Managed Care Era*, New York: Oxford University Press.

Kennedy, I. (2001). *Learning from Bristol: The Report of the Public Inquiry into Children's Heart Surgery at the Bristol Royal Infirmary 1984–95*, London: HMSO, Cm 5207, at p. 366.

—— and Grubb, A. (eds.) (1998). *Principles of Medical Law*, Oxford: Oxford University Press.

Kinney, E. D. (2001). 'The International Right to Health: What Does this Mean for Our Nation and the World?' *Indiana Law Review*, 34: 1457–75.

Law Commission (1995). *Mental Incapacity*, London: Law Commission Report 231.

Lessig, L. (1995). 'The Regulation of Social Meaning', *University of Chicago Law Review*, 62: 943–1045.

Levit, K., Smith, C., Cowan, C., Lazenby, H., and Martin, A. (2002). 'Inflation Spurs Health Spending in 2000', *Health Affairs*, 21: 172–81.

Marmor, T. R., and Boyum, D. (1992). 'American Medical Care Reform: Are We Doomed to Fail?' *Daedalus*, 121: 175–82.

Mills, R. J. (2000). *Health Insurance Coverage: 2000*, Washington: U.S. Bureau of the Census (available at http://www.census.gov).

Monaghan, S. (2002). *The State of Communicable Disease Law*, London: Nuffield Trust.

Newdick, C. (1995). *Who Should We Treat? Law, Patients and Resources in the N.H.S.*, Oxford: Clarendon Press.

Novak, W. J. (1996). *The People's Welfare: Law and Regulation in Nineteenth-Century America*, Chapel Hill, NC: University of North Carolina Press.

Opeskin, B. R. (1998). 'The Architecture of Public Health Law Reform: Harmonisation of Law in a Federal System', *Melbourne University Law Review*, 22: 337–66.

Parmet, W. E., and Daynard, R. A. (2000). 'The New Public Health Litigation', *Annual Review of Public Health*, 21: 437–54.

Sage, W. M. (1999). 'Regulating through Information: Disclosure Laws and American Health Care', *Columbia Law Review*, 99: 1701–829.

Tushnet, M. (1984). 'Talking to Each Other: Reflections on Yudof's When Government Speaks', *Wisconsin Law Review*: 129–46.

Walzer, M. (1983). *Spheres of Justice: A Defense of Pluralism and Equality*, New York: Basic Books.

Weiler, P. C., Hiatt, H. H., Newhouse, J. P., and Johnson, W. G. (1993). *A Measure of Malpractice*, Cambridge, Mass.: Harvard University Press.

CHAPTER 22

GLOBAL DEVELOPMENT AND IMPOVERISHMENT

UPENDRA BAXI

1 INTRODUCTION

THE periodic *reinvention* of impoverishment is now a global ritual (Escobar, 1995). Like all rituals, this at the very least constitutes a mode of legitimation of power. Redescription of conditions of extreme poverty is, indeed, rampant. The richer the articulation of world impoverishment in the global developmental discourse, the less concerted is the ensuing international social action.

At the beginning of the twenty-first century CE, concern with global impoverishment is high on everyone's agenda: from the United Nations system, international financial institutions, Northern state aid and development programmes, supranational regimes (like the European Community (EC) and even the World Trade Organization (WTO)) to transnational and 'glocal' (that is, specific) human rights movements and constituencies. Even chief executive officers (CEOs) of multinationals justify their concern for profits in a globalizing world in the languages of poverty-alleviation and global social progress. And around the forms of reinvention stand clustered and instituted a large variety of practices of global governance and the politics *of* and politics *for* human rights (for this distinction, see Baxi, 2002). These practices

A word of anticipatory appreciation is owed to those readers inclined to take human suffering seriously in the project of fashioning cosmopolitan common law scholarship.

promote conceptions of human development in which the agents and managers of contemporary economic globalization are presented as driven by the moral imperative of poverty alleviation.

But between the word and the deed falls a cruel shadow. The discourse that identifies impoverishment not just in terms of violation of human rights but also of everyone's right *to be and to remain fully human* does not summon forth concerted forms or programmes of global action. Contrary to the United Nations norm stipulating that nations should set a target of 0.7 per cent of GDP for foreign assistance, the actual flow of resources from the North is on the decline, as is well known, amounting to only 0.22 per cent. No international regimes of development policy exist, with the result that assistance programs remain tied to the shifting strategic and policy interests of the major developed societies. Moral exhortations directed towards the escalation of development assistance remain spectacular rhetorical failures. All current efforts to establish a right to human development seem to founder on the shores of contemporary economic globalization. The impoverished of the world are at the same time urged to believe that they may well, after all, constitute the front ranks of the winners in processes of contemporary globalization.

This chapter explores some ways in which forms of contemporary common law scholarship may be said to be related or responsive to global development and global impoverishment. This is a formidable task since common law scholarship lives in conceptual cloisters that often ignore the historic causes of world impoverishment, especially the impact of colonial and imperial common law practices and performances. Common law scholarship is impossible to understand except by reference to conceptual frames that derive from colonialism and imperialism. Yet mainstream common law scholarship remains concerned with explaining what the common law is or ought to be in a particular jurisdiction, in ways that rarely display an articulate concern with these historic world structures. This chapter suggests that scholars should pursue symptomatic and diagnostic practices of reading the many forms of silence in the midst of the speech constituting common law scholarship. If what follows shows the pitfalls, I hope that it also registers some promise for such an enterprise.

The threshold question is, how may we conceptualize the genre, common law scholarship? We need to interrogate the widespread assumption that the common law, and common law scholarship, are singular enterprises. Historians of the formative periods of common law know how diverse the so-called common law tradition was, both in its 'country of origin' and in countries of destination. The tradition has diversified even more since the middle of the last century, which was marked by decolonization and a certain insurrectionary and wholly just measure of juristic and judicial self-determination. In this sense, then, the variegated common law traditions were already profoundly post-modern, though the languages of postmodernism invaded common law scholarship only towards the end of the last century.

'Common law scholarship' now takes many, sometimes incompatible forms. The geography of the common law itself invites attention to maps of power and resistance. May we differentiate the common law and common law scholarship along the axis of the Old and New Commonwealths of the Common Law? Or, do we make our starting-point the narratives of various histories of the reception and imposition of a singular Anglo-American common law tradition? May we speak of a radical divide between the traditions developed in the Euro-American 'North' and the post-colonial 'South'? Or may we trace the 'commonalities' in common law theory and scholarship to certain preferred conceptions of good law (such as the institutions of rights and the rule of law) and of the good life (such as social equality and the secular state) that are firmly held within Euro-American liberal legalism? When we add contexts of larger political histories, how may we describe the multifarious itineraries of common law scholarship during the phases of the early, middle, and late Cold War and the now emerging formations of a common post-Cold-War legality?

2 Hybridities and Hauntologies

Large stories concerning so varied and vast a field of juridical production named as 'common law scholarship' run many a narrative risk. The discursive object constituting forms of scholarship—the 'common law'—needs to be historically understood. That understanding is, in the present opinion, best arrived at from a post-colonial perspective, one that 'commemorates not the colonial but the triumph over it' (Young, 2001: 60). Post-colonial critique seeks to investigate

the extent to which not only European history but also European culture and knowledge was part of, and instrumental in, the practice of colonization and its continuing aftermath . . . identifying fully the means and the causes of continuing international deprivation and exploitation . . . and analysing their epistemological and psychological effects

through transformation of

those epistemologies into new forms of cultural and political production that operate outside the protocols of metropolitan traditions and enable successful resistance to, and transformation of, the degradation and material injustice to which disempowered peoples and societies remain subjected. (Young, 2001: 69)

Common law, and knowledges about it, were an integral aspect of colonization and constitute, in diverse but important ways, its 'continuing aftermath'. Common law doctrine facilitated forceful occupation of territories and societies in diverse ways. The notorious Blackstonian distinction between 'inhabited' and 'uninhabited' colonies led to the destruction of aboriginal peoples and societies in Australia on the one hand and the emergence of common law repertoire of force and fraud, via unequal 'treaties' in dealing with First Nations peoples in the United States and

New Zealand. This then yields two orbits of common law development: common law, as it were, extended to peoples in a 'state of nature', and common law in societies formed by 'social contract'.

The epistemological violence of the common law unfolds further in the distinction between 'settled' colonies and 'dependencies' (now named aptly as 'exploitation colonies'). Drawing on a vast contemporary archive, Professor Robert Young brings to our attention this difference by reference to the two decisive dates that constitute 'British colonial and imperial thinking: 1776 and 1857'. The first signifies the 'War with American Colonies, ending in 1781', that 'led towards ideas of free trade, and a federation of self-governing Anglo-Saxon dominions made up of settlers of the same race: Greater Britain'. The second date, marked by 'the Indian Mutiny of 1857 . . . led to the end of commercial rule, progressive reformist policies, and institution of imperial government with control from the centre, the tenets of which will always over-ride commercial interests if necessary'. British colonization led not just to 'two different kinds of colony' ('exploitation' and 'settler' colonies) but also to two 'imperial systems: not differentiated by form of settlement or trade as in early colonial days, but by the race of settled inhabitants' (Young, 2001: 34–5; Mamdani, 1995). Common law develops, and with it the patterns of common law scholarship, in this hybrid form and ineluctably carries in its development the violent epistemic birthmarks of racism. Indeed, common law manifests its 'pure' form, its quintessentiality, as domination without hegemony through its hybridity.

The not wholly epistemic violence of common law theory and practice is now being archived by contemporaneous, albeit non-mainstream, common law scholarship (Fitzpatrick, 2001; Mamdani, 1995). The mainstream common law scholarship, however, continues to celebrate the *mission civilisatrice*, or more precisely the justification of British imperialism in terms of the White Man's Burden. This coded a double 'moral responsibility': 'first to exploit for the benefit of others ("the civilized world") the available raw materials that would otherwise be left unused, and then to extend the culture of civilization to the society being exploited' (Young, 2001: 40). The post-colonial common law (and with it common law scholarship) provides many histories of 'fulfilment' of this double moral responsibility.

That 'responsibility' may have been performed in ways that perhaps justify Seeley's remark that 'the British Empire' (in contrast with the French) had been acquired in a 'fit of absence of mind (itself a romanticized version of the Earl of Carnarvon's equally implausible claim in 1870 to the House of Lords that the empire was "the child sometimes of accident and sometimes of mistake")' (Young, 2001: 33).

Whatever may be said concerning forms of British imperialism, the imposition or introduction of common law does not allow felicitous description in terms of 'mistake' and 'accident'. The violent birthing of hybrid colonial legality was a fully conscious and planned enterprise. The 'accidents' and 'mistakes' occur in the time-space of post-colony, when common law inheritance continues unmodified in South common law regions. Even so, continuities of common law practices and processes in the New Commonwealth of Nations may not be understood wholly in these terms. In so far as these practices and processes protected and promoted special strategic interests (economic as well as political) their continuation is a planned hegemonic necessity. Elsewhere inertia reigns either because capabilities of imaginative law reform are lacking or because settled adjudicative dispositions (which Pierre Bourdieu names in complex ways as *habitus*) perpetuate dependence on overseas 'wisdom' at the cost of ignoring mass impoverishment. Much of South common law reform emulates models and measures of North common law. Thus, for example, modelling of alternate dispute resolution mimes what happens in the Anglo-American orbit, scarcely cognizing the rich diversity available in national jural experience. When Family Courts are to be instituted, South common law scholarship and law reform bodies create hybrid models drawn from the United States, the UK, and Canada, as if the millennial experience of people's law (the 'informal', 'customary', 'non-state' legal order) did not exist at all! Similarly, and all too often, post-colonial lawyers and justices display common law fetishism; for example, the common law rules of statutory construction and interpretation are routinely implemented, regardless of their unfavourable and unfortunate impact on socially progressive legislation. Post-colonial tutelage of the 'new' common law theory and practice awaits its own future historians.

Imperial governance across forbiddingly vast territories of exploited colonies (as compared with the settled ones) and of insurgent multitudes maps differential trajectories of imposition of hybrid colonial common law's legality. It emerges essentially as predatory legality (Baxi, 2003, and the literature there cited) despite the proud colonial boast that the British Rule of Law was a distinctive 'gift' to the subject peoples and societies (Guha, 1997: 66–72). Still, the politics of imperial law's desire furnishes considerable renovation of the metropolitan common law and jurisprudence. The 'great' Benthamite project of reform, and rationalization, of the common law could only be enacted in colonial India, which furnished a fecund site for its codification. India, as the corpus of Eric Stokes so richly reveals, provided a laboratory of Benthamite ideas for conducting experiments (impermissible at home) in giving contested statutory form to common law principles and doctrines. The Indian Codes (such as the Penal Code, the Codes of Civil and Criminal Procedure, the Indian Evidence, Contract, Acts, for example) travelled to other nascent common law jurisdictions in African colonies, decreeing in enduring ways their own post-colonial legal careers and futures. The intra-colonial imperial transfers of colonial legality await Foucauldian analytical labours.

So do the tasks of understanding the *materiality* of colonial legality. The colonial common law, much like the roads, railways, and communications technology, provides the basic infrastructure for ceaseless exploitation of natural, human, and cultural resources of the colonized peoples. It programs normative software producing legal normative repression: for example, the varieties of unfree labour conferring Roman law-type *patriae potesta* powers, powers over life and death, in the hands of colonial administrators and agents of colonial capitalism, land tenure systems, sedition and treason laws, preventive detention, doctrines of 'crown privilege' and 'sovereign immunity', models of legal education, research, and lawyering that advance the tutelage to metropolitan common law. It also designs the material hardware of law: for example, colonial police, prisons, mechanisms of torture and use of extra-legal fatal force by state agents, sites of preventive detention as well custodial confinement, hierarchical embodiments marking distinctions between 'subordinate' and 'superior' adjudicatory institutions. Much of the software for normative repression and institutional hardware of common law survives long beyond the time of colonial imposition.

Law facilitated the emergence of a 'carefully regulated Empire', in which 'the idiom of conquest was replaced by the idiom of Order'. That idiom was deployed over and over again 'to mobilize manpower' for 'plantations owned by Europeans' in India, indeed to an extent of 'perpetuation of inhumanity'. As Ranajit Guha describes the condition of tea plantation labour in Assam:

No less a person than the Law Member of Government of India admitted that the labour contract authorized by the law was designed to commit a person to employment in Assam even before he knew what he was doing and hold him to his promise for some years on the pain of arrest and imprisonment. 'Conditions like these have no place in the ordinary law of master and servant', he said. 'We made them part of the law of British India at the instance and for the benefit of the planters of Assam'. (Guha, 1997: 27)

Mamdani (1995: 148–65) archives similar practices of feudalism of colonial common law in British Africa. The practices of forced inter-colony migration of indentured labour employs a similar narrative of uses of common law doctrines of property and contract extended to exploitation colonies. Indeed, as Guha witheringly notes: 'In one vital respect the mobilization of coolies for tea plantations differed little from the mobilization of cannon-fodder for the First World War', colonial law and order emerging in the process as an 'idiom of state violence' (1997: 27–8).

That idiom also emerges differently on the register of civil law. Impermissible in the common law metropolis, colonial adjudicatory power and process through the notorious formulae of 'justice, equity, and good conscience' enables colonial judicatures considerable interpretive freedom to modify practices of imported common law (memorably archived by Duncan Derrett in relation to colonial Indian, Anglo-Hindu, and Anglo-Muslim law legal formations). The principle of the 'consent of the governed', scarcely writ large on colonial law, policy, and administration found a convenient and expedient patriarchal articulation in the creation of 'personal law' systems in ways that authorized violent social exclusion of women and social apartheid constituted by the caste-based indigenous law (in the South Asian situation).

Of course, when administrative exigencies so required, the practice of imposition of the common law legislated caste-based law in its 'modern' form. For example, the colonial Indian Criminal Tribes Act stigmatized at birth all human beings as born criminals through the device of enumerating social communities that threatened the

British Indian Empire with potential insurgency. Similarly, colonial legality reproduced hybrid forms of chieftaincy in African societies, and land revenue systems in South Asia, that served the ends of colonial 'decentralized despotism' (cf. Mamdani, 1995) strikingly well.

I mention all this to suggest strongly that the colonial common law was a *sui generis* historic 'cultural' production, constructed along wholly racist lines. It was the 'race of settled inhabitants' (Young, 2001: 35) that made *all* the difference; colonial legal pluralism, even 'multiculturalism', was for an obscene stretch of historic time 'originally intended to be a whites-only affair'. White colonies, like Canada and Australia achieved dominion status in 1867 and 1901 respectively; in contrast 'Home Rule was notoriously impossible to achieve for any "non-whites" who wanted it, such as the West Africans or the Indians' (Young, 2001: 39).

The institutionalized racism of modern common law (and common law scholarship) stands unarticulated in contemporary North and South common law scholarship. Comparative legal studies are no longer unabashedly Eurocentric. Duncan Derrett dedicated his entire life to the creation of a new genre of comparative common law scholarship. His successors (notably Marc Galanter and Werner Menski) have persevered in bringing home the notion that common law may not be understood outside the frames of jural and social experience of the non-European Other. We derive much the same message from the corpus of Max Gluckman, Paul Bohanan, and contemporary students of legal pluralism.

Unfortunately, this genre does not seem to inform teaching and research directed towards the history of common law. The dominant tradition of comparative common law studies concerns itself primarily with the transposition of legal norms and institutional processes as if the common law was a kind of 'brooding omnipresence', unsullied by multifarious modes of domination, exploitation, and racism. The much-vaunted 'spirit of the common law' is a spectre that haunts dominant comparative common law scholarship. Its more egalitarian, and non-complicit, pursuits must go beyond what Jacques Derrida now names (in his *Spectres of Marx*) as 'hauntology'—a historic process which we may describe in our context as the ghosts of colonial common law stalking many a moment of post-colonial legal theory and practice. The 'spirit' of common law needs to be grasped in frankly multicultural dialogic terms. Surely, the common law givers were also law recipients at the same time. But the question 'In what ways did metropolitan common law invite its own transformation through juridical exchange relations in colonial times?' is rarely posed. The posing of the question is inaugural in itself; it invites attention to new ways of performing historiography of the common law. Far from being an esoteric pursuit, the question itself complicates our understanding of colonial continuity and postcolonial legal change and the relation of all this to the production and reproduction of South mass impoverishment.

No matter how we conceptualize the life and times of common law scholarship, its history and present scope do not constitute a single universe but present themselves as a collection of constellations ('pluriverse'). Scholars need to develop narratives of the ways in which common law ideologies and practices promoted human immiseration and entrenched bourgeois legal formations as the arena of struggle for practices of human emancipation. Such accounts are likely to be slow in coming.

3 COMMON LAW SCHOLARSHIP
SOUTH AND NORTH

3.1 Differences

These do not admit any brief summation. Somewhat understandably, North common law scholarship approaches issues of global development and impoverishment in 'slow motion', if at all, while South common law scholarship is animated by 'fast forward' engagement with these concerns, now somewhat mutated by the legal elite's zeal for 'globalization'. This difference shows up in several ways. I archive this here with a scarcity of references imposed by the editorial instruction to limit the range of bibliographical resources. But the *cognoscenti* will surely recognize many unacknowledged epistemic debts.

First, South common law scholarship stands constituted by the intersection of constitutionalism and common law. It invites description as 'constitutional common law scholarship' in the sense that common law inheritance is always cast within, and complicated by, the languages and logics of governance and rights provisions in the constitutional text. Almost all South constitutions stand produced, and develop, within contexts of mass impoverishment, finding some innovative ways to address it. The constitution provides the point of origin for judicial and juridical discourse. But this is at the same time mediated by common law inheritance, especially through the constitutional device of continuing in force, unless amended, the pre-existing legality of classical common law that masks large exercises of public power in the private law orderings created by regimes of property, contract, and tort law. However, overall, the historical circumstances under which South common law scholarship developed have led its proponents to constitutionalize these common law inheritances through the language of 'public law'.

Secondly, South common law scholarship stands marked by distrust of North legal theory, whose (con)founding 'fathers' (because there were no 'mothers' and 'midwives') were never bothered by the injustice of the ways in which colonial legality was produced, and whose contemporary exponents seem unaware (beyond expression of rhetorical anxiety) of the role of law in creating mass impoverishment. All this leads to a rather unmanageable mass of normative contradictions between inherited forms of common law and forms of post-colonial legality. The former valorize exacting solitude for rights of private property; the latter demonstrate a continuing concern with distributive justice. From Jawaharlal Nehru to Robert Mugabe (although the juristic differences that mark the chasm between these iconic figures is radically different in time and space of jural enunciation), post-colonial legality remains tormented by the fractured histories of agrarian and land reform measures. North common law scholarship seems to have little purchase on these histories of mutation of the 'common law' inheritances and their renovation. On the whole, these histories also pass by many a controversy well-beloved of their North conceptual cousins, notably manifest in law and economics, critical legal studies, and a few wholesome developments in 'postmodern' legal theory.

Thirdly, while South justices and jurists endlessly refer to common law precedent and doctrine, they do so rather eclectically, putting the languages of classical and contemporary common law traditions to diverse, often bewildering, uses. The deployment of the *stare decisis* doctrine serves in the main the broadly 'policing' function of control within judicial hierarchy; South appellate justices remain altogether unburdened by whatever residue of judicial self-discipline this doctrine may be said to evoke.

Further, the adaptation of common law judicial custom of *stare decisis* remains incomprehensible outside what Jeremy Bentham named as 'the Judge and company'. The 'company' designates here the role of the appellate legal professionals, the Tenth Wonder (as it were) of the jurisprudential world. Generations of South lawyering elites (which provide a common law South archetype of excellence in lawyering) acquire specialist legal knowledges through Anglo-American circuits of 'higher' legal education. Versatile in dominant North common law discourse, they bring their formative, and formidable, knowledges of comparative precedent to the course of argumentation at home. They thus remain the active carriers of contemporary metropolitan common law to South legislation and adjudication. The North lawyering practices are relatively more self-contained, even to the point of celebration of virtues of Eurocentric insularity. As late as in the 1990s, Justice Antonin Scalia was even heard to say that foreign precedents are of no relevance whatsoever to the doing of justice!

While we ought to appreciate the comparative common law learning thus brought to tasks of South adjudication, we should also pause to notice the fact that the North precedent-happy South lawyering styles, revelling in heavy invocation of foreign precedent, leads many a South Justice to stymie the pro-impoverished aspects of the law and the constitution. A vivid example is furnished by some salient South African constitutional court decisions that, in the result, stand guided by British notions of administrative law and exaggerated notions of separation of powers, which the South African Constitution so remarkably sought to erase by elevating economic and social rights to the status of justiciable, enforceable rights.

On the other hand, it remains equally true that some South jurisdictions generously put Anglo-American precedents to activist uses. For example, the Indian

Supreme Court has renovated the doctrines of 'promissory estoppel', 'legitimate expectations', and prospective overruling to hold state action accountable at the bar of fundamental rights, a performance exceeding the original metropolitan intent. The doctrine of precedent has been used, for weal or woe, to justify (in Robert Cover's memorable distinction) both jurisgenerative and jurispathic uses.

Fourthly, North and South scholars differ markedly over the meaning and import of human rights as ideology and practice. Enunciated earlier in terms of the priority of civil and political rights over social and economic rights, the discord now has shifted to how the protection of these rights may actually empower the impoverished.

Fifthly, necessarily entailed in the preceding are differences in approach concerning judicial power, process, and role. North common law scholarship (especially through the corpus of John Rawls, Jurgen Habermas, Ronald Dworkin, Duncan Kennedy, and Frank Michelman) developed and urged others to adopt universal conceptions of judicial role. This prescriptive theory finds little resonance in South common law scholarship because of the historical circumstances in which proponents of South legal scholarship find themselves, where justices at work are seen as political actors under another name, despite the growing tendency for their occasional, even periodic, cooptation by those who resist unconscionable excesses of power. Future theorizing entails a more nuanced reflexivity concerning the travails of South judicial process and power.

Sixthly, while critical of received notions of the 'rule of law', South common law scholars remain more concerned than their North counterparts with the intersection between the global and national institutional interlinkages that perpetuate mass impoverishment. They read Professor T. E. Holland's quip, at the beginning of the last century, that international law is the vanishing point of the common law rather as meaning that it presents a 'vanishing point' of the common lawyer's intelligence! They continue to pioneer enabling egalitarian and equitable construction of an international rule of law, in ways that endow this notion with adjudicatory policy outcomes.

3.2 Material Conditions of the Production of Legal Scholarship

Differences between the themes pursued and the ideas developed by North and South legal scholarship respectively are related to the material conditions under which scholarship is produced. 'Material conditions' here connote economic, social, and political circumstances affecting ways of production of South common law scholarship. The first refers ineluctably to the minuscule patterns of investment in legal education and research; the second designates iniquitous patterns of access to education in general and legal education in particular; the third categorizes the very possibility of scholarly self-determination in the production of legal and juristic knowledges. The multifarious development assistance programmes (including those notably of the Ford Foundation and the British Council) for regeneration of South legal education and research constitute a fourth material condition, in ways that facilitate, at the end of the day, hegemonic transfers of common law knowledge production. One may only hope that this *Handbook* assists a rounded understanding of these material conditions.

The notion that globalization of common law scholarship provides rough and ready ways of overcoming material conditions warrants a brief re-examination. Even the recent upsurge of interest in and ideas about the effects of cyber-technology on scholarship is unlikely to make much difference because access to legal knowledge will remain unequally distributed between North and South. South law libraries can no longer afford subscriptions to law reports of the Commonwealth and learned legal journals, now heavily proliferating. While they do have recourse to the available free cyber-space materials, very few communities of South common law scholars can afford access to commercial databases such as Lexis and Westlaw!

However, structural inequities in access to global common law scholarship remain a mixed blessing. Differential access provides the theoretical context for emergence of a distinctive form of grassroots, emancipative, and free-standing juristic thought in the South. Yet, and simultaneously, private knowledge-monopolies become repressive because empowering knowledge of effective ways of using law in combating impoverishment remains largely inaccessible. Still, this characterization of the situation may fail to capture the complexity of the material conditions of scholarship to the extent that it attributes to erudite knowledge-production monopolies a certain power over the production of organic and experiential knowledge, and even wisdom. Exploring the complexities and contradictions of the conditions under which legal knowledge about impoverishment is produced is clearly an important endeavour, to be explored in future scholarship.

South legal education differs from the more professional North curricula and pedagogies by its distinctive 'liberal-arts' orientation. When access to legal education is construed almost as the constitutional birthright of every student with a graduate degree, the sheer growth in law school enrolment results in a spectacular decline in the teacher–taught ratio; available resources steadily impoverish the growth of full-time faculty, with the marked impact on dedication of scholarly time to the development of professional scholarship. Also, levels of state and philanthropic funding in the South for law teaching and for the creation of cooperative research networks remain infinitesimally low.

What emerges, then, is the picture of differential South common law scholarship. Academic production stands unevenly distributed: thus marking leadership within South Asia for Indian, within Africa for South African and Tanzanian, within South East Asia for Hong Kong, Singaporean, and Malaysian scholarship. Even on this register, the levels of conversation among these unfortunately remain sub-optimal.

While the avoidance in the South of the North 'publish or perish' syndrome has notable advantages, the low levels of scholarly production generate a deficit both in disciplinary and cross-disciplinary scholarly communication within the South common law regions, and in reflection on the role of law in creating and combating mass impoverishment. The entire South common law scholarship region, for example, produces a minuscule proportion of the common law world's law journals and reviews. While the tradition of sociological and empirical research in law grows apace in some leading South common law regions (e.g. India), as does the tradition of doing South–South comparative legal studies (inspired notably by post-apartheid South African constitutional jurisprudence), overall the landscape of the South common law scholarship remains affected by its historic birthmarks.

Against this background, the existence in common law regions in the North of exiled diasporic communities of South academics, sometimes created by individual decisions to go into exile, sometimes created by forces operating on larger groups, provides a prolific source of critique and renewal. The remainder of this chapter identifies ways in which the activities of South common law scholars in the North may foster the creation of an *egalitarian* mode of production of legal knowledge in ways that actually bring programmatic claims about global development into engagement with the reality of global impoverishment. We need to trace the politics of knowledge-based power on the one hand and, on the other, the politics of insurgent theoretical desire and the philosophies of hope that animate discourse.

The basic causes of impoverishment remain somewhat indifferently addressed by both North and South historians of common law development. Nearly all North 'modern' and 'postmodern' jurisprudence (with some refreshing exceptions: see e.g. Fitzpatrick, 1992, 2001; Santos, 1995) ignores the ways in which 'modern', and now global, common law regimes relate to the circumstances of global impoverishment. Despite some early attempts to address the very possibility of speaking about global justice, this project scarcely informs mainstream North common law legal theory, which is primarily concerned with articulating the nature of lawness, with elucidating notions of obligation to obey the law, and with developing theories about the relative autonomy of adjudication, about rights, and about effective uses of law in 'development'.

This limitation in the scholarly literature seems surprising, given the widespread concern in the last forty years in North common law scholarship with law and poverty, and with the crises of the welfare state in the North. The surprise abates somewhat when we recall that national anti-poverty programmes in the relatively affluent common law regions had few reasons to be concerned with the causes of mass impoverishment in the South common law regions. The paradox of 'poverty amidst plenty' seemed to constitute a good-enough terminal point of enquiry, as if the massive dedication of resources to the many phases of the Cold War, and now the newly emergent discourses of the post-Cold-War period, did not affect mass impoverishment in the affluent common law regions. The almost encyclopaedic genre of

North common-law-and-poverty studies to a great extent mystifies the relationship between local/national and global/South impoverishment. The South common law regions have been, in contrast, understandably more articulate in this respect.

3.3 Understanding South Juridical 'Backwardness'

All this having been fully said, one must also seek to understand endogenous reasons for juristic 'backwardness' of most forms of South scholarship. I refer to 'backwardness' in clinical, diagnostic terms, not as a pejorative marking any comparison with the North scholarship; rather, it marks the distance between understanding of legal development among the social and human sciences epistemic communities as compared with 'black-letter', doctrinal juristic scholarship.

Much refreshing writing on legal history of colonial and post-colonial legality, for example, emanates from cultural and from feminist and eco-history scholarship, *not* from South common law scholarship. Conventional legal historians rarely unveil social meanings of colonial law 'reception' or 'imposition'. Instead, these narratives consist in lifeless technical descriptions of legal institutions and their evolution. These fail even to pose questions concerning why certain institutions and processes of common law (e.g. the jury system) failed to take root in post-colonial societies. What is even more disconcerting is that teaching legal history, for the most part, does not even utilize insights from new historiographies such as subaltern studies.

The same holds true, generally, of the ways of teaching 'legal theory'. Cast in the pedagogically uninspiring reiteration of the 'schools' of jurisprudence, legal theory in South common law teaching (and therefore of research) remains an alienating discourse. A vast amount of legal and social experience of the South remains relatively un- or under-theorized in jurisprudential terms. South common law scholarship interrogates, in rather haphazard ways, North legal theory but fails to identify and develop its own potential for immanent theory about law in society. So profoundly mimetic it remains that it fails to acknowledge the implicit post-colonial theory latent in judicial and juristic endeavours. North common law scholarship remains narcissist in the extreme, failing threshold acknowledgement of the South imagination and experience.

It is pointless to multiply instances. We, however, need to understand reasons for this not-so-benign neglect. How is it that the potential of jurisprudential critique of the common law tradition pioneered, for example, by Sir Dadabhai Naroji's *Poverty and Un-British Rule in India*, Mahatma Gandhi's *Hind Swaraj*, Walter Rodney's *How Europe Underdeveloped Africa*, and the corpus of Touvalou Houenou, Lamine Senghor, Garan Kouyate, Frantz Fanon, Amilcar Cabral, Andre Gunther Frank, Samir Amin, Edward Said, finds so little resonance in South teaching and research? The indictment of 'backwardness' is, at the same time, a summons to theorize South common law experience and imagination.

4 LIMITATIONS OF NORTH COMMON LAW SCHOLARSHIP: THE JURISPRUDENTIAL LEGACIES OF BENTHAM AND MARX

A related, and not wholly historical, question remains: are the genres of North common law scholarship *theoretically indigent*, managing to avoid any serious engagement with the process of understanding the ways in which law performs both causative and ameliorative roles in relation to global impoverishment? If North common law scholarship is theoretically poor in this way, how may we explain and change this situation?

Jeremy Bentham proposed the progressive elimination of indigence as among the four aims of civil law, which he described as subsistence, security, abundance, and equality (1975: 58–95). He carefully distinguished between 'indigence' and 'poverty', describing the former as the 'saddest of all . . . a long catalogue of evils which end in indigence, and consequently in death under its most terrific forms'. This distinction is central to the more recent law-and-poverty programmes in contemporary North common law legal regimes (see Buchanan, 1994, and the literature therein cited). Bentham was resolute in his insistence that indigence should be considered an evil that lay wholly within the power of civil law to redress. To this end Bentham assiduously laboured to establish the constitution of a 'pauper kingdom', and even a 'pauper panopticon'.

Bentham was not, of course, concerned with anything more than reform of the British Poor Law System, but his jurisprudential message, unfortunately much ignored in neo-Benthamite discourse on law, has stayed with us for a very long time in the shape of at least three distinct propositions. First, poverty and indigence remain singular affairs of nation-state law and policy; secondly, modes of bureaucratization of human suffering are considered a necessary evil; and thirdly, the law ought somehow to cope with human deprivation in terms of the Principle of Utility. All these tenets have been criticized on various grounds, yet Bentham did place poverty and indigence within the very core of legal theory and jurisprudence, a message that unfortunately did not appeal to his successors in legal theory from John Austin to H. L. A. Hart, Ronald Dworkin, and Richard Posner or to those who have followed them (of course with the notable exception, no matter how severely North-confined, of John Rawls's representation of the regime of the 'Difference Principle').

In contrast, Marx and Marxian scholarship and theory located impoverishment in both national and global frames. Marxian discourses view colonialism and imperialism as necessary entailments of Western capitalism. Critical legal histories have recognized in vivid images the predatory nature of colonial legality, which systematically underdeveloped whole continents for centuries and is still an active cause of Third World impoverishment. Marxian themes have not been characteristic of

North common law scholarship, with the exception of the critical legal studies movement and (to a limited extent) the law-and-development and law-in-development
movements. Even these movements were ambivalent about the relationship between
law and global development and impoverishment. North common law scholarship
has notably failed to develop a discourse concerning the relationship between local
and national legal doctrine concerning impoverishment on the one hand and, on the
other, forms and practices of global impoverishment. That scholarship has also
ignored the summons to develop an understanding of law's role through studying
the history of ideas and analysing institutional practices.

5 THE LANDSCAPE OF COMMON LAW SCHOLARSHIP

Contemporary North common jurisprudential theory parodies the old division
among 'schools' of jurisprudence. The American and Scandinavian legal realist
approaches, as is well known, dissolved 'schools' into 'movements' of theory and
practice. Yet the 'schools' narratives persist, even in their 'postmodern' and 'post-
metaphysical' moments. Contemporary North common law scholarship divides into
at least four major, and internally highly diverse, movements: law and economics,
critical legal studies, feminist legal theory, and finally the 'old' and the 'new' law-and-
development movements. At the end of the day, these movements present themselves
as the 'schools' of yesteryear, no matter how these chose to self-dissipate!

5.1 Law-and-Economics Movements

The varieties and 'generations' of the North law-and-economics movements offer
some useful post-Weberian insights into the effects of law on economic development
(Mercuro and Medema, 1997; Posner, 1992). These movements address deep and difficult issues entailing at least the following basic assumptions: '... rational agents are self
interested maximizers of utility; ... utility can be best understood ... as a single item
varying only in quantity; ... utility is best analysed in terms of preferences; ... preferences are exogenous i.e. not significantly shaped by law and institutions; and ... ends
adopted by an agent cannot be the subject of rational deliberation, although agents
may deliberate about instrumental means to ends' (Nussbaum, 1997: 1197–8.) These
assumptions have been contested on various grounds (notably by Nussbaum, 2000,
especially based on the notion of 'adaptive preferences'). The issue of distributive

justice does not form a central preoccupation of the law-and-economics movements, barring perhaps the 'deviant' Yale School, which even so shares the general anti-interventionism characteristic of the movements as a whole, framing the case for regulation in terms of correction of specific forms and situations of market failure (Mercuro and Medema, 1997: 79–83).

The principal messages that emerge from the law-and-economics movements provide cause for reasonable anxiety. First, when extended to human rights-based practices of just development of Third World societies, the Coasian notion may suggest that legal rights constitute 'nonsense on stilts', in Bentham's withering, and much misquoted, phrase. Being irrelevant under conditions of nil transaction costs and negotiable under high transaction costs, they have no more value than any other factors of production.

Secondly, the 'catallaxy' approaches to regulation produce the notion (as Posner, following Coase reminds us) that political conduct must be viewed as 'utility maximizing' and 'political parties as firms supplying regulation, with what is supplied . . . being wanted by those groups (or coalitions) which are able to outbid others in the political market'. When such approaches are transferred to the international context, it can accurately be said that the triumph of a rights-based approach to human development—induced by the United Nations and promoting regulation in favour of the impoverished in forms such as agrarian/land reform, human rights to livelihood, and rights for organized and unorganized labour, including migrant labour—must remain liable to progressive outbidding and cancellation by those groups or coalitions that, at a global level, demand free flow of foreign investment.

Thirdly, the insights into non-market behaviour flowing from many versions of public choice theory compel recognition that international, like national, political conduct is not animated by notions of the common good but rather by special interests that most benefit from the production of legal norms and standards (national, supranational, and global) which emerge not as *public* goods but as fungible *private* goods according to the dictates of corporate capital. The situation would no doubt look different were we to move away from the model of utility-maximization and extend the Rawlsian 'Difference Principle' to a global level. The law-and-economics movements do not address in any detail issues of global redistribution and justice. Indeed, conceptions of economic justice arising from the principle of 'wealth maximization' lack even 'an appreciation that people can be dominated, coerced, and constituted by a market plagued with distributional inequalities based on factors such as race, class, gender, religion, and sexual preferences' (Minda, 1989: 1855 at 1864–5).

Fourthly, while the more recent articulation that urges '[s]ystematic resistance to agrarianism' as the primary goal of international economic law (Chen, 2001: 46) is rightly addressed exclusively to the North's tradition of protectionism for agribusiness, it overlooks the fact that millions of South peoples still depend for sustenance and rights on farms rather than factories. North common law scholarship obscures vital issues of this type when that scholarship represents as universal what are only crises of North agriculturalism.

It is unfortunate that South common law scholarship has ignored the messages of the various law-and-economics movements thus forfeiting potential for South-based critique and reconstruction. There is, for example, no notable South-based critique of law as a process of wealth maximization, the allocative role of apex court decisions, and redistributive effect of deregulation, dis-investment, de-nationalization, and even 'corporate citizenship'. Nor is there much debate concerning how we may feminize the discourse of rational choice theory or social contractarianism. The histories of economic rationalities that animate South contributions to the making of 'new' international economic order (especially the WTO, a cruel work in progress) remain in search of gifted raconteurs.

5.2 Critical Legal Studies Movements

Critical legal studies tend towards 'demystification' of the role of law in causing, not always in ways that address, mass deprivation. The movement's principal, and necessarily North-bound, messages remain relevant to the task of understanding law's historical roles in the causation of conditions of mass impoverishment in the South.

First, the categories of 'property' and 'contract' legitimated many a historical formation of intranational mass deprivation. Secondly, these categories were fundamental in the 'de-radicalization' of working class movements. Thirdly, forms of seemingly 'neutral' liberal adjudication preponderantly favour and reproduce social relations of domination inherent in the reproduction of capital accumulation. Fourthly, the subaltern struggles for human rights of the deprived, the dispossessed, and the disadvantaged fashion, in complex and contradictory ways, the formative notions of the rule of law, always tethered, however, to the 'logics' of the maintenance of capitalistic production relations. Fifthly, the logics and paralogics of human rights languages and rhetoric dialectically contribute to the fashioning of practices of liberal democracy in the metropolis, and, in the first phase of colonialism and imperialism, of practices of terror in the colonies. Forms of law emerge as both emancipative and brutally repressive. Although the specific genres of South 'critical legal studies' remain yet unborn, South scholarship now precipitates, by way of creative transposition of these ideas, an emerging global jurisprudence.

5.3 The Feminist Movements

Feminist legal theory movements fortunately cut across the South–North common law scholarship divide. These expose deep patriarchal biases in the evolution of the common law doctrine and practice everywhere. Although historic contexts of women's oppression legitimated by law vary, the jural/juridical forms that sustain patriarchy remain broadly similar. These movements interrogate the very form of law as constitutive of women's oppression, especially by contestation over 'private' and 'public' through which law accomplishes substantial subjugation and oppression of women. The movements have made immense contributions towards the social theory of law. They have nurtured distinctive approaches to the historiography of common law, theory and practice of law reform, legal theory and philosophy, comparative legal studies, and critiques of governance, rights, development, and justice. Based on lived histories of harm and hurt, pain and death, these movements contest common law epistemologies by practices of solidarity-based production of knowledges. Taking fully into account the diversity of women's subjection, the various feminisms (whether liberal, socialist, radical, postmodern) that critique law also strive to recast it in ways that empower struggles for dignity, rights, and justice. Above all, these movements offer a rich arena for addressing forms of impoverishment caused in particular by the contemporary emergence of the sexual division of labour in the global economy, and in general by the political economy of patriarchal knowledge-formations fashioning notions of 'development', 'good governance', and 'participation'.

These feminist movements mark the integrated nature of what Edward Said described in a different context as 'travelling theory'. Acutely marked by a riot of genres, across the 'liberal', 'communitarian', 'socialist', 'radical', and 'postmodern' discursivities, these movements contribute to a powerful articulation of legal theory and scholarship in far-sighted and far-reaching ways, announcing a post-patriarchal human civilization.

The affinities and solidarities being fully recognized, we ought to note the fact that South legal feminist movements confront distinctive problems caused by colonial inheritance. The classical common law, policy, and administration created whole new fields of legal patriarchy named as 'personal law'. These placed outside state concern issues of dignity, rights, and violence against women, leaving these severely to the realm of internal communitarian dominance, reform, and resistance. Post-colonial feminist scholarship has been overwhelmingly concerned with constitutional reversal of pre-existing formations of 'customary' regimes of law. Given the constitutional fact that respects minority rights alongside individual human freedoms, construction of women's right-oriented uniform civil code torments performances of constitutional secularism. Caste, community, and indigenous-custom-based violence against women—from practices of sati, dowry murders, female genital cutting, sexual assault, rape—emerges as another distinctive arena for South feminist scholarship.

Overall, these movements raise, in the present context, at least the following issues for future work:

1. In what ways may legal theory cognize violence against women as a marker of the 'modern' law? What theoretical redescriptions of law (e.g. the 'definition' of law,

'sovereignty', and theories about adjudication) are made possible by feminist legal movements?

2. How may we feminize the dominant patriarchal conceptions of global 'development' and 'impoverishment'? In other words, how may we construct descriptions of the emergent legal patriarchy of contemporary globalization? In what ways does the latter empower as well as disempower voices of women's demands for dignity, equality, and justice?

3. How may feminist jurisprudential discourses relate to the forces of production (digitalization and biotechnology) that profoundly affect relations of production? New practices of embodiment and disembodiment stand created by the TRIPS-driven legal regimes that construe, for example, the human body as a site for fully patented corporate, super-profit exploitation. Are the *Moore Case* languages of body-as-property that resist carceral exploitation via the revival of the ancient languages of tort of conversion the best that the common law inheritance may offer? Common law languages of contract categories heavily complicate (as in surrogate motherhood and artificial insemination situations, and the current regimes of legal justification for human cloning) and invite feminist jurisprudence movements to speak more articulately to the patriarchal and post-patriarchal potential of the new global relations of production.

4. At the plane of high political and legal theory, how may we negotiate, in distinctively feminist ways, the logics of multiculturalism that justify toleration by the state and the law of internal repressive practices instantly violative of individual human rights of women, within logics of identity and difference? How may we read common law imagination in human-rights-friendly ways that respect at the one and the same time group and community rights and the rights of women to be and to remain fully human?

5. How may legal narratives (macro, meso, or micro and national, supranational, or global) be developed in ways that respect, and respond to, the lived and embodied individual and collective histories of the violated selves (individual and collective) of women? In other words, how may we reinstate and reconstitute individual biographies as social texts? How may this movement transform, what must be named as, the 'rape culture' of the common law?

Consideration of these meta-issues holds considerable promise of divesting both North and South common legal scholarship of their patriarchal biases.

5.4 Law-and-Development Movements

5.4.1 *The Old and the New*

The 'old' and the 'new' law-and-development movements (LDM) differ primarily in their formative contexts. The former were constituted and reconstituted in the high phases of the Cold War, while the latter have emerged in the post-Cold-War contexts of contemporary economic globalization. The old LDM harboured North scholarly reworking and extension of the model of legal liberalism, as well as Marxian South critiques of legal imperialism and of neo-colonial relations between core and periphery (Tamanaha, 1995, and the literature therein cited). But the old LDM was typically dominated by an awareness of crises in legal liberalism and by a certain scholarly anxiety, including a somewhat self-indulgent auto-critique (by David Trubek and Marc Galanter in 1974) that manifested itself in forms of disenchantment. Only one survivor, Robert Seidman, came close to a considered revival of the effective uses and potential of law in promoting practices of developmentalism directed to combating mass impoverishment. Robert Seidman and Ann Seidman (1994) invoke narratives of specific Third World experiences to propose consideration of 'development' as a *process* rather than as a *goal*, and to evolve 'a problem-solving methodology to lay a foundation for a more rational, participatory approach to building institutions' (at p. 25; original emphasis omitted). This useful work has met with benign neglect even in the course of transition from the old to the new LDM (*IDS Bulletin*, 2001).

The old LDM remains concerned with the circumstances of post-coloniality while the new LDM necessarily relates to diverse explosions of revived legal liberalism in many post-Cold-War legal regions (e.g. Vietnam: see Rose, 1998), including the so-called 'transitional' post-communist societies. While the Hungarian scholar Guyla Eorsi noted as early as 1975 (in his classic work *Comparative Civil Law*) the phenomenon of convergence in civil law between bourgeois and socialist legal systems, the extension of common law scholarship to the 'transitional' societies marks a very different point of departure. The old LDM remains primarily concerned with problems arising out of colonial legal pluralism. The new LDM defines problems by reference to the relationship between the residual cultures of socialist law and the new cultures of the common law, vaunting the 'virtues' of 'aggressive globalization' (Chen, 2001). The old LDM learnt very little from the legal experience and imagination of post-colonial societies; and if that fact is any guide to the future, one should not expect common law scholarly communities to learn much from the current histories of legal transformation in post-socialist societies.

The discursive terrain of the new LDM remains marked by ideological and programmatic continuities with the old, even when the new LDM identifies specific points on which it departs from the old. But the new LDM must derive the critical wherewithal for its innovations from legal voices of South common law scholarship (e.g. the African critique in Chibundu, 1997). These focus, in ways having crucial bearings on global development and impoverishment, on 'constitutions without constitutionalism', 'coercive nation building', enforced structural adjustment policies, the impact of measures of privatization on the notions of the rule of law, and the various tormented itineraries of the relationship between ethnicity and democracy on the one hand and state and market failures on the other. To all this, we need to add the new LDM insistence on relating South constitutionalism to globalization

(Woodiwiss, 1999) and to the situation of First Nations (the latter concern developed partly out of a New Zealand critique, most notably by Jane Kelsey).

The old law-and-development genre, which celebrated the angst of transposing the paradigm of legal liberalism to 'developing societies', ascribed a province and function to 'lawness' in the process of development. That social construction of 'lawness', in all its forms, simply ignored the formative contexts of the constitution of 'modern' legality in the colonies that constituted the Empire (see Fitzpatrick, 1992, 2001). Accordingly, and unsurprisingly, it encased the logic of human and social 'development' in the languages of semi-autonomous legal orders, only to perish when confronted by the problematic of structural causes of global impoverishment (such as massive 'debt' burdens, structural inequities in global trade relations, and the multifarious and sometimes nefarious roles of international financial institutions). The old LDM ascribed to the law an autonomous existence historically simply unavailable to it.

In contrast, the new LDM grasps the multiple layers of recurrent forms of 'neo-colonialism'. Scholars are now coming to understand that the historic forms of imperialism, colonialism, and neo-colonialism shape the career and the future of post-colonial legality and justice in the processes and relationships of law and development (*IDS Bulletin*, 2001). To this understanding must be added the 'dangerous supplement' of North common law discourse concerning world development programmes.

When we relate law-and-development discourse to international law, we get a more complete measure of radical innovation in doing legal theory. First, what Sir Wilfred Jenks characterized as 'the common law of mankind' and what Wolfgang Friedman named as the 'international law of cooperation' has now attained thresholds of sustainable development, primarily through the critique and reconstruction offered by South common law international lawyers. Secondly, these scholars have also contributed to the renovation of regimes of social, economic, and cultural rights as well as to the establishment of a right to development (to mention here only a few names such as Abi Saab, An-Naim, Chimni, Chibundu, Chua, Ghai, Gathii, Muta, Okafor, Rajagopal). Thirdly, they have made notable contributions to the theory and practice of women's rights as human rights. Fourthly, they have nourished networks of solidarity and social action against agents and managers of contemporary globalization processes, as an aspect of their agenda of struggle against the organized regimes (in terms of Ulrich Beck) of irresponsibility and impunity constituted by transnational corporations (Baxi, 2002). Fifthly, at national levels, as the Indian experience especially demonstrates (Sathe, 2002), they have deployed international standards to nourish forms of insurgent social activism that are addressing issues of mass impoverishment (as archived, for example, by Henry Steiner and Phillip Alston in their valuable anthology *Human Rights in Context*, 2000: 275–99).

Sixthly, cross-border movement of feminist legal studies has further enriched what Santos (1995) calls 'globalized localism'. Whatever may have been the 'original intent' of law-and-development discourse, its migration to the spheres of international law warrants further theoretical exploration.

5.4.2 *Reflexive Issues arising out of the Law-and-Development Movements*

The law-and-development discourse is not of significant concern to the dominant patterns of North common law teaching and research. Despite the intensity of internal critique and dissension, it attracts a minuscule number of North common law scholars, especially when we ignore the cadre of professorial policy experts recruited by governments and research foundations. There is enough evidence to suggest that their engagement with the South common law region is episodic and contingent, and often corrupted (from the worm's eye perspective) by the infinitely, and expediently, shifting agenda of intergovernmental aid agencies, research foundations, and now increasingly by the World Bank. While this limited form of engagement is better than none ('better' if only in terms of faculty improvement and in expanding available resources to law schools via research grants), it fails to promote any serious cosmopolitan understanding of the role of common law theory and practice in the context of global impoverishment.

Despite this, I believe that the issues raised by the old and the new law-and-development movements ought to inform law teaching and research, especially in the South common law regions. These promise a range of curricular and pedagogic fallouts, especially for teaching and research in legal theory and history and South comparative legal studies. I also believe that had the reflexive tradition of law and development studies not been ghettoized, the various movements (explored in Sect. 5.1.4 above) in North common law scholarship would have become more cosmopolitan in their concerns.

The reflexivity of the law-and-development movements raises an array of issues of interest beyond the *cognoscenti*. These include:

1. Will the new LDM experience the same, or at least a similar, trajectory as the Old LDM did, assuming in the first place the theoretical feasibility of drawing bright lines between these genres? How may these possible trajectories relate to the developmental or developmentalist role of law in alleviating mass impoverishment?

2. Does the model of post-Cold-War legal liberalism characterize *any* epistemic break? What strategic and instrumental formations mark the recent histories of transposition of the models of common law legal liberalism to post-Cold-War South societies and post-communist European transitional societies? What messages may these processes be said to carry for a post-socialist 'welfare state' and post-socialist law?

3. From the standpoint of the world's impoverished, we need to ask: in what ways do the developmentalist principles underpinning these processes of transposition of legal and juristic ideologies entail new forms of production of human and social suffering? And what resources remain available in post-Cold-War legal liberalism to ameliorate global mass impoverishment?

4. In particular, how may we relate cause-lawyering and judicial activism to the tasks of social and human rights, activism, empowerment, resistance, and renewal in the South common law regions? What comparative theories emerge about South constitutionalisms, as mediatory forms of common law inheritances, and of human rights (Baxi, 2002)?

5. How may we relate 'ethnicity', 'democracy', and the 'free market', understood at least in substantial part as elements of a 'theology' of neo-liberalism, to the emergent new LDM scholarship? In particular, how may we address the inter-linkages between what Castells called a global criminal economy and the current 'war against terrorism' in terms of the dynamic emergence of a 'networked' international law (Baxi, 2003*a*)?

6. How do the heavily proselytized prescriptions of 'good governance' and 'sustainable development' translate into the here-and-now practical languages for assessing the potential of legal orders (national, supranational, and global) for 'poverty alleviation'? In what ways may recrafting and retooling law provide an effective response to rampant public corruption which aggravates the miseries of the impoverished, both through diversion of public resources into private hands and by fostering cultures of impunity? In what way do the traditions of common law enable struggle against corruption as an abuse of public power and position?

7. How may we understand the roles and relations of *juristic dependencia* (Southern mimicry of dominant North discourse) to any account of mass impoverishment in the South common law regions? Should studies of law and 'poverty' remain wholly informed by policy languages of donor agencies (including the World Bank)? How may we explore the effective use of law in ameliorating mass impoverishment in the low- and middle-income countries (*IDS Bulletin*, 2001 and the literature there cited) from the perspectives of the violated humanity?

6 Globalization and the Privileged Place of Multinational Capital

In the end, the dominant discourse of common law scholarship does not seem to address the creation of the geographies of injustice currently caused by free movements of global capital. While celebrated new regimes of international *lex mercatoria* continue to hold the promise of 'law without the state', such regimes also construct orders of organized irresponsibility and impunity for multinational capital movement that are deeply offensive to notions of human rights. The epistemic practices of common law conflict-of-laws doctrine that persist in the late twentieth and early twenty-first centuries CE (see Baxi, 2001, for a doctrinal map) unabashedly entail colonial ways of short-changing the large masses of South human victims of industrially caused social suffering and disaster, of which the Bhopal catastrophe and Ogoniland provide archetypes. Relegation of victims' claims to the *lex loci delicti* finally signifies that multinational corporations remain free of any order of human-rights responsibilities even when they exacerbate the misfortunes of South communities by intentional acts and policies of international corporate malgovernance. They are liable, if at all, under the law of the place where the delict or the harm occurs; and this ensures substantially lower levels of compensation for human injuries in the South than in the North, especially given the fact that the low rates of industrialization in the South contribute to an underdeveloped theory and practice of tort law.

Further, the common law doctrine poses enormous difficulties for victims of mass social disaster in establishing jurisdiction over foreign multinationals, which evade jurisdiction by creating networks of relatively autonomous subsidiaries. Such contrivances matter (as the Bhopal case shows) even when a South state may sue, *parens patriae*, as a sovereign plaintiff. As if all this were not enough, the law dealing with enforcement of foreign judgments continues to promote regimes of no-recourse and unconscionable 'settlement' of mass tort proceedings that favour and foster, in rather gross ways, the impunity of multinational capital. Foreign plaintiffs suing multinational corporations in courts of the North for their planned acts of mass disaster effectively face a regime of *non liquet*. In this milieu, the daring enunciation of the principle of absolute multinational enterprise liability (fashioned in India in the Bhopal litigation, and already implemented as an aspect of national jurisprudence in relation to ultra-hazardous industry) has attracted painfully little North scholarly attention. Unfortunately, despite their vaunted critical credentials, no genre of law and economics, critical legal studies, or even of feminist theory or old/new LDM, has as yet seriously engaged with this domain of legal doctrine and practice. Nor is discourse on these critical issues concerned with global justice and deliberative democracy.

Yet these rampant and perverse practices of global capital movement should at least attract ethical indictment. Conflict-of-laws doctrine that distinguishes between compensable injuries suffered at home and abroad, and disengages from the latter, becomes genocidally problematic in an era of globalization. Furthermore, such doctrine and practices stand effectively impugned at the bar of contemporary international human rights law and jurisprudence, which at the very least consider human life and bodily and psychic integrity as being equally worthy of juristic and judicial respect in the North and the South. This normative approach disallows racially and ethnically discriminatory constructions of the value of human life and health which, despite all the contrary rhetoric asserting that human rights are universal, indivisible, integral, and interdependent, none the less devalue South forms of human life and livelihood.

7 Approaches to Global Justice

Mainstream common law scholarship displays a deep aversion to abstract theories of justice, a syndrome that needs to be fully diagnosed and treated. John Rawls's germinal work *A Theory of Justice* (1971) has had, indeed, an Aristotle-like (no matter how one wishes that it would have been Marx-like!) impact on the ways of doing moral philosophy and legal theory. But all this scarcely informs practice and research in relation to 'taught law', which Roscoe Pound memorably described as 'tough law'. For the everyday teacher of contract, tort, and property law, whether in the North or the South, the Rawlsian and neo- or post-Rawlsian discourses remain unfortunately distant, dull, and difficult.

This aversion to theorizing about justice feeds the 'production of indifference' for the plight of national and global impoverished, for whom the language of law almost always turns out to be disempowering in the same measure as the language of justice becomes empowering. Rawls's Difference Principle finds little place in common law teaching either in the North or the South; and this greatly undermines the task of accomplishing social justice in the face of globalization. In this light, it is not surprising that discourse about global justice is systemically absent from common law scholarship, despite the fact that anti-colonial and anti-imperial campaigners from Mahatma Gandhi to Nelson Mandela articulated powerful critiques of existing world orderings.

We need now to attend to new approaches that seek to fashion a discourse concerning global justice. This necessity proceeds from recognition that the task of theorizing about justice ought not stop at, or stand enclosed within, arbitrary frontiers of nation-states and societies. In this light, the 'second-order' tasks then emerge as renovating the ethical and legal theory that underlies common law legal scholarship. Such renovations would invite attention to issues such as the following:

1. the very desirability of a 'post-liberal' mode of enunciation of visions of global justice in a globalizing world, a world said to be constituted by the fact that 'there is no alternative';
2. the availability of theoretically feasible means for creative extension of modes of construction of liberal justice found in nation-states to a global scale—for instance, the viability of construction of the First and Second Original Positions and of the globalization of the Rawlsian Difference Principle (Beitz, 1971; Pogge, 1989; Jones, 2000];
3. ethical difficulties of specifying moral duties that nationals may be said to owe to non-nationals (by no means an inconsequential question, as Bhopal and related new forms of multinational catastrophe demonstrate with severest cruelty);
4. the prospects for the elevation of international law's normative standards from the plane of the 'law of nations' to what John Rawls now names as a 'law of peoples'

in a book by that title (1999), and the question of whether international sanctions processes should be invoked, unilaterally or collectively, against regimes that deny human rights;

5. ways of articulating the ethical duties of affluent and 'well-ordered' societies beyond the rather sparse duties of 'development' aid and assistance to the less developed and developing societies, as recently articulated by John Rawls;

6. relating the performance of 'undemocratic', international and regional financial institutions and trade arrangements to the tasks of 'sustainable development' and action programmes for the alleviation of global impoverishment;

7. changing from the ethical languages of human rights to discourses concerning human capabilities and human flourishings.

I have wrestled with these issues elsewhere. But the slenderness and fragility of this discourse on global justice (at the very best one can muster only about a dozen pioneering names in the North and none in South common law scholarship) furnish grounds for urgent moral anxiety.

The aversion of common law scholarship to theorizing concerns constitutes a profound and enduring misfortune for the world's impoverished inhabitants, present and future, wounded, bloodied, and bruised, and so forever socially reproduced in their human and social suffering. Indeed, their re-subjection is an aspect of current common law scholarship, pro-globalization hype, and knowledge-based power, all of which reconstruct them as the objects of development and developmentalism. The analogy between the 'rape' script and the 'globalization' script, and the ways of resistance that this analogy calls to mind, is compellingly demonstrated by J. K. Gibson-Graham, in *The End of Capitalism (As we Knew It)* (1996).

I hope that this discussion contributes to an awareness of the possibility of renewed engagement with the epistemic misfortune that has characterized common law scholarship to this point. New ways of doing common law scholarship in a globalizing epoch remain imperative. At the very least, these might provide us with a fresh start, creating 'minority epistemic enclaves' of albeit-embattled 'indignation entrepreneurs' (as Ullmann-Margalit and Cass Sunstein now name them).

This chapter invites attention to the multiple future potentials for renaissance of common law scholarship in modes that take human and social suffering seriously. Outside this frame, common law scholarship, whether South or North, will remain complicit with that genre of domination that now celebrates colonizations without colonizers, which globally reproduce the more intransigent forms of auto-colonization. Surely, our choices in performative acts of common law scholarship remain located in the frame of *jurisgenerative* and *jurispathic* (in the way in which Robert Cover identified these for us) epistemic practices. The first two years of the twenty-first century already mark the advent of new forms of now globalizing jurispathic human futures. The task then is not just to *explain* this but to *transform* our common law future.

REFERENCES

Baxi, U. (2001). 'The Geography of Injustice: Human Rights at the Altar of Convenience', in R. Craig (ed.), *Torture as Tort: Comparative Perspectives on the Development of Transnational Human Rights Litigation*, Oxford: Hart, 197–212.

—— (2002). *The Future of Human Rights*, Delhi: Oxford University Press.

—— (2003). 'The Colonialist Heritage', in P. Legrand and R. Munday (eds.), *Comparative Legal Studies: Traditions and Transitions*, Cambridge: Cambridge University Press, 46–75.

—— (2003a). 'Operation "Enduring Freedom": Towards a New International Law and Order?' in A. Anghie, B. S. Chimni, K. Mickelson and O. C. Okafor (eds.), *The Third World and International Order: Law, Politics and Globalization*, The Hague: Kluwer Law International (forthcoming).

Beitz, C. R. (1979). *Political Theory and International Relations*, Princeton: Princeton University Press.

Bentham, J. (1975). *The Theory of Legislation*, with an introd. by U. Baxi, Bombay: N. M. Tripathi.

Buchanan, R. M. (1994). 'Context, Continuity, and Difference in Poverty Law Scholarship', *University of Miami Law Review*, 48: 999–1062.

Chen, J. (2001). 'Epiphytic Economics and the Politics of Place', *Minnesota Journal of Global Trade*, 10: 1–61.

Chibundu, M. O. (1997). 'Law in Development: Mapping, Gourding and Preserving Palm Wine', *Case Western Reserve International Law Journal*, 29: 167–258.

Escobar, A. (1995). *Encountering Development: The Making and Unmaking of the Third World*, Princeton: Princeton University Press.

Fitzpatrick, P. (1992). *The Mythology of Modern Law*, London: Routledge.

—— (2001). *Modernism and the Grounds of Law*, Cambridge: Cambridge University Press.

Guha, R. (1997). *Dominance without Hegemony: History and Power in Colonial India*, Harvard, Mass.: Harvard University Press.

IDS Bulletin (2001). 'Making Law Matter: Rules, Rights and Security in the Lives of the Poor', *IDS Bulletin*, 32: 1–104.

Jones, C. (2000). *Global Justice: Defending Cosmopolitanism*, Oxford: Oxford University Press.

Mamdani, M. (1995). *Citizen and Subject: Contemporary Africa and the Legacy of Late Colonialism*, Princeton: Princeton University Press.

Mercuro, N., and Medema, S. G. (1997). *Economics and the Law: From Posner to Postmodernism*, Princeton: Princeton University Press.

Minda, G. (1989). 'Towards a More "Just" Economics of Justice—A Review Essay', *Cardozo Law Review*, 10: 1855–77.

Nussbaum, M. (1997). 'Flawed Foundations: The Philosophical Critique of (A Particular Kind of) Economics', *University of Chicago Law Review*, 64: 1197–214.

—— (2000). *Women and Human Development: A Capabilities Approach*, Cambridge: Cambridge University Press.

Pogge, T. (1989). *Realizing Rawls*, Ithaca, NY: Cornell University Press.

Posner, R. (1992). *An Economic Analysis of Law* (4th edn.), Boston: Little Brown & Co.

Rose, C. V. (1998). 'The "New" Law and Development Movement in the Post-Cold War Era: A Vietnam Case Study', *Law & Society Review*, 32: 93–140.

Santos, B. de Sousa (1995). *Towards a New Common Sense: Law, Science and Politics in a Paradigmatic Transition*, New York: Routledge.

Sathe, S. P. (2002). *Judicial Activism in India: Transgressing Borders and Enforcing Limits*, Delhi: Oxford University Press.

Seidman, A., and Seidman, R. (1994). *State and Law in the Development Process: Problem Solving and Institutional Change in the Third World*, London: Macmillan.

Tamanaha, B. Z. (1995). 'Review Article: The Lessons of Law and Development Studies', *American Journal of International Law*, 89: 470–86.

Woodiwiss, A. (1998). *Globalization, Human Rights and Labour Law in Pacific Asia*, Cambridge: Cambridge University Press.

Young, R. J. C. (2001). *Postcolonialism: An Historical Introduction*, Oxford: Blackwell.

PART IV

BUSINESS AND COMMERCE

CORPORATIONS

BRIAN R. CHEFFINS

1 INTRODUCTION

THIS chapter has two essential objectives. The first is to provide a survey of corporate law's key theoretical themes. The second is to offer an assessment of the manner in which the literature has evolved over time. A key purpose of the enquiry in this instance will be to identify potential future trajectories for corporate law scholarship.

The bulk of the chapter will be devoted to a chronological overview of the major themes dealt with in the theoretical literature on corporate law. To start, there will be a brief description of debates concerning corporate personality that captured a great deal of attention in the early decades of the twentieth century. Next, analysis influenced by a 'separation of ownership and control' thesis Berle and Means (1932) set down will be summarized. After this, there will be an overview of the economically oriented 'contractarian' model of the company that has dominated theoretical analysis of corporate law from the 1980s onwards. Critiques of this approach and interdisciplinary work that takes economic analysis as a point of departure will then be outlined. The foregoing discussion will focus primarily on US material since most of the theoretical contributions concerning corporate law have come from America. Nevertheless, there will also be an overview of input from academics in the UK, Canada, and Australia.

Once the chronological overview is complete, the focus will shift to four potential trajectories for corporate law scholarship. One is based on the idea that knowledge

I would like to thank Ed Rock and Lynn Stout for helpful comments on this chapter.

'accumulates' as part of 'progress' towards a better understanding of the matters under study. The second is the concept of the 'paradigm', derived from work done on the history and sociology of science. The third is a 'cyclical' thesis, grounded in the assumption that legal scholarship consists of discourse on issues that arise on a reoccurring basis. The final potential trajectory we will take into account characterizes academic thought in terms of fads and fashions. As we will see, assumptions one makes about which of these potential trajectories predominates influences considerably predictions one is likely to make concerning the future of corporate law scholarship.

2 CORPORATE PERSONALITY

Beginning in the 1890s and reaching a high point around 1920, there was an intense debate in the legal literature about corporate 'personality' (for background, see Mark, 1987). Three points of view could be discerned. First, the 'fiction' or 'artificial entity' theory held that corporate organizations were mere abstractions that owed their existence and legitimacy to an official grant of authority (a 'concession') from the state. Second, the contractual/association theory implied that a corporation was not a product of sovereign intervention but instead was an association constituted by the aggregation of freely contracting individuals, namely the shareholders. Third, the 'real entity' theory held that a corporation was not fictional but instead had a distinctive personality in the same sense that a human being does. This implied, in turn, that a corporate entity must be conceptually separate and distinct from those owning the equity.

Though the dialogue concerning corporate personality was very spirited, by 1930 the debate had largely ended. By this time, the consensus view was that the corporation was an important legal form that could not be treated, from the law's point of view, as a mere contractual aggregation. Also, though corporate personality had to be taken seriously from a legal perspective, corporate entities could not be analysed as actual persons. Underlying the new orthodoxy was a belief that lawyers should cast aside their interest in abstract concepts and focus instead on 'real' issues.

3 THE BERLE AND MEANS LEGACY: THE SEPARATION OF OWNERSHIP AND CONTROL

As the personification of the corporation faded as a concern, the stage was set for legal academics to assess the corporation in functional terms. Berle and Means's

The Modern Corporation and Private Property (1932) provided an ideal platform for the shift in emphasis. In this highly influential book, the authors analysed the results of a 'corporate revolution' that had occurred in the United States between 1880 and 1930 (for background, see Bratton, 2001). During this period, in many key industries small closely held firms managed by their founders gave way to big publicly traded companies characterized by managerial hierarchies. In these 'quasi-public corporations' (Berle and Means, 1932: 5), widely dispersed shareholders, each lacking a sufficient financial incentive to intervene directly, typically left it to professionally trained executives to deal with matters of importance. The result, according to a phrase Berle and Means made famous, was a 'separation of ownership and control' (1932, p. xli).

An inference that many corporate law scholars drew from Berle and Means's separation of ownership and control thesis was that something was seriously amiss in publicly quoted corporations. More precisely, the managerialist pattern Berle and Means had described implied that those in charge of America's larger business enterprises were not sufficiently accountable to shareholders. A key difficulty allegedly was the manner in which those owning equity voted. Academics noted that executives of a publicly quoted firm could use corporate resources to 'solicit proxies' under the name of the corporation (i.e. contact shareholders and ask them to authorize management to vote on their behalf). This, in turn, allowed corporate officers to secure readily support for resolutions they supported, including those to elect themselves or their allies as directors. Management, then, potentially constituted a self-perpetuating oligarchy.

Academics who were concerned about the balance of power between managers and shareholders advocated various types of reform. One was activating 'shareholder democracy' by fostering more participation by investors in corporate affairs. Another was subjecting the exercise of managerial discretion to tougher equitable standards by strengthening the fiduciary duties top executives owe to their companies. A third was championing a 'monitoring' model for corporate boards, under which 'outside' directors lacking any compromising link with management would supervise corporate executives in an objective manner.

While corporate law scholars invoked Berle and Means's work to advocate stronger protection for shareholders, this was not the only lesson to be drawn from *The Modern Corporation and Private Property*. Instead, the book also cast doubt on the received wisdom under US law that generating profits for shareholders was the objective corporations should pursue (for a critique of this orthodoxy, see Blair and Stout, 1999: 300–4). Berle and Means's analysis was provocative on this count since the concentration of corporate power to which it drew attention implied that the corporation needed to be understood not only as a business entity but also as a social and political institution. Also, their work cast doubt on whether holders of corporate equity were appropriate beneficiaries of the conventional rule that profits derived from the use and sale of property should accrue to its owners. This was because shareholders were seemingly not exercising control in the manner that would be expected from those who own assets.

It is ironic that *The Modern Corporation and Private Property* was a catalyst for debate on whether large business enterprises should be held accountable to constituencies other than shareholders. This is because Berle struggled to resolve in his own mind whether the law was capable of expanding to accommodate the perceived public responsibilities of the modern corporation (Blair and Stout, 1999: 302–3; Bratton, 2001: 761). Nevertheless, in the decades following Berle and Means's proclamation of the separation of ownership and control thesis, various academics invoked the proposition that managers of publicly quoted companies were insufficiently accountable as a basis for advocating changes in the law to address concerns about corporate social responsibility. Proposals that were made included requiring disclosure of corporate activities affecting society and mandating that various key constituencies participate in corporate decision-making.

4 CHALLENGING THE BERLE AND MEANS ORTHODOXY

It has been said that '(n)o field of American law has ever been so totally dominated by one work as the corporation law area by the Berle and Means classic' (Manne, 1987: 223). Indeed, the separation of ownership and control thesis allegedly illustrated the proposition that 'no idea is so strong as one that has no opposition' (Manne, 1987: 228). Still, by the 1960s, a paradox was emerging. This was that the reputed deficiencies in managerial accountability had apparently not created appreciable concern among those most affected, namely the millions of Americans who owned shares in publicly quoted companies. To put matters more starkly, if things were as bad as Berle and Means had described, why did investors continue to put money in the hands of corporate executives?

In a series of articles written in the 1960s, Henry Manne addressed the mystery of investor indifference to a separation of ownership and control and caused the 'first crack(s) in the seemingly unassailable wall of Berlean theory' (Manne, 1987: 228; see more generally Carney, 1999). His crucial point was that executives in widely held public companies are not as unaccountable as they seem. Instead, he argued, various market constraints serve to curb managerial discretion in a way that helps to align the interests of shareholders and executives. One constraint Manne identified was the capital market. To elaborate, since corporations periodically must raise cash to implement business strategies, management potentially becomes subject to close scrutiny at the various points in time when capital is sought from outside investors.

Manne drew attention to various other factors that can have a disciplinary effect on management. One was the market for products and services. The dynamic involved here is that executives will typically not be dishonest or reckless since such misconduct could damage their company's market standing sufficiently to place their jobs at serious risk. Manne also highlighted the potential significance of the market for managerial talent. In very basic terms, it provides executives with an incentive to perform effectively in their current jobs since they will want to impress potential alternative employers.

One further constraint Manne identified was 'the market for corporate control'. When executives running a widely held corporation are incompetent, complacent, overly cautious, or dishonest, this will serve to depress the share price. If the situation deteriorates far enough, a bidder may emerge who will calculate that installing new management will generate sufficient profits to justify the expense of acquiring a controlling interest. Since executives in potential target companies will not want to lose their jobs, the possibility of a bid gives them an incentive to run their companies in a manner that enhances shareholder wealth.

Manne's work constituted a provocative market-oriented critique of the Berle–Means orthodoxy that had come to dominate corporate law scholarship. Still, he was not offering an affirmative theory that explained the modern corporation by reference to the criteria that characterized the economic analysis of markets. Manne was not alone; economists of the time were not addressing the issue either. As the next section will discuss, matters soon changed dramatically.

5 THE CORPORATION AS A NEXUS OF CONTRACTS

5.1 Economic Theory and the Corporation

Prior to the 1970s, economists talked a great deal about business enterprises, typically referred to as firms. Their concern, however, was not firms *per se*. Instead, they were seeking to develop a theory of markets in which firms were important actors. From this angle, the firm was a 'black box' that operated so as to maximize profits. Economists, then, did not concern themselves with how the conflicting objectives of individual participants associated with a particular firm were aligned so as to yield the hypothesized focus on profit maximization.

Ronald Coase's 'The Nature of the Firm' (1937) constituted an exception to the general trend in the economic literature. He opened up the 'black box' other economists ignored by contrasting the distinctive internal hierarchy of a firm with the autonomous, detached nature of the open market. He conjectured that the relative merits of coordinating economic activity within a firm and reliance on the price mechanism would dictate how large particular business enterprises would become. This was a striking insight but Coase's work had little immediate impact on economic theory. The situation did not change until the 1970s, when economists began to acknowledge his analysis and sought to move it forward.

One by-product of the belated interest in Coase's theory of the firm was that his characterization of firms as hierarchical 'islands of conscious power' (Coase, 1937: 388) was subjected to challenge. While Coase emphasized that internal relations within a firm were authoritarian in a way that differed from conventional arm's-length transactions, economists following up on his work stressed that market exchanges did not end at the firm's front door. Instead, the internal organization of business enterprises was the result of voluntary exchanges dictated by market forces. At the same time, market dynamics defined the relationship between a firm and its suppliers, customers, creditors, and so on. As Jensen and Meckling put it: '[t]he private corporation or firm is simply . . . a nexus for contracting relationships [that] . . . serves as a focus for a complex process in which the conflicting objectives of individuals . . . are brought into equilibrium within a framework of contractual relations' (1976: 311).

Within just a few years, economists and economically oriented corporate law academics both began to follow the cue Jensen and Meckling offered and were referring to the firm as a 'nexus of contracts'. This occurred despite the potential for terminological confusion (Rock and Wachter, 2001: 1640–1). When lawyers refer to 'contracts', they normally contemplate agreements that a court will uphold. Economists, on the other hand, use the term more broadly so that it encompasses arrangements to which parties will tend to adhere regardless of legal enforceability (e.g. because of reputational considerations). Economically oriented corporate lawyers were prepared to assume that the corporate nexus encompassed this expanded conception of a contract (e.g. Cheffins, 1997: 32), even though pertinent distinctions between legally binding agreements and 'self-enforcing' arrangements were potentially obscured (Rock and Wachter, 2001: 1629–30).

5.2 Agency Cost Theory

A pivotal aspect of the nexus of contracts model which began to take shape in the 1970s was 'agency cost' theory. Recall that the Berle–Means analysis of the widely held company implied that shareholders potentially might be subjected to the untrammelled whims of powerful executives (Sect. 3). Agency cost theory, which

Jensen and Meckling (1976) first articulated in a systematic fashion, provided a framework for analysing this divergence of interest. From an economic perspective, whenever one individual (the principal) depends upon another (the agent), an agency relationship arises. Since agents do not receive all of the returns from the profit-enhancing activities they engage in on behalf of their principals, they will always be tempted to put their own interests first. When agents in fact do so, the result is 'agency costs'. In a corporation with widely dispersed share ownership, the shareholders, as principals, depend on management, as agents, to operate the business profitably. Self-serving or reckless managerial conduct therefore imposes agency costs on investors.

Agency cost theory did more, however, than characterize in a systematic way the sort of incentive problems which Berle and Means had identified. Instead, it accorded full recognition to market-oriented limitations on the exercise of managerial discretion. More precisely, agency cost theory offered an intellectually elegant account of various constraints that were potentially relevant in a publicly quoted company. These included factors Manne had identified (the capital market, the market for products and services, the market for managerial talent, and the market for corporate control) and others, such as 'internal monitoring' by corporate boards and the adoption of incentive-oriented managerial services contracts.

Those who relied on agency cost theory to highlight constraints on corporate executives drew support from a concept referred to as the efficient capital market hypothesis (ECMH). Financial economists began to formulate and test the ECMH in the 1960s and by the end of the 1970s it was widely assumed that US stock markets were efficient in the 'semi-strong' sense, which implied that shares prices reflected all publicly available information. The explanation typically offered for this state of affairs was that trading by financial professionals, who quickly digest newly available data, causes share prices to incorporate all of the information 'in the market'. A key inference that could be drawn from the semi-strong form of the ECMH was that a corporation's share price would reflect any publicly available evidence of managerial incompetence or dishonesty. Correspondingly, mechanisms that were likely to punish or reward executives in accordance with share price performance (e.g. the market for corporate control, the market for managerial talent, and incentive-oriented services contracts) would have a salutary disciplinary effect on poorly managed firms.

The fact that agency cost theory explicitly made allowances for market-oriented constraints on managerial conduct highlighted an essential tenet of the nexus of contracts model, this being that market forces do not stop functioning at the corporation's front door. Moreover, the theory could be invoked to account for the seemingly paradoxical dominance of the widely held corporation in the US economy. Again, Berle and Means's work implied that this type of business enterprise was afflicted by a lack of managerial accountability. The success of the widely held firm suggested, though, that market dynamics must be addressing the potential difficulties that a separation of ownership and control were posing. At the very least, the advantages the format offered—stock market financing was available if required and executives could be hired solely on the basis of their managerial credentials rather than being required to finance the business—were apparently sufficient to outweigh the disadvantages.

5.3 Reconceptualizing Shareholders

In addition to providing a platform for re-evaluating the position of management, contractarian analysis opened the way for a reconceptualization of the shareholder's status within the corporation. As exemplified by the phrase 'separation of ownership and control', shareholders have often been referred to as 'owners' of a company. Contractarian analysis dispenses with this notion and instead characterizes those who own equity as 'residual claimants' (Cheffins, 1997: 54). From a contractual perspective, shareholders are defined in this way because they are the ultimate beneficiaries of whatever success a company enjoys, in the sense that the return on their investment is based on what is left over after other claims the company is obliged to meet have been satisfied. Hence, while others who are part of a corporate nexus of contracts will contract to receive fixed cash sums (e.g. creditors and employees), the return a company's equity yields is not prescribed in advance and instead is a function of the net cash flow the business generates over time.

For investors, owning equity has a potentially significant downside risk. This is that the fixed claims of other constituencies may end up exceeding the value of corporate assets, thus leaving the shares worthless. Academics who invoked the nexus of contracts model pointed out, though, that those who own equity in publicly quoted companies are potentially well-suited to bear the risks of business failure. One consideration is that shareholders enjoy 'limited liability' and thus will not have to use personal assets to indemnify disgruntled corporate creditors. Moreover, investors can diversify away much of the risk they face by purchasing shares in a large number of companies since the successes will tend to cancel out the failures.

As we have seen, US corporate law has been influenced by the idea that the goal of corporations is to generate profits on behalf of shareholders (Sect. 3). If those owning corporate equity merely constitute one constituency that is part of a nexus of contracts, this 'shareholder primacy' notion seems misguided. Still, contractual analysis has frequently been invoked to support the view that corporations exist for the shareholders. 'Contractarians' have, for instance, sought to justify the pre-eminence of shareholders under corporate law by pointing out that equity investors, as residual claimants, have stronger incentives to encourage maximum corporate achievement than their fixed claim counterparts. This arrangement, it is said, will benefit all concerned since 'maximizing profits for equity investors assists the other "constituencies" automatically. . . . A successful firm provides jobs for workers and goods and services for consumers' (Easterbrook and Fischel, 1991: 38).

Shareholder primacy cannot be defended solely on the grounds that the interests of shareholders and other corporate participants are congruent, since there will be situations where conflicts of interest exist. For instance, shareholders will be likely to support a decision to introduce cost-effective labour-saving technology whereas incumbent employees will fear losing their jobs. Still, for contractarians, the respective bargaining positions of shareholders and non-shareholder constituencies dictates that shareholder primacy is the best arrangement. Equity investors, the argument goes, cannot obtain contractual assurances that managers will seek to maximize profits. This is because the open-ended nature of such a claim makes it very difficult to specify protection at the time of investment and because shares have perpetual life, thus precluding any opportunity to renegotiate. In contrast, creditors, employees, and customers can feasibly bargain to protect their vital interests and may, in the case of workers, be able to secure assistance by political means.

6 CONTRACTARIAN ANALYSIS AS A 'PRAIRIE FIRE'

The emergence of the nexus of contracts model was controversial among corporate law scholars. Indeed, some argued forcefully that the corporation could not be conceptualized properly in contractual terms (for examples, see Easterbrook and Fischel, 1991: 356). Still, the nexus of contracts model quickly became dominant in the legal academy, at least in the United States. The intellectual shift occurred quickly. Indeed, according to one observer, '[l]aw and economics . . . swept the academic corporate law area like prairie fire' (Branson, 1989: 745). Hence, by the late 1990s, the proposition '[t]hat a firm [such as a corporation] can be thought of as a "nexus of contracts" . . . [had become] something of a cliché in the university' (Ramseyer, 1998: 504).

What accounted for the nexus of contracts 'prairie fire'? One explanation was that for many US corporate law academics, contractarian analysis rang true in the sense that 'it capture[d] much of the basic logic at stake' (Ramseyer, 1998: 504). Also important was the intellectual rigour economic analysis offered. According to contractarians, the clear assumptions and testable propositions offered by economics made 'possible a progressive increase in our understanding of corporate structure and behavior' (Johnston, 1993: 239). Even critics were prepared to concede that economic theory had clarified what was at stake and thereby facilitated discussion of key issues (Cheffins, 1997: 713).

The intellectual climate was an additional factor that contributed to the contractarian 'victory'. Coincident with a growing disenchantment with government regulation, during the 1980s and 1990s market-oriented conservatism increasingly characterized theoretical analysis of private law issues in the United States. Contractarian corporate law scholarship fell directly into line with such trends since academics embracing this approach tend to share an overriding trust in contracts and the marketplace. More concretely, they are content to presume that business participants are better positioned to structure arrangements affecting companies than either lawmakers or law professors.

Despite this bias in favour of the market, contractarians do envisage that corporate law can play a productive role by facilitating the private contracting process. Under this view, the starting-point is that contractual arrangements which corporate participants make should be enforced in accordance with the relevant terms. Moreover, to address the various issues that parties will inevitably fail to resolve, lawmakers should offer presumptive 'off-the rack' regulations that match by way of 'hypothetical bargains' what probably would have been agreed to if matters had been thought about in advance. Finally, the state ought to allow corporate participants wide scope to opt out of the 'gap-filling' rules which corporate law provides. A strong bias against mandatory regulation is in order, according to contractarian analysis, because parties often need the option to customize their operating environment to meet distinctive, private requirements.

One further factor contributed to the dominance of the nexus of contracts model. This was that economic analysis stimulated intellectual activity in what had become, from a theoretical perspective, a moribund area of the law (Cheffins, 1999: 208). Even critics of the contractarian approach acknowledged the beneficial influence of fresh thinking. As one said, 'the introduction of perspectives grounded in nonlegal academic disciplines has demonstrably invigorated discussion and deepened analysis' in a field where the literature had been 'uninspiring' and 'parochial' in scope (DeMott, 1996: 1308, 1335).

7 'MARKET FAILURE' AND THE NEXUS OF CONTRACTS

Allegedly, at least in the United States, '[e]very book and journal article in the corporate law field ha[s] to take an economics of law perspective if they [are] to succeed in the marketplace of ideas' (Branson, 2001: 619). Still, concerns about the polemical and 'uncaring' nature of contractarian analysis mean the approach is 'unloved'. As a result, while the nexus of contracts model has changed radically the theoretical study of corporate law, the underlying assumptions have continued to be subjected to critical scrutiny. Correspondingly, in various instances, it has been argued that misplaced faith in the efficacy of market forces has led contractarians to draw erroneous inferences concerning corporate law.

For example, a 'market failure' critique of the economic approach has been offered with respect to the notion of 'efficient' share prices. A proposition associated with contractarian analysis is that strong regulation of managerial behaviour will usually be unnecessary since poor share price performance will activate various market-oriented mechanisms which discipline underperforming executives (see Sect. 5.2). This reasoning presupposes, however, that the prices at which shares trade constitute reliable estimates of the value of corporations as they are being run. If the pricing of corporate equity does not occur in this fashion, market discipline may punish talented executives and be absent when a company is badly managed. There is in fact a substantial body of evidence which suggests that investors trade on the basis of criteria other than the economic prospects of companies ('noise'), including a 'herding' instinct derived from a belief that others making a particular choice cannot be wrong. To the extent that share prices are in fact detached from economic reality, it becomes increasingly open to argue that the law should retain a pivotal residual role as a regulator of managerial misconduct.

Another ground on which questions have been raised about the inferences that should be drawn from the nexus of contracts model relates to the dominance of the widely held corporation in the American economy. From a contractarian perspective, the success of the widely held company implies that this type of business enterprise offers significant advantages, while market dynamics largely address the potential difficulties a separation of ownership and control poses (Sect. 5.2). Going a step further, it would seem arguable that by a process of 'natural selection', the American version of the public corporation emerged as the logical winner of a Darwinian struggle between different forms of corporate structure.

From the 1970s to the early 1990s Germany and Japan seemed to be doing at least as well economically as the United States. This, in turn, cast doubt upon the 'natural selection' story that contractarian analysis seemed to offer. In both Germany and Japan, large business enterprises typically have 'core' investors rather than having the dispersed pattern of share ownership associated with the 'Berle–Means corporation'. The success the two countries were enjoying correspondingly weakened the efficiency explanation for the separation of ownership and control in the United States and opened the way for 'path dependency' analysis conditioned by the assumption that trajectories are heavily shaped by initial starting-points and specific conditions and legacies. Financial services regulation, social democracy, and the legal protection afforded to minority shareholders have all been cited as variables that might have influenced the configuration of the corporate economy in individual countries (for background, see Armour et al., 2002: 1712–14).

The United States enjoyed considerable economic success during the 1990s. This trend implicitly gave a boost to the natural selection hypothesis associated with contractarian analysis. At the same time, though, speculation about how American dynamism might be replicated elsewhere ensured that intellectual debate on the factors influencing national systems of ownership and control was not foreclosed. On the other hand, corporate governance scandals afflicting the United States as the twenty-first century began cast some doubt on the desirability of imitating the American model.

8 Departures from the Contractarian Model

While the notion of market failure has been used to cast doubt on inferences drawn from a contractarian perspective, this is not the only response the economic approach to corporate law has generated. Misgivings concerning the nexus of contracts model have also prompted various academics to develop new ways of looking at the corporation that take due account of the model but use it as a point of departure rather than the analytical focal point. We will now consider some examples.

8.1 Implicit Contracts

At various points in time those associated with companies give informal assurances to which they intend to adhere regardless of legal enforceability. Economists treat such 'self-enforcing' commitments as 'implicit contracts' which are part of the corporate nexus. Economically oriented corporate lawyers tend to do the same (Sect. 5.1). Some corporate law academics have gone a step further. They assert that legislators and the courts need to be prepared, under appropriate circumstances, to create legal rights to support implicit contracts (for discussion, see Daniels, 1993).

Though extra-legal undertakings can be offered in a variety of contexts, the argument in favour of regulation has typically been invoked in relation to employees. It is said that loyal staff develop extensive 'firm-specific' skills throughout the course of employment. Correspondingly, dedicated employees are very much 'at risk' if their employer, having probably offered implicit assurances of job security to inspire commitment, carries out wide-scale 'downsizing'. State intervention, in turn, is justified because workers lack the information and bargaining power required to secure binding contractual protection for their expectations of continued employment.

As we have seen (Sect. 6), those who have characterized corporate activity in contractarian terms recognize that contractual 'gaps' are inevitable and accept that legal rights can be defined by way of 'hypothetical bargains'. Hence, so long as the 'implicit contracts' concept is employed in a 'gap-filling' fashion, it may not constitute a real departure from the 'mainstream' nexus of contracts model. Nevertheless, economically oriented corporate law academics have generally been sceptical of the 'implicit contract' argument made on behalf of regulation favouring the workforce (Daniels, 1993: 326–7). They assert that employees would not contract for protection from 'downsizing' under 'ideal' conditions because other issues are of greater importance. Moreover, they stress that heavy-handed regulation could restrict the ability of companies to create new jobs by responding promptly to changing economic circumstances.

8.2 Norms, Trust, and the Team Production Model

The corporate law academics who have invoked the 'implicit contract' concept have tended to be concerned more about whether regulation is justified than about the precise nature of extra-legal undertakings within companies. Now, however, various corporate law scholars are giving the attributes of 'non-legally enforceable rules and standards' a closer look (on the terminology, see Rock and Wachter, 2001: 1641). Social 'norms', in particular, have emerged as an important topic of study in their own right.

The corporate law literature on norms typically does not seek to refute the nexus of contracts model. Instead, the innovative aspect is highlighting the distinction between legally binding agreements and extra-legal understandings and drawing attention to how the law affects the interplay between the two. The core belief is that the corporation is a prime domain of 'self-enforcing' arrangements (Rock and Wachter, 2001: 1640) since informal rules of conduct do as much or more than legal regulation to shape and determine corporate behaviour. Put even more strongly, corporate law can perhaps be understood best as providing a structure to allow business enterprises to function primarily by way of informal rules of conduct (Rock and Wachter, 2001: 1654). To the extent this is right, norms-oriented analysis can potentially offer a richer understanding of the interface between law and corporate activity than the nexus of contracts model can provide.

It cannot be taken for granted that the newly found appreciation of norms and related concepts will yield a significant redirection of theoretical analysis. Conceptual ambiguity is one reason for scepticism since even experts struggle to offer a fully satisfactory definition of norms and related concepts (Rock and Wachter, 2001: 1641). Another reason why norms-oriented analysis may not generate a major theoretical breakthrough is that it may not be capable of yielding a self-sufficient theory of the corporation that is as elegant and robust as the nexus of contracts model. Correspondingly, the literature may end up simply addressing 'gaps' in contractarian analysis.

Work done on the extra-legal norm or practice of 'trust' in fact addresses, at least partially, the latter caveat about the literature on 'non-legally enforceable rules and standards'. More particularly, Blair and Stout (e.g. 1999, 2001) have relied on the concept of 'trust' to offer an affirmative model that is intended to account in a systematic fashion for key aspects of corporate activity. According to them, the corporation is best understood as a team of people who enter into a complex agreement to work together for mutual gain. The invocation of the notion of 'agreement' indicates that Blair and Stout seek to build upon the nexus of contracts model rather than displace it completely (Blair and Stout, 1999: 319–20). The key point of departure is that they stress that there is much more going on than contractual behaviour.

Blair and Stout argue that, in a company, individuals devote themselves to the firm in the hopes of sharing the benefits flowing from 'team production'. As part of this process, they rely on the board of directors to balance the interests of the constituencies associated with the corporation in an unbiased manner. Since the participants in a corporate 'team' have faith in the board's ability to act as a 'mediating hierarchy', they do not seek full contractual protection for the 'firm-specific' investments they incur. This, admittedly, is somewhat risky since the directors may have little or no stake in the firm and thus may be susceptible to behaviour generating agency costs (Blair and Stout, 1999: 283). Nevertheless, according to Blair and Stout, cultural norms of fairness and trust encourage directors to serve the team faithfully (Blair and Stout, 1999: 315–19). Correspondingly, the benefits arising from board-oriented coordination of team production allegedly exceed the costs (Blair and Stout, 1999: 284).

The team production model, by characterizing the board of directors as a mediating hierarchy for key corporate constituencies, offers a challenge to the idea that 'shareholder primacy' is an appropriate touchstone for corporations (Sect. 3). On this count, the model perhaps does explain certain features of corporate law that cannot be accounted for readily under contractarian theory. An example is the set of duties the legal system imposes on the board. If 'shareholder primacy' was truly a pivotal feature of corporations, the law might be expected to treat directors merely as agents of those owning equity. Instead, directors have duties to a company which are akin to those that a trustee owes to a beneficiary (Blair and Stout, 1999: 290–2).

While the team production model might shed light on some important issues, it suffers from limitations which suggest that it will probably not supersede the nexus of contracts in the corporate law literature. For instance, while the team production model envisages that the board will act as a mediating hierarchy, the fact that those who own equity typically have the power to choose who sits on the board gives directors a powerful incentive to favour shareholders at the expense of other members of the 'team'. Also, though an extra-legal constraint such as trust will become less potent as the relevant community becomes larger and less closely knit

(Bainbridge, 2000: 1051), advocates of the team production model argue paradoxically that it applies more readily to publicly quoted companies than to closely held firms (Blair and Stout, 1999: 281–2).

One further potential difficulty with the team production model is that the characterization of the trust-oriented conduct that allegedly facilitates 'team' coordination is problematic. Blair and Stout assert that 'other-regarding' behaviour by directors will arise as a product of 'internalized' values and beliefs (1999: 315–19). Consistent with this notion, there is experimental evidence on human behaviour that tends to discredit the traditional economic assumption that people act as if they always seek to maximize their own welfare (Blair and Stout, 2001: 439–40). Still, while the experimental data currently available are compelling enough to justify corporate law scholars paying attention to cognitive biases that are inconsistent with mainstream economic thinking, the evidence remains sufficiently equivocal to suggest that a prudent dose of caution is appropriate (Arlen *et al.*, 2002: 5–6, 31–4).

8.3 Asset Partitioning

The team production model does not stand alone as an attempt to incorporate contractarian analysis as part of a more sophisticated conception of the company. Hansmann and Kraakman have also taken steps in this direction by emphasizing the proprietary aspect of business firms (2000). They explicitly acknowledge that a firm constitutes a nexus of contracts but note that business is most often conducted through the medium of legal entities rather than simply via 'contractual cascades' (Hansmann and Kraakman, 2000: 391). Hansmann and Kraakman explain this on the basis that organizational law (of which corporate law is a key subset) permits the formation of a firm that can have ownership of assets of its own.

To illustrate why ownership of assets is important, let us use the example of a company. Corporate law, according to Hansmann and Kraakman's analysis, allows 'affirmative' asset partitioning, which involves assigning to a company's creditors a claim on corporate property that has priority over any rights of the personal creditors of the shareholders. Also, it facilitates 'defensive' asset partitioning, which encompasses shielding the assets of the shareholders from the company's creditors via limited liability. Hansmann and Kraakman acknowledge, consistent with analysis offered from a contractarian perspective, that defensive asset partitioning could be achieved by contract (2000: 428–32). They assert, however, that it is effectively impossible to create affirmative asset partitioning using basic tools of property, contract, and agency law. Legislation authorizing the incorporation of business enterprises correspondingly is 'essential' (2000: 406–23).

Various factors will determine the impact which Hansmann and Kraakman's characterization of business organizations will ultimately have on the theoretical analysis of corporate law. One will be the outcome of historical enquiries devoted to testing their claim that property, contract, and agency law are indeed insufficiently flexible to accommodate affirmative asset partitioning (Hansmann and Kraakman, 2000: 439–40). Another will be the extent to which Hansmann and Kraakman's asset-oriented analysis can be extended and generalized. More specifically, their work is more likely to be influential if areas other than affirmative asset partitioning can be identified where corporate law's contribution is essential. Hansmann and Kraakman, it should be said, only make very modest claims in this regard (2000: 432–8).

An additional factor that could affect the impact which Hansmann and Kraakman's proprietary account of business organizations will have is possible synergies with potentially related analytical constructs. One example might be the 'concession' theory of corporate personality discussed at the beginning of this chapter (Sect. 2). This is because, like Hansmann and Kraakman's work, it implies that the state makes available to those relying on the corporate form something that could not be attained privately. Another example could be work done by economists who have argued that a firm should be defined by reference to 'property rights' (physical or intangible assets subject to common ownership) rather than by a contractual nexus (on the literature, see Rock and Wachter, 2001: 1634–6). Hansmann and Kraakman downplay, however, links between their asset-oriented analysis on the one hand and theories of juridical personality or the 'property rights' version of the firm on the other (2000: 391 n. 5, 438–9).

9 THEORETICAL CORPORATE LAW SCHOLARSHIP OUTSIDE THE UNITED STATES

Readers may have noticed that to this point the discussion has a distinctly American flavour. This is largely a by-product of the literature in other common law jurisdictions. It is fair to say that at least until the beginning of the 1990s the United Kingdom, Canada, and Australia largely lacked an intellectual tradition of placing corporate law scholarship within a broader theoretical framework. As a result, a survey of this sort inevitably must focus primarily on trends in the United States.

Despite historical patterns, theoretical company law scholarship is no longer restricted to the United States. Instead, academics in Australia, Canada, and the UK are now carrying out a growing range of interdisciplinary work (Cheffins, 1999: 209). Since the shift in intellectual focus has been recent in orientation, the nexus of contracts model that has influenced the US literature so strongly has inevitably had an impact on the research that has been carried out. Indeed, observers in Australia, Canada, and the UK generally acknowledge that the nexus of contracts model has dominated the theoretical discourse.

Still, while the sort of economic approach to corporate law that has been so influential in the United States has attracted attention elsewhere, its influence has varied. In Canada, the impact has been substantial. Hence, though the Canadian corporate economy has features that distinguish it from its US counterpart, Canadian scholars regularly look to the law and economics literature to give shape to their analysis of corporate law issues. Likewise, in Australia, the economic approach to law has a growing number of adherents in the corporate law field.

In the UK, on the other hand, contractarian analysis does not currently constitute the mainstream or orthodox approach at the academic level. Instead, in British interdisciplinary corporate law scholarship, there is a tendency to acknowledge law and economics, cite its limitations, and shift to a different theoretical ground. The most typical move UK academics currently make is to discuss the company by reference to its employees and others, such as suppliers, customers, and perhaps society at large, potentially having a 'stake' in the business.

Those adopting a 'stakeholder' perspective often argue that company law should offer explicit protection to the various constituencies associated with companies. This argument is sometimes framed in economic terms, with the logic being that stakeholders need incentives to make firm-specific investments that are allegedly pivotal ingredients of long-term corporate success. In other instances, however, public scrutiny and control of corporate activity is justified on wider grounds. The thinking is that companies are too important to the economy to exist for the benefit of a single constituency, namely the shareholders. Regulation which secures fair treatment for potentially vulnerable stakeholder groups is therefore justified, even if the measures in question may reduce corporate profits.

10 WHERE IS CORPORATE LAW THEORY GOING?

Now that we have considered the major themes in corporate law scholarship, we will consider where matters might proceed in the future. We will do this by discussing four trajectories that potentially account for the manner in which corporate law theory has evolved to this point. As we will see, each can be invoked to forecast the future path of corporate law scholarship. At the same time, though, declaring the 'last word' on how matters will develop is impossible since corporate law does not appear to evolve exclusively in accordance with any of the trajectories we will consider.

10.1 The 'Cumulative' Model

A first potential trajectory for corporate law scholarship is 'cumulative' in nature, with the presumption being that the result is 'progress' in the field. The idea is that the literature develops incrementally within a discipline as new academics resolve existing controversies and expand upon the work of their predecessors by deriving new insights from those resolutions. Natural science is the intellectual endeavour where this accumulation of knowledge is thought of as taking place in its purest form. The classic conception of scientific understanding is that it improves as part of an unfolding story as prior knowledge is used as the foundation to improve our comprehension of the world. Scientists, under this view, 'progress' towards the 'truth' by reliance on 'scientific method', which constitutes objective enquiry founded on the safeguards of explicit theory-building, replication, and corroboration.

The thesis that intellectual enquiry yields a 'better' understanding of the world via the accumulation of knowledge can be applied to the theoretical analysis of corporate law. Essentially, the story that could be told is that our understanding of corporate entities improved when Berle and Means drew attention to the potential separation of ownership and control in large business enterprises. Economic analysis constituted additional 'progress' because it not only offered a cogent account of the separation of ownership and control via agency cost theory but also made full allowances for the market dynamics which influence the manner in which corporations function. More recently, corporate law academics seeking to offer a constructive departure from economic analysis have relied on concepts such as norms, trust, and asset partitioning to tell a 'richer' story of the relationship between law and corporate activity. Looking to the future, 'progress' might continue via further embellishments of the nexus of contracts model. Alternatively, a new conceptual framework might emerge which recognizes that corporations function in a market environment but departs fundamentally from the contractual orientation of economic analysis.

The sort of 'Whig history' just offered needs to be treated with caution. Again, natural science is the field where, via the application of scientific method, 'progress' is conventionally thought to occur in its purest form. This version of progress is potentially relevant to legal scholarship since efforts have been made, most notably at Harvard Law School in the late nineteenth and early twentieth centuries, to depict the legal system as a body of scientifically deducible principles. Academic writing on law, however, is typically too prescriptive and pragmatic in orientation to meet the strict standards of verification and reliability associated with science.

Correspondingly, it seems doubtful that there will be scientific 'progress' with the study of law (Edwards, 1998).

While the 'cumulative' trajectory associated with science is unlikely to prevail in legal scholarship, economic analysis of law might offer a partial exception. The study of economics potentially constitutes a form of scientific enquiry since experts in the field typically seek to generate and test empirically disprovable hypotheses. Given this, and given the economic foundations of the nexus of contracts model, contractarian analysis of corporate law potentially has a scientific aspect (McChesney, 1993). Still, it is not entirely clear whether economics itself is a discipline where the methodology of science is properly invoked and knowledge accumulates (de Geest, 1996). Correspondingly, claims that law and economics can advance our understanding of the legal system in a scientific manner must remain controversial, whether in the corporate context or otherwise.

10.2 Kuhn and Corporate Law Scholarship

Leaving aside the scientific attributes of legal scholarship (or lack thereof), characterizing the evolution of corporate law theory in cumulative terms is problematic. This is because work done on the history, philosophy, and sociology of science has cast doubt on whether even in the natural sciences there is the sort of 'progress' assumed by the conventional wisdom. Thomas Kuhn has offered the most influential reappraisal of scientific knowledge through the invocation of terminology such as 'paradigms' and 'normal science' (Kuhn, 1996; for a helpful summary of Kuhn's work see Hoyningen-Huene, 1993). It is appropriate, therefore to consider whether the trajectory of corporate law scholarship can be characterized appropriately in 'Kuhnian' terms.

According to Kuhn, within a given field, matters begin in a 'pre-consensus', 'immature', or 'pre-paradigm' phase. This means there is competition between intellectual schools addressing the same issues from different, mutually incompatible standpoints. The field subsequently comes together when work is produced that is sufficiently convincing to persuade members of existing schools to defect and to attract the next generation of experts. Once a consensus is in place that is focused on the dominant 'paradigm' or 'disciplinary matrix', researchers are spared the incessant and distracting re-examination of first principles. Instead, they can proceed with confidence to solve 'puzzles' by reference to the dominant mode of thought. Such 'mopping up' activity within a 'mature' field of research is known as 'normal science'.

Kuhn noted that those working in accordance with the precepts of 'normal science' will periodically find inexplicable 'anomalies' that are irreconcilable with the dominant paradigm. Over time, he said, an accumulation of serious anomalies can seriously destabilize the existing consensus and eventually build to a crisis. A fresh competition of ideas will then ensue that could either leave the existing paradigm intact or culminate in a 'scientific revolution' that establishes a new consensus within the discipline. If a 'paradigm shift' does occur, normal science will ultimately recommence under the new world-view, setting the stage for the cycle to repeat itself.

According to Kuhn, such 'paradigm shifts' do not yield the accumulation of knowledge in the manner traditionally associated with scientific progress. Instead, since the preconceptions underlying successive traditions of normal science are radically different, discerning how the relevant paradigms are interrelated is highly problematic. In other words, since comparative evaluation cannot be effected by a neutral, universal set of rules, disciplinary matrixes tend to be 'incommensurable'. Correspondingly, no a priori assumptions can be made as to whether a paradigm shift constitutes a move towards the 'truth' in any objective sense (Kuhn, 1996: 170–3, 206–7). All that can be said is that the relevant academic community is working within an intellectual mind-set that is addressing more successfully the issues deemed pertinent and topical.

If Kuhn is correct that the development of knowledge is not cumulative but instead is organized around paradigm shifts, normal science, and so on, how can his insights be applied to the academic study of corporate law? A Kuhnian sketch of the history and current status of the discipline might proceed as follows. The debate over corporate personality that took place prior to 1930 would qualify as corporate law's 'immature' phase since there was little agreement about how to define the corporation. Berle and Means's separation of ownership and control thesis then marked a decisive break because it was sufficiently convincing to become the dominant paradigm within the field of corporate law. After the emergence of the separation of ownership and control as a pivotal intellectual construct, a period of normal science followed where the focus was on regulatory strategies designed to address the 'core' problem Berle and Means had identified. Manne's subsequent critique of the received wisdom then signalled a 'crisis', which was followed by a 'scientific revolution' that left the nexus of contracts model as the dominant paradigm.

Continuing to the present day, in Kuhnian terms, the academic study of corporate law currently is perhaps in a period of 'normal science' where most theoretical analysis is conducted through the prism of economics. Nevertheless, the work being done on norms, the team production model, and asset partitioning constitute sufficiently ambitious departures from the prevailing mode of analysis to suggest that the existing consensus might be unstable or eroding. The popularity of 'stakeholder' theory in the UK implies likewise. Perhaps, then, a new 'crisis' is imminent which will generate a fresh competition of ideas that will either leave the existing contractarian paradigm intact or culminate in a 'scientific revolution' that yields a new disciplinary matrix.

Relying on Kuhn to think about corporate law scholarship cannot be dismissed as a fanciful endeavour. Indeed, Berle and Means's separation of ownership and control thesis and the nexus of contracts model have both been described on various occasions as 'paradigms' that have dominated corporate law scholarship (e.g. Bratton, 1992: 180–1, 189–90). Nevertheless, it remains at best unclear whether corporate law is a context to which Kuhn's approach can be fruitfully extended. It is important to note that Kuhn was seeking to offer an account of the evolution of scientific thought, not the evolution of legal scholarship. We have seen that drawing parallels between scientific methodology and the study of law is a problematic exercise (Sect. 10.1). Correspondingly, applying Kuhn's analytical framework to legal scholarship requires a potentially problematic leap in logic.

Another difficulty associated with using Kuhn's work to think about legal studies is that the academic work done on law typically lacks the detached tone of scientific enquiry and instead often has a strong prescriptive agenda. Correspondingly, legal researchers may be incapable of achieving the sort of tight research consensus that distinguishes a 'mature' field of research from its 'pre-paradigm' counterpart. Let us translate this into corporate law terms. In contrast with what takes place in scientific disciplines, it might be that neither Berle and Means's separation of ownership and control thesis nor the nexus of contracts model has provided a sufficiently focused research agenda to allow corporate law academics to engage in quasi-scientific 'mopping up' activity. If this is an accurate prognosis, then it is misguided to think about the evolution of corporate law scholarship in Kuhnian terms.

10.3 Intellectual Cycles

If legal scholarship does not 'progress' or evolve via 'paradigm-shifts', then how do matters proceed? A possibility that merits consideration is that the trajectory is, to a substantial extent, cyclical (for an advocate of this thesis, see Allen, 1992). The question 'what is a corporation?' illustrates that this view of legal scholarship as a continuing conversation about pivotal questions is potentially instructive. As we have already seen, there may be links between the old theory that corporate organizations owe their existence to an official grant of authority (a 'concession') from the state and Hansmann and Kraakman's contemporary work concerning asset partitioning (Sect. 8.3). Also, the nexus of contracts model that has been so influential in the past two decades has rhetoric in common with the 'contractual/association' thesis that was offered in the early twentieth century to counter the concession theory (Sect. 2).

'Are managers sufficiently accountable?' and 'on whose behalf are companies run?' qualify as two additional questions that illustrate the potentially cyclical quality of corporate law scholarship. With respect to managerial accountability, as we have seen, Berle and Means's *The Modern Corporation and Private Property* flagged this as a pivotal topic (see Sect. 3). Until the 1980s, the consensus was that state intervention was required to keep corporate executives in line. Contractarians subsequently adopted a more deregulatory posture but nevertheless did continue to focus on managerial accountability via agency cost theory (see Sect. 5.2).

Turning to corporate goals and responsibilities, though Berle was not convinced that a departure from the dominant 'shareholder primacy' view was justified, some inferred from Berle and Means's work that companies must have obligations that extend beyond those owning equity (see Sect. 3). Contractual analysis was subsequently invoked to support the proposition that companies exist for their shareholders (see Sect. 5). In turn, implicit contracts, the team production model, and stakeholder theory have been relied upon to challenge this notion (see Sects 8.1, 8.2, 9).

It may well be that in the area of corporate law there are certain questions which have endured as topics and will continue to do so. Hence, it seems quite likely that in future decades academics will be asking 'what is a corporation?', 'are managers sufficiently accountable?', and 'on whose behalf are companies run?' Still, caution is required so as to avoid attaching undue weight to a cyclical account of corporate law theory.

One reason for caution is that the mere existence of enduring issues does not necessarily displace other trajectories we have considered thus far. Consider the possibility of 'progress' by reference to managerial accountability. Contractarians admittedly explored issues that the separation of ownership and control thesis had already raised. Still, the explicit recognition of market forces arguably constituted an intellectual advance since the resulting scholarship yielded a more fully developed account of the constraints which executives face in the real world. Also, the presence of enduring questions can be consistent with evolution along Kuhnian lines. This is because in order for a paradigm-shift to occur, the new theory must not only be able to cope with the anomalies that caused a crisis for the old theory but also must treat familiar problems with improved accuracy (Hoyningen-Huene, 1993: 241, 259).

An additional reason a cyclical account of corporate law theory should be treated with caution is that uncritical acceptance of this point of view might create a misleading impression of stability and predictability. Academic thinking about corporate law certainly has the potential to evolve in apparently random directions. For instance, if the author of this chapter had been writing at the beginning of the 1970s and forecast that an economically oriented 'prairie fire' was imminent, he or she probably would have been dismissed as foolish. A prediction made a decade or more later about the current interest in the study of social norms might well have yielded similar ridicule. Clearly, then, one cannot outline how corporate law scholarship will evolve in the future simply by considering the past.

10.4 Academic Fads and Fashions

To account for new movements in the academic study of corporate law that are difficult to foresee, it is helpful to turn to consider a fourth potential trajectory for scholarship. This is that fads and fashions influence academic writing about law, thereby yielding intellectual 'cascades' that can produce unpredictable and seemingly random trends in the literature. According to Sunstein, academic lawyers typically lack reliable information about what is 'true' or 'right' (2001: 1254). As a result, choices made by peers and reputational concerns can have a strong influence within the legal academy, as can views adopted by a like-minded group that moves collectively via mutual self-reinforcement towards an extreme position ('group polarization'). Correspondingly, 'polarization entrepreneurs' can rapidly gain followers and thereby create an academic cascade (Sunstein, 2001: 1260–1).

According to Sunstein, some fads 'burn out' quickly because once the relevant points have been raised little can be done with them. Other claims, by contrast, can be developed over a long period (Sunstein, 2001: 1263). Does longevity mean that the relevant ideas are 'good' or 'true'? Sunstein says no (2001: 1263–4). He acknowledges that cogent arguments and contradictory evidence can puncture a faulty set of claims. Still, so long as informational signals, reputational concerns, and 'group polarization' continue to fortify a particular fad, longevity is not out of the question for bad ideas.

The notion of academic fads might well be relevant to corporate law scholarship. On this count, the nexus of contracts model is potentially instructive. According to Sunstein, external shocks constitute a crucial reason why an academic bandwagon might start. Developments in adjacent fields, he says, can be one such catalyst (2001: 1262). Consistent with this analysis, the work which economists began to do in the 1970s on the market dynamics functioning within firms (see Sect. 5.1) helped to prompt the contractarian 'prairie fire' which subsequently swept through corporate law (Sect. 6). Moreover, as we have seen, corporate law scholarship allegedly cannot currently succeed in the marketplace of ideas unless an economics of law perspective has been adopted (see Sect. 7). An inference that can be drawn from this is that reputational pressures and polarization dynamics have helped to guarantee the success and longevity of contractarian analysis. At the same time, Sunstein would say that the durability of the economic approach to corporate law should not be taken as a reliable signal of quality.

To the extent that academic bandwagons do dictate the evolution of corporate law theory, it becomes largely impossible to predict future developments. This is because, as Sunstein says, external shocks can produce unanticipated effects, including seemingly random cascades (2001: 1252). It may therefore be the case that the future contours of corporate law theory are imponderable (DeMott, 1996: 1335). Sunstein has conceded, however, that his analysis of legal scholarship is preliminary. Correspondingly, his arguments do not necessarily refute the proposition that knowledge accumulates nor discredit the Kuhnian account of intellectual activity (Sunstein, 2001: 1252, 1261). Hence, despite Sunstein's analysis of academic fads, other trajectories for legal scholarship remain tenable.

11 CONCLUSION

This chapter has offered an evolutionary account of corporate law scholarship. A chronological overview of key developments in corporate law theory constituted the bulk of the chapter but the relevant scholarship was also described in terms of four different trajectories. These trajectories have, in turn, been drawn upon to forecast how matters might unfold in the years to come.

Admittedly, the predictions outlined here do not offer a fully coherent vision of the future. Instead, to a substantial extent, the prognosis has many contradictory elements. For instance, while the cumulative model of legal scholarship implies that there will be progress towards a better understanding of corporate law, Kuhn's analysis of paradigms and scientific revolutions and Sunstein's account of academic fads both cast doubt on this optimistic assumption. Also, though the cyclical account of corporate law scholarship implies that 'core' questions will endure as the decades pass, if influential schools of legal thought are in fact the product of cascade-driven shifts then random events will largely dictate the future.

Under ideal circumstances, the account of corporate law scholarship offered here might seek to reconcile the predictions tendered. Such an exercise is, however, not feasible within the confines of this chapter. It seems reasonable to assume that, throughout various areas of the law, similar factors dictate how the academic literature is configured. Correspondingly, ascertaining whether corporate law scholarship will evolve in accordance with a cumulative model, a Kuhnian framework, a cyclical process, or a series of fads cannot be done properly without drawing upon the experience in other legal fields. Ultimately, then, it may be necessary to be thoroughly conversant with *The Oxford Handbook of Legal Studies* to be properly positioned to offer predictions on the future direction of corporate law theory.

REFERENCES

Allen, W.T. (1992). 'Our Schizophrenic Conception of the Business Corporation', *Cardozo Law Review*, 14: 261–81.

Arlen, J., Spitzer, M., and Talley, E. (2002). 'Endowment Effects within Corporate Agency Relationships', *Journal of Legal Studies*, 31: 1–34.

Armour, J., Cheffins, B., and Skeel, D. (2002). 'Corporate Ownership Structure and the Evolution of Bankruptcy Law: Lessons from the United Kingdom', *Vanderbilt Law Review*, 55: 1699–783.

Bainbridge, S. M. (2000). 'Mandatory Disclosure: A Behavioral Analysis', *University of Cincinnati Law Review*, 68: 1023–60.

Berle, A. A., and Means, G. C. (1932). *The Modern Corporation and Private Property*, New York: Harcourt, Brace & World.

Blair, M. M. and Stout, L. A. (1999). 'A Team Production Theory of Corporate Law', *Virginia Law Review*, 85: 247–328.

Blair, M. M. and Stout, L. A. (2001). 'Director Accountability and the Mediating Role of the Corporate Board', *Washington University Law Quarterly*, 79: 403–47.

Branson, D. M. (1989). 'A Corporate Paleontologist's Look at Law and Economics in the Seventh Circuit', *Chicago-Kent Law Review*, 65: 745–56.

—— (2001). 'Corporate Governance "Reform" and the New Corporate Social Responsibility', *University of Pittsburgh Law Review*, 62: 605–47.

Bratton, W. W. (1992). 'The Economic Structure of the Post-Contractual Corporation', *Northwestern University Law Review*, 87: 180–215.

—— (2001). 'Berle and Means Reconsidered at the Century's Turn', *Journal of Corporation Law*, 26: 737–70.

Carney, W. J. (1999). 'The Legacy of "The Market for Corporate Control" and the Origins of the Theory of the Firm', *Case Western Reserve Law Review*, 50: 215–44.

Cheffins, B. R. (1997), *Company Law: Theory, Structure and Operation*, Oxford: Oxford University Press.

—— (1999). 'Using Theory to Study Law: A Company Law Perspective', *Cambridge Law Journal*, 58: 197–221.

Coase, R. H. (1937). 'The Nature of the Firm', *Economica* (n.s.), 4: 386–405.

Daniels, R. (1993). 'Stakeholders and Takeovers: Can Contractarianism be Compassionate?' *University of Toronto Law Journal*, 43: 315–51.

De Geest, G. (1996). 'The Debate on the Scientific Status of Law & Economics', *European Economics Review*, 40: 999–1006.

DeMott, D. A. (1996). 'Trust and Tension within Corporations', *Cornell Law Review*, 81: 1308–37.

Easterbrook, F. H., and Fischel, D. R. (1991). *The Economic Structure of Corporate Law*, Cambridge, Mass.: Harvard University Press.

Edwards, C. N. (1998). 'In Search of Legal Scholarship: Strategies for the Integration of Science into the Practice of Law', *Southern California Interdisciplinary Law Journal*, 8: 1–38.

Hansmann, H., and Kraakman, R. (2000). 'The Essential Role of Organizational Law', *Yale Law Journal*, 110: 387–440.

Hoyningen-Huene, P. (1993). *Reconstructing Scientific Revolutions: Thomas S. Kuhn's Philosophy of Science*, Chicago: University of Chicago Press.

Jensen, M. C., and Meckling, W. H. (1976). 'Theory of the Firm: Managerial Behavior, Agency Costs and Ownership Structure', *Journal of Financial Economics*, 3: 305–60.

Johnston, J. S. (1993). 'The Influence of *The Nature of the Firm* on the Theory of Corporate Law', *Journal of Corporation Law*, 18: 213–44.

Kuhn, T. S. (1996). *The Structure of Scientific Revolutions* (3rd edn.), Chicago: University of Chicago Press.

McChesney, F. S. (1993). 'Positive Economics and All That: A Review of the Economic Structure of Corporate Law', *George Washington Law Review*, 61: 272–98.

Manne, H. G. (1987). 'Intellectual Styles and the Evolution of American Corporate Law', in G. Radnitzky and P. Bernholz (eds.), *Economic Imperialism: The Economic Approach Applied outside the Field of Economics*, New York: Paragon House Publishers, 219–41.

Mark, G. A. (1987). 'The Personification of the Business Corporation in American Law', *University of Chicago Law Review*, 54: 1441–83.

Ramseyer, J. M. (1998). 'Corporate Law', in P. Newman (ed.), *The New Palgrave Dictionary of Economics and the Law*, London: Macmillan, i: 503–11.

Rock, E. B., and Wachter, M. L. (2001). 'Islands of Conscious Power: Law, Norms and the Self-Governing Corporation', 149 *University of Pennsylvania Law Review*, 1619–700.

Sunstein, C. R (2001). 'On Academic Fads and Fashions', *Michigan Law Review*, 99: 1251–64.

CHAPTER 24

COMPETITION

DAVID J. GERBER

1 INTRODUCTION

COMPETITION law is a curious mixture. It is both theoretical and intensely procedural, both abstract and embedded in economic experience, and both public law and private law. It claims to seek benefits for consumers, but consumers often have little voice in shaping the law. This mixture of perspectives differs, often dramatically, from one competition-law system to another and from one academic community to another. It also varies over time within competition-law systems and academic communities. As competition-law systems interact more frequently and more intensely, the prominence and practical importance of these differences will increase, and this interaction is likely to restructure competition-law scholarship.

This chapter examines key aspects of competition-law scholarship in the United States and Europe. Its central objective is to reveal contours and conflicts in the legal literature and to provide tools for understanding, interpreting, and evaluating them. I then use this analysis as a basis for considering how competition-law scholarship is likely to develop and where it should go.

Two claims are central. One is that beliefs, arguments, and assumptions about the goals and methods of competition law shape scholarship within each system and thus provide keys to understanding and interpreting the competition-law literature. The second is that the globalization of economic activity and the institutional responses to that process will require increasing interaction between heretofore largely autonomous systems, thereby reshaping not only competition law, but also competition-law scholarship.

The scope of the chapter is limited. First, it deals only with competition law in the antitrust sense, that is, law whose stated function is to protect the process of competition from restraints. It does not refer to what is usually called unfair competition law, a private-law mechanism that provides compensation to parties harmed by 'unfair' methods of competition. Secondly, it refers only to US federal antitrust law and European Union competition law. There are many other competition-law systems, but these two are by far the most influential. Thirdly, it deals only with scholarship that is in some sense analytical rather than merely descriptive.

The chapter first reviews EU and US competition-law scholarship separately. For each system, it looks at the context and dimensions of scholarship, then at debates and issues regarding goals and methods, and finally at conflicts and controversies in specific substantive areas. It concludes by looking at how globalization may, and perhaps should, influence the future development of competition-law scholarship.

2 US Antitrust Law Scholarship: Context and Dimensions

Scholarship is shaped by cognitive, institutional, and social processes, and thus if we want to understand it, we need to know something about who writes, in what contexts, subject to which types of influences, and with what kinds of objectives. Knowledge of how scholarship is produced often provides insight into what it produces.

A high percentage of those who write analytical scholarship about US antitrust law are full-time professors of either law or economics. Law professors predominate, but the economics contingent has grown rapidly in recent years. Legal practitioners occasionally venture analytical comments, but their writings are primarily descriptive. Government officials occasionally also write on the subject, but their writings are generally understood as advocacy of governmental policy decisions rather than as independent contributions to legal analysis, and their influence on court decisions and scholarly debates tends to be limited.

This means that the incentives that shape analytical antitrust scholarship are generally internal to academic communities—that is, they relate to status and advancement within those communities. In general, neither private clients nor government-based incentives play significant roles, although private consulting provides significant incentives in some areas, particularly those relating to the use of economics in litigation. These academic communities are relatively small, and often hierarchic. Moreover, they rarely have more than superficial contact with legal practitioners and judges.

Most of the influential scholarship in the area appears in general-purpose legal journals edited by law students, although there are a few specialized antitrust journals that are professionally edited. In general, law review articles are long (100 or more pages is not uncommon) and heavily footnoted. They frequently focus either on appellate court decisions or on particular legal doctrines or forms of analysis. Articles by economists tend to focus on particular markets or market phenomena. There are relatively few monographs dealing primarily with analytical antitrust issues.

Two modes of discourse dominate this literature. One is the traditional case-law language of US antitrust. Its vocabulary depicts what courts have done, how they have reasoned, and what impact their decisions have had on particular policy goals. It is a factually dense, procedurally embedded, and largely ad hoc language. The other is the theoretical, universalistic, and abstract language of economic science or its law-and-economics variant. There is a sharp tension between these two ways of discussing antitrust issues.

3 GOALS AND METHODS IN US ANTITRUST LAW SCHOLARSHIP

Controversies over goals and methods shape antitrust scholarship. Individuals and groups make decisions in relation to the goals that are considered legitimate within that system, and they articulate the reasons for their decisions in relation to those goals. They also make those decisions within a methodological framework created and maintained by institutions, practices, and expectations. The broad range of choices on these issues leads to much academic controversy about them.

3.1 Goals: The Traditional Case Law Frame

The governing statutes of US antitrust law provide little guidance regarding its goals. Judges have, therefore, developed and articulated those goals in specific cases. In responding to changing circumstances for more than a century, courts have generated a substrate of economic, social, and political values from which later courts have drawn in fashioning and justifying their decisions (e.g. Pitofsky, 1979). At various times, concerns for fairness (particularly for small and medium-sized firms), equality of opportunity, and economic liberty have been deposited in this substrate. The label 'anti-competitive' has been applied to conduct that is seen as harmful to some or all of these goals.

Until recently, antitrust scholarship has aimed primarily to evaluate these court decisions, assessing their consistency with prior decisions, analyzing the reasoning employed, and predicting their consequences. It is a particularistic and procedurally embedded form of scholarship, although abstract concepts are often used in analyzing court decisions.

3.2 The Law-and-Economics Revolution and its Consequences

Since the late 1970s, however, scholars identified with the 'law-and-economics' (L&E) movement have superimposed a different conception of antitrust goals on this decisional background. They have argued that the goals of antitrust should be defined much more narrowly than they traditionally are—that they should be determined *solely* by reference to economic theory (e.g. Bork, 1978). Their ideas about goals quickly won acceptance during the 1980s, thus fundamentally reorienting competition law and competition-law scholarship. This law-and-economics 'revolution' is central to our analysis (Posner, 2000). As with most victories, it is partial and not always what it seems. Other conceptions of antitrust's goals occasionally still surface in the literature.

The rapid victory of this conception of antitrust's goals has had important consequences for competition-law scholarship. First, the battle was fought and won by academics on academic turf. The theoretical writings of what was originally a small group of scholars altered the decisions of prosecutors and judges and thus changed the law. Moreover, the battle was won relatively quickly—within little more than a decade. This experience has given academics in the area a sense of the potential power of their writings: if these ideas can be so successful in such a short period of time, they must be powerful. From here the step to assuming that they are 'right' in a universal sense is easy and often taken.

This experience has also created a kind of post-victory mode of scholarship in which there is generally little willingness to consider perspectives other than those of the victors. The 'big battle' over goals has been won. Once it is accepted that the goals of competition law are defined solely by economic theory, the only remaining issues relate to the contents of that theory. Those that envision other goals become irrelevant. As we shall see, this can create difficulties when US antitrust perspectives encounter perspectives common outside the United States.

It also ties the antitrust debate to issues of political ideology. From the perspective of economics, government actions that affect business decisions are viewed as 'regulation' which 'interferes' with the economy; they are, therefore, presumed to be harmful. This creates an agenda that has much in common with a political ideology that disfavors government action on often quite different grounds.

3.3 Among the Victors: What Kinds of Economic Goals?

Defining antitrust goals solely in terms of economic theory does not mean that no issues about goals remain, but merely that economic theory must be their frame and source. The issues are now about what kind of economics should structure its goals. It is a narrower debate, but not necessarily less intense.

3.3.1 *The Harvard–Chicago Clash*

The debate within economics was initially between the so-called 'Harvard' and 'Chicago' schools. The Harvard school was highly influential prior to the 1980s. Closely related to a branch of economics known as industrial organizational theory, it focused on market structures—that is, the relationships among the participants in markets—as a basis for predicting outcomes and assessing antitrust norms. In its view, the goal of antitrust should be to combat conduct that leads to less competitive market structures. This brand of scholarship tended to be relatively particularistic, emphasizing the details of specific markets rather than the production of theoretical propositions.

The Chicago school, which led the L&E revolution and whose central tenets and assumptions have come to form a kind of orthodoxy within the antitrust community, rejects this analysis. It bases its arguments on a different branch of economics known as price theory. Assessing market relationships in terms of their effect on price, it holds that the sole goal of antitrust should be to combat conduct that at a given point in time restricts output or tends to increase prices—often called the efficiency goal.

3.3.2 *Challenges to Goal Orthodoxy*

This orthodoxy is the focal point of debate about goals. The Chicago school has been challenged on several levels, particularly since the early 1990s. Note that the debate is often historically framed. A central question is often 'What did Congress intend in passing the Sherman Act?'

Some critics argue that efficiency should not be the sole goal of antitrust. For them, the goal should be to protect consumer interests by maintaining the lowest possible prices. This goal is seen as generally, but not entirely, consistent with the efficiency goal. It is based on price theory and is in that sense closely related to the efficiency goal and to Chicago school orthodoxy, but it changes the emphasis and some outcomes.

A second critical thrust is very recent and moves farther from the Chicago-school conception of goals. It is rigorously economic, but fundamentally different from efficiency analysis. Its foremost proponent is Michael Porter, a leading business economist. Porter claims that the Chicago school's efficiency goals represent too narrow a conception of the nature and role of competition in an economy.

For Porter, antitrust law should be used to enhance economic productivity, but the Chicago school's goal of achieving short-run efficiency in price-theoretic terms does this only indirectly, if at all (Porter, 2001).

Porter urges that antitrust analysis be based primarily on the operation of those economic forces that affect productivity in an industry. These include barriers to entry, the intensity of rivalry, customer power, supplier power, and opportunities for substitution. Where conduct significantly impedes productivity improvement in an economy, it should be subject to antitrust scrutiny. His theory is not fully worked out, and he has paid little attention to its applicability by courts, but it represents a direct theoretical challenge to the Chicago school's conception of goals.

3.4 Methods: Claims and Assumptions

The Chicago school's arguments and assumptions—both at the analytical and institutional levels—are also central to the debates about the methods of antitrust law (e.g. Hovenkamp, 2001). Goals and methods are always related, but the importance of that relationship is particularly striking here.

3.4.1 *Case Law as Method*

The traditional methodology of antitrust law has been case-based, not least because the statutes provide so little guidance to decision-makers. Operating in the density of actual conflicts and complex fact patterns, courts have created virtually the entire body of law, and thus case-law methods have shaped antitrust law. This method of decision-making has fostered a multivalent conception of antitrust's goals.

3.4.2 *Chicago: Economics as Legal Method*

The Chicago school calls for a very different conception of legal method. In it, theoretically based propositions about how economic actors make decisions, the consequences of those decisions, and the social value of these consequences are the core of legal method. This concept of method has both conceptual and institutional dimensions.

The conceptual component refers to the forms of analysis used to interpret factual data and to determine whether conduct has caused particular harms. The Chicago school's method is rigorously rationalistic. Assumptions about the conduct of rational actors are used to model and assess real-world decisions. If price theory posits that a rational actor would act in a particular way, courts are to presume that actual decision-makers have in fact acted in such a way. The search for profit in the short run is assumed to be the only significant incentive of market participants.

The institutional focus of the Chicago school's antitrust scholarship is on judicial decisions, largely excluding the messy process of legislation from the law-making picture. It argues that the proper role of courts is to apply theoretical economic principles. Both the principles and their proper application are to be based exclusively on price theory, and those who convey this knowledge (economists and law-and-economics scholars) are to guide the courts. Judges should not be concerned with community values or consider issues such as the political implications of economic power that were part of earlier antitrust methodologies.

3.4.3 *Emerging Conceptions of Antitrust's Methods*

Both the conceptual and the institutional dimensions of Chicago-school methodology have been criticized, particularly since the early 1990s. Its success can be measured in the extent to which virtually all discussion of important issues is located by reference to Chicago analysis. The rational actor assumptions that are critical to Chicago-school methods have been criticized from both theoretical and empirical directions. Critics argue that Chicago-school assumptions diverge from the real world in ways that limit its value for antitrust analysis.

Game theory, which has become particularly fashionable in microeconomic analysis in US universities over the last decade, envisions a more complex set of economic incentives than does the rational actor model. It analyzes incentives not only in relation to given market information such as price movements, but also by reference to the relationships among the actors on the market. It examines the strategies that market participants use to gain advantages in achieving profits (e.g. Carlton *et al.*, 1997). Its approach is theoretical and rational-actor-based, and in that sense it challenges the Chicago school on its own terms; but it countenances a broader set of incentives.

The other main source of criticism of Chicago-school assumptions comes from the relatively new field of behavioral economics, which has become an important force in many leading economic departments over the past few years. Its criticism is largely empirical rather than theoretical. Its adherents claim that economic conduct is often not 'rational' in the Chicago-school sense, but is influenced by psychological and sociological factors. Courts must interpret economic data in applying the antitrust laws, and they cannot do so effectively unless they take such factors into account.

Criticism of the institutional component of the Chicago school's methodology has been less clearly focused, in part because that element of the methodology is less clearly formulated. Nevertheless, there is much academic disquiet over the issue of the role of the judge in antitrust law. The complexity and factual density of antitrust litigation, particularly in a system where a jury may make final decisions about facts, engenders a desire for predictability, and its promise of conceptual clarity has been a factor in the appeal of the Chicago school. On the other hand, the idea that judges should merely apply the economic principles that scholars say they should apply conflicts with strongly held values that support the status and independence of judges in the US legal system.

4 SUBSTANTIVE LAW ISSUES

Competing conceptions of goals and methods often shape the formulation of specific substantive law issues. This section looks briefly at several such issues that are prominent in antitrust scholarship.

4.1 Rule of Reason versus *per se* Analysis

One key issue is how closely courts should look at the effects of agreements that might harm competition. In the Sherman Act of 1890, the central US antitrust statute, Congress prohibited agreements 'in restraint of trade'. Courts quickly recognized that virtually all agreements 'restrain trade' in some sense, and thus they interpreted the Act to prohibit an agreement only where it contained a restraint that was 'unreasonable'. This so-called 'rule of reason' now requires a court to weigh the anti-competitive and pro-competitive effects of agreements against each other. Only where the negative effects outweigh the positive effects is the agreement to be prohibited.

The costs and uncertainties of this extended balancing analysis soon led courts to develop ways of avoiding it—using the concept of *per se* rules. Where the courts were convinced that they had enough collective experience to be confident that a particular type of agreement would virtually always be 'unreasonable', an elaborate rule-of-reason analysis would not be required. The restraint would be considered illegal *per se*. Use of *per se* rules also increases the deterrent force of the law by increasing the probability that a plaintiff (including the US government) will be successful in challenging a particular type of agreement and by significantly reducing the costs of challenging agreements.

The L&E revolution has led, however, to the abandonment or evisceration of most *per se* rules. Economists have succeeded in showing the difficulty of predicting the effects of agreements without looking carefully at the contexts in which they are used, and courts have responded by refusing to class particular agreements as *per se* violations.

This has highlighted a fundamental tension within antitrust law and scholarship. A central argument for adopting Chicago methods has been that it simplifies analysis by giving courts a clearer basis for decision-making. At a conceptual level it does. In practice, however, the enhanced role of economists in antitrust enforcement has had the opposite effect. Given the procedural system within which the concepts are applied, it has often made enforcement of the antitrust laws more costly and uncertain rather than less so.

As a result, courts and scholars have sought ways of formulating rules that appropriately evaluate the facts of a case without requiring a full rule of reason analysis and without relying on *per se* rules. Some argue that a truncated analysis is necessary because without it the risks and costs of antitrust litigation effectively preclude enforcement in most areas. Others claim that judges should be allowed in each case to look as carefully as they wish and that there should be a kind of sliding scale which allows extension of the factual inquiry according to the judges' assessment of what is warranted by the gravity of the allegations and the difficulty of predicting and assessing harm. A recent Supreme Court case (*California Dental Associates v FTC* [1999] 526 US 756) has tried to steer between these positions, leading to extensive and largely critical academic commentary (see e.g. Calkins, 2000).

4.2 Predation

Economic predation is another focus of academic debate. Predation is analyzed as a form of 'monopolization', which is prohibited by the Sherman Act. The basic idea is that a firm harms competition where it sells goods below cost in order to drive rivals from the market and then increases prices to levels that it could not have achieved if the rivals had remained. Pre-Chicago thought took seriously the possibility that dominant firms would engage in such practices. They had incentives to do so, and there was evidence that supported the conclusion that this was their objective.

Chicago scholars argue, however, that such conduct is highly unlikely. They insist that a firm is unlikely to engage in it because it can seldom be confident of recouping its 'losses'. The theoretical analysis assumes that markets are robust and that other firms will enter the market and prevent recoupment. Chicago-school analysts demonstrate that it would normally be irrational for firms to engage in such predatory practices, and thus they insist that antitrust judges should not interpret facts to support such a conclusion absent compelling direct evidence.

The issue goes to the core of Chicago-school methodology and therefore engenders much discussion. Post-Chicago scholars have demonstrated that there might well be situations in which firms have significant strategic incentives to engage in predation. Accordingly, they argue that the Chicago school's assumptions about rationality and short-term profit maximization should be applied here only with great care.

Some scholars go further and argue that the basic legal conception underlying predation and related monopolization issues is too narrow and should be expanded. They claim that the focus on whether a practice eliminates competition misses much anti-competitive behavior. A prominent example of this type of challenge involves the concept of raising rivals' costs, which has been hotly debated for more than a decade (Krattenmaker and Salop, 1986). Its supporters argue that a dominant firm often has incentives to engage in conduct that is designed not to drive competitors from the market in the short run, but merely to increase their costs and thus secure to the dominant firm a competitive advantage unrelated to its performance.

4.3 Mergers

Chicago-school analysis has dramatically altered the standards applied to several types of mergers. Its adherents argue that mergers seldom harm competition, except perhaps where the merging firms are rivals at the time of the merger (so-called 'horizontal' mergers). A rational firm would not acquire another firm if the acquisition were not seen as the most efficient use of the firm's resources. Except where the acquired firm is a former competitor and competition is thereby eliminated, this will normally produce a result that is also efficient from a societal perspective and thus will justify such mergers. As a result of this influence, such mergers are today seldom challenged.

Post-Chicago scholars do not challenge the basic proposition that horizontal mergers are the most likely type to cause antitrust concerns, but they have questioned the assumption that other types of mergers are as problem-free as the Chicago school has assumed. Some have found evidence that the Chicago school's rationality assumptions do not hold in non-horizontal mergers under some circumstances, because firms sometimes enter into mergers for strategic reasons that are not justified by short-term economic-efficiency considerations. Others argue that efficiency should not be the standard of evaluation at all, and propose revamping the intellectual foundations of merger law to foster productivity rather than efficiency. Michael Porter's attack on the inappropriate narrowness of efficiency considerations as the basis for antitrust analysis (noted above) has focused primarily on merger law.

4.4 Microsoft

Another focus of recent US antitrust scholarship relates to the conduct of a single firm—Microsoft. The government's antitrust case against Microsoft is arguably the best known and most talked-about antitrust case in decades (e.g. Cass and Hylton, 1999). It involves numerous technical issues, but much of the discussion revolves around one underlying theme—the extent to which existing conceptual tools should be applied to the 'new' economy.

Microsoft was, and is, a monopolist with respect to important parts of the computer industry. The trial court found, and the appeals court agreed, that it used its dominant position to engage in conduct that was intended to and did impair the capacity of its rivals to compete against it. This meets the basic requirement for a claim of monopolization. Some scholars have argued, however, that in an industry where change occurs so rapidly, the rules and procedures of the antitrust laws cannot be applied effectively. In that context, a monopolistic position can be quickly eroded, and conduct designed to harm rivals may not have a significant economic impact. Some conclude from this that in such rapidly moving technological industries the role of antitrust should be minimal. Others argue that the antitrust laws should be applied, but that new legal tools are needed to analyze such industries appropriately.

4.5 Conclusions

US antitrust law has changed fundamentally over the last two decades, as law-and-economics has reordered its values and reconceived its methods. Scholars have proffered several explanations of why Chicago-school ideas have been so successful, gaining orthodoxy in a very short period of time. But one part of the explanation must be that this analysis has offered to academics, government administrators, and judges ideas that are perceived as more valuable (for varying reasons) than the alternatives. It faces challenges, but the Chicago school sets the agenda in antitrust law; the entire field of scholarship revolves around it.

5 EUROPEAN COMPETITION-LAW SCHOLARSHIP: DIMENSIONS AND DYNAMICS

Competition-law scholarship in the EU presents a very different picture. Its agenda is structured in different ways, and its principal concerns, perspectives, and methods are sometimes dramatically different. As globalization causes US and European institutions increasingly to regulate the same conduct, the significance and ramifications of these differences will increase correspondingly.

5.1 The Competition-Law System

Before looking at EU competition-law scholarship, it is important to note several basic features of the EU's competition-law system. The primary source of the law is the Treaty of Rome that created the entity now called the European Union. Article 81 of that Treaty prohibits agreements that 'prevent, restrict or distort' competition, but it exempts agreements where they meet specific conditions designed to ensure that the restraints produce positive economic effects. Only the European Commission is now authorized to issue such exemptions, but Member States will soon also have that authority. Article 82 prohibits abuse of a dominant position within any market within the EU.

The institutional situation in the EU is about to change in important ways. Currently, the European Commission is almost alone in applying the EU's antitrust provisions, subject to appeal to the two European courts (the European Court of Justice and the Court of First Instance). The European Council has, however, recently adopted a 'modernization' of this arrangement which is designed to encourage more participation by national competition-law authorities and national courts in applying and enforcing EU competition law.

5.2 Who Writes and Why

Those who write analytically about EU competition law form a single community only in a very loose sense. They write about the same subject; they are likely to read more or less regularly one or two English-language journals on the subject; and some will have relatively frequent professional contact with one another. Most of these contacts involve decisions or activities of the Commission.

Beyond that, however, the community is splintered along linguistic and national lines and can best be envisioned as a group of partially integrated sub-communities. There are relatively few competition-law scholars in most Member States, and the members of each sub-group typically know each other and encounter each other frequently. There are also competition-law journals and reference books in most EU languages. While some scholars write exclusively about EU competition law, most also write about their own national competition laws, and this contributes to segmenting the academic competition-law community.

The circumstances and incentives of scholars vary significantly among the Member States. For example, in some countries (e.g. Germany) law professors are not permitted to have private law practices, whereas in others (e.g. Italy) professors in the area generally do maintain such practices. There are also significant differences in the status and roles of administrative officials in academic debates. These factors affect the mix of incentives for scholarship. Where law professors have private law practices, for example, they sometimes become associated with the interests of their clients and potential clients; and where administrators play a central role in scholarship, the incentives for theoretical scholarship are typically lower than where university professors dominate scholarship.

5.3 Forms and Vehicles of Scholarship

The forms of scholarship also differ in important ways from the law-review-centered world of US scholarship. First, there are relatively few journals in the area, and they are edited by legal professionals rather than law students. The articles tend to be far shorter than those in US law reviews, and they tend to be far less theoretical. Treatises are sometimes important, and there are EU competition-law treatises in almost all Member States (e.g. Bellamy and Child, 2001).

A particularly high-status vehicle for competition-law scholarship is the commentary, a civil law form which does not exist in US competition-law scholarship. Commentaries are structured by reference to the provisions of the governing statutory material—in this case, the relevant provisions of the Rome Treaty. A commentary explicates and comments on the texts that are its subject, relating individual provisions to each other, and seeking to provide an integrated picture of the entire textual basis of the law and practice in the area. Often there are two or more authors, each responsible for a part of the commentary.

EU competition-law scholarship is seldom separated into theoretical and case-based modes of expression. The starting-point of analysis is the legislative or administratively generated text which frames the analysis and dialogue. Discussion revolves around the interpretation and application of these texts.

6 GOALS AND METHODS IN EUROPEAN COMPETITION-LAW SCHOLARSHIP

As in the United States, debate about goals and methods pervades competition-law scholarship, and it also structures both the substantive law and the process of decision-making (see e.g. Ehlermann and Laudati, 1998). EU scholarship differs, however, from its US analogue in sometimes striking ways. It focuses on some issues which are of little or no concern to US scholars, while it casts other concerns in very different terms and discusses them from very different perspectives.

6.1 Writing about Goals

Several factors are particularly important in conditioning thinking about objectives. One is the centrality of prescriptive texts. Neither judges nor scholars are seen as having the authority to move outside the framework of the Treaty of Rome in discussing goals. This restricts the range of discourse. A second is the embeddedness of competition law in the larger political discussions of European integration. The overall framework of EU law is still evolving, and competition-law scholarship is necessarily part of that evolution. The role of the Commission in the system is a third factor. The current system revolves around the operations of the Commission. The EU courts can review Commission decisions, but cases are few, and thus the Commission's conceptions of goals guide most decisions.

EU competition law has two stated goals: to protect the competitive process from restraint, and to promote European integration. This duality is a key factor in shaping scholarship in the area. It requires a broader, less well-defined, and less theoretical analysis than that typical of US antitrust scholarship. US antitrust law is charged only with the first of these goals, and this often leads to confusion and misunderstanding regarding EU competition law among US scholars.

6.1.1 *Market Integration as a Goal*

Market integration has been central to the development of EU competition law. Many leading competition-law cases feature integration considerations. Yet integration is a multifaceted, multi-level legal and political process, and thus applying and interpreting it resists abstract theoretical analysis.

This has led to much discussion about the extent to which teleological considerations of what fosters the general goal of market integration can justify competition-law decisions. The lack of precision in market-integration goals has caused some scholars to argue that greater attention should be paid to the limits of interpretation in applying the Treaty provisions, while others have used it to justify a greater role for economic methodology. Those who support the central role of teleology argue that the interpretation and application of competition law demand a politically sensitive perspective that views competition law as part of the project of European integration.

6.1.2 *Protecting Competition*

The second goal—protecting competition—is the central battleground of scholarship. Several conceptions of what it means to protect competition have played roles in the evolution of the system, and they have produced a shifting amalgam of values that often resembles pre-Chicago-school conceptions of competition-law goals in the United States (Gerber, 1998).

Early discussions were heavily influenced by German neo-liberal (or Ordo-liberal) thinking, which focused on the idea of approximating 'perfect competition' (Gerber, 1994). According to this view, the goal of competition law should be to prevent or counteract positions of economic power because these distort the operations of the market (and thereby move it further from a 'perfect' state). This view still resonates in some academic literature.

A second concept of competition protection that gained favor in the 1960s is that of 'workable competition'. Recognizing the limitations of 'perfect' competition as a goal, legal scholars sought a more flexible and pragmatic concept. They found it in the literature of economics and adapted it to the competition-law context. As they saw it, competition law should seek to establish or preserve the conditions for effective competition by combating conduct that eliminated market participants or prevented them from competing effectively.

A third concept of competition protection relates to economic freedom. Rooted in the value structure of classical European liberalism, which has been a source of support and guidance for European integration throughout its history, economic freedom has proved to be an attractive, if elusive, goal. A contingent of scholars, many from Germany, have argued that it should be the anchoring value in the application of the competition laws, while others have argued that it provides little real guidance in making competition-law decisions (e.g. Möschel, 2001).

Current EU scholarship relating to goals focuses on yet another concept of competition protection by asking whether EU competition law should become more efficiency-oriented and thus more like US antitrust. There have long been scholarly voices urging that efficiency should play a greater role in guiding competition-law decisions. Using arguments frequently imported from US scholarship, they have claimed that other goals are too vague to provide guidance and that economic efficiency corresponds most closely to the economic objectives of European integration (e.g. Whish, 2001). Others have rejected the idea that efficiency should play such a central role, claiming that the process of European integration requires a more flexible form of competition-law analysis.

Finally, scholars debate the extent to which goals other than integration and competition protection should play a role in EU competition law. There is reference in some cases and legislation, for example, to the goals of protecting small and medium-sized enterprises (SMEs) and even of protecting the interests of workers and the environment. Some scholars either ignore or disparage such goals, while others argue that under some circumstances they should be considered.

6.1.3 *Interactions: The Identity of Competition Law*

This multiplicity of goals raises a basic issue for scholars: what should EU competition law be? Should it become a generic competition law that is focused primarily on the goal of protecting competition, or should it remain sensitive, as it always has been, to the circumstances and exigencies of the European integration process in which it is embedded and of which it has often been a motor. To the extent that Europe becomes fully integrated both politically and economically, the goal of promoting integration will evaporate. Europe is far from that day, however, particularly in light of the planned expansion to Eastern Europe, and thus the issue is what roles competition law should play in the interim.

6.2 Methods

EU competition-law scholarship about the methods of competition law is structured very differently from its US counterpart. It is not principally about what judges do, as it is in the United States, but is far broader. Its central question is 'How should competition-law institutions operate?' The location of competition law within an evolving political structure—a work in progress—demands attention to this question. This has been particularly true over the last few years, as 'modernization' has occupied the forefront of discussion, and it will undoubtedly continue for years as modernization plans are finalized, implemented, and adjusted (e.g. Ehlermann and Atanasiu, 2001).

6.2.1 *Institutions and Implementation*

Controversies over methods revolve around the issue of what kind of law competition law is. In Europe, competition law has been understood generally as administrative law, to be applied by administrators subject to defined constraints and in accordance with administrative procedures. In some countries such as Germany, however, competition law represents a special form of law that contains elements from both private and public law, and this allows it to be used as the basis for both administrative actions and private claims in the regular courts. The Commission has adhered to the administrative understanding of competition law, but its modernization plans are based on a quite different conception. A central element is the policy of encouraging those harmed by anti-competitive conduct to file private actions in national courts.

The conflict regarding the identity of competition law contains two principal tensions. One is between certainty and discretion. An administrative conception of competition law accommodates a relatively high degree of discretion. Even where administrative acts can be challenged in the courts, administrators make many decisions which in practice are unlikely to be subject to judicial controls. Some scholars argue that this potential for discretion undermines legal security and predictability and should, therefore, be limited. A second tension is between law and politics. Major decisions of the Commission must be approved by the Council of Ministers, which is an overtly political body in which the Member States seek to protect their own national interests. A frequent theme in EU competition-law scholarship is that this political element undermines the 'rule of law' and conflicts with legal mechanisms. Some scholars argue that it should be eliminated, and proposals to establish an independent European cartel office have been widely discussed in the literature (e.g. Ehlermann, 1995).

6.2.2 *Analytical Methods*

The analytical component of EU competition-law methodology is inseparable from the institutional component. Multivalent conceptions of goals and methods fit easily with administrative centrality and significant decisional discretion. They fit less comfortably with a judicially oriented decisional process that calls for greater predictability. It is in this context that the idea of increasing the role of economic analysis, particularly of the Chicago-school variety, has become an important issue in the literature. Proponents of this view have enjoyed some recent successes, as the Commission has moved in that direction on specific issues.

7 Focal Points of European Competition-Law Scholarship

Scholarship regarding substantive law issues often reflects the tensions and debates about goals and methods. Factors such as, for example, the amount of discretion to afford to decision-makers and the role and specific form of economic analysis to be used often play important roles in European competition-law scholarship.

7.1 Analyzing Agreements

One central issue involves the Rome Treaty's prohibition of agreements. The courts have interpreted the concept of 'restrictive agreement' formalistically and broadly, so that a contractual constraint on competitive freedom typically falls within it. This places the weight of analysis and discussion on the exemptions, and there has been much controversy about the merits of this analytical structure. For example, some scholars have called for the introduction of some form of 'rule of reason' which would consider the pro-competitive impact of agreements in determining whether they are restrictive (Korah, 1990). Their objective has typically been to gain a greater role for economic analysis and to reduce accordingly the formalistic characteristics of competition-law analysis. The devolution of authority to the national authorities and courts contained in the modernization proposals is likely to intensify such demands.

Formalism has also been a target for criticism in the context of the Commission's exemption practice. As the European Community began expanding its membership in the 1970s, the Commission increasingly used so-called 'block exemptions' to avoid the need to rule on individual exemptions and to give guidance to firms regarding its policies. These block exemptions typically operate by identifying clauses in particular types of agreements that are considered, respectively, valid, invalid, or questionable. The exemptions are formalistic in the sense that they have little regard for the effects of agreements in particular cases. Many scholars have attacked this formalism and sought a greater emphasis on the economic impact of the agreements (e.g. Hawk, 1995).

These challenges have contributed to major changes in the analysis of agreements, and these changes are likely to be a continuing focus of scholarship in the area. The most prominent changes involve the treatment of vertical agreements. The economic arguments that changed US antitrust law in this area have recently also led to major revisions of EU law. For example, the Commission issued new guidelines on the treatment of vertical agreements in 2000. These revisions do not go as far as US law in relaxing constraints on this type of agreement, and an issue is whether they should go further in that direction. It sets Chicago-school arguments against claims that they are not appropriate in the institutional and political context of EU law. Even more recently, the Commission has moved the law relating to horizontal agreements in the same basic direction.

7.2 Abuse of a Dominant Position

The issue of the character of competition law is particularly prominent in scholarship relating to the concept of abuse of a dominant position. Since its inclusion in the Treaty of Rome, its vagueness has been a source of frequent academic disquiet. Since the late 1960s the Commission and the European courts have been developing case law on the subject, and this represents virtually the sole source of authoritative guidance regarding application of the principle.

This case law is often criticized by scholars. Some see it as too case-specific, providing little guidance for future action. Others claim that it leaves excessive discretion in the hands of administrators. This discretion will become even more troublesome when the modernization plans are implemented, because it will then be exercised primarily by national administrative officials who may be tempted to take national interests into account in exercising it.

Recent scholarship regarding the abuse prohibition has focused on two areas. One is the concept of essential facilities, according to which a firm has a dominant position when it owns rights that other market participants need in order to compete effectively (Microsoft's ownership of computer software is frequently cited as an example). Some scholars have argued that withholding such rights may in some cases represent abuse of a dominant position. The other area is the application of the abuse prohibition to pricing practices. Some who support an aggressive interpretation of the provision argue that it should be applied where a firm sets prices unreasonably high in relation to its costs. Much of this discussion relates to private firms that had previously been part of state monopolies. Other scholars reject this application of the abuse prohibition on the grounds that legal mechanisms cannot effectively and consistently determine when prices are 'excessive'.

7.3 Mergers

Merger law has been highly controversial since the mid-1990s. Much of the discussion has revolved around the basic conceptual mechanism of merger law, which calls for intervention where a merger would lead to the creation or strengthening of a dominant position within the EU. Some have criticized this standard as too narrow. In focusing on dominance, they say, EU law fails to address the most important question, which is the merger's effect on the competitive process. Moreover, in focusing on the dominance *of a particular firm*, the standard is ineffective and unwieldy, because it misses situations where dominance is shared or collective, and leads to tortured attempts to find ways of applying the standard to such situations. This has led to debates about the concept of shared dominance and about whether to adopt the US standard, which calls for intervention where a merger 'lessens competition', regardless of whether dominance is involved.

This brief review of competition-law scholarship in the EU and the United States highlights both similarities and differences. Although the two systems seek the same general goal of fostering competition, there are significant differences in specific goals as well as in methods, and these translate into differences in substance. The focus of scholarship in the EU is on the structure and operations of the system as a whole and its relationship to the process of European integration, while in the United States antitrust-law scholarship focuses on the doctrines and reasoning of the courts.

8 Responding to Economic Globalization: The Path Ahead

Economic globalization and institutional responses to it will increase contacts between these two worlds of scholarship, and in so doing they are likely to change each in fundamental ways. As more markets become global, the norms and procedures of two or more competition-law systems increasingly apply to the same conduct, and at least for the foreseeable future such interaction will be most frequent and most intense between the EU and United States. This increases contacts among competition-law scholars, but as yet relatively little attention has been paid to the implications of these contacts. International encounters among competition-law scholars have become almost commonplace, but they have tended to focus on some aspects of globalization while neglecting others of equal or potentially more importance.

8.1 Restructuring Academic Agendas

Current academic responses to globalization fit generally into three categories. One consists of discussion of the application of national competition-law norms and procedures to conduct on global markets. Issues such as, for example, the extra-territorial application of competition law have been extensively treated (e.g. Waller, 1997). A second category consists of descriptions and analyses of the new international institutions—for example, the World Trade Organization (WTO)—that have arisen to deal with globalization issues. Finally, there is a growing body of scholarship that discusses the procedural aspects of coordination among competition-law officials and the perceived increase in similarities among competition-law regimes—the so-called convergence of competition-law systems (e.g. Fox, 1997).

These issues are important, but other important issues have yet to receive similar attention. Economic globalization creates new issues that call for academic analysis. In order to respond to them effectively, academic agendas will need to be more behavioral, more comparative, more global, and more self-reflective.

8.1.1 *Behavioral Dimensions*

The behavioral dimension is critical. Globalization intensifies contacts between competition-law decision-makers, and thus it calls for tools that have been little developed in national legal settings (Gerber, 2001). In this context, decision-makers relate to each other across institutional, cultural, and linguistic boundaries that influence how they perceive the actions of others, how they interpret facts and statements, and how they react to them. These factors are often central to the decisions of business firms and to the actions of competition-law officials, and thus they deserve increased attention from scholars. The EU's rejection in 2001 of a merger between two very large US companies (GE and Honeywell) is an example. The outcry in the United States, as well as the EU responses to it, made merger law an extraordinarily 'hot' topic. But clearer understanding by each side of the basis for the conduct of the other side could have prevented much misperception and potential harm to international competition-law development.

In fashioning tools to perform these functions, legal scholars will need to draw on other disciplines such as psychology and political science. Such approaches have recently become more common in related areas such as public international law. Yet they continue to be rare in the area of competition law, even though the prominence of this area of law in the globalization process makes them especially important here.

8.1.2 *Global Perspectives*

The need for a more global perspective would seem self-evident, but competition law continues to be discussed in surprisingly national terms. Scholarship relating to

US competition law seldom mentions foreign experience more than in passing. As a result, those discussions assume US institutions, procedures, conceptions of judicial roles, and the like. Discussions of international issues are typically cordoned off from the debates about US antitrust. They inhabit a separate sphere of scholarship, and the scholars who write within that sphere often have marginal status, if any, in domestic debates. EU scholarship tends to have a broader perspective in the sense that it often refers to US law and to the national laws of Member States, but even here the references are often limited to discussion of how particular doctrines might be borrowed or adapted.

What is needed is a global perspective on the phenomenon of competition law itself. The axial questions should be posed as responses to the problems created by market economies operating in a global marketplace. What pressures does the global marketplace create for national decision-makers? To what extent does it call for coordinated action by national decision-makers and how can and should they act to coordinate responses effectively? This does not mean that there should be no discussions of purely national problems, but that those discussions should be understood as part of a larger set of questions about the values, modalities, and interactions of competition law in a global economy.

8.1.3 *Comparative Analysis*

A global perspective should include a comparative perspective, but this is often neglected. Where the central questions are framed in global terms, the differences between competition-law systems demand attention. The starting-point of analysis should be questions such as 'How far apart are the systems in their responses to particular problems? What has led to the differences? and What implications do the differences have?' Little comparative analysis of competition-law systems has gone beyond pure description to reach these types of questions.

Analyzing differences between systems should recognize both objective and subjective elements. Objective analysis looks at the actual differences—in doctrines, procedures, goals, and so on. The subjective element looks at issues such as how individuals and groups within one system perceive what they do, what others do, and what the differences are. These subjective elements are critical influences on decision-making, and thus to the extent that competition-law scholarship excludes them, it fails to understand how decisions are made.

8.1.4 *Self-Reflection, Cooperation, and Communication*

Finally, competition-law scholars as a community need to look at their own domain and its role in the evolution of responses to globalization. The interactions of academic communities will play important roles in the evolution of competition law, but they have been virtually ignored. Which pieces of information or forms of influence in one community affect agendas within others and why? To what extent does scholarship yield results that are useful across systems? How is scholarship understood and evaluated across systems? Answers to such questions can play significant roles in shaping scholarship and influencing its impact.

This raises the further question of whether and to what extent scholars should seek to develop a particular form of discourse for this integrated enterprise. Widespread use of shared analytical tools and conceptual frameworks would facilitate effective communication among scholars and coordination of scholarly enterprises. It would also foster the development of a single community of competition-law scholars. Law-and-economics scholars have expressed the hope that their discipline can provide such a common language, arguing that an abstract language would have the advantage of being more precise and more universalistic than other alternatives. This has attractions, but it would disregard accumulated experience in dealing with competition-law problems. In a global context, such experience should at least be carefully studied.

8.2 Imagining the Path

Many factors will influence the direction of competition-law scholarship, and thus determine the extent to which these goals are achieved. The responses of competition-law scholars to the demands of globalization will be shaped by events and interests external to academic communities as well as by their internal structures and dynamics.

8.2.1 *External Factors*

Competition-law scholarship is subject to both economic and political influences, and often the two are interwoven. Firms, particularly large firms, typically seek to minimize governmental interference with their operations, and thus try to weaken competition laws or avoid their impact. In the context of globalization, however, a 'level playing field'—that is, convergence in the substantive content and/or procedural characteristics of competition-law systems—is a competing value. This is particularly true in areas such as merger law. Political interests—both domestic and geo-political—can also influence competition-law scholarship. Domestically, for example, political leaders often seek to protect domestic economic interests from the strictures of competition law. Internationally, the US and EU competition-law systems often compete for influence in other parts of the world.

The scholarly communities in the United States and Europe are both susceptible to such influences, but in varying degrees. Because US antitrust scholars are typically full-time professors and their principal 'target' audience is the federal courts, such influences tend to have limited impact. In Europe, in contrast, the target audience for competition-law scholarship centers on administrative and political decision-makers, and the community of scholarly writers is less unified and less purely academic. Where, for example, competition-law professors also maintain private law practices, this may tend to influence the issues they address and their opinions on them.

8.2.2 *Internal Factors*

Pressures internal to academic communities have their greatest influence on scholarship where the community that produces the scholarship is tightly woven and where status within it provides the main incentives for scholarship. The more scholars depend on a single, integrated community, the more likely they are to be influenced by its values and incentives. US antitrust scholarship tends to be more influenced by such factors than does its EU analogue.

Under these circumstances, intellectual fashions tend to develop and spread rapidly, and they can quickly both acquire and lose influence. A good example is the extraordinary speed with which law-and-economics perspectives gained ascendancy within US antitrust scholarship. This suggests that US competition-law scholarship may be more subject to rapid change than EU scholarship. There is little basis for predicting the intellectual fashions that may influence this development, but frequent reference in US universities to the value of interdisciplinary methods, and the increasing importance of behavioralism within economics may affect antitrust scholarship.

The socio-professional dynamics of competition-law communities will also influence the direction and speed of change. In general, such communities resist change, particularly where they are tightly knit and where a sub-group with a well-defined ideology has predominant power within the community. Those conditions exist within the US antitrust community, and they may impede change, particularly to the extent that it is seen as harming the prestige, power, and economic status of the dominant group. On the other hand, ambitious younger scholars have incentives to challenge existing paradigms, and this creates a tension whose force and impact in specific situations will depend not only on intellectual and social factors, but also on political and economic ones. In the EU, in contrast, these dynamics are likely to be less evident, because the scholarly competition-law community is less homogeneous, and many of its members are more closely tied to communities outside the university.

There are obstacles in developing scholarly agendas along the lines suggested here. One is its cost in terms of both human capital and money. Any broadening of academic agendas has costs for those within the community. Those costs tend to be particularly high where such broadening includes demands for self-evaluation on the part of the community itself and reassessment of its modes of operation.

Another obstacle may be the attachment to one's own views that is often perceived by others as arrogance. To the extent that members of an academic community are confident that they have the right answers and the best methodo-logy, they are not likely to be interested in learning from the experience and ideas of others. This necessarily impedes development of global and comparative perspec-tives and agendas.

Finally, some perspectives are more open to external input than others. A theoret-ical perspective typically rejects approaches that are inconsistent with its abstract premises. This makes it more difficult for adherents of the theory to consider ideas of a different provenance or to value experience in systems with different methodo-logies. A competition-law regime built on multiple goals and methods does not face these obstacles to developing global and comparative perspectives.

8.3 The Roles of Competition-Law Scholarship

The globalization of markets and the interactions among competition-law scholars that it entails are altering the agendas of competition-law scholarship in both the United States and the EU. They will enable scholars to exchange information and ideas more intensively and more frequently, and they will increase the incentives for doing so. Nevertheless, the roles that competition-law scholarship itself can and should play have been little examined.

In one scenario, competition-law scholars help shape the legal framework of globalization. Their interchanges create a rich set of well-informed analyses that reflect the interests of the various players in the globalization process. They seek to gain insights into the ideas and experience of the participants and assess the relev-ance of those experiences for others. They also provide theoretical perspectives which help to guide political decision-making processes.

Another scenario is less positive. Here scholars look primarily to their own inter-ests and the economic and political interests with which they are associated. Their primary concern is to seek strategic advantage over other scholars both within and outside their own scholarly communities. They pay little or no attention to the experiences or ideas of others, except for the purpose of denigrating them. As a result, scholarship plays a marginal role, at best, in the constructive development of competition law in the global economy.

Elements of both scenarios will undoubtedly accompany the process of com-petition-law development. In the long run, the roles that scholarship plays will depend to a large extent on its perceived value to decision-makers in the globaliza-tion process. Whoever provides the answers and conceptual tools that are the most useful is likely to have the most influence. Scholarship that illuminates the interac-tion of competition-law systems and their relationship to the complex economic and political issues of globalization should be of much potential value for all, but it may be particularly valuable to decision-makers in countries where there is cur-rently little or no competition-law scholarship. During the last decade many new competition-law systems have been created, and moribund laws have been given new roles and status. This has occurred most notably in Eastern Europe, Asia, and Latin America. There is much uncertainty about the future of those systems, but the potential value of insightful competition law scholarship is perhaps nowhere greater than there.

REFERENCES

Bellamy, C., and Child, G. (2001). *European Community Law of Competition* (5th edn.), ed. P. Roth, London: Sweet & Maxwell.

Bork, R. (1978). *The Antitrust Paradox*, New York: Basic Books.

Calkins, S. (2000). 'California Dental Association: Not a Quick Look but not the Full Monty', *Antitrust Law Journal*, 67: 495–557.

Carlton, D., Gertner, R., and Rosenfeld, A. (1997). 'Communication among Competitors: Game Theory and Antitrust', *George Mason Law Review*, 5: 423–40.

Cass, R., and Hylton, K. (1999). 'Preserving Competition: Economic Analysis, Legal Standards & Microsoft', *George Mason Law Review*, 8: 1–41.

Ehlermann, C.-D. (1995). 'Reflections on a European Cartel Office', *Common Market Law Review*, 32: 471–86.

—— and Atanasiu, I. (eds.) (2001). *European Competition Law Annual 2000: Objectives of Competition Policy*, Oxford: Hart.

—— and Laudati, L. (eds.) (1998). *European Competition Law Annual 1997: Objectives of Competition Policy*, Oxford: Hart.

Fox, E. (1997). 'Toward World Antitrust and Market Access', *American Journal of International Law*, 91: 1–25.

Gerber, D. (1994). 'Constitutionalizing the Economy: German Neo-Liberalism, Competition Law and the "New" Europe', *American Journal of Comparative Law*, 42: 25–84.

—— (1998). *Law and Competition in Twentieth Century Europe: Protecting Prometheus*, Oxford: Clarendon Press (paperback, 2001).

—— (2001). 'Globalization and Legal Knowledge: Implications for Comparative Law', *Tulane Law Review*, 75: 949–76.

Hawk, B. (1995). 'System Failure: Vertical Restraints under the E.C. Competition Law', *Common Market Law Review*, 32: 973–89.

Hovenkamp, H. (2001). 'Post-Chicago Antitrust: A Review and Critique', *Columbia Business Law Review*, 2000: 257–337.

Korah, V. (1990). 'From Legal Form toward Economic Efficiency—Article 85(1) of the EEC Treaty in Contrast to U.S. Antitrust', *Antitrust Bulletin*, 34: 1009–37.

Krattenmaker, T., and Salop, S. (1986). 'Anticompetitive Exclusion: Raising Rivals' Costs to Achieve Power over Price', *Yale Law Journal*, 96: 209–93.

Möschel, W. (2001). 'The Proper Scope of Government Viewed from an Ordoliberal Perspective: The Example of Competition Law', *Journal of Institutional & Theoretical Economics*, 157: 3–13.

Pitofsky, R. (1979). 'The Political Content of Antitrust', *University of Pennsylvania Law Review*, 127: 1051–75.

Porter, M. (2001). 'Competition and Antitrust: Towards a Productivity-Based Approach to Evaluating Mergers and Joint Ventures', in *Perspectives on Fundamental Antitrust Theory*, Chicago: American Bar Association, 125–79.

Posner, R. (2000). *Antitrust Law, An Economic Perspective* (2nd edn.), Cambridge, Mass.: Harvard University Press.

Waller, S. (1997). *Antitrust and American Business Abroad* (3rd edn.), Deerfield, Ill.: Clark, Boardman.

Whish, R. (2001). *UK and EC Competition Law* (4th edn.), London: Butterworths.

Other Important Works

Amato, G. (1996). *Antitrust and the Bounds of Power*, Oxford: Hart.

Areeda, P., and Hovenkamp, H. (2000). *Antitrust Law: An Analysis of Antitrust Principles and their Application*, New York: Aspen.

Eisner, M. (1991). *Antitrust and the Triumph of Economics*, Chapel Hill, NC: University of North Carolina Press.

Gifford, D. (1997). 'Antitrust and its Intellectual Milieu', *Antitrust Bulletin*, 24: 333–71.

Goyder, D. G. (1999). *EEC Competition Law*, Oxford: Clarendon Press.

Hovenkamp, H., and Hoskins, G. (1991). *Enterprise and American Law, 1836–1937*, Cambridge, Mass.: Harvard University Press.

Kovacic, W., and Shapiro, C. (2000). 'Antitrust Policy: A Century of Economic and Legal Thinking', *Journal of Economic Perspectives*, 14: 43–60.

Peritz, R. (1996). *Competition Policy in America 1888–1992: History, Rhetoric, Law*, New York: Oxford.

CHAPTER 25

CONSUMERS

GERALD THAIN

CONSUMER law was not considered a discrete area of the law until well into the second half of the twentieth century. Prior to that time, there were legal actions and regulatory decisions that involved what would be called consumer matters today but then were categorized as matters of contract law or tort law or administrative law. The activism of Ralph Nader in the 1960s in the United States eventually led to a recognition that consumer law might exist as a separate branch of legal practice and legal analysis. Although the roots of modern consumer law are found in North America, the concept of such a separate legal arena had spread by the last quarter of the twentieth century to Europe and, to a lesser degree, to much of the rest of the world.

Notwithstanding the general acceptance of consumer law as a field, definition of the term remains somewhat imprecise. It is becoming increasingly accepted to define consumer law as covering the sale or offering for sale of goods or services to consumers (non-business individuals and families) for personal, family, or household use, and the problems that may be faced by consumers in the course of such actions. It is generally recognized that consumer transactions can be viewed as having three stages—offer, purchase, and post-purchase. In the offer stage, issues generally center on the representations made to consumers as to the goods or services that are being offered. In the purchase stage, issues focus on price, including that of any credit or loan involved in the transaction, the quality of the goods or services, and the fairness of any contract terms. In the post-purchase stage, the focus is on performance, that is, whether the product or service has performed as represented or as one might reasonably expect, and whether the seller's promises in the event of consumer dissatisfaction are fulfilled. In all of these areas, attention is often given to the large disparity of power that usually exists between the consumer and the seller and to the difficulty of meaningful recourse for many individual consumers in the absence of an ability to look to regulatory bodies for redress to aggregate a number of similar small claims against a large seller.

All systems of consumer law deal with the three stages in consumer transactions described above. This chapter concentrates on the issues that have arisen in US law which illuminate the kinds of issues that arise in other common law systems, each of which addresses the problems somewhat differently, and in different institutional frameworks. Despite these differences, looking at US law in detail, and some of the controversies about US consumer law, helps identify the kinds of issues that Commonwealth scholarship addresses as well.

Consumer law in the United States and Europe presupposes a market economy, with consumer choice being paramount. It is related to antitrust law in the sense that neither monopoly nor oligopoly allows for meaningful consumer choice. Thus, antitrust advocates often refer to antitrust law as the fundamental element in consumer protection although antitrust law is not classified as consumer law. The market economy, in its ideal theoretical manifestation, allows for meaningful consumer choice not only by the presence of as many competing sellers as a given market will bear but also by access to all the pertinent information that a seller may need or desire to make a truly informed purchase.

Obviously, the market economies of the United States and Europe fall well short of these ideal standards. Yet much consumer law is grounded in the belief that these ideals should be the goal of public policy in shaping and interpreting consumer law. The ideals may be unattainable but the closer to them, the better, in the eyes of many. Political considerations naturally influence the ebb and flow of consumer strength in the legal arena. Alexis de Tocqueville asserted that, in the United States, political issues eventually become legal issues and the history of consumer law does not negate that. In the late nineteenth and early twentieth centuries, when the social theories of Herbert Spencer were widely accepted in the political and legal worlds, efforts on behalf of consumers rarely succeeded. In times of social and political ferment, as during the great depression of the 1930s and the youth-driven reassessments of received political wisdom in the 1960s and 1970s, efforts to protect consumers from what earlier had been legally accepted, if considered 'sharp' business practices, achieved a larger measure of success. However, from the viewpoint of the beginning days of the twenty-first century, it appears that consumer law has become sufficiently established to withstand attacks on its very existence, if not necessarily to flourish regardless of the political climate.

Consumer law, while now an established field, remains very much in flux, subject to shifting not only with the political winds but also with the willingness of individuals to identify themselves as consumers subject to economic abuse from sellers unless laws and rules to protect consumers are established and regularly implemented or enforced. Good economic times accompanied by political stability usually see less interest in the problems of consumers; more uncertain times conversely see more concern since more people then identify with the complaints of dissatisfied purchasers, and consumer purchasers are less likely to shrug off even relatively small losses. The pattern of action leading to reaction is also illustrated in the consumer law arena. Once the concept of consumer law and consumer sovereignty had established a foothold in legal thinking, many of its tenets were attacked in the academy by devotees of the 'law and economics' movement who theorized that an unregulated market was the best means of obtaining consumer justice, in the long run. Debate between those who favor legislation, regulation, and litigation and those who favor leaving most consumer issues to the marketplace has continued for the past thirty-five years.

1 PRE-PURCHASE ISSUES

The area of advertising law and regulation illustrates the changing views of law and politics towards consumer concerns. Historically, misrepresentations in advertising or other marketing practices were rarely the subject of legal action in Great Britain or the United States. Although the tort of deceit was recognized and theoretically could be used by a consumer who had purchased a product in the wake of advertising misrepresentations, such an action was extremely difficult to mount successfully. First, most purchases by individuals were not of a price level that would justify the time and expense of litigation. Secondly, to win an action, a plaintiff needed to prove that there had been a false representation, that the seller had actual knowledge of the falsity, and that the plaintiff had relied, reasonably, upon the misrepresentation in making the purchase:

The purchaser willing to seek recovery of the nominal sum usually involved was likely to be told by the court that scienter [knowledge] had not been adequately proved, that his reliance on the misrepresentation was unreasonable because he should have examined the good or obtained the counsel of impartial and reliable persons, that the representations concerned matters of opinion and thus—as 'puffing'—should have been treated with skepticism, or that in any case he had not sufficiently demonstrated that his purchase was induced by the advertisement. (Note, 1967)

Application of the doctrine of *caveat emptor* ('let the buyer beware') was the norm. The only misrepresentation that was pursued in the courts with some success in those days was that of 'passing off'—the practice of selling one's goods as those of another, more famous seller—and these were actions by the famous seller, not by consumers, against the misrepresenting seller.

The defense of 'puffing' (sometimes referred to as 'seller's talk') has a long history in the law and it remains a defense to actions of misrepresentations today. Puffing has been defined as the right of a seller to lie his head off, on the grounds that no reasonable buyer will believe the statements (Prosser and Keeton, 1984). Such lies, or 'puffs', today must treat some non-measurable attribute, such as an assertion that the product tastes great and the like; a statement that is capable of objective measurement cannot properly be considered a puff. Commentators often wonder why so many sellers spend large amounts of time and money using 'puffing' in advertising if it is not believable (see Preston, 1996).

The earliest English case often cited when a court (or later, an administrative agency) would dismiss a claim of misrepresentation as simple puffing was decided in 1603 (*Chandelor v Lopus*, Exch Chamber Cro Jac 4) and involved a goldsmith defendant who had sold the plaintiff a stone that the goldsmith had affirmed to be a bezar (bezoar in some spellings) stone but was found out not to be such a stone. One judge considered this to be deceit and actionable but all the other 'Justices and Barons' deciding the issue held otherwise. They ruled that a mere affirmation was not a warranty and that the seller therefore was not liable. The purchase price was apparently £100, obviously a significant sum in the early seventeenth century. Many English and American cases since then, down the centuries, have cited *Chandelor* as standing for the proposition that no action lay for a mere affirmation that was not an express warranty or for 'puffing' at least when the seller did not know the representation was false.

It is unclear that the judges in the *Chandelor* case would have endorsed the subsequent extension of that case's holding to other representations as 'puffs' when the decision is examined from the standpoint of the object at issue. A bezar stone was a stone from certain animals that was thought to have magic curative powers. Presumably, the people of that day believed that there were true bezars but also recognized that it could be very difficult to distinguish between a true bezar stone and an imitation. Moreover, the value of the stone might depend on whose hands held it; a believer would consider it extremely valuable but a skeptic might think it of no value whatsoever. Despite the possibility that the actual decision in the case might well be replicated on similar facts in today's world, the broad definition of 'puffing' drawn from the decision seems anachronistic to consumer advocates today. The references to the case as support for the 'puffing' defense in later misrepresentation cases provide a prime example of a legal standard that actually receives no more than limited support for wide application from its putative parent case.

Although there have been occasional calls for reconsideration of the puffing exception to deceptive advertising, the doctrine remains firmly entrenched in the law. Professor Robert Pitofsky, once an FTC Chairman, stated prior to his assuming that position but after service as Director of the agency's Bureau of Consumer Protection that 'puffing' properly was not subject to legal attack and that he interpreted 'puffing' to mean 'those claims which are not capable of objective measurement—for example, claims by cigarette companies that a particular cigarette "tastes milder," as well as those claims that are put forward with no expectation that reasonable people would take them seriously, for example, the claim on behalf of one automobile company that it was "the first automobile on the moon" ' (Pitofsky, 1972).

Some scholars have criticized the protection afforded advertisers under the 'puffing' rule as allowing undue misinformation in the marketplace (see Preston, 1998). Others have asserted that the focus should be on the question of materiality. If an advertising claim is likely to influence a purchasing decision, it should be considered a material claim—and this should include claims that, in context, are claims of comparative superiority for the advertised product, even when the claim may otherwise fall under the 'puffing' exception. For example, a lower federal court in the United States in a case between two pizza companies recently held that an advertisement that asserted 'Better ingredients. Better pizza.' even if considered to be 'puffing' was none the less material and actionable. The Court of Appeals reversed the lower court on this point. In response, a group of professors of law and of marketing urged that the 'better' claims should be considered material claims and that the 'puffing' defense be limited to claims that were clearly opinions incapable of being measured objectively (*Pizza Hut v Papa John's International, Inc*, 227 F 3d 489 (5th Cir 2000), cert denied 532 US 920 (2001)). The refusal of the Court to review this decision indicates the continued vitality of the 'puffing' doctrine notwithstanding the logical force of arguments for limiting the doctrine.

The term 'deceptive advertising' probably is a synonym for 'falsity' in the minds of most people. Certainly, outright falsehoods about a product are found in some advertising messages but a much greater percentage of deceptive advertising actions involve implied rather than overt claims about the advertised product. The law has long held that statements that may be literally true but that are used in a context that is misleading constitute deceptive advertising and cases of this nature are far more common today than cases that involve outright misstatements of fact. An example is an advertisement that truthfully (in the literal sense) states that the advertised food has more 'food energy' than competing products but does not reveal that 'food energy' is another term for calories. Also frequent targets are those advertising messages that note the results of surveys favoring the advertised product's attributes when the surveys in question are based on atypical samples or are otherwise of little or no statistical validity.

Because of the rarity of situations where a misleading advertisement may cause substantial direct and provable injury to an individual consumer, the majority of actions against deceptive advertising or other marketing practices are brought either by a competitor or by a government agency. Regardless of who the plaintiff is, a question may be raised as to the level of gullibility of the audience that is applicable. Should the standard for deception be that of the sophisticated consumer or of the lowest level of sophistication or at some median point? In the United States, the courts have indicated that the criterion should be that of the general populace, including the credulous and unsophisticated. The US Supreme Court has said that allegedly deceptive advertising statements, when challenged in legal proceedings, are not to be read as they would be by an expert but as they would be read by an unsophisticated member of the public. The 'fact that a false statement may be obviously false to those who are trained and experienced does not change its character or take away its power to deceive others less experienced' (*Federal Trade Commission v Standard Education Society*, 302 US 112, 116 (1937)). This has sometimes been criticized as an inappropriate standard that uses 'wayfaring fools' (citing the Biblical prophet Isaiah) as those entitled to protection by the law. Of course, there has always been a limit to the application of this standard; it does not reach to patently preposterous applications, such as insisting that only pastry made in Denmark may be sold as 'Danish' pastry, for example (see *Heinz W. Kirchner*, 63 FTC 1282, affirmed 337 F 2d 751 (9th Cir 1963)). While the law protects the unsophisticated consumer, it does not extend to the literal dunce; some level of limited acumen or 'claimed assininity' is beyond the reach of the law (*Pocket Books, Inc v Dell Publishing Co*, 268 NY Supp 2d 46 (1966)).

In the 1980s, the leadership at the Federal Trade Commission, the major federal regulator of advertising in the United States, announced that it would be applying, in deceptive advertising cases, a standard of 'a consumer, acting rationally under the circumstances' to determine if a challenged representation was deceptive. However, it also noted that the nature of the audience to whom the message was addressed would be taken into account. Thus, a message aimed at a youthful or ill-educated audience would consider the level of the audience's sophistication in determining if the message had a tendency or capacity to mislead. Although many commentators considered the application of the announced new standard to be an indication that some advertisements that could have been challenged by the Commission under the old standard would be allowed under the new standard, virtually all agreed that the new policy would affect no more than a few cases. Moreover, the new interpretation was a matter of administrative discretion being utilized by an agency in interpreting the laws it was charged with administering. As such, it was not insignificant but it did not change either the words of the statutes administered by the agency or the many prior judicial pronouncements upholding the utilization of the standard applying the credulous consumer approach.

The image of the consumer (or consumer stereotype) that is the basis of consumer protection law in the European Union—particularly in the decisions of the European Court of Justice—has been frequently identified as an active or cognitively competent consumer who seeks information aggressively and who makes critical assessments of that information in reaching purchasing decisions. Clearly, this model does not conform to that of the unsophisticated consumer used in the United States. The model of a rational consumer able to make informed choices and to seek rights with a minimum of assistance, especially when matters of health are not involved, underpins EU law and policy directives in the field of consumer law, but the laws of the member states of the EU are more apt to utilize an image of a consumer who is a 'passive glancer' at advertisements and who makes quick, often uncritical purchasing decisions—in short, a consumer who is quite akin to the consumer envisioned by the traditional American approach to misleading advertising (see Howells and Wilhelmsson, 1998: 207, 255–7). An argument once popular in Britain, at least in business circles, as a justification for the rational and competent consumer approach to consumer law was that the 'consumer is not an idiot. She is your wife.' The stereotype of that argument—the consumer being a synonym for housewife—is rarely asserted in today's world. (It is interesting to note, however, that many of today's American university departments of consumer science or the like were originally established as Departments of Home Economics before assuming their present names.)

Although it is easy to deride the standard of the unsophisticated consumer as the benchmark for determining who is entitled to the law's protection, as a misplaced effort to protect those whose ineptness make them beyond protection or to criticize the standard as treating consumers as child-like instead of encouraging critical use of their mental powers, consumer advocates believe that the standard is more realistic than that of the cognitively competent consumer. In a world increasingly characterized by speedy transactions and citizens pressed to find time for reflection, it seems inappropriate to fashion legal remedies that are available only to those who have the time, energy, skill, and resources required to search out pertinent information concerning all their potential purchasing decisions. High-priced items that are purchased infrequently, such as automobiles and houses, may be the subject of more than cursory inquiry by consumers prior to making a decision but life is too short for most consumers to look deeply into the comparative qualities of most products and services—at least without the assistance of some outside reliable source, such as *Consumer Reports* in the United States and *Which?* in England. The unsophisticated consumer standard, while not an incentive for consumers to exercise their analytical powers, does mean that advertisers who make sales pitches designed to take advantage of the credulity and limited time of consumers do so at the peril of legal action against them. Belittling of the standard as one that diminishes consumer status discounts too much the utility, if not necessity, of consumers making quick choices, especially when items of low or moderate cost are involved.

A major issue in advertising regulation has been the appropriate remedy to be invoked when there has been a determination that specific advertising is deceptive or unfair. Most unlawful advertising will not result in a recovery by consumers— often, the amount of loss may be too small to justify an action by individual consumers and, in many cases, there is no satisfactory proof that individual consumers purchased a product specifically in response to an advertising misrepresentation. Most successful pursuits of advertising misrepresentations therefore were undertaken by public agencies and ended with an injunction against continuing the practice or engaging in similar practices. Only if that injunction was later violated would there be any other sanction entered against the advertiser. This situation, in which it has been said that the usual remedy for improper advertising was an admonition to the advertiser to 'go and sin no more' led to efforts to obtain more significant remedies for deceptive or unfair advertising in the many cases where penalties could not be invoked under law or where restitution of injured consumers was impossible or impracticable. The remedy of corrective advertising was designed to fill this gap.

Corrective advertising is posited on the theory that the best means to correct misinformation in the marketplace that has been injected by unlawful advertising is not just to enjoin the unlawful practices of the advertiser in question but also to correct the misinformation caused by it. And what better means to do so than by requiring the advertiser, in advertising of the same type, to tell the public of the facts concerning the misinformation that was earlier spread by it? Although the legal authority of US administrative agencies to order corrective advertising when there was no specific statutory authority for it was once a hotly contested issue, today there is no dispute that corrective advertising is a valid remedy. The argument that the remedy was punitive in nature and not appropriate for use by legal bodies that were empowered only to remedy, not punish, has been rejected. The basic assessment is that a remedy compelling an advertiser to tell the truth about misleading statements in its past advertisements is basically remedial and any punitive aspects are incidental to the primary purposes of the corrective message which are to dissipate the effect of the message on the public and to restore any competitive imbalance that was caused by the success of the improper advertising to the detriment of sellers who did not engage in unlawful selling practices.

Corrective advertising is not a remedy that is used frequently or for misleading advertisements of any type. Corrective advertising is appropriate only in cases where it can be demonstrated that the deceptive message was particularly effective in persuading significant numbers of consumers of its validity. Corrective messages are usually ordered as relief only in cases where there has been a long-standing use of an advertising message, with considerable success and the message is not one whose validity consumers could reasonably be expected to determine from a normal use of the advertised product. A false statement that a candy contained more peanuts or raisins than in fact was the case, for example, while a false representation, is of a type that individual consumers could recognize, following the purchase of a low-cost item, as untrue whereas a misrepresentation about the nutritional value of a food product is not of that type and, if successful, might be the subject of a corrective advertising order.

The cases in which the validity of corrective advertising as a remedy was established in the United States understandably were actions involving extremely successful advertising campaigns over unusually long periods of time that made representations whose validity most consumers were in no position to judge. The claims in Listerine mouthwash advertisements that the product was effective in treating colds had been made for many years and, according to studies, were widely believed by purchasers of the product even though there was no scientific support for the claim; this claim became the subject of the first major corrective advertising case to be reviewed by the American courts. The appellate court, after determining that the claims for the curative powers of the mouthwash were misrepresentations, considered the validity of the Federal Trade Commission's order of corrective advertising. The court found the order justified because to 'allow consumers to continue to buy the product on the strength of the impression built up by prior advertising—an impression which is now known to be false—would be unfair and deceptive' (*Warner-Lambert Co v Federal Trade Commission*, 562 F 2d 749 (DC Cir 1977)). It should be emphasized that consumers had no satisfactory means of testing the truth of the advertised claim. If a cold or its symptoms was overcome by one who used Listerine mouthwash, that did not establish any meaningful relationship between the two events; most colds do not last for long and scientific analysis is necessary to determine if there is any connection between using a medicine and overcoming a disease.

When corrective advertising is sought in a case today, the issue is not whether the remedy is possible but whether it is appropriate in light of the nature of the message, the success of the message in reaching and persuading consumers, and the consequences of consumer action in reliance on the message. Although the corrective message referring to past advertising misrepresentations is a relatively recent development, the concept basically is an extension of a remedy used for many years before the term 'corrective advertising' was coined—the remedy of affirmative disclosure. That remedy was usually applied in situations where representations in advertising were truthful only to a limited degree and therefore could be made only if accompanied by adequate disclosures of the limitations of the claim. For example, in a case involving claims by the makers of Geritol that the product, an iron supplement, was effective in treating tiredness, it was ruled that these claims could continue to be made only if accompanied by a clear and conspicuous disclosure that the product would be effective in treating tiredness only for those who are tired due to iron deficiency anemia and that the vast majority of individuals who experience the symptoms of tiredness do not have iron deficiency anemia. (Advertising for Geritol had used 'tired' and 'anemic' as synonyms although there was no medical basis for that usage.) (*J B Williams Co, Inc v Federal Trade Commission*, 381 F 2d 884 (1967).)

2 THE FIRST AMENDMENT AND ADVERTISING REGULATION

In the United States today, the most lively debate over advertising regulation and litigation is generated by the question of the applicability of the First Amendment to the US Constitution to the specific practices at issue. The First Amendment provides that the Congress (and, via the Fourteenth Amendment, the individual states as well) shall 'make no law' abridging the freedom of speech. Because falsity as such does not receive First Amendment protection and because most actions against advertising practices involved false or misleading statements, it was once accurate to state that advertising received no First Amendment protection (*Valentine v Chrestensen*, 316 US 52 (1942)). However, this was changed, following some individual exceptions in earlier cases, by the US Supreme Court in the mid-1970s, in two cases in which the Court explicitly held that commercial speech was entitled to some First Amendment protection although not to the extent of political or other 'core' speech (*Virginia Pharmacy Board v Virginia Citizens Consumer Council*, 425 US 748 (1976) (prohibition of price advertising of prescription drugs unconstitutional); *Bates v State Bar of Arizona*, 433 US 350 (1977) (ban of all lawyer advertising in state violates First Amendment)). The exact limits of this ruling have not yet been determined. To uphold a restriction on advertising, the Court generally requires that the advertisement at issue not be for an illegal product or service, that the restriction serve a compelling governmental interest that is directly forwarded by the regulation, and that the regulation be narrowly tailored to achieve the government's interest, although it need not be the least restrictive alternative to achieve that goal. Unsurprisingly, the justices are often sharply divided as to whether a specific regulation meets those criteria. The Court has also indicated that misleading speech is unprotected by the First Amendment and not subject to this analysis, but the lower courts have examined the restrictions on misleading advertisements in some cases to determine if they are sufficiently narrowly tailored to pass First Amendment muster.

The 'commercial speech is entitled to some First Amendment protection' argument was first made successfully in the Supreme Court by consumer advocacy groups who argued that consumers and competition were harmed by such practices as bans on price advertising of prescription drugs and of any advertising by lawyers. Ironically, the rulings in recent commercial speech cases have been criticized by many consumer advocates as insufficiently protective of consumers—as when, for example, a closely divided Supreme Court allows a state to limit solicitation by lawyers of potential personal-injury clients (*Florida Bar v Went-For-It*, 515 US 618 (1995)) or strikes down an effort by a state to restrict advertising of tobacco products to minors because the restrictions are held to be too expansive in their scope (*Lorillard Tobacco Co v Reilly*, 121 S Ct 2404 (2001)).

Legal scholars are often at odds over the propriety of First Amendment protection for advertising. Edwin Baker has written that commercial speech ought not be protected because the presence of the profit motive in such speech 'breaks the connection between speech and any vision, or attitude, or value of the individual or group engaged in advocacy. Thus the content and form of commercial speech cannot be attributed to individual value allegiances' (Baker, 1976: 62). This seems consistent with a statement by Justice Black years ago that the protections of the First Amendment did not extend to a pedlar going door to door selling pots and pans. Others have raised questions about the difficulty of countering questionable messages from an industry (advertising) that spends many billions of dollars annually if First Amendment protections are given to the messages (see Shiffrin, 1983: 1281). See also Posner (1986) for the proposition that commercial speech needs little First Amendment protection because the benefits of such speech are obtained by sales of the advertised items. The Supreme Court has agreed with this proposition to the extent of determining that the 'overbreadth' doctrine does not generally apply to commercial speech. That doctrine invalidates laws that restrict too much speech. Its purpose is to negate laws that might have a 'chilling effect' on protected speech because of the uncertainty of its application. Commercial speech is considered hardier than other forms of speech because the profit motive for such speech provides a strong incentive to continue to engage in such speech notwithstanding legal limitations on some forms of it; therefore, the concern about the chilling effect of a specific application of a broader law is not present.

A number of legal scholars challenge the view of commercial speech as outside the mainstream of protected speech, asserting that it is the listener's interests (here, the consumer or putative consumer's interests) that are paramount and that listeners/consumers will act in their own best interests if they are fully informed. Under this approach, listener autonomy becomes a significant free speech value that justifies considerable protection of commercial speech (see Strauss, 1991; Neuborne, 1989; Kozinski and Banner, 1990).

I believe that the supposedly 'absolutist' view of free speech forwarded by the last group of scholars overstates the degree to which the alleged speech in traditional commercial advertising can be separated from its function as one element, usually a first step in contracts or sales, that is indisputably subject to government regulation. The total prohibition of a category of advertising usually raises First Amendment issues because it cuts off any messages to consumers—and by doing so, helps facilitate anti-competitive markets to the detriment of consumers. To extend First Amendment protection beyond that degree raises serious questions of whether the result is the protection of speech or a revival of the concept of economic due process in a new guise.

The most interesting issue in First Amendment commercial speech jurisprudence is probably the legitimacy, under the doctrine, of the American prohibition of cigarette advertisements on television and radio. The question was never raised by the tobacco manufacturers and sellers who did not actively oppose the prohibition but found it to their benefit at the time of its adoption (1971) because it all but eliminated anti-smoking messages on television that, at the time, were required in response to cigarette advertisements at a ratio of one anti-smoking advertisement for every seven cigarette commercials. The prohibition was challenged in court by a group of radio broadcasters whose action was rejected by the lower federal courts and not reviewed by the Supreme Court (*Capital Broadcasting Co v Mitchell*, 333 F Supp 582 (1970), cert denied, 405 US 1000 (1972)). A major point for the court upholding the ban was the special influence of the broadcast media on youngsters. The decision in that case preceded the 1976 rulings of the Supreme Court concerning First Amendment application to commercial speech, so left uncertain whether the law could survive a constitutional challenge today (see Kluger, 1997: 335).

Legal scholars have also raised the question of whether the nature of cigarettes could justify a total ban on all cigarette advertising. Notwithstanding the general invalidity of total bans on advertising, there are some who think that such a prohibition could survive constitutional scrutiny given the scientific evidence that the addictive nature of cigarette smoking causes physiological dependence that justifies regulation beyond that allowed for traditional consumer products (Fallon, 1992). Although the decision of the Supreme Court to strike down the efforts of the state of Massachusetts to limit tobacco advertising in the *Lorillard* case (*Lorillard Tobacco Co v Reilly*, 121 S Ct 2404 (2001)) seems to negate that argument, in the view of most scholars, there remains an argument that a total ban might be justified as an offer to allow the sale of a product of unique dangerousness (a uniquely dangerous product with no utility other than whatever pleasure it may provide its users) in return for a limited waiver of promotion of the product (see Berman, 2002). Although such a conclusion lacks significant judicial support at this point, the argument notes the special case presented by the advertising of cigarettes in the United States and the effort to place tobacco products in a special category due to the unmatched damage they may cause consumers.

A better argument to justify the prohibition of cigarette advertising rests on the addictive nature of the product combined with its unique dangerousness and the fact that over 85-percent of smokers begin smoking before the age of 18. Moreover, tobacco products could not, in their present form, meet the requirements of federal law that food, drugs, and devices must be shown to be safe and efficacious before they can be marketed. The failure to classify nicotine or tobacco products as drugs, in part due to industry lobbying, allowed tobacco products to escape this requirement. Efforts by the Food and Drug Administration to control tobacco products failed, in part, because the agency was held not to have authority to control the product without prohibiting it (see *FDA v Brown & Williamson*, 528 US 120 (2000)). And prohibition of tobacco products would be impractical and probably unworkable. Given all this, why would not a prohibition of advertising for tobacco products constitute a reasonable compromise between an unfeasible ban and a somewhat Pollyannish view that, as long as the product is legal, there should be no prohibitions of speech promoting it? Note that a prohibition of advertising would not prevent anyone's speech concerning his views of tobacco or of the wisdom of an advertising ban in any of the usual channels for speech; only marketing talk would be covered. Having stated this, it must be conceded that it remains highly questionable whether the present Supreme Court would uphold a ban. The belief once expressed that First Amendment protections in the United States do not reach ped-lars selling pots and pans from door to door has been challenged. Will this also become true of the statement of one justice within the past decade that the Court would never give child pornography or cigarette advertising the First Amendment protections granted political speech? That possibility is far from remote even in the face of the significant hazards presented by tobacco products.

3 UNFAIR PRACTICES AND THE CONSUMER

The term 'unfair trade practices' originally referred to unfair competitive practices. A true market economy is posited on the concept that the interests of society, including those of the consumer, are best served by a marketplace of vigorous com-petition, under which those who are unable to compete successfully may find themselves no longer in business. (Of course, business interests have been quite successful in obtaining various kinds of special protections for business enterprises that prevent this model from operating, but that is outside the purview of this essay.) However, the law has long insisted that competition should be conducted in a 'fair' manner. As long ago as 1410, the English courts ruled that, in general, mar-kets should be free from artificial or unnecessary restraints on new entrants to a particular market. It is not unfair competition, under the common law, for a new entrant to 'damage' earlier existing concerns by entering a market and taking cus-tomers away from those who were earlier in that market, even if the new entrant gains a share of the established concern's customers by cutting prices below those prevailing prior to the time of entry. Although the older, established companies almost surely will consider such conduct to be 'unfair' to them, it is not considered such in the eyes of the law because robust competition of this nature benefits the consumer and the public (see *The Schoolmaster's Case*, YB Hilary, 4, f 47, pl 10 (1410), ruling that a school had no legal action against a new school in the area that charged lower prices and thereby enrolled students who otherwise would have attended the other school). However, an entry not based on a desire to compete, but simply to destroy an existing business, even when operating at a loss is needed to achieve that goal, is considered an actionable 'unfair' form of competition (*Tuttle v Buck*, 107 Minn 145 (1909)).

As noted earlier, the most commonly recognized form of 'unfair practice' histor-ically was that of 'passing off', under which a seller 'passed' or 'palmed off' his goods as those of another, more reputable seller. Cases of this nature were brought by the competitors whose goods were supposedly being sold by the defendant. 'Passing off' was sufficiently a synonym for 'unfair trade practices' in the early twentieth century that, when the US Congress passed legislation establishing the Federal Trade Commission and authorizing it to attack and prohibit 'unfair practices' a strong effort was made to define the term statutorily as limited to 'passing off' and perhaps a few similar practices. This effort to limit the definition of 'unfair practices' to a specific list of violations failed and the legislation that emerged included no definition whatever of the term 'unfair'—thereby opening the door to a broad and flexible definition of the term as one that encompassed a wide variety of activities that were injurious to consumers and not just to competitors. The determination of what would constitute an unfair practice under the Act was to be made not by some general definition but by 'the gradual process of judicial inclusion and exclusion' in review of actions of the Commission (*Federal Trade Commission v Raladam Company*, 283 US 643, 648 (1931)). Since most American states eventually adopted statutes that either incorporated or closely tracked the language and interpretation of the Federal Trade Commission Act, this broad scope for defining unfairness had resonance beyond the actions brought by the Commission (see generally *Unfair and Deceptive Acts and Practices*, 2001).

Although it is an unfair practice for a seller to use deception, unfairness may exist outside the traditional legal parameters of deception. In 1964, the Federal Trade Commission, in considering whether to issue a Trade Regulation Rule that would require disclosure of the health hazards of smoking in the labels and advertising of cigarettes, stated that unfairness was not limited to deception. It included situations where the practice contravened some established concept of fairness under public policy or where the practice could be considered 'immoral, unethical, oppressive or unscrupulous' or where the practice caused substantial injury to consumers or competitors or other businesses (29 Federal Register 8324, 8355 (1964)). This statement was later cited with approval by the US Supreme Court in *Federal Trade Commission v Sperry and Hutchinson Co*, 405 US 233 (1972). (The Commission never promulgated the Rule, due to Congressional action.)

It is important to note that the categories of unfairness cited by the Commission and later noted with approval by the Supreme Court were stated in the disjunctive, not the conjunctive; therefore, it was possible to charge a company with an unfair practice, simply because the practice harmed consumers without any need to determine if the practice was 'unethical', for example. Not surprisingly, this broad definition was narrowed by a Commission more conservative than its immediate predecessors in a policy statement in 1980. It announced a new interpretation by the Commission under which the agency's sole focus in future unfairness cases would be whether the practice caused a serious consumer injury that did not have offsetting consumer benefits and could not have been avoided by consumers acting reasonably under the circumstances (see *International Harvester Co*, 104 FTC 949 (1984), holding company committed unfair practice by not warning its customers of dangers of fuel geysering by its gasoline-powered tractors, and *Orkin Exterminating Co, Inc v Federal Trade Commission*, 849 F 2d 1354, cert denied 488 US 1041 (1988), holding that company's breach of contracts with customers as to price of renewal was an unfair practice). However, the broader definition of unfairness approved by the Supreme Court never has been revisited and, presumably, a future Commission could return to that approach, if it felt the political climate would allow such action. Moreover, the definition of unfairness adopted by the Commission does not control that definition for purposes of actions by the individual states of the United States; under the federal system of government, a state may utilize a different standard either narrower or more expansive than that of the federal government, in determining what is an 'unfair practice'. There are strong advantages, from the standpoint of those subject to regulation, as well as more general concerns of efficiency and consistency, for the national government and the individual states to have the same definitions but that outcome is not required by law in a federal system.

Another notable use of the concept of 'unfairness' to consumers was the determination by the Commission, ultimately upheld by the courts, that it was an unfair practice for advertisers to make measurable, verifiable claims in their advertising if they did not have prior, adequate substantiation for the claim. Adoption of this standard placed a greater burden on the defense of advertising claims. Although the burden of proving that the claim was unlawful remained, as always, upon the party asserting unlawfulness (in Federal Trade Commission cases, the Commission staff), once it was noted that there was no substantiation for a particular claim, the burden of going forward to present any evidence that might rebut the allegation was on the advertiser. This is akin to a situation in military law where a soldier is charged with being absent without leave (AWOL). Although the burden of proof is upon the prosecution to show the violation, entry into the trial record of the attendance reports for the soldier's assigned unit, indicating that the soldier was listed as absent on the date(s) in question placed on the defense the burden of going forward with any evidence that might call the report into question. A prima-facie case, one that would compel conviction in the absence of any contradictory evidence, is made upon the receipt of the official roster and attendance report into evidence. Similarly, once it has been demonstrated that advertising representations of verifiable claims were made without substantiation or with inadequate substantiation, a prima-facie case of unfair advertising has been made (*Jay Norris, Inc v Federal Trade Commission*, 598 F 2d 1244 (2d Cir 1979)).

It is also important to note that, under the substantiation approach, it is not relevant to finding a violation, although it may be relevant to what remedy is issued, that the unsubstantiated claim turns out, by chance, to have been truthful. It is not the validity of the underlying claim that is at issue but the support that existed for the claim before it was made. Some critics of the substantiation doctrine have labeled this an inequitable practice but the objection misses the point that the forwarding of a claim without first establishing a basis for it is essence of the unfairness of the practice. A defense should be based on the actual or reasonably determined validity of a claim and not luck (see Thain, 1973).

The utilization of the substantiation doctrine by the Federal Trade Commission and other bodies has waxed and waned with the political climate and its calls for either vigorous or softer enforcement of the laws. At times when government regulation is not strongly favored, substantiation is little used. When consumer issues are at the forefront, there will be greater recourse to it. The significant point is that substantiation has been a tool considered to be available to attack advertising since the concept was first introduced in the early 1970s; there is no question today that it is a lawful approach, even if it is not always used as extensively as possible (see Calkins, 2000).

Philosophically, the substantiation doctrine divides many analysts, including a number who generally are considered consumer advocates. One camp considers it crystal clear that advertising claims that are made without prior, adequate substantiation should not be tolerated and that advertisers who make unsubstantiated claims that are subject to verification obviously should do so at their peril. A contrasting view, while not condoning unsubstantiated claims, counsels caution in attacking unsubstantiated claims. The concern is that too many attacks on unsubstantiated claims may lead some advertisers to abandon altogether, or at least to a considerable degree, the use of verifiable claims in their advertising and turn instead to meaningless 'puffs', thereby reducing the amount of information in advertising to the detriment of consumers (see Note, 1973: 893–8). Some critics argued that substantiation would place too high a cost on advertisers relative to the benefits gained (see BNA Antitrust & Trade Regulation Report No. 1039, p. A-20 (1981), citing the views of then-chairman of the FTC, James C. Miller III, to this effect). This criticism has not led to abandonment of the substantiation requirement, however, as a majority of consumer groups believe that other methods, such as requiring by law or rule that specific information be listed in advertising or labeling, should be used to ensure or encourage the inclusion of meaningful information in advertising and that unsubstantiated claims should not be tolerated in the name of encouraging information. I find the argument that use of substantiation will diminish information to be unpersuasive; when there is sufficient consumer demand for pertinent information, resort to 'puffing' will be limited.

The European Union also recognizes the concept of unfairness to consumers, most notably in its Unfair Terms in Consumer Contracts Directive. However, the exact nature of the controls imposed by the Directive is not yet certain. Unfairness in the Directive is defined as consumer detriment flowing from a contract term which, contrary to the requirements of good faith, causes a significant imbalance in the rights and obligations of the parties. Under this definition, presumably, a consumer must demonstrate a breach of good faith as well as a significant imbalance in the contract terms. The Directive indicates that good faith includes procedural issues such as transparency and clear and understandable language in contract terms, but is not limited to such procedural matters. The Directive provides for a substantive interpretation of good faith or a lack of good faith found by the use of unconscionable provisions in the contract terms. The major concerns of the Directive seem to be about ancillary contract terms that a consumer could not be expected to bargain over; it provides that determination of whether a given contract is unfair under the Directive shall not be made on the basis of terms 'which describe the main subject matter of the contract nor the quality/price ratio' (art. 4 Recital 19 of the Directive). It must be kept in mind, however, that this Directive is considered a minimal directive that builds upon existing law of the member states. In general, the European states have been willing to strike out as inherently unfair certain contract terms—such as waiving the right to receive goods of a certain minimum standard and excusing liability for personal injury caused by negligence. Primarily, however, the concerns about unfairness in consumer contracts in Europe have been focused on procedural impropriety.

In the European states, litigating alleged unfair terms in individual actions is rare and the incentives for individuals and lawyers to bring cases that exist in the United States are not found. Actions are usually brought by ombudsmen or by certain consumer groups authorized under the laws of a member state of the European Union to bring actions seeking injunctive relief of consumers from the challenged terms. The Unfair Terms in Consumer Contracts Directive, consistent with this approach, provides that 'persons or organizations, having a legitimate interest under national law in protecting consumers, may take action according to the national law concerned before the courts or before competent administrative bodies for a decision as to whether contractual terms drawn up for general use are unfair'.

In sum, the concept of actions that are so one-sided, unscrupulous, or unethical in consumer matters, be they in contracts between consumers and non-consumers or in the practices of marketers, is recognized in both the United States and in Europe as actions that should not be allowed by the law. The definition of what constitutes 'unfair' practices to consumers remains flexible but seems certain to become more expansive in future years.

4 CONSUMER CREDIT

Consumer credit was involved in a relatively small portion of transactions (home mortgages aside) until the post-World War II period in the United States. Legislation enacted since the last third of the twentieth century addresses five stages of consumer credit. These are: the information-seeking stage, dealt with by requirements for uniform disclosure of credit terms in advertisements and in credit agreements; the negotiating stage, covered by provisions to assure equal access to consumer credit and to limit the scope of negotiations by restricting the price of

credit and forbidding or requiring specific terms or practices; the formal contracting stage, covered by provisions that specify the content and clarity of the legal
documents obligating consumers; the performance stage, covered by requirements
about billing practices, collection efforts, and credit reporting; and the termination
stage, covered by provisions about the obligations of creditors when consumers
have completed payment (see Johnson, 'Credit Protections', in Brobeck, 1997).

While Ralph Nader is considered the general founder of the US consumer movement of today, Senators Paul Douglas of Illinois and William Proxmire of
Wisconsin were the leaders of the movement to require all those who provided consumer credit to indicate its cost by stating the annual percentage rate (APR) being
charged for it. Although there was considerable opposition to this effort, on the
grounds that the information was too complicated to be meaningful to consumers
or, in some cases, affirmatively misleading, such legislation was passed in 1968. The
legislation, known as the Truth in Lending Act, mandated disclosure of the financial charge in dollars and the APR, in order to provide a standard measure of the
cost of credit. Studies of the impact of this legislation determined, not surprisingly,
that it was not much used by low-income consumers. These consumers were prone
to focus on the size of the monthly payment rather than the rate of interest being
charged. The regulation of rates on interest has remained largely with the individual states, and they have been eliminating rate ceilings and allowing rates to be
set by competition.

The problems of low-income consumers have always been a difficult issue for
consumer advocates. These consumers are obviously the highest risks for credit,
and thus least able to afford the prices charged for high-risk loans. For many years,
these consumers were 'protected' by the imposition of rate ceilings for cash loans.
The result of such ceilings was that low income consumers too frequently were not
protected but rationed out of the legal credit market, compelling them either to do
without credit or, more likely, to obtain it from illegal sources, usually loan sharks.
Although England eliminated all rate ceilings on consumer credit in 1854, usury
laws limiting rates to 6 percent or slightly higher were widely adopted in the United
States from the 1700s to the 1900s. The belief of many religious leaders during that
period that usury, defined as lending at other than low interest rates, was sinful,
caused them, in effect, to join credit predators in opposing the lifting of credit ceilings and delaying their elimination for many years. Unfortunately, elimination has
now led to credit card companies, the major grantors of credit in today's world,
establishing their legal residence in those states with the least restrictions on credit
practices. This has allowed those companies to charge high rates of interest on
unpaid balances on their revolving loans while the companies lure customers with
'low rates' that usually last only for the first few months after obtaining the
company's credit card.

Because a high percentage of low income consumers are also members of
minority groups, their access to credit available to others was sometimes blocked

primarily because of race, religion, color, or national origin. Women often were denied credit solely because of their sex. In the United States, this problem was addressed in 1974 by legislation, the Equal Credit Opportunity Act, which also assisted creditworthy married females to obtain credit under their own names by forbidding creditors from requiring that there be a co-signer or guarantor when there is an application for credit in such cases. Passage of the Equal Credit Opportunity Act led to the development of various statistical bases for the evaluation of credit, both to reduce the possibility of illegal refusal of credit and to provide a basis of comparison that might justify the refusal of credit to a dissatisfied consumer.

The ability of consumers to learn the status of their credit records had been a matter of dispute for some years prior to passage of the Fair Credit Reporting Act. Many instances were cited in which consumers were denied credit based on misinformation in their credit records—records to which consumers did not have access and which many consumers did not know existed. Under the Act, adopted in 1970, consumers who are denied credit on the basis of their credit report must be informed of their right to obtain a copy of the report and to have any inaccurate information corrected.

The virtue of the present US consumer credit disclosure laws is their precision. The requirements of the laws are clear and the penalties for violation are generally also quite definite. The result is that virtually all legitimate credit grantors follow or attempt to follow the rules, and it is now possible for those who compare the annual percentage rates for credit to shop for credit. The downside of these laws is that their very technicality causes many, especially the under-educated and relatively poor, to ignore the information presented and to focus on payment size instead of cost. This may not be a problem that can be addressed successfully short of eliminating poverty. It is not irrational for the poor who live a precarious existence to be more concerned about immediate cost and immediate gratification than to evaluate long-term costs. Credit disclosure laws are beneficial to consumers in general, but are of limited value to those most vulnerable to sharp-credit practices.

The credit laws that require equal opportunity for all creditworthy applicants and those that attack unscrupulous debt-collection practices are of greater value to those of less affluence. Here, the problems are not so much with the laws themselves as with the difficulties of arming consumers with the knowledge of the laws and their rights under them. Much evidence and many cases indicate that it remains common for debt collectors to use harassing tactics in an effort to have low-income and usually debt-ridden consumers pay them first. Laws limiting these practices are useful only when there is knowledge of the laws and of the violations. Action against violators of the debt-collection laws is frequently taken by public agencies when the nature of a company's conduct becomes known. Notwithstanding the specificity of the laws on debt collection, there remain many who will engage in illegal efforts to collect debts while there remain many who have difficulty obtaining credit.

In recent years, there has been a strong movement in the United States to limit the ability of consumers to obtain discharge in bankruptcy proceedings. A huge public relations campaign has been mounted by advocates of such 'bankruptcy reform' to advise the public that the costs to it of bankruptcy filings by consumer 'deadbeats' is immense. These assertions have been demonstrated to be without substance by Professor Elizabeth Warren of Harvard Law School and other legal scholars (see Warren, 2002). The great majority of consumers who declare bankruptcy and receive discharge of their debts are people who have become financially overwhelmed by medical bills, divorce proceedings, or loss of jobs.

The movement for change in the bankruptcy laws has been spurred by banks and credit card companies who have flooded the land with promotions for easy credit, issuing credit cards to virtually anyone who they can encourage to apply, regardless of credit standing. These financial institutions now seek to prevent the debts of those customers from being discharged in bankruptcy when the debts for such easy credit become too large to handle in the face of illness, domestic difficulties, or a slowing economy. These efforts, moreover, continue despite the fact that credit card lending has been shown to be about twice as profitable as other forms of lending (Federal Reserve Board, *The Profitability of Credit Card Operations of Depository Institutions* (Aug. 1997), http://www.federalreserve.gov.bounddocs/RptCongress/creditcard/1997; Ausubel, 1997: 259). Moreover, some economic studies conclude that banks price at the margins for high-risk borrowers, not for all borrowers (Ausubel, 1997: 261). This campaign for bankruptcy 'reform', although it seems quite likely to be successful, is one of the most shameful chapters in the history of American business. It has been promoted by considerable reliance upon a claim that the existing bankruptcy law 'costs every American family $400 a year'. This claim has been widely cited by much of the media, as well as by the supporters of bankruptcy reform, when the truth is that there is no known empirical basis for this figure. In fact, the figure is a mathematical impossibility, based on the number of American families and the number of American bankruptcies. It appears to have been the invention of a lobbyist for the credit industry. Due to constant repetition, the figure has been accepted as a fact by many, in Congress and the press (Warren, 2002: 13–20; Markell, 2000, reviewing Sullivan *et al.*, 2000). This is a classic example of a frequently repeated statement becoming a 'well-known fact' because of its frequency instead of its validity—one definition of propaganda.

5 POST-PURCHASE ISSUES: PRODUCT SAFETY

In the United States, no one individual is more connected with consumer law and consumer advocacy than Ralph Nader. Although he has been involved, over the years, with virtually every matter that could be included in a broad definition of consumer law, he first drew public attention for his criticism of the lack of safety features on automobiles. His book *Unsafe at Any Speed* can be considered the opening statement in the wave of consumer advocacy that began in the 1960s and, to some degree, has continued to the present. It was appropriate that product safety was the issue that first brought him prominence because legal actions seeking recovery for consumer injury due to inadequate product safety standards or practices formed the basis of consumer law in its early stages.

There is a view of the United States, sometimes presented in European and other foreign periodicals but also seen in domestic publications, as a nation of litigation-prone, if not litigation-crazed, citizens who pursue lawsuits that benefit few other than the lawyers who bring them, to the detriment of the general good of the economic system. These criticisms tend to focus on American tort law and the contingent-fee arrangement, under which a lawyer who prevails on behalf of an injured plaintiff takes a percentage of the recovery as his or her fee. There is a strong movement seeking to limit the cases that can be brought or the amounts that may be recovered, a movement usually called 'tort reform'. This movement is essentially the reaction of conservatives and the business community to the increased attention given to product safety in litigation in recent years. Although, as noted earlier, the term 'consumer law' is somewhat amorphous, a private practitioner in the United States who purports to be a 'consumer lawyer' is most likely to be one who represents private parties who allege injury due to inadequate attention by a seller or manufacturer to the safety of a product, whether in product design or other fashion.

The argument for 'tort reform' that would limit recovery for injured consumers can be summarized as follows. It is not possible to produce totally safe products in many categories except at a cost that would be prohibitive for a mass market. The costs of defending against lawsuits, many alleged to be marginal if not frivolous, also burden industry unduly and make less likely the development and offering of new products. The argument is also made that the current state of tort law does not give sufficient weight to individual responsibility for actions that result in individual injury. Among the favorite references by those who promote these arguments are the famous McDonald's hot coffee burn case and the suits by smokers (or their heirs or estates) for the lung cancer or other diseases of smokers. Professor W. Kip Viscusi of Harvard Law School is perhaps the most prominent legal scholar presenting arguments of this nature. He has consistently asserted that efforts to promote consumer safety, in legislation and administrative legislation, as well as in litigation, do not give sufficient attention to the trade-offs of increased cost per reduction of risk (see Viscusi, 1992). He has also criticized warning labels on products as often meaningless, devoting particular attention to the warning messages on cigarette packages (see Viscusi, 2002). Others who have written recent attacks on the US tort system include Walter Olsen and Newt Gingrich. The latter, a former Congressional leader, has written that juries of typical citizens should not be allowed to make determinations of matters that require scientific or other technical knowledge. In response, those economists who emphasize actual, as opposed to theoretical, behavior find that those who urge that market forces should determine the 'risky decisions' of consumers fail to recognize strong evidence that, in an unregulated market, manufacturers may and sometimes do manipulate and deter-mine consumer perception and preferences. The result is that consumer percep-tions of risks are influenced by marketing campaigns that severely underestimate risk (see Hanson and Kyser, 'The Joint Failure of Economic Theory and Regulation', in Slovic, 2001: 229, 258–61; Slovic, 2000).

Defenders of the US tort system note that the attacks on the system and the arguments about litigation-clogged courts are concentrated on actions by individ-uals against large companies. Without the contingent-fee system, almost none of these people would be able to afford legal representation or obtain compensation for their injuries. Empirical studies indicate that the increases in judicial filings so often bemoaned by advocates of 'tort reform' are more attributable to actions by companies than to actions by individuals against companies. Yet, there has been little outcry to limit litigation by companies against other companies. Similarly, a common argument made against personal-injury actions by critics of the contingent-fee system, that these cases too often result in unduly large punitive damages being assessed against companies, hampering innovation by industry and forcing the companies to pass on these costs to consumers by raising the prices of their prod-ucts, is not borne out by the evidence. Punitive damages are in fact awarded in only a small percentage of tort cases and in only a few jurisdictions are punitive dam-ages awarded with any frequency (see papers by, *inter alia*, Michael Rustad, Stephen Daniels, and Joanne Martin in *National Conference on the Future of Punitive Dam-ages: The Incidence of Punitive Damages Claims and Awards* (Institute for Legal Studies, Wisconsin Law School, 1996)). This is not to say that there have been no cases in which a dispassionate observer would find that a verdict against a com-pany in favor of a consumer was either unjustified or unduly large. It is to say that such situations are far less common than the critics of the present system will con-cede. Moreover, the criticisms of many actual awards, such as the McDonald's hot coffee case, attack a jury award of damages lowered considerably by settlements pending appeal or appellate decisions. That case is also typical in that it is one in which the matters before the jury, involving a practice of the company to ignore a widespread pattern of similar injuries, are ignored by the vehement critics of the action.

The dispute between consumer advocates and others over the utility of the contingent-fee system for personal injury cases and the efficacy of punitive damages to control business conduct, is another aspect of the ongoing battle between consumer advocates and those who rely on a rather elementary cost-benefit view of economics in which the result will rarely favor anything other than reliance on the market as the best *modus operandi*. Perhaps the strongest example of a belief by these scholars that intervention in the marketplace is usually unwarranted is the assertion of Professor Viscusi and some others that the actions by individual states resulting in settlements from tobacco companies for all US states could not be justified. These actions sought compensation for the medical and welfare costs borne by the states in the treatment of illnesses that were the result of tobacco use. These critics do not deny the health hazards of smoking tobacco or the costs to the states in treating illnesses due to smoking. In essence, they argue that the expenditure of public funds on treatment of those suffering from tobacco-related diseases was more than offset by the savings of pension payments and subsequent treatment for other illnesses not made by the government because of the relatively early demise of smokers. Tobacco companies were saving the state money by selling products that prevented many citizens from living to their full expected life span. Although this somewhat macabre argument (as one federal judge characterized it at an academic conference on tobacco litigation) has been accepted by some of those especially receptive to a microeconomic approach to legal issues, others have challenged it on various grounds, including that of not giving sufficient weight to the loss to society of fully functioning and productive citizens throughout their working lives (see generally Sugarman, 'International Aspects of Tobacco Control and the Proposed WHO Treaty', in Rabin and Sugarman, 2001: 245, 249).

Attacks on the contingent-fee system used in the United States for personal injury cases, on punitive damages in cases brought by individuals against corporations, and on the alleged unsound and anti-market tort system in general have been raging in the United States for some years. So-called 'tort reform' movements have been successful in a number of states to some degree. The well-known low esteem in which the general public in the United States holds lawyers as a group is, in part, a response to the picture painted by tort reform advocates of aggressive, greedy, unscrupulous lawyers looking for any means to enrich themselves without regard either for the general welfare or the best interest of their clients. Although it cannot be said that there are no lawyers who engage in unsavory tactics—either in the personal injury bar or other types of practice—the assertion that the legal system is unbalanced toward individual consumer plaintiffs and against business is belied by empirical studies. Success as a litigant in the courtroom is highly correlated with being a 'repeat player', and repeat players are almost always business enterprises and not consumers (see Galanter, 1974). Moreover, to the degree that greater resources will bring more experienced, more costly, and possibly more competent legal representation, it is usually not the consumer who is in a position to retain such representation. The contingent-fee system may even the playing field in some small measure, but business interests usually retain significant advantages over consumers in litigation. Most filed cases are settled and usually settled for less than might ultimately be obtained if pursued to completion. Settlement generally is far more attractive to a consumer plaintiff than to a business defendant. The value of a 'bird in the hand' to the individual citizen in lieu of a potentially better result at a much later time tends to be greater than the benefit to a business of simply ending an action, particularly if the settlement prohibits disclosure of the terms and amounts that might be an incentive for more actions by other consumers with similar complaints. Product safety cases are particularly likely to be ones where a consumer is anxious to receive some settlement at hand sooner rather than wait for a better one at a much later time.

There has been progress toward greater consumer redress in matters of product safety through the adoption by courts of strict liability for products—a standard that requires no proof of fault on the part of a seller or manufacturer but makes all sellers in the distributive chain liable for injuries caused by products that are in a defective condition or are unreasonably dangerous to consumers or their property. Products are considered defective and unreasonably dangerous if their dangers exceed the expectations ordinary consumers have of the products. Strict products liability law in the United States therefore operates as a standard akin to the implied warranty of fitness of goods for a particular purpose under the general commercial law (*Greenman v Yuba Products* (Calif 1963), s 402A, Restatement (Second) of Torts). The rationale for strict liability is that it provides a strong incentive for manufacturers to reduce product risks and streamlines litigation by eliminating the evidentiary issues involved when negligence by a manufacturer or seller must be proved. Strict liability, it must be noted, does not mean absolute liability, and issues of design defects and claims that warnings of product hazards were absent or inadequate are most likely to be tried under the traditional standard of requiring negligence to be proved by a plaintiff. Consumer advantages, however, have been offset to a significant degree by the adoption in almost every state—in response to intense lobbying by business interests—of various pro-business legislative provisions that have capped non-economic damages, limited punitive damages, and the like.

A regulatory agency, the Consumer Product Safety Commission, was established in the United States to address some of the injuries and deaths caused by the use of consumer products in and around the home. The Acts administered by the agency authorize it to set standards, ban products, require labeling, and provide for the recall of hazardous consumer products. Congress may also direct the agency to take action on specific products to protect the public from hazards about which the legislature is concerned and for which the agency has not exercised regulatory authority. It should be noted that the agency is expressly forbidden from using its powers as to firearms, tobacco products, or alcoholic beverages, exceptions that were the subject of considerable criticism by consumer advocates but without which, the legislation establishing the agency almost certainly would not have been enacted. Consumer advocates have also questioned the recall procedure as too often coming after too many injuries or deaths and too often being terminated when the safety issues have not been resolved. On the other side, there have been many critics of the agency who have decried some of the actions taken to require labeling of hazards that would seem to be self-evident to many consumers or involve uses for which the product was not designed (see Adler, 1995).

Although the development of product safety law has progressed well beyond the days when consumers were advised that 'buyer beware' was the watchword and that an action for injury caused by an unsafe product required that the plaintiff prove negligence on the part of the defendant, counter-attacks by business have not only stemmed but, in some measure, rolled back the advances of consumers, and the very vigorous 'tort reform' movement in the United States continues to seek further rollbacks of the consumer gains in this area over the last half-century. Some success in these activities appears almost certain. The result will be not only fewer actions by consumers and lower judgments in successful actions but also lowered incentives for business to develop safer products. The Consumer Product Safety Commission has a not insignificant role but its actions, frequently influenced by political concerns, are unlikely to match the incentives from fear of the possibility of a large tort judgment.

Some critics of the tort system argue that it is not the actual number of cases which result in significant verdicts against business that is their true concern but rather the 'shadow of the law', in the sense that fear, even if not well founded, of a large judgment against them leads companies to overreact by producing products with expensive and unnecessary features or even to abandon production of a product line altogether. It is certainly true that the potential for legal action should and will be considered by businesses in making decisions. However, the true shadow of the law will be cast on those actions where business is taking calculated risks, in the hope that the cost benefits gained by ignoring safety matters will not backfire if the safety problem results in serious consumer injury. The classic example is that of the Ford Pinto automobile. There, failing to use equipment costing less than $2 per vehicle was a major factor in deaths and injuries caused by safety failure. The company's action seems to have ignored the shadow of potential legal action. Not all business actions so dramatically ignore that shadow but it takes only a few such examples to make the point that the shadow of the law, at least in the area of product safety, is not so long and so great a deterrent as some suggest. Legal rules that indeed inhibit creativity and stifle product development should be carefully weighed against the benefits to society of those rules. First, it is necessary to be certain of the actual and not the alleged consequences of those rules.

6 CONCLUSION

Consumer law has become a recognized, if not yet fully defined, area of the law. The strength of consumer law is its recognition that individual citizens can and should be protected from misconduct in the marketplace by actions in their own names as well as by public bodies established for those purposes. The weakness of consumer law is that it remains subject to changes in the political climate and the large re-sources that are often used by business interests to campaign against the implemen-tation of consumer rights under the law and to limit those rights. These campaigns have achieved considerable success in the last two decades. None the less, consumer law will not be eliminated, only weakened, and there remains the possibility that the wheel of history and politics will turn more in its favor in the years to come.

REFERENCES

Adler, R. S. (1995). 'Redesigning People versus Redesigning Products: The Consumer Product Safety Commission Addresses Product Misuse', *Journal of Law and Politics*, 11: 79–127.

Ausubel, M. (1997). 'Credit Card Defaults, Credit Card Profits and Bankruptcy', *American Bankruptcy Law Journal*, 71: 249–70.

Baker, C. E. (1976). 'Commercial Speech: A Problem in the Theory of Freedom', *Iowa Law Review*, 62: 1–56.

Berman, M. (2002). 'Commercial Speech and the Unconstitutional Conditions Doctrine: A Second Look at "The Greater Includes the Lesser"', *Vanderbilt Law Review*, 55: 693–796.

Brobeck, S. (ed.) (1997). *Encyclopedia of the Consumer Movement*, Denver: ABC-Clio.

Calkins, S. (2000). 'FTC Unfairness: An Essay', *Wayne Law Review*, 46: 1935–91.

Galanter, M. (1974). 'Why the Haves Come out Ahead', *Law & Society Review*, 9: 95–160.

Howells G., and Wilhelmsson, T. (1998). *Yearbook of European Law 1997*, London: Fitzroy Dearborn.

Kluger, R. (1997). *Ashes to Ashes* (rev. edn.), New York: Vintage Books.

Kozinski, A., and Banner, S. (1990). 'Who's Afraid of Commercial Speech?' *Virginia Law Review*, 76: 626–53.

Law, S. (1992). 'Addiction, Autonomy and Advertising', *Iowa Law Review*, 77: 909–55.

Markell, B. (2000). 'Sorting and Sifting Fact from Fiction: Empirical Research and the Face of Bankruptcy', *American Bankruptcy Law Journal*, 75: 145–55.

Neuborne, B. (1989). 'The First Amendment and Regulation of Capital Markets', *Brooklyn Law Review*, 55: 5–63.

Note (1967). 'Developments in the Law: Deceptive Advertising', *Harvard Law Review*, 80: 1005–163.

——(1973). 'Federal Trade Commission: Developments in Advertising Regulation and Antitrust Policies', *George Washington Law Review*, 41: 880–950.

Pitofsky, R. (1972). 'Consumer Legislation Symposium', *Business Lawyer*, 28-5: 292–7.

Posner, R. (1986). 'Free Speech in an Economic Perspective', *Suffolk Law Review*, 20: 1–154.

Preston, I. (1996). *The Great American Blow-up: Puffery in Advertising & Selling* (rev. edn.) Madison: University of Wisconsin Press.

——(1998). 'Puffery and Other "Loophole" Claims: How the Law's "Don't Ask, Don't Tell" Policy Condones Fraudulent Falsity in Advertising', *Journal of Law and Commerce*, 18: 49–114.

Prosser, W., and Keeton, W. P. (1984). *The Law of Torts* (5th edn.) St Paul, Minn.: West Publishing, 757.

Rabin, R., and Sugarman, S. (eds.) (2001). *Regulating Tobacco*, New York: Oxford University Press.

Sheldon, J. A. (2001). *Unfair and Deceptive Acts and Practices* (5th edn.), Boston: National Consumer Law Center.

Shiffrin, S. (1983). 'The First Amendment and Economic Regulation: Away from a General Theory of the First Amendment', *Northwestern Law Review*, 78: 1212–83.

Slovic, M. (2000). 'Rational Actors or Rational Fools: The Influence of Affect on Judgment and Decision Making', *Roger Williams University Law Review*, 6: 167–212.

—— (ed.) (2001). *Smoking, Risk, Reception and Injury*, Chicago: Sage Publications.

Strauss, D. (1991). 'Persuasion, Autonomy and Freedom of Expression', *Columbia Law Review*, 91: 334–71.

Sullivan, T., Warren, E., and Westbrook, J. (2000). *The Fragile Middle Class: Americans in Debt*, New Haven: Yale University Press.

Thain, G. (1973). 'Advertising Regulation: The Contemporary FTC Approach', *Fordham Urban Law Journal*, 1: 349–71.

Viscusi, W. K. (1992). *Fatal Tradeoffs: Public and Private Responsibilities for Risk*, New York: Oxford University Press.

—— (2002). *Smoke-Filled Rooms: A Postmortem on the Tobacco Deal*, Chicago: University of Chicago Press.

Warren, E. (2002). 'The Market for Data: The Changing Role of Social Science in Shaping the Law', *Wisconsin Law Review*, 1–43.

CHAPTER 26

··

WORKERS

··

MARK BARENBERG

1 INTRODUCTION

··

1.1 The Scope and Ideological Visibility of Labor Law

THE scope of labor and employment law is large. Its core *subject* is the regulation of the employment relationship, workplace governance, and the labor market. The employment relation accounts for a large share of all contractual transactions in the modern market economy; workplace activities comprise much of adults' personal experience outside the household. The regulation may take the *form* of substantive standards protecting individual employees such as wages, hours, non-discrimination requirements, and health and safety rules; procedural mechanisms such as managerial hierarchies, collective bargaining, works councils, and safety committees that transform individual employment contracts into complex systems of authority, democracy, bargaining, and consultation; and labor-market policies such as training, employment subsidies, income tax credits, and social insurance that alter the endowments of the participants to the contractual or authority relations (Deakin and Wilkinson, 1999).

The subject is not only large but also more obviously ideological than many other areas of legal scholarship. The regulation of the workplace and the labor market unavoidably affects the distribution of bargaining power and wealth among workers, investors, and consumers—increasingly, on a global scale. It also influences the division of functions among the workplace, the family, and other social groups that reproduce and socialize workers, social subjects, and political participants. Hence, labor law immediately implicates the political fault-lines of class, gender, personal identity, political citizenship, and inter-state competition.

The subject is not only highly ideological but, for the same reasons, the scope of its legal subject-matter is difficult to limit, and its methods are particularly permeable to social-science disciplines that range widely beyond the doctrinal methods of jurisprudence. To the extent that endowments of workers and investors affect their relative bargaining power, then almost any entitlement in the legal system is relevant to the distributive aims of labor regulation. To the extent that the workplace is imbricated with households, schools, political parties, prisons, the mass media, and other intermediary associations in the functions of social reproduction, social control, and political participation, then almost any social and political regulation is relevant to the boundaries and methods of labor regulation.

Broad matters of political policy and structure also interact closely, albeit unpredictably, with labor regulation. Restrictive macroeconomic policies, for example, have the effect of reducing the bargaining power of workers; conversely, as a means of reducing inflation, state actors may directly weaken labor protections or may include unions in 'social pacts'. Strong labor movements may use their political power to strengthen social rights and welfare states; alternatively, political elites may enact minimum employment standards and social insurance for individual workers as a substitute for workers' collective organization.

1.2 Ideological Stability and Disruption as an Organizing Framework for Exploring Labor-Law Scholarship

These two features of labor law—its obvious ideological implications and the entropic scope of its subject-matter—are useful touchstones for exploring the past and future of scholarship in the field. In the English-speaking countries, identifiable ideological consensus among scholars provides a starting-point in the 1960s. The dominant frameworks are 'collective *laissez-faire*' and 'laborism'—most entrenched in the United Kingdom, Australia, and New Zealand—and 'industrial pluralism'— most evident in the United States and Canada. This early scholarship, described in Section 2, addresses the formation and regulation of individual employment contracts, but its primary concern is the law that enables or disables the transformation of the individual contract into collective bargaining.

After the 1960s, the dominant frameworks' treatment of collective and individual labor relations faced four sources of disruption: chronic failures in the implementation of existing statutes (Sect. 3); legislative enactments that cut against or fall outside the scholarly consensus (Sect. 4); growing disjunctures between existing labor-law regimes and fast-changing political economy (Sect. 5); and insurgent intellectual movements (Sect. 6).

As recounted in Sections 3 and 4, the dominant frameworks are better able to hold their ground in the face of hostile administrative implementation and legislative enactments, since new statutes have a highly uncertain impact and are based on seemingly reversible policy disputes conducted largely in the same vocabulary (even when reaching opposite conclusions) as the scholarly consensus. Section 5 shows that major changes in macroeconomic environment, corporate organization, labor-market participation and intermediation, and globalized capital and product markets are more difficult for conventional frameworks to absorb or deflect—although much depends on the institutional context of the particular country. Sections 6 and 7 recount how insurgent intellectual movements in the legal academy—most notably, law-and-economics, critical theory, feminism, and radical pragmatism—sought to gain footholds within labor law by making sense of some key changes in political economy and by wielding normative and positive concepts that seem, as to some issues, better-honed than the empirical assumptions and policy predispositions of the old frameworks.

The future of labor-law scholarship depends, in part, on whether the economic and political trends sketched in Section 5 transform employment relations in deep and enduring ways. Regardless of the unforeseeable answer to that question, some of the new directions in labor-law scholarship show lasting promise—most notably, those that combine certain large-scale and small-scale methodological strategies. The most promising large-scale strategies seek to identify and promote those emergent legal norms and institutions—at domestic, regional, and global levels— that embody comparative-law innovation, pluralist democratic values, and reflexive legal architectures. The most promising small-scale strategies, inspired by feminism and ethnography, start with workers' and managers' self-understandings in differing production systems and seek to identify legal norms that emerge through the interplay among those actors, legal institutions, and legal scholars themselves. These new directions are discussed in Section 7. Looking back, we see that the virtues of the large-scale and small-scale strategies are latent in the best of the traditional scholarship.

2 THE CONVENTIONAL FRAMEWORKS OF LABOR-LAW SCHOLARSHIP

2.1 The Conventional Frameworks: General Characteristics

In the 1960s, three conventional frameworks predominate in English-language scholarship in the newly consolidated field of labor law. These frameworks are offered here as ideal types cast at a highly general level. They are not found in pure form in the work of any single scholar. All three frameworks coexist, albeit in distinctly differing measure, within each of the national scholarly literatures of the United Kingdom, Australia, New Zealand, Canada, and the United States.

The first, 'collective *laissez-faire*', is most distinctively British. The concept originates with Otto Kahn-Freund, the progenitor of modern English-language and comparative-labor-law scholarship (Kahn-Freund, 1959). Collective *laissez-faire* denotes the voluntaristic collective bargaining grounded in Britain's Trade Disputes Act of 1906. That statute did not codify positive rights of union organization, collective bargaining, or strike action. It merely enacted the 'immunity' of union action from liability to certain economic torts of the common law. British labor relations were therefore governed to an extraordinary degree by the 'autonomous machinery' of collective bargaining and by extra-legal customs and practices, within the space permitted by the 'abstentionism' of labor law. This was the mark of a 'mature' and 'healthy' system of collective self-governance that was peculiarly resistant to intrusive reshaping by state action. The state presided over a pluralist equilibrium between workers' and employers' associations.

Kahn-Freund's conceptualization was shaped by personal experience that reinforced his deep comparative study. The foil for Britain's entrenched voluntarism was German unionism's dependence on legal fortification and its consequent incapacity to resist dismantling by the Nazi regime that Kahn-Freund had fled. His predisposition to find the anti-statist possibilities in labor regimes was compounded by an immigrant's eye for local peculiarities that natives may take for granted. The immigrant scholar's comparativist insight is strikingly repeated in British scholarship on employment discrimination in the 1970s and in US scholarship on union recognition in the 1980s, discussed in Sections 3 and 5 below. It also points, more obliquely, toward contemporary pragmatist scholarship, discussed in Section 7, that seeks to build such disciplined comparativism into the very architecture of labor-law regimes.

Collective *laissez-faire* shared the stage with a second framework—call it 'laborist' or 'social-democratic'—that is deeply grounded in the postwar sociology of industrial relations. The collective *laissez-faire* and laborist frameworks, as with other British legal thinking, strongly influenced Australia's and New Zealand's labor-law literature of the period—although the scholarship of these countries was more doctrinal than Britain's and even less attentive to normative assumptions than Britain's characteristically empiricist method (Sykes and Glasbeek, 1972).

In the framework of laborism, labor law is assigned three primary functions in a presumptively class-riven society. First, labor law establishes institutions of participation and representation in the workplace, where daily rule-making may affect people's vital interests as deeply as the more distant rules of the coercive state. Secondly, the legal restructuring of labor markets—from individual to collective bargaining— shifts relative bargaining power from owners to workers, even if it cannot overcome the fundamental subordination of workers. In this respect, labor law promotes a degree of economic equality at the point of production, a more socially entrenched alternative to redistribution through tax and transfer in a capitalist political economy. Thirdly, political citizenship is promoted by the empowering culture of workplace citizenship and by the economic redistribution that gives substance to formal rights of political participation.

Some laborist scholars in the United Kingdom, Australia, and New Zealand saw Kahn-Freund's anti-statist 'equilibrium' among collective actors as a perilous path for labor law to take—a path that, despite its aim of ensuring the autonomy of collective bargaining, might in fact lead to unions' integration into both managerial and state hierarchies. In radical variants of the laborist framework, labor law's empowerment of workers at the point of production and in political citizenship is a transitional project *en route* to deeper worker control of corporate governance and social control of investment. In variants attuned particularly to the political economy of Australia and New Zealand, it is a form of neo-corporatist social partnership which maintains the preconditions for collective bargaining through incomes policies implemented by social pacts, centralized arbitration and conciliation, or compulsory unionization.

In North American labor-law scholarship predating 1970, the ideology of laborism is tempered by the more moderate framework of 'industrial pluralism'. The original intent of the New Deal labor policy fully encompassed the three key features of laborism (Barenberg, 1993). Leading postwar scholars, however, reinterpreted the National Labor Relations Act (NLRA) of 1935 in tune with prevailing ideologies of interest-group pluralism and, paradoxically, the Cold War's 'end of ideology' (Klare, 1982; Stone, 1981). Interest-group pluralism views workers and investors as two constituencies of workplace self-government represented, respectively, by unions and managers (Cox, 1959). Their interests are aggregated through collective negotia-tion, akin to the interest-aggregating function of pluralist legislatures. A workplace politics of interest-aggregation contrasts with a politics of class-based ideology in which world-views fundamentally collide or, less probably, are fundamentally trans-formed through collective deliberation.

Leading industrial pluralists—including the US Supreme Court—explicitly embraced an 'integrationist' ideology. That is, the interests of workers and managers are 'accommodated' through collective bargaining; and thereafter, the grievances of individual workers are quieted through arbitrators' creation of a common law that is sensitive to the strains in each workplace. Industrial pluralism bears some resemblance to Kahn-Freund's collective *laissez-faire*. In light of the North American preference for bargaining units no larger than a single company or plant, however, US and Canadian labor law do not easily envisage a pluralism of collective associations that are society-wide in scope. Also, in light of its integrationist commitments, industrial pluralism does not sit comfortably with laborist principles of empowering workers as a social or political class.

2.2 The Conventional Frameworks: 'Producerist' Limitations on the Subject-Matter and Concepts of Labor Law

Not surprisingly, these frameworks reflect their political contexts, often because scholars sought to interpret existing workplace institutions with the explicit or implicit purpose of suggesting feasible, incremental reform to elite policy-makers. The frameworks therefore focus on certain features of the social and economic landscape that were historically contingent and, indeed, were soon to change drastically. Aspects of employment relations relegated to the periphery, such as complex systems of regulating individual employment relations, would soon gain salience and challenge the positive and normative assumptions of the core frameworks.

Each of the conventional frameworks was fundamentally 'producerist'. Scholars focused primarily on legal regulation of collective relations internal to unionized workplaces. This had seven implications for labor-law scholarship before the 1970s, some of which are only visible through the lens of hindsight and the focus of 'presentist' concerns.

First, although the literature included precise analysis of the formation and terms of individual employment contracts, the subject was often treated as a mere prologue to understanding the law's obstruction or facilitation of collectivization. 'Legal enactments' directly setting the terms of employment were treated as a 'gloss' to collective bargaining (Kahn-Freund, 1959: 248). The individual's right to a safe and healthy workplace, generally encoded in long-standing rules of tort or in factory legislation, was the exception that highlighted the rule and, in any event, sat comfortably with producerism's implicit emphasis on workplace 'public goods'. (Relevant scholarship on tort law is discussed in Chapter 2 of this volume.)

Secondly, relatively little attention was given to the demographics of labor-market supply—race, gender, age, unemployment, informal-sector employment, and so on—and their potential relevance for individual employment rights in the formal sector, such as anti-discrimination rights or secure pension entitlements in a multicultural and aging society. Thirdly, the legal infrastructure of external labor markets—a wide panoply of rights and policies outside the workplace that affect supply and demand for labor and employees' relative bargaining power, including social insurance and macroeconomic policy—was not well-integrated into the core frameworks.

Fourthly, labor law was viewed as a highly autonomous subsystem within the broader legal sytem. The relationships between labor law and such fields as family law, tax law, bankruptcy law, the law of financial institutions, and even corporate law were occasionally but not deeply explored (Owens, 1995). Fifthly, apart from comparativists' concern about whether national institutions and norms might be effectively 'transplanted' from one country to another, scholars rarely attempted to map transnational phenomena, such as the interaction of multiple state systems of labor law, the indirect effect of international regulation of trade, capital, and labor flows on domestic labor law, or the potential impact of direct supranational rule-making in bilateral, regional, and global instruments.

Sixthly, the broad features of workplace relations seemed relatively stable, in light of the postwar consolidation of mass production, domestic Keynesianism, and the class alignments embedded in the US Democratic Party, the British, Australian, and New Zealand Labour Parties, and the Canadian Liberal Party. Scholarship was not strongly focused on the capacity of labor-law systems to absorb or promote 'adjustment' to rapid changes in production systems, market structures, political commitments to regulatory regimes, and macroeconomic crises.

Finally, the stability of broad features of workplace organization generated little self-examination of the normative foundations of producerist scholarship, however intense and illuminating the debates within those frameworks. Resting their analysis on received pluralist and social-democratic values—based on theories of collective coordination or on class analysis, respectively—labor lawyers did not closely engage with contested concepts regarding, for example, distributive justice and individual rights within liberal political theory; productive, allocative, and dynamic efficiency within economic theory; the cultural and psychological bases of domination based on class, gender, and race within critical social theory; innovation, adaptability, and informal power relations within organization theory; the displacement of collective producerism by mass consumerism within sociological theory; and macroeconomic management and relations between civil society and the state apparatus within state theory (with the important exceptions that Australian scholarship attended to the macro-economic impact of centralized arbitration and that the pluralism of Kahn-Freund and his students explicitly stemmed from close inquiry into state–society theorization) (Collins, 1997).

After the 1960s, four sources of disruption brought each of these features of pro-ducerist labor-law scholarship into relief and challenged the capacity of the core frameworks to sustain the field.

3 FAILURE TO IMPLEMENT EXISTING STATUTES

Union density in the United States began to decline in the late 1950s. That trend accelerated in the 1970s and 1980s—earlier and more rapidly than in the other countries under review—to the point where the crisis of the New Deal labor policy was undeniable. Much of US labor law scholarship in the period is an effort to explain that crisis. While critiques of the industrial pluralist framework were launched by new intellectual currents—law-and-economics, critical legal studies, feminism, and pragmatism—a leading account of the crisis, and an audaciously simple proposal for overcoming it through legal engineering, came from within industrial pluralism.

In the most prominent US labor law article of the 1980s, Professor Paul Weiler adduced empirical evidence that the precipitous decline in union density resulted from unions' decreasing victory rate in National Labor Relations Board (NLRB) elections; and that employers' sky-rocketing rate of unfair labor practices—a tenfold increase in firings of union supporters in the two decades before 1980—was substantially responsible for those election defeats. Weiler argued that there was no administratively and politically feasible means of deterring the violations. Although the NLRB had been an aggressive ally of the industrial unions before the 1950s, the agency's enforcement powers were thereafter neutered by legislative, administrative, and judicial constraints (Gross, 1995). The only solution was to eliminate the employer's opportunity to fire union supporters, which, in turn, required elimination of the campaign period preceding NLRB elections (Weiler, 1983). Weiler's proposal entailed reversal of a single Supreme Court decision requiring that workers demonstrate their majority support for a union by a secret-ballot vote, preceded by an election campaign, rather than by signing union membership cards without the employer's awareness (*Linden Lumber v NLRB*, 419 US 301 (1974)).

In effect, Weiler's argument ascribed the decline of American unionism and the attendant failure of the Democratic Party to maintain its postwar path toward a social democratic politics to a single, obscure rule of labor law—a bold socio-legal claim. Reversal of that rule could revive industrial pluralism. His thesis gained special importance when it became a centerpiece of the Clinton administration's Commission on labor law reform, of which Weiler was chief counsel.

Weiler, a professor at Harvard Law School, had emigrated from Canada, where he was a prominent legal scholar and had served on the provincial labor board of British Columbia. As with Kahn-Freund, his central thesis about his adopted country's labor law draws extensively on a comparison with his homeland. Canada's labor relations and labor law are much the same as the United States', with three exceptions: Canadian workers can choose their majority representative through card majorities or 'snap elections' and therefore need not run the gauntlet of extended election campaigns; Canadian employers do not—and do not have the opportunity to—discharge union supporters at the extraordinary rate of their US peers; and Canada's collective bargaining system is not in free fall.

Weiler's thesis has come under criticism and increasingly so as the crisis of collective bargaining has spread from the United States to many other advanced capitalist economies. An academic industry now debates the accuracy of his empirical arguments about the relations among employer unfair labor practices, union election outcomes, and union decline.

An alternative scholarly response to Weiler accepts his empirical arguments but questions (*a*) whether industrial pluralism for plant-level workforces is well suited to the rapid reorganization and capital mobility that mark contemporary corporate governance, and (*b*) whether 'underground' card-signing by workers can either realize an ideal of deliberative decision-making by workers or dissipate adversarialism on the part of managers who have many means to dispose of unwanted unions other than by firing union supporters during organizing drives.

Effectively abandoning industrial pluralism, this critique calls for such 'radical pragmatic' reforms as: legal facilitation of 'above-ground' fora for deliberation by workers, among themselves and together with other stakeholders; establishing workers' right to choose multi-employer bargaining units defined by geography or by sectoral networks; entrenching workers' entitlement to information and resources that would enable them to choose knowingly among a range of empowering forms of workplace governance, including unions, joint consultative committees, and self-managing teams; and redesigning regulatory systems to provide material and symbolic incentives for workers and managers to adopt labor-empowering and innovative workplace organizations (Barenberg, 1994).

Each set of proposed reforms—the industrial pluralist or the radical pragmatist— faces the paradox that it is designed to remedy the state's failure to enforce existing labor rights, a failure that rests on political opposition to worker empowerment. The same political opposition that accounts for regulatory failure is likely to defeat proposals that would extend and enforce worker rights even more robustly. Significant labor law reform is therefore tied directly to such larger legal initiatives as campaign-finance reform, public access to corporate-dominated mass media, and the like. In this way, the erosion of effective labor-law implementation brings to light not only the weaknesses in industrial pluralist ideology but also the unstable boundaries of labor-law scholarship.

The failure effectively to enforce collective bargaining law and the attendant erosion of union density also had powerful consequences for scholarly debates over individual employment protections. Should direct enactment of the terms of employment contracts—such as rights against discrimination and unjust dismissal—fill the gap left when collectively bargained standards receded? Or should the legal system instead reinforce a trend toward unregulated, individualized labor markets? Responses to these questions are discussed in Sections 5 and 6.

4 ENACTMENT OF NEW LEGISLATION

'Industrial pluralist' scholars in the United States were challenged by administrative failures to effectively enforce legislation they had previously—and painstakingly— reinterpreted in accordance with their conventional framework. Their British, Australian, and New Zealand counterparts faced the more comprehensive task of defending 'collective *laissez-faire*' and 'laborism' against new legislative initiatives that originated in libertarian and utilitarian philosophies radically at odds with their received frameworks.

The British experience can be—very roughly—divided into three phases: legislation of the 1970s; enactments of the Thatcher government; and post-Thatcher initatives of New Labour. In the first phase, British scholars witnessed a kind of unfolding social experiment. In 1969, a Royal Commission, with the participation of leading labor scholars, was the focus of contesting views about the advisibility of state intervention in industrial relations. In 1971, the Conservative's Industrial Relations Act (IRA) implemented an interventionist, juridified program, complete with a new National Industrial Relations Court. In 1974, Labour's 'Social Contract' program swung the pendulum back, restoring the 1906 immunities and moderating though not eliminating the Conservatives' regulation of union recognition.

British scholars debated whether legislative reforms of the 1970s did or should mark a fundamental departure from the tradition of collective *laissez-faire* in the direction of a more statist regime compatible with laborist principles (cf. Kahn-Freund, 1977: 45–6; and Davies and Freedland, 1993: 10, 422–4). This phase helped bring to the surface an idea long emphasized by the American legal realists—that even concepts like 'abstentionism' presume a baseline of complex government regulation difficult to square with a vision of thoroughgoing autonomy of collective actors. That is, the relative power of labor and capital is shaped by the entitlements and endowments protected by the state regime of property, contracts, and tort, not to mention corporation law and many other fields of public regulation. Even union immunity from certain tort liabilities is an affirmative legal initiative of an inevitably state-directed regulatory system (ibid.) Some scholars acknowledged the conceptual strength of the realist position but resisted its full-blooded positivist implications, in light of the manifestly entrenched, anti-statist practices of British unionism. Those social practices indeed proved resistant to the blunt state engineering of the IRA (Hepple, 1995).

The vulnerability of Britain's voluntarist labor relations, however, was demonstrated by Thatcher's more adroit state-led project of market restructuring in the name, ironically, of a different sort of *laissez-faire*. In this second phase, British scholars encountered a 'step by step', anti-collectivist legislative program reflecting the radically libertarian philosophy of Hayek—a program which, according to Hayek himself, required continuous, vigilant state intervention to maintain an individualistic labor market.

This period called for scholars' re-examination and, if possible, fortification of first principles in defense of collective bargaining under conditions of macroeconomic crisis and intensified international competition. In light of producerist assumptions discussed above in Section 2.2, these jurisprudential projects did not come easily to conventional scholars who had long rested their normative case on pragmatic maxims, such as 'labor's power is collective power'. Among the obvious points for research were: the development of more precise *metrics* of power in individual and collective labor markets under contemporary economic conditions; the *consequences* of alternative labor-law regimes for inflation and for effective production systems; and rigorous analysis of the normative *legitimacy* of (*a*) new modes of workplace governance and (*b*) particular *degrees* of relative bargaining power in the new economic environment. By the end of the Thatcher–Major years, these projects were indeed advanced by scholars who effectively brought macroeconomic policy into the center of laborist frameworks (Davies and Freedman, 1993), and by legal economists who extended conventional frameworks into the realm of individual employment relations—and whose work is further described in Section 6.1 (Deakin and Wilkinson, 1999).

In the New Labour phase, scholars were faced with the question whether to try to rebuild collectivist institutions under the conventional frameworks or instead under newly minted conceptions of the role of labor law in a capitalist democracy. From more radical quarters came proposals for the constitutionalization of laborist principles, while realists proposed legislative programs to rebuild collectivism step by step in the fashion it had been successfully dismantled in the previous decade (Ewing, 1995; Hepple, 1995). Further important debates—over programs of social partnership and the increasingly prominent field of individual employment legislation—are entangled with changes in political economy and are therefore discussed in the next section.

In Australian scholarship, the most salient period of regulatory challenge to settled frameworks was symbolized by the Industrial Relations Reform Act of 1993 and the Workplace Relations Act of 1996. The Australian debate focuses in part on the question whether those Acts mark a watershed between an era of centralized arbitration and one of decentralized bargaining *en route* to deregulation, or are instead a large but incremental step in the ongoing transformation of a system always characterized by a laborist hybrid of bargaining and arbitral regulation (Creighton and Smith, 2000: 46). Both views gain credence, paradoxically, from the sheer growth in number of alternative statutory systems of regulated bargaining at national and subnational levels. None the less, there seems little doubt that Australian unions' former 'dependency' on state arbitration systems, followed by the legislative withdrawal of the closed shop and employers' strategic seizing of the opportunity to introduce enterprise and individual bargaining, point in directions that escape the conventional frameworks of labor-law scholarship.

Scholars of New Zealand labor law faced legislative enactments even more stark than their British and Australian colleagues. The Employment Contracts Act of 1991 marked a rapid decline in union density and the installation of individual contracting after decades of collective contracting encouraged by a variety of regulatory instruments.

This section has addressed the challenge to received frameworks posed by legislative reform of collective bargaining and arbitration. The period after the 1960s saw equally important—and equally disruptive—enactments in the area of employment discrimination, unjust dismissal, pension rights, atypical work, and many other aspects of individual employment. These are entwined with changes in the labor market and with new intellectual movements. Scholarly discussion of some of the major statutory developments in the area of individual employment relations is therefore addressed in the next two sections.

5 CHANGES IN THE ECONOMIC AND POLITICAL ENVIRONMENT

The legislative and administrative changes discussed in the previous two sections are, of course, consequence and cause of changes in the economic and political environment of workplaces and labor markets. Legislative and administrative changes, however, pose less decisive challenges to the received frameworks than do transformations in political economy. If legal scholars seek incremental fine-tuning of new legislation or enforcement strategies, then conventional concepts may seem sufficient. If they seek reversal of new legal policy, it may seem adequate to speak in terms of dichotomies grounded in existing scholarship. In either event, conventional legal scholarship is predominantly aimed, implicitly or explicitly, at an audience of labor-law policy-makers—aimed, that is, at decision-makers empowered to manipulate the levers of legislative, administrative, and judicial institutions that directly affect the workplace.

This may be less true when legal scholars must respond to broad changes in political economy. There may be no obvious, pre-existing lever of labor law to grasp in response to complex and novel changes in production systems, international markets, and political alignments that indirectly affect workplaces and labor markets. There may be no obvious policy-makers who speak in the conventional terms of legal scholarship and who occupy positions in the state apparatus that would enable them to act as intermediaries between the scholar and the new political and economic environment. Hence, labor-law scholars must look to new legal institutions and new legal concepts that may well fall outside conventional frameworks. Or scholars may step away from the self-assigned role as technocratic advisors and act instead as critical analysts, legal sociologists, or historians—roles that may entail intellectual distance from existing labor-law regimes and abandonment of conventional frameworks.

After 1970, several disruptions in the political and economic environment of workplace relations and labor markets (in addition to the important macroeconomic shifts mentioned above in Section 4) indeed swept many labor-law scholars in fundamentally new directions.

5.1 New Production Systems and Internal Labor-Market 'Flexibility'

The years of stagflation and oil crisis seemed to usher in new production systems and modes of corporate organization that posed challenges to conventional labor law. According to some analysts, the old 'Fordist' production system—based on centralized mass production and adversarial labor relations—was supplanted in the 1980s and 1990s by a 'post-Fordist' system characterized by decentralized, specialized production and cooperation between workers and managers. Regardless whether the new production systems were diffused more widely in managerial and academic theory than in organizational reality, they provoked debate and reform on the frontier of labor law.

To their proponents, the new collaborative systems empowered workers through self-managing teams, flatter workplace hierarchies, and blurring of the long-standing distinction according to which managers 'conceived' production processes and workers unimaginatively 'executed' work tasks. Their opponents argued that the systems marked no significant break with dehumanizing Fordist assembly lines, but instead merely implemented new modes of speed-up, greater and potentially abusive discretion in managers' allocation of tasks to workers, and heightened integration of workers' collective action into managerial structures.

The debate over the new productions systems arose among scholars in all the countries under examination, inflected by their particular legal frameworks and the political contests of the time. Against the backdrop of New Zealand's aggressive individualization of employment contracts, for example, scholars saw the promotion of labor–management cooperation as a patent program to displace collective bargaining.

In the United Kingdom, exponents of laborist frameworks found the vocabulary of 'post-Fordism' aligned with a broader program of 'social partnership' that in action if not rhetoric opposed workers' collective activity and promoted labor-market individualization in the name of efficiency rather than redistribution. Worse, this program was found lurking in the EU's heralded 'social dialogue' and in New Labour's Employment Relations Act of 1999, which purported to strengthen union rights even if not to alter the main structure of Thatcherite labor law (Wedderburn, 2000).

Another current of scholarship departed explicitly from the traditional discourses of collective *laissez-faire* and laborism. The time had come for British labor law to take seriously a new discourse of 'social justice and integration'. That discourse required attention not only to the microeconomics of labor markets for the sake of social inclusion of non-union and unemployed workers, but also to modes of workplace representation and consultation other than collective bargaining—in fact, if not name, the kind of workplace participation trumpeted by post-Fordism—for the sake of incremental democratization and softening of organizational hierarchies (Collins, 1997).

In the Australian context, economic restructuring raised questions about the capacity of entrenched, centralized arbitration systems to adapt to decentralized production without encouraging labor market segmentation that, as in the otherwise much different British case, threatened to leave the 'peripheral' workforce relatively unprotected. Some scholars saw 'facilitative' forms of arbitral regulation as the most promising route to capture the benefits of flexible production while minimizing the costs of economic dualism (Arup, 1991). As discussed below, labor-law scholars throughout the English-speaking countries increasingly focused on similar 'pragmatist' forms of regulation after the 1980s.

The legal debate raised by the new production systems was most focused, perhaps, in the United States. The spread of the new systems awakened scholars—and the Republican Party—to the surprising fact that section 8(a)(2) of the National Labor Relations Act, originally designed to eliminate the company-dominated unions of the 1930s, also bans nearly all forms of teams and joint committees that anchor the post-1980s collaborative workplace. The predominant view among US industrial pluralists is that section 8(a)(2) is a relic of days when unsophisticated employees could not tell the difference between repressive company unions and beneficial employee committees. As with any other choice afforded consenting adults within a liberal legal order, workers should be free to decide whether they wished to enter collaborative production systems that aligned workers' perceived interests with managers'—a form of cooperation and integration that, in any event, concords with the pacific goals of industrial pluralism (Weiler, 1990).

In all three of the conventional frameworks of English-language scholarship, the new production systems brought to the surface an unacknowledged split between 'adversarialists' and 'cooperationists'. The core concepts of collective bargaining are fluid enough to be conceived in either light. New historical scholarship, provoked by this debate, reveals that the New Deal labor policy in the United States—influenced by the radical-pragmatist philosopher John Dewey—was a sophisticated compound of the two positions: workers' and managers' collective representatives would cooperate and engage in mutually transformative dialogue, but only atop a legally protected foundation of workers' organizational independence and empowerment (Barenberg, 1993).

Today's cooperationists often fail to recognize that their proposed repeal of the ban on collaborative labor organizations would not, in fact, afford workers the freedom to choose collectively whether to enter into collaborative rather than adversarial relations with managers. Managers would instead be entitled to impose unilaterally the collaborative option, as they are in any event doing illegally in great numbers.

If, to the contrary, workers in any of the countries under examination were granted an affirmative entitlement to make that collective choice, then the labor-law regime would move outside the bounds of the three conventional frameworks. That is, labor law would validate workers' right to make a fundamental choice about the organization of production systems, a choice with repercussions for technology, product design, corporate boundaries, marketing, finance, and other long-standing matters of managers' highest strategic prerogative. Labor-law scholars could no longer respect the boundary between their field and the law of corporate governance and financial institutions. The new radical pragmatist framework noted above in Section 3 and discussed further below in Section 7 embraces this broader scope of worker self-governance, taking the new systems of production as an opportunity to make labor law the vehicle for worker-centered corporate design that it has promised but never delivered.

5.2 New Employer–Employee Relationships

In the 1980s and 1990s, new systems of production and organization entailed—or were widely perceived to entail—more fluid and more swiftly changing corporate boundaries, sometimes within networks of firms engaged in vertically or horizontally interrelated processes of production, design, distribution, or service provision. These changes in corporate boundaries, in turn, entail greater instability in the relationship between employer and employee.

This increase in labor-market velocity—and employment insecurity—is reinforced by various forms of strategic behavior by employers. Some strategic behavior is familiar to the conventional frameworks of labor law—such as employers' attempts to rid themselves of unionized workforces through bankruptcy proceedings, sales of company assets, mergers, or other major business reconfigurations.

Some employer strategies are less easily assimilated to the conventional frameworks. For example, one of the hallmarks of 'globalized labor markets' is an increase in outsourcing of production and therefore employment, often across national borders. At the limit, 'manufacturer' or 'retailer' brands of goods and services no longer engage in actual production of their goods and services. Instead, they retain only design and marketing functions in-house, and spin off production processes to low-wage, non-union factories and service centers owned by other, often undercapitalized firms. Other strategies are to convert in-house workforces into temporary workers whose ostensible employer is an intermediary agency—or into 'self-employed', independent contractors.

For labor and employment scholars in all the countries under examination, the new configurations of employment raise obvious, important questions. When a supplier violates labor rights—of the source country, the brand's home country, or international labor standards—should the outsourcing firm be held liable? Should a firm that ultimately controls, uses, or profits from a worker's labor be responsible for labor-rights compliance or should the obligation or risk lie with the intermediary agency or the employee turned independent contractor?

Labor-law scholars responded to these structural changes and strategic behaviors with a wide range of innovative proposals. Whatever the proposed reform, however, the underlying problem is not easily captured in conventional frameworks that assume a collective relationship between a stable workforce and a single managerial hierarchy. This fact is demonstrated by the relative paucity of compelling proposals for restoring full-fledged collective bargaining under such conditions of labor-market entropy and velocity. Instead, the new proposals seek to protect employee rights primarily by using the leverage of international agreements, sovereign standards, or investor and consumer pressure. If effective, that leverage would be transmitted through managerial channels—that is, through the administrative structure of a single firm or through contractual relationships among the managers of firms, suppliers, and employment agencies. The potential role of workers' collective organizations in this new political economy is discussed in Section 7.

5.3 External Labor-Market 'Flexibility' and the Erosion of the Welfare State

Flexibility in 'internal labor markets', associated with the new production methods discussed above in Section 5.1, refers to the heightened discretion afforded employers in assigning workers to do the various tasks internal to the firm. Flexibility in 'external labor markets', by contrast, refers to employers' legal capacity to discharge workers, requiring workers to move from one firm to another through labor markets operating outside the administrative hierarchy of any one employer. The political and economic drive for increased flexibility in external labor markets heightens the importance of legal questions pertaining to individual employment contracts, relative to collective institutions.

The individualization of labor markets raises four salient legal issues: first, the preconditions for the formation and termination of individual employment contracts; secondly, whether the law will impose substantive terms of individual employment; thirdly, whether individual employees may waive any such explicit or implied terms; and fourthly, whether employees' social insurance—formerly attached to presumptively stable employment relationships—will be vested instead in the state, the market, or in new forms of employment-based relationships.

The first three issues are much more significant in the United Kingdom, Canada, Australia, and New Zealand than in the United States. In the United States, the common-law doctrine of 'employment at will' already establishes a baseline of complete flexibility. That is, individual employment contracts have no duration at all, in the sense that the employer may discharge the worker and the worker may quit *at any moment* without either party, for that reason, violating the contract. Also, employers may discharge the worker *for any reason*, even arbitrary or malicious, without violating any explicit or implied term that dismissals must be fair or just.

When British or Australian labor lawyers debate the pros and cons of increasing labor-market flexibility by relaxing restrictions on temporary or part-time work, by shortening the required duration of employment contracts, by diminishing protections against dismissal, and the like, the potential new baseline of employee protection remains so far above that of United States law that it is still nearly unintelligible to US lawyers and market participants—even if US labor markets and ideology set the global horizon for 'flexibilization', at least during the gilded 1990s.

Even in the United States, of course, workers covered by a collective bargaining agreement are generally entitled to protection against unjust dismissal and their incumbency is protected by seniority rules. The near evaporation in the coverage of collective contracts has raised discussion among legal commentators about the need for legal imposition of rules against unjust discharge in individual employment contracts, accompanied by a brief period of innovation by state judges and legislators (Weiler, 1990).

More interesting, perhaps, is another response by US legal scholars to the almost total individualization of employment contracts, the diminution in employment security, and the perceived increase in labor-market velocity. These developments have highlighted the fact that, in the land of the weak welfare state, much if not most social insurance—unemployment compensation, health-care coverage, compensation for disabling injuries, even income subsidies paid in the form of tax credits—has attached in the postwar period not only to the citizen's relationship to the state but also to the worker's relationship to an employer. The US model has been aptly dubbed the 'employee welfare state' (Charny, 1996). One response by respected American legal scholars, perhaps unintelligible to their peers in other advanced economies, is to celebrate the recent erosion of the employee welfare state and to offer intellectual validation of the resulting *laissez-faire* model, in which individuals are ruggedly responsible for purchasing 'social' insurance in the private market —not only for health care, old-age pensions, and disability, but also for such improbably insurable events as unemployment (ibid.). In this view, industrial pluralism is rightly replaced by individual *laissez-faire*. The normative foundation of this program is less the Hayekian libertarianism that undergirds Thatcherist legislation and more an optimistic version of the utilitarianism that underpins welfare economics.

British and Australian scholars have launched powerful critiques of this position, arguing that the institutions of an effective welfare state and of robust macroeconomic management are predicates to equitable outcomes in labor markets and workplaces (Hepple, 1995; Davies and Freedland, 1993). This response itself, however, shifts the debate beyond the producerist bounds of conventional labor-law frameworks.

5.4 New Demographics and Identities in Labor-Market Supply

A change in the political economy with even greater impact than the new production systems and labor-market patterns discussed above is the entry of women into the labor force, and the social pressure to end labor-market segmentation based on race, gender, age, disability, and sexual orientation. Conventional labor-law frameworks rooted in class analysis are shaken, though not necessarily toppled, by new employment rights—and by corporate systems of human resource management that emerge, in part, from the cultural politics of 'identity'.

Legislation against discrimination in employment—apart from its direct effects on labor-market segmentation to be discussed presently—has indirect effects on individual employment relations that may equal in importance the direct effects of unfair-dismissal law and other implied and explicit terms discussed above in Section 5.3. Employers who are legally bound to provide equal treatment to men and women, black and white, old and young, are effectively obligated to implement rationalized systems of 'human resource management'. To avoid liability for discrimination, employers implement procedural systems of record-keeping, warning, and notice, and substantive systems of uniform and merit-based standards. As a practical matter, these systems are applied to all employees, of course, not just 'protected groups' such as women and blacks. Human resource systems implemented on such a wide scale are new to conventional frameworks of labor law and, indeed, are rejected as flatly anti-collectivist by some adherents to the conventional frameworks (Wedderburn, 2000).

The greatest influence of anti-discrimination law on labor-law scholarship comes from the law's direct attack on labor-market segmentation. Some of the most politically effective scholarship on discrimination has been produced by scholars stretching the equality principle beyond the producerist limits of conventional frameworks, as, for example, did the scholars who laid the groundwork for British anti-discrimination legislation. Once again influenced by personal experience in comparative systems, these scholars drew on their deep knowledge of the racial disparities of South Africa (Hepple, 1970).

In all countries, the principle of equality requires, first, that similarly situated workers be treated equally, entailing such fundamental rights as the entitlement to equal pay for men and women and for blacks and whites when they do the same or comparable jobs. A second requirement is the obligation to open jobs to all qualified candidates—that is, the right of equal treatment in hiring, training, and promotion. The implementation of this right entails protracted economic, social, and cultural change. Sex segregation by job, firm, and industry has remarkably deep roots.

The problem of labor-market segmentation has generated—or drawn on—some of the most important feminist, critical-race, and pragmatist scholarship in the legal literature. This scholarship turns to ethnographic, cultural, and psychological methods to explore the resistance of employers and employees to job integration—and the limitations of judicial understandings of discrimination. The 'gendered' nature of job categories is sustained by hostile micro-behaviors in the workplace itself and by conceptions of masculinity and feminity entrenched in the wider culture (Schultz, 1990). The legal system may be capable of uncovering the racial and gendered motivation of employers only through exploration of unconscious intention and the cultural meanings attributed to workplace practices (Lawrence, 1987).

Scholarly exploration of the problem of remediation of wrongful gender or racial segmentation shows that discriminatory practices may also be embedded in organizational pathologies even more generalized than sex or race inequities. For this reason, the most difficult task of anti-discrimination law may begin only after a finding of liability; it is not enough for the legal system to bang its fist on the blameworthy employer's table. Restoring workplace equity may entail more or less comprehensive restructuring of the organization to cleanse the workplace of metastasized patterns of abusive, arbitrary, and perhaps inefficient decision-making (Sturm, 2001). This may require remedial programs in which managers, workers, and external auditors together ensure that corporate compliance programs are effectively integrated into the organization's core functions. In labor-law scholarship, it may require more attention than given by conventional frameworks to the internal compliance programs of human resources departments.

More detailed treatment of scholarship on gender equality is presented in Chapter 11 of this volume.

5.5 Internationalization of Labor Law

Labor law, as much as any other field of scholarship, has been disrupted and redirected by the knot of issues known as 'globalization'. Although transnational analyses of labor law are relatively new and incoherent, these new debates may ultimately prove central to the core issues of domestic as well as international regulation. Two interrelated questions of special interest for the general trajectory of labor-law scholarship are, first, the role of regional and global institutions in the formulation and enforcement of labor rights and, secondly, the capacity of worker organizations to bargain with transnational corporations and commodity chains that stretch across the diverse labor-relations systems of nation-states.

5.5.1 *Regional and Global Labor Regimes—A Critique of 'Core Labor Rights'?*

The questions raised by globalization that seem most easily addressed by the traditional frameworks are issues of social law in such multi-tiered regional institutions as the European Community (EC) and the North American Free Trade Agreement (NAFTA)—that is, labor-law issues that seem most closely analogous to familiar questions of domestic 'labor federalism', the division of governmental powers in the creation of labor norms, and the scope and content of regulatory intervention.

In the event, however, the encounter of European scholars with the particular landscape of EC labor law is more disorienting to traditional frameworks than simply an application of familiar concepts to new terrain. The multi-tiered structure of the EC cannot be understood through traditional models of federalism. The early goal of 'harmonization' of standards across EC countries reached an early impasse, in light of the diversity of national conditions, the distance of European institutions from local collective actors, and the jealousy of nation-states about the politically sensitive subject of collective power relations. But what could meaningfully replace the goal of harmonization? Minimum requirements or juridical definition of individual rights were proposed as alternatives to upward levelling, but these too required convergent legal definitions—of the minima and the rights-in-context—which merely replicate the difficulties of harmonization (Deakin and Wilkinson, 1994; Simitis and Lyon-Cean, 1996). Would standards, whatever their subject-matter scope and content, continue to be defined principally by the European Court of Justice or instead by the administrative-technocratic arms of European institutions (the Commission) or by fortified democratic bodies (the Parliament, the Council, or some novel organs)? This seemingly traditional question of division of powers led scholars more or less directly, in the case of social rights, to the question whether norm-definition and norm-enforcement would take the form of 'hard', juridified law or instead some 'soft' combination of goals, recommendations, reporting, and the like. Many saw the soft-law alternative as a not-so-hidden means of devaluing European social law compared to the hard law creating the common economic market (ibid.). But how could social law be hardened in light of the local diversity and entrenchment of labor-relations institutions that had obstructed the project of harmonization itself? In this light, some saw the dilemma as an opportunity to develop such pragmatist architectures as 'comitology' and 'open methods of coordination' that combine hard law's virtue of regulatory discipline and soft-law's promise of continuous strengthening of substantive social protections adapted to local contexts (see Sect. 7 below).

While scholars have also attempted to apply conventional frameworks of 'labor federalism' to NAFTA's multi-tiered institutions, akin to the analysis of EU social law, this approach is even more difficult to sustain in light of NAFTA's peculiar structure. Indeed, the novelty of NAFTA's labor-side accord generates idiosyncratic questions for research that may challenge scholars' settled understandings of the importance of 'core labor rights'.

Over many decades, the Conventions of the International Labor Organization (ILO) have garnered great legitimacy, culminating in the 1998 Declaration of Fundamental Principles and Rights. Those who believe that labor rights should be enforced through multilateral trade agreements, such as NAFTA and the World Trade Organization (WTO), generally assume that the ILO's core labor rights provide the appropriate international standards. The NAFTA model takes a different tack. It imposes no new supranational obligation on its member states—other than to require, first, that each state effectively enforce its existing domestic labor law and, secondly, that each state commit to improve its existing labor rights. These obligations seem toothless at first blush and, for that reason, NAFTA was opposed by North American labor movements.

In fact, the obligation to effectively enforce domestic labor law is a powerful lever—or could be, if regional institutions were, in turn, empowered effectively to ensure compliance with that obligation. Existing substantive rights in the labor law of each North American state and most other nation-states across the globe are generally quite strong—sufficiently strong, at least, so that genuinely *effective enforcement* of those rights would galvanize workers' collective action much more than would the addition of highly abstract phrases to the substantive rights on the books. This is the implication of Professor Weiler's scholarship, discussed above, demonstrating that the decline of American labor is attributable in large part to the failure to enforce the existing law of unfair labor practices. Similarly, it is likely that effective enforcement of the robust labor rights in Mexican law would cause a virtual social revolution through new organizing by independent union federations in that country.

Secondly, a supranational standard that focuses on effective enforcement *of domestic labor rights* has a double virtue. It is less vulnerable to the charge that powerful countries, perhaps with ulterior geo-political or protectionist motives, are using global trade regimes as a means to impose their interpretation of appropriate rights on less powerful sovereign states. At the same time, domestic rights provide a baseline of finely textured rules adapted to local workplace and labor-market institutions.

It is at this point that a critique of 'core labor standards'—generated by such quirky developments in international political economy as NAFTA—may cut deeply into conventional scholarship about international labor rights. The ILO's core labor rights are phrased in highly abstract terms akin to constitutional rights—workers' 'freedom of association', freedom from 'discrimination', and the like. These abstract rights are extremely susceptible to manipulation or empty application by international or domestic elites. In any event, they give little guidance to regional or global bodies attempting to decide such ambiguous and highly contested questions as—to list three of a thousand examples—whether the closed shop, the pre-hire agreement, or the joint labor–management council violates freedom of association in a specific national or sub-national context. Domestic labor law at least provides a thick web of rights that can serve as a baseline for continuous strengthening of rights-definition and rights-enforcement—again, assuming that the architecture of global, regional, or domestic institutions provides incentives and support for such continuous strengthening, a disruptive problem for conventional scholarship discussed further in Section 7.

5.5.2 *Transnational Collective Bargaining*

The legal capacity of worker organizations to bargain with multinational corporations is a question that scholars have raised for at least thirty years (Wedderburn, 1972). The answer to that question requires, among other things, a comprehensive catalogue of the constraints against transnational organizing, bargaining, and striking embedded in the domestic law of the various nation-states in which each multinational corporation operates. Potential constraints lie in each country's doctrines regulating secondary strikes, definition of bargaining units, employers' duties of recognition and bargaining, extraterritorial application of labor law, agency relationships among unions and their overseas supporters, and many others.

This points to a more general, urgent project facing labor-law scholars, namely, a comprehensive legal-realist mapping of the interaction among multiple labor-law systems and of the economic consequences of that interaction—a project necessary both to assess the legality of multinational collective bargaining and to grasp fully the purported problem of social dumping or 'races to the bottom', through which high-standard countries and corporations 'level down' to their low-standard competitors (Deakin and Wilkinson, 1994). In light of their producerist bias, conventional frameworks may not be well-suited either to extend analysis beyond workplaces and nation-wide collectivism or to explore the interacting legal infrastructures of labor, capital, and product markets.

European scholars' analysis of the role of collective bargaining and 'social dialogue' at the trans-state level of the European Community, of course, directly implicates these substantive questions. That analysis, however, again demonstrates that traditional concepts may be hard-pressed to answer fundamental questions resulting from the internationalization of labor law, such as the legitimate 'representivity' of European-wide union federations and employer associations, in light of the problems of national diversity and institutional distance between regional and national institutions (Bercusson, 1999). While European-wide collective agreements or works councils within multinational enterprises seem assimilable to conventional frameworks, this appears less true of sectoral or economy-wide collective bargaining at the European level. Hopes for European collective bargaining often rest on top-down support for European-wide collective actors by existing European Community institutions, a form of corporatism that does not sit easily with traditional laborism, let alone Kahn-Freund's collective *laissez-faire*.

6 INSURGENT INTELLECTUAL MOVEMENTS IN THE LEGAL ACADEMY

In any academic discipline, as in everyday ideology, conventional frameworks may prove resilient and durable even in the face of changes in hard reality as thorough-going as those discussed in Sections 3, 4, and 5 above. In labor law, new schools of thought, emerging after the 1960s, sought to give more compelling accounts than conventional frameworks of several important changes in political economy and legislation. Certain strands of feminist, pragmatist, and ethnographic scholarship seem the most promising.

6.1 Law and Economics

Within the methodological pluralism of US law faculties, the law-and-economics movement became the predominant school of thought of the 1980s and 1990s. That movement radiated out to other English-speaking countries, if not gaining the pre-eminence it enjoys in the United States. Law and economics is concerned primarily with assessing the impact of legal rules on the microeconomics of wealth maximization (which is taken by scholars, not always self-consciously, as a proxy for utilitarian welfare maximization) and, less frequently, with exposing blockages to libertarian freedoms of individual exchange.

Until recent years, the law of collective bargaining has been guided instead by goals of redistribution and, secondarily, of macroeconomic stabilization and growth. The scholars attracted to the field are largely sympathetic with these aims. For these reasons, it has been one of the last bastions penetrated by the law-and-economics insurgency. The repeatedly cited but one-time foray into the field of collective bargaining by the leading law-and-economics generalist is the exception that makes the point (Posner, 1984).

Ironically, one of the pioneers of transaction-cost economics, Oliver Williamson, developed his theory in large part to explain the existence of workplace hierarchy and unionization, rather than to justify individualized labor markets. His thesis is that protections against unjust dismissal—even unionization—are means by which managers 'credibly commit' to job security and fair distribution of future corporate earnings, thereby inducing workers to enter into efficiency-enhancing relations of subordination (Williamson, 1975). There is a second irony in Williamson's project. He presented his thesis at the precise time when the behavior of corporate managers began to demonstrate strongly that such 'implicit contracts' are not, in fact, credible commitments protecting workers against managerial opportunism and when managers' rhetoric, if not their actions, suggested that traditional managerial hierarchies are not functionally necessary to efficiency.

As the subject of labor law has shifted from its primary focus on collective bargaining to an equal concern for individual rights in employment contracts, especially rights against discrimination and unsafe work, legal economists have entered the field in greater numbers. Some legal economists argue that competition in individualized labor markets has remarkable remedial consequences—such as eroding modes of employment discrimination that rely on criteria other than efficiency to allocate workers to jobs, and compensating workers who choose hazardous jobs with wage premiums. Others more skeptical of the market's magic have used economic tools to illuminate a wide range of labor-market phenomena justifying legal intervention into individual employment relations—from arbitrary dismissal to occupational health to discriminatory testing of job applicants (Deakin and Wilkinson, 1999).

There is overwhelming empirical evidence that labor markets and workplaces do not behave in anything like the manner stipulated by the theory of competitive markets or Darwinian organizations, and are unlikely to be made to so behave by legal intervention. Labor markets are pervaded by information asymmetries, coordination problems, and other market failures familiar to economists. They are also idiosyncratically embedded in status hierarchies and other cultural norm-systems more familiar to the sociologist, historian, or ethnographer. The persistence of sex-segregated jobs, discussed above, is only the most salient example. In this light, the emerging school of 'behavioral law and economics'—both empirically minded and attentive to cognitive psychology—may in the future have more to say in the field of labor law than either transaction-cost or neoclassical economics.

6.2 Critical Legal Studies

The 'critical legal studies' network of scholars emerged at roughly the same time as the law-and-economics movement. The two movements deploy conceptions of law that are in many respects antithetical. Legal economists' theory of law is instrumentalist—that is, the costs and benefits created by legal sanctions are viewed as elements of the opportunity set facing rational actors whose preferences, interests, and endowments are pre-fixed or 'exogenous' to legal entitlements. Critical scholars, on the other hand, are concerned precisely about the way that legal norms, particularly the ideological meaning embedded in legal norms, shape culture and consciousness. For critical scholars, therefore, preferences and interests are 'endogenous' to law. As a normative matter, legal economists focus on wealth maximization, while the touchstone for critical scholars is redistribution and emancipation from subordination.

Labor law is therefore a natural field for attention by critical scholars. Early critical studies of labor law in the United States emphasized two ideological aspects of labor law. First, the potential radicalism of the NLRA was reshaped by the moderate ideology of judges and commentators into the pallid mold of industrial pluralism (Klare, 1982; Stone, 1981). Secondly, the legal doctrines of industrial pluralism, through their ideological effects and their bureaucratization of grievance resolution, constricted the spontaneism and militancy of rank-and-file workers and their leaders (ibid.). The critical scholars made a more compelling case for the ideological content of legal texts than for the ideological effect of the arcane texts on rank-and-file consciousness and behavior; the latter thesis required complex ethnographic and historical research well beyond the range of conventional legal scholarship.

Years earlier, Kahn-Freund had made surprisingly similar arguments about the 'mystification of subordination' that labor law might encode and the consequent dangers to direct democracy and spontaneous action in the workplace. The critical scholars' arguments are, however, differently inflected by their inheritence of American legal realism. Where Kahn-Freund's collective *laissez-faire* sees a realm of autonomous action created by government abstention, the critical scholars see capillaries of social power connected in several distinct ways to the arteries of state coercion. Building upon the research questions raised by the critical scholars, later Gramscian scholarship draws on ethnographic and psychoanalytic evidence to show both the consciousness-shaping power of new production systems and the indirect effects of specific labor laws on the seemingly private actions and attitudes of managers and workers within those systems (Barenberg, 1994).

6.3 Feminist Legal Theory

Since the 1970s, feminist scholarship developed increasingly sophisticated arguments to the effect that family law and labor law, conventionally treated as 'separate spheres', are in fact tightly interrelated. Conventional models of labor law presume full-time employment by workers with no care-giving responsibilities and therefore no justification for flexibility in scheduling of daily work or in seniority-based incumbency and compensation. Traditional employment-based social insurance presumes a household division of labor in which one spouse is a wage laborer and the other a provider of unpaid household labor.

In feminist analysis, separate-spheres ideology has critical effects not just on workplace relations but on family life and gender relations as well. Latent power relations in the traditional family are shaped by differential earnings among spouses and expectations of differential earnings in the event of separation and divorce. The premium placed by the labor market, and by traditional social insurance schemes, on continuity of labor-market participation only deepens such differentials in expected earnings and in life advantages among men and women. Feminist scholarship in all the countries discussed in this chapter animated robust campaigns aimed at reform of labor-market regulation, social insurance law, and divorce law—and reform of legal scholarship and education about these fields (Owens, 1995).

An analogous division of social spheres explains in part the 'invisibility' of a pervasive form of workplace abuse, namely, sexual harassment. The routine acceptance or trivialization of sexual predation throughout social life accounted for labor law's failure to treat it as a grounds for liability within the producerist framework. Once brought to light, however, the effects on the labor market of sexualized abuses of power—by impeding women's job performance and career advancement—were undeniable. The legal regulation of workplace harassment, initiated in large part by legal scholarship, is one of the most striking and socially transformative interventions in individual employment relations in recent years, in national labor-law systems throughout the world (MacKinnon, 1979).

Feminist scholarship is, of course, focused sharply on a range of anti-discrimination norms and principles in addition to those undergirding anti-harassment rules. This scholarship—and its ethnographic attention to the micro-behaviors of the workplace— is discussed above in Section 5.4 and in Chapter 11 of this volume.

7 REFLEXIVE LEGAL THEORY, PRAGMATISM, AND ETHNOGRAPHY—SPECULATION ON FUTURE PROGRAMS FOR LABOR LAW SCHOLARSHIP

Two concepts that increasingly animate legal scholarship—pragmatism and reflexivity—as yet have widely varied meanings and run the risk of meaning little. None the less, among scholars of labor law, these rubrics have more specific meaning and promise fruitful programs of future research. 'Reflexive law' refers to the capacity of legal standards to create and protect 'spaces' or 'subsystems' for the social evolution of extra-legal norms which may reciprocally inform those legal standards. Many adherents of reflexive law embrace the normative goal of promoting social spheres in which people may engage in democratic deliberation about their identities and projects, as groups and individuals. 'Pragmatist law' emphasizes the problem-solving function of legal institutions. When legal tools encounter the hard realities of social problems, the means, ends, and substantive norms of legal regulation are unavoidably and mutually transformed. Abstract social rights are most effective if their specific content is viewed as provisional and revisible—and if built into constitutive legal institutions that encourage such rolling norms to head to the top rather than the bottom.

These concepts have obvious applicability to labor law, particularly labor law's two core rights—the right of association among workers, and the right of equality in workers' individual or collective relations with managers. The legal system's enforcement of these two rights is intentionally designed to create a social space in which employees may freely and equally decide their own fate. It is not surprising, then, that the British concepts of abstentionism and collective *laissez-faire* were debated explicitly in the language of reflexivity long before that concept gained currency as a 'school' of legal thought. In this light, labor law is a prototype of reflexive law and may have lessons for the legal project of embedding egalitarian deliberation in other social spheres.

The potential complexity—and usefulness—of the apparently simple concepts of reflexivity and pragmatism are manifest in the contemporary project of defining and enforcing workers' rights of association and equality in international regimes. How can global or regional institutions use such abstract rights in order meaningfully to carve out local spaces for free and equal action in widely differing workplaces, in countries with varying levels of economic development, and in local cultures embodying distinct visions of hierarchy or equality? How can such local application of rights, in turn, inform the interpretation of abstract, universal norms? What legal institutions can protect national labor standards against destructive downward levelling in competition with other nation-states? As discussed above in Section 5.4, European and North American scholars immediately encounter these difficult questions in their exploration of European Community labor law and NAFTA's labor side-accord. Scholars in all countries face the same issues in contemporary debates about the justification and design of global institutions for implementing international labor standards.

From the point of view of scholars studying and designing supranational regimes, 'macro' architectural features that seem especially promising as the focus of research include: regional or global deliberative bodies that include representatives of multiple parties on a more inclusive basis than traditional tripartite organizations such as the ILO; requirements that the performance of national and sub-national actors in defining and enforcing abstract labor rights be fully transparent; obligations of local actors to justify their disparate performance through comparison with similarly situated actors in other legal regimes; systems for comparative evaluation of local peformance by centralized deliberative bodies; disbursement of positive incentives, material and symbolic, to local actors based on such comparative evaluation; and the continuous reformulation and refinement of abstract rights by centralized bodies based on these disciplined local comparisons.

Legal scholars, drawing on concepts of radical pragmatism, have begun to articulate these institutional features, which embody in practical institutions the virtues of comparative labor scholarship discussed above in Sections 2.1, 3, and 5.4 (Barenberg and Evans, forthcoming). If they are to be politically legitimate and practicable, however, more detailed blueprints of regional and global organizations are likely to emerge not from academic workshops but from 'constitutional' deliberations among states and civil society, including labor unions, business federations, workers and entrepreneurs in the informal and agrarian sectors, women workers, and others with vital interests in the supranational rules of labor markets.

Viewed from the level of scholars studying 'micro' practices that may give concrete content to abstract rights, the most promising projects are inspired by feminist legal theory and elaborated by socio-legal scholars drawing on such ethnographic methods as the 'extended case study'. These projects include contextual study of diverse workplace norms that are 'emergent' in local production systems; the range of feasible variation of norms associated with each production system; the local mechanisms, democratic and undemocratic, by which norms are actually inflected within the feasible range; and the extent and manner of local actors' 'reception' of the discourse of international labor rights, their transformation of such discourse, and its integration into their emergent norm-systems. Because these inquires may call for participant-observer research by legal scholars or their interdisciplinary collaborators, scholars may find themselves engaged with local workers, managers, community members, and others in mutually transformative dialogue about the meaning of labor rights.

Scholarship may most fruitfully focus on regional and global institutions in which the macro- and micro-levels intermesh through tribunals, fact-finding missions, or legal compliance teams that include delegates of regional and local organizations. These are intermediating bodies which may themselves carve out space for reflexive definition of labor rights. That is, the most promising processes of implementation and compliance are likely to embody the same principles of free and equal association which the process aims to entrench as a matter of substantive legal right—processes that ensure egalitarian dialogue between central and local actors about the meaning of universal rights in the given local context.

For both academics and legal officials, the danger to be avoided is the unilateral imposition of their views about the meaning of universal rights, in the absence of (a) comprehensive dialogue with local actors who live out practices and norms within their particular production systems, and (b) horizontal deliberation among local actors about their comparative performance in defining and implementing rights in context. In the best case, through the process of dialogic compliance, local participants will democratically refine and embrace labor rights, and central actors and scholars will reinterpret initially abstract rights in directions that promote the collective projects of local actors.

Paradoxically, the most interesting contemporary experiment in such dialogic compliance is the monitoring of global supply chains by non-governmental consortia—paradoxical, because regional and global regimes would embed such experiments in public international institutions and, if successful, obviate the need for private enforcement aimed now at filling the cracks in sovereign capacity opened by trans-nationalized labor markets. These consortia construct compliance teams that include international specialists—often labor-law scholars—and local participants in deliberative processes of fact-finding, determinations of non-compliance, and development of remediation programs.

This program for labor-law scholarship on multilateral regimes is, of course, highly speculative and one among many possible paths in the uncertain new world confronted by proponents of labor rights. None the less, if it does yield fruit in the international setting, it may also prove useful to the study of domestic labor law. Domestic labor law also faces the old question of applying the abstractions of association, equality, and other employment norms to local contexts. For labor-law scholars, this most fundamental of legal questions erupts anew—and with special difficulty—in an age of individualized and atypical labor markets, blurred lines between family and workplace, decentralized production systems, and the other sources of disruption to conventional frameworks discussed in this chapter.

In the end, the new directions in labor-law scholarship may lead back, perhaps at a higher conceptual pitch, to the reflexivity, pragmatism, and ethnographic detail that characterize the best work of Kahn-Freund and his students.

REFERENCES

Arup, C. (1991). 'Labour Law, Production Strategies, and Industrial Relations', *Law in Context*, 9: 36–69.

Barenberg, M. (1993). 'The Political Economy of the Wagner Act', *Harvard Law Review*, 106: 1379–496.

——(1994). 'Democracy and Domination in the Law of Workplace Cooperation: From Bureaucratic to Flexible Production', *Columbia Law Review*, 94: 753–983.

——and Evans, P. (forthcoming). 'The Impact of the FTAA on Democratic Governance in the Hemisphere', in D. Rodrik and A. Estevadeordal (eds.), *FTAA and Beyond: Prospects for Integration in the Americas*, Cambridge, Mass.: Harvard University Press.

Bercusson, B. (1999). 'Democratic Legitimacy and European Labour Law', *Industrial Law Journal*, 28: 153–70.

Charny, D. (1996). 'The Employee Welfare State in Transition', *Texas Law Review*, 74: 1601–43.

Collins, H. (1997). 'The Productive Disintegration of Labour Law', *Industrial Law Journal*, 26: 295–309.

Cox, A. (1959). 'Reflections upon Labor Arbitration', *Harvard Law Review*, 72: 1482–517.

Creighton, B., and Stewart, A. (2000). *Labour Law*, Sydney: The Federation Press.

Davies, P., and Freedland, M. (1993). *Labour Legislation and Public Policy*, Oxford: Clarendon Press.

Deakin, S., and Wilkinson, F. (1994). 'Rights vs Efficiency? The Economic Case for Transnational Labour Standards', *Industrial Law Journal*, 23: 289–310.

————(1999). 'Labour Law and Economic Theory: A Reappraisal', in G. De Geest, J. Siegers, and R. Van den Bergh (eds.), *Law and Economics and the Labour Market*, Cheltenham: Edward Elgar.

Ewing, K. (1995). 'Democratic Socialism and Labour Law', *Industrial Law Journal*, 24: 103–32.

Gross, J. (1995). *Broken Promise: The Subversion of U.S. Labor Relations Policy, 1947–1994*, Philadelphia: Temple University Press.

Hepple, B. (1970). *Race, Jobs and the Law in Britain*, London: Penguin.

——(1995). 'The Future of Labour Law', *Industrial Law Journal*, 24: 303–22.

Kahn-Freund, O. (1959). 'Labour Law', in M. Ginsberg (ed.), *Law and Opinion in England in the 20th Century*, London: Stevens.

——(1977). *Labour and the Law*, London: Stevens.

Klare, K. (1982). 'Critical Theory and Labor Relations Law', in D. Kairys (ed.), *The Politics of Law: A Progressive Critique*, New York: Pantheon.

Lawrence, C. (1987). 'The Id, the Ego, and Equal Protection: Reckoning with Unconscious Racism', *Stanford Law Review*, 39: 317–88.

MacKinnon, C. (1979). *Sexual Harassment of Working Women*, New Haven: Yale University Press.

Owens, R. (1995). 'The Traditional Labour Law Framework: A Critical Evaluation', in R. Mitchell (ed.), *Redefining Labour Law*, University of Melbourne Centre for Employment and Labour Relations Law Occasional Monograph Series No. 3.

Posner, R. (1984). 'Some Economics of Labor Law', *University of Chicago Law Review*, 51: 988–1011.

Schultz, V. (1990). 'Telling Stories about Women and Work: Judicial Interpretation of Sex Segregation in the Workplace', *Harvard Law Review*, 103: 1749–854.

Simitis, S., and Lyon-Cean, A. (1996). 'Community Labour Law: A Critical Introduction to its History', in P. Davies, A. Lyon-Cean, S. Sciarra, and S. Simitis (eds.), *European Community Labour Law: Principles and Perspectives*, Oxford: Clarendon Press.

Stone, K. (1981). 'The Post-War Paradigm in American Labor Law', *Yale Law Journal*, 90: 1509–80.

Sturm, S. (2001). 'Second Generation Empoyment Discrimination: A Structural Approach', *Columbia Law Review*, 101: 458–568.

Sykes, E. I., and Glasbeck, H. J. (1972). *Labour Law in Australia*, Sydney: Butterworths.

Wedderburn, K. W. (1972). 'Multinational Enterprise and National Labour Law', *Industrial Law Journal*, 1: 12–19.

—— (2000). 'Collective Bargaining or Legal Enactment: The 1999 Act and Union Recognition', *Industrial Law Journal*, 29: 1–42.

Weiler, P. (1983). 'Promises to Keep: Securing Workers' Rights to Self-Organization under the NLRA', *Harvard Law Review*, 96: 1769–827.

—— (1990). *Governing the Workplace: The Future of Labor and Employment Law*, Cambridge, Mass.: Harvard University Press.

Williamson, O. (1975). *Markets and Hierarchies*, New York: Free Press.

CHAPTER 27

....

INTERNATIONAL BUSINESS AND COMMERCE

....

DEBORAH Z. CASS

THE law relating to international business and commerce is an expansive field. It ranges from traditional rules about international trade in its public aspect (GATT (General Agreement on Tariffs and Trade) and WTO (World Trade Organization) law), to private international law rules (conflicts of law), to laws governing international business transactions and commerce generally (including rules regarding the international sales contract, insurance, freight, insolvency, and payment), to national rules on similar subjects. Moreover as its subject is economics, it cannot fail to intersect with that very broad field. This chapter cannot aspire to cover such a farrago of topics. What it can do, however, is to attempt an analysis of some recurrent themes in that portion of the field which is sometimes referred to as international economic law, namely public international law structures that regulate economic relations and exchange between states, with a primary emphasis upon trade. However, in so doing, I remain mindful of the various contributions to international business law and commerce beyond that relatively defined field and will refer to them when relevant and where space permits.

Thanks are due to Damian Chalmers and Gerry Simpson.

In this chapter I will suggest that six features characterize current legal scholarship on international economic law relating to business and commerce:

- a focus on *institutions and on constitutions* as a means to enhance the authority and legitimacy of the rule-making order;
- an interdependence with wider scholarship about *globalization*;
- a general *consensus* about the benefits of liberalization and the international economic law framework which supports it, punctuated by occasional critique;
- a concentration on *regulation* rather than 'law' in the traditional sense;
- a fixation with the problem of *definition* of its own scope;
- a belief in its *transformative* nature capable of facilitating improvements in legal order generally.

The aim of this chapter is to describe and analyse the broad contours of each of these features before critiquing them and suggesting some possible avenues of future research.

1 A FOCUS ON *INSTITUTIONS AND CONSTITUTIONS* AS A MEANS TO ENHANCE THE AUTHORITY AND LEGITIMACY OF THE RULE-MAKING ORDER

In tune with developments in legal theory, writers in the field of international economic law have moved beyond the study of rules alone and emphasized the importance of other mechanisms of obligation. Sometimes these mechanisms of obligation are labelled as *institutions*. Some have drawn on the work of economic historians such as Douglass North who proposed that the evolution and success of divergent economies could best be understood by studying formal and informal constraints on human behaviour as incentives for economic activity, as opposed to technical constraints in the form of technological change, prices, or income (North, 1990). Others (Hoekman and Kostecki, 2001) referred to Krasner's international relations model of a regime with its 'sets of implicit or explicit principles, norms, rules and decision making processes around which expectations converge' (ibid.). Departure from a specifically rules-based focus was reflected in the title of a leading casebook which framed its subject not in terms of 'the law of' the field but instead as legal 'problems' of international economic 'relations' (Jackson *et al.*, 1995). The role and effect of the institution of diplomacy was seen as particularly important by some (Hudec, 1999). More recently, it has been argued that what are critical are not legal rules alone but principles, mechanisms, and actors, and contests between these elements (Braithwaite and Drahos, 2000).

On the other hand, some scholars have engaged more with the notion of *constitutions* than of institutions. This has been used with both a descriptive and prescriptive twist. Descriptively, the term 'constitution' has been used to describe the internal workings of particular legal arrangements in the field such as the WTO (Petersmann, 1997; Jackson *et al.*, 1995); or the European Union (Weiler, 1999), or to compare two organizations such as the WTO and the EU. Prescriptively, also, writers use the term to make a normative claim about an aspect of the field. Europe is said to need a constitution not in order to instantiate a new form of political/economic relationship midway between a confederation and a federation, but in order to conserve a distinctly European way of life based on basic human rights, social welfare, and minimal economic redistribution (Habermas, 2001). Or, international trade law should be constitutionalized so that states recognize the economic right of non-discrimination encapsulated in international trade agreements as a human right, domestic courts can apply it, and citizens can rely on it to challenge state action (Petersmann, 1997). Petersmann has also suggested that liberal international trade rules serve a constitutional function in restraining the powers of national governments, and so basic constitutional principles such as transparency, non-discriminatory market access, competition, and property rights should be extended to apply to the foreign trade powers of states (Petersmann, 1997).

Of course, international economic law has never been restricted merely to a study of rules. It has, almost from its genesis, been cognizant of broader social forces moulding and determining obeisance to its authority. Moreover, this emphasis upon a broad range of mechanisms of obligation (institutions) and the structure of a system of law around those mechanisms (constitutions) has important consequences for the nature of scholarship in the field. The term 'institution' is used to signal the almost open-ended range of public, private, legal, and quasi-legal mechanisms that create obligations for actors. 'Constitutional' language is used to ask where the authority of the law-making source derives from, and to question the system's legitimacy, its levels of participation, representativeness, transparency, and even its democratic credentials. In short, this trend has generated a way of talking about international economic law in which a key question is why states cooperate in the absence of a central legal authority. Hence legitimacy, compliance, and the question of law's authority feature strongly in this field of scholarship.

The emphasis on institutions and constitutionalization sometimes fails to interrogate adequately the particular nature of the legitimacy afforded by constitutions or institutions taking the particular form under discussion. Some critics have argued that focussing on 'good governance' as a foundational institution for the granting of IMF loans and World Bank development assistance has, instead of promoting democracy, undermined it. The very measures and reductions in government spending required to meet the standards of 'good governance' (privatization, tariff reduction,

financial sector restructuring) force governments to reduce spending in areas fundamental to the exercise of democratic rights, such as health, education, and employee
benefits (Gathii, 1999). Or the claim is made that the expansion of Bretton Woods
institutions into poverty alleviation and environment management, and the
increased legitimacy which accompanied that expansion, resulted not from any
natural increase of the ambit of the institutions' jurisdiction, but arose as a result of
direct resistance to the institutions by social movements, especially from the Third
World (Rajagopal, 2000). The legitimacy of the institutions is a by-product not of
internal and graduated institutional reform, but of conflict between institutional
international economic law and social movements. It is the resolution of these
conflicts, often by incorporation of some demands of the social movements, that
ultimately enhances the institutions' social legitimacy.

The constitutionalization literature on international trade raises similar problems
of legitimacy and authority. Is it possible for the EU to be 'constitutional' when it
clearly lacks a polity, or *demos* (Weiler, 1999)? What is meant by labelling the current
transformations of the international trading system into a more powerful force
generally in the international economic order as 'constitutionalization'? Is it 'a step
too far' which will exacerbate legitimacy problems for a WTO lacking sufficient
'democratic contestability' and inclusiveness (Howse and Nicolaidis, 2001)? Does
constitutionalization simply refer to the establishment of a more complex institutional structure—the protection of rights; the existence of an authorizing community
to make international trade law rules—or does the use of the term 'consitutitional'
convey the practice of an adjudicative body generating constitutional norms (Cass,
2001)? Can this constitutionalization process be reconceived so as to take into
account social values as well as economic goals, which have always been an integral
part of the international economic system (Gatthi, 2001)?

The difficulties raised in the critiques of the institutional and constitutional focus
of international economic law suggest a range of new research questions. Foremost
among them is the legitimacy issue: what is the nature of the new legitimacy afforded
by the expanding institutions of international economic law? Will the expansion of
forms of law, and forms of participation, result in a more legitimate international
economic law system? Secondly, and relatedly, are the constitutional questions. What
is the nature of the constitution that is being constructed by changes in the field? Is it
a technical structure, or does it contain some of the principles normally associated
with use of the term. That is to say, does it include notions of separation of powers,
rule of law, or even rights? And what will be the significance of any such inclusions?
Will it lead to the field resembling a supranational structure? What implications arise
for governments and for governance, at both the national and international levels?

Thirdly, there are issues which form a subset of the constitutional questions that
concern the relationship between the international trade regime and human rights.
Included here are not only the obvious question of whether human rights can be
linked to trade, but the question of what sort of human rights we are talking about?
What is the nature of the implicit disagreement between those who advocate a

human rights approach to international economic law (Petersmann, 2002), and those who claim international economic law, in its current form, has only ever incorporated human rights which are conducive to economic goals (Gathii, 1999)? What are the consequences of the view that only those human rights that facilitate repayment of institutional debt by developing countries and encourage foreign capital inflows have been recognized by international business and commerce? Despite the sharing of a common vocabulary, which emphasizes a desire to link trade and human rights, international economic lawyers and human rights lawyers may be talking at cross-purposes. Any further work on trade and human rights and on constitutionalization should address this question.

2 INTERDEPENDENCE BETWEEN INTERNATIONAL ECONOMIC LAW SCHOLARSHIP AND GLOBALIZATION SCHOLARSHIP

The second characteristic of international economic law scholarship is its emphasis on globalization. Business regulation is deemed 'utterly global' (Braithwaite and Drahos, 2000). Whole studies are christened 'global business regulation' (ibid.) or 'global legal pluralism' (Snyder, 1999). At the same time, these very studies are replete with discussion of the inherent uncertainty of the concept of globalization, which is conceived of as a porous, complex concept with an uncertain landscape. It is described as 'messy' and 'non-linear' (Braithwaite and Drahos, 2000) and this echoes a view beyond legal scholarship that describes current processes of change as a 'decentred and deterritorializing apparatus of rule that progressively incorporates the entire global realm within its open, expanding frontiers' (Hardt and Negri, 2000). Power in a globalized world is conceptualized less as a matter of domination than as a complex and contingent process, a matter of 'webs of influence' (Braithwaite and Drahos, 2000) or 'global business and regulatory networks' (Picciotto and Mayne, 1999). (US power is a result of the triumph of this mode of network power (Hardt and Negri, 2000).) Nevertheless, a strong strand of scholarship, associated with social movements and opposed to market-driven corporate globalization continues to utilize a domination model of globalization, pointing to the continuing increase in the size, economic power, and political influence of transnational corporations (George, 2001).

As a result of the instability of globalization, the law bred in its wake is a diffuse, fragmented creature. Global economic relations are governed by global legal pluralism which is the 'totality of strategically determined, situationally specific and often episodic conjunctions of a multiplicity of institutional, normative, and processual sites throughout the world' (Snyder, 1999: 371). Globalization has led to the development of law labelled as 'neo-spontaneous' (Teubner, 2000) because it derives not from the ordinary processes of legislative development but instead appears to emerge, semi-autonomously, from new sources, commercial, institutional, and non-public. It is therefore 'peripheral', characterized by the location of its making, in private fora, and at the 'edge' of law, where law intersects with other social sectors such as science, media, or transport (ibid.).

Characteristic also of the fuzziness of globalization and the law that both produces it and is produced by it, is the breakdown of the traditional separation between economics and politics. The various 'sites' which produce law can be market or polity based (Snyder, 1999). Indeed globalization itself is new to the extent that the power it produces is a conflation of economic and political power (Hardt and Negri, 2000).

Paradoxically perhaps, the inherently unstable nature of globalization and globalized economic law is neither good nor bad and consequently there are not good or bad outcomes. Scholars are generally agnostic about the benefits or otherwise of globalization—even those whose previous work implicitly questioned this premise. Good institutions and more regulation can temper the harsher effects of liberalization (Picciotto and Mayne, 1999). Globalization alone cannot be 'blamed' for underregulation (Braithwaite and Drahos, 2000: 5); the weak can prevail in a globalized world and citizen sovereignty may emerge (Braithwaite and Drahos, 2000: 35; Hardt and Negri, 2000). The very fluidity of the process provides grounds for optimism about the possibilities offered by globalization for the making of positive linkages similar to those that have been made between trade and intellectual property. Perhaps trade and the environment will be the next (Picciotto and Mayne, 1999: 221). Ultimately, the picture is one of neither absolute improvement in general welfare brought about by increased flows of trade, transport, communication, investment, and information, nor rampant destruction of national sovereignty over economic policy-making. Globalization is a question of degree and intensification.

In short, the loosening of the parameters of international economic law referred to in Section 1 above has made the scholarship amenable to linkage with much broader debates about globalization. Institutional discourse was a precursor of sorts to the globalization debate, in its emphasis on non-legal mechanisms of behaviour, and inter-state and non-state forms of cooperation. Constitutional discourse was a natural companion of the globalization debate because it sought to describe the deep underlying structure of interdependence among states. Moreover the open-ended emphasis on institutions and constitutions in international economic law resembled a similar fuzziness in descriptions of globalization.

One way of thinking about this association between the field of international economic law and globalization might be to ask: what are the consequences for the field of the expanded globalization of business regulation of a law which is 'neo-spontaneous' and 'peripheral' in nature, site-specific, decentred, and porous? Is the fuzziness of the globalization debate good or bad for international business and commerce? Does it matter? In what ways do the traditional categories of national and international law remain relevant, if at all? What of the fact that general international law has largely ignored the developments in international economic law despite the affinity between the fields, and between international law and globalization?

3 General *Consensus* about the Benefits of Liberalization and the International Economic Law Framework that Supports it, Punctuated by Occasional Critique

In addition to agnosticism about globalization, a general consensus about the benefits of liberalization pervades the literature, coupled with a desire to make the international economic order more egalitarian. International economic law can be a valuable vehicle for liberalization and, when subject to appropriate limits, liberalization (and so international economic law) will contribute to an overall increase in economic welfare. The challenge is, therefore, to improve international institutions; tame financial flows and volatility; create better mechanisms of accountability by managing the interaction between layers of regulation; and strengthen state regulation through flexible linkage to internationally agreed standards (Picciotto and Mayne, 1999). Strategies for improvement of global business regulation are pragmatic (Kennedy, 1994) and include: harnessing management philosophies such as 'continuous improvement' and 'best practice'; strengthening competition law; increasing health and environmental standards; building 'global epistemic communities' to assist in competition enforcement; and transforming the consumer movement into a watchdog of monopolies (Braithwaite and Drahos, 2000). Even human rights can be harnessed to the promotion of economic welfare through international trade law and this can be achieved by exploiting 'synergies' between the fields (Petersmann, 2002). As noted in Section 4 below, 'pure' free trade is off the agenda (if it was ever there at all).

As a consequence of this pervasive consensus about the benefits of international economic liberalization, *general* critiques of international economic law are rare. This is not to say that there is not a wide and vigorous debate about specific aspects of the field, or about how liberalization should proceed. Arguments about what subjects to include within the ambit of the WTO; how to constitutionalize the field; and how to improve the voting structure of the IMF; all contribute to a rich and vigorous discussion about improving international economic law. But voices that challenge the underlying structure of the field are few and far between.

In contrast, the period of 1960 to 1980 marked a break in the general consensus in the scholarship with a burst of strong critique. Coincident with decolonization in the third world, and the emergence of dependency theory in international relations, a critique arose in law, which was labelled the New International Economic Order (NIEO) critique. This inquiry was aimed not only at particular aspects of the field of international economic law, but also at the field's very existence, its place within public international law, and its legitimacy. One of the strongest and most influential of the dissenters was Mohammed Bedjaoui, later judge of the International Court of Justice, whose views were summarized in a volume written toward the end of the 1970s entitled *Towards a New International Economic Order*. Bedjaoui challenged traditional principles of international economic law, and indeed international law generally, as pro-Western and biased in relation to its formation, content, and practical application.

As part of this general environment of critique, legal structures changed. Judicial decisions reflected the influence of the NIEO arguments in relation to matters such as sovereignty and acquisition of territory (Western Sahara Advisory Opinion, ICJ Reports, 1975, 12) and expropriation (*Texaco v Libya* ILR 389 (1997)). Sources doctrine in public international law was minimally modified to take account of new actors and forms of participation in law-making (*Nicaragua v US*, ICJ Reports, 1984, 392). A new principle was proclaimed declaring that states possessed permanent sovereignty over their natural resources (GA Res 1803 (XVII), GAOR, Seventeenth Session, Supp 17, 15). Controversial legal instruments were passed by the General Assembly including one which, arguably, modified the standard of compensation due from states for expropriation of foreign assets (Charter of Economic Rights and Duties, GA Res 3281 (XXIX), 14 ILM 251 (1975)). A right to development emerged (GA Res 41/128, GAOR Forty-First Session, Supp 53, 186 (1986)) and, interpreted by the Southern states, this right imposed some legal responsibility upon Northern states to compensate them for the formers' lack of wealth (Seidl-Hohenveldern, 1999). Most noteworthy of all, the GATT 1947 was amended with the inclusion of Part IV that provided for special and differential treatment for developing countries in trading matters. Therefore, unlike the pre-1960s period where consensus largely prevailed, this period was characterized by strong debate about the nature of international economic law, about the types of rights it should protect, and the types of obligations it recognized. The interplay between economic fact, legal scholarship, and law-creation, was particularly vigorous and visible, with consequences for economic policy as well as law. In the wake of the intellectual foment of the NIEO, developing countries adopted policies of import substitution and infant industry protection in order to extend their economies beyond traditional primary production toward the building of stronger manufacturing bases so that they could compete successfully in the international economic order.

Despite the relative success of the NIEO critique, ultimately it fell into decline. The United Nations Conference on Trade and Development (UNCTAD) which was formed in 1964 and was strongly associated with ideas of the NIEO lost much of its power. Economically significant subjects such as intellectual property were transferred from UNCTAD to World Intellectual Property Organization (WIPO), an organization dominated by producer interests, and not explicitly concerned with the relationship between trade and development. East Asian countries, such as South Korea and Singapore, successfully pursued export-led growth after abandoning policies of import substitution, albeit while retaining strongly interventionist governments. And development economists began to argue against the intellectual tradition of the NIEO, and the insights of the 1950s literature. They moved away from the position, associated with the Singer–Prebisch thesis, which held that gains from international trade and foreign investment accrued mainly to developed countries. They began to question the view that foreign investment in developing states, which occurred in primary production and minerals, lacked multiplier effects. They challenged arguments that free trade diverted domestic resources from other areas of economic development leading to an increase in import of manufactures and, ultimately, to an imbalance in terms of trade. Now instead, a leading developing country economist, Jagdish Bhagwati, calculated the high cost of protectionism for developing countries and, bringing a political economy perspective to the debate, demonstrated that vested interests sought to entrench protectionism despite evidence of its economic inefficiency. The intellectual and factual power of these arguments was such that Bhagwati is credited with influencing India to move from a policy of import substitution towards export promotion (Balasubramanyam, 1997).

Allied to the economic arguments that trade protectionism reduced economic welfare, were the legal critiques. These argued that the differential status accorded to developing countries, especially in the form of non-reciprocity and preferential treatment in trade concessions, was a one-sided system. It was impractical to implement, and would cause more internal harm than good to the domestic economies of developing countries (Hudec, 1987). Even though developing states might be able to increase some exports to developed states, in the long run increased exports in these sectors would be offset by increased non-tariff measures in others. Moreover, the failure of domestic producers to restructure in order to compete successfully with foreign rivals would, overall, reduce internal welfare. According to another writer, international economic law did not include the demands of the NIEO because of the suspicion, deeply held by the North, that the goal of compensating inequality would necessitate the very thing which international economic law sought to protect against, namely, it would require a planned economy and a world organization to plan it, rather than the relatively free flow of market forces (Seidl-Hohenveldern, 1999).

What is interesting about victory of this counter-critique is that it returned the field to a state of *relative* stasis where the consensus about the benefits of liberalization was revived, but the consensus was now conditioned in subtle ways. In the main, the counter-critique quietened the voices calling for dismantling, or wholesale rewriting, of the international economic law, and it reinforced the original insights of the field, namely that liberalization could lead to an increase in general welfare. The economic and legal environment became more hospitable to international business and international commercial transactions generally. But the new environment, whilst favouring deeper liberalization and international economic integration, did so in a different register. In this new register, two strands of thinking are clear. First, the *legacy of the NIEO* became deeply embedded in the scholarship and in the law; and secondly, the *anti-liberal impulses of developed states* came in for increasing criticism.

The first subtle deviation from the earlier consensus on the benefits of trade liberalization, was that the NIEO argument for differential status for developing states was incorporated into the new liberalization agenda. Hence the legacy of the NIEO persists today, even if it is unacknowledged or unrealised. The 'special status' approach persisted in key principles of the WTO/GATT system. It was enshrined as a non-binding principle in Part IV of the GATT. It later re-emerged with even more vigour during the Uruguay Round of trade negotiations, where, for the first time, in 1994, a large number of states signed a single package of trade agreements, covering a broad range of subjects including subsidies, dumping, health-related measures, agriculture, intellectual property, and dispute resolution. Included in most of these 'covered' agreements were special rules for developing states. But special and differential treatment was present not just in the agreements themselves. It became more evident in almost every policy discussion within the key public institutions of international economic order, the WTO, IMF (International Monetary Fund), and World Bank. Key institutions focused more and more on development, as an end in itself. The World Bank shifted its objective from one of specific lending for reconstruction after World War II to one of development. Its project lending changed from 'hard' projects such as transport or electricity, and to 'soft', more generalized purposes of development, including legal reform, infrastructure, and even political development. IMF lending, to an extent, reflected the basic insight that structural inequalities persisted between economies and it was the responsibility of the international economic institutions to assist in alleviating those inequalities.

Secondly, as well as the NIEO legacy, subsequent scholarship became more concerned with the anti-liberal impulses of developed states. The counter-critique to the NIEO had partially refuted some of the latter's claims. But it had also unsettled the previous consensus on liberalization in one further aspect. The old consensus on liberalization largely assumed that it was developing states which had the most work to do in relation to achieving that goal. While exploding the myth of developing country special status, the NIEO counter-critique also exposed the hypocrisy and double standards inherent in developed states' attitudes to liberalization. The developed states may have been committed to liberalization, but, according to the counter-critique, they were equally committed to the 'practice of imposing new restrictions that limit developing exports once they begin to cause discomfort' (Hudec, 1987). The cumulative effect of the NIEO critique and its counter-critique punctuated the old consensus on liberalization, and laid the groundwork for the assault on the 'new protectionism' of developed states (Hudec, 1999). Together, they led to an attack on a new set of policies which had arisen in the 1970s and 1980s, partly in response to the success of export-led growth in South East Asia. These policies were characterized by an increased use, by developed states mainly, of non-trade barriers and trade remedies such as anti-dumping, and countervailing duties.

Scholarship now focused on these new protectionist methods and criticized the heavy use of anti-dumping law, and the use of safeguards against competitive import surges. It condemned the 'dressing up' of the new intellectual property regime of the WTO as trade liberalizing when, in practice, it constituted a strongly protectionist regime which extended monopoly rights throughout the trading world. It focused on granting greater access to markets in which developing states would have had a comparative advantage, namely agriculture, textiles and clothing, and steel, were it not for the continuation of practices of trade discrimination.

The tenor of the current scholarship is, thus, fairly optimistic. It takes a pragmatic approach to globalization, counsels the benefits of liberalization, and criticizes departures, by both North and South, from that goal. Nevertheless, strong disagreement with this consensus comes from two or three quarters, namely social activist, post-colonial, and Third World scholarship. These critiques are situated at the intersection with other disciplines such as economics, anthropology, and international relations, and none are central interlocutors with international economic law scholarship, in the same way that the NIEO critique was. A brief account of some of their key arguments follows.

A position associated with social movement activism aims at what it refers to as market-driven corporate globalization. It suggests that the international financial system is dominated by industrial and financial transnational corporations which make enormous profit at expense of others, through, for example, demands for complete freedom of investment, capital, goods and services, including intellectual property, and education. The antidote to this state of affairs includes: fair trade incorporating recognition of social and environmental concerns; taxing of international capital movements and mergers and acquisitions; corporate responsibility for environmental and other social damage; and cancellation of developing country debt (George, 2001).

Another group of scholars, variously associated with Third World scholarship and post-colonial critique, challenges the institutional arrangements, coverage, and outcomes of international economic law. The role and functions of the international economic law institutions such as the World Bank have been shaped by resistance between those institutions and Third World social movements and not by gradual legal change (Rajagopal, 2000). Examples given include the extension of the World Bank's mandate to cover environment regulation and poverty alleviation. The new international economic law rule of good governance, with its emphasis on human rights and democracy combined with liberal economic solutions, undermines the achievement of social justice because it forces states to limit and reduce delivery of public goods such as education and health. The real agenda of good governance is to facilitate repayment of sovereign debts to institutional lenders and secure unhindered influx of foreign capital into developing states (Gathii, 1999). The World Bank encourages promotion of only those human rights that are consistent with increasing corporate investment, growth, and profit and neglects the social-welfare aspects of human rights (Gatthi, 1999). Attempts to expunge corruption from developing states legitimizes a strong police power in the state, and emphasizes market economic reforms such as privatization and tariff reduction, which were precisely the reforms which caused the corruption and social dislocation in the first place (Rajagopal, 1999). Finally, and relatedly, in political science a vast field of cultural studies scholarship intersects with the exact same interests of international economic law, and questions the basic assumptions of the scholarship. The global cultural economy is characterized by 'disjuncture and difference' in which markets in money, commodities, and people are deterritorialized, and which can no longer be understood in terms of existing models of centre and periphery, surplus and deficit, consumers and producers (Appadurai, 1990).

In sum, a general consensus on the benefits of liberalization characterizes this field of scholarship, although this is challenged occasionally by outside critiques. In a sense, the field has been constituted by the contest between liberal economic consensus and partial critique—with apologies to Stephen Jay Gould, a kind of 'punctuated equilibrium' characterizes the evolution of the scholarship.

4 A CONCENTRATION ON *REGULATION* RATHER THAN 'LAW' IN THE TRADITIONAL SENSE

The fourth theme of international economic law scholarship is its increasing emphasis on regulation. If naming is important in constructing and reflecting ideas then the idea of regulation has truly taken hold of the academic consciousness of the twenty-first century international economic lawyer. It is the central organizing principle of many texts including: *The Regulation of International Trade* (Trebilcock and Howse, 1995, 2nd edn., 1999); *Global Business Regulation* (Braithwaite and Drahos, 2000); *Regulating International Business* (Picciotto and Mayne, 1999). Academic programmes are structured around regulation (MSc in Regulation at the London School of Economics) and entire academic centres of research specialize in it (Centre for Risk and Regulation at the London School of Economics; the Regulatory Institutions Network (RegNet) at the Australian National University).

As the current catchword of the field, regulation is perceived as *the* critical phenomenon of study. The international body which oversees trade rules, the WTO, is said to 'regulate . . . the regulators' (Hoekman and Kostecki, 2001). Modernity itself cannot be understood without understanding regulation (Braithwaite and Drahos, 2000: 9).

For international business and commerce this has various consequences. The range of forms of obligation are greater, although the forms of regulation businesses will be subject to are often 'softer' than rigid rules; they may be voluntary in the guise of codes of conduct and guiding principles. In the European context, a focus on subsidiarity, as a means of mediating the intensity of levels of European law, takes hold. Enforcement may be less important than in strict legal systems. And non-state interests, such as business and commercial organizations, as well as interest groups focused on specific issues, may be involved in the making of such forms of regulation. Conflicts between systems of regulation may be both easier to avoid because the jurisdiction of regulatory systems does not obviously collide, and more difficult to resolve because of an absence of clear rules for system-conflict resolution.

The emphasis on regulation, as a process, rather than on law as a matter of substantive values, has another significant consequence. It focuses attention upon the *way* in which things are done rather than on *what* is being done. In other words, the focus on regulation, over law, is accompanied by a focus on procedural solutions rather than particular outcomes. How states 'manage' relations between national and international regulation will be the key to the success of the GATT/WTO system (Jackson *et al.*, 1995). 'Accommodation' of competing interests will resolve the ' "trade-and-" ' labour, environment or competition debates (Hudec in Bhagwati and Hudec, 1997: 13). GATT has been successful in offering inducements to lower tariffs because a rule-based system is superior to a results-based one (Hoekman and Koestecki, 2001).

Here we can see clearly another feature of this trend towards regulation—the emphasis on process has affiliations with the procedural school of liberal democratic theory, and highlights important democratic questions about legitimacy again. International economic law is thus connected to wider concerns about the nature of democracy. In the face of increasing variety between states, and diversity of interests within them, international economic law scholarship emphasizes the procedurally democratic aspects of regulation in order to emphasize the legitimacy aspect of the field. The themes of the new (democratized) international economic law become openness, transparency, public communication, and participation. In the context of the European Community, what is most important in deciding whether a national rule is valid is not whether freedom of goods is supposed to merely limit states' protectionist impulses or whether it was intended to enable inter-state operators to trade completely free of any regulation. What is important is not the resolution of that particular polarity, but whether the state imposing a potentially discriminatory measure took sufficient account of interests beyond the state when doing so

(Maduro, 1997). What is important is who is at the table, not what they decide. So instead of tackling the question of links between trade and other issues such as the environment in terms of a discussion of what is 'fair' (Bhagwati and Hudec, 1996), scholarship focuses on procedural solutions, on the 'interface' between national economies (Jackson *et al.*, 1995)—in part because those earlier studies had recognized the difficulties of identifying a normative baseline for what constitutes 'fairness'. Agreement being impossible on the particular outcomes or 'critical' in relation to 'even normative starting points' (Hudec, 1997), the focus moved to method. Improvements in participation (for other states and non-state groups); increases in the representative nature of the body making decisions, whether it be the WTO, the IMF, or the World Bank; and improved communication and transparency will improve and safeguard the legitimacy and authority of international economic law regulation and decision-making.

Here we can also see how a softer, more flexible notion of regulation, through subtle alterations to the idea of what is being studied (process not outcome), and links with other areas of scholarship (democratic theory), has come not only to stand in for 'law', but also to code for deeper notions associated with societal order. Moreover, the concept evokes changes in law to take account of greater participation, and representativeness, and engages other aspects of the language of democratic theory, so that regulation becomes associated with notions of governance, government, and, perhaps even, a state (Picciotto and Mayne, 1999: 4; Braithwaite and Drahos, 2000: 475). And if the particular form of regulation substituting for the state is international economic law regulation, then the structures of international economic law are seen by some as constituting new structures of international governance. This link between international economic legal regulation and ideas about international governance has led to an increasing focus on constitutions and institutions in the scholarship of the field, and has been accompanied by strong public demonstrations at international economic institution meetings, beginning with the WTO's failed launch of a new trade round in Seattle in 1999. Public concern about international economic legal regulation reflects the field's shift towards regulation, and the association of regulation with notions of governance.

Finally, in relation to regulation, this shift in focus to process has allowed writers to recognize *non-state* forms of regulation, and *non-law* forms of obligation as key components of the field. Major (US) corporations are shown to have been highly influential in the formation of new international agreements and indeed in persuading public officials to link aspects of international economic law such as trade and intellectual property (Braithwaite and Drahos, 2000: 218). State regulation itself is, literally, written by private interests, usually in their capacity as participants in key standard-setting organizations in areas such as air transport and telecommunications (Braithwaite and Drahos, 2000: 218, 488–91).

The difficulty with refracting the discussion of international business and commerce away from law and towards regulation is that it focuses attention on management rather than on policy itself. The GATT becomes a tool for massaging differences between economies and cultures, and all problems are reduced to procedural ones (Kennedy, 1994). According to this view, of John Jackson's scholarship in particular, international economic law can never provide a strong system of international order. In Jackson's work, a 'spirit of liberal trade' is more important than constructing a particular international regime. One of Jackson's key contributions to the field—his notion of international trade law as constituting an 'interface' with which to negotiate differences between states about trade policy—is reduced to a mechanistic tool of management. So whereas law conceived of as rules might provide a structure for a new international regime, law conceived of as regulation does not (Kennedy, 1994: 99). The very strength of regulation as opposed to law, namely its focus on process rather than values, is also its weakness. And regulation which is overly procedural in nature avoids the hard questions of what sorts of values the international trade should encompass, or what an earlier generation thought of as a discussion about what is 'fair' in trade. Future research might therefore focus more deeply on the types of regulation being proposed, and what is meant by regulation. It might consider what are the underlying values promoted under the auspices of a neutral system of regulation as opposed to law? How are conflicts among systems of regulation being resolved? In whose interests are regulators acting? If the interests being represented are not those of the state, with its limited apparatus of democracy, then by what methods of accountability are we to assess the new regulatory arrangements?

5 A FIXATION WITH THE PROBLEM OF *DEFINITION* BOTH OF THE FIELD AND ITS SUB-PARTS

The next characteristic of the field of law relating to international business and commerce is that it is fixated with the problem of defining its own scope. The problem of definition is present, first, in relation to how to conceptualize a broad field provisionally labelled international economic law. What should be its name? What topics should fall within its range? How should we decide what is within and what is without? Is it a part of a broader field of public international law, or does it exist as its own discipline? Early scholars using the term 'international economic law', distinguished it from another growth area of 'transnational' law, and described it as 'embedded' within public international law, albeit with a broader range of subjects (multinational enterprises) and sources (for example, the law merchant which consisted of international commercial customs as recognized and applied between states) (Seidl-Hohenveldern, 1999). Later, others made a distinction between the private *transactional* aspects which included matters such as private contract law, customs law, law relating to shipping, and *regulatory* aspects which involved government regulation at the national (import and export controls) and international (WTO, IMF, and WB rules and policies) levels and focused primarily on the latter (Jackson *et al.*, 1995: 3). To others still, public international law is not central to the examination and instead they mixed a number of topics under the label 'international trade law', including some from the transactional and some from the regulatory categories. Particular examinations of, say, GATT dispute resolution are prepared under the heading 'transnational economic law' (Petersmann, 1997). Other studies organize the field under the subject of international business transactions, or, as discussed above (Sect. 4), they bundle together a collection of instruments, trends, and acts, which are labelled as 'regulation'. Clearly the self-image of the discipline is uncertain. In part this self-doubt is a product of the discipline's (relative) novelty compared to public international law proper, or particular aspects of international legal studies. But the problem of definition is also a result of the inherent implausibility of separating economic and business transactions from other aspects of social life, and is a product of the proliferation of new mechanisms of obligation generally (see above at Sect. 1). Nowhere are these three factors of novelty, economic/social separation, and extension of forms of control more apparent, and therefore the problem of self-definition more acute, than in relation to the correct ambit of the field of WTO law.

The problem of definition in relation to specific sub-parts of the field such as the law of the IMF and WTO, is born, in part, of a need to respond to the challenge to its authority. This problem of what is the correct and authorized scope of international economic law in relation to institutions such as the WTO or the IMF takes two forms—one related to the geographical jurisdiction of these bodies and the other to the subject-matter of their jurisdiction. First, what is the appropriate geographical scope of the field? Is its authority confined solely to economic behaviour on the international plane? Does it extend into the nation state, and, if so, to what extent, or is the intersection of national and international the correct focus for international economic law? Numerous articles and books have been written with this underlying problem of self-definition at their core.

Some scholarship begins from a narrow point of departure but leads to a similar question of how to define the field from a geographical perspective. Writers may discuss what the correct role of the World Bank is in determining national policy; how interventionist the IMF should be in setting conditions for loans; what standard of review the WTO Appellate Body should adopt in reviewing national agency decisions in relation to, say, health, or environment matters; how this should differ from the standard of review of national agencies in relation to dumping decisions; what should be the respective powers of the WTO's 'legislative' arm, the Ministerial Council/General Council, as opposed to its 'judicial' arm, the Dispute Settlement Body; what authority the WTO's superior tribunal (the Appellate Body) has to accept *amicus* briefs, as compared to the authority of its legislative body (the General Council) to decide when to accept briefs. In each of these works, the key underlying issue, behind the question of the extent of competence and power of the body in question is the question of geographical jurisdiction, namely what is the correct and authorized definition of the field? How far into national state competence can the field of international economic law intrude?

The second and related aspect of the definitional problem concerns the scope of subject-matters covered by international economic law, and in particular the law of the WTO. What subjects should fall within its field of regulation? One obvious starting-point would be to assume that international trade law should be about free trade. But this turns out not to be the case. As one noted commentator remarked, it is doubtful whether 'a perfectly free market economy existed anywhere else than in the minds of some liberal philosophers' (Seidl-Hohenveldern, 1999). The Havana Charter, the original constitutional agreement of the first international trade organization, which was never adopted by the international community after rejection by the US Congress, was not restricted to purely free trade issues and included chapters on restrictive business practices, and even international labour standards. The founding legal instrument of the discipline, GATT 1947, includes many departures from the basic principle of non-discrimination, including allowance for duties on dumping of products and in response to state subsidization; permission for adjustments to protect a state's balance of payments situation; conditional licence to impose safe-guard measures in the event of import surges causing injury to domestic industry; and general exceptions to non-discrimination for health, environment, and national security reasons. Indeed, the form of liberal free trade embodied by the GATT was not classical free market liberalism in any pure sense (Hudec, 1987), but embedded liberalism, to use John Ruggie's term (Gathii, 2001). In this modified form of free trade, or managed trade, an international regime for liberalization was mandated in the form of compulsory tariffication and the imposition of binding levels of tariffs, but modified or conditioned by allowance for state intervention where necessary to protect critical national interests.

Consistent with this approach of managed, rather than free, trade, the history of the discipline has been one of incremental expansion of subject-matter of GATT/ WTO law. It began in 1947 by focusing on tariff barriers. It gradually accommodated new issues, most notably non-tariff barriers and subsidies after the 1979 Tokyo Round of negotiations. The subject-matter continued to extend after the 1995 Uruguay Round, explicitly linking non-trade issues such as intellectual property to the trade regime. Current candidates for inclusion in the WTO agreements are environment, labour, investment, competition, and trade facilitation.

In the light of this variegated and expanding background, it is not surprising that a key concern of the scholarship is what should be within and what should be outside of its subject-matter ambit? Sometimes this question takes the form of the 'fair trade and harmonization' debate (Hudec in Bhagwati and Hudec, 1997). To what extent can states impose trade measures for actions they perceive to be 'unfair' because the comparative advantage of the other state is based on weak labour, environment, or competition policies and standards? To what extent should the international community be attempting to harmonize these matters? Is it possible, in any case, to decide matters of 'fairness' in relation to international trade, when there are so many competing conceptions of appropriate models for economic development nationally, and when no normative baseline can be identified (Hudec, 1999)? More recently, writers have characterized this problem as one of 'linkage' and have come up with a variety of methods for deciding how, when, and what should be linked to trade. Others challenge conventional wisdom which assumes it is necessary to ask which social issues should now be 'added on' to the mandate of international trade, by arguing that social issues have always been inextricably linked with the GATT system (Gathii, 2001).

The problem of linkage leads directly to the crucial question of what level of integration is embodied in any legal arrangements in international economic matters. In European law, the question of integration has long been a topic of discussion. In relation to the GATT/WTO system, and particularly since the agreement on intellectual property initiated introduction of internationally set legal standards into domestic systems (in addition to the rule against non-discrimination) the question of integration has become more prominent. Does the system mandate negative integration, encapsulated by the non-discrimination principle—states should not do certain things—or is it better represented as promoting positive integration—states should introduce these particular standards into their domestic legal systems (Hoekman and Kostecki, 2001: 413)?

Allied to the integration debate is the question of harmonization, and whether or not the GATT/WTO system should facilitate the production of global norms, or protect nation-state norm-diversity. It has always been an article of faith of the field that nation states retain full autonomy to regulate domestic issues in whichever way they deem appropriate (Roessler in Bhagwati and Hudec, 1997). This view is, of course, carefully hedged with the condition that states lose national power if their actions result in inter-state discrimination in trade. However, the autonomy of the position about retention of the full complement of national competence is subject to encroachment from a variety of angles including: the expansion of international economic law into areas formerly within the domestic domain such as health; adoption of more stringent standards of review; discussion of extension of existing agreements on services; and expansion into new areas such as investment and competition.

Once again we have come full circle. The problem of 'what is international economic law?' turns out to be related to the starting-point of our inquiry, namely its focus on institutions, constitutions, and globalization. Both the subject-matter ambit and jurisdictional scope of international economic law raise questions concerning the harmonization of international norms and whether to move to a deeper level of integration. Once this link is established, it becomes clear that the question of what the appropriate scope of the field is (the definitional question) is a constitutional one, both in the technical sense that it raises issues about how the system is being constituted, and in the normative sense in that it leads us to questions about who decides (its scope), where those decisions take place, and on whose authority.

6 A *TRANSFORMATIVE* NATURE CAPABLE OF FACILITATING IMPROVEMENTS IN LEGAL ORDER GENERALLY

The final characteristic I want to discuss concerns the transformative nature of international economic law scholarship. In its early manifestation the transformative potential of the discipline was thought to assist in understanding economic change and thus improving social life. Douglass North argued that the institutional theory of economics made it easier to understand 'the endless struggle of human beings to solve the problems of cooperation so that they may reap the advantages not only of technology, but also of all the other facets of human endeavor that constitute civilization' (North, 1990: 133). More recently, it has been suggested that the improved institutional arrangements of WTO law, post-Uruguay, could be used as a model for international order more generally (Petersmann, 1999). Based on the WTO experience, the UN could link human rights to security matters and establish a stronger centralized and binding dispute-resolution system. In between understanding and modelling, the transformative urge of international economic law scholarship takes the form of a Kantian equation of international trade harmony with international peace and security. Simply put, states that trade together rarely, if ever, go to war against each other. Linked to this is the view that democratic states rarely, if ever, go to war with each other. Hence we see the conflation of the three ideals of free market, democracy, and peace, and the return to our recurring theme about the constitutional issues implicated in international economic law change. Perhaps the best example of the argument that international economic law is constitutional is Ernst Ulrich Petersmann's suggestion that international trade rights be re-characterized as human rights with all the conceptual baggage that the latter connotes (Petersmann, 2002).

The problem with the transformative urge of international economic law is that it may be too transformative in one sense and not very transformative in another. At one end of the scale is the work that suggests that international economic law can transform world systems (Petersmann, 1999). Others have criticized the claim that international economic law is transformative, arguing instead that it is 'quasi-mechanical and facilitative, focusing on communication and correspondence between systems rather than construction of a new international legal order' (Kennedy, 1994: 95). A further criticism is that international economic law is not transformative at all and is a revisiting of standard liberal arguments for free trade which create a legal structure for liberal economic principles which perpetuates pre-existing inequalities of access and wealth (Gathii, 1999). Globalization by any other name is (unequal) liberalization still. One way out of this conundrum would be (*a*) to begin to analyse the precise ways in which international economic law is contributing to redistributive change, as opposed to reinforcing existing situations; (*b*) to identify the particular values which are being promoted by current trade transformations, and (*c*) to examine the neutrality and structure of the international economic law system. In other words, international economic law scholarship could usefully address the nature of specific transformations, which are, by any measure, undoubtedly occurring; and also stand back, and examine the system as a whole. For instance, the question of China and the WTO becomes interesting at both the micro-level (what particular changes will its entry facilitate in China and in international trading rules) and at the macro-level where wider transformations might be taking place (how might the fundamental structures of international trade law be altered by China's participation?). Similarly, while studying developing countries in international trade, one could look at the effects of the introduction of competition policy on the particular internal economies of those states. But one might also think about the reconfiguration of the basic dynamics of the relationship between developing and developed which will occur. Researching the specific in combination with the general will help illuminate the particular ways in which the field has transformative potential, if at all.

7 CONCLUSION

International business and commerce operates within a fascinating and sprawling array of legal developments, particularly in respect of international trade. Nested within these expanding borders are important issues confronting internationalized law and public order. In order to tackle those issues, future research will consider specific aspects of the package of arrangements envisaged for a system of global economic relations, the role of scholarship within those arrangements, and the overall architecture of the field. The role of institutions and constitutions in international economic law; their association with globalization; the forms, locations, and content of law and regulation; and the investigation of consensus and critique about these matters will be critical parts of the research agenda of international economic law.

References

Appadurai, A. (1990). 'Disjuncture and Difference in the Global Cultural Economy', *Public Culture*, 2: 1–24.

Balasubramanyam, V. N. (ed.) (1997). *Jagdish Bhagwati—Writings on International Economics*, Delhi: Oxford University Press.

Bedjaoui, M. (1979). *Towards a New International Economic Order*, Paris: UNESCO; New York and London: Holmes and Meier Publishers.

Bhagwati, J. N., and Hudec, R. E. (1997). *Fair Trade and Harmonization, Volume 2: Legal Analysis* (2nd print., 1997), Cambridge, Mass.: MIT Press (1st pub., 1996).

Braithwaite, J., and Drahos, P. (2000). *Global Business Regulation*, Cambridge: Cambridge University Press.

Cass, D. Z. (2001). 'The "Constitutionalization" of International Trade Law: Judicial Norm-Generation as the Engine of Constitutional Development in International Trade', *European Journal of International Law*, 12: 39–75.

Gathii, J. T. (1999). 'Good Governance as a Counter Insurgency Agenda to Oppositional and Transformative Social Projects in International Law', *Buffalo Human Rights Law Review*, 5: 107–74.

—— (2001). 'Re-Characterizing the Social in the Constitutionalization of the WTO: A Preliminary Analysis', *Widener Law Symposium Journal*, 7: 137–73.

George, S. (2001). 'Corporate Globalisation', in E. Bircham and J. Charlton (eds.), *Anti-Capitalism: A Guide to the Movement*, London: Bookmarks Publications.

Habermas, J. (2001). 'A Constitution for Europe?' *New Left Review*, 11: 5–26.

Hardt, M., and Negri, A. (2000). *Empire*, Cambridge, Mass.: Harvard University Press.

Hoekman, B., and Kostecki, M. (2001). *The Political Economy of the World Trading System* (2nd edn.), Oxford: Oxford University Press.

Howse, R., and Nicolaidis, K. (2001). 'Legitimacy, and Global Governance: Why Constitutionalizing the WTO is a Step too Far', in P. Suave, R. B. Porter, A. Subramanian, and A. B. Zampetti, *Equity, Efficiency and Legitimacy: The Multilateral Trading System at the Millennium*, Washington: Brookings Institution.

Hudec, R. E. (1987). *Developing Countries in the GATT Legal System*, London: Gower Publishing Co.

—— (1999). *Essays on the Nature of International Trade Law*, London: Cameron May.

Jackson, J. H., Davey, W., and Sykes, A. (1995). *Legal Problems of International Economic Relations* (3rd edn.), St Paul, Minn.: West Publishing Co.

Kennedy, D. (1994). 'The International Style in Postwar Law and Policy', *Utah Law Review*, 1: 7–103.

Maduro, M. P. (1997). *We the Court: The European Court of Justice and the European Economic Constitution: A Critical Reading of Article 30 of the EC Treaty*, Oxford: Hart.

North, D. C. (1990). *Institutions, Institutional Change and Economic Performance* (1995 repr.), Cambridge: Cambridge University Press.

Petersmann, E. U. (1997). *International Trade Law and GATT/WTO Dispute Settlement System 1948–1996*, London: Kluwer.

—— (1999). 'Constitutionalism and International Adjudication: How to Constitutionalize the U.N. Dispute Settlement System', *New York Journal of International Law and Politics*, 31: 753–90.

—— (2002). 'Time for a United Nations "Global Compact" for Integrating Human Rights into the Law of Worldwide Organizations', *European Journal of International Law*, 13: 1–30.

Picciotto, S., and Mayne, R. (1999). *Regulating International Business: Beyond Liberalization*, Basingstoke: Macmillan; New York: St Martin's Press.

Rajagopal, B. (1999). 'Corruption, Legitimacy and Human Rights: The Dialectic of the Relationship', *Connecticut Journal of International Law*, 14: 495–507.

—— (2000). 'From Resistance to Renewal: The Third World, Social Movements and the Expansion of International Institutions', *Harvard International Law Journal*, 41: 529–78.

Seidl-Hohenveldern, I. (1999). *International Economic Law* (3rd edn.), The Hague, London, and Boston: Kluwer.

Snyder, F. (1999). 'Governing Economic Globalisation: Global Legal Pluralism and European Law', *European Law Journal*, 5: 334–74.

Teubner, G. (2000). 'Global Private Regimes: Neospontaneous Law and Dual Constitution of Autonomous Sectors?' http://www.uni-frankfurt.de/fb01/teubner/

Trebilcock M., and Howse, R. (1995). *The Regulation of International Trade* (2nd edn., 1999), London and New York: Routledge.

Weiler, J. (1999). *The Constitution of Europe*, Cambridge: Cambridge University Press.

PART V

TECHNOLOGY

CHAPTER 28

INTELLECTUAL PROPERTY

WENDY J. GORDON

1 INTRODUCTION

1.1 Defining the Field

1.1.1 *Overview*

THIS chapter concerns a group of doctrines that bear a family relation to each other. Doctrines usually included under the rubric of 'Intellectual Property' (IP) include, among others, copyright, patent, trademark, trade secrecy, so-called 'moral' rights, rights in the topography of integrated circuits, rights in industrial design, plant breeder rights, rights of publicity, database rights, and rights against misappropriation. Not all nations recognize or enforce all the doctrines, but because of international obligations, most nations must recognize much of this list.

Each doctrine involves restraining people from using or duplicating a pattern that is owned by, or associated with, another party. The range of potentially covered

Copyright 2003 by Wendy Gordon. I thank Paula Baron, Robert Denicola, Estelle Derclaye, Rochelle Dreyfuss, Gail Evans, Mike Meurer, Malla Pollack, Richard Posner, David Vaver, and Richard Watt for generous suggestions, and Allan Axelrod for helping me to see that IP (and intentionality) is everywhere. Finally, I would like to express my appreciation to F. Scott Kieff who contributed substantial ideas and expression to my discussion of patent law. Responsibility for all error of course rests with me.

patterns is wide, including, for example, patterns in words, symbols, gene segments, the settings on computer switches, physical structures, processes, colors, and sounds. The patterns are thought of as valuable intangibles, capable of being embodied in, and replicated by, physical media.

There are five key parts to each such law. An IP law will specify the kinds of subject-matters (patterns) covered; it will define the nature of the restraints (rights) associated with the covered subject-matters and specify the corresponding remedies; it will state the criteria that give rise to ownership or other ability to assert the rights; it will specify privileges, limits, and defenses to the rights; and it will specify whether and how the rights and privileges are transferable.

1.1.2 *Can 'Intangible' or 'Intellectual' Serve as Unifying Concepts*

As noted, the conventional label for the field has become 'Intellectual Property', but the label is not fully accurate. One difficulty is that the label presumes that a 'thing' exists that can be owned. However, the 'thing' around which rights are organized in IP—the intangible product—is simply a conceptual construct. Most IP doctrines can be reconceptualized in ways that dispense with the notion of intangible 'things'. For example, instead of seeing trademark law as allocating rights in a 'thing' called a 'trademark', one can rather see trademark doctrines as an elaboration of rights against fraud. For another example, copyright law can be seen as a legal device that simply enables authors to charge different prices for identical copies (Gordon in Symposium on the Internet and Legal Theory, 1998). Another difficulty is that the term 'intellectual property' is drastically overbroad, for virtually any interest can be conceived of as a 'valuable intangible'. For example, a decrepit factory can, without causing any physical damage, injure the property values of its residential neighbor. The factory's ugliness is an 'intangible'—but that does not make zoning law a branch of IP.

The word 'intellectual' in 'intellectual property' does not only refer to the intangibility of the 'things' involved. The word 'intellectual' is usually taken to indicate that the patterns protected by IP doctrine have been produced by human mental activity. For example, the painter deliberately creates the patterns of brushwork and colors that make up the mural or portrait. Yet here, too, the language is deceptive, for in some IP fields it can be very hard to see the role of mental activity. For example, the 'right of publicity' attaches to famous faces—and although the celebrity's career may be a deliberate artefact, the face probably is not. Similarly, trademarks can be protected even if the companies using them did not originate them. For another example, many English-speaking nations give copyright or *sui generis* protection to databases that are a product more of physical than mental labor. Perhaps it would be better to say that the 'intellectual' component can be either in the mode of creation, *or* in the way that product is used.

Such an alternative formulation has possibilities: after all, the celebrity face, the trademark, and the database can all serve as sources of meaning or information. However, although that approach to definition has the merit of embracing more IP doctrines, it has the vice of over-breadth. All things can be invested with meaning, and even the most physical of values may depend on knowledge (e.g. water increases in value once we know that water is for drinking). If 'intellectual' refers to the fact that some aspect of creation, distribution, or use employs the mental faculty, virtually nothing would be excluded.

1.1.3 Is it 'Property'?

The 'property' portion of the 'intellectual property' label has caused practical as well as conceptual difficulties. Too many courts have assumed that all things called 'property' should be treated similarly, ignoring the important physical, institutional, and statutory differences that distinguish intellectual 'property' from the tangible kind. For example, it has become standard in the study of IP to note that patent and copyright reflect a *balance* between two effects on society: (1) providing incentives to authors and inventors, and (2) providing access to the members of the public, both as consumers and as potential new authors and inventors who need to copy in order to implement their own creativity and skill. The first goal (incentives) is served by giving rights to IP proprietors. The second goal (access) is served by giving liberties to the public, which involves limiting IP owners' rights in ways quite foreign to ordinary property. Yet those limits are as crucial to IP as are the rights that IP grants. (Or at least the limits should be as important. The dynamics of public choice sometimes result in special interests having a greater impact on IP legislation than does the interest of the general public (see Litman, 2001).)

Another difficulty with the 'property' label is that, even more obviously than with ordinary property, the essence of IP law is person-to-person, not person-to-thing. This relational focus might have been better captured by the label that the US bar employed for the field during the first half of the last century, 'unfair competition'. In my view, that was a better phrase (albeit still imperfect) to unite the various doctrines. The core and most justifiable part of the essence of the IP cause of action is to restrain some act of duplication or free riding that, if widespread, would be wrongful ('unfair') because it is immoral and/or economically costly. Economic cost in IP usually stems from the danger that free riding will cause a loss of incentives, leading to under-production, or from the danger that fraud and confusion will result from too many entities using the same symbol. However, 'unfair competition', too, is inadequate as a label.

Most obviously, it is misleading as a descriptive matter. IP owners today have rights against persons who are neither competitors nor cause effects like those caused by competitors. It is even a bit misleading to use 'unfair competition' as a normative model. That is because competitors are not the only persons who can use strangers' patterns in ways that have deleterious social effects.

Today, the phrase 'unfair competition' tends to be reserved for a particular subset of IP causes of action, particularly passing off (the tort of mislabeling one's goods to deceive consumers into thinking they are made by someone else, a tort recognized historically in virtually all countries) and misappropriation (a controversial tort recognized by some state jurisdictions in the United States). Passing off and misappropriation typically require a plaintiff to prove that a defendant's behavior is of a type likely to cause harm to the public (e.g. is likely to confuse, or likely to leave the plaintiff's customers without a source for the contested good or service). By contrast, neither copyright nor patent law requires proprietors in the ordinary case to offer proof that the defendant's behavior will be socially harmful. (In fact, copyright and patent typically allow proprietors to succeed even if they can show no *private* harm.)

As mentioned, many subfields in IP require judges to impose liability without allowing inquiry into whether granting the relief sought by the plaintiff will further the public interest. This, too, is characteristic of 'property'. Whether rooted in a belief that owners' pursuit of their self-interest can serve the public good, in an esteem for owners' autonomy interests, or in a desire to increase certainty and decrease litigation costs, causes of action of the property type usually require a judge to defer to an owner's will. By contrast, the approach found in 'unfair competition' was conditional. With a conditional right, the plaintiff can prevail only by proving some fact (such as likelihood of confusion, still used today in traditional trademark actions) that the doctrine takes to indicate that a plaintiff's victory would serve the public interest.

There are some economic advantages to rejecting conditional approaches and instead choosing deference to an owner. For example, the deference that is characteristic of 'property' can simplify administration, make use of decentralized information via pricing signals, and decrease the transaction costs involved in disseminating works. Some markets may well be 'perfect' enough to allow the Invisible Hand to guide owners to serve the public interest while pursuing private gain. Therefore, so long as the subject-matters protected by IP were narrowly defined, and the scope of rights were also narrow, the benefits of using the 'property' formulation clearly outweighed the costs. That is because the narrow definitions made it likely that any prima-facie violation of the IP right would also be an act that hurt the public. Dispensing with the need for a plaintiff to show a particularized personal or social harm reduced the cost of adjudication, increased certainty, and made it easier to buy and sell rights—and, so long as the IP was sufficiently narrow, may have done so without significantly chilling the socially desirable use of created works by third parties.

However, over the years, the definitions of both subject-matters and protectable rights have expanded. (For example, under early copyright statutes, the proprietor typically had rights only against slavish duplication and sale of the copyrighted manuscript. She had no right to veto, for example, a creative adaptation of her work that served a different market. By contrast, today a copyright proprietor's rights extend over creative uses that others may wish to make of her work.) With this expansion, a lack of fit between private and public interest has become increasingly likely to occur in given IP cases.

At least, so is the view of this writer, and of the growing academic consensus. Various devices exist to ameliorate this situation. More IP rights could be put into a conditional form, such as 'unfair competition', where the plaintiff would have to show some indicia that the public interest would be served by stopping the defendant's behavior, or making the defendant pay. Another possibility is to retain the property form, but alter its remedies, perhaps eliminating injunctions in a significant class of cases (Reichman in Dreyfuss *et al.*, 2001; on separating the inquiries into behavior and compensation, see Gordon in Elkin-Koren and Netanel, 2002). There are many ways in which the scope and subject-matter of IP could be trimmed back to a narrower and more easily justifiable compass.

As mentioned, one salient alternative might be to modify the strict property form with procedures or defenses that make IP rights more conditional. The US defense of 'fair use' is one such possibility. It can be employed as a sorting device. When the defendant cannot plausibly claim fair use, that may indicate that her case can safely be decided via formal deference to an owner. When by contrast, the defendant can make out a plausible fair use claim, that may be a case worth the high cost of a judge doing a case-by-case, fact-intensive evaluation of whether the defendant's use should go forward. Such defenses can be structured so that the defendant has to make some special showing to trigger their application, thus potentially reserving the complexity of non-property conditional inquiry to a manageable subset of cases.

Copyright and patent are unlike ordinary tangible property in a number of ways. From an economic perspective, the subject-matters of copyright and patent are more like inexhaustible 'public goods' that are ordinarily un-owned, than they are like exhaustible 'private goods'. Further, there are both personal and public interest components to many IP doctrines, leading the law to give less market control to 'owners' than to most owners of ordinary tangible property. However, over time, IP is becoming more like ordinary tangible property.

Constraining the growth of IP is conceptually attractive but politically difficult, in part because of international agreements and industry pressures, and in part because, ironically, the 'property' label itself seems to reassure some judges and legislators that the expansions in IP have legitimacy. Nevertheless, serving the public good by constraining IP is a fruitful area in which much scholarly work is being done, particularly under the rubrics of expanding the public domain, and investigating the possibilities of commons-based institutions.

In sum: although copyright and patent do not require proof in *individual* cases that the defendant has done harm or behaved badly, the rationales typically given to justify copyright, patent, and most of the other IP doctrines are the same as those underlying 'unfair competition', namely, a desire to restrain behavior that is either immoral or likely to damage the public. Under the rubric of 'Intellectual Property', unfortunately, the grant of rights often outruns its rationale.

1.1.4 *Is Similitude the Key to IP?*

As a penultimate try at unifying the field, I will return to the notion of 'pattern' with which this chapter began, and suggest that IP concerns *similitude among patterns*. (Instead of 'similitude', one could say 'resemblance' or 'likeness'. The central conception of similitude is the quality of two things being identical or similar in essential respects, either in function or as perceived.) Plaintiffs in a trademark, copyright, patent, right of publicity suit are usually suing because someone has made, sold, or employed a pattern that in essential ways is *similar to* something the plaintiffs made or something associated with them.

'Similitude' is hardly a perfect unifier. First, similitude serves different functions as one travels from doctrine to doctrine. Secondly, not all the branches of IP require a showing of similitude; notably, 'moral rights' can be concerned with protecting original paintings and sculptures from distortion. In the European countries where moral rights originated, however, moral rights extend to distorted copies (similitudes) as well. Moreover, as the scope of IP rights expands (particularly in copyright and rights of publicity), the test for infringement threatens to go far beyond similitude. Suits have been successful because the defendant has done something that could *remind* the audience of plaintiff, or had the same *concept and feel* as what plaintiff made, or somehow borrowed a luster associated with plaintiff. Nevertheless, I suggest it is the role of similitude that has led the courts and the academy to see the various doctrines now known as Intellectual Property as belonging together.

1.1.5 *Externalities: The Beneficial and Harmful Effects one Causes without Experiencing*

A final unifying concept remains to be considered: the notion of 'externality'. Those effects that flow from an act that do not affect the actor herself are said to be 'external' to her. An effect becomes 'internal' when law (or the law of nature) brings the impact to bear on an actor who had a role in causing it.

The externality notion is applicable to that subset of IP concerned with copying. This subset comprises the largest part of IP. For example, a copyright suit can be won only if copying is proved, and even in patent and trademark suits—where coincidental similitude can give rise to liability—many important cases involve copying. To copy is to reap a benefit from the efforts of the person copied. Thus, most of IP law is concerned with internalizing positive externalities: when someone copies or adapts a book or invention without paying the originator, the benefit remains 'external' to the originator and is thus unlikely to affect her incentives. When IP requires the copier or adapter to pay, part of the benefit is 'internalized' to the originator.

In this respect, IP can be visualized as tort law turned upside down: ordinary tort law, governing unintentional injury, encourages persons to take precautions by making them bear some of the costs their risky behavior imposes on others. IP law encourages persons to become more productive by allowing them to capture some of the benefits their useful behavior gives to others. Thus, just as ordinary accident law internalizes negative externalities to discourage carelessness, IP law internalizes positive externalities to encourage productivity.

However, note an important caveat: no one would suggest that IP should internalize *all* the benefits that flow from an intangible. For example, imagine how odd the world would be if a young person had to pay the authors of his textbooks for all the benefits that, over a lifetime, the books generated for him. Therefore, 'externality' merely provides a mode for beginning one's analysis, and does not provide a self-defining answer to how far IP should extend. Among other things, IP must be as concerned with the follow-on innovator as with originators. In the year 2003, every originator is a borrower as well. Many IP doctrines recognize this need to serve new generations, and accommodate it by techniques such as limiting the duration of the copyright or patent term, limiting the scope of rights, or shielding some subject-matters from ownership. (To illustrate the latter technique, readers are free to build upon the ideas they learn in copyrighted books because 'expression' but not 'ideas' can be owned under copyright law.) As in accident law a careless pedestrian can 'cause' an accident, a copier or adapter of someone else's work can 'cause' benefits to arise for the public. Both plaintiff and defendant need to bear and capture some of the costs and benefits of their activities.

1.2 Implications of the Doctrinal Divisions

Just as there is dispute on how to characterize the field, there is a great deal of inter-penetration among the categories. For example, analogies from trademark law have helped expand the right of publicity, and once the right of publicity was established, lawyers representing plaintiffs in trademark cases used analogy to borrow some attri-butes from the new right of publicity to expand trademark law further (Denicola, 1994, esp. 617–27).

Scholars dispute not only the normative basis of the various doctrines (morality and natural law? consequentialism? consistency?), but also the boundaries between doctrines (both patent and copyright can cover aspects of computer programs), the institutional tools in which the various doctrines are instantiated (property rights? personal rights? conditional tort rights?), and the institutional sources (judges? legislatures? constitutions? custom?) that are best suited to create IP rights.

The battle of labels is oddly important, since the increased economic importance of intellectual products has made the scope of IP a major political issue. The 'prop-erty' analogy helps the law of IP expand much as, in earlier days, the more pejorative but equally descriptive label 'monopoly' helped keep IP from expanding. Behind the labels are some obvious functional queries. The debate over 'property' versus 'tort' usually centers on the extent to which an IP 'owner' can sue to restrain or obtain com-pensation for a non-harmful use. (Since free riding by definition always creates *some* benefit—someone is getting a ride, after all—the question of whether an IP plaintiff need prove harm can be an essential issue.) The debate over 'personal' versus 'property' characteristics usually centers on the question of whether a given right is waivable, alienable, or descendible/heritable. And so on. Despite a century of Legal Realism, the functional issues are often obscured by labels.

1.3 Overview of Developments in IP Theory

It is often said that on the European Continent, IP is perceived as having its roots in natural law and natural right, while in Anglo-American jurisdictions the basis of IP is utilitarian (Kase, 1967). For example, the dominance of consequentialist reasoning in the United States is indicated by the language of the constitutional clause authorizing Congress to grant copyrights and patents: 'To promote the Progress of Science and the useful Arts' (art. I, cl. 8, para. 8). Nevertheless, intimations of both rights-based and utility-based claims can be found in most countries. For example, both rights-types of analysis and consequentialist forms of analysis can be found in the revolutionary settings of both the United States and France (Ginsburg, 1990).

IP theorizing was sparse in legal academia until the second half of the twentieth century. Despite an occasional lapse into illogic on the part of courts and legislatures, theorizing on intellectual property law has flowered as IP has become more economically important. So far, the theoretical approaches have derived largely from the models used for analyzing the common law. Theories of torts (involving physical harms), property (of the tangible type), and restitution (unjust enrichment) have been extended into IP, with useful results.

The most profitable lines of analysis for copyright and patent have been drawn from economics, where the most influential writing has so far come out of the United States. However, the US law and economics movement has tended to take a pro-property position. It is only recently that the economic virtues of common ownership have begun to be explored there, by scholars such as Benkler (2002), Eisenberg (in Dreyfuss *et al.*, 2001), and Rose (1998). Much of the literature exploring the virtues of common ownership for IP has come from Australia and Canada (see Drahos, 'Introduction', and articles by Mandeville and others in Drahos, 1999, and Coombe, forthcoming). However, with the formalization of the 'anti-commons' model the United States is catching up. See, for example, Heller and Eisenberg (1998).

On the philosophical side, theories developed from a Lockean base have been the most influential in IP. John Locke argued that persons who mixed their labor with an object from the common—such as someone who caught a fish, or picked an apple from a wild apple tree—should have property in it, subject to the proviso that the person seeking property has left 'enough, and as good' in the common for others to use. Lockean theory has been used as a basis for 'justifying' IP and, via the Lockean proviso, as a basis for curtailing its reach (Drahos, 1996; Gordon, 1993; Hettinger in Drahos, 1999).

For example, some have questioned the fairness of the rule adopted by most countries that gives patent owners the power to enjoin even coincidental and independent invention. Yet 'fairness' is a slippery concept. The Lockean proviso provides one fruitful logic for examining this aspect of patent doctrine. When a patent owner is entitled to restrain a third party who happens to have independently duplicated his work, the restraint leaves the third party without 'enough and as good'. Therefore if the patent rule is to be justified in fairness terms, investigation is needed into whether there is empirical support for alternative formulations of fairness, such as whether all persons involved in a patent race *consent* to the winner-take-all patent system—or, perhaps, whether the short duration of patents suffices to keep 'enough, and as good' for the re-inventor (Sherman and Bently, 1999; Gordon, 1993).

For a potential application of the Lockean proviso drawn from copyright, consider an influential work of authorship that has deeply affected its audience. A broad copyright law could give that work's author the power to restrain new authors who are hostile to the first work's point of view from making substantial but necessary quotation from that first work. Such suppression could leave persons affected by the first work worse off than they would have been had they never seen the first work. This harms them, and violates the essential equality that the proviso seeks to protect. Accordingly, the hostile use of the first work should be permitted (either by employing a doctrine of 'fair use' or 'fair dealing', or by limiting the first author's prima-facie claim rights), lest second comers lack tools to deal with their culture that are 'enough, and as good' as the tools the first author had at her disposal.

A difficulty with Locke's argument is that it focuses on 'labor', and many of the IP doctrines distinguish between (1) physical work and mental work, and between (2) creative mental work and merely arduous mental work. Although countries and doctrines differ on the importance of the 'kind' of labor employed, and modern IP law sometimes seeks to look at the created 'thing' separately from the process that brought it forth, it is clear that the kind of labor or creativity often matters a great deal (Sherman and Bently, 1999). Locke's philosophy does not readily explain why the type of labor should matter.

Economics does not provide a ready explanation either. Goods produced by both physical and mental labor, and by both creative and non-creative mental labor, can suffer from public-goods-type fencing difficulties. (For example, even a non-creative database can be cheaply copied, as can a non-creative layout of type on a page, or a restored movie.) Nevertheless, nations typically reserve the initial grant of IP rights to products involving at least some mental labor, and some doctrines and nations give greater protection to the creative and inventive.

To explain the dominance of this trend, and the fact that most observers are more comfortable with 'property'-like protection for intangibles tinged with personality, one explanation might be technological history: most physical work, such as laying out type, did not become open to free riding until recently. (In prior centuries, each typesetter had to set his own type; today, a typeset manuscript can be quickly scanned into a computer and duplicated.) However, more than path dependence may be at work. For investigation of whether and how the 'personal' element *should* be important, we probably should look to sources such as Hegelian and Kantian philosophy. At least in the English-speaking world, although some valuable work has been done (see Drahos, 1996; Hughes, 1998), application of those schools of thought to IP is still at an early stage. Another possible explanation for the respect given the 'personal' may be a romantic vision of authorship that understates the author's need to use and build upon her predecessors (Boyle, 1996) (criticizing the notion of romantic authorship). Nevertheless, all accounts that lay stress upon the 'personal' element have to face the awkward fact that most copyrights and patents are owned not by the authors and inventors, but by their employers or assignees.

Some work has been done on the basic question of when and whether products of the mind should be commodified (Elkin-Koren and Netanel, 2002). The empirical fact that something has value too often leads judges and lawgivers to give it property status. Property need not and should not automatically flow from value (Dreyfuss, 1990). There are many reasons for this—notably, privatizing individual value flows can threaten a larger but less-appropriable stream of social value (Drahos, see e.g., 'Introduction', in Drahos, 1996).

The commodification literature can be helpful with this basic issue. For example, many of the policies that counsel against making body parts alienable also help explain the copyright policy that allows people to use the ideas they may have integrated into their thinking as a result of reading others' work. Ideas of human dignity have played a role in the disputes over the patenting of gene sequences, and the issue of patenting genetically altered mice and other live beings. They may also play a role in the special devices that many nations embed in their statutes for protecting authors as against the publishers and entrepreneurs who exploit their work, such as the non-waivable right of termination that the United States gives all authors outside the work-for-hire context or the Canadian right of reversion. (See Cornish, 2002 (overview of the publisher-author issue, including treatment in France and Germany); also see Hansmann and Santilli in Towse and Holzhauer, 2002, vol. 1 (arguing that giving artists non-waivable, inalienable moral rights to safeguard their work's integrity can also serve the public's economic interest).)

Similarly, IP ramifications arise out of the familiar commodification debates about whether it is better to identify distinct 'spheres' of activity (or distinct types of goods) that should be segregated from the market, or whether all activities and all goods could in some contexts benefit from non-market treatment. The 'sphere' approach supports using bright line tests such as excluding certain intangibles from possible ownership, while the contextual approach supports using flexible devices such as 'fair use'. Nevertheless, as with the anti-commons in economics, the anti-commodification arguments and their application to IP are still in a fairly early stage of development.

Another area that is attracting study, but needs much more development, is the study of what kinds of environment foster the best and most diverse creative work. Most of the valuable work is likely to come from social psychologists. Consider, for example, the work of Theresa Amabile and colleagues (1996). Their experiments tentatively suggest that it is intrinsic motivation that makes for the best creative work, as opposed to extrinsic motivators such as money. How should that possibility influence our view of the extrinsic motivator that IP provides? One implication may be remedial: a full property right, complete with injunction, may feel more natural to artists, and thus less extrinsic, than would a remedy limited to monetary relief. Amabile herself admits the tentative nature of her research, and although a great deal of work is done on the psychology of creativity, more of it should be aimed at discovering how law can (or cannot) be of assistance. One complicating difficulty is the fact that many of the actors in the IP field are corporations and persons with purely business motives.

Meanwhile, as intimated, international developments and industry pressures move ahead of sound theorizing. Increased protection is being mandated virtually everywhere. This pro-property movement has created two major problems that cut across virtually all areas of IP (copyright, patent, trade secret, and so on): developing nations (Reichman in Towse and Holzhauer, 2002; and Braga in ibid.), and public domain (Boyle, 1996; Lange in Drahos, 1999).

Regarding developing nations, most observers agree that Third World populations need both access to technology, and some ability to control and profit from their ecological and cultural assets. As for the first issue, the most prominent debate is on reasonably priced access to AIDS drugs. As for the second issue, much debate concerns issues of legal technique: how can a nation exclude outsiders from its treasures of communally developed age-old medical and cultural information, particularly given the individualistic bent and limited duration of Western models of IP.

In developed nations, the converse problem appears: the need to keep a strong public domain. There is an ironic tension between the two problems: for distributional justice reasons, many favor the developing nations keeping control over their assets, but these may be the same assets that in developed nations need to be kept free for all to use. So far, the conflict has been under-theorized, with the same scholars favoring both results without addressing the contradiction (Boyle, 1996). Part of the solution may lie in the anthropology of groups: sharing *within* a group has different implications than sharing *outside* it. Rose (1998) calls this 'limited common property'. Part of the difficulty is the tension between group and national claims of distributive justice, and individual claims of corrective justice.

Another important issue is 'fit' with free speech principles. In the United States through the First Amendment and in England and many Commonwealth countries through the Declaration of Human Rights, free speech has the potential to trump IP rights. Whether or not that potential can be fulfilled is a subject of much debate and, in the United States, recent litigation. Ironically, although publishers in England initially obtained functional protection against copyists by serving the Crown's desire for censorship, copyright came to maturity in the first copyright statute as opposed to censorship (Patterson in Drahos, 1999).

IP law is not the only mode of excluding non-payors from creative products. Locked drawers and drawn curtains can do so as well, just as sometimes the practicalities of production can give a first comer a substantial lead-time advantage over potential copyists (Breyer in Towse and Holzhauer, 2002). While tangible space has always provided some modes of excluding non-payors, Lessig (1999) has suggested that the architecture of cyberspace is uniquely controllable. For example, the law will never face the issue of whether public policy supports giving the public a right to read and copy a particular work if the work is so encrypted that the affected public does not know enough about what is behind the barrier to challenge it. Much argument suggests that we need to import public policy—for example, providing access to ideas, avoiding unconscionability, fostering fair use—into the regulation of privately developed computer code, and into the way our courts enforce shrinkwrap and Internet contracts (Fisher in Symposium on the Internet and Legal Theory, 1998). However, the legislatures have so far tended to go in the opposite direction, enacting legal prohibitions to discourage hacking and encourage acceptance of encryption.

The next section of the chapter describes the primary areas of IP. It is followed by an outline of some of the dominant economic approaches, as economics provides the most developed line of systematic scholarship thus far.

2 IP SUBSTANCE: OVERVIEW OF PARTICULAR DOCTRINES

As mentioned above, the various doctrines of IP have at most a 'family resemblance', in Wittgenstein's sense: no one defining characteristic is necessary or sufficient for making something 'intellectual property', but there will be many common characteristics between any two of the doctrines, and when the group is viewed together a family resemblance may be perceived. For example, copyright and rights of publicity involve free riding, that is, copying. By contrast, a patent or a trademark can be infringed even by someone who has not copied. (Nevertheless, the ordinary patent and trademark case probably involves copying.) In the United States, copyright and patent are alike in protecting products that result from some intellectual (more than merely laborious) effort, while in the Commonwealth nations the 'originality' needed for copyright may be sufficiently provided by sweat of the brow. There are other exceptions to the apparent importance of 'intellectual' content to 'intellectual property'. Notably, database rights in the European Union attach to labor and funds invested independently of creativity; trademark law requires neither intellectuality nor originality in choosing or devising a mark; and trade secrecy can protect even the most routine of productions, such as lists of customers.

As a matter of positive law, sources of Intellectual Property rights (IPRs) vary from country to country and from doctrine to doctrine. In the United States, for example, copyright and patent are federal and statutory, the right of publicity is state-based and most often judicially created, and trademark law is oddly ubiquitous: concurrently state and federal, judicial and statutory. In Europe, complexity is similar. For example, a trademark can be registered in a particular nation, in the EU, or both. Not only may local, national, and EU law and administrative bodies have an impact on

European IP rights, but also aspects of the Declaration of Human Rights—such as its protection for free speech—can play a role.

Copyright, patent, and trademark laws constitute the three main areas of IP. It will be useful to highlight some of the similarities and differences among them, and to mention some of the other areas where IPRs appear.

Copyright subsists in any work of original authorship once the work is fixed in a tangible medium of expression. (This is US language, but generally applicable in English-speaking countries. Other countries may not require fixation as a pre-requisite.) When someone writes a letter, takes a photograph, or makes a record of her band playing an old folk tune, she has a copyright. Prior to 1978, federal copyright in the United States applied only when an author had complied with particular formalities, but with the US desire to join the primary international convention on copyright, the Berne Convention, the US approach began to de-emphasize formalities.

Some creative efforts do not result in a copyright, or the copyright does not apply to all aspects of what has been created. For example, a book may contain original ideas or facts that the author has discovered by diligent and imaginative research, but ideas and facts are not usually copyrightable. (The UK is more generous to uncreative compilers than is the United States, however.) Short words or phrases are typically too trivial to be 'works of authorship', although if they serve to indicate a product's source they can be protected under trademark law. Perhaps the most contested limit on copyrightability has to do with attractive designs of useful objects (attractive bicycle racks, lamp bases, plastic copies of sculpted torsos used as fashion mannequins). Countries have widely varying approaches to design protection. Ordinarily, copyright law will have various limits to cabin the extent to which useful designs can be monopolized under its protection. This occurs because virtually all nations try to keep a border between patent law, which gives hard-to-achieve and short-lived protection to functional inventions, and copyright law, which gives easy-to-obtain and long-lived protection to works of expression.

This is related to the more general issue of how to provide appropriate but not over-large incentives for sub-patentable invention (Reichman in Dreyfuss *et al.*, 2001). Many countries are more hospitable to industrial design and sub-patentable invention than is the United States. Sherman and Bently (1999) suggest that, in Britain, design protection came to maturity early, as its own category and not as a hybrid between copyright and patent.

The United States is a dominant exporter of copyrighted works, but until recently viewed copyright as a dangerous incursion on public right, justifiable only to the extent that it served the public benefit, and to be narrowly construed. At least, that was how the law seemed to operate. For example, unless copyright notices of a particular type were attached to works when published, the work went into the public domain. Even today, a defendant in the United States can defeat a copyright suit by proving that the plaintiff's work was publicly distributed without notice before March 1989. As the United States abandoned formalities to come into compliance with the Berne Convention, the question has been raised whether it has also come to adopt some of the 'authors' rights' or 'natural rights' conceptions which have been particularly popular on the Continent.

Most copyrights last for the life of the author plus some number of years, usually fifty or seventy. After that time, the entire public shares the liberty to use the copyrighted work. Duration in virtually all countries has continually increased via legislation, and many debates currently focus on the wisdom and constitutionality of those extensions (Vaver, 2000).

During the 'copyright term' (i.e. the period during which a copyright is still valid), the copyright owner can obtain damages from, and enjoin, anyone who violates one or more of her exclusive rights. Many nations in their copyright acts give different rights to different kinds of works. For example, in the United States, 'musical works' (compositions) are a kind of subject-matter that has more rights than do 'sound recordings' (the sounds produced by singer and orchestra). Similarly, most nations have exceptions that favor particular industries. Some commentators, most notably Litman (2001) in the United States, have examined the public-choice dimension of copyright legislation, noting that the major players tend to be industries who obtain narrowly worded exceptions to protect themselves, leaving the public's liberty insufficiently protected.

Most copyright owners have exclusive rights over reproduction, public performance, public display, distribution, and the making of derivative works. In all cases, the plaintiff will have to prove that the defendant copied from the copyrighted material in a way that is qualitatively or quantitatively substantial. That is, copyright is only valid against those who 'free ride', and not against fully independent creators. In the United States, it is not an infringement to make a 'fair use' of copyrighted material, and what constitutes a 'fair use' is much debated. One interpretation sees 'fair use' as a response to occasions when the market may fail to serve social goals because, for example, significant transaction costs prevent desirable transactions or because non-monetizable interests are at stake (Gordon in Towse and Holzhauer, 2002, vol. 1). Other nations have more limited 'fair dealing' privileges, restricted to special types of dealing, such as research or criticism.

Copyrights can be bought, sold, licensed, subdivided, and inherited. There are limits on the freedom of disposition, however. For example, as mentioned above, both the United States and Canada give authors (not in a work-for-hire situation) rights to recapture copyrights they have assigned away. The Canadian right is automatic, and is triggered twenty-five years after the author's death. The US right has to be actively exercised, and is available much earlier. Both countries limit the author's ability to divest herself of this right.

Conflicts can arise requiring a choice of law. This is obvious when cyberspace crosses national boundaries. Jurisdictional issues, and issues of legitimacy, can arise within nations as well: for example, because of conflicts between layers of a federal state, or (in common law countries) between enacted legislation and common law.

In the United States, federal law will *pre-empt* state attempts to give subject-matter covered by the federal copyright statute rights equivalent to what the federal copyright statute grants. Thus, for example, pre-emption would invalidate a state law that tried to give the books written by resident authors a perpetual right against copying.

Probably the most important practical issue of the current day is private copying and copying for educational use (Litman, 2001). For example, to what extent should copyright liability attach to activities such as viewing a copyrighted work on the Internet, privately trading MP3 music files, videotaping movies, or photocopying? Some countries have established compulsory licenses for some of these uses. Others have turned to technological strategies, such as requiring that electronic devices be built in ways that inhibit copying, or giving copyright owners legal rights to discourage hackers from bypassing cryptography and other forms of electronic fencing. Other crucial issues are the potential conflict between copyright and free speech, and the extent to which copyright should be applicable to *standards* in computer software and elsewhere. Disciplines brought to bear on these issues include, for example, the economics of network effects, philosophies of commodification, and contested notions of human flourishing. For a guide to the law and society literature, see Coombe (forthcoming).

Patents are granted only to inventions that make some advance over prior art. There are several categories of patents, such as design patents intended for items that are ornamental rather than useful, and plant patents (see Reichman in Dreyfuss *et al.*, 2001). Most scholarly attention, however, is given to utility patents as the most economically significant category. (When this chapter uses the term 'patent', it generally will be referring to utility patents.) Issues here include matters such as the proper length of patent terms (David and Olsen and other works in Towse and Holzhauer, 2002, vol. 2), how to encourage follow-on innovation (see Scotchmer in ibid.), the scope of the patent right (see Merges and Nelson in ibid.), and whether first-to-invent or first-to-file should obtain patents.

In virtually all countries, to obtain a patent, it is not enough to have a breakthrough. No matter how meritorious one's invention might be, the inventor cannot obtain a patent unless she applies for one in a timely manner. This is quite different from the majority rule in copyright law, for a copyright arises automatically and is valid even if not registered with the applicable office.

Drafting patent claims is a demanding skill. In most nations, the examination process is costly (largely in attorney fees), cumbersome, and lengthy. Some applications are denied, often on the ground that the proffered inventions are not 'novel' or do not constitute a 'non-obvious' advance over the prior art. In many nations, even patents that are granted are likely to be invalidated by the courts. Some interesting statistical work has investigated the workings of patent systems (Lemley in Towse and Holzhauer, 2002, vol. 3).

There are several incentive-based theories underlying the patent system's grant to the patent applicant of the right to exclude others from practicing her invention if she can show that her invention satisfies the conditions for patentability. These include theories based on the incentives to invent, disclose, design around, and organize post-inventive activity. For each of these theories, discussed immediately below, it is argued that the patent system provides some incentive that would be present at sub-optimal levels absent the patent system.

The incentive to invent theory suggests that a patent is granted to encourage invention. Under this theory, it is postulated that without the inducement of a patent, inventors might not invest sufficiently in the inventive process. One objection to this theory is that the incentive may be too great, resulting in an inefficiently high level of pre-inventive activity or an unnecessary deadweight loss during the patent grant. This theory also raises questions about how to measure what would constitute an appropriate incentive. Questions also persist as to whether alternative tools such as subsidies, cash prizes, reputational advantage, or tax credits might be better than, or reduce the need for, a patent system.

The incentive to disclose theory suggests that a patent is granted to encourage an enabling disclosure of the invention claimed in the patent. This is related to a notion of patent as 'bargain': the government gives the possibility of exclusivity and in exchange the patent applicant gives disclosure. This teaching function is achieved upon publication of the issued patent, which in most regimes takes about three years after the application is filed, or upon publication of the application itself, which in most situations occurs 18 months after filing. (In the United States, an inventor who chooses a US-only patent can avoid having the application made public until and unless the patent issues.)

The incentive to disclose theory rests on two primary assumptions. First, it assumes that, without patents, inventors could profit from their work while concealing the knowhow or other information necessary to the enterprise. This assumption has difficulties. For example, many inventions bear their techniques on their face, so that secrecy is impossible. (Consider, for example, the design of an innovative paper clip.) The second assumption on which the incentive to disclose theory rests is that a patent's enabling disclosure actually teaches. It has been argued that the enabling disclosure of the patent application is often not enabling at all. In addition, many inventors are driven by fame and other non-pecuniary rewards at least as much as by money, and thus even without a patent may already be sufficiently motivated to make their advances public.

The incentive to design around theory suggests there are advantages in encouraging competitors to circumvent a patent's scope by inventing substitutes. As the market for a patented product becomes increasingly tight, the patent provides an increasingly strong incentive for third parties to invent non-infringing substitutes, or even infringing improvements. It is a live question whether such secondary inventive activity involves primarily redundancy and waste, or whether on balance such secondary inventive activity may be desirable: a second-generation product may be better than the first, perhaps being cheaper, more effective, or having fewer or even different collateral costs or side-effects.

The primary theory that focuses on organizing post-inventive activity is called the prospect theory. Related theories focus on the incentive to invest, incentive to innovate, or incentive to commercialize. Such theories focus not on how to encourage initial invention but rather on how to make an invention practicable and useful—much as claim systems in mineral prospecting are concerned not with creating gold or silver but with coordinating its extraction (see Kitch in Towse and Holzhauer, 2002, vol. 2). The patent holder can centralize the exploitation and development of the prospect. Without the exclusivity and public announcement provided by a patent, the theory argues, wastefully duplicative expenditures could ensue. The patent also solves the Arrow paradox (the notion that without a legal right, inventors will fear disclosing their invention lest it be copied, yet may need to disclose in order to sell or license it). For the prospect theory, the signaling function of the patent is especially important. The 'prospect' notion suggests that with a patent's issuance, venture capitalists, developers, advertisers, and product sellers can all begin to make the necessary investments to ensure that consumers will eventually be offered the invention's commercial embodiment. The prospect theory and its cousins have their critics as well, of course. For example, it is sometimes argued that apparently duplicative expenditures on research and development (R&D) are more likely to produce useful variations than they are to be wasteful. (This is, in fact, an assumption underlying the incentive to invent around theory.) Further, even a patent does not allow coordination of all follow-on innovation. For example, since the holder of an 'improvement patent' can cross-license with an original patent holder, independent experimentation to refine an invention can prove profitable. Moreover, many legal regimes are explicitly concerned with giving incentives to 'inventors', rather than to the entrepreneurs who may make inventions more publicly available.

If the government issues a patent, in most nations it is valid for twenty years from the application date. (In the United States, for patents pending when TRIPs (Trade-Related Aspects of Intellectual Property Rights) went into effect, one can get the longer of the twenty years or seventeen from issuance. Most countries do not have the seventeen-year option.) After that time, the entire public shares a liberty to use the patented invention. Many Supreme Court cases in the United States have emphasized that the public's liberty to share in an unpatented invention, or an invention whose patent has expired, is a crucial part of patent law.

During the period that a patent is valid, the patent owner can obtain damages from, and enjoin, anyone who makes, uses, sells or offers to sell or import into the United States a product or process that is covered by the patent claims, or that is considered equivalent thereto. It does not matter whether the identity between the patented and accused items results from copying or from coincidence, although many nations have a prior user defense that provides some shelter for prior and independent inventors. Nevertheless, in most if not all nations, an inventor who *independently* makes a product that duplicates the patented product cannot defend simply on the basis that he has not copied.

The usual justification for this is economic: given the high likelihood of parallel invention in the sciences, allowing an independent inventor to practice his invention will reduce the value of the patent 'prize' that is given to the winner of the patent race. (However, if the prize is small, innovation may not occur; if the prize is large, rent-seeking may erode the patent's value.)

Several aspects of patent law remain topics of debate. Some examples are discussed below.

(*a*) Some see patents on processes to be too much of an impingement on personal liberty to do whatever one wants, but see patents on products as acceptable. Others see patents on products to be too much of an impingement on personal liberty to use whatever one wants, but see patents on processes to be acceptable. Manifestations of these debates appear, for example, in today's debates about whether patents should be allowed to cover medically important drugs and techniques, computer hardware and software, and business methods.

(*b*) Often a company takes out patents for the sake of using them defensively in the event the company is itself sued for patent infringement. Some industry participants cooperate in 'patent pools'. Patents can be sold, licensed, and inherited. A plaintiff's 'misuse' of his patent is a defense to patent infringement in the United States and some other jurisdictions, and the nature of misuse is much debated.

(*c*) In many countries, including the United States, patent law exists side by side with trade secrecy law. This complicates research on incentives: if the lure of one regime decreases, persons seeking exclusivity may turn to the other.

Trademarks are protected for their role in marketing, rather than for their creativity. Unlike copyrighted works, therefore, a trademark need not be a full 'work of authorship' and need not be original. Thus, for example, trademark status is available for short words and phrases and trivial graphics. All a trademark need do is identify a product, service, or company to the public. Nevertheless, there is some overlap between the doctrines of copyright and trademark. Both deal with communicative activity, so that disputes in each realm can implicate similar free speech principles. The overlap can also cause tension. The same cartoon or drawing can be both a copyrightable work of authorship, and, if the public recognizes it as a source-identifier, as a trademark. If the copyright goes into the public domain before the trademark loses its capacity to identify source, a court may have to choose which set of policies should have priority.

Many countries do not require that trademarks be registered as a prerequisite for validity, although registration can give definite advantages.

Sometimes the source-identifying nature of a word or symbol is obvious because it is inherently distinctive. Arbitrary words such as 'Kodak' are clearly there to serve a source-identifying function. If, by contrast, a word or phrase is descriptive of the product to which it is attached (consider 'Excellent' toiletries or 'Big Red' fire-trucks), the word or phrase may be understood by the public as merely a piece of information regarding a product's quality or other characteristics. Therefore, descriptive words and symbols attain trademark status only after the public comes to understand the mark as indicating the source of the product. At that stage, a descriptive mark is said to have acquired 'secondary meaning'. Trademark proprietors can usually succeed in lawsuits only by showing that the defendant's use of the mark is likely to cause confusion in the marketplace. Suit in trademark law can be brought even if there is no copying. Coincidental duplication can confuse as much as intentional duplication does, and, as mentioned, the essential test for infringement is whether the accused use causes confusion.

Recently, there has been an additional cause of action available to 'famous' marks, and sometimes available even to those that are not famous: the right to prevent 'dilution' and 'tarnishment' of marks. Under 'anti-dilution' statutes, owners of famous marks can sue for unauthorized uses that 'dilute' the strength of the marks. Thus, for example, the company that markets Pillsbury baking products might sue under an anti-dilution cause of action if a magazine parody showed the 'Pillsbury dough boy' engaged in sexual activity. Anti-dilution, unlike ordinary trademark law, can be sued upon where there is no consumer confusion, and is of more doubtful legitimacy than ordinary trademark law.

Trademarks are typically words or symbols attached to goods. Often the phrase 'trademark law' is also used to embrace several related categories, such as 'trade dress' (which is the term for distinctive packaging or product design) and 'service marks' (which are applied to services). In all these instances, the marks, names, or designs primarily serve to identify the item's source to the public, and similar but not identical legal principles apply. In addition, marks can be used for certification purposes.

Trademarks can last as long as they retain their source-identifying function, which can be forever. The United States takes the position that when marks lose their source-identifying function in public discourse, exclusivity is lost. This happens, most notably, when a mark becomes 'generic': when people use a work as a generic term, they mean a kind of product rather than a source. 'Aspirin', 'cellophane', and 'linoleum' began as trademarks and are now generic.

Trademarks can be sold, licensed, inherited, and so on, so long as they are not separated from the goodwill they represent. The latter is an important qualification, at least under US law. To sell or license a trademark without an accompanying business, or at least a set of quality-control requirements, can invalidate the trademark. This is one of the main reasons why it is misleading to call trademarks a kind of 'property right'. Another reason is that trademarks could, traditionally, only be sued upon when they cause confusion, so that intentional use for a wide range of non-confusing purposes is not actionable.

Many practical and legal dilemmas arise out of the awkward intersection between trademarks and Internet domain names. In the 'real world' of ordinary streets, a hundred different enterprises can display the same or similar word as their trademark. So long as there is no confusion, there is no lawsuit, and there may be a large amount of concurrent use. For example, the purchaser of an Apple record has no illusion that it comes from the same source that makes Apple computers. The purchaser of an Apple computer is similarly free of any belief that his computer comes from the record company. Therefore, both the record company and the computer company can have trademark rights in the word 'Apple'. However, the 'virtual world' of the Internet is not so flexible. There are relatively few high-level domains, such as '.com', '.edu' and '.org'. Although the number of high-level domain names is increasing, some have more market punch than others do. There can be only one 'Apple.[dot]com'. It has, and will probably continue to have, more punch than 'Apple.[dot]name'.

Cybersquatting can be seen as a branch of blackmail. Just as blackmail is illegal because it is wasteful to encourage people 'to dig up information just to bury it again' (Richard Epstein's wonderful phrase), it is wasteful to encourage people to purchase domain names just to sell them again. Also like blackmail, cybersquatting is a non-productive behavior aimed at extracting money, a form of preferring one's self over others rather than respecting their equality. When cybersquatting first appeared, courts sometimes stretched existing doctrine to find methods to restrain it. In the United States, cybersquatting has been made subject to a federal statute.

Rights of publicity are granted by many but not all states in the United States, and many but not all nations on the Continent and elsewhere. Typically, a celebrity who possesses a right of publicity can sue anyone who uses the celebrity's name or likeness in a commercial fashion. Rights of free expression raise intriguing questions in this context, and much controversy centers on whether a right of publicity should survive beyond the death of the famous person. In addition to covering name and likeness, the label 'right of publicity' is sometimes given to someone's claim of right over a performance. One such case involved a circus performer who made his living by being shot out of a cannon; he won a 'right of publicity' suit seeking damages—not an injunction—against a news station that broadcast his act in full.

Misappropriation is an unfair competition cause of action recognized by some but not all jurisdictions. Typically, the plaintiff must show that he made a substantial investment in creating an intangible product, that the defendant substantially appropriated it, and that the appropriation will harm the plaintiff and, if left unredressed, the public. Much debate centers on whether, to succeed in a misappropriation cause of action, the plaintiff must show that he and defendant are in competition. Only if the parties are in competition is there likely to be harm from the defendant's behavior, and public benefit from restraining the defendant. Sometimes the gravamen of the tort is described as 'reaping where one has not sown', as if free riding were itself wrongful. In that guise, misappropriation is inconsistent with the common law approach to restitution, under which it is ordinarily not actionable to reap a benefit. The tort of misappropriation often treads on the toes of copyright or patent (courting pre-emption or other invalidation), and its lack of clear boundaries poses great difficulties. The tort is thus controversial, with different nations and even different states within the United States coming to differing conclusions. One of the crucial determinants is attitude toward judicial (rather than legislative) creation of IP rights. In Commonwealth countries, the tort of misappropriation is rejected.

Trade secrets developed by common law, and have also come to be recognized by statute in many jurisdictions. Essentially, if someone has commercially valuable information and takes reasonable steps to keep it secret, and it *is* secret, the state will assist that entity in preserving the secrecy against improper behavior. For example, imagine that third parties bribe the employee of a soft-drink company to give them the company's secret recipe. The company can use trade secret law to stop the third parties from profiting. An invention too obvious for patenting can be a trade secret, and can be something as mundane as a list of customers. However, trade secrecy has many limits. Most importantly, it is usually lawful for third parties to reverse-engineer a non-patented product to discover and use its secrets. In the general growth of pro-property sentiment, trade secrecy law has begun to change. Some statutes cast doubt on the reverse-engineering principle. There are many competing rationales for trade secrecy law, with some jurisdictions emphasizing the immorality of the defendant's behavior (the defendant will be liable if he, for example, trespassed to spy on plaintiff's industrial processes, or bribed an employee), other jurisdictions stressing the ability of trade secrecy to act as a spur to innovation in conjunction with patent law, and still others treating trade secrecy as a way to keep down waste: without trade secrecy law, both spies and spied-upon would invest in an ever-escalating arms race (Friedman; and Friedman, *et al.*, both in Towse and Holzhauer, 2002, vol. 3).

Moral rights. The category refers to legal rights concerned with protecting predominantly non-economic interests. For example, in some countries the 'moral right' of 'integrity' might protect the interest an author might have—independent of and perhaps even in conflict with his desire for profit—to keep versions of his work faithful to the original. Moral rights usually apply to works of art, but many countries give designers or inventors a small 'right of paternity'—the right to be cited in the application for a design or patent.

'Moral right' is the conventional but awkward translation of the French term, *droit moral.* A more accurate translation might be 'incorporeal rights'. Perhaps because the term 'incorporeal rights' is over-broad (it could refer to all of IP), the alternative phrase, 'moral rights' has come into frequent use. The term's use of the word 'moral' gives the doctrine the connotation of unquestionable justifiability. The doctrine does not deserve this connotation, given the way so-called moral rights can interfere with the free speech rights of iconoclasts, dissidents, and humorists.

Moral rights are recognized by several European countries, and are included in the most significant international copyright treaty, the Berne Convention. Typically, moral rights stay with the author even after copyright is sold. The most significant moral rights are the 'right of paternity' that allows the author to control who is named as the author of her work, and a 'right of integrity' that allows the author to forbid distortions of her work. In the United States, some equivalent rights exist within copyright, trademark, and unfair competition law, and contract law allows artists the ability to retain equivalent rights if they negotiate for them. However, despite the United States having signed the Berne Convention, concerns with both free speech and commercial practicality have kept that nation from wholesale adoption of the moral rights approach. In addition to their role in potentially vindicating personal interests, moral rights may have some useful economic functions (Santilli and Hansmann in Towse and Holzhauer, 2002).

Database rights. The EC has passed a directive for database rights which creates both a copyright (for the creative aspects of database compilations) and a *sui generis* right (for the information contained in the database) (Directive 96/9/EC of the European Parliament and of the Council of 11 March 1996 on the Legal Protection of Databases, 1996 OJ (L 77) 20). So far, the various nations of the Union have implemented the directive's *sui generis* protection in differing ways and to differing extents. Protection attaches if substantial investment has been made, and exclusivity extends even to persons not making wholesale copying. The economic wisdom of this law has been questioned by many. Because the EC directive has a reciprocity provision, it may have the effect of encouraging the United States to give protection to data, but this has so far been resisted. Under current US law, federal copyright can be given only to the creative 'selection and arrangement' of facts, and not to the facts themselves.

Conflicts can arise among the doctrines, and jurisdictions decide on priorities. In the United States, it is fairly clear that patent policy has priority. In order to give the public free use of functional but unpatented objects, otherwise-available copyright and trademark protection may be denied.

3 THE CENTRAL ECONOMIC ARGUMENTS

3.1 Monopoly Analysis

The standard way to analyze the economics of IP is via monopoly analysis. To the extent that intellectual products will be under-produced without IPRs, exclusivity may be necessary to raise price above marginal cost. However, when price is above marginal cost, there will be some 'deadweight loss'. The most important component of this loss is the benefit forgone by people who would have paid the marginal cost for the product, but who do not purchase it at the monopoly price. The goal of an IP system is to maximize the net of incentives, deadweight loss, and administrative and other costs (Landes and Posner in Towse and Holzhauer, 2002; Fisher in Symposium on the Internet and Legal Theory, 1998).

The monopoly is argued to be productive for intangibles because without an exclusion right, there may be no way for the author/inventor/investor to earn a return on her investment.

Liebowitz (1986) has made an important contribution to the usual monopoly analysis by suggesting that the 'deadweight loss' that should be counted against a copyright system is solely the deadweight loss attributable to works that did not need the particular system as incentive. For works that by contrast did require the particular system as incentive to come into being, there is no 'competitive level of price and quantity' with which to compare; therefore, to say that such works generate 'deadweight loss' is to partake of a Nirvana Fallacy. Different copyright systems, and different durations, will have different deadweight losses. Liebowitz has shown how this analysis of deadweight loss can explain the limited durational provisions of both copyright and patent law.

3.2 Centralization

Kitch (in Towse and Holzhauer, 2002, vol. 2) has argued that one reason for giving inventions patent protection is to create an exclusive right capable of coordinating follow-on research and development, and avoid duplicative costs. From the same perspective, it can be argued that one reason why general ideas cannot be 'owned' under copyright law is that they are best developed in a *decentralized* and diverse way.

3.3 Internalizing Externalities

Copyright, database rights, and to a lesser extent, patent law can be explained as a mode of 'internalizing externalities'. As mentioned, just as ordinary tort law seeks to bring negative effects to bear on those who cause them, in order to discourage overly risky activity, so IP law seeks to bring positive effects to bear on those who cause them, in order to encourage productive activity. As with tort law, the hardest questions arise with 'joint causation': how to allocate as between joint contributors to a result. Increasing copyright protection to one generation of authors raises the cost of creation to the next generation of authors (Landes and Posner in Towse and Holzhauer, 2002; Reichman in Dreyfuss *et al.*, 2001). Doctrinal alternatives are many. Copyright in some countries (like the United States) gives no copyright to anyone who has used another's copyrighted work unlawfully, regardless of the creativity of the second author's adaptation. The inventors of improvements to patented inventions, by contrast, in many countries can have patents on their improvements. This encourages bargaining between the improver (who has a patent but cannot use it without the original patentee's permission to use the original invention) and the original patentee (who can use his original invention but not the improvement, unless he obtains permission) (Merges in Towse and Holzhauer, 2002).

3.4 From a Game Theory Perspective

Property theorists are accustomed to using 'The Tragic Commons', Garret Hardin's multi-person prisoner's dilemma, to illustrate the dangers that come from insufficiently privatizing a resource. The basic notion is that if persons can appropriate benefits privately, but externalize the costs of resource use to their other co-owners, the use (and costs) will grow excessive. The opposing perspective is that of the 'tragic anti-commons': if too many people have private claims, it may be impossible to get consent from everyone concerned: the use of the resource (and benefit) will be too small. Empirical work, while so far scant, is investigating the extent to which these different effects prevail (see the articles in Towse and Holzhauer, 2002, vol. 3).

One can use the prisoner's dilemma in another way, both to illuminate the case for giving exclusive rights over inexhaustible intangibles, and to illuminate the case for *not* giving such rights. Assume that, in a world without copyright, there are two players. Each can choose to invest in becoming an author (which we will denote the 'cooperate' option), or in becoming a printer who copies what others write (the 'defect' option). Under certain conditions, a prisoner's dilemma presents itself (see Fig. 28.1).

To minimize risk (the worst result, C, losing all one's savings), the dominant strategy is to defect (become a printer). As a result, the society arrives at D: both parties defect. No one goes to the poor-house, but no one has a decent standard of living, either. More to the point: at D, if both parties become printers, and neither becomes an author, there are no books.

	If Person Two cooperates	If Person Two defects
If Person One cooperates	**Pay-off A** [*both write their own books, and each attains a decent standard of living*]	**Pay-off C** [*cooperator loses his shirt: after the author spends a year writing instead of earning other money, his work is copied and sold at price equaling marginal cost by the printer*]
If Person One defects	**Pay-off B** [*defector becomes rich: as a printer who pays nothing to create the book, he can sell copies cheaply, and prosper*]	**Pay-off D** [*two people with print shops have nothing to print; each goes to work flipping burgers at McDonald's*]

Fig. 28.1. Pattern of pay-offs *A, B, C, D* to Person One (with the assumption that Person Two's pay-offs are symmetrical)

The moral of the tale seems to be the advisability of adopting a law to change the pay-off structure, here, a copyright law. But note how many conditions need to be met before the above prisoner's dilemma structure will actually characterize the relations between author and potential copyist:

(1) The cost of authorship (independent creation or production) is very high.

(2) A second party is able to copy the creation/production from its originator at a cost lower than the cost of independent creation, and no other restraint (e.g. a sense of fair play) adds significantly to the copier's reasons for refraining from making copies.

(3) These copies are perfect substitutes for the originator's product, being identical to the originator's product in regard to all characteristics that affect consumer preferences. Such characteristics include, *inter alia*: quality, reliability, number and quality of distribution networks, authenticity and associational value, and support services provided in connection with the product.

(4) Consumers perceive the two products to be perfect substitutes. (Arguably, if this condition is met, it does not matter if the copies indeed *are* perfect substitutes.) The originator cannot rely on lead-time advantage, willingness to provide support services, or brand loyalty to distinguish his goods from the imitators' goods.

(5) The difference between the cost of copying and the cost of independent creation is high enough that the price the copyist charges will be significantly less than the price the originator would have to charge in order to recoup his costs of independent creation.

(6) In the absence of an opportunity to recoup the costs of independent creation, no one will invest in creative activity. That is, non-monetary remuneration (such as prestige, or the desire for artistic satisfaction) plays no role in inducing the originator's creation or production.

(7) The independent creator or producer can recoup her costs only by means of selling or licensing copies, and in doing so, she has no effective recourse to price discrimination (see Gordon and Bone in Towse and Holzhauer, 2002, vol. 1).

Where one or more of these are absent—and the simultaneous appearance of all will be fairly rare—there may be no prisoner's dilemma (see Breyer and Palmer, both in Towse and Holzhauer, 2002, vol. 1). For example, if the costs of independent creation are low, even a small lead time or reputational advantage can give the author as much leverage as she needs to obtain adequate incentives. Similarly, there will be no prisoner's dilemma if the customer perceives the copies as being 'inauthentic' or otherwise inferior—and in many fields (e.g. computer software) an author can provide convenience, updating, and support services that distinguish her product from that of copyists. Much of the current growth in IP law ignores these facts, as Vaver (2000) suggests, with the lobbyists and legislatures instead calling on 'incentives' as if IP were the only source of incentives.

3.5 The Role of the Personal

Another reason presented to explain the outsize growth in IP law is the role of the 'personal': the romanticization of the Author and, to a lesser extent, of the Inventor. The role of the romantic image may also explain the growth of the right of publicity. Much scholarship criticizes the unrealistic conception of both the authorship/inventor process, and the lack of connection between 'high authorship' and the typical created work (Lemley in Drahos, 1999; Boyle, 1996).

3.6 Price Discrimination

Lawyers tend to see the various rights under IP as separate 'things' to be bought and sold. That tendency, coupled with the field's increasing use of the 'property' label, makes it difficult to see that the basic way that copyright operates is to enable authors to discriminate between different purchasers of copies (Gordon in Symposium on the Internet and Legal Theory, 1998). Copyright is primarily a legal device for provoking self-selection by customers who plan commercially significant uses: they must identify themselves and bargain separately from ordinary purchasers, or face legal penalties for carrying out their plans without permission.

One can visualize the problem faced by an author in a world without copyright as a need to be able to distinguish the customers who want a copy of her work for its intrinsic purpose (e.g. customers who want to purchase a book to read it), from customers who want to buy a copy for other purposes, such as reproducing and publishing it, publicly performing it, broadcasting it, making it into new products, and so on. Copyright makes it unlawful for publishers to print, publicly perform, and so on, copyrighted works when they lack a license from the copyright owner to do so. This forces the publishers to identify themselves as high-value users and pay more than an ordinary user would. Copyright law by the same device prevents high-value users from employing 'arbitrage' to evade the price discrimination: Even though a publisher can buy an inexpensive copy from an ordinary reader, he cannot reproduce it without entering into further negotiations with the copyright owner. Copyright law thus empowers the author to charge a publisher more than she charges a reader. By engaging in this price discrimination, the author may be able to cover her costs of creation.

It has long been recognized (Demsetz, 1970), that if a monopoly is necessary for incentives, coupling it with price discrimination can serve the purpose of giving the author the needed inducements without reducing output as much as would occur under a monopoly that lacked price discrimination. In the Internet and computer context, click-through or shrinkwrap contracts sometimes purport to restrain copying of public domain materials, or to allow such copying only upon the payment of additional fees. Some commentators suggest that it is desirable to enforce contracts that create more price discrimination (Fisher in Symposium on the Internet and Legal

Theory, 1998). However, price discrimination does not always reduce the cost of the copyright monopoly, and (if incentives are otherwise provided) monopoly plus price discrimination imposes a higher social cost than does pure competition.

Price discrimination also operates without using the law as a lever. Thus, under US law, libraries are permitted to do a great deal of photocopying without paying. But journals price-discriminate by charging libraries much more money for subscriptions than private subscribers are asked to pay. Liebowitz (in Towse and Holzhauer, 2002, vol. 1) suggests that this price discrimination may make clearing-house charges redundant, for photocopying yields significant indirect revenues through indirect appropriability. Price discrimination also has implications for 'fair use' and the operation of many other IP doctrines, particularly in regard to private and family use of copyrighted material (Bakos *et al.*, 1999; Meurer, 1997).

So viewed, copyright can learn from the literature that addresses the extent to which the law should enforce 'restraints on alienation' and other restraints on the use of chattels after they are sold.

3.7 Empirical Work

Empirical work is increasing in all areas of IP law (Lemley and others in Towse and Holzhauer, 2002, vol. 3), but so far the simple question of whether copyright and patent help more than hurt has not been answered. In trademark law, most observers probably think that traditional trademark law is economically desirable, for it saves consumers search costs and enables producers of desirable goods to capitalize on their investments in quality. Nevertheless, money is doubtless wasted on advertising to create barriers to entry, so even for traditional trademark law the empirical evidence is not yet conclusive. As for the new 'anti-dilution' trademark law, which permits suit even when the user of the mark is causing no confusion, it is hard to see any significant public benefit (Dreyfuss, 1990; Carter in Towse and Holzhauer, 2002, vol. 3). The same can be said for the right of publicity, but that doctrine has its primary roots in personality rather than economics, and is thus less embarrassed by the lack of social product.

4 To the Future Agenda of IP: Looking at Gifts and Interdependence

Most IP scholarship has focused on the potential justifications for the author or inventor's rights, focusing either on arguments drawn from morality and natural law, or from consequentialism. Gradually, a shift is occurring toward investigating the negative consequences that can arise from overly enthusiastic grants of property.

For example, Eisenberg (in Dreyfuss *et al.*, 2001) has suggested that the culture of science may require, for full flowering, a free flow of information, and less balkanization than patent law will permit. (For a response to this suggestion, see Kieff, 2001 (collecting literature).) Mandeville (in Drahos, 1996) similarly suggests that for uncodified information, flows unblocked by exclusive rights may be necessary. Benkler (2002), Scotchmer (in Towse and Holzhauer, 2002), and others similarly explore arenas where economic welfare can be maximized by the lack of exclusivity. In other words, the very progress that patent law seeks to encourage may be undone by patent law itself.

Something similar may occur in the arts. Lewis Hyde in his evocative book, *The Gift*, suggests that an important part of the aesthetic process is the living relation between the artist and what she receives. The beauty of the physical world and the life within predecessor artists' work create in the receiving artist a sense of gratitude. The artist repays the gift by his own creation—so that gratitude becomes a catalyst (or better, a nutrient fluid) fostering new creativity. Hyde points out at least two things that can interfere with this necessary gratitude: monetary payment, and a sense of calculation. In my mind, the danger lies less in a need to pay, than in a need to calculate. Imagine a composer inspired by a book that she read as a child to make an opera of it. It is hard to imagine her genuine impulse of creativity surviving a process of calculating which children's book has the best cost-benefit ratio between license fee and likely revenue flow. Much writing from artists of all kinds indicates that those whose motivation is intrinsic are not fully free to calculate, to search for the cheapest license or the author's heir who does not object to his ancestor being reinterpreted and criticized.

Economists usually say there are two things distinctive about IP: that works of authorship and invention are not easily fenced, and that they can be used by large numbers of people without being used up. While the fencing notions have been well developed, a crucial area remains in need of more explicit theorizing: that is, the inexhaustibility of IP. Scholarship needs to move into analyzing that aspect on its own. My own intuition is that we need to spend more time thinking about the gift relationship and interdependence. What makes a community are the exchanges and reciprocity for which its members do not demand explicit and calculating payment. To demand too much payment may erode the sense of gratitude that is at the bottom of so many of our institutions, such as trust, and willingness to obey law.

Shareable goods are a traditional source of binding groups together: not only standard 'public goods' such as highways and defense, but also folk tales, art, songs, and symphonies. The same is true on the technological side: even to drink a glass of water is to benefit from generations before us that learned how to temper glass, how to direct liquid flows, how to disinfect. We can never pay for everything we have—but we may, if forced to pay too often for too much, begin to have the illusion that we have paid for everything. The illusion of independence is dangerous when we are in reality interdependent. IP is a magnificent resource for building community, but the new movements to 'enclose' IP threaten to waste that potential. Even from a purely consequentialist perspective, therefore, the possibilities of gift relations need to be systematically explored.

References

Amabile, T. M., Collins, M. A., Conti, R., Phillips, E., Picariello, M., Ruscio, J., and Whitney, D. (1996). *Creativity in Context: Update to the Social Psychology of Creativity*, Boulder, Colo.: Westview Press.

Bakos, Y., Brynjolfsson, E., and Lichtman, D. (1999). 'Shared Information Goods', *Journal of Law and Economics*, 42: 117–55.

Benkler, Y. (2002). 'Coase's Penguin, or Linux and The Nature of the Firm', *Yale Law Journal*, (Winter), 112: 369–446.

Boyle, J. (1996). *Shamans, Software, and Spleens: Law and the Construction of the Information Society*, Cambridge, Mass.: Harvard University Press.

Coombe, R. J. (forthcoming). 'Commodity Culture, Private Censorship, Branded Environments, Global Trade Politics and Alternative Articulations: Intellectual Property as a Topic of Law and Society Research', in A. Sarat (ed.), *Companion Guide to Law and Society*, Oxford: Blackwell.

Cornish, W. (2002). 'The Author as Risk-Sharer', *Columbia Journal of Law and the Arts*, 26: 1–16.

Demsetz, H. (1970). 'The Private Production of Public Goods', *Journal of Law and Economics*, 13: 293–306.

Denicola, R. (1994). 'Institutional Publicity Rights: An Analysis of The Merchandising of Famous Trade Symbols', *North Carolina Law Review*, 62: 603–41 esp. 617–27.

Drahos, P. (1996). *A Philosophy of Intellectual Property*, Aldershot: Dartmouth/Aldershot.

——(ed.) (1999). *Intellectual Property: The International Library of Essays in Law and Legal Theory, Second Series*, Aldershot: Ashgate/Dartmouth.

Dreyfuss, R. C. (1990). 'Expressive Genericity: Trademarks as Language in the Pepsi Generation', *Notre Dame Law Review*, 65: 397–424.

——Zimmerman, D. L., and First, H. (eds.) (2001). *Expanding the Boundaries of Intellectual Property: Innovation Policy for the Knowledge Society*, Oxford and New York: Oxford University Press.

Elkin-Koren, N., and Netanel, N. W. (eds.) (2002). *The Commodification of Information*, The Hague: Kluwer Law International.

Ginsburg, J. (1990). 'A Tale of Two Copyrights: Literary Property in Revolutionary France and America', *Tulane Law Review*, 64: 991–1023.

Gordon, W. J. (1993). 'A Property Right in Self-Expression: Equality and Individualism in the Natural Law of Intellectual Property', *Yale Law Journal*, 102: 1533–609.

Heller, M. A., and Eisenberg, R. S. (1998). 'Can Patents Deter Innovation? The Anticommons in Biomedical Research', *Science*, 280: 698–701.

Hughes, J. (1998). 'The Philosophy of Intellectual Property', *Georgetown Law Journal* 77: 287–365.

Hyde, L. (1979). *The Gift: Imagination and the Erotic Life of Property*, New York: Vintage Books.

Kase, F. J. (1967). *Copyright Thought in Continental Europe: A Selected Bibliography*, South Hackensack, NJ: Fred B. Rothman & Co.

Kieff, F. S. (2001). 'Facilitating Scientific Research: Intellectual Property Rights and the Norms of Science—A Response to Rai & Eisenberg, *Northwestern University Law Review*, 95: 691–705.

Lessig, L. (1999). *Code and Other Laws of Cyberspace*, New York: Basic Books.

Liebowitz, S. J. (1986). 'Copyright Law, Photocopying, and Price Discrimination', in J. Palmer and R. O. Zerbe, Jr. (eds.), *Research in Law and Economics: The Economics of Patents and Copyrights*, 8: 181–200.

Litman, J. (2001). *Digital Copyright*, Amherst, NY: Prometheus Books.

Meurer, M. J. (1997). 'Price Discrimination, Personal Use and Piracy: Copyright Protection of Digital Works', *Buffalo Law Review*, 45: 845–98.

Rose, C. M. (1998). 'The Several Futures of Property: Of Cyberspace and Folk Tales, Emission Trades and Ecosystems', *Minnesota Law Review*, 83: 129–82.

Sherman, B., and Bently, L. (1999). *The Making of Modern Intellectual Property Law: The British Experience 1760–1911*, Cambridge and New York: Cambridge University Press.

Symposium on the Internet and Legal Theory. (1998). *Chicago-Kent Law Review*, 73.

Towse, R., and Holzhauer, R. (eds.) (2002). *The Economics of Intellectual Property*, vols. 1–4 Cheltenham: Edward Elgar.

Vaver, D. (2000). 'Intellectual Property: The State of the Art', *Law Quarterly Review*, 116: 621–37.

CHAPTER 29

....

THE MEDIA

....

EDWIN BAKER

AUTHORITARIAN regimes regularly rely on murdering journalists, jailing editors, and censoring the media to remain in power and to carry out their objectives. In 2001, thirty-seven journalists were reportedly killed in connection with their work, two-thirds apparently by governments or their supporters who did not like to take the heat of criticism. Ruling elites in market-economy democratic states primarily rely instead on owning or controlling the media or creating conditions in which the media naturally represent the world in a manner congenial to these elites' interests (Herman and Chomsky, 2002). Section 1 of this chapter describes debates concerning the normative premises for freedom of the press, premises that reject the censorship required by authoritarian regimes and occasionally imposed by democratic states. Section 2 describes the more pragmatic controversies centering on legal responses to the more indirect democratic threats posed by ruling elites in democratic market societies. Beyond the rejection of overt censorship, it discusses the debates over what legal treatment of the press best supports democracy while appropriately taking account of other societal needs.

The chapter largely ignores a third important area. A central issue of media law concerns how (or even whether) the law should specially provide for the needs and practices of journalists. Many democratic countries with a recognizably free press have press codes that deal extensively with journalists. In other countries, such as the United States, a commonly asserted view is that specialized legal regulation of journalism signifies an unfree press. (This view ignores the many ad hoc legal rules, ranging from regulation of the provision of press passes and press facilities to grants

I wish to thank Yochai Benkler and Michael Madow for helpful comments on this chapter.

of privileges protecting journalists against compelled disclosure of confidential sources, that provide journalists with special rights within particular regulatory contexts.) Both approaches are surely consistent with a commitment to a free press. The specifics of appropriate regulation of and rights for journalists are subject to scholarly debate as well as variation among countries (Lahav, 1985).

Also, possibly the most vital matter concerning media legal policy is merely assumed, not reviewed, here. The fundamental, instrumental importance of a free press for a democracy is subject to little serious scholarly dispute. Both democracy and a free press may even be central to people's material welfare, even their survival. Amartya Sen has described functional mechanisms that lead to his famous claim that no serious famine has occurred in a country that has a multi-party democracy supported by a free press. The logic of this scenario involves two empirical assertions. First, large-scale famines always reflect problems that arise in the distribution of wealth. Famine results from the inability of those who starve to pay for food, not from the absence of food. Many countries experiencing famine at the same time actually export food. Secondly, in the face of a free press able to report the existence and human dimensions of a developing famine and given electoral competitors promising a response to starvation, no ruling party can maintain its power without itself taking the steps necessary to distribute resources in a manner that alleviates the problem.

Sen's account of a dynamic of responding to media-informed public opinion merely illustrates the centrality of a free press to the *minimal* functioning of a democratic process. The media structure obviously can also be vital for the *quality* of democracy. The specifics of a desirable structure for this purpose are much less clear. Since we are so much the product of the media we consume, it is difficult to guess whether the media's insistent but not persuasively supported claim that the American people were impatient for a quick result encouraged the US Supreme Court to put an end to the normal legal process of choosing between Gore and Bush in the 2000 presidential election. It is similarly difficult to know how much American media's theme of 'America under attack' and, within hours after the destruction of the World Trade Center Towers on 11 September 2001, its drumbeat for a forceful response contributed to President Bush's decision to bomb Afghanistan and to use military methods in addition to police actions to fight criminal terrorism. Would a different media structure have produced different content with better democratic consequences?

Finally, possibly because of the ideological attraction of the First Amendment and a long experience with judicial enforcement (although the US Supreme Court first invalidated a federal statute on free speech grounds only in 1965), American theoretical free speech scholarship has been particularly rich. It will be the focus in Section 1. This scholarship should have general relevance as other countries and international bodies since World War II have increasingly developed their free speech jurisprudence under common law, national constitutional law, or international instruments such as the European Convention on Human Rights, article 10. For example, multiple national court decisions and international scholarly debates concerning free speech limitations on defamation law show the influence of the American decision in

New York Times v Sullivan, 376 US 254 (1964), even as most countries give somewhat greater protection to people's dignitary interest in reputation. In any event, references here to US Supreme Court constitutional decisions will serve only as illustrative of general theoretical issues. On the other hand, possibly because less constrained by worries about its consistency with a judicially enforced First Amendment but also possibly in part because of a clearer recognition that media freedom must be understood in an institutional context, such as public broadcasting, rather than an individual rights framework (Barendt, 1993), policy-oriented scholarship, especially by communications as opposed to legal scholars, may be more plentiful and creative outside the United States (Curran, 2000; Humphreys, 1996).

1 SPECIAL PROTECTION OF COMMUNICATIONS

Governments continually want to regulate specific communicative content for a huge number of presumptively legitimate reasons. Multi-billion dollar military budgets testify to the legitimacy of maintaining national security. Governments sometimes restrict communications to promote the same goal. A person's dignity as a person may be central to her identity; her reputation may be one of her most valued possessions. Governments sometimes restrict speech to protect these dignitary values. Physical security of person and property is almost universally valued, providing a central Lockean reason for having a state. Governments sometimes restrict speech that advocates, threatens, stimulates, or aids violations of these interests. Communications are crucial constituents of the human environment in which we live. Some restrictions on public speech might help prevent degradation of this environment. Fraudulent or otherwise false speech can manipulate people and frustrate their aims. The law often restricts such false or misleading speech so that people's choices will have greater integrity and their activities will be more likely to succeed. People value communications—for example, as information or entertainment. Restrictions on certain communications by some people (e.g. copyright violators) may provide an economic incentive to produce valued commodified communications. Governments occasionally restrict opinion or even truthful speech out of a concern that it will lead listeners to unwarranted premises or undesirable actions. Alternatively, content regulation of even truthful commercial speech sometimes reflects a conclusion that these commercial entities' market-oriented communications should play a lesser role in people's decision-making or in the practices that lead to the creation of the common social world. The law often restricts or allows restrictions on communicative activities not out of any concern with the message but merely to prevent the *activity* of communicating from interfering with other activities at the particular time or place. Finally, governments sometimes compel certain speech, for example, to obtain information or to symbolize and hopefully reinforce patriotic values.

This list is hardly complete. Still, the question arises: how should people think about the legitimacy of such regulations? The commitment—at least officially asserted by most countries and many international legal agreements—to freedom of speech and of the press and to related human rights implies that the issue is not merely whether a restriction reasonably serves some legitimate purpose. At least two inquires are centrally relevant for responding to the question. First, what rationale(s) justify this virtually universal commitment to special protection of expression? Secondly, what do the rationale(s) imply for acceptability of various regulatory initiatives?

1.1 Rationale(s) for Protection

Surely, the most influential modern characterization of the rationale for constitutional protection is Thomas Emerson's proposal that the system of freedom of expression serves four central functions or values. 'Freedom of expression is essential [(1)] as a means of assuring individual self-fulfillment' or 'self-realization'; (2) 'for advancing knowledge and discovering truth'—basically the marketplace of ideas rationale that held virtually unchallenged dominance in American scholarly literature up until the 1970s; (3) 'to provide for participation in decision-making by all members of society', including participation 'in the building of the whole culture'; and (4) for 'achieving a more adaptable and hence a more stable community' by 'maintaining the precarious balance between healthy cleavage and necessary consensus' (Emerson, 1970: 6–7).

Although arguably encompassed within Emerson's broad categories, other scholars have proposed alternative or additional normative or functional rationales for constitutional protection of expression. Most prominently, Alexander Meiklejohn asserts that freedom of speech is a deduction from the idea that we are a self-governing people. This view led him to conclude that the constitutional guarantee should apply fully but only to speech relevant for the project of self-government. Only in respect to this speech did Meiklejohn believe that the First Amendment was an absolute (Meiklejohn, 1965).

Alternatively, even without a belief in fundamental values or a belief that democratic majorities should be stymied in carrying out their will even in respect to fundamental values, pragmatic theorists offer somewhat different arguments. Some offer systemic reasons to doubt the likelihood that even democratic governments will make appropriate judgments about when speech, or at least some types of speech, should be restricted. A more nuanced development of this point suggests that even a democratic country needs mechanisms to keep a close watch on the possibility of abuse of power by the government in office. Despite a commitment to democratic rule, government should not be entrusted with power to gag the watchdog—hence the practical need for constitutional protection of speech that performs this 'checking function' (Blasi, 1977).

An alternative pragmatic account observes that idealized scholarly accounts of democracy involving people actually participating in government or of democracy really being responsive to deliberative popular opinion are largely civic fantasies. In contrast, the right to dissent may be key to people's notion of living in a democratic rather than an authoritarian society (Shiffrin, 1990). Moreover, the modern world inevitably relies heavily on inegalitarian, hierarchical institutional structures to meet people's material and other needs. Maintaining a culture of dissent, where people assume a right to object to whatever they see as wrong or to deviate in favor of self-perceived better alternatives, greatly improves the chance that these structures will serve rather than unjustly oppress people (Shiffrin, 1999). In contrast, reasoned, civil discourse aimed at agreement has no need for the constitutional protection that dissent both needs and merits. Majority forces will short-sightedly want, and unjust hierarchies will calculatedly choose, to suppress deviance which they often see as the virtual embodiment of 'unreason' (Karst, 1990).

1.2 Further Specification of Values

Apparent agreement on the centrality of particular values or functions is insufficient if theorized in dramatically different ways. These differences can affect the appropriateness of objections to government intervention as well as the identification of needed government media policy. Some of the most provocative scholarly debates occur here. Two examples serve to illustrate.

First, many scholars find the basis for special protection of expressive freedom lies in its contribution to democracy. Democracies' pretensions at being egalitarian, deliberative or civic, and inclusive lead some to argue that the democratic order justifies or requires regulatory interventions to promote the inclusiveness and possibly the deliberative or civic nature of political communications (Sunstein, 1993), a conclusion that even has constitutional status in parts of Europe. In contrast, Robert Post, who claims that First Amendment jurisprudence primarily 'concerns the articulation of democratic aspirations' (Post, 1995: 187) and observes that the implications of this observation depend on the meaning given to democracy, argues that, at least in the United States, democracy aims at people being self-governing, giving law to themselves. The centrality of autonomy, he says, is inseparable from this aspiration. Democracy is simply the attempt to reconcile law with individual autonomy by subordinating government decisions to public discourse (ibid.: 273). From this perspective, Sunstein's arguments for governmental intervention must be rejected for impermissibly introducing an element of heterogeneity into public discourse, which

Post asserts must be maintained as a realm of autonomy. Rather, democracy requires protection for a morally ascribed expressive autonomy.

Post's arguments against managerial interventions related to *individuals'* expressive freedom might be accepted. Or to reverse the derivation, democracy can be understood as the political form that best embodies respect for individual autonomy. However, even granting Post's conception of democracy, his opposition to government intervention may be incoherent in the context of property rights. Even more so, it is incoherent as to corporate-based institutions involving multiple persons. These institutions constitute entirely socially and legally constructed systems of rights— 'heterogeneity' is implicit in their existence. Media entities are necessarily legally structured, presumably for instrumental human ends; and it is these institutions that were, for the most part, the focus of Sunstein's reform recommendations. Given that different property or corporate legal regimes inevitably favor some communicative practices over others, it seems indefensible not to structure such rights in ways that best serve human ends, including democratic discourse.

Of course, even granting the propriety of conscious decision-making about structuring *media entities* to make them provide better service, that conclusion does not identify the more specific goals of the structuring. For this, a favored conception of democracy must be further specified. Sunstein implicitly recommends a form of civic republican democracy. Some major constitutional scholars base their recommendations concerning First Amendment rights on a more elitist conception of democracy (Blasi, 1977). Finally, others recommend what is variously called a theory of 'discourse' or 'complex' democracy, which consciously combines elements of republican and liberal pluralist theories and places special emphasis on meeting the internal communication needs of marginal or subaltern groups (Habermas, 1996; Baker, 2002).

Secondly, over the last thirty years, increasing numbers of scholars have substituted a notion of autonomy (or liberty) for the formerly dominant marketplace of ideas or search for truth theories as the central premise of freedom of speech. This change might respond to an increased popularity of more Kantian over utilitarian value frameworks. In any event, an autonomy conception might imply that a person be allowed to choose for herself what to say (and maybe to choose for herself whether to listen). Robert Post, for example, argues that such an ascribed sense of autonomy is 'the transcendental precondition for the possibility of democratic self-determination' (Post, 1995: 283; see also Baker, 1989). Nevertheless, the more common scholarly approach merely gives an autonomy spin on the traditional marketplace of ideas concern with people's access to information and ideas. The claim is that listeners instrumentally need information or ideas in order to know how best to act (Scanlon, 1972). Speech supplies people with information that helps their choices better serve their autonomous aims. The emphasis here is on a particular understanding of listener autonomy—fully consistent with Meiklejohn's assertion that 'what is essential is not that everyone shall speak, but that everything worth saying shall be said' (Meiklejohn, 1965: 26).

A demand that a legal order respect people as self-determining, self-governing agents might seem—it does to me—to require the first, ascribed sense of individual autonomy over expressive (and listening) choices. For example, whenever US Supreme Court Justices have invoked a notion of liberty or speech freedom as an end in itself or the notion of speech freedom as inviolate, they seem to refer to this conception. Thus, why the dichotomy? And, if both 'ascribed speaker autonomy' and 'empirical instrumental contributions to listener autonomy' have relevance for the system of freedom of expression, how are the two related? Social-engineering policy-oriented theorists who place central importance on people's actual capacities could conclude that the 'ascribed' conception of autonomy is merely a metaphysical diversion. The pragmatic concern for people's actual opportunities to successfully and meaningfully author their lives correctly recognizes the vital importance of their having the resources necessary to do so. Communicative inputs—information, ideas, and inspiration—are clearly among the necessary elements. Of course, these are only among the important inputs. Sometimes providing for these will 'cost' so much in terms of other valuable goals, other material and psychic resources needed for leading a successful self-authored life, that restricting expression would apparently be the more sensible policy. Sometimes, depending on both the content and context of a communicative input, receipt of additional or low quality communications can even be dysfunctional from the perspective of the recipient's actual capacity for fulfilling self-authorship. Thus, clearly the notion of autonomy that focuses on the value of communicative inputs for people's actual empirical capacity to act autonomously requires some balancing approach to expressive freedom.

In contrast, the ascribed conception of autonomy sees expressive freedom as a matter of acting—of choice of expressive action—rather than a provider of an (only sometimes) valuable resource. This view strongly suggests treating government respect for expressive freedom as a foundational principle. Respect for autonomy operates as a side-constraint limiting the state's choice of methods of pursuing its legitimate aims. Of course, even fully implementing this requirement does not impeach the central importance of people's actual empirical ability to lead meaningful, robust, self-authored lives—although the conditions that are most enabling will be politically contested. Any theorist advancing an ascribed conception of autonomy as foundational could and presumably should also manifest passion for the more empirical conception of autonomy for which communications serve as valuable inputs. This combination requires a prohibition on laws aimed at restricting individual speaker autonomy but, in addition, could support any of three, not necessarily mutually exclusive stances toward other legal regulation in the communications sphere. First, as long as the side-constraint is respected, the theorist might conclude that the concern with providing for communications that serve people's capacity to lead self-authored lives should generally be left to the legislative, policy-making arena which can make the necessary trade-offs—as it has by providing for freedom of information acts or financial support for public broadcasting. Secondly, this concern might still serve as an additional constitutional consideration where relevant. Courts (or legislative bodies self-consciously acting to advance constitutional mandates) could revise (or mandate) policies that affect how well the communications order provides these resources (Benkler, 2001). This approach self-consciously combines the two conceptions of autonomy within the constitutional or fundamental human rights framework.

A third response, however, has special relevance to the distinct legal treatment of the mass media. Different parts of the constitutional or fundamental rights frame-work could be understood to respond primarily to one or the other formulation of autonomy. Freedom of *speech*—an individual activity—suggests the ascription of autonomy to the individual, while the value of any institution or economically organized structures embodying bureaucratic organization (in contrast to purely voluntary associations within the lifeworld) presumably lies in how they serve human needs and values—that is, how they serve the second sense of autonomy (Baker, 1994*b*). Thus, unsurprisingly, much of the historical emphasis on freedom of the press relates not to how it is implied by any abstract or ascribed notion of indi-vidual autonomy but on how it serves various democratic functions, including pro-viding an independent source of information and vision. Under this view, issues raised by regulation of media entities would be quite different from those involved in directly regulating the speech of individuals.

1.3 Protective Implications of Rationales

If all values served by expressive freedom pointed to the same conclusions regarding legal protection, debates concerning theoretical rationales for protection might be of mere scholastic importance. Legal reasoning could proceed on the sanguine view that at least one of the values adequately justifies the fundamental status of speech freedom. This approach is common. In considering the propriety of some doctrinal approach to regulation of speech, the typical American scholarly article during the last quarter of the twentieth century first catalogues theories concerning the basis of the First Amendment. The author, apparently wishing to avoid determining which theory is most persuasive (and thereby implicitly demonstrating a belief in the ultim-ate irrelevance of such theoretical endeavors), then rather woodenly shows that each theory supports the author's favored doctrinal or (anti-)regulatory view.

This common rhetorical strategy is fundamentally flawed. The author's demon-stration often required a distorted interpretation of at least some of theories consid-ered. For at least two reasons, many important issues concerning expressive freedom turn precisely on the justification(s) accepted for protecting expression.

First, different justifications cover different expressive activities. For example, in a famous case invalidating a requirement that schoolchildren salute the flag, Justice Frankfurter's dissent argued that the mandatory salute did not impair the marketplace of ideas—the search for truth—since the rule left the children and their parents unrestricted in their right to speak out and condemn the compelled flag salute. Frankfurter's point, however, did not speak to the majority's rationale. The majority emphatically proclaimed that the liberty protected by freedom of speech was as much at stake in the choice not to speak as in the choice to speak (*West Virginia State Board of Education v Barnette*, 318 US 624 (1943)).

Similarly, as one group of Justices emphasized, a marketplace of ideas theory objects to regulation of corporate political speech since the 'inherent worth of the speech in terms of its capacity for informing the public does not depend on the identity of its [source]'. Relying on a liberty theory, other Justices prevailed in a second case where the US Supreme Court upheld such a law. They argued that these corporate communications do not further 'the use of communications as a means of self-expression, self-realization and self-fulfillment'. They concluded that 'ideas which are not a product of individual choice are entitled to less First Amendment protection' (*First National Bank of Boston v Bellotti*, 435 US 765 (1978); *Austin v Michigan Chamber of Commerce*, 494 US 652 (1990)).

Or consider obscenity. Given the view that expressive freedom 'was fashioned to assure unfettered interchange of ideas', and thus all 'ideas having even the slightest redeeming social importance ... have ... full protection', Justice Brennan could conclude that the government could ban sexually explicit materials but only if the material lacks any ideas (*Roth v United States*, 354 US 476 (1957)). Later in dissent, Brennan abandoned the attempt to legally prohibit obscenity because this was unworkable within constitutional standards. However, he also indicated a changed perspective on freedom of speech. Emphasizing the 'willing, adult recipient'—code words for notions of liberty—Brennan suggested that a person had a right to receive information 'regardless of [its] social worth', and that this right was allied to freedom in relation to 'the decision whether to bear a or beget a child', and to 'autonomous control over the development and expression of one's intellect, interests, tastes, and personality' (*Paris Adult Theatre v Slaton*, 413 US 49 (1973)).

Secondly, the rationale for protection can affect the form protection takes. Some rationales are merely important *interests* that (arguably) merit special protection. Truth is useful, as is information that empirically serves our autonomy. Expression is instrumental in achieving various goals, but we have other important goals that should be weighed in considering the validity of any particular regulation. Other rationales purportedly represent *constitutive premises*. The legitimacy of the legal order, the point of democracy, assertedly depends on the law viewing or treating people as autonomous, self-governing agents. Any regulation that contradicts this premise is presumptively impermissible.

Depending on which rationale(s) provide the basis for the fundamental status of communicative freedom, the circumstances that justify its abridgement can vary. Scholars who implicitly assume the first (instrumental) category of rationales routinely recommend forms of pragmatic balancing, while those accepting the second (constitutive) rationales usually argue for more absolutist protection. Just as with the prohibition on torture, speech-abridging *means* would be off limits in the government's

pursuit of even important social objectives. As Justice Brennan remarked, 'in a democracy like our own...autonomy of each individual is accorded...incommensurate
respect'. A third view, uncommon in academic scholarship but recognized by
Brennan, is to combine the two approaches. Thus, he adds to the first point the claim
that other social and democratic values, such as the search for truth, justify more qualified protection. Here, Brennan concludes that 'a broadly defined freedom of the press
assures the maintenance of our political system and an open society' (*Herbert v Lando*,
441 US 153 (1979) (Brennan, dissenting)). In this view, while some premises, where
applicable, make 'freedom of expression...inviolate', those premises are not always
applicable. Other premises, however, lead to less 'categorical assurance' for instrumentally valued rights, such as 'the correlative freedom of access to information'
(*Richmond Newspapers v Virginia*, 448 US 555 (1980) (Brennan, concurring)).

The contextual quality of the instrumental rationales should not be understated. If
speech freedom contributes empirically to a search for truth or to empirical autonomy or to democracy rather than being ascribed as constitutive of them, not only
will other values sometimes outweigh their value but also the freedom itself will sometimes be dysfunctional. Too much expression by rich, powerful entities not only distorts the marketplace of ideas but arguably deters expressive political participation
by larger numbers of people. Although subject to severe feminist critique (cf. Meyer,
1994), Catherine MacKinnon's arguments for regulating pornography include the
claim that pornography silences women. Does speech that drowns out or deters other
expression merit protection or restriction? The first group of theorists argue that,
given the (contestable) empirical facts, restriction can serve the same generic values
as justify protection while the second object to use of improper 'means'.

Similarly, some theorists argue that the empirical support that information provides
to people's autonomous decision-making may justify a purported 'right to know'.
However, restrictions on information availability serve interests in personal privacy,
national security, regulation of currency markets, law enforcement, and a huge number of other legitimate interests. The routine importance of keeping information secret
or private suggests that any 'right to know' would not provide a very persuasive basis to
ground the right of free speech. Certainly, few think that a broad right to know justifies
a person's fundamental right to require that another private individual unwillingly
speak. Scholars debate the implications of the US Supreme Court's repeatedly stated
view that the government cannot stop the media from publishing the very information
that the Court also asserts the government can, arguably should, keep secret. This combination of views places greater weight on intrinsic speech-act autonomy than on the
instrumental justifications. Still, in the case of governmentally held information, the
bureaucratic instinct towards privacy *might* justify an independent body—a judicial
tribunal—having authority to find secrecy not merited in particular cases.

Further discussion of specific issues would show other consequences of accepting one
or another rationale for expressive freedom. Different rationales lead to different

conclusions about whether a particular restriction is objectionable authoritarian censorship or, instead, permissible state advancement of people's welfare or respect for their dignity. Those inquiries must be left aside here. Moreover, different rationales largely determine the legal treatment of the state interest invoked to prohibit the expression. Many leading US Supreme Court decisions protecting expression seemed virtually unconcerned with the state interests advanced by the invalidated restriction. This inattention is as it should be if the rationale for protection is of, as Robert Post put it, a form of autonomy that is a 'transcendental precondition' of our democracy. If protection is premised on the necessity that the legal order respect this 'ascribed' autonomy, then the *purpose* to restrict a category of expression is an impermissible choice of means. On the other hand, in more 'interest'-based accounts, the question always exists whether a legal restriction's detrimental *effect* on expressive interests is more or less significant than the social interests that the restriction advances. Here is not the place to resolve these questions—they are the meat of the scholarly debates referred to here.

One point in the above discussion, building on the observation that alternative rationales lead to different doctrinal approaches to protection, has direct relevance for Section 2. The point is that the ascribed autonomy rationale has force only in the context of individuals or voluntary, solidarity associations but that the instrumental rationales have direct and possibly their primary application to media entities. This point provides guidance to the next topic: government power to engage not in censorship but structural regulation of the media.

2 Structural Issues

Described as the wealthiest man in Italy, Silvio Berlusconi rode his media empire to political power, becoming Prime Minister of Italy. His electoral victories in 1996 and again in 2001 put a human face on the most serious issue of media law of the next century: how, if at all, should law regulate the structure of media industries. Once the battle against ideological state censorship has been (largely) won, structure clearly becomes the dominant issue. Regulations that determine who makes content decisions are crucial. And what incentives operate, and how powerfully do they operate, on the decision-makers—on owners, executives, editors, reporters, and organizations? Despite more scholarly emphasis on content issues, these structural issues may be more important for the nature of society and the future of democracy. Media scholarship should shed light on the advantages and disadvantages of alternative structures and on the role of law in encouraging, prohibiting, or requiring alternative arrangements.

Possibly the central scholarly (and political) debate is whether or not society should rely almost exclusively on comparatively unregulated market entities to provide and distribute media content. Two broad positions have competed globally for both scholarly approval and legal implementation. On the one hand, some scholars (especially in the United States) conclude that reliance on the market ought to be virtually complete. On the other, fears of the potential ill effects of concentrated private power and recognition of the inadequacies of commercial market processes lead others to favor a variety of policy-guided government interventions specifically directed at the communications realm. The first group generally makes three broad claims: Intervention is contemptuously paternalistic, ignoring people's preferences for media content. The market properly provides for people's actual preferences and for all the diversity that people desire and democracy needs. Intervention, in contrast, risks (or, worse, ensures) partisan (undemocratic) government manipulation of the communication order.

During the last twenty years, both scholarship and policy in the United States—on which I will focus—and, increasingly, policy internationally have moved dramatically toward an extreme pro-market stance. For example, public service broadcasting's virtual monopoly position in much of Europe (and elsewhere) has been largely abandoned in favor of major, sometimes dominant, reliance on commercial, mostly advertising-supported broadcasting. Even with this change, in some countries, especially Germany, the inadequacies of the market are recognized to be so great that public broadcasters have a constitutional status.

Controversy about commercialized media is not new even in the United States. In a now largely forgotten history, the late 1920s and early 1930s saw commercial interests only narrowly win the battle to develop broadcasting as a commercial advertising-supported system rather than a non-commercial system (McChesney, 1993). Nevertheless, American intellectual exploration of problems with the market-based media order awaited its most influential development in a landmark 1947 report, *A Free and Responsible Press*, of a privately funded Commission on Freedom of the Press chaired by Robert Hutchins. Seeing both trends toward concentration and ill effects of an exclusive focus on profits, the Hutchins Commission famously argued that the press ought to recognize its social responsibilities to a democratic order. Beyond that, the report and supplementary books written by individual commission members, especially one by Zechariah Chafee, Jr., stimulated the modern debate about what forms of government intervention would be both consistent with press freedom and helpful in making the media more consistent with democratic needs. The resulting discussion focused on three types of structural interventions.

2.1 Proposed Structural Interventions

First is government funding or subsidies. Media products have economic qualities —especially non-rivalrous use (or zero or low copy costs) which is a constitutive element of public goods and varying degrees of positive and negative externalities—that predictably lead markets to massively short-change important communications needs (Baker, 2002). These factors helped stimulate the commitment of Europe, Canada, and other countries to public broadcasting. America's constantly underfunded public broadcasting received a major intellectual as well as political boost with the publication of the report of the Carnegie Commission on Educational Television (1967). Most countries, including the United States, have also provided a variety of public subsidies for both commercial and other non-commercial media and cultural endeavors. Interestingly, media subsidies seem comparatively unproblematic constitutionally. This indicates that, despite occasional scholarly and judicial assertions to the contrary, neither the law nor dominant scholarly opinion recognizes the need (or possibility) of any neutral or 'undistorted' private market-based marketplace of ideas. In fact, in Europe, often the opposite is assumed in relation to broadcasting. There the issue is whether, given the creative and journalistic distortions introduced by markets, public broadcasting is mandatory. Thus, in Germany, constitutional principles not only require public broadcasting and require its independence from both state and commercial control but also mandate adequate economic support for it to perform its responsibilities (Barendt, 1993).

Second is the issue of ownership and concentration. Many scholars, especially on the left, worry that concentrated corporate ownership of the dominant media outlets is inherently dangerous and bad for democracy (Bagdikian; Herman and McChesney). Historically, the US Federal Communications Commission (FCC) agreed. It prohibited most cross-ownership of broadcast and other media within the same community, restricted ownership of multiple broadcast facilities within a single community, and favored local ownership and control. In order to maintain programming control in the hands of individual owners as opposed to being concentrated in the hands of huge corporate entities, the FCC adopted, and the US Supreme Court upheld, rules that restricted permissible terms of network affiliation agreements (*National Broadcasting Co v United States*, 319 US 190 (1943)). Moreover, with thousands of broadcast stations operating nationally, the FCC long limited ownership to no more than seven in any classification (AM radio, FM radio, and television).

Although some ownership restrictions served antitrust concerns with abuse of 'economic' market power, clearly market power was not the dominant policy concern. There was never a serious claim, for example, that ownership of a single broadcast station in each of a number of geographically dispersed cities created monopoly economic power. The limitations responded instead to other policy goals, most obviously preventing concentration of power within the marketplace of ideas and increasing in absolute numbers the people or entities that could participate as media owners within that communications realm. Ownership policy, approved as unproblematic by the US Supreme Court (e.g. *United States v Storer Broadcasting Co*, 351 US 192 (1956); *FCC v National Citizens Committee for Broadcasting*, 436 US 775 (1978)), reflected concerns of democratic process, not economic efficiency. Prevention of concentrated control over 'editorial' voices, not a concern with economic market power, was also the recognized rationale of media-specific legislative intervention in the newspaper industry. Under defined circumstances, the Newspaper Preservation Act (1970), 15 USCA §§ 1801 ff., allowed two newspapers within a community to gain monopoly (economic) market power by combining all the commercial parts of their operations. In return, the policy bargain required the two papers to maintain separate operation of their journalistic or editorial endeavors. Similar policy concerns have animated media policy in many democratic countries. Sweden, for example, long viewed competing partisan local newspapers as the virtual *sine qua non* of democracy. Still, not just in the United States but elsewhere, the issue of whether it is important to provide special legal and administrative limits on media concentration beyond those mandated by general concentration (antitrust) policy is on the table.

Third is providing access to major media for speakers or categories of programming content. Many scholars and reformers have viewed such access as an important means of promoting diversity and popular exposure to content not adequately provided by the market or as a matter of simple fairness to the person allowed access (Barron, 1967). Regulations of this sort are ubiquitous but are also ubiquitously critiqued by pro-market advocates. Although constitutionally required in some circumstances in some European countries, both access and right of reply requirements are regularly challenged in the United States as violations of the First Amendment. Two cases, one upholding the Fairness Doctrine's provision for limited mandated access to broadcasting (*Red Lion Broadcasting v FCC* (1969)) and the other rejecting mandated access to daily newspapers under similar circumstances (*Miami Herald Publishing v Tornillo*, 418 US 241 (1974)) purportedly represent two opposing models of media regulation (Bollinger, 1976). Most scholars routinely assert that *Red Lion* represents a limited broadcasting exception, purportedly based on the scarcity of broadcast channels, to the standard rule of constitutionally protected editorial autonomy, represented by *Miami Herald*. In fact, they may have it backwards (Baker, 1994b). Censorship is condemned in all media. Intrusions into editorial autonomy, however, have been imposed and upheld as to most media including cable, satellite TV, and telephone. An old law, upheld against First Amendment attack before the development of modern doctrine, effectively required newspapers to publish periodically the identity of their owners and to identify advertising as such (*Lewis v Morgan Publishing*, 229 US 283 (1913)). And despite current abandonment of the Fairness Doctrine, other intrusions into editorial control in broadcasting remain, including requirements that broadcasters provide at least minimum amounts of children's educational programming and reasonable opportunities for political candidates to buy advertising time.

Thus, although most scholarship has advocated a deregulatory standard (that advances the media's commercial interests), the US Supreme Court has upheld most regulations. The Court understood the media as being constitutionally protected as an industry serving the public interest in a robust range of uncensored content. This constitutional policy, as famously spelled out in *Associated Press v United States*, 326 US 1, 20 (1945), does not restrict government power to regulate or structure the industry so that it would better serve this end. In fact *Red Lion*, the purported exception, relied heavily on this newspaper case in adopting an instrumental view of the media and in concluding that the people's 'collective right to have the medium function consistently with the ends and purposes of the First Amendment [and] ... the right of the viewers and listeners, not the right of the broadcasters ... [are] paramount'. The US Supreme Court found that public 'access to social, political, esthetic, moral, and other ideas and experiences ... is crucial here'.

Pro-market scholars highlight *Miami Herald*'s emphasis on editorial autonomy, analogizing the challenged law's mandate to print what editors would choose not to print to a censorious prohibition of publication. Actually, the US Supreme Court gave two grounds for striking down the statute. It did invoke protection of editorial autonomy. It also identified as a constitutional problem that, since access was required only because of the paper's prior decision to publish criticism of a candidate, the law operated as a content-based penalty on that earlier decision to publish, creating the risk of deterrence of critical expression. Of course, on this issue, the European experience with newspaper right of reply requirements combined with anecdotal reports of actual deterrence in broadcasting shows what an economic understanding of the two media would predict—deterrence of critical newspaper as opposed to commercial broadcasting expression is unlikely. In any event, later cases, which have allowed intrusions into editorial autonomy, have explained *Miami Herald* as based on the second deterrence rationale. Most prominently, given the Court's acceptance of the questionable view that cable operators should count as editors in the *Miami Herald* sense, its approval of a rule requiring a cable company to carry local broadcast station's programming would be a clear violation of any editorial autonomy principle. The Court, however, interpreted *Miami Herald* as based on the law, there being a penalty on particular content, that is, as censorious, and thus not really being a case of structural regulation (*Turner Broadcasting v FCC*, 512 US 622, 653–5 (1994)).

2.2 Scholarly Opposition to Interventions

Opponents of media-specific regulation have developed five claims that have gained increasing hegemony. First, absent concentration of the sort already prohibited by efficiency-based antitrust laws, the market best provides the media people want. It will also supply any diversity that people actually want or need (Fowler and Brenner, 1982). Mark Fowler, famous for his characterization of television as just a 'toaster with pictures' and (as FCC chair) for being the father of deregulation of the media, explains that the market is the only proper means of identifying the public's media interests.

Although diversity is often offered as a reason for structural regulation, market advocates regularly raise a much debated issue of what type of diversity is of concern. From a perspective of democratic participation and a more egalitarian distribution of power, both maximal numbers of owners who can act as speakers and ownership by individuals or entities connected to and representative of the broad pluralism of societal groups are obviously important goals *irrespective* of whether these multiple speakers choose to say different things. The distribution of power and voice, not the production of content, clearly animated much of the early FCC regulation of owner-ship. With tin ears for these claims, market advocates quickly conclude that the ul-timate concern must be with supplying the public with diverse content—or with toasters. From this commodity rather than participatory perspective, concern with any type of ownership diversity is hardly coherent except as an empirically justified proxy for some desirable content diversity. (Of course, to their surprise, empirical support is often available.) The market advocates, however, argue that the market will best supply the actual content diversity that people want. More boldly, they some-times argue that greater concentration can serve diversity. An owner of multiple outlets, not wanting to compete against itself, will have a profit-based incentive efficiently to use its different outlets to serve content interests of diverse segments of the population. That is, the market induces concentration that increases desirable content diversity much better than the 'ruinous competition' caused by too many separate owners who all compete for the same dominant or mainstream audience. This advantage of concentration is merely one point—efficiencies of scale is another —that justifies opposition to legal limits on ownership beyond those required by antitrust principles.

Secondly, market advocates suggest that, ultimately, proponents of intervention are simply dissatisfied with the choices people make. Interventionists wish to pater-nalistically impose on the public the cultural and public affairs content that this elite (purportedly 'liberal' elite) thinks they need. Given that the market, like democracy, respects individual freedom and choice, intervention is fundamentally undemocra-tic. Market advocates favor a rule or constitutional principle that forbids these pater-nalistic regulatory interventions—even if elite judgements could be permitted as a basis for subsidies. Of course, this anti-interventionist argument depends on its assessment of the market. If the market does not provide what people want, the charge of paternalism should be reversed. Any rule would be paternalistic if it denies people the opportunity to act politically to legally restructure or regulate the market as a means to get closer to what they want.

Thirdly, some market advocates insist that, even though economic markets are not perfect, what they like to call 'political markets' are equally or more prone to failure. Political biases, if not outright partisan corruptions, are believed not only likely to occur—they represent appealing temptations—but also likely to be more objectionable, especially to democracy, than any inadequacies of economic markets. More theoretic-ally inclined commentators recognize that the market itself relies on consciously adopted legal rules—that define, for example, property, contract, and the nature of the corporation. These rules necessarily affect opportunities for profits and expres-sion of preferences in the market and, hence affect (bias?) media content. However, they are not likely to reflect political corruption or failure, certainly of a form particu-larly dangerous to the functioning of the media. Thus, typical market advocates accept application of general legal rules to media entities—in the end only objecting to the *media-specific* structural regulations.

Fourthly, the pro-market advocates have savagely critiqued the existing order's purported two model regulatory regime (with broadcasting being the deviant model), including a critique of the view that the two models sensibly respond to the media's multiple democratic functions (cf. Bollinger, 1976). Instead, the same First Amendment principles should apply to all media (Krattenmaker and Powe, 1995). Despite the US Supreme Court's continued allegiance to *Red Lion*, a widespread aca-demic consensus rejects the scarcity argument for broadcast regulation. Scarcity will always exist for desired goods if priced at zero, but if made available at its market price, supply will naturally equal demand. This will be no less true for broadcast licenses than for newspapers. Given lack of other persuasive reasons for government regulation, commentators argue that broadcast licensing is itself presumptively unconstitutional—spectrum should be fully privatized (Spitzer, 1989).

Fifthly, much can turn on whether press freedom is seen as an institutional right, as has been quite clear in Europe (Barendt, 1993), or an individual right, presumably of an 'owner'. Early scholarly and judicial discussions in the United States also implicitly assumed the first, finding the value of media freedom lay in its service to democratic or social needs—for example, 'to secure the widest possible dissemination of informa-tion from diverse and antagonistic sources'. Rights of media entities, as Justice Hugo Black suggested in *Associated Press*, were *only* those that served this instrumental role. Nevertheless, at least in the United States, there seems to have been an observable but possibly unconscious shift, usually undefended and rarely critiqued, in background assumptions. The new view, already embodied in US lower court decisions, sees media entities as themselves 'rights bearing entities'. Instrumentally valuable institutions in this account receive the same respect, the same rights, as do individuals. This change of assumptions could be as consequential for legal and scholarly treatment of the media as the recent enthusiasm for the market.

For example, historically, First Amendment scholars defended and the US Supreme Court protected an individual in attempting to reach as large an audience as she can with the resources she commands. She can leaflet, knock on doors, or speak on top of her soapbox—and she has a right not to speak if she does not want. If she has enough money, she might place ads (subject to the media entities' 'right' to reject them) in media covering the entire country. Media entities, however, were always different. Democratic or other First Amendment values require that they, like individuals, not be censored. Censorship is inconsistent with the instrumental rationale of the press's status. Purposeful suppression, however, is distinguished from 'suppression' that results merely from rules distributing material opportunities. Since the media company was not the bearer of an *autonomy-based* right to speak, it had no right to speak to all the people of the country by owning multiple media outlets. It was surely enough that a media entity (exactly like non-media-owning individuals) could try to reach more people by placing ads. And often it had no right to refuse to speak, at least in the sense of carrying the other's speech.

In contrast, the new vision sees the media company itself as the rights bearer. Its right to speak to as large an audience as it can, and over as many microphones as possible, is infringed by a law that restricts it to owning only 30 percent of the country's cable systems (over 10,000 systems) or that requires it to lease some of its channels to independent speakers (*Time Warner Entertainment Co v FCC*, 240 F. 3rd 1126 (DC Cir 2001)). Similarly, a common species of cross-ownership regulation—a restriction on cross-ownership of a telephone and cable system within the same geographic area—abridges the telephone company's First Amendment right to speak (*Chesapeake and Potomac Telephone Co v United States*, 42 F 3d 181 (4th Cir 1994), *vacated*, 516 US 415 (1996)).

After long treating structural regulation as a relatively unproblematic means to serve individuals' interest in media that provide for a robust communication order, the US Supreme Court recently gave arguable support to the view of the media as a repository of rights on its own behalf. It did so by adopting a standard of review that still permits structural regulation (i.e. purportedly 'content-neutral' regulation) but only if the regulation 'furthers an important or substantial governmental interest . . . and if the incidental restriction on alleged First Amendment freedoms is no greater than essential to the furtherance of that interest' (*Turner Broadcasting System v FCC*, 512 US 622 (1994)). Many scholars have uncritically employed this judicial standard, combined with the new view of the media entity as the bearer of basic speech rights, to attack government regulations. This new burden of proof allows activist courts, skeptical of the rationality of deviations from reliance on markets, to block much media regulation.

Sixthly, market advocates routinely insist that any problems with concentration, inadequate diversity, access, or other failures of the old media that might justify legal intervention are eliminated by the communicative abundance created by the Internet. Now anyone with something to say can be both an author and publisher to the world.

2.3 Responses Favoring Structural Regulation

Non-academic challenges to this new, hegemonic view of media structural regulation are common. The continual stream of media mergers and the increasing concentration of media power is a common target of criticism in the popular press. Communications scholars as well have discussed the problems of concentration and the market in popular books (Bagdikian; Herman and McChesney). Nevertheless, defenders of intervention have mostly been on the defensive in legal scholarship. Still, they have elaborated policy-relevant responses to each of the market advocates' claims, responses which I believe market advocates have yet to answer.

2.3.1 *Market Failures*

Admittedly some advocates of intervention are paternalistic, believing that existing social conditions do not allow undistorted development of people's 'true' preferences. That, however, is not the primary response to market advocates' paternalism critique. Putting aside general critiques of markets as unresponsive to people's values or preferences, at least five arguments show why specific features of media products make media markets especially likely to fail dramatically to respond appropriately to people's preferences (Baker, 2002).

First are consequences of the typically high cost of creating the first copy of media products and the virtual costlessness of subsequent copies. Any commodity with this 'public good' quality—non-rivalrous use—will be predictably under-produced by a market unless the producer/seller is able to fully and costlessly price discriminate. Market competition can exacerbate the problem. Given that the availability of one media product affects the demand for an alternative, sometimes competition from media products that produce less consumer surplus will cause media products that generate greater consumer surplus to become unprofitable. This competition-based inefficiency predictably favors large-audience products over products primarily valued by smaller groups—namely, it disfavors those products that often add more to diversity and cultural pluralism. Finally, this market-based inefficiency increases to the extent that, as is predictable, large audience products are better positioned to effectively price discriminate.

Secondly, markets only work on the assumption that products are properly priced. Unregulated markets under-price and over-produce products with negative externalities. Those with positive externalities are over-priced, resulting in inadequate production. For example, the press's properly discharged watchdog or 'fourth estate' role produces huge positive externalities—benefitting all members of a political community whether or not they purchase (or consume) the media product. Other knowledge and behavioral effects of media products on their consumers—ranging from stimulating intelligent or misguided political participation to stimulating pro- or anti-social behavior or generating a rich or banal culture—can hugely affect the lives of those other than the purchasers. Media goods may greatly outpace smoke-stack industries in terms of producing large externalities, positive as well as negative. Importantly, often these negative and positive externalities will not flow from the same media products. The result is that the market predictably provides much more of some media products and much less of others than people would want if the market properly priced the products.

Thirdly, that advertisers are a joint or primary provider of revenue for many media products means that to a significant degree advertisers' interests determine media content and price. This has two primary consequences for media content creation and distribution. First, often the advertiser will 'subsidize' content that diverges from that more desired by the audience. Advertisers typically want content that leaves audiences receptive to their advertising appeals (content that creates a 'buying mood'), that praises or glamorizes the advertiser's product rather than showing the product's underside, and that conforms to rather than undermines the advertisers' political agendas. The result is that content of this sort will be more widespread than if the market merely responded to audience preferences. And except when audiences' preferences are particularly strong, these products may not merely supplement but will replace media content that audiences would prefer.

Equally or more important, advertisers' definition of their targeted audience has major structural and content consequences. The availability of advertising revenue hugely affects the success or failure of different types of media enterprises. For example, advertisers use daily city newspapers to target the financially non-marginal, general population. Newspapers' consequent attempt to appeal equally to all elements of this audience was arguably a major cause of the development of an objective style of journalism. Since competition in declining-cost products typically requires strong product differentiation, illustrated by partisan but much less by 'objective' papers, objective journalism, in turn, helped create one-newspaper cities. Alternatively, where the target is a particular population subgroup, as it often is for magazine advertisers, advertising and not people's independent interests largely determines the fissures along which media content is created and packaged. Finally, although all markets unequally favor the preferences of the wealthy (because the wealthy can most easily pay), advertising greatly increases this distortion, subsidizing media products that appeal to those the advertisers want as customers. Since news media consumption is a major stimulate of political participation, the consequent inattention to the poor can operate as one of the forces effectively disenfranchising the poor (Baker, 1994a).

Fourthly, markets only respond to market-expressed and money-backed preferences—the 'willing and able to pay' standard. There is absolutely no reason to assume that the preference that a rich person will back with a $100 is more socially valuable (certainly not ten times more) than the preference that a poor person will back with $10. Moreover, people express very different preferences under different conditions and in different contexts. There is no reason to believe that those expressed in one context, say within the market, are more valid or objectively real than those expressed in other contexts, for example, within the political sphere or other interpersonal non-commodified realms. Of course, plausible pragmatic reasons lead all market societies regularly to rely on market expressions of preferences for distributing many goods. All societies, certainly all democratic societies, also use alternative methods—usually, more egalitarian methods—of identifying and responding to desires or preferences for other goods or opportunities. Media products straddle the line between goods typically distributed by markets—for example, entertainment—and goods often distributed through more egalitarian mechanisms—for example, education, culture, and resources needed for basic political participation. In any event, the choice among methods of identifying and measuring preferences cannot be resolved on the basis of which method is most objectively accurate. Rather, the choice is a value-based, necessarily collective self-definitional decision among alternative structures. In a democracy, this choice should be made politically, with one caveat. Two central liberal premises are that people should not be barred from expressing their preferences within any structural arena available in society and that the state should not purposely suppress the existence of possible arenas—even if some policy choices inevitably favor greater or lesser robustness of a particular arena.

Fifthly, usually market competition in products that sell at their marginal cost effectively enforces a profit-maximizing (efficiency) orientation on all firms. Little discretion is left for value choices by producers who wish to continue to participate in the market. This market pressure to use resources most efficiently to satisfy market demand is the meaning of 'consumer sovereignty'. Of course, even for these products, unprofitable 'gentleman' farmers illustrate that owners can sometimes subsidize their personal values in their economic activities. However, the nature of monopolistic competition (which is typical of products that sell above their marginal cost) means that *successful* products often have the capacity to generate huge operating profits—a fact evident in the highly profitable nature of monopoly daily newspapers. In this situation, discretion to pursue different alternatives exists. An individual or firm can attempt to maximize these potential profits by its prices and responses to audience preferences or it can 'spend' them on providing products that embody the owner's values. On the bright side of the second alternative, this 'expenditure' of profits can benefit the public—for example, by supporting products that are unprofitable to the seller but which have substantial positive externalities. Family book publishing enterprises' devotion to quality literature purportedly once led many publishers to 'spend' profits on supporting publication of unprofitable but worthy authors. Local family-owned newspapers sometimes spent these 'profits' to subsidize good journalism. Some journalists claim this also commonly occurred within media corporations dominated by people who held to the professional commitments of journalism rather than the currently more common goal of maximizing stock values. Or these profits can be spent to advance an ideological agenda—including, as the Berlusconi example illustrates, the owner's personal political ambitions. Without objecting wholesale to this use, the point explains why a democracy should be committed to a wider distribution of media ownership.

2.3.2 *Other Arguments*

If one accepts this response to the market advocates' simplistic economic model, responses to their other five points are quite straightforward. Rather than being paternalistic, only intervention can respond to preferences otherwise frustrated by predictable, systematic, and massive market failures. Any (constitutional) prohibition on governmental interventions in the market treats people paternalistically in relation to their political capacities.

Market advocates can be credited with rightfully viewing government as a potential threat to liberty if not merely a (potentially) corrupt cartel. Historical examples are plentiful. However, the inadequacies of even a perfectly working market suggest that any hope for better results must rely on government intervention. This observation supports two directives. First, human welfare requires intellectual, legal, and political efforts to make government work better—not to abandon reliance on it. Secondly, judicial doctrine should be designed to restrict government abuse but not by disabling means. Thus, constitutional doctrine or interpretive methods should invalidate content-based censorship and limit government practices that undermine the integrity of media institutions. Exemption of journalists from compulsory disclosures of their confidential sources or their work-product, protections now common in Europe, might illustrate such a desirable legal doctrine.

The critique of a US constitutional distinction between print and broadcast can be largely accepted. However, as noted earlier, the conclusion that a hands-off, deregulatory approach represents the standard constitutional mandate corresponds neither to case law nor good theory. As the Europeans recognize, there may still be good grounds to subject different media to different policy-based legal regimes. And given the historically developed role of print media, many structural interventions *there* may turn out to be hard to justify on policy grounds. On inspection, some of these might be interpreted as (unconstitutionally) undermining the integrity of the press.

Treating media corporations as the fundamental bearers of rights should be rejected as mere ideological mystification. Rights of institutional entities must be derivative and instrumental. Of course, media entities properly represent the public interest in a free press when they challenge censorship or challenge denial of journalistic rights that contribute to its effective functioning. However, there should be no constitutional objection to structural regulation that represents a plausible, even if debatable, public choice about how to increase media entities' contribution to a society's open and democratic political and cultural life.

Finally, the Internet and digital communications raise a host of important policy issues that are not taken up here (Lessig, 1999). Still, the same issues concerning what communicative content should be allowed to circulate and why remain virtually unchanged. Section 1 described the theoretical underpinning that underlies positions different scholars take on this matter. However, by dramatically reducing copy and distribution costs and changing the nature of search efforts, as well as merely increasing the ease of certain forms of both individual interpersonal conversations and group conversation/notification activities, digital technologies undoubtedly have a major impact on the communications environment. More than anyone, copyright theorists and policy-makers are debating how to take these changes into account within their regulatory efforts. Nevertheless, the costs of making the first copy of *quality* content remain. Reducing copy and distribution costs can sometimes encourage greater monopolization of production. For these and other reasons, digital communications eliminate none of the inadequacies of the market described above. New structural issues of great importance arise. Serious scholarly treatment of the opportunities that digital communications open up and how legal structural policy affects the likelihood of alternative paths of development is beginning. Although largely beyond the scope of this chapter, the point here is that thoughtful responses should not be prevented by knee-jerk reliance on markets.

2.4 Other Structural Issues

The dominant American scholarly focus on showing that media regulation is misguided—or on responding to these claims—has left little time to imaginatively investigatie the best forms of intervention. Much of the best policy scholarship comes from other countries. An example is James Curran's recognition that different media organizational structures both respond to different media-related societal needs and protect against different forms of government and private corruption. Based on this insight, Curran thoughtfully proposes that the media be loosely organized in five sectors—a core public service, civic media, professional media, private enterprise, and social market sectors, each with different organizational forms and with different bases of financial viability (Curran, 2000; cf. Bollinger, 1976).

More generally, as discussed in Section 1 above, since a central premise concerning a free press is its fundamental role as a constituent element of democracy, the appropriate forms of media regulation will inevitably reflect the theory of democracy adopted. This creates a need for self-conscious debate about democratic theory and how different media policies respond to different conceptions of democracy (Baker, 2002; Sunstein, 1993; Barron, 1967).

Finally, there is a vitally important, under-analyzed issue relating to law's differential impact on two realms of communication. Jürgen Habermas has distinguished between the lifeworld, where people coordinate behavior based on communicative agreement, and systems realms—the economy and the bureaucratic state—which rely on the mediums of money and power to steer behavior (Habermas, 1987). He famously described the role of the commercial mass media—with one foot in the systems realm and the other in the lifeworld—as contributing crucially to the non-commercial, non-market-oriented discourse of a democratic public sphere. In a sense, Habermas's point suggests both the (possible) distinction between constitutional protection of speech and of the press suggested in Section 1 and the discussion of structural regulation in Section 2, which implicitly assumed that policy should aim at enhancing the quality of the media's contribution to democratic public sphere(s). As long as legal rules do not affect non-commodified communications or affect them and the commodified mass media in the same way—for example, defamation is prohibited in both contexts—this aim is fine. Increasingly, however, media policy, especially as related to copyright and to the Internet, differentially affects commodified mass media and private or non-commercial or non-commodified public sphere communications—positively affecting one sphere at the cost of negatively affecting the other (Benkler, 1999). Although usually not stated in these terms, media policy has actually faced this issue often. It is an underlying issue (along with efficiency questions related to elasticity of demand that have consequences for pricing strategies) involved in choosing rules controlling cross-subsidies of self-supporting telephone and mail systems. Historically, newspapers in the United States received tremendously important postal subsidies paid for by other mail users. Mandated cable system subsidies for public access programming involve the same issue.

Ultimately, the value of commodified mass media lies in its contribution to people's non-commodified discourses, to their discursive development of democratic public opinion, and to their cultural appreciation and experiences. Thus, it might seem that in cases of conflict, policy should always favor non-commodified communications. This conclusion comes much too fast. The commodified realm's valuable contributions to the quality of discourse and to participation in public and cultural spheres must not be sacrificed. Still, given policies that have opposing consequences for the expense or difficulty of communications in the non-commodified lifeworld as compared to the realm of commercial media, scholarly investigations and policy outcomes should be sensitive to these policies' empirical consequences for and the normative value of both realms. Here, economics provides no traction for thinking through the central normative issues. Unfortunately, however, given the incentives for organized lobbying to favor the commodified side of most policy disputes, standard theories of interest group politics predict that legislative policy-making will over-protect the commodified mass media in any conflict with non-commodified communication spheres. New scholarship, now developing among copyright scholars, needs to further investigate this danger.

References

Baker, C. E. (1989). *Human Liberty and Freedom of Speech*, New York: Oxford University Press.
—— (1994*a*). *Advertising and A Democratic Press*, Princeton: Princeton University Press.
—— (1994*b*). 'Turner Broadcasting: Content-Based Regulation of Persons and Presses', *Supreme Court Review*, 57–128.
—— (2002). *Media, Markets, and Democracy*, Cambridge: Cambridge University Press.
Barendt, E. (1993). *Broadcasting Law: A Comparative Study*, Oxford: Oxford University Press.
Barron, J. (1967). 'Access to the Press—A New First Amendment Right', *Harvard Law Review*, 80: 1641–78.
Benkler, Y. (1999). 'Free as the Air to Common Use: First Amendment Constraints on Enclosure of the Public Domain', *New York University Law Review*, 74: 354–446.

—— (2001). 'Siren Songs and Amish Children: Autonomy, Information, and Law', *New York University Law Review*, 76: 23–113.

Blasi, V. (1977). 'The Checking Value in First Amendment Theory', *American Bar Foundation Research Journal*, 521–649.

Bollinger, L. (1976). 'Freedom of the Press and Public Access: Toward a Theory of Partial Regulation of the Mass Media', *Michigan Law Review*, 75: 1–42.

Curran, J. (2000). 'Rethinking Media and Democracy', in J. Curran and M. Gurevitch, *Mass Media and Society* (3rd edn.), London: Arnold.

Emerson, T. I. (1970). *The System of Freedom of Expression*, New York: Random House.

Fowler, M. S., and Brenner, D. L. (1982). 'A Marketplace Approach to Broadcast Regulation', *Texas Law Review*, 60: 207–57.

Habermas, J. (1987). *The Theory of Communicative Action*, ii, Boston: Beacon Press.

—— (1996). *Between Facts and Norms*, Cambridge, Mass.: MIT Press.

Herman, E. S., and Chomsky, N. (2002). *Manufacturing Consent: The Political Economy of the Mass Media* (2nd edn.), New York: Pantheon.

Humphreys, P. J. (1996). *Mass Media and Media Policy in Western Europe*, Manchester and New York: Manchester University Press.

Karst, K. L. (1990). 'Boundaries and Reasons: Freedom of Expression and the Subordination of Groups', *University of Illinois Law Review*, 95–149.

Krattenmaker, T. G., and Powe, Jr., L. A. (1995). 'Converging First Amendment Principles for Converging Communications Media', *Yale Law Journal*, 104: 1719–41.

Lahav, P. (ed.) (1985). *Press Law in Modern Democracies*, New York: Longman.

Lessig, L. (1999). *Code and Other Laws of Cyberspace*, New York: Basic.

McChesney, R. W. (1993). *Telecommunications, Mass Media, and Democracy: The Battle for the Control of U.S. Broadcasting, 1928–1935*, New York: Oxford University Press.

Meiklejohn, A. (1965). *Political Freedom: The Constitutional Powers of the People*, New York: Oxford University Press.

Meyer, C. (1994). 'Sex, Sin, and Women's Liberation: Against Porn-Suppression', *Texas Law Review*, 72: 1097–201.

Post, R. (1995). *Constitutional Domains: Democracy, Community, Management*, Cambridge, Mass.: Harvard University Press.

Scanlon, T. A. (1972). 'A Theory of Freedom of Expression', *Philosophy & Public Affairs*, 1: 204–26.

Shiffrin, S. H. (1990). *The First Amendment, Democracy, and Romance*, Cambridge, Mass.: Harvard University Press.

—— (1999). *Dissent, Injustice, and the Meaning of America*, Princeton: Princeton University Press.

Spitzer, M. L. (1989). 'The Constitutionality of Licensing Broadcasters', *New York University Law Review*, 64: 990–1071.

Sunstein, C. R. (1993). *Democracy and the Problem of Free Speech*, New York: Free Press.

CHAPTER 30

ABORTION AND REPRODUCTIVE RIGHTS

JANE MASLOW COHEN

1 INTRODUCTION

THIS chapter will discuss critical debate about individual control over the beginnings of life that has sprawled across the fields of academic law, philosophy, politics, religion, the life sciences, and the self-christened field of bioethics from the 1960s up to the present. The subject has formed in and around a cascade of popular pressures; biomedical advances; legislative, judicial, and public policy initiatives; media attention; and the boiling politics in which, at least in the United States, the whole series of enterprises has been bathed. The present undertaking will train on the law.

The normative tensions that have formed the basis of critical inquiry dilute the emphasis that might alternatively have been placed on the loose but resilient partnership that has developed amongst regulators; market actors—especially those in the pharmaceutical industry; and the multi-millions of individuals who have endorsed one or more of the reproductive choices that we will explore. It is these forces, not, as some court critics would have it, constitutional decision-making or 'judicial legislation', that have generated a consistent and progressively forward line of march toward ever-more-comprehensive varieties of life-cycle control, including reproductive control, for individuals in the American and European democracies to choose. Despite the emphasis on critique that will cause us to attend primarily to the resistant edge of these developments, the shaping forces of industry and market demands have hardly been banished from this account. Nor could they be, for they have been highly influential and genuinely irrepressible. And so will be their presence, in and out.

I should introduce an additional grab-bag of elements that have played a substantial role in the construction of this chapter. First, the actual controversies that have swirled around the topics we will consider have tended to attract single-issue debaters. Secondly, within each precinct of authorial interest, commentators have tended to lavish their attentions on the law and policy of a single sovereign state: comparative work across the subjects we will consider has been stingy, to say the least. Thirdly, academic commentators have articulated their claims largely to members of their own disciplines. Few have tried to influence discussion across fields, let alone to guide the public's views. Taken together, these forms of insularity have reinforced cultural, disciplinary, and subject-matter divides, lending an untidy disunity to the kind of sharp-profile analysis that best suits the short-essay form. More crudely: I am not able to reconstruct in these pages a singular debate about reproductive regulation in the developed democracies simply because there isn't one. I have substituted, instead, a sampling of related topics with my own version of their cross-cutting ties. These ties consist of the popular recognition, in the developed democracies, that reproductive control for men and women alike should be a matter of personal choice that is not subject to the overriding control of the state—an understanding that has fostered, even as it has been fostered, by the marketplace development and distribution of safe, cheap, and effective, though still imperfectly reliable, aids to that end. Together with these features of a common landscape has come the recognition in law of a right to abortion—especially, to early abortion—that has, as of this writing, succeeded in surmounting moral and religious critique as well as oppositional political force. Lastly, it is a fact that, while the ideal of self-sovereignty, shaped around concerns for autonomy and privacy, together with a practical concern for women's economic freedom and equality have helped to sculpt into democratic culture a sense of ungendered entitlement to reproductive freedom, the legal warrant for abortion has required considerable intervention by the courts. Beyond these commonalities, lies a region of private and public thought and action that has been rendered highly susceptible to divisive political choice.

Even more awkward is the size and shape of the US abortion debate. Not just its bloated presence within both politics and law but its tentacular quality accounts for its aggressive presence here. Why so bloated? In part, because both national parties cater to single-issue constituencies by maintaining a major ideological divide over abortion when, on an increasingly wide swath of issues, their positions tend to converge—this, while polls have steadily demonstrated wide support amongst voters for early abortions, at the least. Single-issue groups can swing close elections; efforts by the parties to woo them over the abortion issue have mesmerized the process of federal (and in some states) judicial selection for many years. This long-standing interjection of the politics of abortion into the judicial selection process is widely understood to have distorted the relationship between politics and law. Hence, a major cause of bloat.

Why tentacular? Not only because abortion issues have breached the divide (for those who believe that there is one) between law and politics, but because abortion has come to represent so much to so many: a matter of moral principle; distributive justice; gender justice; social policy; constitutional decision-making gone right or gone wrong; liberalism or libertarianism or populism, translated from theory to application in the right way or the wrong; federalism, correctly understood or mis-applied, and so on. And on. In the United States, abortion is a free-standing issue—in some ways, the isolate of all isolates in its ability to dwarf other social policy debates. But the many fragments that the subject has fallen into have also managed to intertwine themselves with a host of other concerns.

Two last items warrant mention. One is that I have not sought to disguise my identity as a liberal-progressive feminist, albeit one of a contrarian stripe. The sec-ond item is that the saga of life-cycle choice, including reproductive choice, that has been enacted as a significant chapter in contemporary social history and institu-tional life within the Western democracies has come about largely because the baby-boom generation has made insistent demands on the social and political institutions of our times to make life-cycle choices possible. It is no accident of his-tory that the contemporary law and policy of reproductive choice was launched as our generation came to be of reproductive age, or that the technologies that have extended the age of female child-bearing have been discovered in time to benefit our generation's range of choice. Nor is it an accident that the 'second wave' of feminism—the liberal feminism that predominated from the 1960s until the 1980s—remained highly identified with the relationship between economic inequality, coercive construction of the family and women's role in it, and reproductive choice.

Indeed, feminist theorizing moved on to its current, more expansive and self-critical phase only when the basic value of reproductive choice seemed well-established within democratic life. Despite the congeniality of the market for reproductive control and the regulatory lenity that has accompanied it—the two secure, and, therefore, unexamined background conditions of this account—my 1960s feminist conditioning and the highly perturbed state of abortion law and politics within the United States have left me hyper-vigilant toward the subject of reproductive legal and policy developments, overall. These elements—a liberal-progressive-feminist historical allegiance, the occasional contrarian tendency, and a hyper-vigilant attitude borne of abortion-related strife—have combined to produce interpretive biases that must have influenced this account.

2 CONTRACEPTION IN THE UNITED STATES: INTRODUCTORY REMARKS

From an Olympian view, the law and policy of contraception in the United States consists of two diachronic episodes. The first, like its English analog, was about a century long. It blended the regulation of contraception into a host of efforts, made in the name of collective morality, to regulate intimate social relations, including sexual conduct and reproductive choice.

The second episode, which took place during the 1960s and 1970s, thoroughly disrupted the prior regime. On the reproductive front, it consisted of an attempt—waged in bedrooms; in a slightly farcical way, in the streets; and, more soberly, in the courts—to cast off the regulatory yoke so that a safe and effective oral contraceptive for women, embracingly referred to as 'the pill', could be easily acquired and used.

Looking back on these events, the late English novelist Angela Carter is said to have remarked that there were only ten years in human history when sex was both safe and fun—the ten years when the pill first became available and before the advent of AIDS. Her compatriot, the poet Philip Larkin sought to capture the zeitgeist still more closely with the news: 'Sexual intercourse began | In nineteen sixty-three'.

In the United States, the mood was neither as insouciant nor as elegiac as the English literati cared to suggest. The sexual revolution, as we who were in its infantry preferred to heroize it, was accompanied by the senseless tragedy of the Vietnam War. 'Make love, not war', we demanded. But the first half of our incantation proved easier to accomplish than the second, since the Supreme Court proved an ally only of our bid for reproductive freedom, but not of our efforts to end the war. The state regulatory regime the Court spent a strenuous decade dismantling included the wholesale derogation of entire groups of people—'illegitimate' children and 'miscegenating' couples, among them—quite apart from those aspects that reflected exertions of intended power and influence over sexual relations in the name of the post-Victorian secular state. The undoing of these excesses of moralistic zeal by the least democratic, though arguably the least dangerous branch of government divided the ranks of close observers into enthusiasts as well as abiding critics of the Court's work. Contraceptive freedom rode in on this controversial reformist wave.

2.1 The Historical Underpinnings of Contraceptive Law and Policy in the United States

The law and policy of contraception have their chronological beginnings in the nineteenth century in both England and the United States, when efforts to enforce community morality, most especially, the link between extra-marital sex and sinful behavior, were widely enacted. These measures included the criminalization of adultery; a civil law bar on alimony for adulterous wives in the event of divorce—this, without regard to financial need or the possibility of bilateral marital wrongs; and a wide range of statutory enactments and common law rules intended to visit hardship and opprobrium on children born out of wedlock, and, thus, on their mothers in sin.

To discourage extra-marital sex still further—amongst other rationales—moral reformers successfully campaigned for the criminalization of abortion in England and throughout the United States; and, in 1873, the same efforts accomplished the federal passage of a law named for the legendary zealot Anthony Comstock that prohibited the dissemination of information about abortion or contraception through the mail.

Together with a long and wide skein of laws aimed at the maintenance of two classes of children—the legitimate and the illegitimate; laws intended to derogate the status of women relative to men; and, in a strong minority of states, laws designed to prohibit interracial marriage, these laws contravening reproductive autonomy for women stood the test of legislative and popular acquiescence for almost one hundred years.

2.2 The Legal Regulation of Contraception: The Supreme Court's Response

The regulation of reproductivity by the states went unchallenged as an aspect of American federalism and the regulatory invocation of collective morality from the mid-nineteenth century until 1937, when its initial constitutional challenge went up in flames. Throughout this long period, the states enacted laws shaped by local and, especially in the South, by regional tastes. The regimes that eventuated included several types of laws that pertained to reproduction alone. Three of these types are presented below, in chronological order of adoption. A fourth type—anti-abortion legislation—is, as previously noted, nearly as old as the Type One legislation with which I begin. But its complex unfolding, in the American context, requires separate development in Section 3.

Type One laws criminalized the distribution and use of contraceptive devices, on the foundational premise that contraception was (is) an immoral act. Type Two laws were enacted by the Southern states, primarily, following the Civil War. Their purpose was to criminalize and void marriages between white persons and 'those of the colored race'—anyone who, according to the statutory definition of racial purity, was insufficiently white. Type Three laws permitted the involuntary sterilization of individuals based on the weak science, but strong social ideology of eugenics. There were two varieties of these. The common one created the authority for mentally retarded individuals to be sterilized after a civil proceeding. A second, uncommon variant called for the sterilization of individuals who were repeat felons—but only those who had engaged in one particular crime. A challenge to each of these types was eventually brought on constitutional grounds.

The Court's initial re-casting took up both variants of legislation within Type Three. The first to be heard was the civil involuntary sterilization issue, decided in *Buck v Bell*, 274 US 200 (1927), where, in the first flush of the Court's re-positioning toward generous deference to legislatures, the procedural regularity built into the sterilization statute left the Justices unmoved by its cruel extremity, while its scientific rationale was treated to no examination at all.

This turn toward legislative deference became the essence of the Court's New Deal and post-New Deal stance, occasioning what became known as rational basis review. Yet, the constitutional challenges of the remaining regulatory types that came after the decision in *Buck* all managed to attain more careful scrutiny—each, on a different theoretical ground. By 1942, when the Court decided *Skinner v Oklahoma*, 316 US 535 (1942), the criminal sterilization case from Type Three, its opinion served amply to signal a more flexible, if inchoate, normative stance. Unlike the flaccid response to involuntary sterilization offered in *Buck*, the *Skinner* Court was able to opine that '[m]arriage and procreation are fundamental to the very existence and survival of the race'—here, the human race. The Court worried aloud, moreover, about involuntary sterilization as being in the nature of a deprivation of a 'basic liberty'. The Court invalidated the law in the context of an unarticulated standard of review.

By the time the Court decided *Loving v Virginia*, 388 US 1 (1967), the landmark representative of Type Two, its agenda had come to include a separate major turn toward basic justice for the racially oppressed. In striking down Virginia's criminal 'miscegenation' ban, the Court negated the very idea that state supervention over the legitimacy of marriage and marital offspring could be grounded on race, consistent with the Equal Protection clause of the Fourteenth Amendment. To demonstrate the force of its conviction—as of the time of its decision, some sixteen states still maintained a ban on interracial marriage—the Court added to its Equal Protection holding an alternative one based on a substantive due process theory of liberty. The Court re-attached the ideas of a 'natural' right to marry and to procreate—*Skinner*'s 'basic civil rights of man'—to the substance of liberty that, on due process grounds, must be constitutionally guarded from unwarranted deprivation by the states.

The Court's move toward a natural rights-based justification for 'heightened' scrutiny served as the grounding of its analytically unguarded opinion in *Griswold v Connecticut*, 381 US 479 (1965), the case that finally choked Type One legislation to death. In *Griswold*, the Court struck down a Connecticut statute that banned the use of 'any drug, medicinal article or instrument for the purpose of preventing contraception'. For the purpose, Justice Douglas infamously pasted together an ungainly pastiche of a rationale, reliant on a vision of 'specific guarantees in the Bill of Rights [which] have penumbras, formed by emanations from those guarantees that help give them life and substance' (367 US at 480). Far clearer than this hazy abstraction was the fact that the state's long-standing reach toward the imposition of a governing reproductive orthodoxy offended the liberal majority on the Court.

2.3 Critical Responses to the Contraception Cases

The Supreme Court's pre-abortion reproductive jurisprudence includes one case— *Buck v Bell*—that amounts to a clear embarrassment to the liberal ideal of equal individual regard. Yet, never having been overruled, *Buck* has not been formally repudiated by the Court. Perhaps its outcome is best understood strictly as a period piece, the personal triumph of Justice Holmes, whose paean to legislative deference in his dissent in *Lochner v New York*, 198 US 45 (1905) was simply ahead of its time. Still, the unfeeling disdain of Holmes's eugenics-based rationale ('Three generations of imbeciles are enough', 274 US 200, 207 (1927)) remains a monument to poor judgment that Holmes's many adulators have had to step around. Together with his non-adulators, they can focus, instead, on the procrustean analytic sensibilities of the late nineteenth-through-early-twentieth-century Court.

The jurisprudence we have considered includes two cases, *Skinner* and *Loving*, that fill the modern liberal bill by treating as the basis of heightened scrutiny, whether or not called by that name, instances of a narrow, overbearing, and fundamentally unfair use of the state's coercive machinery against 'discrete and insular minorities', to borrow an earlier constitutional phrase (*United States v Carolene Products Co*, 304 US 144 fn 4 (1938)). The anti-miscegenation statutes held unconstitutional in *Loving* represent the apotheosis of that approach. Even the Warren Court's most devotedly hostile detractors—including those who attack *Griswold* root, branch, and stalk—tend to leave *Loving* alone (see Berger, 1977; Bork, 1990; and Ely, 1980).

Griswold commonly falls prey to charges of Warren Court result-driven ad hockery, in that the spasmodically deployed statute at its base, aimed, as it was, at the general populace, held no discrete or insular groups in its scope. Fittingly, a Yale Law School theorist has risen to the task of defending the Court's honor in the *Griswold* case, while serving to conjoin this example of Type One unconstitutionality with those of Types Two and Three. His position is that the Court should stand willing to patrol for statist abuses signaled when 'one's life [may be] too totally determined by a progressively more normalizing state' (Rubenfeld, 1989). The fact that this idea trades off its raw intuitive appeal, rather than any crisp theoretical bounds, renders it liable to being considered the perfect descriptor of the Warren

Court's jurisprudence, whatever one's critical take. Yet, the cautionary stance this scholar offers towards an overly supine version of legislative deference may yet demonstrate the best posture available to defenders of the Warren Court, which has developed, over time, few abidingly cheerful friends. Perhaps, too, this is the normative stance that will best fortify those who must next defend the abortion right in the United States, should it become (as seems likely at the time of this writing) prone to heightened judicial and legislative attack.

It might be supposed that the American legal academy's libertarians would embrace the Court's apparent hostility toward the regulation of individual life. (For rhetorical effect, at the least, Justice Douglas funneled into his *Griswold* opinion a vision of police invading the 'sacred precincts' of the marital bedroom. Shades of *1984*!) But the most energetic libertarians in legal academe have maintained an unmitigated repugnance toward *Roe v Wade*, 410 US 113 (1973), to which the contraceptive rights cases can now be seen to have led (see e.g. Epstein, 1973). These days, it seems, legal academics tend to present themselves as populists more than they do as libertarians, even when libertarianism has served as their usual calling card. (I myself find this crossover puzzling, without the intervention of some theory, as yet unoffered, of the second-best.) Their obvious objections to *Griswold* can be seen simply as target practice for *Roe*. (See also discussion in Subsect. 3.2 below.)

As curious as is the missing libertarian defense of the contraception cases is the absence of a feminist defense of *Griswold*. Anti-contraception statutes operated significantly to the detriment of women, while touching far less the lives of men. The Connecticut law at issue in the case had been interpreted to permit the interdiction of *prescription* contraceptives. These consisted, in the main, of the diaphragm and 'the pill'. One-size-fits-all contraception, such as the condom, does not require a physician's aid. Condom distribution was, correspondingly, impossible to interdict, giving men far more latitude—let's call it freedom—than women about whether or not to engage in contraceptive use. Given the barriers to safe abortion that were also a part of the regulatory regime, the lack of female contraceptive availability served to reinforce for women a lack of reproductive control, absent travel for this clandestine purpose to a more liberal state (a further cost, in itself). Then again, so what? From the standpoint of liberal progressivism, the social relations branch of libertarianism, and even feminism, the *Griswold* decision joins *Skinner, Loving*, and a host of other demise-of-collective-morality cases in coming out the right way. The 'so what' coda to this thought experiment goes, however, like this: an honest confrontation with the differential impact that contraceptive non-availability—the medically prescribed versions, at least—played in the lives of women might have provoked an awareness of the relationship between sexual autonomy and economic opportunity for women a great deal earlier than when it finally came about (see discussion in Subsect. 3.2 below).

At a minimum, the issue of women's sexual autonomy would have been able to breathe free, for as much as a decade, of the moral complexities of fetal life. Would a woman-oriented version of *Griswold* have made any difference at all? If one takes at all seriously the didactic value of the Court's work (West, 1990; but see Eisgruber, 1992), an equal protection analysis of women's right to contraception, coupled with a recognition of the constitutional value of reproductive autonomy, might have had an early, perhaps a profound influence over the seemingly perdurable reproductive rights debate.

The contraception case law trilogy we have considered undeniably set the stage for the recognition of an abortion right by the Supreme Court, albeit without benefit of a feministically inspired foundation. Beginning with *Roe v Wade* (1973), the Court went on to deconstruct the final pillar of the four types of sexual regulation that we have revisited here. That much has hardly prevented efforts to rebuild the regime. Indeed, a respectable bevy of critics have opined that the politics of the anti-abortion movement received a ferocious strengthening on account of the Court's work.

3 ABORTION LAW AND POLICY
IN THE UNITED STATES

The most turbulent and divisive issue in American domestic politics from the close of the McCarthy era until the close of the twentieth century has also been the most painful and relentless issue in contemporary US law. This involves the Supreme Court's decision, in *Roe v Wade* (1973), to recognize a federal constitutional right of abortion for women, a decision the Court has been called upon to reject or reconsider or remake from the time of its issuance to the present. The peculiar dominance of abortion as a question of constitutional right was, on first emergence, so massively overdetermined that an endless stream of American commentators has descended into the arena of debate without pausing to observe the one feature that has long entertained observers from abroad: the very peculiarity of the issue's dominance itself.

The right to abortion has been a matter of sustained controversy in the United States for an extraordinary variety of reasons. First, its recognition as a federal constitutional matter is contested on the ground that it constitutes a usurpation of states' rights (the federalism issue). Secondly, its legitimacy as an exercise of the judicial power is contested on the ground that it violates the constitutional separation of powers (the judicial supremacy/counter-majoritarian issue). Thirdly, its status both as a matter of right and as a right of evolving dimension and scope is contested by a variety of durable constituencies. Fourthly, its grant of decisional autonomy to women upsets the traditional balance of power between men and women, on the patriarchal-conservative view. Fifthly, its grant of decisional autonomy to women is contested on the (unconsolidated) moral or religious ground that it subserviates the fetus to a pregnant woman's self-determined interests and needs in the absence of a sufficiency of regard for the fetus's countervailing right to life.

3.1 The Constitutionalization of an Abortion Right: *Roe v Wade*

Roe held that a woman's decision to abort a first-trimester pregnancy should be a matter of constitutionally protected liberty, in that the decision falls within the ambit of privacy the Court had begun to inscribe into constitutional case law in *Griswold*. However, the Court continued, pregnancy itself is not a sphere of activity as to which regulatory intrusions should be taken as entirely 'unwarranted'. Rather, the state is to be understood to have two separate interests in pregnancy which constitute independent and, on an increasing basis during gestation, 'compelling' regulatory grounds. The first is maternal health. The second is the development of fetal life. The Court found no justification for regulation by the state during the first trimester of pregnancy on either ground, thus leaving the decision to terminate or maintain an early pregnancy as entirely a woman's choice. Beginning in the second trimester, the Court found the state entitled to regulate to oversee maternal health. But during the final trimester of pregnancy, the state should be entitled to regulate pregnancy both to protect the welfare of the pregnant woman and to protect the welfare of the fetus—a potentially conflictual regime.

A considerable amount of the body of the decision is given over to the reconstruction of the historical status of abortion. At the time that most, if not all, of the states had codified their criminal codes during the mid-nineteenth century, the dominant practice had been to enact the common law crime of 'foeticide' with—at least for practical, largely evidentiary reasons—a 'quickening' distinction intact. (The fetus was considered legally protectible only after a pregnant woman was likely to be able to feel the fetus move—roughly, the gestational fourth month.) But later in the century, a powerful branch of the medical profession became persuaded that quickening was the basis of a 'ridiculous distinction'. Instead, it concluded, ' "[T]o extinguish the first spark of life is a crime of the same nature . . . as to destroy an infant, a child, or a man" ' (Witherspoon, 1985). A protracted lobbying effort by doctors of this persuasion caused a considerable number of states to revise their foeticide statutes, criminalizing the intentional causation of any pregnancy termination. These strict and comprehensive criminal abortion statutes matured prior to the ratification of the Fourteenth Amendment. Several had stood largely or entirely unmodified as of the time of *Roe*.

A second group of states had, during the 1960s and early 1970s, liberalized their abortion statutes, instead. Their purpose was to permit abortion if, as a matter of medical judgment, the life or the health (not statutorily defined) of the pregnant woman so required. The conflict into which the *Roe* Court proceeded involved, then, a deep schism between a type of abortion regulation designed to protect fetal welfare at the potential expense of the welfare (though never the life) of the pregnant woman and a second type, designed to recognize the primacy of the woman's interests, if not precisely her rights.

What these statutes all had in common, however, framed the issue of their constitutionality more profoundly than that which divided them: All of them together take the state to be the arbiter of the individual woman's interests in her reproductivity and her health and all of them leave to the state the articulation of a balancing of any interests outstanding, when those of more than one juridical entity are found to be at stake. When, in *Roe*, the Court annexed an abortion right to the other personal rights it had earlier announced in Types One through Three of the regulatory variants we have considered, it not only terminated the states' legislative capacity to balance the interests implicated in the earliest stage of pregnancy, but it allowed women to take their place amongst the rights-holders whose reproductive decisions and actions were entitled to protection above and—during the first trimester, at least—beyond the control of the state. Despite Justice Blackmun's protestation that the Court intended to adopt no 'theory of life', fetal rights advocates, then to now, have refused to take the Court at its word.

3.2 Criticisms of *Roe*

The abortion right announced in *Roe* has drawn vast negative attention. Critics of a federalist persuasion have dined on the position that the Court's decision usurped states' rights. Originalists have argued that the drafters and ratifiers of the Fourteenth Amendment must have intended to validate the multitude of anti-abortion statutes then in place, of which the Texas statute at issue in *Roe* was one (Ely, 1973, 1980; Epstein, 1973). Critics of judicial activism on counter-majoritarian grounds have rejected Justice Blackmun's attempt to make capital out of historic divisions regarding the moral status of the fetus. They would have left to the states all relevant choices, including the recognition of 'the rights of the unborn child' (Epstein, 1973).

Religious groups, most notably the Catholic Church, had already gone on the attack against abortion liberalization in the various states; had contributed in numbers to the amicus briefs filed with the *Roe* Court; and had urged on the Court the understanding that life deserves the state's protection from the moment of conception forward—a substantive posture different from the federalist notion that each state should remain constitutionally unconstrained in its choice of a 'theory of life'.

American social conservatives—most especially, extremists within this camp—have been galvanized, since *Roe* was handed down, by the residuum of power granted to the woman *qua* individual to decide without a male's supervention, let alone that of the state, the fate of early fetal life.

Feminist theorists, amongst others in legal academe, have expressed dissatisfaction with the *Roe* majority's privacy-based rationale. While others have criticized 'privacy' as devoid of a textual home or as an unsuitable, even hypocritical descriptor of a decision the Court itself had opined should be made by a woman in concert with others, the basal dissatisfaction of the feminist theorists has been the Court's lack of willingness to embrace an equality-driven rationale. On this account, it is only by acknowledging the transcendent unfairness of uncontrollable pregnancy in relation to women's opportunities for employment and other social and economic advance that the Court could have put the abortion right on the appropriate normative track.

This, the primary feminist-theoretical complaint about the abortion decision, draws unacknowledged moral sustenance from the intuition that women should not be held responsible for maintaining the life of fetuses that just happen to be inside them for reasons for which the women are not necessarily responsible. Contraceptive failure is an example. Rape is a second. Incest may constitute a third. This view is taken to hold—at least during early pregnancy—even if we grant that the fetus is a person (Thomson, 1971). It is a view that does not distinguish between pregnancies for which women are completely without responsibility (e.g. rape) and pregnancies that are the result of a woman's partial responsibility (e.g. the use of a contraceptive with a substantial failure rate, when more highly successful types are available). Nor does it invite a close factual analysis of such potentially dense moral thickets as incest. Still less does it guide the moral reckoning that might be called for in the case of intended pregnancies as to which the pregnant woman changes her mind. Instead, the no-moral-responsibility position is consistent with (and would seem to appeal for practical purposes) to the idea that either: (1) there is no satisfactory way for the liberal democratic state to determine the moral responsibility of each and every woman for each and every pregnancy or (2) more fundamentally, an intrusive inquiry of this kind is not the liberal state's job, even if it has strong interests in the matter—a straightforward libertarian view.

As the chief exponent of this claim made clear at the time that her now-famous essay first appeared, the intuitive basis for the no-responsibility position is time-dependent: a woman who allows her pregnancy to progress in the ordinary course (nothing being said about significantly deformed fetuses and the like) would seem to grow increasingly responsible for its existence and, therefore, no longer as free of constraint (Thomson, 1971). This turn of the moral screw has sizeable implications for position (2): as a fetus draws closer to birth—the point at which legal person-hood has clearly attached throughout the history of American law—the less obvious it becomes that the state's interest in fetal protection is unwarranted, even if its intrusiveness remains. Feminist equality theorists have consistently avoided ack-nowledging such differences in the moral significance of pregnancy on account of its development over time.

At the end of the day, those who believe that the fetus is entitled, uncontingently, to both the moral and the legal status of a person will not be swept off their perch by claims in favor of a woman's right to liberty or equality—still less, to privacy. Indeed, not. Galvanized by the *Roe* decision, anti-abortionists of many stripes formed the Moral Majority—a voting bloc that helped to put Ronald Reagan and (to a lesser extent) George H. W. Bush in the White House for three successive pres-idential terms. This same bloc, now heavily associated with the religious right in the United States, has continued to advance an anti-abortion agenda both in Congress and the states, producing a steady stream of legislation that has spawned constitu-tional challenges to this day.

The women's movement of the 1960s was also galvanized by the effort to secure a constitutional right to abortion for women. But, unlike the anti-abortion forces, which have solidified their base of popular support, the emphasis by the women's movement on abortion rights has been undermined by critical legal theorists and radical feminists for its association with what is taken to be a middle-class vision of welfare rights, one that is seen to have kept a more sweeping agenda of distributive justice for women from gaining support. Equality theory has thus become both a shield on which abortion rights have been defended and a sword used by feminist theorists against other feminists when wider issues of justice are put in play.

This unpretty state of affairs within feminism cannot be said to have yielded a productive dispute. Rather, it seems to have led to a state of near-exhaustion, at times, within the remnants of the women's movement. One consequence is that the feminist-theoretical development of abortion as a right has had but a single significant flowering in the aftermath of *Roe*—the energetic re-visioning of equal opportunity, especially equal economic opportunity, rather than liberty or privacy, as abortion's just constitutional ground (Ginsburg, 1975; Law, 1984; Siegel, 1992).

Liberty and equality theorists tend to converge in their belief that there is, in-deed, a normatively funded relationship between persons and the liberal state. Within American feminism, the centrality of this issue is generally treated by assump-tion. As noted earlier, libertarians divide over it, when the counter-majoritarian 'difficulty', as it is known, sticks in their craws. For conservative theorists of a differ-ent stripe, the American attachment to rights and to rights discourse is understood to be extravagant, causing the achievement of a European-style 'compromise' at the legislative level over such highly fraught issues as abortion to get blocked. This is taken to be a matter of national regret—a situation that has been compared unfavorably to the legislative treatment of abortion and other matters in England,

France, and Germany (Glendon, 1987, 1991; but cf., Epstein, 1992). Other populists, including apparent converts from left-liberalism, see voters and their legislative proxies as capable of—indeed, likely to make—satisfactory decisions about political life (the nature of politics, here, going undefined), if unconstrained by judicial review (Tushnet, 1999).

The core issue of whether or not abortion deserves to be treated as an implied (non-textual) constitutional right has, from well before the Supreme Court's decision in *Roe v Wade*, functioned as a legal, social, and political Rorschach test—an inkblot, the interpretation of which depends on a deep and wide diversity of other predisposing concerns. There was obviously no way for the Supreme Court to appease all of these tastes and preferences, or, indeed, many of them, when it extended the constitutional right to reproductive freedom to abortion as a woman's choice.

3.3 *Roe*'s 'Progeny'

Since the Supreme Court's decision in *Roe v Wade*, a steady stream of constitutional challenges involving abortion has been taken up by the Court. These are often referred to, collectively (and without irony), as '*Roe*'s Progeny'. Their diversity represents efforts by individual litigants to extend the abortion right but, more consistently, efforts by various state legislatures either to extinguish it altogether, or to whittle away at its availability, thereby causing it to attrite. These legislative re-castings have practical significance on the ground, though empirical studies of their effects have been both partial and slight. The most provocative of them have borne a special invitation to the evolving membership of the Supreme Court to repudiate *Roe v Wade*. The brief catalog below represents the most significant of this capacious inventory of moves.

3.3.1 *Abortion Funding*

Shortly after *Roe v Wade* (1973), the Court made clear its unwillingness to treat the abortion right as more than a bare prerogative. In *Maher v Roe*, 432 US 464 (1977) and, again, in *Harris v McRae*, 448 US 297 (1980), the Court considered the claim that the already-recognized abortion right ought to be extended so as to include a constitutional right to have the procedure paid for by the state under conditions of indigency or medical hardship. The Court refused these opportunities to expand abortion into a welfare entitlement, regardless of individual privation or the state's willingness to fund either indigents' medical needs, in general, or their pregnancy and childbirth-related expenses, in particular. For normative theorists who have disputed the widespread view that the US Constitution protects only 'negative' rights (in Isaiah Berlin's famous phrase, 'freedom from' rather than 'freedom to'), and for those who have argued more pointedly that the Constitution embraces a positive sphere of welfare rights, the abortion funding cases offer nothing by way of support.

The vanguard of critics of the abortion funding cases has been filled with more than those who have argued for the protection of positive liberties on largely philosophical grounds. Welfare rights advocates argue that the cases demote the welfare of the most economically helpless women below that of their fetuses, thereby inverting the intended significance of *Roe v Wade*. European critics of American health and social policy have used the abortion funding cases to underscore the peculiarity, and even the perversity, of US policy, given apparent public reluctance to subsidize poor women's abortions in the midst of further reluctance to provide adequate welfare assistance for their children. (Here, the relative glare of Congressional activity helps to hide the diversity of state actions, some of which now provide for the public funding of early abortion for the indigent, though less often for the merely poor.)

For its own part, the Supreme Court has gone on to extend its commitment to the line of reasoning introduced in *Maher* and *Harris*. In the highly controversial case of *Rust v Sullivan*, 500 US 173 (1991), the Court accepted the federal government's administrative interpretation of a statute which denied federal funding to agencies which even permit the discussion by doctors or other counselors of abortion as a method of family planning. This 'gag rule', as it immediately became known, was condoned despite clear evidence of its negative implications for women's health; the obviousness of its purpose (to circumvent *Roe*'s maternal health-related commitments); and its effects on the first amendment rights (not under attack for the only time) of government-paid workers to freedom of speech. Freed from constitutional concerns, Congressional conservatives have extended the outcome of *Rust v Sullivan* to the international sphere, rendering the receipt of American foreign aid for family planning programs conditional on compliance by each recipient program and facility with the identical rule.

3.3.2 *Regulatory Constraints on Abortion*

State responses to *Roe v Wade* and to the trimesterized framework of interests and interest-balancing that it announced have come to differ widely. These differences have become encapsulated within regulatory policy, as they are at the federal level as well. On the whole, a greater number of states than at the time of *Roe* now have liberal abortion regimes, undertaken to ease access to early abortion, in particular, and to provide funding for the indigent. But all of the states have engaged in time, place, and manner regulation and, in a number of them, the resultant restrictions have been designed to be harsh. Amongst a small number of states that have acted as provocateurs, moreover, either by skating as close to constitutional limitations as possible or by purposefully seeking to incite legal challenges to the schema in place, the blockages to abortion access have become severe. The actions of the provocateur states, in particular, have forced an array of constitutional challenges into the courts, where abortion-sensitive judicial appointments within the federal circuits and on state court benches, as well as on the Supreme Court, have been responsible for the creation of a patchwork of results.

Through all of this, the constitutional right to a first-trimester abortion, for a non-adolescent woman who can afford to pay, has remained essentially safe, though the paucity, in many parts of the country, of medical personnel willing to perform even early abortions constitutes just one consequence of the vigilante tactics of some anti-abortionists and the bitter controversy that has continued to rage. While most of the social welfare democracies have folded *early* abortion into their national health-care regimes, women who choose to terminate their pregnancies in the United States have to bob and weave around obstacles that the federal government, the states, and the medical community have been free to impose. (Until recently, most medical schools across the country had ceased to provide abortion instruction. It would be contrary to medical ethics for the state to require any physician who was conscientiously opposed to abortion to perform the act. But nothing explains why medical students who *are* willing to perform abortions should not be so trained. In France, by contrast, the law requires that an abortion provider be available within a designated small unit of geographic measure, country-wide.)

3.3.3 *Decisional versus Deliberative Autonomy*

Roe v Wade was meant to secure autonomy for women over the abortion decision during the first trimester of pregnancy, with regulatory interventions by the state being permitted later, if justified to protect maternal, and, after viability, fetal health. In *Planned Parenthood of Southeastern Pennsylvania v Casey*, 505 US 833 (1992), a plurality of the Court sustained the constitutionality of the abortion right, but went on to dismember the trimester-based framework of *Roe*, adopting, instead, a standard that protects pregnant women from the 'undue burdens' a state might attempt to impose on her right to abortion, a standard that opens the door to state interventions at any gestational stage, subject to judicial review of their due or 'undue' effects.

Applying its new formulation, the three-Justice coalition responsible for this outcome let stand the statutory sections under challenge that authorized a twenty-four-hour waiting period, except under emergency conditions, thereby necessitating two trips to accomplish the intended result and—at least as controversially—the authorization of at least some effort by the states to persuade every pregnant woman of the value of fetal life. Thus, to the consternation of at least some critics, the *Casey* plurality pledged its ongoing fealty to women's *decisional* autonomy over abortion, while retracting the protection of their *deliberative* autonomy at the same time (Cohen, 1992).

What had been widely predicted was that the Court would use *Casey* as the vehicle to 'gut' *Roe*. Refusing to be disappointed, critics of the Court, feminists amongst them, still insist that *Casey* gutted *Roe*. I simply don't agree. The abortion right lives a precarious existence in the United States. But, after and on account of *Casey*, it lives.

3.3.4 *Adolescent Abortion*

Three lines of common law doctrine and three further lines of constitutional doctrine have come to converge—at best, uneasily—in the regulation of abortion procedures for girls below the legal age of majority, an area into which the Supreme Court has now waded more than a half dozen times. The oldest and broadest line of authority inscribed in the common law is the recognition that children are under the general jurisdiction of their legal custodians, usually, therefore, their parents. Accordingly, it is a legal wrong, in the absence of specific exception, for a medical procedure to be performed on a minor child without prior custodial consent. A second line of doctrine traces out the exceptions to this rule. The traditional exception allows for the provision of emergency care in the absence of custodial consent. A more recent exception permits 'mature' minors to give or, in some instances, to withhold authorization for medical interventions, bypassing adult consent. The maturity that need be demonstrated in relevant instances has not been subject to close definition by the courts; rather, it has been fashioned as an impressionistic test. In a third line of cases, those involving private-actor disqualification, the state has adopted the primary decisional role.

In particular circumstances, the Court has recognized that minors are legal persons within the meaning of the Bill of Rights and, thus, may be rights-holders on their own. Still later, the Court began to fudge on the scope and significance of minors' constitutional rights, allowing the interests of their parents to outweigh those of the child.

Enter into this already unwieldy mix the complex issue of what right or rights ought to belong to pregnant girls, a category that must span the youngest females capable of becoming pregnant as well as those who are but weeks or even days away from the age of majority; girls who are entirely dependent on their parents or other legal custodians and those who, though minors, are functionally or legally emancipated; those who could reasonably benefit from parental guidance, assuming the parents are reasonable, and those for whom any parental or custodial notification could constitute the basis of grievous harm. Add, too, those girls who have already been subjected to abuse and those whose pregnancies are its direct outcome. Then, add pregnancies due to rape. Lastly, add in the troubling fact that adolescents in the United States tend to ignore or deny their pregnancies, becoming galvanized to take action only when their fetuses are near or past the mid-term.

On its first stride into this complex arena, the Supreme Court held unconstitutional a statute that required the written consent of at least one parent for any first-trimester abortion involving an unmarried minor—a legislative attempt to drive a clear wedge between this group—still, despite avoidance techniques, the largest subset of pregnant minors—and the uncompromised right to early abortion that the Court had announced in *Roe*. The Court declared this blanket parental veto authorization to be an 'undue burden' on the constitutional right to privacy, which, following *Roe*, it here found to include an abortion right for girls (*Planned Parenthood of Central Missouri v Danforth*, 428 US 52 (1976)).

Since that time, the Court has stuck by its initial positions that a constitutional right to abortion exists for under-age girls and that states may not unduly burden it. But the Court has let slip normative guidance with exceeding sparseness in this arena, effectively stepping into the framework of state-by-state regulation only to declare specific enactments outside constitutional bounds.

The Court's willingness to extend an abortion right to minors hardly begins to describe the chaos, moral and otherwise, that attends adolescent pregnancy in the United States. In some states, judges have liberally consented to abortions after parental bypass hearings that they speed through. In other states, especially where judges stand for election, doubt has been raised—by judges themselves—that they will ever grant their consent.

In many states, the abortion question is effectively decided by the dearth of providers willing to perform abortions on girls or abort the mid-term pregnancies that girls so commonly present. Of the 1.1 million adolescents who have become pregnant in the United States each year during recent decades, some 60-percent maintain their pregnancies to term. Courtesy of the confluence of the mature minor rule in relation to medical consent and the willingness of many states to pay for childbirth, girls may receive both pregnancy and childbirth subsidies, even when their parents do not believe that pregnancy and childbirth are in their daughter's interests (and when the parents may bear secondary support obligations to the child).

The decrease in stigma that has come to attend births out of wedlock has helped to foster a second trend: significantly reduced relinquishment for adoption, along with retention of their babies by adolescent girls. At the same time, old-style favoring of shotgun weddings is in severe decline. The retention phenomenon, in particular, has generated potentially fatal effects on the further education of adolescent mothers. Amongst the older ones, the effects on educational opportunity and economic advancement have been generally found severe, and the heavy statistical tilt toward pregnancy, childbirth, and retention amongst black and hispanic adolescents adds a multiplier effect to the potential for career derailment and resultant economic loss (Rosenheim and Testa, 1992). There seems to be no controversy (though rather little study) concerning these effects. Whereas pregnancy prevention programs are commonplace throughout the social welfare democracies, such programs have been held hostage within local politics in the United States to abortion hostility on the part of political and religious groups, most often in the name of parental prerogative and family autonomy. The trends toward high adolescent pregnancy and child-retention rates are often thus disabled from being effectively countered at the source.

Disputes over the empirics of adolescent pregnancy help to keep the fires burning in this precinct of the abortion conflict (Lawson and Rhode, 1993). Commentators who believe that 'easy' abortion encourages teenage promiscuity do not need to rely on empirics for guidance: theirs is a normative stance (Carlson, 1988). Allies of these anti-abortion normativists point to studies that suggest that the psychological sequelae of childbirth, at least for older teens, may be less severe than the guilt that may attend abortion, especially if it is undertaken without parental notice or support—a hypothesis dependent largely upon anecdotal evidence involving multiple variables that have not generally been pulled apart.

Those who represent the other side of this conflict use extant empirical studies to support the opposite normative outcomes. The mildest of these studies are offered for the position that, in general, adolescents weather the abortion experience with considerably less damage to their health and welfare than they do childbirth (Melton, 1986). The most denunciatory argue from studies of racial and ethnic minority teenagers that early childbirth permanently stunts their lives (Elders, *et al.*, 1989–90).

None of the studies that point to optimistic or pessimistic outcomes for the girls goes so far as to provide longitudinal examinations of personal and social outcomes for the children of those who have not chosen abortion (assuming that control variables could be designed). The stark fact that teenage mothers in the United States have increasingly stopped surrendering their offspring for adoption merely takes us to the door of what deserves to be known. On an altogether different side, a recent and controversial, if not incendiary, study proffers evidence that decreases in crime within the United States, and the state-by-state emergence of its decline, correlates directly with variations in the states' abortion restrictions over time (Donahue and Levitt, 2001).

3.4 Normative and Practical Implications of the Contraception and Abortion Cases

The contraception cases have come to reinforce the baby-boom generation's sense that sexual liberty is a personal entitlement and that procreative liberty is, on account of the responsibilities that children entail, an *a fortiori* case of that entitlement. So far and so fast had these understandings become incorporated into the general body of knowledge (if not of social truths) that an argument made by the state's attorney in *Griswold* to the effect that community morals are enhanced by the harsh penalties that pregnancies impose, was not even trotted into view on the state's behalf barely a decade later in *Roe*.

Left lingering is the question of whether this normative ground has been gained in virtue of its never having been lost: marital, procreative, or, for that matter, sexual liberty are sometimes conceptualized as rights that are inherently pre-political, which the Court, prior to the abortion cases, had more than once proclaimed to be the 'basic civil rights of man'. Does the oxymoronic notion of a pre-political right help to dissolve the issue of pedigree for the rights in question? Or, does the image of a just pre-political order act merely as an instruction to look away from law in the direction of metaphor—or common sense—for validation of the interpretive judgment at hand? The fact is, the 1960s generation which reaped the whirlwind on account of the contraception cases treated them simply as acts of avuncular good sense. And polls continue to demonstrate the American public's (albeit mild) support for at least an early abortion right, despite the continual blitz of more extreme views from the anti-abortion right.

Some combination of normative allegiance and normative drift have settled in, in support of the position that abortion is, indeed, a woman's *right*. Does that mean that, thirty years downstream of *Roe*, this right would garner legislative recognition across the states if a change in the Supreme Court's current fragile balance were to effectuate the total repudiation of *Roe* (and *Casey*) and return the abortion issue to the states, *tout court*? I find it difficult to opine on this, the ultimate predictive question. What does seem reliable is that the few states that have acted as abortion provocateurs would outlaw the practice quite thoroughly, though what even they might fashion, in cases of rape, incest, severe threats of injury to maternal health, and the youngest girl-pregnancies seems considerably insecure. More reliable is the prediction that the states with the most populous urban centers and concomitantly liberal populations would install liberal abortion regimes, or retain those that they now have. Just the divergence between these liberal and illiberal states would recreate the checkerboard legislative pattern in existence at the time *Roe* was decided. This would be likely to re-instigate the pre-*Roe* phenomenon of abortion tourism, as it had become known—well beyond the amount that exists now—giving rise to obvious distributive concerns. In other respects, the three decades of activity since *Roe* was handed down seem likely to have caused certain predictably durable practical effects.

One such effect involves the number of abortions women would have. A position taken by court critics (including critics of the Supreme Court) is that the constitutional jurisprudence of abortion turns out to have been, at best, irrelevant, as a matter of practical significance (Rosenberg, 1993). The crudest evidence asserted is that, from the years before *Roe* was decided to the present, the number of abortions performed in America each year has remained about the same. This much may well be true: the 1.3 to 1.5 million annual abortions statistic seems remarkably obdurate to change. But evaluating the practical effects of the abortion decisions requires an examination of more than statistical trends.

The first practical effect that I assume would perdure is that, by outlawing the criminalization of abortion, the *Roe* decision hastened the demise of an illegal industry—the provision of abortion to girls and to women under often horrendous conditions deleterious to their lives, their future fertility, and their health. It should be a fact to be reckoned with, quite apart from anything else, that the mortality and morbidity factors that were associated with illegal abortion—thousands of deaths and serious injuries per year—have been almost entirely eliminated in the United States in the epoch that has followed *Roe*. This effect is attributable not only to the circumstance that abortion providers are now entirely above ground, where they can easily provide safe and sanitary procedures. In addition, a technique for the performance of early-to-mid-term abortion, the use of suction curettage under ultrasound guide, gained rapid use, once the sale of standard medical equipment to providers who were not on the run was able to be uncoupled from fear. The relatively modest cost of the equipment involved has assured no sacrifice in safety of the early-to-mid-term procedure, across reputable facilities where it is performed. This and the low level of capital investment involved has permitted clinics to out-compete hospitals on cost to an extent that has continued to encourage providers to enter and remain in the market for abortion services, at least in areas where the locale proves accepting, on a basis that has helped to keep the costs of early medical (surgical) abortion low. One may hope that even a major resurgence of checker-board legislation would not provoke a resurgence of illegal and unsafe abortions in its wake.

Indeed, the swiftness of the procedure, lack of health complications, and low cost of suction curettage have so far enabled it to survive handily against the recently introduced, much-heralded alternative: pharmaceutical (non-surgical) abortion using the progesterone antagonist RU-486. (In the case of the earliest procedures this regimen makes possible, the term 'abortion' is inapt: implantation is impeded and the unimplanted embryo is shed.) For present purposes, the complicated, secretive introduction of this product into the American marketplace has accrued mostly symbolic effects: out of the 2.6 million abortions performed in the period since the drug was made available to US women in November 2000, approximately 100,000 nationwide have employed RU-486—a far lower response rate than had been predicted heretofore, but one that may well mirror the relative novelty of the procedure; its newness to market; its greater cost, inconvenience, and its risk of complications; and, on account of risk, physician reluctance to prescribe. What was supposed to provide a strong, new incentive for the earliest post-fertilization intervention—and, therefore, the greatest possible insulation against moral attack—has amounted, in the United States, at least, to a promise unfulfilled.

What must remain a matter of pure speculation is whether a woman's *use* of an early intervention procedure like RU-486 can and does affect her relation to the decision to terminate her pregnancy, and whether, as well as how, each type of available procedure might influence her attitude toward the early embryo or the later fetus itself. Would a cheap, easy, and reliable method of expelling the earliest embryos increase moral hazard by discouraging contraceptive use? Is there a minimum of moral suffering that *should* accompany the disuse of embryos, instead? The private aspects of pregnancy are necessarily that, and they are likely, therefore, to be immunized from most forms of reliable empirical research. (Extant studies that compare grief and regret over abortion with grief and regret over child-birth fail to satisfy reasonable methodological concerns.) Even in attempting to consider the practical consequences of abortion techniques, we find ourselves back in the normative realm.

4 Contraception and Abortion in Europe and the United Kingdom

The general, developmental arc of the law and policy of contraception and abor-tion in much of Europe and in the United Kingdom is, at the crudest level, similar. Most countries began with highly restrictive—indeed, prohibitory—policies, as did the United States. Indeed, countries with heavy Catholic majorities followed the church's teachings and landed on abortionists with force.

In France, by the mid-1970s, widespread contraceptive use, the commonplace—and dangerous—level of illegal abortion, and the phenomenon of abortion 'tourism' to countries that had already enacted reforms led to major legislative change. The interesting result was a statute that required a single consultation and a week's wait but gave pregnant women discretion over the first trimester abortion decision if they considered themselves 'in distress'.

In England, in a 1939 case that marked the beginning of the turn away from the criminal sanction of abortion and toward a more liberal regime, a judge read an exception to save the life of the woman into the statute at issue in the case. Sweeping parliamentary reform of England's abortion law came about in 1967. The terms of the new Abortion Act were far more encompassing in their generosity toward women's welfare and realistic toward the totality of circumstances that may sur-round the abortion decision than any statute or judicial ruling that has appeared, to this day, on US shores. (The Act permits a physician to perform an abortion, *inter alia*, where taking a pregnancy to term would create risk to the life or mental or physical health of the pregnant woman *or* to any of her children. The statute and its politically benign enactment were mentioned by Justice Blackmun in his opinion for the majority in *Roe* as an indicator of the direction of developments with which the United States should become aligned. The didactic salience of this brief part of the opinion appears to have been nil.)

The German story of abortion reform was more wrenching than the English or the French. An invariant criminal abortion prohibition was first enacted in 1871, being subjected to slightly liberal amendment, first by statute, then by judicial exception. The Nazis, however, abolished all reform, reinstituting harsh criminal penalties, except on the basis of eugenic determinants, to aid in the purification of the Aryan 'race'. At the end of the war, when Germany was split into two, West Germany re-adopted the pre-Nazi Weimar law. Communist East Germany, meanwhile, went on to enact a law permissive of abortion virtually without limit—a rather ugly showcase, as promulgated, for the ideal of gender equality under law.

The substantive difference between the laws of the two Germanys created a substantial market in abortion tourism, West to East. This undermined whatever efficacy the West German abortion regime might have had. Around the same time as the major French statutory reform, and just a few years after the English, a bitter and divisive change was enacted, one that had, amongst its effects, the decriminalization of first trimester abortions and the provision of excusing conditions for later abortions, too.

The new German and new French laws were challenged on constitutional grounds for what, suddenly, they were attempting to do. The Conseil Constitutionnel held that the French statute, with its self-determinative 'distress' provision, did not violate the 1789 Declaration of the Rights of Man or the 1946 Preamble to the Constitution, which states: 'The nation guarantees protection of health to all, notably, to children and mothers' (French Constitution of 1947, Preamble). Rather, the Court interpreted the concept of 'distress' to satisfy the principle of respect for life by limiting abortion, here and in the later provisions of the statute, on grounds of necessity—a creative, if instrumental, result.

The German challenge bit more deeply and painfully into the relationship between West Germany and its Nazi past. The postwar constitution was drafted to effectuate, as well as to symbolize, that country's break with fascist ideology and its horrific social instruments: the destruction of the handicapped ('unworthy' life); and the liquidation ('Liquidierung') of 'races' outside the Volk in accord with the 'final solution': genocide. The Basic Law (the Constitution) contains individual rights, including a right to freely develop one's 'personality'. Its stratified text contains higher-order principles and public values which, for the sake of the community, are intended to be strongly observed. In this latter portion is found the guarantee of a right to life for 'everyone'—a command the Constitutional Court interpreted so as to impose positive obligations on the state—obligations meant to reach as far as the embrace of fetal protection as a form of developing life, from and after the fourteenth day after conception.

The West German Parliament had debated between two statutory models before narrowly enacting one. The rejected 'indication' model treated gestation after the fourteenth day as a continuous process—one that a pregnant woman would require a good and sufficient reason (indication) to interrupt. The chosen 'periodic' model bore similarities to the *Roe* Court's trimester framework, as did East Germany's law.

The German Constitutional Court struck down the statute in 1975 by asserting the primacy of communal protection for what it broadly interpreted to be all human life-forms after the initial fourteen days, a decision that allowed the Court to side-step the question that Justice Blackmun had placed at the center of his analysis: whether a fetus as well as a woman has legally cognizable rights. Instead, it elevated communal obligation toward the fetus to a level above a woman's rights.

The constitutional demand on which the Court insisted was not, however, that all or even that most fetuses be brought to term. It was that the legislature create a statutory scheme out of the alternative model that it had rejected, a decision that mandated the re-criminalization of abortion, subject to specific exceptions. The loosest of these, conceptually, permitted abortion on the basis of social or medical necessity, including under circumstances where it would be 'unreasonable' to expect the woman to take the pregnancy to term. But this compromise proved unstable. Ultimately, the Court demanded a provision requiring that a state-sponsored counselor put a serious case for fetal protection to pregnant women whenever abortion is contemplated.

The terms of the enactment in the German Parliament followed the letter of these demands. But the Court's concerns fell in a different direction than the East German population's, which came close to causing the suspension of reunification in 1990, until a statute more generous to the interests of women was laid out. The political compromise that was reached blended a periodic basis for abortion such as the East Germans had had, with the mandatory counseling provisions from the West.

As with the prior enactment, the losing parliamentary parties took their case to the Constitutional Court. The Court handed down a ruling insisting that, in the interest of unborn life, abortion must remain illegal but that, if the counseling obligation were fulfilled, abortion during the first three months of fetal life would go unpunished and, thereby, excused. Thus, every abortion for any reason has been made to take place directly in the shadow of the German Criminal Code. And a powerfully managerial Court.

After its insistence that the abortion decision be authored under an umbrella of wrongdoing, the Court liberalized the counseling requirement so as to rest the ultimate decision about her pregnancy in the woman's hands. Moreover, the Court insisted upon the provision of meaningful social subsidies, in the form of public support for the willing pregnant woman and, later, for her child. Even beyond the matter of monetary support, the Court insisted on gender non-discriminatory workplace rules. In regard to the payment for abortions out of state funds, the Court permitted some; outlawed others; and required still others, treating the funding decision not as a matter of legislative discretion, but as the Court's alone. Recently, the individual states have acquired greater discretion in regard to funding, especially regarding later than first-trimester abortions.

From the period shortly after both the French and the German litigations wound down until the present, the abortion controversy in both countries has leveled out, such that major political turmoil over abortion cannot be said to exist. The English experience, has stayed calm, to boot. This then—to the first approximation, a decades-long end to social perturbation—unites the English, French, and German developmental arcs. And it unites them, too, with the political response to abortion that has long been maintained in the other European welfare states.

Because these are *welfare* states, their similarity, one to another, does not end with the brute fact of a bare abortion 'compromise' (Glendon, 1987) having been achieved. Yet, the critical commentary from comparative law scholars has tended to focus not on the welfare deficiencies of the US position on abortion but on an institutional critique that views the US abortion conflict as the fault of the Supreme Court.

4.1 Comparative Critiques of US Abortion Law and the Counter-Critical Response

Two of the most prominent comparative law scholars in the United States have written extensively and enthusiastically about the value to an American audience of attention to European abortion law (Glendon, 1987, 1991; Kommers 1977, 1993). Both scholars praise the decisions of the German Constitutional Court, in particular. Both decry the Supreme Court's efforts in *Roe*. Both set the stage for what turns out to be a heavily one-sided match, as a comparative constitutional exercise. Both avoid focus on the extraordinary degree of judicial activism that the German Court exhibited in dictating a set of demands to the national legislative body—not once, but twice—demands that created a rare and bitter split on the Court itself and unintentionally encouraged a political schism that almost paralyzed reunification.

Given the vilification that has been heaped on the *Roe v Wade* majority for taking decisional authority out of the state legislatures' hands, it is surprising that these observers have chosen the German example through which to extol the virtues of communitarianism and populism (Glendon, 1987) without shouldering the high burden of persuasion that, on balance of power grounds alone, an American jurisprudential audience might require. Indeed, it is difficult to treat the case that is enthusiastically mounted (especially by Glendon, 1987) for a single, Euro-centered approach to abortion as much beyond a subtle and sophisticated form of advocacy for her deeply committed pro-life views (Cohen, 1989; see also Hertberg, 1993; Werner, 1996; and Miedel, 1994).

4.2 The European Subsidy of Abortion and Contraception

The most striking feature of much of the comparative scholarship in relation to contraception and abortion, as issued from the American side, is how court-skeptical it tends to be and how formalist analytically, besides. What eventually gets nudged into view, but with a denial of permission to parade is that, for some twenty to thirty years, all of the developed democracies of Europe and North America have reached a point of stasis regarding the legitimacy of abortion during the first trimester of pregnancy, though the process and the justification of legal legitimation have taken several different forms. The point that has been reached throughout the developed European and North American democracies is that the continuation or termination of her pregnancy is a woman's choice. With the exception of the United States, two other facts are widely in place: one is that abortions are and, by clear inference, should be performed in publicly supported health facilities, with consultative counselors who are state paid, rather than being isolated in sole-function clinics on the metaphorical edge of town. The other is that, when the procedural conditions that de-limit regulatory control are properly followed, all early abortions and certifiedly therapeutic late-term abortions are and, by clear inference, should be paid for by the state. The national health-care delivery system in the true welfare democracies both makes abortion available and subsidizes the cost.

This general incorporation of pregnancy and pregnancy termination into the national plan for public health was what fueled the decision of the French government not only to invest in the development of the pharmaceutical abortifacient RU-486 but to demand its distribution, when the company which had manufactured it, fearing a threatened American boycott, held back. As the French Minister of Health announced to his nation and to the world, 'From the moment government approval ... was granted, RU-486 became the moral property of women' (Greenhouse, 1988).

Where the normative implications of this coherentist approach have become powerful is in the formulation of legal and policy goals for women throughout the developing world. There, one tends to see concerns about the remaining prevalence of unsafe abortion framed within similarly coherentist terms—terms that are far in advance of the rhetoric of rights and political action in the United States in linking population planning to reproductive health to individual, autonomous choice on the family planning front. (See e.g. *Reproductive Rights 2000: Moving Forward*, 2000.)

While Europe has been in the vanguard of the move to understand personal health and population planning as co-dependent and their support by the state as, at least in part, a public good, there is another side to the present situation throughout Western Europe that currently resides somewhere between a puzzle and a mystery. It involves the fact that, even with the substantial pregnancy, childbirth, and child subsidies that many European countries pay, virtually all of them have, for almost two decades, had childbirth rates that are below the level of population replacement, even as average life expectancy has grown high, as concerns about immigrant populations have spiked, and as long-term political worries about who will fill the borders of Europe, whether or not it develops into a single union, have become rife.

What recent population studies report in the cases of France, Germany, and Italy is that government support for contraceptive use and abortion provision remains in place, but that the officially reported governmental 'view on fertility level' is that it is 'too low' (*World Population Prospects*, 2002). The puzzle, if not the mystery, becomes: if generous subsidies haven't been able to nudge fertility rates upward, what further blandishments might be adopted in coming years? Will Europe simply continue to treat reproductive choice as the moral property of women and learn to revise its anxieties and its goals? The anxieties are clearly potent. It is a given that the population is aging within most of the European welfare democracies, while birth rates are continuing to fall. Guest-worker policies and welcome berth to citizens of the host country's former colonies have helped to fill needed workers' ranks. But anti-immigrant sentiment is on the rise. How will national and pan-European family policy formation accommodate labor needs, high welfare costs, and (if they continue) falling birth trends?

Questions such as these are not currently generating reliable answers at the level of policy or principle within the nation-states that are giving rise to them. In the case of Europe, one can only hope that the welfare democracies will remain welfarist, but not to such an extent that the pressures to support rising numbers of aged persons will heavily distort their attractive liberal values and their ways. In the United States, one must similarly hope that the liberal values that have become encoded within the law of reproductive choice—autonomy and equality, to the fore—survive any coming paroxysmic moments so that, apart from an atmosphere of crisis, they can gracefully evolve and mature.

5 CONCLUSION

During the past thirty to forty years, the right to use contraception and the right of women to choose to terminate especially their early pregnancies have received consistent acknowledgement as matters of policy and law. These outcomes have depended on differing, though generally substantial amounts of intervention on the part of constitutional courts. The instability that persists in regard to the status of the abortion right may be a function of its judicial supervention in the United States, as its domestic critics are given to conclude. But a host of other factors have been at work. Whether abortion rights can survive and develop despite these pressures defies present prediction. Their incorporation within the scope of European social philosophy and welfare entitlement seems more readily capable of granting the twinned fortunes of contraception and abortion a secure—though not an imperturbable—life. Despite the obvious threats of legal and political upheaval in the

United States, the ties that bind reproductive choices to liberal values and embed them in economic and social life may yet drive the same result.

References

Berger, R. (1977). *Government by Judiciary: The Transformation of the Fourteenth Amendment*, Cambridge, Mass.: Harvard University Press.

Bork, R. (1990). *The Tempting of America*, New York: Free Press.

Carlson, A. (1988). *Family Questions: Reflections on the American Social Crises*, New Brunswick, NJ: Transaction.

Cohen, J. (1989). 'Comparison Shopping in the Marketplace of Rights', review of Mary Ann Glendon, *Abortion and Divorce in Western Law*, Yale Law Journal, 98: 1235–76.

——(1992). 'A Jurisprudence of Doubt: Deliberative Autonomy and Abortion', *Columbia Journal of Gender and Law*, 3: 175–246.

Donahue, J., and Levitt, S. (2001). 'The Impact of Legalized Abortion on Crime', *Quarterly Journal of Economics*, 116: 379–420.

Eisgruber, C. (1992). 'Is the Supreme Court an Educative Institution?' *New York University Law Review*, 67: 962–1028.

Elders, J., Hui, J., and Padilla, S. (1989–90). 'Adolescent Pregnancy: Does the Nation Really Care?' *Berkeley Women's Law Journal*, 5: 170–80.

Ely, J. (1973). 'The Wages of Crying Wolf: A Comment on *Roe v. Wade*', Yale Law Journal, 82: 920–49.

——(1980). *Democracy and Distrust*, Cambridge, Mass.: Harvard University Press.

Epstein, R. (1973). 'Substantive Due Process by Any Other Name: The Abortion Cases', *Supreme Court Review*, 1973: 159–85.

——(1992). 'Rights and Rights Talk', review of Mary Ann Glendon, *Rights Talk: The Impoverishment of Political Discourse*, Harvard Law Review, 105: 1106–23.

Ginsburg, R. (1975). 'Gender and the Constitution', *University of Cincinnati Law Review*, 44: 1–42.

Glendon, M. (1987). *Abortion and Divorce in Western Law*, Cambridge, Mass.: Harvard University Press.

——(1991). *Rights Talk: The Impoverishment of Political Discourse*, New York: Free Press.

Greenhouse, S. (1988). 'France Ordering Company to Sell its Abortion Drug', *The New York Times*, 29 Oct., A1.

Hertberg, B. (1993). 'Resolving the Abortion Debate: Compromise Legislation, an Analysis of the Abortion Policies of the United States, France and Germany', *Suffolk Transnational Law Review*, 16: 513–70.

Kommers, D. (1977). 'Abortion and Constitution, U.S. and West Germany', *American Journal of Comparative Law*, 25: 255–85.

——(1993). 'The Constitutional Law of Abortion in Germany: Should Americans Pay Attention?' *Journal of Contemporary Health Law and Policy*, 10: 1–32.

Larkin, P. (1993). *Collected Poems: Philip Larkin*, New York: Farrar, Straus and Giroux.

Law, S. (1984). 'Rethinking Sex and the Constitution', *University of Pennsylvania Law Review*, 132: 955–1040.

Lawson, A., and Rhode, D. (1993). *The Politics of Pregnancy*, New Haven: Yale University Press.

Melton, G. (1986). *Adolescent Abortion*, Lincoln, Nebr.: University of Nebraska Press.

Miedel, F. (1994). 'Is West Germany's 1975 Abortion Decision a Solution to the American Abortion Debate?: A Critique of Mary Ann Glendon and Donald Kommers', *New York University Review of Law and Social Change*, 20: 471–515.

Reproductive Rights 2000: Moving Forward (2000). New York: Center for Reproductive Law and Policy.

Rosenberg, G. (1993). *The Hollow Hope*, Chicago: Chicago University Press.

Rosenheim, M., and Testa, M. (1992). *Early Parenthood and Coming of Age in the 1990s*, New Brunswick, NJ: Rutgers University Press.

Rubenfeld, J. (1989). 'The Right to Privacy', *Harvard Law Review*, 102: 737–807.

Siegel, R. (1992). 'Reasoning from the Body: A Historical Perspective on Abortion Regulation and Questions of Equal Protection', *Stanford Law Review*, 44: 261–381.

Thomson, J. (1971). 'A Defense of Abortion', *Philosophy and Public Affairs*, 1: 47–66.

Tushnet, M. (1999). *Taking the Constitution away from the Courts*, New Jersey: Princeton University Press.

Werner, U. (1996). 'The Convergence of Abortion Regulation in Germany and the United States: A Critique of Glendon's Rights Talk Thesis', *Loyola of Los Angeles International and Comparative Law Journal*, 18: 571–602.

West, R. (1990). 'Foreword: Taking Freedom Seriously', *Harvard Law Review*, 104: 43–106.

Witherspoon, J. (1985). 'Re-examining Roe: Nineteenth-Century Abortion Statutes and the Fourteenth Amendment', *Saint Mary's Law Journal*, 17: 30–77.

World Population Prospects: The 2000 Revision, Volume III (2002). New York: United Nations Department of Economic and Social Affairs, Population Division.

CHAPTER 31

THE ENVIRONMENT

LISA HEINZERLING

1 INTRODUCTION

ENVIRONMENTAL law scholarship grew up with environmental law itself. Before the 1970s, when most of the first major environmental statutes were passed in the developed countries, environmental law as a separate discipline, and a separate topic of scholarly inquiry, essentially did not exist. Although many of the early laws have since been amended, some significantly, the laws written during the 1970s still provide the basic framework for environmental protection in many countries.

This history has had at least three important implications for environmental law scholarship. First, the nearly simultaneous passage of the major environmental laws meant that legislators often had no time to react to the experience under one law before enacting another; thus several mistakes were made in the early environmental laws, and many of these mistakes were repeated from one statute to the next. A large strand of legal scholarship on the environment has taken critical aim at these early mistakes. To this day, environmental law scholars focus much of their attention on issues of statutory design.

Secondly, environmental law came of age during a period of great flux in the relationships between the legislature, the executive, and the courts. In the United States, the major environmental laws were part of a cascade of new social legislation enacted in the 1970s and aimed at protecting consumers, workers, the environment, and other interests left out of the first New Deal. The answers to questions such as how to interpret statutes, how broadly to review agency decision-making, who should be able to participate in the administrative process, and the like, all critically important to the shape and scope of environmental protection, entered a period of ferment while the major environmental laws were being passed, and to a large extent this ferment is with us still. Indeed, in many ways, environmental law itself has been responsible for many changes in our understanding of the institutional relationships between legislatures, the executive branch, and the courts. The questions of 'horizontal' institutional design occasioned by what in the United States is sometimes called the 'second New Deal' have been another large focus of environmental law scholars in the United States and elsewhere. Indeed, a substantial portion of the growing literature in comparative environmental law focuses on national differences in horizontal institutional design.

Finally, environmental law has come of age during a period in which opinions about 'vertical' institutional design—what in the United States comes under the umbrella of 'federalism' and what in the European Union comes under the umbrella of 'subsidiarity'—have changed quite substantially. Environmental law began at a time when, in the United States at least, the national role in developing social policy, and agreement about the appropriateness of that role, were at their height. Now, thirty years later, federalism is all the rage, and many environmental law scholars are casting about for ways to enlist other decision-making bodies, including states, regions, towns, and more informal associations, in decisions about the environment. Some are even questioning the appropriateness of the national government's own role. Likewise, in the European Union, national environmental laws arose almost simultaneously with the recognition of enhanced power for the European Union to develop laws to govern member countries. Thus questions of 'vertical' institutional design permeate current legal scholarship on the environment.

These three strands of environmental law scholarship frame the bulk of the discussion that follows. Before exploring these specific concerns, however, it may be useful to consider some of the general characteristics of environmental law scholarship and the ways in which this scholarship is distinctive from legal scholarship in other fields.

1.1 Interdisciplinarity

Environmental law scholarship is pervasively interdisciplinary. Indeed, it is almost impossible to imagine a first-rate environmental law scholar who is not comfortable with, and whose work does not touch upon, scholarly disciplines beyond law. Toxicology, ecology, public health, statistics, economics, sociology, psychology, philosophy, and more—these fields have as much to do with environmental law, and environmental law scholarship, as 'law' itself (assuming that law is an autonomous discipline in any event). Outside of several constitutional issues that have special relevance to environmental problems (such as the 'takings' issue in the United States), traditional modes of legal scholarship—doctrinal analysis, case parsing, analogical reasoning—have relatively little place in cutting-edge environmental law scholarship. Most of the heavy labor is done only with the help of other scholarly disciplines. For example, to look ahead for a moment, the astonishingly popular scholarly trend in favor of market-based mechanisms for pollution control came, not from law, but from economics. In environmental law scholarship, interdisciplinarity is not a trend; it's a way of life.

1.2 Concreteness

Environmental law scholarship also differs from many other kinds of legal scholarship in so far as it tends toward concreteness; it tends to avoid the high-level abstractions, without obvious practical significance, found in some other fields of legal inquiry. Many excellent environmental law scholars are, to be sure, first and foremost theoreticians. But even they tend to press their theoretical claims into a concrete framework. They tend to ask how the environmental law system can be made to *work*; they tend not to rest content with carrying on an abstract and exclusive conversation among themselves. In fact, one challenge faced by many top-notch environmental law scholars is to stay engaged in scholarly debates while at the same time trying to satisfy the inevitable demands placed on them by non-scholarly pursuits, such as litigation, legislative reform, and the like. At the same time, one of the great fears of many legal scholars—irrelevance—is not as much of a concern for deeply engaged environmental law scholars, who not infrequently see their own ideas become part of the law.

1.3 Fragmentation

Environmental law scholarship tends to straddle several different fault lines, for both historical and practical reasons. Perhaps the most important dividing line is between 'brown' and 'green' scholarship, brown having to do with pollution control and green having to do with natural resources protection. Few legal scholars cross over the line separating major pollution control laws, such as those controlling air and water pollution, from natural resources laws, such as laws governing the management of forests, grazing lands, and mineral resources. Even law school courses typically do not cross this divide; the 'environmental law' survey course offered in most US law schools, for example, is brown, not green. One reason for this divide, at least in the United States, is historical: the pollution control laws were part of the wave of social legislation enacted in the 1970s, whereas the natural resources laws have developed over a longer period of time and indeed have their origins in the resource-extractive policies of the nineteenth century (Wilkinson, 1992).

Another kind of fragmentation also occurs in environmental law scholarship, and that is between different environmental media and their associated problems. There are 'air' scholars and 'water' scholars, 'wetlands' scholars and 'toxics' scholars. Of course, not all environmental law scholars are so narrowly focused, and indeed, the best in the field range beyond one discrete area of interest. And of course, most fields of legal scholarship have their specialties. But in a field where a solution to one problem (say, air pollution) can literally create another problem (say, water pollution), scholarly fragmentation can have consequences that range well beyond the academy. In settling themselves into environmental niches to promote the healthy development of specialized knowledge, legal scholars can at the same time open up large gaps in understanding and create the potential for a wide range of unintended consequences.

Finally, and least surprisingly, environmental law scholars have tended to be fragmented along national lines; US scholars, for example, write about US environmental law. But the comparative work that exists shows exceedingly promising avenues for further research and analysis. For example, although many countries have converged on technology-based regulation as the primary means of pollution control, and have also, at present, converged on market-oriented regulation as an alternative to technology-based control, countries differ markedly in their approaches to administrative law and regulatory compliance. Countries also differ in their particular choices of market-oriented regulatory instruments; in the United States, pollution trading is probably the instrument of choice for scholars and regulatory reformers, whereas in Europe, pollution taxes have enjoyed a bigger role. Comparative research on these differences might yield important discoveries for the next wave of environmental law scholars.

1.4 Conclusion and Preview

Contributors to this volume were asked to limit their essays to scholarship published after 1960. In the case of legal scholarship on the environment, this is an easy requirement to meet: such scholarship, in essence, did not exist until the 1970s (despite the long existence of laws governing the disposition of natural resources). Since then, legal scholars have focused much of their attention on questions of statutory design, institutional arrangements, and vertical institutional design. In doing so, they have marshaled the lessons of other disciplines and have asked concrete questions about how the existing legal framework can be improved. This is all to the good.

Nevertheless, as I will explain, environmental law scholars' interdisciplinarity has often been marked by an uncritical acceptance of research from other fields and by an unduly hearty embrace of reform proposals from other disciplines. Faced with environmental problems of daunting complexity and stunning variety, environmental law scholars have tended too often to be comforted by the possibility that one simple idea—say, pollution trading—will fix everything that is broken. The problems are more complex, and more multifarious, than that.

Specialization in one or two environmental fields—forests or wetlands or clean air—has also permitted environmental law scholars to grapple with the legal, scientific, and economic challenges of environmental law without taking on every one of the many laws in this complex field. But this specialization, too, comes at a cost. The fact is that environmental law scholarship is too fragmented today between brown and green, between air and water and land, and, more abstractly, between regulators and anti-regulators. Age-old stand-offs between different philosophical camps in the environmental law academy have become unproductive, even dull.

What is needed, for the next generation of environmental law scholarship, are ideas that break the log-jam by trying something different. Some of these ideas are already in place, in our laws, but their potential remains largely untapped. Others are discernible, in broad and shadowy outline, in existing scholarly work and some-times in existing law. To bring these innovations into the light of day, the next generation of environmental scholars must be unintimidated by the jargon and culture of other disciplines, unapologetic about insisting upon practical applications for their academic work, and unembarrassed by the possibility that some of their ideas might turn out to be mistakes.

2 STATUTORY DESIGN

Most environmental protection derives from statutes rather than from the com-mon law. Certainly, the common law of nuisance, negligence, and strict liability has played some role in addressing environmental problems. In some jurisdictions, moreover, common law doctrines have been reshaped to facilitate compensation for victims of environmental torts. Yet for the most part, addressing environ-mental problems through the tort system is made almost impossible by transactional and doctrinal hurdles. The statutory system for environmental protection arose, in part, in self-conscious rejection of the common law as a means of protecting the environment. The predominant focus of scholars in the field of environmental law has been the environmental statutes, not tort doctrine. Statutes will be our focus as well.

In designing statutes for environmental protection, two large questions immedi-ately present themselves: what goal should the law aim to achieve, and what means should it use to carry out that goal? Much of the best environmental law scholarship addresses one of these two questions. Less well covered, but equally important and rising in prominence of late, is the question of how to implement a statute once its ends and means have been set.

2.1 Ends

Generally speaking, environmental laws can serve one of three broad goals: they can bring environmental risk down to a level deemed acceptable by the relevant decision-makers; they can ensure the utilization of the best available technology (or other means) for pollution control; or they can strive to achieve a balancing between competing interests, most often between environmental protection and economic cost. Some of the fiercest debates in environmental law scholarship have concerned this basic choice about statutory design.

2.1.1 *Acceptable Risk*

'Acceptable' risk has a range of meanings. It could reach all the way down to zero or it could go much higher. Environmental laws in the United States have in fact spanned this wide range, giving ample material to critical environmental law scholars. Although most scholars in theory agree that it would be wonderful if the law could limit its protections to ensuring an acceptable level of risk, most scholars also criticize, from various perspectives, the acceptable risk laws that have existed to date.

Acceptable risk might, for starters, mean zero risk. This is not a common standard in environmental law. Indeed, the only true zero risk statute even in the United States—which is known for having, at least in form, the most absolutist environmental statutes of all of the common law countries—was the Delaney Clause, which prohibited carcinogenic pesticide residues on processed food and which has now been repealed as applied to pesticides. Scholars loved to hate the Delaney Clause; so popular was the Delaney Clause as a topic of scholarly scorn that one continually sees reference to it to this day as an example of misguided environmental legislation, though it has been dead and buried for over five years. The problem, as scholars saw it, was that, in aiming for 'zero risk', the Delaney Clause actually created more risk than it avoided. New pesticides were subject to the Clause's exacting anti-carcinogen standards, whereas old pesticides—which could be far more dangerous than new pesticides—enjoyed an informal system of grandfathering that allowed them to stay on the market even if new information revealed their carcinogenic potential. The Clause thus inspired its own eponymous paradox—the 'Delaney Paradox'—used to describe a situation in which aiming for zero risk can badly misfire and create more risk rather than less. In scholarly debates, the case in favor of the Delaney Clause never really got off the ground, and it seems fair to say that today, no substantial scholar argues for a reinvigoration of a zero-risk regime. Nevertheless, the Delaney Clause hangs around as a kind of poster child for regulation gone wrong, and environmental law scholars critical of regulation often charge environmental advocates with supporting a zero-risk regime. Never a large part of environmental law, and now long defunct, the Delaney Clause and zero-risk standards primarily live on as rhetorical devices deployed, in most cases unfairly, against advocates of stricter environmental protection.

Acceptable risk might, alternatively, mean a level of risk that public health professionals and other experts deem acceptable. Regulatory standards would then be set to ensure that the designated level of risk is not exceeded. The most prominent US example of this kind of regime comes from the federal Clean Air Act, which requires national air quality standards to be set at a level that protects the public health and welfare with an adequate margin of safety. The idea is that standards will be set to prevent adverse and significant effects on public health, and will be set strictly enough so that vulnerable subpopulations—such as children, the elderly, and people who are ill—will be protected. Germany sets similarly health-based standards for air pollution. Environmental scholars have long argued against cost-blind, nationally uniform environmental standards such as these (Krier, 1974). To be sure, some environmental scholars love public health standards; but for the most part they do so in the privacy of their own minds. Most published writing on the US Clean Air Act, and on public health standards generally, questions the wisdom and even the possibility of setting standards without regard to costs. The authors of these works believe that an administrator will inevitably peek at costs when she sets standards, and if she does, she should say so. Thus, on this view, cost-blind standards carry potential not only for enormous inefficiencies, but for large-scale disingenuousness as well. Again, however, as with the Delaney Clause, the debate has veered into an area of relatively little concrete significance for environmental law. Few environmental standards are cost-blind; even in the United States, with its uniquely stringent environmental laws, the Clean Air Act standards are an exception. And costs *are* carefully considered in choices about how to implement these standards. Thus, not only do cost-blind standards play a relatively minor role in environmental protection; even where they exist, they are set in motion only through regulatory frameworks that are exquisitely sensitive to economic costs. In these circumstances, the amount of critical scholarly attention paid to health-based, cost-blind standards seems disproportionate indeed.

A final model for a risk-based regulatory regime comes from the US Occupational Safety and Health Act, which has been interpreted by the US Supreme Court to require the Occupational Safety and Health Administration (OSHA) to determine whether a risk is 'significant' before regulating it. The determination of 'significance' here is fluid, intuitive, subjective. The important feature of this regime is not the process of attaching the label 'significant' to a particular numerical risk, but rather the requirement that the risk be described quantitatively rather than qualitatively in the first instance. The requirement of quantification has been embraced by numerous legal scholars, who appear to share the Supreme Court's pre-analytic assumption that the only way to think rationally is to think quantitatively. Others have noted that the insistence on quantification has led to regulatory delay without improving either the quality of regulation or even, in many cases, the quality of information undergirding regulation. In the European Union, the issue of risk assessment surfaced in the free trade challenge to the EU's prohibition on beef from cattle treated with bovine growth hormone. In that dispute, the EU's dominant preference for 'precautionary' regulation—which may be imposed before a risk can be quantified or known with certainty—gave way to a requirement of risk assessment imposed by the appellate body of the World Trade Organization.

The questions of whether to quantify environmental risks and, if so, what role numerical probabilities of harm should play in environmental decision-making, have become staples of environmental law scholarship. At this point, it is possible to discern a trend in favor of two potentially conflicting ideas: (1) it is important to quantify environmental risks so far as possible, even when this involves many assumptions that cannot themselves be validated by science (Pildes and Sunstein, 1995); and (2) 'risk', appropriately defined, involves more than numerical probabilities of harm, and includes such considerations as the voluntariness, controllability, familiarity, immediacy, and distribution of the potential for harm (Hornstein, 1992; Krier and Gillette, 1990).

Few scholars have adequately appreciated, however, the tensions created by this general agreement on the importance of the quantitative and qualitative features of risk. First, in practice, once numerical estimates of harm are generated, they tend to dominate all further debate; qualitative variables are typically given lip-service, nothing more. Secondly, if the qualitative features of risk were to play a substantial role in decision-making about the environment, one might then have to wonder about the utility of spending large amounts of time and money generating precise numerical estimates of risk, when those estimates can be trumped in the end by vague but readily accessible notions about which risks are worth reducing. Finally, a focus on quantifying risk in the presence of extreme scientific uncertainty has often created what Wendy Wagner has called a 'science charade', in which political decisions masquerade as scientific ones (Wagner, 1995). An important agenda item for future environmental law scholarship will be to try to reconcile intuitions about the necessity of quantification with intuitions about the importance of values like autonomy, community, and equity, in addressing risk—or, alternatively, to explore whether one or the other of these intuitions should be reconsidered.

2.1.2 Best Available Technology

The most pervasive goal in environmental statutes is to achieve the widespread use of effective technology for controlling pollution. Obviously, this goal is fundamentally subordinate to a broader goal of achieving an acceptable level of environmental risk; but technology-based standards do not directly aim at any particular environmental outcome. Instead, they aim to achieve a cleaner environment more indirectly, through application of the most sophisticated available approaches to pollution control.

Technology-based standards permeate environmental law. In the United States, laws on air pollution, water pollution, hazardous waste remediation, and toxic chemicals, all employ technology-based requirements as their primary means of pollution control. Even where laws set risk-based goals, those goals are predominantly met through technology-based standards; here, risk-based goals get all the credit, but technology-based standards do all the work. Indeed, one little-noticed historical trend in environmental law is for health-based standards to be changed into technology-based standards once it becomes apparent that little regulation will occur under a health-based framework; the toxic pollutant programs in the United States for air and water both followed this path. Other countries, such as England and Germany, also rely pervasively on technology-based standards.

Technology-based standards are another example of standards environmental law scholars love to hate. Stalinist, command-and-control, central planning—these are the kinds of descriptors associated with technology-based pollution control (Ackerman and Stewart, 1985). The lack of a tight connection between precisely correct environmental outcomes and technology-based requirements, and the variance in control costs across firms, have convinced the bulk of environmental law scholars that there is something presumptively suspicious about environmental law's primary means of doing its work. Common misunderstandings of the nature of technology-based regulation have also contributed to its unpopularity among legal scholars. Many reputable scholars, for example, continue to assert that technology-based regulation is cost-blind. It is not. Even in the United States, where technology-based standards are often designed to 'force' technology to become more effective in preventing pollution, costs are considered in setting such standards.

Technology-based regulation does have its scholarly defenders. These scholars are worried about the large informational demands of alternative environmental standards (risk-based and balancing standards), and, armed with evidence of unexpected innovations and cost savings that often occur after regulation is in place (but are not accounted for in estimating the costs of regulation before the fact), they worry less about technology-based standards being excessively costly (Latin, 1985). With their emphasis on informational demands and the excessive delay such demands can bring to the regulatory process, it is perhaps no surprise that some of the same scholars who have defended technology-based regulation also have devoted a good deal of energy to trying to identify ways in which the regulatory system might become less 'ossified' (McGarity, 1992). If the administrative process were not so slow and cumbersome, these scholars would say, the record of technology-based regulation would appreciably improve: it is the process, not the substantive decision-making framework, that is unacceptably inefficient.

2.1.3 Balancing

The current darling of many environmental law scholars is balancing: either a rough-hewn, all-things-considered kind of balancing, or a more formal, cost-benefit analysis where the relevant variables are quantified and monetized. In the most current debates, the second kind of balancing has morphed into the first; no one anymore seems to want to say publicly that he is in favor of completely precise, quantified cost-benefit analysis that leaves no room for subjective judgment. Thus the cost-benefit balancing of environmental law scholarship has, in recent years, been softened around the edges, to include consideration of factors that no one has managed to quantify or monetize (like fairness) and to reflect some ambivalence about quantification and monetization even where it is possible (as when the benefits in question are human lives). Here, however, there is quite a large divide between theory and practice. While in theory, qualitative considerations like fairness are relevant in the cost-benefit equation, in practice, anything that cannot be counted is not likely to figure very prominently in regulatory decision-making.

A now-predictable set of arguments is offered in favor of cost-benefit balancing. Some of these arguments—such as the claim that any other regulatory framework requires a zero-risk regime or does not allow economic costs to be taken into account—are simply wrong, and obviously so to any careful student of environmental policy. Others are equally wrong, but the mistakes underlying them are harder to uncover. For example, one of the most prominent arguments for cost-benefit balancing is that such balancing will restore a sense of proportion and sensible prioritization to the environmental laws. Current laws have no sense of proportion, it is argued, and the evidence for this lack of proportion in the United States, for example, often requires the expenditure of a huge amount of money, sometimes billions of dollars, to save a single human life through environmental regulation. In a related vein, some scholars have claimed that rearranging life-saving priorities would save not just money, but lives; if resources were shifted from, say, toxin control to, say, prenatal care, thousands more lives could be saved every year with the same amount of money.

These are powerful claims, and they have had a powerful effect on environmental law scholarship, particularly in the United States. Few articles that go to the basic design of environmental statutes do not refer to this literature on regulatory costs and priority-setting in one way or another. Even fewer refer to this literature with any kind of skepticism. Yet the literature is deeply misleading. Many of the US 'regulations' it targets for reform were never implemented, and some never even proposed. Moreover, the rather complex numerical calculations that lead to the fantastic estimates of costs per life saved are pervaded by value judgments (such as judgments about the relative worth of present and future lives) that are not acknowledged by the scholars who rely on this literature as the empirical premise for large-scale regulatory reform. Here, legal scholarship on the environment has been slipshod and credulous, and the widespread acceptance of dubious estimates of regulatory costs has led to a pervasive skepticism about the efficacy of environmental protection that has dominated environmental law scholarship in the United States and elsewhere in the last decade (Heinzerling, 1998).

Stripped of the dubious premise of enormous regulatory costs, the case for cost-benefit balancing loses much of its charm. Information-intensive, expensive, time-consuming, contentious, and ultimately indeterminate, cost-benefit balancing has never made for a successful environmental regime. Indeed, the two long experiences the United States has had with balancing regimes—the Toxic Substances Control Act and the Federal Insecticide, Rodenticide, and Fungicide Act—are widely considered by legal scholars to be among the biggest failures of US environmental policy in the last three decades. Moreover, the latest addition to the balancing provisions—in the Safe Drinking Water Act—led to one of the biggest brawls of the early Bush (II) administration, concerning the regulation of arsenic in drinking water. Oddly, one of the most ardent defenders of cost-benefit balancing in the legal literature has generated estimates of the benefits of strengthening the standard for arsenic in drinking water that cover such a wide range (from $0 to $500 million) that, if one accepts these estimates, cost-benefit analysis can only be regarded as hopelessly indeterminate—the very thing critics of cost-benefit analysis have been saying for decades (Sunstein, 2002).

Scholars outside the United States have sometimes expressed bewilderment over the controversy generated by cost-benefit balancing in the United States In England, for example, environmental standards are typically set for individual sources based on consideration of many factors including costs, thus leading some scholars to conclude that cost-benefit analysis is built into the very framework of English environmental law (Vogel, 1986). Nevertheless, there remains an important difference between setting standards with attention to economic costs—the prevailing approach not only in England but also, as we have seen, in the United States—and setting standards by attempting to quantify all relevant variables and reduce them to monetary terms. This form of balancing continues to generate controversy not only in the United States but in other countries as well.

2.2 Means

To put into place a system of environmental protection, it is not enough to state one's goals. One must have a way of operationalizing those goals, of reaching them through the application of enforceable limits on the hundreds or thousands of sources responsible for the pollution one is trying to address. This is where the choice of regulatory means comes in. Here, too, one can discern a decided scholarly trend in favor of the most market-oriented of the possibilities, yet here, too, that preference is based at least in part on a misapprehension of the relevant facts.

2.2.1 Design

The first two ways of operationalizing environmental standards are both technology-based. The first, design standards, requires sources of pollution to install particular devices or other means of controlling pollution. The most infamous example of such a standard, widely cited in the literature on environmental law, is the Environmental

Protection Agency's decision two decades ago effectively to require scrubbing technology for power plants to control their emissions of sulfur dioxide. Design standards not only require firms to reduce their pollution by a certain, fixed amount, consistent with the capabilities of the pollution control equipment in question; they also forbid firms to find another way to reduce that pollution. Because of their inflexibility, design standards are the most widely reviled of the different forms of technology-based regulation. They are fast disappearing from the scene of environmental regulation. Yet critics of technology-based regulation seem not to have noticed.

2.2.2 *Performance*

Performance standards are another kind of technology-based system. Here, the idea is to set a numerical pollution limit for sources of pollution, a limit that is in most cases based on an assessment of available technologies for controlling pollution, and then to allow the sources to decide for themselves how to meet that numerical limit. Performance standards are pervasive in environmental law. They combine a degree of flexibility (inherent in the sources' choice about how to meet the numerical limits) with predictable limits on sources of pollution. In much of the scholarly literature on environmental law, however, performance standards are lumped in the same category as, and thrown into the intellectual dustbin with, design standards. Their achievements, and their potential promise for the future, are thus under-remarked in environmental law scholarship. Interestingly, this is so even though one of the great policy successes of the last decade—the sulfur dioxide controls imposed by the US Clean Air Act Amendments of 1990—has so far achieved its cost savings and pollution reductions in substantial part through the flexibility of performance-based measures rather than through the more glamorous trading program that has excited environmental law scholars around the country and the world. This trading program is one of several market-based mechanisms for pollution control that have caught on in environmental law scholarship, as discussed in the next section.

2.2.3 *Market Mechanisms*

Market-based environmental requirements attempt to enlist the market in the service of environmental protection. Pollution trading programs, for example, give an incentive to firms to clean up their pollution so that they can either refrain from buying pollution permits or even sell their extra permits to other firms. Pollution taxes offer much the same incentive structure. Informational requirements, such as disclosure of toxic chemical releases or warnings about carcinogens in consumer products, attempt to correct market imbalances in information and thus to help consumers and citizens respond to information about firms' varying environmental profiles. All of these kinds of requirements are enjoying a long honeymoon in legal scholarship. And with some reason: the US sulfur dioxide program has met with considerable success, and many hope to replicate that success in other regulatory settings. Likewise, disclosure requirements such as the US Emergency Planning and Community Right-to-Know Act have been credited with leading to substantial reductions in chemical use and chemical releases, at a fraction of the cost of more traditional regulatory programs.

Here, too, however, well-founded enthusiasm has a way, in legal scholarship, of spiraling into irrational exuberance. From the well-documented and sound point that market-based regulation is a good approach to take for *some* environmental problems, many scholars have jumped to the conclusion that it is the *only* approach to take to environmental problems. Against this tide stands a handful of scholars who have taken the time to look carefully, and critically, at market-based programs in operation, and have found much to worry about. Some examples of cause for concern: technologies for emissions monitoring, essential to validating compliance with pollution trading programs, are unavailable for many pollutants; many pollutants produce adverse and serious localized harms that make liberal trading of pollutants from one place to another problematic in distributional and public health terms; interpollutant trading often relies on crude and incomplete estimates of the relative harms caused by the covered pollutants; and so on. In this more cautious scholarship, pollution trading emerges as one, but not the only, promising possibility for pollution control, to be used with sensitivity to the individual circumstances in which it is proposed.

Here again, therefore, the most fruitful course for future environmental law scholarship is to combine careful empiricism with cautious experimentalism: try out new regulatory ideas, to be sure, but do not promote them everywhere at once, and pay attention to contextual differences that make a good idea in one setting a very bad idea in another (Cole and Grossman, 1999; Rose, 1991). Perhaps even more promising are proposals for combining different regulatory instruments to address the same environmental problem (Gunningham and Grobosky, 1998). At this time, it seems fair to say that legal scholars in Australia and other countries are well ahead of legal scholars in the United States in this area, as US scholars still tend, unreasonably, to press a quite limited set of solutions for any given environmental problem.

2.3 Compliance

Although, as discussed, many developed countries have settled upon some form of technology-based regulation as their primary framework for environmental standard-setting, the same countries differ markedly in their approaches to regulatory enforcement. Given the extensive 'slippage' between the environmental standards set by the legislature in collaboration with administrative agencies and the standards firms are actually required to meet once enforcement practices and priorities are taken into account (Farber, 1999), and given the disheartening statistics on government resources available for enforcement (Steinzor, 2000), a large future task for environmental law scholars will be to develop approaches to regulatory compliance that rely less heavily on traditional government coercion.

At least two standard answers to the enforcement problem already exist. One is that adequate monitoring, coupled with reporting requirements, takes care of the problem. To some extent this is true. The US sulfur dioxide trading program, for example, has been—amazingly—self-enforcing; there has not been a single reported violation of the requirements of this program. But without the monitoring technology that exists for sulfur dioxide—which does not exist for all pollutants—this regime would likely not have worked as well as it has. A second common answer to the enforcement problem is to provide for citizen suits—designed both to take the pressure off overworked government enforcement offices and to put the pressure on the units of government that are themselves responsible for environmental problems. In the United States, a good bit of legal scholarship in recent years has been devoted to the construction (or refutation) of arguments designed to keep the citizen suit constitutionally afloat in the wake of several Supreme Court decisions cutting back significantly on citizens' ability to sue. Elsewhere, as in scholarship on German environmental law, attention has been directed to the more basic question of whether standing should be granted at all to citizens to challenge environmental decisions (mostly standing has been denied in such cases in Germany). Relatively less effort has been devoted to figuring out whether, even with citizen suits, environmental laws are being adequately enforced or, if not, what else can be done about it. As a result, many legal scholars have been casting about for new ways to achieve compliance with environmental laws.

In the growing literature on regulatory compliance, several writers have observed what they call the 'American Paradox': the strange fact that the United States has the most formally strict environmental laws in the world while at the same time enjoying less environmental success than countries with more lenient laws. Some scholars have suggested that the American propensity for adversarial approaches to regulation, including frequent resort to litigation, have created this paradox, and they compare the United States unfavorably to countries, such as England and Germany, in which regulators and regulated work out solutions to pollution problems together and in which litigation is viewed as a failure (Hawkins, 1984; Verweij, 2000; Vogel, 1986). Other scholars, in contrast, have criticized the cozy and secretive relationships between government and industry that develop in such a collaborative rather than adversarial setting, and have suggested that a country such as Germany, where the administrative system is characterized by coziness and secrecy, could learn from the openness and accountability offered by the American system of administrative law (Rose-Ackerman, 1995).

In these circumstances, it seems reasonable to conclude that the truth must lie somewhere in-between, and that an important task for future legal scholarship on the environment will be to identify innovative ways in which regulatory compliance might be achieved. The existing work on this subject is creative and promising. Corporate self-governance through environmental auditing and enlistment of third-party commercial actors (such as banks and insurance companies) in the service of environmental protection are two especially intriguing proposals—the former widely discussed in the United States and elsewhere and the latter just emerging in scholarship, mostly outside the United States (Gunningham and Grobosky, 1998). It is hard to predict whether the Enron and other corporate scandals revealed recently in the United States will promote or retard the development of alternative regulatory compliance strategies within the United States. Nevertheless, it is tempting to specu-late that the most recent work on regulatory compliance—concluding that corpor-ate profitability and corporate environmental management style are as helpful in explaining regulatory compliance as are national regulatory differences (Kagan *et al.*, forthcoming)—may dovetail with the current focus on corporate govern-ance in a way that promotes new insights into and developments in strategies for regulatory compliance.

3 HORIZONTAL INSTITUTIONAL DESIGN

Environmental law is as much about the relationships among the branches of government as it is about risk, pollution control technology, cost-benefit tradeoffs, and market incentives. These relationships determine the shape and scope of environmental protection. Likewise, environmental laws have helped give new con-tent to legal doctrines concerning the duties and powers of the different branches of government. Indeed, many of the important legal decisions in the United States in the last three decades concerning the relationships among the branches have emerged from environmental cases; especially important here have been legal doc-trines and institutional frameworks designed to constrain agency discretion. The experience in the United States puts into sharp focus some issues of institutional design that arise everywhere in slightly different forms, depending on the particular nation's governmental structure. Nevertheless, despite the importance of the question of institutional design to environmental law, environmental law scholar-ship has been surprisingly unproductive here. For every yin suggesting one kind of institutional design or posture, there is a yang proposing quite the opposite. The debate has been left in a kind of gyrating stalemate. Even so, if one digs deep enough into the literature, one can find institutional success stories that could pave the way for more progressive and fruitful scholarship in the future.

3.1 Legislatures

Happily for them, most elected representatives probably do not spend their time reading legal scholarship on the environment. If they did, they would discover that they are doing pretty much everything wrong—and that if they try to fix it, they will run into opposite but equally vociferous objections.

In discussing institutional design in so far as legislatures are concerned, environmental law scholars have focused most of their attention on two basic issues legislatures face in passing environmental legislation: how specific should legislatures be in their directives to the agencies or ministries responsible for implementing their commands? And, how sensitive should legislatures be to the preferences of their political constituencies? In both realms, many environmental law scholars have given legislatures a failing grade, but have given very different reasons for doing so.

On the question of specificity of legislative guidance to agencies and ministries, legal scholars have fallen mostly into one of two camps. Many have criticized legislatures for being unduly vague and general in their commands, for delegating controversial and complicated political and scientific judgments to agencies without giving the bureaucracies adequate direction. Thus, these scholars have argued, legislatures can take credit for environmentally protective legislation without having to do the difficult and contentious work of actually protecting the environment in concrete cases. Some scholars have attributed the aspirational features of many US environmental statutes to this dynamic: Congress embraces lofty-sounding, but ultimately unattainable, environmental goals in its statutes, and then, if necessary, blames the agencies for failing to live up to them (Dwyer, 1990). The solution, on this view, is for legislatures to give more rather than less guidance to the administrative agencies.

Other scholars say just the opposite. They argue that one large problem in environmental law has been a lack of intelligent priority-setting. In the United States, this problem is compounded by Congress's tendency, when it amends the environmental laws, to become ever more prescriptive—to set precise deadlines for the agency to meet and to direct the agency to regulate specific pollutants in a specific manner. This tendency leads, in the view of some scholars, to a 'pollutant of the month' syndrome which ties the agency's regulatory hands and which may require the agency to address trivial environmental problems. The solution, here, is for legislatures to give the bureaucracies freer rein.

A similar kind of stand-off exists with respect to the question of how responsive elected representatives should be to their various political constituencies. On the one hand, a large vein of legal scholarship on the environment has argued for the past decade or so that elected representatives are far too responsive to the public's desires for strong environmental laws. The public, on this view, is unduly hysterical about environmental threats, while ignoring many other kinds of hazards (such as automobile accidents) that produce many more human fatalities than environmental risks do. The result is a system which spends extravagant amounts to save lives through environmental laws and at the same time spends little or nothing on larger yet less salient kinds of risks. The solution is to wrest environmental protection from the hands of the public, and to place it in the hands of technocrats educated in science, economics, and public policy, who will take a clear-eyed, rational view of risk and allocate life-saving resources to the places where they are most needed and most effective. This solution, offered by US Supreme Court Justice Stephen Breyer in his book, *Breaking the Vicious Circle*, resembles regulatory frameworks already in place in some European countries, such as Germany (Breyer, 1993). Nevertheless, in the United States, Breyer's proposal was widely criticized as anti-democratic at the time, even by scholars who generally shared Breyer's critical perspective on environmental regulation. Yet the basic outlines of Breyer's proposal are quietly being implemented within the United States, most prominently by White House officials in charge of reviewing agencies' regulatory proposals. Given the ascendancy of a vision of risk regulation dominated by technocrats rather than citizens in policy debates within the United States, US legal scholars, in particular, would do well to look to the experience of other countries, such as Germany, with the kind of technocracy—focused on expertise and quantification, directed away from citizens and the qualitative features of risk—Breyer and others have proposed (Rose-Ackerman, 1995).

While this academic to-and-fro-ing continues, lawmakers have quietly been experimenting with institutional designs that aim to constrain agencies somewhat while at the same time giving agency expertise room enough to maneuver. Two successful US legislative examples of this kind of middle ground come to mind. First, California's 'Proposition 65', which requires warning labels on consumer products containing carcinogens that pose a significant risk, avoided the paralysis that has stricken so many other regulatory regimes dependent on scientific findings of risk by shifting the burden of proof to industry to show that a carcinogen posed an insignificant risk. More risk-based standard-setting occurred within a couple of years after this statute had passed than has occurred under all of the federal environmental laws put together, over thirty years. A second example comes from the US Resource Conservation and Recovery Act, which governs hazardous waste treatment and disposal. In this law, Congress banned all land disposal of hazardous waste—*unless* the waste was either pre-treated according to standards to be issued by the EPA or was shown not to be capable of migrating through soil and groundwater for 10,000 years. Congress established precise dates on which land disposal would be banned unless the pre-treatment regulations or no-migration showings were in place. These so-called 'hammer' provisions tied the EPA's hands while at the same time leaving the EPA free to establish its own pre-treatment regulations, using its expertise. And they worked: the EPA met virtually all of the deadlines under the statute, a rare event in the annals of environmental law.

Environmental law scholarship in the coming years would benefit from closer inspection of legislatures' most recent experiments with institutional design. Scholars could perform an important service by identifying successful (or failed) experiments, and trying to find ways to duplicate them, with appropriate adjustments, in other settings. The idea would be to create a menu of options for making the most of the ongoing collaboration between legislative politics and agency expertise.

3.2 Courts

Environmental law scholarship on the role of courts in constraining agency or ministerial discretion is as polarized and mostly unsatisfying as scholarship on the role of legislatures. Here I concentrate on the US literature, in which the issues are well-developed.

On the wisdom and propriety of intensive judicial scrutiny of agency action, there is a large scholarly divide. Many environmental scholars view aggressive judicial policing of agency action as essential to an effective regime of environmental protection. US scholars point, in particular, to a series of landmark decisions from the federal court of appeals in Washington, DC, as showing how the courts can effectuate environmental protection even in the face of recalcitrant administrative agencies. The National Environmental Policy Act, for example—probably the most-copied of all US environmental laws, in the United States and abroad—was turned into a powerful environmental litigator's tool essentially overnight, in one famous decision by the federal appeals court in Washington. Other US decisions in the 1970s, in the first wave of litigation following the passage of the major federal environmental statutes, scrutinized the newly created EPA's actions closely, but in the end managed to uphold many of the most important of these actions. Indeed, one of the most-cited law review articles of all time is a piece by Judge Harold Leventhal, a member of the 1970s-era federal court of appeals in Washington, defending his view that judges should, in reviewing agency decisions that are based on scientific expertise, strive to become somewhat expert themselves, in order to give the decisions the close scrutiny they warrant (Leventhal, 1974). Active judicial involvement in agency decision-making became, for many early environmental law scholars, an integral part of the institutional arrangements surrounding environmental protection.

The very judicial involvement that some scholars have thought critical to environmental protection has, recently, become a subject of criticism by other scholars, who blame it for the 'ossification' of the administrative rule-making process in the United States. Widely accepted in this circle of scholars is the notion that a large portion of what US agencies spend their time and resources on—from making progress in our scientific understanding of environmental problems to writing the explanations for the rules the agencies announce—is driven by a fear of invalidation by US courts, not by scientific or technical necessity. Major environmental rules today are years in the making at US agencies, following the development of administrative records that frequently run into the tens of thousands of pages. These rules can then be overturned by an appeals court that finds something inadequately thorough about the agency's reasoning or explanation. The result is perhaps not so much ossification as osteoporosis—in which an apparently stable structure is vulnerable to the smallest blow.

Many scholars are exploring alternative administrative processes that promise less rigidity. Regulatory negotiation and collaborative decision-making are two prominently discussed, and widely exercised, alternatives. Here, too, more comparative work might yield important insights. The United States system of administrative law has, since at least the 1970s, been characterized by wide public participation and quite intense judicial policing of agency procedures (Stewart, 1975). This approach sharply contrasts with the approach of, for example, England and Germany, where environmental decision-making largely takes place outside the public eye and outside the range of judicial invalidation (Vogel, 1986; Rose-Ackerman, 1995). In the best case, comparative scholarship might well help US scholars in their quest for more agile administrative processes and might help scholars outside the United States to transcend some of the coziness that appears to attend more informal, collaborative decision-making frameworks elsewhere.

4 VERTICAL INSTITUTIONAL DESIGN

In the United States, the passage of the major environmental laws in the 1970s came on the heels of the passage of the civil rights and Great Society legislation of the 1960s. At the time, the case for federal protections was quite straightforward, even if not universally accepted: states had done essentially nothing on the important fronts, and it was time someone (the federal government) stepped in. The legislative histories of the major environmental statutes are filled with references to the failure of states to shoulder the burden of protecting their citizens and natural resources from environmental harms. Legislators also worried that leaving standard-setting to the states would encourage states to compete for business by relaxing environmental protections. Few seemed to think it was a good idea that states be able to do this. Even fewer thought the laws they were enacting might be unconstitutional infringements on states' power. None, it seems fair to say, predicted that their laws could eventually be undone by an international tribunal specializing in issues of free trade.

Now much has changed. Devolution of authority from the federal government to the states is much in vogue, supported by powerful political constituencies and a recent change of constitutional course by the US Supreme Court in the area of federal–state relations; collaborative decision-making by interested persons, outside the traditional process of agency rule-making, is celebrated both for national rule-making proceedings and for decisions regarding more localized matters, such as the proper management of a particular forest or watershed; and, finally, looming over every environmentally protective regulation today is the possibility that it will be overturned in the name of free trade. Many issues relating to these broad matters have been fully aired in environmental law scholarship, but some are only now starting to emerge in the environmental law literature. The potential implications of free trade agreements for domestic environmental protection, in particular, are quite under-developed in the mainstream literature on environmental law. Here, again, a kind of fragmentation in environmental law scholarship exists—in this instance, between domestic and international specialists—and it has so far impeded a full understanding of the ramifications of trade law for environmental law. Even in countries with weaker national governments, the question of vertical institutional design arises if they are parties to free trade agreements that may threaten their local environmental laws.

4.1 Devolution

In the wake of the US Supreme Court's newly aggressive posture in federalism cases, some environmental law scholarship has begun to focus on defending (or attacking) federal environmental laws on constitutional grounds. This scholarship is important in practical terms from a litigator's perspective, but it has tended to break little new theoretical ground. More interesting, and potentially more fundamentally threatening to federal law in the end, is a raft of legal scholarship concerning a basic premise of federal environmental legislation—the idea that in the absence of such legislation there will be a 'race to the bottom' in which states individually relax their environmental standards to encourage economic growth in a way that makes the states collectively worse off (Revesz, 1992). A similar idea, and similar scholarship, exists with respect to the relationship between the European Union and its member states (Bird and Veiga-Pestana, 1993).

The US scholarship, though theoretically engaging, has been characterized by an unfortunate disengagement with facts concerning states' capacity to take on the role of environmental protection. Complicated mathematical equations purporting to show social improvements from devolution have not come to terms with more prosaic statistics revealing the inadequacy of state resources for environmental protection. Future environmental law scholarship on devolution would do well to engage both the theoretical and empirical dimensions of this debate. Future US scholarship in this area would also be well served by considering the experience of other countries, such as Germany, that have relied more heavily than has the United States on state rather than federal environmental regulation and, in the view of some, have stumbled as a consequence (Rose-Ackerman, 1995).

4.2 Collaborative Decision-Making

Just as regulatory negotiation has been promoted as an antidote to rule-making ossification, so collaborative models of decision-making have recently caught on as an
antidote to the top–down, nationally driven, elitist modes of decision-making that
have traditionally pervaded environmental law (Freeman, 1997). The collaborative
model of decision-making has been deployed in the United States in two quite different circumstances, with two very different political valences.

In one incarnation, collaborative decision-making has been employed in contexts
where choices must be made about use and management of a particular natural
resource, one with (arguably) predominantly local effects, such as a forest or watershed. Collaborative processes have sprung up all over the place recently, with some
legal scholars enthusiastically embracing the trend. Others, who have had actual
experience participating in such collaborations, worry about the time and resources
required to participate effectively, and worry that such collaborations inevitably end
up caving in to the lowest common environmental denominator. Between these
poles, there seems room for fruitful scholarship on ways to make collaborative
arrangements more inclusive, less unwieldy, and less tilted against environmental
protection. Again, the idea would be to experiment, but cautiously.

In another incarnation, collaborative decision-making is one way to describe the
kind of decision-making process many advocates for environmental justice envision.
In the elaborate administrative proceedings that attend environmental decision-
making in the United States, one important concern that has traditionally been quite
completely overlooked is the cumulative and disproportionate effect of pollution
sources on low-income communities, communities of color, and politically weak
communities (Lazarus, 1992). Environmental law scholarship uncovering this gap in
protection has begun to exert a large influence on environmental law. One of the ways
often suggested for filling this gap is a kind of collaborative decision-making, in
which local communities disproportionately affected by environmental hazards are
allowed to participate in environmental decisions that affect them, such as the siting
of new hazardous waste facilities within their borders. In general, a large challenge for
future environmental law scholarship is to seek ways to incorporate insights from the
environmental justice movement into a regulatory regime that is, archaically, still
mostly focused on one pollutant, or one polluting facility, at a time, without consideration of the cumulative effects pollutants and facilities might have in communities
disproportionately exposed to a variety of pollutants from a variety of sources.

As students of American law rush to embrace collaborative decision-making,
some students of the environmental experience in other countries have been more
hesitant. 'Collaboration' can quickly degenerate into a kind of quiet conspiracy to
undermine environmental values; some scholars have suggested that this lesson
might be taken from Germany's approach to administration (Rose-Ackerman,
1995). Others have suggested that collaboration is exactly what makes some formally

less stringent environmental regimes ultimately more effective (Vogel, 1986; Verweij, 2000).

4.3 International Governance

Historically, most environmental law scholars have made a choice between expending their scholarly energy on domestic or international law; most scholars have not managed to be experts in both. This is changing, and with good reason. Domestic environmental laws have become vulnerable to challenges grounded in international law, particularly international trade law, and at the same time environmental problems, more than ever, are coming to be understood as global problems requiring global attention. Thus international law must enter every environmental law scholar's range of vision. Environmental law scholars can contribute to ongoing debates over free trade, for example, by pointing out the special vulnerabilities of domestic environmental laws to broadly worded prohibitions in trade agreements. Chapter 11 of the North American Free Trade Agreement (NAFTA), for example, provides a right of financial compensation to foreign investors harmed by government actions that are 'tantamount to expropriation'—a standard inviting enough for potential plaintiffs that numerous lawsuits are now pending against NAFTA signatory states. Given that such broadly worded trade agreements exist, and given that international trade tribunals have been comfortable about questioning environmental protections under these broad agreements, there will continue to be plenty of constructive (or re-constructive) work to be done by environmental law scholars on the intersection of domestic environmental protections and free trade aspirations.

5 CONCLUSION

The handiwork of environmental law scholars can be seen all over environmental law—from the decline of design standards and the rise of market-based measures for pollution control to the influence of concerns about environmental justice on regulatory policy and the rise of collaborative decision-making. But environmental law scholars could do a better job along several dimensions, all related to the distinctive features of environmental law scholarship with which I began this essay.

First, environmental law scholars' interdisciplinarity is admirable and even necessary in a field like environmental law, but environmental law scholarship is at the same time unduly uncritical in the face of empirical and theoretical claims from other disciplines. Many claims about the inefficiency and extravagance of environmental protection, repeated over and over again by leading environmental law scholars, turn out on close inspection to be thick with dubious factual assumptions and contestable moral judgments. Environmental law scholars need to take interdisciplinarity to the next level, and instead of taking claims from other disciplines at face value, they need to become even more comfortable in the fields from which they are borrowing their ideas.

Secondly, environmental law scholars' practical inclinations could also be extended. Many scholars write for practical effect and then do not test the real-world consequences against their own predictions and theories. They also sometimes do not bother to notice when the legislature, or the agencies, or another relevant actor actually changes course and gets things 'right' according to prevailing scholarly views. Thus, for example, we continue to see a debate over zero-risk and technology-based regulation that targets regulatory practices that mostly have gone the way of the dodo bird.

Finally, and most fundamentally, environmental law scholars should aim to reduce the fragmentation that characterizes the field. Brown and green, court lovers and court haters, domestic and international—the fault lines in environmental law scholarship run deep, deep enough so that it is often impossible to peek over one's own narrow trench and see what damage one has wrought elsewhere. Opportunities for improvement, coming from outside one's own narrow boundaries, are also often overlooked. The growing literature on environmental justice, risk trade-offs, and the lessons of pollution control for natural resources law, all attempt to cross the divides that have historically marked environmental law scholarship. This border crossing should continue and grow in the next generation of environmental law scholarship.

References

Ackerman, B., and Stewart, R. (1985). 'Reforming Environmental Law', *Stanford Law Review*, 37: 333–65.

Bird, I., and Veiga-Pestana, M. (1993). 'European Community Environmental Policy and Law: An Introduction', in R. Folsom, R. Lake, and V. Nanda (eds.), *European Community Law after 1992*, Deventer, Netherlands: Kluwer Law and Taxation Publishers.

Breyer, S. (1993). *Breaking the Vicious Circle: Toward Effective Risk Regulation*, Cambridge, Mass. and London: Harvard University Press.

Cole, D., and Grossman, P. (1999). 'When is Command-and-Control Efficient? Institutions, Technology, and the Comparative Efficiency of Alternative Regulatory Regimes for Environmental Protection', *Wisconsin Law Review*, 887–938.

Dwyer, J. (1990). 'The Pathology of Symbolic Legislation', *Ecology Law Quarterly*, 17: 233–316.

Farber, D. (1999). 'Taking Slippage Seriously: Noncompliance and Creative Compliance in Environmental Law', *Harvard Environmental Law Review*, 23: 297–325.

Freeman, J. (1997). 'Collaborative Governance in the Administrative State', *University of California at Los Angeles Law Review*, 45: 1–98.

Gunningham, N., and Grabosky, P. (1998). *Smart Regulation: Designing Environmental Policy*, Oxford: Clarendon Press.

Hawkins, K. (1984). *Environment and Enforcement: Regulation and the Social Definition of Pollution*, Oxford: Clarendon Press.

Heinzerling, L. (1998). 'Regulatory Costs of Mythic Proportions', *Yale Law Journal*, 107: 1981–2070.

Hornstein, D. (1992). 'Reclaiming Environmental Law: A Normative Critique of Comparative Risk Analysis', *Columbia Law Review*, 92: 562–633.

Kagan, R., Gunningham, N., and Thornton, D. (2003, forthcoming). 'Explaining Corporate Environmental Performance: How Does Regulation Matter?' *Law & Society Review*.

Krier, J. (1974). 'The Irrational Air Quality Standards: Macro and Micro-Mistakes', *University of California at Los Angeles Law Review*, 22: 323–42.

—— and Gillette, C. (1990). 'Risk, Courts, and Agencies', *University of Pennsylvania Law Review*, 138: 1027–109.

Latin, H. (1985). 'Ideal versus Real Regulatory Efficiency: Implementation of Uniform Standards and "Fine-Tuning" Regulatory Reforms', *Stanford Law Review*, 37: 1267–332.

Lazarus, R. (1992). 'Pursuing "Environmental Justice": The Distributional Effects of Environmental Protection', *Northwestern University Law Review*, 87: 787–857.

Leventhal, H. (1974). 'Environmental Decision-Making and the Role of the Courts', *University of Pennsylvania Law Review*, 122: 509–55.

McGarity, T. (1992). 'Some Thoughts on "Deossifying" the Rulemaking Process', *Duke Law Journal*, 41: 1385–462.

Pildes, R., and Sunstein, S. (1995). 'Reinventing the Regulatory State', *University of Chicago Law Review*, 62: 1–129.

Revesz, R. (1992). 'Rehabilitating Interstate Competition: Rethinking the "Race-to-the-Bottom" Rationale for Federal Environmental Regulation', *New York University Law Review*, 67: 1210–54.

Rose, C. (1991), 'Rethinking Environmental Controls: Management Strategies for Common Resources', *Duke Law Journal*, 1–38.

Rose-Ackerman, S. (1995). *Controlling Environmental Policy: The Limits of Public Law in Germany and the United States*, New Haven and London: Yale University Press.

Steinzor, R. (2000). 'Devolution and the Public Health', *Harvard Environmental Law Review*, 24: 351–463.

Stewart, R. (1975). 'The Reformation of American Administrative Law', *Harvard Law Review*, 88: 1669–813.

Sunstein, C. (2002). 'The Arithmetic of Arsenic', *Georgetown Law Journal*, 90: 2255–309.

Verweij, M. (2000). 'Why is the River Rhine Cleaner than the Great Lakes (Despite Looser Regulation)?' *Law and Society Review*, 34: 1007–54.

Vogel, D. (1986). *National Styles of Regulation: Environmental Policy in Great Britain and the United States*, Ithaca, NY and London: Cornell University Press.

Wagner, W. (1995). 'The Science Charade in Toxic Substance Regulation', *Columbia Law Review*, 95: 1613–723.

Wilkinson, C. (1992). *Crossing the Next Meridian: Land, Water, and the Future of the West*, Washington: Island Press.

PART VI

PROCESSES

CHAPTER 32

LEGISLATION AND RULE-MAKING

ROBERT BALDWIN

GOVERNMENTS seek to influence behaviour by employing a variety of rule types. These range from formal statutes to rules made under delegated powers to the most informal of administrative prescriptions. These different kinds of rules, in turn, are reinforced with very different responses—from penal threats to administrative sanctions, to mere exhortations.

Such variety in rule use has long attracted the attention of legal scholars who have sought to explain and justify rule-making practices, to evaluate processes as well as to explore the implications of choosing different strategies of rule use. Scholarly debates in this area have never been more compelling as the legislators and rule-makers of the new millennium seek to devise fresh approaches in order to meet new governmental and regulatory challenges.

This chapter looks at developing scholarly debates clustered around three themes: explaining choices between rule types; issues of legitimation surrounding governmentally produced rules; and the challenge of making rules that are attuned to new modes of government. Particular attention is then paid to a number of rule-making issues that are likely to be prominent in forthcoming scholarly and policy concerns.

1 CHOICES BETWEEN RULE TYPES

It is possible to think of rules as divided into primary, secondary, and tertiary kinds. Primary rules are exemplified by legislative enactments that possess the full force of law. Secondary rules have legal force and are produced in exercise of a power to legislate that is itself conferred by a statute of legal force. Tertiary rules do not create rights that are directly enforceable through civil or criminal proceedings although they may produce indirect legal effects. They may or may not be made in exercise of a statutory power and, like secondary rules, are promulgated by governmental bodies rather than elected legislatures.

A question that legal scholars have approached from a variety of perspectives is one of motivation—why governments increasingly elect to regulate behaviour by relying on secondary and tertiary (or 'governmental') rules rather than primary legislation.

Commentators who have adopted functionalist or public interest approaches have stressed the considerable practical advantages of relying on governmentally pro-duced rules rather than legislative provisions. Legislatures, it has been noted, have neither the technical expertise nor the time to pass laws on matters of detail and it is far more useful for legislators to focus on questions of broad principle or framework and to rely on the executive to promulgate more precise rules (Baldwin, 1995). It has, secondly, been argued that the practicalities of consulting various constituencies on the contents of rules are far better managed by delegating rule-making to the execu-tive. A third point often made is that, in the real world, rules cannot be used to lay down blueprints for future actions and, accordingly, the public interest is best served by relying on governmental rather than primary rules so that flexibility is ensured and new rule formulations can be developed quickly and without adherence to lengthy legislative procedures. An associated advantage of governmental rule-making is that emergencies can be reacted to with speed.

Such public interest visions have, however, come under scholarly attack on a number of fronts particularly in the United States. Notably, it has been contended that such visions tend to underplay the role of interests (private, bureaucratic, or group), in shaping rule-making choices, and that they exaggerate the disinterestedness of legis-lators, politicians, and bureaucrats who, in fact, often pursue selfish ends in the shape of such desiderata as power, votes, influence, money, and job satisfaction (Stigler, 1971). Consistent with such attacks on public interest accounts is the view that politi-cians in power, as well as agency bureaucrats, tend to favour governmental rule-making, and build such rule-making into new statutory regimes of regulation because it gives them very considerable, and continuing, control over policy developments. From their perspective, this is infinitely preferable to implementing the will of an elected legislature and having to return to that legislature when changes are required. A further cited reason why members of governments will be attracted to delegated legislation is that this sidesteps awkward parliamentary scrutiny on difficult issues.

Legal and other scholars who have espoused 'economic', 'private interest', or 'public choice' visions have been in the forefront in countering public interest accounts by suggesting that legislative developments and choices of rule type are driven by the tendency of politicians and legislators to act in pursuit of their own private interests and preferences. Governmental behaviour, on this view, can be understood by seeing all actors as rational individual maximizers of their own welfare. Movements towards greater reliance on governmental or even industry-produced rules are, in turn, seen as encouraged by perceptions on the part of bureaucrats, regulators, or politicians that their own utilities are served by delegation of rule-making functions to the executive, to independent regulators, or to business and professional organizations. This is a line of analysis often countered by assertions that parties involved in government may act for altruistic or ideological reasons, not merely self-serving ones, and by allegations that certain historical developments (e.g. periods of deregulation) are difficult to explain in terms of the economic theory. The impact of institutional factors, the limitations of information, and the influence of pressure groups are matters also said to pose problems for such theory.

Scholars putting forward interest group theories have, in turn, contributed to the above debate by contending that rule-making choices are often dictated by deals that have been made between competing groups. The impulse to delegate legislative functions is explained, in such accounts, by reference to the value of delegation in appeasing interest groups or even in avoiding confrontations between different interests. Primary legislation is accordingly seen as a means of establishing a framework for rules, but the pain of steering contentious issues through democratic institutions is seen as being managed most easily by leaving an executive department or an agency to negotiate compromises and solutions with interested groups. The contribution of 'regulatory space' theory here has been to draw attention to the complex interplay of interests that may attend particular regulatory issues and choices of legislative strategy (Hancher and Moran, 1989).

Another sort of account is in turn offered by the 'civic republican theory' of regulation which sees rule-making processes as shaped not so much by competing preferences as by the willingness of involved parties (public and private) to engage in dialogue and to behave in an open-minded and other-regarding fashion. Within this vision, regulatory rule-makers act as mediators and translators in an effort to facilitate deliberative processes. Outcomes represent not 'victories' for certain interests, but compromises enjoying wide support from many of the participants. Choices of rule type would be influenced, according to such theories, by desires to maximize possibilities for deliberation. Resort to governmental rather than primary rules would be accounted for on this basis. Support for the civic republican approach can thus be derived from the growth of negotiated rule-making processes in the United States under the Negotiated Rulemaking Act of 1990 and Executive Order No. 12,866 of 1994 (instructing the use of 'consensual mechanisms' in rule-making).

This vision, however, does encounter difficulties in both its descriptive and normative aspects. Some of these difficulties stem from its assumptions concerning access to deliberations; the public-spiritedness of relevant actors, and their motives to act unselfishly; the conditions under which deliberative processes will produce desired results rather than deadlock; and the capacity of deliberation to deal with irreconcilable differences in values, perceptions, and preferences.

In the last twenty years 'institutional' approaches have raised a series of new and provocative issues concerning the relationships that exist between legislators and those bodies who are given tasks to perform in accordance with the law. From this perspective, there is more to shaping legislative strategies than the detached pursuit of public interests, or aggregations of personal interests, or clashes between groups. Actors involved in legislative processes are seen by institutionalists as having preferences that are influenced by institutional procedures, principles, expectations, and norms—as where politicians' actions are shaped by various assumptions about the nature of agencies and their relationships to central government departments (Powell and Di Maggio, 1991). Legislative choices have thus been seen as moulded by institutional factors that are embedded in cultural and historical frameworks. Institutional factors may produce regimes of governance in which rule-making powers are extensively delegated to agencies. Institutionalists, however, may also point to the tendency of elected officials to attempt to ensure that delegated powers are used in ways that are consistent with the compromises and agreements that underpinned the initial legislation (McCubbins *et al.*, 1987). A key debate here concerns agency problems—whether and how institutional frameworks, and the policy or rule-making processes that are set up in primary legislation, can be structured or 'stacked' in order to limit the propensity of implementing bureaucrats to depart from the legislative will.

Institutionalist approaches are clearly seen in studies of European Union legislative strategies—notably in discussions of Directives and 'soft laws'. Directives are a form of secondary or delegated EU legislation (the Treaties being viewed as EU primary laws). Directives instruct Member States to take action to achieve certain results and are binding as to the results to be achieved while leaving Member States the 'choice of form and methods' (article 189 EC). It is the role of one institution, the EC Commission, in developing a 'New Approach' to the use of Directives that has attracted the special attention of legal scholars (Pelkmans, 1987). As will be seen below, such developments in European legislative styles have prompted considerable scholarly debate concerning the legitimacy and effectiveness of different strategies for using rules and the various ways of harmonizing Member State laws and regulations across Europe.

Note should also be taken of explanations that give pride of place to ideas as shapers of institutions, rule strategies, and legal relationships. In the field of regulation (and notably in accounts of deregulation) a number of scholars have seen developments as being driven, not by interests but by the force of ideas—'conceptions of how and why the government ought to control' (Harris and Milkis, 1996). Similarly, it can be argued, that ideas about the respective constitutional roles of primary, secondary, and tertiary rules, or about the appropriate balance between constitutional proprieties and efficient government will affect choices of rule-making strategy. In the British context, for instance, it could be argued that since the early Thatcher years a particular idea about legislation has grown in force (at least within government) to the effect that the needs of modern government demand, and justify, a shift away from predominantly primary law and in the direction of governmentally produced rules. More recently, in the United States, it could be argued that 'post-bureaucratic' ideas about the need to 'reinvent government' (discussed below) have underpinned a shift away from the use of command-based rules.

All ideas-based accounts, of course, face the challenge of explaining how ideas can be said to translate into practical force—a challenge that is often difficult to meet without invoking the support of interest, functionalist, or other accounts. Ideas about the propriety of governmental rules may, indeed, have gained sway at least in part because of factors best understood in functionalist or interest terms; but that is not to deny that ideas can play a catalytic role and, at times, can galvanize action. As for the evidence that such ideas may have affected legislative forms in the last decades of the second millennium, it is clear in the UK both that the practice of using primary legislation as a mere framework for governmental rules has developed almost to the point of being a standard point of departure (Ganz, 1987) and, also, that governments appear to have accepted this as a norm for some time. In the United States, numerous scholars have reviewed examples of recent choices of rule-making style and high-lighted their consistency with developing ideas about 'reinvented' or 'deliberative' government (Osborne and Gaebler, 1992; Dorf and Sabel, 1998). In 1993, moreover, Vice President Al Gore chaired the National Performance Review, which led to the Clinton administration's Reinventing Government campaign—a movement that embraced many of the ideas associated with 'reinvented' government and brought to popular attention by David Osborne and Ted Gaebler.

That ideas can shape legislative strategies can also be seen within the European Union. Ideas about the tactics and proprieties of using Directives in different ways have been a focus of discussions in the Commission, Council, and elsewhere since before the 'New Approach' was adopted in the Commission's 1985 White Paper (EC Commission, 1985). The attendant issues, in turn, have offered a focus for socio-legal scholars (Pelkmans, 1987). Particular attention has been paid to matters of democratic legitimation, and this is a topic that will be discussed in the next section.

2 THE LEGITIMACY OF GOVERNMENTAL RULES

The case for resorting to governmental rules, rather than relying on primary legislation or open-ended discretions, has been built on a number of different scholarly foundations. Over the years, moreover, it can be argued that there has been a progression in approaches.

A starting-point for modern discussions of the role and legitimacy of governmental rules was the case made in terms of justice as presented by K. C. Davis in his 1971 book *Discretionary Justice*. Davis argued that one of the greatest hopes for improving justice for individuals in the government and legal systems was to eliminate all unnecessary discretionary power. This could be done by confining discretion with standards, by using checking arrangements (whereby an official would monitor another's use of discretion), but, above all, by earlier and more elaborate administrative rule-making.

Some later scholars, however, came to see the Davis approach as excessively legalistic—as too concerned with justice for individuals and as underplaying the importance in public decision-making of values beyond individual justice such as efficiency, adaptability, and the furtherance of public rather than private interests. For such critics, there exist valued interests beyond those of individuals and there is a role for administrative rules in protecting those broader interests—notably in facilitating the pursuit of 'non-justice' values and public objectives. Rules, they stressed, could be used not merely to control discretions and abuses (a 'red light' concept) but for the positive achievement of governmental objectives (a 'green light' notion) (Harlow and Rawlings, 1997).

Running parallel to such scholarly discussions were debates about the value of seeking to further justice in terms of the rule of law. Dicey's legacy was seen as producing a stereotypical 'lawyer's view' of the world that generally favoured regulating human activity with legal rules and that looked to deal with problems by filling in 'gaps' in the rules (Lacey, 1992). Critics of this view urged, again, that there is more to fairness than individual justice and that a liberal democracy should pursue an array of values other than justice. As for the use of rules to solve governmental and regulatory problems, a body of scholars writing in the United States in the 1970s and 1980s launched an attack on 'command-based' approaches to regulation and the tendency of regulators to produce dense thickets of rules (Bardach and Kagan, 1982).

Scholars concerned to evaluate rule use by looking to values other than justice began to look to desiderata such as efficiency and accountability within government. With regard to the former, the key question was whether using governmental rules achieved desired results in a lower cost manner than alternative modes of action. To this end, the law and economics school explored such issues as the costs and benefits associated with the use of different rule types and rules of different degrees of precision. The governmental use of cost-benefit testing in appraising regulatory rules itself became a distinct area of study. Socio-legal scholars, in turn, considered the different dimensions that administrative rules may possess (such as precision, transparency, accessibility, scope, status, sanction) (Diver, 1983). Design choices concerning the various dimensions of rules were then related to questions of efficiency and investigations were mounted into such issues as: whether precise or general rules were more conducive to efficient enforcement (Black, 1997); whether certain formulations of rules produced particular problems of inclusiveness, indeterminacy, or interpretation—and whose coverage or implications could only be identified with difficulty; and whether particular types of rules are more vulnerable than others to 'creative compliance'—the process whereby those regulated do not break the rules but circumvent the scope of the rule by sidestepping its coverage (McBarnet and Whelan, 1991).

In contrasting primary legislation and governmental rules on efficiency grounds, socio-legal scholars have noted that, although governmental rules might lack the symbolism and authority of primary legislation, they tend to be more flexible and adaptable; cheaper to produce and change; more amenable to specialist drafting; more accessible and especially useful in encouraging consistency in bureaucratic decision-making (Baldwin, 1995). Measuring and comparing the efficiency of different rule types has, however, been observed to present huge difficulties. A body of scholarship dealing with the use of different rules across the European Union has sought to come to grips with the problems encountered in seeking both to ensure and to evaluate the even-handed and effective implementation of (particularly secondary) EU rules (Cappelletti *et al.*, 1986).

The question of who should be given the task of making governmental rules is a further issue that has attracted the attention of scholars. This raises issues of efficiency (as well as of fairness, accountability, and transparency) and will be discussed in the next section when the fragmentation or decentring of government is considered.

It is on the accountability issue, however, that the most urgent debates about the legitimacy of governmental rules have centred. Governmental rule-making processes have provoked concerns on a number of fronts. Frequently made criticisms are that secondary and tertiary rules operate under regimes that allow scant scrutiny by elected institutions; are only sporadically and weakly reviewed by the courts; and are produced by a bewildering array of procedures. A further serious worry has been that the status and legal effects of many governmental rules are often difficult to discern or predict, and that such vagueness itself produces poor accountability.

How governmental rule-making processes can be regulated so as to ensure proper access, transparency, and accountability has been a fruitful area of scholarly investigation, and a good deal of work has looked at the requirements of the US Administrative Procedure Act 1946 and compared these with control strategies adopted in other jurisdictions. Key comparative issues have been how different legal systems, constitutions, and courts decide legislative competences and set out to define what constitutes a rule to which mandated procedures apply. A related question is how different varieties of rule can be classified and identified for the purposes of deciding their legal effects and the proper processes to be adopted for their promulgation (Ziamou, 2001).

If transparency and accessibility are seen as key aspects of rule-making processes, then other worries should also be noted: that in many jurisdictions consultations concerning governmental rules are largely unregulated and, again, only weakly supervised by the courts; that access to rule-making processes is not guaranteed to affected parties; and that, in many instances, there is no obligation on the applier of a rule to disclose the existence or content of the rule.

European Union rule-making, in particular, has been attacked on the grounds that there is a 'democratic deficit' constituted by the gap between the legislative powers being deployed and the controls being exercised over such powers by the elected European Parliament or the Member State parliaments. Numbers of legal scholars have cautioned that rule-making processes within Europe are considerably distanced and insulated from democratic oversight because rules tend to be produced deep within the Commission or the extensive committee structures of the EU and because there is bureaucratic rather than democratic domination of rule-making processes (Lodge, 1989). The delegation of rule- and standard-setting powers to private bodies such as CEN (Comité Européen de Normalisation) and CENELEC (Comité Européen de Normalisation Electro-technique) has been seen by some as creating further barriers to access and accountability within the EU's New Approach to the technical harmonization of rules. This has prompted debates concerning the value of introducing more formal procedures to regulate access to rule-making processes—such as EU provisions along the lines of the US Administrative Procedure Act 1946 (APA).

To return to the theme of different values and perspectives on the legitimacy of governmental rules, the scholarly trend, as noted, has been to move away from approaches based on furthering 'rule of law' objectives towards multiple-value accounts that look to efficiency, accountability, and accessibility as well as to substantive justice or fairness. This has prompted numbers of legal scholars to come to grips with the issue of how trade-offs between such values can be evaluated and resolved—how, for instance, society is to judge whether and to what extent greater efficiency in rule use should be achieved at the price of lower accountability or accessibility.

A further strand of legal scholarship has, furthermore, cautioned that in evaluating the legitimacy or propriety of rules, it is necessary to move away from traditional approaches to governmental rule-making that see governmental action as quintessentially taking place in centralized locations such as ministerial departments and public agencies. Much recent thinking has thus pointed to the way that modern governmental functions tend to be (and should be) spread both across an array of bodies, public and private, and across various layers of government.

The new debates and challenges, it can be said, have to deal with the roles of primary legislation and governmental rules within such orderings. Further problems may also have to be faced—many socio-legal commentators have stressed that needs for legitimation have to be met in a world where government has to be ever faster-moving, and increasingly responsive. They, accordingly, look to focus on new ways of legitimating through deliberations and processes modelled on market relationships rather than through old-fashioned notions of accountability (Osborne and Gaebler, 1992; Dorf and Sabel, 1998). The challenges posed by some of these new approaches to government are ones to which we now turn.

3 Rules and the Challenges of Decentred Government

What might be called a 'decentred' view of government moves away from traditional perspectives in two important ways. First, as noted, it sees governmental functions as being carried out by a variety of bodies and, secondly, it sees legal rules and regulations as merely one element within a web of potential constraints or influences on behaviour. On this view, 'governmental' control may be exercised by, say, harnessing private corporate capacities for self-regulation as much as by the issuing of state commands.

Before considering how rules and rule-making processes can be attuned to decentred government, it is worth exploring in a little more detail what such decentring comprises. Here it is possible to point to a number of depictions. One way of portraying governmental activity flows from the idea of regimes or networks (Hood *et al.*, 2001). If, for instance, we ask how government acts to deal with a particular risk or mischief it may be possible to identify a system of control in which a host of public institutions and private bodies exert influence. To give an example, the quality of legal service that a litigant enjoys in a British court is governed by the actions of more than twenty bodies—including the Law Society, Bar Council, Lord Chancellor's Department, solicitors' firms, the Legal Services Commission, and Parliament. The influences exerted by such bodies may or may not overlap—or, indeed, operate harmoniously. Various bodies of rules and other kinds of control may operate and the rules may vary in status (some may be statutory, some administrative, some contractual). Moreover, various sanctions, commands, incentives, and other inducements may be incorporated in rules dealing with the activity, and those rules may vary in status and formality.

A second but related vision of decentring notes how governmental control functions can be divided between public and private bodies and may operate through public or private law frameworks. Consistent with this vision are studies of the extent to which states contract out regulatory and operational functions, and research projects that examine different ways in which the state does or could operate so as to harness the self-regulatory capacity of corporations. Numerous scholars, in addition, have been concerned to explore how controls can be seen as an interaction between traditional state constraints and the processes of corporate governance and risk management. A further, but highly influential, variant on decentring stresses the gains to be achieved by 'reinventing government' so as to encourage an 'entrepreneurial' approach to the public sector—one based on missions, markets, and community empowerment rather than the bureaucratic application of rules (Osborne and Gaebler, 1992).

A third view of decentring points to the phenomenon of multi-layered government and stresses how controls may operate at many levels, involving (in Europe, for instance) actions by the following bodies: international organizations, the European Union institutions, individual Member State governments, devolved governmental bodies, and regional or local authorities.

How, then, have these various notions of decentring given new impetus to scholarly debates about rule-making? The notion that government controls do in practice operate through various networks brings to the fore a host of questions about the role of governmental rules. Legal scholars have examined many such questions, notably: how consistency between different bodies of rules can be ensured; how different sets of rules (or different types of rules) interact; how displacement effects may occur and unanticipated consequences can flow when numerous sets of rules apply simultaneously to an activity; how particular types of rule (e.g. public laws) can be used in order to encourage the constructive use of other types of rule (e.g. contracts); how the effects of rule interactions can be predicted and managed so as to produce fairer, more efficient and more accountable government.

It is similarly the case that turning the research spotlight on linkages between 'public' and 'private' governmental rules has promoted an impressive body of scholarly activity. One line of research has focused on the 'contracting state' (Harden, 1992) and the special problems of ensuring that rule-making activity is fair, transparent, and accountable when bodies of rules that are based on private contractual models are used for public purposes. Such inquiries, moreover, have, as noted, prompted scholars to investigate whether traditional, or 'democractic', notions of accountability have to be reformulated in order to take on board both the private law or market-based structuring of relationships and the combining of different types of rules—some emanating, perhaps, from central departments of government and public in nature, others flowing from relationships between private contracting parties. How accountability can be ensured by different mechanisms which overlap and act simultaneously (the 'redundancy' issue) is a particular area of study. Where, moreover, the operational functions of government are hived-off to agencies, and novel forms of public management are adopted, new rule-forms have developed and, again, prompted research. The 'Next Steps' agencies that developed in the UK in the 1980s are a case in point. These bodies were established in the belief that the delivery of services was a task that could be separated from policy-making and given to agencies with remits to operate managerially under a Chief Executive. These providers of service were to be subjected to 'market-based' rather than 'public' models of accountability but policies were to be guided by a new form of rule—the framework document. These documents are issued by Ministers and set out jurisdictional and organizational matters as well as terms of reference for the executive agencies. They are, however, informal in nature and this has raised questions about the ability of the courts to review them. On this point they contrast with systems of statutory policy guidance which are clearly viewed by the courts as reviewable—as has been seen in cases such as *Laker Airways v Department of Trade* ([1977] QB 643).

The governmental strategy of delegating regulatory rule-making functions to private sector bodies has raised issues that Australian socio-legal scholars, in particular, have been concerned to explore. The model of 'enforced self-regulation' is an example of such a strategy. It envisages that in some regulatory contexts it is 'more efficacious for the regulated firms to take on some or all of the legislative, executive, and judicial regulatory functions' (Ayres and Braithwaite, 1992: 103). Such firms might thus devise their own regulatory rules, monitor themselves for non-compliance, and indulge in enforcement activity; but the exact allocation of functions would depend on the industry's structure and its past record of compliance. The pursuit of 'smart regulation' is similarly concerned to set up the best mix of regulatory instruments, with business, commercial, or third parties acting 'as surrogate or quasi-regulators, complementing or replacing government regulation' (Gunningham and Graboski, 1998: 15).

Such efforts to obtain the best mixes of public and private, and legislative as well as enforcement, strategies raise, in turn, a host of further issues that scholars have investigated. These include such questions as: how it is possible to identify optimal mixes of strategy; the conditions under which particular strategies (such as enforced self-regulation) are more desirable than others; how dangers of capture can be controlled in 'mixed' arrangements; how the courts should view privately produced rules; and how we might assess the likelihood that a given institution will be able to operate such a strategy in the public interest.

A more dramatic way of moving government away from a reliance on traditional forms of rules is to institute new 'post-bureaucratic' modes of government—an approach exemplified by Osborne and Gaebler's bestseller *Reinventing Government* (Osborne and Gaebler, 1992). This work points to a host of examples of 'entrepreneurial' government to be found at locality, city, state, and federal levels. This is a style of public management that is said to differ from, and to offer more than, traditional governmental methods in a number of ways. The old style of government (on the bureaucratic model) is said to have developed in the industrial era and to be sluggish, centralized, preoccupied with rules and regulations and marked by hierarchical chains of command. It is ill-fitted to the modern world and is cumbersome, expensive, and unresponsive. Entrepreneurial governments, in contrast, do not focus on rules and regulations—they are driven by goals or *missions*. In addition, they promote competition between service providers; place controls in the hands of communities rather than bureaucracies; measure outcomes and performance rather than inputs; and redefine their clients as customers who are to be offered choices. Osborne and Gaebler also note how entrepreneurial approaches seek to prevent problems from emerging (rather than react to these); they seek to generate income (rather than merely spend); they decentralize authority by adopting participatory modes of management and they prefer market to bureaucratic mechanisms. Public services, in this approach, should not simply be provided by public bureaucracies but should result from strategies of catalysing all sectors, public, private, and voluntary so that community problems are solved. Government thus is seen as a process of 'steering' rather than 'rowing.'

An example demonstrates the contrast between traditional and entrepreneurial (or bureaucratic and post-bureaucratic) government. In the former, a federal housing and development department operates public housing with reference to a voluminous book of regulations; in the latter, a non-profit subsidiary is set up with a comparatively small staff and a broad-ranging discretion to use contracting-out or a variety of other methods to achieve its mission (Osborne and Gaebler, 1992: 108–9).

The claims made on behalf of entrepreneurial government are numerous. It is said by its proponents to be more efficient, effective, innovative, flexible, and rewarding than traditional rule-driven government. Such a movement away from rules does, however, confront legal and other scholars with an acute set of issues. The discretions and decentrings involved in entrepreneurial government demand that a good deal of faith is placed in markets and new approaches to accountability—in particular, on the potential of information technologies and performance measurement devices to offer transparent and effective modes of holding to account. High levels of participation and decentring in government raise questions about the coordination of inputs from different sources and the equal treatment of these. Where, moreover, performance measurers look to consumer responses, some observers may worry that imbalances of consumer access and power may distort evaluations. A further serious issue is whether democratic control over objectives can be achieved in the face of the market orientation and economic incentives that entrepreneurial government embraces, or by focusing on outcomes that are defined in terms of broad missions. Finally, it should be noted that tensions exist within entrepreneurial government—a movement, for instance, away from state service delivery and in the direction of contracting out or regulated private service delivery may itself produce strong pressures to develop new rule-based regimes of control.

Numerous other scholars have developed the post-bureaucratic line of argument and given it their own imprint. Influential amongst these approaches is the notion of 'democratic experimentation' (Dorf and Sabel, 1998). This strategy involves a change in rule use so that the central state legislative body does not lay down detailed command-based standards but authorizes and finances experimental reforms by states and sub-national jurisdictions. These bodies are broadly free to set goals and choose the means to attain them. Authorization to set such goals is conditional on the experimenters declaring their objectives and performance measures and refining these through deliberative processes. Information on performance is to be made openly available and the courts are to protect the process and constitutional rights of individuals. Comparisons with the performance of other governmental bodies would be mandated and this would generate debates about the relative success of different experimental strategies. In the regulatory context, agencies would set out, and ensure compliance with, national objectives by means of best-practice performance standards based on information that regulated entities provide in return for the freedom they are given to experiment with solutions they prefer. Governmental institutions and affected parties gain information by monitoring and comparing the actions and techniques of different bodies. They thus engage in a new form of deliberation based on experimentation and benchmarking and this, it is claimed, enhances accountability and participation as well as adaptability, learning, and efficiency.

As with the entrepreneurialism of Osborne and Gaebler, democratic experimentalism's revised approach to rules makes a number of assumptions that socio-legal scholars will be concerned to scrutinize. Some notable issues are: whether experimentation will simply favour the already well-placed and powerful; the conditions under which the ill-placed will be adequately protected; and whether the approach will reproduce familiar problems of legalism. Further questions are whether such regimes will generate information for benchmarking that is adequate, accurate, and accessible; whether (and when) governmental and private bodies will possess incentives to participate in information and strategic exchanges; whether they will do so in good faith; whether the system will produce a 'race to the bottom' and a lowering, rather than a raising, of standards; whether new experimental modes of public management will be generated rather than familiar strategies defended; and whether the system will lead to excessive fragmentation, poor coordination, and uncertainty in governmental rule-making.

Turning to the notion of decentring as multi-layered government, European lawyers have for some time investigated how European laws, and Directives in particular, can be used to achieve the best of two worlds—on the one hand, to give Member States freedom as to the way in which domestic legislation is used to achieve EU-mandated objectives and, on the other, to create regimes of rules in which there is overall effectiveness combined with a degree of harmony across Europe. Scholars have examined developments in EU rule use with special vigour since the Commission adopted the New Approach to technical harmonization in 1985. They have looked *inter alia* at the numerous harmonization strategies that are encountered in the EU; the difference between the challenge of harmonizing Member State's transformations of EU law into domestic law and that of harmonizing the enforcement of those domestic laws; the influence of the subsidiarity principle on allocations of legislative functions; and the various legitimacy issues surrounding EU rule-making.

The progression of harmonization strategies and the introduction of innovative techniques of rule use is thus a fruitful area of study for European legal scholars and it is an area of interest that has echoes in studies of intra-state devolution. British scholars, for instance, have looked at the devolution of powers to Northern Ireland, Scotland, and Wales and (particularly regarding the latter) have explored how new forms of quasi-legislation have been developed in order to manage the devolved constitutional structure of the United Kingdom. Thus, it has been argued that 'concordats' have come to serve a key role within new legislative regimes. These new forms of quasi-legislation or 'bureaucratic law' are reinforced with further levels of guidance and offer codifications of the previously internal processes of government. They establish the ground rules for administrative cooperation as well as for information exchanges between Whitehall and the devolved bureaucracies. They have been called the 'glue of a reinvented Union State' (Rawlings, 2000). They are, however, devised and applied at a distance from external inputs and scrutiny and, as a fresh species of rules, raise newly framed issues of transparency and accountability as well as of effectiveness in managing jurisdictional interfaces.

4 DIRECTIONS AND AGENDAS

Legal scholars will continue to wrestle with many of the above issues for as long as governmental rules are used. Important ongoing debates will deal with such matters as whether notions of legitimacy and accountability have to be revised in order to cope with developments in rule types, rule use, and choices of rule-maker; how rules can best be used within networks of regulators and other governmental actors; how rules can both cope with and facilitate the operation of government at a variety of levels—from local to supranational; and how best to divide rule-making and en-forcement activities across public and private bodies.

Recent scholarly discussions, moreover, point to a number of issues that are likely to occupy a special and growing prominence in forthcoming academic and policy concerns. Three can be focused on here: the question of how participation can be made to work; the place of economic appraisals in rule-making; and the special problems of using rules to manage risks.

4.1 Making Participation Work

A salient issue in many jurisdictions is how to ensure that rule-making processes can be designed so as to cope with apparently ever-growing popular appetites for access and participation. What is already clear from existing studies is that a wide variety of approaches to participation can be seen across states. In the United States, for instance, there is a long history of negotiated rule-making (Harter, 1982) and this is a process that has been legitimized in the Negotiated Rulemaking Act of 1992. Negotiated rule-making procedures combine with those set down in other US legislation, such as the APA, to institutionalize broad participation in a way that is not reflected in other states such as Britain, where negotiatory and participatory processes are often informal, or Germany, where formal regulations tend to be pro-mulgated in processes that do not allow wide access (Ziamou, 2001: 103–21).

As for making participation work, there is an increasing scholarly awareness that this requires more than allowing a wide variety of parties to have their say. 'Democratic experimentation' offers, as noted, one canvassed route to enhanced participation and deliberation and a large number of commentators have discussed the potential of various 'proceduralist' approaches to the design of deliberative processes. In certain of these accounts, a distinction is drawn between 'thin' and 'thick' proceduralization. In the former, procedures are aimed at producing bargains and compromises but they offer little assistance in helping parties involved in regulation to understand each other's world-views or languages. In 'thick' proceduralization, participation is 'oriented towards the mutuality, consensus and inter-subjective understanding of deliberative democracy' (Black, 2000: 599). This is where greater hope is seen to lie—in developing processes that enable and enhance deliberations involving parties with very different perspectives. Central here is the potential of processes of deliberation that seek to deal with the difficulties that arise when participants from different interpretive communities use different codes, logics, and languages. The answer, according to such approaches, is not to assume that a Habermasian ideal speech situation is possible but to confront the impediments to such ideal situations, to deal with divergent forms of communications, and to come to grips with scenarios in which there will be manipulation by communicants, and parties who lack sincerity and trust in others.

This approach demands that in regulators' and governmental deliberations on rules, discourses between participants may need to be 'mediated' so that differences between the positionings of participants are mapped out and strategies deployed to overcome them. Such mediation will involve 'translation', which is not simply the imposition of an official or dominant language but a process of finding ways of explaining and reflecting on the different logic of various systems or groups in such a way that others can understand.

Proceduralization, as described, offers an approach to making participatory rule-making processes work. But the further issue, for scholars and practitioners, is whether (and under what conditions) this is an approach that can be implemented productively on the ground. If government officials, regulators, or private sector rule-makers are looked to as mediators and translators, questions arise as to their orientation and potential commitment and their ability to work schemes of proceduralization to the general advantage. It can be assumed that these parties will have their own world-views, rationalities, areas of expertise, and technical limitations. Fulfilling the role of translator would demand receptiveness to the world-views of other actors affected by rules (e.g. consumers or service providers). This may make unrealistic assumptions about the disinterestedness of these rule-makers and their commitment to open discourse—their mind-sets may blind them to the rationalities of other parties, never mind impede their acting successfully as translators.

A second danger is that even if rule-makers are committed to the mediation role, they may not possess the knowledge or expertise required in order to unpack and translate the arguments of various groups into forms that others can understand. Nor will they always be able to manage the mediation process in a way that is fair to all parties (who may possess different abilities to participate). They may not have the ability to recognize inclusionary and exclusionary effects or to clamp down on manipulations by the powerful, or other forms of distortion in deliberation. They may, in addition, not be capable of managing deliberations in a manner that is consistent with efficient policy and decision-making. We cannot, for instance, always be confident that such deliberations will produce agreement rather than dissent, or lead to action rather than deadlocks and stultification. Rule-makers, moreover, may be hindered by (and parties may be suspicious of) tensions between their status as rule-makers and their adopted positions as mediators. To be a rule-maker is, after all, associated with possession of legal authority to devise rule-based solutions and to ensure that an ordained regulatory outcome is achieved. Mediation, by contrast, involves making arrangements so that the parties involved in a deliberation can determine the ends and the contents of rules. Critics who are happy for elected legislatures to delegate rule-making powers to specified actors may take the view that the loss of legislative grip involved in proceduralizing is unacceptable.

Much, then, depends on the skill, expertise, and open-mindedness of the rule-maker who adopts proceduralist or deliberative procedures. Here there are ongoing and pressing issues for legal scholars who can be expected to develop our understandings of the bureaucratic, regulatory, and governmental conditions that allow deliberative processes to be incorporated within rule-making. A related concern is to analyse the potential of the various strategies adopted to expand participation while keeping within the rule-makers' democratically endorsed remits. Here legal scholars are likely to draw on other disciplines (notably political science and public management) where foundational studies already exist.

Work in point is that of Mark Moore who has echoed proceduralist as well as post-bureaucratic concerns in putting forward a strongly managerial approach to government (Moore, 1995). Moore's method of pursuing public value is seen in terms of a 'strategic triangle' which, first, declares the overall mission of the organization (cast in terms of public values); secondly, offers an account of the sources of support or legitimacy to be tapped in order to sustain society's commitment; and, thirdly, explains how the enterprise will be organized and operated in order to achieve declared objectives. Within this method, emphasis is placed on the need for public managers (e.g. rule-makers) to diagnose political environments, to mobilize support and resources for their organization, and to enlist the aid of others beyond their organizational boundaries who can help them achieve the results for which they are held accountable.

As for the techniques of political management, Moore describes five, all of which can be applied in rule-making scenarios. *Entrepreneurial advocacy* involves identifying key players and finding ways to mobilize support for the specific choices that managers want to be made. *Managing policy development* is characterized not so much by the advocacy of a particular policy but by managing a policy-making process so as to invest decisions or policies with a high degree of legitimacy, power, and accuracy. *Negotiation* involves persuading others to go along with a policy. *Public deliberation, social learning, and leadership* is a strategy closer to proceduralization and places less emphasis on acting to ensure that public managers' preferred options will be adopted. Instead of using government authority to make policy decisions, this method creates environments in which the citizens who face collective problems can decide together what they would like to do. Finally, *public sector marketing and strategic communication* seeks to advance particular policies by making them comprehensible and enlisting the support and cooperation of those who must work together to produce intended results.

Such strategies offer ways in which officials can exert a degree of influence over public enthusiasm, expectations, divisions of opinions, changes of attitude, lay irrationalities, and even ideas relevant to rule-making strategy. As for whether such techniques are likely, in any given context, to produce acceptable modes of participation in rule-making, it is as well to be aware of their attendant dangers and general weaknesses. Entrepreneurial advocacy may offer policy control but it (and to a lesser extent negotiation) brings the considerable danger that individual officials or groups of experts will advance their own views without due regard for the opinions of others or of the lay public. Moore's other three techniques involve public managers being more open to counter-opinions; but all of these processes (and negotiation) may encounter difficulties when entrenched and opposing views are sought to be reconciled through procedural devices of different kinds. As with proceduralization, there are dangers that parties will not be cooperative, honest, and constructive and that deliberative processes may produce stalemates, bullying, manipulation, dishonesty, and confrontation rather than agreed policies for rules.

Whether rule-making is likely to be improved by such endeavours depends on a number of factors. One such factor is the likelihood that the rule-maker will be able, and disposed, to deploy (and combine) such approaches effectively, and sensitively. Here different strategies make different demands. If entrepreneurial advocacy is used, for instance, a central issue is the openness of the rule-maker and their willingness to adjust the policy to accommodate the voices of others. If, on the other hand, negotiation or public deliberation is employed, a key concern is whether the issues involved lend themselves to the production of a collectively acceptable policy for encapsulation in a rule. Similarly, the parties must be appropriately committed and arranged—they may be too uncooperative or dispersed to allow effective deliberation.

Space here does not allow this discussion to be extended further but enough has been said to indicate that the search for ways to make participation work is one that raises issues of acute concern across disciplines. The questions involved are likely to grow rather than diminish in urgency in the forthcoming years as new approaches to government burgeon and the public becomes ever more interested in making its voice heard within rule-making and other public management processes.

4.2 The Place of Economic Appraisals in Rule-Making

Scholars and governmental bodies have in recent years become increasingly ready to apply a range of values in assessing the quality of government rules. Bodies such as the British Better Regulation Task Force routinely list the need for transparency, proportionality, targeting, consistency, and accountability in governmental and regulatory rules. They also stress the need (explicitly or implicitly), for technical efficiency in the pursuit of mandated ends.

More contentious, however, is the use of cost-benefit testing in (particularly regulatory) rule-making. Many legal scholars have pointed to the array of assumptions that underpin cost-benefit testing and to the dangers inherent in allowing policy to be driven by considerations of allocative efficiency. Elected bodies, it is commonly pointed out, often instruct rule-makers to act in ways that are not wealth-maximizing but are concerned with distributive justice. To override such instructions in the name of allocative efficiency, they argue, counters the democratic voice. Such a mixture of academic debate and government commitment to economic appraisals presents a considerable challenge to ongoing legal scholarship—how to devise methods of incorporating cost-benefit testing into rule-making so that economic appraisals inform but do not drive rule-making processes. This, moreover, is a debate that links to the participation question already discussed. The broad task is to devise participatory processes that not only balance concerns for democratically established objectives, social justice, accountability, and access but which involve deliberations capable of taking on board economic arguments. To this end, suggestions have been made for combining cost-benefit analyses with 'ethical weighting' and other procedures (Shrader-Frechette, 1991), but this is a line of argument with a considerable way to run.

Cost-benefit analyses of rules, it is often pointed out, necessarily involve injustice through their biases in favour of conferring more benefits on those parties who already enjoy favoured positions. This philosophy of 'to those who have, give more' is unavoidable, it is argued, because the best way to maximize wealth or pass a cost-benefit test is to allocate rights to those who already have rights.

Running counter to such arguments, however, are scholarly voices that stress the necessity of bearing costs and benefits in mind when rules are made. If costs and benefits are not considered, it is pointed out, rule-users tend to set out to achieve objectives without knowing the social costs involved or the size of any benefit being aimed for—the basis for action is some kind of blind intuition (Shrader-Frechette, 1991). For their part, many governments have followed the US lead and have committed themselves to using some sort of cost-benefit assessment procedure in their regulatory rule-making processes.

4.3 Rules and Risks

Much governmental and regulatory activity is now seen as concerned with risks. If rule-making is viewed in this way, light is thrown on a series of issues that are of growing concern to scholars. A first return from looking at rule-making through a risk lens is that this spotlights the special difficulties of making governmental rules when problems (or risks) are seen differently by different parties. The rapidly growing literature on risk tells us that perceptions of risks vary from actor to actor and are influenced by a host of factors. It is widely accepted in the socio-legal literature (and increasingly in government circles) that risk assessments cannot be reduced to mechanical, technical, or wholly rational processes—that what counts as acceptable or unacceptable, serious or less serious depends on such factors as social position, degree of perceived control over the risk, and whether a party is exposed to the risk voluntarily or not. Experts, moreover, are confronted with the reality that the lay public possesses 'irrational' attitudes to risks. These impact on rule-making when experts are involved in making rules about risks but when those holding 'irrational' lay opinions also demand that their voices be heard. In the existing literature there are different views on how such expert versus lay, or rational versus irrational, tensions can be managed when rules are to be made. Proponents of the expert/rational approach might be expected to sympathize with Stephen Breyer's proposals that the regulatory rule-making processes should be 'depoliticised' in favour of allowing small groups of experts within government to devise rational priorities for writing rules within risk control programmes (Breyer, 1993). A number of scholars, however, might be expected to object that experts are no more 'rational' than lay persons and that risk priorities have to be seen as perceptual, distributional, and political matters that must be negotiated through exchanges of views rather than laid down from on high by experts making hidden value judgements.

The ongoing challenge, again, is to devise rule-making processes that can cope not merely with all the 'normal' challenges posed by deliberation but also with differences in risk perceptions. Existing work on risk, moreover, tells us that certain risks may produce special problems for those who would negotiate or deliberate on rules. Joyce Tait, for instance, has distinguished between 'interest-based' conflicts about risks and 'value and ethics-based conflicts' (Tait, 2001). The former conflicts are debated through the currency of scientific evidence, while the latter are founded on arguments formulated mainly on the basis of fundamental values or ethical judgements. Tait argues that whereas 'interest-based' conflicts can usually be resolved by the provision of information, compensation, or negotiation, 'value and ethics' conflicts are very difficult to resolve since, within these, information tends to be viewed as propaganda, compensation as bribery, and negotiation as betrayal.

Designing rule-making procedures that can cope with 'value and ethics' conflicts is thus a particularly severe challenge. It is also one that is likely to grow in scholarly and practical importance as the precautionary principle continues to grow in political influence and as this, in turn, contributes to the construction of an increasing number of risk conflicts on a 'value and ethics' basis.

5 CONCLUSION

This chapter has focused on three themes: choosing between primary and governmental rules; issues of legitimation; and the attuning of rule-making processes to new governmental challenges. The themes, it has become clear, are inextricably linked. A broad thread runs through them all—the need to devise strategies for rule choices and rule-making that can be seen as legitimate and which are capable of dealing with fast-developing modes of government and public management. The challenges involved have been mapped out and include those presented by growing expectations concerning participation; by governmental and other pressures to incorporate economic appraisals into rule-making; and by the increasing need to devise rules that can manage risks acceptably. These newer challenges do not replace, but add to, those longer-established issues that scholars of rule-making have sought to address. Current developments do, however, demand that consideration is given to new ways of thinking about such matters as modes of legitimation and models of accountability. The good news for socio-legal scholars is that our studies of these questions bring us closer to work in other disciplines and that there is no shortage of insights to be drawn from (and, indeed, offered to) those disciplines. Rule-making and its alternatives is a subject of scholarship that should be viewed not as a field increasingly ploughed by the same legal approaches and techniques but as a fast expanding territory calling for new imaginations.

REFERENCES

Ayres, I., and Braithwaite, J. (1992). *Responsive Regulation*, Oxford: Oxford University Press.

Baldwin, R. (1995). *Rules and Government*, Oxford: Oxford University Press.

Bardach, E., and Kagan, R. (1982). *Going by the Book*, Philadelphia: Temple University Press.

Black, J. (1997). *Rules and Regulators*, Oxford: Oxford University Press.

—— (2000, 2001). 'Proceduralising Regulation Part I', *Oxford Journal of Legal Studies*, 20: 597–614; Part II *Oxford Journal of Legal Studies*, 21: 33–58.

Breyer, S. (1993). *Breaking the Vicious Circle*, Cambridge, Mass.: Harvard University Press.

Cappelletti, M., Seccombe, M., and Weiler, J. (eds.) (1986). *Integration through Law*, Berlin: De Gruyter.

Commission of the EC (1985). *Completing the Internal Market*, COM (85) 310 Final, Luxembourg: CEC.

Davis, K. C. (1971). *Discretionary Justice*, Chicago: University of Illinois Press.

Diver, C. (1983). 'The Optimal Precision of Administrative Rules', *Yale Law Journal*, 93: 65–109.

Dorf, M. C., and Sabel, C. F. (1998). 'A Constitution of Democratic Experimentalism', *Columbia Law Review*, 98: 267–473.

Ganz, G. (1987). *Quasi-Legislation*, London: Sweet and Maxwell.

Gunningham, N., and Graboski, P. (1998). *Smart Regulation*, Oxford: Oxford University Press.

Hancher, L., and Moran, M. (eds.) (1989). *Capitalism, Culture and Regulation*, Oxford: Oxford University Press.

Harden, I. (1992). *The Contracting State*, Buckingham: Open University Press.

Harlow, C., and Rawlings, R. (1997). *Law and Administration* (2nd edn.), London: Weidenfeld.

Harris, R., and Milkis, S. M. (1996). *The Politics of Regulatory Change* (2nd edn.), New York: Oxford University Press.

Harter, P. (1982). 'Negotiating Regulations: A Cure for Malaise?' *Georgetown Law Journal*, 71: 1–18.

Hood, C., Rothstein, H., and Baldwin, R. (2001). *The Government of Risk*, Oxford: Oxford University Press.

Lacey, N. (1992). 'The Jurisprudence of Discretion: Escaping the Legal Paradigm', in K. Hawkins (ed.), *The Uses of Discretion*, Oxford: Oxford University Press, 361–88.

Lodge, J. (ed.) (1989). *The European Community and the Challenge of the Future*, London: Pinter.

McBarnet, D., and Whelan, C. (1991). 'The Elusive Spirit of the Law', *Modern Law Review*, 54: 848–73.

McCubbins, M., Noll, R., and Weingast, B. (1987). 'Administrative Procedures as Instruments of Political Control', *Journal of Law of Economics*, 3: 243–77.

Moore, M. (1995). *Creating Public Value*, Harvard, Mass.: Harvard University Press.

Osborne, D., and Gaebler, T. (1992). *Reinventing Government*, Reading, Mass.: Addison-Wesley.

Pelkmans, J. (1987). 'The New Approach to Technical Harmonisation and Standardisation', *Journal of Common Market Studies*, 25: 249–69.

Powell, W., and Di Maggio, P. (eds.) (1991). *The New Institutionalism in Organisational Analysis*, Chicago: University of Chicago Press.

Rawlings, R. (2000). 'Concordats of the Constitution', *Law Quarterly Review*, 116: 257–86.

Shrader-Frechette, K. (1991). *Risk and Rationality*, Berkeley: University of California Press.

Stigler, G. (1971). 'The Theory of Economic Regulation', *Bell Journal of Economics*, 2: 3–21.

Tait, J. (2001). 'More Faust than Frankenstein', *Journal of Risk Research*, 4: 175–89.

Ziamou, T. (2001). *Rule-Making, Participation and the Limits of Public Law in the USA and Europe*, Aldershot: Ashgate.

CHAPTER 33

CIVIL PROCESSES

JUDITH RESNIK

1 FROM CIVIL PROCESS TO CIVIL PROCESSES

FOR much of the twentieth century, the term 'procedure' served as a reference to the processes by which courts made decisions. Courts were assumed to be institutions focused singularly on adjudication, and proceduralists were, in turn, focused exclusively on courts. But by the end of the twentieth century, courts no longer provided only adjudication but also offered an array of other processes. Further, through professionalization and administrative expansion, judiciaries had developed into corporate actors capable of pressing specific agendas about their own forms and charters. Scholars interested in civil processes were no longer able to cluster about a single topic, Procedure, nor could they focus solely on the processes for adjudication. Rather, they had come to understand that many venues (including administrative agencies in the public sector, arbitration in the private sector, and transnational bodies) were central sources of procedural rule-making and invention.

This chapter charts and analyzes the shifts in civil processes during the twentieth century by examining sequences of reformation and critique during which calls have been made for more, for less, and for different forms of process. I begin by contrasting different modes of process and by exploring the increasingly diverse paradigms of conflicts, which have prompted choices about what kind of process to provide for which kinds of disputes. Through examples from the United States, England, and

Thanks for thoughtful advice are due to Dennis Curtis, Kevin Clermont, Geoff Davies, Diane Orentlicher, Adrian Zuckerman, and Cori Van Noy.

Wales, I examine aspirations for and the critiques of civil processes, which are, in turn, embedded in debates about substantive liability rules, the role of and the market for lawyers, empirical effects, and political conceptions of the utility and propriety of regulation.

A predicate to this discussion is the recognition that changes in legal, political, and economic regimes far-afield from procedural rules often influence the use of civil processes. For example, during the first half of the twentieth century, some jurisdictions required owners of homes and automobiles to carry insurance. Those injured learned to seek compensation, both through their own policies and from defendants with the capacity to pay. The quest for recoupment, in turn, helped to spur a market for lawyers who (when permitted by ethical rules) financed small-scale cases in anticipation of returns on loans through contingent fee arrangements (Yeazell, 2001). And, just as substantive and procedural rules create incentives for certain forms of lawyering, so does the legal profession's structure (policing access to lawyers) influence the shape of procedural rules (Abel and Lewis, 1995).

Assessing the effects, in turn, of procedural reforms also requires sensitivity to a range of non-procedural rules as well as to the political institutions and social movements that spawn them. For example, in many countries, efforts are ongoing to restructure procedural opportunities in the name of reducing complexity, cost, and delay. In some jurisdictions, that struggle comes against a backdrop of an independent and entrepreneurial bar with substantial authority over procedure. Entities opposed to the use of litigation to enforce or create government regulation seek procedural reform in an effort to limit their own liability. In other countries, a minimal tradition of lawyer independence exists, and most of a population lacks access to government-based dispute resolution processes. Reformers want to revamp process to make litigation a means of implementing legal norms. Thus, even when calls for change in different countries are comparable, the implications of restructuring civil processes differ—requiring understanding of political understandings of the import of reforms, the resources available to support them, technical challenges to their implementation, and economic interests seeking expansion or constraint of procedural opportunities.

Assessing procedural debates not only requires sensitivity to particular jurisdictions (Damaska, 1997). Awareness of transnational movements is also needed. Worldwide commitments to—as well as unhappiness with—civil processes can be seen in international and regional treaties and in research from the academy. Increasing interaction among professional classes, driven by both political and economic transactions, are diminishing the structural distinctions between civil and common law countries in professional training, career paths, and tasks for lawyers and judges. Some features of the civil law system (such as extended fact-finding without a concentrated time for a trial and the reliance on a judge to supervise the gathering of information) are beginning to be incorporated in the common law system (relying on exchanges in discovery and the increasingly managerial stance of judges).

Further, initiatives are under way to create procedural norms and sometimes processes that cross jurisdictional lines (Goldstein, 1999; Langbein, 1985). A series of covenants, promulgated through the United Nations, announce rights to fair and public hearings, aimed at protecting economic and personal security and at ensuring equality before the law. Reliance is placed on impartial and independent judges as the iconic protectors of the rule of law, working through transparent processes to which the public has access.

But those judges are also seen as vulnerable. In 1985, in an effort to protect judges against the very governments that deploy them, the United Nations issued twenty 'basic principles on the independence of the judiciary'. Hoping for 'effective implementation', the UN appointed a special rapporteur to monitor compliance through yearly reports addressing corruption, accountability, and independence. In addition, private organizations are forging links among jurists worldwide. Significant foundation support (from the Open Society Institute, the Ford Foundation, and others) has promoted judicial independence projects in efforts to use legal processes to enable societal and political development (*Monitoring the EU Accession Process*, 2001). Courts have also lent their voices through rulings—predicated upon a mixture of constitutional and natural law—holding that a judiciary has a right to independence. Some decisions have required budgets for courts to be insulated from politics or that terms of service for judges be fixed to limit executive and parliamentary control.

In addition to developing a shared jurisprudence of 'the judicial', the UN, region al organizations, the World Bank, and other entities have created new dispute-resolution mechanisms for specific problems (some stemming from treaties on trade, others focused on equality rights) that rely either on court-based or arbitral models (Petersmann, 1999). And, in the late 1990s, the American Law Institute (ALI), working in conjunction with UNIDROIT, launched an effort to draft principles and rules of 'transnational civil procedure', adoptable by a country for adjudication of disputes arising from commercial transactions (ALI, Discussion Draft, 2002). Building on earlier attempts by European procedural scholars (many involved with an international association of procedural law) to harmonize different legal regimes, ALI/UNIDROIT seeks to negotiate differing legal traditions (most prominently those of civil and common law procedures). The proposed regime bears some resemblance to model rules for arbitration but aspires to be court-based—standing in contrast to the proliferation of mini-procedural codes detailed through individual contracts in which parties opt out of government-based dispute resolution either by turning to arbitration organizations or by crafting their own dispute-resolution mechanisms. Thus, unlike traditional comparativist conceptions of 'transplantation' of a distinct feature from one system to another, the newer efforts can be understood as forms of domestication and homogenization.

Some read such developments as the proliferation and juridification of processes, attesting to the corporate power of judges and lawyers, enabled by administrative structures that facilitate their influence in legislatures and their control over process.

But, while transnational political and professional organizations are linking political rights and commerce with formal court-based processes, many of the same institutions are also raising questions about the utility of process, examining the political economy of disputants, lawyers, and judges, and crafting alternatives to reduce formality.

In 2002, for example, a team of academics undertook cross-country comparisons of how, in 109 countries, law processed two kinds of creditor–debtor disputes—one that involved evictions of tenants for failure to pay rent, and another about collection on bounced checks (Djankov *et al.*, 2002). Surveying what it described as the 'largest international association' of law firms, the group sought to measure the effects of 'formalism' in dispute processing, defined as including a rule-based process, staffed by professional judges who were required to accept written arguments, to limit their information through rules of evidence, and to provide legal justification for rulings for appellate review. The researchers concluded that, from the perspective of creditors, formal processes predicted slow processes. Formalism also predicted less judicial efficiency, less access to justice, and lower degrees of honesty and consistency.

Through different research techniques in one country (England), a parallel finding —that simple contracts are not readily enforceable in courts—has been made, there coupled with concern that current reforms of civil processes do not relate to the bedrock problem that most potential disputants have no means of access to any court-based remedy, regardless of levels of formality (Genn, 1999). Such non-disputants are rarely the source of procedural reform because pressures for change in process come, in large measure, from those with the resources to use procedural systems repeatedly—the 'repeat players' who have the capacity to and the interest in playing for the rules (Galanter, 1972). Given the incentives of such repeat players, the concern is that their proposals are either irrelevant, non-responsive, or harmful to those not participating in shaping the process.

Thus, site-specific and global contests emerge from within the particulars of each country and from transnational agreements on process, responding to debates about the role of regulation as contrasted to private ordering, the function of the legal profession, and the capacity and desirability of law to create enforceable rights. Civil processes are one site of the struggle between public and private governance and between state-based redistribution efforts and market-focused mechanisms (Ewick and Silbey, 1998). For some, civil processes ought to be a beacon of justice and embody a society's ideals about equal opportunities and fair allocation of resources. Conflict is, under this rubric, neither pathological nor inefficient but a means for public norms to be understood, applied, and generated (Fiss, 1979). As the materials in Cover, Fiss, and Resnik exemplify, the public derives utility both from being able to bring claims and from being able to watch others in dispute, since the processes themselves express social values (Cover *et al.*, 1988). In this vein, lawyering is a form of social service, and reforms are needed to increase access and to render civil processes more transparent.

For others, reliance on civil processes is evidence of the failure of private ordering; the less such processes are used, the healthier the society. From this vantage point, goals for reform include the internalization of disputes to the immediate participants and a reduction in the visibility of conflict through privatization of processes. Yet other commentators see the use of civil processes as a palliative offered by legal liberalism, committed to sustaining the power of professional and propertied classes while dampening down distress about that very social order. Given such deep conflicts about the utility and propriety of reliance on civil processes, it is not surprising that the current era is filled with disagreement about the import and shape of such processes.

2 MODES OF PROCESSING DISPUTES AND PARADIGMATIC CONFLICTS

2.1 Adjudication, Private Dispute Resolution, and State-Based Incorporation of Private Processes

One mode of civil processes—adjudication—focuses on the state and relies on the personage of the professional judge, sometimes working in conjunction with lay judges or with juries. Such decision-makers are charged with gaining a sufficient quantum of reliable information about a given dispute to render a decision that imposes a rule of law to legitimate the transfer of assets or the imposition of obligations. An alternative mode—private dispute resolution—promotes party-based consent as preferable to adjudication on the theory that parties possess the requisite information and can, at lower costs, obtain appropriate resolutions of their disputes. Under this approach, the parties or their advocates negotiate directly or authorize a third party to mediate or arbitrate their disagreement.

Both of these forms have been familiar long before the twentieth century but the paradigmatic disputes that fell within their respective domains shifted during that century. Private dispute resolution used to be identified with commercial controversies or with conflicts arising inside self-contained communities, sometimes delineated by religion or ethnicity. During the second half of the twentieth century, however, the state embraced private dispute resolution as appropriate for a broad range of disputes. A third mode of civil processing is thus emerging, in which governments require disputants, coming to court, to use non-adjudicatory mechanisms that resemble private dispute resolution but that stem from state-based rules of process rather than from contractual agreements. One might understand this development as the legalization of private processes (with risks of professional domination and greater complexity) or as the privatization of public processes (with risks of diminished transparency and decline in regulatory potential).

2.2 Kinds of Conflicts

Paradigmatic disputes are implicit in modes of civil processes. As noted, private dispute resolution once focused on resolving conflicts among those with pre-existing and ongoing relationships developed through contracts or community. Adjudication, in turn, responded to disputes either among strangers or neighbors claiming rights under law. During the twentieth century, however, the dominance of those images was reduced by several shifts in political and economic organization—the emergence of understandings that the state itself was subject to regulation, the increase in trans- actions among larger-scale economic conglomerates, the conception of women as rights-holders both in and outside of their families, and the availability of technolo- gies illuminating patterns of injuries experienced by large numbers of individuals. New prototypes of disputes have came to the fore (Trubek *et al.*, 1983).

2.2.1 *Civil Disputes between Individuals and the State*

With the growth of regulation and of social welfare programs came efforts by the state to alter the status of individuals—for example, by seeking to terminate parental rights or to reduce state-funded benefits. Individuals, in turn, sought to require the state to meet regulatory obligations—for example, by arguing that state programs violated statutory constitutional mandates. Because such contests pit individuals against their governments, disputants argued that such civil litigants were similar to criminal defendants, and therefore that the state ought to provide civil opponents with formal procedural protections (and, when necessary, state subsidies) to make more equal the capacities and resources of the adversaries.

2.2.2 *Civil Claims Transcending the Nation-State*

In the latter part of the twentieth century, through increasing transnational trade and the nomenclature of 'human rights', the framing of conflicts between individuals and states moved beyond the boundaries of the nation-state. Corporate actors in transnational settings wanted reliable legal regimes. Political theorists conceptual- ized a small subset of claims as premised on rights of personhood to be enforceable domestically or through international bodies. Moreover, from within the boundaries of some nation-states came groups of 'First Nations', arguing that their sovereignty entailed control over their own dispute-resolution processes as well as rights to pro- ceed through national or international processes.

The human rights paradigm incorporated both substantive rights and ideals of fair process, including adjudicatory processes conducted by impartial judges accord- ing defendants (civil as well as criminal) notice of their rights in their own language and, when needed, subsidized legal representation. But adjudication was not the sole mode relied upon for conflicts freed from territorial specificity. International and regional treaties, some related to human rights and others focused on commercial transactions, deploy an array of dispute-resolution mechanisms, ranging from adjudication (at the behest of either nation-states and, increasingly, individual complainants) to arbitration or settlement-focused processes.

2.2.3 *Aggregate Claims*

The increasing dominance of large-scale political and economic units and the visibility of group-based injuries has generated another paradigm of civil disputes: the aggregate claim. One set of exemplary cases involves individuals subjected to state-based regulatory frameworks (prisons, schools, or licensure provisions) and seeking structural reforms. Other cases come from widespread injuries—some involving a single event (a fire or plane crash) and others stemming from long-standing exposure to toxic substances (asbestos or nicotine). Commercial transactions generated yet other species of claims, some between corporate actors and others involving small sums but thousands of injured individuals (fraud or illegal overcharges).

As technology facilitated both knowledge of such harms and identification of the numbers involved, some advocates, scholars, and judges pushed for civil processes to respond. They urged reconfiguration to serve regulatory ends, with private actors and the state posited as potential defendants in adjudicatory proceedings that rely on representatives to bring claims and on the loyalty of lawyers to spearhead and finance them. Some focus on how to turn group-based disputes into group-based settlements, sometimes accompanied by mechanisms to disaggregate and individualize the remedies provided.

In some countries, such aggregate problems seem too far afield from civil processes and more appropriately handled through government regulation, ombudspersons, or state-based law reform. And in others, scholars have used examples of widespread harms to press for radical reconfiguration of dispute processes, to imagine more transformative possibilities—termed healing, restorative, problem-solving, or therapeutic justice (Braithwaite, 2002).

3 DIVERSIFYING DEMANDS AND RESPONSES

Civil processes have had to take into account this mushrooming array of demands—of disputes involving intra-family conflict, small-scale disputes between individuals and the state, grand-scale claims between corporate opponents or by those seeking either major structural changes or damages, and sometimes pressing beyond state boundaries. Responses have varied depending on a country's political structure and culture, the flexibility of its civil processes, attitudes toward social welfare, and its traditions about financing lawyers.

3.1 Manufacturing More Judges in Courts and Using Agencies as Courts

In the United States, for example, the constitutionally inscribed role of the federal courts as a vehicle for promoting national norms and traditions of lawyers as entre-preneurial activists created the backdrop for conceiving of private civil litigation as a part of the regulatory apparatus. Congress created hundreds of new statutory causes of action and increased the number of judgeships protected by guarantees, in Article III of the Constitution, of life-tenure and non-diminution of salary. The number of such 'constitutional judges' grew from around 100 in the early 1900s to more than 800 by the century's end. Yet such growth was insufficient to meet adjudicatory demands, so political invention and constitutional reinterpretation generated new sets of federal judges. Congress authorized life-tenured judges to appoint two groups of 'statutory judges' (magistrate and bankruptcy judges) to serve within the Article III judiciary for renewable terms but without the constitutional attributes of independence—thereby adding a corps of trial judges about equal in number to the life-tenured.

Further, agencies became an important site of adjudication. In 1946, Congress enacted the Administrative Procedure Act, licensing a cadre of 'administrative law judges' and protecting them through a civil service model. Yet others, grouped under titles such as 'hearing officers', 'administrative judges', or 'presiding officers', hold a more ad hoc status. By the beginning of the twenty-first century, within the federal system, about four statutory or administrative judgeships existed for every one life-tenured trial judgeship, and a career ladder for judges began to take shape.

Administrative adjudication also blossomed in England and Wales, where, begin-ning in the 1950s, reliance on administrative tribunals increased with the growth of government programs (Galligan, 1996). Proponents thought that court-based judges, identified with upper-class interests, were wedded to inflexible and overly com-plex procedures. Specially constituted tribunals might instead avoid over-burden-ing courts, unnecessarily involving lawyers, and imposing costs on losers. Founded on hopes of informality and accessibility, more than sixty different types of tribunals came into being to offer specialized decision-making for small-scale claims. By the cen-tury's end, some 2,000 institutions, working through a mixture of reliance on lay and professional decision-makers, rendered a volume of decisions many multiples of that produced by common law courts. Further, the Parliamentary Commissioner Act of 1967 established the office of Parliamentary Ombudsman; in 1974, a local equivalent, the Commissioner for Local Administration, was created.

3.2 Endorsing Alternatives to Adjudication and Multiplying the Sources of Process

Atop full-time additions to the judicial corps and the development of agency-based tribunals, other personnel became central participants in and redefined adjudicatory processes. In 1925, in the United States, Congress enacted the Federal Arbitration Act (FAA), mandating federal courts to enforce arbitration contracts. But judges remained leery of limiting their role in monitoring adherence to national norms, and they declined to enforce *ex ante* agreements to arbitrate federal statutory rights.

Towards the last decades of the century, however, US courts embraced alternatives both from within and from without. Judges lauded arbitration as a flexible, inexpensive method of dispute resolution, and focused on its similarity to adjudication, now reconceived as one of several techniques for resolution of disputes. Judges enforced contracts mandating arbitration programs created by employers, manufacturers, and providers of goods and services. Further, a movement in and beyond the United States developed to bring 'alternative dispute resolution' (ADR) inside courts. Through judicial rule-making and statutory mandates, both court and agency-based services expanded to include arbitrators, mediators, 'neutrals', and other para-judicial officers giving advice to lawyers and litigants or making initial determinations about the validity of claims.

England, with London's dominance as a 'seat' of commercial arbitrations, had long been welcoming of arbitration. During the twentieth century, it revisited the law of arbitration. Debate centered on the degree to which parties were free to craft arbitration regimes or courts were to superintend such contracts for compliance with government-based norms on processes and outcome. The Arbitration Act of 1950 enabled parties to create their own procedural template but licensed judicial oversight to ensure that arbitrators' substantive decisions not result in a commercial law different from that of the English courts. Amendments in 1979 provided some buffer by giving parties the power to forbid, by contract, appeals on the law and by creating presumptions in favor of enforcing awards.

More substantial revisions came through the 1996 Arbitration Act, responding to criticism that English arbitration law had become too cumbersome and inaccessible, too judge-controlled, and hence too uninviting, putting London's historic centrality to international commercial disputes at risk (Mustill and Boyd, 2001). Commentators described the change as transformative in its insistence on party autonomy and its imposition of a 'judicial minimalism' that restricts court intervention. (Judges retain some control over consumer arbitrations by having the power not to enforce 'unfair contraction terms', sometimes defined as those not negotiated individually or creating a significant imbalance of rights between contracting parties.) The hope is for London to remain an attractive venue, welcoming to domestic and international users by permitting parties to seat an arbitration in England, Wales, or Northern Ireland regardless of where the actual arbitration occurs, and appealing to arbitrators by conferring statutory immunity from liability for failures in the services rendered.

The changes in England follow and interact with the creation—through the UN Commission on International Trade (UNCITRAL)—of a model arbitration law, promulgated in the mid-1980s and aimed at harmonizing provisions for international arbitration. UNCITRAL provided what some describe as an 'internal' law of arbitration, creating the format for selecting arbitrators, developing the case, and the terms of awards but neither addressing the governing principles nor the coercive authority of nations to enforce contractual terms. In contrast, the 1996 Arbitration Act provided a code detailing some mandatory and default rules to clarify expectations in the absence of specific tailoring through contract.

Such interactions exemplify the growing influence of federalism and transnationalism on civil processes, formerly conceived to be internally driven (Ladeur, 2002). Both the United States and the United Kingdom have systems in which subnational units (states, or Scotland and Northern Ireland) control their own procedural systems. The United States has been reluctant to permit 'outside' legal regimes to affect domestic requirements (Chase, 2002), whereas the UK has been more welcoming of regional and international regimes. In 1998, Parliament passed the Human Rights Act, making the European Convention on Human Rights (ECHR) the domestic law of the UK as of 2000. Questions are now being posed about the likely effects of ECHR and European Union law, including whether rights of public hearing will have applicability in arbitrations and whether EU understandings of judicial independence, speedy process, and access to justice will prompt court-based constitutional remedies. Further, while aggregate litigation has taken a back seat in the UK to specially commissioned public inquiries or direct government regulation, the increasing presence of EU law and of transnational legal professionals is producing pressures to use such processes for claims once understood as more appropriately subjects of political reform. Proposals for 'representative claims', circulated in 2001, were prompted by the need to implement the European Directive on Unfair Terms in Consumer Contracts. For some, such developments are appropriate reconceptions of common law capacities, while others warn of the specter of 'gouvernement des juges'. The layers of federated legal norms may, in turn, make private venues attractive for those with the resources to shop.

4 TWENTIETH-CENTURY PROCEDURAL REFORMS IN THE UNITED STATES, ENGLAND, AND WALES

As the market for adjudicatory services has expanded (in terms of demand and supply) and as it has diversified (in terms of the kinds of disputes eligible for legal resolution, the range of tasks for third parties, the kinds and quality of processes provided, and the remedies envisioned), choices emerge about which disputes deserve what form of process. Many countries—often invoking the language of 'crisis'—have taken on projects reorganizing their courts, retooling their civil processes, reallocating disputes across venues, and reconfiguring rules on costs and attorneys' fees. In England, the United States, and elsewhere, state-based civil dispute resolution systems are pushing litigants to rely on administrative tribunals and also to settle cases, either through private or court-based non-adjudicatory methods (*Hume Papers*, 1997, 1999). These systems are imbuing judges with discretion to ration procedural opportunities (including appeals) and with authority to engage in techniques other than adjudication—such as management, advice-giving, and mediation. Debates have ensued about which processes are optimal for what kinds of disputes, about whether government ought to subsidize litigants, and about how much access to courts should be permitted.

4.1 The United States

4.1.1 *Trans-substantive Aspirations for Adversarial Process*

The baseline for late twentieth-century critique was established by the great procedural reform project during the first half of the twentieth century, the Federal Rules of Civil Procedure. Under the governing 1934 statute, the Supreme Court gained the power to promulgate rules of practice and procedure that, absent an affirmative legislative override, became effective nationwide. To create those rules, the Court turned to experts—lawyers and judges. The resultant 1938 civil rules eschewed formal procedural distinctions in favor of functional delineations, aimed at easing access and focusing on the substantive issues in dispute. By spanning the country, the new rules created national processes that united federal judges through shared daily practices, which in turn promoted their identity as a distinctive cadre of legal actors. The rules gave those judges a good deal of discretion, and, when courts subsequently adopted individual calendar systems, judicial authority over case processing resulted in the embrace of managerial judging.

The 1938 Rules thus represented a commitment to nationalization, to uniformity, to simplification, and to expertise. The scholarly and legal currents that supported this project have been conceptualized (at least in hindsight) as part of a progressive project promoted by individuals having faith in facts and government. The reworkings of procedure were concurrent with a larger movement committed to governance through increasing reliance on federal courts and agencies to enforce national norms in a milieu appreciative of managerial expertise. Constitutional interpretation looked favorably upon court-based processes; statutory provisions were understood as preferring adjudication to other forms of disposition, and courts were committed to streamlining and 'modernizing' their processes to meet growing demands (Resnik, 2000).

For several decades, this model was admired and its aegis expanded. More than half of the states formatted rules to resemble the federal system. Further, during the 1960s and 1970s, the template provided by the Federal Rules was applied to the administrative context. The Supreme Court—borrowing Professor Charles Reich's insight that statutory entitlements were forms of 'property' to be protected from state deprivation by 'due process of law'—required agencies making decision about individual entitlements to employ judicial modes of process to ensure fairness (Reich, 1964).

4.1.2 Problems of Access and Equipage: Individual and Aggregate Responses

Equality problems haunt all procedural systems, and those that rely on party-based fact gathering and preparation are especially dependent upon the capacities of adversaries. As more individuals and groups (and specifically those who were poor or subject to other forms of subordination) came to be understood as rights-holders, their lack of resources tested a procedural system that sought to justify outcomes based on information generated by disputants. During the 1960s and early 1970s, some efforts were made toward equipping litigants with resources. The Supreme Court interpreted the constitutional guarantee of counsel for criminal defendants as requiring government to provide indigent defendants with lawyers, funds for expert evidence, and transcripts to enable appellate review. Scholars and activists offered theories of why constitutional mandates of due process and equal protection ought similarly to protect at least some civil litigants. They found a judiciary occasionally sympathetic to a specific example—such as poor litigants seeking to divorce spouses but unable to pay filing fees. But advocates could not convince the federal judiciary to analogize problems of inequality based on poverty to those based on race, to which equal protection analysis applied. Moreover, the federal judiciary was leery of understanding due process guarantees as requiring subsidies for the many litigants handicapped by having fewer resources than their opponents.

But claims about the problems of unfair limitations on access to justice—linked more generally to a 'war on poverty' and the advancement of civil rights—obtained support for a few decades in the legislature. In 1974, Congress created the Legal Services Corporation to provide lawyers for community-based offices and for 'back-up centers' charged with thinking about how legal regimes affected the poor. Congress also denominated certain kinds of plaintiffs as serving public ends and thereby deserving of reimbursement for litigation fees and costs, often through one-way shifts from losing defendants to victorious plaintiffs.

Procedural rule-makers also played a role in facilitating access. For example, revisions in 1966 to the class action rule authorized self-appointed individuals (and their lawyers) to bring cases on behalf of hundreds or thousands of others, similarly situated, who might not know or be able individually to pursue claims of right.

For some attorneys, working on behalf of litigants seeking institutional reform, statutory fee-shifts would fund their work, if successful. Others hoped to obtain large court-awarded fees through the equitable doctrine that co-plaintiffs, gaining monetary benefits through the work of representatives, had to pay those lawyers a 'percentage of the fund' generated. While the contingent fee system had provided a modicum of access for individual plaintiffs, the growth of aggregate damage litigation spurred the market for large-scale plaintiff-based tort work. As tort lawyers began to form collectives, they gained—for the first time—the economic resources to challenge industry practices.

These changes in civil and social processes both reflected and contributed to different understandings of the possibilities of adjudication. Court-based enforcement of federal law appealed to Congress, which authorized litigants to bring a widening array of lawsuits, and caseloads grew (Heydebrand and Seron, 1990). Sometimes the new statutory regimes came with built-in processes, often located in agencies. Statutes often created specified procedures for a particular kind of lawsuit, departing from the framework of trans-substantive procedures controlled by the courts. Further, the class action rule, complemented by other forms of aggregation, spawned the development of the 'big case', a genre of its own, prompting 'manuals for complex litigation' to detail methods of handling such litigations. At the other end of the spectrum, special procedures were developed for prisoners, claimants under federal benefit systems, and *pro se* litigants.

Legal scholarship debated whether the changing case-load included new forms of litigation or whether familiar templates had been adapted to handle new groups of claimants. For some, the civil rights injunction represented an innovation, no longer bi-polar, no longer retrospective, no longer party-driven because the judge was at the helm (Chayes, 1976). For others, such configurations resembled familiar formats used for probating wills, reorganizing railroads, and proceedings in bankruptcy. The novelty came from their adaptation for newly endowed groups of claimants (prisoners, welfare recipients, and schoolchildren) seeking future-looking decrees to restructure institutions, and for groups of tort victims, seeking to share large settlements to remunerate a cohort suffering comparable injuries. Moreover, such scholars argued, the increasing centrality of the judge to the processes of litigation was not a phenomenon limited to the 'big case' or the structural injunction. Rather, the managerial model was becoming a familiar facet of all federal cases (Resnik, 1982).

Legal scholarship thus attended to right, remedy, and scale of civil litigation but focused less on the structural implications of other profound shifts in civil processes, such as the proliferation of the kinds of judges. As Congress was authorizing more and varying kinds of lawsuits, Congress was also authorizing more and differing kinds of judges, many of whom did not enjoy much by way of the structural or individual independence that had been a signature of federal adjudication. The life-tenured judges, in turn, shaped legal doctrines accepting of administrative judging, of diminishing roles for juries, and of replacing both judge and jury by publicly sponsored and privately based ADR programs.

4.1.3 *Failing Faith in Adjudicatory Procedure*

During the last decades of the twentieth century, the celebration of the processes embodied in the 1938 Rules was replaced with the language of crisis, coupled with calls for restricted entry, limited access to information, and shifting litigants away from adjudication and towards other forms of dispute resolution. The critiques stem from a range of intellectual and political traditions.

Insufficient Fairness and Equality. Some objections came from those committed to the rubric of adjudicatory civil processes but wanting to take better account of economic disparities, discrimination against individuals based on their identity, and the many challenges of rendering legitimate judgments. The procedural system was faulted for not doing enough to facilitate rights-claiming, not only for the poor but also for large segments of the middle class. But legislatures refused to respond with sufficient subsidies. Further, well-heeled opponents convinced Congress to impose severe restrictions on lawyers for the poor. Similarly, courts narrowed fee-shifting rights, refused to compensate attorneys for the risk of taking contingent claims, and curbed access enabled through class actions.

Others worried that courts were populated by governing elites inhospitable to claimants identified as occupying disfavored statuses. Although the demography of court users (both voluntary and involuntary) had shifted, the composition of judiciaries and of the legal profession had not changed as much, resulting in judiciaries often more than 80 percent white and male. The response, begun in state courts during the 1980s and 1990s, were projects to identify sources of 'bias' in the courts and to redouble efforts to enhance 'fairness', in terms of drafting codes and rules focused on civility in courtroom interactions, providing more translators, changing employment practices, and to a much lesser extent, altering substantive legal practices (Ninth Circuit Gender Bias Task Force, 1994).

Yet another source of friendly concern came from social science empiricism on cognitive processes. Psychologists explored how individuals and groups make decisions and interrogated procedural forms to assess whether to alter modes of presentation, rules of evidence, and the numbers and background knowledge of decision-makers. Some courts turned to scientific panels, admitted or refused expert testimony, or attempted to change procedures for juries.

Insufficiently Inclusive, Relaxed, or Creative Process. Another critique moved away from the 1930s adjudicatory mode but did not debate its aspirations for easy access to process. Rather, under an umbrella of humanism, communitarianism, and social welfare concerns, commentators objected to the depersonalization, objectification, and distance that they associated with courtroom formality and its dependency on legal professionals. Arguing for more user-friendly, less adversarial processes, posited as capable of producing more useful remediation, these critics sought to re-center process on the disputants' voices and goals. The movement embraced ADR as more generative than adjudication. While one form of critique sought to supplement adjudication by opening 'many [other] doors', another saw trial as requiring extravagant investments of resources to yield imperfect states of knowledge and unhappy participants.

This movement's success, if measured through formal rule changes, institutionalization, and support from lawyers and judges, has been substantial. The 1938 Rules were amended to direct judges to promote ADR; new statutes were written to authorize court-annexed arbitration, and legislatures mandated the use of ADR in agencies. Institutions supporting ADR proliferated, convening conferences, proffering services, teaching law school classes, and shaping model rules, including, in 2001, a Uniform Mediation Act.

An alternative metric is empirical, attempting to ascertain the use of ADR processes and their costs, speed, and responsiveness to disputants' needs. Surveys of lawyers found that, aside from case-management and judge-run settlement conferences, courts in fact provided relatively few ADR services. Studies also found that ADR imposed costs (in terms of lawyers' time and energies) and—through strategic exploitation—could slow negotiations. Whether more lawyer or judicial investment yielded better process or outcomes has been difficult to measure, spawning a debate about why and when to advocate various kinds of ADR. Further, research on litigants undercut the claim that adjudicatory proceedings were as alienating as some had posited. Studies found that litigants liked to 'tell their stories' and preferred more formal processes, identified as dignifying the participants and treating them impartially (Lind and Tyler, 1988).

Too Much Process. A different kind of critique worried that the system has provided too many opportunities for process. These concerns regard twentieth-century aspirations for lawyer-based production of information to yield good and reliable outcomes as simplistic, superseded, or wrong. Game theorists and economists analyzed such processes and their efficiencies (Shavell, 1982). Critics pointed to rules of discovery, crafted before photocopying and computers were commonplace, which could not have envisioned the massive amounts of information generated, stored, or hidden. Such rules enabled lawyers to garner profits from production and obfuscation and created incentives to build large law firms fueled by associates clocking hourly bills. Commentators argued that aggregation rules were overly optimistic about the capacity to group similarly situated individuals in collectives that could be adequately represented through a single or small numbers of self-elected or designated advocates. Critics argued that strategic acting by attorneys for plaintiffs and by defendants in search of 'global peace' yielded judgments protecting both sets of interests at the expense of either those injured or the public.

Undersupervised Processes and Lawyers. Another critique fastened on sloppiness, inattention, ineptitude, inexperience, and misuse, attributed to lawyers engaged, with a range of motives and skills, in strategic interaction. As pre-trial and discovery rules made these problems more transparent, judges argued that they should take on a managerial role. Through formal redrafting of rules and energetic teaching programs, judges and other court personnel gained control over the pre-trial phase.

Managerial judges found themselves intrigued by the possibility that their oversight could not only reduce waste on the way to trial but also produce settlements, aborting litigation altogether. Court-based settlement efforts, once termed 'extra-judicial', became regular features of civil processes. The definition of the 'good judge' came to be the judge focused on and able to achieve dispositions, and trials came to be described as 'failures' of the system that ought to be producing settlements. Although popular culture proliferated images of trials, in legal civil processes they became increasingly rare. By the century's end, fewer than 3 percent of all federal civil proceedings ended with a trial by either judge or jury. The data for state courts were similar—that juries reach verdicts in fewer than 5 percent of contract and tort disputes.

4.1.4 *Civil Processes Reconfigured*

Thus, a range of constituencies produced critique, and a subset succeeded in reformatting processes. The aspiration for trans-substantive uniformity of the 1938 Rules has been rejected—through amendments made by the judiciary, carving out special processes for different kinds of cases and detailing local and varying rule regimes; by Congress, requiring that certain litigants use subject-matter-specific processes; by contract, creating a multitude of dispute-resolution programs. Within the academy, the plausibility of such aspirations have been undermined as the image of public-spirited expert judges and lawyers, presumed able to craft processes neutral as between opposing litigants, has eroded during the sixty years of practicing under the rule-making regime. Strategic repeat players within the litigation system have learned to lobby such rule-makers or to go to Congress to intervene at their behest. For example, while misuse of the discovery system was documented in only a small segment of cases, critics harnessed images of exploitative lawyers and of overwhelming quantities of data and successfully argued for rule revisions reducing access to information and increasing court authority over its exchange. Similarly, while class actions have a complex track record, opponents focused attention on those cases in which lawyers were paid vast sums of money in contrast to negligible recoveries of individual plaintiffs, and succeeded in limiting class action opportunities in federal courts. Of course, just as the expansion of civil processes had not been founded exclusively on premises about process, so the efforts at constriction have not come solely through interest in civil processes. The attack on the adjudicatory mode of the Federal Rules has been coupled with efforts to restrict liability for torts, environmental and consumer injuries, and civil rights.

While I have focused on civil processes at the trial level, changes in appellate process have followed a similar pattern. The right of appeal became enshrined in the later part of the nineteenth century and actualized in the twentieth century through expansion of the number of judges dedicated to appellate work and the development (in both federal and state systems) of intermediate appellate courts, hearing all who filed. A third tier—the highest court—then selected a subset for additional review. The volume of appeals grew, as well as skepticism about its utility. By the later part of the twentieth century, substantial revisions were in place. While appeal as of right remained the law, some scholars argued that, in fact, a discretionary system of review had been put into place. Appellate courts relied on staff attorneys to screen cases; many cases were decided without argument, and fewer than 20 percent of the rulings in the federal system resulted in published decisions. Other scholars worried that the freedom gained by the Supreme Court during the twentieth century to select the cases it would decide had negative effects on the Court's jurisprudence, prompting an inappropriate set of rules for lower courts, too ready to oversee Congress and too constrained to remediate in individual cases.

4.2 England and Wales

England has had a long history of self-consciousness about its own procedures. By one calculation, during the twentieth century, some sixty official reports were commissioned to evaluate civil processes, and specifically problems of access, cost, delay, and complexity. Further, England was in the forefront of conceiving of access to civil justice as a right. In 1949 legal aid became available as an entitlement for individuals seeking to use civil processes (Regan *et al.*, 1999). During the late 1990s, England substantially revised both its civil and appellate rules and its legal aid system. As noted, England also expanded its reliance on administrative adjudication, enacted new arbitration legislation, and made the ECHR a document with domestic legal application. Commentators see these reforms as aimed at the costs of disputing, attributed both to party control over and to the complexity of process. Responses have been to limit state-funded lawyering, to direct attorneys towards settlement and ADR, and to give judges more authority over the pace and shape of litigation.

4.2.1 *Lawyers' Services and Access to Civil Processes*

The 1949 Legal Aid Program, termed by scholars as the 'most ambitious' in the world, was initially responsive to need. Upon obtaining certificates of eligibility based on means, clients could obtain assistance from the private bar, paid according to a schedule of fees and protected against the 'English rule' requiring reimbursement of victorious opponents. According to one study, within the first four years of the 1980s, the legal aid budget grew from some £100 million to more than £250 million, with most certificates related to family matters. By the mid-1990s, civil legal assistance cost about £600 million. Public funds represented significant percentages of private lawyers' incomes.

But the growing budget also made visible the high costs of using civil justice processes. One response was to limit eligibility, which fell from 80 to 40 percent of the population. In the 1990s, two more fundamental changes occurred. Through legislation styled 'The 1999 Access to Justice Act', the open-ended features of England's Legal Aid system ended. And, based on a 1996 report, also labeled *Access to Justice* (called the Woolf Reforms), civil processes were revised in an effort to constrain cost and delay.

The 1999 Access to Justice Act abolished the Legal Aid Board and created in its stead a Legal Services Commission (LSC) to work through decentralized groups, Community Legal Services (CLS) and the Criminal Defense Service (CDS), charged with assessing local needs, identifying lawyers eligible for providing services, and requesting funding. Budgets came with annual caps, resulting in the rationing of services and further restrictions on eligibility. Criminal defense services headed the priorities, followed on the civil side by lawyers for disputes involving children, housing, and personal violence in homes. The 1999 Act also identified a few new areas of need (such as immigration proceedings) and attempted to enhance use of technologies (such as a website for the Citizens' Advice Bureaux (CAB)) to provide information on legal processes and rights.

Through 1999 revisions of ethical rules, some claimants unable to obtain Legal Aid gained a new means to obtain lawyers' assistance. England relaxed its ban on contingent fees by permitting 'conditional fee agreements' (CFAs) that enabled solicitors to take cases despite a risk of non-payment upon losing. 'After the Event' (ATE) insurance became available so that, if necessary, losers could pay victorious opponents, entitled under English fee-shifting rules to indemnification for fees and costs. The incentive to take such work was enhanced by entitling a lawyer for a prevailing plaintiff to the fees paid by the loser and to a bonus, paid directly by the client but limited to no more than 100 percent of the hourly fees and, under rules of the Law Society, presumptively capped at no more than 25 percent of client's damages. Revisions in 1999 permitted the victorious lawyer to recover that 'success fee' from the loser; the client recovers the insurance premium.

Revised legal aid rules and conditional fee agreements may alter the pool of lawyers in the market for representing claimants unable to pay directly. The reforms enhanced the power of LSC, CLS partnerships, and insurance companies, reduced the relevance of legal aid, and increased the focus on the monetary costs of litigation. Some commentators argue that, by changing the pool of lawyers eligible for legal aid payments, quality will suffer and the cadre of lawyers identified with an impoverished clientele will become marginalized. According to these scholars, despite being named the Access to Justice Act, the 1999 reforms restrict entry. Proponents see the utility of the new legal aid rules in developing specialization among lawyers, in turn gaining expertise that will improve quality and reduce delay. Others see the conditional fee system as responsive to the concern about the declining role for legal aid but note that the new conditional fee system may have decreased incentives to reduce overall costs while itself being a source of litigation about fees. Commentary also links the reforms to shifting attitudes towards social welfare, labeled during the 1990s as the 'Third Way' in reference to efforts (under the Blair Labour government in England and the Clinton Democratic administration in Washington) to reduce government spending on entitlement programs.

4.2.2 *The Woolf Reforms*

As noted, revisions in the financing of litigation occurred in tandem with revisions of civil procedure. A 1996 inquiry, chaired by Lord Harry Woolf, argued that a major reorientation was required to curb adversarialism by shifting control over the pace and quantum of litigation away from individual lawyers, by calling for increased use of ADR, by focusing on settlement, and by giving greater authority to judges to manage cases (Woolf, 1996). The 1996 report proposed that lawyers 'front load work' by requiring them, pre-filing, to avoid the need for litigation through discussions with opponents. The report urged that judges, in turn, be given managerial powers to make the costs of proceedings 'proportionate' to the amount at stake. To do so, the report called for detailed 'protocols' (to be developed for different kinds of cases through bench/bar committees) for how to proceed before filing and for assigned 'tracks' with proposed timetables for cases once filed. The report also proposed empowering judges to police compliance and to sanction misbehavior, in part by allocating costs based on assessments of the reasonableness of positions taken during proceedings. In 1999, pre-action protocols and new rules became effective in England and Wales that require claimants to serve pre-filing demands on opponents, who are charged with investigating and replying. Once filed, cases are assigned to one of three tracks ('small claims', 'fast', and 'multi-track').

4.2.3 *Representative and Appellate Processes*

In 2000, civil procedural rules were amended to permit a cluster of claims to proceed under a group litigation order (GLO) for decisions on common law or fact (Andrews, 2001). In 2001, the Lord Chancellor's Department circulated proposed procedures for 'representative claims', prompted in part to enable consumer organizations to challenge systemic unfairness, as required by EU directives. Eighty respondents debated whether the proposal would—for better or worse—import US-style class actions.

Turning to the appellate level, in the late 1990s, a committee chaired by Sir Jeffery Bowman filed its report, Review of the Court of Appeal (Civil Division, Sept. 1997) on civil appellate procedures. Like the Woolf Report, that committee worried about expense, delay, and complexity, and focused on enhancing efficiency. Concerned about rising numbers of appeals, the Bowman Report concluded that leave for appeal was too leniently granted. Opining against any 'automatic right of appeal', the report called for a change in culture through court management, a fast track for certain appeals, and constraints on appeal rights—all to result in process deemed proportionate to the scope of a given controversy. In 2001, restrictions were put into place, requiring permission for almost all civil appeals and cross-appeals and making the decision to permit appeals final. Applicants need to show a real chance for success or 'some other compelling reason'. Grants can be limited to specific issues and accompanied by conditions, such as requiring security for payment of opponents' appellate costs or for the judgment itself.

4.2.4 *Debating the Utility and Rationales for Change*

Academic concerns include opposition to the increased authority and discretion accorded judges, suspicion about the shift away from adjudication, and skepticism about the degree to which reforms will produce change. For some, the revisions are too radical, undoing the best of English practices (Zander, 2000). For others, the new rules have failed to alter the incentives of lawyers and therefore will not constrain the fundamental problem of the cost of process. Further, they predict that the rules will have little impact on the culture of lawyers and judges. Unaddressed, for example, were concerns about the closed nature of the legal profession, the lack of diversity of the judiciary, and the limited routes to appointment of judges, controlled by the Lord Chancellor's office. Work by researchers based at University College London and the National Centre for Social Research suggests a different critique—that, while ordinary individuals believed that law was relevant to their lives, almost none used court-based processes to remediate the many problems they encountered. Eight out of ten surveyed used neither ADR, nor courts, nor sought assistance from ombudspersons. For them, the Woolf and Bowman Reforms have no direct ameliorative effect.

Critics have also focused on administrative tribunals. Just as England has produced numerous reports on court-based procedures, it has also chartered several commissions to review administrative processes. Recent empirical work investigated the claimed advantages and distinctiveness of administrative tribunals (Richardson and Genn, 1994). A study of the Social Security Appeals Tribunals (SSATs) revealed poor first-tier decision-making, a lack of independence of decision-makers, and high error rates that went unchallenged due to claimants' general confusion, lack of knowledge, sense of powerlessness, and stress. Another surveyed the Immigration Appeal Tribunal and concluded that its greater formality and the provision of state-funded representation played a significant role in claimants' success. Researchers found that speed and reduced expenses were associated with losses in fairness, in accuracy of decisions, and reduced consistency—stemming in part from the complexity of regulations. The researchers argued that specialist tribunals were not havens from but depended upon legalism, and that claimants' lawyers appropriately used legalisms as a buffer against inaccurate and unfair decision-making, thereby checking state power.

5 Ambivalence towards Process

This review reveals several cross-currents. First, dissatisfaction with civil processes has become commonplace (Zuckerman, 1999), resulting in a language of 'crisis' that outlasts temporal dimensions implied by that term. A proliferation in the sources and forms of processes has been accomplished, accompanied by sense of a failure to make the kinds of changes required. What is 'required', however, varies substantially with one's vantage point (Zuckerman and Cranston, 1995). The language of law and economics has shifted discussion toward incentives and efficiencies, as those modeling process and empiricists play significant roles in reform activities. However, the simplification entailed in modeling often fails to capture the complexity, variety, and the many constituencies that actual disputing involves. Further, adequate data collection requires both substantial resources and sophistication to identify the import of many variables. And the metrics by which to assess findings are not shared. Some critics rest concerns on usage rates (too much or too little), while others on the distribution of usage, or on costs (variously measured and charged), and yet others on the forms of remediation possible and achieved.

Secondly, given the long menu of civil processes available, choices are in the forefront, and the domain of civil processes is now widely perceived as an arena of social contest. Repeat players—both governmental and non-governmental—understand that civil processes affect regulatory capacity and therefore participate actively in shaping the content and scope of rules. The capacity for endless claims of crisis stems in part from the built-in instability of efforts that express conflicting social and political values. Economy, for example, is in tension with oversight, and the benefits of any particular form of process are not evenly distributed across disputants.

Thirdly, the cost of process—made vivid, in part through efforts to subsidize the poor—has prompted interest in limiting its availability, at both first instance and appellate levels. But expense is not only translated in dollar terms; critics of appellate filings argue that they produce 'too much law'—costly in terms of predictability and consistency. That demands outstrip capacity at the conceptual level can also be seen through concerns about the feasibility of processing small claims. The last century has made vivid the tension between highly individualized inquiries undertaken by relatively visible and costly government actors and the need to produce millions of judgments about disputed claims of obligation and right. An early response was to vest decision-making authority in government institutions other than courts, yet recent analyses worry about the adequacy of agency processes. Another response was to turn to aggregate processing. Experiences with large-scale litigation have, however, exposed both its utility in redressing adversarial imbalances and the temptations for overuse and abuse. Questions focus on the degree of relatedness of claims, the quality of representation, the loyalty of agents often holding economic stakes larger than individual claimants, and the capacity of judges to monitor risks to the absentees—raising problems about the legitimacy of according finality to the outcomes so obtained (Hensler *et al.*, 2000).

Fourthly, substantial pressures exist to shift away from adjudicatory processes, both by turning judges into settlement brokers and by turning to more privatized resolutions (Fiss, 1984). Yet when those processes are heavily used, pressures develop to regularize them through law. Earlier in the twentieth century, agency-based civil processes were seen as a useful addition or alternative to adjudication; critiques resulted in efforts to formalize those processes. Later in the century, court-based and private arbitrations came into vogue, and likewise, some saw these inventions as too unbridled. Repeat players have begun to call for more formality, precedent, and rules, promising predictability. Yet others now criticize ADR as too much subjected to legal constraints and urge a shift to mediation. And, concurrent with privatization come calls for more state-based civil processes, linked to economic and political stability. Federated governments rely on such processes to mediate internal disputes and to implement both national and subnational rules, while private actors use flourishing government-based processes as a metric of a well-functioning social order.

Fifthly, reforms have underscored the centrality of lawyers and judges to developing process and the interdependence of civil processes and the legal and juridical professions. The turn, for example, in the United States, England/Wales, Australia, Canada, and Scotland towards 'case management' comes from a desire to manage lawyers as much as cases. Rules of civil process become prescriptions to lawyers for providing client services and responding to court demands. Merging, thus, are rules of process and lawyers' ethics. Less subjected to constraint—at least under current iterations—are judges, dispatched to superintend the process, imbued with substantial discretion, and largely immune from appellate oversight. The practice of judging has itself shifted, with the increase in reliance on staff, the development of administrative infrastructures, and increasing focus on goals for disposition. Higher status judges retain (and, in some instances, have gained) significant autonomy.

These developments in turn are subject to competing assessments. For some, judicially based civil processes are anachronistic, predicated on an obsolete nineteenth-century individualistic model. As societies organize through bureaucracies and lawyers move toward aggregate practices, judges were still peculiarly functioning as solo practitioners, inefficiently engaging in labor-intensive craft-like work. The judiciary is thus belatedly shifting gears to generate corporate capacity, and from this vantage point, higher court judges are appropriately becoming administrators, overseers, and employers—selecting and dispatching their juniors and rationing court attention. First-tier judges are, in turn, seen as properly engaged in multi-tasking, molding processes and interpersonal techniques to fit needs. Declining percentages of trials and formal appellate rulings become measures of success.

For others, the move to management is a retreat from the promise that, through transparent processes, shared norms will be developed and applied. That faith in governance and expertise persists is evident in professional efforts to format sets of transnational rules to make processes accessible at least to some strata of society. Further, a massive socialization project remains intact that, through television, film, news, and international activities, focuses on the centrality of court-based processes. Yet others, relying on empirical work about usage of public and private process, see both early and late century self-styled 'reforms' as unresponsive and therefore irrelevant to many disputants, who are without the ability to participate in any mode of civil processes.

The changes are also starting to stimulate interest in new sets of questions. For example, given the shift away from common law courts—promoted and supported by common law courts—will judges be able to control their own dockets by attracting the cases they deem 'important'? As the market of dispute providers expands, what institutions will become dominant? Perhaps, in light of infinite volume (or government control over volume through its power over legal claims) and political and economic reliance on government-based processes, courts will retain control. Further, in the twentieth century, some kinds of disputes (workers' compensation, car accidents, and divorce) have cycled into and others out of courts. On the other hand, as judges themselves press to alter juridical modes and resemble other governmental workers engaged in an array of tasks, it is not clear how they will or why they should sustain claims on resources or rights of independence from political oversight.

The proliferation of venues also prompts question about what inventions await. Some argue that all these reforms are just variations on a legal theme, professionally dominated and capable of sustaining its own legitimacy. Others see a natural law of trans-substantive procedure—based in democratic theory and psychological needs—that consistently produces a format involving a hearing, framed by rules of transparency, with an impartial decision-maker limited in its powers. Whether predicated upon state or private authority, civil processes repeatedly shape comparable means by which to enable interaction among parties, the development of information, and the constrained power of decision-makers. But others see this template as culturally specific, missing understandings of justice and remediation that could prompt imagining new forms of proceeding.

A final note is the reminder that a focus on proceduralism ought not to imply an autonomy that does not exist. Reforms of the past century were never 'only' about procedure but were related to the creation of professionalized judiciaries, to the institutionalization of courts as corporate actors within governments, to the development of agendas by academic and practicing lawyers, and to the goals of court users, all as part of country-specific and of transnational social movements.

REFERENCES

Abel, Richard L., and Lewis, Philip S. C. (1995). *Lawyers in Society: An Overview*, Berkeley: University of California.

Andrews, Neil (2001). 'Multi-Party Proceedings in England: Representative and Group Actions', *Duke Journal of Comparative & International Law*, 11: 249–67.

Braithwaite, John (2002). *Restorative Justice & Responsive Regulation*, Oxford and New York: Oxford University Press.

Chase, Oscar (2002). 'American "Exceptionalism" and Comparative Procedure', *American Journal of Comparative Law*, 50: 277–302.

Chayes, Abram (1976). 'The Role of the Judge in Public Law Litigation', *Harvard Law Review*, 89: 1281–316.

Cover, Robert M., Fiss, Owen M., and Resnik, Judith (1988). *Procedure*, Westbury, NY: Foundation Press.

Damaska, Mirjan (1997). *Evidence Law, Adrift*, New Haven: Yale Press.

Djankov, Simeon, La Porta, Rafael, Lopez-de-Silanes, Florencio, and Shleifer, Andrei (2002). 'Courts: The Lex Mundi Project', Harvard Institute for Economic Research (HIER), Discussion Paper No. 1951, Mar.

Ewick, Patricia, and Silbey, Susan S. (1998). *The Common Place of Law*, Chicago: University of Chicago Press.

Fiss, Owen (1978). 'The Forms of Justice', *Harvard Law Review*, 93: 1070–90.

—— (1984). 'Against Settlement', *Yale Law Journal*, 93: 1073–93.

Galanter, Marc (1972). 'Why the "Haves" Come Out Ahead: Speculations on the Limits of Legal Change', *Law & Society Review*, 9: 95–160.

Galligan, D. J. (1996). *Due Process and Fair Procedures: A Study of Administrative Procedures*, Oxford and New York: Clarendon Press.

Genn, Hazel (1999). *Paths to Justice: What People Do and Think about Going to Law*, Oxford and Portland, Ore.: Hart.

Goldstein, Stephen (1999). *The Utility of the Comparative Perspective in Understanding, Analyzing, and Reforming Procedural Law*, Institute of European and Comparative Law, Oxford: University of Oxford.

Hensler, Deborah R., Dombrey-Moore, Bonnie, Giddens, Beth, Gross, Jennifer, Moller, Erik, and Pace, Nicholas M. (2000). *Class Actions Dilemmas: Pursuing Public Goals for Private Gain*, St Monica, Calif.: RAND.

Heydebrand, Wolf, and Seron, Carroll (1990). *Rationalizing Justice: The Political Economy of Federal District Courts*, New York: New York State Press.

Hume Papers (1997). *Hume Papers on Public Policy: The Reform of Civil Justice*, ed. Joelle Godard and David Guild, Edinburgh: Edinburgh University Press.

—— (1999). *Hume Papers on Public Policy: Justice and Money*, ed. Joelle Godard and David Guild, Edinburgh: Edinburgh University Press.

Ladeur, Karl H. (ed.) (2002). *Europeanisation of Administrative Law: Transforming National Decision-Making Procedures*, Aldershort and Burlington, UK: Ashgate.

Langbein, John (1985). 'The German Advantage in Civil Procedure', *University of Chicago Law Review*, 52: 823–66.

Lind, E. Allan, and Tyler, Tom R. (1988). *The Social Psychology of Procedural Justice*, New York: Plenum Press.

Monitoring the EU Accession Process: Judicial Independence in the EU Accession Process (2001). Open Society Institute.

Mustill, Michael J. and Boyd, Stewart C. (2001). *Commercial Arbitration: 2001 Companion Volume to the Second Edition*, London: Butterworth.

Ninth Circuit Gender Bias Task Force, The Effects of Gender: The Final Report of the Ninth Circuit Gender Bias Task Force (1993), repub., *Southern California Law Review*, 67 (1994), 727–1106.

Petersmann, Ernst-Ulrich (1999). 'Dispute Settlement in International Economic Law— Lessons for Strengthening International Dispute Settlement in Non-Economic Areas', *Journal of International Economic Law*, 189–248.

Reich, Charles A. (1964). 'The New Property', *Yale Law Journal*, 73: 733–87.

Regan, Francis, Paterson, Alan, Goriely, Tamara, and Fleming, Don (eds.) (1999). *The Transformation of Legal Aid: Comparative and Historical Studies*, Oxford: Oxford University Press.

Resnik, Judith (1982). 'Managerial Judges', *Harvard Law Review*, 96: 374–448.

—— (2000). 'Trial as Error, Jurisdiction as Injury: Transforming the Meaning of Article III', *Harvard Law Review*, 113: 924–1037.

Richardson, Genevra, and Genn, Hazel (1994). *Administrative Law and Government Action*, Oxford and New York: Oxford University Press.

Shavell, Steven (1982). 'Suit, Settlement, and Trial: A Theoretical Analysis under Alternative Methods for the Allocation of Legal Costs', *Journal of Legal Studies*, 11: 55–81.

Trubek, David M., Sarat, Austin, Felstiner, William F., Kritzer, Herbert M. and Grossman, Joel B. (1983). 'The Costs of Ordinary Litigation', *University of California at Los Angeles Law Review*, 31: 72–127.

Woolf, Sir Harry (1996). *Access to Justice: Final Report*, London: HMSO.

Yeazell, Stephen C. (2001). 'Re-Financing Civil Litigation', *DePaul Law Review*, 51: 183–218.

Zander, Michael (2000). *The State of Justice*, London: Sweet & Maxwell.

Zuckerman, Adrian A. S. (1999). *Civil Justice in Crisis*, Oxford: Clarendon Press.

—— and Cranston, Ross (eds.) (1995). *Reform of Civil Procedure: Essays on Access to Justice*, Oxford: Clarendon Press.

CHAPTER 34

....

CRIMINAL
PROCESS

....

KENT ROACH

1 INTRODUCTION

....

A CASE can be made that the high point of criminal process scholarship was in the 1960s. Inspired by the legal process paradigm of scholarship and the activism of the American Warren Court in criminal procedure, Herbert Packer constructed contrasting due process and crime control models that continue to influence criminal process scholarship to this day. The crime control model described the criminal process as an 'assembly line' run by police and prosecutors resulting in guilty pleas, while the due process model described the criminal process as an 'obstacle course' dominated by defence lawyers and judges who were prepared to acquit accused persons in order to protect their rights (Packer, 1968: 159, 180). The 1960s also saw the development of scholarship, official reports, and teaching materials that eschewed the traditional divide between substantive criminal law and criminal procedure to examine the entire criminal process from the investigation of crime through to its punishment. The focus was on the discretion exercised by various public officials from the police to correctional officials and on various law reforms to better govern that discretion. This approach is sometimes still followed today, but is often criticized for failing to place the criminal process into its broader social, organizational, and political contexts (McConville and Bridges, 1994).

Much contemporary criminal process scholarship reflects less a theoretical or conscious criminal process paradigm, but more a focus on social problems as they affect criminal justice. These social problems are varied and include racism and sexism in the administration of criminal justice. Contemporary criminal process scholarship also features case studies of specific crimes, political cases, and wrongful convictions. Comparative criminal justice scholarship and official public inquiries into criminal justice are also often drawn to the study of the multiple stages of the criminal process. An issue that may at first appear to affect only part of the criminal process frequently implicates other stages. To some extent, examination of the entire criminal process is inevitable whenever scholars and policy-makers attempt to understand criminal justice.

Although criminal process scholarship will continue as an inevitable result of the frequent need to examine the entire criminal justice system and its administration, it will not regain prominence within the academy without two major changes. The first is the development of a more self-conscious and theoretically rich understanding of the objectives and methodologies of criminal process scholarship. Criminal process scholarship needs to regain its sense of identity, including its linkages with the scholarship of the entire legal process. Unfortunately, much criminal process scholarship still eschews theory or relies on the problematic assumptions and limited vision of Packer's due process and crime control models. Criminal process scholars should rethink traditional models and develop new theories of the political, legal, social, and organizational factors that affect the investigation and prosecution of crime.

The second needed change is to expand the boundaries of what constitutes the criminal process. Traditional criminal process scholarship has focused on the police, defence lawyers, prosecutors, judges, and correctional officials. These public officials continue to play important roles that deserve study, but an exclusive focus on them will result in a dated and impoverished approach to the criminal process and one that is excessively oriented to law and organizational reform. There is a need to examine other actors and systems that affect the investigation and prosecution of crime. They include the private police, insurance companies, schools, the media, non-governmental organizations, legislators, immigration officials, and various international bodies. The very notion of what constitutes and shapes the criminal process, as well as the disciplinary range of criminal process scholarship, should expand. A broader approach will not only enrich the empirical study of the criminal process, but also force scholars to examine the limitations of existing theories of the criminal process and to develop new ones.

2 ORIGINS OF THE CRIMINAL PROCESS APPROACH

If criminal process scholarship is to have a better sense of identity and a more vibrant future, it must first understand its past. Criminal process scholarship should be placed into the evolving traditions of legal scholarship.

2.1 Sociological Jurisprudence and Legal Realism

The origins of criminal process scholarship lie in sociological jurisprudence and legal realism. Sociological jurisprudence examined the administration of the law or the 'law in action'. In a number of his writings about criminal justice, Roscoe Pound called attention to the important role of discretion in all phases of the criminal process and the danger of abuse in the exercise of the discretion. He argued that a lack of coordination between the multiple actors of the system resulted in 'administrative anarchy' (Pound, 1930: 177). His answer was to advocate centralization and apolitical expertise in the administration of criminal justice. Pound's optimistic faith in expertise and proper institutional design persisted into the 1960s, but is now rejected by most criminal process scholars. Nevertheless, his work established the need for studying the administration of criminal justice from policing through to corrections with particular attention to the exercise of discretion by criminal justice actors.

Some scholars influenced by legal realism in the 1930s and 1940s continued to study discretion in the administration of criminal justice, but took a more critical approach to institutional failures by focusing, for example, on how various actors contributed to wrongful convictions. Karl Llewellyn took an even more creative approach. Drawing on his study of dispute resolution among an aboriginal tribe, Llewellyn constructed contrasting 'parental' and 'arm's length' models of criminal justice. The purpose of the parental model as reflected in aboriginal societies was 'to bring the erring brother, now known to be such, to repentance, to open confession and to reintegration with the community of which he is, was and still is regarded as an integral part' (Llewellyn, 1962: 448). In contrast, the arm's length model was based on the ideal of due process and adversarial individualism in its insistence on trial before an impartial tribunal on a narrow range of relevant evidence. As will be seen, subsequent generations of scholars have continued Llewellyn's task of building contrasting ideal models. The common objective has been to use models to understand the values behind the criminal process. At the same time, very little criminal process scholarship has yet embraced Llewellyn's interest in legal pluralism or the study of law or systems outside of official law or institutions. Llewellyn's work should inspire criminal process scholars to be bolder in their use of other disciplines and more creative in their research strategies.

2.2 Legal Process

Although they made only rare references to criminal justice, the influential legal process teaching materials prepared by Henry Hart Jr. and Albert Sacks in the 1950s laid important foundations for criminal process scholarship. Their ambition was to examine the legal process as a whole, including legislative, administrative, and judicial decision-making. Hart and Sacks were also concerned about private ordering because of their recognition that most cases settle, something that was stressed in much early criminal process scholarship in the 1960s (Blumberg, 1967). Hart and Sacks identified the exercise of prosecutorial discretion as a key issue in the criminal process (Hart and Sacks, 1994: 1048–60). Again, early criminal process scholars focused on police and prosecutorial discretion as the key entry points into the criminal process (Skolnick, 1966). Hart and Sacks also called for an examination of alternatives to the criminal sanction by criticizing 'the classic pattern of unthinking, unscientific legislation: if you want to stop something from happening, make it a crime'. In their view 'the systematic study of sanctions—criminal penalties, private rights of actions of various kinds, licensing and license revocation, and the like—is one of the most neglected fields in the science of the law' (Hart and Sacks, 1994: 35, 124). Many of these themes were subsequently developed by Herbert Packer who readily acknowledged that his 'general views about law have been greatly influenced by Henry M. Hart and Albert Sacks, *The Legal Process* (Tent ed., 1958)' (Packer, 1968: 369). Packer's willingness to situate his work on the criminal process in the broader field of legal process scholarship was one of its many strengths.

3 MODELS OF THE CRIMINAL PROCESS

A good deal of criminal process scholarship has revolved around models or ideal types of the criminal process. Models have been used, as in the sciences, as 'a hypothetical but coherent scheme for testing the evidence' (King, 1981: 12). For example, much empirical research tested the validity of the due process or adversarial model of the criminal process and found it did not match the evidence of high rates of guilty pleas in the lower criminal courts. Unlike in science, however, multiple models have been used because they 'legitimately account in different ways for various aspects of the system's operation' (ibid. 122). For example, the due process model may still reflect the aspirations of criminal justice and the doctrine of the appellate courts even though it does not describe the operation of the lower criminal courts. Multiple models are also valuable in articulating conflicting values in the criminal process such as due process, crime control, and victims' rights.

Ideal models of the criminal process allow scholars to step back and gain perspective 'from the welter of the more or less connected details that make up an accurate description of the myriad ways in which the criminal process does operate or may be likely to operate' (Packer, 1968: 152; Damaska, 1986: 3, 10). Models can be used to transcend the details of criminal procedure scholarship and assess overall trends, themes, and values in the investigation and prosecution of crime. The most successful and enduring models—Packer's crime control and due process models—have become terms of art reflected in academic and even popular discourse. As will be seen, however, the leading models have been criticized for not representing the full range of relevant values and for making false assumptions about the operation of the criminal justice system. Despite these critiques, it is undeniable that abstract models have played a crucial role in criminal process scholarship.

3.1 Packer's Models

Although they constitute perhaps the most significant and enduring piece of criminal process scholarship ever, Packer's models were reflective of the time and place in which they were written. It is an open question how applicable Packer's models are outside of the United States of the 1960s.

In the crime control model, the criminal process functioned as an 'assembly-line conveyor belt' (Packer, 1968: 159) dominated by expert police and prosecutorial officers who screened out the innocent. The main product of the assembly line was the efficient entry of a guilty plea. The ultimate authority was the legislature which enacted the criminal law to protect people, but also to pursue the conservative project of maintaining public decency even with respect to illicit consensual transactions. The emphasis was on factual guilt, and the only justified restraints on the police were those necessary to ensure that evidence was reliable. Packer's crime control model was influenced by empirical studies demonstrating considerable police discretion, high rates of pre-trial detention, and high rates of guilty pleas. It was also influenced by governmental enthusiasm for the use of the criminal sanction even at the cost of 'spending billions of dollars . . . on improving the capacity of the nation's criminal justice system to deal with gamblers, narcotics addicts, prostitutes, homosexuals, abortionists and other producers of illegal goods and services' (ibid. 366). Packer concluded that the crime control model approximated the operation of the American criminal process 'in the large majority of cases . . . the real world criminal process tends to be far more administrative and managerial than adversary and judicial' (ibid. 239).

In the due process model, the criminal process functioned as an 'obstacle course' in which defence counsel and judges could conclude that prosecutions should be rejected because the accused's rights had been violated. The ultimate authority was the United States Supreme Court interpreting the American Bill of Rights in terms both of its specific protections of due process and its concern with the equality of African-Americans and other disadvantaged groups disproportionately caught up in the criminal process (ibid. 180, 243). The driving force was the Warren Court which was turning the criminal process 'from an assembly line into an obstacle course' by rejecting prosecutions, and excluding relevant evidence when accused were not given access to defence lawyers at trial or during pre-trial interrogation, or when evidence was seized without prior judicial authorization. The Court was willing to restrict police discretion with broad quasi-legislative rules that attempted to ensure that suspects were treated equally regardless of financial status (ibid. 194, 219–20). The due process model was based on liberal values that were sceptical about 'the morality and utility of the criminal sanction' especially with regards to 'victimless crimes' based on consensual transactions (ibid. 170, 151).

Packer's models reflected the traditional legal process concern about 'how the rules shall be implemented' by administrators and courts. An important difference between the crime control and due process models was not so much the rules, but how they were enforced. The crime control model required separate civil, criminal, or disciplinary proceedings to address police and prosecutorial misconduct, while the due process model was based on the view that unpopular and poor suspects in the criminal process would be unable to obtain effective remedies except through the use of deterrent exclusionary rules in the criminal trial, even at the cost of 'the release of the factually guilty' (ibid. 18, 168).

Packer was also sensitive to the distinction between the law in the books and the law in action that had influenced Pound and others concerned with sociological jurisprudence. Like many empirical scholars, he recognized that 'the real world criminal process tends to be far more administrative and managerial than adversary and judicial' (ibid. 239). The ideal was that the accused would be presumed innocent and represented by a lawyer prepared to insist that the state act fairly and prove its case beyond a reasonable doubt. The reality, however, was that the accused was presumed guilty by the police and prosecutors and often pleaded guilty at the first opportunity. This insight, however, did not make Packer despair of reforming the criminal process to make it look more like its due process ideal (ibid. 239). It only produced 'an interesting paradox: the more we learn about the Is of the criminal process, the more we are instructed about its Ought' (ibid. 150).

A strength of Packer's models was their ability to capture much of the politics of criminal justice. The rise of the due process model was 'a judge-made revolution' (ibid. 365) that was vulnerable to public and legislative resistance because 'reform in the criminal process has very little political appeal' (ibid. 241). Indeed, Packer's models reflected the struggle between the courts and legislatures in the United States at the time over due process and crime control (Bradley, 1993). The conflict between crime control and due process values makes Packer's models useful in describing public discourse about criminal justice, but it opens the question of the extent to which such discourse has evolved since the 1960s.

Packer's models were constructed to assist in answering the classic legal process question of the appropriate role of law, in this case criminal law. His answer reflected a liberal agenda of the 1960s including decriminalization of gambling, abortion, consensual sexual crimes and narcotics, and a nuisance-based approach to obscenity and prostitution. Restraint in the criminal law was required because emerging due process standards made it less possible to rely on the 'low-cost, high-speed' crime control model (ibid. 245). The 'rational legislator' would have to explore alternatives to costly criminal law. This should produce 'a workable jurisprudence of sanctions' based on the relative strengths and weaknesses and cost and benefits of various forms of regulation such as licensing, regulation, and the criminal law (ibid. 251). Many scholars in the 1960s agreed with Packer that legislatures should place less reliance on the criminal sanction, especially with respect to difficult-to-detect consensual crimes. In retrospect, much of this scholarship seems naive in its confidence that crimes based on consensual transactions were 'victimless' and that decriminalization would occur. Although gambling and abortion has frequently been decriminalized, narcotics have not; and the war on drugs in the United States has produced substantial increases in prison populations (Tonry, 1995). Some feminist scholars have argued that obscenity and prostitution are not victimless crimes and should not be decriminalized. It is also unlikely that the massive decriminalization advocated by Packer would have produced compliance with due process norms in the administration of the remaining criminal law. Nevertheless, Packer's scholarship can be praised for drawing connections between the decisions of legislatures to enact criminal law and the effects of such decisions on the other institutions of the criminal process from policing to corrections.

3.2 Critiques of Packer's Models

A number of empirical researchers questioned Packer's assumption that defence lawyers and judges act as agents of due process. One provocative early argument was that defence lawyers were engaged in a 'confidence game' in which they acted as 'double agents' not so much on behalf of their clients and their due process rights, but on behalf of organizational interests that they shared with prosecutors, judges, and correctional officials (Blumberg, 1967: 110, 113). Other empirical research suggested that Packer's vision of due process was largely irrelevant as defence lawyers frequently recommended guilty pleas in exchange for more lenient treatment of the accused (Bottoms and McClean, 1976; Ericson and Baranek, 1982). Much of this empirical research suggested that the due process model was irrelevant, at least to the functioning of the lower criminal courts.

Other researchers questioned Packer's assumption that the due process and crime control models were at odds with each other. In the United Kingdom, Doreen McBarnet (1981) and in Canada, Richard Ericson and Patricia Baranek (1982) examined the law of criminal procedure. They found that the formal law often enabled and legitimated the crime control activities of police and prosecutors. Although their findings may reflect the absence at the time of bills of rights in the jurisdictions that they studied, they also raised larger questions about Packer's assumptions about conflict between due process and crime control. Due process could be for crime control in the sense that the 'rhetoric of justice' (McBarnet, 1981: 6) could coexist and even help legitimate the routine imposition of punishment as described in the crime control model. This scholarship revealed how Packer's models were centred on the particular American experience; how 'two tiers' of justice could coexist; and perhaps how the image of a lenient due process model could provide an illusion of fair treatment throughout a criminal process that mainly resulted in guilty pleas. At the very least, due process in the rare case litigated on appeal and in official discourse about the law was not inconsistent with increased crime control in the form of more criminal laws, more guilty pleas, and more people in jail. These critiques of Packer's models raised important empirical and ideological points, but they remained focused on Packer's contrast between due process and crime control and did not account for other values that might affect the criminal process.

3.3 Alternative Models

From the start, scholars have presented alternative models to supplement Packer's exclusive focus on crime control and due process. John Griffiths argued in 1970 that although the crime control model favoured the state and the due process model favoured the individual, they were united by a 'battle model' that assumed 'the inevitability of a state of irreconcilable hostility between the individual and the state' (Griffiths, 1970: 368, 413). Griffiths presented a third 'family' model of the criminal process that rejected the distrust of governmental officials and assumption of conflicting interests found in both of Packer's models. The family model of the criminal process was holistic and reintegrative. 'When a parent punishes his child, both parent and child know that afterward they will go on living together as before' (ibid. 376). Its closest parallel was the juvenile court movement based on the best interests of the child. Griffiths acknowledged the failure of that movement, but attributed it to the ideological strength of a battle model that made the juvenile court a site for struggle between crime control and due process. Griffiths's work is exceptional in its early argument that the criminal process cannot be understood without attention to issues of 'political philosophy' and 'ideology' (ibid. 412–13).

John Braithwaite (1989: 56) has more recently expanded on Griffiths's work to argue in favour of restorative justice as a new model of criminal justice. His argument is that criminal justice officials and citizens can learn from successful families. They should encourage 'reintegrative shaming' to respond to wrongdoing rather than the isolation and stigmatization that results from traditional criminal processing under either the due process or crime control models. Braithwaite advocates institutional arrangements such as family conferences and aboriginal healing circles that bring offenders, victims, their supporters, and community representatives together to discuss the effects of crime and propose means of redress and reconciliation. His approach reflects an interest in what happens outside of courtrooms. It also sets up an ambitious hypothesis that restorative justice can be more successful than the due process model in respecting individuals, and more successful than the crime control model in controlling crime. Unlike Packer and Griffiths, however, Braithwaite argues this hypothesis can only be proven or disproven by empirical research into restorative dispute resolution in a wide variety of settings (Braithwaite, 1999). Griffiths's and Braithwaite's scholarship demonstrates the need to explore the political and institutional assumptions behind Packer's models and to examine other sites in civil society for the resolution of conflicts caused by crime.

A number of commentators have criticized Packer's models for their neglect of crime victims (Sanders and Young, 2000). Packer's assumption that crimes such as pornography and drugs are victimless has been challenged, as has his assumption that criminal justice will always be defined as a matter between the state and the accused. Victimization studies have also demonstrated that Packer was wrong to assume that the enforcement of the criminal law and in particular the pre-trial process can effectively control crime (Ashworth, 1998: 27). Some attempts have been made to construct new models of the criminal process which include crime victims. They include a 'circle' model of criminal justice involving the use of restorative justice proceedings and crime prevention, and a 'roller coaster' model that accounts for growing political and legal conflict between the rights of the accused and rights claimed by crime victims (Roach, 1999). This later model explains 'the new political trial' (Fletcher, 1995: 1) which pits the accused not only against the state, but also against the claims of crime victims and groups of potential crime victims such as women, children, and minorities vulnerable to hate crimes. It also seeks to explain dissatisfaction with the inability of the existing system either to prevent crime victimization or to treat victims in a respectful manner, as well as attempts to make the existing system more conducive to victim participation.

Other alternative models of the criminal process argue that the goal is not crime control or due process, but 'surveillance' and 'knowledge production for the efficient risk management of suspect populations' (McConville and Bridges, 1994: 140). This approach accounts for linkages between the police and insurance companies, as well as the movement of data between various state agencies. It also describes the increasing emphasis in the criminal process on the construction of data banks and the notification of communities of the presence of high risk offenders (Scheingold et al., 1994). 'Risk management techniques do not invoke the form of sovereign power linked to the criminal law' and can be used by corporations and the private police (Simon, 1997: 179). Surveillance and risk management models of the criminal process are well placed to expand the vision of criminal process scholars beyond the traditional criminal justice actors to other state bureaucracies and the private sector. They may also be particularly helpful in assessing the increased concern about security in many countries since the terrorism attacks of 11 September 2001.

4 The Evolution of Criminal Process Scholarship

4.1 Self-Conscious Criminal Process Scholarship

The high point of self-conscious criminal process scholarship in American law schools was the 1960s. Much scholarship produced in the law schools follows the cases. The activism of the Warren Court encouraged the development of scholarship and teaching materials that went beyond the traditional subjects of substantive criminal law and criminal procedure to study the administration of the entire criminal process. Particular attention was paid to the exclusionary rules imposed on the police and the disclosure obligations imposed on prosecutors. Criminal process scholarship following the cases also explains a similar but smaller revival of criminal process scholarship in the United Kingdom and Canada in the 1980s and 1990s, as the courts, armed with new legislation and new bills of rights, decided more cases concerning the conduct of police, prosecutors, and trial judges (Ashworth, 1998; Sanders and Young, 2000).

Another source of the 1960s American criminal process boom was the civil rights movement and civil unrest in many American cities. The focus of much concern was the behaviour of the police, as well as high rates of pre-trial detention. An important research project was undertaken by the American Bar Foundation to produce 'a series of volumes which will, in the aggregate, cover the major stages in criminal justice administration from the time a crime is committed until the offender is finally released from parole supervision'. It was based on the premise that 'it is important for the legal profession and for law teaching and law research to assume greater responsibility for the total process of criminal justice administration than they have in the past' (LaFave, 1965, p. xv). Much criminal process scholarship in the 1960s involved empirical on-site observations of the police, and focused on police discretion whether to invoke the criminal process and the various ways in which the police could neutralize or avoid court-imposed rules (Skolnick, 1966). A number of studies found high rates of pre-trial detention and the frequent use of money as bail. They also related pre-trial detention to the eventual outcome of cases (Friedland, 1965).

Much of the early 1960s criminal process scholarship tended to focus on divergences between due process norms and actual behaviour, and proceeded on what later generations of socio-legal researchers would see as the somewhat naive assumption that the law in action could and should follow the law on the books. In later decades, scholars drawing on more detailed empirical studies of the lower criminal courts, would take a more critical approach that would be less concerned with identifying and attempting to narrow gaps between the law on the books and in action and more intent on explaining the reasons for such persistent gaps.

4.2 Empirical Studies of the Criminal Process

The next wave of criminal process scholarship was a series of empirical studies of the lower criminal courts. These studies were often methodologically more sophisticated than earlier criminal process studies which relied heavily on qualitative observations of the police. British and Canadian studies found not only high rates of guilty pleas, but various organizational and legal factors that encouraged the entry of guilty pleas, as opposed to the invocation of due process rights. They argued that accused were dependent on previous decisions made by police, prosecutors, and defence lawyers and rarely acted as autonomous agents asserting their rights (Bottoms and McClean, 1976; Ericson and Baranek, 1982).

Malcolm Feeley's study of the lower criminal courts in New Haven confirmed high rates of guilty pleas and plea bargaining and explained these findings with the provocative conclusion that the 'process is the punishment'. By this, he meant that the costs of pre-trial detention, obtaining a lawyer, and procedural delay often were greater to the accused than those of the quick entry of a guilty plea. Many offenders already had a criminal record and would receive a lenient sanction for a minor offence. 'Ironically, the cost of *invoking* one's rights is frequently greater than the loss of the rights themselves, which is why so many defendants accept a guilty plea without a battle' (Feeley, 1979: 277). All of these empirical studies significantly complicated the dichotomy between crime control and due process posited by Packer by finding that due process was not generally relevant in the lower criminal courts (Ericson and Baranek, 1982: 224).

4.3 Official Policy Studies of the Criminal Process

It would be a mistake to confine any examination of criminal process scholarship to academic journals and monographs. Criminal process scholarship is characterized by a practical policy orientation as compared to the often more philosophical explorations of the substantive criminal law, technical explorations of criminal procedure, and sociological explorations of criminology. The practical and policy orientation of criminal process scholarship helps explain why it is often commissioned by official inquiries into the criminal justice system and why criminal process scholarship itself can become part of public and reform discourse about criminal justice.

The US President's Commission on Law Enforcement and Administration of Justice commissioned a large number of studies on various aspects of the criminal process (United States, 1967: 312). Its final report took a legal process approach with chapters on policing, courts, and corrections, as well as on particular phenomena such as organized crime and drugs. Not surprisingly, it called for increased research both within governments and the universities (ibid. 273–7). A similar criminal process approach was taken two years later in a major inquiry in Canada that focused on sentencing and corrections, but also examined police powers, bail, legal aid, and the lower criminal courts (Canada, 1969). The criminal process scholarship of the 1960s laid the foundation for such comprehensive official studies of the criminal justice system. As will be seen, however, the task of studying the entire criminal process would become more complicated and often less satisfying by the 1990s.

In the United Kingdom, the Runciman Royal Commission on Criminal Justice was appointed in 1991 on the same day that the wrongful convictions of the 'Birmingham Six' for terrorist bombings were quashed. Like the earlier American commission, it had an ambitious research programme which sponsored studies into policing, defence representation, forensic evidence, trials, and appeals. Its final report took a traditional criminal process approach and was based on the premise that '[a]ny recommendation to change the rules and procedures governing one part of the criminal justice system will have a consequential effect on the others' (United Kingdom, 1993: 3). The report, however, was criticized for its proposals to expand police powers and legitimate plea bargaining. The report was also criticized for its preoccupation with balancing crime control and due process values and its narrow focus on the criminal justice system as a means to control crime (Ashworth, 1998: 315–16). Perhaps most importantly, the report was criticized for its dated methodology in failing to place the criminal process in its larger social, organizational, and political contexts (McConville and Bridges, 1994). These criticisms were influenced by the studies of the 1970s and 1980s that had revealed the limitations of studying the criminal process apart from its broader contexts and the limitations of Packer's models. The almost unanimous scholarly criticism of the Runciman report was a watershed that cast doubt on the continued viability of a traditional organizational and law reform approach to the criminal process.

In Canada and Australia, a number of public inquiries have been appointed in response to wrongful convictions, police misconduct, and concerns about the treatment of aboriginal people and racial minorities in the criminal justice system. In order to explain phenomena such as the dramatic overrepresentation of aboriginal people in prison or among deaths in custody, these inquiries have invariably found it necessary to take a criminal process approach which examines the treatment of such groups by police, prosecutors, defence lawyers, judges, and correctional officials. Studies of wrongful convictions have led to moratoriums on the use of the death penalty in some jurisdictions in the United States. As was the case with the Runciman Commission, many public inquiries into wrongful convictions have recommended the creation of a new institution to investigate allegations of wrongful convictions. This represents a continued reformist streak in criminal process scholarship which sees the addition of new institutions and more due process rights as a solution to the failures of existing institutions. As the empirical studies examined above suggest, however, the determinants of behaviour in the criminal process are often more complex and resistant to reform.

Although they take a reformist approach that many criminal process scholars see as unduly optimistic, official reports into the criminal justice system affirm the importance of the criminal process approach by their attention to the multiple actors and phases in criminal justice. They can also play an important role by commissioning scholarship and empirical research that might otherwise not be undertaken. As official reports, however, they can be criticized for taking a limited and traditional approach to the range of criminal justice actors; for an overly optimistic approach to the possibilities of organizational and law reform; and for not situating the criminal process in its political, social, and organizational contexts.

5 Contemporary Criminal Process Scholarship

With some notable exceptions (Ashworth, 1998; Sanders and Young, 2000), much contemporary criminal process scholarship is not self-consciously defined as criminal process scholarship. The focus is often on specific problems, crimes, and cases. This work has been valuable in increasing our understanding of parts of the criminal process, but its failure to examine the criminal process as a whole may have contributed to a decline in the prominence and prestige of criminal process scholarship and a neglect of theoretical issues concerning the operation and nature of the criminal process.

5.1 Bias Studies

The growing overrepresentation of African-Americans in prisons in the United States and aboriginal people in prisons in Canada and Australia has sparked scholarship attempting to explain and suggest remedies for this problem. Some of this scholarship follows a traditional criminal process framework as it examines the role of police, juries, and judges (Kennedy, 1997; Cole, 1999). A danger is that this scholarship may fall into the traditional habit of focusing on the exercise of discretion and proposing law and organizational reform. This could lead criminal process scholarship away from examining the larger political, social, historical, and economic contexts of racism and its effects on the criminal process.

A promising aspect of bias scholarship is the identification of 'the war on drugs' as a central cause for disproportionate African-American imprisonment (Tonry, 1995; Kennedy, 1997, ch. 10; Cole, 1999). This not only provides a useful focus on particular crimes, but also requires an examination of the legislative process that produces mandatory sentencing laws or narrow sentencing guidelines (Tonry, 1995; Cole, 1999). From the start, criminal process scholars such as Packer have recognized the importance of the legislature's decision to criminalize certain activities, but contemporary racial bias studies underline the need to employ the insights of political science in understanding not only the criminal process but also tendencies to 'govern through crime' (Simon, 1997). In a similar vein, political science can make an important contribution to understanding the impact that the victims' rights movement is having on the criminal process, again primarily through the legislature (Fletcher, 1995; Scheingold et al., 1994).

Another promising feature of bias scholarship are the linkages drawn between the overrepresentation of African-Americans and aboriginal people in prison and their overrepresentation among the victims of crime (Tonry, 1995; Kennedy, 1997). This scholarship demonstrates an interest in social, economic, and environmental factors that may affect the criminal process. The next step may be to draw on disciplines such as public health and urban studies to examine the variety of causes of high rates of both victimization and incarceration among many disadvantaged groups. Systems not traditionally associated with the criminal process may have a role to play in providing remedies for problems associated with criminal justice.

Unfortunately, less scholarship has examined the role of sexism than racism in the criminal process. A somewhat similar methodological approach may be appropriate with a focus on linkages between the criminal process and the larger political, social, and economic environment and between the victimization of women by crime and the criminalization of women. As Carol Smart (1977: 185) has argued, 'an isolated study of court-room procedure or police attitudes to female offenders would be meaningless without an analysis of attitudes towards women in general'. Feminist criminal process scholarship might attempt to relate patterns of victimization of women to female criminality; to compare how the criminal process responds to both phenomena; and to relate these responses to larger political, social, and economic issues.

5.2 Case Studies

A popular means to cope with the complexity of the criminal process is to take a micro approach that examines particular cases or classes of crimes. Although case studies can be criticized for focusing on the atypical and even the sensational, they also provide a manageable means to explore how various factors, including personalities and the media, affect the criminal process. Several American studies have examined the politicization of controversial cases and have demonstrated the important role that the media, politicians, and community activists may play in the criminal process (Fletcher, 1995). Studies of specific crimes such as terrorism or hate crimes should also include issues such as immigration, citizenship, and identity politics. Studies of particular cases and crimes have started the much-needed task of expanding the boundaries of criminal process scholarship.

Scholarship on wrongful convictions has traditionally been dominated by case studies. Such scholarship has neglected the systemic factors that may contribute to wrongful convictions as well as the political saliency of wrongful convictions. Some recent scholarship, however, goes beyond both individual case studies and a focus on the traditional actors in the criminal process to explore wrongful convictions 'as a site of various systems of communication' in the media, forensic science, jury trials, and appeals. This scholarship also avoids a rationalist focus on institutional reform found in the Runciman Report in favour of an approach that focuses on how various systems manage the inevitability of wrongful convictions (Nobles and Schiff, 2000: 7).

5.3 Comparative Scholarship

Much comparative work to date has focused on contrasting adversarial and inquisitorial systems of criminal justice. The work of Mirjan Damaska has played an influential role by constructing contrasting models of hierarchical inquisitorial justice and decentralized coordinate adversarial justice. These models, like Packer's due process and crime control models, are a conscious attempt to reduce the complexity of the criminal process into 'intelligible', 'manageable', and 'ideal' patterns, even at the acknowledged cost of creating 'fictitious creatures, seldom if ever found in reality, but under certain conditions useful for analyzing it' (Damaska, 1986: 3, 5, 10). Like Packer's models, Damaska's models continue to influence scholarship (Kagan, 2001) with many of the same virtues and weaknesses.

Damaska's models are helpful because they focus on broad trends and values and can identify both inquisitorial and adversarial elements in the same system. They are also valuable in linking adjudicative models to larger patterns of governance in a way that Packer's models do not. Building on Damaska's work, Robert Kagan has argued that the particularly adversarial and punitive nature of the American criminal process is related to that country's populist and decentralized politics (Kagan, 2001, chs. 4 and 5). Damaska's work also relates the more centralized nature of governance in many countries with inquisitorial systems to a broader desire to manage and order social, economic, and political life. The decline of communism and the spread of capitalism in many countries with inquisitorial systems provide an excellent opportunity to test Damaska's theory linking legal and governmental styles. The type of empirical work that cast doubt on Packer's models remains to be done with Damaska's models.

In the absence of detailed studies, Damaska's models run the risk of idealizing or reifying the differences between inquisitorial and adversarial systems. Much comparative criminal process scholarship has stressed the differences between

Continental and American criminal processes, frequently at an abstract level that is superficial from a sociological or organizational perspective. The point has often been to illustrate the excesses of American reliance on due process litigation (Kagan, 2001). Optimistic assumptions about the operation of inquisitorial systems (ibid.) and the virtues of greater reliance on legislation to govern conduct in the criminal process (Bradley, 1993) have been made. This scholarship has revealed comparative studies as a promising venue for research, but much work remains to be done. There is an urgent need for more fine-grained and empirical comparisons about the operation of actual criminal justice systems in different countries. This will require a return to the empirical studies that were conducted in the 1970s and 1980s to test Packer's models, but this time complicated by having research sites in two or more countries. The difficulties and costs of such research should not be underestimated.

Comparative scholarship should also examine growing convergence in terms of supranational and national rights protection instruments while also paying attention to perhaps enduring differences in terms of governance structures and local legal culture. One thesis that should be critically explored is that of American exceptionalism (Simon, 1997: 180). For better or worse, much comparative work has compared the criminal process in the United States to the criminal process in Continental Europe, the United Kingdom, or Canada. The result has often been a stress on the uniqueness of the American experience in its reliance on the death penalty, juries, unrestricted media coverage, and adversarial due process litigation (Kagan, 2001). Although the political economy of research suggests that the United States will remain a frequently used comparator, there may be limits to this type of research precisely because of distinctive features of the American experience. Nevertheless, comparative studies should play an important role in the future of criminal process scholarship.

6 THE FUTURE OF CRIMINAL PROCESS SCHOLARSHIP

Although some contemporary criminal process scholarship is quite promising, its overall state is not. Some of the most interesting work about the criminal process does not define itself as criminal process scholarship. In itself, this loss of identity can be liberating and expand the boundaries of what is understood as part of the criminal process. At the same time, however, it is not surprising that scholarship that does not define itself as criminal process scholarship does not attempt to assess or advance general theories of the criminal process or relate itself to the evolving traditions of such scholarship.

6.1 A More Theoretical and Self-Conscious Approach

One strategy for a more self-conscious criminal process scholarship is to revive the traditions of texts and teaching materials that focus on the entire criminal process. One impetus for this revival will be the increasing attention that is being paid in many countries to issues of compliance with domestic and international rights-protection norms. Scholarship in the United Kingdom is leading the way in reviving texts that concern themselves with the entire criminal process as distinct from substantive criminal law and criminal procedure (Ashworth, 1998; Sanders and Young, 2000). Care must be taken, however, to ensure that this scholarship escapes traditional conceptions of what constitutes the criminal process. This danger can be avoided by building on the robust tradition of empirical studies of the criminal process, and by examining institutions such as the media and the private police that have not traditionally been seen as part of the criminal process. In the United States, current problems such as the dramatic overrepresentation of African-Americans among prisoners, wrongful convictions in death penalty cases, and high rates of imprisonment in general should force policy-makers and scholars to take a criminal process approach as they rethink the very basics of criminal justice. The particular importance of crimes based on drugs, guns, and most recently terrorism in the United States may also provide a basis for reviving a tradition of examining the criminal process in light of particular crimes (United States, 1967). Again, the challenge will be not to fall back on a narrow vision of the criminal process.

New models of the criminal process would respond to the theoretical deficit and would help reconstitute criminal process scholarship as an identifiable genre of legal scholarship. New models must, however, incorporate the criticisms of the limitations of the existing models. They should include a broader range of actors and systems than Packer's models. In particular, they should include the role of the legislative process and various non-governmental actors that affect the investigation and prosecution of crime. They should incorporate an increased emphasis on surveillance and risk-management strategies that may not be aimed at prosecution and punishment. They should also be sensitive to the sociological context of crime in which only a small minority of crimes are officially investigated and prosecuted. New models should be designed not only to assess the operation of the traditional criminal process, but also public discourse about criminal justice. They should also incorporate new developments such as restorative justice that do not fit easily under the rubric of the investigation and punishment of crime by public officials. If the past is any indication, much of the future of the criminal process scholarship may depend on the construction, testing, and subsequent criticism of models. Although there is a danger that new models of the criminal process will embrace their own problematic assumptions and limit the range of inquiry, they are a necessary means to focus and advance criminal process scholarship.

6.2 Expanding the Boundaries of Criminal Process Scholarship

Simply reviving the criminal process paradigm will not be enough to enrich and revitalize criminal process scholarship. A nostalgic desire to return to the heyday of criminal process scholarship in the 1960s and its focus on the problem of discretion exercised by public law enforcement officials and law and organizational reform should be resisted. Attempts to take such a limited approach will rightly meet with sustained scholarly criticism (McConville and Bridges, 1994). It will also discount the contemporary impediments to law reform by experts and the wider range of constituencies that now assert influence over criminal justice.

Fortunately, valuable work has already been done in expanding the boundaries of criminal process scholarship. It includes work on the role that private police, the media, and insurance companies play in the criminal process. The retreat of the state also makes it more necessary to study how private actors such as insurance and private security companies may influence the investigation and prosecution of crime. There should be a conscious and vigorous attempt to incorporate the insights of legal pluralism so as to escape the traditional focus on official state bureaucracies and processes of criminal justice. Scholars must be bold and innovative and study institutions and actors that have not traditionally been studied as part of the criminal process.

An expansion of the boundaries of criminal process scholarship will require it to become more methodologically diverse and sophisticated. Although a self-consciously defined 'new legal process' scholarship (Hart and Sacks, 1994, pp. li–cxxxvi) has made a revival in other areas of public law, it has so far had minimal impact on criminal justice scholars in law schools and departments of criminology. New legal process scholarship has integrated the insights of feminism, critical race theory, and economic models of the legislative process with a traditional legal process interest in the making and application of the law. New legal process scholarship is also sensitive to the reality of legal pluralism and the manner in which most grievances are resolved without official intervention. Criminal process scholarship that is better integrated into a broader framework of new legal process scholarship will not only have a richer sense of identity and place in the academy, but will also be better prepared to expand the boundaries of criminal process scholarship.

Criminal process scholarship has traditionally been influenced by the insights of sociology and criminology, but scholars should be prepared to employ insights and methodologies from other disciplines. In order to understand the role that city design, the media, drugs, guns, immigration, and international law have on criminal justice, it will be necessary for scholars to draw on insights of diverse disciplines including urban studies, media studies, public health, political science, and international relations. Criminal process scholarship should become even more multidisciplinary. A risk, however, is that the addition of other disciplines will eclipse the need to reclaim a theory and vision of the criminal process.

An expanded conception of criminal process scholarship should also change its reformist orientation. There will be less emphasis on proposing legal and organizational reforms to better govern the discretion of public officials. The focus of the scholarly enterprise will often be simply on understanding the various social, political, and organizational systems that affect the investigation and prosecution of crimes rather than reform (Nobles and Schiff, 2000). This will bring criminal process scholarship closer to other social sciences, but also perhaps marginalize the important role that it has played in official reform discourse about the criminal process.

The two conceptual changes advocated here should be complementary and mutually reinforcing. Deliberate decisions to study institutions and processes that have not traditionally been seen as part of the criminal process will place pressures on criminal process scholars to justify their choices. This should encourage them to question traditional models of the criminal process that focus on the public police, prosecutors, judges, and correctional officials. As scholars find that the existing models do not account for the phenomena that they observe as affecting criminal justice, they will hopefully construct new and richer theories of the criminal process.

6.3 Possible Research Topics and Strategies

The final issue is what research subjects and strategies will contribute to the development of a more theoretical, self-conscious, and expansive approach to criminal process scholarship. Criminal process scholarship has always been characterized by its interest in the particular legal, social, and political controversies of the times and this engagement should continue. Thus current concerns about terrorism, wrongful convictions, crime victims, and globalized and international elements of the criminal process have the potential to generate criminal process scholarship that is both innovative and relevant.

Globalized aspects of the criminal process and the development of international criminal law provide an opportunity to expand the boundaries of the criminal process, as well as to reflect on fundamental norms that should be part of an international criminal process. It will be important, however, not to replicate the traditional focus on state actors, but also to assess the role of non-governmental organizations and more informal forms of ordering. Scholars should be sensitive to the interplay between domestic and international law and the fundamental choice between dealing with international crimes through an international court-based process or through a more informal reconciliation-based approach. Criminal process scholars should attempt not only to understand the emerging international criminal process, but also the complex forces that are making international criminal law assume a greater importance in governance. They should also examine patterns of convergence and divergence between criminal justice in different countries.

Criminal process scholars should take an interest in the incidence of crimes and the decisions that crime victims and corporations take to use alternatives to the official criminal process. Traditional criminal process scholarship has only examined the processing of the small minority of crimes that are reported to the police or prosecuted by the state. The study of crimes not reported to or cleared by the police should also be part of the scholarship. In the case of corporations especially, this may also inspire scholars to examine risk-management strategies that do not rely on the formal criminal process. The examination of alternatives to the formal criminal process should be informed by an appreciation of legal pluralism.

Criminal process scholars should take an interest in state bureaucracies that are not traditionally seen as part of the criminal justice system. The study of dispute resolution in schools or various regulatory systems may not only identify how cases are transferred to the formal criminal process, but also produce studies of informal justice systems. The effects of deregulation and the retreat of the state on the criminal process should be examined, including the transfer of disputes between criminal and civil processes of dispute resolution. Study of terrorism should provide a venue for examining the interactions between immigration, criminal justice, and international relations systems (Roach, 2003). Criminal process scholars should not be deterred by traditional distinctions between criminal, administrative, and civil process; between adjudication, regulation, and alternative forms of dispute resolution; or between domestic and international law. Criminal process scholars should expand their vision to the entire legal process as it affects criminal justice.

Studies of the legislative process are also needed to place frequent criminal law reform and public discourse about crime into the larger context of governance. Scholars should explore the thesis that Western countries are increasingly 'governing through crime' (Simon, 1997) or engaging in a 'criminalization of politics' (Roach, 1999) in which crime is becoming a more important instrument of governance and public discourse. Criminal process scholars should examine whether criminal justice issues are taking on increased importance as the state retreats in other areas and as social, cultural, and economic divisions among the population increase. Criminal process scholars should expand their vision to all forms of governance as they affect criminal justice.

7 CONCLUSION

Criminal process scholarship will survive as an inevitable by-product of the need to understand criminal justice in all its complexities. Nevertheless, it will not thrive without some significant changes. It must first regain its sense of identity through scholarship that examines the entire criminal process. A return to a traditional focus on the multiple phases and state bureaucracies of the criminal process will not, however, be sufficient to revitalize criminal process scholarship. There must be a willingness to go beyond the traditional focus on police, prosecutors, defence lawyers, judges, and correctional officials and examine other institutions such as corporations, the private police, the media, non-governmental organizations, immigration officials, and international bodies that also affect criminal justice. Expanding the range of actors and systems studied as part of the criminal process will also require some methodological changes. There is a need for criminal process scholarship to become more multidisciplinary and better integrated with the broader fields of legal process and social science scholarship.

There is a need to develop new theories or models of the criminal process, both to focus criminal process scholarship and to make sense of its expanded vision. The old models of the criminal process should be recognized for their vital contributions to the scholarship; but their assumptions and limitations require new models of the criminal process. Like the influential models of Packer and Damaska, any new models will one day be seen as dated and inadequate. Nevertheless, the vital contribution of abstract models to criminal process scholarship must be acknowledged and the absence of new models can have a debilitating effect on scholarship. Without models or theories, the scholarship can become lost in the details and lack a focus for comparisons over time and between jurisdictions.

Fortunately, the moves towards theory and expansion of what constitutes the criminal process advocated in this essay can have mutually reinforcing effects. As scholars study the role of non-traditional actors in the criminal process, they will be forced to question traditional theories of what constitutes the criminal process. This should provide both a theoretical need and an empirical basis for developing new theories of the criminal process. The goal should be a new criminal process scholarship that examines much more than the traditional state actors and phases of the criminal process. A new criminal process scholarship should develop both empirical and theoretical understandings of the multiple actors and process that constitute and shape criminal justice.

REFERENCES

Ashworth, A. (1998). *The Criminal Process: An Evaluative Study* (2nd edn.), Oxford: Oxford University Press.
Blumberg, A. (1967). *Criminal Justice*, Chicago: Quadrangle Books.
Bottoms, A., and McClean, J. (1976). *Defendants in the Criminal Process*, London: Routledge.
Bradley, C. (1993). *The Failure of the Criminal Procedure Revolution*, Philadelphia: University of Pennsylvania Press.
Braithwaite, J. (1989). *Crime, Shame and Reintegration*, Cambridge: Cambridge University Press.
—— (1999). 'Restorative Justice: Assessing Optimistic and Pessimistic Accounts', in M. Tonry (ed.), *Crime and Justice: A Review of Research*, xxv, Chicago: University of Chicago Press.
Canada, (1969). *Report of the Canadian Committee on Corrections Toward Unity: Criminal Justice and Corrections*, Ottawa: Queens Printer.
Cole, D. (1999). *No Equal Justice*, New York: The New Press.
Damaska, M. (1986). *The Faces of Justice and State Authority*, New Haven: Yale University Press.
Ericson, R., and Baranek, P. (1982). *The Ordering of Justice: A Study of Accused Persons as Dependants in the Criminal Process*, Toronto: University of Toronto Press.
Feeley, M. (1979). *The Process is the Punishment: Handling Cases in a Lower Criminal Court*, New York: Russell Sage Foundation.
Fletcher, G. (1995). *With Justice for Some Victims' Rights in Criminal Trials*, Reading, Mass.: Addison-Wesley.
Friedland, M. L. (1965). *Detention before Trial*, Toronto: University of Toronto Press.
Griffiths, J. (1970). 'Ideology in Criminal Procedure or a Third "Model" of the Criminal Process', *Yale Law Journal*, 79: 359–417.
Hart, H., and Sacks, A. (1994). *The Legal Process: Basic Problems in the Making and Application of the Law* (Westbury: Foundation Press tentative unpub. edn., 1958).
Kagan, R. (2001). *Adversarial Legalism: The American Way of Law*, Cambridge, Mass.: Harvard University Press.
Kennedy, R. (1997). *Race, Crime and the Law*, New York: Vintage Books.
King, M. (1981). *The Framework of Criminal Justice*, London: Croom Helm Publishers.
LaFave, W. (1965). *Arrest: The Decision to Take a Suspect into Custody*, Boston: Little, Brown and Company.
Llewellyn, K. (1962). *Jurisprudence: Realism in Theory and Practice*, Chicago: University of Chicago Press.
McBarnet, D. (1981). *Conviction, Law, the State and the Construction of Justice*, London: Macmillan.
McConville, M., and Bridges, L. (eds.) (1994). *Criminal Justice in Crisis*, Aldershot: Edward Elgar.
Nobles, R., and Schiff, D. (2000). *Understanding Miscarriages of Justice: Law, the Media and the Inevitability of Crisis*, Oxford: Oxford University Press.
Packer, H. (1968). *The Limits of the Criminal Sanction*, Stanford: Stanford University Press.

Pound, R. (1930). *Criminal Justice in America*, New York: Da Capo Press.

Roach, K. (1999). 'Four Models of the Criminal Process', *Journal of Criminal Law and Criminology*, 89: 671–716.

—— (2003). *September 11: Consequences for Canada*, Montreal: McGill Queens Press.

Sanders, A., and Young, R. (2000). *Criminal Justice* (2nd edn.), London: Butterworths.

Scheingold, S., Olson, T., and Pershing, J. (1994). 'Sexual Violence, Victim Advocacy and Republican Criminology', *Law and Society Review*, 28: 729–63.

Simon, J. (1997). 'Governing through Crime', in L. Friedman and G. Fisher (eds.), *The Crime Condundrum*, New York: Westview Press, 171–89.

Skolnick, J. (1966). *Justice without Trial: Law Enforcement in Democratic Society*, New York: John Wiley and Sons.

Smart, C. (1977). *Women, Crime and Criminology*, London: Routledge.

Tonry, M. (1995). *Malign Neglect: Race, Crime, and Punishment in America*, New York: Oxford University Press.

United Kingdom (1993). *The Royal Commission on Criminal Justice*, London: HMSO.

United States (1967). *The Challenge of Crime in a Free Society*, Washington: Government Printing Office.

CHAPTER 35

....

LAWYERS AND
LEGAL SERVICES

....

RICHARD L. ABEL

ALL legal professions must answer the following questions: (1) What barriers must entrants overcome, who sets them, and how does and should this affect the number of lawyers? (2) What is the appropriate relationship between the ascribed characteristics of lawyers and the larger society, and how should this be pursued? (3) How does and should the profession limit competition, both among lawyers and by outsiders? (4) What does and should the profession, government, and philanthropy do to stimulate demand for legal services and deliver services to those unable or unwilling to buy them? (5) How does and should the profession, government, and others regulate lawyer behavior? (6) How does and should the profession govern itself in order to perform these tasks?

1 CONTROLLING THE PRODUCTION OF PRODUCERS: NUMBERS

....

Labor markets vary from the most free (e.g. household, agricultural, and unskilled factory work) to the most constrained (e.g. succession to the British throne)

(Larson, 1977; Abel and Lewis, 1988–95). All professions, including law, limit entry. A French *notaire* once could transmit one of the limited number of positions to a child or sell it to a stranger. The English Lord Chancellor keeps Queen's Counsel at 10 percent of the practicing Bar. By contrast, any white man could call himself a lawyer in many American states in the decades following the Jacksonian attack on privilege.

Traditional professions unapologetically restricted entry to maintain members' social and economic status, ostensibly to ensure the integrity essential to their fiduciary relationship with clients. Modern professions justify entry barriers as warrants of technical competence. Professions never tested either claim. We must attempt this essential, if difficult, task, validating performance at each entry barrier against lifetime skill and integrity as a lawyer. (Of course, we can never know whether those who fall at the barriers, or are discouraged from trying, would perform better than those who succeed.) We should also ask whether clients are better off with *no* lawyer than a less well-trained one. What is the justification for a professional paternalism that prevents clients from making price–quality trade-offs? Are there ways of ensuring minimum quality other than entry barriers? Do all legal tasks require identical preparation?

Shortfalls of supply (during wartime or when women became half of new entrants and sought to combine work with child-rearing) or demand (the collapse of the English housing market in the late 1980s, the bursting of the American dot-com bubble a decade later, contraction of the English legal aid budget), as well as fluctuations in the business cycle, lead professions to intervene to restore equilibrium. But manpower planning is very difficult because of the impossibility of predicting demand, the length of time it takes to qualify, and the investment of those in the pipeline. We should study the occasion, justifications, and success of such market interventions.

1.1 Academic Education

Although universities in Continental Europe (and its former colonies) have trained lawyers for centuries, academic legal education became dominant only after World War I in the United States and World War II in other common law countries, perhaps because it articulates more naturally with the theoretical approach of civil law. American law schools responded by developing the case method. With the globalization of some sectors of law practice, common and civil lawyers are having to learn each other's styles of practice. This offers an ideal opportunity to test the virtues and deficiencies of different pedagogies in transmitting knowledge, inculcating skills, and reinforcing integrity. Findings could be used to refine continuing education requirements.

Because higher education is overwhelmingly public, government funding controls numbers. Universities maximize enrollment (sometimes of foreigners, who pay higher tuition and return home to practice). Legal education is cheap: large lectures, little feedback, no laboratories. Rather than limiting numbers, governments are shifting the financial burden through educational loans repaid by high-earning professionals. We should study the effect on class recruitment and career choice. In the United States, where private universities predominate, law schools are accredited by their own professional association (the Association of American Law Schools) and the American Bar Association (voluntary membership and no regulatory authority), which forced most part-time evening programs to close. Now, although the very few proprietary schools may have an incentive to enroll more students, an influential ranking of the nearly 200 schools (by *US News*) has motivated many to shrink enroll-ments in order to boost their median LSAT (law school admission test) scores and thus their rank. Only in a few states (e.g. California) do significant numbers of students attend unaccredited schools (and most do not graduate). Thus, the require-ment of a law degree (absent in England, where students may do a one-year law course after reading another subject) allows numbers to be influenced by university enrollments and tuition, government funding, educational indebtedness, profes-sional associations of lawyers and law schools, and private rankings. We should study how each player seeks to shape entry, its relative influence, and the consequences for fluctuations in supply.

1.2 Professional Courses

Most legal professions require university law graduates to take a practical course, often preparing them for a professional examination. In England, these were con-ducted by the two branches, which could thereby limit entry (though they have since lost their monopolies to each other and universities). In the United States, proprietary courses are regulated only by the market. Because providers are motivated to max-imize enrollment and examination success, the profession has sometimes sought (unsuccessfully) to reassert control. We need to investigate the relationship between course content and pedagogy, exam success, and ultimate performance as a lawyer.

1.3 Professional Examinations

Although some legal professions admit all who complete the university (and usually the professional) course, most set an additional examination. (Nineteenth-century solicitors had to pass *three* exams.) These differ greatly in difficulty: less than 2 percent traditionally passed the examination to enter the Japanese Institute for Legal Training and Research and become *bengoshi* (other law graduates entering peripheral professions, like judicial and administrative scrivener); virtually all pass the Canadian examinations. We need to test the relationship between examination scores and professional performance (although we cannot know how good those who fail would have been as lawyers). We should consider whether a single examination continues to make sense as lawyer work diversifies. We should see what explains variation in pass rates between jurisdictions (e.g. North Dakota and California) and over time (in response to business cycles, wars).

1.4 Apprenticeship

Common law professions (but not civil law) traditionally qualified through apprenticeship. This has been displaced (United States) or complemented (other common law countries) by academic education. The profession believes the academy is excessively theoretical and preoccupied with scholarship; the academy suspects the profession of subordinating teaching to earning. We need to test empirically the strengths and weaknesses of each pedagogy and explore the incentives of academics and practitioners. Although professions do not collectively determine the number of apprenticeships (as they can the difficulty of examinations), lawyer refusals to mentor limit entry. Student investment of time and money in formal legal education increases pressure on the profession to guarantee apprenticeship places to all graduates and pay a minimum wage. We need to study how apprenticeship constrains numbers and shapes composition and allocation to professional roles.

1.5 First Position

Although American lawyers can practice alone immediately after passing the bar examination, most professions impose further restrictions. English assistant solicitors must be employed for three years; minimum salaries facilitate survival but reduce numbers. Barristers must obtain a seat in chambers (which used to be limited, in London, to the Inns of Court). These requirements created subordinated categories of solicitors employed as paralegals and barrister 'floaters' without a permanent seat. We need to evaluate the knowledge, skills, and socialization of assistant solicitors. The Bar's requirement is patently anti-competitive (absent in Scotland); we need to see whether it biases entry.

1.6 Lateral Mobility

In divided professions (like England), each branch regulates transfer from the other. In federal polities (like the United States, Canada, Australia), each state or province regulates transfer from others. With increasing globalization (accelerated by regional integration, such as the EU), members of one national profession seek entry to others. Since most transferees are experienced, we need to study the relationship between the additional hurdles and competence.

2 CONTROLLING THE PRODUCTION OF PRODUCERS: COMPOSITION

All entry barriers influence composition as well as numbers. Traditional professions restricted entry ascriptively (class and gender) to enhance collective status and ensure integrity and altruism (without testing the latter correlations); demands for technical competence were minimal. Character and fitness committees are a vestige (we should study whom they exclude and whether that population is any less ethical than the one they admit). Such exclusivity was first challenged by calls for formal equality, in the name of efficiency, under the banner of meritocracy, through the vehicle of academic education. The warrant of professional legitimacy has begun to change from exclusivity to representativeness in terms of class, gender, race, sexual orientation, and disability. The profession is under pressure to demonstrate equality of outcome (rather than just opportunity) because it enjoys social and economic privilege, members exercise state power (obviously judges but also lawyer legislators and executives), and some believe ascriptive identity between lawyer and client improves the quality of representation (an empirically testable proposition). Making entry more representative increases pressure for representativeness up the career ladder: law firm partners, Queen's Counsel, judges. Indeed, the greater the position's visibility, privilege, and power, the more intense the demands for representation (sometimes appeased through tokenism and figureheads). But just as exclusivity resisted meritocracy (as an index of both competence and desert), so does representativeness. Members of underrepresented categories fear the stigma of affirmative action (suggested by English suspicion of 'reverse discrimination'). (We should study whether it actually stigmatizes.) And pressure for representativeness also undermines control over numbers. Both tensions contribute to backlash (another research question).

2.1 Class

The English Bar not only recorded the occupations of applicants' fathers (usually 'gent' in the nineteenth century) but also prohibited newly qualified barristers waiting years for briefs from engaging in a variety of 'disreputable' trades. Articled clerks had to pay enormous premiums (£500) for the privilege of serving an uncompensated five-year apprenticeship (once spent making 'fair copies', now photocopies). Although meritocracy and (free) university education facilitated social mobility, they also reproduced class privilege, now transmitted through human capital rather than financial or land. Although class no longer bars entry, we need to understand how it influences locus in the professional hierarchy, mediated by school and university attended, grades, apprenticeship, and first position.

2.2 Gender

Few women entered law before the second wave of feminism in the 1970s, although the first wave had abolished *de jure* barriers half a century earlier. Their increasing numbers explain most of the profession's expansion during the last thirty years; now that women have achieved parity, growth will slacken and may reverse if they interrupt their careers for child-rearing. Greater gender equality may have intensified class bias by increasing competition for entry (which could be studied). Although women (after the pioneering generation) embarked on careers similar to men's, they remain underrepresented further up the hierarchy and undercompensated compared with male peers (Epstein, 1993; Hagan and Kay, 1995; Thornton, 1996; Sommerlad and Sanderson, 1998). Maternity leave and positions that make fewer time demands on those caring for young children (but offer less responsibility) perpetuate gender inequality (Epstein *et al.*, 1998). We need to understand why working hours have risen dramatically and how lawyering can be reconciled with family (and other) life. Some observers claim to find gendered differences in lawyering styles (and are criticized for essentialism). We need to understand how and why men and women lawyers differ in career choice and behavior.

2.3 Race

Whereas all legal professions face issues of gender equality, national histories of racism are unique: American slavery and segregation, Australian treatment of Aborigines, distinctive responses to immigration. Unlike gender, race overlaps with class disadvantage. And significant proportions of minority lawyers serve their own communities (like earlier American ethno-religious minorities, but unlike most women). Consequently, the experience of minority lawyers has been very different from that of women. It took a century for American law schools to address the effects of slavery and segregation through affirmative action. Beneficiaries have been strikingly successful, despite law schools' failure to confront the pedagogic requirements of a more diverse student body (Lempert *et al.*, 2000). Nevertheless, such programs never achieved full racial representation and recently have been drastically curtailed through referenda and judicial decisions. Subtle racism—mentoring, socializing, opportunities for rain-making, and intra-professional referral networks—keep minorities underrepresented at higher ranks. We need to identify the mechanisms reproducing racial hierarchy and evaluate the remedies.

3 CONTROLLING PRODUCTION
BY PRODUCERS

Professions that successfully control entry also limit competition from outsiders and among members (Dezalay and Sugarman, 1995; Parker, 1999). Traditionally, they just called it unseemly (the taint of trade). Contemporary lawyers offer a number of self-serving, inconsistent, and empirically untested justifications. Markets are said to erode the 'professionalism' that ensures integrity (through independence) and altruism (through *noblesse oblige*). Monopoly rents (from conveyancing) are said to cross-subsidize unprofitable work (such as legal aid) (although it is unclear why this would be good if true). Competition is said to tempt lawyers to cut corners (although every-where else market forces are supposed to promote quality). Critics have suggested lawyers really seek to extract monopoly rents, protect market share, defend social status, dominate competitors, preserve self-regulation, and guard esoteric knowledge. Both sets of propositions can be tested. Once any restrictive practice is discredited, all become harder to defend. *Laissez-faire* is truly hegemonic. And yet professions are partly a response to market failure: the quality of services cannot be evaluated until *after* they are consumed; and even then informational asymmetries make it difficult for most consumers to do so accurately. We should evaluate various mechanisms for ensuring quality and integrity and promoting altruism.

3.1 Jurisdictional Boundaries

Legal professions define their monopolies very differently—laypersons can sell legal advice and even represent parties in court (without pay) in England but not the United States—suggesting that the boundaries reflect historical accident, cultural variation, and power relationships rather than essential consumer protections. American lawyers succeeded (embarrassingly) in preventing an independent paralegal from assisting clients with name changes and uncontested divorces but failed to close websites offering legal information. English solicitors fought licensed conveyancers (although laypersons transfer property in the United States and Australia), will writers, claims adjusters, and divorce mediators. Some lawyers have encouraged the devolution of functions to laypersons and clients by 'unbundling' legal services. Lay competitors have the competitive advantage of being allowed to solicit business. Some subordinated occupations have sought to professionalize (although the experience of health-care providers reveals the obstacles). The credibility of objections to lay providers is undermined by lawyers' growing use of minimally supervised paralegals to increase profits. We need empirical studies of the quality of services provided by those with different levels and kinds of training.

Elite lawyers also face external competition. Tax is a highly lucrative staple of American large firm practice, but City of London firms lost much of it to accountants and the Bar. Stringent entry restrictions by French *avocats* and Japanese *bengoshi* generated parallel professions serving business (*conseils juridiques*) and providing tax advice (tax scriveners). Arbitrators have captured a great deal of international business litigation from courts (and hence judges) (Dezalay and Garth, 1996). American and English lawyers (and to a lesser extent Canadian, Australian, Dutch, and German) have penetrated leading financial centers (London, New York, Tokyo, Hong Kong, Frankfurt). National professions have sought to limit such intruders to foreign law, and some (like India) banned them. But the most desirable destinations are eager for reciprocity from many of those seeking entry. We need to compare quality across national and disciplinary categories and evaluate the ability of corporate consumers to make accurate judgments.

3.2 Intra-professional Competition

The greatest competitive threats, and hence the most vigorously resisted, come from other lawyers. Professions traditionally prohibited all forms of business generation, regulating even the names under which lawyers could practice and the typeface on their business cards. The large cohort of younger lawyers competing against elders with established reputations and the increasing dominance of market ideology led most professions to relax or eliminate these restrictions. Firms seek individual clients through mass advertising and corporate clients through networking and public relations. But they remain disadvantaged in competing with accountants, who can actively solicit business clients. Legal professions traditionally set minimum fees; but the claim that these protected consumers (by ensuring quality) was undermined by the profession's refusal to set and police maximum fees. The dramatic drop in prices when these patently anti-competitive schedules were abolished exposed monopoly rents. House counsel increasingly monitors the quality and price of the firms they retain, forcing competition through beauty contests. We need to study the anti-competitive effects and justifications of remaining restrictive practices.

Professions also control competition between categories of lawyers. Federal polities restricted practice to the subdivision of admission—impossible to justify given the minimal differences in substantive and procedural law. Where the profession is formally divided (England and some former colonies), branches challenge each other's exclusive jurisdiction. Threatened with loss of their conveyancing monopoly (less by the new occupation of licensed conveyancer than large lenders), solicitors aggressively sought the higher court audience rights of barristers, also coveting the Bar's superior status and monopoly of appointments to the higher judiciary. Barristers responded by unilaterally offering direct access, first to other professionals and then to lay clients, eliminating solicitor intermediaries. Each branch argued (persuasively, if against self-interest) that one lawyer was cheaper than two. Although the government promptly eliminated legal barriers (having fomented inter-branch rivalry in order to cut costs, especially to its own Legal Aid Board), actual practice changed little. Few solicitors qualified for higher court advocacy and even fewer do it, partly because the requisite court time conflicts with the need to be available to clients. And the Bar has categorically declined to conduct the preliminaries of litigation because it does not want to deal directly with difficult clients or handle their money. Habit (or path dependence) is a powerful inertial force. We need to evaluate the efficiency and quality of alternative allocations of legal tasks.

Just as the legal profession exemplifies the division of labor, so it is fragmented by further specialization, first self-identification and then formal certification, based on experience, training, and examination (Carruthers and Halliday, 1998). Specialists seek to increase market share and profits by claiming superior expertise (advertising, titles), negotiating better contractual terms with major consumers (franchises and bulk contracts for legal aid), and ultimately asserting the same kind of exclusive jurisdiction lawyers defend against lay competitors (only specialists can do some kinds of legal aid in England). Generalists naturally resist, invoking professional solidarity. But as the knowledge base grows and functions and clienteles diversify, further fissions seems inevitable (Abbott, 1988). We need to chart the fracture lines and evolutionary sequence and evaluate the contenders' competitive strategies.

Because some legal professions (e.g. barristers, *avoués*) elevated the historical accident of solo private practice to an ideal, they view employment with suspicion. (In civil law systems, employed lawyers—typically a third of law graduates—are a different profession.) Private practitioners rightly fear employment as both subordination (lower status and income and less autonomy—compare large firms with house counsel) and competition (economies of scale, capital and labor substitution). American lawyers opposed legal expenses insurance, claiming third-party payers would interfere with representation (fears substantiated by doctors' experience with managed care). English solicitors adamantly resisted 'corporate conveyancing' by lenders and estate agents, who could not only do it more cheaply but also reach house sellers and buyers first. English barristers vigorously opposed higher court audience rights for lawyers employed by the Crown Prosecution Service (CPS) (or barristers who were partners in, or employed by, solicitors' firms) and the creation of a Criminal Defence Service (CDS). Solicitors claim that lawyers employed by lenders cannot give borrowers independent financial advice (but clients do not seek it from private solicitors). Barristers claim solo practice is essential to independence (thereby insulting all solicitors) and (inconsistently) that CPS lawyers are too close to their client (the state) but CDS lawyers too distant from their client (the accused). We need both a normative theory about the right balance between loyalty to and independence from clients and empirical studies of how different practice structures affect this balance.

Multinational and multidisciplinary partnerships (MNPs and MDPs) are the most recent threats. MNPs let foreign lawyers, forbidden to practice domestic law, partner with domestic, challenging local firms lacking foreign competence. Some nations also fear domination by more aggressive foreign rivals (England by the United States, France by England). English lawyers initially responded by demanding that all MNP members, even those practicing exclusively in foreign countries, purchase (prohibitively expensive) English legal malpractice insurance. MDPs allow firms to combine law with complementary disciplines—pre-eminently accounting—while attracting the best lawyers with the lure of partnership profits, power, and status. MDPs can also aggressively seek business (unlike lawyers) and use the mandatory audits they perform to get and retain legal clients. Moreover, the largest accounting firms are both more global than law firms and much larger (more than ten times). Although some jurisdictions have permitted MDPs, often with stringent regulations, others (notably American states and the Securities and Exchange Commission) have refused, claiming that lawyer–client confidentiality is fundamentally incompatible with the accountant's obligation to disclose. Since the largest accounting firms have already hired thousands of lawyers and become the largest law firms in some countries, we need to assess the dangers to clients (breach of confidence) and society (compromise of auditor independence) and devise suitable prophylactics.

3.3 Relations of Production

Restrictions on relations of production profoundly affect lawyers and clients. Solo practice may be mandatory for higher court advocates or confer a competitive edge (New Zealand and some Australian states). This significantly disadvantages new entrants, who cannot borrow reputational capital from established lawyers to get clients and may depend on the goodwill of the clerk of chambers for briefs. The English Bar has adamantly refused to allow private practitioners to enter partnerships or employment (although it failed to stop employed barristers from doing advocacy). Solicitors' firms were limited to twenty partners until 1967; now Clifford Chance, by merging with American and German firms, has become the world's largest, with nearly 3,000 lawyers. Although economies of scale, comprehensive service, cross-referrals of business among departments and branches, and competition for visibility (a powerful signal of quality in a world of highly imperfect information) have fueled several decades of rapid growth through hiring and mergers, conflict of interest rules prevent law from becoming as concentrated as accounting. Furthermore, legal professions limit access to capital for expansion by forbidding the sale of equity to non-lawyers on the ground that this would compromise autonomy. We need to study the effect of size and organizational structure on law practice.

Whereas lawyers used to join a firm for life, large firms have become more like advertising agencies: rapid mobility of individuals and departments; mergers and dissolutions. Firms increasingly mirror the capitalist clients they serve. Personnel are structured in a steep hierarchy of remuneration, power, and status: senior partners and executive committees; equity and non-equity partners; senior, junior, and permanent associates; contract and temporary lawyers; paralegals; and clerical and support staff. Equity partners' extraordinary incomes depend on billing subordinates at hourly rates approximately three times their salaries and retaining a third as profit— an obvious incentive to maximize leverage (the ratio of subordinates to partners). Although some have described this as payment of rent for partners' surplus human capital, these commentators offer no independent measure of human capital and ignore the fact that partners prevent associates from accumulating human capital (Galanter and Palay, 1991). Because large American firms start inadequately trained law graduates at extraordinary salaries (exceeding $150,000), they make them bill more than 2,500 hours annually through the tournament for partnership, lasting up to ten years, which only about one in ten will win. The costs are fraud (bill padding), dissatisfaction, and dysfunctionality (depression, failed relationships, substance abuse), and attrition (especially of women). Public sector lawyers have unionized but gained little clout, either because they cannot strike (prosecutors) or nobody cares (public defenders). Older lawyers wax nostalgic about a golden era in which protection from competition ensured them even greater profits by exploiting clients rather than subordinates. We need to study the effect of exploiting subordinated labor on job performance and satisfaction and life outside work.

4 CREATING DEMAND

Traditional professionals responded passively to demand, displaying an English contempt for trade or a German idealization of *honoratiores*. Many inherited status and wealth; all were protected from competition. The public also is more ambivalent about legality than health care or education. Does the assertion of rights advance justice or express a litigiousness that is at least selfish and perhaps frivolous or vindictive? Is access to justice a right, protected by constitutions and treaties; or should law be a commodity, allocated by the market? Disagreement about the answer explains why government and philanthropy have been slow and stingy in funding law. Third-party payment also raises difficult questions about the power of government, lawyers, and clients to ration and control services. We need to understand the sources, strength, and substance of government commitment to equal justice.

4.1 Private Demand Creation

Until recently professionalism mandated passivity: lawyers who aggressively sought clients were maligned as ambulance chasers and both disciplined and prosecuted (although markets usually reward such behavior). Because most jurisdictions still prohibit lawyers from targeting prospective clients (the most efficient way to disseminate information), the limited advertising permitted under constitutional (US) or *laissez-faire* (UK) principles is profitable only if it creates mass clienteles for routine work, such as wills, uncontested divorces, or minor workplace injuries (Seron, 1996; Van Hoy, 1997). England (but not the United States) allows non-lawyers to solicit legal work and sell contacts to lawyers. We need to specify the advantages and disadvantages of rights assertion and study empirically the consequences of encouraging it through advertising and solicitation by both lawyers and law brokers.

Because advertising effectively educates about rights and gives purchasers name recognition only if it is extensive and intensive, lawyers have sought to pool resources. The English Law Society engaged in 'Make a Will' campaigns and created the Accident Legal Advice Scheme; local American bar associations operate lawyer referral services to distribute cases randomly. But most lawyers (who finance these activities through dues) gain little and resent those who do get clients. Entrepreneurs perform similar promotional functions for a fee, allocating to subscribers all referrals within exclusive territories. Alternatively, *clients* can be aggregated through legal expense insurance and voluntary associations (trade unions and civil rights, consumer and environmental organizations). Collective action creating rights valuable to a larger population has free-rider problems; legal expense insurance, like all other, creates moral hazard. We need to study the ways in which lawyers, brokers, insurers, and clients have sought to rationalize the market for legal services and the inefficiencies these efforts may introduce.

Philanthropy also redistributes legal services. Lawyers provide *pro bono* (or *pro deo*) services at the behest of intermediaries, often hoping for future paying business from the client or referral source. Law firms fund such programs in response to the commitment of powerful partners, to recruit law graduates and to compete for status. Some firms fund extensive public interest activities from private client fees. Foundations pursue social change agendas but tend to be fickle in their commitment to institutions. We need to understand the incentives for altruism (intangible and material) and how these influence which clients receive what kinds and quality of services from which lawyers.

4.2 Public Demand Creation

Lawyers and clients have selfish reasons to promote rights assertion (interests that can undermine the legitimacy of such efforts). The state's motives for subsidizing legal services are more complex, especially since it may be the beneficiary's adversary (Abel, 1985). Most countries acknowledge an accused's right to representation, while rarely funding it adequately. We need to scrutinize this boundary critically and explore civil claims to which the right might be extended.

Legal aid programs must choose between (or combine) private and salaried lawyers. Only the United States chose not to reimburse private lawyers, fearing 'socialization' of the profession. (American doctors opposed Medicaid and Medicare but have become heavily dependent on them.) Other legal professions claim that salaried lawyers lack sufficient independence (but critics also fear losing market share to state employees). Salaried specialists may have superior expertise, but private practitioners may be more motivated (to retain repeat-players, such as professional criminals, although most legal aid clients are unsophisticated one-shot consumers). The two systems have been converging. The United States now reimburses private practitioners, not only when it must because salaried lawyers have conflicts of interest but also when it wants to cut costs and reduce government dependence on a single provider. England has expanded salaried services for similar reasons (reimbursement schemes are demand driven, making budgets unpredictable). Low reimbursement rates force private practitioners to specialize in legal aid to achieve the economies of scale needed to make a profit. Governments encourage specialization, ostensibly to ensure quality (through franchising based on process variables or certification based on experience) but also to increase provider dependence and thus government's ability to control costs. Lawyers have resisted concentration in the name of client choice (disregarding information imperfections). Compared with salaried schemes, reimbursement involves a much higher proportion of the profession, which therefore supports legal aid more strongly; but lawyer self-interest may undermine public sympathy; and the majority of lawyers who do little or no legal aid may be disaffected. We need to study empirically the independence, cost, and quality of alternative delivery systems.

Legal aid can be a universal benefit like education (English legal aid originally covered 80 percent of the population) or target the poorest (roughly 10 percent in the United States). The profession seeks to expand client eligibility for reimbursement schemes and contract it for salaried lawyers (whom it sees as competitors). Universal benefits enjoy broader popular support (American social security, the British National Health Service); but it is hard to justify subsidizing legal services for wealthy individuals (much less businesses). Governments have made broader programs contributory to cut costs, reducing take-up. Eligibility contracts over time since governments fail to index means tests for inflation. Some countries exclude non-citizens. We need to understand political pressures for inclusion and exclusion.

Services vary by type and distribution. Because criminal defense is a right, civil representation often gets only the money left over. Private practitioners offer poor people services similar to those they offer the middle class (predominately family matters). But salaried lawyers who creatively expand rights are condemned as political and restrained or defunded. Legal aid may not cover administrative proceedings. Political opponents may persuade the state to exclude categories of cases: voting rights, reapportionment, abortion, school desegregation, prisoners, even the eviction defense of public housing tenants charged with drug use. Legal aid may also forbid certain activities: demonstrations, lobbying, class actions. We need to understand the politics of such limitations and consider whether they are consistent with lawyers' ethical responsibilities to their clients.

As employer or monopsonistic consumer, the state sets salaries and remuneration levels. Although starting salaries for American legal aid lawyers were two-thirds those of large firm lawyers in the 1970s, they are less than a third today, sometimes just a fifth, a gap that can widen to twenty to one with age. Similarly, the near-market rates English legal aid paid in the 1950s have eroded drastically (partly because inadequately indexed for inflation). England has further reduced legal aid costs by replacing hourly rates with standard fees, introducing bulk contracts, and making lawyers engage in competitive tendering. All these cost-saving measures adversely affect quality. Lawyers enjoy less legitimacy when seeking money for themselves rather than wider eligibility and broader services for clients. They have less political or economic power than doctors or teachers, since most of the public cares little about the quality or even survival of legal aid, and they are reluctant to wield their limited leverage through industrial actions that hurt clients (boycotts, strikes). We need to study the politics of legal aid funding and the consequences of the widening income gap for who enters and remains and the quality of their work.

Governments have adopted other strategies to reduce costs. As in medicine, they have paid non-professionals to advise clients and even represent them before tribunals and in uncontested court hearings. Governments have encouraged and educated clients to represent themselves in small claims courts. And governments have shifted the financial burden to lawyers and parties through conditional fees and legal expense insurance (creating potential conflicts of interest between clients and both lawyers and insurers). We need to evaluate the relative quality of services provided by professional, lay, and self-representation.

The combination of inadequate salaries, heavy case-loads, and repetitive work, the difficulty of imbuing cases with significance, and the experience of constant defeat demoralizes many lawyers, who disengage or drop out (Katz, 1982; Stover, 1989). We need to consider how to attract, retain, and motivate public interest lawyers and clarify what they can do on behalf of their clients to discipline the power of state and capital, redress ascriptive biases (race, gender, sexual orientation, disability), represent inchoate interests (the environment, consumers), and enforce legal entitlements (Sarat and Scheingold, 1998, 2001).

5 SELF-REGULATION

Professions offer members immunity from external control in exchange for engaging in self-regulation, advancing the same justification they gave for restrictive practices: the specialization necessary to acquire essential expertise makes lawyers the only ones equipped to evaluate their behavior. But like all self-regulatory regimes (e.g. police of violence and corruption, entrepreneurs of pollution), professions are torn between dissatisfied clients and member resentment of unwarranted grievances. The legal profession's response is further complicated by deepening and proliferating divisions, some of which parallel differences in clients and their complaints. Lawyers dominate individual one-shot clients, who feel mistreated; but lawyers are dominated by corporate repeat-player clients, causing injuries with no obvious victims (cf. McConville *et al.*, 1994; Sarat and Felstiner, 1995; Eekelaar *et al.*, 2000; and Mather *et al.*, 2001 with Nelson, 1988). We need to understand how to combine the independence necessary to inspire public trust with the expertise necessary to convince lawyers to submit to regulation.

The profession's reason for insisting on self-regulation is the very information asymmetry that generates complaints. Clients are unhappy about lawyers' failures to keep them informed and answer questions promptly, handle matters expeditiously, disclose fees in advance and stay within cost estimates, achieve the best results, and of course account for client money. Market forces fail to correct these deficiencies because one-shot individual consumers cannot evaluate services before using them, learn from experience, or credibly threaten to defect or damage the lawyer's reputation. Some professions have sought to anticipate these problems and resolve disputes without resort to formal procedures. England requires solicitors to give advance fee quotations (which corporations routinely demand) and operate internal grievance mechanisms (which clients must exhaust before initiating a formal complaint). We need to consider ways of aggregating individual consumers so they, like corporate clients, can mobilize market mechanisms to enhance quality.

The ethical issues that preoccupy lawyers are tangential to common client grievances. Lawyers refine conflicts of interest rules (which may help to create work, for instance by requiring separate representation of mortgage lenders and borrowers); but firms also devise mechanisms to circumvent those rules (e.g. Chinese walls) when they want to accept or retain clients. Lawyers elevate client confidentiality above responsibility to those their clients endanger (thereby gaining a competitive advantage over accountants). Lawyers disclaim moral responsibility for accepting clients (the English Bar's cab rank rule denies them any choice) and even for strategic decisions (e.g. using homophobia in a custody dispute or exposing a woman's prior sexual activity to establish consent in a rape case). We need to investigate which categories of lawyers dominate the drafting of ethical rules and whether unrepresented interests (clients, the public) should have a voice.

Reputation may have been a powerful influence when the London Bar and Circuit messes were small and uniform, but as professions have grown and diversified they have had to formalize social control. Regulatory mechanisms must distinguish between misconduct and incompetence and choose whether to discipline or educate (in law school as well as after qualification). They must identify and address emotional problems and substance abuse. Some disciplinary processes award clients nominal compensation. Unlike most forms of regulation, professions are largely reactive (although some regularly inspect accounts); we need to consider whether they should be more proactive and, if so, how. We should consider how regulators could be encouraged to apprise complainants of the investigation's progress and outcome. They are torn between seeking to protect lawyers against unfounded accusations (false positives) and present and future clients against misconduct (false negatives). We need to consider whether non-lawyers can acquire sufficient expertise to participate in regulation and how to protect them from lawyer domination.

Client discontent with their lawyers is compounded when regulators are also unresponsive, secretive, and slow. Because lawyers (especially in large firms, whose clients rarely make formal complaints) resent the cost of regulation (a large part of their annual membership or practicing certificate fee), disciplinary mechanisms are seriously underfunded. When a growing backlog prevented the English Office for the Supervision of Solicitors from opening new files for six months, it closed intake, provoking the Lord Chancellor to threaten to take over regulation. Some lawyers want the profession to jettison regulatory responsibility, becoming a pure trade union (although it would probably continue to pay the cost). Regulators may lack the resources, expertise, and incentive to investigate thoroughly. The vast majority of complaints are dismissed at an early stage; and clients and the public feel the rare penalties imposed are excessively lenient, suspecting the profession of protecting its own. In federal polities, disbarred lawyers may gain admission to other jurisdictions. We need to explore the funding, staffing, incentives, transparency, and accountability of lawyer self-regulation.

Malpractice and financial misconduct pose distinctive problems. Some legal professions do not require lawyers to carry malpractice insurance, leaving injured clients uncompensated. Partnership liability usually ensures repayment of client funds (although an increasing number of large firms have dissolved recently, some without sufficient assets to cover their debts). Not all professions take collective responsibility for bankrupt solo practitioners, and those that do risk resentment of the cost of compensation funds. By aggregating risk to guarantee compensation of malpractice victims and spread the burden widely, insurance confronts an obvious dilemma. If premiums are not experience rated, those rarely sued for malpractice subsidize the frequent targets. This fuels the anger of large firm lawyers towards solo and small firm practitioners, and of advocates (who do not handle client funds) towards transactional lawyers (who do—English conveyancers, for instance). But if premiums *are* proportioned to risk, lawyers in the high-risk pools object to the stigma and cost (and may even be priced out of practice). Malpractice insurers may police their insureds to reduce liability exposure and premium levels (eroding professional self-regulation). We need to study how politics distorts the insurance market and how risk allocation affects professional divisions and lawyer behavior.

Although professional associations are unlikely to lose all regulatory power, other institutions are taking more responsibility. Governments establish ombudsmen to investigate and publicize the failure of professional self-regulation and even order professions to compensate clients. Large firms have reputations to protect and both the resources to supervise members and the power to change behavior. As lawyers seek to enter new markets, such as financial services (in response to increased internal competition), they expose themselves to new forms of regulation (often governmental). Multinational practice may increase the power of foreign or regional bodies at the expense of domestic regulators. Multidisciplinary practice may subject lawyers to oversight by other professional bodies. Greater specialization may make it more difficult for large mandatory generalist associations to monitor all lawyers; smaller voluntary specialist associations may impose more stringent rules, have a greater stake in their collective reputation, and better understand member behavior. Third-party payers (both government legal aid and private legal expense insurance) have an interest in quality as well as price and may be more willing to expel lawyers from those limited markets than professions are to exclude them from practice entirely. Courts and administrative agencies control lawyers who appear before them and may report misbehavior to professional regulators, impose liability for costs and fines, or use the contempt power. We need a more capacious and nuanced view of the range of regulatory authorities and the different controls they exercise.

6 SELF-GOVERNANCE

Occupations become professions through the kinds of collective action described above. This generates several classic problems: free riders if action is voluntary, violations of autonomy if it is compelled; powerlessness if groups are coherent but small, dissensus if they are large but diverse.

Although professional associations begin as voluntary, exclusive clubs, usually at the instance of elites seeking to enhance or protect their status (frequently by barring undesirables or controlling disreputable behavior), they soon seek government power in order to compel universal membership (to enhance legitimacy and increase political efficacy) and collect dues (to finance activities). Some members may disagree with the body's goals or strategies, invoking rights of free speech or association and seeking to have their dues reduced or the association's activities curbed. Alternatively, government may attack the association's views or actions. California Governor Pete Wilson was so infuriated by the State Bar's liberal positions on social issues (abortion, sexual orientation, the death penalty) that he vetoed its annual authorization to levy dues, forcing it to shut down for months until the state Supreme Court issued an emergency plea for dues and Wilson was succeeded by a governor with views closer to the Bar's. When the English Law Society spent £700,000 to oppose Lord Irvine's Access to Justice Bill (especially its substitution of conditional fees for legal aid in money cases) the Lord Chancellor added a clause empowering him to strip the Society of all but its regulatory and educational functions. We need further thought about how to reconcile coercion and autonomy, voluntarism and responsibility.

As legal professions grow and diversify, associations find it increasingly difficult to represent the interests of their multiplying fractions. For nearly a century, observers have pointed to the profound differences between the two hemispheres of the American profession serving individual and business clients (Heinz and Laumann, 1994). English solicitors are similarly divided by firm size and relative dependence on conveyancing and legal aid. Voluntary associations intensify these differences: the British Legal Association and Sole Practitioners Group on one side, the City of London Law Society on the other; the New York County Lawyers Association and the Association of the Bar of the City of New York (Powell, 1988). Other groups emerge to serve lawyers dependent on a single source of payment (Legal Aid Practitioners Group), practicing in particular courts (London Criminal Courts Solicitors Association), employed (prosecutors, Bar Association for Commerce, Finance and Industry, Law Society's Commerce & Industry and Local Government groups), specialized by substantive area (Solicitors Family Law Association, Association of Personal Injury Lawyers) or even sides of the adversary system (management and union), grouped geographically, or sharing ascribed characteristics (gender, race, ethnicity, religion, age, sexual orientation, disability). We need to study these fracture lines, which can herald future stages in the division of labor.

These centrifugal forces not only spawn competing associations but also shape politics within the official body. Populist demagogues can seek control, hoping to turn the association to the advantage of their faction: limiting the number of lawyers by reimposing entry controls, abolishing anti-discrimination rules, fixing prices, minimizing or ending regulatory responsibility. More commonly, the association is so paralyzed by the need to reach consensus that members lose interest, rarely voting in elections or attending meetings and increasingly resentful of dues, which seem to produce few tangible benefits. Lawyers fail to join voluntary associations (the ABA has never enrolled half the profession). Because elected officials are little more than figureheads, professional associations (like most organizations) are actually run by staff who alone know how to get things done (or prevent them from happening). We need to study the sources and consequences of apathy and engagement.

The professional associations of lawyers, even more than those of other occupations, are obsessed with public image, perhaps because it is perennially bad and always seems to be worsening. Many efforts—*pro bono* activities, educational programs, celebrations of law and lawyers—seek to enhance that image. We need to understand how and why lawyers seek to burnish their image and what difference such efforts make. Unfortunately, most people view lawyers through their personal experience of the law, which is usually unhappy (always for the losing party in litigation, often for the winner too), and firmly believe lawyers produce *injustice* (clients want to win, not lose to vindicate an ideal). We need to understand how clients interpret their encounters with law and lawyers and how these shape their overall conceptions. Since most people have little personal experience with law (the average American sees a lawyer about twice in a lifetime), the media plays a much larger role in shaping popular views. Lawyers are news: in criminal and civil trials, major deals and bankruptcies; as members of the executive, legislature, and of course judiciary; and when charged with misconduct. In recent decades, lawyers have displaced doctors as the favored professionals in television and film, which both glamorize and demonize their character, behavior, and lifestyles (Chase, 2002). We need to study both popular representations of lawyers and how audiences read them.

Professional associations also seek to reform substantive and procedural law and legal and political institutions (Halliday, 1987). Some of these efforts clearly reflect the self-interests of lawyers (opposing no-fault divorce or compensation for injury, which reduce the need for legal representation) or their clients (diluting regulation, creating tax loopholes). But associations also offer opinions about judicial nominees, controversial legal issues (the death penalty, gun control, decriminalization of drugs), and political questions about which lawyers can claim little or no distinctive expertise (immigration, wars). We need to understand when and why professional associations enter the political arena and how effective they are.

7 THE FUTURE OF LEGAL PROFESSIONS

Like all social institutions, professions change slowly; lawyers are especially resistant (partly because law's authority rests on history, precedent). Nevertheless, I can suggest some likely directions. Legal professions will be less able or willing to control numbers. Those at the top of the hierarchy are relatively protected from imbalances between supply and demand, though some may experience downward mobility. Those on the bottom, especially if dependent on a few, volatile sources of work, may be forced out. Professions will feel greater pressure to reflect demographic divisions within the larger society (limiting the ability to control numbers). They will have less difficulty admitting women than those disadvantaged by race, ethnicity, or class; but all four will encounter obstacles further up the career ladder, especially in positions that depend on generating business. Honorific categories, like Queen's Counsel, may be abolished if they do not become representative (since it is easier to justify exclusivity produced by 'market forces'). Restrictive practices will continue to be attacked by forces inside the profession (newer entrants seeking to enlarge their market share) and outside (competitors seeking to invade lawyers' turf, large consumers and third-party payers seeking to reduce costs). It will become more difficult to defend anti-competitive practices in the name of professionalism, independence, or paternalism. Although the state will still pay lip-service to the ideal of equal justice, the gap will widen between the representation and advice that can be bought and what the state, philanthropy, and *pro bono* activities make available. Professional associations will increasingly share regulatory powers with fora (courts, administrative agencies), other professions, supranational bodies, consumers, public and private third-party payers, and the state. Scandalous failures in policing will generate pressure for the reform and even the end of self-regulation. Compulsory comprehensive associations will be paralyzed and either lose their ability to speak for the profession or be challenged or supplanted by voluntary groups representing professional fractions (which will seek the power to compel membership and dues). Law cannot escape the commodification that is transforming other services.

REFERENCE

Abbott, A. (1988). *The System of Professions: An Essay on the Division of Expert Labor*, Chicago: University of Chicago Press.

Abel, R. (1985). 'Law Without Politics: Legal Aid under Advanced Capitalism', *UCLA Law Review*, 32: 474–642.

——and Lewis, P. (eds.) (1988–95). *Lawyers in Society* (4 vols.), Berkeley: University of California Press.

Carruthers, B., and Halliday, T. (1998). *Rescuing Business: The Making of Corporate Bankruptcy Law in England and the United States*, Oxford: Clarendon Press.

Chase, A. (2002). *Movies on Trial: The Legal System on the Silver Screen*, New York: New Press.

Dezalay, Y., and Garth, B. (1996). *Dealing in Virtue: International Commercial Arbitration and the Construction of a Transnational Legal Order*, Chicago: University of Chicago Press.

——and Sugarman, D. (eds.) (1995). *Professional Competition and the Social Construction of Markets*, New York: Routledge.

Eekelaar, J., Maclean, M., and Beinert, S. (2000). *Family Lawyers: How Solicitors Deal with Divorcing Clients*, Oxford: Hart.

Epstein, C. (1993). *Women in Law* (2nd edn.), Urbana, Ill.: University of Illinois Press.

—— Seron, C., Oglensky, B., and Sauté, R. (1998). *The Part-time Paradox: Time Norms, Professional Life, Family and Gender*, New York: Routledge.

Galanter, M., and Palay, T. (1991). *Tournament of Lawyers: The Transformation of the Big Law Firm*, Chicago: University of Chicago Press.

Hagan, J., and Kay, F. (1995). *Gender in Practice: A Study of Lawyers' Lives*, New York: Oxford University Press.

Halliday, T. (1987). *Beyond Monopoly: Lawyers, State Crises, and Professional Empowerment*, Chicago: University of Chicago Press.

Heinz, J., and Laumann, E. (1994). *Chicago Lawyers: The Social Structure of the Bar* (rev. edn.), Evanston, Ill.: Northwestern University Press and Chicago: American Bar Foundation.

Katz, J. (1982). *Poor People's Lawyers in Transition*, New Brunswick, NJ: Rutgers University Press.

Larson, M. (1977). *The Rise of Professionalism: A Sociological Analysis*, Berkeley: University of California Press.

Lempert, R., Chambers, D., and Adams, T. (2000). 'Michigan's Minority Graduates in Practice: The River Runs through Law School', *Law & Social Inquiry*, 25: 395–505.

McConville, M., Hodgson, J., and Bridges, L. (1994). *Standing Accused: The Organization and Practices of Criminal Defence Lawyers in Britain*, Oxford: Oxford University Press.

Mather, L., McEwen, C., and Maiman, R. (2001). *Divorce Lawyers at Work: Varieties of Professionalism in Practice*, New York: Oxford University Press.

Nelson, R. (1988). *Partners with Power: The Social Transformation of the Large Law Firm*, Berkeley: University of California Press.

Parker, C. (1999). *Just Lawyers: Regulation and Access to Justice*, Oxford: Oxford University Press.

Powell, M. (1988). *From Patrician to Professional Elite: The Transformation of the New York City Bar Association*, New York: Russell Sage Foundation.

Sarat, A., and Felstiner, W. (1995). *Divorce Lawyers and their Clients: Power and Meaning in the Legal Process*, New York: Oxford University Press.

—— and Scheingold, S. (eds.) (1998). *Cause Lawyering: Political Commitments and Professional Responsibilities*, New York: Oxford University Press.

—— —— (2001). *Cause Lawyering and the State in a Global Era*, New York: Oxford University Press.

Seron, C. (1996). *The Business of Practicing Law: The Work Lives of Solo and Small-Firm Attorneys*, Philadelphia: Temple University Press.

Sommerlad, H., and Sanderson, P. (1998). *Gender, Choice and Commitment: Women Solicitors in England and Wales and the Struggle for Equal Status*, Aldershot: Ashgate.

Stover, R. (1989). *Making it and Breaking it: The Fate of Public Interest Commitment in Law School*, Urbana, Ill.: University of Illinois Press.

Thornton, M. (1996). *Dissonance and Distrust: Women in the Legal Profession*, Melbourne: Oxford University Press.

Van Hoy, J. (1997). *Franchise Law Firms and the Transformation of Personal Legal Services*, Westport, Conn.: Greenwood Press.

CHAPTER 36

INTERNATIONAL LEGAL SANCTION PROCESSES

JORDAN PAUST

1 THE NATURE OF INTERNATIONAL LEGAL SANCTION OR REMEDIAL PROCESSES

In this chapter, international legal sanction processes are viewed as richly varied and dynamic, involving numerous types of participants, with various sanction objectives, operating in both formal and less formal fora or processes, utilizing various types of resources, with varied effects and long-term consequences. Scholars of a realist orientation tend to focus on such aspects (e.g. McDougal *et al.*, 1980: 1–142, 161–363). More generally, there is increased recognition of a growing interaction and interdependence of individuals, groups, and public and private institutional arrangements in all social, economic, and political sectors and processes (e.g. ibid.; Chen, 2000: 3–81). Sanction processes are sometimes categorized as those involving primarily political, diplomatic, economic, and military or related power tactics (and these general categorizations might be convenient for some forms of future scholarship), but realistic inquiry demonstrates that sanction efforts are not always so neatly compartmentalized (Chen, 2000: 245–322). One focus for future realist or pragmatic scholarship might involve greater attention to a richer array of categories, or at least awareness of various types of sanction processes and strategies that are available and that are actually being utilized by various actors in the international community.

Too many rigid state-oriented (often positivist) theoretical constructs still inhibit thinking about the availability of sanctions for violations of international law outside state-to-state or international organizational processes. For example, some British-trained or influenced writers assume incorrectly that international law merely binds states and state actors. A minority of scholars still questions whether international law exists outside state-to-state and international organizational processes. Further, confusion is still evident among such writers concerning the availability of individual remedies required by or based in international law, whether private individuals and private entities have duties under international law, and whether such rights, duties, and sanction possibilities existed prior to the twentieth century or even prior to World War II (compare Brierly, 1955; Simma and Alston, 1989: 99–100 with McDougal *et al.*, 1980: 73–5; Paust *et al.*, 2000*b*: 7–27; Paust, 1996: 167–210).

Such unrealistic theoretic preferences, never 'traditional' and always opposed (especially by French, German, Italian, and US scholars), are especially unhelpful in a world lacking formal institutional arrangements that are often (but improperly) associated with 'law' in a domestic setting, that is, in a world lacking an effective world government, a world police force, world jails, or a world court with global jurisdiction. They can inhibit realistic awareness of functional legal processes and the full range of sanctions available for more effective realization of legal policies at stake.

The goal of this chapter is not merely to identify certain areas of debate, but also to suggest a future scholarly agenda. With that in mind, it is evident that increasing attention to the creation, shaping, and efficacy of international law outside such traditional institutional settings should be part of a future scholarly agenda regardless of one's jurisprudential bias. Moreover, there is a lack of adequate awareness in some scholarship of the often primary and interpenetrating roles of domestic courts in international legal processes, even though domestic courts are among the formal institutional fora often associated with domestic 'law' and sanctions. Further attention to the identification, clarification, incorporation, application, and shaping of international law through domestic criminal prosecutions and civil litigation will be beneficial for scholarly consideration of 'sanctions' regardless of one's jurisprudential orientation.

2 PARTICIPANTS IN SANCTION PROCESSES

2.1 Governmental

Perhaps most people consider that state governments are the primary initiators and targets of international sanction processes. This appears incorrect, however, given the widespread and continuous participation of numerous other actors in international legal processes, especially as initiators and targets of sanction strategies. Further, governments participate through the actions and omissions of governmental actors, and not all governments are those of states as opposed to regions, nations, belligerents, insurgents, and so forth. Future scholarly inquiry should give increased attention to the role of such non-state governmental actors. Additionally, governments often press claims of various private individual and group actors either directly or indirectly in various formal and less formal sanction processes. Thus, increased attention to the actual roles and objectives of various governmental actors and their association with numerous other actors (including special interest entities and groups locally, regionally, and globally) with respect to sanction strategies would be helpful.

One ongoing (but not 'hot') debate in the area of international criminal law is whether states should be liable to criminal prosecution (e.g. Paust *et al.*, 2000a: 14–15). States and other organizations could be labeled as criminal, have 'state responsibility' under international law (leading to political, diplomatic, and economic sanctions and lawsuits), and be subject to criminal fines; but some scholars ask whether other sanctions might be available against a criminal state.

For example, expansion of 'state responsibility' for supporting international crimes, environmental degradation, denials of human rights, and consequences of economic sanctions is worth attention. Future debate might consider whether, if sanctions become more effective against various private actors, state responsibility for private actor liability should continue or be lessened. Beyond the focus in continual drafts on state responsibility published by the International Law Commission, will the contours of state responsibility be expanded? What sanction objectives and processes will best assure state compliance, and are new institutional arrangements needed or should others be improved?

2.2 International Organizations

It is well known that international organizations such as the United Nations can and do engage in numerous forms of sanction strategies with respect to the promotion and shaping of international law and in response to various violations of international law. After the end of the Cold War, scholarship began to focus on new powers of the UN Security Council, especially with respect to security and peace. Scholarship is likely to continue to focus on new powers and proffered limits of the authority of the Security Council to authorize or mandate economic, military, and other sanction efforts in response to threats to the peace, breaches of the peace, and acts of aggression. There has been debate about whether the Security Council is bound to serve (and thus not to thwart) the major purposes of the UN Charter identified, for example, in the Charter's preamble and article 1. Scholars disagree about whether the

International Court of Justice should review decisions of the Security Council for compliance with these purposes (e.g. Caron, 1993; Franck, 1992: 519–23).

The recent self-defense efforts of the United States in its war on terrorism, with some approval from NATO, and the broad sanction requirements mandated for states in recent Security Council resolutions (e.g. UNSC res 1373 (28 Sept 2001)) and broad authorizations to use military force offer a rich set of issues for future legal scholarship. There have been debates about permissible use of military force (as opposed to diplomatic and economic sanctions) against states that merely 'harbor' or 'tolerate' non-state terrorists and these are likely to continue (e.g. Reisman *et al.*, 1999). Scholars disagree about whether UN-authorized or mandated economic sanctions are always policy-serving (Addis *et al.*, 2001: 23–7). Newer unilateralist claims of pre-emptive self-defense, which most consider to be impermissible under the UN Charter, will also stimulate debate.

2.3 Private Individuals

Private individuals have been both initiators and targets of sanction strategies for at least the last two hundred years. In an increasingly interdependent world, scholarship is likely to pay increasing attention to the role of private individuals as initiators of various sanction strategies and to the use of various sanction strategies against private or public individuals. Of current interest, for example, is the use of various sanction strategies against non-state terrorists. Given increased attention to Bin Laden and his Al Qa'ida followers after September 11, 2001, it is likely that writings addressing sanctions involving the use of military force against, capture of, prosecution of, and civil lawsuits against non-state terrorists in various domestic and international fora will be prominent in near future legal literature.

What will and should the international community expect with respect to sanctions against private individuals and groups that finance or provide other material support for terrorists or for various international crimes such as genocide and other crimes against humanity? Will ordinary criminal prosecutions of complicitous behavior be sufficient or will new crimes have to be created? Will civil suits in domestic legal processes more adequately reach the financiers of international terrorism, narcotics trafficking, genocide, and other crimes against humanity? Are changes needed in domestic laws or processes in particular countries? Additional comparative studies of incorporation of international law in various domestic legal processes could be helpful (e.g. ILA 1996: 570–90 (identifying forms of and trends in incorporation in a large number of states and on all continents); Stein *et al.*, 1997: 289–307).

Future scholarship should consider what roles women have played in the shaping of international law and with respect to various sanctions, and with what sort of consequences. What additional roles or strategies are likely or possible (Askin and Koenig, 2000)? The United States, in contrast to countries like Australia and the United Kingdom, has refused to ratify the Convention on the Elimination of All Forms of Discrimination Against Women. Such a refusal rests partly on the realization that human rights duties based in the treaty can reach the family and various private actors. If the United States does not ratify the treaty, what other sanction strategies are available to women who seek greater effectuation of their human rights? In Australia, the United Kingdom, and other countries that have ratified the treaty, what sanction strategies should be pursued for more effective implementation of the treaty? Debate continues whether failures of protection in some countries are due to permissible cultural relativism or whether generally shared core values and normative content are being violated.

2.4 Corporations and Companies

Recent litigation in Canada, Great Britain, and the United States has focused on the liability of private corporations under human rights law, and debates in law review literature have begun to reflect on the human rights responsibilities of such private actors (McDougal *et al.*, 1980: 103–4; Paust, 2002b: 802–10; Stephens *et al.*, 2001: 42–9; cf. Raday, 2000: 103), some arguing that private duties either do not or should not exist. Courts of Canada, the UK, and other countries have recognized the responsibility of private corporations concerning human rights, especially with respect to equality in employment and working conditions (e.g. *Johnson v Unisys Ltd* [2001] UKHL 13, at [37] (Lord Hoffmann); *Puspanathan v Canada* (1998) 160 DLR (4th) 193, 231 (private violations of human rights can amount to persecution, also noting a related practice by Australia); *Janzen v Platy Enterprises Ltd* [1989] 1 SCR 1252; *Hevra Kadisha, Jerusalem Burial Company v Kestenbaum* (1992) 46 (2) PD 464, 530 (Barak J)).

Since many large corporations and companies wield significant power, wealth, and respect (some wielding more of each than many states) and their acts and omissions can impact greatly on human rights, the environment, and the efficacy of other international laws, it is likely that there will be increasing debate concerning the roles and responsibilities of private corporations and companies under international law. In a simplified form, part of the debate in the United States has focused on whether corporations have human rights duties. Further debate can address how the exercise of power by some multinational corporations impacts on human rights, the environment, international trade, employment, and rights of indigenous peoples and what sanction objectives (see Sect. 3) might be pursued for the greater promotion of international law. Debate has also focused on tensions between human rights and trade and development, and these are worth reconsidering in terms of sanction efforts by and sanctions against corporations.

2.5 Other Groups

As mentioned, with increasing attention to non-state terrorist activities, it is likely that scholarship will involve further inquiry into the role of terrorist groups as targets of sanction strategies. Such groups, depending on their claims, can also be initiators of sanction strategies. More attention might be paid to the type of claims made by terrorists as well as the various sanction strategies used by terrorist groups to achieve various goals. Questions include whether such claims are viable under international law, whether terrorist strategies are always impermissible (e.g. terroristic targetings of enemy combatants during war), whether there are alternative strategies that even terrorist groups might more adequately pursue, and whether there are ways of removing conditions that might spawn terrorism or other forms of impermissible social violence.

The role of non-governmental organizations (NGOs) in efforts to increase the efficacy of human rights, humanitarian law (e.g. the law of war), environmental protection, protection of children, and so forth, is well known (e.g. Chen, 2000: 65–73, 325–6, 334–9, 354–5; Lord *et al.*, 2001). Study of similar roles played by other groups in the shaping of international law and achieving of greater compliance would be useful. For example, increased inquiry into how various private groups use the 'sanctions' of public opinion, public protest, diplomacy, education, various media including websites, networking, lobbying, advising, drafting, testifying, investigating, reporting of violations, and so forth would be helpful, as would examination of how private groups might use such sanction strategies or tactics more effectively.

Scholarship might pay increasing attention to the roles that various groups organized primarily in terms of power, wealth, respect, religion, ethnic or cultural origin, language, skills, and so forth, can play in realizing sanction objectives, as well as to the likely consequences of group participation. Can additional strategies be devised for more effective group participation?

3 SANCTION OBJECTIVES

3.1 General Prevention

As an objective of sanctions, prevention can involve general efforts to discourage impermissible conduct. With respect to terrorism, new treaty and UN Security Council requirements, for example, that states prevent and suppress the financing of terrorist acts, criminalize collection of funds for terrorist acts, freeze such funds, and refrain from providing any form of support for entities or persons involved in terrorist acts, will provide bases for new scholarly inquiry and debates concerning such forms of economic and criminal sanction strategies for prevention and other sanction objectives. Exploration of other methods of preventing terrorism may involve identification of various conditions that spawn terrorism and creative recommendations for prevention. Will more adequate promotion of human rights and dignity for all peoples lessen terrorism? If so, can states be convinced of the need to engage in longer-term preventative efforts as opposed to unilateralist responsive efforts when terrorism strikes? Should international organizations be strengthened or provided with even more support for such preventative efforts?

3.2 Deterrence

Deterrence as a sanction objective, unlike more general prevention, can involve effort to prevent impermissible conduct that has been clearly and imminently threatened. Efforts by some scholars after September 11 to revisit debates about the use of military force to prevent imminent terroristic 'threats' (which logically are not even threats), as opposed to waiting for a process of 'armed attack' to occur which justifies self-defense under article 51 of the UN Charter, will undoubtedly raise concerns about the propriety of the use of unilateral military force for deterrence objectives. European scholars especially debate whether US 'unilateralism' is generally preferable to 'multilateralism' in meeting sanction objectives. Such scholars and others might address how both such efforts can be usefully accommodated.

3.3 Restoration

Restoration as a sanction objective can involve use of sanction tactics to compel a violator of international law to reduce or stop unlawful conduct and to restore situations to those obtaining before violations occurred. September 11 will spawn new scholarly inquiry into the meaning of self-defense under the UN Charter, the roles of the UN Security Council and regional organizations such as NATO and the Organization of American States with respect to terrorist attacks, and issues of proportionality. Debates still continue concerning the permissibility of humanitarian intervention to stop international crimes such as genocide and other crimes against humanity occurring in foreign territory. Future inquiry might identify what forms of political, diplomatic, economic, or military intervention are best suited in what sort of contexts to stop violence, especially private violence, against women and children.

With respect to economic sanctions, scholars debate whether economic reprisals are in need of further regulation. Tensions and violence in the Middle East might spark further attention to use of economic weapons. Debate also continues whether some forms of economic coercion are proscribed by article 2(4) of the UN Charter (Lillich, 1976). Are some tactics, such as the use of food or water as an economic weapon, ripe for more general outlawry? Should some economic sanctions authorized by the UN Security Council be subject to review by the International Court of Justice or other judicial bodies in view of their impact on UN Charter purposes such as self-determination of peoples and the duty to ensure respect for and observance of human rights?

3.4 Reparation and Rehabilitation

Reparation and rehabilitation as sanction objectives can involve money or other reparations with respect to actual losses suffered by victims of violations, and further efforts at rehabilitation of victims in various ways, including provision of long-term medical and psychological treatment. Debates about the need for adequate compensation, punitive damages, access by victims to courts, and effective rights to a remedy for violations of international law will continue. Human rights law has been particularly attuned to the need for access to courts and rights to a remedy, and the Statute for the new International Criminal Court (ICC) allows reparations for victims of international crimes covered by the Statute. Terrorist acts continue to spawn interest in civil sanctions in domestic courts (Carter et al., 2002). Will other international crimes, such as war crimes, genocide, and other crimes against humanity be more adequately addressed and subjected to civil sanctions in domestic courts? How can and should awards of international human rights courts or the International Criminal Court be executed in various domestic legal processes? Will new legislation or administrative rules be needed in some states?

If access to courts, effective judicial remedies, and effective prosecution are blocked or frustrated by state elites (including cooperative judges) and inhibiting doctrines, will victims and other claimants shift attention to economic, political, or other power-related sanction strategies (e.g. social violence)? Scholars might investigate this type of phenomenon and consider more adequately the consequences likely to follow from blocking or hindering of effective judicial remedies or prosecution (see also Sects. 6.1–6.2). Access to courts can also serve to control governmental abuses of power, but there are notable exceptions (e.g. *United States v Alvarez-Machain* 504 US 655 (1992) (narrow reading of bilateral treaty so as not to exclude kidnappings, a reading without traditional use of other international law as interpretive background); *Korematsu v United States* 323 US 214 (1944) (race-based area exclusions and concentration camps); *Garcia-Mir v Meese* 788 F 2d 1446 (11th Cir 1986) (detention of aliens without trial); *Ireland v the United Kingdom*, ECHR, Ser A, No 25 (13 Dec 1977) ('margin of appreciation' regarding detention without trial)). For example, increased attention should be paid to fulfillment of the human right to judicial review of such forms of detention. Greater scholarly attention should be paid to judicial responsibility and restraints on governmental abuse of power, especially in connection with various new laws and practices authorizing detention of terrorist suspects without trial. As part of such effort, there should also be more inquiry into corruption of the judiciary in various countries and the conditions that produce it; and into the need for judicial reforms and more active judicial involvement in efforts to restrain governmental abuse and illegality.

With respect to economic sanctions, there is debate about whether restraints of trade designed to achieve general reparations should be subject to further legal limits. Consequences of some forms of economic sanction strategies are likely to engender further debate about their propriety, for example, with respect to economic sanctions arising out of prior Cuban expropriations (Lowenfeld *et al.*, 1996).

3.5 Long-Term Reconstruction

Long-term reconstruction as a sanction objective in response to violations of international law can involve, for example, efforts to avoid recurrence of violations by modifying particular social, political, or governmental structures or processes or by eliminating 'causes' of violations. Debates still occur with respect to outside military support for self-determination struggles against dictatorial regimes, and the full meaning of self-determination of peoples and the human right to democracy (Paust *et al.*, 1992: 126–41; D'Amato, 1994: 367–80). Issues concerning regime change in Afghanistan and Iraq are also relevant. Certain economic policies of the International Monetary Fund and other economically oriented organizations have been sufficiently thwarting of human rights and self-determination to cause debate about whether goals or policies of the various organizations need to be revisited (e.g. whether they should include greater attention to such consequences).

3.6 Correction

Correction as a sanction objective can involve efforts to influence the behaviour of particular violators. For example, corrective sanctions involving criminal fines or incarceration are well known. A continuing debate concerns the permissibility of the death penalty and in particular, efforts by the United States to retain the death penalty for some persons who were below the age of 18 at the time of commission of an offense. Even with creation of the International Criminal Court, is there an increasing need for more regional international criminal courts with jurisdiction over various international crimes? There is debate in a few countries about whether to ratify treaties creating the International Criminal Court or such regional courts; and about whether local amnesties, formal or functional, serve the needs for justice and accountability as well as peace. Recent claims to new immunity for sitting heads of state and state ministers have stirred debate concerning short- and long-term sanction needs with respect to human rights and international criminal law (see also Sect. 6.2). The recent decision of the Inter-American Court of Human Rights in *Chumbipuma Aguirre, et al v Peru (Barrios Altos Case)*, Inter-Am Ct Hum Rts (14 Mar 2001), concerning the invalidity of local amnesty laws is likely to shift scholarly attention back to the need for accountability and away from self-protecting claims of state elites. Future scholarship might provide recommendations concerning criminal and civil sanctions against sitting heads of state to reinvigorate customary liability and to promote more adequately respect for and observance of international criminal law and human rights.

4 Formal Fora

4.1 Civil Litigation and Related Measures

4.1.1 *International*

Various formal institutional arrangements are available for certain forms of civil sanction strategies. For example, the International Court of Justice (for advisory opinions and state-to-state disputes), the European Court of Human Rights, and the Inter-American Court of Human Rights will continue to play constructive roles. Future scholarship might address whether these institutions need to be strengthened and, if so, how. Should human rights courts be created in Africa (as contemplated), the Middle East, and Asia? Since some of these international fora are inadequate for directly effective sanctions against various non-state violators of international law, should new international institutions be created for more direct and effective civil sanctions against non-state violators? Scholars should address the prospect of an international civil court. Additionally, scholars should address the functioning and prospects of Article 75 of the treaty creating the International Criminal Court (ICC), which allows the ICC to order criminal perpetrators to pay 'reparations to, or in respect of, victims' for the purposes of 'restitution, compensation and rehabilitation' and obligates state signatories to 'give effect' to such a decision.

4.1.2 *Domestic*

Most direct forms of civil sanction effort involving litigation occur in domestic fora. Are rights of access to domestic courts and to effective remedies being adequately implemented? Should states that deny such rights, thus implicating state responsibility, be subject to new sanction strategies at the international or regional levels? Should more detailed procedural guarantees concerning civil litigation be identified (cf. art. 14 of the International Covenant on Civil and Political Rights, 999 UNTS 171 (9 Dec 1966)) and form part of international and regional human rights instruments? How might more adequate mutual legal assistance (beyond service of process or the taking of evidence) be stimulated (Paust *et al.*, 2000*b*: 713–38)?

The increasing internationalization of private rights and duties may be met with new forms of backlash or opposition. In the United States, a radical conservative agenda to change the reach of international law domestically is evident, especially in relation to human rights and the prohibition of genocide (compare Bradly and Goldsmith, 1997*a*, 1997*b* with Paust, 1999, 1996: 167–210).

4.2 Criminal Prosecution

4.2.1 *International*

The new International Criminal Court will be functioning soon, thus providing a major development of international criminal law enforcement at the international level. Scholarly attention will continue to address the ICC's jurisdictional reach with respect to certain crimes (for example, it will not reach all crimes against humanity and war crimes) and to nationals of non-signatories in certain circumstances, the workings and refinements of complementarity or coordination of jurisdiction with that of various states, its refined rules of evidence and procedure, rulings that clarify individual responsibility for and defenses concerning various crimes, and so forth (Paust *et al.*, 2000*a*: 708–16). (For additional attention to developments in the International Criminal Tribunal for the Former Yugoslavia (ICTY), see McDonald and Swaak-Goldman, 2000.)

The United States seems to be increasingly opposed to institutional arrangements that it cannot control (such as those under the UN Law of the Sea Convention). This is apparently part of the US justification for its opposition to ratification of the treaty creating the International Criminal Court. Scholars might pay further attention to this trend and to likely consequences on the one hand for effective international legal sanction processes and the serving of more general short- and long-term foreign policy interests of countries like the United States, and on the other hand for the international community.

4.2.2 *Domestic*

Domestic fora will continue to be the primary fora for prosecution of international crimes. Have states adequately implemented international criminal law? Comparative studies are needed, for example, concerning domestic legislation and practices designed to implement the many international criminal law treaties that exist. Why have some states, like Australia, been so reluctant to prosecute international crimes such as genocide, other crimes against humanity, and war crimes?

In the United States and abroad, controversy has arisen over the recent US proposal to create military commissions for prosecution of alleged non-state terrorists and the lack of adequate attention to due process and equal protection guarantees under the 1949 Geneva Conventions, Protocol I thereto, human rights law, and other international laws. Some countries (like the UK, France, and Spain) have refused extradition of accused to the United States or warned of such a consequence unless the United States applies due-process guarantees required under international law. In various countries, should military commissions, as opposed to ordinary domestic courts or regional and international fora, be used for such prosecutions? What forms of due process and equal protection are and should be guaranteed under various international laws (Paust, 2002*a*)?

5 Less Formal Processes

Less formal sanction processes can include certain political, diplomatic, economic, and ad hoc military arrangements. Scholars should address the question of whether direct military or economic sanctions are preferable in efforts to seek compliance by states with international law or whether diplomatic sanction strategies should be used instead, such as those seeking to identify mutual self-interests (i.e. common interests) and to utilize various cooperative and negotiation processes for agreed solutions to problems (Chayes and Chayes, 1995). Should private individuals and groups have greater formal roles in shaping economic and political sanction processes (Strauss *et al.*, 2001).

6 More Specific Sanction Strategies or Problems

6.1 Strategies for Accountability and Efficacy

6.1.1 *Universal Jurisdiction and Responsibility*

Under customary international law, it is the responsibility of states alternatively (1) to initiate prosecution of, or (2) to extradite all persons reasonably accused of crimes under customary international law (Paust *et al.*, 2000*a*: 132–6, 140–7, 170–1, 175; *United States v Arjona* 120 US 479 (1887); *United States v Klintock* 18 US 144, 147–8 (1820); *Talbot v Janson* 3 US 133, 159–61 (1795); *Demjanjuk v Petrovsky* 776 F 2d 571 (6th Cir 1985); *Ex p dos Santos* 7 F Cas 949, 953 (1835); *United States v bin Laden* 92 F Supp 2d 189, 222 (2000); *Flatow v Islamic Republic of Iran* 999 F Supp 1, 14 (1998); 1 Op Att Gen 68, 69 (1797); *Polyukhovich v Commonwealth* (1991) 172 CLR 501). This customary and universal, mandatory but alternative duty is reflected in the phrase *aut dedere aut judicare* and in UN Security Council and General Assembly resolutions and other international organizational practices. A significant number of international criminal law treaties expressly include the obligation and stress that it applies without exception whatsoever, thus reflecting its continual affirmation and consistent patterns of legal expectation relevant to the duty's continued base in customary international law.

However, as the relevance and actual reach of international criminal law has grown, some state elites (perhaps fearful of their own responsibility and the reach of international law in an increasingly interdependent world) and some text-writers have begun to question whether universal jurisdiction should continue to provide a competence for every state to bring into custody and initiate prosecution of all who are reasonably accused of international crimes (see also Sect. 6.2.1). Debates in the legal literature have begun to address such efforts to cut back universal jurisdiction and responsibility. Further attention to such claims, likely consequences of acceptance of any cutbacks, and the need for more adequate accountability for all who are reasonably accused of international crimes, should be part of a future scholarly agenda. Much is at stake.

Another problem involves efforts by some state elites, judges, and text-writers to change the customary definitions, and thus the customary reach, of certain international crimes. Threats to accountability are evident, for example, when attempts are made to change customary definitions of crimes against humanity by adding limiting phrases such as a putative need for 'systematic' or 'widespread' patterns of conduct. This is evident even in the statute for the new International Criminal Court, which adopts only a limited jurisdictional coverage over some crimes against humanity. The phenomenon has been part of the debate in legal literature in the last several years, and attention to continued attempts to limit accountability by definitional limitations or exclusions should be part of a responsible future scholarly agenda. Egregious cases include: *R v Imre Finta* [1994] 28 CR (4th) 265 (SCt Canada); *Matter of Touvier* Cour de Cassation (Criminal Chamber) (France) (1992); *Matter of Barbie* Cour de Cassation (Criminal Chamber) (France) (6 Oct 1983 and 26 Jan 1984); see also Paust *et al.*, 2000*a*: 876–909).

6.1.2 *Incorporation of International Law*

International law has been incorporated in domestic legal processes both (1) directly as the basis for a civil claim or defense or for prosecution, and (2) indirectly through domestic constitutions or other laws or as an interpretive aid with respect to the meaning, content or reach of domestic laws (ILA, 1996; Paust *et al.*, 2000*b*, chs. 1–3; Paust, 1996, chs. 1–5). Such forms of incorporation have been the focus of scholarly inquiry in the past and will be a necessary part of any future scholarly agenda given increased interdependence and increased litigation and prosecution of violations of international law. Especially important will be research into legislation and trends in judicial decision involving incorporation of international law for both civil and criminal sanctions.

With respect to civil sanctions, increased attention needs to be given to effective implementation of the rights of individuals to access to courts and to effective remedies for violations of international law. What problems remain, how can they best be solved? Is there a need for further legislation in particular countries? If so, what particular forms of legislation are needed or would be helpful?

6.2 Strategies for Avoidance of Sanctions

6.2.1 *Immunity*

The reach of jurisdiction over violations of customary international law for both civil and criminal sanctions is also universal with respect to the status of perpetrators. For example, with respect to international crimes, there is absolutely no head-of-state, diplomatic, or public-official immunity under customary international law or any international criminal law treaty or instrument (Paust *et al.*, 2000*a*: 27–34, 38, 132–4, 136, 170–1, 741–8). As recognized by the International Military Tribunal at Nuremberg: 'The principle of international law, which under certain circumstances protects the representatives of a state, cannot be applied to acts which are condemned as criminal by international law. The authors of these acts cannot shelter themselves behind their official position', and one 'cannot claim immunity while acting in pursuance of the authority of the State if the State in authorizing action moves outside its competence under international law' (Opinion and Judgment of the IMT at Nuremberg (1 Oct 1946)). Thus, acts in violation of international law are beyond the lawful authority of any state and are *ultra vires* (Paust *et al.*, 2000*b*: 25, 303–4, 313–14, 574–5, 592–3, 651, 676, 709–11).

Some state elites are clearly uncomfortable with these principles of customary international law and some text-writers have also begun to challenge non-immunity for violations of international law (Paust *et al.*, 2000*a*: 34–8, 338–9; Paust *et al.*, 2000*b*: 653–71). Some countries, like Australia and the United States, openly refuse to prosecute former Nazis accused of international crimes, thus providing a functional immunity and continual failure to comply with the obligation *aut dedere aut judicare* with respect to certain accused (Paust *et al.*, 2000*a*: 151–5). In partial contrast, the United Kingdom has recently convicted a Nazi war criminal, Mr Sawoniuk, the first person to be prosecuted under the War Crimes Act 1991 (ibid. 284; *R v Sawoniuk* [2000] 2 Cr App Rep 220). Such failures need further scholarly attention. More generally, since elites are likely to push for various cutbacks in non-immunity, and a recent majority opinion of the International Court of Justice (*Case Concerning the Arrest Warrant of 11 April 2000 (Democratic Republic of the Congo v Belgium* (2002) ICJ) provides a new cutback in sharp contrast with the decision of the International Criminal Tribunal for Former Yugoslavia in *The Prosecutor v Milosevic* (8 Nov 2001), it is likely that future scholarship will address such claims and the validity and likely consequences of the ICJ decision.

6.2.2 *Domestic Amnesty and Related Practices*

Non-immunity under international law for violations of international law is also reflected in the recognition that domestic amnesties, pardons, immunities, statutes of limitation, and limiting laws or orders are not valid internationally or binding in other states (*Chumbipuma Aguirre, et al v Peru (Barrios Altos Case)*, Inter-Am Ct Hum Rts (14 Mar 2001); Paust *et al.*, 2000*a*: 133–6, 140, 170–1). Nevertheless, some text-writers have argued that interests other than the need for accountability and justice, such as interests in peace and stability, justify changes in the rule of non-immunity (ibid. 20–5, 136–40, 144). Elites interested in obtaining immunity are likely to push similar claims. Thus, future scholarship is likely to address such claims for cutbacks in accountability, as well as tensions evident at times between accountability and justice on the one hand and peace and stability on the other; although scholars have rightly asked whether the dichotomy is real (e.g. whether such non-immunity is merely one more form of oppression, and whether peace is actually possible without justice).

6.2.3 *Statutes of Limitation*

There are no statutes of limitation under customary international law either for civil or criminal sanctions. Further, as far as I am aware, no international criminal law instrument or relevant treaty contains a statute of limitation, and article 29 of the treaty creating the International Criminal Court expressly denies applicability of any statute of limitation. It is therefore evident that, under international law, sanctions against violations of international law should not be subject to any statute of limitation.

Nevertheless, when international law claims have been raised in domestic civil litigation some courts have borrowed domestic statutes of limitation to bar effective sanctions against international law violations. This has occurred in the United States with respect to some civil claims under the Alien Tort Claims Act (ATCA) (28 USC § 1350) despite the fact that ACTA contains no statute of limitations and was meant to incorporate international law and provide causes of action and adequate remedies. Some US legislation providing causes of action for certain international law violations also contains statutes of limitation (e.g. the Antiterrorism Act, 18 USC §§ 2333, 2335 (four years), and the Torture Victim Protection Act (TVPA), Public Law 102–256, 100 Stat 73, section 2(c) (ten years)). Tolling of statutes of limitation (while a defendant is outside the territory of the forum state and thus outside its enforcement jurisdictional competence under international law) is allowed either under equitable judicial doctrine (e.g. regarding the ATCA or the TVPA) or specific legislative provisions (e.g. the Antiterrorism Act). Scholars should give more attention to these and other domestic limitations on sanctions against violations of international law. Have such limits had negative consequences for access to courts and the right to effective remedies for violations of international law? What interests are served by statutes of limitation? Should these be addressed in international agreements instead of by domestic courts or legislators?

6.3 Strategies for Cooperation or Accommodation

6.3.1 *Mutual Legal Assistance*

Mutual legal assistance treaties and arrangements are increasing in number (Paust *et al.*, 2000*a*: 724–35). The functioning of such arrangements is ripe for further scholarly attention. With increasing litigation and prosecution of international law, how have mutual legal assistance arrangements impacted on effective sanctioning of international law violations? What needs arise and how can mutual legal assistance be more effective?

6.3.2 *Extradition*

Extradition of persons accused of international crimes was the focus of much scholarly attention in the latter half of the twentieth century. Issues still being debated include: the appropriate reach of the political offense exception to extradition; the need for non-application of the political offense exception to international crime; resolution of conflicting claims to extradition by states and international tribunals (especially with the creation of the new International Criminal Court); and the need for greater inquiry into foreseeable deprivations of the human rights of persons accused if they are extradited to certain countries. This last issue has achieved recent prominent attention as Spain, the United Kingdom, and France have either refused, or expressed concerns about, extradition of alleged terrorists to the United States for trial in military commissions that will involve violations of human rights to due process and of other international norms.

Canada, Mexico, and various European countries also refuse to extradite criminal accused to countries such as the United States that impose the death penalty, at least without assurances that the death penalty will not be imposed against a particular extraditee. How have such claims impacted extradition processes? The failure of some states to notify foreign accused of their right to communicate with their consulate (under the Vienna Convention on Consular Relations) and various domestic and international judicial decisions regarding such rights have led to disagreement in the law review literature and courts.

6.3.3 *Facilitation of Execution of Judgments*

Given increased use of domestic courts for litigation of international legal claims, increased scholarly attention to facilitation of transnational execution of judgments would be useful. As noted, article 75 of the treaty creating the International Criminal Court imposes obligations on signatories to give effect to decisions of the ICC awarding reparations. Other treaties attempt to facilitate execution of certain domestic legal judgments, although they leave a great deal of discretion in each state as to whether a particular judgment will actually be executed (Paust *et al.*, 2000*b*: 736–8). What factors have inhibited greater facilitation? How can such factors and relevant problems be addressed? Is there a need for changes in existing treaties, or to create new treaties to facilitate execution regionally or internationally?

6.3.4 *Treaty Allocations of Primary Jurisdiction*

Certain international agreements allocate primary jurisdiction over various criminal matters among state signatories and/or between states and international criminal courts. NATO Status of Forces Agreements concerning military accused and the Statutes of the International Criminal Tribunal for Former Yugoslavia (art. 9) and for Rwanda (art. 8) concerning certain persons accused of international crimes are examples. Complementarity-of-jurisdiction provisions also appear in the treaty creating the International Criminal Court (art. 17 and 20). Scholars might pay further attention to the workings, conditions, and consequences of primacy and complementarity, and of concurrent jurisdiction more generally under such international agreements. Is there a need for refinement of the agreements or of their actual functioning? What problems are predictable in the implementation of articles 17 and 20 of the Statute of the ICC?

REFERENCES

Addis, A., Stark, B., Slaughter, A., Atik, J. C., and Reisman, W. M. (2001). Panel: 'Does Method Matter?' *Proceedings, American Society of International Law*, 95: 23–7.

Askin, K. D., and Koenig, D. M. (2000). *Women and International Human Rights Law*, i–ii, New York: Transnational Publishers.

Bradly, C. A., and Goldsmith, J. L. (1997*a*). 'Customary International Law as Federal Common Law: A Critique of the Modern Position.' *Harvard Law Review*, 110: 815–76.

Bradly, C. A., and Goldsmith, J. L. (1997b). 'The Current Illegitimacy of International Human Rights Litigation', *Fordham Law Review*, 66: 319–69.

Brierly, J. (1955). *The Law of Nations* (5th edn.), London: Oxford University Press.

Caron, D. (1993). 'The Legitimacy of the Collective Authority of the Security Council', *American Journal of International Law*, 87: 552–88.

Carter, B. E., Gerson, A., Scharf, M., and Sofaer, A. (2002). Panel: 'The Judicial Response to Terror', *Proceedings, American Society of International Law*, 96: 250–9.

Chayes, A., and Chayes, A. H. (1995). *The New Sovereignty: Compliance with International Regulatory Agreements*, Cambridge, Mass.: Harvard University Press.

Chen, L. (2000). *An Introduction to Contemporary International Law* (2nd edn.) New Haven: Yale University Press.

D'Amato, A. (1994). *International Law Anthology*, Cincinnati: Anderson Publishing Co.

Franck, T. M. (1992). ' "The Powers of Appreciation": Who Is the Ultimate Guardian of UN Legality?', *American Journal of International Law*, 86: 519–23.

ILA (1996). 'Report of the Committee on International Law in National Courts', in *International Law Association, Sixty-Seventh Conference, Helsinki* 570–90.

Lillich, R. B. (1976). *Economic Coercion and the New International Economic Order*, Charlottesville, Va.: Michie Co.

Lord, J., Greenberg, M. E., and Diller, J. M. (2001). Panel: 'On the Possibilities and Limitations of NGO Participation in International Law and its Processes', *Proceedings, American Society of International Law*, 95: 295–309.

Lowenfeld, A., Clagett, B. M., Leigh, M., Rubin, A. P., Byers, M., Strauss, A., Trooboff, P., Fauteux, P., Stern, B., and Rockwood, B. L. (1996). Panel: 'Cuba and U.S. Sanctions and Extraterritoriality', *Proceedings, American Society of International Law*, 90: 368–79.

McDonald, G. K., and Swaak-Goldman, O. (2000), *Substantive and Procedural Aspects of International Criminal Law*, i, The Hague: Kluwer Law International.

McDougal, M. S., Lasswell, H. D., and Chen, L. (1980). *Human Rights and World Public Order*, New Haven: Yale University Press.

Paust, J. J. (1996). *International Law as Law of the United States*, Durham, NC: Carolina Academic Press.

—— (1999). 'Customary International Law and Human Rights Treaties are Law of the United States', *Michigan Journal of International Law*, 20: 301–36.

—— (2002a). 'Antiterrorism Military Commissions: Courting Illegality', *Michigan Journal of International Law*, 23: 1–29.

—— (2002b). 'Human Rights Responsibilities of Private Corporations', *Vanderbilt Journal of Transnational Law*, 35: 801–25.

—— Bassiouni, M. C., et al. (2000a). *International Criminal Law* (2nd edn.), Durham, NC: Carolina Academic Press.

—— Fitzpatrick, J. M., and Van Dyke, J. M. (2000b). *International Law and Litigation in the U.S.*, West Group, American Casebook Series, St Paul, Minn.: West Publishing.

—— Schloh, B., van Boven, T., Franck, T. M., Qureshi, A. H., Halberstam, M., Masahiko, K., and Hohmann, H. (1992). 'Democracy and Legitimacy', in *Contemporary International Legal Issues: Sharing Pan-European and American Perspectives*, Dordrecht: Martinus Nijhoff, 126–41.

Raday, F. (2000). 'Privatising Human Rights and the Abuse of Power', *Canadian Journal of Law and Jurisprudence*, 13: 103–35.

Reisman, W. M., Damrosch, L. F., and Turner, R. F. (1999). 'Symposium: Legal Responses to International Terrorism', *Houston Journal of International Law*, 22: 3–91.

Simma, B., and Alston, P. (1989). 'The Sources of Human Rights Law: Custom, Jus Cogens, and General Principles', *Australian Yearbook of International Law*, 12: 99–100.

Stein, E., Frowein, J. A., Danilenko, G. M., and Iwasawa, Y. (1997). *Proceedings, American Society of International Law*, 91: 289–307.

Stephens, B., Crow, M., Herz, R., and Myles, K. L. (2001). Panel: 'Alien Tort Claims and Business Liability', *Proceedings, American Society of International Law*, 95: 42–9.

Strauss, A., Falk, R., and Franck, T. M. (2001). Panel: 'Citizens in the International Realm: The New Participatory Demands', *Proceedings, American Society of International Law*, 95: 162–72.

PART VII

RESEARCH AND RESEARCHERS

CHAPTER 37

A TRANSNATIONAL CONCEPT OF LAW

H. PATRICK GLENN

MOST of the legal theory of the last four centuries, in the Western world, has been state-centered. It has justified the existence of states, facilitated their expansion, conceptualized their sources and structures, sought to resolve their conflicts, and developed their law. The state has even been taken, in much of this writing, as the exclusive source of law. There are indications, however, that this theoretical pre-occupation with state structures, state institutions, and state laws may now be in decline. This would be a significant development, an historical shift in emphasis in the conceptualization of Western law. It would not, however, mean the end of states or of state law, but rather their contextualization. States and state law would exist in a larger field of normativity. This would entail recognition of a wider range of sources of law and a wider range of relations between laws and between peoples. To attempt to understand these processes, and the extent of their progression, it may be useful first to examine what we know, or think we know, of the relations between law and the state, before turning to current efforts to develop a transnational concept of law.

The research assistance of Vinay Shandal and the financial support of the Wainwright Foundation of the McGill Faculty of Law are gratefully acknowledged.

1 LAW AND THE STATE

Law prior to the state did not bind, but was available to those who might have need of it. The common law was thus suppletive law for most of its existence (*stare decisis* emerging only in the nineteenth century), and the jurisdiction of the royal courts was an option amongst many. This was also the case for Roman law, and for the *ius commune* of Continental Europe. What we know as custom was much more present in the lives of ordinary folk, but this was not conceptualized as binding obligation. It was rather simply a way of life, and one was expected to live the life one had chosen to live. That which bound in medieval Europe was religion, from the Latin *relegare*, to bind or collect together, and we may see, in this earlier model of obligatory grouping of people around a higher ideal, a model for later ideas of state law. The notion of 'binding' was to be pressed into service once again.

It would be inappropriate to think of pre-state law as transnational law, since there were as yet no nation-states to transcend. Yet both the common and civil laws were overarching, in their ability to speak to different peoples in different places, and to attract some form of adherence from them. They were also open laws, not conceived as closed systems, such that the lawyers and judges of the common law in England both informed, and were informed by, the maritime, ecclesiastical, and Equity practice of the civilians of Doctors' Commons.

1.1 Nationalization of Law

Turning law into state law, even theoretically, was a very long process. It first involved Christianity which, unlike other religions, contemplated a world of Caesar in which the human person, in the image of God, could act as God's delegate in the exercise of dominium over the world. It involved political theory, which constructed a model of political organization to offset the hazards of a natural world perceived, at least in the circumstances of Europe, as brutal. It involved scientific epistemology, itself perhaps religiously derived, which portrayed the world as real, capable of inspection, analysis, and even redirection. And it involved the particular form of thought which is Western philosophy, notably a form of binary rationality derived from Aristotle and a healthy scepticism towards universals.

The state is thus profoundly embedded in many streams of Western thought, which is why its disappearance is unlikely and why its decline will be a very slow process. The detailed work of state construction was of course the work of lawyers, who undertook the task of construction without a master plan or theory. They simply built from the ground up, developing whatever theory they needed as they ascended. The first state, in the sense of contemporary international law, was

England. It possessed, by virtue of the hazards of geography and military conquest, an effective government exercising authority over a defined territory. As such it existed from the eleventh century, though it was only in the twentieth century that a full theory of a national legal system emerged. The same pattern was replicated on the Continent, piecemeal construction and expansion being followed by more developed, justificatory theory. States were created, in Europe, at the same time as worldwide colonization occurred and the two derived essentially from the same process of expansion. Within Europe the process of expansion ended when other territorial ambitions were met, and national boundaries thus drawn (*uti possidetis juris*) (Glenn, 2003). Outside Europe, in the absence of organized resistance, the process took longer (the expanding frontier) but the process was essentially the same, if you can discount the suffering. Law was an essential element, eventually, of national construction and national expansion. The Civil Code of France may be seen as bringing France together in 1804 as it came into force, by virtue of its own article 1, on successive days in a series of concentric circles radiating out from Paris, each a day's ride further than the last. In England, the language of 'binding' national law began to be used with some frequency in the first decades of the nineteenth century. This was also the century of development of the notion of *stare decisis* and of creation of vertical, national structures of courts in common law jurisdictions.

State law is introspective law, but the new states were unable to ignore the rest of the world. They *were* able, however, to transform the world into one dominated by concepts of statehood. This came about primarily through colonization, as a result of which state structures were imposed on the entire globe, only the uninhabited continent of Antarctica escaping this hegemonic process. It also resulted from the development of the three legal disciplines of public international law, private international law, and comparative law. Each of these has played a part in the construction and maintenance of states. Each is profoundly rooted in Western, statist theory.

Public international law came into being with the creation of states, and served as the principal justification for their individual existence and recognition. As state structures were imposed on the world by Western colonialism, so public international law came to be seen as global in importance. Public international law is meant to limit states, at least to the extent that it is recognized by them, but it is first and foremost a creation of Western states, meant to exist for their mutual advantage.

Private international law also exists to facilitate the inter-national, and according to state criteria. Thus, private international cases can be dealt with only according to state law, which is presumed complete for every case. Cases are referred to state law, for resolution, according to criteria which are geographic (connecting cases with state territory) or interpretive (defining the reach of state legislation). Differing concepts of justice can thus have application only in accordance with state rules.

Comparative law, in contrast, would entail examination of the respective merits of substantive rules. In the Western tradition, this is what comparative law initially did, and it was widely engaged in, with great resonance, from the sixteenth century. The timing is important, since this is, once again, the era of the construction of states. So comparative law became an intellectual tool in the construction of state law, an instrument in the nationalization of law. Canon law, customary law, Roman law, all were exhaustively researched in the pursuit of the better rule, which could then be incorporated into formal state law. When this task could be seen as at or near completion, with the codes, exhaustive treatises, and binding case law of the nineteenth century, comparative law could assume a more specialized, and marginal, role. Through the nineteenth and twentieth centuries, comparative law, as a discipline, dedicated itself principally to the amelioration of state law and the construction of taxonomies of national legal systems. Only specialists could perform these functions. They were in no way subversive of state legal orders.

Western legal theory came to a developed articulation of state law and national legal systems in the nineteenth and twentieth centuries. In the civil law world, Kelsen explained state law as descending from a presumed basic norm that state constitutions should be followed. The panoply of state law was thus rooted in a larger (through presumed) national normative order. In the common law world Hart refined earlier notions of law as sovereign command and explained national legal systems as a combination of primary rules of obligation, directed to citizens, and secondary rules of recognition and change (of state primary rules) and adjudication. Hart was sufficiently confident of state law that he could present his analysis as simple description (justification being no longer required) and as general or universal in character.

In spite of the enormous influence of these ideas on the role of states and state law, they have been less influential in the world than commonly supposed, at least by legal theorists in their countries of origin. There has been considerable correspondence between statist legal theory and actual legal practice in Europe and the United States, but elsewhere it has been taken *cum grano salis*. States in the colonized world (the rest of the world) lived through the eighteenth, nineteenth, and twentieth centuries in a delicate equilibrium between local law (often in non-state form) and the metropolitan law of the colonial power. Identities here were complex and shared, law was conceived in a pluralistic manner, state law was necessarily limited, and conquered peoples played an active role in the determination of the law applicable to them. Even the independence of former colonies did not end these phenomena, and the ongoing use of 'persuasive authority', particularly in the common law world but not limited to it, is an indication of ongoing resistance to exclusivist, statist concepts of law (Glenn, 1987). Law here has been conceived for centuries in a transnational manner.

1.2 Denationalization of Law

The process of denationalization of law resembles that of the nationalization of law. It is proceeding incrementally, differently in different fields, with no established master plan or theory.

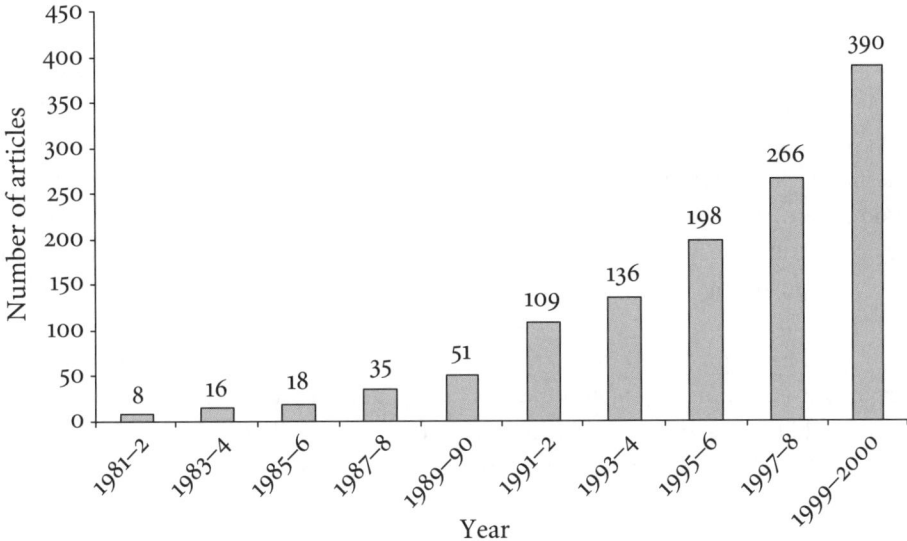

Fig. 37.1. Articles containing global(ization) in title

Source: Index to Legal Periodicals, searched 21 Aug 2001.

The major factor contributing to the denationalization of law would be the declining role of the state in the world. There is now a large literature dealing with this subject. The decline of the state, paradoxically, would result both from the collapse of the colonial empires and subsequent rejection of Western models (failed or dysfunctional states) and from the 'globalization' of Western commercial, technological, and legal methods. The latter process has received the greater attention (Held *et al.*, 1999; Braithwaite and Drahos, 2000) and Western legal periodical literature has seen a remarkable expansion in writing on the subject, as Figure 37.1 indicates. The state would thus be increasingly rejected on the ground and increasingly transcended in cyberspace. Its importance and role for citizens would also be in decline, given a decline in the exclusivity of citizenship (captured in such concepts as 'transnational membership', 'cosmopolitan citizenship'), the use of residence as opposed to citizenship as a criterion for entitlement to state benefits, migration which eludes state regulation ('transnational migration'), and the increasing incidence of minority populations (diasporas) which increasingly invoke and abide by non-state law which defines their (non-state) identity. Even the territorial integrity of states comes to be questioned as the notion of the 'frontier' begins to reappear in discussion of the environment and resource management. Frontier zones surround national boundaries, providing a geographical area of diminished national sovereignty, and collaboration. States must therefore themselves decide on their commitment to state law.

Contemporary theories of state or positive law appear to offer little resistance to these processes. To an important extent, Western state law even encourages them. The globalization process is founded in large measure on the freedom of contracting parties to create their own normativity, beyond that of the state. State law authorizes this party autonomy, seen initially as freedom to choose amongst state laws, but its exercise has now reached the point where it is said that parties may contract without reference to state authority. States have also, faced with massive case-loads in state courts over the last half-century, come to authorize arbitration and various forms of alternative dispute resolution and this process has also weakened the grip of state law, as non-state adjudicators cast their net widely for appropriate law (Goode, 1999: 46). Regional and international trade agreements also impose negative as opposed to positive constraints on states, enlarging the space for private legal modelling or 'contractualization'.

In a still more profound manner, however, the positive law of states, even where it purports to be mandatory, offers little effective resistance to other forms of normativity. This should not be exaggerated, since it is perfectly conceivable that in particular cases state agencies or state judges will bring about a significant measure of state control. The problem is rather at the level of conceptualization of state or positive law. Hart's formulation of a state legal system was intended to be both general and descriptive. The effort to be general meant sacrifice of reasons underlying national particularities. The effort to be descriptive meant that national legal systems were conceived as founded on fact, and a general phenomenon of social obedience. In classical Western analysis, however, obligation cannot be derived from fact (no 'ought' from 'is') and contemporary theorists of legal positivism, such as Joseph Raz, draw the necessary conclusion that there is no obligation to obey state law. The language of 'binding' is rhetorical, for public consumption. 'Binding' law thus can cease to bind, as religion has often ceased to bind, and contractual practice can therefore withdraw itself from state regulation, whatever state law may say. This is confirmed by the law of arbitration. More generally, however, contemporary positivist theory provides no reasons for maintaining state structures or state law. If states fail, this is because the social fact of obedience to them no longer exists. This is what contemporary positivism is able to tell us. States outside the Western world are now failing, since positivism is singularly unconvincing to those not already aware of the reasons which underly it.

In a denationalizing legal world, the traditional international legal disciplines find themselves challenged. Comparative law, with its traditional state-centered bias (an instrument for improvement and reinforcement of state law), is now perceived as narrow and inadequate (Vining, 2000: 186) and calls are being made for a 'renaissance' in comparative law. This would entail an approach which 'focuses on practices more than rules, links legal to economic and political fields, incorporates both "international" and "domestic" factors, stresses the dynamics of fields, and highlights the strategies of key actors' (Trubek *et al.*, 1994: 497). Comparative law would thus abandon the taxonomic function, and become a generalized method of normative reasoning, within and across state law.

Private international law, the law of laws of the nineteenth and twentieth centuries, also sees its position challenged, even by its own experts. The nineteenth-century nationalization of laws, with conflicts arbitrated by private international law, is thus seen as 'a modern day aberration, entirely inadequate for the modern business community, and out of date' (Dalhuisen, 2000, p. vii). Choice of law is a costly and inefficient process, particularly weak in cases of second-order conflict of conflict rules and in cases of tripartite relationships involving mixed proprietary and contractual features (ibid. 8). Given a remarkable increase in cross-border transactions, its generalized application would threaten entire court systems, unfamiliar with the application of foreign law. The general direction of reform is towards substantive rules of law adequate for cross-border transactions and cases.

The effect of the denationalization of law on public international law is more complex. Where states fail, or disappear, public international law has in principle no response and no obvious ongoing role. Where states remain, and find they are individually unable to control transborder problems, they increasingly collaborate, such that there is a recognizable phenomenon of 'internationalization', consisting of heightened levels of formal, interstate collaboration. This is occurring, for example, with respect to trade, the law of children (the Hague Child Abduction Convention), intellectual property, the environment, refugees, and crime. Other fields, such as labor law, are lagging behind in this process.

Where 'internationalization' takes place there are two identifiable consequences. First, states become agencies of implementation of rules of extra-state origin. They may not even have participated in the elaboration of the rules, for example, in matters of air safety regulation (Braithwaite and Drahos, 2000: 3; Wiener, 1999: 82, 98, 184). Secondly, there may be formal assignment of elements of national sovereignty to supranational organizations, international judicial persons whose decisions and rules can be practically enforced. Where such organizations are regional, a new form of regional law may be the result, such as the law of the European Union. Here the developing regional law may essentially eliminate notions of international law.

Internationalization is thus state-based, but may effectively weaken the role of states. It is also the case, however, that the process of 'internationalization' may weaken the concept of public international law itself. This occurs when public international law, with a view to heightened efficacy, opens itself to individual, non-state claimants and parties. This is notably the case for human rights, trade (in some measure), and crime. The law applied in many such cases is not a law which can properly be described as 'inter-national'. It does not regulate the relations between states, but rather determines individual rights and obligations. International criminal tribunals must develop general principles of criminal procedure and substantive criminal law, and must rely on general principles of substantive law, of nation-states, in order to do so. A new form of normative comparative law emerges in this process. The line between the international and the national, or substantive, thus blurs. The judge plays an important role in this process, national legislators become background personae. The pressure towards substantive law beyond states appears irresistible. In environmental matters there is discussion of 'duties beyond borders' because of the 'more interconnected' nature of the world. Public international law is thus lured by the prospect of solving particular problems for particular people. In so doing, it risks losing its own identity as international. Law which runs, substantively, across borders, is transnational law.

1.3 The Development of Transnational Law

The notion of transnational law appears to have been first given prominence in the mid-twentieth century by the US international lawyer Philip Jessup, for whom transnational law included 'all law which regulates actions or events that transcend national frontiers. Both public and private international law are included, as are other rules which do not wholly fit into such standard categories' (Jessup, 1956: 2). Jessup's own treatment of the subject, however, was classic and statist, cross-border cases being in principle controlled by 'choice of law' of state origin (ibid. 3–5). The residual category of 'other rules' appears as an afterthought and is not developed or even illustrated in any significant way. It would apply, however, to relations between private persons or corporations and foreign states, which could not be seen as strictly 'international'. It is, however, this residual category of 'other rules' which has now expanded to become the most dynamic feature of a current process of 'denational-ization of transnational relationships' (Pinheiro, 2001) or 'transnationalization'.

Two distinct features of 'transnationalization' are apparent. In the first, as has been indicated, traditional public international law becomes open to private actors, and particularly those operating in a transnational manner. This is both a qualitative and a quantitative shift in the nature of public international law and is due in large part to the increase in mobility, size, and influence of non-state organizations in the world. In the 1990s, the majority of the hundred largest economies in the world were those of corporations rather than states (Braithwaite and Drahos, 2000: 492). Yet non-governmental organizations other than corporations (NGOs) have also increased greatly in both number and influence and now operate on a worldwide, transnational basis (TANGOs). These transnational, private actors 'interact in a variety of public and private, domestic and international fora to make, interpret, enforce, and ulti-mately internalize rules of transnational law' (Koh, 1996: 183–4). States thus are losing their 'gatekeeping' capacity as interstate or international dispute resolution becomes transnational. Public international law is becoming open, however, not only to organizations, but to individuals in need, and the growth in international human rights and humanitarian law is also therefore a fundamental element in the trans-nationalization process. European and Inter-American human rights tribunals are the best evidence of this. The developing humanitarian law has been also described as 'cosmopolitan' (Held et al., 1999: 70–4).

However, transnationalization does not only occur within the framework of an expanding, though increasingly ambiguous, notion of public international law. It also occurs in a more radical manner through non-governmental formation of substantive transnational law. Private parties here make their own law, or have resort to law of non-state origin. The new *lex mercatoria* is the best evidence of this, as standardized contract practice becomes the norm for increasing levels of international commerce. National substantive law and national private international law would thus already be of only residual application (Dalhuisen, 2000: 6; Goode, 1999: 46). The change is particularly radical for states, such as those of Latin America, having previously adhered to a notion of an 'import substitution economy', which generally precluded resort to all law other than local, state law. There is also multiplication of statements, or restatements, of 'soft' law, those prepared by private or non-state organizations as a suppletive law of transnational legal transactions. The best examples are the UNIDROIT Principles of International Commercial Contracts and the Lando Principles of European Contract Law, which are already being very favourably received in transborder practice. A non-profit, private corporation, the Internet Corporation for Assigned Names and Numbers (ICANN), also plays an essential role in assignment of domain names on the Internet. There is a new Central Transnational Law Database (http://www.tldb.de), of university origin, to track this emerging form of non-state law.

The increase in non-state activity over national boundaries places states, and international law, in a less controlling position than has previously been the case. There are therefore shifts in understanding of international relations, from the vertical to the horizontal. Historically, states themselves have been thought of as vertical structures, with the conduct of foreign relations concentrated at the apex of the structure. Beyond states, above them, are supranational organizations, regional forms of government, and, for some, at least potentially, world government. Each of these levels of a conceptual vertical hierarchy is now, however, challenged. The exclusive authority of a state sovereign to control external affairs is challenged by a new 'transgovernmentalism', characterized by horizontal relations amongst sub-units of national governments, which form in the absence of centralized and authoritative national decisions (Slaughter, 2001). Between states there would be not so much a process of world government but 'global governance', characterized by its 'complex, non-hierarchical, overlapping, interlocking and evolutionary character' (Harding, 2000: 128). A particular form of 'low level' international governance would flow simply from a pattern of gradual convergence of municipal laws (Wiener, 1999: 10, 20). There is discussion of a 'new medievalism'. Lawyers and judges, as opposed to political authorities, are playing an important role in these developments.

1.4 Transnational Actors

Professor Goode has written, with respect to development of transnational law, that it is 'practising lawyers who are making the running' (Goode, 1999: 57). This follows from the increasing frequency of transnational legal relations, which must be founded on an enlarged view of potentially applicable national laws or on a new and more appropriate set of transnational rules. The structures and techniques of legal practice are changing to accommodate these new necessities. Historically, the legal professions and their units of practice have been organized on a very local and frequently individual basis. Secondary offices in another locale have been prohibited. We are now witnessing, however, units of practice which function at a national and even transnational level. This is historically important, since we now see, for the first time, the intellectual resources of lawyers being deployed at a supranational level (Glenn, 2001). National law becomes contextualized at this level of practice, 'foreign' law is more immediately accessible, the occasions for choice of law are multiplied, the need for transnational law is more evident. Information technology plays an important role in this process, as does comparative legal reasoning. The challenge for the professions is to ensure self-regulation in an efficient and responsible manner. A new and important role has been created for international federations of lawyers.

Much of the transnational work of lawyers has been in commercial law. It also takes place, however, in lesser volume, before international criminal tribunals, international or regional human rights tribunals, and, most interestingly, before national courts in both international and domestic cases. Private international law may still play a role here, but it is increasingly relegated to a secondary function in favour of a more active process of conciliation of laws. Judges are now increasingly involved in this process. Particularly in the common law world, they may cite, and even call upon counsel to produce, relevant foreign material. While this has been common practice in much of the world (persuasive authority), it has acquired a new legitimacy and a new frequency in many areas of law such as human rights (McCrudden, 2000) or the relations between law and fast-moving technology. Even in jurisdictions most committed to national sources, forms of judicial dialogue, in judgments, are now being explored (Slaughter 2000a: 1112–23, for the United States, Lenoir, 2000: 163, for France). Transnational judicial collaboration has now, however, gone beyond simple judicial acknowledgment of foreign sources of domestic law. It extends to regularly programmed, transnational judicial meetings and study groups (McCrudden, 2000: 511; Slaughter, 1994: 103), online cross-border talk shops amongst judges (Judicial Assistance Information Networks), and the working out of joint protocols and even joint teleconferenced judicial hearings on transborder cases, notably those involving complex forms of bankruptcy administration (Glenn, 2001: 1000; Slaughter, 2000a: 1114).

The legal academic world is, perhaps more slowly, adjusting to transnational legal phenomena. This is more evident in legal writing and research than in legal education. There have thus been major recent statements of transnational commercial law (Dalhuisen, 2000) and of the 'common core' of European private law in the cadre of the Trento project of mapping commonalities of European law. Major treatises have been written on the pan-European (civil and common) law of contracts and torts, and major pan-European casebooks are being produced at Maastricht University. This work, however, is at the level of development of substantive law and not at the level of legal theory. In legal education, there has been much circulation of law students, less of legal professors, and still less actual teaching of transnational law, which has provoked criticism (Reimann, 2001; Kozolchyk, 1998: 169, 170). Transnational teaching has, however, begun to develop (programmes of Maastricht, Hanse Law School, McGill) and will slowly expand. The traditional teaching of comparative law stands in some measure as an obstacle to this process, suggesting, as it does, that domestic law is somehow not fashioned in a comparative manner and therefore need not engage in cross-border dialogue. The model of transborder teaching of law is, however, already evident, and consists of teaching discernible transnational principles of law with domestic law taught as exemplifications or exceptions to such general principles. The conceptual anchoring of this process remains to be developed and examined.

2 A Transnational Concept of Law?

There has thus been considerable development of transnational law and there are increasing numbers of transnational legal actors. As has been the case with the nationalization and the denationalization of law, however, this process has been occurring more rapidly than the development of its theoretical justification. In the European context, it has thus been observed that '[w]hat we are facing today with the multiplicity of projects is the emergence of a European and truly global legal culture which is developing outside the constraints of the domestic or EU-lawmaking process. . . . We are faced with the question as to the dogmatic and methodological basis of the emerging doctrine of transnational law' (Berger, 2001: 27). Other calls have been made for the development of a new conceptual edifice to replace ageing if not obsolete doctrines of sovereign statehood. Progress, however, is being made and, since lawyers have long memories, we are seeing both ancient and original justifications for law beyond the state. There are also interesting combinations of the two.

Ancient justifications for law beyond the state are once again of relevance since transnational law is not (generally) considered to be binding law. We will see that there are exceptions to this general position. Pre-state and post-state law, however, share the general characteristic of being suppletive law, law which is at the disposition of parties as opposed to binding them. The notion of binding people together was necessary for purposes of construction of collective identities, as in the case of organized religion or the state. The world of transnational law, however, assumes that peoples already exist, in state or other form, and seeks to build bridges between them. In so doing, their particular identity will weaken, as the role of states is weakening, but there is no evident, worldwide need for construction of new identities built on a notion of binding law, though there is debate on this question in Europe.

So transnational law, like pre-state law, can address legal problems with no, or fewer, systemic concerns. It must be adequate to solve the problems it addresses and need respond to no higher organizational concerns.

The major source of law beyond the state is legal tradition. There are various ways in which this is manifested.

2.1 Legal Tradition and Transnational Law

A. W. B. Simpson has written that '[l]aw is essentially a tradition, that is to say something which has come down to us from the past' (Simpson, 1988: 23). The laws of the world thus exist as living traditions and highly normative ones (Glenn, 2000). This is as true for Western law, often conceived as modern or even postmodern, as it is for non-Western law. The oldest law of the world, that of chthonic or aboriginal peoples, exists most clearly as oral tradition, since it is neither articulated nor supported by formal institutions. It is nevertheless highly normative (though not usually said to be 'binding'). The religious laws of the world also exist, even given revelatory origins, as ongoing accumulations of normative traditions derived from the past. They may, or may not, provide effective and immediate forms of sanctions for their violation. This is not considered essential to their legal or normative character.

Western state law is said to be exclusive, positive, binding law, though we have seen that contemporary positivist legal theory denies its ability to create obligations, to effectively bind. It would exist as simple fact. Yet the existence of the fact of an efficient legal system does not somehow float, like a bubble, free of all forms of normative support. Positive, statist theory is a result of a long Western tradition (see Sect. 1.1) and if it tells us of the fact of the existence of a national legal system there is a long (normative) tradition which tells us that we should believe in the existence of this fact. State law is traditional law, though often denying its traditional character. This is why there are states, because there is a powerful normative tradition in favour of their creation and maintenance. This tradition is a transnational one, so it may be said that states themselves are the product of transnational law. It is thus entirely appropriate, and even inevitable, that European courts look to the 'constitutional traditions common to the Member States' in their articulation of supranational European law (Lenoir, 2000: 165).

Tradition is thus the major source and justification of transnational law. It will rarely, however, be invoked as such. This is because Western lawyers (unlike other lawyers) are not accustomed to thinking of law as tradition. It may also be because there is genuine originality in some justifications being offered for transnational law. More usually, however, it is because there are particular (ancient) traditions, which go by their own names and not by that of tradition itself, which are powerful justifications for transnational law.

2.2 Transnational Traditions of Law

Some transnational traditions of law are genuinely transnational. They have existed only since the time of states, yet beyond them. Others are pre-state, yet are now seen as transnational since they have always been overarching. Both types are now being pressed into contemporary service, often with new refinements.

2.2.1 *Persuasive Authority*

The notion of persuasive authority, designated as such, appears to have developed within the common law tradition during and after the period of English colonialism (Glenn, 1987). Persuasive authority does not designate itself as 'binding', as state law generally does, but provides an explicitly suppletive source of law. The persuasiveness of the authority may flow from its content or the inherent authority of its source. At least one South Pacific jurisdiction has thus adopted the common law, not as it existed in English form at a given date, but as it exists *from time to time*. Trust, as well as specific content, may therefore be an essential element of persuasive authority.

Persuasive authority has never been limited exclusively to the common law tradition, however, and is now expanding well beyond its colonial and post-colonial settings. That which constitutes persuasive authority may thus be foreign state law, used in a transnational manner by the courts of other countries, international law or treaties, which may be followed without explicit incorporation into domestic law, or new forms of specifically transnational (non-state, non-international) law. All of these instances of actual use of persuasive authority are inconsistent with exclusivist theories of state law. The ultimately persuasive (non-binding) character of state law is thus declining in efficacy in the face of other, more persuasive sources of law in the contemporary state of the world.

There is also a current process of rethinking the nature of persuasive authority. It is now seen as a process of 'coordinate persuasion' involving multiple actors in an ongoing process of collaboration; or as a process of 'judicial parallelism' which may be acknowledged or unacknowledged by the courts involved (Goode, 1998: 92); or as a form of 'transjudicial' communication in dialogical, monological, or intermediated form (Slaughter, 1994: 101). The language of 'reception' is being replaced by that of 'dialogue', since subsequent closure is no longer contemplated. The process is occurring on a global basis but also, and perhaps more intensively, within regions such as the European Union or NAFTA where the circulation of ideas accelerates with the circulation of goods, people, and services. In the European Union in particular, there is a process of dialogue between the European Courts and the national courts, not controlled or limited by vertical hierarchies.

The shift in theoretical attention towards persuasive authority has provided a more nuanced and subtle appreciation of it, as well as of state law. The distinction between 'binding' state law and 'persuasive' authority would thus be too 'starkly drawn' and such a binary opposition between them would be giving way to a continuum of strength of authority. In the area of human rights, 'binding' national precedent would thus be weaker than in other areas of law and would itself be closer to persuasive authority, thus more readily justifying resort to extra-national guidance (McCrudden, 2000: 512). 'Binding' state law would simply 'offer reasons which justify ignoring the countervailing substantive arguments in favour of any alternative decision' (Bell, 2000: 30). Application of state law thus has to be justified, in the face of alternative persuasive authority. Persuasive authority itself is present as a matter of degree and some persuasive authorities, such as the US Restatements within the United States, would be recognizably 'strong' in character (Dalhuisen, 2000: 78). Persuasive authority must be acknowledged and dealt with because, as a matter of fairness, similar cases should be similarly treated and 'similarity . . . can and does obtain across . . . national borders' (McCrudden, 2000: 513, citing Bronaugh).

The renewed importance of persuasive authority is being recognized as compatible with long-standing (and non-national) conceptions of the common law and the civil law. Common law judicial decisions are thus 'provisional statements of fundamental common law principles which have to be reviewed and developed over time' and which 'cross national boundaries' (Bell, 2000: 13). Increasingly lawyers look to 'internationally accepted principles and standards to make good perceived deficiencies in domestic law' (Goode, 1999: 46). In difficult human rights cases, there would be 'conflicting principles which need to be resolved in conversation with judges in other countries' (McCrudden, 2000: 528). Similar reconceptualizations are occurring in civil law jurisdictions. The Preamble to the new Quebec Civil Code thus states that it governs private law relations 'in harmony with . . . the general principles of law' such that Quebec judges will continue to elaborate such principles in collaboration with other judges of the civil law world, and beyond.

2.2.2 *The* Ius Commune

The common law maintained its recognizable existence through the period of state constructions, though its transnational dimensions came to be recognized as that dimension of the common law which is 'persuasive authority'. In the civil law world of Europe, the Continental common law, or *ius commune*, was taken generally as having disappeared in the process of nationalization of law. Yet it is now re-emerging as a transnational tradition of law.

The European *ius commune* was originally elaborated over centuries by scholarly work on the Digest of Justinian. The canon law of the Christian church was a partner in the endeavour. The law was thus essentially a doctrinal construction, found in the great glosses and treatises, and its role was independent of the power and sanctions of legislators and judges. Both would look to it as required, and legal education throughout the Continent was almost entirely based upon it, but it had no official, governmental, or national status. Its authority was persuasive, and though there was great resistance to it on the part of adherents to local or customary law, it eventually came to govern wide areas of private law, notably the law of obligations. There were clearly local variations in its application, but it was a common law because of the commonality of the questions it inspired, and the large consensus which emerged as to the answers. It has been referred to as essentially a way of thought, as opposed to a fixed corpus of rules. With the nationalization of law, many of its principles came to ground in national codifications, and subsequent interpretation thereafter was exclusively in terms of national law, expressed in national languages. As a *ius commune* it became disaggregated, '*territorial zersplittert*'.

Since law in Europe is going through the same process of denationalization as elsewhere, the same problem of justification of transnational law is raised. The European legal landscape is 'increasingly transnational and supranational' (Harding, 2000: 145) and the *ius commune* could be reaggregated as a form of transnational European law. Its content would have great authority as the embodiment of continental European legal tradition. Yet there is great debate as to how the *ius commune* could be revived. Some, projecting nineteenth and twentieth century ideas of state law and positivism into the future, assert that the *ius commune* should now take codified form. This view has received support at high political levels, and in much distinguished academic writing. Though much is said in favor of a European Civil Code, however, the idea presents little theoretical interest from the perspective of transnational law. It involves thinking in terms of entities 'institutionally substitutable for the state' (Harding, 2000: 145, citing Ruggie), if not simply in terms of a larger, perhaps federated, state. Genuinely transnational law could emerge in Europe only in the absence of formal legal unification. The *ius commune* would have to be resurrected in a way somehow resembling its original form.

A number of conceptual justifications are now being advanced in Europe as a means of bringing this about. They are remarkably similar to justifications for the transnational character of the common law, in the form of persuasive authority. Thus the *ius commune* would be suppletive law and there is vigorous criticism of the idea that a common, transnational law could be seen as binding, in a way incompatible with local particularity. 'Authoritative imposition' of rules or principles would thus be unacceptable and there should be freer movement of legal rules across national borders. Law in Europe should be conceived not in 'monist' terms but according to an 'interactionist' view requiring '*comparative evaluation* of prescriptions and values and their interpretations according to a general rule of *integrity*'. This process, moreover, would be 'ongoing' (La Torre, 1999: 193, 194; emphasis in original) in a way comparable to the provisional character of common law decisions. European law would contain, again in a way similar to the common law, 'general principles' of a transnational character and the goal of the Trento Common Core project is not to impose new rules and categories but to find existing, similar solutions, the hidden form of European transnational law. There is also explicit reliance on the concept of 'European legal tradition'.

2.2.3 *The* Lex Mercatoria

The *lex mercatoria* developed originally in the medieval circumstances of Europe, with no state structures to obstruct the horizontal, pan-European development of commercial norms. It was the product of its practitioners, and drew freely on other commercial models, notably those of Talmudic and Islamic law. Commercial law was more resistant to nationalization than private law generally, since so much commercial activity looks beyond borders, but the nationalization movement was nevertheless remarkably successful in commercial matters. National Codes of Commerce are the best indication of this. Yet transnational commerce has today reached such a volume of intensity that national regulation of it, even through the techniques of private international law, is seen as increasingly inadequate. There has therefore been a revival, in the second half of the twentieth century, of the tradition of a (relatively) autonomous *lex mercatoria*. This constitutes today a 'transnational commercial law' drawn from a wide array of international and transnational sources (Goode, 1998: 88). It is said that the development of these transnational sources 'requires a rethinking of the traditional theory of legal sources' (Berger, 2001: 24).

What is the justification offered for contemporary transnational commercial law? It is generally the justification offered for the separation of commercial law from general civil or private law—the need for speed, flexibility, and adaptability to commercial circumstance. The pressures of commercial globalization now require the separation of transnational commercial law from national commercial law, given 'global time and space compression' and the requirements of a 'high-speed economy'. Only the informal methods of transnational law-making allow for on-time adaptation of the law to new transnational developments (ibid. 24). Its informal adoption would not require consent of states of radically different economic circumstances; it would provide norms which are 'politically neutral, anational, and thus detached from the law of either of the contestants' (Goode, 1999: 53).

Transnational commercial law may result from contractualization of business practices, from industry-specific or transaction-specific formulation of general norms, and most recently from international 'restatements', which may involve some 'pre-statement', of transnational law. These documents both formulate transational law and improve access to it. The content of these international restatements, such as those of the Lando Principles of European Contract Law or the UNIDROIT Principles of International Commercial Contracts, is in the form of general principles of transnational commercial law, common to the law of states, or of accepted transnational commercial usage (ibid. 48). The existence of such 'fundamental legal principles' (Dalhuisen, 2000: 65) is increasingly acknowledged by international treaty law as well as by transnational doctrine. The notion of 'general principles' would thus play the same role here, in commercial law, as it is playing with respect to the transnational dimensions of the common law and the *ius commune* generally (Sects. 2.2.1, 2.2.2 above).

Transnational commercial law is often referred to as 'soft' law, yet it would have 'a force independent of contract' (Goode, 1999: 48) and the effect of the new transnational restatements is already said to be 'quite remarkable' (Goode, 1998: 93). Their force would be based 'on influence, not on power' (ibid.); it would be a question of their 'comparative persuasiveness' (as stated in http://www.tldb.de). The restatements are clearly suppletive in character; they yield to the 'mandatory' provisions of national law. Their adaptability is ensured by their formulation according to a technique of 'creeping' or ongoing codification, which is a process not of creeping towards codification but of codifying in an informal, constantly updated, and never completed manner (http:www.tldb.de). This is a reversal of the traditional codification process (Berger, 2001: 21). The development of international restatements is now being extended beyond substantive commercial law to international litigation, under the joint auspices of the American Law Institute and UNIDROIT. Legal scholars and legal practitioners collaborate usefully in their articulation.

2.2.4 *Natural Law*

General principles are thus perceived as a constitutive element of persuasive authority, the *ius commune* and the new *lex mercatoria*. It has been said, however, with respect to contested principles in the field of human rights law, that foreign judgments should not be looked to as 'laying down a discovered truth or interpreting higher law' (McCrudden, 2000: 528). This would be incompatible with the dialogical and provisional nature of common law decision-making, particularly in relation to human rights adjudication. Natural law is not entirely absent, however, from current thinking about transnational forms of law. Jan Dalhuisen has suggested that 'natural law revival stands at the beginning of any new age when a reassessment of fundamental principle and the deduction of new rules from new needs overtake the established order' (Dalhuisen, 2000: 34). Natural law is here conceived, however, in an open-ended manner and 'may mean religion-inspired, human rights inspired law, or equitable or rational law' (ibid. 35). The notion of natural law here becomes more a source of critique of custom, practice or positive law, since 'the law is always moving and can never be entirely predetermined in a set of written rules' (ibid. 35). Any more substantive reliance on natural law has been criticized elsewhere as being overly ambitious and unrealistic (De Ly, 2001: 167).

2.2.5 *Personal Laws*

Personal laws, which apply by virtue of personal adherence as opposed to territorial control, may be explicitly religious in origin, as with Talmudic law, Islamic law, or Hindu law. These laws are revelatory in origin and were not originated in transnational terms but in terms of the relation between the human person and a God, or gods. With the development of the state, however, and contemporary global patterns of human migration, the transnational character of these religious laws has become evident. This is also the case for indigenous or chthonic law and adherents to these different types of personal law adhere to normative texts or principles which are applicable in many parts of the world. Adherence to personal law must be compatible with state law, and the reconciliation of personal laws with state law is now an increasing preoccupation in the world.

2.3 Contemporary Justifications of Transnational Law

Since the growth of transnational law may be seen as a new phenomenon (the world not having previously known a process of declining state authority), there are interesting contemporary efforts to justify transnational law afresh, in its current circumstances. These contemporary justifications can be broadly situated within a tradition of Western rationality, in its various manifestations, but they do not invoke the tradition and do not explicitly rely upon the traditions of transnational law (see Sect. 2.2). Their persuasive authority is thus yet to be established, though it is reinforced in some instances by reliance on concepts of law which are well known in other circumstances.

2.3.1 *Community-Based Norms*

Since communities can only exist by virtue of principles or rules of coherence of some type, the existence of communities is an indication of the existence of such principles or rules. Since transnational rules are often not the object of formal articulation, easily identifiable transnational communities may be more visible than the normativity upon which they depend. A number of contemporary justifications of transnational law thus rely on the coherence and efficacy of transnational groups as an indication of underlying, justifiable, normativity.

Modern, electronic forms of communication have contributed greatly to these community-based justifications for transnational law. One of the earliest of such justifications to emerge was that of 'epistemic communities', defined generally as 'loose collections of knowledge-based experts who share certain attitudes and values and substantive knowledge, as well as ways of thinking about how to use that knowledge' (Braithwaite and Drahos, 2000: 501, 504, with references). These epistemic communities exist across national boundaries, thanks to contemporary means of communication. They have the potential to bring together adversaries, frequently develop around professionals such as lawyers, and would be capable of generating highly influential modes of analysis of problems as well as specific rules or principles. Their 'software' type of structure would even be capable of hijacking the 'hardware' of institutional order (ibid. 501). Soft power would be the only effective power, particularly over time.

The notion of 'epistemic communities' is a large and expansive one and has been used in a number of different contexts. Dalhuisen justifies his notion of a new *lex mercatoria* because of the existence of an 'independent and professional commercial and financial order [which] is now a sufficient reality for its own normativity to be accepted' (Dalhuisen, 2000: 63). Others doubt the existence of a *societas mercatorum* 'institutionalized within an autonomous legal order' but admit the possibility of autonomous orders within 'given sectors' (Pinheiro, 2001: 441). Slaughter relies on epistemic communities within and across state structures in the form of 'intergovernmental networks'. It is their effectiveness which gives rise to the phenomenon of 'transgovernmentalism' (Slaughter, 2001). Within such networks '[p]ersuasion is the dominant currency' (Slaughter, 2000b: 532). Judges would also be engaged in a 'common enterprise', particularly in human rights adjudication, and this would allow them to place national differences within a broader perspective (Slaughter, 1994: 132; McCrudden, 2000: 528, 529).

The notion of epistemic communities also underlies the notion of 'dialogic webs' which play a fundamental role of issue definition, the initial prerequisite of any global regime (Braithwaite and Drahos, 2000: 553). These dialogic webs are more fundamentally 'webs of persuasion' or 'webs of influence' than 'webs of control' and in their totality would be replacing any notion of a 'master of the world' or 'master mechanism' (ibid. 7, 553). Within such epistemic communities or dialogic webs, there would be cosmopolitan projects and cosmopolitan citizens. The cosmopolitan citizen would be a person 'capable of mediating between national traditions, communities of fate and alternative forms of life'. They would be capable of reasoning 'from the point of view of others' (Held *et al.*, 1999: 449).

Epistemic communities are criticized, however, as being elitist, technocratic, and undemocratic. Their law is often difficult to access (Berger, 2001: 29). There is truth in all of these criticisms, which could be overcome in part by specific measures of visibility and transparency (Slaughter, 2001: 363). Their justification rests ultimately on their contribution to transnational justice.

2.3.2 *Transnational Contract*

State law allows parties the autonomy to choose the terms of their contract and, in considerable measure, the autonomy to choose the state law applicable to their contract. The contract is thus founded on, and limited by, state law. Yet contracts existed prior to the state, in all legal traditions including those of the common and civil laws. Contracts could therefore exist above and beyond, independently of, state law. We are now seeing re-emergence of the idea of contract founded only on its constituent elements, at least as perceived in a transnational concept of contract and by those charged with its implementation.

The transnational contract is visible in at least two circumstances. In the first, the parties choose non-state law as the law governing their contract. Their choice may be negatively expressed, as where they state simply that the contract shall not be governed by any state law. This is sometimes referred to as the phenomenon of the '*contrat sans loi*' but it is more precisely a contract without *state* law. More frequently, parties positively choose a transnational formulation of contract law, such as the UNIDROIT Principles, to govern their contract. There is opposition to recognition of the validity of such party choice, since transnational law is said not to be law (Goode, 1999: 51) but such choice is increasingly recognized by arbitrators and now by national courts.

The second type of transnational contract is evident in new forms of 'electronic formalism' where parties participate in transactions governed by a framework contract or '*contrat cadre*', the content of which is established in uniform, computer-controlled language. This type of transnational contract is increasing rapidly in importance. Parties are bound to the contract because of 'their willingness to join the transnational stream of pre-established terms and conditions' (Kozolchyk, 1998: 152, 153).

2.3.3 'Binding' Custom

The notion of binding people to norms appears to have been first a religious phenomenon (Sect. 1) and was then taken up again with the rise of state law. That which Western law knows as 'custom' is not usually described as of binding effect. Custom is rather repeated conduct, or repeated adherence, under a sense of obligation, but what is important is the ongoing, repetitive character of adherence to whatever the custom might be. Both the content of the custom, and its inherent normativity, are largely irrelevant to this process. So custom has largely fallen by the wayside as a source of law, which of course was a necessary conceptual step in the ascendancy of state law. Custom, or usage, however, is now undergoing conceptual revival as a source of transnational law. The revival means the content of custom is once again of consequence, as is its inherent normativity. The notion of 'binding' is once again being pressed into service.

Customs and usage of international trade would thus be a binding source of international contract law, since the parties may have agreed to particular usages or established given practices between themselves (Kozolchyk, 1998: 170, citing art. 1.8 of the UNIDROIT Principles). Such mandatory custom would even be at the apex of a hierarchy of sources of transnational law (Dalhuisen, 2000: 74). Parties may deviate from them but they will apply if one of the parties does not wish to do so. 'True mandatory custom is more likely to emerge in non-contractual aspects or in contractual aspects that, like issues of validity, cannot be freely determined or changed by the parties' (ibid. 110). Contrary to what one might ordinarily suppose, trade usage would be in practice a higher norm than an international private law convention, which is usually suppletive in character and yields to the agreement of the parties (Goode, 1998: 90). Such customary rules would thus be in force 'autonomously' and 'independently of their reception by a national legal order' (Pinheiro, 2001: 442).

2.3.4 *Best Practices*

Custom or usage, like tradition, requires some measure of acceptance over time. In a high-speed economy, however, there is need for normativity in new circumstances, where the test of time cannot be met. Here the criteria for choice of normativity becomes explicitly comparative and normative. There is no ignoring the content of that which one is evaluating, or its relative advantages or disadvantages. The 'best practices' of transnational trade are those developed by leading practitioners and those most suitable for the creation of objective and internationally uniform standards (Kozolchyk, 1998: 155). There are therefore substantive requirements for the emergence of best practices. They must incorporate marketplace standards of fairness and will usually reject the arm's-length or 'stranger' standard in regulating contract relations, in favor of altruistic requirements of watching out for the other party's best interests. This would be the case since merchants seldom engage in a practice because its outcome is assured by enforceable and formal legal sanctions. They prefer practices and standards which are extra-judicial and self-enforcing (ibid. 168). Formal, abstract, state law does not meet these requirements and it is far from being self-enforcing. It is therefore in the process of being abandoned by the international commercial community, which looks to normativity more appropriate to its circumstances.

Transnational law is thus in the process of development and its justification has been conceptually undertaken in some measure. There remain questions as to the relations between transnational law and state law, and also as to the relations between state laws, given the existence of transnational law.

2.4 Convergence, Divergence, and Transnational Law

Transnational law is built on a process of convergence of ideas, across national boundaries. It is very close to a process of convergence of national laws, but may develop in the absence of such convergence, in the face of ongoing, conflictual diversity of state laws. Analysis of law in economic terms, using economic criteria of comparison, demonstrates major phenomena of convergence in the fields of financial regulation and commercial transactions. There is less convergence, and more path dependency (ongoing reliance on the substance of national traditions) in the field of corporate governance. State laws can thus be seen as in competition with one another and there may, or may not, be agreement on the efficiency of different national models. The analysis remains, however, statist in character, so the convergence, if it exists, is still perceived in terms of state law. Where convergence is resisted, as it often is, because of different concepts of efficiency, national culture, or incompatible values, the analysis also remains statist, and is often conflictual in character. This is the ongoing legacy of the nationalization of law in a time of heightened communication.

Transnational law thus adds a new form of normativity to Western law in bridging national laws. The law is no longer national, but nations share in its application. It is, moreover, substantive law, and not a law which is inter-national. Nations thus sacrifice some of their law in adhering to transnational law or in allowing their citizens to adhere to it. There would be no danger for essential national interests in this process, however, since transnational law, unlike state law, does not purport to exclude other sources of normativity. States recognize this internally even with respect to the application by state institutions of (transnational) personal laws, which state law can accommodate in a process of 'reasonable accommodation'. The essentially suppletive character of transnational law means that it should generally been seen as an ally and an aid, as opposed to a competitor or opponent. This explains its current ascendancy.

3 CONCLUSION

There is no uniformity in the emergence of transnational law. There is no unicity of its sources and no systemic form of justification. It does not conform to a general or universal model, other than speaking to contemporary need on the basis of some measure of past experience. It may be religious, commercial, humanitarian, or other, in character. Since it is compatible with great diversity, this diversity in its own nature is entirely appropriate. In a world where convergence and diversity must somehow be (peacefully) reconciled, transnational law appears an increasingly relevant and useful legal instrument.

REFERENCES

Bell, J. (2000). 'Sources of Law', in P. Birks (ed.), *English Private Law*, i, Oxford: Oxford University Press, 3–46.

Berger, K. (2001). 'The Principles of European Contract Law and the Concept of the "Creeping Codification" of Law', *European Review of Private Law*, 1: 21–34.

Braithwaite, J., and Drahos, P. (2000). *Global Business Regulation*, Cambridge: Cambridge University Press.

Dalhuisen, J. (2000). *Dalhuisen on International Commercial, Financial and Trade Law*, Oxford and Portland, Me.: Hart.

De Ly, F. (2001). 'Lex Mercatoria (New Law Merchant): Globalisation and International Self-Regulation', in R. P. Appelbaum, W. L. F. Felstiner, and V. Gessner, *Rules and Networks: The Legal Culture of Global Business Transactions*, Oxford and Portland, Me.: Hart, 159–88.

Glenn, H. P. (1987). 'Persuasive Authority', *McGill Law Journal*, 32: 261–98.

—— (2000). *Legal Traditions of the World*, Oxford: Oxford University Press.

—— (2001). 'Comparative Law and Legal Practice: On Removing the Borders', *Tulane Law Review*, 75: 977–1022.

—— (2003). 'The Nationalist Heritage', in P. Legrand and R. Munday (eds.), *Comparative Legal Studies: Traditions and Transitions*, Cambridge: Cambridge University Press.

Goode, R. (1998). *Commercial Law in the Next Millenium*, London: Sweet & Maxwell.

—— (1999). 'International Restatements and National Law', in W. Swadling and G. Jones (eds.), *The Search for Principle: Essays in Honour of Lord Goff of Chieveley*, Oxford: Oxford University Press, 45–58.

Harding, C. (2000). 'The Identity of European Law: Mapping out the European Legal Space', *European Law Journal*, 6: 128–47.

Held, D., McGrew, A., Goldblatt, D., and Perraton, J. (1999). *Global Transformations: Politics, Economics and Culture*, Stanford, Calif.: Stanford University Press.

Jessup, P. (1956). *Transnational Law*, New Haven: Yale University Press.

Koh, H. (1996). 'Transnational Legal Process', *Nebraska Law Review*, 75: 181–207.

Kozolchyk, B. (1991). 'On the State of Commercial Law at the End of the 20th Century', *Arizona Journal of International and Comparative Law*, 13: 1–32.

—— (1998). 'The UNIDROIT Principles as a Model for the Unification of the Best Contractual Practices in the Americas', *American Journal of Comparative Law*, 46: 151–79.

La Torre, M. (1999). 'Legal Pluralism as Evolutionary Achievement of Community Law', *Ratio Juris*, 12: 182–95.

Lenoir, N. (2000). 'The Response of the French Constitutional Court to the Growing Importance of International Law', in B. Markesinis (ed.), *The Clifford Chance Millennium Lectures: The Coming Together of the Common Law and the Civil Law*, Oxford and Portland, Me.: Hart, 163–94.

McCrudden, C. (2000). 'A Common Law of Human Rights? Transnational Judicial Conversations on Constitutional Rights', *Oxford Journal of Legal Studies*, 20: 499–532.

Pinheiro, L. (2001). 'The "Denationalization" of Transnational Relationships—Regulation of Transnational Relationships by Public International Law, European Community Law and Transnational Law', in J. Basedow, U. Drobnig, R. Ellger, K. J. Hopt, H. Kötz, R. Kulms, and E.-J. Mestmacher (eds.), *Aufbruch nach Europa: 75 Jahre Max-Planck-Institut für Privatrecht*, Tübingen: Mohr Siebeck, 429–46.

Reimann, M. (2001). 'Beyond National Systems: A Comparative Law for the International Age', *Tulane Law Review*, 75: 1103–19.

Simpson, A. W. B. (1988). *Invitation to Law*, Oxford: Blackwell.

Slaughter, A.-M. (1994). 'A Typology of Transjudicial Communication', *University of Richmond Law Review*, 29: 99–137.

—— (2000a). 'Judicial Globalization', *Virginia Journal of International Law*, 40: 1103–24.

—— (2000b). 'Agencies on the Loose? Holding Government Networks Accountable', in G. Bermann, M. Herdegen, and P. Lindseth, *Transatlantic Regulatory Cooperation: Legal Problems and Political Prospects*, Oxford: Oxford University Press, 521–46.

—— (2001). 'The Accountability of Government Networks', *Indiana Journal of Global Legal Studies*, 8: 347–67.

Trubek, D., Dezalay, Y., Buchanan, R., and Davis, J. (1994). 'Global Restructuring and the Law: Studies of the Internationalization of Legal Fields and the Creation of Transnational Arenas', *Case Western Reserve Law Review*, 44: 405–98.

Vining, W. (2000). *Globalisation and Legal Theory*, London, Edinburgh, and Dublin: Butterworths.

Wiener, J. (1999). *Globalization and the Harmonization of Law*. London/New York: Pinter.

CHAPTER 38

HISTORICAL RESEARCH IN LAW

DAVID IBBETSON

LEGAL history is not a topic that lends itself easily to a simple survey. In so far as law is inextricably woven into the social and political fabric of states, it follows that much historical writing could be treated as falling within a broadly defined genre of legal history. Equally, in so far as the common law has developed as a case-law system, where the fact that something has been done in the past is a prima-facie reason for doing it in the present, it follows that much legal writing could be said to fall within this same broadly defined genre. Such a treatment of legal history would be far too all-encompassing to be useful; consequently, somewhat arbitrary boundaries have to be placed on what counts as legal history for present purposes: studies whose primary focus is the development or functioning of legal ideas or institutions at some time in the past. A second problem is that even if the common law in its different manifestations can be regarded as a unitary system or a set of closely related systems, it is not at all obvious that the concerns of legal historians are the same throughout the common law world. The legal historian in the United States might see slavery as a central topic in the subject, the legal historian in Australia or Canada might give far greater weight to the interaction between the legal ideas of indigenous peoples and colonial laws, the legal historian in England might be concerned with the problems of land tenure in the thirteenth century. Inevitably, though, there is something of a bias towards England since it was the already well-established English common law that was transplanted elsewhere. English legal history is a strand in the legal history of every part of the English-speaking world.

Legal history is by no means a unitary discipline. A convenient and conventional division can be made between 'internal' and 'external' legal history. The former, we might say, is the history of lawyers' law, of legal rules and principles. Its sources are predominantly those that are thrown up by the legal process: principally statutes and decided cases, supplemented where possible with lawyers' literature expounding the rules and occasionally reflecting on them. The latter is the history of the law in practice, of legal institutions at work in society rather than legal rules existing in a social, economic, and political vacuum. The former, defined by its own terms, is bounded within its own field of reference; the latter, in its very nature, is necessarily unbounded. The division runs deep within contemporary legal historiography. Its most obvious effect is that while internal legal history can be summarized more or less adequately within the compass of a traditional textbook, external legal history cannot.

1 THE HISTORICAL FOUNDATIONS OF LEGAL HISTORIOGRAPHY

The foundations of much modern legal history were laid at the end of the nineteenth century and in the first years of the twentieth. Two writers in particular set the agenda: Frederic William Maitland, Downing Professor at Cambridge, in England, and James Barr Ames, Dane Professor at Harvard, in the United States. Both were positivists, essentially legal archaeologists who saw their functions as unearthing the past and attempting to describe it for the present. At the same time, both believed that law's past and law's present were connected: they were not merely antiquarians looking at the past for its own sake. Both, in fact, wrote works of the highest quality on contemporary law as well as purely historical studies.

Characteristic of the approach taken by Ames and Maitland was that legal history was something to be written with close attention to the primary sources; the fact that Blackstone in the middle of the eighteenth century or Coke at the beginning of the seventeenth might have propounded some historical point of view, purporting to describe or explain the law of the Middle Ages, was not in itself a good reason for believing it to be true. Historical authority and legal authority were to be separated. For Ames, 'primary sources' meant predominantly the printed case law of the English and American courts from the Middle Ages to his own time. He was deeply immersed in this material, and showed independence of mind in its analysis; but he did not have any real opportunity to go beyond it. Maitland was far more wide-ranging, for in England he had access to manuscripts, and not simply the printed materials available to Ames in Harvard. Most notably, in his work on medieval English law, whose principal product was the *History of English Law* (Pollock and Maitland, 1895), he pioneered the use of Plea Rolls—the records of the central courts of common law from the end of the twelfth century onwards—as well as moving outside the traditional sources of (legal) authority into such materials as private charters.

Maitland, too, pioneered the editing and dissemination of legal texts. He was by no means the first to see the importance of the bringing into print of materials which had remained dormant in manuscript from the Middle Ages; an important start had been made in the first half of the nineteenth century by the Record Commission (which had published among other things the medieval Rolls of Parliament and a reliable edition of the Statutes of the Realm), and in the Rolls Series in the second half of the century. The editorial standards of the latter series were very low; in particular, no real attempt had been made properly to collate the available manuscripts. Maitland was especially coruscating in his criticism of the edition of the most valuable of the medieval legal treatises, Bracton's *Of the Laws and Customs of England*, by Sir Travers Twiss, an edition which he described in a letter to Melville M. Bigelow as 'six volumes of rubbish' (Fifoot, 1965: 16). His own standards were of a vastly higher order. He began his editorial work with a volume of criminal pleas in 1884, followed closely by the three volumes of *Bracton's Note Book*. Most important, though, was his work for the Selden Society; he was one of its founder members in 1887, the dominant force within it until his death in 1906, and the editor of eight of its first twenty-one volumes as well as the active supervisor of the editors of the other volumes (Yale and Baker, 1987: 9). The Society's publications, still governed by the editorial principles laid down by Maitland, make up the spine of publications in English legal history linking the historiography of the end of the nineteenth century to that of the present day.

Maitland, and perhaps to a greater extent Ames, were lawyers who used history as a tool in their exegesis of contemporary law. Maitland's lectures on Equity, for example, are shot through with history. His history is not simply an elegant gloss on dry modern law, either; the whole treatment of the subject is thoroughly historicized. More telling is Ames's essay on a superficially arcane aspect of the history of contract law, 'Implied Assumpsit' (Ames, 1913: 149). In this he analysed certain situations pleaded as contract, but in which no contract had to be proved, as properly to be analysed in terms of a principle of unjust enrichment (transparently borrowed from Roman law). The historical sources provided no justification whatsoever for such an approach, though from a purely analytical point of view it had a lot to recommend it. What is interesting is that in Ames's eyes doctrinal analysis and history were so intermingled that his rigour as to the former resulted in his substantial misrepresentation of the latter. Other writers similarly mixed law and history: notable among these were the American Oliver Wendell Holmes and the English Frederick Pollock. Both in their own writings, and in the letters written between them, the elucidation of modern legal doctrine is time and again locked into their perception of the historical grounding of the law.

At the heart of this lay the historicism or pseudo-historicism of common law thought. Though few lawyers (presumably) would have held to the extreme position that the common law was an unchanging body of rules and principles, equally few could have failed to notice its strong dependence on its historical roots. At the start of the twentieth century, the forms of action, with all their historical baggage, were only just buried—in Maitland's words, they were still ruling from their graves—and no lawyer (at least, no lawyer in England) could afford to disdain an acquaintance with them. Moreover, even at a theoretical level, a lawyer like Pollock could openly hold to the position that the lawyers' authorities were like the data of natural scientists, with the result that just as the natural scientists' laws were based upon an observed congruity of single instances, so the lawyers' rules were to be discovered from the observation of similar results in similar lawsuits (Pollock, 1961). Such a parallel with the natural sciences played firmly in the direction of a synchronic analysis of legal materials: leaving aside the hierarchy of courts, all cases, whenever decided, were of equivalent value. In such a world, legal history really was the handmaid of the law.

A second way in which thinking about contemporary law affected the approach to legal history is visible in the predominantly Anglocentric view of the legal history of the common law world. When the Association of American Law Schools sponsored the publication of the three-volume series of *Select Essays in Anglo-American Legal History* in 1907, the great majority of the contributions focused heavily on England: only nine of the ninety-seven essays reprinted have any substantial American dimension at all. None the less, this did not prevent the (American) editorial committee describing them as 'a welcome enlargement of the horizon of *our* law' (i, p. vi). Legal history was the history of the organic common law system, not the history of the law in any particular place. As late as 1973 it could be said that American legal history was a rather neglected field (Friedman, 1973: 9); it was not until 1995 that there appeared the first substantial history of Australian law, albeit one protesting that it was not attempting to provide a comprehensive history of the subject (Kercher, 1995, p. ix); and it is only very recently that Canada has begun to follow this lead (Guth and Pue, 2001).

'We have all of us been nationalists of late. Cosmopolitanism can afford to wait its turn' (Maitland, 1901: 8). Maitland's description of legal historical studies at the beginning of the twentieth century—and he was not referring simply to the common law world—is very revealing. Legal history was the history of particular systems (though we should qualify his statement so as to recognize the unity of the different manifestations of the common law), and there was relatively little concern for the connexions between them or their mutual influences. But this did not mean that legal historical scholarship was insular. Ames had studied in Germany, for example, and Maitland was acutely conscious of German scholarship (he translated Gierke's *Deutsche Genossenschaftsrecht* into English (Maitland, 1900)); and both men had a familiarity with continental European writing on law. This, though, did not make the substance of their legal history any less insular. There is a direct analogy here with contemporary common law method: however much English or American lawyers might have been familiar with legal developments outside the common law world, and perhaps even have mimicked them from time to time, it would have appeared an absurd heresy to deny the independence of the common law.

This curious balance of cosmpolitanism and nationalism is well brought out in the preface to the first volume of the *Cambridge Studies in English Legal History* by the general editor of the series, Harold Dexter Hazeltine, who had recently been appointed to Maitland's chair. The series was to be concerned with *English* legal history, albeit with English legal history as a worldwide phenomenon in so far as the English common law spread through the British Isles, to America, to the dominions and to the colonies, and to India. But in intellectual terms, English legal history was seen in the context of the European world of scholarship, the world of legal historians such as Eichhorn, Savigny, Ihering, Mitteis, Brunner, Gierke, Karlowa, Esmein, Viollet, Brissaud, Pertile, and Hinojosa (Winfield, 1921, pp. viii, xii). Hazeltine himself was part of this world: his doctorate, on the history of the English mortgage, had been completed not at Oxford or Cambridge but in Berlin. World War I, though, knocked a nail into the coffin of this transnationalism; so too did the growth of the Americal law school. Increasingly common law history became not merely common law centred but almost exclusively Anglophone. English legal historians wanting to study abroad turned their eyes to the West rather than to Germany and the European Continent.

2 THE PROFESSIONALIZATION OF LEGAL HISTORY

Ames and Maitland, Holmes and Pollock, were lawyers who also did legal history. Not that their legal history was amateurish—very much the reverse—but, except in the case of Maitland, it was not their primary concern. The second quarter of the twentieth century marked the rise of the professional legal historian, the scholar whose academic life was firmly anchored in the history of the law. Most significant of these was Sir William Holdsworth, Vinerian Professor in Oxford, whose multi-volume *History of English Law* appeared between 1903 and (posthumously) 1972. Holdsworth did not follow Maitland in immersing himself in manuscript sources, though he was not an unoriginal thinker. None the less, the main characteristic of the *History of English Law* was its magisterial synthesis of the work of others. The work marks the great watershed in twentieth-century English legal historiography. Legal practitioners who wanted or needed a historical dimension to their work (and the gradual fading of the forms of action made this in reality increasingly unnecessary) could invariably satisfy their needs by consulting Holdsworth; and legal historians wanting to go beyond Holdsworth had to look further than the readily available printed sources which had formed the basis of his work. There was, of course, much room for debate about the proper interpretation of the printed sources, but for the generation of legal historians emerging after World War II it was clear that the debate could only usefully be advanced—at least so far as the Middle Ages and the early modern period were concerned—by following Maitland's lead and looking at the manuscripts. Central areas of controversy were revivified and the terms of the controversy redefined by such an approach. To take one single example from among many, the whole debate about the reorientation of the English law of tort in the fourteenth century associated with the appearance of the action of trespass on the case was raised to a completely new level by the publication in the 1950s of the work of Kiralfy and Milsom (Kiralfy, 1951; Milsom, 1958).

Holdsworth's work meant that legal history was perforce professionalized. The historian working in the traditional heartland of the subject, the development of legal doctrine, was drawn to the use of technical sources raising vastly greater problems than those that had had to be faced by earlier scholars: problems of geography, for the sources were no longer available in every reasonably stocked law library (it is a matter of wonder that so much top-flight English legal history has been written by Americans condemned repeatedly to spend 'vacations' living out of suitcases while digging away in the Public Record Office); problems of palaeography and linguistics; and problems of interpretation. Maitland had already pointed to the use of Plea Rolls as the best way to explore the law before the end of the thirteenth century, and after Holdsworth scholars made considerable use of them as a crucial supplementary source in studying the law of the fourteenth, fifteenth, and sixteenth centuries. Other genres of legal manuscript began to be explored, too. Lawyers' notebooks of cases, especially from the sixteenth century, proved especially rewarding as a means of tracking the way in which English law developed in the crucial period of transformation from the mystifying period of the Year Books (essentially from 1300 to 1500) into the discernibly modern world of Sir Edward Coke and the so-called nominate reports; and scholars began to quarry the seam of learning to be found in pedagogic material, particularly that associated with the Inns of Court, bringing to the fore the mind-numbing complexity of the pre-modern common law.

This increasing use of technically difficult legal sources, the characteristic of internal legal history in the second half of the twentieth century, was not the only feature of the substantial professionalization of the subject. External legal history changed, too, as scholars came to adopt different intellectual methodologies in their approach to the history of the law. Nor were these simply the methods of economics and sociology. Cultural and literary theory might bring a new dimension to the analysis of legal texts, for example, and anthropological approaches contributed to the understanding of law in pre-literate societies.

A further consequence of the professionalization of legal history was its gradual divorce from the mainstream of law (it might be noted in passing that exactly the same phenomenon was visible with Roman law in the English legal world in the second half of the twentieth century), though it did not of course follow that the cutting free of legal history from contemporary legal issues meant that legal historians were immunized against a concern with such topics. No longer is legal history (in any form) seen as playing a fundamental role in legal education: few (if any) law courses in the English-speaking world have it as a compulsory component. Nor is law historicized in the same way that it was a century ago: the apparently rigid doctrine of precedent has been softened; legal reasoning has become far more dependent on considerations of 'policy' than would once have seemed appropriate; there is a greater sense that the law has social functions that need to be recognized, that lawyers have a responsibility to do more than manipulate an ever more complex set of rules handed down by earlier generations.

Another consequence, perhaps, though one contributed to by political changes and shifts in intellectual fashion too, was the increasing willingness of legal historians to break away from their traditional nationalism. Fuelled by the growing European dimension of modern English law, English legal historians have come to look more closely at the European dimension of its history. This has not so much taken the rather stale form of just trying to identify places where Roman legal ideas have influenced the substantive common law, but more in looking at the way in which common law developments reflected contemporaneous or near-contemporaneous developments in Continental Europe. To some extent this is an issue of legal form; it has been most notable in the demonstration that the same processes of intellectualization affected all European legal systems in the sixteenth century, questioning the facile distinction once drawn between an isolated English law and Continental legal systems suffering some form of 'reception' of Roman law. No less interesting are the applications of this type of comparative study to substantive legal institutions. Already by the middle of the century it was being suggested that Bracton's Roman law was of an altogether higher quality than Maitland had thought; by the end of the century it had been demonstrated that the foundation document of common law ideology, the Magna Carta, borrowed a good deal from the contemporary Continental legal tradition. At the other end of the historical timescale, it has been argued that the Protestant Natural law writers of the seventeenth and eighteenth centuries played just as important a part in the shaping of modern English law as they did in France and Germany; equally, it has been said that Roman law was an important element in the shaping of the nineteenth-century American legal consciousness. And it has been suggested that legal institutions apparently unique to the common law, such as the trust, owe far more to the continental *ius commune* than would have been imaginable to a legal historian half a century ago.

This cosmopolitanism is not simply an Anglo-European phenomenon. In the United States, legal historians have turned their attention to the way in which state laws were moulded by influences from outside the common law, especially by French and Hispanic ideas. Different considerations have brought about a different sort of legal cosmopolitanism in such places as Australia and Canada: here the increasing concern with the rights of pre-colonial groups has led to a shift of the spotlight on to the friction between common law ideas and those of aboriginal peoples, especially in so far as ideas of property ownership and land use are concerned. The same approach is visible in external legal histories, where comparative studies of such topics as the nature of feudalism in the Middle Ages or of industrialization in the nineteenth century have been no less pregnant in their implications.

3 INTERNAL LEGAL HISTORY: FORMS AND METHOD

It is probably foolish to attempt to categorize different types of legal history; it would certainly be misguided to treat such categories as rigid boxes into which works of legal history fall. None the less, it is a convenient way to bring out the different facets of the discipline. It should also be noted that different areas of law are susceptible to different styles of analysis: constitutional history meshes well with political history and the history of ideas, for example, crime benefits from the methods of the social historian, private law is perhaps best dealt with from the point of view of the lawyer.

Just as legal positivism has continued to exercise considerable sway over legal thinking in the common law world, so too has Maitland's and Ames's positivist approach to legal history remained a dominant force. It provides the standpoint for the leading modern textbook on the subject (Baker, 2002). The earlier the focus of study, the truer this becomes; perhaps inevitably so, for the relatively slow pace at which the study of legal history has moved over the last century has meant that there is still an enormous amount of work to be done to establish the most basic data on which a theoretically more sophisticated model could be erected. It has recently been said that the estimate (made in 1971) that at the current rate of progress the Year Books—lawyers' case reports from the late thirteenth century to 1535—will finally be available to historians in a usable and reliable edition by the year 2750 looks to be wildly optimistic (Baker, 2000: 76). Small wonder, then, that much of the legal historian's endeavour is spent simply describing what happened.

It would, though, be wrong to think of such a positivist approach to legal history as something inherently undesirable to which scholars have been driven for want of any better approach being practically feasible. Before the introduction of printing, it is not at all obvious that legal development occurred in the same self-conscious way that typified the world in which legal decisions were made by reference to an accepted corpus of materials from the past which could be freely consulted by all with the technical skill to interpret it. No such accepted corpus existed; nor, in the absence of reliably accessible written texts, should we suppose that there was any institutional memory of decisions that had been made more than a very short time earlier. If the assumption cannot be made that law is a continuous fabric woven through time, there is little that the historian can do but describe the events as they happened without succumbing to the temptation of over-interpreting them.

Positivist legal history may be descriptive, but it none the less raises interpretive problems in so far as its raw data consist largely in the progress and outcome of individual lawsuits. Information derived from the official records of the courts, the Plea Rolls, may be supposed to reflect the different stages of the action—it is, after all, the purpose of legal records accurately to record what occurred within the legal process— but all too frequently the pleadings mislead if they are taken too literally as statements of what the case was in fact about. At best they represent *ex parte* statements by the litigants of what they would like the court or the jury to think had happened; at worst they are so riddled with legally sanctioned fictions that historians have no choice but to use their imaginations to reconstruct a plausible sequence of events that could possibly have been described in the form in which the pleadings are found.

Information derived from the Year Books raises rather different problems. These early reports are made up of fragments of dialogue between advocates and judges, and although they can provisionally be treated as meaning what they say, they can only safely be read as statements of what one individual—in the artificial context of legal argument—wanted to argue that the law was, not as statements of law that were uncontroversially true. They are, moreover, often so opaquely expressed as practically to deny comprehension. Before they can be understood, therefore, both Plea Rolls and Year Books require a substantial amount of background knowledge; in particular, they are apt to be especially misleading to the historian with an inadequate grasp of the rules and practices of pleading and procedure and a sensitivity to the way in which these changed through time. A further difficulty arises when the legal data come to be contextualized: it can never be assumed that an individual decision was in any sense typical. No lawsuit ever existed in the abstract, independent of its social setting; though occurring against a background of the legal fabric, political factors— the power relationship between the parties, their influence in the community or their popularity, the favour or disfavour with which they were viewed by the elite—cannot fail sometimes to have played a significant part in the outcome of the dispute.

Fewer problems of interpretation are raised by pedagogical literature. In the main, for the period before 1600 this consists of moots (students' learning exercises) and readings (lectures) given at the Inns of Court. It is only very recently that the potential locked up in this type of material has begun to be recognized, and it has as yet hardly been tapped as a substantial source of legal data (Baker, 2001: 73–81). Its enormous advantage is that it gives the historian relatively reliable information about what the law was taught to be and hence thought to be; and in the period before printed sources were widely available to be consulted, it may well be that no real distinction could be drawn between lawyers' generally held beliefs as to what the law was and what the law 'really' was. The disadvantage of this material, as it appears to the historian in the twenty-first century, is that the law that it depicts is quite dispiritingly complex. The revelation of the significance of these non-formal sources therefore provides both an opportunity and a challenge for pre-modern legal historians. In addition, it necessitates a rethinking of the nature of medieval law and its relation to political authority. One step beyond this it raises similar questions, yet to be explored, about the nature of law in post-medieval times, by which time the binding authority of judicial decisions had come to be accepted and the views of law teachers were treated as having no authority whatsoever.

Once the sixteenth-century watershed of the introduction of printing has been passed, and increasingly as we approach the present day, positivistic legal history loses its dominance, though it still represents an important strand in legal historical research. The raw legal data is relatively easily accessible and raises relatively fewer interpretative problems, so that other approaches become more practicable. There is perhaps relatively little that can be added to Holdsworth's wide survey, though there of course remains enormous scope for different, or differently nuanced, interpretations and there is much work that can be (and some that has been) done to place the legal developments tracked by Holdsworth into their political and socio-economic context. Some contextualization of this sort seems essential: with the emergence of a self-conscious doctrinal literature—essentially a product of the first part of the nineteenth century—purely descriptive legal history can all too easily degenerate into something akin to simply copying out footnotes from old books.

A close relative of the positivist legal history that continues to dominate the pre-printing era is the editing of texts. Both the Selden Society in England and the Ames Foundation in the United States have in hand the editing of Year Books (the former beginning with those of Edward II, the latter concentrating on the unprinted texts of the reign of Richard II), though progress in bringing the texts into print has been leisurely. Legal records of various sorts (and not just in England) are in the process of being printed under the auspices both of private societies (principally, local history societies and societies devoted to the publication of official records) and of national bodies. The process, though, is relatively haphazard and progress is inevitably very slow, for accurate transcription requires very painstaking care and the rewards for doing it are very slight. Little work has yet been done to edit the Readings from the Inns of Court, though the second half of the twentieth century did see editions of a range of important medieval tracts which probably originally had an educational function. Finally, a start has been made on the editing (or, for a later period, reprinting) of more straightforwardly professional literature, spanning the range from Glanvill and Bracton in the twelfth and thirteenth centuries to the institutional writings and practitioners' manuals of the eighteenth and nineteenth.

The appearance in 1969 of Milsom's *Historical Foundations of the Common Law* marked the fully-fledged emergence of a rather different strand of legal historiography, idealist or doctrinal legal history. The genre can be traced back to Oliver Wendell Holmes in the late nineteenth century, but it was only with Milsom's work that it was freed from the Whiggish assumptions of progress towards some ideal (usually a recently achieved ideal) that marred a good deal of the early work of this type. Doctrinal legal history aims not so much to identify what happened but to articulate the intellectual framework of the substantive ideas giving shape to the legal domain. It was only in the late eighteenth century that this framework was made explicit; before this time the Milsomian historian is aiming to articulate the unspoken assumptions that held together concrete legal rules. Since these unspoken assumptions were mental constructs and not real entities, it follows that any attempt to identify them must inevitably be hypothetical. Moreover, since different lawyers could use different frameworks around which to order the same basic material, the historian is always faced with the problem of having to operate with a range of competing possibilities. The main consequence of this is that doctrinal legal history has been at its most effective over long timescales, where the friction between different models can be treated as an important force in the generation of legal change rather than as an inconvenience blurring what might otherwise have been a sharply defined picture.

As a general observation, this form of legal history requires considerable imagination. It is only very rarely that the Year Books or early reports give anything more than a veiled hint of the principled assumptions lying behind specific legal propositions; it is even rarer that a hint gets into the Plea Rolls, whose concern was with the accurate recording of the stages in legal process and not at all with the reasons for which decisions were made. Given that before the eighteenth century the lawyers' art was primarily concerned with the way in which questions were raised rather than with the answers that should be given to them, it may legitimately be questioned whether substantive legal doctrine (in the modern sense) can meaningfully be talked about at all; but abstract ideas can be discerned operating beneath the surface of the specific decisions, and it seems unlikely that they are purely the product of historians' fantasies. Moreover, however tempting it is to conclude that the later common law was little more than a set of highly complex technical rules without any principled underpinning, it seems highly improbable that this was the case when the common law began to emerge out of customary practices in the twelfth century.

Perhaps the most important contribution of doctrinal legal history to the earlier history of the common law has been to demarcate the sort of questions that are not capable of being answered with any degree of precision. The more that questions were left to decision by a jury with a significantly unchecked range of discretion, the less sharply determined was the law. It was only when judicial control began to increase, in civil matters (outside the Court of Chancery) from the second half of the eighteenth century, that the law began to take on the degree of precision that characterizes the modern common law system. Outside the analysis of traditional legal thinking, doctrinal history has played its part in the exploration of competing paradigms stemming both from the friction between conflicting cultures (such as that between aboriginal peoples and colonial administrators) and from the conscious adoption of different philosophical models to explain existing legal systems (as where English and American lawyers of the eighteenth and early nineteenth centuries turned to natural law writings to provide a coherent intellectual framework for many branches of the common law).

The real difficulty with doctrinal legal history is that its primary focus is ideas rather than facts or events. The legal frameworks with which it is concerned were not real entities simply waiting to be described by legal historians with sufficient stamina and imagination to join the dots together in the right way. At any moment in time, there might have been, and almost certainly would have been, competing frameworks held by different lawyers—perhaps even by the same lawyers, for we cannot even assume that individuals were self-consistent. The point is well illustrated by the competing positions taken on the question of the emergence of property rights over land in the twelfth century. For Maitland, working back from the thirteenth century, the structure of remedies available in the later twelfth century was explicable in terms of a duality between ownership and possession. Milsom, working forward from the earlier twelfth century, analysed the same remedies in terms of claims by feudal tenants to be treated with due process by their feudal lords. The contrast is apparently stark, but can be resolved straightforwardly if it is recognized that there might have been competing paradigms, one visible in the fragmentary sources of the early twelfth century and one in the sources of the early thirteenth. It is not even necessary to suppose that one paradigm replaced the other, though that may have happened; it may simply be that the individuals responsible for the production of the earlier data happened to have thought in terms of one abstract framework while the individuals responsible for the later data thought in terms of another.

4 EXTERNAL LEGAL HISTORIES

Positivist and doctrinal legal history represent, *par excellence*, internal legal history. Their practitioners have been predominantly trained lawyers, their primary materials the sources generated within the legal process, predominantly statutes and decided cases. Such internal legal history has been accused of conservatism, though it is perhaps fairer to say that it reflects uncritically the bias built in to the legal materials themselves: it concentrates on the law of the landowner and businessman, of the rich rather than the poor, of men rather than women. Behind it lurks the assumption that law constitutes a sufficiently autonomous field of experience or discourse that it can legitimately be described by reference to its own sources. This may be defensible—it is still strongly disputed among legal philosophers—but from the first half of the twentieth century there were mutterings that it was not obviously tenable (Smith and McLaren, 2001). At first these doubts generated little of positive value in the way of external legal history, where law was analysed within its context without giving any credence to its claims to autonomy or objectivity; too much of what was written was facile, easily controverted by historians concerned to preserve legal history in its traditional mould. A highly intelligent preliminary sally in a new direction was fired by Roscoe Pound (Pound, 1923), but he did not push the implications of his ideas far enough, and the great turning-point was the publication in 1950 of Willard Hurst's *Growth of American Law* (Hurst, 1950). This was followed by a number of other books centring on the nineteenth century, most notably his minute analysis of the working of the law in the Wisconsin lumber industry (Hurst, 1964). Against the background of American legal pragmatism, and under the influence of Felix Frankfurter (for whom he acted as research assistant) and of the progressive Supreme Court justice Brandeis (whose clerk he was), Hurst shifted his focus away from legal rules and doctrines on to institutional frameworks—looking at legal practitioners and administrators, not just at judges—and the highly complex factual situations within which the rules operated. Hurst's work loosed legal history from its traditional positivist dominance, spawning a phantasmagoria of external legal histories, most notable among them Morton Horwitz's work on the transformation of American law from the mid-eighteenth to the mid-nineteenth century (Horwitz, 1977). For all that Hurst's work represented a radical break with the past, there was none the less a strong conservative dimension to it: its focus remained fixed on the elite—in his case, substantially on business interests—rather than on the underclass of hidden legal subjects, and he continued to place considerable reliance on the law as it operated through decided cases. More recent writers have tended to shift their focus away from both of these, redressing the traditional historiographical bias by disinterring the law (in the broad institutional sense favoured by Hurst) as it applied to disadvantaged groups such as slaves, ethnic minorities, and women, and consequently weakening the hold of formal legal sources on the historical narrative. A noteworthy spin-off of this type of writing has been the emergence of a distinct Australian–Canadian legal history, concerned with the functioning of law in a colonial or post-colonial context rather than with the niceties of (English) legal doctrine.

Critics and sympathetic commentators alike have pointed to the methodological difficulties commonly thrown up for external legal histories. The more ambitious the work, the more acute these difficulties become. The historian needs a careful and accurate grasp of the legal materials as well as a proper understanding of their context; and there needs to be a plentiful supply of data from both within the law and from outside it. The risk of selecting sources in order to support a predetermined thesis is both obvious and avoidable, but it is less easy to solve the interpretive problems that arise. The adoption of a legal rule that appears to have favoured some particular group—industrialists, members of trades unions, landowners, slaves—in no way demonstrates that it was adopted in order to favour that group; nor, in the converse situation, can we show with any degree of certainty that some combination of legal rules did in fact have a particular effect on the social or economic framework in which it operated. One way through this thicket is consciously to fit the historical analysis into some explicitly theorized framework; alternatively, the historian can adopt a sceptical or agnostic standpoint and simply point to suggestive parallels without drawing any definite conclusions from them.

Many topics—one could point to such subjects as the law relating to the exploitation of land, water, and other natural resources, the development of corporations, or the law of commercial contracts—have benefited from the external approach; but in two areas in particular, the history of the family and the history of crime, the social context of the law has been very much to the fore.

Historians of the family, needing large bodies of data to examine so as to be able to distinguish between the typical and the untypical, have made considerable use of legal materials. As well as purely administrative records, such as parish registers, court rolls—especially the rolls of manor courts—have proved highly valuable as sources of demographic data. In addition, legal disputes can shed light on family matters, so long as it is borne in mind that the lawsuit itself will almost certainly reveal a dysfunction within the family relationship rather than the norm. Legal materials relating to marriage and divorce are, unsurprisingly, revealing as to the legitimate expectations of husband and wife, and actions relating to guardianship and custody provide considerable information about the position of children. Less directly, but no less importantly, disputes over property and inheritance can cast illumination over frequently hidden matters relating to the whereabouts of economic power within the family (including here extended family groups), and more generally between men and women. Legal records can be no less valuable as sources of data, even where the law itself is not the historian's concern. One example out of very many is the way in which defamation actions in London church courts in the early seventeenth century—nearly all of which involved women as both complainant and defendant—have been used to reconstruct the world and language of women, when practically all other writing which has survived was written by men to be read by men (Gowing, 1996).

Criminal law, it has been argued, was relatively unsophisticated in the pre-eighteenth century common law as a result of the exclusion of lawyers from the trial process (Langbein, 2002). While this did not entirely rule out the development of formal legal rules, it did militate against their articulation with the degree of complexity that characterized real property and other branches of the civil law. Moreover, the relative absence of lawyers led to the relative absence of law reports, so that legal historians used to working with case law have found themselves hamstrung by a dearth of source material. There do survive reports of major political prosecutions—the State Trials—but such cases are likely to be so atypical that it is acutely hazardous to derive from them any principles of general application. The purely legal sources that do exist, from which a sharper history of criminal law could be written, are primarily the readings in the Inns of Court; but, as has been said above, research based on these is still very much in its infancy. This has both left the field relatively free for social historians, and more importantly meant that researchers into the early history of criminal law have frequently found it worthwhile (and perhaps sometimes even necessary) to put their work in its social context in order to make some sense of it. The history of crime, too, is the opposite side of the coin to the history of social control, a matter of obvious centrality in the broader context of social history. Fashion has also played its part: perhaps the most interesting insights into legal history from a Marxist perspective have had as their focus the operation of the criminal law (see e.g. Hay, 1975); and non-verbal legal history (such as provided by museums) has concentrated almost exclusively on crime and its social context, for reasons both of popularity and of the accessibility of appropriate material. Even after the eighteenth century, as the criminal trial became increasingly legalized, the continued dominance of the jury has operated as a brake on legal development through case law; as a result, lawyers interested in the history of legal rules and doctrines have tended to shy away from the subject, while the greater availability of source material has made the topic yet more attractive to examination from a social-historical dimension.

Any legal topic can gain from its contextualization, though. This is clearly visible in the multifarious studies which have been made of particular legal events, such as the enactments of individual pieces of legislation or the making of individual legal decisions. Historians have produced careful studies of specific statutory provisions from the sixteenth century onwards, that is, from as early as evidence can be found in personal and parliamentary papers from which it is possible to do something more than guess as to the reasons and competing pressures influencing the form in which the statute was eventually passed. The nineteenth and twentieth centuries lend themselves particularly well to such studies, sometimes combined with analyses of the way in which the statutes were applied and interpreted, given the mass of documentation to be found in parliamentary papers and in the working documents of the department or departments of government responsible for drafting the legislation and steering it through parliament. Studies of individual decisions can be divided into those examining the formal legal materials (counsels' arguments and judges' reasons) and those examining the factual background to disputes. Works of the former type may be motivated by the desire to deconstruct a case which has come to be regarded as authority for some legal proposition which, properly analysed, it might not support. More positively, they can be used to uncover the doctrinal sources—from within the common law tradition or outside it—from which legal rules or principles were ultimately derived. Works of the latter type can highlight the sometimes contorted factual circumstances of cases that appear straightforward from the sanitized version of the 'facts' appearing in the law reports, and point to the extra-legal factors which pulled in the direction of some particular outcome. By drawing back from the formal legal reasons, whose function is invariably to show why the decision reached is the legally correct one in terms of abstract legal doctrine, and concentrating on the uniqueness of the individual case, this type of study is most congenial to historians of a sceptical or postmodernist bent. In the hands of their admitted master (Simpson, 1995), these analyses of cases can also be hugely entertaining.

Finally, putting across the artificial boundary between internal and external history, and constituting a very important strand in modern legal historiography, are institutional studies. In so far as the law is the product of the activities of lawyers operating in a professional context through properly constituted courts, the examination of the history of these institutions, as well as being important in itself, sheds a good deal of light on the development of the law. By looking at the courts, their administration, and their staffing it is possible to trace the way that formal mechanisms have played their part in nudging the law in a particular direction, and the in-depth study of superior courts over a period brings up to the surface the importance of judicial ideology in the generation both of substantive rules and—often more importantly—legal method. Biographical and prosopographical studies of lawyers can have similar functions; and biographical works derived from lawyers' own papers can additionally reveal otherwise hidden dimensions of the legal process. As well as contributing to the building up of a balanced picture of the history of the legal profession, by examining the education and training of lawyers the institutional historian can provide a valuable corrective to legal history written from a formal legal perspective: taught law both reflects and creates the solid core of apparently uncontroversial rules, principles, and doctrines which lie at the heart of the legal system at any particular moment. Analogous results can be obtained by focusing on legal literature, looking both at individual works and at the development of different genres.

Institutional works of these types are not only valuable on their own terms and for the way in which they feed in to the mainstream of the history of law; they also serve to bring the law into the broader field of view of intellectual history. They are a reminder that law is not a purely autonomous discipline standing aloof from the rest of life, but something locked in to a society's culture.

REFERENCES

Ames, J. B. (1913). *Lectures on Legal History and Miscellaneous Legal Essays*, Cambridge, Mass.: Harvard University Press.

Association of American Law Schools (1907). *Select Essays in Anglo-American Legal History*, Boston: Little, Brown & Co.

Baker, J. H. (2000). 'Why the History of English Law has not been Finished', *Cambridge Law Journal*, 62–84.

—— (2001). *The Law's Two Bodies*, Oxford: Oxford University Press.

—— (2002). *An Introduction to English Legal History* (4th edn.), London: Butterworths.

Fifoot, C. H. S. (1965). *The Letters of Frederic William Maitland*, Cambridge: Cambridge University Press.

Friedman, L. (1973). *A History of American Law*, New York: Simon and Schuster.

Gowing, L. (1996). *Domestic Dangers*, Oxford: Clarendon Press.

Guth, D. J., and Pue, W. W. (2001). *Canada's Legal Inheritances*, Winnipeg: Canadian Legal History Project, Faculty of Law, University of Manitoba.

Hay, D. (1975). 'Property, Authority and the Criminal Law', in D. Hay, P. Linebaugh, J. G. Rule, E. P. Thompson, and C. Winslow (eds.), *Albion's Fatal Tree*, London: Allen Lane.

Holdsworth, W. S. (1903–72). *A History of English Law*, London: Methuen.

Horwitz, M. (1977). *The Transformation of American Law, 1780–1860*, New York and Oxford: Oxford University Press.

Hurst, J. W. (1950). *The Growth of American Law*, Boston: Little, Brown & Co.

—— (1964). *Law and Economic Growth: The Legal History of the Lumber Industry in Wisconsin, 1836–1915*, Cambridge, Mass.: Belknap Press.

Kercher, B. (1995). *An Unruly Child: A History of Law in Australia*, St Leonard's, NSW: Allen and Unwin.

Kiralfy, A. K. R. (1951). *The Action on the Case*, London: Sweet and Maxwell.

Langbein, J. H. (2002). *The Origins of Adversary Criminal Trial*, Oxford: Oxford University Press.

Maitland, F. W. (1900). *Political Theories of the Middle Age*, Cambridge: Cambridge University Press.

—— (1901). *English Law and the Renaissance*, Cambridge: Cambridge University Press.

Milsom, S. F. C. (1958). 'Trespass from Henry III to Edward III', *Law Quarterly Review*, 74: 195–224, 407–36, 561–90.

—— (1969). *Historical Foundations of the Common Law*, London: Butterworths.

Pollock, F. (1961). 'The Science of Case-Law', in *Essays in Jurisprudence and Ethics*, London: Macmillan, 169–84.

—— and Maitland, F. W. (1895). *The History of English Law before the Time of Edward I*, Cambridge: Cambridge University Press.

Pound, R. (1923). *Interpretations of Legal History*, Cambridge: Cambridge University Press.

Simpson, A. W. B. (1995). *Leading Cases in the Common Law*, Oxford: Clarendon Press.

Smith, K. J. M., and McLaren, J. P. S. (2001). 'History's Living Legacy: An Outline of "Modern" Historiography of the Common Law', *Legal Studies*, 21: 251–324.

Winfield, P. H. (1921). *The History of Conspiracy and Abuse of Legal Procedure*, Cambridge: Cambridge University Press.

Yale, D. E. C., and Baker, J. H. (1987). *A Centenary Guide to the Publications of the Selden Society*, London: Selden Society.

CHAPTER 39

···

EMPIRICAL
RESEARCH IN LAW

···

JOHN BALDWIN

GWYNN DAVIS

1 INTRODUCTION

···

IN this chapter we consider the contribution to legal scholarship which has been and
is being made by research strategies which fall under the broad heading of 'empirical'.
Empirical research may be defined by reference to what it is not, as well as to what it
is. It is not purely theoretical or doctrinal; it does not rest on an analysis of statute and
decided cases; and it does not rely on secondary sources. What empiricists do, in one
way or another, is to study the operations and the effects of the law. This leaves a great
many decisions still to be taken. The focus of attention may be upon professional
actors or it may be upon consumers; it may be upon the practice of law or upon
measures of outcome; it may be upon legal processes which are in any event highly
visible, even iconic, or it may be upon aspects of the law which normally remain
subterranean; and finally it may involve collecting data on large numbers of cases,
each subject to a predetermined scheme of categorization and reporting, or it may
involve the painstaking examination of a relatively few interactions. All we can say,
therefore, is that empirical research in law involves the study, through direct methods

We are indebted to Julie Vennard, Julian Rivers, and John Parkinson, each of whom made helpful
suggestions from within their own fields of expertise, and to Anne Griffiths for secretarial support.

rather than secondary sources, of the institutions, rules, procedures, and personnel of the law, with a view to understanding how they operate and what effects they have. It is not a synonym for 'statistical' or 'factual', and its intellectual depth and significance are not determined by the empirical label but can only be judged by reference to the same standards and the same yardsticks as would be applied to any other academic endeavour.

There is one distinctive feature of the empirical research enterprise to which we should draw attention at the outset. This is that empirical research in law is not the preserve of the academic lawyer alone, but has attracted scholars from across the social sciences, especially sociologists, economists, and psychologists. This is desirable in principle since the workings of law and legal institutions have such profound social, economic, and political consequences that they ought not to be treated as the monopoly interest of lawyers. In keeping with this, we find that even long-established principles governing the analysis of legal reasoning have been subject to challenge by 'realist' scholars (Twining, 1973). However, it is principally through empirical study of the *practice* of law (especially of the preliminary and apparently more mundane aspects), and in studying the way legal processes and decisions impact upon the citizen, that the disciplines of sociology and, to a lesser degree, philosophy, psychology, and economics have entered into and enriched the study of law. This multidisciplinary research has, in turn, influenced many aspects of legal practice, albeit the insights gained may be conveyed imperfectly and in such a manner as barely to do justice to the complexity of the originating ideas. Even the rules and procedures of the law, which can seem arcane and specialist, reflect this influence.

Whilst 'black letter' legal scholars engage in painstaking analysis of decisions taken in the courts, especially at appellate level, other social science disciplines have contributed to a widespread recognition that the study of what law *does* can be as stimulating and intellectually challenging as the study of what the law *says*, and furthermore that traditional legal scholarship should not be regarded as a separate world but is itself enriched through a fuller understanding of law in its social context. So it is that many distinguished legal scholars, whilst they may not conduct empirical research themselves, engage with the evidence contributed by empiricists as to how law works and how it affects people's lives. Their definition of the scope of their subject now includes these elements.

2 BURGEONING ACTIVITY

In the period since World War II growing numbers of academic lawyers and social scientists have become interested in applying empirical research methods to the study of legal processes. It is possible to trace the origins of the empirical approach to a much earlier time, for example, to the work of Quetelet and Guerry in Continental Europe in the early nineteenth century (see Radzinowicz, 1966: 29–42), but it was not until the advent of the so-called 'realist' school of jurisprudence in the middle of the last century that empirical enquiry became an accepted basis for legal analysis. Realist scholars maintained that judicial decisions were influenced by a host of personal and social factors, and that they ought therefore to be analysed not only with reference to statute, precedent, and established legal principle, but also with reference to judges' social backgrounds and political beliefs. Research on the politics of the judiciary conducted in the UK by Griffith (1997) and Robertson (1998), and in the United States by writers such as Levin (1977) and Estreicher and Sexton (1986), indicates that this tradition is still very much alive. The questions posed by these researchers, and their starting assumptions, have in turn influenced the work of other legal scholars who are not themselves inclined to pursue empirical strategies, thereby contributing to a reorientation in legal thinking and helping to change the nature of legal scholarship.

These developments have not, however, been uniform, either geographically or substantively. Despite the altered profile of legal research in the common law world following the widespread adoption of an empirical approach, there are some law schools—and some disciplines—within which empirical study continues to be regarded as a peripheral and perhaps even a downmarket interest, and certainly the dominant ethos remains doctrinal. However, virtually all law schools contain at least a smattering of empiricists, and some legal disciplines have been transformed through their influence. These include, most obviously, criminal law and criminal justice, family law, and parts of regulatory or 'public' law. There is also a burgeoning interest in empirical study of developments within the legal profession.

One factor not intrinsic to the subject itself which has stimulated the empirical approach within law schools has been the income which universities have been able to secure by this means. In the UK all universities have been driven to seek funds beyond their core government grant. Empirical research in, for example, criminal justice has proved attractive to potential sponsors—including government departments—and universities have found it in their interests to sustain empirical researchers who are capable of generating this income. Also, as external audit and monitoring of academic activities have become increasingly prominent in the drive to make these institutions more publicly accountable, the capacity to undertake large-scale empirical research has come to be regarded as one of the hallmarks of a diverse and academically vibrant law school. Similar processes occur in the United States, where the expenditures of public universities may be reviewed by state legislatures, and national grant agencies may require universities to account for their spending. This external auditing, coupled with pressures to extend universities' funding base, has contributed to a situation where empirical research is now central to the life of many law departments—something that would have been unthinkable a few decades ago.

These developments have gone hand in hand with the recruitment of non-lawyers into law schools, and also with collaboration across disciplinary and institutional boundaries. Indeed, it is striking how many prominent empirical researchers in law have a background in other disciplines. Some took their first degree in the humanities, but most were trained in one or other of the social sciences. It is probably fair to say that there has not been a coherent intellectual vision underlying this recruitment and collaboration. It has tended, rather, to be haphazard and serendipitous, reflecting perhaps the fact that scholars happened to be working in the same institution, or a chance convergence of interests. Many non-lawyers working in law schools were recruited in the first instance as contract researchers, employed on projects devised by academic lawyers. Sometimes the process of recruitment has worked the other way, with lawyers being approached by colleagues in the social sciences who were intent on examining some aspects of the legal process and who recognized the need for legal expertise on their research team.

Some of the non-lawyers recruited in this way have a firm grounding in the core discipline of sociology; others have some training in the methods of empirical invest-igation; but it is a very mixed picture, and many empirical research projects in law, even those with nominal 'social scientists' on board, cannot lay claim to intellectual roots located in another discipline. They may be referred to as 'interdisciplinary' but reflect only the most basic sociological precepts—for example, that rules do not necessarily determine behaviour, or that the conduct of actors and institutions cannot be understood simply by reference to their officially declared purposes.

So intellectual depth and coherence may sometimes be lacking, but over a period many of these non-lawyers have established a foothold in law schools, following which they have expanded the scope of their activities. For example, some now contribute as teachers of 'fringe' legal subjects—for example, criminology, sociology of law, socio-legal studies—which grew in popularity in the 1970s and 1980s as a means of extending a narrowly based law curriculum. Meanwhile, perhaps influ-enced by this cross-fertilization, some academic lawyers have themselves become interested in the study of legal processes, including the behaviour of professional actors, the strategies of bargaining and negotiation, and the degree to which legal endowments determine formal outcome. The sociological underpinning may be rudimentary, but some of these untutored investigators have proved themselves to be talented, intuitive commentators upon a world which they have chosen to view not as professional insiders but with an outsider's critical eye and an enthusiasm for the great themes exemplified in the practice of law.

This burgeoning interest in the study of legal processes has contributed to the cre-ation of a number of research institutes dedicated to the empirical study of law and legal institutions. Whilst many of these centres are generalist in character, in which case the generic label 'socio-legal' may be applied to them, others are more specialist, devoted, for example, to the study of criminal justice, penology, judicial administration, civil justice, or family law. Some of these research centres are long-established, being supported by grants from charitable trusts or foundations, or by government departments; others lead a more precarious existence, being dependent upon their own host institution for financial support. Whilst only a minority of the academic researchers who engage in empirical research in law are employed within these centres, they are none the less important, both practically and symbolically, as demonstrating an institutional commitment to this kind of research and in raising its profile.

Similar observations might be made in relation to the publication of the results of empirical research. In some fields of law it is empirical researchers, rather than doctrinal scholars, who are cited most frequently in the legal literature. Some of the most venerable and prestigious legal journals have proved ready recipients of material with an empirical content. In addition, journals with a distinctly 'socio-legal' orientation (e.g. *Law and Society Review* and *Journal of Law and Society*) have flourished in this period and provide an invaluable outlet for socio-legal scholarship, including the empirical. Finally, some mainstream legal publishers have committed themselves to producing substantial monographs which present the fruits of empirical enquiry on a range of legal topics, and we have even seen the advent of distinctively 'socio-legal' publishers (for example, Sage Publications and Hart Publishing), much of whose output has an empirical component.

3 Why is Empiricism Found in Some Fields of Law but Not Others?

Whilst some areas of law have been transformed by the empirical approach, others (such as contract) have remained largely untouched by it. It is important to ask why this is, and to consider the implications for legal scholarship generally. One possible starting-point is the observation that empirical strategies reflect the influence of non-lawyers, and it is probably the case that some legal subjects are more accessible to the non-lawyer, and hold greater intuitive appeal, than do others. The technical intricacies of the law relating to trusts or contract, for example, inevitably act as a deterrent to anyone outside the narrow band of legal scholars who have mastered the complexities of the subject. Criminal law is also complex, but it is not 'law' as such that has attracted the interest of criminologists and other criminal justice scholars. The focus of attention has tended to be upon legal institutions—for example, the police and prosecuting authorities—rather than upon legal doctrine, and some sociologists have contributed ground-breaking studies of these institutions which in turn have deepened our understanding of legal phenomena (see e.g. Reiner, 1992; Rock, 1993).

Accessibility to non-lawyers is important because the empirical approach is only likely to appeal, and to seem relevant, when law is conceived as an instrument of social policy, and this is not the way in which doctrinal lawyers are taught to approach their subject. The legal scholar who operates in the common law tradition is primarily interested not in the social policy of the law, or the translation of that policy into effective practice, but rather in the coherence and logic of legal argument applied to a given set of facts. Admittedly, most legal scholars in common law countries would say that their work is informed to some degree by the social sciences, and by theoretical or policy-orientated writing. However, that does not mean that they themselves engage in empirical research, or even that they consume the fruits of others' investigations. Criminal justice and, to a lesser extent, the tort system are perhaps the two areas in which there has been the most effective cross-over—see, for example, the work of Dewees *et al.* (1996); the series of surveys conducted in the 1970s for the Pearson Commission (Royal Commission, 1978), and by the Oxford Centre for Socio-Legal Studies; Genn's work on tort settlements (1987); and research sponsored by the Rand Corporation in the US (Hensler *et al.*, 2000).

Despite this important work, there lies buried deep within the traditions of the common law an alternative view of the legal enterprise, one in which 'policy' emerges through the application of legal precedent. This is not to say that the academic lawyer is uninterested in broader themes, or in empirical investigation as a means of exploring those themes, but such exploration will tend to be regarded as a parallel activity, one that is undertaken by scholars from other disciplines. In fact, there are many fields of law in which academic lawyers tend not to conduct empirical research, but where their approach is none the less socio-legal in the sense that they draw upon a parallel literature which addresses many of the same issues, but from a sociological or economic perspective. Company law provides one example. This is a field in which there are strong interdisciplinary links and in which the fruits of empirical research are routinely employed by academic lawyers to enrich their view of the subject. There is, for example, a substantial empirical literature on the economic effects of take-overs. However, this empirical investigation tends not to be something that company lawyers carry forward themselves; nor is it defined as falling within the 'law' component of the subject.

There are other fields however—and criminal justice is the most obvious example—in which there is no separation of the legal and social policy dimensions and therefore no gulf to bridge. This is partly because the legal dimension is reasonably accessible to the non-lawyer, and partly because lawyers working in these areas tend themselves to be enthused by issues of policy and practice. So it is that in criminal justice (and to a lesser extent in tort, public and family law) academic lawyers have tended to address many of the same issues as social scientists and they have a literature which is at the very least overlapping. They also tend to regard empirical investigation as an essential tool, and one that confers academic prestige and other benefits upon its most skilled and inventive practitioners.

4 MAIN QUESTIONS AND PREOCCUPATIONS

To say that empirical researchers are interested in issues of social policy which are reflected in the law, and in the implementation of that policy through legal practice, leaves much still to be explained about the nature of empirical work. One possible starting-point is with the observation that empiricists aim to describe the legal world as it is, not as it is meant to be, with many studies emphasizing the disparity between textbook depictions of legal and judicial processes and their everyday reality. It was Roscoe Pound in the early years of the last century who first drew the distinction between 'law in the books' and 'law in action', the essential point being that the study of statute and decided cases is not sufficient as a means of discovering how legal institutions and legal practitioners conduct themselves (Pound, 1910). Many aspects of legal process are characterized by the exercise of discretion, and by the development of working practices which do not figure in any account of legal rules. The settlement culture which pervades the civil courts, and plea bargaining within criminal justice, are two examples of this.

This 'gap' between legal texts and the day-to-day reality of legal practice has become a preoccupation of the empirical researcher. Studies have been conducted which demonstrate, for example, that the way in which police officers arrive at arrest and detention decisions is often at odds with legal rules; that decision-making in the courtroom reflects the attitudes and prejudices of the judge who hears the case as well as the clinical application of the law; and that the way in which lawyers dispose of their cases frequently departs from legally prescribed procedures. The 1960s, in particular, witnessed a considerable reorientation of criminal justice research, with studies such as those conducted by Piliavin and Briar (1964), Skolnick (1966), and Blumberg (1967) focusing on decision-making at different stages of the justice process. These studies revealed that police officers' arrest decisions reflected their assessments of the character and demeanour of the individuals concerned; that informal interactions between defence and prosecution lawyers were commonly at odds with legally prescribed procedures; and that courtroom decisions reflected, at least in part, the personal attributes of the judge. A typical observation was that of Piliavin and Briar (1964: 214), who concluded that '[t]he official delinquent, as distinguished from the juvenile who simply commits a delinquent act, is the product of a social judgment . . . he is a delinquent because someone in authority has defined him as one, often on the basis of the public face he has presented to officials rather than of the kind of offence he has committed'. These studies represent landmarks in the empirical investigation of legal procedures, and some indication of the scale of the endeavour is provided by the criminal justice bibliography compiled by Radzinowicz and Hood in 1976 which gives 10,000 references to criminal justice research and runs to 400 pages. As those of us embarking on research careers in this period appreciate, this literature had a profound impact, serving to inspire empirical researchers throughout the common law world.

One abiding characteristic of this research was its critical edge, with the authors generally taking a negative view of legal actors' casual approach to rule observance. The disparity between law in the books and law in action was most evident in relation to pre-trial criminal procedures, with legal practitioners being seen to concentrate their energies on avoiding trial rather than preparing for it. The US literature on plea bargaining, focusing upon the inducements offered to criminal defendants to forgo their right to jury trial, would itself fill several shelves in any law library, with most of this work being critical in tone.

As far as civil justice is concerned, empirical research has developed more slowly, but it has still proved influential in certain areas, with US scholars again leading the way. These civil justice studies have been concerned with matters such as case settlement procedures (Rosenberg, 1964); access to justice (Cappelletti and Garth, 1978); small claims adjudication (Yngvesson and Hennessey, 1975); and developments in the legal profession (Abel, 1989). As with criminal justice research, many of these authors have highlighted the disparity between formal rules and textbook accounts of process and procedures on the one hand and the reality of legal practice on the other.

The now commonplace observation that the standard means of disposal of both criminal and civil cases is through informal out-of-court negotiation and settlement is derived principally from this research. Although still not reflected in some textbooks, the literature on plea bargaining, and on the settlement of civil claims, has contributed greatly to what is now a general acceptance of the view that in order to understand the justice process it is necessary to observe it at every stage and not to focus exclusively on set-piece courtroom dramas. It is also vital to tap the experience of lay actors and not to view the operation of legal processes solely from the perspective of the powerful and the privileged.

This brings us to a second characteristic of empirical research, which is that it tends to give considerable prominence to the voice of the consumer of legal services. In the best work of this kind, the consumer (whether litigant, witness, victim, or defendant) is not regarded as the sole arbiter of the value and effectiveness of legal services, but the consumer perspective is seen as having its own validity, which means that it can be a useful corrective both to some rule-based accounts and to the voice of the professional practitioner. Some of the most influential research of this kind has achieved its impact precisely because it has demonstrated that the experience of those on the receiving end of legal processes was not understood or adequately represented by the legal practitioners whose job it was to safeguard their interests and who saw themselves as doing this in good faith (Baldwin and McConville, 1977; Felstiner *et al.*, 1981; Davis *et al.*, 1994). So the view that legal processes can only be described and evaluated by practitioners and professional commentators—or even that they are *best* evaluated by these professional insiders—is one that has been effectively challenged through empirical research.

A third feature of the empirical approach is that it tends to be focused upon lower level and preliminary legal processes. It is true that some empirical legal researchers have been concerned with decision-making at more rarified levels, but the main focus tends to be upon those parts of the legal process which are high volume, routine, largely hidden from public view, and which are dealt with cursorily if at all within legal texts. This focus upon routine decision-making is characteristic of empirical studies in both criminal and civil justice. So also is the preoccupation with the early stages of legal proceedings—the so-called 'low visibility' part—this being the point at which the future trajectory of both civil and criminal cases is often determined. Empirical researchers have examined, for example, how the police make decisions on the streets; the processes by which the police and prosecuting authorities decide whether an alleged offender should be prosecuted, and on what charge; the settlement strategies of civil and criminal litigators; the significance of procedure, including the part played by preliminary hearings in civil cases, and why these cases typically settle at a late stage. Other studies have examined the interactions between lawyers and their clients, and the impact of lawyers' work management strategies. None of these subjects is intrinsically more (or less) interesting than the preoccupations of the doctrinal legal scholar, but they reflect a view that the practice of law is an important subject for study in its own right, and that this practice needs to be observed in all its 'minute particulars' if it is to be accurately described and understood.

Low visibility is also a feature of the mechanisms intended to ensure that organizations comply with the regulations governing their practice, and these regulatory regimes have provided another target for empirical study. This work, which has been conducted in many parts of the common law world, has focused upon the role of inspectorates of various kinds and on the extent to which organizations comply with their own regulatory standards. The studies cover, for example, the work of factory inspectors (Baldwin, 1995), environmental health officers (Hutter, 1988), occupational health and safety officers (Gunningham and Johnstone, 1999), and business and financial services regulators (Grabosky and Braithwaite, 1986; Black, 1997). A unifying theme of this literature is the significance of negotiation in delivering compliance.

Another 'driver' of empirical research, prominent under the recent New Labour administrations in the UK, is the (laudable) impulse to monitor legal innovation by government and to evaluate its consequences. Monitoring and evaluating innovation have provided a great deal of work for the socio-legal community, which perhaps explains why it is seldom questioned, but we have certain reservations about it as the dominant empirical research model. The first arises from the fact that this research may be used essentially for presentational purposes. It is hard to imagine that the government department which commissions the research is seeking totally independent assessment and conclusions: to some degree at least the policy is already formed. The tensions around this issue are reflected in the tussles which occasionally occur between government departments and researchers over the right to publish (see below). A second reservation concerns the 'reformist' nature of evaluative research. Neither the practitioners who participate in the initiative nor the researchers who study it can claim that they are addressing the fundamental causes of social problems. As Pawson and Tilley put it: 'Evaluations are … patently petty political'. In other words, government-sponsored initiatives treat certain social and political configurations as given, so that 'the programmes which get evaluated are directed at reducing problems with systems, or ensuring the better operation of those systems' (Pawson and Tilley, 1997: 12). A third and final reservation concerns the short-term agenda that inevitably drives empirical research on this model. The agenda is that of the commissioning government department—which means the minister and his or her civil servants—and their thinking will tend to be dominated by immediate political considerations.

A distinctive form of evaluative research is that which sails under the 'what works?' banner. This question, which can of course be asked of almost anything, has come to function as a label applied to interventions which are geared to changing attitudes or behaviour. It tends to be asked especially of government-sponsored initiatives which, it is hoped, will have therapeutic effects—say, in diverting offenders from whatever patterns of behaviour (such as drug-taking) or whatever modes of thought (such as denying responsibility for their own actions) are deemed to underlie their offending behaviour. Research on this model is designed to test the cost-effectiveness of the intervention, for example, by examining changes in reconviction rates, or by interviewing the relevant population in order to gauge changes in behaviour and attitude.

Whilst each of the above is an immediately recognizable research stimulus, and between them they underpin much of the empirical research undertaken within law schools, it would be a mistake to imagine that empirical research necessarily falls into any one of these categories. Indeed, it is possible to conclude that the very best work transcends all of them, aiming as it does at a fundamental re-evaluation of the operation of a given area of law. In that sense it may not be designed to measure anything in particular, but rather to assist our understanding of the way law works, including the contribution it makes to addressing social problems and its impact upon the citizen. Accordingly, it will tend to explore many of the same themes as underpin the finest works of literature, or the great political debates. It may to some extent engage with the social policy agenda of the government of the day, but it will not be defined by it.

5 RESEARCH METHODS

There are a host of different approaches to the task of gathering empirical research data, each reflecting different assumptions concerning what questions are worth asking, and what might constitute valid answers to those questions. Whilst the choice of research methods will reflect the researcher's views as to what knowledge is worth acquiring, those views will not necessarily be made explicit. Often they will be implicit in the choice of method and in the way in which evidence is presented. The natural scientist's preoccupation with rigorous scientific method is seldom paralleled in socio-legal research, most of which is conducted by academics who were not educated within that tradition and who, in any event, may doubt whether those techniques would serve their purpose. Thus, for example, the randomized controlled trial, which has long been the gold standard in medical research, hardly figures in research into legal processes. This is partly on ethical grounds, but also because empirical researchers in law are seldom concerned to explore the long-term impact of one specific intervention.

Much empirical legal research is descriptive in character, the aim being to examine the operation of legal processes and to demonstrate how these are perceived by all the parties concerned, perhaps especially by 'consumers' who do not normally have much opportunity to explain how the legal world feels to them. But empirical legal research is at least as much about providing explanations for social phenomena as it is descriptive. These explanations vary considerably in the level of sociological sophistication that is brought to bear, and readers may on occasion be tempted to ask whether the implicit value judgements which lie buried within them are ones which they would share. None the less, an explanation of sorts is being offered. Other empirical research is self-consciously evaluative, in which case there may be explicit design and delivery requirements which can be examined with a fair degree of objectivity.

As far as technical research skills are concerned, it is likely that few empirical legal researchers will have done more than dip into the various methodological texts that have been published in recent years. Research skills are picked up by observing more experienced colleagues, and there is nothing particularly complex or technical about the methods employed. This is not to say that these researchers lack skill, only that their skill does not lie in a mastery of research techniques. Essentially, it lies in their understanding of the fundamental purposes of the legal enterprise and their ability to deploy Wright Mills's 'sociological imagination' in order to re-describe and re-evaluate it. The creativity lies in marrying some aspects of the insider's legal knowledge with the sociologist's ability to discern the wider themes underlying the individual dramas of the law—or, in Wright Mills's terms, to discern the public issue within the private trouble (Wright Mills, 1959). The methods by which this is achieved—observing, interviewing, perusing documents—can have a somewhat homespun or improvised feel to them, but this is not necessarily a matter for regret, provided that the methods employed are appropriate as a means of exploring the issues which the researchers say they are trying to explore.

It is important, therefore, to recognize that empirical research in law is a creative process—as, probably, we would find is also true of research in the physical sciences, if only we understood it better. The difference is that one tends not to find within legal research any equivalent of the pure science model of hypothesis formulation, testing, and re-testing, leading to a finding which can then be further explored by means of other studies. Legal researchers seldom identify specific hypotheses which they mean to test, nor is there much enthusiasm for replicating earlier work. This is for three reasons: first, as we have said, most socio-legal research is essentially descriptive and explanatory, rather than evaluative; secondly, it is understood that the researcher's own value judgements lie buried within the research—so there is little enthusiasm for re-testing a 'finding' which everyone understands to be subjective to some degree; and thirdly, because much socio-legal scholarship tends to be focused upon process rather than outcome, it is only to a limited extent that its practitioners see themselves as building on earlier studies, thereby playing their part in a gradual accumulation of knowledge. The metaphor of 'pushing back the frontiers' tends to be employed only ironically within the socio-legal world. Rather, research is seen as a means of developing more satisfying descriptions and explanations of complex institutions and interactions—in which case it is not essential to replicate earlier methodologies, and indeed it can seem rather unexciting to do so.

5.1 Qualitative versus Quantitative Methods

The main distinction within empirical legal research is that between 'qualitative' and 'quantitative' approaches. The former involves an attempted in-depth exploration of legal processes, typically focusing on a modest number of interactions but viewing these from a variety of perspectives and perhaps over time. The strength of this approach lies in its capacity to reflect the complexity of legal processes, and the complexity of the relationship between process and outcome. It is also well suited to exploring the meaning which people place on legal events (Miles and Huberman, 1994). The research instruments (interview schedules, checklists, and so on) may be rudimentary, perhaps comprising no more than a few prompts for the observer, or reminders to the interviewer. This is a research style favoured by many experienced socio-legal researchers, including the authors, although it has to be accepted that the approach may raise questions as to the researchers' underlying attitudes and assumptions, and hence the validity and generalizability of their findings.

Qualitative research calls for fine judgement in deciding what significance to attach to elements of practice and to fleeting interactions within the individual dramas of the law, and this is a potential weakness as well as a strength. Qualitative researchers would claim that the accounts which they offer reflect the entirety of their research evidence, but this can never be proved given that it is not feasible to present more than snippets of that evidence, essentially for illustrative purposes in any published work. This is a research style in which the researchers first inform themselves and then seek to convey the fruits of that understanding to others. It follows that qualitative research, if it is to be of any value, cannot be conducted at second hand, for example, by a survey company; the aim is to improve understanding, not to gather evidence, and that improved understanding can only be achieved through immersion.

Quantitative approaches appear, at least on the face of it, to conform more closely to the pure scientific model. The objectives will usually be clearly identifiable within the research instruments. The study will be carried out on a large scale, possibly employing the services of a survey company such as the National Centre for Social Research, and the information recorded may allow complex statistical analysis. This approach has been adopted, for example, in the large-scale victimization studies that are now routinely conducted in very many countries in an effort to provide more reliable measures of crime than are to be found in official police records (e.g. van Dijk and Mayhew, 1997). So, provided the research questions can be answered by means of this kind of standardized interrogation, the social survey may, if well designed (i.e. with efficient sampling techniques and intelligible, discriminating questions), reveal much about the weight of experience and/or opinion within a given population. Another example of what can be achieved by this approach is the community survey designed to explore the extent of unmet legal need. A recent study of this type in the UK was the investigation conducted by Hazel Genn and the National Centre for Social Research into people's experience of 'justiciable problems' (Genn, 1999).

At the same time one should acknowledge the limitations of quantitative research methods, at least in respect of certain topics. First, such methods are not necessarily any more 'objective' than qualitative approaches in that the researcher's prior assumptions will, inevitably, be embedded in the design of questionnaires and other research instruments. Furthermore, there is no possibility of these biases being corrected as the research proceeds, as is at least possible when researchers are trying to educate themselves in the nuances of a subject. Secondly, surveys are only useful when they focus upon issues concerning which the informants have experience and can respond authoritatively. There is no point asking people about matters of which they have no direct experience and therefore nothing to offer beyond prejudice and received opinion. Yet that is sometimes done, and the resulting 'findings' reported as if they were of some value.

Increasingly, empirical legal researchers are employing a combination of qualitative and quantitative techniques, seeking to harness the strengths of both. For example, in-depth interviews may be conducted with comparatively few informants where there is need to explain the results of an earlier survey. Essentially, the data collection methods should reflect the focus of the research. A combination of qualitative and quantitative approaches may or may not offer greater 'explanatory completeness' (Pawson and Tilley, 1997). One instance where this was achieved was in a recent study of bail decisions and plea bargaining (Kellough and Wortley, 2002) which employed a variety of methods, including tracking some 1,800 criminal cases through the courts and, in methodological contrast, face-to-face interviews with a limited number of offenders. The various data sources allowed for statistical identification of the factors that influence bail decisions, but the study also gave insight into the various ways that remands in custody may affect plea decisions and the prosecution's decision to withdraw charges.

5.2 Research Access

One difficulty which characteristically faces the socio-legal researcher is that of securing access to data. Even if funding is secured, access may be denied, or permission to study an organization's work will be granted only on restrictive conditions. There are considerable differences between institutions in this respect, with some having proved more open to research than others. For example, the police have been quite receptive to external research over the years, even though some of that research has been highly critical of their practice, but the judiciary (especially at the most senior levels) have been less welcoming. It is important to recognize, therefore, that empirical research may be conducted in circumstances that are far from ideal. Legal researchers may find that it is not possible for them to examine certain subjects, or not in the way that they would wish. Studies of sensitive subjects will often proceed on the basis of second-best approaches. Other topics are ruled out altogether, the jury's deliberations being one obvious example.

There are two ways of viewing this admittedly frustrating state of affairs. The first is that powerful institutional forces are conspiring to thwart independent academic enquiry. The second is that some empirical researchers are liable to abuse the privilege of research access in order to attack groups or institutions which they have long viewed in a critical light. We think both explanations contain an element of truth. Some legal institutions are beleaguered and respond in a defensive manner; but also, empirical researchers may pursue an agenda which is not rooted in their data, or not in the data upon which they claim to rely, and this in turn may make it more difficult for other members of the academic community to secure the access they need. Researchers who are granted privileged access to confidential material bear a heavy responsibility—first, to respect that confidentiality, but secondly, just as important, to represent their evidence faithfully, in all its complexity. Equally, major legal institutions ought to accept, as most, including the police, seem to do, that they are publicly accountable. One aspect of that accountability lies in their opening themselves up to reputable academic study.

6 THE RELATIONSHIP TO THEORY

Few empirical researchers in law make any claim that their research is located within some overarching theoretical framework derived from one of the core social science disciplines. In most legal research monographs there is seldom more than a polite nod in the direction of those explanatory frameworks, and when that happens there all too often appears to be no meaningful connection between the theory and the empirical investigation. Of course, all research is influenced by ideas about how groups and

institutions function, or about ways in which individuals react to certain life circumstances. However, it is not clear whether we should refer to this knowledge as 'theory'
or whether we should regard it as part of the store of wisdom which (to some degree)
we all acquire as we move through life. Perhaps we should allow that researchers draw
on a mix of folk wisdom and academic insights.

Unfortunately, those academic insights may be as contentious as the folk wisdom,
so it is helpful if academic researchers are clear about their own core beliefs, and if
they are prepared to articulate these. As we have already observed, this seldom
happens, and the reader is left attempting to fathom the researcher's ideological
stance and starting assumptions. We each have our favoured explanations of motive
and behaviour, and there is virtually no research in law which is uninfluenced by this
tendency to favour some explanations over others, and to apply a normative colouring
to whatever actions are being described.

These sympathies and antipathies, favoured explanations and discarded explanations, underpin all socio-legal writing. Commonly, they will be reflected in the
researchers' choice of subject, and even more so in their choice of informants,
although it is not unknown for researchers to rely upon interviews with one set of
respondents in order to construct accounts which are critical of almost every aspect
of that group's professional practice. We should concede that 'bias' is inevitable in the
sense that the researcher will feel more sympathy towards some informants than
others, and will favour some explanations over others. It is impossible to determine
what would constitute a neutral stance when interviewing or observing a given group
of actors—for example, court officials, legal practitioners, police officers, judges,
divorcing parents, criminal defendants, prisoners, or civil litigants. The question—
'whose side are you on?'—is one that is inevitably raised (Becker, 1967). The lesson
that we draw from this is that it is important for the empiricist to be enthusiastic
about evidence, and to want to be surprised by that evidence in the interests of developing an account which offers fresh insight. So far as possible 'theory' should grow
out of the research data; it should not be the other way around. If the story of the
research does not emerge from the data, one may question the decision to undertake
empirical research in the first place. The research becomes little more than a cosmetic
exercise, designed to add weight to an already well-honed series of descriptions and
explanations.

Having said that, describing the world 'as it is' is inevitably a problematic undertaking, and empirical researchers do not begin with a clean slate. They will have, from
the outset, at least a rudimentary conceptual framework. This will include the main
actors and activities to be examined, key relationships to be explored, and questions
that they hope to answer. This early conceptualizing of the subject-matter is necessary
in order to give clarity and focus, and also to avoid indiscriminate data collection
(Miles and Huberman, 1994). This, however, is only the beginning of the interpretative
task. The essence of the empirical approach lies not only in collecting relevant materials
through the development of appropriate research techniques, but in making sense of

that material as it is being collected. All interviews, all observations, and all documentary materials have to be given meaning by the researcher. It is only if empirical research is understood to be interpretative that it has some prospect of being anything other than ephemeral. If, on the other hand, empirical research is conceived as an attempt to keep pace with the latest changes in law and procedure in order to describe the impact of these changes, then it may be of some immediate interest to policy-makers and practitioners but that interest will not be sustained. This is because legal processes tend not to change very rapidly, and in many of their more fundamental aspects they hardly change at all. Accordingly, empirical research is devalued if it is regarded primarily as a means of monitoring and evaluating new initiatives. It *ought* to be seen, instead, as a means of exploring those aspects of law and legal practice which are enduring and which lie at the heart of the enterprise.

The following passage, taken from the final paragraph of a research monograph exploring one 'hidden' area of family law—the settlement of financial disputes by the parties' lawyers—is the kind of research output we have in mind:

> For the foreseeable future some elements at least of these disputes will continue to be handled by lawyers. But the system was not designed to cope with the present volume of cases and, unsurprisingly, it has many weaknesses. We have identified, in particular: the very great premium which is placed on the energy and inventiveness of individual practitioners; the ponderousness of the process and the opportunity, if either party is so minded, to create delay at every stage; the failure, in many instances, to rectify the bargaining endowments conferred by an ability to conceal resources or to tolerate a postponed resolution; the way in which a settlement culture can override traditional legal values so that the negotiation process becomes no more than a search for compromise; the failure to distinguish between two distinct objectives—advancing the process and promoting settlement—so that these are conflated; and, finally, courts' reluctance or inability to enforce their own procedural orders. (Davis *et al.*, 1994: 273)

This analysis is not located within some overarching sociological theory; but nor is it ephemeral. The researchers have drawn on the evidence of a large number of interactions in order to capture, as they see it, the fundamentals of legal practice in this area. It is questionable whether empiricism can deliver more than this. These authors might have attempted a different level of explanation, perhaps one that was rooted in an overarching theory of professionalism, but it would have been difficult for them in that case to assert that the explanation emerged from their data.

7 INFLUENCE UPON LAW AND SOCIAL POLICY

Given that empirical researchers are interested in the social policy of the law, an obvious question arises as to whether empirical research findings do indeed exert some influence, partly in relation to reform of the substantive law, but also in relation to practice and procedure. It has been claimed that the direction of family law, in particular, has been *over*-influenced by empirical research findings of dubious validity (Deech, 1984), and no doubt the same point could be made in relation to other areas of legal practice. However, the more generally accepted view appears to be that the relationship between research and policy, or research and law reform, is extremely tenuous (Thomas, 1985). This is despite the fact that much empirical research is, either directly or indirectly, state-funded, in which case it might be anticipated that researchers would wish to address issues that are of immediate concern to government, and furthermore that government would be interested in this research evidence and would use it to inform their policies in relation to legal and social issues. We suspect that both sides to this 'contract' would like to believe that this is what happens. On the government side, successive administrations of every hue have been heard to claim that their policies are 'evidence-led', whilst empirical researchers, for their part, like to feel that they are of some use, and that they exert influence. Many engage in the business of empirical research because they want to bring about social change.

We suspect that the limitations of the empirical approach lie at least as much with the paucity of imagination displayed by some researchers as they do with a slavish adherence to the government's agenda. The relationship between the government 'customer' and the empirical research 'contractor' has, over the past forty years, proved something of a disappointment to both. Social policy research has struggled to exert its influence alongside all the other forces bearing upon government, and researchers whose principal motivation has been to influence policy often feel, if not ignored, then manipulated and abused. This is despite the fact that it sometimes suits both sides to pretend that the research in question has made a difference.

Difficulties in the relationship between researchers and policy-makers are perhaps most apparent in disputes which centre on the publication of results. The problems can be acute when the research findings are embarrassing to the government or are believed to offer a distorted and misleading view of the activities of a particular organization. Hostility to publication plans is by no means uncommon, and both authors have experienced it on occasions. A challenge to research findings, whether in private or in public, is invariably an unpleasant experience for the researcher in question and can lead to severe personal and professional difficulties (Baldwin and McConville, 1977). When government, or government agencies, attempt to suppress publication of research findings, the academic community has an obligation to resist. This is why contractual arrangements entered into when research is commissioned need to be considered very carefully lest the right to publish be compromised. Government will often find it uncomfortable to allow publication, but that discomfort cannot be avoided. Of course, those who are on the receiving end of research, whether as subjects or as funders, have a right to see drafts prior to publication, and they may wish to comment in uncompromising terms or ultimately to distance themselves from the research findings as these are presented. But, if the integrity and independence of the researcher are to be maintained, that right must fall short of the power of veto.

Partly this problem reflects the way in which research is commissioned in the first place. Government is not always skilled in determining what it needs to know and what kind of research might fit the bill. In fact, research can be commissioned for a number of disreputable, as well as reputable reasons. The work of Thomas and Weiss suggests that research in law and the social sciences is employed for a number of purposes that cannot be openly acknowledged (Thomas, 1985; Weiss, 1978). These are some of the reasons suggested by Carol Weiss:

- as political ammunition;
- to delay action;
- to avoid taking responsibility for a decision;
- to win kudos for a successful innovation;
- to discredit a disliked policy;
- to maintain the prestige of a government department by supporting well-regarded researchers.

Experienced socio-legal researchers will recognize most of the above list, and they could probably add other equally disreputable items from their own experience. However, it seems to us inevitable that the relationship between research and policy will seldom be direct or straightforward. Government will always use research to serve political ends, and it will likewise do its best to ignore those findings which are politically inconvenient. We would prefer to emphasize independence rather than influence. The key for empirical researchers is to maintain their independence of government (and of any other research customers) in order fully to do justice to the research evidence.

This independence needs to be jealously guarded by the academic community, and for the most part we believe it is. Empirical research in law is often critical of existing policy and practice, and that is appropriate since the research 'story' ought to provide an alternative to the accounts which emerge from government or, indeed, from practitioners. Empirical research, in other words, has a debunking tendency. This, in turn, may bring it under attack (sometimes in private, less often in public) from members of the legal profession, the judiciary, or government representatives. This is what one comes to expect. There is inevitably some tension within these relationships, so it is important that those agencies which are liable to be criticized (or to be presented in a light not entirely consistent with the way they choose to present themselves) accept that this is a legitimate academic function and one that is, ultimately, in the public interest.

This brings us back to influence. Most empirical researchers of any experience appreciate that research findings which reinforce the prevailing thinking of the commissioning government department are more likely to be referred to, and therefore to appear to be influential, than are those which run counter to it. Where the research evidence points in an uncomfortable direction it is not difficult for policy-makers to ignore it.

To gain some impression of how limited the influence of researchers can be if their results do not suit the prevailing mood, and how easy it is for policy-makers to dis-regard their work if they are so minded, one need only consider what has happened in the criminal justice arena in the past twenty years. Punitive law and order policies have been adopted by many Western governments, notwithstanding the empirical research evidence that points to the dangers of such policies. The overwhelming weight of the research and writing produced by generations of criminologists, most of it funded by governments, points to the ineffectiveness of 'crackdowns' on crime, 'wars' on drugs, tough deterrent sentencing, and the like. Yet none of this evidence has succeeded in dissuading governments from following their own tough 'law and order' policies. The fact is that policies based on 'common-sense' solutions to crime problems (mandatory sentencing, deterrent sentencing for drug offenders, more liberal use of imprisonment, and so on) carry great electoral appeal, however much they may fly in the fact of empirical research findings. Garland observes that 'Policy measures [in the United States and the UK] are constructed in ways that appear to value political advantage and public opinion over the views of experts and the evidence of research' (2001: 13), and he offers a long list of contemporary penal pol-icies (including 'prison works', 'three-strikes-and-you're-out', 'no frills prisons', and 'zero-tolerance') to illustrate the point. Nor have protests about these policies in criminological journals cut much ice with policy-makers. It is instructive in this con-text to consider the reaction of a UK government minister in the 1980s to a research finding that prosecutors at a certain court were sometimes able to secure the listing of a particular trial before a particular judge. He responded: 'It does not happen, and if it does, it should not'. Another frequent response by policy-makers who wish to dis-miss unpalatable research findings is to concede that the research may have been accurate at the time it was carried out, but to assert that practice has since changed in some fundamental way, so that the researchers' conclusions are no longer valid.

We regard this evidence of tension between government and members of the aca-demic community as an inevitable consequence of the proximity of some research to the political process: researchers cannot control the reception of their work by policy-makers, and should not become too agitated if that reception is not as they would wish. Policies that carry electoral appeal, or which are congenial to ministers for ideological reasons, are routinely pursued in the face of contrary advice from aca-demic experts who contend that the available evidence points in a different direction.

The conclusion that we draw from this is not necessarily dispiriting. It is inevitable that the development of social policy in contentious areas will reflect prejudice, gut instinct, and vested interests, as well as the accumulated wisdom of practitioners and researchers over many years. The fact that this research wisdom is 'accumulated', and not just the product of the latest monitoring exercise, is in our view a key feature. This is consistent with Weiss's 'enlightenment' or 'knowledge creep' theory, under which the most common mode of research use 'is the diffuse and undirected infiltration of research ideas into [decision-makers'] understanding of the world' (Weiss, 1978).

It is essential, therefore, to take a long-term view of the profound social issues which confront policy-makers in, for example, criminal justice and penology. We would prefer empirical researchers also to take this long-term view, in order to address the fundamentals of law and practice in these areas. Of course there are tensions here with the political imperatives with which ministers and civil servants must wrestle on a daily basis. But it would be deeply regrettable were empirical research in law to be conceived as a series of short-term evaluations. One has to hope that government will continue to sponsor research, whilst at the same time accepting that it is not well placed to determine what kinds of evidence will ultimately prove to be of greatest value. This calls for a continuing dialogue between researchers and policy-makers, and a constructive spirit on the part of both.

REFERENCES

Abel, R. L. (1989). *Criminal Lawyers*, New York: Oxford University Press.

Baldwin, J., and McConville, M. (1977). *Negotiated Justice*, London: Martin Robertson.

Baldwin, R. (1995). *Rules and Government*, Oxford: Clarendon Press.

Becker, J. S. (1967). 'Whose Side are We On?' *Social Problems*, 14: 239–47.

Black, J. (1997). *Rules and Regulators*, Oxford: Clarendon Press.

Blumberg, A. S. (1967). *Criminal Justice*, Chicago: Quadrangle Books.

Cappelletti, M., and Garth, B. (1978). *Access to Justice, Vol. 1: A World Survey*, Alphenaandenrijn: Sijthoff and Noordhoff.

Davis, G., Cretney, S., and Collins, J. (1994). *Simple Quarrels*, Oxford: Clarendon Press.

Deech, R. (1984). 'Matrimonial Property and Divorce: A Century of Progress?' in M. D. A. Freeman (ed.), *The State, the Law, and the Family*, London: Tavistock, 245–61.

Dewees, D., Duff, D., and Trebilcock, M. (1996). *Exploring the Domain of Accident Law: Taking the Facts Seriously*, Oxford: Oxford University Press.

Estreicher, S., and Sexton, J. (1986). *Redefining the Supreme Court's Role*, New Haven: Yale University Press.

Felstiner, W., Abel, R., and Sarat, A. (1981). 'The Emergence and Transformation of Disputes— Naming, Blaming and Claiming', *Law and Society Review*, 15: 631–54.

Garland, D. (2001). *The Culture of Control: Crime and Social Order in Contemporary Society*, Oxford: Oxford University Press.

Genn, H. (1987). *Hard Bargaining*, Oxford: Clarendon Press.

—— (1999). *Paths to Justice: What People Do and Think about Going to Law*, Oxford: Hart.

Grabosky, P., and Braithwaite, J. (1986). *Of Manners Gentle: Enforcement Strategies of Australian Business Regulatory Agencies*, Melbourne: Oxford University Press.

Griffith, J. A. G. (1997). *The Politics of the Judiciary* (5th edn.), London: Fontana.

Gunningham, N., and Johnstone, R. (1999). *Regulating Workplace Safety*, Oxford: Clarendon Press.

Hensler, D. R., Page, N. M., Dombey-Moore, B., Giddens, E., Gross, J., and Moller, E. (2000). *Class Action Dilemmas: Pursuing Public Goals for Private Gain*, Santa Monica, Calif.: Rand.

Hutter, B. (1988). *The Reasonable Arm of the Law? The Law Enforcement Procedures of Environmental Health Officers*, Oxford: Clarendon Press.

Kellough, G., and Wortley, S. (2002). 'Remand for Plea: Bail Decisions and Plea Bargaining as Commensurate Decisions', *British Journal of Criminology*, 42: 186–210.

Levin, M. A. (1977). *Urban Politics and the Criminal Courts*, Chicago: University of Chicago Press.

Miles, M. B., and Huberman, A. M. (1994). *Qualitative Data Analysis* (2nd edn.), London: Sage.

Pawson, R., and Tilley, N. (1997). *Realistic Evaluation*, London: Sage.

Piliavin, I., and Briar, S. (1964). 'Police Encounters with Juveniles', *American Journal of Sociology*, 70: 206–14.

Pound, R. (1910). 'Law in Books and Law in Action', *American Law Review*, 44: 12–36.

Radzinowicz, L. (1966). *Ideology and Crime*, London: Heinemann.

——and Hood, R. (1976). *Criminology and the Administration of Criminal Justice: A Bibliography*, London: Mansell.

Reiner, R. (1992). *The Politics of the Police* (2nd edn.), Hemel Hempstead: Wheatsheaf.

Robertson, D. (1998). *Judicial Discretion in the House of Lords*, Oxford: Clarendon Press.

Rock, P. (1993). *The Social World of an English Crown Court*, Oxford: Clarendon Press.

Rosenberg, M. (1964). *The Pretrial Conference and Effective Justice: A Controlled Test in Personal Injury Litigation*, New York: Columbia University Press.

Royal Commission on Civil Liability and Compensation for Personal Injury (1978). *Report*, Cmnd 7053–1, London: Her Majesty's Stationery Office.

Skolnick, J. H. (1966). *Justice without Trial: Law Enforcement in Democratic Society*, New York: John Wiley.

Thomas, P. (1985). *The Aims and Outcomes of Social Policy Research*, London: Croom Helm.

Twining, W. (1973). *Karl Llewellyn and the Realist Movement*, London: Weidenfeld and Nicolson.

van Dijk, J. J. M., and Mayhew, P. (1997). *Criminal Victimisation in Eleven Industrialised Countries: Key Findings from the 1996 International Crime Victims Survey*, The Hague: Ministry of Justice.

Weiss, C. H. (1978). *Using Social Research in Public Policy Making*, New York: Teakfield.

Wright Mills, C. (1959). *The Sociological Imagination*, New York: Oxford University Press.

Yngvesson, B., and Hennessey, P. H. (1975). 'Small Claims, Complex Disputes: A Review of the Small Claims Literature', *Law and Society Review*, 9: 219–74.

CHAPTER 40

LEGAL EDUCATION

JOHN BELL

1 INTRODUCTION

1.1 Legal Education and Training

IT is important to distinguish education from training. Training is concerned with providing a person with the knowledge and skills required to undertake a specific and immediate task. It is focused and utilitarian. Education is concerned with enabling an individual to understand and reflect upon knowledge and processes and to be able to act in a critical and responsible manner. It is concerned with critical self-awareness. The two are, in reality, on a spectrum between doing and being. They are also located in the spectrum between short-term and long-term development. This chapter will deal with legal education. It will deal with the purposes of legal education and the methods of supporting student learning.

1.2 Research on Legal Education

Legal education is subject to research in a number of ways. The writing is predominantly of three types: theoretical, historical, and empirical.

Theoretical writing debates the purposes of legal education in the context of the purposes of higher education. It is often difficult to distinguish between *research* in this field and *programmatic discussion*. Writing may be characterized as research if it involves engagement with and the development of received ideas and the subjection of trends to analysis. *Programmatic* discussion, reflecting on experience of teaching law or a branch of it, may provide the raw material for a deeper theoretical discussion.

Historical writing is common. Like any history, it involves the study of ideas and data about the way in which legal education has developed. This may be in relation to a particular law school or in relation to law schools generally (see Twining, 1994).

Empirical research involves an analysis of particular instances of legal education. On the whole, there has been a limited amount of structured observational study of how students learn law, and how different methods work. Typically, law teachers lack the necessary training in such empirical methods. Writing about how students learn frequently draws upon general educational research (see D. Tribe, in Webb and Maughan, 1996: 5). Less structured empirical research often involves an account of and reflection upon the teacher's own experiences of legal education. This may involve case studies of experiments that have been conducted or considered reflection by an established teacher on the nature and methods of teaching a branch of law. The strength of the work as research depends on the analytical character of the reflections and their ability to engage with debates in legal education. But there is a danger that such writing is anecdotal or unduly descriptive of a single instance.

This diversity of research has two principal foci: the broad purposes of legal education, and the content of education.

2 THE PURPOSES OF LEGAL EDUCATION

2.1 Who is Legal Education for?

The European tradition, followed in Australasia, has been for university legal education to be part of the general provision of basic higher education. Unlike in North America, the students are undergraduates. This has an important impact on the ambitions of law courses and the style of scholarship that underpins it. Although European students will often have vocational reasons for having chosen to study law, the programme of study is offered as part of general education, a tendency accentuated by the growth of mass higher education. By contrast, the graduate character of American law schools has made them traditionally dominated by the vocational aspirations of students and the need to retain close links with the legal professions, though this is now under strain (see J. H. Langbein in Birks, 1996: 3).

The social role of university education in general sets an important context for legal education. In a mass higher education system, the role of the university is not just to train the elite who may go into the professions of doctor, lawyer, senior civil servant, or manager. Many students will be part of a broader, flexible labour market, engaging in a variety of paid and unpaid roles (Scott, 1995: 113–14; Le Brun and Johnstone, 1994: 23–6). Any undergraduate programme of study has to equip students with the resources, intellectual and personal, which will be appropriate to a variety of activities. Where law is taught at undergraduate level, its place as part of a general education has an impact not merely on the content of the programme, but also on its character. The diversity of career aspirations of students requires a generalist education. In many European countries, a substantial number of law students do not intend to enter specifically legal professions, but intend to enter the civil service.

Two features are connected with this 'massification' of university education. The first is the importance of the skills and employability aspects of the education programme, since these provide a general range of opportunities for students. The second issue concerns access. If university education is effectively the gatekeeper to a range of employment opportunities, then it becomes part of an agenda of social inclusion. The social responsibilities of universities are now more likely to be expressed in terms of their duty to accommodate students from less privileged social backgrounds (the working class) or from minority ethnic or religious groups in their own societies (Scott, 1995: 114; Le Brun and Johnstone, 1994: 63–6). Both of these features generate issues for legal educational research.

The American experience of law as a graduate subject provides a different perspective. Law is chosen more heavily for vocational reasons. Since 1921, when the American Bar Association (ABA) adopted the Reed Report (*Training for the Public Professions of Law*), education at law school has been an obligatory prerequisite for entry into the legal profession, even if state bar examinations are administered by the professions. This has a major impact on the law programme (Stevens, 1983, chs. 7 and 13). In more recent years, skills development has become part of the programme as a result of a focus on the work of lawyers (MacCrate Report, 1992). The focus is on lawyering skills, rather than general transferable skills, as will be discussed later. Since law schools are the gatekeepers to the important social role of being a lawyer, then issues of access also arise. In America, there has long been a concern that the law school entry (and thereby the legal profession) is not representative of society at large. A further consequence is that the law school curriculum itself has become a contested subject. There has been a move to understand the law from the distinctive perspectives of different social groups. For example, there are studies of the feminine perspective on law and legal studies (e.g. Guinier, 1994; Thornton, 1996, esp. chs. 1 and 3), which build a discussion of law on the experiences of women. The approach can be extended to the perspectives of racial groups, those from the Third World, or lesbian and gay groups. A pluralism of perspectives can reflect the plurality of the subjects of national or international law, or of the student body within the law school.

The other social development which affects legal education is the increased juridification of society. The role of law in society has given rise to an increased variety of legal activities. Many of these lie outside the traditional preserve of the legal professions. The growth of new professions practising law to deal with new kinds of work is not a modern problem. But the broad definitions of legal services required by modern society can be seen in new groups of people engaged in legal work in areas such as consumer advice, marriage advice, refugee work, human rights work, social protection, and so on. Because of this greater diversity of ways in which individuals may work professionally with the law, the whole idea of legal education has to be broadened. It is not sufficient that legal education prepares students for the classical professions (in the UK for professions of barrister and solicitor, in Germany and Sweden for the role of judge). Rather, there needs to be something generic that is capable of helping students to progress into a number of different career paths which involve the law (Le Brun and Johnstone, 1994: 50–4).

Universities are international institutions, contributing to the universal discussion of issues. By nature, they focus on the international scholarly community, rather than the agendas of national governments or of national or, in the United States, state legal professions. Much of the writing on legal education relates to these national or state contexts, but there is now an increasing focus on globalization.

2.2 Legal Education and Liberal Education

The literature on legal education has not contributed significantly to the broad debates about the purposes of university education in general. Rather, writing on legal education typically draws from the stock of general writing on the purposes of universities. The distinction between 'education' and 'training' in relation to professional subjects has typically been made by emphasizing the mission of the university to provide liberal education.

There is considerable debate about the link between university legal education and liberal education. In order to fulfil the mission of the university and to gain credibility as an *academic* subject, the liberal aspects of legal education have been stressed (Twining, 1994, ch. 2). The importance of liberal education was relatively easy to stress in the period before mass higher education. At a time when very few students undertook a full law degree before entering the legal profession, it could be argued that the purpose of legal education should involve a study of the law, but not education towards entry into the professions.

Such a broad liberal function is supported by Twining who argues that it is difficult to justify a specifically *legal* focus in education and the development of skills:

Many of the so-called 'transferable' skills of reading, writing, talking, thinking clearly, enquiring, analysing and arguing and, in the modern jargon, 'learning to learn' can be developed through the study of any number of subjects. The idea of a liberal education relates to how and in what spirit one studies a particular subject matter. The 'case for law'... is not that it is superior to other disciplines, but rather that it can claim to be potentially as good a vehicle for a general education as English or History or Politics or Sociology. (Twining, 1994: 60)

But even if the academic ambitions of intellectual and skills development are part of the general pattern of liberal education, the core of legal education lies in a distinct subject-matter and distinct methods of dealing with it. Legal education is not just the study of law, but a study which also inculcates the ability to make use of law, to analyse it, and to criticize it as a member of the legal community.

The other facet of liberal education is what Barnett describes as the 'enlightenment' function, of developing the ability to generate new understandings, even to 'unlearn' what has been inherited from the past (Barnett, 2000). The function of universities is to challenge presently perceived social reality. They should want to be seen at least as useless, if not actually as dangerous, in the eyes of the present holders of political power.

2.3 Legal Education and Professional Education

In Europe, the separation between liberal university education and professional training has been maintained. University legal education (outside England) is a prerequisite for professional study, but largely controlled by the professors, who, in many countries, have a constitutional right to independence. Professors may well be engaged in legal practice, but this does not impact directly on the law curriculum. Legal professions (judge, advocate, or notary) traditionally had aptitude tests, focusing on knowledge of legal rules, and an apprenticeship system. A pedagogy of professional education has been developing since the 1970s, but is largely underdeveloped in many countries. Continuing professional development has been given increasing emphasis in the 1990s, but is still not compulsory for many professions in many countries. The issue of how to link academic and professional pedagogy has been studied more in North America and Australia.

In European systems, the content of degree programmes has been set by universities with the approval of the minister. The professions have had no direct standing in this process. In common law legal systems, on the other hand, the professional bodies have set out a framework of what they will recognize. As law schools have tried to establish their academic credentials, there was a phase in which they wished to distinguish their function from vocational training. The result was a constant debate about the relationship between professional and academic educational requirements (see Twining, 1994, ch. 2; Stevens, 1983, ch. 13; Stevens in Birks, 1995, ch. 9). That picture is changing, both because of the move from an elite to a mass higher education system, and because of the development of a sophisticated pedagogy of professional education.

In a system of mass education, vocational utility is inevitably emphasized. Government expects a return for the substantial amount of public funding which is being put into education. The same is true for the increasingly large amounts of private money invested by students, parents, and employers in post-compulsory education. They are keen to see a return on their investment, particularly in programmes of study, such as law, which are avowedly connected to entry into professions (Scott, 1995: 111–13). The general educational literature has made use of the idea of the 'reflective practitioner' and sought to understand her or his attributes (Schön, 1987). The legal educational literature, particularly in the United States, has sought to articulate what is meant by 'thinking like a lawyer' or the skills of a lawyer. Educational literature now focuses on how to develop those kinds of attributes.

One bridge between liberal and critical educational analysis and professional education lies in the area of law reform. It has been argued strongly that legal education should also focus on the processes of legal change (Lasswell and McDougall, 1943). In this way, it can be a vehicle for law reform in the widest sense, which can include critical debate about the social objectives which law is to serve. Liberal education both within law and outside offers a number of perspectives from which the need for change and its potential impact can be analysed. In this analysis, the so-called 'liberal' education agenda is connected to the broader needs of the profession. This requires an ability to understand and evaluate how law relates to its wider setting. The difference between this agenda and liberal education would be the connection made between the law and its broader setting.

3 MODELS OF LEGAL EDUCATION

There are a number of models of the higher education process available in the general educational literature.

3.1 Model 1: Knowledge Transmission

One model particularly influential in the past has been the idea that the university is the guardian of knowledge. Students come to acquire knowledge which, once they are proficient, can then be applied independently. At the higher levels, the student is able also to acquire new knowledge themselves. The function of the (legal) education process is to ensure that the students have acquired at least the minimum knowledge to be proficient.

In legal education, this model is particularly powerful, since law has been conceived as a tradition. In the early medieval university, the core of the activity in learning the law was acquisition of knowledge about the texts which had been handed down. At the same time, learning involved reinterpretation. In the first place, the glosses on the received texts had as their objective the updating of the tradition by application to new situations. So the tradition was embellished. In the second place, the students would acquire the ability to undertake this process themselves and to become advisers on the law or judges. In the contemporary period, law is similarly conceived not as a static tradition, but as requiring continual updating.

Within the common law, the emphasis on knowledge transmission and acquisition was strongest in the examinations for entry into the legal profession until the 1970s (Arthurs Report, 1983; Parker and Goldsmith in Bradney and Cownie, 1998: 16–17, 27–8, 34–6). The style of professional examinations also emphasized the learning of material. Similarly, basic legal education in Europe has traditionally focused on learning the professor's course.

The core activities for the universities in this model are knowledge conservation, knowledge development, and knowledge transmission, whilst the students are measured by their acquisition of knowledge. There is a conventional idea that research is about creating new knowledge and that this is transmitted to students through teaching. This model of knowledge transmission has long been criticized, and it can be rejected in relation to law for four reasons: it is not appropriate to *education*; it takes no account of how legal knowledge develops and what professions do; it is no longer appropriate to a situation of explosion in both knowledge and in legal norms; and it does not provide students with the skills necessary for lifelong learning.

Academic writers have typically argued that the knowledge transmission model was incompatible with a proper understanding of education. Education is about encouraging critical thinking, rather than simply learning received knowledge, as in the older model of the crammers for the professional examinations. The development of a capacity for analysis, synthesis, and critical judgement are central. A knowledge-centred core is even less appropriate to modern conditions (Twining, 1994: 162–6).

Another reason for rejecting the 'knowledge transmission' model of legal education is that neither the academic nor the professional communities have a monopoly of developing doctrinal knowledge. New information is generated by government, Parliament, the courts, and the professions at a phenomenal rate. This parallels the variety of sources of knowledge in modern society (Scott, 1995: 148). The most pressing need for lawyers is to analyse, order, and evaluate the information about the law that already exists, rather than discover new information. The academic lawyer performs her most valuable role by engaging in critical thinking and in putting together available information in a way which offers insight. Rather than generating new facts, legal researchers have the principal role of making sense of the materials which we already know or have available to us. The product of this critical thinking is new knowledge in its own right. Such critical thinking reflects the importance of seeing connections and developing new opportunities through the law that is characteristic both of legal practice and of legal research more generally.

Although legal doctrinal scholarship has predominated within universities, especially within Europe, other research focuses on knowledge about the law. Philosophy, political science, and sociology have all provided a focus for the study of the law in terms of its ultimate objectives or its social setting. While for some this involved engagement with the perspectives of other disciplines—philosophy, politics, and sociology—for many the important thing was for lawyers to be more critical in their analysis of the law in terms of its coherence and conceptual structure (Kahn-Freund, 1966: 123–7). They were to be less deferential to the profession and especially the judges. The extent of such interdisciplinary literature varies between the university traditions of different countries and the kind of scholarship which is fashionable in non-legal disciplines within the academy. For example, empirical work is more common in North America than in many European countries.

Particularly where empirical work is undertaken, there is a body of information to be learnt and reflected upon. It is also difficult for students to engage first-hand in gathering the material for empirical research in a way which is parallel to the way they study doctrinal topics. These features affect the kind of pedagogy which is appropriate for such aspects of the curriculum.

3.2 Model 2: Skills and Techniques

A contrast is often drawn between propositional knowledge (knowing that) and process knowledge (knowing how). The knowledge which a professional needs includes both aspects. The same is true for the student. Knowing how to apply knowledge is an essential test of how well the information is understood. In relation to professional education, the emphasis has been on how the individual can act proficiently and responsibly in the role of a professional. For this, it was necessary to learn the arts of the trade, such as drafting and advocacy. It became clear in the 1970s that the content of law was changing rapidly, and that the practitioner would need to develop and adapt practices in the future. This was noted in the Cramton Report in 1979 which argued for a stronger emphasis on legal skills within the law curriculum (Stevens, 1983: 240). This was then developed in a series of reports on legal education across the common law world in the 1980s and 1990s. Equally, greater professionalism in the use of skills and techniques became required. In terms of educational theory, the emphasis on the integration of skills and techniques with knowledge forms part of the conception of the 'reflective practitioner', the ideal construct of the active learner at work (Schön, 1987).

The distinction between generic skills and specifically legal skills was recognized by the Marre Report in England (Marre Report, 1988, ch. 12). But the origins lie in the

Arthurs Report (1983) in Canada and the Pearce Report of 1987 in Australia. The US MacCrate Report of 1992 identified ten generic skills and four values which were fundamental to the competence of a lawyer. The skills were problem-solving; legal analysis and reasoning; legal research; factual investigation; oral and written communication; counselling or advice; negotiation; understanding procedures for litigation and alternative dispute resolution; organization and management of legal work; and recognizing and resolving ethical dilemmas. The four values were providing competent representation (responsibility to clients); striving to promote justice, fairness, and morality (public responsibility for the legal system); maintaining and improving the profession (responsibility to the profession); and professional self-development (responsibility to oneself). Such a list is fairly representative of skills and values recognized in the common law world, and which are the subject-matter of theoretical and empirical research.

Experience of teaching such skills suggests that an abstract introduction to skills is unsuccessful. There is a need to introduce skills and knowledge together so that the two can be integrated. Indeed, it is questioned how far skills can be effectively demonstrated in the abstract (Webb and Maughan, 1996, ch. 8; Jones, 1994: 23–5; Le Brun and Johnstone, 1994: 71–80).

Many of the skills identified by MacCrate and others are not specific to law. These are often labelled 'general transferable skills'. Among these might be classed teamwork, communication, problem-solving, personal effectiveness, ability to learn, analysis, synthesis, evaluation, and creativity, to which might be added professional responsibility (Bell, 1996: 11–14). A significant question about so-called 'transferable' skills is the way in which they are transferable (ibid. 5–6). Merely because a skill is acquired in one context does not mean that it will be applied in another context. If, for example, English students are presented with an unknown legal system, would they be able to demonstrate the analytical and reasoning skills which have been learnt in relation to English law? The context of training and development has to be taken into account. A person needs support to be able to use their skills in a substantially different context.

3.3 Model 3: Supercomplexity

The idea of legal education as 'engagement in critical thinking' reflects both the modern phenomenon of the 'knowledge explosion' and the more local problem of 'legislative inflation'. In relation to the former, Van Kinkel (Paul Hamlyn Foundation, 1994: 81) has argued:

I must stress that nowadays as knowledge doubles every five years and the shelf value of all knowledge is so short, the knowledge content of disciplines is probably less important for university programmes. You need some content in order to help students study a discipline or to learn from example. We should try to make programmes shorter and allow more time for research-style activity.

The capacity to deal with new legal and social developments, and relate these to legal principle and existing solutions is a critical feature of being a good lawyer. But the concern is not simply the need to engage in lifelong learning. The professions recognize this both in the various updating and training opportunities, which they provide in-house, and in the professional requirement to engage in continuing education. In this view of legal education, students have to be prepared to cope with diversity and change. They have to be able to work with the tradition and reinvent it more radically than in the past.

A more fundamental analysis is described by Ron Barnett as 'supercomplexity'. On this view, 'the world is radically unknowable. *Every* framework for knowing and every sense of our world, of ourselves, of our relationships to the world and to each other is contestable' (Barnett, 2000: 77). Rather than education being a process of knowledge transmission or handing down a tradition, university education is about coming to terms with uncertainty: 'The wider world is looking for three things from its universities: a continuing flow of new stories to add to those we already have in the world; a critical interrogation, and even rebuttal, of existing ideas; and the development of the human capacities to live both at ease and purposively amid such uncertainty' (ibid. 71). This ability may include the ability to unlearn established ways of looking at things (ibid. 127).

The concept of 'law' is analysed by some writers not as an ordered system unified into a coherent hierarchy, but as a 'chaos', with competing elements which potentially push legal development in a number of different ways. The movements such as critical legal studies and feminism have called into question existing paradigms and understandings of the law. There are competing frameworks within which law can be viewed.

The operation of the markets for legal services has forced reconsideration of the way in which lawyers practise. In the commercial sphere, the focus on serving the client has encouraged the development of multidisciplinary partnerships. Certain types of advice and the conduct of certain transactions is no longer the preserve of the traditional professional lawyer. Similar trends are evident in private client work. In such a setting, legal education has to be able to prepare individuals for an uncertain and changing future. Among the abilities required are the willingness to question existing frameworks, rather than just content or ways of working, also to be able to cope with rapidity of change and the potential for reinventing oneself and one's organization. Perhaps more than ever before, there is no single model of professional legal activity.

The need for lawyers to live with such uncertainty comes from the radical changeability of the law and of legal practice. Legislative innovation and judicial decisionmaking can reshape the landscape within which lawyers operate. Jurists and practitioners can make contributions to the legislative process, but the ultimate decision is out of their hands. Legal practice is changing profoundly. Europe and Canada have followed the United States in giving an increasing emphasis to fundamental rights. Big bang, globalization, and changes in government funding for legal aid are changing the face of professional practice (Watt and Savage in Birks, 1996: 50). The core of legal learning is perceived less as 'knowledge' and more as the ethical and value standards which constitute 'professionalism' in taking decisions in the new world (ibid. 47; Barnett, 2000: 159). Education has the ambition of preparing people for this situation.

4 THE CONTENT OF LEGAL EDUCATION

4.1 Learning Outcomes

The debate about skills and knowledge in the law curriculum brings to the fore both the articulation of what student learning is supposed to achieve and how this is demonstrated.

Inspired by the Council for National Academic Awards in the United Kingdom, there has been a move to identify learning outcomes of programmes. Compared with Continental European approaches to student learning, this has a number of advantages. Instead of defining a programme in terms of the number of teaching hours or the number of years studied or even the content of what is taught, focusing on the outcomes of a programme pays attention to the student achievement that is required by the end of the course. It is more explicit in showing what students are expected to be able to do, and it provides a framework for reviewing the appropriateness of learning tasks and assessment. But there are limits. In the first place, the idea of learning outcomes seems predicated on a linear, even technocratic, model of the learning process. The course team sets its objectives—the learning outcomes—designs learning activities, and then assesses the student achievement that results. Such a perspective obviously simplifies the student learning process. The learning environment of the institution more generally will influence learning, as will the social environment within which the student lives—peer pressure, family pressures, and so on. The mere fact that learning activities take place with a particular designed objective does not ensure that this will be fulfilled in the student learning. The importance of the unplanned and unexpected cannot be underestimated. Furthermore, the achievement of the student may not be in any direct correlation to the planned learning activities. As Jones (1994: 48) has suggested, a programme of student learning might well have as its objective to give the student a certain kind of learning experience:

Within higher education . . . the organisation of the learning experience comes first [. It] has its own internal set of concerns and imperatives. The specification of learning outcomes or 'competences' comes second. They are used to provide a means of articulating different curriculum elements, to shift the perspective from the needs of the discipline to those of the students, to provide a focus on active forms of learning and to derive principles against which student achievement can be assessed.

This focus on the learning experience is particularly important in activities such as clinical skills education, discussed below.

4.2 Study Methods

The understanding of student learning is shaped, in particular, by four theories of learning. The first is Entwistle's distinction between surface and deep learning (Entwistle, 1988, chs. 4 and 5). This encourages educators to focus on learning activities which promote understanding and deep learning. The second theory is that of Kolb's learning cycle. There is a continual process of action, experience, reflection, and planning which is involved in any learning activity. The learning process has to be designed to incorporate and foster each element, rather than focusing on a linear process of imparting, learning, and reproducing information. The third element is 'the reflective practitioner' idea developed by Schön (Schön, 1987). The fourth is the 'capability' approach promoted by the Royal Society of Arts through the work of John Stephenson (Stephenson and Weil, 1992: 2; Webb and Maughan, 1996, ch. 13).

The work of Schön is particularly important for understanding professional learning. Schön contrasts two models of professional knowledge. A 'technocractic model', which sees professional knowledge in terms of facts, rules, and procedures that have to be applied instrumentally to problems. The purpose of instruction on this model is to ensure that technique is properly demonstrated and applied. Certain aspects of legal practice lend themselves to this, such as filling out forms correctly for the Land Registry. But the 'reflective practitioner' model focuses on the ability that the practitioner acquires to reflect in action and to adjust behaviour to new situations. 'If we see professional knowing in terms of "thinking like a" manager, lawyer, or teacher, students will still learn relevant facts and operations but will also learn the forms of inquiry by which competent practitioners reason their way, in problematic instances, to clear connections between general knowledge and particular cases' (Schön, 1987: 39).

The emphasis is not on rules of conduct, but developing 'artistry', a sense of the right way of doing things, which is capable of adjusting to changing and novel circumstances. Schön draws the analogy with teaching tennis. If the coach is able to help the player to get the feeling for hitting the ball correctly, then the player will be able herself to correct actions when she hits the ball wrongly (ibid. 24). Within a profession like law, the student is inducted into the traditional practices of the profession, its routines and knowledge. But the student also has to learn from this world of practitioners 'a kind of reflection-in-action that goes beyond the statable rules—not only by devising new methods of reasoning . . . but also by constructing and testing new categories of understanding, strategies of action, and ways of framing problems' (ibid. 39). The methods he identifies for developing such ability involve apprenticeship or a more limited 'practicum', an environment which constitutes a simplified practice world in which students can learn through doing, even though their activity falls short of the real world of work. As Jones comments, the kind of practitioner which this tries to develop is 'thoughtful, wise and contemplative, not just "skilful" or "competent" but one whose work involves intuition, insight and "artistry" ' (Webb and Maughan, 1996: 291). But Jones also insists that the knowledge element remains important, and is perhaps underplayed by Schön's presentation (1987: 301). The key characteristic of the reflective practitioner as a critical and not a technical ideal is that he or she is someone who can imagine things differently.

The emphasis on reflection as reflective practice in Kolb and Schön helps to explain the representation of the skills and competences developed in students in the form of 'capability'. Capability involves the ability to act. It involves both knowledge and the ability to do something with that knowledge. At the same time, capability is different because it focuses on the future. Competence focuses on past achievement, and is usually measured by producing evidence of having performed relevant component elements in the past. Capability is more difficult to measure in that it involves a confidence that the person will be able to act effectively in the future.

The ideas of learning styles, the reflective practitioner, and capability provide frameworks for judging the value of particular learning activities.

4.3 Specific Learning Activities

Some studies examine particular forms of learning support. Two particular forms of learning, legal clinics and problem-based learning, attract attention because they represent learning experiences in which integration of knowledge and skills can be fostered and in which capability and learner autonomy can be demonstrated. There is a substantial range of work that has been undertaken in relation to specific legal subjects and how these may best be taught. Much of the writing in the United States has concerned the 'Socratic method' and its support through books of legal materials. The concern in Australia, Hong Kong, and the United Kingdom has more recently been on 'active learning' methods which try to encourage understanding and deep learning, rather than the kind of superficial learning associated with large lecture classes. Experiments have been tried which look at features such as group work and projects to support student learning. Many of these experiments are assessed by student and staff evaluation of enjoyment and learning. The experiences of law schools both apply and mirror the general educational literature. The purpose of much of the writing is to provide concrete examples from which other teachers can draw. Journals such as the *Journal of Legal Education* in the United States and the *Law Teacher* in the

United Kingdom contain many such articles. A few topics raise rather specific and central issues about the shape of legal education.

4.3.1 *Legal Clinics*

Legal clinics represent one important mechanism by which students can be placed in a setting, not too dissimilar to a professional work context, in which they are required to learn by doing. Students are engaged with real clients and problems and have to resolve these under supervision. Students are required to demonstrate not only their knowledge, but also their skills in being able to make use of the knowledge. In this sense, the learning experience is holistic in its integration of aspects of student ability (Webb and Maughan, 1996, ch. 5; Grimes *et al.*, 1996). It also enables the student to study the legal activity as an integrated whole, since it involves a study both of the practical context for the application of legal rules, as well as the activity of lawyers including the ethical issues (Jones, 1994, ch. 7). The value of this kind of exercise formed part of the legal realist agenda (see Frank, 1933), but has risen to prominence with the importance attached to active and action-based learning in higher education.

Assessment of clinical education poses particular difficulties. Schön notes that much 'background learning' takes place that may not be evident in the performance of the task at hand (Schön, 1987: 168). A second concern is that assessment criteria tend to focus on specific competences which are demonstrated in the task, rather than on the way in which they are integrated (Jones, 1994: 107–8). Inevitably judgement is required, even if this brings with it an element of subjectivity. All the same, Schön (1987: 168–9) argues that one can map student performance against a number of dimensions, for example, on a line between unitary procedures and holistic grasp, between narrow and superficial understanding and broad and deep understanding. In this way, one can report on performance in a more detailed way than a mere 'hunch', but without resorting to an objective 'tick-list'. There is also the need to recognize that there are several levels of ability to be demonstrated in this form of task. The ability expected of the second-year law student is different from that of the practitioner. The practicum is a mechanism for recognizing this by devising an appropriate kind of task and setting for the student. But the criteria for assessing what is a 'competent' performance also have to be adapted.

4.3.2 *Problem-Based Learning*

This active student learning task takes place in a more hypothetical setting, but the focus is similar to clinical education in that the students are required to integrate knowledge and skills at a level of complexity appropriate to their level of development. Inevitably, there will need to be induction into this way of learning, but the approach encourages a degree of autonomy in learning and making use of the material learnt, rather than reproducing it (Cruickshank, in Webb and

Maughan, 1996, ch. 7). Naturally, this is not easy to structure and to take part in. There is less margin of comfort and the students may resist the approach in comparison with other, traditional, and more predictable learning activities. At the same time, it provides encouragement for deeper forms of learning (Le Brun and Johnstone, 1994: 92–7, 303–4).

4.3.3 Assessment

A large amount of student learning time and staff time is spent on assessment. Two major issues arise. In the first place, how far does the assessment task contribute to the learning which has been planned as part of the course? Secondly, how can the marking become more objective? On the whole, it is recognized that producing objective judgements is possible only to a limited extent. Even if one has criteria, these have to be interpreted and weighed. The complex and interactive nature of the features which have to be assessed—knowledge and understanding, subject skills, general skills—make assessment a task for trained individuals. Processes also need to be in place to promote common understandings among such individuals.

Assessment is linked primarily to the appropriateness of awards. Outcomes may be specified as a way of identifying the levels of achievement appropriate to a particular award. But these outcomes may be linked only partially to the design of a programme of student learning. A major function of assessment should be to assist students to develop the capacity to evaluate their own performance and engage in future planning as reflective learners and practitioners. To this end, assessment practices may be designed not only to provide a formative or summative assessment of achievement from a tutor, but to encourage students to make use of criteria in evaluating their own progress (see Le Brun and Johnstone, 1994, ch. 4).

The use of competence criteria to judge skills is a particular concern in research. Competence statements are prevalent in assessment for vocational qualifications generally, and have also been important both in North America and in vocational courses in the UK for identifying whether a person is fit to practise. The research literature in this field raises two problems with this approach. The first is whether a competence-based approach actually does capture what is required for a person to be fit for practice. In order to produce a list of competences, it is necessary to break the professional activity into describable units. But this runs the danger of being both overly atomistic and failing to capture the important dimension that the competent professional is one who is able to relate knowledge to practice in original ways (Winter in Webb and Maughan, 1996, ch. 11). Secondly, the assessment of competences tends to be approached in terms of a checklist, based on the accumulation of past evidence. Boon has argued that this is unduly behaviourist and runs counter to the emphasis on independent student learning and originality which legal education is also wishing to secure (Webb and Maughan, 1996: 109). The objectivity secured in assessment comes at the price of a narrow methodology and a failure to attend to whether the student will be able to perform in the future. A demonstration of under-standing and a capacity to develop is critical.

4.4 Legal Skills

Professional skills courses have engendered a literature on the nature and develop-ment of lawyering skills, such as those identified by the MacCrate Report (1992; see Sect. 2.1 above). Identifying such skills requires research on the work of practising lawyers. Research is then needed to identify educational objectives and pedagogic practices to prepare students for such work.

There is a substantial literature on what these different skills involve. The focus on how the profession operates connects academic lawyers to two strands of literature. The first strand involves sociological research into the character of the legal profes-sions and how they work. By researching the professions, insights can be gained on how best to prepare students at the vocational stage. Maughan and Webb (1995: 9–10) identify a number of clusters of skills. For example, in advocacy, there are communi-cation skills, but also organizational skills in preparing the material, and cognitive skills in assessing a situation and sorting out relevant issues. It does not matter that many of the skills involved are not peculiar to lawyers; it suffices that they are appro-priate to the activity of professional lawyering.

A second strand is the study in educational theory of practitioners in general, particularly Donald Schön's concept of the 'reflective practitioner' (Schön, 1987; Le Brun and Johnstone, 1994: 26–8). His concepts such as 'artistry' involve a capacity for holistic learning and the application of skills and knowledge in an integrated fashion as professional activity takes place (Schön, 1987: 11). The emphasis here is less on developing specific skills than on the opportunity to enable students to integrate the different features of legal education.

There is a significant debate about the place of *legal* skills within the curriculum. There are those who consider that the whole skills agenda is selling out the academic educational values to an instrumental employment and vocational agenda which is inappropriate (Toddington in Birks, 1996: 75–6). Others would argue somewhat dif-ferently that the claimed specificity of *legal* skills is overdrawn. For example, Twining (1994: 176) suggests that many of the skills of a lawyer are shared with other profession-als. Indeed, the broad range of demands on individuals in professional practice makes the claim to the specificity of legal skills rather fragile. Despite these reservations, there has been significant attention paid to the content and pedagogy of legal skills.

4.5 Legal Ethics

The relationship between legal education and professional concerns has been shown in recent years through the study of legal ethics. Paterson (in Cranston, 1994, ch. 8) suggests that the study of legal ethics represents an important dimension of contemporary preparation for legal practice and of legal education generally. Ethics introduce the moral problems of applying the law in practical contexts. Presenting ethical dilemmas sharpens understanding of the purposes of law and lawyers. They are not simply to be seen as technicians or 'the hired gun', but as having their own responsibilities for the operation of law in the service of society. The problem of teaching this topic lies in the need for materials which will adequately present the issues and offer the students a rigorous intellectual experience. There has also been reluctance from professions to see this as an appropriate university activity, since they have preferred to educate students about the topic themselves as part of professional socialization (O'Dair, 2001, ch. 5). One can legitimately ask how far legal education should help students understand and call into question professional legal dilemmas, values, and practices, or how far the role is to strengthen the codes of practice operated by the professions and their effective observance. Simon (1998) and Nicolson and Webb (1999) offer such a critique of professional education. For these reasons, legal ethics has been a latecomer in the range of legal subjects.

Viewed narrowly, the topic of legal ethics is about the legal values of the professions in a particular jurisdiction. Viewed more generally ethics is about encouraging a self-critical awareness that is appropriate to any reflective professional. Viewed in this way, ethics, like skills, represents a dimension to the study of law, not a bolt-on extra. The work of Hyams et al. (1998) represents an attempt to integrate the reflective moral dimension into the study of legal skills. This offers a perspective from which the ethical issues can be studied outside the context of professional induction in a way that encourages broader critical thinking.

5 Conclusion

Legal education is (properly) becoming ever more professional, both in law schools and in professional training colleges. This will generate further literature. Undoubtedly, a major aspect will remain the study of the practice of the legal professions with a view to better initial and continuing education. Because legal information and legal rules change so rapidly, the emphasis will be on the skills which lawyers will need for their work. Inevitably, the use of technologies will be a major feature of such a study of skills, particularly in research. But law will remain a practice of personal interactions, such that the issues of relating to and understanding clients and colleagues will be significant. A major change will be the increasing mobility of lawyers across the boundaries of jurisdictions. The ability to relate to different jurisdictions and to be able to cope with the legal complexity involved will be a major part of the agenda for lawyers and legal educators. The diversity of legal sources will make pluralism significant in terms of norms. The heterogeneity of societies will also make pluralism a major issue in terms of the pedagogy required to support the learning of a diverse student body. There are thus a number of agendas for research: the skills and knowledge necessary to operate as a person using the law professionally (not necessarily in conventional legal professions), the appropriate range of perspectives for studying the law in a pluralistic society, and the pedagogical strategies required, as well as measures for their effectiveness.

References

Arthurs Report (1983). Arthurs, H. W. (Chairman), Consultative Group on Research and Education in Law, *Law and Learning: Report to the Social Sciences and Humanities Research Council of Canada*, Ottawa: Social Sciences and Humanities Research Council of Canada.

Barnett, R. (2000). *Realising the University in an Age of Supercomplexity*, Buckingham: Open University Press.

Bell, J. (1996). 'General Transferable Skills in the Law Curiculum', *Contemporary Issues in Law*, 2: 1–11.

Birks, P. (ed.) (1995). *Reviewing Legal Education*, Oxford: Oxford University Press.

—— (ed.) (1996). *What are Law Schools for?* Oxford: Oxford University Press.

Bradney, A., and Cownie, F. (eds.) (1998). *Transformative Visions of Legal Education*, Oxford: Blackwell.

Cranston, R. (ed.) (1994). *Legal Ethics and Professional Responsibility*, Oxford: Oxford University Press.

Entwistle, N. (1988). *Styles of Learning and Teaching*, London: David Fulton.

Frank, J. (1933). 'Why Not a Clinical Lawyer-School?' *University of Pennsylvania Law Review*, 81: 907–23.

Grimes, R., Klass, J., and Smith, C. (1996). 'Legal Skills and Clinical Legal Education—A Survey of Undergraduate Law School Practice', *Law Teacher*, 30: 44–67.

Guinier, L., Fine, M., and Balin, J. (1994). 'Becoming Gentlemen: Women's Experiences at One Ivy League Law School', *University of Pennsylvania Law Review*, 143: 1–110.

Hyams, R., Campbell, S., and Evans A. (1998). *Practical Legal Skills*, Melbourne: Oxford University Press.

Jones, P. A. (1994). *Competences, Learning Outcomes and Legal Education*, London: IALS Working Paper.

Kahn-Freund, O. (1966). 'Reflections on Legal Education', *Modern Law Review*, 29: 121–36.

Lasswell, H. D., and McDougal, M. S. (1943). 'Legal Education and Public Policy: Professional Training in the Public Interest', *Yale Law Journal*, 52: 203–95.

LeBrun, M., and Johnstone, R. (1994). *The Quiet (R)evolution: Improving Student Learning in Law*, Sydney: Law Book Co.

MacCrate Report (1992). *Legal Education and Professional Development*, Chicago: ABA.

Marre Report (1988). *A Time for Change: Report of the Committee on the Future of the Legal Profession*, London: HMSO.

Maughan, C., and Webb, J. (1995). *Lawyering Skills and the Legal Process*, London: Butterworths.

Nicolson, D., and Webb, J. (1999). *Professional Legal Ethics*, Oxford: Oxford University Press.

O'Dair, R. (2001). *Legal Ethics: Text and Materials*, London: Butterworths.

Paul Hamlyn Foundation (1994). *Universities in the Twenty-First Century*, London: Heinemann.

Pearce Report (1987). Pearce, D., Campbell, E., and Harding, D., and Commonwealth Tertiary Education Committee, *Australian Law Schools: A Disciplinary Assessment for the CTEC*, Canberra: Australian Government Publishing Service.

Schön, D. (1987). *Educating the Reflective Practitioner*, San Francisco: Jossey-Bass.

Scott, P. (1995). *The Meanings of Mass Higher Education*, Milton Keynes: Open University Press.

Simon, W. (1998). *The Practice of Justice: A Theory of Lawyers' Ethics*, Cambridge, Mass.: Harvard University Press.

Stephenson, J., and Weil, S. (1992). *Quality in Learning: A Capability Approach to Higher Education*, London: Kogan Page.

Stevens, R. B. (1983). *Law School: Legal Education in America from the 1850s to the 1980s*, Chapel Hill, NC: University of North Carolina Press.

Thornton, M. (1996). *Dissonance and Distrust: Women in the Legal Profession*, Melbourne: Oxford University Press.

Twining, W. (1994). *Blackstone's Tower: The English Law School*, London: Sweet and Maxwell.

Webb, J., and Maughan, C. (1996). *Teaching Lawyers' Skills*, London: Butterworths.

CHAPTER 41

....

THE ROLE OF
ACADEMICS IN THE
LEGAL SYSTEM

....

WILLIAM TWINING

WARD FARNSWORTH

STEFAN VOGENAUER

FERNANDO TESÓN

1 INTRODUCTION

....

IN considering the ways in which legal scholars relate to and participate in practical legal affairs, several points need to be borne in mind. First, full-time university scholar-teachers of law constitute a small minority of people involved in law teaching; not all law teaching takes place in universities or university law schools; not all law teachers are full time; not all full-time law teachers are 'research active'; as befits a learned profession, not all legal scholarship is undertaken by academic lawyers. Many of these other categories of people who are involved in law teaching make significant, often unsung, contributions to legal administration and development.

The authors of this chapter contributed the following sections: Sections 1 and 2 (William Twining), Section 3 (Ward Farnsworth), Section 4 (Stefan Vogenauer), and Section 5 (Fernando Tesón).

Secondly, many prominent public figures in the common law world, including prime ministers, chief justices, senior judges, attorneys-general, heads of public bodies, and leading practitioners, have spent a significant part of their careers as full-time scholar-teachers of law, but they have made their most direct practical contributions to legal life after moving on. This mobility may be one of the most important channels of influence of law schools on practical legal affairs and vice versa, but this also falls outside this chapter.

Thirdly, no legal scholar can today confine her attention to just one jurisdiction and, by situation rather than training, 'we are all comparatists now' (Twining, 2000: 255). Traditionally, public international law has provided more opportunities than most fields for scholars to be involved in practical affairs. Regionalization, transnationalization and so-called 'globalization' are extending such outlets to many other fields, including both private and public law—for example, in respect of commercial law or human rights or European Union affairs, and unification and harmonization of laws. There are also opportunities for constitution mongering and 'expert' consulting in societies in transition or the Third World. The potential for contribution and practical involvement by legal scholars is not confined to domestic municipal law.

Finally, as a discipline law is not easily characterized, because it is so varied. In universities and higher education policy, law is generally lumped in with the social sciences and humanities, sometimes sitting uneasily between them. There is a general tendency for undergraduate law students to be more vocationally oriented than their teachers. Becher suggested that academic law's main tendency is 'soft-applied' (Becher, 1989). However, nearly all scholar-teachers of law are specialists and different specialisms are spread quite widely along the continuums of pure/applied, hard/soft, urban/rural, and normative/empirical. Academic law generally is pulled in several different directions. This can result in obsessive introspection, debilitating controversy, and creative tension. For legal scholarship, questions about audience are crucial in resolving these tensions.

2 OUTSIDE WORK: AUDIENCES AND INFLUENCE OF LEGAL SCHOLARS IN THE UNITED KINGDOM

In 1975, an international committee on legal education in the world as a whole advanced a quite explicit vision of the potential contributions of university law schools to the societies in which they are located:

Law schools, perceived as multipurpose centers, can develop human resources and idealism needed to strengthen legal systems; they can develop research and intellectual direction; they can address problems ranging from land reform to criminal justice; they can foster the development of indigenous languages as vehicles for the administration of law; they can assist institutions involved in training paraprofessionals; they can provide materials and encouragement for civic education about law in schools and more intelligent treatment of law in the media; they can organize, or help organize, advanced specialized legal education for professionals who must acquire particular kinds of skills and expertise. (International Legal Center, 1975: 39)

This ambitious statement contrasts sharply with standard discussions of the contributions of academic lawyers outside the academy. These tend to focus almost entirely on relations with the legal establishment: their status within the legal profession, their role in expounding the law, commenting on judicial decisions and legislation, participating in law reform and, above all, on the quite close, but uneasy, relations between 'judge and jurist' (e.g. Fifoot, 1959; Goff, 1983; Duxbury, 2001). Apart perhaps from the National Law School of India University at Bangalore, it might be said that no law school in the common law world has even aspired to emulate this model of a multifunctional institution serving all levels of society. However, if this 'ILC model' is taken as a metaphor for a national legal education system seen as a whole, the picture is different: in the United Kingdom, for example, continuing professional development, the training of judges, magistrates, paraprofessionals, and the police, and, until recently, even primary pre-qualification training have taken place largely in institutions other than universities.

2.1 The Institutional Context

In the United Kingdom, university law schools were relatively late developers and for most of the twentieth century they were essentially academic primary schools, focusing very largely on three- or four-year undergraduate law degrees for the 18-plus age group. Most scholars chose to research in areas in which they taught. Since the undergraduate curriculum was constrained, narrow, overloaded, and conventional, for a long time the range of legal research was correspondingly limited. Vast swathes of legal life and most aspects of professional development were largely neglected by legal scholars, notable examples being civil procedure, professional ethics, taxation, international finance, intellectual property, arbitration, negotiation, and the sociology of the legal professions. This is now changing. In recent years, two significant steps have been taken away from 'the primary school model': first, postgraduate legal studies have increased, greatly broadening the range of scholarly work; secondly, some universities have taken responsibility for offering courses at the second 'vocational' stage, but to date these for the most part have not yet been fully integrated into the university and have made significantly less impact on the nature and scope of legal scholarship.

There are other institutional channels for the individual and collective contributions of legal scholars. In Britain, these include learned societies, such as the British Academy, the Society of Legal Scholars (formerly the Society of Public Teachers of Law), the Socio-Legal Studies Association, and the British Institute of International and Comparative Law; the Association of Law Teachers; the Heads of University Law Schools; and non-governmental organizations such as Justice, Liberty, and Amnesty International. These organizations tend to be uncoordinated with loosely overlapping memberships and aims, but taken together they can be said to be concerned with four main functions: cooperation and coordination within and between disciplines; improving legal education; influencing government policy and law reform; and fostering public awareness and understanding of law. There is, as yet, no strong non-governmental organization at national level concerned with the improvement and reform of the law, such as the American Law Institute.

2.2 Individual Scholars

The ILC Report recognized that nearly all law teachers are specialists and that there should not be a single prototype of law teachers, but rather a variety of specialists with quite varied academic credentials, skills, and experience. By and large the modern academic profession fits these prescriptions, but traditionally law had the lowest number of holders of Ph.D.s of any university discipline. That, too, may be changing.

The standard contracts of employment of full-time university teachers of law are almost identical to those of full-time academic staff in other disciplines in the humanities and the social sciences. The criteria of promotion to senior academic posts similarly emphasize international reputation in respect of scholarly research and publication, excellence in teaching, and contributions to institutional administration. There are some differences between institutions in respect of the relative emphasis placed on teaching, administration, and research, but requirements for appointment and promotion are fairly uniform in universities in the United Kingdom and throughout most of the Commonwealth. These requirements both symbolize and provide evidence of the almost complete integration of law schools into the university. They are one concrete embodiment of 'the academic ethic' that the mission of universities is the advancement and dissemination of learning through teaching and research (Twining, 1994).

What are the main contributions of academic lawyers to the practical administration and development of the law? This is a familiar question, but an odd one. It is familiar through a fairly extensive literature. It is odd because, except in relation to scholarly publications, almost no direct contributions are part of the normal duties of academic lawyers. There is a puzzle because clearly both collectively and individually academics are perceived as making some quite significant contributions to the practical operation and development of the law and to public life through a variety of activities, but these are not carried out as part of their normal duties. Almost all of the following activities are generally treated as 'outside work', whether or not they are paid: private practice, voluntary legal aid and advice, law reform, membership of government or other commissions or committees, consultancy, involvement in local or national politics, journalism, serving as an arbitrator, member of a tribunal or parole board, justice of the peace or mediator, and even part-time teaching in continuing professional development, legal awareness, and extra-mural courses. Some of these activities may be permitted, or even encouraged, but if they substantially interfere with the primary tasks of departmental teaching and scholarly research they are likely to be rationed or even to be regarded as 'moonlighting'. Yet my impression from reading hundreds of résumés and sampling various directories and obituaries is that a substantial majority of established full-time scholar-teachers of law have been involved in one or more kinds of 'outside work', some to a very considerable extent. For example, an inspection of the entries in *Who's Who* for current members of the British Academy's law section indicates that at least 80 per cent of law Fellows report involvement in public service activities of some kind and this is probably an underestimate of the scale of such involvement. Similarly, almost without exception the holders of Chairs of Jurisprudence in Oxford, London, and Edinburgh during the twentieth century made some significant contribution to public affairs in the United Kingdom or abroad—Pollock, Goodhart, Hart, Lloyd, Dworkin, and MacCormick have all been influential public figures. Thus, even our leading theorists hardly fit the old image of the retiring academic monk cloistered in an ivory tower. Nearly all such activities involve the use of legal academics' specialist expertise and cumulatively they almost certainly constitute their most important direct contributions to practical legal affairs. Yet hardly any of these activities have been performed as part of their ordinary academic duties.

There are, of course, some 'grey areas'. For example, writing to or for newspapers, appearing on television, or contributing to professional journals or intellectual publications, such as *The Times Literary Supplement* or *Prospect*, academics can be said to take on the role of public intellectuals and to be exerting intellectual, if not academic, leadership. Yet such contributions are often not counted as scholarly publications for the purposes of promotion or as performance indicators in university league tables or bureaucratic evaluations of the 'products' of research. A similar ambivalence is sometimes exhibited towards involvement in law reform activities, writing case notes and commentaries on draft Bills and recent legislation. It is 'good experience', but for the most part the products do not count as 'scholarship'. So, even in respect of writing, many of the most direct contributions of academic lawyers to practical legal affairs count as 'outside work'.

The most systematic attempt to analyse what scholar-teachers of law do by way of research is still the Arthurs Report on *Law and Learning* in Canada (Arthurs, 1983). Although the details are local and are now out of date, some general lessons from this exercise are still pertinent. Quebecois distinguish between *recherche sublime* and *recherches ponctuelles*. The terms might suggest a sardonic view of all research, but in the context the latter category was described as 'isolated, narrowly focused and rather random' and was dismissed as ephemeral. The Arthurs Report advanced a fourfold classification of non-ephemeral research: conventional texts and articles (expository work); legal theory (an inexact translation of the French 'doctrine'); 'law reform research'; and 'fundamental research' ('designed to secure a deeper understanding of law as a phenomenon, typically involving interdisciplinary work'). The taxonomy was crude and controversial, but it formed the basis for some striking findings in respect of Canada. The main conclusion of the report was that there was a serious imbalance between applied and fundamental research: 'Scholarly research, and especially fundamental and theoretical research, has been consistently undervalued by the legal community, and even by legal academics; whereas it has an essential contribution to make to legal education, to the legal profession and the practice of law, and to the evolution of law and society' (Arthurs, 1983: 157).

Arthurs criticized Canadian academics for devoting too much time and effort to doctrinal commentary and exposition, and even to law reform work. By contrast, a few years later, two American judges who were former academics, Richard Posner and Harry Edwards, berated law schools for being too concerned with 'theory' and argued forcefully for a return to 'practical doctrinal scholarship' as the core of the discipline (Posner, 1987; Edwards, 1992). The controversy continues. In the United Kingdom, the bureaucratization of higher education has, perhaps ironically, pushed academic lawyers quite strongly in the direction advocated by Arthurs. For the past fifteen years or so, the national Research Assessment Exercises (RAE) have dominated thinking about research in British universities. The definition of research for RAE purposes emphasizes the advancement of knowledge: originality and innovation are in, *recherches ponctuelles* are clearly out. Emphasis is put on refereed journals, international reputation, and other indicators that are closer to social science research than legal practice. It is true that the guidelines include 'work of direct relevance to the needs of commerce, industry, and public and voluntary sectors' and that the Law Panel has recognized case notes, loose leaf works, and books written for the legal or other professions, 'provided that they exhibit significant scholarly material'. However, such statements have been treated with understandable caution, so that there is a widespread perception that articles are preferred to case notes, refereed journals to practitioners' journals, scholarly monographs to practitioners' works, and an international 'scientific' audience to a local one. However, a five-year cycle is widely thought to be too short for much fundamental research.

Thus the most direct written channels of communication to practitioners, judges, and law reformers are not generally recognized as 'scholarly' for the purposes of academic appointment, promotion, and bureaucratic performance indicators of research output. Moreover, the information needs (for law reports, up-to-date information, basic reference works) of practitioners, judges, and other legal actors are largely met by non-academics, especially specialist legal publishers and other agencies. This is illustrated by law publishing in Northern Ireland. The aim of the Servicing the Legal System Programme (SLS) is based on a systematic assessment of the information needs of the main users of Northern Ireland law. The services include works of reference, regular information about recent legal developments in law and practice in Northern Ireland, information technology (IT) publication and training, continuing legal development, and public legal awareness. While the Court Service and practicing lawyers are the main customers, SLS also addresses the legal information needs of civil servants, other professionals, business, students, and the public at large. SLS was conceived and initiated by members of the Faculty of Law of the Queen's University, Belfast. In the early years, much of the work was done by full-time academics. Today it is still physically situated at the university, but SLS Legal Publications is an independent corporation, with full-time staff, and a Board of Directors with representatives of the Bar, the Law Society, the Court Service, and the university, chaired by a senior judge. Whilst academic lawyers continue to contribute to SLS publications and courses, and SLS in turn provides a publishing outlet for academic books and articles, there is a tension between the perceived information needs that SLS tries to meet and the kinds of scholarship that satisfy academic criteria.

SLS can be seen as a prototype of legal information provision not only in a small jurisdiction, but also in any modern legal system. The main needs for information of participants in the legal system, both professional and lay, are not and cannot be met systematically by scholar-teachers of law as part of their normal duties. At different times, academic lawyers have contributed to law reporting, updating services, continuing professional development, commentaries on recent legislation, do-it-yourself works, and the compilation and writing of practical treatises and reference works. To a limited extent they still do, especially in respect of those kinds of publication in which practical utility is enhanced by scholarly values. Many of the best-known legal treatises in common law countries are erudite, precise, accurate, comprehensive, and more or less systematic. Some are treated as authoritative by the courts and the practising profession. But other scholarly values relating to originality, creativity, theoretical and historical depth, breadth of vision, and above all criticism do not fit so easily with the immediate practical needs of participants in a legal system.

2.3 'Influence'

Assessing 'influence' with any exactitude is almost impossible in this context. In his Presidential Address to the Society of Public Teachers of Law in 1980, Professor (now Sir) John Smith told a story that nicely illustrates the elusiveness of 'influence' and the ambiguities surrounding the public role of legal scholars (Smith, 1981: 21–2). In 1978, Smith read a transcript of a judgment in the Court of Appeal, in which it was indicated that 'it cannot be said that one who has it in mind to steal only if what he finds is worth stealing has a present intention to steal'. 'Here, I said to myself, is a burglar's charter. If that is right, many burglars have no intention to steal' (ibid.). He wondered whether he should keep this insight to himself or draw attention to a loophole by a case note in the *Criminal Law Review*. He chose the latter course. Within a short time, burglars or their counsel were raising the point and sufficient acquittals followed to cause disquiet to the police and prosecuting authorities. Had he done the right thing? After reflection, Smith's conclusion was robust:

Notwithstanding the doubts I have entertained from time to time, my opinion is that we must write what we think to be the truth about the law, however inconvenient it may be and however unpopular it may make us in some quarters. If reported cases—and we can only rely on the words reported—do appear to create a burglar's charter, it is right to say so. If legislation fails, on any reasonable construction, to achieve its intended effect, that must be said. The immediate effect may be a worsening of the functioning of the law; but it cannot be right that the law should be administered on false premises; and we cannot get the law right unless we expose what it is now. (ibid. 124–5)

Sir John Smith is widely perceived, along with Sir Rupert Cross and Professor Glanville Williams, to have made a significant impact on the development of English criminal law, an area in which academics have made a more visible contribution than usual. This may in part be because of the existence of the *Criminal Law Review*, which is widely read by judges, practitioners, and the police, yet—perhaps grudgingly—is acknowledged to be a scholarly publication. Few other law journals have this status.

This story not only raises issues about the proper role of academics in practical affairs, but it also illustrates the elusiveness of 'influence'. It seems unlikely that a latter-day Raffles subscribed to the *Criminal Law Review* and passed on the information about Smith's loophole to his professional colleagues; it seems more likely that one or more members of the Bar took note of the point and used it on behalf of their clients; but it is equally likely that some barrister or judge reached the same conclusion independently or would have done so had not Smith pointed it out. Smith claimed to have indulged 'in this form of legal journalism' (his words) precisely because he wished to address directly the participants in the criminal justice system who read the *Criminal Law Review*. Except for law students, the audience of most academic legal writing is both small and indeterminate and 'influence' is even harder to trace.

To what extent do scholar-teachers of law have influence outside the academy through performance of their normal duties? Common sense suggests that the most important single channel of influence of academic lawyers is through teaching future practitioners. Such influence is naturally difficult to gauge, especially in a system in which universities only contribute systematically to the first stage of a four-stage process of professional formation, they do not have a monopoly over this stage, and a large percentage of their students do not pursue a career in legal practice. Nevertheless, primary legal education is almost certainly the most important arena through which scholar-teachers of law contribute in the longer term to overall legal culture—attitudes, values, competencies, and knowledge.

There are two main reasons why the impact of scholarly legal writing is even harder to assess: it is extraordinarily diverse and a high proportion of it is not intended to have a direct or immediate impact on practical affairs. If one leafs through publishers' catalogues, one is immediately struck by the diversity in terms of subject-matters, styles, perspectives, and putative audiences. Specialist law publishers tend to draw fairly sharp lines between markets: practitioner, student, and (academic) library. Unlike some disciplines, such as history, general publishers tend to shy away from academic books with 'law' in the title. In the United Kingdom, very few law books by academics, however well written, reach a general audience.

The principal audiences for scholarly writing about law, in a probable descending order of salience, are law students, fellow academics, legal practitioners, judges, civil servants, NGO activists, politicians, and the public at large. Not all of these are in a single jurisdiction. Of those outside the academy the last category seems the hardest to reach. This is typified by the annual Hamlyn Lectures which are meant to enlighten 'the Common People of the United Kingdom of Great Britain and Northern Ireland'. Despite the best efforts of lecturers and publishers, the lectures tend to draw an exclusively legal audience and the resultant self-effacing little red books end up in the remotest corners of bookshops. Law in the United Kingdom is not a part of 'general culture' and, unlike in some countries, very few British academic lawyers are recognized as public intellectuals.

In the areas of public policy and law reform, legal scholars almost certainly have more direct influence through membership of Law Commissions, public committees, or activist pressure groups than through their published writings. In their chapter on empirical research, John Baldwin and Gwynn Davis have described the vagaries of 'influence' even in respect of government-sponsored research (this volume, p. 895 ff). If in the future grand plans emerge for major codification or unification of laws, academics may expect to play a more significant role, for they are better situated than others to be involved in large-scale projects.

In common law systems, there is a complex symbiotic relationship between the senior judiciary and established legal scholars. This is because, as Lord Goff and others have pointed out, judges and jurists have a shared concern for the development of the law through case-by-case decision on the basis of principle (Goff, 1983). There is an extensive literature, especially in the United States, on judge–jurist relations and the frequency and significance of judicial citation of academic writings (see generally, Duxbury, 2001). For an academic to be cited by the House of Lords is an accolade; it is even recognized as 'an indicator of esteem' in the RAE. Judicial conventions concerning citation have varied between jurisdictions and over time. Clearly, in England, judges have become more receptive to some kinds of academic writing and explicit citation is more common than it once was. As legal practice becomes more cosmopolitan, legal scholars in their role as comparatists may be listened to even more closely, as Professor Basil Markesenis has eloquently argued that they should (Markesenis, 1997). However, neither bibliometrics nor explicit citation are reliable indicators of influence. Judges need not and do not always openly acknowledge what they read—indeed, there is a well-established tradition of 'licensed plagiarism' by both Bar and Bench; when an academic writer is cited, it may be to dissent from her views or to bolster an argument; some judges are more generous in acknowledgement than others; individual judges follow different conventions.

After a careful study, Neil Duxbury concluded persuasively that it is impossible to assess the extent and weight of the influence of jurists on judges in England, but it is probably much greater than external indicators suggest and it may be no less than in France or the United States (Duxbury, 2001: 115). The crux of the matter was pointed out by Lord Goff: despite their shared concern for principle, jurists write at large, while judges are more sharply focused on the facts and issues of particular cases and they have both power and responsibility to decide. It is not for academics to try to do the judges' job for them (Goff, 1983).

Scholars lack direct power and responsibility. They owe no duty to clients, they are free to set their own agenda, to criticize and subvert, to be curious, and to develop dreams and visions of a better law. They may adopt the role of critic or expositor, explorer, innovator, or conscience of the profession. Echoing Judge Posner, Neil Duxbury suggests that 'legal scholarship is a high-risk, low return activity' (Duxbury, 2001: 114). That might be true, if the central concern was to make an immediate impact. But that is to miss the point of any scholarship, including legal. Jurists have little to risk but their reputation, because they are in an important sense irresponsible, in the spirit that John Smith elegantly articulated.

3 THE UNITED STATES

The relationship between the American legal academy and the institutions it studies is a bit estranged, particularly by comparison to where matters stood a few decades ago. There still are direct encounters between academy and profession—doctrinal scholarship and restatement projects that lawyers appreciate, and occasional first-hand involvement by academics in legal and political life. But the high-status, high-profile work in the legal academy nowadays tends to be increasingly critical, theoretical, interdisciplinary, interesting to other academics, and useless to courts. Many judges and lawyers understandably are nonplussed by the resulting cascade of literature that has no apparent application to their work; meanwhile academics spend perhaps 7 million man-hours annually on scholarship—as much labour each year as it took to construct the Empire State Building—yet usually see little sign that anything they write is valued by the legal system or makes an impact on it. The consequences of this estrangement probably are less important than they appear, but now we are getting ahead of our story.

3.1 Courts and Scholars

The most natural meeting place for the work of the academy and the work of the profession has long been thought to be the judicial branch, where a judge confronted with a hard case might repair for guidance to scholarship that points the way to its resolution. But only a narrow type of academic work can serve this purpose. It has to be pitched at a relatively low level of generality; it has to take a discrete problem that arises in an adversarial setting and produce a recommendation about it; the recommendation has to be presented as a way that legal materials can be nudged around within the rules of the judging game, where radical rethinking is discouraged as a matter of norm and practice; and the setting must be one where existing tools for resolving the problem seem unsatisfactory, thus causing a judge to be interested in outside guidance (Cass and Beermann, 1993). As a practical matter, this generally means that an academic trying to make a direct impact on judicial decisions needs to achieve a particular mix of descriptive and normative elements in his work—largely descriptive and only modestly normative. The best examples of the mix are found in successful treatises and restatements, where recommendations to courts are embedded in large efforts at description and are stated in the language of legal principle, not interdisciplinary talk. Courts welcome the results and often find them useful. Their influence in any given case typically is small but can be large in the aggregate and sometimes very large in particular areas; the American Law Institution's restatements of tort law, for example, suggested frameworks for several causes of action that took hold in many jurisdictions that had not previously adopted them. Law review articles can strike the same balance and be useful in similar ways, and until perhaps thirty years ago this was the conventional understanding of the primary purpose of legal scholarship: the best of it was most helpful to courts and other legal institutions.

Since around 1970 there has been a gradual shift of the norms within the legal academy about what work counts as valuable. The most prized legal scholarship is now likely to employ tools of economics or other social sciences; more likely to view the legal system from perspectives external to it, such as feminism; and more likely to pitch normative theories at a high level of generality—theories of interpretation or efficiency or equality that are ever further removed from the practical details of the decisions judges make in their cases. Various reasons for this trend can be offered from the standpoint of intellectual, social, or economic history. The legal realist movement reoriented scholars towards analysis of whether legal doctrines were serving useful purposes; it was only natural for such enquiries to employ tools from other disciplines, as 'legal reasoning' is an internal sort of analysis that supplies no answers to questions about the relationship between law and the world it governs. Meanwhile a generation of students dissatisfied with American public institutions in the 1960s and 1970s grew into a generation of academics bored by questions about how they could help courts do their jobs a little better, and more interested in grander critical enquiries into the system's structure and operation.

Then there is the economic account: the legal profession and the wealth attainable by lawyers have both grown dramatically since the 1960s, and this has translated into greater demand for legal education and a corresponding infusion of wealth into the law schools. The wealth in turn has increased the number of law professors, raised their salaries, and made it easier for them to treat scholarship as their only concern. Earlier in the century, law professors were much more likely to be part-time practitioners, which increased their likely interest in the same matters that concerned other lawyers and made it less likely that they would have the time or inclination to pursue ambitious interdisciplinary projects. As both a consequence of these developments and a spur to them, Ph.D.s in disciplines other than law became more common on law school faculties. So did academic lawyers without graduate degrees in other disciplines who saw it as their task to combine insights from various social sciences with their own intimate knowledge of legal institutions to create a distinctive intellectual product.

Whatever the cause of these developments, the result is that the standards of value within the academy and outside it have diverged markedly. The law review articles courts cite the most tend to be cited in scholarly work only rarely and are not well-known to academics. Likewise, the legal scholarship most famous and influential within the academy over the past thirty years generally is of little interest to courts, sometimes being cited hundreds of times by academics but not once in a judicial opinion (Merritt and Putnam, 1996). The trend is illustrated by the Supreme Court's declining interest in citing law review articles. There were 0.86 such citations per opinion in the early 1970s, but only 0.47 in the late 1990s; the *Harvard Law Review* was cited 169 times in 1971–3 (0.15 cites per opinion) but only 30 times in 1996–8 (0.052 cites per opinion) (Sirico, 2000). The decline has not been met with any particular alarm in the academy. It is a case of mutual indifference. When a recent survey asked academics who they considered the primary audience for their work, the most common answer by a wide margin was other academics (Merritt, 1998). Many of the most illustrious figures in the legal academy have had no perceptible influence at all on the legal system, instead achieving prominence by saying things that impress and influence other professors.

3.2 The Extent and Significance of the Disconnection

Some judges and lawyers infer from the output of leading law faculties that academics lack interest in the practical challenges faced by legal professionals. They long for the days when there was a stronger sense of partnership between academy and profession (Edwards, 1992). But the enlargement of the distance is not as consequential as might first appear—or at least not consequential in the *way* that first appears. First, legal academics still produce enormous amounts of doctrinal scholarship. It may be a smaller share of legal scholarship than it used to be (yet even this is not clear; see

Gordon, 1992); but there are more than twice as many law professors now as there were in 1970 and more than twice as many law journals, so a declining share need not indicate an absolute decline. Secondly, it is not clear that the *influence* of legal scholarship on the profession has declined, because that influence never has been great. We saw that the Supreme Court cites the *Harvard Law Review* less now than it once did, but in the old days, and today as well, most of the citations to it were ornamental anyway—a dash of erudition at the end of a string of citations listing cases and articles that discuss the point the Court is dealing with, but with no indication that the academic discussion cited actually affected the Court's analysis. Scholarship may have stimulated the thinking of judges in ways not visible in their opinions, of course, but then that is still true even when no scholarship is cited at all. And while restatements and treatises have sometimes had considerable influence on courts, that also remains so today.

What may be true is that work towards the doctrinal end of the spectrum has lost prestige within the academy. This takes a psychological toll on the profession's sense of camaraderie with the law schools. Judges and lawyers don't want to feel that the academy has relegated their concerns to a second rank; and meanwhile they look at what academics are writing instead and much of it seems frivolous. These problems do not seem serious. They are matters of image and pique. The more troubling complaint occasionally offered is that the quality of doctrinal work is slipping precisely because it is no longer the preoccupation of the best minds in the academy. The reasons for this view seem just to be that the work isn't appearing in elite law journals as often as it used to and that elite law schools aren't hiring as many doctrinalists as they once did. But it would be fallacious to infer from this that the quality of doctrinal work is dipping. It may instead be that the academy has redefined the meaning of 'best minds' to make producers of useful doctrinal work less likely to qualify—but that the quality of the thinking brought to bear on doctrinal problems is as good as ever. The work of the thousands of doctrinalists in the legal academy should not be disparaged just because their work is less to the taste of the elite law schools than it used to be. Or less to the taste of the elite law reviews, which are almost all edited by students.

Even if it is not as consequential as it appears, however, we might ask whether anything can or should be done about this redistribution of labour and prestige within the academy and the resulting sense of disconnection between academy and profession. The shift represents a trade-off. Whereas doctrinal scholarship has the potential to make a modest but visible difference in the legal system, academics engaging in higher levels of theory are aiming for a larger impact that is less likely to occur or to be clearly visible if it does. They are operating as wholesalers, relying on others to turn their ideas into concrete possibilities for legislation, regulation, or judicial decision. Any single piece of writing in this vein is unlikely ever to make any difference, but it may contribute to a body of work that infects the thinking of other academics, which in turn affects the milieu in which their colleagues talk and their students are trained.

The ideas gradually may be imported into public life by students or colleagues who venture into government service as law clerks, judges, regulators, and so forth. The final impact may be hard to discern or trace to its source, yet still be greater than the impact of an idea retailed directly to judges in a law review article.

It should be stressed that usually the impact of *either* type of work is nil. Doctrinal scholarship specific enough to be useful to courts is the academic equivalent of a scratch-off lottery ticket. Relatively soon the author learns whether he has won anything; probably he hasn't; if he has, the returns are modest but satisfying. The more theoretical and abstract legal academic writing, like basic research in many fields, is akin to the bigger lotteries where the potential pay-off and the odds against achieving it are both larger by orders of magnitude. Failure is the norm either way; nobody has yet found a way to generate good ideas, large or small, except by creating a system that also generates a lot of bad or trivial ones (see Posner, 1995). Thus most legal scholarship, doctrinal or otherwise, is read by hardly anyone and has no impact on anything. Indeed, many academics abjure any interest in whether their work has a practical impact. They seek to understand the legal system for the intrinsic satisfaction of it; impact on anyone else is just a happy by-product of their labours. For all that appears, the practical pay-off of this approach may end up as high as, or higher than, that of more direct efforts to make a difference.

In any event, there is no question that the creation of the larger theoretical scholarship, however motivated, *can* have a large impact. The law and economics movement has had a few specific triumphs in various areas of doctrine, but its greatest success has been a transformation of the way not only many academics but also many legal officials, especially in the regulatory arena, think about law. Arguments about the efficiency of a rule are more common and influential now than thirty years ago, and this must be attributed in significant part to the rise of law and economics as an analytical approach. In the 1960s it barely existed; by the 1990s it accounted for a substantial share of all legal scholarship. Much of that scholarship seems pointless, just like any other type, but the overall effect of the movement must be counted as high even if little of it has ever been directly useful to courts.

3.3 Outlook for the Future

Might the gap between academy and profession be narrowed partly by movement on the profession's part? Perhaps judges should be more open to some of the interdisciplinary work academics generate. But the legal system is resistant to the direct influence of such work, and with good reason. The law developed into its current form at times when powerful contributions from the academy weren't available. Think of the legal system, and especially the judicial branch, as if it were a many-brained organism that evolved into its current form by learning to survive on the materials at hand: principles, concepts, and customs that judges could use to make satisfactory decisions with little time and information. Constraints on their knowledge caused courts to decide one case at a time, keeping the resulting decisions close to the facts at bar; efforts to do more were to be scorned as judicial legislation. Whatever legal pronouncements courts did make were supposed to be based on cases, statutes, or regulations, or the Constitution—not on academic work. Those understandings about the proper size of decisions and about what counts as valid authority persist to this day.

Now that a large legal academy exists with millions of hours of analysis to contribute every year, it might seem appropriate for the legal system to make more room for the contributions academics have to offer. But the powerful tools of analysis that didn't exist when the law was growing up still don't quite exist. Analysts of law have economic and philosophical tools that were not available one or two or three hundred years ago, but those tools still tend not to produce clear, decisive guidance. They generate disagreement among their users, and when the users do agree, the normative strength of the methods isn't great enough to command deference from judges or legislators. Compared to an academic, the judge has relatively few hours to spend on a question, but the hours an academic can spend are dwarfed in their own way by the hours of experience and judicial consideration that may be impounded in an old and durable doctrine that the judge in a case is called upon to nudge forward. And judges who do attempt to take academic work into account may find it hard to distinguish the good from the bad, or to apply the good work competently once it is found. A judge who admits that academic scholarship influenced his decision invites ridicule from judicial colleagues, who will cite this as evidence that his position is flimsy; or from the academy, which may be quick to complain if a court relies on work that turns out to be flawed, or inapposite, or that the judge fumbled in trying to apply. The most celebrated use of extra-legal scholarship by an American court came in *Brown v Board of Education*; while the result of the case is considered a great success, the Supreme Court's use of social science scholarship received a mixed reception (see Cahn, 1955). Most courts would still be more comfortable citing an obscure judicial opinion from another jurisdiction than a hundred-page law review article as support for a holding.

The limits of the direct impact academics usually have on the legal system can be illuminated by considering an exceptional case where the impact has been large: antitrust. A number of important ideas in antitrust law were pressed by scholars in the 1960s and 1970s and then adopted fairly quickly by courts. Maybe the changes would have occurred anyway, but then that can always be said; at the very least, the scholarship greatly hastened the advance of certain ideas. But the reasons for the influence of some antitrust scholarship help explain why most other legal scholarship is not so influential. Antitrust is a relatively new set of legal doctrines. It does not have centuries of doctrinal development behind it that courts can use as a comfortable foundation for decision. It is also relatively technical, calling on courts to serve as regulators of commercial organization in complex industries. Most judges don't know much about economics, so it is natural for them to welcome guidance from those who do. In addition, antitrust litigation in the 1960s and afterwards became especially complex and time-consuming, justifying investment by the parties in research into any academic work that might be useful. And academics have played a large role in antitrust enforcement, taking tours of duty in the Justice Department and bringing with them various ideas from the academy.

Economic analysis as well as other movements have generated large amounts of scholarship in other areas, too, but usually without making a comparable impact on doctrine. The economic analysis of contract law, for example, has consumed thousands of pages in legal journals over the past twenty years, but a recent study of the influence of those studies on contract law concluded that there had been none (Posner, 2003). The reasons for this can be seen by looking at the supply and demand sides of the production relationship. Contract law is old, and mostly was built from customary and fairly simple ideas that were refined in small increments over a long period of time. The resulting edifice is sturdy if imperfect, and seems to serve its purposes tolerably well. Judges feel at home with it and competent to apply it. So when an academic appears with a new argument that some alternative regime of remedies would be more efficient than the existing one, or better from some other perspective, courts pay no attention; academics do not have a comparative advantage that judges feel they need. Thus the big developments in the academic treatment of an area need not, and often do not, bear any connection to developments in the practice of it.

A final point is that the law and economics agenda in antitrust was at least roughly in keeping with the political temper of the times when it took hold; that is one reason *why* it took hold. More commonly, hot academic fads are driven by or accompany a politics unpalatable to the legal system. The figure at the political median of the legal academy is well to the left of the median in the profession, and this is another reason for the distrust of the academy's output by legal professionals (Lindgren, 2002): to the extent that the output is normative rather than informative, it is likely to advance a political vision shared by too few judges and lawyers to be appealing.

4 CIVIL LAW SYSTEMS

Conventional wisdom has it that one of the salient features distinguishing 'the common law' and 'the civil law' is the respective significance accorded to legal scholars in the different legal families (van Caenegem, 1987). As has been demonstrated within the preceding two sections of this chapter, major differences occur even between various countries belonging to the common law world. It will not come as a surprise that the same holds true for civil law systems if the term 'civil law' is used—as it usually is—as the somewhat inexact generic term for those legal orders within the Western tradition that do not belong to the common law, that is, to use another set of collective terms necessarily bedevilled with imprecision, the 'Romanistic', the 'Germanic', and the 'Nordic' legal systems. While it is true that all those legal orders share a common juristic legacy based partly on the medieval reformulation of Roman law and partly on Germanic custom, it is also true that today most of them have developed a distinctive legal culture of their own, which makes it almost impossible to group them together within one and the same category. However, the limitations inherent in a handbook like this call for simplification. All that can be done is to emphasize the common traits of the respective legal systems, providing some illustrative, but inevitably somewhat arbitrarily chosen, instances and omitting a great amount of detail at the expense of occasional overgeneralization. With this proviso in mind, it can certainly be said that academics play a pre-eminent role in civil law countries. They exert an enormous influence on the law-making process, be it statutory or judicial.

With respect to legislation, admittedly, the days are long gone when the fathers of the *Code civil* took over whole passages from the works of Domat and Pothier verbatim, the leading German Pandectist Windscheid was the guiding influence behind the first draft of the *Bürgerliches Gesetzbuch* (BGB), Bern law professor Huber single-handedly drafted the Swiss Civil Code, Professor Meijers of Leyden did the same with the first parts of the New Dutch Civil Code, and Paris dean Carbonnier prepared a number of important acts on family law. Today, even smaller legislative proposals are considered to be too complex to be entrusted to a single person. However, academics' advice is still eagerly sought. Frequently, either a commission of experts dominated by law professors is set up, or academics are asked to contribute to hearings of the relevant legislative bodies. When, for instance, the German legislature recently undertook the most sweeping reform of the BGB to date, it could rely on more than twenty years of preparatory work by some of Germany's most distinguished scholars.

As far as judicial exposition and development of the law is concerned, some of the modern codes explicitly require the judge, in 'hard cases', to have regard to 'the common and constant opinion of learned persons' (Code of Canon Law of 1983, canon 19) or to 'approved legal doctrine' (Swiss Civil Code, art. 1.3). It is important to note that the terms *la doctrine* or *Rechtslehre* do not only refer to the entire body of legal writings apart from judicial opinions, but are also used to designate, collectively, the persons who are engaged in analysis, synthesis, and evaluation of legal materials. In most civilian systems, doctrinal writings undisputedly do not represent a formal 'source of law' and they do not possess any binding force for the courts, but it is equally agreed upon that they are of eminent importance in the judicial process. This can be seen in at least three different situations. First, judges use legal literature to find a specific answer when dealing with new statutes or new circumstances. It is well known, for instance, that, as to certain cases of breach of contract, the German *Reichsgericht* in 1903 simply adopted the solution suggested by a law professor a couple of months earlier. The French *Conseil d'État*, in a 1951 landmark-case on administrative law, made use of a proposition that had been made in a law review article in 1948. Secondly, legal writings function as a sort of watchdog for the courts. Each important decision is commented upon in case notes or doctrinal articles, and civilian authors are, in general, much bolder in their criticism of judicial opinions than their English counterparts. Overwhelming disapproval of a judicial solution might induce a court to re-examine its holding. The French *notes d'arrêt*, which appear alongside the actual case report, are famous for the feedback they give to judges and for their suggestions as to a further refinement or a partial retreat from a judge-made rule (Duxbury, 2001). They do not only explain the rationale of a decision or of a line of decisions, but normally make a constructive effort as to the future development of the law as well. By this means they transcend the is/ought divide, something that the traditional English case note regularly stops short of.

Thirdly, legal writings structure and organize entire subject areas of the law. This is of the utmost importance in those disciplines which have never been comprehensively codified or have been codified only relatively recently, such as administrative law or labour law. Here the system was essentially created by case law, guided by learned writings. The systematizing function of legal doctrine is also particularly relevant as long as a code is relatively new. Usually, the first commentaries and treatises appear immediately after a code's enactment, so that the conceptual and structural scheme for that particular area has already been shaped before the courts have the first occasion to interpret a specific provision. But even in areas that have been codified for a long time any practitioner, when faced with a legal problem, will immediately look for a synthesis of the relevant legal rules and of their relation to fundamental legal principles and, indeed, to the legal system as a whole. For that purpose, he will turn to a textbook or, especially in the Germanic countries, to one of the 'commentaries', which follow the sections of the relevant code and offer thorough discussion as well as massive references to further writings and to case law. As in all civil law countries, therefore, there is ample justification for regarding the 'prevailing doctrine', *la doctrine dominante* or *die herrschende Lehre*, as a '*de facto*' or 'indirect' source of law with strong persuasive authority. A specific opinion is all the more persuasive, the more authors (dead or alive) subscribe to it and the better their academic reputation.

The dominant role of academics within the legal system, the pervasion of the whole legal process by 'doctrine', can only be explained historically. Today's civil law professor is the inheritor of a proud tradition, reaching back to pre-classical and classical Roman law, the very hallmark of which was its character as 'jurists' law' (Kaser, 1971). There, legal issues were decided by the *praetor*. Although he was even entitled to grant new actions or new exceptions in 'hard cases', he was not a trained lawyer and therefore regularly followed the advice given by those 'experienced in the law', the *iures prudentes*. By this means, the jurists became a veritable law-making power. By the post-classical period, the opinions and writings of the ancient jurists were regarded as a binding source of law and had become so predominant that authoritative status was restricted, by imperial enactment in AD 426, to the writings of five classical jurists. Roughly

a century later a number of fragments of the ancient juristic works were even formally accorded legal validity when Emperor Justinian, in order to restate the law,
arranged them according to subject-matter and enacted them as a Code. In the formative era of modern civil law systems, from the twelfth century onwards, Roman law
became the subject of systematic studies at the emerging universities. This 'learned
law' filled the legal vacuum arising from the absence of a centralized and unified state
with strong and prestigious legislative and judicial organs (Wieacker, 1995). Its influence on the judicial process was secured by a number of procedural factors. First, the
prevalent written procedure required the advocates to produce extensive briefs with
citations guiding the judges to the relevant literature. Secondly, professors were
frequently involved in litigation by providing *consilia* to the parties; and, at least in
Germany, the common practice of sending the records of complex cases to benches
of professors at the nearest law faculty with a request for an opinion on the legal issues
(*'Aktenversendung'*) provided for consistency of judicial decisions with prevailing
academic opinion. Thirdly, every judge could be personally held liable for wrong
judgments by the losing party. This could be avoided if he had followed the *com-
munis opinio*, which was taken to be the view of the majority of the most authoritative writers. Thus he had a strong incentive to peruse the handbooks and indices
created for the very purpose of finding the prevalent strand in legal writing, and to
supply his judgment with an endless collection of citations.

It does not come as a surprise, therefore, that the most distinguished pieces of
medieval scholarship were granted normative force. Thus it was said to be useless to
go to court without knowledge of the glossator Azo's works (*'chi non ha Azzo non
vada in palazzo'*) and it was considered a rule that the courts would not recognize
anything which was not recognized by the gloss of Accursius (*'Quidquid non agnoscit
glossa nec agnoscit forum'*). Later, various territorial legislators even ordered the
judges to have recourse to the writings of prominent commentators such as Bartolus
and Baldus in 'hard cases'. In Portugal, for instance, these provisions remained in
force until well into the eighteenth century.

But even in those territories where the learned commentary of Roman law was
not formally elevated to a source of law, prominent legal writings retained strong
persuasive authority. This, incidentally, is still the position in civil law and mixed legal
systems whose laws have remained uncodified, such as San Marino, Scotland, where
the works of the 'institutional writers' enjoy a special authority said to be just inferior
to a House of Lords decision, or South Africa, where the view of the most distinguished authors of Roman–Dutch law agreeing on a particular question is binding
even for a modern court (Dainow, 1974). But even the enactment of codes purporting
to provide for a coherent and conclusive settlement of all legal issues did not diminish the academics' role. True, the French revolutionaries closed the law faculties for a
decade, and German legislators tried to guard themselves against the apprehended
scholarly 'corruption' of their texts with bans on all legal commentary. But soon the
new codes themselves required exposition and solutions for unprovided cases, and

they were to be applied by lawyers who had acquired their training and experience under the older system and thus were steeped in traditional learning. Moreover, the need to intellectualize, rationalize, and systematize the law was still felt, so that the traditional roles, in the creative development of the law, of the jurist as senior partner, and the judge as junior partner were quickly resumed (Stein, 1985).

It is precisely because the main features of this tradition are still alive that the professorial character of civilian systems persists. First, legal knowledge is still almost entirely acquired at the university. It is impossible to enter the legal profession without a degree that requires, as a rule, four or five years of studies in a law faculty. Even the second phase of legal education, which mainly consists in practical training, regularly involves a substantial amount of theoretical coursework. As a consequence of the monopoly of university teaching, the law fresher begins his discovery of the law with abstract and conceptual reflections, of the sort that might be taught to English finalists in their jurisprudence course, for instance, on the distinction between 'the objective law' and 'subjective rights', and on the nature of 'absolute' and 'relative' rights. He studies the various theories about the distinctions between private law and public law and between general private law and commercial law. He becomes acquainted with the various categories of crimes and learns to distinguish sharply between justification and excuse. By this means, he acquires a structural foundation and a conceptual system at an early stage that later enables him to classify any new legal phenomenon and to integrate it somehow into that system. As a result, every practising lawyer is, in principle, a 'learned lawyer' whether he works in a law firm (the renowned law firms in Germany expect their applicants to hold a doctorate), in a court, or anywhere in the legislative process. He will never dismiss academic opinion out of hand, let alone simply ignore it.

Secondly, with respect to the judiciary, that attitude is reinforced by some simple sociological facts. In most civilian systems, judges are appointed straight after the end of their legal education, when they are still imbued with university training. As civil servants, those career judges enjoy a relatively modest social standing and salary. In addition, the traditional role of the civil law judge is much more modest than that of his common law counterpart. Usually, it is not openly acknowledged that he has a creative function or even anything coming close to real law-making power. Judgments are given in the name of the court as a unit and not in the name of a specific judge. Dissenting opinions are not admitted. Individual judges are simply not widely known within the legal community. Contrast this to the prestigious position of law professors whose names are associated with legal innovations, whose views are widely debated, and who, especially in Italy and France, have close connections to the political sphere and often get elected to the highest offices. They might not necessarily be better compensated than judges, and are definitely worse off than leading advocates, but the path to a chair is so extraordinarily arduous that it is unthinkable to allege, as has sometimes been done in England, that a person might have gone into academia because he could not make a success of the bar.

Thirdly, the pervasion of civil law systems with legal doctrine can be explained by the enduringly close cooperation between academics and other actors within the legal profession. On the one hand, professors do not only participate in the drafting of legislation. They may also engage in private practice, provide expert opinions, act as counsel in litigation, work as arbitrators, or even serve as part-time judges, as frequently happens in German courts of second instance. In the Netherlands, there is a long tradition of academics being appointed as fully entitled judges to the highest court, and they now make up roughly a quarter of its members. The French *Cour de cassation* counts some former professors amongst its judges, and their proportion is even higher in the constitutional courts that have been introduced in many civil law countries since World War II. On the other hand, legal practitioners, including judges, frequently enter into the academic arena by publishing law journal articles, commentaries, or even textbooks. Some of the leading treatises on French public law have been prepared by members of the *Conseil d'État*. The most widely used commentary on the BGB, the *Palandt*, is almost entirely written by judges. It is no exaggeration to speak of an 'integrated community' between the academic and the non-academic legal world (Bell and Boyron, 1998).

Fourthly, from a methodological point of view, the academics' influence depends to a large extent on the 'constructive' nature of legal scholarship that has already been referred to with respect to case notes. Academics traditionally do not confine themselves to analysis and critique of isolated cases. They try to anticipate further developments and endeavour to contribute to the improvement of the legal system as a whole.

Whether the established role of academics within civilian systems can be maintained is open to question. To be sure, there is no acute danger of a growing disjunction between scholarship and the profession as can currently be witnessed in the United States. Civil law writing remains of a rather 'doctrinal' nature. But there are signs of a creeping de-academization of legal culture. The more openly the law-making function of the courts is admitted, the less important seems the role of legal doctrine in developing the law. The continuous change of modern legislation and the inflation of information encourage breathless, descriptive, technical, and positivistic surveys and reports on new and supposedly attractive issues. Often this research is pursued at the expense of the critical analysis and the thorough examination of the context of the whole legal system that is so characteristic of civilian scholarship. This might be seen as a welcome adaptation to the needs of modern life, but if legal scholarship should one day be no longer of a different kind than legal practice, it might easily be asked what it is needed for. However, anyone who has only a cursory look at the pages of the *Revue trimestrielle de droit civil* or of a German *Habilitationsschrift* will not be too worried about traditional legal scholarship. Very soon it might even find itself at the very forefront of legal development again. Probably the dominant issue in the law today is its rapid Europeanization which, against the background of a variety of legal cultures, is very difficult to achieve by legislation, let alone by judge-made law.

Arguably, there is a strong need for a common European legal science that provides future lawmakers and judges with a common stock of systematic and conceptual tools that can, as the learned law did before the age of codification, provide a legal grammar for further development of the law (Zimmermann, 1996).

5 INTERNATIONAL LAW

5.1 The Nature of International Legal Scholarship

Modern international law scholarship has been shaped by two congenital character-istics of the international system. First, as is well known, the international commun-ity is not organized as a super-state. There are no international legislatures, courts, or executive powers. While the United Nations Charter resembles a sort of international constitution, the analogy should not be stretched too far. There is a generalized sense that sovereign governments pay only lip-service to international law, and that, when they do refer to international rights and duties, their apparently public-spirited statements are not statements of law, but self-serving utterances cloaked in legal language. National interest, and not a desire to comply with the law, is still the guiding force in international relations. There are no similar infirmities in muni-cipal law, at least in the legal systems of modern democracies. Citizens in those democracies, while of course often acting, like states, in their self-interest, gener-ally acknowledge that they live under the rule of law. That is why municipal legal scholarship can safely rest on authoritative sources such as written constitutions, judicial decisions, and legislation. Judicial decisions are regularly enforced, people go to jail when they commit crimes, and so on. This disanalogy between the domestic and international legal systems causes many people to doubt that international law really is or can be, 'law'.

The second feature is the relative indeterminacy of many international law rules—most specifically customary international law. It is not simply that international law rules underdetermine behaviour, that is, that they are often too abstract to yield normative results in concrete cases. More fundamentally, the concept of customary law itself is incoherent (Goldsmith and Posner, 1999: 1116–20). Because international practice is mostly chaotic and contradictory, any attempt to find normative patterns of international behaviour will be result-oriented. Routinely, courts and comment-ators identify rules they like (for whatever reason: fairness, efficiency, or political viability) and declare them to be 'custom' (Tesón, 1998: 85–92). They either cite state practice selectively or omit citing that practice altogether. The corollary is that it is perfectly possible to make customary-law types of argument for and against almost any particular view—say, whether or not there is a right of humanitarian intervention, to cite a current controversial topic. To be sure, this problem may also arise in municipal legal systems, but in international law it is compounded by the incoherence of the concept of customary law and by the lack of institutional mechanisms to decide among conflicting interpretations of the law. The problem is obviously less acute with respect to treaty law; but here too, self-serving interpretations of treaty language are common, and disputes about treaty interpretation are not usually submitted to authoritative settlement. This marks, here again, a noticeable contrast with municipal legal systems.

This harsh reality of international politics creates a problem for academics. Perhaps an observer could have predicted, from the infirmities summarized above, that international law would be a fertile ground for intellectual creativity, where scholars would fill the normative gaps with various forms of policy analysis. That prediction, however, would have been mistaken: international law scholars have done exactly the opposite. Their task has almost uniformly consisted in attempts to show that international law is as 'legal' a discipline as tort, or property, or constitutional law. To do this, international law academics have resorted to a kind of positivist doctrinalism, that is, a dry, seemingly value-free analysis of international rules, and, conversely, a general distrust of theory (until recently) and other non-doctrinal, interdisciplinary ways of looking at international law and relations (Slaughter-Burley, 1993). This is usually coupled with an unreflective form of cultural relativism, a reluctance to criticize regimes or cultures, again, with the presumed aim of keeping international law separate from politics and values.

These scholarly attitudes reflect two impulses that are somewhat in tension. First, mainstream scholarship locates the principle of sovereignty at the centre of theoretical thinking. A primary expression of this emphasis on sovereignty is the well-known principle of effectiveness, according to which governments that succeed in establishing their authority over a territory are internationally legitimate (Brownlie, 1998: 70–7; Shearer, 1994: 85). The international law scholar simply looks at whether a ruler, any ruler, has succeeded in exacting obedience. If so, the ruler will be regarded as enjoying sovereign prerogatives and as protected by the principle of non-intervention and similar doctrines. (In other areas of the law, e.g. constitutional law, such endorsement of naked power would be unthinkable.)

Secondly, however, international law scholars have traditionally stood for the international rule of law. Whatever their political or theoretical views, they usually recommend that governments exercise restraint in the pursuit of national interest by observing international rules and procedures. This recommendation is normally coupled with support for more international courts, more international institutions, and various kinds of legal procedures. Their apparent goal is, of course, to enhance compliance with international law. (However, I suggest another, less charitable, explanation below.) It is hard to quarrel with the aim of enhancing respect for international law. However, as things are, that task is highly problematic. For one thing, its realization is complicated by the undecidability of legal principles of rules. States should observe human rights, but does this include respecting freedom of the press? States should comply with the prohibition on the use of force, but does this prohibition include invading another state to stop genocide or to apprehend terrorists? The examples could be multiplied. So international scholarship suffers, I think, from a defective approach to legal reasoning (pretending there is legal certainty where there is not) which in turns leads to recommendations for compliance that turn out to be empty and ineffective. If governments do not know *what* international law prescribes, they will either assert self-serving rules (they will make up their own version of international law, as it were), or will feel free to act as they wish.

But most importantly, the ambition to institutionalize collective decision-making, for example, by enlarging the kinds of cases that require approval of the United Nations Security Council or that can be heard by the International Court of Justice and other bodies, is open to a serious moral objection. Many governments lack legitimacy, and thus it is odd to support a version of 'the rule of law' where undemocratic, dictatorial, or otherwise objectionable regimes are important participants in decisions that affect millions of persons. The institutionalist approach (multiplying international institutions) works reasonably well when participating governments genuinely represent their citizens. Likewise, where there are 'good neighbourhoods', involving the 'bad neighbours' in regional institutions can have important moderating effects (Keohane, forthcoming). But the democratic and law-abiding aspirations that undergird *global* institutionalist ambitions are mere appearance. The world-view favoured by mainstream international scholars countenances a *faux* respect for the rule of law that ends up favouring incumbent regimes regardless of their democratic credentials. Because of its pro-sovereignty bias and its ties to foreign-policy bureaucracies, conventional legal scholarship is, most of the time, highly conservative.

Mainstream international law scholarship, with its dominant emphasis on doctrine, differs from legal scholarship in other areas, such as constitutional law, criminal law, or private law, where moral, political, and economic analyses have become common currency (at least in the common law world). The reason for this difference is hard to pinpoint, but a plausible conjecture is that international law academics want to earn the respect of their conventional colleagues. Because others (and especially their colleagues on law faculties) see international law as standing on weak ground, international legal scholars seek respectability for international law as true 'law', and for international legal scholarship as a serious academic discipline. A way to do that is for international law academics to prove that they also occupy themselves with law as an object of study, and not merely with power politics under the pretence of law. A body of doctrine that refers back to treaties, resolutions, declarations, governments' statements, and so on, *looks like* the kind of doctrinal analysis undertaken in conventional areas of the law. Of course, it is often not so, because statements and declarations are often just that—words. They rarely reflect binding rules.

Paradoxically, this peculiarity of international legal scholarship has kept many scholars, until recently, away from cosmopolitan values. The concept of sovereignty is central to the doctrinal task just described. It is no surprise, therefore, that many international lawyers have resisted reliance on universal, cosmopolitan values, as these are, of course, in conflict with pro-sovereignty values. With the end of the Cold War, the picture changed somewhat. The relative success of free markets and the spread of democratic values throughout the world have made sovereignty somewhat less popular, and a good part of the more recent scholarship reflects this trend.

5.2 The Influence of International Legal Scholars on International Law

There have been important changes in international law in the past fifteen years or so. In general, since the end of the Cold War, international rules reflect a certain retreat from the principle of sovereignty and a corresponding tendency to locate important sectors of social life in transnational contexts. It is quite difficult, however, to ascertain whether legal changes have occurred as a result of scholarly influence or simply as a result of world opinion and grass-roots movements. In the area of human rights, for example, there has been increased attention to the rights of women and children. Certainly, scholarship has moved in that direction as well, but scholarly writing followed, or coincided with, powerful lobbying and currents of opinion. Likewise, the progress made in international environmental law and international trade law owes more to the environmental movement and the economic literature, respectively, than to the writings of publicists. The principles governing the use of force, and humanitarian law, have evolved in interesting ways, but here again, the end of the Cold War and the September 2001 attacks against the United States have had much more influence than scholarly thinking (Commission Report, 2001). My sense is that most of the time, scholarly thinking follows international events, rather than the other way around. This is not surprising, given that traditional international scholarship relies on the practice of states as the cornerstone of international doctrine. International law scholars are positivists, and as such, uncomfortable with reform.

International scholars from time to time are called upon to serve in government, or in international courts and other international institutions. However, here again, the number of professional academics in government and international institutions is relatively small, and whatever influence they might have is diluted by national interest. Of the fifteen judges of the International Court of Justice, only three (Buerghental, Higgins, and Parra-Aranguren) were noted academics before joining the Court. The rest have backgrounds as diplomats, judges, or politicians.

A disturbing fact is that no one can possibly be appointed to the International Court of Justice (or any other major international court) if the person lacks support from his or her government. This fact may explain the pro-government bias of many of the decisions of international courts.

It has been quite some time since an academic has occupied the Legal Adviser position in the United States Department of State. Career officials, and not academics, likewise occupy the offices of the legal adviser at the United Kingdom Foreign Office and at their Australian and Canadian counterparts. At any rate, it is uncertain whether an academic who joins government will attempt to exercise influence with the power of her ideas, as it were. When a scholar joins the government, it is more likely that his scholarship will be adapted to the political agenda of the administration, rather than the other way around. Given the structure of incentives that a high-ranking government official faces in a modern democracy, his scholarship will be most likely put at the service of the government's political goals, and it will become, for that reason, corrupted. Legal academia (international and otherwise) rewards people who alternate between government and teaching. Such practice may be salutary for a number of reasons, but concern for the disinterested search for the truth is certainly *not* one of them.

It cannot be denied, however, that the many thousands of pages published annually in international law journals have an influence on the actual rules enforced and articulated in the legal arena. Again, that influence cannot be easily quantified, yet this much can be said: scholars sometimes help to make the agenda of important international law issues more concrete and well defined. To be sure, that agenda is ultimately the reflection of the various converging interests and conflicts that governments happen to have. Still, there is no doubt that the systematic scholarly presentation of an issue contributes to the discussion of that issue and the sharpening of the respective positions in non-academic settings. Just as governments shift the object of their concern, so do scholars. Two decades ago, the main concern was with state power: the aggressive use of force, governmental violations of human rights. Later, the attention shifted to issues of minority rights and ethnic rivalries, secession and state succession, the environment, and the various consequences of the liberalization of world markets. Today, concerns seem to have shifted to terrorism, war crimes and crimes against humanity, the status of non-state actors, and the possibility of using force collectively or unilaterally for purposes other than self-defence.

International courts vary in the citation of publicists. The International Court of Justice almost never does (curiously, the dissenting opinions rely more on scholarly writings), notwithstanding the fact that it is expressly authorized by its statute to do so. Other courts (e.g. the European Court of Human Rights) ignore scholars completely. This omission is somewhat surprising, given that judicial treatment of customary law itself is so deficient. Perhaps courts believe that scholarship is mere opinion, whereas 'custom' is not. For an international court, deciding that its preferred international rule is 'custom' will sound more objective. Even invented

legal rules will presumably have, unlike the opinions of publicists, some sort of onto-
logical reality.

Is international legal scholarship more ideological than conventional legal scholarship? I do not believe so. Rather, the ideological lines are drawn somewhat differently,
depending on the issue. On certain issues, such as protection of the environment, the
contending sides (pro-environmental regulation and pro-free markets) will replicate
similar divisions in domestic legal scholarship. But on other issues this is not the case.
For example, pro-interventionist positions and anti-interventionist positions will
cut across the left–right divide (Keohane and Holzgrefe, forthcoming). In general,
left-of-centre views tend to be more favourable to positions favoured by developing states, and (somewhat mysteriously) critical of the West, and especially of the
United States. But, even here, there are anomalies unique to international legal scholarship. Women's rights advocates tend to be on the left, and for that reason to sympathize with the causes championed by developing nations. But many of them
are caught off-guard when they find that the governments they defend mistreat
women in various, and sometimes horrible, ways. The problem here is that international legal scholars are sometimes committed to a cause, but this is incompatible
with cultural relativist positions that, as indicated above, they also tend to endorse.
The question of self-determination and secession lends itself particularly well to ideological manipulation, aggravated by the fact that the law, here again, is incoherent.
The question of secession, in particular, cannot be resolved in individual cases without evaluating the moral and political claims advanced by the parties (Buchanan,
1991). Scholars who favour sovereignty will normally resist secession and favour its
opposite, territorial integrity. This position, however, will sometimes clash with a
commitment to respect the diversity of cultures—a position better served by the
principle of self-determination.

There are, of course, more technical yet important issues of international law
where the positions cannot be clearly located by reference to an ideological divide. It
is unclear, for example, whether a view that allows more discretion by states to object
to treaty reservations is related to ideology, except in the general sense that such a
view seems to favour state sovereignty more than the opposing view. Perhaps a divide
unique to international legal scholarship is that between pro-sovereignty and cosmopolitan positions, and it is unclear in what sense such a divide is ideological.

An interesting question for international law scholars is whether they should be
committed to giving special weight to scholarly views held by their counterparts in
other parts of the globe. This is an issue unique to international legal scholarship
because international law purports to be universal. The idea here is that one should
give special weight to views from foreign scholars *because* they are foreign, and thus
active participants in the generation of ideas by the world community. Not doing so,
it is thought, would be unduly provincial (Pellet, 2000). Thus, for example, in the
human rights field there is a literature that examines 'the Asian view' (usually unsym-
pathetic to expanding human rights) with special care because it is supposed to be

Asian, independently of whether or not the view is intrinsically appealing, morally or legally. It is worth noting that, in this debate, scholars usually seek the opinion of rulers, not of citizens, and especially not of victims of governmental abuse. This approach embodies a fake notion of tolerance. A better position is that a scholar with integrity should consider fairly and thoroughly *all* competent scholarly views on issues, including those published by scholars overseas, and accept or reject them on their merits.

Yet, for all these weaknesses, there is no doubt that a world with law, where both governments and the general public share a sense of acceptable and unacceptable behaviour, is preferable to a world without law. International legal scholars strive to convey this message. The enterprise is not intellectually satisfying, but this is more due to the particular methodology that dominates the discipline than to the intrinsic worth of the aim pursued. More precisely, it is not possible to identify international legal rules by the conventional doctrinal methods. If international legal scholarship is going to advance humane values and not simply serve those in power, it must supplement legal doctrine with international relations theory and political philosophy. Otherwise, it will continue to be an exercise in futility.

REFERENCES

Arthurs, H. W. (Chairman) (1983). *Law and Learning: Report to the Social Sciences and Humanities Research Council of Canada*, Ottawa: Social Sciences and Humanities Research Council of Canada.

Becher, T. (1989). *Academic Tribes and Territories*, Milton Keynes: Open University Press.

Bell, J., and Boyron, S. (1998). 'Sources of Law', in J. Bell, S. Boyron, and S. Whittaker (eds.), *Principles of French Law*, Oxford: Oxford University Press, 13–36.

Brownlie, I. (1998). *Principles of Public International Law* (5th edn.), Oxford: Oxford University Press.

Buchanan, A. (1991). *Secession: The Morality of Political Divorce from Fort Sumner to Quebec*, Boulder, Colo.: Westview Press.

Cahn, E. (1955). 'Jurisprudence', *New York University Law Review*, 30: 150–69.

Cass, R., and Beermann, J. M. (1993). *Throwing Stones at the Mudbank: The Impact of Scholarship on Administrative Law*, Administrative Law Review, 45: 1–19.

Commission Report (2001). *The Responsibility to Protect: Report of the International Commission on Intervention and State Sovereignty*, Ottawa: International Development Research Centre.

Dainow, J. (ed.) (1974). *The Role of Judicial Decisions and Doctrine in Civil Law and in Mixed Jurisdictions*, Baton Rouge, La.: Louisiana State University Press.

Duxbury, N. (2001). *Jurists and Judges: An Essay on Influence*, Oxford: Hart.

Edwards, H. T. (1992). 'The Growing Disjunction between Legal Education and the Legal Profession', *Michigan Law Review*, 91: 34–78.

Fifoot, C. H. S. (1959). *Judge and Jurist in the Reign of Victoria* (Hamlyn Lectures), London: Sweet and Maxwell.

Goff, Robert (Lord) (1983). 'Appendix: The Search for Principle', in W. Swadling and G. Jones (eds.), in *The Search for Principle: Essays in Honour of Lord Goff, of Chieveley*, Oxford: Oxford University Press, 313–29. Maccabean Lecture originally delivered in 1983.

Goldsmith, J. L., and Posner, E. A. (1999). 'A Theory of Customary International Law', *University of Chicago Law Review*, 66: 1113–77.

Gordon, R. W. (1992). 'Lawyers, Scholars, and the "Middle Ground"', *Michigan Law Review*, 91: 2075–112.

International Legal Center (1975). *Legal Education in a Changing World*, New York: International Legal Center.

Kaser, M. (1971). *Das römische Privatrecht*, i (2nd edn.), Munich: C. H. Beck.

Keohane, R. O. (forthcoming). 'Political Authority after Intervention', in Keohane and Holzgrefe (forthcoming).

—— and Holzgrefe, J. (eds.) (forthcoming). *Humanitarian Intervention: Ethical, Political, and Legal Challenges*, Cambridge: Cambridge University Press.

Lindgren, J. (2002). 'Measuring Diversity' (unpublished manuscript; on file with the author).

Markesenis, B. (1997). *Foreign Law and Comparative Methodology: A Subject and a Thesis*, Oxford: Hart.

Merritt, D. J. (1998). 'Preliminary Results of a Survey of Law Professors who Began Tenure-Track Teaching 1986–1991 and who Remained on the Tenure Track in Fall 1997' (unpublished manuscript; on file with the author).

—— and Putnam, M. (1996). 'Judges and Scholars: Do Courts and Scholarly Journals Cite the Same Law Review Articles?' *Chicago-Kent Law Review*, 71: 871–99.

Pellet, A. (2000). 'Book Review', *American Journal of International Law*, 94: 419–21.

Posner, E. A. (2003). 'Economic Analysis of Contract Law after Three Decades: Success or Failure?' *Yale Law Journal*, 112: 829–880.

Posner, R. (1987). 'The Decline of Law as an Autonomous Discipline: 1962–87', *Harvard Law Review*, 100: 761–80.

—— (1995). *Overcoming Law*, Cambridge, Mass.: Harvard University Press.

Servicing the Legal System (SLS) (2001). *Annual Report*, Belfast: SLS Publications.

Shearer, I. A. (1994). *Starke's International Law* (11th edn.), London: Butterworths.

Sirico, L. J., Jr. (2000). 'The Citing of Law Reviews by the Supreme Court: 1971–99', *Indiana Law Journal*, 75: 1099–39.

Slaughter-Burley, A.-M. (1993). 'International Law and International Relations Theory: A Dual Agenda', *American Journal of International Law*, 87: 205–39.

Smith, J. C. (1981). 'An Academic Lawyer and Law Reform' (Presidential Address, The Society of Public Teachers of Law), *Legal Studies* 1: 119–30.

Stein, P. (1985). 'Judge and Jurist in the Civil Law: A Historical Interpretation', *Louisiana Law Review*, 46: 241–57.

Tesón, F. R. (1998). *A Philosophy of International Law*, Boulder, Colo.: Westview Press.

Twining, W. (1994). *Blackstone's Tower: The English Law School* (Hamlyn Lectures), London: Sweet and Maxwell.

—— (2000). *Globalisation and Legal Theory*, London: Butterworth.

van Caenegem, R. C. (1987). *Judges, Legislators and Professors: Chapters in European Legal History*, Cambridge : Cambridge University Press.

Wieacker, F. (1995). *A History of Private Law in Europe, with Particular Reference to Germany*, Oxford: Clarendon Press.

Zimmermann, R. (1996). 'Savigny's Legacy: Legal History, Comparative Law, and the Emergence of a European Science', *Law Quarterly Review*, 112: 576–605.

Additional Important Works

Dawson, J. P. (1968). *The Oracles of the Law*, Ann Arbor: University of Michigan Law School.

Kötz, H. (1990). 'Scholarship and the Courts: A Comparative Survey', in D. S. Clark (ed.), *Comparative and Private International Law: Essays in Honour of John Henry Merryman*, Berlin: Duncker & Humblot, 183–95.

Symposium on Legal Education (1993). *Michigan Law Review*, 91: 1921–2119.

CHAPTER 42

....

A CENTURY OF
LEGAL STUDIES

....

NEIL DUXBURY

1

....

So far as the study of law is concerned, the twentieth century was a century for the
exploration of grand schemes and ideas. But it would be strange to characterize this
period as one during which many such schemes and ideas were discovered. During
the twentieth century juristic speculation became a fully-fledged professional activity, and those engaged in this profession—like the glossators of the early European
law schools with their reverence for the *Corpus Iuris Civilis*—generally conceived
their task to be one of honouring the past. That twentieth-century legal scholars
should have gone about their business thus is entirely understandable. History—and
fairly recent history at that—had a great deal to teach them about the conceptualization of law; it would have been strange had they not looked to the past for inspirational
ideas and agenda. Nor should the general absence of grand discoveries throughout
this period be mistaken for unoriginality. Twentieth-century legal scholars tended to
run with the ideas of their forebears, but this is not to say that they never arrived
anywhere interesting.

Earlier versions of this chapter were presented at the law schools of the Universities of Minnesota,
Virginia, and Wisconsin. Besides being grateful for feedback to participants at those events, I am also
indebted to Brian Bix and Martin Loughlin for comments on earlier drafts. The inferences to be drawn
from these signals should be obvious.

The basic purpose of this chapter is to identify and consider the principal destinations of these scholars. It focuses primarily on developments in legal studies since 1960 in the United States and England (meaning England specifically, rather than the United Kingdom). As regards the United States, legal scholarship of the first half of the twentieth century forms an important backdrop to what happened during the second half of the century, and so it is almost inevitable that there is contextual work to be undertaken. English legal scholarship of the first half of the twentieth century has received less attention, perhaps because the study of law there remained—certainly in comparison with developments in the United States—a fledgling professional activity until after World War II. That law as an academic discipline was slow to evolve in England does not mean that nothing of interest could have occurred there during the first half of the twentieth century. The difficulty is, certainly for the purposes of an essay such as this one, that hardly anything systematic occurred during this period: early twentieth-century English legal studies seemed largely to hang on to the coat-tails of the great Victorian jurists, to whom most early twentieth-century English legal scholars were resolutely deferential. And so, in general terms, 1960 is perhaps a fair point at which to take up the story of English legal studies in the twentieth century.

There run throughout this chapter a number of arguments. In the next section, some of these arguments are developed with regard to legal scholarship in the United States. The rather unimaginative yet almost unavoidable starting-point is legal realism, which is regarded as significant primarily for the responses it evoked rather than the propositions it supported. From there, we offer various local, low-key observations on the ways in which legal studies have developed in the United States in the wake of legal realism. Besides noting the principal juristic tendencies to have emerged in the United States during the twentieth century, we also note the main characteristics of American academic-legal inquiry. What is especially noticeable is the extent to which American juristic culture has emphasized originality and counter-intuitiveness, and how, in the quest to exhibit these qualities, American legal academics—much as they often purport to behave otherwise—have tended increasingly to value legal scholarship by how visible and in vogue it happens to be.

In England, which is the primary focus of Section 3, the style is different. Late-twentieth-century English legal scholarship has not evolved against a backdrop of intense juristic activity and ambition—there is no danger of modern English legal scholars being eclipsed by an earlier generation of jurists, because that earlier generation hardly existed. In so far as that generation did exist, furthermore, it was itself largely overshadowed by the achievements of Austin, Maine, Maitland, Dicey, Pollock, and various other jurists of the Victorian era. The beginnings of modern English juristic identity can be dated to around the start of the 1960s—the publication of H. L. A. Hart's *The Concept of Law* symbolizes the inception of the modern period, even if it is not a definitive starting-point. *The Concept of Law* remains an influential text to this day, and charting the evolution of modern English jurisprudential thought is largely an exercise in identifying the reactions that the book elicited. Understanding English theoretical legal scholarship also demands an appreciation of the fact that, during the later stages of the twentieth century, it assimilated some of the trends which had emerged or were emerging in the United States. 'Socio-legal studies', as it developed in England, may have owed much to Eugen Ehrlich and other Continental pioneers of the sociology of law, but it was also indebted to the sociological jurisprudence of Roscoe Pound; English enthusiasm for economic analysis of law was inspired in the main by Coase, Calabresi, and Posner; and the most visible strand of critical legal scholarship to emerge in England, although primarily inspired by Continental European philosophy, to some extent paralleled the deconstructivist dimension of that movement as it evolved in the United States. Legal studies in England become more intriguing when one shifts away from theoretical initiatives and focuses on traditional doctrinal scholarship, which, whatever its pitfalls and limitations, remains the English academic lawyer's preferred form of inquiry.

2

American legal realism is the great enigma of twentieth-century jurisprudence. Throughout the twentieth century, English law students have, as a matter of course, studied something called 'American legal realism' on the jurisprudence syllabus. But the concoction that tends to be served up—usually a mixture of themes from Oliver Wendell Holmes, Roscoe Pound, Karl Llewellyn, and Jerome Frank—is hardly more authentic than spaghetti from a tin. The concoction can be quite easily explained. Within the British context, the great antithesis of realism has been not formalism but positivism: realism, that is, has been presented as offering an alternative perspective on the value and purpose of legal rules—an inferior perspective, indeed, since realist rule-scepticism turns out to be a weak position to take once it is conceded that many rules are of the power-conferring variety. As Hart explained, although 'rule-scepticism ... can make a powerful appeal to a lawyer's candour ... the assertion that there are decisions of courts cannot consistently be combined with the denial that there are any rules at all', since 'the existence of a court entails the existence of secondary rules conferring jurisdiction on a changing succession of individuals and so making their decisions authoritative' (Hart, 1994: 136). Within the modern English jurisprudential tradition, legal realism has served admirably as a stooge—a rather ironic state of affairs, considering that the most ambitious, subtle, and sympathetic study of realism to be produced during the twentieth century was the work of an Englishman (Twining, 1973).

The expectation, of course, is that we might look to the United States to find legal realism subjected to better treatment. And at a certain level the expectation is fulfilled. American academic lawyers of the twentieth century showed how realism connected with the social sciences, the New Deal, pragmatism, the economic credo of the *Lochner* court, the Langdellian revolution, and more. All American law professors seem to have within them, even if they have not typed it up, an essay entitled 'American Legal Realism and What it Means to Me'. One consequence of this is that legal realism is not the intriguing jurisprudential topic that it once was: an American legal academic without a perspective on legal realism is as improbable as an American legal academic without a word processor. Trying to offer a profound insight on the subject is rather like trying to say something insightful about a major sporting event: anyone who does not care does not count, and anyone who does care is an expert.

Perhaps this is inevitable. American law professors seem to have created among themselves the expectation that they never be short of an opinion on more or less anything. Journals and workshops, particularly at the major law schools, are full of genuinely bright sparks striving to be original, even though most American law professors seem—with good reason—to regard originality as a rare commodity. In this context, the quest for originality usually means trying to move forward, to extend research horizons, to develop new ideas, projects, even movements. Looking back at legal realism, even looking back with revisionist aspirations, is likely, in this brave new world, to appear quaint and outmoded. Perhaps, then, we should draw a veil over legal realism, concluding that it is a subject that invites banality, that there can be nothing particularly new or interesting to say about it.

The problem, however, is that there are still elements of the realist jurisprudential tradition that appear to have been neither satisfactorily explored nor explained. For a better understanding of twentieth-century legal studies, indeed, it might be the case that we should be exploring a number of questions relating to realism.

First, there is the simple if not trite question of whether there is much more to be gained from examining the history of realism. In-depth studies of particular realist figures, for example, have sometimes provided interesting insights into mid-twentieth-century American jurisprudential culture; and, while the most important work of this type has probably already been done, there remain a number of curiosities who perhaps deserve scrutinizing. One example would be Wesley Sturges, dean at the Yale Law School during the 1940s and 1950s and author of some of the most uncompromising, indeed nihilistic, doctrinal critique of the realist era.

Secondly, there is a question of jurisprudential objectives. Within the European tradition, legal philosophers have been concerned by and large with the notion of legal validity. European positivists, for example, have been concerned primarily with demonstrating that the validity of law does not depend, or depends only minimally, upon the moral content of law. Also of concern to these positivists has been the relationship between validity and efficacy: although laws will usually be effective as well as valid, Kelsen and others have contended, the validity of law is something more than its effectiveness. Within the American tradition, realist jurists—the label 'legal philosopher' seems inappropriate to many of them—have tended to be concerned with the effectiveness rather than with the validity of law. Although the question of what makes for legal validity is crucial to constitutional law scholarship (and indeed constitutional adjudication) in the United States, the question never seemed particularly to interest realist jurists. Formally valid laws, after all, can be ineffective: that a particular law is valid does not mean that citizens, or even courts, will necessarily follow it.

This was hardly a unique realist insight. Holmes had intimated in 'The Path of the Law' that the so-called bad man might consult his lawyer for advice on whether it may be advantageous to disobey a valid law—'how strongly', this man seems to be asking, 'might the state come down on me if my disobedience is detected?' During the late nineteenth and early twentieth centuries, Holmes's Supreme Court brethren demonstrated—often quite ruthlessly—that the fact that a statute had been passed did not guarantee its being treated as a valid law: such treatment depends on how the Court approaches the task of constitutional adjudication. The disjunction between validity and efficacy was further noted by American lawyer-economists of the 1960s and 1970s who, inspired by seminal studies of the economics of punishment (see e.g. Becker, 1968), attempted to demonstrate that the valid laws which deter crime in an optimal fashion are those which impose high penalties but entail low levels of monitoring. Throughout twentieth-century American legal studies, the separation of validity and efficacy was never really a source of controversy.

Legal realism, however, did cause controversy. Why? The vilification that legal realism received in certain quarters during the second half of the twentieth century seemed to stem from the view that so-called realists regarded the limitations of legal rules as a cause for celebration. Yet realism seems largely to have been an exercise in telling it as it is. Law in action is a very different phenomenon from law in books, and judges, in the process of decision-making, will often be guided primarily by their instincts or preferences rather than by established rules—these and other observations, so-called realists seemed to be saying, are not endorsements but merely statements about how things really are. When various twentieth-century commentators on the realist tradition observed that many so-called realists never truly escaped the clutches of legal formalism, they were missing the point. The fact that Thurman Arnold, as head of the Antitrust Division, ensured that antitrust rules worked fairly effectively, or that Jerome Frank, as a judge on the Second Circuit, disliked juries because '[t]o comprehend the meaning of many a legal rule requires special training' (Frank, 1949: 116) does not mean that either renounced their realist roots. For it appears never to have been a realist tenet that rules cannot work as they are supposed to work, only that rules often do not work as they are supposed to work.

Those who failed to heed this last message were, not surprisingly, keen in the main to denigrate the realist tradition. Whether the more extreme opponents of realism—those who detected in realism a disdain for the rule of law—were ever taken seriously seems doubtful. During the second half of the twentieth century, however, at least two responses to realism were especially noteworthy.

The first was what we might term the process jurisprudence response. For representatives of process jurisprudence, legal realism problematized adjudication; but to the problem these representatives had a solution. The proper way to decide cases was neither to be completely bound by rules nor to improvise according to instinct, but to be guided by appropriate principles. By articulating and elaborating principles, judges render themselves accountable, determine rights, provide future courts and commentators with a plot upon which to build, and reduce the likelihood of bias. 'I put it to you that the main constituent of the judicial process is precisely that it must be genuinely principled,' Wechsler wrote in 1959, 'resting with respect to every step that is involved in reaching judgment on analysis and reasons quite transcending the immediate result that is achieved' (Wechsler, 1959: 15).

To see this glorification of principle simply as a response to legal realism would, of course, be wrong. Realism, after all, did not unequivocally endorse judicial activism. Some realists did offer such endorsement, and process jurisprudence was in part a reaction to realist-inclined judges—William O. Douglas is the obvious example—who fell into this category. But other realists—particularly those who had lamented the Supreme Court's social-Darwinist reading of freedom of contract into the US Constitution—could see only too well that activism is a double-edged sword. Whereas this latter group of realists recognized and analysed the problem, representatives of the process tradition tried to solve it.

Process jurisprudence would become especially significant in the second half of the twentieth century not because of the responses that it offered but because of the responses that it provoked. Most of these responses, as is well known, revolve around the jurisprudential project of Ronald Dworkin, who, in developing his notion of law as integrity, faced head-on the key problem highlighted by opponents of the process tradition—that of resolving conflicts of principle (see Dworkin, 1986: 176–275). Many of these responses also highlight just how much the American jurisprudential project changed throughout the twentieth century. Whereas the realists were trying to describe how judges really decide cases, representatives of the process school were making claims about how judges ought ideally to decide cases.

By the end of the twentieth century, claims that courts ought to seek fearlessly to root out and elaborate the best available principles were being attacked not because they were considered incoherent but because they were considered to be the wrong type of exhortation. Extensive deliberation about best possible principles, argued one law professor who grew up in the shadow of the process tradition, is likely to prove time consuming, possibly even divisive, for multi-member decision-making bodies; perhaps the better judicial strategy is to try to eschew deliberative ambition and extensive quests for principle (Sunstein, 1999). Other American law professors went further still, questioning the value of any normative jurisprudential agenda (see e.g. Schlag, 1996).

One of the reasons that the legal process tradition endured is that it was very much a jurisprudence of constitutional adjudication. A striking feature of American legal scholarship to many an outsider is the intense preoccupation of American legal academics with constitutional law. While one often senses that a good deal of American constitutional law scholarship represents the height of normative redundancy—student notes suggesting how the Supreme Court might best interpret the Fifth Amendment, and so on—this preoccupation is not particularly puzzling. The counter-majoritarian implications of constitutional adjudication—classically identified by Learned Hand in his Holmes Lectures of 1958—have ensured that American academic lawyers have been at pains to show that the Supreme Court is more than that dreaded third legislative chamber in which judges give effect to their preferences when reviewing administrative action. The process tradition in American jurisprudence was an attempt to allay this fear of judicial supremacy, as indeed have been most of the constitutional law theories—originalism, textualism, translationism, civic republicanism, and so on—which have evolved throughout the twentieth century.

Parenthetically, we might observe that the most interesting question to be asked about constitutional law scholarship at the beginning of the twenty-first century is how it will evolve not in the United States but in Europe. The elaboration of a European constitution—whereby countries and regions retain everyday self-government but vest responsibility for defence, foreign policy, protection of human rights, currency, and other common interests in a higher federal authority—will be, indeed is already, a task for legal theorists. There are likely to be few lessons that these theorists will draw from US constitutional history and jurisprudence, since constitutionalism in the European context is not, primarily, about constitutional adjudication, but about the difficulties of solving conflicts between member state constitutions and the European legal order. Indeed, the British—and in this context it seems necessary to use 'British' as opposed to 'English'—debate over constitutionalism in the European context has for the past thirty years revolved in the main around the implications of EU membership and the supremacy of EC law for parliamentary sovereignty. It will be interesting to see just how legal theorists conceptualize Europe in the twenty-first century. One would hardly be going out on a limb in predicting that this is an area in which a good deal of innovative jurisprudence will evolve.

Returning to the United States, if one response to legal realism was to vilify it, and another, the legal process response, was to try to render it less of a worry, the final response was to regard it with a general air of indifference. The most popular articulation of this response—which it seems fair to attribute to Richard Posner—has it that legal realism can be credited with nothing original, since so-called realist insights on the nature of adjudication and legal rules are actually attributable to Holmes and other pragmatists, and the decline of law as an autonomous discipline was prompted not by realism but primarily by the law and economics movement during the 1960s. The generality of pragmatism means that many ideas and movements might plausibly be traced to it. Legal theorists as diverse as Posner, Margaret Radin, and Jules

Coleman all claim to be pragmatists (though by no means pragmatists of the same stripe), and even realism might be presented as but an instance of pragmatist jurisprudence. Pragmatism has clearly been massively influential on many facets of twentieth-century life, and to find academic lawyers identifying with one or another pragmatist agenda is only to be expected. More intriguing is the fact that pragmatism clearly permits of more than one agenda. Politically, pragmatism attaches importance to civil liberties and tolerance and to experimentation in the discussions and institutions that shape social arrangements; methodologically, it emphasizes open-mindedness and debate in the sciences, humanities, and arts; philosophically, it opposes the idea that knowledge can be grounded on absolute foundations (see Kramer, 1999a: 94). American jurists have been variously committed to each of these agenda: Coleman's pragmatism, for instance, is rigorously philosophical (see Coleman, 2001: 6), while Posner argues that what has proved especially valuable to judges is pragmatism as an attitude rather than as a philosophy (see R. Posner, 1999: 240–2). For many American legal academics, and no doubt many others, pragmatism has been an angle for all seasons.

The argument that legal realism was eclipsed by pragmatism during the twentieth century is largely attributable to the belief that, as between these two perspectives, pragmatism is the more expansive and accommodating. The argument that legal realism was eclipsed during the same period by economic analysis is premised on the belief that law and economics delivered the interdisciplinary ethos that so-called realists never pushed much beyond the planning stage.

Interdisciplinarity is a difficult theme to assess within the context of twentieth-century American legal studies. There is certainly a danger, in considering the theme, of unduly denigrating what American academic lawyers have achieved. The fact is that the imaginativeness, particularly the capacity for lateral thinking, demonstrated by some American jurists with interdisciplinary leanings has often been an inspiration for legal academics based outside the United States and frustrated by what they consider to be the narrowness of focus pervading their own juristic cultures. But it is also a fact that during the latter decades of the twentieth century, it became possible to detect—it still is possible to detect—an astonishing amount of cross-disciplinary chutzpah in the American law reviews. American law professors, one commentator observed almost forty years ago, are remarkably willing and confident to wander into disciplinary domains within which they have no professional training (Bergin, 1968). Nothing has changed. Think of a theory or philosophy—phenomenology, chaos theory, Taoism, whatever—and the likelihood is that somewhere there is a law review carrying an article purporting to apply it to law in some way or another. A law professor with no formal qualifications in philosophy might undertake a project of remarkable philosophical ambition and publish it in a journal edited by individuals who not only are equally unlikely to have any philosophical qualifications but who have yet to become qualified in law. By the 1980s, if not before then, this tendency of many law professors to wander unself-consciously into other disciplinary domains was beginning to demoralize many of their doctrinally oriented colleagues, who felt that regular black-letter scholarship was being undervalued: it seemed that law professors had an incentive to neglect that body of knowledge over which they had some expertise and begin professing on matters about which they had little or no expertise. Many an American law professor articulated this sense of demoralization, but it required a judge to make the point (see Edwards, 1992) before it began to surface as regularly in the American law reviews as it did in the faculty lounges.

Plenty of commentary appeared in the later stages of the twentieth century denouncing self-indulgence in the American law reviews—denouncing, in some instances, the institution of the student-edited law review itself. The general argument had some resonance to it (notwithstanding that it was often made within the pages of student-edited law reviews!): student editors rarely have the training or experience to determine what makes for good interdisciplinary scholarship, and will often (usually through the addition of footnotes) increase the length of an already over-long article when they should really be urging excision. However compelling this argument may sometimes appear, however, it tends, for at least three reasons, to have a distorting effect.

First of all, part of the complaint about the student-edited law journal is that it eschews that guarantor of good scholarship that most other disciplines take for granted: peer review. Leaving aside the question of whether peer review guarantees the publication of the best work submitted—while it often will do, various studies (see e.g. Cole *et al.*, 1981) indicate that it sometimes will not—the fact is that a form of peer review is widely used by American law professors nowadays. One variant of a recent trend in American legal scholarship—social norms theory—has it that by cooperating with others and conforming to social norms we are sending out the signal that we belong, as it were, to the good type (E. Posner, 2000). American lawyers have generally acquired the habit of sending out early versions of their research to colleagues for feedback before seeking to publish, and nowadays it is unusual for an article not to carry an opening footnote acknowledging a list of academics for comments on earlier drafts. The obvious point about such footnotes is that they usually send out a positive signal about the academic company that one keeps and one's willingness to be appraised by one's peers: one improves one's prospects of belonging to the good academic type by sending out one's work to, and acknowledging the help of, other academics (preferably recognized names) engaged in similar projects. The process is not tantamount to conventional peer review: there is no anonymity—if there were, the value of signalling the circulation of earlier drafts would diminish significantly—and publication does not depend on addressing the objections of those who have provided comments. Something akin to peer review is being undertaken in such instances, all the same. The most interesting question here—and the one to which it is most difficult to formulate an answer—is why American law professors are nowadays so committed to this signalling strategy whereas forty or so years ago they were not. A charitable answer would be that these professors have become more courteous, or at least more publicly courteous, than their forebears. A far less charitable answer would be that many of these modern professors seem as if drenched by a wave of self-doubt.

The second problem with the general argument about law review self-indulgence is that the law reviews do not accurately reflect interdisciplinary initiatives in the law schools themselves. Many of the best law schools have reputations and pay salaries that attract renowned political scientists, literary theorists, philosophers, and other exotica. One particularly dynamic law professor (trained in law, but also with a doctorate in English) appeared to spend the 1990s studying notions such as humiliation, disgust, cowardice, and courage. Law professors with non-legal research agenda generally have little incentive, and so tend not, to publish much in law reviews. Their presence on American law faculties seems indicative of how the American law school displays some of the characteristics of Luhmann's cognitively open but normatively closed autopoietic system (see Luhmann, 1987). The system of American legal scholarship, that is, processes the 'energy' generated within a wider environment— generated by other disciplines—and uses it to reproduce itself: law as an academic discipline evolves, in other words, largely by extracting resources (data, theories, even the occasional academic) from other disciplines and using those resources to its own ends. Law gathers in a great deal from other disciplines—more than is reflected in the American law reviews—though it seems unlikely that many of these other disciplines, certainly throughout most of the twentieth century, gathered in all that much from law.

Not that there has been a complete absence of symbiosis. The third problem with the argument about law review self-indulgence is that it shines the spotlight away from those American law journals that are genuinely interdisciplinary and peer reviewed. That curious movement called 'law and society' spawned one such journal, the *Law and Society Review*, in the mid-1960s. One of the interesting characteristics of the law and society movement—as the contributions to the journal have always made clear—is that it has endeavoured to emulate the academic projects and norms of the wider social sciences: law and society scholars have never seemed interested in fitting into—and seem, indeed, never really to have fitted into—the academic-legal mainstream in America. Certainly some of their lessons—about the dynamics of litigation (see e.g. Galanter, 1974), say, or the marginal significance of legal remedies for the purpose of ensuring compliance with contractual terms (see e.g. Macaulay, 1963)— have resonated (if only, at times, superficially) with American law professors. But generally the law and society movement has marched to the beat of its own drum, remaining doggedly empirical throughout a period when American legal academics became increasingly attracted to abstract theorization. It is sometimes the case with certain film directors, musicians, and other artists that they are widely recognized to be technically accomplished and impressive, but for one reason or another they are simply not fashionable. Within American legal scholarship, the law and society movement holds a similar status: much of the research, particularly that showing how the operation of law is very different from what one would expect were one only to study the law itself, has been impressive and important. But for some reason—perhaps because most law and society scholars have been happy to be 'out there', doing sociology, distanced from mainstream American legal scholarship with all its trends and fads—its contributions to legal understanding have been undervalued.

The achievements of the law and society movement have been steady and un-spectacular; yet when we look back over what that movement achieved during the second half of the twentieth century, it seems fair to say that it moved beyond that planning stage which represented the pinnacle of the realist interdisciplinary project. While Richard Posner may, as we noted earlier, have been indifferent to legal realism, he recognized that the law and society movement has played a significant if under-estimated role in modern American legal studies (see R. Posner, 1999: 212–15). For Posner and many others, however, the main interdisciplinary achievement of twen-tieth-century American legal studies is certainly not law and society—that distinc-tion belongs instead to the law and economics movement.

Part of Chicago law and economics folklore has it that the movement was, during its early days, considered the 'lunatic fringe' of American legal studies. Were this ever really the case, then the relentless rise to power and growth in influence of the law and economics ethos would—particularly given that some of its detractors have publicly prayed for its death—make a particularly heroic story. It seems more likely, however, that law and economics sat comfortably with many academic lawyers more or less from its inception. Economic analysis provides legal academics with almost instant perspectives—rarely is it regarded with indifference, and over the past forty years it has stimulated various styles of scholarship, from advanced game theory applied to law to uncompromising polemics against the notion of wealth-maximization. Those within the mainstream tend to ignore what they believe to be lunatic fringes, but lawyer economists were listened to from the moment they started to popularize Aaron Director's line on antitrust. Even the famous article contemplating a partially deregulated market in adoptions (Landes and Posner, 1978) was recognized by its critics to be an important and challenging piece of work. Law and economics may have been widely disliked, but it has never been widely regarded as crackpot.

A good deal of modern law and economics scholarship would not look out of place in microeconomics journals. Indeed, the research published in the major law and economics journals is as often the work of economists as it is of lawyers. Much of the research seems to speak only to the already converted. Anyone who receives the many series of law and economics workshop papers delivered electronically by the Legal Scholarship Network will know how formulaic the titles to those papers can be, and how interchangeable their contents can sometimes seem. Not that we should be dis-missive: law and economics is a highly active subdiscipline which has advanced our general understanding of many legal issues. The interesting question is that of how the development of this subdiscipline has affected the general direction of modern legal studies.

The guiding impulse behind law and economics is counter-intuitiveness. Law and economics is not the only legal research agenda to have placed a premium on counter-intuitive claims, but is surely the one which has done so most relentlessly and successfully. Over and again, lawyer-economists want to warn us that things are not as they might at first appear. The tone was set by the work of an American-based Englishman, published at the beginning of the 1960s (Coase, 1960). The so-called Coase theorem simultaneously appeals to and offends against basic juristic sensibilities. The theorem offers the academic lawyer the prospect of interdisciplinarity without tears: here is a form of economics which, unlike much economic theory, is both comprehensible and relevant to many academic lawyers and which can be entered into without the requirement of any distinct disciplinary expertise (such as an understanding of sophisticated economic models or of complex mathematical reasoning). Coasian economics appeals to theoretically inclined academic lawyers not only because of the insights that it offers but also because it is easily assimilated into the sorts of discourse that many of them produce.

Academic lawyers are often fascinated by the Coase theorem, however, not because they find it persuasive but because it seems to them to be alien. Part of the problem is that legal academics sometimes perceive the theorem to diminish the significance of law within the process of dispute resolution. One of the insights of the theorem, after all, is that the importance of legal rules for the purpose of remedying disputes regarding rights and entitlements will in effect be eradicated where transaction costs are not so high as to deter disputing parties from negotiating for themselves a more efficient allocation of resources. Not that academic lawyers always consider application of the theorem to result in an undervaluation of legal rules: indeed, one of the most innovative twentieth-century works in law and economics suggests that Coase actually exaggerates the potential influence of law (see Ellickson, 1991).

Perhaps the greater problem that academic lawyers have had with the Coase theorem is its failure to connect causation and responsibility. Lawyers do not, by and large, treat causation and responsibility as synonymous—that somebody causes my business to fail by setting up in competition with me, for example, does not mean that they will be held legally responsible for my downfall. None the less, lawyers do not generally treat the two concepts as wholly distinct: often, they recognize, one ought to be legally responsible for harms which one causes. Yet Coase appears not to accept the common law notion of causation as a means of assigning responsibility. That someone 'causes' a nuisance (as determined by common law principles) does not, in his view, imply the efficiency of holding that person liable. If sparks from the railroad engine start a fire in the woods, one ought not simply to conclude that the railway has caused the fire; rather, in determining with whom responsibility for preventing such accidents should rest, one might, among other things, ask whether the social cost of cutting down trees near the railway tracks would be less than the cost of installing new safety devices in railroad engines (the assumption here being, of course, that positive transaction costs require an allocation of legal rights for efficiency purposes).

This manner of thinking does not really work for lawyers, especially when they attempt to apply it to areas other than tort. When you punched me in the face, is it correct to characterize the incident thus, or was it more reciprocal than that: was I somehow at fault for making my face available to be punched? Coase, of course, is concerned specifically with the reciprocal nature of social costs in relation to incompatible forms of land use. Lawyers, however, tend to conceive of such reciprocity problems not as an economist might conceive of them—as problems, that is, of determining the least costly harm and of deciding, on that basis, who should be allowed to harm whom—but as legal problems. Conceived thus, such problems require that one attends to the issue of causation. Coase, however, is not interested in causation; his reasoning is not legal reasoning.

After Coase, the counter-intuitive impulse spread throughout American law and economics and, indeed, throughout American legal scholarship generally. Whereas law professors of the realist era wanted to show how things really were, many law professors writing in the aftermath of law and economics have wanted to show that 'how things really are' is often very different from how they may appear to be. Indeed, trying to show that things are not as one would expect them to be became, during the closing decades of the twentieth century, a dominant scholarly strategy within the American law schools. Consider, as an illustration of the point, the development of 'cyberlaw' scholarship. That legal study of the Internet should have flourished over the past two decades is hardly surprising. Equally unsurprising, however, is the fact that 'cyberlaw' scholarship is generally counter-intuitively oriented. Two of the most popular legal books on the subject, books authored by lawyers with connections to the Chicago law and economics tradition, endeavour to show that, contrary to expectations, the Internet accommodates rather than defies regulation (Lessig, 1999) and that, again contrary to expectations, increased reliance on the Internet, particularly on its capacity as an information-filtering device, might lead many citizens to become insulated from those with different concerns, experiences, and opinions from themselves—such insulation having potentially damaging consequences for democratic deliberation (Sunstein, 2001). In short, 'cyberlaw' scholarship typifies the American taste for a counter-intuitive argument.

Also in the ascendancy during the last decades of the twentieth century were a number of jurisprudential perspectives which, in one way or another, posed a challenge to mainstream juristic values. Feminist jurisprudence and critical legal studies were crucial to this general development, and it seems odd, at the beginning of the twenty-first century, to find that both of these movements have failed to capitalize on their early momentum to the degree that might have been expected. Feminist legal scholarship has by no means become irrelevant within the American law schools, nor is it the case that there has been an exhaustion of challenging and original research agenda. Such scholarship has scored some notable successes—in areas such as affirmative action, sexual harassment, maternity rights, and pornography—and the reason that it seems to have become less visible by the end of the twentieth century may be largely due to the fact that so many of its lessons have been absorbed. But there is also a sense in which American feminist legal scholarship seems to have become a victim of its own success: such work is nowadays more often than not to be found in the various American journals of law and feminism, a consequence of which is that the enterprise itself has become not just less visible but more insular.

With critical legal studies, the problem is rather different. It has been suggested already here that legal realism was, at various points throughout the twentieth century, vilified, treated as a solvable problem, and ignored. It was also—and perhaps this should be classed as another significant response to the realist project—considered inspirational. Critical legal scholarship took the realist lesson about indeterminacy in judicial decision-making and overtly politicized it: of course the realists were right to draw attention to the fact that adjudication is a matter of instinct, so the argument went, but it is just as important to recognize that those instincts are political—that deciding according to 'hunch', or whatever we want to call it, is the way in which judges make the law represent their political preferences. Critical legal scholars, as well as feminist and critical race theorists (although these last two groups were perhaps understandably less keen regularly to declare their indebtedness to dead white males), also politicized the realist lesson about the oxymoronic status of freedom of contract: of course the realists were correct to point out that freedom of contract is freedom of the economically powerful to coerce the economically weak into accepting their contractual terms; but again, so the argument went, the politics of this insight ought to be spelled out and elaborated. Freedom, in this context, is the freedom of one group of private citizens to use its position of advantage to restrict the opportunities of others—thus it is that we find the rich governing the poor, men governing women, whites governing minorities. And when courts refuse to interfere with such freedoms, when they preserve what is invariably a far from neutral status quo, they are making political choices.

The politicization of realist insights by critical legal scholars made for heady reading. But then, in its early days, critical legal studies generally made for heady reading. To return to early critical legal studies literature is to smell cordite—this movement, with its samizdat newsletters, its proclaimed distaste for hierarchy, and its explicit alignment with the politics of the left, was genuinely on the fringe. Movements of this type invariably suffer burn-out, and it seems ironic that when one of the movement's principal representatives eventually produced a highly ambitious and carefully thought-out critique of legal decision-making (Kennedy, 1997), many of the reviews and responses—even the reviews and responses of scholars sympathetic to the critical legal agenda—considered it not as an effort to develop a systematic critical jurisprudence but as an occasion to reflect on the critical legal project as an exercise in either spent or inauthentic radicalism.

The conclusion that critical legal studies did burn out—that it withered for want of an enduring agenda, or whatever—may be unhelpful in more ways than one. First, what seems to matter most about critical studies is the manner of its life, not the circumstances of its decline: critical legal studies not only offered insightful and controversial arguments about liberalism, rights, legal education, adjudication, and politics, but developed those arguments in ways that seemed new and powerful (and sometimes, of course, exasperating) to those who did not share the faith. Secondly, claims about burn-out count for little in the context of modern American legal studies, since it is exceptional to discover a jurisprudential perspective which does not, sooner or later, burn out. Even law and economics has periodically undergone substantial reinvention—the late twentieth century turn towards game theory, the marriage of economic analysis and behavioural psychology, the development of social norms jurisprudence, and so on—in order to keep its flame alive.

Thus it is that we find ourselves pulled towards a rather pessimistic conclusion. The phenomenon of burn-out evokes that image of fifteen minutes of fame: in the United States over at least the past two decades, various academic-legal perspectives have enjoyed periods of intense popularity before attention has generally shifted elsewhere. The fact is that there was a good deal of faddishness about American legal scholarship of the late twentieth century. This tendency to follow trends may be partly attributable to a lack of discernment and confidence on the part of many student editors, who, given their typical age and the brevity of their editorial tenure, are probably often insensitive to long-term scholarly trends and inordinately enthusiastic about research which draws upon theories, themes, and cultural referents which are popular right at this moment. Blaming the editors in this instance, however, is rather like shooting the messenger. What explains the fact that this type of scholarship is being produced in the first place?

One answer may be that too many law professors seeking tenure or fresh pastures are happy to produce the type of fashionable scholarship—complete with the cute title, the epigraphs, the fusion of high theory and popular culture, and so on—which, experience tells them, will appeal to the average editor of a major law review. Another answer—to revisit an earlier theme—seems to be that American academic lawyers, particularly at the best law schools, place upon themselves an immense burden to be original. Anyone who has sat through law school workshop presentations, witnessing law professors striving to be smart and audiences striving to be smarter, is likely to be aware of this. Scholarship offering collar-grabbing, counter-intuitive lessons is very much what is desired; and the more that scholars seek to produce such work, the more difficult it becomes to produce. One way in which some American law professors have dealt with this difficulty has been to seek out a readership with less demanding standards. Thus it is that more and more American legal academics seek audiences outside the academy. Consider, for example, the writing of 'trade books' and journalism on current issues of legal controversy. American academic lawyers have never been strangers to such writing, and there seems to be no doubt that it is often motivated by a genuine belief that academics have a duty to try to enlighten a wider audience and contribute to public affairs. But the simple point to be emphasized for our purposes is that, by the end of the twentieth century, such lawyers seemed to be producing more of this type of work than ever before.

It should not be assumed that grandiosity fatigue explains the burn-out of just about any late-twentieth-century American jurisprudential perspective. Some such perspectives seem as if designed to burn out. This would seem to be the case, for example, with the argument about the normative redundancy of legal scholarship. Academic lawyers can either ignore the argument or take it to heart. If they take it to heart, there is a simple yet (for any normative legal scholar) devastating message to be absorbed. Whether or not one heeds the message, it is one which does not open up any research agenda—one which can and sometimes seems to be endlessly repeated, but which not only needs little but allows for little elaboration. It is too early to tell whether the same might be true of the various forms of so-called outsider scholarship. Certainly many of these forms of scholarship seem thus far to have relied on theoretical manoeuvres which will bear only so much reiteration before they lose their shine. By no means, however, is this fated to happen. Gay-legal, latino, critical-race, and other outsider theories could acquire fresh impetus were they, for example, to evolve—as is by no means inconceivable—into ambitious empirical projects. Whether the term 'outsider scholarship' will continue to make sense during the twenty-first century is, of course, anybody's guess: as we all become more vulnerable, more alienated, more aware of the fact that somewhere in the world—and not necessarily at a safe distance—there are those who despise what we are, the proposition that we are all outsiders now will perhaps begin to resonate.

3

The major developments in the American law schools from the 1870s to the 1960s are well known and documented. The principal difference between England and the United States throughout this period is not that England had no similar developments; rather it is that England had very few law schools. The first professorship of English law may have been established at Oxford in 1758, but, two centuries later, membership of the Society of Public Teachers of Law (the United Kingdom's equivalent of the United States' Association of American Law Schools) only just exceeded 200. It was not until well into the second half of the twentieth century that the study of law began to develop significantly within the English universities.

Not that nothing at all happened in the first half of the century. Legal realism may never have become established in England during this period, but some of the most notable legal scholars of the time—figures such as Harold Laski, Ivor Jennings, and Otto Kahn-Freund—were at least partially inspired by realist and sociological jurisprudential concerns. Realism aside, furthermore, the great Victorian jurists had left their successors with a great deal to think about. What is especially notable about the Victorian jurisprudential legacy is how little its handful of inheritors was able to use it to their profit. By the 1940s, English jurisprudence was still dominated by Austinian positivism. Indeed, the main late-nineteenth- and early-twentieth-century jurisprudential initiatives seem to fall into three categories. First, there are numerous restatements of Austin: exemplary works are T. E. Holland's *Elements of Jurisprudence* (1880), W. W. Buckland's *Some Reflections on Jurisprudence* (1945), and the various jurisprudence treatises by the now long-forgotten Sheldon Amos. Secondly, there is the effort—attributable mainly to Paul Vinogradoff and (to a lesser extent) to Frederick Pollock—to establish historical and comparative jurisprudence as an enduring juristic project. The effort proved unsuccessful, and to this day the principal achievements of this tradition as developed in England belong to Henry Maine. Finally, there are those 'jurisprudence' books—often written by professors of jurisprudence—which dwell little upon legal philosophy but heavily upon the principal features of common law systems: works typical of this category are Pollock's *A First Book of Jurisprudence for Students of the Common Law* (1896), C. K. Allen's *Law in the Making* (1927), and A. L. Goodhart's *Essays in Jurisprudence and the Common Law* (1931). In short, late-nineteenth- and early-twentieth-century jurisprudence was uninspiring and basically moribund. Not until the intervention of yet another Englishman at the beginning of the 1960s did anything change.

Why did *The Concept of Law* have the impact that it did? Part of the reason may be that it was the right book for the era, as the study of law within universities and polytechnics began to expand. Academic lawyers looking to marry vocational and intellectual approaches to law could hardly have wished for a book which better combined serious philosophical analysis with down-to-earth doctrinal illustrations. The main reason for the book's success, however, is probably that it is simply a pleasure to read. Though it loses its momentum in the later chapters, the quality of writing is inspirational throughout; and the critique of the notion of habit for the purpose of explaining obedience to law, the distinguishing of habits from social rules, social from legal rules, primary from secondary rules, and the explication of the rule of recognition make for one of the high points of legal philosophy, so skilled is Hart at maintaining analytical rigour while retaining lightness of touch. During the 1970s and 1980s, there was something of a backlash against *The Concept of Law* in England. In some quarters, its author was more or less made to don jackboots: 'Hart follows squarely in the Austinian tradition of legal analysis', one particularly severe commentator insisted, 'and consequently endeavours both to steer the questions of existence and acceptance [of legal authority] away from the mirky [*sic*] clutches of the ignorant plebeian and simultaneously to reassert, without argument, the unity or hegemony of a governing or official elite, in the form of the legal personification of state power' (Goodrich, 1987: 49). As the century drew to a close, nevertheless, serious legal philosophers began to return to the book and appreciate afresh the quality and complexity of Hart's achievement.

'In the balmy days of the 1950s', Tony Honoré recalls, 'Hart was a central and I a peripheral figure in the movement called linguistic philosophy. The movement has since passed from fashion but lawyers can still learn much from it. Its adherents stressed that we should pay close attention to the way people speak and write. We repeated the salutary maxim that everything is what it is and is not something else' (Honoré, 1987: 88). The type of linguistic philosophy with which Hart and Honoré were concerned may well have lost much of its shine—though, as was indicated in the previous paragraph, analytical jurisprudence enjoyed a late-twentieth-century revival—but it is notable that linguistic philosophies of one brand or another have been the inspiration for various late-twentieth-century English jurisprudential projects. These later efforts at linguistics-based philosophy of law—poststructuralist jurisprudence and the semiotics of law are perhaps the two most obvious examples—never really captured the English jurisprudential imagination. There are at least two possible reasons for this: modern linguistics-based legal philosophy is not only highly technical, and therefore forbidding to the uninitiated, but is also often narrowly focused on semantics. Legal positivism, too, was to some degree concerned with such matters; but linguistics-based jurisprudence has been concerned with leaving behind 'basic' positivist exercises such as distinguishing being obliged and having an obligation, or considering the open-textured quality of 'no vehicles in the park', much as modern game-theoretic jurisprudence has been about progressing beyond the non-repeated prisoners' dilemma. The problem with this narrowness of focus has been that modern linguistics-based legal philosophy has offered no significant advance on, or revision of, positivist jurisprudence.

Within the English jurisprudential tradition, all critiques of legal positivism pale alongside that which has been developed by Ronald Dworkin—who, in England, has been accorded an identity somewhat different from that which he has in the United States (where he is considerably more than just a detractor from legal positivism). Late-twentieth-century English jurisprudence scholars—and their students—found little fault with Dworkin's claim that legal principles cannot be identified by anything akin to Hart's rule of recognition. Indeed, it was Hart himself, posthumously, who inspired a reappraisal of the Dworkinian critique (Hart, 1994: 238–76). Only at the end of the twentieth century did legal philosophers begin to develop robust defences of Hart against Dworkin (see e.g. Kramer, 1999b: 128–92).

Although it would be wrong to suggest that sociological concerns have never been of interest to English academic lawyers, jurisprudence in England has been influenced only minimally by the social sciences. 'Socio-legal studies' has thrived in areas such as corporate governance, family law, and criminal justice; but sociological jurisprudence has never really thrived at all. There are, inevitably, exceptions to this claim, but generally socio-legal scholarship has been practised and regarded in England as something distinct from jurisprudence. The principal area in which the two types of inquiry came head to head was critical legal studies. In so far as England ever developed a critical legal studies movement, it centred around a struggle between more sociologically minded legal theorists and legal philosophers inspired primarily by poststructuralism and deconstructivism. And in so far as this was a struggle to appropriate critical legal studies as a jurisprudential project, the latter group—as should be clear from a perusal of the British critical legal studies journal, *Law and Critique*—has been the more successful. Oddly enough, some of the most jurisprudentially intriguing questions of modern times—questions concerning the changing meaning of law, and the failure of legal theorists to reconceptualize law, in the face of evolving technologies of administrative and political governance—have been raised within the socio-legal tradition (see, in particular, Murphy, 1997).

In certain areas, legal studies in England have largely followed in the path of legal studies in the United States. To some extent this was the case with critical legal studies, though in truth English critical legal studies developed an identity distinct from its American correlate. Much the same is true of feminist legal studies in England, which, rather than having been painted into a corner, have become embedded in mainstream areas of legal scholarship such as health-care ethics, criminal justice, and human rights law. Whereas feminist legal scholarship in the United States seems to have moved inwards, in England it has generally moved outwards. Law and economics in England, however, is a somewhat different matter. Having emerged initially as a sub-field of the socio-legal studies movement, law and economics was employed, and is still employed, to good effect in fields such as competition law, social and economic regulation, and corporate governance. But the English tendency has been largely to replicate, rather than to develop variants on, what lawyer-economists achieved in the United States. Europe more generally is a different matter again: over the past ten or so years, there has emerged throughout Continental European countries not only considerable enthusiasm for the economic analysis of law, but also a good deal of legal-economic scholarship which, in terms of theoretical rigour and ambition, stands shoulder to shoulder with much of that which has been produced in the United States.

We have noted already how doctrinal legal scholars in the United States have sometimes felt demoralized and undervalued. Legal theorists, the sentiment seems to be, generally get the better breaks. Perhaps a similar pattern is emerging in England. Current research assessment norms encourage academics to place a premium upon scholarship with international visibility. Certain forms of doctrinal scholarship—often being jurisdictionally specific, often published by specialist law journals or publishers lacking international presence—are less likely than is theoretical work to straddle boundaries and establish international reputations for scholarly excellence. This is not true of all types of doctrinal work, obviously: international lawyers, along with specialists in areas such as comparative law, EU law, and environmental law will often produce scholarship, the significance of which transcends national boundaries. But many areas of law generate scholarship which, in the main, is relevant only to a specific legal system. The problem, for those working within such areas, is not only the lack of a supra-jurisdictional *lingua franca*. There is also a problem of audience. Legal theorists are often writing for one another, and have some notion of their audience, however esoteric it might be. Public international and EU lawyers, furthermore, tend not only to work within and write with the aim of being read by distinct academic-legal networks, but also benefit from a considerable degree of willingness on the part of relevant courts to take account of academic opinion. Within international law, for example, judicial resort to academic opinion is positively condoned: article 38(1)(d) of the Statute of the International Court of Justice permits the Court to apply 'the teachings of the most highly qualified publicists of the various nations, as the subsidiary means for the determination of rules of law'. Traditional black-letter English lawyers, however, might generally be less confident about finding an audience, or certainly a desired audience.

Throughout the twentieth century, English judges largely abided by a restrictive citation convention which operated so as to obscure any influence that academic commentators might have on judicial decision-making. Even as late as 1980 it is possible to find concern being expressed in the House of Lords over 'the dangers, well perceived by our predecessors but tending to be neglected in modern times, of placing reliance on textbook authority for an analysis of judicial decisions' (*Johnson v Agnew* [1980] AC 367, 395, per Lord Wilberforce). It is widely recognized that there has been change—that today's appellate judges are considerably more receptive to and willing to acknowledge academic opinion than was the case, say, forty years ago. But it is still the case that most academic commentary is unlikely to make an impression upon those whom the commentators would most like to impress. This is not to say that such commentary is useless: students often profit, for example, from reading good notes on important cases. As a scholarly enterprise, however, doctrinal commentary seems often to invite its own neglect. It would be inappropriate to pursue this matter further here, since it is addressed more carefully in Chapter 41. But we should at least note one basic point: that it is no longer realistic to assume—and it was not too long ago that many legal theorists did assume—that while theoretically oriented legal scholars are more often than not marginalized within the English law schools, their black-letter colleagues hold all the best cards. As in the United States, so too in England: certainly in the early decades of the twenty-first century it is, crudely speaking, the doctrinalists rather than the theorists whom we might anticipate feeling undervalued and demoralized within the university system.

The emphasis on counter-intuitiveness to which we drew attention in the United States appears not to be so pronounced in England. A good deal of doctrinal scholarship, for example, seems to be about asking for more: hence the case-note writer's familiar lament that the court did not dig deeper or tie up loose ends, that relevant legal sources were not considered, or that reasons adduced for decisions were insufficiently clear, elaborated, or compelling. This lament might itself be subjected to counter-intuitive appraisal. In judicial decision-making, more is not necessarily better: reasoning comes at a price. It may be the case that a court will do better to deal expeditiously with one dispute in order to ensure that it has time to attend to others. Perhaps it is not surprising that we should now and again find American jurists—with ingrained counter-intuitive instincts (and sometimes with experience in

practice or on the bench)—berating academic lawyers for theorizing about adjudication and second-guessing courts without taking account of the fact that judges are
often burdened by temporal constraints. One reason Dworkinian idealism struck a
chord in England may be that English academic lawyers so often express disappointment when judges fail to exhibit Herculean aspirations—when, for example, they do
not ask the questions and provide the reasoning that one would expect to be asked and
provided by the author of an incisive case note or article. For most of the twentieth
century English jurists seemed generally content to assume that, as regards judicial
reasoning, more will invariably be better. And for any English law graduate who never
had the benefit of a good comparative law tutor—which means, of course, the vast
majority of us—the terseness and formality of the opinions of the *Cour de Cassation*
and other major Continental European courts has tended to seem as strange and
incomprehensible as siestas or Roman traffic norms. How, we wonder, can other
systems cope with such odd practices? In particular, how can anyone assume the
integrity of the courts when judges seem so unwilling to elaborate principles?

The one area in which English academic lawyers have made a big issue of counter-
intuitiveness is that of rights: following very much in the footsteps of many of their
North American and Canadian counterparts, various academic lawyers based in
England have explored in a number of ways the proposition that ambitious schemes
for the enactment of fundamental rights do not necessarily bring the benefits that
might reasonably be expected of them. Much of this work is highly topical (see e.g.
Campbell *et al.*, 2001), often having as its primary point of focus the incorporation
of the European Convention of Human Rights into English law under the Human
Rights Act 1998. What is perhaps most intriguing about this body of work is how,
having evolved as an argument against orthodoxy, it has itself become the orthodoxy.
In short, it would be unusual today to find a human rights lawyer in an English law
school who was not, in one way or another, resolutely sceptical about rights discourse.
There is, perhaps, an easy explanation for this state of affairs. The phenomenon
of rights scepticism, having featured significantly in legal studies across the Atlantic
for at least the past three decades, is almost impossible to ignore. Any English academic lawyer seeking to run against the grain on the subject of individual rights would
probably do best to start from the premise that they matter fundamentally.

Counter-intuitive argumentation usually requires a good deal of self-confidence.
Law review culture in the United States tends to breed such argumentation, whereas
in England there has always been a tendency towards caution, indeed a widespread
suspicion of grandiose theorizing. Sometimes, this cautiousness can prove irksome.
During the last two decades of the twentieth century there evolved in England a tendency in certain quarters to develop projects which certainly hinted at imaginativeness and (now and again) cross-disciplinarity—sports law, law and art, law and
popular culture, and the like—but which usually turned out to be conventional
discussions of recognized legal categories (torts, contract, criminal justice, intellectual property, insurance law, and so on) as relevant to sport, art, film, or whatever.

In England, 'Law and' was not always such a disappointing category. In the 1970s and 1980s, there existed a genuine eagerness to connect law with something else—notwithstanding that the specifics of that 'something else' were rarely stable. Marxism was the most popular source of otherness, and although studies demonstrating the evils of law as an instrument of class oppression may have gone out of fashion, there was, twenty or so years ago, no denying the adventurous, visionary quality to arguments which had it that the withering away of law would change social consciousness so that law as it had existed would no longer be missed. Roberto Unger's great achievement—and the reason, one suspects, that his work became popular for a time among English legal theorists—was that he retained this style of argumentation but replaced an increasingly unfashionable Marxist vision with something more congenial: with non-alienated consciousness would come superliberalism.

The basic problem with grand visionary jurisprudence is much as it has ever been: that it entails a manner of conjecture which is impervious to reasoned counter-argument. Those who prefer their legal philosophy to be grounded in the here and now—who want to explain legal rights, or the validity of legal systems, or what makes for good judicial decision-making—may not accept, but are still unlikely to be able to disprove, the prognostications of the visionary; and since such prognostications are rarely susceptible to a hard-wired legal philosopher's criteria of proof, they are unlikely to hold his attention for very long.

Although visionary jurisprudence tended to occupy the margins of twentieth-century legal studies, something less grandiose but similarly motivated—predictivism—became central to Anglo-American juristic thought. We may have lost interest in prophesying the consequences of the withering away of the state apparatus, but more modest forms of ball-gazing—anticipating the consequences of, say, the increased availability of mediation or shifts to incentive-based regulatory schemes—are currently popular on both sides of the Atlantic. In this respect, a number of essentially American lessons—originating in the best-known works of Holmes and Coase—have made their mark upon English academic-legal consciousness.

But it is important not to overemphasize this point. Within the English juristic tradition, ambitious theoretical agenda have rarely taken root. Even economic analysis of law, a perspective which one might expect most English academic lawyers to consider congenial, has remained at the margins of this tradition. By and large, English legal scholarship has evolved rather like the English common law: instead of embracing grand systems and ideas, our tendency has been to approach the evolution of juristic thought in a fatalistic fashion. Rather than rely on one-size-fits-all theories, we prefer ad hoc solutions to local problems, and, if we are to place faith at all in general theoretical frameworks, we prefer those frameworks which have evolved and proved trustworthy over time (thus it is that so much modern constitutional law scholarship remains fundamentally Diceyan) rather than the ambitious schemes of some contemporary juristic innovator. Frederick Pollock exalted this juristic mindset at the beginning of the twentieth century: 'Our bent is not to think of ourselves as setting an example to the world, . . . but to take up the day's work . . . and handle it as best we may . . . [O]n the whole it is less likely to end in crushing disaster than the far-reaching ambition which lays out new worlds for itself, and thinks to build them by forcing the hand of Providence' (Pollock, 1904: 58–9). The mind-set remains very much in evidence throughout English legal studies to this day.

And so we do not find very much evidence in England of that preoccupation with originality and ambitious argumentation which is such a strong feature of American legal scholarship. Indeed, it is both notable and somewhat dispiriting that, over the past two decades, some of England's most original legal thinkers have sought out academic careers abroad. The lure of better academic resources elsewhere no doubt partially explains this drift. In this context, however, the idea of resource disparity can be exaggerated. Much has been made in the past, for example, of how English legal academics lack the research resources enjoyed by their counterparts in the United States. While this proposition seems in general to be true, there are a number of significant factors that militate against it. The proliferation of easily accessible academic websites and electronic databases, for example, means that increasingly we share the same library. And the surplus of certain resources in the United States is not necessarily to be envied. For example, although there are many more law journals in the United States than there are in England, to have one's work published in any other than the most prestigious of those journals is more or less to ensure that it will not be read. Most American academic lawyers probably stand less chance of being published in the very best American law journals than most English academic lawyers stand of being published in the very best English ones. It is nowadays probably the case, moreover, that one more easily finds a publisher for an academic-legal monograph in England than one does in the United States.

Although some of the differences as between legal scholarship in the United States and in England may be exaggerated, the fact is that many differences do exist. Contrasting cultures, professional priorities, and academic norms more or less guarantee as much. Legal studies in both systems seem to have become ever more specialized—hence the fondness of many academics within both systems for carving out new subdisciplines—but in England the objective of specialization has generally been to produce useful local knowledge of the type that Pollock would have commended, rather than to produce grand agenda or overarching frameworks. To put the point crudely, the English have preferred the microscope to the telescope, the Americans vice versa; both preferences can be commended, and both can be criticized.

It is tempting to ask to what extent English legal scholarship is likely to become more like legal scholarship in the United States. Certainly English academic lawyers increasingly asked this question about themselves over the second half of the twentieth century. That they should have done so is not surprising. The belief that England becomes ever more like America is a recognizably English belief anyway, and in the realm of legal scholarship it seems largely sustainable. During the twentieth century, as this chapter has attempted to show, English academic lawyers followed their American counterparts in developing critical legal, socio-legal, and (to a lesser degree) legal-economic agenda, even if the English usually brought to these projects some features of their own. We might wonder to what extent, during the twenty-first century, English academic lawyers will come to share the American obsession with visibility—with the ranking of law schools, with the number of times an article has been cited (or, to note the current obsession, downloaded), with the number of web hits yielded by one's name, and so on. The more interesting speculation, however, concerns not how much the English might come to emulate the Americans, but how much American legal scholarship will become oriented towards the rest of the world. Many of the principal legal dilemmas facing the United States today are international dilemmas. They are dilemmas, furthermore, in which the United States is fated to play a pivotal role. American legal scholarship will no doubt remain committed to its current main doctrinal, constitutional, and theoretical perspectives. But we might anticipate the emergence of another perspective. The twenty-first century, we might predict, will see many American law professors becoming ever more preoccupied by problems which are best described not as doctrinal or constitutional or theoretical, but global.

REFERENCES

Becker, G. (1968). 'Crime and Punishment: An Economic Approach', *Journal of Political Economy*, 76: 169–217.

Bergin, T. (1968). 'The Law Teacher: A Man Divided against Himself', *Virginia Law Review*, 54: 637–57.

Campbell, T., Ewing, K. D., and Tomkins, A. (eds.) (2001). *Sceptical Essays on Human Rights*, Oxford: Oxford University Press.

Coase, R. (1960). 'The Problem of Social Cost', *Journal of Law and Economics*, 3: 1–44.

Cole, S., Cole, J.R., and Simons, G. A. (1981). 'Chance and Consensus in Peer Review', *Science*, 214: 881–6.

Coleman, J. (2001). *The Practice of Principle: In Defence of a Pragmatist Approach to Legal Theory*, Oxford: Oxford University Press.

Dworkin, R. (1986). *Law's Empire*, London: Fontana.

Edwards, H. (1992). 'The Growing Disjunction between Legal Education and the Legal Profession', *Michigan Law Review*, 91: 34–78.

Ellickson, R. (1991). *Order without Law: How Neighbors Settle Disputes*, Cambridge, Mass.: Harvard University Press.

Frank, J. (1949). *Courts on Trial: Myth and Reality in American Justice*, Princeton: Princeton University Press.

Galanter, M. (1974). 'Why the "Haves" Come out Ahead: Speculation on the Limits of Legal Change', *Law and Society Review*, 9: 95–160.

Goodrich, P. (1987). *Legal Discourse: Studies in Linguistics, Rhetoric and Legal Analysis*, London: Macmillan.

Hart, H. L. A. (1994). *The Concept of Law* (2nd edn.; 1st edn. pub. 1961), Oxford: Clarendon Press.

Honoré, T. (1987). *Making Law Bind: Essays Legal and Philosophical*, Oxford: Clarendon Press.

Kennedy, D. (1997). *A Critique of Adjudication (fin de siècle)*, Cambridge, Mass.: Harvard University Press.

Kramer, M. (1999a). *In the Realm of Legal and Moral Philosophy: Critical Encounters*, Basingstoke: Macmillan.

—— (1999b). *In Defense of Legal Positivism: Law without Trimmings*, Oxford: Oxford University Press.

Landes, E., and Posner, R. (1978). 'The Economics of the Baby Shortage', *Journal of Legal Studies*, 7: 323–48.

Lessig, L. (1999). *Code, and Other Laws of Cyberspace*, New York: Free Press.

Luhmann, N. (1987). 'The Unity of the Legal System', in G. Teubner (ed.), *Autopoietic Law: A New Approach to Law and Society*, Berlin: De Gruyter, 12–35.

Macaulay, S. (1963). 'Non-contractual Relations in Business: A Preliminary Study', *American Sociological Review*, 28: 55–63.

Murphy, W. T. (1997). *The Oldest Social Science? Configurations of Law and Modernity*, Oxford: Clarendon Press.

Pollock, F. (1904). *The Expansion of the Common Law*, London: Stevens & Sons.

Posner, E. (1999). *Law and Social Norms*, Cambridge, Mass.: Harvard University Press.

Posner, R. (2000). *The Problematics of Moral and Legal Theory*, Cambridge, Mass.: Belknap Press.

Schlag, P. (1996). *Laying Down the Law: Mysticism, Fetishism, and the American Legal Mind*, New York: New York University Press.

Sunstein, C. (1999). *One Case at a Time: Judicial Minimalism on the Supreme Court*, Cambridge, Mass.: Harvard University Press.

—— (2001). *republic.com*, Princeton: Princeton University Press.

Twining, W. (1973). *Karl Llewellyn and the Realist Movement*, London: Weidenfeld & Nicolson.

Wechsler, H. (1959). 'Toward Neutral Principles of Constitutional Law', *Harvard Law Review*, 73: 1–35.

LAW AS AN AUTONOMOUS DISCIPLINE

BRIAN H. BIX

1 INTRODUCTION

THE 'autonomy of law' refers to a number of related but distinct claims: (1) that legal reasoning is different from other forms of reasoning; (2) that legal decision-making is different from other forms of decision-making; (3) that legal reasoning and decision-making are sufficient to themselves, that they neither need help from other approaches nor would they be significantly improved by such help; and (4) that legal scholarship should be about distinctively legal topics (often referred to as 'legal doctrine') and is not or should not be about other topics.

While there had been prominent advocates for the autonomy of law in the nineteenth and early twentieth centuries, the strong trend of recent decades has been away from seeing law as an autonomous discipline. The consensus in scholarly circles is that legal reasoning cannot be adequate without supplement, and that, in any event, law has much to learn from other disciplines, and has in fact been successful, at least in part, in adapting and adopting other forms of knowledge. If anything, there is now

I am grateful to Neil Duxbury, William A. Edmundson, and David McGowan for their comments and suggestions.

some risk that scholars will underestimate the autonomy of law—not give enough attention to what is specific to law and to legal reasoning. It remains valuable to focus on what is distinctive to law—that it is, in most legal systems, guidance through general rules; that it may involve an interaction of law-making and law-applying institutions (e.g. courts applying the rules passed by legislatures); and that (in common law systems) the application of rules will be done through a judicial system that both authorizes judicial law-making and has important rules of *stare decisis* (rules of hierarchy and rules about the way that later decisions are constrained by earlier decisions). All of these features may contribute to a form of reasoning that is distinctive, if not entirely autonomous.

A claim about the autonomy of law could be understood in three different ways: descriptively, analytically, and prescriptively. Descriptively, the question is what level of autonomy is assumed or encouraged by current practices within a particular legal system. The form of judicial reasoning and the approach to legal education within a community may be more or less autonomous. As has already been noted, and will be discussed in greater detail below, the general trend in both England and the United States, in both legal reasoning and legal education, has been *away from* legal autonomy, towards a more interdisciplinary approach. Analytically, the question is whether law, by its nature, either *must be* or *cannot be* autonomous. For an analytical claim, one would investigate the ways in which legal reasoning is purportedly autonomous, and see whether such claims stand up to close scrutiny. Prescriptively, one can argue that current practices should (or should not) be changed to incorporate greater or lesser dependence on other disciplines, either in judicial decision-making or in legal education. (A desire for greater use of other disciplines can be, but need not be, connected with an argument about the autonomy of legal reasoning and the value of traditional doctrinal legal scholarship. One could argue that legal doctrinal analysis *requires* no supplement, but would none the less be improved by ideas from other disciplines.)

Obviously, there are connections between, on the one hand, the analytical claim regarding autonomy and the descriptive and prescriptive claims on the other hand. If one believes that legal reasoning either *must be* or *cannot be* autonomous, then this obviously constrains what one can sensibly prescribe for the practice, and must also affect the description of the practice (e.g. it may be, as some of the American legal realists argued, that judges portray their decisions as autonomous when (according to the realists' analytical view) that cannot be the case, and thus the judges must be attempting to deceive others, or at least are unintentionally deceiving themselves (e.g. Frank, 1931)).

2 LEGAL REASONING

Claims about the autonomy of law (or its absence) are usually made in one of two contexts: (1) in legal reasoning (one must be careful not to equate legal and judicial reasoning; while judicial reasoning is often considered the paradigmatic site of legal reasoning, it is not the only place where legal reasoning takes place, and it is unwise to assume that all forms of legal reasoning are merely some sort of imitation of what judges do (Raz, 1994: 310–11)); or (2) in legal education. As regards legal reasoning, 'autonomy' should be understood in a relative way. No one has ever seriously claimed that law is a way of thinking entirely of its own category, and legal reasoning, even when most autonomous, does not shun (for example) basic rules of logic and inference. While there are times when the legal profession seems to depend on a language and a way of thinking entirely foreign to common sense and common language, this is only the appearance of the extremes of the practice. As Joseph Raz has pointed out (Raz, 2002: 1–2), the fact that many words are used in a legal context with their conventional meaning entails that certain forms of conventional inference also apply (if one says that the object is 'yellow', it follows, by the nature of the term ascribed, that object is 'colored'). At the other extreme, those who claim that legal reasoning is in no way distinct do not necessarily claim that there is no need for legal experts, and no such thing as legal expertise. For even if there is no special way of reasoning legally, decisions about what the law requires would need a knowledge of the sources of law, a set of rules, principles, and procedures that (in most societies) are extensive and separate from the standards and practices of other normative systems (e.g. conventional morality or religion).

Those who argue for the substantial autonomy of law see the form(s) of reasoning and decision-making used within the law (whether this means in *all* legal systems, due to the 'essential nature' of law, or in a particular legal system) as being distinctly different from the forms of reasoning and decision-making of, for example, practical reasoning, moral theory, and politics. When King James I argued that since law was grounded on reason, the King could decide cases as well as any judge, Lord Edward Coke responded that legal disputes 'are not to be decided by natural Reason but by the artificial Reason and Judgment of Law, which Law is an Act which requires long Study and experience, before that a Man can attain to the Cognizance of it ...' (Coke, 1907: 1343). This 'artificial reason' has often been equated with the use of analogical reasoning and precedent within law (e.g. Fried, 1981). If there is an argument to be made for an approach to decision-making that is distinctively legal (both separate from non-legal forms of decision-making, and common from one legal system to the next), it would likely be one that emphasized certain aspects of (most) legal systems: institutional decision-making, a hierarchy of decision-makers, and an effort to systematize the rules (Raz, 2002). And because law is intended as a practical guide for action, there is a pressure in the interpretation and application of legal norms towards consistency, coherence, stability, predictability, and finality. Those pressures are sometimes at tension with the desire that the outcomes be fair and just (with 'justice' here referring to those aspects of justice that go beyond 'following the rules laid down', that is, going beyond meeting reasonable expectations and reasonable reliance). These tend to combine into rules of 'precedent', 'statutory interpretation', and 'constitutional interpretation'. Though such rules vary from one legal system to another, rough convergences can be found, and the form of reasoning can be contrasted with other social practices and social institutions that do not operate under similar constraints and pressures.

One can come towards a similar conclusion from a different approach: what is distinctive about legal reasoning and legal decision-making is that the law involves primarily, though not exclusively, guidance by way of rules (Raz, 2002). The peculiar normative status of rules (and promises, agreements, and undertakings) is that when there is a reason to be governed by and through rules, one has a reason to do as the rule states independently of the content of the rule (though this is only a presumptive conclusion, which can be overcome when contrary reasons of a sufficient weight are present—thus, one has reasons to disobey an unjust rule, just as one has reasons to disregard a promise to do an evil act). In situations like common law judging, where the rule-applier also has the power to modify the rule, the tensions between the moral force of following the rule earlier laid down, even when not optimal, and the moral force of changing the law to a more optimal rule, lead to a distinctive structure and style of analysis and argumentation (though other rule-governed institutions will be likely to have similar forms of argument and decision).

One way in which legal reasoning can differ from other forms of reasoning, and the reasoning of one legal system can differ from others, is the extent to which analogies can be extended. There are rarely self-evident ways of distinguishing 'persuasive' from 'unpersuasive' (or 'clearly unpersuasive') analogies; instead, this tends to be a form of judgment learned in the course of legal training and experience within the profession (Bell, 1986). This is a sense of 'judgment' that can become crucial to good legal counseling, because it is central to the accurate prediction of how judges are likely to decide cases.

3 THE AMERICAN LEGAL REALISTS AND THE FORMALISTS

As regards the limits of legal reasoning, the American legal realists, in the early decades of the twentieth century, famously fought against what they called 'formalism', an extreme approach to legal reasoning which depended on a strong assertion of autonomy for law. 'Formalism' and 'mechanical jurisprudence' (Pound, 1908) were then, as now, terms of criticism, even abuse; there were no self-proclaimed 'formalists' in the early years of the twentieth century, though there are today a few modern contrarian thinkers willing to take on that label (e.g. Summers, 1997; Weinrib, 1988).

However, the views the American legal realists were attacking were not straw men. Formalism was the belief that legal reasoning was a form of logical deduction from first principles or from general (legal) concepts. Harvard Law School Dean Christopher Columbus Langdell, who popularized the Case Method of legal education, was almost certainly a formalist, as was Professor Joseph Beale, perhaps best known for his 'vested rights' theory in Conflict of Laws (Sebok, 1998: 83–104; Grey, 1983). Additionally, there were numerous court decisions, including some crucial decisions by the US Supreme Court, which were vulnerable to the criticism of 'formalism', in the way they derived conclusions to difficult legal (and social) disputes from the purported eternal meanings of general legal concepts (like 'property' or 'corporation').

The realists argued that legal reasoning was insufficient of itself, and required supplementation by policy science (a neutral social science, that could teach us which legal rules or political practices would help us most efficiently to achieve our social goals). The realists tended to make two quite different claims, which were not always clearly distinguished: (1) that the reasoning of judges of their time, though it purported to exemplify autonomous legal reasoning, in fact smuggled in views from outside law; and (2) that legal reasoning can never be entirely autonomous, because of a basic indeterminacy in the meaning or application of words or rules (Fisher et al., 1993). The first line of critique—that judicial reasoning (and legal commentary) tended to have unstated biases, policy preferences, and value judgments—was inevitably more convincing than the second line of critique. The realists had a good sense of when judicial opinions contained unstated logical gaps, and when doctrinal arguments could be manipulated for contrary results, but they did not have the training necessary to make cogent arguments about foundational aspects of language, meaning, rules, and interpretation that would be necessary to prove the indeterminacy of language or rules.

Sometimes the realist critique was phrased in terms of the application of general principles: for example, Supreme Court Justice Oliver Wendell Holmes, Jr.'s famous assertion that '[g]eneral propositions do not decide concrete cases' (Holmes, 1905: 76). Justice Holmes was said once to have challenged his brethren on the US Supreme Court, when they were conferring about a case, 'to name any principle they liked, and he would use it to decide the case under consideration either way' (Menand, 2001: 340).

The problem with formalist reasoning, according to the realists, was that it could result in legal doctrines and legal rules that were *too* autonomous—too abstracted from the conditions of life. Felix Cohen described the formalist thinking of his day as 'an autonomous system of legal concepts, rules, and arguments . . . independent both of ethics and of such positive sciences as economics or psychology. In effect, it is a special branch of the science of transcendental nonsense' (Cohen, 1935: 821). The realists preferred a picture of law as a human product meant to serve social needs and subject to criticism and reform when it fails to serve those needs or fails to serve them well. This view now seems so obvious and so much a matter of common sense that it is hard to comprehend how it could once have been controversial. However, it continues to be a sharp challenge to the core of any claim about the autonomy of law: if legal reasoning is somehow autonomous from both facts and values, why should it be preferred to forms of reasoning that *are* tied to normative and empirical forms of analysis? (If there is a response, it is in the way that a rule system can serve moral ends *indirectly*, by being entirely, or relatively, formalist in its application. This is just a larger-scale version of the argument that legal rules will more securely attain their instrumental ends if individual judges apply them *as written* rather than each judge modifying those rules in individual cases in light of what he or she thinks will best serve the rules' purposes.)

As noted, the realist critique was strongest when pointing out the unstated biases present in the judicial reasoning at the time. Whether the critique sufficed to show that law *could not* be autonomous (as contrasted e.g. with an argument that though law *could* be autonomous, it *should* not be) is far from clear, though this argument would be taken up again by later critical theorists, as discussed below. And the realist assumption that social science could be as neutral and uncontroversial as the physical sciences would eventually be shown to be highly problematic. Despite those doubts, the realist critique should be viewed as largely successful, and this can be seen, at least in the United States, in the way legal scholarship in particular, but also legal education and judicial reasoning, are *far* more interdisciplinary now than they were at the time the realists wrote.

4 THE LEGAL PROCESS SCHOOL

While the American legal realist critique could be said to have prevailed (and to have done so more or less completely), some of the effects of that critique were largely blunted for a generation or two in American academic thought. During that period, judges, academics, and law students were aware that the legal materials by themselves were inadequate to decide at least the most difficult and most important legal disputes, but it was thought that a well-rounded lawyer (or judge) of wisdom, insight, and experience would have all the additional material needed to either decide legal disputes or evaluate the merits of the law (Posner, 1987: 762–4). Another force that mollified the effect of the realist critique was a school of thought known as 'legal process'. The legal process school conceded many of the realists' criticisms of formalism—that legal materials were frequently indeterminate, and that some extra-legal values or norms would be required to decide many legal disputes—but argued that there was none the less room for a distinctively *legal* response to disputes. Legal process saw the distinctive legal response as involving understanding the relative strengths and weaknesses of different institutions and decision-making processes ('institutional competence'), and thus being able to determine whether (for example) it would be best to use adjudication, arbitration, agency rule-making, or public legislation to resolve a particular dispute. Additionally, legal process offered a picture of adjudication in which courts *had* discretion, but this discretion was bounded by a proper understanding of the judicial role (e.g. Hart and Sacks, 1994; Duxbury, 1995: 205–99).

The 'process studies' of the legal process school eventually shared the fate of the 'policy science' underlying the American legal realists' positive programme: both faltered because they assumed a neutrality in the social sciences and an ability of the social sciences to answer substantive questions of governance, assumptions that turned out to be untenable. There are various problems with the assumption that questions of social structure or questions of justice could be decided by a fully objective or fully neutral approach. First, too much depends on the ultimate objective—what one values and what one considers valuable—and there is no 'neutral' approach to that question. Secondly, the analysis of data too often depends on contestable and value-laden assumptions about human nature (some of which may possibly yet be resolved by further study in sociology or cognitive science or evolutionary psychology, but at the least we are far from that point now). Thirdly, the social sciences—whether sociology, economics, or psychology—remain at so undeveloped a state that they have been unable to come to clear consensus answers even to relatively straightforward law questions (e.g. whether the death penalty deters and whether the move from a fault to a no-fault divorce regime in the United States caused an increase in the divorce rate).

5 RECENT DEVELOPMENTS

In legal scholarship, American scholars have traveled far from viewing law as an autonomous discipline. Doctrinal work is still done, but it is has been overshadowed (particularly in 'high status' law journals) by interdisciplinary and theoretical work of various kinds. Economic analysis of different forms (now including game theory and public choice theory) pervades 'legal' analysis in most fields, and sociology, history, moral philosophy, and literary theory make regular appearances in legal scholarship and legal education, and also, if far less frequently, in judicial opinions. Other common law countries and much of Continental Europe seem to be traveling a similar path, though they are less far along it. England has its own well-developed mixture of law and sociology, known variously as 'law and society', 'socio-legal studies', and 'law in context' (e.g. Twining, 1991), though such work seems to be marginalized there ('law and society' is similarly marginalized in the United States, and has failed to be anywhere near as successful as the less empirically grounded work of law and economics, a situation not easily understood. See further Ch. 42).

The law and economics movement is entrenched in many parts of American legal academia, and in American scholarly commentary on legal matters (Posner, 1998). For some commentators within that tradition, the question of the autonomy of law has been inverted: the presumption being that all legal doctrines should be understood as proxies for the promotion of 'efficiency' or 'wealth maximization', and to the extent that the existing rules do not in fact promote these goals, they should be reformed (by judicial decision or legislative action) to do so. There are some commentators within this school who seem to require convincing that there are values other than economic ones, and valid forms of analysis outside that discipline. It is mysterious why law and economics has become so pervasive, and in many places dominant, in American legal scholarship, and equally mysterious why this phenomenon has not been replicated in other countries (the growth of law and economics in Commonwealth countries seems fairly slow, but there are places in Continental Europe where its influence, and its sophistication, seems to be increasing quickly (Ch. 42)). It may just be that Americans are at the cutting edge of a trend that will eventually occur everywhere, or (perhaps more likely) there may be something in the American character (a mixture of pragmatism and a deference to anything that appears to be 'scientific') that makes American scholars especially vulnerable to the rhetoric and claims of economic analysis.

At the other end of the political spectrum from the (usually) conservative legal economists, the skeptical (and Leftist) 'critical legal studies' (CLS) movement frequently summarized its approach to law in the slogan, 'law is politics'. This slogan expresses a sharp rejection of the autonomy of law: that all reasoning in and about the law is, and must be, political reasoning (or, one could just as well have said, 'moral reasoning', except that the critical legal theorists were often skeptics about objective moral truth). In the United States, the political nature of law, at least in the sense that judges appointed by conservatives tend to decide controversial cases differently than do judges appointed by liberals, is widely accepted. There is a fair amount of skepticism about the autonomy or neutrality of law, even in mainstream thought (with lawyers perhaps being even more skeptical than non-lawyers). However, CLS took more radical positions even than the skeptical mainstream, arguing, for example, against the neutrality and objectivity of legal reasoning even in 'easy' cases (e.g. Kelman, 1987: 242–68).

While CLS had a relatively short life as a 'movement' (see Kennedy, 1997: 8–11), lasting roughly from the mid-1970s to the late 1980s, many of the critical arguments put forward by its adherents still warrant close attention, and the radical challenge to the autonomy of law is probably one area where this is true. Critical legal studies saw itself as applying and extending some of the critiques of the American legal realists (e.g. Kennedy, 1997: 73–96). In particular, CLS theorists argued for the radical inde-

terminacy of law: the argument that legal materials do not determine the outcomes of particular cases. CLS theorists generally accepted that the outcomes of most
cases were *predictable*; but this was, they claimed, not because of the determinacy of
the law, but rather because judges had known or predictable biases. The legal materials,
on their own, were said to be indeterminate, because language was indeterminate, or
because legal rules tended to include contradictory principles which allowed judges
to justify whatever result they chose (Kelman, 1987). The CLS critiques have generally
been held to be overstated (Solum, 1987); though there may well be cases for which
the legal materials do not give a clear result, or at least not a result on which everyone
could immediately agree, this negates neither the easiness of the vast majority of possible disputes nor the possibility of right answers even for the harder cases.

One area which might once have been thought to have been a core example of
'legal autonomy', textual interpretation, has become a highly contested area. While
some academics continue to believe that law has a distinctive approach that brings
determinate answers to the meaning of legal texts (in particular, statutes, but also
constitutional provisions, contracts, wills, and trusts), other academics purport to
have learned from social choice theory, public choice theory, and literary theory, that
the issues are more complex and less determinate than had been earlier believed
(Posner, 1987: 773–8).

6 Professional Legal Education

Legal education is relevant to questions about the autonomy of law, not only in the
sense that this is the context in which forms of legal reasoning are passed on within
the profession, but also because the training itself may express the forms of knowledge and decision-making that are considered distinctive for law, or at least for one
particular legal system. Additionally, the way legal training is structured indicates a
great deal about the legal profession's view of itself, including its view about the
methods of reasoning and decision-making appropriate within the profession.

In most countries, becoming a lawyer involves a number of years of professional
education and/or significant time apprenticing with practicing lawyers. The implication is that being a lawyer requires the acquisition of substantial skills. What is it students learn in their legal studies? Is it another way of reasoning? Is it a peculiar kind
of moral or policy analysis? Or perhaps it is merely a special vocabulary, idiosyncratic
procedures, and a long list of statutes and case names, with the basic form of analysis
and argument actually being no different from other forms of private or institutional
decision-making. Those being trained in a legal system who have previously had no
legal training, or have been trained in another legal system, recognize from the effort

required to gain mastery that there is *something* distinctive to a (any) legal system's approach to problems. Sometimes the effort may be required because the legal system is so irrational, with a vast number of arcane and inexplicable rules, and heroic exertions are required to learn this 'strange game' of legal practice. In fact, it may be that most legal systems have some element of this sort of irrationality—a residue of the long history of Western law (both in the common law and civil law/Roman law traditions).

There is a sense in which every legal system is a whole *culture*, with its own sense of acceptability and form: not just the priority of different kinds of authority and different kinds of arguments, but, as already mentioned, also a sense of how far analogies can be stretched and still considered potentially persuasive (Bell, 1986). In this way, there is a measure of autonomy not only in legal reasoning generally, but also some autonomy in the reasoning of each individual legal system.

American legal education long ago accepted the basic core of the legal realist critique. It is a consensus with few dissenters that law students should be taught the current doctrine, but, along with the doctrine, 'policy' and moral arguments that could be used (e.g. in appellate advocacy) either to support the current doctrine, argue for an exception to its application, or urge its reform. The idea that legal truth is something 'discovered' or 'discerned' as a type of truth independent of human interests would only be raised to be ridiculed. And while there are still occasional references to 'thinking like a lawyer' (even here, the references are as often satiric as serious), this more often refers to a rigor and clarity of thought rather than a special form of reasoning. The transformation of English legal education has been more tentative and sporadic: one can find a growing number of courses which emphasize interdisciplinary work and contextual analysis, yet teaching which rarely ventures beyond traditional doctrinal analysis seems still to be far too common.

7 OTHER FORMS OF LEGAL AUTONOMY

There are other theorists who have argued for some recognition of the autonomy of law: for example, Hans Kelsen, the neo-formalists, and the legal autopoeisis theorists.

Hans Kelsen's 'Pure Theory of Law' (*reine Rechtslehre*) (Kelsen, 1992), written around the same time as the American legal realists were publishing, but coming from a quite different tradition, can be seen as advocating a form of autonomy of law. Kelsen is trying to apply something like Immanuel Kant's Transcendental Argument to the normative reasoning of law: investigating what follows (as an analytical matter) from the fact that citizens treat the acts and comments of certain individuals ('legal officials', 'legal institutions') as valid legal norms (Paulson, 1992). Whatever the ultimate merits of Kelsen's influential approach to legal theory, it can be seen as portraying law autonomously in the sense that it views law as a form of cognition or knowledge which can and should be studied separately from other forms of investigation (e.g. the sociology, ethics, or history of law)—thus, Kelsen's reference to a 'pure theory'.

The argument of the neo-formalists is that certain areas of doctrine (e.g. tort law) have an essence, which current practices roughly express, but the law should be reformed to express that essence more fully (Weinrib, 1995). Sometimes the argument is made on a broader scale—that the law *as a whole* has an eternal and essential form (Summers, 1997; Weinrib, 1988). Here one must be careful not to confuse the historical claim from the conceptual or prescriptive claim. One could accept that there is, for example, a certain connection between various aspects of private law (tort, contract, restitution), as they have developed over time in both the common law and civil law traditions, and different aspects and conceptions of corrective and distributive justice (e.g. Fried, 1981), without going a step further and arguing that any reform of (for example) the tort law system (e.g. to allow a greater use of strict liability: cf. Weinrib, 1995: 171–203) would be necessarily improper, unjust, or unjustifiable.

'Autopoiesis' is the idea that many systems (both biological and social) have significant feedback or recursive mechanisms that allow the self-regulation of the system. 'An autopoietic system produces and reproduces its own elements by the interaction of its elements' (Teubner, 1988: 3). 'Autopoietic law' is the idea that legal systems often are significantly self-regulating, self-reinforcing, and self-sustaining, that there is a 'recursive reproduction of legal acts' that results in a 'self-reproductive system of communication' (ibid. 4). This is an autonomy of law in the sense that, under this approach, law is viewed as being, contrary to the claims of many, relatively immune to social and political forces.

8 CONCLUSION

There are a variety of ways in which law is or can be an autonomous discipline. To the extent that the autonomy of law reflects only archaic jargon and outdated rules of a practice and profession with a long history, the autonomy of law is hardly worth defending or maintaining. Similarly, when law's distinctive form of reasoning and decision-making becomes entirely separated from conventional forms of normative argument and empirical studies, as seemed to occur with the formalist judges and commentators of a century ago, this separate approach seems harmful rather than valuable. However, a *relatively* autonomous discipline of law may be defensible, where law's distinctive approach to reasoning and decision-making is understood as deriving from the type of practice law is: a behavior-guiding practice, where the guidance is done primarily through general rules, and the rules are interpreted and applied by a hierarchical court system that gives precedential weight to earlier decisions. Within this sort of structure, legal discourse is distinctive, but can also be seen as merely a *particular application* of moral and political reasoning, rather than entirely abstracted from such reasoning.

One can see the 'autonomy' or 'formality' of law as analogous to the 'autonomy' or 'formality' of rules that operate *within* law (Fish, 1994: 141–79). The idea of guidance by rules (in law and elsewhere) is that ultimate objectives will be better achieved when the rules are generally applied 'formally', as written, with little to no consideration of the short-term consequences. However, there will always be pressures to interpret rules according to the rule's ultimate purposes and to do justice (all things considered) between the relevant parties. Within many legal systems, one can see the way rules of evidence, rules of contract, principles of statutory interpretation and other standards tend, over the decades, to oscillate between more and less formal treatment. On a broader level, legal systems, like rules, probably work best when they are treated, to some extent, as a formal system, almost a kind of logic, which should be applied according to its terms and its own standards. However, legal systems are in fact intended to serve human purposes, and the pressures to serve moral and functional ends inevitably occasionally push law from its formal and formalist path. One may reason *about the law* (purely doctrinal analysis) in a largely formalistic way, but when it comes to deciding disputes in the world *according to law* (judicial decision-making that involves the manipulation of doctrine, but goes far beyond that), the decisions are best seen as (a subcategory of) general moral reasoning, as legal officials are deciding what ought to be done, all things considered, with the legal rules being part of the 'all things' that are being considered (Raz, 1994: 313–19).

REFERENCES

Bell, J. (1986). 'The Acceptability of Legal Arguments', in N. MacCormick and P. Birks (eds.), *The Legal Mind*, Oxford: Clarendon Press, 45–65.

Cohen, F. (1935). 'Transcendental Nonsense and the Functional Approach', *Columbia Law Review*, 35: 809–49.

Coke, E. (1907). 'Prohibitions del Roy', *Coke Reports, Part 12* (1608), repr. in *English Reports*, 77: 1342–3.

Duxbury, N. (1995). *Patterns of American Jurisprudence*, Oxford: Clarendon Press.

Fish, S. (1994). *There's No Such Thing as Free Speech . . . And it's a Good Thing, Too*, New York: Oxford University Press.

Fisher, W. F., III, Horwitz, M. J., and Reed, T. A. (eds.) (1993). *American Legal Realism*, New York: Oxford University Press.

Frank, J. (1931). 'Are Judges Human?' *University of Pennsylvania Law Review*, 80: 17–53, 233–67.

Fried, C. (1981). 'The Artificial Reason of the Law or: What Lawyers Know', *Texas Law Review*, 60: 35–58.

Grey, T. C. (1983). 'Langdell's Orthodoxy', *University of Pittsburgh Law Review*, 45: 1–53.

Hart, H. M., Jr. and Sacks, A. M. (1994). *The Legal Process: Basic Problems in the Making and Application of Law*, W. N. Eskridge, Jr and P. P. Frickey (eds.), Westbury, NY: Foundation Press.

Holmes, O. W., Jr. (1897). 'The Path of the Law', *Harvard Law Review*, 10: 457–78.

—— (1905). Dissenting Opinion, *Lochner v New York*, 198 US 45: 74–6.

Kelman, M. (1987). *A Guide to Critical Legal Studies*, Cambridge, Mass.: Harvard University Press.

Kelsen, H. (1992). *Introduction to the Problems of Legal Theory*, trans. B. L. Paulson and S. L. Paulson, Oxford: Clarendon Press (original work pub. 1934).

Kennedy, D. (1997). *A Critique of Adjudication (fin de siècle)*, Cambridge, Mass.: Harvard University Press.

Menand, L. (2001). *The Metaphysical Club*, New York: Farrar, Straus and Giroux.

Paulson, S. L. (1992). 'The Neo-Kantian Dimension of Kelsen's Pure Theory of Law', *Oxford Journal of Legal Studies*, 12: 311–32.

Posner, R. A. (1987). 'The Decline of Law as an Autonomous Discipline: 1962–1987', *Harvard Law Review*, 100: 761–80.

—— (1998). *Economic Analysis of Law* (5th edn.), New York: Aspen Law & Business.

Postema, G. (1996). 'Law's Autonomy and Public Practical Reason', in R. P. George (ed.), *The Autonomy of Law: Essays on Legal Positivism*, Oxford: Clarendon Press, 79–118.

Pound, R. (1908). 'Mechanical Jurisprudence', *Columbia Law Review*, 8: 605–23.

Raz, J. (1994). *Ethics in the Public Domain: Essays in the Morality of Law and Politics*, Oxford: Clarendon Press.

—— (2002). 'Reasoning with Rules', in M. D. A. Freeman (ed.), *Current Legal Problems 2001, Volume 54*, Oxford: Oxford University Press, 1–18.

Sebok, A. J. (1998). *Legal Positivism in American Jurisprudence*, Cambridge: Cambridge University Press.

Solum, L. (1987). 'On the Indeterminacy Crisis: Critiquing Critical Dogma', *University of Chicago Law Review*, 54: 462–503.

Summers, R. S. (1997). 'How Law is Formal and Why it Matters', *Cornell Law Review*, 82: 1165–229.

Teubner, G. (1988). 'Introduction to Autopoietic Law', in G. Teubner (ed.), *Autopoietic Law: A New Approach to Law and Society*, Berlin: Walter de Gruyter, 1–11.

Twining, W. (1991). 'Reflections on Law in Context', in P. Cane and J. Stapleton (eds.), *Essays for Patrick Atiyah*, Oxford: Clarendon Press, 1–30.

Weinrib, E. J. (1988). 'Legal Formalism: On The Immanent Rationality of Law', *Yale Law Journal*, 97: 949–1016.

—— (1995). *The Idea of Private Law*, Cambridge, Mass.: Harvard University Press.

Index

INDEX 1037

labour law (*cont.*)
economic environment, changes in the 574–84
employer–employee relationships 577–8
enforcement 583
ethnography 588–91
European Union 202, 581–2, 589
Evans, P 589
Ewing, K 573
external labour market flexibility 578–9
feminist legal theory 587–8, 589
flexibility 575–9
Fordist production system 575
Freedland, M 572–3, 579
gender 581, 587–8
Germany, trade unions in 566
global labour regimes 581–3, 589–90
globalization 581
Gross, J 570
harmonization 582
Hayek, FA 572, 579
Hepple, B 572, 573, 580
human resource systems 580
human rights 301
ideology 563–5, 586–7
immunities 566
individual rights 585–6
industrial pluralism 564, 567, 568–71, 576, 579,
586
institutions 589–90
integration 567, 581, 590
intellectual movements 584–8
interest groups 567
International Labour Organization conventions
582–3, 589
internationalization 581–4
Kahn-Freund, Otto 566–7, 568, 570, 572, 587,
591
Klare, K 567, 586
labour market supply 580–1
labourism 564, 566–7, 572, 575–6
law and economics movement 585–6
Lawrence, C 581
legal realism 24, 584
legislation
enactment of new 571–4
failure to implement existing 569–71
Lyon-Cean, A 582
MacKinnon, C 588
management 575, 585
mass production 575
multinationals 584
NAFTA 581–3, 589
national institutions 584
National Labor Relations Board 570
neo-corporatism 567
New Deal 567, 569–70
New Zealand 564, 566–7, 571–3, 575–6

labour law (*cont.*)
Owens, R 568, 587
political environment, changes in the 574–84
Posner, R 585
pragmatism 588–91
producerist limitations 568–9
production systems, new 575–7, 589–90
race discrimination 581
reflexive legal theory 588–91
regional institutions 584
regional labour rights 581–3, 589–90
regulation 563–4
scholarship 564–5
conventional frameworks of 565–9, 587
future programmes for 588–91
Schultz, V 58
scope of 563–4
segmentation 579–80
sex discrimination 581
sexual harassment 588
Simitis, S 582
social partnership 567, 575
South Africa 580
standards 301, 563, 581–3, 588
statutes 569–71
Stone, K 567, 586
Sturm, S 581
subject matter of, limitations on 568–9
trade unions 566–7, 569–70, 572–6, 585
transnational collective bargaining 583–4
unfair dismissal 579
United Kingdom 564, 566–7, 571–2, 578
collective bargaining 566, 575
collective *laissez faire* 572
flexibility 579
immunities 566
trade unions 572–3, 575
United States 564, 566–7, 583
collective bargaining 570–1, 579
critical legal studies 586
flexibility 578–9
law and economics movement 585
National Labor Relations Board 570
New Deal 567, 569–70
trade unions 569–70, 576
unfair dismissal 579
universal rights 590
voluntarism 566
wealth maximisation 585
Wedderburn, KW 575, 583–4
Weiler, Paul 570–1, 576, 579, 583
welfare state, erosion of the 578–9
Wilkinson, F 563, 573, 582, 584, 586
Williamson, Oliver 585
Lacey, Nicola 217, 218–20, 237, 239, 245, 732
Lacharrière, Ladreit de 283, 286
Ladeur, KH 757

legal education (*cont.*)
  executive action, judicial review of 155–7
  feminist studies, legal education and 903
  Frank, J 914
  funding 906
  general transferable skills 905, 909
  global development and impoverishment 464–7
  Grimes, R 914
  higher education, 'enlightenment' function of 905
  historical 869, 878, 902
  Hong Kong 913
  Hyams, R 917
  innovation 910–11
  interdisciplinary study 908
  Johnstone, R 903, 904, 909, 915
  Jones, PA 911, 913, 914
  journals 913–14
  juridification of society 903
  Kahn-Freund, Otto 907
  knowledge transmission 906–8, 910
  Kolb's learning cycles 912
  Lasswell, HD 906
  law reform 906
  law schools 798
  learning outcomes 911–12
  LeBrun, M 903, 904, 909, 915
  legal change 906
  legal clinics 914
  legal ethics 909, 911, 916–17
  legal skills 903–4, 906, 908–9, 911, 914, 916
  liberal education 904–5, 906
  MacCrate Report 909, 916
  Marre Report 908–9
  'massification' of 903, 906
  Maughan, C 902, 909, 912, 913, 914–16
  McDougal, MS 906
  models of legal education 906–11
  Nicolson, D 917
  O'Dair, R 917
  oral communication 909
  Pearce Report 909
  pluralism 903
  problem-based learning 914–15
  problem-solving 909
  process knowledge 908
  professional legal education 798–9, 905–6, 907, 908, 983–4
  professors 905, 907
  programmatic discussion 901
  propositional knowledge 908
  purposes of legal education 902–6
  reflective practitioner 906, 908, 912, 916
  research 901–2, 909, 916
  Schon, Donald 906, 908, 912–14, 916
  Scott, P 903, 906, 907
  Simon, W 917
  social backgrounds 903

legal education (*cont.*)
  Socratic method 913
  specific learning activities 913–16
  Stephenson, J 912
  Stevens, RB 903, 905, 908
  study methods 912–13
  supercomplexity of legal education 909–11
  technocratic model 912
  theoretical 901–2
  training and 901, 904
  transferability of skills 904–5, 909
  transnational concept of law 848–9
  Twining, William 902, 904–5, 907
  United Kingdom 911, 913–15
  United States 155–8, 902–5, 909, 910, 915–16
  utilitarianism 901
  vocational legal education 902–3, 906, 915–16
  Webb, J 902, 909, 912, 913, 914–17
  Weil, S 912
  welfare state 411
legal positivism
  contract 4
  criminal law 226–30
  executive action, judicial review of 154–5
  historical research in law 864, 870–2, 874
  international legal order 272–4, 282–9, 294–5
  legal studies 953–4, 966, 967
  parliamentary sovereignty, judicial review and 168
  transnational concept of law 844, 850, 853
legal process
  autonomous discipline, law as an 980–1
  executive action, judicial review of 155–6
  legal studies 955–7
  United States 155–6
legal profession *see* lawyers and legal services
legal realism
  academics in the legal system 930
  autonomous discipline, law as an 975–6, 978–80, 984
  criminal process 775
  empirical research in law 881
  England 158
  executive action, judicial review of 158
  international legal order 273, 282, 286–7, 289
  international legal sanction processes 817–18
  labour law 584
  legal studies 951–7, 960, 963, 965–6
  tort 24
legal reasoning
  academics in the legal system 930, 943
  autonomous discipline, law as an 976–80, 984–6
  empirical research in law 881
  judiciary 976–7, 980
Legal Scholarship Network 960
legal services *see* lawyers and legal services
Legal Services Commission 765

United Kingdom (*cont.*)
  international legal sanction processes 821, 830–1
  journals 400–2
  labour law 564, 566–7, 571–3, 575, 578–9
  law schools 411
  legal education 911, 913–15
  legislation, judicial review of 176
  liberalization 109
  neo-liberalism 209
  new public management 110, 123
  parliamentary sovereignty 108
  Poor Law 405, 407
  private military companies 16
  privatization 104–5, 108–9, 123–4
  procurement 113
  public choice model 103
  public health 449
  public law 407
  public utilities 112
  regulation 121, 123–4, 126
  rule-making 730–1, 735, 739–40, 743–4
  Social Fund 406–7
  social insurance, introduction of 399
  Social Security Commissioners 401–2
  state, nature and functions of the 103–5, 108–10,
      112–14, 116
  tax credits 410
  taxation scholarship 379–82, 386–7, 395
  textbooks 399–402
  therapeutic relationship 444–7
  trade unions 572–3, 575
  tribunals 401–2, 406
  trusts 84
  welfare system 399–403, 405–7, 409–11
United Nations
  academics in the legal system 943
  civil processes 750
  Charter 819–20, 823–4
    constitutionalism and 274, 281, 283, 287
  Compensation Commission 278
  Declaration of Human Rights 299, 302
  General Assembly 829
  Global Network on Crime 265–8
  human rights 280, 301–2
  Human Rights Committee 280
  international legal order 274, 281, 283, 287
  international legal sanction processes 819–20,
      823–4
  Law of the Sea Tribunal 281
  Security Council 281, 819–20, 823–4, 829, 943
  UNCTAD 601
United States *see also* September 11, 2001 terrorist
      attacks
  abortion 673–4, 676, 680–93, 696–9
  academics in the legal system 928–35
  adjudication 761–3
  administrative law 161–2

United States (*cont.*)
  Administrative Procedure Act 1946 148–9, 156,
      733–4, 740
  adversarial process 768–9
  advertising 538, 540–8
  air pollution 712
  alien tort claims 831–2
  arbitration 756
  Australia 161–2
  autonomous discipline, law as an 975–87
  best available technology 708–9
  capital gains tax 394
  citizenship 195, 196–7, 755, 757
    adjudication 761–3
    adversarial process 768–9
    arbitration 756
    fairness and impartiality 761
    judges 758, 760–4
    legal profession 759–63
    reform 758–64
  collective bargaining 570–1, 579
  competition law 525, 527, 530–2
  complex polities 357–8, 358–60, 363, 368
  constitutional structure in 202
  consumer credit 555
  consumers 536–7, 649–50, 552
  contingent fee arrangements 43, 556–8
  contraception 675–80
  contract 3–7, 9–10, 13–16, 18
  contracting out 115
  copyright 629–31, 639
  corporate tax 390–1
  corporations 487–506
  courts 718–19
  criminal law 228–30, 237
  criminal process 773–88
  criminology 253–4, 356, 260–1, 267–8
  critical legal studies 156, 586
  Cuba 825
  data protection 447
  death penalty 825, 832–3
  Delaney Clause 706, 707
  devolution 720–1
  disclosure 713
  discrimination 202, 204–5, 209
  double tax 391
  due process 140, 156, 405, 828
  Due Process Clause 43
  empirical research in law 882, 887
  environment 701–2, 704, 706–11, 715
    air pollution 712
    balancing 710–11
    best available technology 708–9
    collaborative decision-making 721–2
    courts 718–19
    Delaney Clause 706, 707
    devolution 720–1